The Ultimate Guide to College Football

Sport and Society

Series Editors
Benjamin G. Rader
Randy Roberts

A list of books in the series appears at the end of this book.

The Ultimate Guide to College Football

Rankings, Records, and Scores of the Major Teams and Conferences

James Quirk

University of Illinois Press

Urbana and Chicago

Library of Congress Cataloging-in-Publication Data

Quirk, James P.
The ultimate guide to college football : rankings, records, and
scores of the major teams and conferences / James Quirk.
p.   cm. — (Sport and society)
ISBN 0-252-07226-X (pbk. : alk. paper)
1. Football—Records—United States. 2. College sports—Records—
United States. I. Title. II. Series.
GV956.8.Q85Q85   2004
796.332'63—dc22   2004009450

To my wife, Shirley; to my kids, Elizabeth De Ford, Jim Quirk, Janice Ratliff, Jill Powell, Colleen Stone, and Tom Quirk; to my grandkids, Jennifer Holst, Nicole Jaycox, Mike Jaycox, Will Delehanty, James Delehanty, Kevin Powell, Julie Powell, Chris Stone, and Katie Stone; and to my great-grandkids, Taylor Donner, Megan Donner, and Nicole Donner, for all the fun and happiness they have given me.

Contents

Introduction   1

PART I: A Summary History of College Football

PART II: Records of Division 1-A Football Teams

University of Akron   29
University of Alabama at Birmingham   31
University of Alabama   32
Arizona State University   34
University of Arizona   36
Arkansas State University   38
University of Arkansas   40
Auburn University   42
Ball State University   44
Baylor University   46
Boise State University   48
Boston College   49
Bowling Green University   51
Brigham Young University   53
University of Buffalo   55
University of California   57
University of Central Florida   59
Central Michigan University   60
University of Cincinnati   62
Clemson University   64
Colorado State University   66
University of Colorado   68
University of Connecticut   70
Duke University   72
East Carolina University   74

Eastern Michigan University   76
Florida State University   78
University of Florida   80
Fresno State University   82
Georgia Tech   84
University of Georgia   86
University of Hawaii   88
University of Houston   89
University of Idaho   91
University of Illinois   93
University of Indiana   95
Iowa State University   97
University of Iowa   99
Kansas State University   101
University of Kansas   103
Kent State University   105
University of Kentucky   107
University of Louisiana at Lafayette   109
University of Louisiana at Monroe   111
Louisiana State University   112
Louisiana Tech   114
University of Louisville   116
Marshall University   118
University of Maryland   120
University of Memphis   122

CONTENTS

Miami University   124

University of Miami (Florida)   126

Michigan State University   128

University of Michigan   130

Middle Tennessee University   132

University of Minnesota   134

Mississippi State University   136

University of Mississippi   138

University of Missouri   140

University of Nebraska   142

University of Nevada at Las Vegas   145

University of Nevada   146

New Mexico State University   148

University of New Mexico   150

North Carolina State University   152

University of North Carolina   154

North Texas University   156

Northern Illinois University   158

Northwestern University   160

University of Notre Dame   162

Ohio State University   165

Ohio University   167

Oklahoma State University   169

University of Oklahoma   171

Oregon State University   174

University of Oregon   176

Penn State   178

University of Pittsburgh   180

Purdue University   182

RICE University   184

Rutgers University   186

San Diego State   188

San Jose State   190

University of South Carolina   192

University of South Florida   194

University of Southern California   195

Southern Methodist University   197

University of Southern Mississippi   199

Stanford University   201

Syracuse University   203

Temple University   205

University of Tennessee   207

Texas A & M   209

University of Texas at El Paso (UTEP)   211

Texas Christian University   213

Texas Tech University   215

University of Texas   217

University of Toledo   219

Troy State University   221

Tulane University   223

University of Tulsa   225

University of California
   at Los Angeles   227

United States Air Force Academy   229

United States Military Academy   230

United States Naval Academy   232

Utah State University   234

University of Utah   236

Vanderbilt University   238

Virginia Tech   240

University of Virginia   242

Wake Forest University   244

Washington State University   246

University of Washington   248

West Virginia University   250

Westen Michigan University   252

Texas Christian University   254

University of Wisconsin   256

University of Wyoming   258

PART III: Records of Other Major Football Teams

Brown University   263

Carlisle Institute   265

Carnegie Tech   266

University of Chicago   267

Colgate University   268

Columbia University   270

CONTENTS

Cornell University   272

Dartmouth College   274

University of Denver   276

Drake University   278

Duquesne University   279

Fordham University   280

Georgetown University   281

Hardin-Simmons University   282

Harvard University   284

College of Holy Cross   286

Lafayette College   288

Marquette University   290

University of Montana   291

New York University   293

University of the Pacific   295

University of Pennsylvania   297

Princeton University   299

University of San Francisco   301

Santa Clara University   302

St. Mary's College   303

Villanova University   304

Virginia Military Institute   306

Washington and Lee   308

Washington University   309

The College of William and Mary   310

Yale University   312

PART IV: Records of Service Teams During World War II

1942 Season   317

1943 Season   320

1944 Season   323

1945 Season   327

PART V: Major College Football Conferences

Atlantic Coast Conference (ACC)   335

Big East Conference   340

Big Eight Conference   343

Big Ten   350

Big Twelve Conference   362

Big West Conference   365

Border Conference   369

Conference USA   373

Ivy League   375

Mid-America Conference (MAC)   380

Missouri Valley Conference (MVC)   387

Mountain States Conference
   (Skyline Conference)   394

Mountain West Conference   397

Pacific-10 Conference (Pac-10)   399

Southeastern Conference (SEC)   408

Southern Conference   418

Southwest Conference (SWC)   429

Sun Belt Conference   438

Western Athletic Conference (WAC)   439

PART VI: Records of Bowl Games

Alamo Bowl   447

Capital One Bowl   447

Citrus Bowl   447

Continental Tire Bowl   447

Cotton Bowl   447

Fiesta Bowl   447

Gator Bowl   447

GMAC Bowl (Mobile Bowl)   448

Hawaii Bowl (Aloha Bowl)   448

Hawaii Bowl (Oahu Bowl)   448

Holiday Bowl   448

Houston Bowl (Gallery Furniture.com
   Bowl)   448

Houston Bowl   448

Humanitarian Bowl   448

Independence Bowl   448

CONTENTS

Insight.com Bowl   448

Las Vegas Bowl (California Bowl)   448

Las Vegas Bowl   448

Liberty Bowl   448

Motor City Bowl   449

Music City Bowl   449

New Orleans Bowl   449

Orange Bowl   449

Outback Bowl (Hall of Fame Bowl)   449

Peach Bowl   449

Rose Bowl   449

San Francisco Bowl   450

Silicon Valley Classic   450

Sugar Bowl   450

Sun Bowl   450

John Hancock Bowl   451

Tangerine Bowl   451

All American Bowl   451

Aviation Bowl   451

Bacardi Bowl   451

Bluebonnet Bowl   451

Bluegrass Bowl   451

Camelia Bowl   451

Cherry Bowl   451

Christmas Festival   451

Cigar Bowl   451

Delta Bowl   451

Dixie Classic   451

Eastern Bowl   451

East-West Bowl   451

Elks Bowl   451

Freedom Bowl   451

Garden State Bowl   451

Glass Bowl   451

Grape Bowl   451

Gotham Bowl   451

Great Lakes Bowl   451

Harbor Bowl   451

Lions Bowl   451

Independence Bowl   451

Little All American Bowl   451

Mercy Bowl   451

Micron.com Bowl (Blockbuster Bowl)   451

Micron.com Bowl (Carquest Bowl)   451

Micron.com Bowl   452

Mineral Water Bowl   452

Mirage Bowl   452

Oil Bowl   452

Optimist Bowl   452

Palm Festival   452

Paper Bowl   452

Pasadena Bowl   452

Pecan Bowl   452

Pioneer Bowl   452

Pineapple Bowl   452

Presidential Cup   452

Raisin Bowl   452

Refrigerator Bowl   452

Salad Bowl   452

Shrine Bowl   452

Turkey Bowl   452

PART VII: All American Teams (1883–2003)

Walter Camp Teams   455

Grantland Rice Teams   457

Consensus Teams   459

AP Teams   465

PART VIII: Player Awards

Heisman Trophy   471

Maxwell Award   471

Outland Trophy   471

Ray Guy Award   472

CONTENTS

Dick Butkus Award   472

Fred Biletnikoff Award   472

Davey O'Brien Award   472

Doak Walker Award   472

Lombardi Award   472

Jim Thorpe Award   472

Lou Groza Award   472

Chuck Bednarik Award   472

Johnny Unitas Award   472

Sammy Baugh Award   472

Walter Camp Award   473

Ted Hendricks Award   473

John Mackey Award   473

Bronko Nagurski Award   473

Rimington Trophy   473

Moisi Tatupu Award   473

PART IX: National Rankings of Teams (1883–2003)

PART X: Changes in the Rules of College Football

Introduction

This book is intended as a basic reference source for college football fans, for coaches, for players, for sports reporters, and for researchers in the field of sports—in brief, for anyone interested in the history of college football.

The book is organized so that the central chapters of the book present the won-loss records, over each team's history, for all teams qualifying for Division I-A status in the 2003 season. There were 117 Division I-A teams in 2003, 113 of which were members of some Division I-A conference, with four independent teams. For each team, the team's location, its nickname, and the school colors are given, along with the capacity of the team's stadium. A brief history of each team's conference affiliations is given as well.

The main body of the report for each team gives the overall end-of-season won-loss-tied record for each year of the team's history, together with points scored by team (PF = points for) and points scored against the team (PA = points against), for each season. For any year in which the team was a member of a major football conference, the conference won-loss-tied record is given as well, together with the rank of the team within the conference for that season. In addition, the team's won-loss-tied record over its history in any major conference is also provided in the table. (The conference records shown are the records of teams in conference play; non-conference games are excluded from those totals.)

The team tables also include the national rank-ing (if any) for the team, for each season, under the columns headed "AP Other," under the super heading "Nat'l" (for national ranking). "AP" refers to the end-of-season ranking of teams in the poll of sports writers that has been conducted by the Associated Press each season, beginning in 1936. The "other" column refers to three different rankings at differing times. Prior to the 1924 season, what is reported under the "Other" head-ing is only the mythical national champion for that season, as determined by the Helms Athletic Foundation. For seasons from 1924 through 1940, the number shown under "Other" is the national rank for that season, in the ranking system devel-oped by Professor Frank Dickinson of the Univer-sity of Illinois. Dickinson published a list of the top eleven teams for each year between 1924 and 1940. (Prior to 1941, when the number one team in the Helms ranking differs from the number one team in Dickinson's ranking, both teams are as-signed a ranking of number one.)

The AP ranking was the only nationally recog-nized ranking between 1941 and 1949, so the "Other" column is blank for those years. Begin-ning in 1950, the number shown in the "Other" column is the ranking from a poll of college coaches. This poll was initiated by UPI in 1950, and continued by that organization through the 1990 season. In 1991, the poll was taken over by CNN and *USA Today*. In the late 1990s, CNN dropped out and was replaced by ESPN. The AP ranking covered the top 20 teams in the country from 1936 through 1961. From 1962 through 1967, the AP cut back to listing only the top 10 teams in its poll. Beginning with 1968, the AP returned to listing the top 20 teams and continued to do so through the 1988 season. In 1989, the AP began listing the top 25 teams in the country, and it also provides a vote count on teams not making the top 25. Between 1950 and 1989, the UPI poll ranked the top 20 teams in the country. Starting in 1990, the CNN/*USA Today* poll (and later the ESPN/*USA Today* poll) began listing the top 25 teams in the country.

The team tables also include the won-loss-tied records of the team, under each coach of the team, beyond the early years of the history of teams, when coaching was essentially a hobby activity, with the coach typically being a faculty member, and when there was a rapid turnover of coaches.

Finally, the team's overall won-loss-tied record by decades is shown, along with the historic record of the team, that is, the team's overall won-loss-tied record over its history, through the 2003 season. This is followed by a listing of the team's post-season record, including the game scores of all post-season games played by the team, including conference championship games. (It should be noted that the year listed for the post-season game is determined by when the game was played, and not by the season.) Players and coaches who have been elected to the College Football Hall of Fame through the 2003 class of inductees are listed, along with the names of players who have been awarded certain nationally recognized player trophies or awards.

Following the section dealing with Division I-A teams is a section that lists comparable information, over their major college football histories, for thirty-two teams that were at some time in the past nationally ranked, or in other ways qualified for major college football status, even though the schools no longer field major college teams. The list of teams includes all of the Ivy League schools, together with Carlisle Institute, Carnegie Tech, University of Chicago, Colgate University, University of Denver, Drake University, Duquesne University, Fordham University, Georgetown University, Hardin-Simmons University, College of the Holy Cross, Lafayette College, Marquette University, the University of Montana, New York University, University of the Pacific, University of San Francisco, St. Mary's College (California), Santa Clara University, Villanova University, Virginia Military Institute, Washington University (St. Louis), Washington and Lee, and the College of William and Mary. The records for these teams cover only the years in which the teams were playing major college schedules; their records at Division I-AA or lower are not included here.

Finally, team records (including the scores of all games) are provided in the book for some 130 military camps or bases that sponsored football teams during World War II. The schedules of the World War II service teams ranged from playing other military teams or junior college teams, up through scheduling the strongest college teams in the country. Some service teams even scheduled games against NFL teams. The best of the service teams—Great Lakes, Iowa Pre-Flight, Randolph Field—were as good as the best college teams, and they had the coaching talent to match, with individuals like Bernie Bierman, Paul Brown, Jim Crowley, Jim Tatum, and Don Faurot coaching service teams.

In 1942, the sports editors at AP decided that the numbers of ex-college and ex-pro stars studding the lineups of the best service teams made comparisons with college teams unfair, and, for that year, sportswriters were asked to rank college teams, disregarding the games played against service teams. At the end of the 1942 season, there were two separate AP polls taken of sportswriters, one for college teams, and one for service teams. Following this, the AP changed its approach, and there was just one AP poll, covering both college and service teams, for the 1943, 1944, and 1945 seasons.

The service teams made a significant impact on college football during the war years through 1944. This is reflected in the AP polls for the war years. In 1945, no service teams were listed among the AP top 20.

1942 College	Service	1943 Combined Poll	1944 Combined Poll
1. Ohio State	1. Great Lakes	1. Notre Dame	1. Army
2. Georgia	2. Iowa P-F	2. Iowa P-F	2. Ohio State
3. Wisconsin	3. Georgia P-F	3. Michigan	3. Randolph Field
4. Tulsa	4. N. Carolina P-F	4. Navy	4. Navy
5. Georgia Tech	5. California P-F	5. Purdue	5. Bainbridge NTS
6. Notre Dame	6. Jacksonville NAS	6. Great Lakes	6. Iowa P-F
7. Tennessee	7. Camp Grant	7. Duke	7. USC
8. Boston College	8. Pensacola NAS	8. Del Monte	8. Michigan
9. Michigan	9. Manhattan Beach	9. Northwestern	9. Notre Dame
10. Alabama	10. Corpus Christie	10. March Field	10. March Field
11. Texas	11. Second Air	11. Army	11. Duke
12. Stanford	12. Fort Knox	12. Washington	12. Tennessee
13. UCLA	13. Lakehurst NAS	13. Georgia P-F	13. Georgia P-F
14. Wm. & Mary	14. Fort Monmouth	14. Texas	14. Norman P-F
15. Santa Clara	15. Fort Riley	15. Tulsa	15. Illinois
16. Auburn	16. Camp Davis	16. Dartmouth	16. El Toro Marines
17. Wash. State	17. March Field	17. Bainbridge NAS	17. Great Lakes
18. Miss. State	18. Mather Field	18. Colorado	18. Fort Pierce
19. Minnesota	19. Fort Totten	19. Lafayette	19. St. Mary's P-F
19. Holy Cross	19. Spence Field	20. Penn State	20. Second Air Force

The next major division of the book provides the final season rankings, for each year of their history, for all the major college conferences in the history of college football. Included in the list of major college conferences are the eleven Division I-A conferences active in the 2003 season: Atlantic Coast Conference, Big East Conference, Big Ten Conference, Big Twelve Conference, Conference USA, Mid-American Conference, Mountain West Conference, Pacific Ten Conference, Southeastern Conference, Sun Belt Conference, and the Western Athletic Conference. In addition to these conferences, records are provided for major college football conferences that had disbanded before the 2003 season: the Big Eight Conference (disbanded after the 1995 sea-son); the Big West Conference (disbanded after the 2000 season, with most members transferring to the new Sun Belt Conference); the Border Conference (disbanded after the 1961 season); the Missouri Valley Conference (disbanded after the 1985 season); the Mountain States (Skyline) Conference (disbanded after the 1961 season); and the Southwest Conference (disbanded after 1995 season). Two other conference histories are also included in this section of the book, the Southern Conference (through the 1981 season), and the Ivy League. The Southern Conference was a major college football conference through most of its history, and it was ex-members of the Southern Conference that organized the Southeastern Conference (in 1933), and the Atlantic Coast

Conference (in 1953). By the 1970s, most members of the Southern Conference were small college teams, and, in 1981, the Southern Conference was classified as a Division I-AA conference. The record of the Southern Conference is given through the 1981 season. The Ivy League, organized in 1956, is included here because as late as the 1950s, Ivy League teams were still being accorded national ranking in the AP and UPI polls. In addition, the important role played by members of this conference in the early history of college football argued for inclusion of this conference among those college football conferences of interest to fans and to historians of the sport.

For each conference, end-of-season won-loss-tied records are given for each year in the history of the conference as a major conference, together with the end-of-season won-loss-tied records of conference members. The scores of conference championship games are also given. Certain conferences, including the Big Ten and the Missouri Valley Conference, ignored ties in determining conference standings and win percents, in the early years of play (in the Big Ten this was the rule until 1946). The win percents and conference standings shown here follow conference rules concerning the treatment of ties, insofar as they are known. When there is ambiguity or a lack of evidence to the contrary, ties are treated as half-a-win, half-a-loss. The record of conference teams in total against non-conference teams is also shown for each season. Conference championship games, as in the Big Twelve, MAC, and Southeastern Conference, are not included in end-of-season conference won-loss records, but are included in overall records. Also, when games are forfeited, which usually comes after a season is concluded, the records here are the records after forfeits.

After the year-to-year conference standings, there is a summary page for each conference, giving the decade-by-decade won-loss-tied records (in conference games, and not including conference championship games) of all member teams, through the 2003 season. The summary page also gives the conference titles won by members, for each decade, and over the history of the conference. Any team winning a conference title outright is assigned a "1" for the season. If the conference title was shared between two teams, each team receives a score of one-half (.5) for the season, etc. Thus, in the table showing the titles won by decades, the totals will add up to the number of season the conference has been in existence.

The final section of the book provides supplementary information on the history of major college football. There is a listing of the game scores of all the bowl games that have been played, over their histories, for the twenty-eight bowls that were active in the 2003 season. There also are scattered scores given for games played in bowls that are now defunct or inactive. In particular, the listing given here covers all of the major bowl games played by any of the 149 teams whose major college playing history is given in this book. Of the inactive bowls, the listing given here is complete for the All American Bowl, the Bluebonnet Bowl, the Freedom Bowl, and the Micron.com bowl. The histories of the other inactive bowls are fragmentary and incomplete. The national rankings of teams by the various sources noted earlier are given for all seasons from 1924 through the 2003 season, along with the listing of the national champions between 1883 and 1935 as chosen by the Helms Hall of Fame. This is followed by a listing of the game scores of all the bowl games that have been played, over their histories, for the twenty-eight bowls that were active in the 2003 season. There also are scattered scores given for games played in bowls that are now defunct or inactive. In particular, the listing given here covers all of the major bowl games played by any of the 149 teams whose major college playing history is given in this book. Of the inactive bowls, the listing given here is complete for the All

American Bowl, the Bluebonnet Bowl, the Freedom Bowl, and the Micron.com Bowl. The histories of the other inactive bowls are fragmentary and incomplete.

The first All American team was selected in 1889. For years, it was assumed that the selection of that team was by Walter Camp. However, in 1950, research revealed that the first All American team had in fact been selected by a friend of Camp's named Casper Whitney. It was not until 1897 that a team picked by Camp appeared in print. Following this year, Camp published his selections (first, second, and third teams) every year through 1924. Camp died in 1925. When Camp died, sportswriter Grantland Rice was chosen by Colliers magazine to continue on the Camp tradition, by selecting an All American team each year. Rice did this from 1925 through 1947, and Rice's teams, like Camp's before him, were the most prestigious teams chosen. In the All American section of this book, the Camp (or Camp-Whitney) selections from 1889 through 1924 are given, followed by the Grantland Rice teams from 1925 through 1947. For the period 1948–1994, the consensus All American teams picked by David Wilson are listed. The AP All American teams are listed for the period 1995 through 2003.

Supplementing the All American section is one dealing with a listing of those players who won distinction as recipients of nationally recognized player awards. The awards or trophies included in this book were voted to the most outstanding player of the season in the following categories:

Sammy Baugh Trophy	passer
Dick Butkus Award	linebacker
Walter Camp Award	player
Lou Groza Award	place kicker
Ray Guy Award	punter
John Heisman Trophy	player
Ted Hendricks Award	defensive end
Vince Lombardi Award	lineman
John Mackey Award	tight end
Maxwell Award	player
Bronko Nagurski Award	defensive player
Davey O'Brien Award	quarterback
Outland Trophy	interior lineman
Dave Rimington Trophy	center
Mosi Tatupu Award	special teams player
Jim Thorpe Award	defensive back
John Unitas Award	senior quarterback
Doak Walker Award	running back

Following the player awards section, there is a listing of the national rankings of teams for each year from 1924 through 2003, together with a listing of the Helms Hall of Fame mythical national champions between 1883 and 1935. The final topic covered in the book is a summary of some of the more significant rules changes that have taken place over the history of college football.

The focus of the book is on the won-loss records of teams, conferences, and coaches, and the idea behind the book was to collect in one place the all time won-loss records of every major college team and every major college conference in the history of the sport. This is admittedly a "bare bones" approach to the recorded history of college football, and one that does not attempt to look at the records of the great players of the game, or at the many important non-quantitative aspects of the history of the sport. To partially compensate for this, and to provide an introduction to the collection of team and conference records, a very brief "summary history" of college football is provided following this introduction.

The main sources for the data presented here are the media guides published annually by all major college teams, and the media guides published by the major college football conferences. I wish to express my appreciation for the generosity of the many athletic departments and conferences that provided media guides when they were informed of the nature of the research that was being undertaken. George Rudd, curator of the

INTRODUCTION

Joyce Sports Library at Notre Dame, was especially helpful in unearthing comparable information for those schools no longer fielding major college teams, and Kent Stephens of the College Football Hall of Fame was of great assistance in this matter as well. Personal visits to a number of those schools always met with complete cooperation, which is much appreciated. The information on service team records comes from the *Official NCAA Football Guides* for the years 1942 through 1945, copies of which are held at the Joyce Sports Library. Data on the most recent season records are from the NCAA football Web site, and the most recent bowl results also come from that Web site.

Other helpful sources were the many team Web sites, the NCAA Directory of member teams and conferences and the Directory of the American Football Coaches Association.

Earlier compilations of data on team and conference records that were drawn on for this volume include Dr. H. L. Baker, *Football: Facts and Figures*, New York: Farrar and Rinehart, 1945, and Harold Claassen and Steve Boda,*The Encyclopedia of Football, 3rd edition*, New York: Ronald Press, 1963. Among the team histories that were also valuable in compiling the information here should be mentioned John S. Steckbeck, *Fabulous Redmen: The Carlisle Indians and Their Famous Football Teams*, Harrisburgh, PA: J. Horace McFarland, 1951, and Robin Lester, *Stagg's University*, Champaign-Urbana, Illinois: University of Illinois Press, date unknown. Other helpful sources include John D. McCallum and Charles Pearson, *College Football USA, 1869–1971, Official Book of the National Football Foundation*, Hall of Fame Publishing, 1971, and Tug Wilson and Jerry Brondfield, *The Big Ten*, Englewood Cliffs, N.J.: Prentice Hall, 1967. The Helms Foundation selections of national champions come from the 1991 *Information Please Sports Almanac*, Mike Meserole, editor, Burlington, Mass.; Houghton Miflin. The AP and UPI rankings are those compiled by Patrick Dunn and Chris Stassen, as they appear on the Internet home page of RSFC. Bowl game histories are taken from the team media guides, supplemented by the information compiled by David Krysakowski that appears on the RSFC home page. Information on membership in the College Football Hall of Fame is from the Hall of Fame Internet Web site.

As noted, those final sections of the book summarizing historical data on rankings, All American teams, and player awards, are for the most part taken directly from Dave Wilson's authoritative and carefully researched Web site, RSFC home page, a gold mine for any student of college football history. An especially valuable source for early All American teams is Bernie McCarty, *All America: The Complete Roster of Football's Heroes, Volume One: 1889–1945*, privately printed, University Park, Illinois, 1991, a book provided to me by Dick Parker.

In the earliest stages of the research on this book, Dick Parker's help was invaluable in providing data sources that got me over the first hurdles in collecting material for this book. I also want to thank Ray Schmidt, President of the College Football Historical Society, for his suggestions. Quentin Quirk's editorial comments, encouragement and work on the non-Division I-A teams are much appreciated, and Bill Quirk also helped out with the Service Teams. I also want to express my thanks to Dick Wentworth and Kris Ding of the University of Illinois Press, and their cohorts, for their valiant work in shepherding the manuscript through the publication process.

My wife, Shirley Quirk, took on the thankless and time-consuming job of proofreading the many tables that appear in the book. I am pretty sure this was not what she was thinking of when she said that the two of us should spend more time together, but she did a careful and conscientious job that added immeasurably to the book. It couldn't have been written without her.

PART I

A Summary History of College Football

The history of college football begins with that famous first game between Rutgers and Princeton, back on November 6, 1869. But the game that was played on that memorable day had only a nodding acquaintance with football as we know it today, being played with a rugby ball and with rules against running with the ball or throwing it. The history of college football is in part a history of the changes in the rules for playing the game that have transformed football since that initial Rutgers-Princeton game. Some of the more notable of those rules changes are listed in a later section of this book. But, more importantly, the history of college football is a history of the great teams that have played the sport, and of the players, coaches, and others, who have had a significant impact on the development of the game. Beyond this, there are political, economic, and social factors that, in some striking instances, have also acted to shape the game and the way it is played. In a brief history such as this, it is not possible to go into much detail concerning these matters, but it is hoped that at least a broad outline of the history of college football can be sketched out.

For the first fifteen years or so of college football history, football was pretty much an Ivy League thing, with a few other Eastern schools, such as Rutgers and NYU, fielding teams as well. Even within the Ivy League, schedules were short—four or five games a season until the 1880s—and these were definitely student-run teams, with the team captain taking on any coaching chores. During this development period, the rules of the game of football were being written by student-players from the Ivy League schools. By 1883, most of the essential elements of the modern game of football had been incorporated into the rules of the game. At the most fundamental level, the other Ivy schools accepted part at least of Harvard's version of football, one that allowed running with the ball, however, passing was still illegal. Teams fielded eleven players on a side, rules were in place for maintaining possession of the ball (three downs to make five yards), dimensions of the playing field (close to the present day ones) had been established, points had been assigned to scoring plays, and games were to be played subject to a time limit (90 minutes at the time), introducing the tension and excitement of time pressures into play. And, as proof that the players knew what they were doing in their rules-making, the game of football began to spread across the entire country.

One of the student-athletes who had a hand in writing the early rules was an individual named Walter Camp, who had captained his Yale team in the early 1880s. Camp became the first designated coach of a Yale team in 1888 and compiled an almost impeccable 67-2-0 record in his five years of coaching the Elis. Of all team sports, college football is arguably the one best described as a "coach's sport," and Walter Camp became the first in the honored line of great college football coaches. But Camp was much more than that. He was the leading architect of the rules changes that took place in football over the next thirty years, and he also produced his annual selection of an All American team of college players, the most prestigious All American teams of his era. The Camp All American selections (1889–1924) are given later in this book.

Much later on, the Helms Foundation selected mythical national champions for the early years of college football. Three of Camp's five Yale teams (1888, 1891, 1892) appear on the Helms Foundation list. These were impressive teams. Among Camp's players was the first true superstar of college football, "Pudge" Hefflefinger, a lineman of such ability that, for the next fifty years and more, Heff was a shoo-in choice at guard on any All-Time, All American team. Hefflefinger is credited with inventing the "pulling guard" maneuver, was the first documented pro player in an 1892 game, coached briefly at Cal and at Minnesota, and, most notably, kept suiting up to play football and play it well, usually for charity events, until his last appearance in a game in Minneapolis in 1933, when he was a hale and hearty sixty-five. Also on Camp's teams were two individuals who would go on to become among the finest of the college coaches of the next generation—Amos Alonzo Stagg, who made his reputation in an historic forty-one-year career at the University of Chicago, and Henry Williams, whose powerful Minnesota Gopher teams of the first decades of the 1900s featured innovations such as Williams' "Minnesota shift."

Despite the fact that the sport was dominated by the elite Ivy League schools, the game that was being played up to the turn of the century was flat out brutal. Prior to a rules change in 1894, there was no requirement of a minimum number of players on the scrimmage line. This permitted formations such as the "flying wedge," in which ten players lined up in the backfield in a wedge surrounding a backfield man, with the center at the point of the wedge. The players in the wedge would lock arms and legs, and moved as a unit once the ball was centered. A favorite ploy for the center was to slug anyone in the jaw who tried to get at the ball carrier. In the melee that followed, both offensive and defensive players got mauled, injured, and sometimes killed.

Rules changes from 1894 on, setting limits on the number of players who could line up off the line of scrimmage, and rules outlawing linking of arms and legs in formations, acted over time to eliminate the wedge and the mayhem it was causing. Nonetheless, injuries and deaths continued to occur, because the essence of the game under the "three downs to make five yards" rule was to run rugby type "scrum"—direct over-the-center—plays with every player involved in pileups that were difficult for officials to police and were where most injuries occurred.

By the mid- to late-1880s, Ivy League schedules had expanded to eight or nine and up to fifteen games per season as the popularity of the sport grew for students, alums, and the general public. In the Midwest, the large publicly funded universities began to field teams—Michigan in 1879, Minnesota in 1882, Purdue in 1887. In 1896, seven of the leading Midwest universities—Chicago, Illinois, Michigan, Minnesota, Northwestern, Purdue, and Wisconsin—combined to form the first major college athletic conference, the Western Conference, with football being the featured attraction. Indiana and Iowa were added in 1900, and Ohio State in 1913, to make up what later became known as the Big Ten. In the South, college football came on the scene in the early 1890s, at Alabama, Georgia, and Georgia Tech, among other major Southern colleges. Football was even spreading to the West Coast, where California and Washington were fielding teams already by the late 1880s. By the early 1900s, most colleges in the country, major or minor, had football teams, and high school football was becoming a big spectator sport. Fall Saturdays became college football days, with Fridays reserved for the high schools. On Fall Sundays, semi-pro football teams (the so-called "independents") were beginning to stage their own games, in large cities and smaller ones, featuring ex-college and ex-high school stars, and before growing audiences. The Sunday metropolitan papers were adding sports sections, featuring detailed descriptions of football games involving local teams, as well as games of nationally recognized teams.

Given this rising public popularity of college football, President Theodore Roosevelt's condemnation of the brutality of the sport in a powerful speech given in 1905 was a bombshell. It triggered action to change the game to reduce the injuries and deaths that football, and especially college football, was causing. A number of the leading colleges in the country organized into a group called the Intercollegiate Athletic Association of the United States (name changed in 1910 to the National Collegiate Athletic Association). In January 1906, this group met with the football rules-making group headed by Walter Camp to devise changes in the rules to meet the objections raised by Roosevelt.

The 1906 changes to the rules of college football were truly revolutionary—football was a different game from this date on. The best known of the changes was the legalization of the forward pass, but actually the restrictions imposed on passing under the new rules, enumerated later in the book, were so severe that, initially at least, passing still represented only a minor part of the sport. More important at the time was the change from "three downs to make five yards" for a first down, to "three downs to make ten yards." This new provision forced teams to open up their games, because relying strictly on over-the-center plunges to gain five yards per play didn't make football sense. In addition, the new rules spelled

out roughness offenses and their penalties, designed to eliminate from the game the most dangerous actions of players.

There were other consequences of Roosevelt's criticisms. The Western Conference elected to de-emphasize football by mandating five-game schedules for all conference members. (Minnesota had played 13 games in 1904 and 11 in 1905, and Michigan had played 13 in 1905 and 10 in 1904.) In 1907, Fielding Yost took Michigan out of the Western Conference, in part because of the restrictive new scheduling regulations, not to return until 1917. A number of major teams dropped football entirely for a period of time. Northwestern dropped football for 1906 and 1907; California replaced football with rugby between 1906 and 1914, and Stanford also fielded a rugby team in place of its football team, from 1906 through 1917. For those schools that continued to field football teams, there was a difficult adjustment period. Scoring was down, as coaches searched for offensive strategies to meet the difficult new ball possession rules. (In fact, the possession rule of "three plays to make ten yards" caused so many problems that it was replaced by the present "four plays to make ten yards" in 1912.)

Prior to the enactment of the 1906 rules, the standard offensive formation used by essentially all college teams was the T-formation, with the quarterback over the center and the other backfield men lined up a couple of yards behind him. Line bucks and off tackle plays were most teams' bread and butter plays. With the new rules in place, there was a need to add more variety to the offense, and there were new offensive formations available to meet this need, the most important being an invention of Glenn "Pop" Warner, one of the most creative offensive thinkers in the history of football. The new formation was the single wing, a formation that effectively replaced the T as the leading offensive formation in college football for the next forty years.

In the single wing to the right formation, the tailback (usually the left halfback) stood three to five yards directly behind the center, with the fullback a step or two to his right and a yard or so ahead of him. The quarterback was positioned a yard or so behind the right guard, and the right halfback (the wingback) was stationed a yard or so behind the right end. Play started with a direct snap from the center, usually to the tailback, who could run an off-tackle play to the right, or an end sweep, or he could fade back and pass the ball to an end or a backfield man, or hand the ball off on a reverse to the right half or to an end on an end-around play. One advantage of the single wing over the T is that it concentrated the blocking power of the team on the side of the field where most of the plays were run. To add to that power, some teams, including Williams' Minnesota teams, used an unbalanced line with four or sometimes even five linemen to the right of the center, with a pulling guard plus the three non-ball carrying backfield men available for blocking as well. For the era, one in which field position was deemed critical to victory, another advantage of the single wing was that it was an ideal formation for a "quick kick" by the tailback, in an attempt to catch the defense unaware, to put them deep in their own territory.

Pop Warner devised the single wing (and the double wing as well) while he was coaching at Carlisle Institute, one of the first small schools to make its mark in the history of college football. Carlisle played a major college schedule during Warner's years with the team (1899–1903, 1906–14), and featured at halfback one of the storied American athletes of all time, Jim Thorpe. Warner's success at Carlisle led to a nine-year stint at Pittsburgh (1915–23), where he had two mythical national championship teams (1916, 1917); and this was followed by another highly successful tour of duty at Stanford (1924–32), where he won yet another national championship (1926),

and coached another backfield legend, Ernie Nevers.

But, right up to World War I, Ivy League teams continued to dominate college football, under outstanding coaches such as George Woodruff at Penn (1892–1901) and Percy Haughton at Harvard (1908–16). Ivy League schools were Helms Foundation selections for all the mythical national championships between 1883 and 1899, were awarded six for the 1900–1909 decade, and six more for the decade between 1910 and 1919. The schools breaking through the Ivy League lock were Michigan (1901 and 1902), Chicago (1905), Army (1914), Georgia Tech (1918), and Warner's two Pittsburgh champions. Fielding Yost's 1902 Wolverine team became famous as the "point a minute" team, scoring 644 points to 12 for its opponents. Between 1901 and 1905, Yost had a record of 55-1-1, the tie coming in an historic 1903 game against Minnesota, 6-6, and the 1905 loss was to Amos Alonzo Stagg's national championship University of Chicago team, 2-0. Meanwhile, out on the West Coast, there was another coach, Gil Dobie, making a reputation for himself. Dobie coached at Washington for nine years (1908–16) and posted a never-to-be-surpassed record of 58-0-3, nine undefeated seasons in a row. If it is thought that this might have been due solely to the relatively weak schedule that the Dawgs played, this was put to rest when Dobie went on to coach Cornell to three undefeated seasons in a row (1921–23), winning two national championships (1921, 1922) along the way.

The Dobie championships at Cornell marked the end of the road for Ivy League domination of football, with Midwestern and Western schools emerging as national powers. Bob Zuppke's Illini teams of the 1920s still played T-formation football, but with wacky plays with names like "the Flying Trapeze," which ". . . involved a man in motion, a direct snap from center, a shovel pass, a lateral, and then a long forward pass downfield—often for a touchdown" (Tug Wilson and Jerry Brondfield, *The Big Ten*, Englewood Cliffs, NJ: Prentice Hall, 1967, p. 91). Zuppke managed to parlay his inventiveness into two national championship teams in the 1920s (1923, 1927), although, of course, it helped that the first title team featured one of the best backs of all time, and certainly among the most charismatic, number 77, Red Grange. Meanwhile, down in Tuscaloosa, Alabama, the South was heard from, as Wallace Wade coached the Crimson Tide to the first of the school's many national championships, with undefeated seasons in 1925 and 1926. Wade went on to more successes in the 1930s, when his Duke Blue Devils dominated the Southern Conference.

Most importantly, the 1920s saw the emergence of the Notre Dame Fighting Irish as a major power in college football under coach Knute Rockne. It might have been because of its great record, it might have been because it was a small school, it might have been because of Rockne's appeal, and it might have been because of the "Irish" nickname (in our family, we say that everyone either is Irish or wishes they were Irish). In any case, almost overnight, Notre Dame became the favorite of everyone who didn't already have a favorite college team, and Rockne became the standard by which all other coaches were measured. In 1919, George Gipp became the first Notre Dame player to be chosen a Walter Camp All-American, and then there was the 1924 team featuring a backfield of the Four Horsemen (christened by sportswriter Grantland Rice)—Harry Stuhldreher, Elmer Layden, Don Miller, and Jim Crowley—and the first Irish national championship. Rockne's 1929 team put together another undefeated season, most impressive because the team played all of its games on the road due to the stadium construction going on in South Bend. Notre Dame won back-to-back mythical national championships in 1929 and 1930, using a running attack featuring Rockne's "Notre Dame box" formation, a balanced line, and the "Notre Dame shift" involving the backfield men and the flaring of the ends. The Rockne era came to a tragic end in early 1931 when Rockne was killed in a plane crash.

Out on the West coast, Andy Smith brought California an undefeated team in 1920 and followed that with undefeated seasons in 1921, 1922, and 1923. But in the mid- to late-1920s and early 1930s, the rising power on the Pacific coast was Southern California. Coach Howard Jones had won a national title at Yale in 1909, and had produced two undefeated Big Ten title teams at Iowa in 1921 and 1923. While coaching at USC (1925–40), Jones won national titles in 1928, 1931, 1932, and 1939, setting winning standards that John McKay (1960–75) and John Robinson (1976–82) carried on in future years.

In the East, the dominant team in the 1920s and 1930s was the Pittsburgh Panthers, under coach Jock Sutherland, who had compiled an impressive record at Lafayette before taking over for Pop Warner at Pitt. The Panthers played the toughest schedule in college football during the Sutherland years (1924–38), featuring games with powerhouses of the time such as Notre Dame, Fordham, Minnesota, and Nebraska. Despite this, Sutherland's teams managed to win more than 80 percent of their games over his years at the school. Pitt was an independent during an era in which player eligibility rules and player compensation arrangements were determined, not by the NCAA, but by conferences or by independent schools themselves, and Sutherland's era at the school was marred by controversy concerning this. Pittsburgh was the undisputed national champion in 1937 and was invited to the January 1, 1938 Rose Bowl. A scandal erupted when it was reported that the Pitt players were striking to demand extra pay to play the post-season game, and an investigation by the *Saturday Evening Post* revealed that Pitt had been paying its players all through the Sutherland years. Sutherland left for the NFL after the 1938 season, following the announcement that the University of Pittsburgh had decided to operate the football program under the strict Big Ten rules, which, among other things, forbade pay for players.

Even with USC and Pittsburgh in the picture, the depression years of the 1930s leading up to World War II were the years when the Big Ten took over the spotlight in college football. Fielding Yost was now the athletic director and not the coach, but his student, Harry Kipke, coached the Wolverines to two national titles (1932, shared with USC, and 1933), using his "a punt, a pass, and a prayer" offense and a bone-crushing defense. Over in Minneapolis, it was Henry Williams's protégé, Bernie Bierman, returning to Minnesota from a very successful stay at Tulane (1927–31), and bringing with him a reputation for hard-nosed, close to the vest, single wing football. Actually, Bierman had a few tricks in his offense, too, including his "buck lateral" sequence off the single wing, something that was a predecessor of sorts to the ball handling in the split-T of the future. Bierman's Golden Gophers won five national championships in just eight years (1934, 1935, 1936, 1940, 1941), and the 1934 Gopher squad is still ranked among the best in the history of football.

Beyond the seven national titles between 1932 and 1941, the strength of the Big Ten also showed in the Heisman Trophy selections, which were inaugurated in 1935. The first winner of the Heisman was Jay Berwanger of the University of Chicago, a star on an out-manned team coached by the peripatetic Clark Shaughnessy (1933–39), another of Henry Williams' ex-players. Shaughnessy replaced Amos Alonzo Stagg when Stagg was forced to retire by University of Chicago president Hutchins because of his age. Stagg went on to coach at the College of the Pacific (1933–

46), doing well enough that he was named college football coach of the year in his last year at that school, still performing as a head coach when he was 81 years old. Big Ten players went on to win the Heisman in 1939, 1940, and 1941—Nile Kinnick of Iowa in 1939, Tommy Harmon of Michigan in 1940, and Bruce Smith of Minnesota in 1941.

Generally speaking, the Big Ten teams of the pre-World War II years featured single wing running attacks, with passing pretty much a rare and relatively ineffective part of the offense, although there were some exceptions. During Francis Schmidt's years as coach at Ohio State (1934–40), the Buckeyes ran a wide-open offense including a strong passing attack, and Cecil Isbell of Purdue and Otto Graham of Northwestern were noted passers even in their college days, both out of a single wing formation. But the days of the single wing were numbered as the 1930s came to an end. The University of Chicago had dropped football after the 1939 season, and Clark Shaughnessy, whose list of coaching jobs seems endless, took his impressive offensive skills out to the Pacific Coast Conference for 1940. What he brought with him was a new-old formation, the (modern) T-formation, as played by the Chicago Bears, with some wrinkles that Shaughnessy had added to the Bear offense.

The modern T-formation resembled the old in that the focus was shifted from the tailback in the single wing, to the quarterback in the T. The backfield lined up with the quarterback directly over the center, and with the three other backs lined up a couple of yards in back of the quarterback. The quarterback took the ball from the center, and spun to hand the ball off to one of the backs, or faded back to pass the ball, or ran the ball himself, perhaps on an option play. What was different from the old fashioned T of the early 1900s was that, on almost every play, a backfield man went in motion before the ball was snapped, to be ready for a pitch from the quarterback, or to catch a pass from him. Shaughnessy's contribution to the offense was to line one end split out from the tackle, to put a backfield man in motion in the opposite direction, and then to run plays toward the side of the split end. This version of the T caused havoc for defenders because of its quick opening plays, and it created problems in trying to find out who had the ball, and where it was going to go. With Frankie Albert at quarterback and Norm Standlee at fullback, Shaughnessy's 1940 Stanford team tore up the Pacific Coast Conference, and beat a very good Nebraska team in the 1941 Rose Bowl game.

The success of the 1940 Stanford team, combined with the Chicago Bears' 73-0 rout of the Washington Redskins in the 1940 NFL championship game, had college and pro coaches alike making plans to learn the modern T, especially when they discovered that, beyond the enhanced speed and deception of the plays of the new formation, another big advantage was that it was much easier to teach, especially with regard to blocking assignments. The handwriting was on the wall for the single wing, but the changeover to the T in college football was delayed because of the disruptions caused by the entry of the United States into World War II.

World War II brought on some fundamental changes in college football. In the pre-war years, college football was still operating under "limited substitution" rules, which at the time prevented a player from returning to the game in the same quarter in which he was replaced by a substitute. In the rules committee meetings in early 1941, before Pearl Harbor, it was already recognized that the supply of players was going to be curtailed because of the ongoing military draft. To help solve this problem, the substitution rule was changed to allow a player to return after one play at any time in the game. Along with the change to "unlimited substitution," the long-standing and

almost unenforceable rule against communication between a substitute and his teammates on the field was also effectively dropped. From now on, it would be the coaches and not the players who would call the plays, and the game would be controlled from the bench. Needless to say, coaches were almost universally in favor of the new substitution rule.

Perhaps the NFL owners could foresee what was coming and were aware of the potential increase in player costs, because the NFL was more reluctant about the matter and didn't change its rules to permit unlimited substitution until the 1943 season. Two years later, in 1945, Michigan became the first team to use the new rule to institute "two-platoon" football, fielding specialized offensive and defensive teams, a move that is generally credited to Biggie Munn, at the time an assistant to head coach Fritz Crisler. Most pro teams were playing two-platoon football a year or two later.

During World War I, a number of major colleges had dropped their football programs, in part because of problems caused by the draft, and later because of the 1918 flu pandemic. There were some major colleges that dropped football in World War II for a time as well, including Stanford (1943–45), Tennessee (1943), and Syracuse (1943), but most major college programs continued to operate, albeit with ongoing problems in staffing coaching positions and fielding respectable teams. One solution to the player-manpower problem for favored schools was the Navy V-12 program, inaugurated in 1943. This was a program for developing officer candidates, under which recruits were provided with a speeded-up college education along with naval science courses. The Navy permitted and even encouraged intercollegiate athletic activities by recruits, including playing college football. Favored schools, such as Notre Dame, Northwestern, and Michigan, ended up with star student-athletes as transfers from other major teams. Adding to the benefits of the V-12 program, eligibility rules were generally relaxed during the war to permit essentially any registered student-athlete to suit up for play. Thus, for example, in 1943, Bill Daley, who had played three years at Minnesota, was assigned to a V-12 program at Michigan, and earned All-American honors there in his fourth year of play.

Another feature of the war years was the organization of football teams at military bases and training facilities around the country. The schedules of these teams ran the gamut from games with the teams from other military bases, through games against junior college teams and the B teams of four-year colleges, to a schedule of games against the top college teams in the country. Some service teams even included one or two pro teams on their schedules. The best of the service teams, teams such as Great Lakes, coached by Tony Hinkle and later by Paul Brown, and the Iowa Seahawks, coached by Bernie Bierman and later by Don Faurot and Jack Meagher, vied for the national championships during the war years of 1942 through 1944. There is a listing, later in this book, of the records of roughly 130 service teams during the World War II years.

The war years, with 13 million young men in the service, saw a drastic decline in attendance at college football games. Still, even with so many men in the armed services, the war years and their immediate aftermath produced some outstanding teams, headed by Earl Blaik's Army teams of 1944, 1945, and 1946, starring Glenn Davis, Doc Blanchard, Barney Poole, and Arnold Galiffa. These teams chalked up a combined record of 27-0-1, along with two national championships (1944, 1945). At South Bend, Frank Leahy had replaced Elmer Layden in 1941, after two years at Boston College, where Leahy put together a 20-2-0 record, including an undefeated 1940 season. Leahy's career at Notre Dame spanned

eleven years, and included four national championship years in the 1940s (1943, 1946, 1947, and 1949) along with a winning percentage of .855, just below Knute Rockne's record with the Irish, and earned against tougher opponents.

The post-war years saw a resurgence of interest in college football with attendance records being broken at many major colleges. There also was a new source of revenue for the major college teams from the sale of television rights to games. The added revenue helped to offset a big increase in expenses for football programs, because, by 1947 or 1948, most major teams were playing "two-platoon" football, football squads were doubling in size (and more), and coaching staffs were expanding as well. For the big schools, this was just an inconvenience. For the small independents, football got priced out of the picture by the increased cost of fielding a team, coupled with the loss of ticket sales because of competition from the televising of major college games. To add to the independents' problems, for the first time in its history, the NCAA announced and began enforcing national standards for recruiting, eligibility, and compensation of players, standards much stricter than those that had been employed by a number of the smaller independents.

Carnegie Tech, which had been a power in the East in the 1920s and 1930s, and had played some memorable games against Notre Dame, went to a small school schedule in 1946. Duquesne, another Pittsburgh independent, had had nationally ranked teams in the 1930s, under coaches Clipper Smith and Buff Donelli, but the Dukes dropped football after the 1950 season. Fordham, a pre-war Eastern power under coach Jim Crowley, was out of football after the 1954 season. Georgetown cancelled its football program after the 1950 season, and NYU's football team was gone by 1953. On the West coast, St. Mary's, famed for its long-term rivalry with Fordham, dropped football after the 1950 season, and its neighbor in the Bay Area, Santa Clara, followed after the 1952 season.

San Francisco, with an undefeated team under Joe Kuharich that was ranked fourteenth in the country in 1951, gave up the ghost after that season. Two-platoon football, TV, and the new NCAA rules had wreaked havoc on the small school independents.

Between 1940 and 1949, Minnesota won two national titles, Army won two, Notre Dame four, and the remaining two were won by Big Ten teams under Hall of Fame coaches, Ohio State in 1942 under Paul Brown, and Michigan in 1948 under Bennie Oosterbaan, in Oosterbaan's first year after succeeding Fritz Crisler. It is of interest that, while Notre Dame was definitely a T-formation team, the other teams were still primarily single wing teams, using the T-formation sparingly. In the main, Oosterbaan was still using Crisler's interesting variant of the single wing, in which there were two tailbacks, the fullback and a halfback, stationed three or four yards behind the center. After the ball was centered to one of these, each would spin towards the other, hiding the ball from defenders. Crisler's double-spin offense was particularly effective with two multi-talented backs (say, as in 1940, with Bob Westfall and Tommy Harmon as tailbacks).

Thus the single wing wasn't quite dead as the decade of the 1940s came to an end, but the T-formation was being used by more and more teams, and, in another important development, passing was coming to the fore. In the pre-war days, passing was often a desperation tactic, so that, when passes were attempted, there was little deception concerning what was going to happen, and passes tended to be long bombs, with low completion rates. In the offenses that were gearing up in the early post-war years, passing was being used simply to make first downs, not just to win ball games, and the T, with its deception and its quick opening plays, was ideally suited to short passing plays.

The decade of the 1950s was a particularly interesting one for college football. After experimenting with unlimited substitution for twelve years, college football returned to limited substitution rules and "one-platoon" football, beginning in the 1953 season, and restrictions were also imposed on the televising of games, both moves being designed as responses to the financial problems that were being experienced by the small independents, and by lower division teams as well. One-platoon football would be the rule for twelve years. In 1965, college football dropped one-platoon rules for good, going back to two-platoon football, in response to the competition that pro football, playing under two-platoon rules, was posing for ticket sales and TV rights dollars at major college football programs around the country.

The 1950s are of interest as well because of the wide variety of approaches to the game that were being applied successfully, by a new crop of bright young coaches, at schools, none of which had won a title before. Moreover, signaling a regional shift in the distribution of football strength, schools from the Plains States and from the South were in the list of title winners. Out in the Plains, it was Bud Wilkinson at Oklahoma, a Bernie Bierman product, simply running away with the Big Seven Conference with his split-T offense, something he had learned while assisting Don Farout at Iowa Pre-Flight back in 1943. Wilkinson's Sooners won thirteen Big Seven titles in a row (1947–59), and were national champions in 1950, 1955, and 1956. Turning to the West Coast, Red Sanders at UCLA was proving that there was still some life left in the old single wing, as his Bruin teams were ranked in the top ten from 1952 through 1955, winning a national title in 1954. Another more eclectic approach was taken by Biggie Munn at Michigan State (1947–53). Munn's teams used a multiple offense, mixing in T-formation and single wing plays, including a liberal use of Bierman's buck lateral plays, to confuse defenses. Michigan State was the national champion in 1952 and had continuing success under Munn's successor, Duffy Daugherty (1954–72). There was one other new face in Big Ten coaching ranks. After putting in two years at Miami (Ohio), the "cradle of coaches," Woody Hayes arrived at Ohio State in 1951 to provide Buckeye fans with twenty-eight years of "three yards and a cloud of dust" winning football, including national titles in 1954, 1957, and 1968. And, in the East, it was Ben Schwartzwalder's Syracuse Orangemen winning a title in 1959.

For the first time since the mid-1920s, when Alabama won two successive titles, the 1950s saw Southern national champs, four of them in all—Tennessee in 1951, Maryland in 1953, Auburn in 1957 shared with Ohio State, and LSU in 1959. Bud Wilkinson got his chance at Oklahoma because the previous coach, Jim Tatum, had left after just one year to take a job at Maryland. Tatum stayed with the Terrapins for nine years (1947–58), and coached an undefeated team in 1951 together with that national championship team in 1953. Auburn's coach was the legendary Shug Jordan, who coached at the school for twenty-five years, producing an undefeated team in 1957 and outstanding teams in most other years as well. At LSU, it was Paul Dietzel who won a national title in 1958 during his relatively short stay in Baton Rouge (1956–61).

Finally, the 1950s also saw a national title for an old timer who, like Red Sanders, still coached single-wing football. This was General Robert Neyland, whose coaching career at Tennessee spanned twenty-one years, broken up by service in World War II. Neyland's last three years with the Vols (1950–52) involved teams that had top ten national rankings, to cap off one of the most illustrious coaching careers in the history of college football, and to establish a winning tradition at the school that has been carried on to the present.

The 1950s also saw the beginnings of the civil rights movement that finally destroyed publicly enforced segregation in the American South. Among the many consequences of the new social and political order, universities—both public and private—were opened up for the first time to enrollment by blacks and other racial minorities. The elimination of segregation did not end racism, but it was an essential first step in moving towards that elusive goal.

The shameful racism of professional sports up to World War II and beyond is well documented. Blacks were barred from baseball until 1947, when Branch Rickey of the Dodgers brought Jackie Robinson up from Montreal to break baseball's color barrier. In pro football, there were black players in the 1920s, but later, supposedly because of the racial attitudes of George Marshall, owner of the Washington Redskins, the NFL instituted an unofficial ban on black players. This ban was only lifted in the early post-war years because of the competition posed for the NFL by a new pro league, the All American Football Conference, which featured star black players.

The history of college football is a little more mixed. There were a handful of great black players in the early history of college football, including College Football Hall of Famers Bobby Marshall of Minnesota, a second team Walter Camp All American in 1906; Fritz Pollard of Brown, a 1916 first team Walter Camp All American; Paul Robeson of Rutgers, a first team Walter Camp All American in 1918, Duke Slater of Iowa, a second team Walter Camp All American in 1922, Brud Holland of Cornell, an All American in 1938; and Kenny Washington of UCLA, All American in 1939. Iowa in particular was known in the 1920s and 1930s as a school that made black players welcome. But almost all of the major Southern schools had lily-white student bodies and lily-white teams.

What was particularly shameful about the pre-war years was that, when Southern schools played

Northern schools, the universal practice was for the Northern schools to bench any black players, so as to not offend the Southern teams. In 1935, when national champion Minnesota played Tulane in Minneapolis, first string Minnesota end Dwight Reed, a black player, was announced as being "injured." Instead of playing, he acted as a spotter for a radio announcer. A year later, Minnesota played Texas in Minneapolis, and both Reed and guard Horace Bell, the two black players on the Gopher team, were benched. In an interview fifty years later, Reed said that he had gone to Athletic Director Frank McCormick to complain about the practice, and he said that McCormick promised him it would never happen again. Reed went on to say that, even before he left school in 1937, the Gophers had again withdrawn black athletes, this time in a track meet involving a Southern school.

After the 1940 season, Boston College was invited to play in the Sugar Bowl on January 1, 1941. BC, under coach Frank Leahy, accepted the invitation, as well as the condition imposed on the team of benching a star black player. Even the coaches at the very top of their profession, heading nationally ranked teams, and with no bias against using black players themselves, coaches such as Bierman and Leahy, simply caved in to the demands of the Southern schools. But this, of course, pales in comparison with events such as "the Johnny Bright incident." Johnny Bright was a black player, a star halfback at Drake, and the national college rushing leader in 1949 and 1950. On October 20, 1951, Drake played Missouri Valley Conference rival Oklahoma State at Stillwater, Oklahoma. For a week before the game, there were reports in the local newspaper about the possibility of racial flare-ups. Early in the game, Bright was tackled by an Aggies player. While Bright was down, the player slugged him in the face so hard that he broke Bright's jaw. As luck would have it, there was a cameraman

filming the play, and he caught all of the action. The picture of the slugging was published throughout the country and won the cameraman a Pulitzer prize. Drake withdrew from the MVC after the incident, which was clearly racially motivated. The good thing about the incident is that it brought to the fore the racial problems that plagued college football at the time and put pressures on universities around the country to reform their racial attitudes and racial practices, including those involving their football programs. Johnny Bright went on to a record-breaking career in the Canadian Football League.

Besides the return of two-platoon football, the 1960s saw the emergence of a group of coaches who would dominate the sport around the country over the next twenty years and more. Heading the list is Bear Bryant, who played football at Alabama and began his coaching career with a one-year job at Maryland (1945). From 1946 through 1953, Bryant coached at Kentucky, posting a 60-23-5 record there. From Kentucky, Bryant moved to Texas A&M, coaching there from 1954 through 1957, with a record of 25-14-2. In 1958, Bryant came back home to Alabama, and coached at his alma mater for 25 years, 1958–82, winning national titles in 1961, 1964, 1965, 1973, 1978, and 1979, with a won-loss record of 232-46-9. Bryant's 323 career wins topped the previous record for a major college coach, held by Amos Alonzo Stagg, and his six national titles remain the most earned by any coach in the history of college football.

Prior to the 1960s, the Southwest Conference had never won a national title. That changed when Darrell Royal was hired as coach of the Texas Longhorns in 1957. Royal had been Bud Wilkinson's quarterback on his Sooner teams of the late 1940s, and he had put in time coaching at Mississippi State, Edmonton of the CFL, and the University of Washington before coming to Texas. Royal spent twenty years as a coach in

Austin, winning eleven SWC titles, and three national championships (1963, 1969, 1970). The 1960s also saw a resurgence of Trojan football under John McKay, who coached at USC for sixteen years (1960–75). McKay's teams became famous for their outstanding tailbacks—Mike Garrett and O. J. Simpson being the best—running those "student body right" and "student body left" plays. USC won the national title four times under McKay, in 1962, 1967, 1972, and 1974.

The other four national championship teams in the 1960s were from the Midwest. Woody Hayes won his third and final title in 1968, Duffy Daughtery led Michigan State to a national championship in 1965, and Murray Warmath won a title for Minnesota in 1960, to account for the three Big Ten national titles, the last the conference would win for thirty years, until the 1997 season. And Notre Dame, under coach Ara Parseghian, won a championship in 1966 (and then added another for the Irish in 1973). Parseghian joined Woody Hayes in the list of outstanding coaches who had gotten their start in coaching at Miami of Ohio. After his years at Miami, Parseghian moved on, first to Northwestern, and then to Notre Dame.

We might also mention several other coaches who became nationally known in the 1960s without winning a title in that decade, but who fashioned long, highly successful careers. The most impressive of these, of course, is Joe Paterno. Paterno played his college ball at Brown, but has done all of his coaching at Penn State. After years as an assistant to Rip Engle, Paterno took over the Nittany Lions in 1966, and, thirty-eight years later, was still the head coach in State College. His lifetime record after the 2003 season was 339-109-3, for a winning percentage of .755, with nationally ranked teams in thirty-one of thirty-eight years, and with national championships in 1982 and 1986. For a brief time at least, Paterno had the most wins ever for a major college coach, and, as of late 2003, the curtains had not yet been drawn on his career.

A second of these coaches bursting onto the scene in the 1960s was Bo Schembechler, someone who, like Hayes and Parseghian, had a Miami (Ohio) coaching background. Schembechler came to Michigan in 1969 and coached the Wolverines through the 1989 season. While Michigan did not win a national championship during his years at the school, Schembechler's teams were nationally ranked in twenty of his twenty-one years at Michigan and won outright or tied for fourteen Big Ten titles.

Another coach who would make his impressive mark on the game was Bob Devaney. Devaney first made himself known to football fans while coaching at Wyoming (1957–61), winning four Skyline Conference titles in his five years with the Cowboys. In 1962, Devaney moved to Nebraska and completely turned around a program that had been in the doldrums for twenty years. In the 1920s and 1930s, Nebraska had been a national power, under coaches such as Dana X. Bible (1929–36) and Biff Jones (1937–41). By the time Devaney came to Lincoln, it had been twenty years since Nebraska had won a Big Eight (or Big Seven) title. His second year at Nebraska, Devaney had the Cornhuskers ranked fifth in the country, and he went on to win two national titles, in 1970 and 1971. He also deserves credit for the fact that, when he retired to the athletic director's post, he picked Tom Osborne to succeed him.

One thing that should be noted about the national championship teams of the 1960s is that, for the first time, black players were playing a prominent role on most of them. Murray Warmath's Southern background and contacts enabled Minnesota to recruit star black players on all of his teams, with Carl Eller, Bobby Bell, and Sandy Stephens being notable examples. Ernie Davis of Syracuse, and Mike Garrett and O. J. Simpson of USC were black Heisman Trophy winners in the

1960s, and the All American ranks of the decade were loaded with outstanding black players. The years since the 1960s have seen a complete turnaround from the past, with the number of black players on major college squads rising year after year, and with black players dominating the All American lists. The growing importance of black players, together with the integration of Southern universities and the high black population densities of Southern states, goes a long way towards explaining why it is that the South has overtaken the Midwest and the West in the production of championship football teams.

One other important factor impacting college football, beginning in the early 1960s, was the rise in the popularity and profitability of pro football. Prior to the 1960s, few college players, star players included, aimed at a career in the pros. The pros didn't pay very well, and the typical pro football career is a notoriously short one. But football, college or pro, is an ideal sport for television, and it was television money that changed the face of pro football in the early 1960s. Financed in large part by a lucrative TV contract, the American Football League came on the scene in 1960 as a rival to the NFL, which expanded its list of franchises to compete with the AFL. The NFL-AFL war more than doubled the demand for pro players and introduced some vigorous competition into the football player market. Added to that, the rise in TV and gate revenues also pushed player salaries up. Coupled with the fact that discrimination in the job market at the time limited the options of black players, more and more college players, especially black players, viewed their years at college as a kind of apprenticeship for their hoped-for career as a pro. Among other things, this played into the decision of the colleges to go back to two-platoon football in 1965, to provide training for a pro career in which the player would be a one-way specialist. The changeover of college football to an apprenticeship for the pros would also have consequences for

competitive balance in college football conferences, as we shall see.

In the 1970s, Bob Devaney started things off with his two national championship teams, playing a game that centered on the option play, behind a set of huge, tough Nebraska linemen. John McKay's USC teams, also built around a running attack, won titles in 1972 and 1974; and, after McKay had left for the pros, his successor, John Robinson, won a title in 1978 with a running team that included two future Heisman Trophy backs, Charles White and Marcus Allen. Hayes ended his career at Ohio State with a win percent of .755 (205-61-10), thirteen outright or tied Big Ten Titles, and three national titles.

At the administrative level, in 1975, the NCAA set up a divisional structure for college athletics, and in 1978, created Division I-A and Division I-AA in football. For the first time, teams had to make decisions as to whether they would meet the new NCAA requirements to qualify as "major" (Division I-A) football teams, or instead play what amounted to "small college" football. Similarly, new requirements were specified for classification as an I-A conference. One prominent conference, the Southern Conference, a major for much of its history, decided on a I-AA classification. NCAA requirements for I-A status were based on stadium size, average attendance at games, quality of schedule, number of athletic scholarships offered, and other matters. Teams have the option of applying for a change in classification at any time, and a number of teams have made the move to I-A status since 1978, including Marshall, Akron, Connecticut, Central Florida, Idaho, and Boise State, among other schools. One interesting difference between Divisions I-A and I-AA is that in Division I-AA, the national championship is decided by a post-season tournament, while the BCS (Bowl Championship Series) format (plus the national polls) determines the national champion for Division I-A.

In the 1980s, the South accounted for half of the national championships. Georgia, under Vince Dooley, won the 1980 title, behind the hard running Herschel Walker, who won the Heisman two years later. Dooley coached the Bulldogs for twenty-five years, and had just one losing season, despite coaching during a period when Bear Bryant's Alabama team was dominating the Southeastern Conference. Danny Ford took Clemson to the national title in 1981 with an undefeated season, in a twelve-year tour of duty that was marred by two years of NCAA suspensions (1983 and 1984).

Most importantly, the 1980s were the years when Florida-based teams began to dominate college football, with the Miami Hurricanes making the first moves in that direction. Miami was a latecomer to college football, fielding its first team in 1926. In the early post-World War II years, Andy Gustafson (1948–63) coached the first Miami teams that made the national rankings, but it was Howard Schnellenberger (1979–83), who put everything together for the 1983 undefeated season that won Miami its first national title. And then Schnellenberger was gone, taking at job at Louisville, and being replaced by Jimmy Johnson (1984–88), who turned out four top ten teams in his five years at Miami, including the 1987 national champion. But then Johnson was also gone, to the Dallas Cowboys. Johnson's successor, Dennis Erickson (1989–94), had had an unbroken record of success at Idaho and Washington State before coming to Miami. Johnson had put up a .852 winning record, and Erickson did even better, with an .868 mark, and two national titles, in 1989 and in 1991.

The other team with multiple national titles in the 1980s was Penn State, with Joe Paterno winning the mythical championship in 1982 and 1986. In 1984, the mountain states finally had a championship, when LaVell Edwards' BYU team, with its wide-open passing attack, put to-gether an undefeated season. Edwards had taken over a struggling program in 1972, and coached through the 2000 season. In his twenty-nine years in Provo, Edwards' teams had just one losing season, and won twenty conference titles. Barry Switzer won the last of his national titles at Oklahoma in 1985, retiring from college football after the 1988 season. Finally, Notre Dame won a title in the 1980s as well, under Lou Holtz (1986–96), whose 100 wins for the Irish were just five less than Rockne's record at the school. Holtz had had earlier success at North Carolina State, and Arkansas, and would move on later to coach South Carolina.

College football was as popular as ever during the 1980s, but there were problems festering. The NCAA had stepped in, back in the early 1950s, to restrict the televising of games and the number of appearances of major schools on television, in part to protect the interests of the small college teams. In 1984, the University of Oklahoma and the University of Georgia brought an anti-trust suit against the NCAA, to eliminate the NCAA restrictions. The case went to the U.S. Supreme Court, which ruled against the NCAA, opening up the marketing of television games to individual conferences and/or schools. The number of games on TV skyrocketed briefly, but the elimination of the monopoly power of the NCAA actually decreased the total amount that was spent on the sport by the networks and independent TV stations. By the end of the 1980s, ABC had managed to sign contracts with essentially all of the major conferences, in the process adding a restriction on the televising of conferences games during periods when ABC is showing a nationally televised game, a return to something approaching the old NCAA rule. The single major team not covered by the agreement, of course, is Notre Dame, which has its own TV contract covering the televising of home games for the Irish.

The most disturbing development that came to

the surface in the 1980s was a rash of NCAA recruiting and player compensation and eligibility violations by several leading major colleges, something that hit the Southwest Conference and the Southeastern Conference especially hard. The worst of the cases involved multiple violations at SMU during the early 1980s. SMU was given an NCAA "death sentence," under which the school cancelled the 1987 and 1988 seasons and had severe restrictions imposed on recruiting. Football was resumed in 1989, but SMU has had only one winning season since that time. Texas A&M was ineligible for the Southwest Conference title in 1988 because of its NCAA violations, and then was hit with NCAA penalties in 1994, which tarnished its 10-0-1 record for that season. TCU ran into NCAA penalties in the 1986 season for earlier violations. In 1989, it was Houston that was on probation. Arkansas left the conference for the SEC after the 1991 season, presumably because of the problems the SWC was having with the NCAA. After the 1995 season, the SWC was disbanded.

In the Southeastern Conference, Clemson's problems surfaced early in the 1980s, and Florida was on NCAA probation in 1985, after having its conference title in 1984 vacated because of recruiting violations; to make things worse, Florida was back on probation in 1990. The 1990s were nightmare years for the SEC, with Alabama, Auburn, Arkansas, and Ole Miss on probation at various times. Alabama in particular has been on and off probation several times, and seems to have systemic problems with NCAA violations that were still under investigation in early 2004. At the root of the wave of violations, of course, are the vast benefits that a coach and a school can enjoy with a winning team - bowl bids, sold out games, television exposure of players, recruiting advantages, and just plain old-fashioned American dollars. The NCAA is trying to run a system in which every party except the players makes

money from the system, so that it is not surprising that stopping violations is the football equivalent of plugging holes in a leaky dike, and everything about the system indicates that the violations will continue in the future.

Between 1990 and 2003, the South accounted for more than half the national titles, with the state of Florida - Miami (1991 shared with Washington, 2001), Florida State (1993, 1999), and Florida (1996) - accounting for five of these, and with Alabama (1992), Tennessee (1998), and Georgia Tech (1991 shared with Colorado) winning the others. The Big Ten won two titles, Michigan in 1997 (shared with Nebraska), and Ohio State in 2002, being overshadowed by the Big Twelve, with Nebraska's three titles (1994, 1995, 1997 shared with Michigan), together with titles by Colorado (1990 shared with Georgia Tech), and Oklahoma (2000).

The list of coaches making their mark in the 1990s begins with Bobby Bowden at Florida State, who has coached the Seminoles since 1976, winning 80 percent of his games, with his teams being ranked in the top ten nationally 18 times in his 28-year career at the school, and with those two national titles in the 1990s. During the 2003 season, Bowden passed Joe Paterno for the lifetime lead in wins as a major college football coach. Florida State joined the ACC in 1992 and has won or tied for the ACC title 11 years out of 12, a mark approaching that of Bud Wilkinson's early years in the Big Seven. The Seminoles have combined a dominating defense with a powerful and balanced offense, featuring star players such as Deion Sanders, Terrell Buckley, Charlie Ward, and Chris Weinke.

A few miles away, in Gainesville, Steve Spurrier was coaching the Florida Gators from 1990 through the 2001 season, with a win percent just a fraction better than Bowden's at .815. Spurrier's teams were top ten nationally in ten of his twelve years with Florida, with one national title (1996).

As a Heisman Trophy winner himself as a passer, it is not surprising that Spurrier's teams featured explosive offenses with an emphasis on passing and high scoring games, providing the most sensational football being played during the 1990s. Spurrier was gone to the pros, for a short stay, after the 2001 season.

And then there is Bob Devaney's successor, Tom Osborne, who coached Nebraska from 1973 through 1997, a twenty-five year period in which the Huskers were nationally ranked in every year, and in the top ten nationally nineteen years out of the twenty-five. Osborne's success during a time when a "balanced attack" has become one in which a team passes 50 percent or more of the time, shows that college football is still a sport in which there are many avenues to success. Osborne's teams were running teams, option teams, and teams with overpowering defenses. Looking at things from a long run point of view, his teams, playing solid fundamental football, have been among the most consistently successful teams in the history of football, ranking with Bear Bryant's Alabama teams in this regard.

The Washington Huskies won their first and only national championship in 1991, under coach Don James, who spent 18 years at the Seattle school. U Dub's history records some outstanding coaches, including Gil Dobie in the early years, Enoch Bagshaw in the 1920s, Jimmy Phelan in the 1930s, and Jim Owens from 1957 through 1974. This makes it all the more impressive that Don James managed to put together the best record in the history of the school, excluding only Gil Dobie's mark, of course, and during years when USC and UCLA were running wild in the Pac-10.

With all of the attention centered on the Florida schools, it is easy to overlook the impressive record that has been fashioned by Phil Fullmer at Tennessee. Fullmer took over from Johnny Majors in mid-season in 1992 and has had nationally ranked teams in eleven of twelve seasons at Tennessee. His teams have produced Tennessee's first Heisman winner, in Peyton Manning, and, in the tough SEC with Alabama and Florida around, Fullmer's Vols have won four titles and three second place finishes. The 1998 national title was the first since General Neyland's title in 1951.

Other first time winners of national titles were Bobby Ross at Georgia Tech, and Bill McCartney at Colorado, whose 1990 teams shared the national title. Ross spent five years at Tech, and then left for the pros. McCartney was at Colorado for 13 years (1982–94), taking over at a time when Colorado was in a slump. The last six seasons for McCartney were nationally ranked years, and Colorado has been a power in the Big Twelve since his retirement.

Perhaps the biggest news in college football in the 1990s was the creation of the Bowl Championship Series for determining a national champion. Just before the 1998 season, an agreement was reached between the four leading bowls—the Orange Bowl, the Sugar Bowl, the Rose Bowl, and the Fiesta Bowl—and the six leading college conferences—the ACC, Big East, Big Ten, Big Twelve, Pac-10, and SEC,—and with Notre Dame as well. Under this agreement, a computerized system was created to rank major college teams during the season, based on poll results, leading independent rankings, strength of schedule, and other factors. At the end of the season, the two teams ranked highest in the BCS computerized rankings play in a "championship game" in one of the four bowls, with the location of the game rotating among the bowls. The participants in the other bowls are determined in part by the agreements the bowls have with conferences, and in part by the bowl managers themselves. So far as the leading bowls are concerned, the conference-bowl alignments are: Big-10 and Pac-10, Rose Bowl; Big Twelve, Fiesta Bowl; SEC, Sugar Bowl; ACC and Big East, Orange Bowl. The BCS agreement is to last through the 2005 season (and January, 2006 bowl games). The coaches' poll run by *USA Today* is committed to declaring the winner of the BCS championship game the national champ. Nonetheless, the BCS approach has not eliminated the controversies over which team is in fact the best team in college football - with the sharing of the 2003 title between LSU and USC a prime example - and further tinkering with the BCS rules was going on in early 2004. Despite calls by fans and sports reporters for a post-season tournament in Division I-A, the coaches almost to a man oppose this, so such a drastic change in the present system for choosing a national champion seems unlikely.

Beyond other matters, the BCS has brought a clearer focus on the importance of the leading football conferences in determining the way in which college football is organized in the 21st century. For much of the history of college football, independent teams teams such as Pittsburgh, Penn State, Florida State, Miami, Army—played major college schedules without committing to a particular conference. This is now a thing of the past. Of the 117 Division I-A teams in 2003, only four were independents, and in the 2004 season, barring further developments, this will drop to just three—Army, Navy, and Notre Dame. The move of teams out of independent status and into conferences began in the late 1980s and has continued since, because of the spate of contracts that have been signed between conferences and television networks, and between conferences and the bowls. TV income forms an increasingly important share of the financial picture for college football programs, and conferences are in a better position to bargain with television networks and cable channels than are teams, excepting only Notre Dame. The ability to participate in bowl games also offers financial rewards, along with recruiting advantages, and with more and more bowls signing agreements with conferences, bowl slots become set aside for conference members, with independents being locked out.

In 1991, the Big East Conference was organized, bringing together eight previously independent leading East coast powers. After the SWC disbanded in 1995, four ex-members joined with members of the Big Eight Conference to form the Big Twelve. In 1996, Conference USA was organized. In 1999, it was the Mountain West Conference, and in 2001, the Sun Belt Conference. Certainly one of the most important motivations for these moves was the prospective increase in TV and bowl game income from the new conference alignment. In 2003, the spat between the ACC and the Big East over the move of Miami, Boston College, and Virginia Tech from the Big East into the ACC arose because of the TV and bowl income that will be lost to Big East members and gained by ACC members. There are other related dollar matters involved. Connecticut is joining the Big East football conference in 2004 and has spent millions of dollars on a stadium to meet Big East (and NCAA) requirements. With three leading teams leaving the Big East, Connecticut can no longer look forward to sharing in the revenues these teams brought in the conference. Moreover, the move by the ACC has given rise to a domino effect that will be felt over the next few years, with the Big East announcing the acquisition of Louisville, South Florida, and Cincinnati from Conference USA as replacements. In turn, Conference USA has recruited Rice, SMU, and Tulsa from the WAC, along with Marshall and Central Florida from the MAC, to offset its losses, forming a twelve-team league. The WAC added Utah State and New Mexico State from the Sun Belt Conference, which added Troy State for the 2004 season, and then chose two Division I-AA teams, Florida International and Florida Atlantic, as future members, after a probationary period. These have been by far the most tumultuous conference changes in the history of college football. Meanwhile, the non-BCS schools are raising what might become a potential antitrust issue, because of their apparent exclusion from the big dollars being made by the BCS schools.

Looking over the history of the last forty years or so of college football, the change back to two-platoon football in 1965, the rise of pro football beginning in the 1960s, and the increasing importance of TV and bowl income to schools, have together radically changed the environment of college football. Football programs have become much more expensive to maintain than in the days before two-platoon football, so that colleges are forced to be more concerned about the revenues that can be generated by football programs than in the past. Star players now look forward to high paying pro careers and presumably choose to attend the colleges that offer the best chances to sign a lucrative pro contract. As compared to earlier periods, this means that colleges with winning coaches, and those offering more television and other media exposure to players, have a built in advantage in recruiting, which in turn spells more wins in the future. So decisions by athletic departments as to which conference to join and which coach to hire, decisions by coaches as to which jobs to accept, and decisions by players as to where to enroll, all are driven by money considerations much more strongly than in the past. One consequence of this is that it is harder and harder than in earlier years for second level schools to compete with the top schools for coaching talent and playing talent. The big program schools—Ohio State, Michigan, and Penn State in the Big Ten, Oklahoma, Nebraska, and Texas in the Big Twelve, USC, UCLA, and Washington in the Pac-10—have been more dominant since the return of two-platoon football and the rise of pro football in the mid-1960s, than they were before that time.

Taking two thirty-year periods (1935–64) and (1965–94), centered on the change back to two-platoon football, as the "before" and "after" periods, in the Big Ten, Ohio State, and Michigan won 42 percent of the titles in the before period, and 72 percent in the after period. In the Big Eight, where there was much more dominance by the two teams, Oklahoma and Nebraska won 77 percent of the titles in the before period, and 83 percent in the after period. (Note that dominance has increased in the "after" period even though the "before" period here included Oklahoma's thirteen titles in a row in the Wilkinson years.) In the Pac-10, USC and UCLA won 52 percent of the titles in the before period, and 64 percent in the after period. More general measures, such as Gini coefficients of concentration, show similar results—there is less competitive balance in college football conferences since the mid-1960s than earlier. The long-term effects of this are problematic, but it does raise questions as to whether the future might see a "super conference" or a new NCAA division restricted to the big program schools, who would then be able to capture more of the money they generate that is now shared with their fellow conference members. There also have been some radical suggestions made as to changes in the way that college football operates, ranging from instituting pay-for-play under which players get to share in the income generated by college football, to the other extreme of a return to one-platoon football. The jury is out on these and other proposals for reforming college football.

College football has problems because of the massive amounts of money that flow through the college football system, but the money is there because college football, with all of its problems, fills a unique niche in American life, for fans and players alike. College football always has been, and remains, a fascinating and always controversial part of American life.

PART II

Records of Division 1-A Football Teams

UNIVERSITY OF AKRON, Akron, Ohio; nickname "Zips"; Rubber Bowl (35,202); Mid-American Conference. Akron began play in 1891 as an independent. In 1916, Akron joined the Ohio Athletic Conference (OAC) and played in that conference until 1936, when it reverted to independent status. In 1948, Akron rejoined the OAC and remained there until the 1966 season, when it again became an independent. In 1978, Akron joined the Midwest College Conference and then transferred to the Ohio Valley Conference in 1980, a Division 1-AA conference. In 1987, Akron attained Division 1-A status as an independent and then joined the MAC in 1992.

Early years as an independent (1891-1915)

Year	Coach	W-L-T	PF	PA	Pct.	Year	Coach	W-L-T	PF	PA	Pct.
1891	none	1-3-0	22	94	.250	1902	Forest Firestone	2-5-0	34	163	.286
1892	Frank Cook	3-4-0	69	180	.429	1903	Alfred Pace	0-2-0	0	43	.000
1893	John Heisman	5-2-0	276	82	.714	1904-1907	no team				
1894	John Heisman	1-0-0	12	6	1.000	1908	Dwight Bradley	3-4-0	32	80	.429
1895	none	3-2-0	42	62	.600	1909	Clarence Weed	4-4-0	54	69	.500
1896	Harry Wilson	0-1-0	0	32	.000	1910	Frank Haggerty	7-2-0	136	83	.778
1897 and 1898	no team					1911	Frank Haggerty	3-4-1	80	24	.438
1899	Archie Eves	2-1-0	26	11	.667	1912	Frank Haggerty	5-2-1	105	36	.688
1900	none	2-3-1	55	66	.417	1913	Frank Haggerty	3-4-0	87	103	.429
1901	no team					1914	Frank Haggerty	4-4-1	122	134	.500

Member of the Ohio Athletic Conference (1915-1935, 1948-1965) 130-113-13 .533

Fred Sefton (1915-1923) 34-33-4 .507

	Nat'l	Overall				Conference				Nat'l	Overall				Conference		
Year	AP Other	W-L-T	PF	PA	Pct.	W-L-T	Pct.	Rank	Year	AP Other	W-L-T	PF	PA	Pct.	W-L-T	Pct.	Rank
1915		1-7-1	20	39	.167	1-6-0	.143		1920		4-4-0	99	93	.500	2-4-0	.333	
1916		2-7-0	90	183	.222	2-4-0	.333		1921		5-3-0	117	69	.625	4-3-0	.571	
1917		5-3-0	143	84	.625	3-1-0	.750		1922		5-3-0	141	53	.625	5-3-0	.625	
1918		2-2-1	69	47	.500	1-2-1	.375		1923		4-3-1	92	37	.562	2-3-1	.417	
1919		6-1-1	139	38	.812	5-1-1	.786										

James Coleman (1924-1925) 6-10-0 .375

Year	AP Other	W-L-T	PF	PA	Pct.	W-L-T	Pct.	Rank	Year	AP Other	W-L-T	PF	PA	Pct.	W-L-T	Pct.	Rank
1924		5-3-0	89	75	.625	3-2-0	.600		1925		1-7-0	17	150	.125	1-6-0	.143	

George Babcock (1926) 5-2-2 .667

Year	AP Other	W-L-T	PF	PA	Pct.	W-L-T	Pct.	Rank
1926		5-2-2	109	74	.667	4-2-2	.625	

Red Blair (1927-1935) 43-30-5 .583

Year	AP Other	W-L-T	PF	PA	Pct.	W-L-T	Pct.	Rank	Year	AP Other	W-L-T	PF	PA	Pct.	W-L-T	Pct.	Rank
1927		5-3-0	145	79	.625	4-3-0	.571		1932		2-4-3	37	91	.388	1-4-3	.312	
1928		5-4-0	158	94	.556	3-4-0	.429		1933		5-3-1	97	50	.611	5-2-1	.688	
1929		9-1-0	158	21	.900	7-1-0	.875		1934		3-4-1	65	48	.438	3-4-0	.429	
1930		7-1-0	130	38	.875	5-1-0	.833		1935		6-3-0	81	70	.667	6-3-0	.667	
1931		1-7-0	39	114	.125	0-6-0	.000										

Akron reverts to independent status (1936-1947)

James Aiken (1936-1938) 19-7-1 .722

Year	AP Other	W-L-T	PF	PA	Pct.				Year	AP Other	W-L-T	PF	PA	Pct.			
1936		6-2-1	150	87	.722				1938		6-3-0	117	94	.667			
1937		7-2-0	139	53	.778												

Thomas Dowler (1939-1940) 7-9-2 .444

Year	AP Other	W-L-T	PF	PA	Pct.				Year	AP Other	W-L-T	PF	PA	Pct.			
1939		5-4-0	122	132	.545				1940		2-5-2	90	106	.333			

Otis Douglas (1941-1942) 5-10-3 .361

Year	AP Other	W-L-T	PF	PA	Pct.				Year	AP Other	W-L-T	PF	PA	Pct.			
1941		5-3-1	114	76	.611				1942		0-7-2	26	186	.111			

No team (1943-1945)

Paul Baldacci (1946-1947) 7-10-0 .412

Year	AP Other	W-L-T	PF	PA	Pct.				Year	AP Other	W-L-T	PF	PA	Pct.			
1946		5-4-0	122	134	.556				1947		2-6-0	44	162	.250			

Akron returns to the Ohio Athletic Conference (1948-1965)

William Houghton (1948-1951) 7-27-1 .214

Year	AP Other	W-L-T	PF	PA	Pct.	W-L-T	Pct.	Rank	Year	AP Other	W-L-T	PF	PA	Pct.	W-L-T	Pct.	Rank
1948		2-6-0	46	146	.250	1-4-0	.200		1950		2-7-0	131	185	.222	1-3-0	.250	
1949		2-6-1	114	257	.278	0-3-1	.125		1951		1-8-0	116	252	.111	1-3-0	.250	

Red Cochrane (1952-1953) 8-9-1 .472

Year	AP Other	W-L-T	PF	PA	Pct.	W-L-T	Pct.	Rank	Year	AP Other	W-L-T	PF	PA	Pct.	W-L-T	Pct.	Rank
1952		2-6-1	121	156	.278	2-2-1	.500		1953		6-3-0	198	210	.667	4-2-0	.667	

Joe McMullin (1954-1960) 30-28-3 .516

Year	AP Other	W-L-T	PF	PA	Pct.	W-L-T	Pct.	Rank	Year	AP Other	W-L-T	PF	PA	Pct.	W-L-T	Pct.	Rank
1954		3-5-0	169	213	.375	3-4-0	.429		1958		6-2-1	166	82	.722	6-2-0	.750	
1955		6-2-0	245	73	.750	6-2-0	.750		1959		4-5-0	111	155	.444	4-3-0	.571	
1956		3-5-1	216	171	.388	3-5-1	.388		1960		1-8-0	70	269	.111	1-6-0	.143	
1957		7-1-1	208	87	.833	5-1-1	.786										

Gordon Larson (1961-1972) 74-33-5 .689

Year	Record	PF	PA	Pct	Conf	Pct		Year	Record	PF	PA	Pct	Conf	Pct
1961	6-2-0	185	57	.750	6-1-0	.857		1964	6-3-0	116	109	.667	4-3-0	.571
1962	7-2-0	261	65	.778	7-1-0	.875		1965	5-3-1	110	94	.611	4-1-0	.800
1963	6-3-0	201	102	.667	5-2-0	.714								

Akron becomes an independent again (1966-1977)

Year	Record	PF	PA	Pct		Year	Record	PF	PA	Pct
1966	6-3-0	137	116	.667		1970	7-3-0	259	92	.700
1967	4-4-1	162	155	.500		1971	8-2-0	193	119	.800
1968	7-3-1	327	172	.682		1972	3-4-2	193	148	.444
1969	9-1-0	316	103	.900						

Jim Dennison (1973-1985) 80-62-2 .562

Year	Record	PF	PA	Pct		Year	Record	PF	PA	Pct
1973	6-5-0	289	203	.545		1976	10-3-0	282	144	.767
1974	5-5-0	162	197	.500		1977	6-4-1	234	170	.591
1975	7-4-0	189	166	.636						

Member of the Midwest College Conference (1978-1979) 7-3-0 .700

Year	Record	PF	PA	Pct	Conf	Pct		Year	Record	PF	PA	Pct	Conf	Pct
1978	6-5-0	221	232	.545	4-1-0	.800		1979	6-5-0	232	223	.545	3-2-0	.600

Member of the Ohio Valley Conference (1980-1986) 27-25-1 .519

Year	Record	PF	PA	Pct	Conf	Pct		Year	Record	PF	PA	Pct	Conf	Pct
1980	3-7-1	134	183	.318	2-4-1	.358		1983	8-3-0	210	104	.727	5-2-0	.714
1981	5-5-0	132	183	.500	4-4-0	.500		1984	4-7-0	205	158	.364	2-5-0	.286
1982	6-5-0	188	144	.545	5-2-0	.714		1985	8-4-0	258	186	.667	5-2-0	.714

Gerry Faust (1986-1994) 43-53-3 .449

Year	Record	PF	PA	Pct	Conf	Pct
1986	7-4-0	291	188	.636	4-3-0	.571

Akron becomes a Division 1-A independent (1987-1991)

Year	Record	PF	PA	Pct		Year	Record	PF	PA	Pct
1987	4-7-0	204	273	.364		1990	3-7-1	233	263	.318
1988	5-6-0	233	214	.455		1991	5-6-0	257	308	.455
1989	6-4-1	296	241	.591						

Member of the Mid-American Conference (1992-2003) 41-56-0 .423

Year	Record	PF	PA	Pct	Conf	Pct	Fin		Year	Record	PF	PA	Pct	Conf	Pct	Fin
1992	7-3-1	218	186	.682	5-3-0	.625	3		1994	1-10-0	145	404	.091	1-8-0	.111	9
1993	5-6-0	192	222	.455	4-4-0	.500	4									

Lee Owen (1995-2003) 40-61-0 .396

Year	Record	PF	PA	Pct	Conf	Pct	Fin		Year	Record	PF	PA	Pct	Conf	Pct	Fin
1995	2-9-0	141	428	.182	2-6-0	.250	7		1999	7-4-0	315	314	.636	5-3-0	.625	4
1996	4-7-0	175	269	.364	3-5-0	.375	6		2000	6-5-0	333	295	.545	5-3-0	.625	3
1997	2-9-0	218	435	.182	2-6-0	.250	10		2001	4-7-0	281	360	.364	4-4-0	.500	8
1998	4-7-0	265	299	.364	2-6-0	.250	9		2002	4-8-0	325	379	.333	3-5-0	.375	9
									2003	7-5-0	435	353	.583	5-3-0	.625	6

Won-loss record by decades:

Decade	Record	Pct	Decade	Record	Pct	Decade	Record	Pct
1891-99	15-13-0	.537	1930-39	47-33-6	.581	1970-79	64-40-3	.612
1900-09	11-18-1	.383	1940-49	18-37-6	.344	1980-89	56-52-2	.518
1910-19	38-36-6	.512	1950-59	40-44-4	.477	1990-99	40-68-2	.373
1920-29	48-33-3	.589	1960-69	57-32-3	.636	2000-03	21-25-0	.457

Historic record: 455-431-36 .513

Post-season won-loss record 2-3-0 .400

1968: Grantland Rice Bowl, Louisiana Tech 33, Akron 13
1976: Division II Playoff, Akron 27, UNLV 6
1976: Knute Rockne Bowl, Akron 29, North Michigan 26
1976: Pioneer Bowl, Montana State 24, Akron 13
1985: Division I-AA Playoff, Rhode Island 35, Akron 27

Hall of Fame: John Heisman, coach, 1893-94.

UNIVERSITY OF ALABAMA AT BIRMINGHAM (UAB), Birmingham, Alabama; nickname "Blazers"; colors forest green and old gold; Legion Field (83,091); Conference USA. UAB began play as a Division III independent in 1991. In 1993, UAB moved up to 1-AA independent status. UAB became a Division 1-A independent in 1996 and then joined Conference USA for the 1999 season.

Year	Nat'l AP Other	Overall W-L-T	PF	PA	Pct.	Conference W-L-T	Pct.	Rank	Year	Nat'l AP Other	Overall W-L-T	PF	PA	Pct.	Conference W-L-T	Pct.	Rank
Early years as an independent (1991-1998)																	
Jim Hillyer (1991-1994) 27-12-2 .683																	
1991		4-3-2	170	196	.556				1993		9-2-0	356	213	.818			
1992		7-3-0	271	163	.600				1994		7-4-0	301	258	.636			
Watson Brown (1995-2003) 47-54-0 .465																	
1995		5-6-0	273	261	.455				1997		5-6-0	222	238	.455			
1996		5-6-0	266	279	.455				1998		4-7-0	237	309	.364			
Member of Conference USA (1999-2003) 20-16-0 .556																	
1999		5-6-0	248	279	.455	4-2-0	.667	2	2002		5-7-0	268	370	.417	4-4-0	.500	5
2000		7-4-0	277	153	.636	3-4-0	.429	5	2003		5-7-0	245	287	.417	4-4-0	.500	6
2001		6-5-0	265	206	.545	5-2-0	.714	2									

Won-loss record by decades:
1991-99	51-42-2	.547
2000-03	23-23-0	.500
Historic record	74-65-2	.532

UNIVERSITY OF ALABAMA, Tuscaloosa, AL; nickname "Crimson Tide"; colors crimson and white; Bryant-Denny Stadium (83,818); Southeastern Conference. Alabama began play in 1892, and joined the Southern Conference at its founding in 1922. Alabama left the SC after the 1932 season, as a founding member of the new Southeastern Conference. Alabama has played in the SEC since that time.

Early years as an independent (1892-1921)

Year	Coach	W-L-T	PF	PA	Pct.	Year	Coach	W-L-T	PF	PA	Pct.
1892	E.B. Beaumont	2-2-0	96	37	.500	1906	J.W.H. Pollard	5-1-0	97	82	.833
1893	Eli Abbott	0-4-0	24	74	.000	1907	J.W.H. Pollard	5-1-2	70	64	.750
1894	Eli Abbott	3-1-0	60	16	.750	1908	J.W.H. Pollard	6-1-1	108	31	.812
1895	Eli Abbott	0-4-0	12	112	.000	1909	J.W.H. Pollard	5-1-2	68	17	.750
1896	Otto Wagonhurst	2-1-0	56	10	.667	1910	Guy Lowman	4-4-0	65	107	.500
1897	Allen McCants	1-0-0	6	0	1.000	1911	D.V. Graves	5-2-2	153	31	.667
1898	no team					1912	D.V. Graves	5-3-1	156	55	.611
1899	W.A. Martin	3-1-0	39	31	.750	1913	D.V. Graves	6-3-0	188	40	.667
1900	M. Griffin	2-3-0	52	99	.400	1914	D.V. Graves	5-4-0	211	64	.556
1901	M.H. Harvey	2-1-2	92	23	.600	1915	Thomas Kelley	6-2-0	250	51	.750
1902	Eli Abbott	4-4-0	191	49	.500	1916	Thomas Kelley	6-3-0	156	62	.667
1903	W.B. Blount	3-4-0	60	114	.429	1917	Thomas Kelley	5-2-1	168	29	.688
1904	W.B. Blount	7-3-0	100	62	.700	1918	no team				
1905	J. Leavenworth	6-4-0	178	113	.600						

Xen Scott (1919-1922) 29-9-3 .744

Year	W-L-T	PF	PA	Pct.	Year	W-L-T	PF	PA	Pct.
1919	8-1-0	280	22	.889	1921	5-4-2	241	104	.545
1920	10-1-0	377	35	.909					

Member of the Southern Conference (1922-1932) 60-15-3 .788

	Nat'l		Overall				Conference				Nat'l		Overall				Conference		
Year	AP	Other	W-L-T	PF	PA	Pct.	W-L-T	Pct.	Rank	Year	AP	Other	W-L-T	PF	PA	Pct.	W-L-T	Pct.	Rank
1922			6-3-1	300	81	.650	3-2-1	.650	8										

Wallace Wade (1923-1930) 61-13-3 .812

Year	AP	Other	W-L-T	PF	PA	Pct.	W-L-T	Pct.	Rank	Year	AP	Other	W-L-T	PF	PA	Pct.	W-L-T	Pct.	Rank
1923			7-2-1	222	50	.750	4-1-1	.750	6	1927			5-4-1	154	73	.550	3-4-1	.438	10
1924			8-1-0	294	24	.889	5-0-0	1.000	1	1928			6-3-0	187	75	.667	6-2-0	.750	5
1925	1		10-0-0	297	26	1.000	7-0-0	1.000	1	1929			6-3-0	196	58	.667	4-3-0	.571	11
1926	1		9-0-1	249	27	.950	8-0-0	1.000	1	1930		3	10-0-0	271	13	1.000	8-0-0	1.000	1

Frank Thomas (1931-1946) 115-24-7 .812

Year	AP	Other	W-L-T	PF	PA	Pct.	W-L-T	Pct.	Rank	Year	AP	Other	W-L-T	PF	PA	Pct.	W-L-T	Pct.	Rank
1931			9-1-0	360	57	.900	7-1-0	.875		1932			8-2-0	200	51	.800	5-2-0	.714	7

Member of the Southeastern Conference (1933-2003) 326-142-20 .689

Year	AP	Other	W-L-T	PF	PA	Pct.	W-L-T	Pct.	Rank	Year	AP	Other	W-L-T	PF	PA	Pct.	W-L-T	Pct.	Rank
1933			7-1-1	130	17	.833	5-0-1	.917	1	1940			7-2-0	166	80	.778	4-2-0	.667	4
1934		6	10-0-0	316	45	1.000	7-0-0	1.000	2	1941	20		9-2-0	263	85	.818	5-2-0	.714	3
1935			6-2-1	185	55	.722	4-2-0	.667	5	1942	10		8-3-0	246	97	.727	4-2-0	.667	5
1936	4	5	8-0-1	168	35	.944	5-0-1	.917	2	1943	no team								
1937	4	4	9-1-0	225	33	.900	6-0-0	1.000	1	1944			5-2-2	272	83	.667	3-1-2	.600	3
1938	13	9	7-1-1	149	40	.833	4-1-1	.750	2	1945	2		10-0-0	430	80	1.000	6-0-0	1.000	1
1939			5-3-1	101	53	.611	2-3-1	.417	8	1946			7-4-0	186	110	.636	4-3-0	.571	6

Red Drew (1947-1954) 54-28-7 .643

Year	AP	Other	W-L-T	PF	PA	Pct.	W-L-T	Pct.	Rank	Year	AP	Other	W-L-T	PF	PA	Pct.	W-L-T	Pct.	Rank
1947	6		8-3-0	210	101	.727	5-2-0	.714	3	1951			5-6-0	263	188	.455	3-5-0	.375	7
1948			6-4-1	228	170	.591	4-4-1	.500	6	1952	9	9	10-2-0	325	139	.833	4-2-0	.667	4
1949			6-3-1	227	130	.650	4-3-1	.562	6	1953	13	11	6-3-3	178	152	.625	4-0-3	.786	1
1950	16	17	9-2-0	328	107	.818	6-2-0	.750	3	1954			4-5-2	123	104	.455	3-3-2	.500	5

Ears Whitworth (1955-1957) 4-24-2 .167

Year	AP	Other	W-L-T	PF	PA	Pct.	W-L-T	Pct.	Rank	Year	AP	Other	W-L-T	PF	PA	Pct.	W-L-T	Pct.	Rank
1955			0-10-0	48	256	.000	0-7-0	.000	12	1957			2-7-1	69	173	.250	1-6-1	.188	11
1956			2-7-1	85	208	.250	2-5-0	.286	9										

Bear Bryant (1958-1982) 232-46-9 .824

Year	AP	Other	W-L-T	PF	PA	Pct.	W-L-T	Pct.	Rank	Year	AP	Other	W-L-T	PF	PA	Pct.	W-L-T	Pct.	Rank
1958			5-4-1	106	75	.550	3-4-1	.438	6	1971	4	2	11-1-0	368	122	.917	7-0-0	1.000	1
1959	10	13	7-2-2	95	59	.727	4-1-2	.714	4	1972	7	4	10-2-0	406	150	.833	7-1-0	.875	1
1960	9	10	8-1-2	183	56	.818	5-1-1	.786	3	1973	4	1	11-1-0	477	113	.917	8-0-0	1.000	1
1961	1	1	11-0-0	297	25	1.000	7-0-0	1.000	1	1974	5	2	11-1-0	329	96	.917	6-0-0	1.000	1
1962	5	5	10-1-0	289	39	.909	6-1-0	.857	2	1975	3	3	11-1-0	374	72	.917	6-0-0	1.000	1
1963	8	9	9-2-0	227	95	.818	6-2-0	.750	3	1976	11	9	9-3-0	326	140	.750	5-2-0	.714	3
1964	1	1	10-1-0	250	88	.909	8-0-0	1.000	1	1977	2	2	11-1-0	380	139	.917	7-0-0	1.000	1
1965	1	4	9-1-1	256	107	.864	6-1-1	.812	1	1978	1	2	11-1-0	345	168	.917	6-0-0	1.000	1
1966	3	3	11-0-0	301	44	1.000	6-0-0	1.000	1	1979	1	1	12-0-0	384	67	1.000	6-0-0	1.000	1
1967	8	7	8-2-1	204	131	.773	5-1-0	.833	2	1980	6	6	10-2-0	352	98	.833	5-1-0	.833	2
1968	17	12	8-3-0	184	139	.727	4-2-0	.667	3	1981	7	6	9-2-1	296	151	.767	6-0-0	1.000	1
1969			6-5-0	314	268	.545	2-4-0	.333	8	1982		17	8-4-0	338	216	.667	3-3-0	.500	6
1970			6-5-1	334	264	.542	3-4-0	.429	7										

Ray Perkins (1983-1986) 32-15-1 .667

Year	AP	Other	W-L-T	PF	PA	Pct.	W-L-T	Pct.	Rank	Year	AP	Other	W-L-T	PF	PA	Pct.	W-L-T	Pct.	Rank
1983	15	12	8-4-0	366	229	.667	4-2-0	.667	3	1985	13	14	9-2-1	318	181	.767	4-1-1	.750	2
1984			5-6-0	226	208	.455	2-4-0	.333	7	1986	9	9	10-3-0	351	163	.769	4-2-0	.667	2

Bill Curry (1987-1989) 26-10-0 .722

| 1987 | | | 7-5-0 | 268 | 213 | .583 | 4-2-0 | .667 | 4 | 1989 | 9 | 7 | 10-2-0 | 357 | 217 | .833 | 6-1-0 | .857 | 1 |
| 1988 | 17 | 17 | 9-3-0 | 297 | 188 | .750 | 4-3-0 | .771 | 4 | | | | | | | | | | |

Gene Stallings (1990-1996) 62-25-0 .713*

1990			7-5-0	260	161	.583	5-2-0	.714	2	1994	5	4	12-1-0	305	190	.923	8-0-0	1.000	2
1991	5	5	11-1-0	324	143	.917	6-1-0	.857	2	1995**21			8-3-0	260	188	.727	5-3-0	.625	12
1992	1	1	13-0-0	366	122	1.000	8-0-0	1.000	1	1996	11	11	10-3-0	286	143	.769	6-2-0	.750	2
1993 * 14	13		1-12-0	316	158	.077	0-8-0	.000	12										

*1993 record before NCAA forfeit action was 9-3-1; Stallings record would be 70-16-0 .814, before forfeits of eight games.
** Not eligible for conference title in 1995.

Mike DuBose (1997-2000) 24-23-0 .511

| 1997 | | | 4-7-0 | 246 | 248 | .364 | 2-6-0 | .250 | 9 | 1999 | 8 | 8 | 10-3-0 | 380 | 265 | .769 | 7-1-0 | .875 | 1 |
| 1998 | | | 7-5-0 | 251 | 287 | .583 | 4-4-0 | .500 | 6 | 2000 | | | 3-8-0 | 228 | 246 | .273 | 3-5-0 | .375 | 10 |

Dennis Franchione (2001-2002) 17-8-0 .680

| 2001 | | | 7-5-0 | 318 | 232 | .583 | 4-4-0 | .500 | 7 | 2002* 11 | | | 10-3-0 | 367 | 200 | .769 | 6-2-0 | .750 | * |

Mike Shula (2003) 4-9-0 .308

| 2003* | | | 4-9-0 | 331 | 333 | .308 | 2-6-0 | .250 | * | | | | | | | | | | |

*Not eligible for league title in 2002 or 2003.

Won-lost record by decades:

1892-99	11-13-0	.458	1930-39	79-11-5	.858	1970-79	103-16-1	.863
1900-09	45-23-7	.647	1940-49	66-23-4	.731	1980-89	85-32-2	.723
1910-19	50-24-4	.667	1950-59	50-48-10	.509	1990-99	83-40-0	.675
1920-29	72-21-6	.758	1960-69	90-16-4	.836	2000-03	24-25-0	.490

Historical record: 758-292-43 .713

Post-season won-lost record: 31-22-3 .580

1926: Rose Bowl, Alabama 20, Washington 19
1927: Rose Bowl, Alabama 7, Stanford 7
1931: Rose Bowl, Alabama 24, Washington State 0
1935: Rose Bowl, Alabama 29, Stanford 13
1938: Rose Bowl, California 13, Alabama 0
1942: Cotton Bowl, Alabama 29, Texas A&M 21
1943: Orange Bowl, Alabama 37, Boston College 21
1945: Sugar Bowl, Duke 29, Alabama 26
1946: Rose Bowl, Alabama 34, USC 14
1948: Sugar Bowl, Texas 27, Alabama 7
1953: Orange Bowl, Alabama 61, Syracuse 6
1954: Cotton Bowl, Rice 28, Alabama 6
1959: Liberty Bowl, Penn State 7, Alabama 0
1960: Bluebonnet Bowl, Alabama 3, Texas 3
1962: Sugar Bowl, Alabama 10, Arkansas 3
1963: Orange Bowl, Alabama 17, Oklahoma 0
1964: Sugar Bowl, Alabama 12, Mississippi 7
1965: Orange Bowl, Texas 21, Alabama 17
1966: Orange Bowl, Alabama 39, Nebraska 28
1967: Sugar Bowl, Alabama 34, Nebraska 7
1968: Cotton Bowl, Texas A&M 20, Alabama 16
1968: Gator Bowl, Missouri 35, Alabama 10
1969: Liberty Bowl, Colorado 47, Alabama 33
1970: Bluebonnet Bowl, Alabama 24, Oklahoma 24
1972: Orange Bowl, Nebraska 38, Alabama 6
1973: Cotton Bowl, Texas 17, Alabama 13

1973: Sugar Bowl, Notre Dame 24, Alabama 23
1975: Orange Bowl, Notre Dame 13, Alabama 11
1975: Sugar Bowl, Alabama 13, Penn State 6
1976: Liberty Bowl, Alabama 36, UCLA 6
1978: Sugar Bowl, Alabama 35, Ohio State 6
1979: Sugar Bowl, Alabama 14, Penn State 7
1980: Sugar Bowl, Alabama 24, Arkansas 9
1981: Cotton Bowl, Alabama 30, Baylor 2
1982: Cotton Bowl, Texas 14, Alabama 12
1982: Liberty Bowl, Alabama 21, Illinois 15
1983: Sun Bowl, Alabama 28, SMU 7
1985: Aloha Bowl, Alabama 24, USC 3
1986: Sun Bowl, Alabama 28, Washington 6
1988: Hall of Fame Bowl, Michigan 28, Alabama 24
1988: Sun Bowl, Alabama 29, Army 28
1990: Sugar Bowl, Miami (FL) 33, Alabama 25
1991: Fiesta Bowl, Louisville 34, Alabama 7
1991: Blockbuster Bowl, Alabama 30, Colorado 25
1992: SEC Championship, Alabama 28, Florida 21
1993: Sugar Bowl, Alabama 34, Miami (FL) 13
1993: SEC Championship, Florida 28, Alabama 13
1993: Gator Bowl, Alabama 24, North Carolina 10
1994: SEC Championship, Florida 24, Alabama 23
1995: Citrus Bowl, Alabama 24, Ohio State 17
1996: SEC Championship, Florida 45, Alabama 30
1997: Outback Bowl, Alabama 17, Michigan 14
1998: Music City Bowl, Va. Tech 38, Alabama 34
1999: SEC Championship, Alabama 34, Florida 7
2000: Orange Bowl, Michigan 35, Alabama 34
2001: Independence Bowl, Alabama 14, Iowa State 3

College Football Hall of Fame: Pooley Hubert, fullback, 1922-25; Johnny Mack Brown, halfback, 1923-25; Wallace Wade, coach, 1923-30; Frank Sington, tackle, 1928-30; John Cain, fullback/quarterback, 1930-32; Frank Thomas, coach, 1932-46; Don Hutson, end, 1932-34; Riley Smith, quarterback, 1933-35; Don Whitmire, tackle, 1941-42; Harry Gilmer, halfback, 1944-47;; Vaughn Mancha, center, 1944-47; Bear Bryant, coach, 1958-82; Lee Roy Jordan, center 1960-62; Johnny Musso, halfback, 1969-71; John Hannah, guard, 1970-72; Ozzie Newcombe, wide receiver, 1974-77; Billy Neighbors, tackle, 1959-61.

Awards: Butkus Award, 1988: Derrick Thomas; Lombardi Award, 1986: Cornelius Bennett; Jim Thorpe Award, 1993: Antonio Langham; Outland Trophy, 1999: Chris Samuels; Unitas Award: 1994, Jay Barker; Baugh Trophy: 1965, Steve Sloan.

ARIZONA STATE UNIVERSITY, Tempe, Arizona; nickname "Sun Devils"; colors maroon and gold; Sun Devil Stadium (73,379); Pac-10 Conference. ASU joined the Border Conference in 1931 and played in that conference until it disbanded after the 1961 season. ASU moved into the newly formed Western Athletic Conference where it played through the 1977 season. In 1978, ASU joined the Pac-10 and has played in the conference since that time.

Early years as an independent (1897-1930)

Year	Coach	W-L-T	PF	PA	Pct.	Year	Coach	W-L-T	PF	PA	Pct.
1897	Fred Irish	0-1-0	20	38	.000	1906	Fred Irish	0-2-0	6	22	.000
1898	no team					1907-1913	no team				
1899	Fred Irish	3-0-0	23	2	1.000	1914	George Schaefer	4-3-0	143	87	.571
1900	Fred Irish	1-1-0	5	5	.500	1915	George Schaefer	3-2-0	125	36	.600
1901	no team					1916	George Schaefer	0-3-0	13	51	.000
1902	Fred Irish	2-1-0	73	12	.667	1917-18	no team				
1903	Fred Irish	2-0-0	33	0	1.000	1919	George Cooper	0-2-0	3	104	.000
1904	Fred Irish	4-0-0	116	0	1.000	1920-21	no team				
1905	Fred Irish	0-3-0	8	28	.000	1922	Ernest Wills	0-3-1	31	74	.125

Aaron McCreary (1923-1929) 25-17-4 .587

Year	W-L-T	PF	PA	Pct.	Year	W-L-T	PF	PA	Pct.
1923	4-2-0	152	102	.667	1927	2-3-1	63	50	.417
1924	6-1-1	160	85	.812	1928	3-2-1	133	72	.583
1925	6-2-0	154	59	.750	1929	0-6-0	13	143	.000
1926	4-1-1	97	42	.750					

Ted Shipley (1930-1932) 12-10-2 .542

Year	W-L-T	PF	PA	Pct.
1930	3-5-1	111	94	.438

Member of the Border Conference (1931-1961) 76-54-5 .581

Year	Nat'l AP	Other	Overall W-L-T	PF	PA	Pct.	Conf. W-L-T	Pct.	Rank	Year	Nat'l AP	Other	Overall W-L-T	PF	PA	Pct.	Conf. W-L-T	Pct.	Rank
1931			6-2-0	170	66	.750	3-1-0	.750	1	1932			3-3-1	83	92	.500	2-2-0	.500	3

Rudy Lavik (1933-1937) 13-26-3 .345

Year	Nat'l AP	Other	Overall W-L-T	PF	PA	Pct.	Conf. W-L-T	Pct.	Rank	Year	Nat'l AP	Other	Overall W-L-T	PF	PA	Pct.	Conf. W-L-T	Pct.	Rank
1933			3-5-0	73	125	.375	2-2-0	.500	3	1936			4-5-0	83	109	.444	2-5-0	.286	5
1934			4-3-1	91	113	.562	1-2-1	.375	4	1937			0-8-1	32	140	.055	0-5-0	.000	7
1935			2-5-1	29	66	.312	2-3-1	.417	4										

Dixie Howell (1938-1941) 23-15-4 .595

Year	Nat'l AP	Other	Overall W-L-T	PF	PA	Pct.	Conf. W-L-T	Pct.	Rank	Year	Nat'l AP	Other	Overall W-L-T	PF	PA	Pct.	Conf. W-L-T	Pct.	Rank
1938			3-6-0	89	98	.333	0-4-0	.000	6	1940			7-2-2	198	100	.727	3-0-1	.875	1
1939			8-2-1	212	56	.773	4-0-0	1.000	1	1941			5-5-1	111	137	.500	2-4-1	.357	7

Hilman Walker (1942) 2-8-0 .200

Year	Overall W-L-T	PF	PA	Pct.	Conf. W-L-T	Pct.	Rank	Year	
1942	2-8-0	53	236	.200	2-4-0	.333	7	1943-1945	no team

Steve Coutchie (1946) 2-7-2 .273

Year	Overall W-L-T	PF	PA	Pct.	Conf. W-L-T	Pct.	Rank
1946	2-7-2	93	313	.273	1-4-1	.250	8

Ed Doherty (1947-1950) 25-17-0 .595

Year	Overall W-L-T	PF	PA	Pct.	Conf. W-L-T	Pct.	Rank	Year	Overall W-L-T	PF	PA	Pct.	Conf. W-L-T	Pct.	Rank
1947	4-7-0	168	234	.364	3-4-0	.429	6	1949	7-3-0	342	204	.700	4-1-0	.800	2
1948	5-5-0	276	192	.500	3-2-0	.600	3	1950	9-2-0	404	154	.818	4-1-0	.800	2

Larry Siemering (1951) 6-3-1 .650

Year	Overall W-L-T	PF	PA	Pct.	Conf. W-L-T	Pct.	Rank
1951	6-3-1	308	176	.650	4-1-0	.800	2

Clyde Smith (1952-1954) 15-13-1 .534

Year	Overall W-L-T	PF	PA	Pct.	Conf. W-L-T	Pct.	Rank	Year	Nat'l	Overall W-L-T	PF	PA	Pct.	Conf. W-L-T	Pct.	Rank
1952	6-3-0	247	121	.667	4-0-0	1.000	1	1954		5-5-0	178	228	.500	3-1-0	.750	2
1953	4-5-1	207	203	.450	1-3-0	.250	5									

Dan Devine (1955-1957) 27-3-1 .887

Year	Overall W-L-T	PF	PA	Pct.	Conf. W-L-T	Pct.	Rank	Year	Nat'l	Overall W-L-T	PF	PA	Pct.	Conf. W-L-T	Pct.	Rank
1955	8-2-1	343	107	.773	4-1-0	.800	2	1957	12-12	10-0-0	397	66	1.000	4-0-0	1.000	1
1956	9-1-0	306	83	.900	3-1-0	.750	2									

Frank Kush (1958-1979) 173-57-1 .751

Year	Overall W-L-T	PF	PA	Pct.	Conf. W-L-T	Pct.	Rank	Year	Overall W-L-T	PF	PA	Pct.	Conf. W-L-T	Pct.	Rank
1958	7-3-0	271	131	.700	4-1-0	.800	1	1960	7-3-0	223	120	.700	3-2-0	.600	3
1959	10-1-0	272	150	.909	5-0-0	1.000	1	1961	7-3-0	287	163	.700	3-0-0	1.000	1

Member of the Western Athletic Association (1962-1977) 71-18-0 .798

Year	AP	Other	Overall W-L-T	PF	PA	Pct.	Conf. W-L-T	Pct.	Rank	Year	AP	Other	Overall W-L-T	PF	PA	Pct.	Conf. W-L-T	Pct.	Rank
1962	18		7-2-1	304	126	.750	1-1-0	.500	*	1970	6	8	11-0-0	405	148	1.000	7-0-0	1.000	1
1963	13		8-1-0	249	122	.889	3-0-0	1.000	*	1971	8	6	11-1-0	462	201	.917	7-0-0	1.000	1
1964			8-2-0	230	125	.800	0-2-0	.000	*	1972	13	13	10-2-0	562	296	.833	5-1-0	.833	1
1965			6-4-0	132	142	.600	3-1-0	.750	2	1973	9	10	11-1-0	519	171	.917	6-1-0	.857	1
1966			5-5-0	166	174	.500	3-2-0	.600	2	1974			7-5-0	267	163	.583	4-3-0	.571	3
1967	20		8-2-0	350	210	.800	4-1-0	.800	2	1975	2	2	12-0-0	347	127	1.000	7-0-0	1.000	1
1968			8-2-0	414	163	.800	5-1-0	.833	2	1976			4-7-0	223	241	.364	4-3-0	.571	3
1969			8-2-0	383	179	.800	6-1-0	.857	1	1977	18	18	9-3-0	399	196	.750	6-1-0	.857	1

* Ineligible for conference title because ASU played fewer than qualifying number of games.

Member of the Pac-10 Conference (1978-2003) 98-94-4 .510

Year	AP	Overall W-L-T	PF	PA	Pct.	Conf. W-L-T	Pct.	Rank	Year	Overall W-L-T	PF	PA	Pct.	Conf. W-L-T	Pct.
1978	19	9-3-0	347	236	.750	4-3-0	.571	4	1979**	0-5-0	118	55	.000	0-3-0	.000

**Kush resigned in mid-season. Three wins were forfeited. Pre-forfeits, Kush record was 3-2-0 overall, 2-1-0 in Pac-10.

Bob Owens (1979) 1-6-0 .143

Year			W-L-T	PF	PA	Pct	Conf	CPct	Fin
1979***			1-6-0	188	153	.143	0-4-0	.000	10

***Took over in mid-season. Two wins were forfeited. Pre-forfeits, Owens record was 3-4-0 overall, 1-3-0 in Pac-10

Darryl Rogers (1980-1984) 37-18-1 .670

Year			W-L-T	PF	PA	Pct	Conf	CPct	Fin	Year	W-L-T	PF	PA	Pct	Conf	CPct	Fin
1980			7-4-0	311	216	.636	5-3-0	.625	4	1983	6-4-1	320	200	.591	3-3-1	.500	6
1981	16		9-2-0	394	193	.818	5-2-0	.714	2	1984	5-6-0	297	203	.455	3-4-0	.429	6
1982	6	6	10-2-0	294	145	.833	5-2-0	.714	3								

John Cooper (1985-1987) 25-9-2 .722

Year			W-L-T	PF	PA	Pct	Conf	CPct	Fin	Year		W-L-T	PF	PA	Pct	Conf	CPct	Fin
1985			8-4-0	285	168	.667	5-2-0	.714	2	1987	20	7-4-1	334	259	.625	3-3-1	.500	4
1986	4	5	10-1-1	379	167	.875	5-1-1	.786	1									

Larry Marmie (1988-1991) 22-21-1 .511

Year			W-L-T	PF	PA	Pct	Conf	CPct	Fin	Year	W-L-T	PF	PA	Pct	Conf	CPct	Fin
1988			6-5-0	192	277	.545	3-4-0	.429	5	1990	4-7-0	272	294	.364	2-5-0	.286	8
1989			6-4-1	241	258	.591	3-3-1	.500	5	1991	6-5-0	218	210	.545	4-4-0	.500	5

Bruce Snyder (1992-2000) 58-45-0 .563

Year			W-L-T	PF	PA	Pct	Conf	CPct	Fin	Year			W-L-T	PF	PA	Pct	Conf	CPct	Fin
1992			6-5-0	235	185	.545	4-4-0	.500	6	1997	14	14	9-3-0	324	210	.750	6-2-0	.750	3
1993			6-5-0	282	248	.545	4-4-0	.500	5	1998			5-6-0	333	338	.455	4-4-0	.500	5
1994			3-8-0	242	347	.273	2-6-0	.250	8	1999			6-6-0	285	311	.500	5-3-0	.625	4
1995			6-5-0	308	330	.545	4-4-0	.500	5	2000			6-6-0	313	307	.500	3-5-0	.375	5
1996	4	4	11-1-0	488	201	.917	8-0-0	1.000	1										

Dirk Koetter (2001-2003) 17-20-0 .459

Year			W-L-T	PF	PA	Pct	Conf	CPct	Fin	Year	W-L-T	PF	PA	Pct	Conf	CPct	Fin
2001			4-7-0	374	361	.364	1-7-0	.125	9	2003	5-7-0	298	328	.417	2-6-0	.250	8
2002			8-6-0	452	407	.571	5-3-0	.625	3								

Won-lost record by decades:

1897-99	3- 1-0	.750	1930-39	36-44-6	.453	1970-79	85-33-0	.720	
1900-09	9- 6-0	.600	1940-49	32-37-5	.466	1980-89	74-36-4	.667	
1910-19	7-10-0	.412	1950-59	74-25-3	.740	1990-99	62-51-0	.549	
1920-29	25-20-5	.550	1960-69	72-26-1	.732	2000-03	23-26-0	.469	

Historical record (1997-2003) 502-315-24 .611

Post-season won-lost record 10-9-1 .525

1940: Sun Bowl, ASU 0, Catholic University 0	1978: Garden State Bowl, ASU 34, Rutgers 18
1941: Sun Bowl, Case Western 26, ASU 13	1983: Fiesta Bowl, ASU 32, Oklahoma 21
1950: Salad Bowl, Xavier 33, ASU 21	1985: Holiday Bowl, Arkansas 18, ASU 17
1951: Salad Bowl, Miami (O) 34, ASU 21	1987: Rose Bowl, ASU 22, Michigan 15
1970: Peach Bowl, ASU 48, North Carolina 26	1987: Freedom Bowl, ASU 33, Air Force 28
1971: Fiesta Bowl, ASU 45, Florida State 38	1997: Rose Bowl, Ohio State 20, ASU 17
1972: Fiesta Bowl, ASU 49, Missouri 35	1997: Sun Bowl, ASU 17, Iowa 7
1973: Fiesta Bowl, ASU 28, Pittsburgh 7	1999: Aloha Bowl, Wake Forest 23, ASU 3
1975: Fiesta Bowl, ASU 17, Nebraska 14	2000: Aloha Bowl, Boston College 31, ASU 17
1977: Fiesta Bowl, Penn State 42, ASU 30	2002: Holiday Bowl, Kansas State 34, ASU 27

College Football Hall of Fame:
Dan Devine, coach, 1955-57; Frank Kush, coach, 1958-79; Danny White, quarterback, 1971-73; Michael Haynes, cornerback, 1972-75, Ron Pritchard, linebacker, 1966-68; John Jefferson, wide receiver, 1974-77.

Awards: Lombardi Award: 2002, Terrell Suggs; Nagurski Award: 2002, Terrell Suggs; Hendricks Award: 2002, Terrell Suggs.

UNIVERSITY OF ARIZONA, Tucson, Arizona; nickname "Wildcats"; colors cardinal and navy; Arizona Stadium (56,002); Pac-10 Conference. Arizona began play in 1899. Arizona was a founding member of the Border Conference in 1931 and played in that conference through the 1960 season. Arizona played as an independent in the 1961 season and then joined the newly organized Western Athletic Conference for the 1962 season. It played in the WAC through the 1977 season and then, together with Arizona State, joined the Pacific-8 Conference, which was renamed the Pacific-10 Conference.

Early days as an independent (1899-1930)

Year	Coach	W-L-T	PF	PA	Pct.	Year	Coach	W-L-T	PF	PA	Pct.
1899	Stuart Forbes	1-1-1	24	16	.500	1907	no team				
1900	William Skinner	3-1-0	131	6	.750	1908	H. Galbraith	5-0-0	136	5	1.000
1901	William Skinner	4-1-0	115	19	.800	1909	H. Galbraith	3-1-0	71	23	.750
1902	Leslie Gillett	5-0-0	134	0	1.000	1910	George Shipp	5-0-0	87	8	1.000
1903	no team					1911	George Shipp	3-1-1	16	3	.700
1904	Orin Kates	3-1-2	66	48	.667	1912	R. Quigley	2-1-0	65	30	.667
1905	W. Ruthrauff	4-2-0	84	96	.667	1913	Frank King	2-2-0	26	42	.500
1906	no team										

J. F. "Pop" McKale (1914-1930) 80-32-6 .703

Year		W-L-T	PF	PA	Pct.	Year		W-L-T	PF	PA	Pct.
1914		4-1-0	72	20	.800	1923		5-3-0	146	127	.625
1915		5-3-0	133	34	.625	1924		2-4-0	40	93	.333
1916		5-3-0	247	93	.625	1925		3-3-1	77	88	.500
1917		3-2-0	118	41	.600	1926		5-1-1	143	59	.786
1918	no team					1927		4-2-1	165	59	.643
1919		7-1-0	253	19	.875	1928		5-1-2	152	110	.750
1920		6-1-0	381	65	.857	1929		7-1-0	182	22	.875
1921		7-2-0	418	68	.778	1930		6-1-1	122	33	.812
1922		6-3-0	109	53	.667						

Member of the Border Conference (1931-1960) 65-48-4 .572

Year	Nat'l AP Other	Overall W-L-T	PF	PA	Pct.	Conference W-L-T	Pct.	Rank	Year	Nat'l AP Other	Overall W-L-T	PF	PA	Pct.	Conference W-L-T	Pct.	Rank
								Fred Enke (1931) 3-5-1 .389									
1931		3-5-1	72	149	.389	1-1-1	.500	2									
								Gus Farwick (1932) 4-5-0 .444									
1932		4-5-0-	82	106	.444	3-2-0	.600	2									
								Tex Olivier (1933-1937) 32-11-4 .723									
1933		5-3-0	113	35	.625	3-2-0	.600	3	1936		5-2-3	190	54	.650	3-0-1	.875	1
1934		7-2-1	138	54	.750	2-1-1	.625	3	1937		8-2-0	194	88	.800	3-1-0	.750	3
1935		7-2-0	218	45	.778	4-0-0	1.000	1									
								Orian Landreth (1938) 3-6-0 .333									
1938		3-6-0	75	146	.333	0-3-0	.000	6									
								Miles Casteel (1939-1942, 1945-1948) 46-26-3 .633									
1939		6-4-0	109	113	.600	1-2-0	.333	4	1944	no team							
1940		7-2-0	204	83	.778	3-1-0	.750	2	1945*		5-0-0	193	12	1.000			
1941		7-3-0	253	146	.700	5-0-0	1.000	1	1946		4-4-2	218	136	.500	2-2-1	.500	4
1942		6-4-0	189	139	.600	4-2-0	.667	4	1947		5-4-1	223	241	.550	3-2-0	.600	4
1943	no team								1948		6-5-0	167	246	.545	3-2-0	.600	3

*The Border Conference did not operate from 1943 through 1945.

Year	Nat'l AP Other	Overall W-L-T	PF	PA	Pct.	Conference W-L-T	Pct.	Rank	Year	Nat'l AP Other	Overall W-L-T	PF	PA	Pct.	Conference W-L-T	Pct.	Rank
								Bob Winslow (1949-1951) 12-18-1 .403									
1949		2-7-1	118	298	.250	2-4-0	.333	6	1951		6-5-0	246	270	.545	4-3-0	.571	4
1950		4-6-0	214	257	.400	2-4-0	.333	6									
								W. Woodson (1952-1956) 25-22-2 .531									
1952		6-4-0	285	155	.600	3-2-0	.600	3	1955		4-4-1	184	169	.500	1-2-1	.375	5
1953		4-5-1	234	181	.450	3-1-0	.750	3	1956		4-6-0	180	182	.400	1-3-0	.250	5
1954		7-3-0	385	215	.700	3-2-0	.600	4									
								Ed Doherty (1957-1958) 4-15-1 .225									
1957		1-8-1	125	297	.150	0-4-0	.000	5	1958		3-7-0	83	276	.300	2-1-0	.667	3
								Jim LaRue (1959-1966) 41-37-2 .538									
1959		4-6-0	118	211	.400	2-1-0	.667	2	1961*	18	8-1-1	288	131	.850			
1960		7-3-0	233	152	.700	3-0-0	1.000	2									

*Arizona left the Border Conference after the 1960 season, and was independent in 1961.

Member of the Western Athletic Association (1962-1977) 50-43-0 .538

Year	Nat'l AP Other	Overall W-L-T	PF	PA	Pct.	Conference W-L-T	Pct.	Rank	Year	Nat'l AP Other	Overall W-L-T	PF	PA	Pct.	Conference W-L-T	Pct.	Rank
1962		5-5-0	134	171	.500	2-2-0	500	2	1965		3-7-0	77	172	.300	1-4-0	.200	6
1963		5-5-0	136	165	.500	2-2-0	.500	2	1966		3-7-0	192	250	.300	1-4-0	.200	5
1964		6-3-1	147	76	.650	3-1-0	.750	1									
								Darrell Mudra (1967-1968) 11-9-1 .548									
1967		3-6-1	162	231	.350	1-4-0	.200	5	1968		8-3-0	186	149	.727	5-1-0	.833	2
								Robert Weber (1969-1972) 16-26-0 .381									
1969		3-7-0	210	276	.300	3-3-0	.500	5	1971		5-6-0	191	213	.455	3-3-0	.500	3
1970		4-6-0	168	213	.400	2-4-0	.333	5	1972		4-7-0	226	271	.364	4-3-0	.571	4

Jim Young (1973-1976) 31-13-0 .705

Year			W-L-T	PF	PA	Pct	Conf	Pct		Year			W-L-T	PF	PA	Pct	Conf	Pct	
1973			8-3-0	295	219	.727	6-1-0	.857	1	1975	18	13	9-2-0	330	169	.857	5-2-0	.714	2
1974			9-2-0	264	174	.818	6-1-0	.857	2	1976			5-6-0	283	273	.455	3-4-0	.428	5

Tony Mason (1977-1979) 16-18-1 .471

| 1977 | | | 5-7-0 | 256 | 250 | .417 | 3-4-0 | .429 | 5 |

Member of the Pac-10 Conference (1978-2003) 101-97-6 .510

| 1978 | | | 5-6-0 | 245 | 205 | .455 | 3-4-0 | .429 | 6 | 1979 | | | 6-5-1 | 244 | 243 | .542 | 4-3-0 | .571 | 3 |

Larry Smith (1980-1986) 48-28-3 .627

1980			5-6-0	215	275	.455	3-4-0	.429	6	1984			7-4-0	272	192	.636	5-2-0	.714	3
1981			6-5-0	253	205	.545	4-4-0	.500	6	1985			8-3-1	252	146	.708	5-2-0	.714	2
1982			6-4-1	311	219	.591	4-3-1	.562	5	1986	11	10	9-3-0	352	204	.750	5-3-0	.625	4
1983			7-3-1	353	118	.692	4-3-1	.562	5										

Dick Tomey   (1987-2000) 95-64-4 .595

1987			4-4-3	263	220	.500	2-3-3	.438	7	1994	20	20	8-4-0	278	190	.667	6-2-0	.750	2
1988			7-4-0	179	171	.636	5-3-0	.625	3	1995			6-5-0	207	199	.545	4-4-0	.500	5
1989	25		8-4-0	248	178	.667	5-3-0	.625	2	1996			5-6-0	310	280	.455	3-5-0	.375	5
1990			7-5-0	267	311	.583	5-4-0	.556	5	1997			7-5-0	317	285	.583	4-4-0	.500	5
1991			4-7-0	248	361	.364	3-5-0	.375	6	1998	4	4	12-1-0	439	236	.923	7-1-0	.875	2
1992			6-5-1	232	118	.542	4-3-1	.562	5	1999			6-6-0	339	364	.500	3-5-0	.375	6
1993	10	9	10-2-0	294	161	.833	6-2-0	.750	1	2000			5-6-0	254	237	.455	3-5-0	.375	5

John Mackovic (2001-2003) 10-18-0 .357

| 2001 | | | 5-6-0 | 320 | 377 | .455 | 2-6-0 | .250 | 8 | 2003* | | | 1-4-0 | 82 | 186 | .200 | 0-1-0 | .000 | |
| 2002 | | | 4-8-0 | 227 | 310 | .333 | 1-7-0 | .125 | 9 | | | | | | | | | | |

Mike Hankwitz (2003) 1-6-0 .143

| 2003* | | | 1-6-0 | 99 | 243 | .143 | 1-6-0 | .243 | 10 |

*Mackovic coached the first five games of the 2003 season, and Hankwitz coached the last seven.

Won-lost record by decades:

1899-09	28- 7-3	.776	1940-49	42-29-4	.587	1980-89	67-40-6	.619
1910-19	36-14-1	.716	1950-59	43-54-3	.445	1990-99	71-46-1	.606
1920-29	50-21-5	.691	1960-69	51-47-3	.520	2000-03	16-30-0	.348
1930-39	54-32-6	.620	1970-79	60-50-1	.545			

Historical total (1899-2003) 518-370-33 .580

Post-season won-lost record 5-7-1 .423

1921: East-West Christmas Classic, Centre College 38, Arizona 0
1949: Salad Bowl, Drake 14, Arizona 13
1968: Sun Bowl, Auburn 34, Arizona 10
1979: Fiesta Bowl, Pittsburgh 16, Arizona 10
1985: Sun Bowl, Arizona 13, Georgia 13
1986: Aloha Bowl, Arizona 30, North Carolina 21
1989: Copper Bowl, Arizona 17, NC State 10

1990: Eagle Aloha Bowl, Syracuse 28, Arizona 0
1992: John Hancock Bowl, Baylor 20, Arizona 15
1994: Fiesta Bowl, Arizona 29, Miami (Fl) 0
1994: Freedom Bowl, Utah 16, Arizona 13
1997: Insight.com Bowl, Arizona 20, New Mexico 14
1998: Holiday Bowl, Arizona 23, Nebraska 20

College Football Hall of Fame:
Warren Woodson, coach, 1952-56; Darrell Mudra, coach, 1967-68; Jim Young, coach, 1973-76; Rickey Hunley, linebacker, 1980-83.

Awards: Jim Thorpe Award, 1990: Darryl Lewis; Lou Groza Award, 1994: Steve McLaughlin; Outland Trophy, 1993: Rob Waldrop; Chuck Bednarik Award, 1993: Rob Waldrop; Tatupu Award: 1998, Chris McAlistor; Nagurski Award: 1993, Rob Waldrop.

ARKANSAS STATE UNIVERSITY, Jonesboro, Arkansas; nickname "Indians"; colors scarlet and black; Indian Stadium (33,410); Sun Belt Conference. ASU began play in 1911 as an independent. In 1975, ASU became a Division 1 independent and in 1979 the team was awarded 1-A status. In 1982, ASU became a 1-AA team. ASU reverted to 1-A status in 1992 as an independent and then joined the Big West Conference in 1999. When this conference disbanded after the 2000 season, Arkansas State joined several other Big West teams in moving to the newly formed Sun Belt Conference.

Early years (1911-1941)

Year	Coach	W-L-T	PF	PA	Pct.	Year	Coach	W-L-T	PF	PA	Pct.
1911	F. T. Parks	1-1-0	12	11	.500	1927	Herbert Schwartz	4-3-0	61	56	.571
1912	F. T. Parks	3-1-0	39	20	.750	1928	Herbert Schwartz	3-3-1	105	65	.500
1913	Clinton Young	3-1-1	157	30	.700	1929	Herbert Schwartz	1-5-0	61	137	.167
1914	Earl Brannon	4-3-0	85	94	.571	1930	Herbert Schwartz	1-4-3	20	84	.312
1915	Earl Brannon	4-1-1	100	13	.750	1931	Jack Dale	6-2-0	98	53	.750
1916	Earl Brannon	4-3-0	72	51	.571	1932	Jack Dale	3-4-0	98	73	.429
1917	Earl Brannon	4-2-1	158	54	.643	1933	E. T. Renfro	2-4-2	34	79	.375
1918	no team					1934	Tommie Mills	2-5-1	31	80	.312
1919	Foy Hammons	2-5-0	27	101	.286	1935	Tommie Mills	2-7-0	38	198	.222
1920	Foy Hammons	3-3-0	56	97	.500	1936	Leslie Speck	3-5-0	54	188	.375
1921	Foy Hammons	3-2-1	47	33	.583	1937	Leslie Speck	1-5-0	16	267	.167
1922	Tom Dandelet	0-7-0	0	401	.000	1938	Leslie Speck	3-3-0	54	68	.500
1923	Tom Dandelet	0-6-1	0	164	.072	1939	Bill Adams	4-3-0	65	98	.571
1924	Bill Stanley	4-4-0	95	56	.500	1940	Bill Adams	1-4-2	45	98	.286
1925	Herbert Schwartz	4-3-1	65	118	.562	1941	Bill Adams	0-7-0	0	308	.000
1926	Herbert Schwartz	4-3-1	60	71	.562	1942-1944	no team				

Ike Tomlinson (1945) 2-4-1 .357

Year	W-L-T	PF	PA	Pct.	Year	W-L-T	PF	PA	Pct.
1945	2-4-1	51	95	.357					

Frosty England (1946-1953) 49-21-9 .677

Year	W-L-T	PF	PA	Pct.	Year	W-L-T	PF	PA	Pct.
1946	4-3-3	99	103	.550	1950	6-3-0	200	179	.667
1947	4-2-3	159	91	.611	1951	10-2-0	456	98	.833
1948	4-4-1	131	186	.500	1952	8-3-0	351	117	.727
1949	5-4-0	111	149	.556	1953	8-0-2	239	65	.900

Glenn Harmeson (1954) 1-8-0 .111

Year	W-L-T	PF	PA	Pct.	Year	W-L-T	PF	PA	Pct.
1954	1-8-0	74	349	.111					

Gene Harlow (1955-1957) 15-12-0 .556

Year	W-L-T	PF	PA	Pct.	Year	W-L-T	PF	PA	Pct.
1955	6-3-0	202	127	.667	1957	4-5-0	138	180	.444
1956	5-4-0	193	170	.556					

Bones Taylor (1958-1959) 7-11-0 .389

Year	W-L-T	PF	PA	Pct.	Year	W-L-T	PF	PA	Pct.
1958	4-5-0	162	176	.444	1959	3-6-0	171	214	.333

King Block (1960-1962) 13-14-0 .482

Year	W-L-T	PF	PA	Pct.	Year	W-L-T	PF	PA	Pct.
1960	4-5-0	116	138	.444	1962	6-3-0	146	96	.667
1961	3-6-0	84	179	.333					

Bennie Ellender (1963-1970) 52-20-4 .711

Year	W-L-T	PF	PA	Pct.	Year	W-L-T	PF	PA	Pct.
1963	2-6-0	159	174	.250	1967	4-5-0	126	116	.444
1964	7-0-2	148	61	.889	1968	7-3-1	245	172	.682
1965	6-3-0	157	107	.667	1969	8-1-1	262	140	.850
1966	7-2-0	222	109	.778	1970	11-0-0	360	134	1.000

Bill Davidson (1971-1978) 51-32-1 .613

Year	W-L-T	PF	PA	Pct.	Year	W-L-T	PF	PA	Pct.
1971	4-4-1	174	147	.500	1975	11-0-0	355	81	1.000
1972	3-8-0	163	198	.273	1976	5-6-0	274	221	.455
1973	7-3-0	249	166	.700	1977	7-4-0	184	214	.636
1974	7-3-0	215	122	.700	1978	7-4-0	163	144	.636

Larry Lacewell (1979-1989) 69-58-4 .542

Year	W-L-T	PF	PA	Pct.	Year	W-L-T	PF	PA	Pct.
1979	4-7-0	167	188	.364	1985	9-4-0	322	169	.692
1980	2-9-0	129	269	.182	1986	12-2-1	452	210	.833
1981	6-5-0	177	159	.545	1987	8-4-1	395	277	.654
1982	5-6-0	170	244	.455	1988	5-6-0	261	245	.455
1983	5-5-1	195	226	.500	1989	5-6-0	261	265	.455
1984	8-4-1	347	187	.654					

Al Kincaid (1990-1991) 4-17-1 .205

Year	W-L-T	PF	PA	Pct.	Year	W-L-T	PF	PA	Pct.
1990	3-7-1	200	313	.318	1991	1-10-0	189	361	.091

Ray Perkins (1992) 2-9-0 .182

Year	W-L-T	PF	PA	Pct.
1992	2-9-0	118	402	.182

Member of the Big West Conference (1993-1995, 1999-2000) 7-21-0 .250

John Bobo (1993-1996) 13-30-1 .307

Year	Nat'l AP	Other	Overall W-L-T	PF	PA	Pct.	Conference W-L-T	Pct.	Rank	Year	Nat'l AP	Other	Overall W-L-T	PF	PA	Pct.	Conference W-L-T	Pct.	Rank
1993			2-8-1	122	274	.227	1-5-0	.167	10	1995			6-5-0	265	270	.545	3-3-0	.500	4
1994			1-10-0	123	316	.091	0-6-0	.000	10										

Arkansas State reverts to independent status (1996-1998)

| 1996 | | | 4-7-0 | 272 | 365 | .364 | | | | | | | | | | | | | |

Joe Hollis (1997-2001) 13-43-0 .232

| 1997 | | | 2-9-0 | 201 | 394 | .182 | | | | 1998 | | | 4-8-0 | 216 | 385 | .333 | | | |

Arkansas State rejoins the Big West Conference (1999-2000)

| 1999 | | | 4-7-0 | 246 | 332 | .364 | 2-3-0 | .400 | 5 | 2000 | | | 1-10-0 | | | .091 | 1-4-0 | .200 | 4 |

Member of the Sun Belt Conference (2001-2003) 8-11-0 .421

| 2001 | | | 2-9-0 | 177 | 357 | .182 | 2-4-0 | .333 | 4 | | | | | | | | | | |

Steve Roberts (2002-2003) 11-14-0 .440

| 2002 | | | 6-7-0 | 259 | 361 | .462 | 3-3-0 | .500 | 3 | 2003 | | | 5-7-0 | 242 | 401 | .417 | 3-4-0 | .429 | 4 |

Won-loss record by decades:

1911-19	25-17-3	.589	1950-59	55-39-2	.583	1980-89	65-51-4	.558
1920-29	27-39-5	.415	1960-69	54-34-4	.609	1990-99	29-80-2	.270
1930-39	27-42-6	.400	1970-79	66-39-1	.627	2000-03	14-33-0	.298
1940-49	20-28-10	.431						
Historic record	382-402-37	.488						

Post-season won-loss record 9-7-1 .559

1951: Refrigerator Bowl, ASU 46, Camp Breckenridge 12
1952: Tangerine Bowl, Stetson 35, ASU 20
1952: Refrigerator Bowl, Western Kentucky 34, ASU 19
1954: Tangerine Bowl, ASU 7, East Texas State 7
1968: Pecan Bowl, North Dakota State 23, ASU 14
1969: Pecan Bowl, ASU 29, Drake 21
1970: Pecan Bowl, ASU 38, Central Missouri 21
1984: I-AA Playoffs, ASU 37, Tennessee Chattanooga 10
1984: 1-AA Playoffs, Montana State 31, ASU 14

1985: 1-AA Playoffs, ASU 10, Grambling 7
1985: 1-AA Playoffs, Nevada 24, ASU 23
1986: 1-AA Playoffs, ASU 48, Sam Houston State 7
1986: 1-AA Playoffs, ASU 55, Delaware 14
1986: 1-AA Playoffs, ASU 24, Eastern Kentucky 10
1986: 1-AA Championship, Ga. Southern 48, ASU 21
1987: 1-AA Playoffs, ASU 35, Jackson State 32
1987: 1-AA Playoffs, Northern Iowa 49, ASU 28

UNIVERSITY OF ARKANSAS, Fayetteville, Arkansas; nickname "Razorbacks"; colors cardinal and white; Donald W. Reynolds Razorback Stadium (72,000); Southeastern Conference. Arkansas began play in 1894, and then joined the Southwest Conference as a founding member in 1915. Arkansas played in the SWC through the 1991 season and then left to join the Southeastern Conference, beginning with the 1992 season.

Early years as an independent (1894-1914)

Year	Coach	W-L-T	PF	PA	Pct.	Year	Coach	W-L-T	PF	PA	Pct.
1894	John Futrall	2-1-0	80	54	.667	1905	A.D. Brown	2-6-0	32	50	.250
1895	John Futrall	1-0-0	30	0	1.000	1906	F.C. Longman	2-4-2	45	71	.375
1896	John Futrall	2-1-0	16	36	.667	1907	F.C. Longman	3-4-1	73	110	.438
1897	B.N. Wilson	2-0-1	42	6	.833	1908	Hugo Bezdek	5-4-0	214	120	.556
1898	B. N. Wilson	2-1-0	37	42	.667	1909	Hugo Bezdek	7-0-0	184	18	1.000
1899	Colbert Searles	3-1-1	37	21	.700	1910	Hugo Bezdek	7-1-0	221	19	.875
1900	Colbert Searles	2-1-1	36	23	.625	1911	Hugo Bezdek	6-2-1	268	23	.722
1901	Charles Thomas	3-5-0	98	52	.375	1912	Hugo Bezdek	4-6-0	149	179	.400
1902	Charles Thomas	6-3-0	138	73	.667	1913	E.T. Pickering	7-2-0	137	43	.778
1903	D.A. McDaniel	3-4-0	50	63	.428	1914	E.T. Pickering	4-5-0	83	187	.444
1904	A.D. Brown	4-3-0	62	55	.571						

Member of Southwest Conference (1915-1991) 249-195-16 .557

Year	Nat'l AP Other	Overall W-L-T	PF	PA	Pct.	Conference W-L-T	Pct.	Rank	Year	Nat'l AP Other	Overall W-L-T	PF	PA	Pct.	Conference W-L-T	Pct.	Rank
					T.T. McConnell (1915-1916) 8-6-1 .567												
1915		4-2-1	121	55	.643	1-1-0	.500	2	1916		4-4-0	261	123	.500	0-2-0	.000	5
					Norman Paine (1917-1918) 8-3-1 .708												
1917		5-1-1	118	27	.786	0-1-1	.250	6	1918		3-2-0	41	121	.600	0-1-0	.000	6
					J. B. Craig (1919) 3-4-0 .428												
1919		3-4-0	55	164	.428	1-2-0	.333	5									
					G.W. McLaren (1920-1921) 8-5-3 .594												
1920		3-2-2	42	22	.571	2-0-1	.833	2	1921		5-3-1	144	48	.611	2-1-0	.667	3
					Francis Schmidt (1922-1928) 42-20-3 .669												
1922		5-4-0	138	123	.556	1-3-0	.250	6	1926		5-5-0	179	88	.500	2-2-0	.500	3
1923		6-2-1	158	40	.722	2-2-0	.500	4	1927		8-1-0	218	76	.889	3-1-0	.750	3
1924		7-2-1	227	69	.750	1-2-1	.375	7	1928		7-2-0	251	63	.778	3-1-0	.750	2
1925		4-4-1	95	62	.500	2-2-1	.500	4									
					Fred Thomsen (1929-1941) 49-69-9 .480												
1929		7-2-0	230	93	.778	3-2-0	.600	3	1936 18		7-3-0	178	87	.700	5-1-0	.833	1
1930		3-6-0	78	154	.333	2-2-0	.500	4	1937 15		6-2-2	186	89	.700	3-2-1	.583	3
1931		3-5-1	82	126	.389	0-4-0	.000	7	1938		2-7-1	128	125	.250	1-5-0	.167	6
1932		1-6-2	58	133	.222	1-4-0	.200	7	1939		4-5-1	115	118	.450	2-3-1	.417	5
1933*		0-11-0	213	61	.000	0-5-0	.000	*	1940		4-6-0	112	174	.400	1-5-0	.167	6
1934		4-4-2	95	76	.500	2-3-1	.417	5	1941		3-7-0	118	149	.300	0-6-0	.000	7
1935		5-5-0	152	109	.500	2-4-0	.333	5									

*Arkansas forfeited all 1933 games. The record before forfeits was 7-3-1; Thomsen's overall record before forfeits was 56-61-10.

					George Cole (1942) 3-7-0 .300												
1942		3-7-0	88	228	.300	0-6-0	.000	7									
					John Tomlin (1943) 2-7-0 .222												
1943		2-7-0	105	192	.222	1-4-0	.200	5									
					Glen Rose (1944-1945) 8-12-1 .405												
1944		5-5-1	120	161	.500	2-2-1	.500	3	1945		3-7-0	112	222	.300	1-5-0	.167	7
					John Barnhill (1946-1949) 22-17-3 .560												
1946 16		6-3-2	136	92	.583	5-1-0	.833	1	1948		5-5-0	227	146	.500	2-4-0	.333	5
1947		6-4-1	191	145	.591	1-4-1	.250	5	1949		5-5-0	147	175	.500	2-4-0	.333	6
					Otis Douglans (1950-1952) 9-21-0 .300												
1950		2-8-0	156	163	.200	1-5-0	.167	7	1952		2-8-0	166	282	.200	1-5-0	.167	7
1951		5-5-0	178	162	.500	2-4-0	.333	5									
					Bowden Wyatt (1953-1954) 11-10-0 .524												
1953		3-7-0	116	161	.300	2-4-0	.333	5	1954 10	8	8-3-0	195	90	.727	5-1-0	.833	1
					Jack Mitchell (1955-1957) 17-12-1 .583												
1955		5-4-1	126	115	.550	3-2-1	.583	4	1957		6-4-0	187	134	.600	2-4-0	.333	5
1956		6-4-0	160	155	.600	3-3-0	.500	4									
					Frank Broyles (1958-1976) 144-58-5 .707												
1958		4-6-0	147	150	.400	2-4-0	.333	5	1968	6 9	10-1-0	334	187	.909	6-1-0	.857	1
1959	9 9	9-2-0	149	94	.818	5-1-0	.833	1	1969	7 3	9-2-0	376	76	.818	6-1-0	.857	2
1960	7 7	8-3-0	179	80	.727	6-1-0	.857	1	1970	11 12	9-2-0	402	144	.818	6-1-0	.857	1
1961	9 8	8-3-0	180	87	.727	6-1-0	.857	1	1971	16 20	8-3-1	343	155	.708	5-1-1	.786	2
1962	6 6	9-2-0	246	88	.818	6-1-0	.857	2	1972		6-5-0	228	227	.545	3-4-0	.429	4
1963		5-5-0	179	96	.500	3-4-0	.428	4	1973		5-5-1	124	184	.500	3-3-1	.500	4
1964	2 2	11-0-0	221	57	1.000	7-0-0	1.000	1	1974		6-4-1	285	164	.591	3-3-1	.500	4
1965	3 2	10-1-0	324	104	.909	7-0-0	1.000	1	1975	7 6	10-2-0	305	113	.833	6-1-0	.857	1

— 40 —

Year			W-L-T	PF	PA	Pct	Conf	Pct		Year			W-L-T	PF	PA	Pct	Conf	Pct	
1966	13		8-2-0	218	73	.800	5-2-0	.714	2	1976			5-5-1	220	204	.500	3-4-1	.438	6
1967			4-5-1	200	149	.450	3-3-1	.500	5										

Lou Holtz (1977-1983) 60-21-2 .735

Year			W-L-T	PF	PA	Pct	Conf	Pct		Year			W-L-T	PF	PA	Pct	Conf	Pct	
1977	3	3	11-1-0	358	95	.917	7-1-0	.875	2	1981		16	8-4-0	298	188	.667	5-3-0	.625	4
1978	11	10	9-2-1	326	137	.792	6-2-0	.750	2	1982	9	8	9-2-1	275	115	.792	5-2-1	.688	3
1979	8	9	10-2-0	275	108	.833	7-1-0	.857	1	1983			6-5-0	204	172	.545	4-4-0	.500	5
1980			7-5-0	238	221	.583	3-5-0	.375	6										

Ken Hatfield (1984-1989) 55-17-1 .760

Year			W-L-T	PF	PA	Pct	Conf	Pct		Year			W-L-T	PF	PA	Pct	Conf	Pct	
1984			7-4-1	253	138	.625	5-3-0	.625	3	1987			9-4-0	283	199	.692	5-2-0	.714	2
1985	12	12	10-2-0	305	129	.833	6-2-0	.750	2	1988	12	13	10-2-0	346	173	.833	7-0-0	1.000	1
1986	15	16	9-3-0	303	142	.750	6-2-0	.750	2	1989	13	13	10-2-0	358	199	.833	7-1-0	.875	1

Jack Crowe (1990-1991) 9-14-0 .391

Year			W-L-T	PF	PA	Pct	Conf	Pct		Year			W-L-T	PF	PA	Pct	Conf	Pct	
1990			3-8-0	263	360	.273	1-7-0	.125	7	1991			6-6-0	160	179	.500	5-3-0	.625	2

Member of the Southeastern Conference (1992-2003) 45-49-2 .474
Joe Kines (1992) 3-6-1 .350

Year			W-L-T	PF	PA	Pct	Conf	Pct		Year			W-L-T	PF	PA	Pct	Conf	Pct	
1992			3-6-1	172	209	.318	3-4-1	.438	8										

Danny Ford (1993-1997) 26-29-1 .473

Year			W-L-T	PF	PA	Pct	Conf	Pct		Year			W-L-T	PF	PA	Pct	Conf	Pct	
1993*			6-4-1	165	208	.591	4-3-1	.562	*	1996			4-7-0	174	267	.365	2-6-0	.250	10
1994			4-7-0	212	213	.364	2-6-0	.250	8	1997			4-7-0	181	284	.365	2-6-0	.250	9
1995			8-4-0	274	283	.667	6-2-0	.750	3										

* Arkansas not eligible for SEC title.

Houston Nutt (1998-2003) 48-27-0 .640

Year			W-L-T	PF	PA	Pct	Conf	Pct		Year			W-L-T	PF	PA	Pct	Conf	Pct	
1998	16	17	9-3-0	390	227	.750	6-2-0	.750	3	2001			7-5-0	294	279	.583	4-4-0	.500	7
1999	17	19	8-4-0	353	214	.667	4-4-0	.500	6	2002			9-5-0	370	277	.643	5-3-0	.625	6
2000			6-6-0	264	258	.500	3-5-0	.375	9	2003			9-4-0	436	305	.692	4-4-0	.500	7

Won-lost record by decades*:

1894-99	12- 4-2	.722	1930-39	35-54-9	.403	1970-79	79-31-5	.709
1900-09	37-34-4	.520	1940-49	42-56-4	.431	1980-89	85-33-2	.717
1910-19	47-29-3	.614	1950-59	50-51-1	.495	1990-99	55-56-2	.496
1920-29	57-27-6	.667	1960-69	82-24-1	.771	2000-03	31-20-0	.608

Historic record 612-419-39 .590
*These data reflect the forfeit loss of all games in the 1933 season because of use of an ineligible player.

Post season won-loss record: 10-22-4 .333

1934: Dixie Classic, Arkansas 7, Centenary 7
1947: Cotton Bowl, Arkansas 0, LSU 0
1948: Dixie Bowl, Arkansas 21, Wm. & Mary 19
1955: Cotton Bowl, Georgia Tech 14, Arkansas 6
1960: Gator Bowl, Arkansas 14, Georgia Tech 7
1961: Cotton Bowl, Duke 7, Arkansas 6
1962: Sugar Bowl, Alabama 10, Arkansas 3
1963: Sugar Bowl, Ole Miss 17, Arkansas 13
1965: Cotton Bowl, Arkansas 10, Nebraska 7
1966: Cotton Bowl, LSU 14, Arkansas 7
1969: Sugar Bowl, Arkansas 16, Georgia 2
1970: Sugar Bowl, Ole Miss 27, Arkansas 22
1971: Liberty Bowl, Tennessee 14, Arkansas 13
1976: Cotton Bowl, Arkansas 31, Georgia 10
1976: Orange Bowl, Arkansas 31, Oklahoma 6
1978: Fiesta Bowl, Arkansas 10, UCLA 10

1980: Hall of Fame Bowl, Arkansas 34, Tulane 15
1980: Sugar Bowl, Alabama 24, Arkansas 9
1981: Gator Bowl, North Carolina 31, Arkansas 27
1982: Bluebonnet Bowl, Arkansas 28, Florida 24
1984: Liberty Bowl, Auburn 21, Arkansas 21
1985: Holiday Bowl, Arkansas 18, Arizona State 17
1987: Orange Bowl, Oklahoma 42, Arkansas 8
1987: Liberty Bowl, Georgia 20, Arkansas 17
1989: Cotton Bowl, UCLA 17, Arkansas 3
1990: Cotton Bowl, Tennessee 31, Arkansas 17
1991: Independence Bowl, Georgia 24, Arkansas 15
1995: SEC Championship, Florida 35, Arkansas 24
1995: Carquest Bowl, North Carolina 20, Arkansas 10
1999: Florida Citrus Bowl, Michigan 45, Arkansas 31
2000: Cotton Bowl, Arkansas 27, Texas 6
2000: Las Vegas Bowl, UNLV 31, Arkansas 14
2001: Cotton Bowl, Oklahoma 10, Arkansas 3
2002: SEC Championship, Georgia 30, Arkansas 3
2002: Music City Bowl, Minnesota 29, Arkansas 14
2003: Independence Bowl, Arkansas 24, Missouri 21

College Football Hall of Fame:
Hugo Bezdek, coach, 1909-12; Francis Schmidt, coach, 1922-28; Wear Schoonover, end, 1927-29; Clyde Scott, halfback, 1944-48; Wayne Harris, guard/linebacker, 1958-60; Lance Alworth, halfback, 1959-61; Frank Broyles, coach, 1960-76; Lloyd Phillips, defensive tackle, 1964-66; Chuck Dicus, wide receiver, 1968-70; Billy Ray Smith, defensive end, 1979-82.

Awards:
Outland Trophy: 1954, Bill Brooks; 1966, Lloyd Phillips.

AUBURN UNIVERSITY, Auburn, Alabama; nickname "Tigers"; colors burnt orange and navy blue; Jordan-Hare Stadium (85,063); Southeastern Conference. Auburn was a founding member of the Southern Conference in 1922 and then left that conference after the 1932 season to join the newly formed Southeastern Conference.

Early years as an independent (1892-1921)

Year	Coach	W-L-T	PF	PA	Pct.	Year	Coach	W-L-T	PF	PA	Pct.
1892	George Petrie	2-2-0	42	98	.500	1898	John Heisman	2-1-0	47	47	.667
1893	D.M. Balliet	1-0-0	32	22	1.000	1899	John Heisman	3-1-1	148	11	.700
1893	G.H. Harvey	2-0-2	116	62	.750	1900	Billy Watkins	4-0-0	148	0	1.000
1894	F.M. Hall	1-3-0	106	48	.250	1901	Billy Watkins	2-3-1	50	74	.417
1895	John Heisman	2-1-0	70	15	.667	1902	Robert Kent	2-4-1	46	45	.357
1896	John Heisman	3-1-0	135	18	.750	1903	Billy Bates	4-3-0	125	92	.571
1897	John Heisman	2-0-1	40	4	.833	1907	W.S. Klienholz	6-2-1	185	30	.722

Mike Donahue (1904-1906, 1908-1922) 99-35-5 .730

Year		W-L-T	PF	PA	Pct.	Year		W-L-T	PF	PA	Pct.
1904		5-0-0	73	11	1.000	1914		8-0-1	193	0	.944
1905		2-4-0	38	96	.333	1915		6-2-0	182	24	.750
1906		1-5-1	24	41	.214	1916		6-2-0	201	56	.750
1908		6-1-0	158	10	.857	1917		6-2-1	199	102	.722
1909		5-2-0	116	39	.714	1918		2-5-0	84	116	.286
1910		6-1-0	176	9	.857	1919		8-1-0	132	33	.889
1911		4-2-1	85	45	.643	1920		7-2-0	332	49	.778
1912		6-1-1	164	45	.812	1921		5-3-0	163	52	.625
1913		8-0-0	223	13	1.000						

Member of Southern Conference (1922-1932) 20-40-7 .351

Year	Nat'l AP	Other	Overall W-L-T	PF	PA	Pct.	Conference W-L-T	Pct.	Rank	Year	Nat'l AP	Other	Overall W-L-T	PF	PA	Pct.	Conference W-L-T	Pct.	Rank
1922			8-2-0	276	48	.800	2-1-0	.667	6										

Boozer Pitts (1923-1924, 1927) 7-11-6 .417

Year	Nat'l AP	Other	Overall W-L-T	PF	PA	Pct.	Conference W-L-T	Pct.	Rank	Year	Nat'l AP	Other	Overall W-L-T	PF	PA	Pct.	Conference W-L-T	Pct.	Rank
1923			3-3-3	96	58	.500	0-1-3	.375	16	1924			4-4-1	46	40	.500	2-4-1	.357	16

Dave Morey (1925-1927) 10-10-1 .500

Year	Nat'l AP	Other	Overall W-L-T	PF	PA	Pct.	Conference W-L-T	Pct.	Rank	Year	Nat'l AP	Other	Overall W-L-T	PF	PA	Pct.	Conference W-L-T	Pct.	Rank
1925			5-3-1	81	114	.611	3-2-1	.583	9	1927*			0-3-0	6	42	.000	0-2-0	.000	*
1926			5-4-0	123	85	.556	3-3-0	.500	10										

Boozer Pitts (1927)

Year	Nat'l AP	Other	Overall W-L-T	PF	PA	Pct.	Conference W-L-T	Pct.	Rank
1927*			0-4-2	24	82	.167	0-4-1	.200	22

*Morey resigned after three games of the 1927 season, and Pitts coached the last six games.

George Bohler (1928-1929) 3-11-0 .214

Year	Nat'l AP	Other	Overall W-L-T	PF	PA	Pct.	Conference W-L-T	Pct.	Rank	Year	Nat'l AP	Other	Overall W-L-T	PF	PA	Pct.	Conference W-L-T	Pct.	Rank
1928			1-8-0	37	154	.111	0-7-0	.000	21	1929**			2-3-0	22	80	.400	0-3-0		

John Floyd (1929) 0-4-0 .000

Year	Nat'l AP	Other	Overall W-L-T	PF	PA	Pct.	Conference W-L-T	Pct.	Rank
1929**			0-4-0	6	122	.000	0-4-0	.000	22

**Bohler resigned after five games of the 1929 season, and Floyd coached the last four games.

Chet Wynn (1930-1933) 22-15-2 .591

Year	Nat'l AP	Other	Overall W-L-T	PF	PA	Pct.	Conference W-L-T	Pct.	Rank	Year	Nat'l AP	Other	Overall W-L-T	PF	PA	Pct.	Conference W-L-T	Pct.	Rank
1930			3-7-0	101	135	.300	1-6-0	.143	21	1932			9-0-1	275	54	.944	6-0-1	.929	2
1931			5-3-1	114	78	.531	3-3-0	.500	8										

Member of the Southeastern Conference (1933-2003) 250-201-18 .552

Year	Nat'l AP	Other	Overall W-L-T	PF	PA	Pct.	Conference W-L-T	Pct.	Rank
1933			5-5-0	133	104	.500	2-2-0	.500	6

Jack Meagher (1934-1942) 48-37-10 .558

Year	Nat'l AP	Other	Overall W-L-T	PF	PA	Pct.	Conference W-L-T	Pct.	Rank	Year	Nat'l AP	Other	Overall W-L-T	PF	PA	Pct.	Conference W-L-T	Pct.	Rank
1934			2-8-0	58	107	.200	1-6-0	.143	10	1939			5-5-1	71	69	.500	3-3-1	.500	5
1935			8-2-0	201	46	.800	5-2-0	.714	4	1940			6-4-1	170	153	.591	3-2-1	.583	5
1936			7-2-2	160	63	.727	4-1-1	.750	3	1941			4-5-1	123	115	.450	0-4-1	.100	11
1937			6-2-3	127	36	.682	4-1-2	.714	3	1942	16		6-4-1	174	133	.591	3-3-0	.500	7
1938			4-5-1	110	88	.450	3-3-1	.500	7	1943			no team						

Carl Voyes (1944-1947) 15-22-0 .405

Year	Nat'l AP	Other	Overall W-L-T	PF	PA	Pct.	Conference W-L-T	Pct.	Rank	Year	Nat'l AP	Other	Overall W-L-T	PF	PA	Pct.	Conference W-L-T	Pct.	Rank
1944			4-4-0	181	137	.500	0-4-0	.000	10	1946			4-6-0	132	210	.400	1-5-0	.167	10
1945			5-5-0	172	129	.500	2-3-0	.400	7	1947			2-7-0	78	204	.222	1-5-0	.167	11

Earl Brown (1948-1950) 3-22-4 .172

Year	Nat'l AP	Other	Overall W-L-T	PF	PA	Pct.	Conference W-L-T	Pct.	Rank	Year	Nat'l AP	Other	Overall W-L-T	PF	PA	Pct.	Conference W-L-T	Pct.	Rank
1948			1-8-1	68	262	.150	0-7-0	.000	12	1950			0-10-0	31	255	.000	0-7-0	.000	12
1949			2-4-3	134	188	.389	2-4-2	.375	8										

Shug Jordan (1951-1975) 176-83-6 .675

Year	Nat'l AP	Other	Overall W-L-T	PF	PA	Pct.	Conference W-L-T	Pct.	Rank	Year	Nat'l AP	Other	Overall W-L-T	PF	PA	Pct.	Conference W-L-T	Pct.	Rank
1951			5-5-0	180	212	.500	3-4-0	.429	6	1964			6-4-0	123	91	.600	3-3-0	.500	6
1952			2-8-0	139	208	.200	0-7-0	.000	12	1965			5-5-1	172	175	.500	4-1-1	.750	2
1953	17		7-3-1	270	173	.682	4-2-1	.643	5	1966			4-6-0	104	162	.400	1-5-0	.167	8
1954	13		8-3-0	276	86	.727	3-3-0	.500	5	1967			6-4-0	237	123	.600	3-3-0	.500	7
1955	8	8	8-2-1	224	123	.773	5-1-1	.786	2	1968	16		7-4-0	257	159	.636	4-2-0	.667	3
1956			7-3-0	174	117	.700	4-3-0	.571	5	1969	20	15	8-3-0	370	173	.727	5-2-0	.714	3
1957	1	2	10-0-0	207	28	1.000	7-0-0	1.000	1	1970	10	9	9-2-0	390	177	.818	5-2-0	.714	3
1958	4	4	9-0-1	173	62	.950	6-0-1	.929	2	1971	12	5	9-2-0	335	182	.818	5-1-0	.833	2
1959		15	7-3-0	174	58	.700	4-3-0	.571	5	1972	5	7	10-1-0	209	141	.909	6-1-0	.857	2

Year			W-L-T	PF	PA	Pct	Conf	Pct		Year			W-L-T	PF	PA	Pct	Conf	Pct	
1960	13	14	8-2-0	155	80	.800	5-2-0	.714	4	1973			6-6-0	170	193	.500	2-5-0	.286	8
1961			6-4-0	174	137	.600	3-4-0	.428	7	1974	8	6	10-2-0	287	122	.833	4-2-0	.667	2
1962			6-3-1	173	168	.650	4-3-0	.571	6	1975			4-6-1	174	243	.419	2-4-0	.333	6
1963	5	6	9-2-0	196	116	.818	6-1-0	.857	2										

Doug Barfield (1976-1980) 29-25-1 .536

Year			W-L-T	PF	PA	Pct	Conf	Pct		Year			W-L-T	PF	PA	Pct	Conf	Pct	
1976			4-7-0	194	267	.364	3-3-0	.500	6	1979	16		8-3-0	330	238	.727	4-2-0	.667	3
1977			6-5-0	204	243	.545	5-1-0	.833	3	1980			5-6-0	235	238	.455	0-6-0	.000	9
1978			6-4-1	238	191	.591	3-2-1	.583	3										

Pat Dye (1981-1992) 99-39-4 .711

Year			W-L-T	PF	PA	Pct	Conf	Pct		Year			W-L-T	PF	PA	Pct	Conf	Pct	
1981			5-6-0	186	166	.455	2-4-0	.333	6	1987	7	7	9-1-2	314	132	.833	5-0-1	.917	1
1982	14	14	9-3-0	274	197	.750	4-2-0	.667	3	1988	8	7	10-2-0	308	92	.833	6-1-0	.857	1
1983	3	3	11-1-0	311	186	.917	6-0-0	1.000	1	1989	6	6	10-2-0	284	131	.833	6-1-0	.857	1
1984	14	14	9-4-0	360	254	.692	4-2-0	.667	3	1990	19	19	8-3-1	283	217	.708	4-2-1	.643	4
1985			8-4-0	344	208	.667	3-3-0	.500	5	1991			5-6-0	233	214	.455	2-5-0	.286	8
1986	6	8	10-2-0	395	122	.833	4-2-0	.667	2	1992			5-5-1	228	205	.500	2-5-1	.312	9

Terry Bowden (1993-1998) 47-17-1 .731

Year			W-L-T	PF	PA	Pct	Conf	Pct		Year			W-L-T	PF	PA	Pct	Conf	Pct	
1993	4		11-0-0	353	192	1.000	8-0-0	1.000	*	1996	24	25	8-4-0	398	277	.667	4-4-0	.500	5
1994	9		9-1-1	359	199	.864	6-1-1	.812	*	1997	11	11	10-3-0	340	250	.769	6-2-0	.750	2
1995	22	21	8-4-0	438	283	.667	5-3-0	.625	4	1998**			1-5-0	68	129	.167	1-4-0	.200	**

*Auburn ineligible for conference title.
** Bowden resigned after first six games of 1998 season, and Bill Oliver coached the remaining games of the season

Bill Oliver (1998) 2-3-0 .400

Year			W-L-T	PF	PA	Pct	Conf	Pct	
1998			2-3-0	98	106	.400	0-3-0	.000	11

Tommy Tuberville (1999-2003) 38-24-0 .613

Year			W-L-T	PF	PA	Pct	Conf	Pct		Year			W-L-T	PF	PA	Pct	Conf	Pct	
1999			5-6-0	212	243	.455	2-6-0	.250	9	2001			7-5-0	254	281	.583	5-3-0	.625	3
2000	18	20	9-4-0	319	263	.692	6-2-0	.750	2	2002	14	16	9-4-0	388	231	.692	5-3-0	.625	4
										2003			8-5-0	342	212	.615	5-3-0	.625	6

Won-lost record by decades:

1892-99	18- 9-4	.645	1930-39	54-39-9	.574	1970-79	72-38-2	.652
1900-09	37-24-4	.600	1940-49	34-47-7	.436	1980-89	86-32-2	.725
1910-19	60-16-4	.775	1950-59	63-37-3	.626	1990-99	72-40-3	.639
1920-29	40-43-7	.483	1960-69	65-37-2	.635	2000-03	33-18-0	.647

Historical record (1892-2003) 634-380-47 .620

Post-season won-lost record: 16-13-2 .548

1936: Bacardi Bowl, Auburn 7, Villanova 7
1938: Orange Bowl, Auburn 6, Michigan State 0
1954: Gator Bowl, Texas Tech 35, Auburn 13
1955: Gator Bowl, Auburn 33, Baylor 13
1956: Gator Bowl, Vanderbilt 25, Auburn 13
1964: Orange Bowl, Nebraska 13, Auburn 7
1965: Liberty Bowl, Ole Miss 13, Auburn 7
1968: Sun Bowl, Auburn 34, Arizona 10
1969: Astro Bluebonnet Bowl, Houston 36, Auburn 7
1971: Gator Bowl, Auburn 35, Ole Miss 28
1972: Sugar Bowl, Oklahoma 40, Auburn 22
1972; Gator Bowl, Auburn 24, Colorado 3
1973: Sun Bowl, Missouri 34, Auburn 17
1974: Gator Bowl, Auburn 27, Texas 3

1982: Tangerine Bowl, Auburn 33, Boston College 26
1984: Sugar Bowl, Auburn 9, Michigan 7
1984: Liberty Bowl, Auburn 21, Arkansas 15
1986: Cotton Bowl, Texas A&M 36, Auburn 16
1987: Citrus Bowl, Auburn 16, USC 7
1988: Sugar Bowl, Auburn 16, Syracuse 16
1989: Sugar Bowl, Florida State 13, Auburn 7
1990: Hall of Fame Bowl, Auburn 13, Ohio State 14
1990: Peach Bowl, Auburn 27, Indiana 23
1996: Outback Bowl, Penn State 43, Auburn 14
1996: Independence Bowl, Auburn 32, Army 29
1997: SEC Championship, Tennessee 30, Auburn 29
1998: Peach Bowl, Auburn 21, Clemson 17
2001: Citrus Bowl, Michigan 31, Auburn 28
2001: Peach Bowl, North Carolina 16, Auburn 10
2003: Capital One Bowl, Auburn 13, Penn State 9
2003: Music City Bowl, Auburn 28, Wisconsin 14

College Football Hall of Fame:
John Heisman, coach, 1895-1899; Mike Donahue, coach, 1904-06, 1908-22; Jimmy Hitchcock, halfback, 1930-32; Walter Gilbert, center, 1934-36; Shug Jordan, coach, 1951-75; Tucker Fredrickson, halfback, 1962-64; Tracy Rooker, defensive tackle, 1965-68; Pat Sullivan, quarterback, 1969-71; Terry Beasley, split end, 1969-71; Bo Jackson, halfback, 1982-85.

Awards:
Heisman Trophy: 1971, Pat Sullivan; 1985, Bo Jackson; Lombardi Award: 1988, Tracy Rocker; Outland Trophy: 1958, Zeke Smith; 1988, Tracy Rocker; Camp Award: 1971, Pat Sullivan; 1985, Bo Jackson; Baugh Trophy: 1970, Pat Sullivan.

BALL STATE UNIVERSITY, Muncie, Indiana; nickname "Cardinals"; colors cardinal and white; Ball State Stadium (22,500); Mid-American Conference. Ball State began play in 1924 and joined the Mid-American Conference in 1975.

Early years (1924-1974)

Year	W-L-T	PF	PA	Pct.	Year	W-L-T	PF	PA	Pct.
Paul Williams (1924-1925. 1929) 3-13-0 .188									
1924	1-3-0	11	87	.250	1925	2-5-0	52	132	.286
Norman Wann (1926-1927) 10-3-2 .733									
1926	5-1-1	127	56	.786	1927	5-2-1	151	108	.688
Paul Parker (1928) 3-2-2 .571									
1928	3-2-2	88	50	.571					
Paul Williams (1929)									
1929	0-5-0	24	92	.000					
Lawrence McPhee (1930-1934) 15-23-1 .397									
1930	6-1-0	130	38	.857	1933	1-6-1	20	90	.188
1931	2-6-0	65	161	.250	1934	2-6-0	58	100	.250
1932	4-4-0	102	90	.500					
J. Magnabosco (1935-1952) 68-46-14 .586									
1935	3-4-1	77	66	.438	1944	2-2-0	58	51	.500
1936	3-4-1	78	55	.438	1945	4-1-1	119	27	.750
1937	5-2-1	135	38	.688	1946	3-4-1	101	68	.438
1938	6-1-1	131	48	.812	1947	5-1-2	100	53	.750
1939	6-2-0	112	69	.750	1948	6-2-0	155	73	.750
1940	3-4-1	78	69	.438	1949	8-0-0	276	61	1.000
1941	3-2-2	98	26	.571	1950	2-4-1	81	129	.357
1942	6-2-0	178	58	.750	1951	0-6-1	94	176	.071
1943	no team				1952	3-5-1	164	167	.688
George Serdula (1953-1955) 14-9-1 .604									
1953	5-2-1	163	125	.688	1955	3-5-0	97	144	.375
1954	6-2-0	218	113	.750					
Jim Freeman (1956-1961) 18-28-2 .396									
1956	4-4-0	116	203	.500	1959	1-7-0	66	172	.125
1957	2-5-1	119	209	.312	1960	3-5-0	102	113	.375
1958	6-2-0	140	69	.750	1961	2-5-1	68	179	.312
Ray Louthen (1962-1967) 37-13-3 .726									
1962	4-3-1	138	107	.562	1965	9-0-1	309	150	.960
1963	5-3-0	156	115	.625	1966	7-1-1	207	152	.833
1964	5-3-0	175	139	.625	1967	7-3-0	276	112	.700
Wave Myers (1968-1970) 15-14-0 .517									
1968	5-4-0	189	218	.556	1970	5-5-0	146	226	.500
1969	5-5-0	178	201	.500					
Dave McClain (1971-77) 46-25-3 .642									
1971	4-5-1	136	155	.450	1973	5-5-1	226	201	.500
1972	5-4-1	235	180	.550	1974	6-4-0	265	177	.600

Member of the Mid-American Conference (1975-2003) 123-101-3 .548

Year	Nat'l AP Other	Overall W-L-T	PF	PA	Pct.	Conference W-L-T	Pct.	Rank	Year	Nat'l AP Other	Overall W-L-T	PF	PA	Pct.	Conference W-L-T	Pct.	Rank
1975		9-2-0	244	171	.818	4-2-0	.667	3	1977		9-2-0	377	169	.818	5-1-0	.833	3
1976		8-3-0	262	124	.727	4-1-0	.800	1									
Dwight Wallace (1978-1984) 40-37-0 .519																	
1978		10-1-0	251	82	.909	8-0-0	1.000	1	1982		5-6-0	177	207	.455	4-4-0	.500	8
1979		6-5-0	272	191	.545	3-5-0	.375	4	1983		6-5-0	247	302	.545	4-4-0	.500	5
1980		6-5-0	239	198	.545	5-4-0	.556	5	1984		3-8-0	134	275	.273	3-5-0	.375	6
1981		4-7-0	157	218	.364	2-6-0	.250	8									
Paul Schudel (1985-1994) 60-48-4 .554																	
1985		4-7-0	203	283	.364	3-6-0	.333	6	1990		7-4-0	204	121	.636	5-3-0	.625	3
1986		6-5-0	199	201	.545	4-4-0	.500	5	1991		6-5-0	159	150	.545	4-4-0	.500	5
1987		4-7-0	226	255	.364	3-5-0	.375	8	1992		5-6-0	171	243	.455	5-4-0	.556	6
1988		8-3-0	288	170	.727	5-3-0	.625	3	1993		8-3-1	334	307	.708	7-0-1	.938	1
1989		7-3-2	274	239	.667	6-1-1	.813	1	1994		5-5-1	276	296	.500	5-3-1	.611	5
Bill Lynch (1995-2002) 37-53-0 .411																	
1995		7-4-0	204	187	.636	6-2-0	.750	3	1999		0-11-0	157	361	.000	0-8-0	.000	11
1996		8-4-0	311	228	.667	7-1-0	.875	1	2000		5-6-0	212	349	.455	4-3-0	.571	7
1997		5-6-0	239	260	.455	4-4-0	.500	6	2001		5-6-0	199	191	.455	4-3-0	.571	6
1998		1-10-0	150	343	.091	1-7-0	.125	11	2002		6-6-0	278	333	.500	4-4-0	.500	7
Bradley Hoke (2003) 4-8-0 .333																	
2003		4-8-0	261	386	.333	3-5-0	.375	9									

Won-lost record by decades:

1924-29	16-18-4	.474	1950-59	32-42-5	.437	1980-89	53-56-2	.486
1930-39	38-36-5	.513	1960-69	52-32-4	.587	1990-99	52-58-2	.473
1940-49	40-18-7	.669	1970-79	67-36-3	.646	2000-03	20-26-0	.435

Historical record (1924-2003): 370-322-32 .533

Post-season won-lost record: 0-4-1 .100

1965: Grantland Rice Bowl, Ball State 14, Tennessee State 14

1967: Grantland Rice Bowl, Eastern Kentucky 27, Ball State 13

1989: California Raisin Bowl, Fresno State 27, Ball State 6

1993: Las Vegas Bowl, Utah State 42, Ball State 33

1996: Las Vegas Bowl, Nevada Reno 18, Ball State 15

BAYLOR UNIVERSITY, Waco, Texas; nickname "Bears"; colors green and gold; Floyd Casey Stadium (50,000); Big Twelve Conference. Baylor started play in 1899 and joined the Southwest Conference when it began play in 1915. When the Southwest Conference disbanded after the 1995 season, Baylor moved into the newly organized Big Twelve Conference.

Early years as an independent (1899-1914)

Year	Coach	W-L-T	PF	PA	Pct.	Year	Coach	W-L-T	PF	PA	Pct.
1899	R.H. Hamilton	2-1-1	26	33	.625	1907	Luther Burleson	4-3-1	91	105	.562
1900	R.H. Hamilton	3-0-0	44	6	1.000	1908	E.J. Mills	3-5-0	48	164	.375
1901	W.J. Ritchie	5-3-0	174	61	.625	1909	E.J. Mills	5-3-0	112	41	.625
1902	J.C. Ewing	3-4-2	71	89	.444	1910	Ralph Glaze	6-1-1	211	12	.812
1903	R.N. Watts	4-3-1	46	69	.562	1911	Ralph Glaze	3-4-2	103	53	.444
1904	Sol Metzger	2-5-1	34	106	.312	1912	Ralph Glaze	3-5-0	78	123	.375
1905	Archie Webb	1-6-0	20	153	.143	1913	Norman Payne	3-4-3	57	208	.450
1906	no team										

Bubs Mosley (1914-1919) 30-18-4 .615

1914		3-5-2	70	159	.400

Member of the Southwest Conference (1915-1995) 221-250-25 .471

	Nat'l		Overall				Conference				Nat'l		Overall				Conference		
Year	AP	Other	W-L-T	PF	PA	Pct.	W-L-T	Pct.	Rank	Year	AP	Other	W-L-T	PF	PA	Pct.	W-L-T	Pct.	Rank
1915*			7-1-0	188	22	.875	3-0-0	1.000	*	1918			0-6-0	19	92	.000	0-2-0	.000	6
1916			9-1-0	317	27	.900	3-1-0	.750	2	1919			5-3-1	146	73	.611	0-3-1	.125	7
1917			6-2-1	221	41	.722	2-1-0	.667	2										

*Baylor ineligible for league title for using ineligible player.

Frank Bridges (1920-1925) 35-18-6 .644

1920			4-4-1	65	89	.500	1-2-1	.375	5	1923			5-1-2	104	39	.750	1-1-2	.500	4
1921			8-3-0	214	83	.727	2-2-0	.500	4	1924			7-2-1	159	66	.750	4-0-1	.900	1
1922			8-3-0	295	128	.727	5-0-0	1.000	1	1925			3-5-2	79	115	.400	0-3-2	.200	7

Morley Jennings (1926-1940) 84-59-6 .584

1926			6-3-1	103	93	.650	3-1-1	.700	2	1934			3-7-0	91	140	.300	1-5-0	.167	7
1927			2-7-0	74	139	.222	0-5-0	.000	7	1935			8-3-0	122	69	.727	3-3-0	.500	3
1928			8-2-0	219	54	.800	3-2-0	.600	3	1936			6-3-1	128	90	.650	3-2-1	.583	3
1929			7-3-1	286	106	.682	2-2-1	.500	4	1937			7-3-0	178	64	.700	3-3-0	.500	4
1930			6-3-1	233	90	.650	3-1-1	.700	2	1938			7-2-1	165	89	.750	3-2-1	.583	3
1931			3-6-0	100	134	.333	1-5-0	.167	6	1939			7-3-0	136	81	.700	4-2-0	.667	2
1932			3-5-1	77	92	.389	1-4-1	.250	5	1940			4-6-0	109	114	.400	0-6-0	.000	7
1933*			7-3-0	84	85	.700	5-1-0	.833	1										

*Record reflects the forfeit by Arkansas of win over Baylor in 1933.

Frank Kimbrough (1941-1942, 1945-1946) 15-23-3 .402

1941			3-6-1	106	161	.350	1-4-1	.250	6	1945			5-5-1	178	141	.500	2-4-0	.333	6
1942			6-4-1	148	116	.591	3-2-1	.583	4	1946			1-8-0	50	175	.111	0-6-0	.000	7
1943-44		no team																	

Bob Woodruff (1947-1949) 19-10-2 .629

1947			5-5-0	128	138	.500	1-5-0	.167	7	1949	20		8-2-0	230	126	.800	4-2-0	.667	2
1948			6-3-2	167	125	.636	3-2-1	.583	3										

George Sauer (1950-1955) 38-21-3 .637

1950	15		7-3-0	183	128	.700	4-2-0	.667	2	1953			7-3-0	219	166	.700	4-2-0	.667	3
1951	9	9	8-2-1	231	148	.773	4-1-1	.750	2	1954	18		7-4-0	250	174	.636	4-2-0	.667	3
1952			4-4-2	187	181	.500	1-3-2	.333	5	1955			5-5-0	140	143	.500	2-4-0	.333	5

Sam Boyd (1956-1958) 15-15-1 .500

1956	11	11	9-2-0	202	73	.818	4-2-0	.667	3	1958			3-7-0	159	181	.300	1-5-0	.167	7
1957			3-6-1	80	125	.350	0-5-1	.083	7										

John Bridgers (1959-1968) 49-53-1 .481

1959			4-6-0	106	154	.400	2-4-0	.333	4	1964			5-5-0	162	176	.500	4-3-0	.571	3
1960	12	11	8-3-0	181	91	.727	5-2-0	.714	2	1965			5-5-0	156	171	.500	3-4-0	.429	4
1961			6-5-0	212	183	.545	2-5-0	.286	6	1966			5-5-0	168	140	.500	3-4-0	.429	5
1962			4-6-0	159	169	.400	3-4-0	.429	4	1967			1-8-1	101	199	.150	0-6-1	.071	7
1963		20	8-3-0	205	120	.727	6-1-0	.857	2	1968			3-7-0	206	322	.300	3-4-0	.429	5

Bill Beall (1969-1971) 3-28-0 .097

1969			0-10-0	87	347	.000	0-7-0	.000	8	1971			1-9-0	74	236	.100	0-7-0	.000	8
1970			2-9-0	133	259	.182	1-6-0	.143	7										

Grant Teaff (1972-1992) 128-105-6 .548

Year			Record	PF	PA	Pct	Conf	Pct	Pl	Year			Record	PF	PA	Pct	Conf	Pct	Pl
1972			5-6-0	180	156	.455	3-4-0	.429	4	1983			7-4-1	339	290	.625	4-3-1	.562	3
1973			2-9-0	192	359	.182	0-7-0	.000	8	1984			5-6-0	248	261	.455	4-4-0	.500	6
1974	14	14	8-4-0	252	223	.667	6-1-0	.857	1	1985	17	15	9-3-0	293	156	.750	6-2-0	.750	2
1975			3-6-2	181	235	.364	2-5-0	.286	5	1986	12	13	9-3-0	325	207	.750	6-2-0	.750	3
1976	19		7-3-1	209	183	.682	4-3-1	.562	4	1987			6-5-0	221	228	.545	3-4-0	.429	5
1977			5-6-0	228	220	.455	3-5-0	.375	6	1988			6-5-0	232	196	.545	2-5-0	.286	4
1978			3-8-0	242	242	.273	3-5-0	.375	6	1989			5-6-0	245	190	.455	4-4-0	.500	4
1979	15		8-4-0	258	147	.667	5-3-0	.625	4	1990			6-4-1	225	202	.591	5-2-1	.688	2
1980	14	13	10-2-0	317	189	.833	8-0-0	1.000	1	1991			8-4-0	282	204	.667	5-3-0	.625	2
1981			5-6-0	252	245	.455	3-5-0	.375	6	1992			7-5-0	344	242	.583	4-3-0	.571	2
1982			4-6-1	233	261	.409	3-4-1	.438	5										

Chuck Reedy (1993-1996) 23-22-0 .511

Year			Record	PF	PA	Pct	Conf	Pct	Pl	Year			Record	PF	PA	Pct	Conf	Pct	Pl
1993			5-6-0	265	331	.455	3-4-0	.429	4	1995			7-4-0	273	166	.636	5-2-0	.714	2
1994			7-5-0	362	277	.583	4-3-0	.571	1										

Member of the Big Twelve (1996-2003) 5-59-0 .078

Year			Record	PF	PA	Pct	Conf	Pct	Pl
1996			4-7-0	266	320	.364	1-7-0	.125	11

Dave Roberts (1997-1998) 4-18-0 .182

Year			Record	PF	PA	Pct	Conf	Pct	Pl	Year			Record	PF	PA	Pct	Conf	Pct	Pl
1997			2-9-0	200	375	.182	1-7-0	.125	11	1998			2-9-0	195	323	.182	1-7-0	.125	11

Kevin Steele (1999-2002) 9-36-0 .200

Year			Record	PF	PA	Pct	Conf	Pct	Pl	Year			Record	PF	PA	Pct	Conf	Pct	Pl
1999			1-10-0	137	414	.091	0-8-0	.000	12	2001			3-8-0	205	357	.273	0-8-0	.000	12
2000			2-9-0	139	397	.182	0-8-0	.000	12	2002			3-9-0	202	496	.250	1-7-0	.125	11

Guy Morris (2003) 3-9-0 .250

Year			Record	PF	PA	Pct	Conf	Pct	Pl
2003			3-9-0	191	455	.250	1-7-0	.125	11

Won-lost record by decades:

1899-09	32-33-6	.493	1940-49	38-39-5	.494	1980-89	66-46-2	.588
1910-19	45-32-10	.575	1950-59	57-42-4	.573	1990-99	49-63-1	.438
1920-29	58-33-8	.569	1960-69	45-57-1	.442	2000-03	11-35-0	.244
1930-39	57-38-4	.595	1970-79	44-64-3	.410			

Historical record (1899-2003) 502-482-44 .510

Post-season record 8-8-0 .500

1948: Dixie Bowl, Baylor 20, Wake Forest 7
1952: Orange Bowl, Georgia Tech 17, Baylor 14
1955: Gator Bowl, Auburn 33, Baylor 13
1957: Sugar Bowl, Baylor 13, Tennessee 7
1961: Gator Bowl, Florida 13, Baylor 12
1961: Gotham Bowl, Baylor 24, Utah 9
1963: Bluebonnet Bowl, Baylor 14, LSU 7
1975: Cotton Bowl, Penn State 41, Baylor 20

1979: Peach Bowl, Baylor 24, Clemson 18
1981: Cotton Bowl, Alabama 30, Baylor 2
1983: Bluebonnet Bowl, Oklahoma State 24, Baylor 14
1985: Liberty Bowl, Baylor 21, LSU 7
1986: Bluebonnet Bowl, Baylor 21, Colorado 9
1991: Copper Bowl, Indiana 24, Baylor 0
1992: Sun Bowl, Baylor 20, Arizona 15
1994: Alamo Bowl, Washington State 10, Baylor 3

College Football Hall of Fame:
Morley Jennings, coach, 1926-40; Barton Koch, guard, 1928-30; Jim Ray Smith, tackle, 1952-54; Bill Glass, guard, 1954-56; Larry Elkins, wide receiver, 1962-64; Grant Teaff, coach, 1972-92; Mike Singletary, linebacker, 1977-80.

Awards: Jim Thorpe Award: 1986, Thomas Everett; Baugh Trophy: 1962 and 1963, Don Trull.

BOISE STATE UNIVERSITY, Boise, Idaho; nickname "Broncos"; colors blue and orange; Bronco Stadium (30,000); Western Athletic Conference. Boise State became a four-year college in 1968, and the record below is shown only for the seasons as a four-year college. After two years as an independent, Boise State joined the Division I-AA Big Sky conference. The team played in that conference through the 1995 season and then opted for I-A status, joining the Big West Conference. When that conference disbanded after the 2000 season, Boise State joined the Western Athletic Conference.

Year	Nat'l AP Other	Overall W-L-T	PF	PA	Pct.	Conference W-L-T	Pct	Rank	Year	Nat'l AP Other	Overall W-L-T	PF	PA	Pct.	Conference W-L-T	Pct.	Rank

Tony Kanp (1968-1975) 71-19-1 .786

Years as an independent (1968-1969)

| 1968 | | 8-2-0 | 324 | 14 | .800 | | | | 1969 | | 9-1-0 | 391 | 94 | .900 | | | |

Member of the Big Sky Conference (1970-1995) 114-61-1 .651

1970		8-3-0	293	129	.727	2-2-0	.500	4	1973		10-3-0	470	221	.769	6-0-0	1.000	1
1971		10-2-0	351	247	.833	4-2-0	.667	2	1974		10-2-0	497	138	.833	6-0-0	1.000	1
1972		7-4-0	345	240	.636	3-3-0	.500	3	1975		9-2-1	401	265	.864	5-0-1	.917	1

Jim Krier (1976-1982) 59-21-1 .735

1976		5-5-1	283	197	.500	2-4-0	.333	5	1980		10-3-0	317	179	.769	6-1-0	.857	1
1977		9-2-0	317	181	.818	6-0-0	1.000	1	1981		10-3-0	298	206	.769	6-1-0	.857	1
1978		7-4-0	269	182	.636	3-3-0	.500	4	1982		8-3-0	302	211	.727	4-3-0	.571	4
1979		10-1-0	347	140	.909	7-0-0	1.000	1									

Lyle Setenich (1983-1986) 24-20-0 .546

| 1983 | | 6-5-0 | 281 | 194 | .545 | 4-3-0 | .571 | 3 | 1985 | | 7-4-0 | 288 | 211 | .636 | 5-2-0 | .714 | 3 |
| 1984 | | 6-5-0 | 256 | 227 | .545 | 4-3-0 | .571 | 3 | 1986 | | 5-6-0 | 262 | 183 | .455 | 3-4-0 | .429 | 5 |

Skip Hall (1987-1992) 42-28-0 .600

1987		6-5-0	361	261	.545	4-4-0	.500	4	1990		10-4-0	382	258	.714	6-2-0	.750	2
1988		8-4-0	280	274	.667	5-3-0	.625	3	1991		7-4-0	355	197	.636	4-4-0	.500	4
1989		6-5-0	261	245	.545	5-3-0	.625	3	1992		5-6-0	220	286	.455	3-4-0	.429	5

Pokey Allen (1993-1996) 24-15-0 .615

| 1993 | | 3-8-0 | 210 | 319 | .272 | 1-6-0 | .143 | 7 | 1995 | | 7-4-0 | 361 | 265 | .636 | 4-3-0 | .571 | 2 |
| 1994 | | 13-2-0 | 433 | 291 | .867 | 6-1-0 | .857 | 1 | | | | | | | | | |

Member of the Big West Conference (1996-2000) 16-10-0 .615

| 1996* | | 1-1-0 | 52 | 96 | .500 | 1-1-0 | .500 | * | | | | | | | | | |

Tom Mason (1996) 1-9-0 .100

| 1996* | | 1-9-0 | 188 | 366 | .100 | 0-3-0 | .000 | 5 | | | | | | | | | |

*Tom Mason coached the first ten games of the 1996 season and then Pokey Allen coached the last two games.

Houston Nutt (1997) 5-6-0 .455

| 1997 | | 5-6-0 | 285 | 358 | .455 | 3-2-0 | .600 | 3 | | | | | | | | | |

Dirk Koetter (1998-2000) 26-10-0 .722

| 1998 | | 6-5-0 | 329 | 350 | .545 | 2-3-0 | .400 | 4 | 2000 | | 10-2-0 | 532 | 274 | .833 | 5-0-0 | 1.000 | 1 |
| 1999 | | 10-3-0 | 430 | 277 | .769 | 5-1-0 | .833 | 1 | | | | | | | | | |

Member of the Western Athletic Conference (2001-2003) 22-2-0 .917

Dan Hawkins (2001-2003) 33-6-0 .846

| 2001 | | 8-4-0 | 411 | 280 | .667 | 6-2-0 | .750 | 3 | 2003 | 16   15 | 13-1-0 | 602 | 239 | .929 | 8-0-0 | 1.000 | 1 |
| 2002 | 15   12 | 12-1-0 | 593 | 240 | .923 | 8-0-0 | 1.000 | 1 | | | | | | | | | |

Won-lost record by decades:

1968-69	17- 3-0	.850	1980-89	74-43-0	.626	2000-03	43-8-0	.843
1970-79	83-28-2	.748	1990-99	68-52-0	.567			

Historical record (1968-2002) 285-134-2 .679

Post-season won-lost record: 14-7-0 .667

1971: Camelia Bowl, Boise State 32, Chico State 28
1973: Division II Playoffs, Boise State 53, So. Dakota 10
1973: Division II Playoffs, Louisiana Tech 38, Boise State 34
1974: Division II Playoffs, Central Michigan 20, Boise State 6
1975: Division III Playoffs, Northern Michigan 24, Boise State 21
1980: Division IAA Playoffs, Boise State 14, Grambling 9
1980: IAA Championship, Boise State 31, Eastern Kentucky 29
1981: Division IAA playoffs, Boise State 19, Jackson State 7
1981: IAA Playoffs, Eastern Kentucky 24, Boise State 17
1988: IAA Playoffs, Northwestern State 22, Boise State 13

1990: IAA Playoffs, Boise State 20, Mid. Tenn. State 13
1990: IAA Playoffs, Boise State 20, Northern Iowa 3
1990: IAA Playoffs, Nevada 59, Boise State 52
1994: IAA Playoffs, Boise State 24, North Texas 20
1994: IAA Playoffs, Boise State 17, Appalachian St. 14
1994: IAA Playoffs, Boise State 28, Marshall 24
1994: IAA Championship, Youngstown St. 28, Boise St. 14
1999: Humanitarian Bowl, Boise State 34, Louisville 31
2000: Humanitarian Bowl, Boise State 38, UTEP 23
2002: Humanitarian Bowl, Boise State 34, Iowa State 16
2003: Fort Worth Bowl, Boise State 34, TCU 31

College Football Hall of Fame:
Randy Trautman, defensive tackle, 1978-1981

BOSTON COLLEGE, Newton, Massachusetts; nickname "Eagles"; colors maroon and gold; Alumni Stadium (44,500); Big East Conference. BC began play as an independent in 1893 and remained an independent through the 1990 season. In 1991, BC became one of the founding members of the Big East Conference. After the 2003 season, BC announced its move to the ACC for the 2005 season.

Years as an independent (1893-1990)

Year	Coach	W-L-T	PF	PA	Pct.	Year	Coach	W-L-T	PF	PA	Pct.
1893	Joseph Waters	3-3-0	24	34	.500	1902	Arthur White	0-7-1	11	134	.062
1894	William Nagle	1-6-0	20	110	.143	1903-1907	no team				
1895	Joseph Lawless	2-4-2	36	86	.375	1908	Joe Reilly and				
1896	Frank Carney	5-2-0	54	60	.714		Joe Kenne	2-4-2	30	54	.375
1897	John Dunlop	4-3-0	54	40	.571	1909	Charles McCarthy	3-4-1	71	42	.438
1898	John Dunlop	2-5-1	22	41	.312	1910	Jim Hart	0-4-2	16	73	.167
1899	John Dunlop	8-1-1	85	18	.850	1911	Joseph Courtney	0-7-0	33	72	.000
1900	no team					1912	William Joy	2-4-1	33	157	.357
1901	John Dunlop	2-7-0	22	108	.222	1913	William Joy	4-3-1	166	73	.562

Year	Nat'l AP	Other	W-L-T	PF	PA	Pct.	Year	Nat'l AP	Other	W-L-T	PF	PA	Pct.
Stephen Mahoney (1914-1915) 8-8-0 .500													
1914			5-4-0	119	80	.556	1915			3-4-0	45	69	.429
Charles Brickley (1916-1917) 12-4-0 .750													
1916			6-2-0	167	66	.750	1917			6-2-0	208	33	.750
Frank Morrissey (1918) 5-2-0 .714													
1918			5-2-0	142	35	.714							
Frank Cavanaugh (1919-1926) 48-14-5 .754													
1919			5-3-0	78	62	.625	1923			7-1-1	167	14	.833
1920			8-0-0	161	16	1.000	1924			6-3-0	198	74	.667
1921			4-3-1	85	90	.562	1925			6-2-0	140	54	.750
1922			6-2-1	134	58	.722	1926			6-0-2	222	31	.875
Leo Daley (1927) 4-4-0 .50 0													
1927			4-4-0	101	105	.500							
Joe McKenney (1928-1934) 44-18-3 .700													
1928			9-0-0	282	39	1.000	1932			4-2-2	73	59	.625
1929			7-2-1	202	65	.750	1933			8-1-0	169	50	.889
1930			5-5-0	167	63	.500	1934			5-4-0	64	72	.556
1931			6-4-0	102	87	.600							
Dinney McNamara (1935) 3-1-0 .750													
1935*			3-1-0	50	33	.750							
Harry Downes (1935) 3-2-0 .600													
1935 *			3-2-0	96	44	.600							

*McNamara coached the first four games of the 1935 season, and Downes coached the last five games.

Year	Nat'l AP	Other	W-L-T	PF	PA	Pct.	Year	Nat'l AP	Other	W-L-T	PF	PA	Pct.
Gil Dobie (1936-1938) 16-6-5 .685													
1936			6-1-2	109	55	.778	1938			6-1-2	186	87	.778
1937			4-4-1	109	68	.500							
Frank Leahy (1939-1940) 20-2-0 .909													
1939	11		9-2-0	216	46	.818	1940	5		11-0-0	339	65	1.000
Denny Myers (1941-1942, 1946-1950) 35-27-4 .561													
1941			7-3-0	235	106	.700	1942	8		8-2-0	282	111	.800
Moody Sarno (1943-1945) 11-7-1 .605													
1943			4-0-1	156	18	.900	1945			3-4-0	79	171	.429
1944			4-3-0	131	134	.571							
Denny Myers (1946-1950)													
1946			6-3-0	234	123	.667	1949			4-4-1	196	200	.500
1947			5-4-0	184	134	.556	1950			0-9-1	77	263	.050
1948			5-2-2	131	141	.667							
Mike Holovak (1951-1959) 49-29-3 .623													
1951			3-6-0	135	198	.333	1956			5-4-0	142	98	.556
1952			4-4-1	106	115	.500	1957			7-2-0	158	129	.778
1953			5-3-1	137	139	.611	1958			7-3-0	229	127	.700
1954			8-1-0	196	74	.889	1959			5-4-0	162	123	.556
1955			5-2-1	176	79	.688							
Ernie Hefferle (1960-1961) 7-12-1 .375													
1960			3-6-1	146	146	.350	1961			4-6-0	117	189	.400
Jim Miller (1962-1967) 34-25-0 .576													
1962			8-2-0	250	123	.800	1965			6-4-0	209	117	.600
1963			6-3-0	179	119	.667	1966			4-6-0	142	203	.400
1964			6-4-0	112	110	.600	1967			4-6-0	227	212	.400

Joe Yukica (1968-1977) 68-37-0 .648

1968	6-3-0	253	196	.667		1973	7-4-0	311	172	.636
1969	5-4-0	218	245	.556		1974	8-3-0	365	154	.727
1970	8-2-0	307	142	.800		1975	7-4-0	227	146	.636
1971	9-2-0	259	117	.818		1976	8-3-0	238	126	.727
1972	4-7-0	241	258	.364		1977	6-5-0	242	269	.545

Ed Chlebek (1978-1980) 12-21-0 .363

1978	0-11-0	153	294	.000		1980	7-4-0	199	186	.636
1979	5-6-0	229	231	.455						

Jack Bicknell (1981-1990) 59-55-1 .517

1981			5-6-0	243	298	.455		1986	19	18	9-3-0	338 233 .750
1982			8-3-1	271	212	.708		1987			5-6-0	244 281 .455
1983	19	20	9-3-0	351	190	.750		1988			3-8-0	248 315 .273
1984	5	4	10-2-0	449	296	.833		1989			2-9-0	207 253 .182
1985			4-8-0	222	307	.333		1990			4-7-0	207 217 .364

Member of the Big East Conference (1991-2003) 41-44-2 .483

Year	Nat'l	Overall				Conference			Year	Nat'l	Overall				Conference		
		W-L-T	PF	PA	Pct.	W-L-T	Pct.	Rank			W-L-T	PF	PA	Pct.	W-L-T	Pct.	Rank

Tom Coughlin (1991-1993) 21-13-1 .614

Year	Nat'l	W-L-T	PF	PA	Pct.	W-L-T	Pct.	Rank	Year	Nat'l	W-L-T	PF	PA	Pct.	W-L-T	Pct.	Rank
1991		4-7-0	246	247	.364	2-4-0	.333	7	1993	13 12	9-3-0	408	240	.750	5-2-0	714	3
1992	21 21	8-3-1	330	228	.708	2-1-1	.625	3									

Dan Henning (1994-1996) 16-19-1 .458

Year	Nat'l	W-L-T	PF	PA	Pct.	W-L-T	Pct.	Rank	Year	Nat'l	W-L-T	PF	PA	Pct.	W-L-T	Pct.	Rank
1994	23 22	7-4-1	288	152	.625	3-3-1	.500	5	1996		5-7-0	264	364	.417	2-5-0	.286	6
1995		4-8-0	207	322	.333	4-3-0	.571	3									

Tom O'Brien (1997-2003) 48-36-0 .571

Year	Nat'l	W-L-T	PF	PA	Pct.	W-L-T	Pct.	Rank	Year	Nat'l	W-L-T	PF	PA	Pct.	W-L-T	Pct.	Rank
1997		4-7-0	237	314	.364	3-4-0	.429	5	2000		7-5-0	301	26 4	.583	3-4-0	.429	5
1998		4-7-0	308	276	.364	3-4-0	.429	5	2001	21 23	8-4-0	337	227	.667	4-3-0	.571	3
1999		8-4-0	298	309	.667	4-3-0	.571	3	2002		9-4-0	392	253	.692	3-4-0	.429	4
									2003		8-5-0	370	331	.615	3-4-0	.429	5

Won-loss record by decades:

1893-99	25-24-4	.509	1930-39	59-27-7	.672	1970-79	62-47-0	.569
1900-09	7-22-4	.273	1940-49	57-25-4	.686	1980-89	62-52-1	.544
1910-19	36-35-4	.507	1950-59	49-38-4	.560	1990-99	57-57-2	.500
1920-29	63-17-6	.767	1960-69	52-44-1	.541	2000-03	32-18-0	.640

Historical record (1893-2002) 561-406-37 .577

Post-season won-loss record 9-6-0 .600

1940: Cotton Bowl, Clemson 6, BC 3	1993: Hall of Fame Bowl, Tennessee 38, BC 23
1941: Sugar Bowl, BC 19, Tennessee 13	1993: Carquest Bowl, BC 31, Virginia 13
1943: Orange Bowl, Alabama 37, BC 21	1994: Jeep Eagle Aloha Bowl, BC 12, Kansas State 7
1982: Tangerine Bowl, Auburn 33, BC 26	1999: Insight.com Bowl, Colorado 62, BC 28
1983: Liberty Bowl, Notre Dame 19, BC 18	2000: Jeep Eagle Aloha Bowl, BC 31, Arizona State 17
1985: Cotton Bowl, BC 45, Houston 28	2001: Music City Bowl, BC 20, Georgia 16
1986: Hall of Fame Bowl, BC 27, Georgia 24	2002: Motor City Bowl, BC 51, Toledo 25
	2000: San Francisco Bowl, BC 35, Colorado State 21

College Football Hall of Fame:
Frank Cavanaugh, coach, 1919-26; Gil Dobie, coach, 1936-38; Frank Leahy, coach, 1939-40; Charlie O'Rourke, quarterback, 1939-41: Chester Gladchuck, center, 1939-41; Gene Goodreault, end, 1939-41; George Kerr, guard, 1939-41; Mike Holovak, halfback, 1940-42.

Awards: Heisman Trophy: 1984, Doug Flutie; Maxwell Award, 1984: Doug Flutie; Walter Camp Award, 1984: Doug Flutie; Davie O'Brien Award, 1984, Doug Flutie; Outland Trophy, 1985, Mike Rush, nose tackle; Camp Award: 1984, Doug Flutie.

BOWLING GREEN UNIVERSITY, Bowling Green, Ohio; nickname "Falcons;" colors orange and brown; Doyt L. Perry Stadium (30,599); Mid-American Conference. Bowling Green began play in 1919, joined the MAC in the 1952 season, and has played in the conference since that time.

Early years (1919-1951)

Year	W-LT	PF	PA	Pct.
1919	0-3-0	0	28	.000
1920	1-4-0	41	138	.200
1921	3-1-1	178	34	.700
1922	4-3-1	98	46	.563
1923	3-5-0	68	131	.375
1924	3-4-0	60	73	.428
1925	3-1-3	34	28	.643
1926	4-3-1	88	70	.563
1927	5-1-1	52	14	.786
1928	5-0-2	84	18	.857
1929	4-2-1	76	54	.643
1935	1-6-0	25	246	.143
1936	4-2-3	66	60	.611
1937	3-4-1	56	80	.438
1941	7-1-1	173	40	.833
1942	6-2-1	135	55	.722
1943	5-3-1	194	104	.611
1944	5-3-0	133	117	.625
1945	4-3-0	79	81	.571
1946	5-3-0	95	39	.625

John Stitt (1919) 0-3-0 .000

Walter Jean (1920) 1-4-0 .200

Earl Krieger (1921) 3-1-1 .700

Allen Snyder (1922) 4-3-1 .563

R.C. McCandless (1923) 3-5-0 .375

Warren Steller (1924-1934) 40-21-19 .619

Year	W-L-T	PF	PA	Pct.
1930	6-0-2	107	38	.875
1931	3-1-4	31	21	.625
1932	3-3-1	33	77	.500
1933	2-3-2	44	91	.429
1934	2-3-2	36	54	.429

Harry Ockerman (1935-1940) 20-19-9 .510

Year	W-L-T	PF	PA	Pct.
1938	3-2-3	95	41	.563
1939	6-1-1	159	46	.812
1940	3-4-1	62	122	.438

Robert Whittaker (1941-1954) 66-50-7 .565

Year	W-L-T	PF	PA	Pct.
1947	5-5-0	134	149	.500
1948	8-0-1	230	100	.944
1949	4-5-0	206	161	.444
1950	3-4-2	134	188	.444
1951	4-4-1	150	178	.500

Member of the Mid-American Conference (1952-2003) 219-129-13 .625

Year	Nat'l	Overall W-L-T	PF	PA	Pct.	Conf. W-L-T	Pct.	Rank
1952		7-2-0	257	155	.778	2-2-0	.500	4
1953		1-8-0	119	252	.111	0-4-0	.000	7
1954		2-7-0	125	196	.222	0-6-0	.000	8

Doyt Perry (1955-1964) 77-11-5 .855

Year	Nat'l	Overall W-L-T	PF	PA	Pct.	Conf. W-L-T	Pct.	Rank
1955		7-1-1	224	53	.833	4-1-1	.750	2
1956		8-0-1	311	99	.944	5-0-1	.917	1
1957		6-1-2	167	55	.778	3-1-2	.667	2
1958		7-2-0	218	91	.778	4-2-0	.667	3
1959		9-0-0	274	83	1.000	6-0-0	1.000	1
1960		8-1-0	196	61	.889	5-1-0	.833	2
1961		8-2-0	194	78	.800	5-1-0	.833	1
1962		7-1-1	204	91	.833	5-0-1	.917	1
1963		8-2-0	201	116	.800	4-2-0	.667	3
1964		9-1-0	275	87	.900	5-1-0	.833	1

Bob Gibson (1965-1967) 19-9-0 .679

Year	Nat'l	Overall W-L-T	PF	PA	Pct.	Conf. W-L-T	Pct.	Rank
1965		7-2-0	123	107	.779	5-1-0	.833	1
1966		6-3-0	187	124	.667	4-2-0	.667	3
1967		6-4-0	131	130	.600	2-4-0	.333	5

Don Nehlen (1968-1976) 53-35-4 .598

Year	Nat'l	Overall W-L-T	PF	PA	Pct.	Conf. W-L-T	Pct.	Rank
1968		6-3-1	267	147	.650	3-2-1	.583	3
1969		6-4-0	179	146	.600	4-1-0	.800	2
1970		2-6-1	118	178	.278	1-4-0	.200	5
1971		6-4-0	263	207	.600	4-1-0	.800	2
1972		6-3-1	184	127	.650	3-1-1	.700	2
1973		7-3-0	266	209	.700	2-3-0	.400	3
1974		6-4-1	249	203	.591	2-3-0	.400	4
1975		8-3-0	278	166	.727	4-2-0	.667	3
1976		6-5-0	292	249	.545	4-3-0	.571	5

Denny Stolz (1977-1985) 56-45-1 .553

Year	Nat'l	Overall W-L-T	PF	PA	Pct.	Conf. W-L-T	Pct.	Rank
1977		5-7-0	275	296	.417	4-3-0	.571	4
1978		4-7-0	277	267	.364	3-5-0	.375	5
1979		4-7-0	194	265	.364	4-4-0	.500	7
1980		4-7-0	189	186	.364	4-4-0	.500	7
1981		5-5-1	155	132	.500	5-3-1	.611	4
1982		7-5-0	265	199	.583	7-2-0	.778	1
1983		8-3-0	277	242	.727	7-2-0	.778	2
1984		8-3-0	327	198	.727	7-2-0	.778	2
1985		11-1-0	355	223	.917	9-0-0	1.000	1

Moe Ankney (1986-1990) 20-31-3 .398

Year	Nat'l	Overall W-L-T	PF	PA	Pct.	Conf. W-L-T	Pct.	Rank
1986		5-6-0	148	222	.455	5-3-0	.625	2
1987		5-6-0	215	249	.455	5-3-0	.625	2
1988		2-8-1	159	333	.227	1-6-1	.188	8
1989		5-6-0	233	319	.455	5-3-0	.625	5
1990		3-5-2	138	163	.400	2-4-2	.375	6

Gary Blackney (1991-2000) 60-50-2 .545

Year	W-L-T	PF	PA	Pct	Conf	Pct	Rank
1991	11-1-0	279	168	.917	8-0-0	1.000	1
1992	10-2-0	324	235	.833	8-0-0	1.000	1
1993	6-3-2	268	173	.636	5-1-2	.750	3
1994	9-2-0	391	174	.818	7-1-0	.875	2
1995	5-6-0	226	228	.455	3-5-0	.375	6
1996	4-7-0	176	240	.363	3-5-0	.375	6
1997	3-8-0	191	341	.273	3-5-0	.375	7
1998	5-6-0	292	312	.455	5-3-0	.625	4
1999	5-6-0	296	312	.455	3-5-0	.375	9
2000	2-9-0	174	289	.182	2-6-0	.250	9

Urban Meyer (2001-2002) 17-6-0 .739

Year	W-L-T	PF	PA	Pct	Conf	Pct	Rank
2001	8-3-0	333	215	.727	5-3-0	.625	3
2002	9-3-0	490	304	.750	6-2-0	.750	4

Greg Brandon (2003) 11-3-0 .786

Year	W-L-T	PF	PA	Pct	Conf	Pct	Rank
2003	11-3-0	470	304	.786	7-1-0	.875	2

Won-loss record by decades:

Decade	Record	Pct		Decade	Record	Pct		Decade	Record	Pct
1919-29	35-26-10	.563		1950-59	54-29-7	.639		1980-89	60-50-2	.545
1930-39	33-25-19	.552		1960-69	71-23-2	.750		1990-99	61-46-4	.568
1940-49	52-29-5	.645		1970-79	54-49-3	.524		2000-03	30-18-0	.625

Historical record   450-295-52 .597

Post-season won-loss record 3-3-0 .500

1961: Mercy Bowl, Fresno State 36, Bowling Green 6
1982: California Bowl, Fresno State 29, Bowling Green 28
1985: California Bowl, Fresno State 51, Bowling Green 7
1991: California Raisin Bowl, Bowling Green 28, Fresno State 21
1992: Las Vegas Bowl, Bowling Green 35, Nevada 34
2003: Motor City Bowl, Bowling Green 28, Northwestern 24

College Football Hall of Fame:
Doyt Perry, coach, 1955-64.

Awards: Baugh Trophy: 1985, Brian McClure.

BRIGHAM YOUNG UNIVERSITY, Provo, Utah; nickname "Cougars"; colors dark blue, white, and tan; LaVell Edwards Stadium (65,000); Mountain West Conference. BYU began play as an independent in 1922. In 1938, BYU joined the Mountain States (Skyline) Conference and played there until that conference disbanded in 1961. BYU then joined the newly organized Western Athletic Conference and played in that conference through the 1998 season. In 1999, BYU left the WAC to join the newly organized Mountain West Conference.

Years as an independent (1922-1937)

Year	W-L-T	PF	PA	Pct.	Year	W-L-T	PF	PA	Pct.
					Alvin Twitchell (1922-1924) 5-13-1				
1922	1-5-0	10	183	.167	1924	2-3-1	44	61	.417
1923	2-5-0	47	156	.286					
					C.J. Hart (1925-1927) 6-12-2 .350				
1925	3-3-0	69	81	.500	1927	2-4-1	105	118	.357
1926	1-5-1	49	115	.214					
					G. Ott Romney (1928-1936) 42-31-5 .583				
1928	3-3-1	75	56	.500	1933	5-4-0	81	67	.556
1929	5-3-0	140	115	.625	1934	4-5-0	144	150	.444
1930	5-2-4	170	150	.636	1935	4-4-0	78	90	.500
1931	4-4-0	69	104	.500	1936	4-5-0	123	123	.444
1932	8-1-0	188	50	.889					
					Eddie Kimball (1937-1941, 1946-1948) 34-32-8 .514				
1937	6-3-0	164	41	.667					

Member of the Skyline Conference (1938-1961) 41-79-13 .357

	Nat'l	Overall				Conference			Nat'l	Overall				Conference	
Year	AP Other	W-L-T	PF	PA	Pct.	W-L-T	Pct.	Rank	Year	AP Other	W-L-T	PF	PA	Pct.	W-L-T Pct. Rank
1938		4-3-1	93	49	.562	3-2-1	.583	2	1940		2-4-2	79	93	.375	2-3-1 .417 4
1939		5-2-2	110	90	.667	2-2-2	.500	4	1941		4-3-2	136	100	.556	3-1-2 .667 2
								Floyd Millet (1942) 2-5-0 .286							
1942		2-5-0	55	133	.286	1-4-0	.200	6	1943, 1944, 1945	no team					
								Eddie Kimball (1946-1948)							
1946		5-4-1	94	119	.550	3-2-1	.583	4	1948		5-6-0	135	199	.455	1-3-0 .250 5
1947		3-7-0	168	182	.300	1-5-0	.167	7							
								Chick Atkinson (1949-1955) 18-49-3 .279							
1949		0-11-0	105	372	.000	0-5-0	.000	6	1953		2-7-1	172	228	.250	1-5-1 .214 7
1950		4-5-1	169	292	.450	1-3-1	.300	5	1954		1-8-0	96	188	.111	1-6-0 .143 8
1951		6-3-1	215	181	.650	2-3-1	.417	5	1955		1-9-0	104	300	.100	0-7-0 .000 8
1952		4-6-0	154	240	.400	3-4-0	.429	5							
								Hal Kopp (1956-1958) 13-14-3 .483							
1956		2-7-1	157	232	.250	1-5-1	.214	7	1958		6-4-0	189	152	.600	5-2-0 .714 3
1957		5-3-2	134	138	.545	5-1-1	.786	2							
								Tally Stevens (1959-1960) 6-15-0 .286							
1959		3-7-0	101	163	.300	2-5-0	.714	5	1960		3-8-0	102	207	.273	2-5-0 .286 5
								Hal Mitchell (1961-1963) 8-22-0 .267							
1961		2-8-0	130	289	.200	2-4-0	.333	5							

Member of the Western Athletic Association (1962-1998) 187-70-2 .726

1962		4-6-0	197	170	.400	2-2-0	.500	2	1963		2-8-0	91	222	.200	0-4-0 .000 5
									Tom Hudspeth (1964-1971) 39-42-1 .482							
1964		3-6-1	173	210	.350	0-4-0	.000	5	1968		2-8-0	179	247	.200	1-5-0 .167 7
1965		6-4-0	229	178	.600	4-1-0	.800	1	1969		6-4-0	186	158	.600	4-3-0 .571 3
1966		8-2-0	269	163	.800	3-2-0	.600	2	1970		3-8-0	138	255	.273	1-6-0 .143 7
1967		6-4-0	278	215	.600	3-2-0	.600	3	1971		5-6-0	227	199	.455	3-4-0 .429 4
									LaVell Edwards (1972-2000) 257-101-3 .717							
1972		7-4-0	251	227	.636	5-2-0	.714	2	1986		8-5-0	310	236	.615	6-2-0 .750 2
1973		5-6-0	337	245	.455	3-4-0	.429	4	1987		9-4-0	350	293	.692	7-1-0 .875 2
1974		7-4-1	303	199	.625	6-0-1	.857	1	1988		9-4-0	421	281	.692	5-3-0 .625 3
1975		6-5-0	244	228	.545	4-3-0	.571	4	1989 22 18		10-3-0	523	369	.692	7-1-0 .875 1
1976		9-3-0	372	231	.750	6-1-0	.857	1	1990 22 17		10-3-0	524	350	.692	7-1-0 .875 1
1977 20 16		9-2-0	433	165	.818	6-1-0	.857	1	1991 23 23		8-3-2	433	321	.692	7-0-1 .938 1
1978		9-4-0	304	176	.750	5-1-0	.833	1	1992		8-5-0	375	298	.614	6-2-0 .750 1
1979 13 12		11-1-0	484	163	.917	7-0-0	1.000	1	1993		6-6-0	411	435	.500	6-2-0 .750 1
1980 12 11		12-1-0	606	243	.923	6-1-0	.857	1	1994 18 10		10-3-0	388	300	.769	6-2-0 .750 2
1981 13 11		11-2-0	503	256	.846	7-1-0	.875	1	1995		7-4-0	308	268	.636	6-2-0 .750 2
1982		8-4-0	375	214	.667	7-1-0	.875	1	1996 5 5		14-1-0	590	277	.933	8-0-0 1.000 1
1983 7 7		11-1-0	505	247	.917	7-0-0	1.000	1	1997		6-5-0	250	254	.545	4-4-0 .500 8
1984 1 1		13-0-0	456	183	1.000	8-0-0	1.000	1	1998		9-5-0	402	290	.643	7-1-0 .875 1
1985 16 17		11-3-0	442	286	.785	7-1-0	.875	1							

Member of the Mountain West Conference (1999-2003) 21-14-0 .600

1999		8-4-0	335	241	.667	5-2-0	.714	1	2000		6-6-0	280	315	.500	4-3-0 .571 3

Gary Crowton (2001-2003) 21-17-0 .553

2001	25	24	12-2-0	618	424	.857	7-0-0	1.000	1	2003		4-8-0	196	310	.333	3-4-0	.429	4
2002			5-7-0	272	333	.417	2-5-0		.286	7								

Won-loss record by decades:

1922-29	19-31-4	.389	1950-59	34-59-6	.374	1980-89	102-27-0	.791
1930-39	49-33-7	.590	1960-69	42-58-1	.421	1990-99	86-39-2	.685
1940-49	21-40-5	.356	1970-79	71-43-1	.622	2000-03	27-23-0	.540

Historical record (1922-2003) 451-353-26 .559

Post-season won-loss record: 7-15-1 .32

1974: Fiesta Bowl, Oklahoma State 16, BYU 6
1976: Tangerine Bowl, Oklahoma State 49, BYU 21
1978: Holiday Bowl, Navy 23, BYU 16
1979: Holiday Bowl, Indiana 38, BYU 37
1980: Holiday Bowl, BYU 46, SMU 45
1981: Holiday Bowl, BYU 38, Washington State 36
1982: Holiday Bowl, Ohio State 47, BYU 17
1983: Holiday Bowl, BYU 21, Missouri 17
1984: Holiday Bowl, BYU 24, Michigan 17
1985: Citrus Bowl, Ohio State 10, BYU 7
1986: Freedom Bowl, UCLA 31, BYU 10
1987: All American Bowl, Virginia 22, BYU 16

1988: Freedom Bowl, BYU 20, Colorado 17
1989: Holiday Bowl, Penn State 50, BYU 39
1990: Holiday Bowl, Texas A&M 65, BYU 14
1991: Holiday Bowl, BYU 13, Iowa 13
1992: Aloha Bowl, Kansas 23, BYU 20
1993: Holiday Bowl, Ohio State 28, BYU 21
1994: Copper Bowl, BYU 31, Oklahoma 6
1997: Cotton Bowl, BYU 19, Kansas State 15
1998: Liberty Bowl, Tulane 41, BYU 27
1999: Motor City Bowl, Marshall 21, BYU 3
2001: Liberty Bowl, Louisville 28, BYU 10

College Football Hall of Fame:

LaVell Edwards, coach, 1972-2000; Gifford Nielsen, quarterback, 1975-77; Jim McMahon, quarterback, 1977-81; Marc Wilson, quarterback, 1977-1979; Steve Young, quarterback, 1981-83.

Awards: Heisman Trophy: 1990, Ty Detmer; Davey O'Brien Award: 1981, Jim McMahon; 1983: Steve Young; 1990: Ty Detmer; Maxwell Award: 1990, Ty Detmer; Outland Trophy: 1986, Jason Buck; 1989, Mohamed Edelwomibi; Doak Walker Award: 2001, Luke Staley; Baugh Trophy: 1974, Dary Scheide; 1979, Marc Wilson; 1981, Jim McMahon; 1983, Steve Young; 1984, Robbie Bosco; 1991, Ty Detmer; 1996, Steve Sarkisian.

UNIVERSITY OF BUFFALO, Buffalo, New York; nickname "Bulls"; colors royal blue and white; UB Stadium (31,000) Mid-American Conference. Buffalo began play in 1894, as an independent and played leading Eastern independents until football was dropped after the 1970 season. Football began again in 1977. Buffalo became a member of the MAC beginning with the 1999 season.

Year		W-L-T	PF	PA	Pct.	Year		W-L-T	PF	PA	Pc.t
1894	no coach	0-1-1	6	12	.429	1900	no coach	1-1-2	10	17	.500
1895	no coach	0-1-1	10	12	.250	1901	no coach	4-2-0	38	145	.667
1896	no coach	1-0-2	18	17	.667	1902	no coach	2-4-1	34	68	.357
1897	C.W. Dibble	7-0-0	144	12	1.000	1903	Ray Turnbull	3-3-0	41	96	.500
1898	no coach	4-1-0	100	37	.800	1904-1914	no team				
1899	no coach	6-0-0	126	0	1.000	1915	Frank Pleasant	3-3-0	32	62	.500
Art Powell (1916-1921) 13-22-5 .388											
1916		3-5-2	24	88	.400	1919		0-5-1	12	114	.083
1917		4-4-0	122	59	.500	1920		1-4-0	17	60	.200
1918		3-1-0	141	31	.750	1921		2-3-2	73	101	.429
Jim Batterson (1922) 1-5-0 .167											
1922		1-5-0	35	85	.167						
James Bond (1923) 2-5-1 .312											
1923		2-5-1	66	112	.312						
Russ Carrick (1924-1928) 5-30-2 .162											
1924		1-7-0	27	139	.125	1927		0-6-1	7	212	.083
1925		3-4-1	18	121	.438	1928		1-6-0	18	178	.143
1926		0-7-0	21	231	.000						
Jay Lee (1929-1930) 8-7-0 .533											
1929		5-2-0	92	74	.714	1930		3-5-0	79	210	.375
Bill Pritchard (1931) 2-6-0 .250											
1931		2-6-0	64	171	.250						
Jim Wilson (1932-1933, 1950-1951) 12-15-3 .450											
1932		1-5-1	19	208	.214	1933		2-3-2	38	95	.429
G. Van Bibber (1934-1935) 4-10-1 .409											
1934		2-4-1	35	106	.357	1935		2-6-0	26	213	.250
Jim Peelle (1936-1942, 1946-1947) 39-34-1 .534											
1936		6-3-0	121	127	.667	1941		3-4-1	55	75	.438
1937		4-4-0	89	94	.500	1942		6-2-0	215	52	.750
1938		2-6-0	81	156	.250	1943-1945	no teams				
1939		0-7-0	7	126	.000	1946		7-2-0	224	90	.778
1940		3-5-0	47	116	.375	1947		8-1-0	258	79	.889
Frank Clair (1948-1949) 12-4-1 .735											
1948		6-1-1	235	105	.812	1949		6-3-0	183	95	.667
Jim Wilson (1950-1951)											
1950		5-3-0	191	129	.625	1951		4-4-0	144	189	.500
Fritz Febel (1952-1954) 4-19-1 .188											
1952		1-7-0	59	201	.125	1954		2-7-0	72	247	.222
1953		1-5-1	44	181	.214						
Dick Offenhamer (1955-1965) 58-37-5 .605											
1955		4-4-1	186	118	.500	1961		4-5-0	136	163	.444
1956		5-3-0	227	122	.625	1962		6-3-0	159	148	.667
1957		5-4-0	108	98	.556	1963		5-3-1	120	85	.611
1958		8-1-0	236	101	.889	1964		4-4-1	166	97	.500
1959		8-1-0	279	93	.889	1965		5-3-2	145	78	.600
1960		4-6-0	213	238	.400						
Doc Urich (1966-1968) 18-12-0 .600											
1966		5-5-0	220	172	.500	1968		7-3-0	195	183	.700
1967		6-4-0	241	191	.600						
Bob Deming (1969-1970) 8-12-0 .400											
1969		6-3-0	174	89	.667	1970		2-9-0	128	299	.182
1971-1976 no team											
Bill Dando (1977-1989) 59-64-1 .480											
1977		0-3-1	36	87	.125	1984		6-4-0	192	140	.600
1978		3-6-0	164	211	.333	1985		4-6-0	188	206	.400
1979		4-5-0	116	177	.444	1986		9-2-0	264	182	.818.
1980		6-5-0	138	241	.545	1987		3-7-0	151	204	.300
1981		5-5-0	187	168	.500	1988		2-8-0	148	237	.200
1982		5-5-0	291	180	.500	1989		4-6-0	198	217	.400
1983		8-2-0	232	150	.800						
Sam Sanders (1990-1991) 5-15-0 .250											
1990		2-8-0	188	330	.200	1991		3-7-0	231	304	.300

Jim Ward (1992-1994) 8-24-0 .250

Year	W-L-T	PF	PA	Pct	Year	W-L-T	PF	PA	Pct
1992	4-6-0	298	395	.400	1994	3-8-0	154	331	.273
1993	1-10-0	190	359	.091					

Craig Cirbus (1995-2000) 19-47-0 .288

Year	W-L-T	PF	PA	Pct	Year	W-L-T	PF	PA	Pct
1995	3-8-0	198	259	.273	1997	2-9-0	229	421	.182
1996	8-3-0	271	241	.727	1998	4-7-0	315	340	.364

Member of the Mid-American Conference (1999-2003) 4-36-0 .100

Year	Nat'l AP	Other	Overall W-L-T	PF	PA	Pct	Conference W-L-T	Pct.	Rank	Year	Nat'l AP	Other	Overall W-L-T	PF	PA	Pct.	Conference W-L-T	Pct.	Rank
1999		0-11-0		130	426	.000	0-8-0	.000	11	2000			2-9-0	177	512	.182	2-6-0	.250	9

Jim Hofher (2001-2003) 5-30-0 .143

Year	Overall W-L-T	PF	PA	Pct	Conference W-L-T	Pct.	Rank	Year	Overall W-L-T	PF	PA	Pct.	Conference W-L-T	Pct.	Rank
2001	3-8-0	205	286	.273	1-7-0	.125	12	2003	1-11-0	177	445	.083	1-7-0	.125	12
2002	1-11-0	214	416	.083	0-8-0	.000	14								

Won-loss record by decades:

1894-99	18- 3-4	.800	1930-39	24-49-4	.338	1970-79	9-23-1	.288
1900-09	10-10-3	.500	1940-49	39-18-2	.678	1980-89	52-50-0	.510
1910-19	13-18-3	.426	1950-59	43-39-2	.524	1990-99	30-77-0	.280
1920-29	16-49-5	.264	1960-69	52-39-4	.568	2000-03	7-39-0	.152

Historical record 313-414-28 .433

UNIVERSITY OF CALIFORNIA, Berkeley, California; nickname "Golden Bears"; colors blue and gold; Memorial Stadium (75,028); Pac-10 Conference. California began play in 1897 and joined the Pacific Coast Conference as a founding member in 1915. California has remained in the conference (including its successor conferences) to the present.

Early years (1886-1915)

Year	Coach	W-L-T	PF	PA	Pct.	Year	Coach	W-L-T	PF	PA	Pct.
						1897	Charles Nott	0-3-2	8	58	.200
1887	no coach	4-0-0	66	12	1.000	1898	Garrett Cochran	8-0-2	221	5	.900
1888	no coach	6-1-0	104	10	.857	1899	Garrett Cochran	7-1-1	142	2	.833
1889	no team					1900	Addison Kelly	4-2-1	53	7	.643
1890	no coach	4-0-0	45	4	1.000	1901	Frank Simpson	9-0-1	106	15	.950
1891	no coach	0-1-0	0	36	.000	1902	James Whipple	8-0-0	168	12	1.000
1892	spring, no coach	4-2-0	82	24	.667	1903	James Whipple	6-1-2	128	12	.778
1892	fall, T. McClung	2-1-1	44	34	.624	1904	James Hopper	6-1-1	75	24	.813
1893	Pudge Hefflefinger	5-1-1	110	60	.786	1905	J. W. Knibbs	4-1-2	75	12	.714
1894	Charles Gill	0-1-2	12	18	.333	1906-1914	rugby substituted for football				
1895	F. Butterworth	3-1-1	46	10	.700	1915	James Schaeffer	8-5-0	242	184	.615
1896	F. Butterworth	6-2-2	150	56	.722						

Member of the Pacific Coast Conference (1916-2003) 246-286-22 .464

	Nat'l		Overall				Conference				Nat'l		Overall				Conference		
Year	AP	Other	W-L-T	PF	PA	Pct.	W-L-T	Pct.	Rank	Year	AP	Other	W-L-T	PF	PA	Pct.	W-L-T	Pct.	Rank

Andy Smith (1916-1925) 74-16-7 .799

Year	AP	Other	W-L-T	PF	PA	Pct.	W-L-T	Pct.	Rank	Year	AP	Other	W-L-T	PF	PA	Pct.	W-L-T	Pct.	Rank
1916			6-4-1	192	103	.591	0-3-0	.000	4	1921			9-0-1	312	33	.950	4-0-0	1.000	1
1917			5-5-1	149	104	.500	2-1-0	.667	2	1922			9-0-0	398	34	1.000	4-0-0	1.000	1
1918			7-2-0	187	62	.778	2-0-0	1.000	1	1923			9-0-1	182	7	.950	5-0-0	1.000	1
1919			6-2-1	147	64	.722	2-2-0	.500	3	1924		2	8-0-2	162	51	.900	2-0-2	.667	2
1920		1	9-0-0	510	14	1.000	3-0-0	1.000	1	1925			6-3-0	192	56	.667	2-2-0	.500	5

Nibs Price (1926-1930) 27-17-3 .606

Year	AP	Other	W-L-T	PF	PA	Pct.	W-L-T	Pct.	Rank	Year	AP	Other	W-L-T	PF	PA	Pct.	W-L-T	Pct.	Rank
1926			3-6-0	105	167	.333	0-5-0	.000	9	1929		4	7-1-1	155	78	.833	4-1-0	.800	3
1927			7-3-0	184	64	.700	2-3-0	.400	5	1930			4-5-0	87	170	.444	1-4-0	.200	8
1928		2	6-2-2	141	36	.700	3-0-2	.800	2										

Bill Ingram (1931-1934) 27-14-4 .644

Year	AP	Other	W-L-T	PF	PA	Pct.	W-L-T	Pct.	Rank	Year	AP	Other	W-L-T	PF	PA	Pct.	W-L-T	Pct.	Rank
1931			8-2-0	106	41	.800	4-1-0	.800	2	1933			6-3-2	161	39	.636	2-2-2	.500	6
1932			7-3-2	169	89	.667	2-2-1	.500	5	1934			6-6-0	176	110	.500	3-2-0	.600	5

Stub Allison (1935-1944) 58-42-2 .578

Year	AP	Other	W-L-T	PF	PA	Pct.	W-L-T	Pct.	Rank	Year	AP	Other	W-L-T	PF	PA	Pct.	W-L-T	Pct.	Rank
1935		5	9-1-0	163	22	.900	4-1-0	.800	1	1940			4-6-0	84	128	.400	3-4-0	.429	6
1936			6-5-0	147	74	.545	4-3-0	.571	4	1941			4-5-0	107	71	.444	3-4-0	.429	7
1937	2	7	10-0-1	214	33	.955	6-0-1	.929	1	1942			5-5-0	98	107	.500	3-4-0	.429	7
1938	14		10-1-0	219	44	.909	6-1-0	.857	1	1943			4-6-0	99	143	.400	2-2-0	.500	2
1939			3-7-0	93	134	.300	2-5-0	.286	8	1944			3-6-1	78	149	.350	2-5-0	.286	4

Buck Shaw (1945) 4-5-1 .450

Year	AP	Other	W-L-T	PF	PA	Pct.	W-L-T	Pct.	Rank
1945			4-5-1	93	107	.450	2-4-1	.357	7

Frank Wickhorst (1946) 2-7-0 .222

Year	AP	Other	W-L-T	PF	PA	Pct.	W-L-T	Pct.	Rank
1946			2-7-0	112	169	.222	1-6-0	.143	9

Pappy Waldorf (1947-1956) 67-32-4 .670

Year	AP	Other	W-L-T	PF	PA	Pct.	W-L-T	Pct.	Rank	Year	AP	Other	W-L-T	PF	PA	Pct.	W-L-T	Pct.	Rank
1947	15		9-1-0	275	111	.900	5-1-0	.833	2	1952			7-3-0	247	127	.700	3-3-0	.500	4
1948	4		10-1-0	291	100	.909	6-0-0	1.000	2	1953			4-4-2	220	170	.500	2-2-2	.500	4
1949	3		10-1-0	319	131	.909	7-0-0	1.000	1	1954			5-5-0	249	177	.500	4-3-0	.571	4
1950	5	4	9-1-1	224	90	.864	5-0-1	.917	1	1955			2-7-1	107	216	.250	1-5-1	.214	8
1951	12	12	8-2-0	307	166	.800	5-2-0	.714	3	1956			3-7-0	135	181	.300	2-5-0	.286	9

Pete Elliott (1957-1959) 10-21-0 .323

Year	AP	Other	W-L-T	PF	PA	Pct.	W-L-T	Pct.	Rank	Year	AP	Other	W-L-T	PF	PA	Pct.	W-L-T	Pct.	Rank
1957			1-9-0	109	176	.100	1-6-0	.143	7	1959			2-8-0	115	223	.200	1-3-0	.250	4
1958	16	16	7-4-0	207	200	.636	6-1-0	.857	1										

Marv Levy (1960-1963) 8-29-3 .244

Year	AP	Other	W-L-T	PF	PA	Pct.	W-L-T	Pct.	Rank	Year	AP	Other	W-L-T	PF	PA	Pct.	W-L-T	Pct.	Rank
1960			2-7-1	93	195	.250	1-3-0	.250	4	1962			1-9-0	143	247	.100	0-4-0	.000	6
1961			1-8-1	118	268	.150	1-3-0	.250	5	1963			4-5-1	195	213	.450	1-3-0	.250	5

Ray Willsey (1964-1971) 40-42-1 .488

Year	AP	Other	W-L-T	PF	PA	Pct.	W-L-T	Pct.	Rank	Year	AP	Other	W-L-T	PF	PA	Pct.	W-L-T	Pct.	Rank
1964			3-7-0	152	187	.300	0-4-0	.000	8	1968			7-3-1	243	114	.682	2-2-1	.500	4
1965			5-5-0	125	194	.500	2-3-0	.400	5	1969			5-5-0	180	182	.500	2-4-0	.333	6
1966			3-7-0	131	197	.300	2-3-0	.400	5	1970			6-5-0	272	249	.545	4-3-0	.571	4
1967			5-5-0	155	195	.500	2-3-0	.400	6	1971			6-5-0	186	262	.545	4-3-0	.571	3

Mike White (1972-1977) 34-31-1 .523

Year	AP	Other	W-L-T	PF	PA	Pct.	W-L-T	Pct.	Rank	Year	AP	Other	W-L-T	PF	PA	Pct.	W-L-T	Pct.	Rank
1972			3-8-0	228	314	.272	3-4-0	.429	5	1975	14	15	8-3-0	330	233	.727	6-1-0	.857	1
1973			4-7-0	245	380	.364	2-5-0	.286	5	1976			5-6-0	230	226	.455	3-4-0	.429	4
1974			7-3-1	276	213	.682	4-2-1	.643	3	1977			7-4-0	300	211	.636	3-4-0	.429	5

Roger Theder (1978-1981) 17-28-0 .378

Year	AP	Other	W-L-T	PF	PA	Pct.	W-L-T	Pct.	Rank	Year	AP	Other	W-L-T	PF	PA	Pct.	W-L-T	Pct.	Rank
1978			6-5-0	236	289	.545	3-4-0	.429	6	1980			3-8-0	194	328	.272	3-5-0	.375	9
1979			6-6-0	257	194	.500	5-4-0	.556	5	1981			2-9-0	197	287	.182	2-6-0	.250	8

Joe Kapp (1982-1986) 20-34-1 .373

Year			W-L-T	PF	PA	Pct	Conf	Pct	Rk
1982			7-4-0	220	233	.636	4-4-0	.500	6
1983			5-5-1	242	227	.500	3-4-1	.438	8
1984			2-9-0	150	264	.222	1-8-0	.111	10
1985			4-7-0	233	265	.364	2-7-0	..222	10
1986			2-9-0	145	325	.182	2-7-0	.222	9

Bruce Snyder (1987-1991) 29-24-4 .544

Year			W-L-T	PF	PA	Pct	Conf	Pct	Rk
1987			3-6-2	239	267	.364	2-3-2	.429	7
1988			5-5-1	243	244	.500	1-5-1	.214	10
1989			4-7-0	200	288	.364	2-6-0	.250	10
1990			7-4-1	325	341	.625	4-3-1	.562	4
1991	8	7	10-2-0	443	239	.833	6-2-0	.750	2

Keith Gilbertson (1992-1995) 20-26-0 .435

Year			W-L-T	PF	PA	Pct	Conf	Pct	Rk
1992			4-7-0	284	284	.364	2-6-0	.250	9
1993	25	24	9-4-0	411	303	.692	4-4-0	.500	5
1994			4-7-0	212	248	.364	3-5-0	.375	6
1995			3-8-0	244	286	.272	2-6-0	.250	7

Steve Mariucci (1996) 6-6-0 .500

Year			W-L-T	PF	PA	Pct	Conf	Pct	Rk
1996			6-6-0	344	365	.500	3-5-0	.375	7

Tom Holmoe (1997-2001) 16-39-0 .291

Year			W-L-T	PF	PA	Pct	Conf	Pct	Rk
1997			3-8-0	295	339	.272	1-7-0	.125	9
1998			5-6-0	183	251	.455	3-5-0	.375	7
1999			4-7-0	180	254	.364	3-5-0	.375	7
2000			3-8-0	246	295	.272	2-6-0	.250	10
2001			1-10-0	201	431	.091	0-8-0	.000	10

Jeff Tedford (2002-2003) 15-11-0 .577

Year			W-L-T	PF	PA	Pct	Conf	Pct	Rk
2002			7-5-0	427	318	.583	4-4-0	.500	4
2003			8-6-0	457	341	.571	5-3-0	.625	3

Won-loss record by decades:

1887-89	10-1-0	.909	1930-39	69-33-5	.668	1970-79	58-52-1	.527	
1890-99	39-13-12	.706	1940-49	55-43-2	.560	1980-89	37-69-4	.355	
1900-09	35-5-7	.827	1950-59	48-50-4	.490	1990-99	55-59-1	.483	
1910-19	32-18-3	.632	1960-69	36-61-4	.376	2000-03	19-29-0	.396	
1920-29	73-15-7	.805							

Historical record (1886-2001) 566-448-50 .555

Post-season won-loss record 6-7-1 .464

1921: Rose Bowl, California 28, Ohio State 0
1922: Rose Bowl, California 0, Wash. & Jeff. 0
1929: Rose Bowl, Georgia Tech 8, California 7
1938: Rose Bowl, California 13, Alabama 0
1949: Rose Bowl, Northwestern 20, California 14
1950: Rose Bowl, Ohio State 17, California 14
1951: Rose Bowl, Michigan 14, California 6
1959: Rose Bowl, Iowa 38, California 12
1979: Garden State Bowl, Temple 28, California 17
1990: Copper Bowl, California 17, Wyoming 15
1992: Citrus Bowl, California 37, Clemson 13
1993: Alamo Bowl, California 37, Iowa 3
1996: Aloha Bowl, Navy 42, California 38
2003: Insight.com Bowl, California 52, Va. Tech 49

College Football Hall of Fame:
Andy Smith, coach, 1916-25; Walter Gordon, guard/tackle, 1916-18; Stan Barnes, center/tackle, 1918-21; Dana McMillan, tackle, 1920-21; Brick Muller, end, 1920-22; Babe Horrell, center, 1922-24; Bill Ingram, coach, 1931-34; Bob Herwig, center, 1935-37; Vic Bottari, halfback, 1936-38; Sam Chapman, halfback, 1935-37; Buck Shaw, coach, 1945; Rod Franz, guard, 1946-49; Jackie Jensen, fullback, 1946-48; Pappy Waldorf, coach, 1947-56; Les Richter, guard, 1949-51; Matt Hazeltine, center, 1951-54; Craig Morton, quarterback, 1962-64; Ed White, middle guard, 1966-68.

Awards: Tatupu Award: 1999, Deltha O'Neal.

UNIVERSITY OF CENTRAL FLORIDA, Orlando, Florida; nickname "Golden Knights"; colors black and gold; Florida Citrus Bowl (70,188). UCF began play in 1979 as a Division III team and has been Division IA since 1996. UCF played as an independent until joining the Mid-American Conference for the 2002 season.

Year	Coach	W-L-T	PF	PA	Pct.	Year	Coach	W-L-T	PF	PA	Pct
					Division III (1979-1981) 13-13-1 .500						
					Don Jonas (1979-1981) 13-13-1 .500						
1979		6-2-0	104	96	.750	1981		4-6-0	142	130	.400
1980		3-5-1	156	175	.389						
					Division II (1982-1989) 39-49-0 .443						
					Sam Weir (1982) 0-10-0 .000						
1982		0-10-0	109	356	.000						
					Lou Saban (1983-1984) 6-12-0 .333						
1983		5-6-0	283	306	.455	1984*		1-6-0	154	270	.143
					Jerry Anderson (1984) 1-3-0 .250						
1984*		1-3-0	55	128	.250						

*Saban coached the first seven games of the 1984 season, and Anderson coached the last four.

Year	Coach	W-L-T	PF	PA	Pct.	Year	Coach	W-L-T	PF	PA	Pct
					Gene McDowell (1985-1997) 86-61-0 .585						
1985		4-7-0	266	386	.364	1988		6-5-0	267	288	.545
1986		6-5-0	293	217	.545	1989		7-3-0	256	168	.700
1987		9-4-0	401	210	.692						
					Division I-AA (1990-1995) 44-25-0 .638						
1990		10-4-0	444	280	.714	1993		9-3-0	414	277	.750
1991		6-5-0	278	230	.545	1994		7-4-0	399	263	.636
1992		6-4-0	416	249	.600	1995		6-5-0	283	280	.545
					Division I-A (1996-2001) 36-30-0 .545						
1996		5-6-0	277	261	.455	1997		5-6-0	374	303	.455
					Mike Kruczek (1998-2003) 36-30-0 .545						
1998		9-2-0	393	209	.818	2000		7-4-0	333	221	.636
1999		4-7-0	277	318	.364	2001		6-5-0	333	204	.545

Member of the Mid-American Conference (2002-2003) 8-8-0 .500

		Nat'l	Overall				Conference						
Year	AP	Other	W-L-T	PF	PA	Pct.	W-L-T	Pct.	Rank				
2002			7-5-0	.391	315	.583	6-2-0	.750	4	2003*	3-7-0	196	296	.300	10

Alan Gooch (2003) 0-2-0 .000

Year			W-L-T	PF	PA	Pct.	W-L-T	Pct.
2003*			0-2-0	28	77	.000	0-2-0	.000

*Kruczek coached the first ten games of the 2003 season, and Gooch coached the last two games.

Won-loss record by decades:
1979-89	52-62-1	.465	1990-99	67-46-0	.593	2000-03	23-23-0	.500

Historical record (1979-2003) 142-131-1 .520

Post-season won-loss record 3-3-0 .500
1987: Division II Playofffs, UCF 12, Indiana (Pa) 10
1987: Division II Playoffs, Troy State 31, UCF 10
1990: Division I-AA Playoffs, UCF 20, Youngstown State 17
1990: Division I-AA Playoffs, UCF 52, Wm & Mary 38
1990: Division I-AA Playoffs, Georgia Southern 44, UCF 7
1993: Division I-AA Playoffs, Youngstown State 56, UCF 30

Awards: Sammy Baugh Trophy: 1998, Duante Culpepper.

CENTRAL MICHIGAN UNIVERSITY, Mount Pleasant, Michigan; nickname "Chippewas"; colors maroon and gold; Kelly/Shorts Stadium (30,199); Mid-American Conference. Central Michigan began play in 1896 and joined the MAC beginning with the 1975 season.

Early years (1896-1974)

Year	W-L-T	PF	PA	Pct.	Year	W-L-T	PF	PA	Pct.
Pete McCormick (1896) 3-1-0 .750									
1896	3-1-0	62	22	.750					
Carl Pray (1897-1899) 6-5-0 .545									
1897	2-1-0	10	18	.667	1899	3-2-0	45	22	.600
1898	1-2-0	37	32	.333					
Unknown coach (1900) 1-0-0 1.000									
1900	1-0-0	20	5	1.000	1901	no team			
Charles Tambling (1902-1905, 1918) 18-2-0 .900									
1902	4-0-0	82	0	1.000	1905	7-1-0	126	14	.875
1903	6-0-0	57	11	1.000	1906	no team			
1904	0-1-0	6	60	.000					
Ralph Thacker (1907) 2-4-0 .333									
1907	2-4-0	18	129	.333					
Hugh Sutherland (1908) 4-3-0 .571									
1908	4-3-0	26	16	.571					
Harry Helmer (1909-1912) 14-7-2 .652									
1909	4-3-0	63	58	.571	1911	3-2-0	17	6	.600
1910	6-1-1	106	33	.812	1912*	1-1-1	0	0	.500

*Scores not reported for two games in 1912.

No team from 1913 through 1915

Year	W-L-T	PF	PA	Pct.	Year	W-L-T	PF	PA	Pct.
Blake Miller (1916) 1-5-0 .167									
1916	1-5-0	39	139	.167					
Fred Johnson (1917) 1-2-0 .333									
1917	1-2-0	7	71						
Charles Trambling (1918)									
1918	1-0-0	41	6	1.000					
Garland Nevitt (1919) 2-2-3 .500									
1919	2-2-3	82	88	.500					
Joe Simmons (1920) 4-3-1 .562									
1920	4-3-1	94	41	.562					
Wallace Parker (1921-1923, 1926-1928) 32-10-6 .729									
1921	5-1-1	143	7	.786	1923	5-1-2	167	24	.750
1922	6-0-2	179	13	.875					
Lester Barnard (1924-1925) 11-2-3 .781									
1924	7-1-0	158	19	.875	1925	4-1-3	96	20	.688
Wallace Parker (1926-1928)									
1926	3-4-1	66	90	.438	1928	6-3-0	126	64	.667
1927	7-1-0	124	37	.875					
A.J. Nowak (1929-1930) 8-5-2 .600									
1929	2-3-2	71	80	.429	1930	6-2-0	108	81	.750
George Van Bibber (1931-1933) 12-9-2 .565									
1931	4-3-0	95	58	.571	1933	5-2-1	162	66	.688
1932	3-4-1	97	66	.438					
Alex Yunevich (1934-1936) 10-13-1 .479									
1934	5-3-0	81	82	.675	1936	3-4-1	89	135	.438
1935	2-6-0	39	95	.250					
Ron Finch (1937-1946) 53-18-1 .743									
1937	6-2-0	200	42	.750	1942	6-0-0	93	21	1.000
1938	7-1-0	270	44	.875	1943	2-3-0	19	70	.400
1939	7-1-0	119	40	.875	1944	5-2-0	150	106	.714
1940	4-3-1	88	60	.562	1945	6-1-0	98	26	.857
1941	4-3-0	44	82	.571	1946	6-2-0	233	67	.750
Lyle Bennett (1947-1949) 8-15-1 .354									
1947	2-5-1	136	125	.312	1949	3-4-0	106	103	.429
1948	3-6-0	127	139	.333					
Warren Schmakel (1950) 6-4-0 .600									
1950	6-4-0	210	125	.600					

Bill Kelly (1951-1966) 91-58-2 .609

Year	W-L-T	PF	PA	Pct.		Year	W-L-T	PF	PA	Pct.
1951	5-3-0	228	158	.625		1959	7-3-0	233	155	.700
1952	7-2-0	285	85	.778		1960	3-5-0	161	165	.375
1953	7-1-1	244	129	.833		1961	2-8-0	95	214	.200
1954	8-2-0	321	107	.800		1962	6-4-0	191	171	.600
1955	8-1-0	327	79	.889		1963	4-5-1	209	195	.450
1956	9-0-0	313	92	1.000		1964	4-5-0	117	148	.444
1957	4-6-0	220	222	.400		1965	5-5-0	193	143	.500
1958	7-3-0	216	204	.700		1966	5-5-0	213	159	.500

Roy Kramer (1967-1977) 83-32-2 .718

Year	W-L-T	PF	PA	Pct.		Year	W-L-T	PF	PA	Pct.
1967	8-2-0	247	154	.800		1971	5-5-0	183	181	.500
1968	7-2-0	256	132	.778		1972	5-5-1	265	190	.500
1969	7-3-0	254	147	.700		1973	7-4-0	197	151	.636
1970	7-3-0	263	190	.700		1974	12-1-0	450	127	.923

Member of the Mid-American Conference (1975-2003) 135-95-10 .583

		Overall				Conference						Overall				Conference		
Year	Nat'l	W-L-T	PF	PA	Pct.	W-L-T	Pct.	Rank	Year	Nat'l	W-L-T	PF	PA	Pct.	W-L-T	Pct.	Rank
1975		8-2-1	309	102	.773	4-1-1	.750	2	1977		10-1-0	317	155	.909	7-1-0	.875	2
1976		7-4-0	223	219	.636	4-3-0	.571	5									

Herb Deromedi (1978-1993) 110-55-10 .657

Year	Nat'l	W-L-T	PF	PA	Pct.	W-L-T	Pct.	Rank	Year	Nat'l	W-L-T	PF	PA	Pct.	W-L-T	Pct.	Rank
1978		9-2-0	331	119	.818	8-1-0	.889	2	1986		5-5-0	258	284	.500	4-4-0	.500	5
1979		10-0-1	291	133	.955	8-0-1	.944	1	1987		5-5-1	222	203	.500	3-4-1	.438	6
1980		9-2-0	218	127	.818	7-2-0	.778	1	1988		7-4-0	287	176	.636	5-3-0	.625	3
1981		7-4-0	223	131	.636	7-2-0	.778	3	1989		5-5-1	228	182	.500	5-2-1	.688	4
1982		6-4-1	228	199	.591	5-3-1	.611	4	1990		8-3-1	283	146	.708	7-1-0	.875	1
1983		8-3-0	257	136	.727	7-2-0	.778	2	1991		6-1-4	205	157	.727	3-1-4	.625	2
1984		8-2-1	282	141	.773	6-2-1	.722	3	1992		5-6-0	247	170	.455	4-5-0	.444	7
1985		7-3-0	194	143	.700	6-3-0	.667	3	1993		5-6-0	275	244	.455	5-4-0	.556	4

Dick Flynn (1994-1999) 30-37-0 .448

Year	Nat'l	W-L-T	PF	PA	Pct.	W-L-T	Pct.	Rank	Year	Nat'l	W-L-T	PF	PA	Pct.	W-L-T	Pct.	Rank
1994		9-3-0	400	315	.750	8-1-0	.889	1	1997		2-9-0	282	479	.182	1-7-0	.125	11
1995		4-7-0	255	276	.363	2-6-0	.250	7	1998		6-5-0	na	na	.545	5-3-0	.625	4
1996		5-6-0	351	353	.455	4-4-0	.500	5	1999		4-7-0	229	344	.364	3-5-0	.375	9

Mike DeBord (2000-2003) 12-34-0 .261

Year	Nat'l	W-L-T	PF	PA	Pct.	W-L-T	Pct.	Rank	Year	Nat'l	W-L-T	PF	PA	Pct.	W-L-T	Pct.	Rank
2000		2-9-0	137	366	.182	2-6-0	.250	10	2002		4-8-0	267	384	.333	2-6-0	.200	11
2001		3-8-0	251	346	.273	2-6-0	.250	10	2003		3-9-0	277	428	.250	1-7-0	.125	12

Won-loss record by decades:

1896-99	9-6-0	.600	1930-39	48-28-3	.627	1970-79	80-27-3	.741
1900-09	28-12-0	.700	1940-49	41-29-2	.583	1980-89	67-37-4	.639
1910-19	15-13-5	.530	1950-59	68-25-1	.729	1990-99	54-53-5	.504
1920-29	49-18-12	.696	1960-69	51-44-1	.536	2000-03	12-34-0	.261

Historical record (1896-2003) 522-326-36 .611

Post-season won-loss record: 3-2-0 .600

1974: Division II Playoffs: CMU 20, Boise State 6
1974: Division II Playoffs: CMU 35, Louisiana Tech 14
1974: Division II Championship: CMU 54, Delaware 14

1990: California Raisin Bowl, San Jose State 48, CMU 24
1994: Las Vegas Bowl, UNLV 52, CMU 24

UNIVERSITY OF CINCINNATI, Cincinnati, Ohio; nickname "Bearcats"; colors red and black; Nippert Stadium (35,000); Conference USA. Cincinnati began play in 1885 as an independent. In 1910, Cincinnati joined the Ohio Conference and played in that conference through the 1924 season. The Bearcats joined the Buckeye Conference in 1925 and then reverted to independent status in 1936. In 1947, Cincinnati joined the Mid-American Conference dropping out to independent status after the 1952 season. Cincinnati was in the Missouri Valley Conference from 1957 through the 1969 season and then again became an independent until the 1996 season when it became one of the founding members of Conference USA.

Early years as an independent (1885-1909)
No coach (1985-1893)

Year	W-L-T	PF	PA	Pct.	Year	W-L-T	PF	PA	Pct.
1885	1-0-1	26	6	.750	1890	2-1-1	22	20	625
1886	2-0-0	26	12	1.000	1891	4-2-1	129	46	.643
1887	1-0-0	8	4	1.000	1892	1-2-0	20	52	.333
1888	1-0-1	8	6	.750	1893	0-6-0	12	120	.000
1889	1-1-0	12	34	.500					

Year		W-L-T	PF	PA	Pct.	Year		W-L-T	PF	PA	Pct.
1894	W.D. Berry	3-3-0	64	44	.500	1902	Anthony Chez	4-2-2	58	45	.625
1895	W.D. Berry	3-3-0	54	46	.500	1903	Anthony Chez	1-8-0	39	141	.111
1896	William Reynolds	4-3-1	88	68	.562	1904	Amos Foster	7-1-0	182	10	.875
1897	Tom Fennell	9-1-1	146	22	.864	1905	Amos Foster	4-3-0	87	91	.571
1898	Frank Cavanaugh	5-1-3	143	40	.722	1906	William Foley	0-7-2	5	162	.111
1899	Dan Reed	5-2-0	88	60	.714	1907	no team				
1900	Dan Reed	3-4-1	51	155	438	1908	Ralph Inott	1-4-1	69	74	.562
1901	Henry Pratt	1-3-1	10	47	.300						

Robert Burch (1909-1911) 16-8-2 .654

1909	4-3-1	69	74	.562

Member of the Ohio Conference (1910-1924) 26-40-8 .405

Year	Nat'l AP Other	Overall W-L-T	PF	PA	Pct.	Conference W-L-T	Pct.	Rank	Year	Nat'l AP Other	Overall W-L-T	PF	PA	Pct.	Conference W-L-T	Pct.	Rank
1910		6-3-0	122	59	.667	2-1-0	.667		1911		6-2-1	79	34	.722	2-1-1	.625	

Lowell Dana (1912-1913) 8-7-2 .529

| 1912 | | 3-4-1 | 251 | 145 | .438 | 0-3-1 | .125 | | 1913 | | 5-3-1 | 177 | 61 | .611 | 4-2-1 | .643 | |

George Little (1914-1915) 10-8-0 .556

| 1914 | | 6-3-0 | 164 | 44 | .667 | 4-2-0 | .667 | | 1915 | | 4-5-0 | 110 | 158 | .444 | 3-3-0 | .500 | |

Ion Cortright (1916) 0-8-1 .055

| 1916 | | 0-8-1 | 10 | 124 | .055 | 0-6-1 | .072 | | | | | | | | | | |

Frank Marty (1917) 0-6-0 .000

| 1917 | | 0-6-0 | 0 | 189 | .000 | 0-4-0 | .000 | | | | | | | | | | |

Boyd Chambers (1918-1921) 12-15-3 .450

| 1918 | | 3-0-2 | 45 | 13 | .800 | 0-0-2 | .500 | | 1920 | | 4-5-0 | 125 | 96 | .444 | 3-2-0 | .600 | |
| 1919 | | 3-4-1 | 73 | 102 | .438 | 1-3-1 | .300 | | 1921 | | 2-6-0 | 164 | 107 | .250 | 0-4-0 | .000 | |

George McLaren (1922-1926) 16-26-3 .389

| 1922 | | 1-7-1 | 35 | 174 | .167 | 1-3-1 | .300 | | 1924 | | 2-6-1 | 54 | 164 | 278 | 1-4-0 | .2000 | |
| 1923 | | 6-3-0 | 157 | 71 | .667 | 5-2-0 | .714 | | | | | | | | | | |

Member of the Buckeye Conference (1925-1935)

| 1925 | | 4-5-0 | 65 | 122 | .444 | 1-3-0 | .250 | | 1926 | | 3-5-1 | 96 | 152 | .389 | 0-3-1 | .125 | |

George Babcock (1927-1930) 12-21-3 .375

| 1927 | | 2-5-2 | 81 | 105 | .333 | 0-3-1 | .125 | | 1929 | | 4-4-1 | 75 | 133 | .500 | 0-4-1 | .100 | |
| 1928 | | 1-8-0 | 32 | 247 | .111 | 0-5-0 | .000 | | 1930 | | 5-4-0 | 91 | 138 | .556 | 2-3-0 | .400 | |

Dana King (1931-1934) 25-10-1 .708

| 1931 | | 5-4-0 | 187 | 115 | .556 | 2-1-0 | .667 | | 1933 | | 7-2-0 | 111 | 22 | .778 | 3-1-0 | .750 | |
| 1932 | | 7-2-0 | 151 | 69 | .778 | 2-2-0 | .500 | | 1934 | | 6-2-1 | 163 | 71 | .722 | 2-0-1 | .833 | |

Russ Cohen (1935-1937) 8-11-3 .432

| 1935 | | 7-2-0 | 237 | 49 | .778 | 2-2-0 | .500 | | | | | | | | | | |

Cincinnati reverts to independent status (1936-1946)

| 1936 | | 1-5-3 | 57 | 124 | .288 | | | | 1937* | | 0-4-0 | 6 | 87 | .000 | | | |

Red Woodworth (1937) 0-6-0 .000

| 1937* | | 0-6-0 | 12 | 127 | .000 | | | | | | | | | | | | |

*Russ Cohen resigned during the 1937 season, replaced by Red Woodworth for the remainder of the season.

Joe Meyer (1938-1942) 27-16-3 .620

1938		4-5-0	81	137	.444	1941		6-3-0		194	45	.667
1939		4-3-2	87	65	.556	1942		8-2-0		197	95	.800
1940		5-3-1	132	48	.611	1943, 1944	no team					

Ray Nolting (1945-1948) 23-15-1 .603

| 1945 | | 4-4-0 | 132 | 88 | .500 | 1946 | | 9-2-0 | | 221 | 93 | .818 |

Member of the Mid-American Conference (1947-1952) 19-3-0 .864

| 1947 | | 7-3-0 | 182 | 168 | .700 | 3-1-0 | .750 | 1 | 1948 | | 3-6-1 | 106 | 193 | .350 | 3-1-0 | .750 | 2 |

— 62 —

Sid Gilman (1949-1954) 50-13-1 .789

1949	7-4-0	237	181	.636	4-0-0	1.000	1	1951		10-1-0	345	112	.909	3-0-0	1.000	1
1950	8-4-0	258	169	.667	3-1-0	.750	2	1952		8-1-1	275	72	.850	3-0-0	1.000	1

Cincinnati reverts to independent status (1953-1956)

1953	9-1-0	354	58	.900	1954	8-2-0 249 107	.800

George Blackburn (1955-1960) 25-27-6 .483

1955	1-6-2	97	199	.222	1956	4-5-0 156 140	.444

Member of the Missouri Valley Conference (1957-1969) 23-25-3 .480

1957	5-4-1	130	101	.550	1-3-0	.250	4	1959		5-4-1	193	148	.550	0-3-1	.125	5
1958	6-2-2	139	104	.700	1-1-2	.500	2	1960		4-6-0	113	150	.400	1-2-0	.333	3

Chuck Studley (1961-1966) 27-33-0 .450

1961	3-7-0	97	142	.300	1-2-0	.333	3	1964		8-2-0	211	99	.800	4-0-0	1.000	1
1962	2-8-0	142	202	.200	1-2-0	.333	3	1965		5-5-0	163	172	.500	2-2-0	.500	3
1963	6-4-0	238	138	.600	3-1-0	.750	1	1966		3-7-0	141	201	.300	2-2-0	.500	3

Homer Rice (1967-1968) 8-10-1 .447

1967	3-6-0	111	189	.333	2-2-0	.500	3	1968		5-4-1	300	327	.550	3-2-0	.600	3

Ray Callahan (1969-1972) 20-23-0 .465

1969	4-6-0	192	329	.400	2-3-0	.400	3

Cincinnati reverts again to independent status (1970-1995)

1970	7-4-0	229	108	.636	1972	2-9-0 138 323	.182
1971	7-4-0	225	188	.636			

Tony Mason (1973-1976) 26-18-0 .591

1973	4-7-0	210	109	.364	1975	6-5-0 209 182	.545
1974	7-4-0	227	175	.636	1976	9-2-0 204 114	.818

Ralph Staub (1977-1980) 14-28-2 .341

1977	5-4-2	250	121	.545	1979	2-9-0 156 281	.182
1978	5-6-0	279	224	.455	1980	2-9-0 122 271	.182

Mike Gottfried (1981-1982) 12-10-0 .545

1981	6-5-0	171	187	.545	1982	6-5-0 276 206	.545

Watson Brown (1983) 4-6-1 .409

1983	4-6-1	208	234	.409

Dave Currey (1984-1988) 19-36-0 .345

1984	2-9-0	198	424	.182	1987	4-7-0 234 314	.364
1985	5-6-0	199	261	.455	1988	3-8-0 201 379	.273
1986	5-6-0	267	345	.455			

Tim Murphy (1989-1993) 17-37-1 .318

1989	1-9-1	111	379	.136	1992	3-8-0 199 276	.273
1990	1-10-0	172	460	.091	1993	8-3-0 302 197	.727
1991	4-7-0	201	293	.364			

Rick Minter (1994-2003) 53-63-1 .457

1994	2-8-1	159	301	.227	1995	6-5-0 252 197	.545

Member of Conference USA (1996-2003) 23-30-0 .434

1996	6-5-0	228	212	.545	2-3-0	.400	3	2000		7-5-0	289	285	.583	5-2-0	.714	2
1997	8-4-0	321	252	.667	2-4-0	.333	4	2001		7-5-0	336	290	.583	5-2-0	.714	2
1998	2-9-0	259	456	.182	1-5-0	.167	7	2002		7-7-0	409	329	.500	6-2-0	.750	1
1999	3-8-0	275	289	.273	0-6-0	.000	9	2003		5-7-0	303	319	.417	2-6-0	.250	9

Won-loss record by decades:

1885-89	6- 1-2	.778		1930-39	36-29-6	.538		1980-89	38-70-2	.355
1890-99	36-24-7	.590		1940-49	49-27-2	.641		1990-99	43-67-1	.392
1900-09	25-35-8	.426		1950-59	64-30-7	.668		2000-03	26-24-0	.520
1910-19	36-38-7	.488		1960-69	43-55-1	.439				
1920-29	29-54-6	.360		1970-79	54-54-2	.500				
Historic record	495-518-51	.489								

Post-season won-loss record 3-4-0 .429

1947: Sun Bowl, Cincinnati 18, Virginia Tech 6
1949: Glass Bowl, Cincinnati 33, Toledo 13
1951: Sun Bowl, West Texas State 14, Cincinnati 13

1997: Humanitarian Bowl, Cincinnati 35, Utah State 19
2000: Motor City Bowl: Marshall 25, Cincinnati 14
2001: Motor City Bowl: Toledo 23, Cincinnati 16
2002: New Orleans Bowl, North Texas 24, Cincinnati 19

College Football Hall of Fame:
Frank Cavanaugh, coach, 1898; George Little, coach, 1914-15; Sid Gilman, coach, 1950-54.

Awards: Lou Groza Award: 2000, Jonathan Ruffin.

CLEMSON UNIVERSITY, Clemson, South Carolina; nickname "Tigers"; colors Northwestern purple and burnt orange; Memorial Stadium (81,473). Atlantic Coast Conference. Clemson began play in 1896 and joined the newly formed Southern Conference in 1922, playing there through the 1952 season. Clemson then joined with other Southern Conference teams to organize the Atlantic Coast Conference and has played in that conference since that time, beginning with the 1953 season.

Year	W-L-T	PF	PA	Pct.	Year	W-L-T	PF	PA	Pct
					Years as an independent (1896-1921)				
					Walter Riggs (1896, 1899) 6-3-0 .667				
1896	2-1-0	36	18	.667					
					W. M. Williams (1897) 2-2-0 .500				
1897	2-2-0	30	58	.500					
					John Penton (1898) 3-1-0 .750				
1898	3-1-0	110	20	.750					
					Walter Riggs (1899)				
1899	4-2-0	109	50	.667					
					John Heisman (1900-1903) 19-3-2 .833				
1900	6-0-0	222	10	1.000	1902	6-1-0	152	22	.857
1901	3-1-1	190	38	.700	1903	4-1-1	167	22	.750
					A. B. Shealy (1904) 3-3-1 .500				
1904	3-3-1	50	45	.500					
					Eddie Coochems (1905) 3-2-1 .583				
1905	3-2-1	101	63	.583					
					Bob Williams (1906, 1909, 1913-1915) 21-14-6 .585				
1906	4-0-3	38	4	.786					
					Frank Shaughnessy (1907) 4-4-0 .500				
1907	4-4-0	67	45	.500					
					John Stone (1908) 1-6-0 .143				
1908	1-6-0	26	104	.143					
					Bob Williams (1909)				
1909	6-3-0	93	43	.667					
					Frank Dobson (1910-1912) 11-12-1 .479				
1910	4-3-1	106	54	.562	1912	4-4-0	177	123	.500
1911	3-5-0	71	108	.375					
					Bob Williams (1913-1915)				
1913	4-4-0	112	98	.500	1915	2-4-2	113	48	.375
1914	5-3-1	168	123	.611					
					Wayne Hart (1916) 3-6-0 .333				
1916	3-6-0	81	147	.333					
					Edward Donohue (1917-1920) 21-12-3 .625				
1917	6-2-0	183	64	.750	1919	6-2-2	152	55	.700
1918	5-2-0	198	101	.714	1920	4-6-1	98	146	.409
					Doc Stewart (1921-1922) 6-10-2 .389				
1921	1-6-2	48	187	.222					

Member of the Southern Conference (1922-1952) 66-53-7 .552

	Nat'l	Overall				Conference				Nat'l	Overall				Conference		
Year	AP Other	W-L-T	PF	PA	Pct.	W-L-T	Pct.	Rank	Year	AP Other	W-L-T	PF	PA	Pct.	W-L-T	Pct.	Rank
1922		5-4-0	170	109	.556	1-2-0	.333	11									
						Bud Saunders (1923-1926) 10-22-1 .318											
1923		5-2-1	91	65	.688	1-1-1	.500	14	1925		1-7-0	27	160	.125	0-4-0	.000	20
1924		2-6-0	80	96	.250	0-3-0	.000	19	1926		2-7-0	20	169	.222	0-3-0	.000	20
						Josh Cody (1927-1930) 29-11-1 .720											
1927		5-3-1	73	84	.611	2-2-0	.500	8	1929		8-3-0	236	110	.727	3-3-0	.500	12
1928		8-3-0	192	77	.727	4-2-0	.667	7	1930		8-2-0	239	82	.800	3-2-0	.600	9
						Jess Neely (1931-1939) 43-35-7 .547											
1931		1-6-2	19	164	.222	1-4-0	.200	20	1936		5-5-0	98	95	.500	3-2-0	.600	5
1932		3-5-1	89	111	.389	0-4-0	.000	21	1937		4-4-1	128	64	.500	2-0-1	.833	3
1933		3-6-2	50	98	.364	1-1-0	.500	5	1938		7-1-1	145	56	.833	3-0-1	.875	2
1934		5-4-0	89	85	.556	2-1-0	.667	5	1939	12	9-1-0	165	45	.900	4-0-0	1.000	2
1935		6-3-0	147	99	.667	2-1-0	.667	4									
						Frank Howard (1940-1969) 165-118-12 .580											
1940		6-2-1	182	73	.722	4-0-0	1.000	1	1947		4-5-0	206	146	.444	1-3-0	.250	12
1941		7-2-0	233	90	.778	5-1-0	.833	3	1948	11	11-0-0	274	76	1.000	5-0-0	1.000	1
1942		3-6-1	100	138	.350	2-3-1	.417	9	1949		4-4-2	232	216	.500	2-2-0	.500	7
1943		2-6-0	94	185	.250	2-3-0	.400	71	1950	10 12	9-0-1	344	76	.950	3-0-1	.875	2
1944		4-5-0	165	179	.444	3-1-0	.750	3	1951	20	7-3-0	196	97	.700	3-1-0	.750	5
1945		6-3-1	211	73	.650	2-1-1	.625	4	1952		2-6-1	112	157	.278	0-0-0	*	*
1946		4-5-0	147	174	.444	2-3-0	.400	10									

* Played no conference games in 1952.

Member of the Atlantic Coast Conference (1953-2003) 202-111-6 .643

1953			3-5-1	139	172	389	1-2-0	.333	6	1962			6-4-0	168	130	.600	5-1-0	.833	2
1954			5-5-0	193	121		.500	1-2-0	.333	5	1963			5-4-1	181	140	.550	5-2-0	.714	3
1955			7-3-0	206	144		.700	3-1-0	.750	3	1964			3-7-0	105	135	.300	2-4-0	.333	7
1956	19		7-2-2	167	101		.727	4-0-1	.900	1	1965			5-5-0	117	137	.500	4-3-0	.571	3
1957		18	7-3-0	216	78		.700	4-3-0	.571	3	1966			6-4-0	174	177	.600	6-1-0	.857	1
1958	12	13	8-3-0	169	138		.727	5-1-0	.833	1	1967			6-4-0	166	128	.600	6-0-0	1.000	1
1959	11	11	9-2-0	295	103		.818	6-1-0	.857	1	1968			4-5-1	184	179	.450	4-1-1	.750	2
1960			6-4-0	197	124		.600	4-2-0	.667	4	1969			4-6-0	178	250	.400	3-3-0	.500	3
1961			5-5-0	199	126		.500	3-3-0	.500	3										

Hootie Ingram (1970-1972) 12-21-0 .364

1970			3-8-0	164	313	.273	2-4-0	.333	6	1972			4-7-0	143	245	.364	2-4-0	.333	5
1971			5-6-0	155	202	.455	4-2-0	.667	2										

Red Parker (1973-1976) 17-25-2 .409

1973			5-6-0	231	263	.455	4-2-0	.667	3	1975			2-9-0	177	381	.182	2-3-0	.400	5
1974			7-4-0	246	250	.636	4-2-0	.667	2	1976			3-6-2	172	237	.364	0-4-1	.100	7

Charley Pell (1977-78) 18-4-1 .804

1977	19		8-3-1	228	163	.773	4-1-1	.750	2	1978*	6	7	10-1-0	351	116	.917	6-0-0	1.000	1

Danny Ford (1978-1989) 96-29-4 .760

1978*			1-0-0	17	15	1.000	0-0-0			1984			7-4-0	346	215	.636	5-2-0	.714	**
1979			8-4-0	205	116	.667	4-2-0	.667	2	1985			6-6-0	244	222	.500	4-3-0	.571	3
1980			6-5-0	217	222	.545	2-4-0	.333	4	1986	17	19	8-2-2	296	187	.750	5-1-1	.786	1
1981	1	1	12-0-0	338	105	1.000	6-0-0	1.000	1	1987	12	10	10-2-0	333	176	.833	6-1-0	.857	1
1982	8		9-1-1	289	147	.864	6-0-0	1.000	1	1988	9	8	10-2-0	342	157	.833	6-1-0	.857	1
1983	11		9-1-1	338	200	.864	7-0-0	1.000	**	1989	12	11	10-2-0	368	138	.833	5-2-0	.714	3

* Pell resigned after the regular season, and Ford coached Clemson in the Gator Bowl.
** Clemson on NCAA suspension, ineligible for the ACC title.

Ken Hatfield (1990-1993) 31-13-1 .700

1990	9	9	10-2-0	333	109	.833	5-2-0	.714	2	1992			5-6-0	261	213	.455	3-5-0	.375	7
1991	18	17	8-2-1	317	185	.792	6-0-1	.929	1	1993*	23	22	8-3-0	184	179	.750	5-3-0	.625	3

Tommy West (1993-1998) 31-28-0 .525

1993*			1-0-0	14	13	1.000	0-0-0			1996			7-5-0	245	241	.583	6-2-0	.750	2
1994			5-6-0	164	188	.455	4-4-0	.500	6	1997			7-5-0	292	219	.583	4-4-0	.500	5
1995			8-4-0	303	219	.667	6-2-0	.750	3	1998			3-8-0	218	272	.273	1-7-0	.125	8

*Hatfield coached the first eleven games of the 1993 season, and West coached the final game.

Tommy Bowden (1999-2003) 38-24-0 .613

1999			6-6-0	322	253	.500	5-3-0	.625	2	2002			7-6-0	315	294	.538	4-4-0	.500	5
2000	16	14	9-3-0	416	253	.750	6-2-0	.750	2	2003	22	22	9-4-0	365	250	.692	5-3-0	.625	3
2001			7-5-0	368	339	.583	4-4-0	.500	4										

Won-loss record by decades:

1896-99	11- 6-0	.647	1930-39	51-37-7	.574	1970-79	56-54-3	.509
1900-09	40-21-7	.640	1940-49	51-38-5	.569	1980-89	87-25-4	.767
1910-19	42-35-6	.542	1950-59	64-32-5	.658	1990-99	69-47-1	.594
1920-29	41-47-5	.468	1960-69	50-48-2	.510	2000-03	32-18-0	.640

Historical record (1986-2003) 594-408-45 .589

Post-season won-loss record 13-12-0 .520

1940: Cotton Bowl, Clemson 6, Boston College 3
1949: Gator Bowl, Clemson 24, Missouri 23
1951: Orange Bowl, Clemson 15, Miami (Fl) 14
1952: Gator Bowl, Miami (Fl) 14, Clemson 0
1957: Orange Bowl, Colorado 27, Clemson 21
1959: Sugar Bowl, LSU 7, Clemson 0
1959: Bluebonnet Bowl, Clemson 23, TCU 7
1977: Gator Bowl, Pittsburgh 34, Clemson 3
1978: Gator Bowl, Clemson 17, Ohio State 15
1979: Peach Bowl, Baylor 24, Clemson 18
1982: Orange Bowl, Clemson 22, Nebraska 15
1985: Independence Bowl, Minnesota 21, Clemson 17
1986: Gator Bowl, Clemson 27, Stanford 21
1987: Citrus Bowl, Clemson 35, Penn State 10

1988: Citrus Bowl, Clemson 13, Oklahoma 6
1989: Gator Bowl, Clemson 27, West Virginia 7
1991: Hall of Fame Bowl, Clemson 30, Illinois 0
1992: Citrus Bowl, California 37, Clemson 13
1994: Peach Bowl, Clemson 14, Kentucky 13
1996: Gator Bowl, Syracuse 41, Clemson 0
1996: Peach Bowl, LSU 10, Clemson 7
1998: Peach Bowl, Auburn 21, Clemson 17
1999: Peach Bowl, Mississippi State 17, Clemson 7
2001: Gator Bowl, Virginia Tech 41, Clemson 20
2001: Humanitarian Bowl, Clemson 48, Louisiana Tech 24
2002: Tangerine Bowl, Texas Tech 55, Clemson 15
2003: Peach Bowl, Clemson 27, Tennessee 14

College Football Hall of Fame: John Heisman, coach, 1900-1903; Jess Neely, coach, 1931-39; Banks McFadden, halfback, 1937-39; Frank Howard, coach, 1940-69; Terry Kinard, safety, 1979-82.

COLORADO STATE UNIVERSITY, Fort Collins, Colorado; nickname "Rams"; colors green and gold; Hughes Stadium (30,000); Mountain West Conference. Colorado State began play in 1893 as a member of the Intercollegiate Athletic Association of Colorado. In 1912, the Rams joined the Rocky Mountain Athletic Conference and played in that conference through the 1937 season. The Rams were one of the founding members of the Mountain States (Skyline) Conference in 1938 and played there until the conference disbanded in 1961. Between 1962 and 1967, Colorado State played as an independent. Beginning with the 1968 season, Colorado State became a member of the Western Athletic Conference and played there through the 1998 season. In 1999, Colorado State joined with other members of the WAC to form the Mountain West Conference.

Early years (1893-1911)

Year	W-L-T	PF	PA	Pct.		Year	W-L-T	PF	PA	Pct.
No coach (1893-1894)										
1893	2-4-0	110	164	.333						
						1894	0-1-0	0	67	.000
No team (1895-1898)										
W. J. Forbes (1899) 1-2-1 .375										
1899	1-2-1	22	117	.375						
George Toomey (1900) 1-3-0 .250										
1900	1-3-0	16	109	.250						
C. J. Griffith (1901-1903) 7-7-2 .500										
1901	1-3-0	15	83	.250						
1902	1-3-2	47	62	.333		1903	5-1-0	67	24	.833
John McIntosh (1904-1906) 4-9-2 .333										
1904	0-4-1	6	125	.100						
1905	3-3-0	67	71	.500		1906	1-2-1	4	21	.375
Claude Rothgeb (1907-1910) 2-14-0 .125										
1907	0-4-0	17	77	.000		1909	1-2-0	38	91	.333
1908	1-3-0	30	58	.250		1910	0-5-0	6	110	.000
Harry Hughes (1911-1941) 125-95-18 .563										
1911	0-6-0	0	216	.000						

Member of the Rocky Mountain Athletic Conference (1912-1937) 104-58-11 .633

Year	Nat'l AP	Other	Overall W-L-T	PF	PA	Pct.	Conference W-L-T	Pct.	Rank	Year	Nat'l AP	Other	Overall W-L-T	PF	PA	Pct.	Conference W-L-T	Pct.	Rank
										1925			9-1-0	228	79	.900	8-0-0	1.000	1
1912			3-2-0	68	40	.600	2-2-0	.500	3	1926			6-2-1	149	44	.722	5-2-0	.714	4
1913			3-2-0	115	43	.600	3-2-0	.600	3	1927			7-1-0	76	26	.875	7-1-0	.875	1
1914			3-4-0	127	106	.429	3-3-0	.500	4	1928			6-2-0	151	70	.750	6-2-0	.750	3
1915			7-0-0	243	32	1.000	7-0-0	1.000	1	1929			5-4-0	118	88	.556	4-4-0	.500	8
1916			6-0-1	172	45	.929	6-0-1	.929	1	1930			3-5-1	67	104	.389	3-3-1	.500	5
1917			0-7-1	51	148	.062	0-7-0	.000	8	1931			5-4-0	137	138	.556	5-2-0	.714	2
1918			0-2-0	13	30	.000	0-2-0	.000	3	1932			4-3-1	100	45	.562	4-3-1	.562	5
1919			7-1-0	218	30	.875	5-1-0	.833	1	1933			5-3-1	78	26	.611	5-3-1	.611	1
1920			6-1-1	152	14	.812	4-0-1	.900	1	1934			6-2-1	173	67	.722	6-1-1	.812	1
1921			2-3-1	66	115	.417	2-2-1	.500	4	1935			3-4-1	58	75	.438	2-4-1	.357	9
1922			5-2-1	179	38	.688	5-1-1	.786	2	1936			4-4-1	67	74	.500	3-4-1	.438	7
1923			5-2-1	121	35	.688	5-1-1	.786	2	1937			1-7-0	6	182	.125	1-6-0	.143	11
1924			4-2-0	81	63	.667	3-2-0	.600	2										

Member of the Skyline Conference (1938-1961) 57-67-8 .462

Year	Nat'l AP	Other	Overall W-L-T	PF	PA	Pct.	Conference W-L-T	Pct.	Rank	Year	Nat'l AP	Other	Overall W-L-T	PF	PA	Pct.	Conference W-L-T	Pct.	Rank
1938			1-5-2	37	103	.250	0-4-2	.167	7	1940			3-5-2	85	131	.400	1-3-2	.250	6
1939			2-7-0	89	120	.222	2-4-0	.333	6	1941			4-2-1	109	77	.643	3-2-1	.583	4
Julius Wagner (1942, 1945-1946) 8-15-1 .354																			
1942			4-3-0	97	99	.571	2-3-0	.400	4	1945			2-5-1	89	179	.312	no conference		
1943, 1944 no team										1946			2-7-0	50	183	.222	1-5-0	.167	6
Bob Davis (1947-1955) 54-33-2 .618																			
1947			5-4-1	159	182	.550	2-3-1	.417	5	1952			6-4-0	177	137	.600	5-2-0	.714	3
1948			8-3-0	244	138	.727	4-1-0	.800	2	1953			4-5-0	157	149	.444	3-4-0	.429	5
1949			9-1-0	206	86	.900	4-1-0	.800	2	1954			3-7-0	93	248	.300	3-4-0	.429	6
1950			6-3-0	215	141	.667	4-1-0	.800	2	1955			8-2-0	175	108	.800	6-1-0	.857	1
1951			5-4-1	242	158	.550	3-3-1	.500	4										
Don Mullison (1956-1961) 19-40-1 .325																			
1956			2-7-1	156	314	.250	2-4-1	.357	5	1959			6-4-0	123	147	.600	5-2-0	.714	2
1957			3-7-0	109	24	.300	2-5-0	.286	6	1960			2-8-0	92	240	.200	1-6-0	.143	7
1958			6-4-0	178	110	.600	4-3-0	.571	4	1961			0-10-0	74	249	.000	0-6-0	.000	7

Independent (1962-1967)

Mike Lude (1962-1969) 29-51-1 .324

Year	W-L-T	PF	PA	Pct.		Year	W-L-T	PF	PA	Pct.
1962	0-10-0	66	269	.000		1965	4-6-0	264	264	.400
1963	3-7-0	118	299	.300		1966	7-3-0	275	178	.700
1964	5-6-0	111	199	.455		1967	4-5-1	219	149	.450

Member of the Western Athletic Conference (1968-1998) 100-111-2 .474

Year	W-L-T	PF	PA	Pct.	Conf W-L-T	Pct.	Rank	Year	W-L-T	PF	PA	Pct.	Conf W-L-T	Pct.	Rank
1968	2-8-0	133	262	.200	1-2-0	.333	6	1969	4-6-0	218	288	.400	0-4-0	.000	8

Jerry Wampfler (1970-1972) 8-25-0 .242

| 1970 | 4-7-0 | 206 | 256 | .364 | 1-3-0 | .250 | 6 | 1972 | | 1-10-0 | 128 | 413 | .091 | 1-4-0 | .200 | 7 |
| 1971 | 3-8-0 | 177 | 276 | .273 | 1-4-0 | .200 | 7 | | | | | | | | | |

Sark Arsianian (1973-1981) 45-47-4 .490

1973	5-6-0	250	333	.455	2-4-0	.333	7	1978		5-6-0	238	247	.455	2-4-0	.333	5
1974	4-6-1	295	266	.409	2-3-1	.417	6	1979		4-7-1	177	238	.375	3-4-0	.429	4
1975	6-5-0	172	234	.545	4-2-0	.667	3	1980		6-4-1	232	300	.591	5-1-1	.786	2
1976	6-5-0	205	186	.545	2-4-0	.333	7	1981*		0-6-0	71	210	.000	0-3-0	.000	9
1977	9-2-1	310	223	.792	5-2-0	.714	3									

Chester Caddas (1981) 0-6-0

| 1981 | 0-6-0 | 93 | 292 | .000 | 0-6-0 | .000 | 9 |

*Arsianian coached the first six games of the 1981 season, and Caddas coached the remaining six games.

Leon Fuller (1982-1988) 25-55-0 .313

1982	4-7-0	220	267	.364	3-5-0	.375	7	1986		6-5-0	266	237	.545	4-4-0	.500	4
1983	5-7-0	222	340	.417	4-4-0	.500	5	1987		1-11-0	245	352	.083	1-7-0	.125	8
1984	3-8-0	230	360	.273	3-5-0	.375	7	1988		1-10-0	192	348	.091	1-7-0	.125	8
1985	5-7-0	249	332	.417	4-4-0	.500	5									

Earle Bruce (1989-1992) 22-24-1 .479

| 1989 | 5-5-1 | 351 | 304 | .500 | 4-3-0 | .571 | 5 | 1991 | | 3-8-0 | 265 | 375 | .273 | 2-6-0 | .250 | 8 |
| 1990 | 9-4-0 | 332 | 300 | .692 | 6-1-0 | .857 | 2 | 1992 | | 5-7-0 | 281 | 334 | .417 | 3-5-0 | .375 | 7 |

Sonny Lubick (1993-2003) 91-44-0 .674

1993		5-6-0	230	268	.455	5-3-0	.625	4	1996			7-5-0	380	356	.583	6-2-0	.750	2
1994	16	14	10-2-0	400	269	.833	7-1-0	.875	1	1997	17	16	11-2-0	477	193	.846	7-1-0	.875	1
1995		8-4-0	339	254	.667	6-2-0	.750	1	1998			8-4-0	345	263	.667	5-3-0	.625	5

Member of the Mountain West Conference (1999-2003) 26-9-0 .743

1999		8-4-0	345	269	.667	5-2-0	.714	1	2001		7-5-0	298	274	.583	5-2-0	.714	2
2000	14	15	10-2-0	363	225	.833	6-1-0	.857	1	2002		10-4-0	418	352	.714	6-1-0	.857	1
									2003		7-6-0	381	318	.538	4-3-0	.571	3

Won-loss record by decades:

1893-99	3- 7-1	.318	1930-39	34-44-8	.442	1970-79	47-62-3	.433
1900-09	14-28-4	.348	1940-49	37-30-5	.549	1980-89	36-76-2	.325
1910-19	29-29-2	.500	1950-59	49-47-2	.510	1990-99	74-46-0	.617
1920-29	55-20-5	.719	1960-69	31-69-1	.312	2000-03	34-17-0	.667

Historical record 443-475-33 .483

Post-season won-loss record 4-6-0 .400

1949: Raisin Bowl, Occidental 21, Colorado A&M 20
1990: Freedom Bowl, Colorado State 32, Oregon 31
1994: Holiday Bowl, Michigan 24, Colorado State 14
1995: Holiday Bowl, Kansas State 54, Colorado State 21

1997: Holiday Bowl, Colorado State 35, Missouri 24
1999: Liberty Bowl, Southern Mississippi 23, Colorado State 17
2000: Liberty Bowl, Colorado State 22, Louisville 17
2001: New Orleans Bowl, Colorado State 45, North Texas 20
2002: Liberty Bowl, TCU 17, Colorado State 3
2003: San Francisco Bowl, Boston College 35, Colorado State 21

College Football Hall of Fame: Thurman McGraw, tackle, 1946-49; Earle Bruce, coach, 1989-92.

Awards: Jim Thorpe Award: 1995, Chris Myers

UNIVERSITY OF COLORADO, Boulder, Colorado; nickname "Buffaloes"; colors silver, gold, and black; Folsom Field (50,942); Big Twelve Conference. Colorado began play in 1890 and joined the Colorado Football Association in 1893. In 1910, Colorado became a member of the Rocky Mountain Athletic Association and played there through the 1937 season. In 1938, Colorado became one of the founding members of the Mountain States (Skyline) Conference. Colorado left that conference after the 1947 season, to join the Big Six Conference (then renamed the Big Seven Conference) and played in that conference (and the successor Big Eight) until 1995, when the Big Eight joined with four members of the disbanded Southwest Conference to form the Big Twelve Conference.

Year		W-L-T	PF	PA	Pct.	Year		W-L-T	PF	PA	Pct.
						Early years (1890-1909)					
						No Coach (1890-1893)					
1890	No coach	0-4-0	4	217	.000	1899	Fred Folsom	7-2-0	210	34	.778
1891	No coach	1-4-0	30	106	.250	1900	T.W. Mortimer	6-4-0	15	78	.600
1892	No coach	3-2-0	178	64	.600	1901	Fred Folsom	5-1-1	87	31	.786
1893	No coach	2-3-0	62	76	.400	1902	Fred Folsom	5-1-0	87	22	.833
1894	Harry Heller	8-1-0	288	32	.889	1903	David Cropp	8-2-0	359	28	.800
1895	Fred Folsom	5-1-0	158	32	.833	1904	David Cropp	6-2-1	187	58	.722
1896	Fred Folsom	5-0-0	171	6	1.000	1905	Willis Keinholtz	8-1-0	359	28	.889
1897	Fred Folsom	7-1-0	188	10	.875	1906	Frank Castleman	2-3-4	28	32	.444
1898	Fred Folsom	4-4-0	150	73	.500	1907	Frank Castleman	5-3-0	127	64	.625
					Fred Folsom (1895-1899, 1901-1902, 1908-1915) 78-23-2 .767						
1908		5-2-0	96	35	.714	1909		6-0-0	141	0	1.000

Member of the Rocky Mountain Athletic Association (1910-1936) 101-49-9 .664

	Nat'l	Overall				Conference				Nat'l	Overall				Conference		
Year	AP Other	W-L-T	PF	PA	Pct.	W-L-T	Pct.	Rank	Year	AP Other	W-L-T	PF	PA	Pct.	W-L-T	Pct.	Rank
1910		6-0-0	121	3	1.000	3-0-0	1.000	1	1913		5-1-1	82	33	.786	3-0-1	.875	1
1911		6-0-0	88	5	1.000	4-0-0	1.000	1	1914		5-1-0	111	22	.833	4-1-0	.800	2
1912		6-3-0	147	81	.667	2-2-0	.500	3	1915		1-6-0	45	168	.143	0-5-0	.000	6
					Bob Evans (1916-1917) 7-7-1 .500												
1916		1-5-1	40	162	.214	1-5-0	.167	6	1917		6-2-0	114	56	.750	4-2-0	.667	3
					Joe Mills (1918-1919) 4-6-1 .409												
1918		2-3-0	43	42	.400	1-2-0	.333	3	1919		2-3-1	87	96	.417	2-3-1	.417	5
					Myron Witham (1920-1931) 63-26-7 .693												
1920		4-1-2	99	28	.625	3-1-2	.667	3	1926		3-5-1	77	103	.389	2-5-1	.313	8
1921		4-1-1	65	63	.750	4-0-1	.900	2	1927		4-5-0	136	195	.444	4-4-0	.500	5
1922		4-4-0	56	79	.500	3-2-0	.600	5	1928		5-1-0	110	57	.833	5-1-0	.833	2
1923		9-0-0	280	27	1.000	7-0-0	1.000	1	1929		5-1-1	78	69	.786	4-1-1	.750	2
1924		8-1-1	237	13	.850	5-0-1	.917	1	1930		6-1-1	120	68	.812	5-1-1	.786	2
1925		6-3-0	156	45	.667	5-2-0	.714	4	1931		5-3-0	111	94	.625	3-2-0	.600	3
					William Saunders (1932-1934) 15-7-2 .667												
1932		2-4-0	63	46	.333	2-4-0	.667	8	1934		6-1-2	167	40	.778	6-1-0	.857	1
1933		7-2-0	183	51	.778	5-2-0	.714	2									
					Bunnie Oakes (1935-1939) 25-15-1 .662												
1935		5-4-0	140	47	.556	5-1-0	.833	1	1937 17		8-1-0	262	54	.889	5-0-0	1.000	1
1936		4-3-0	99	43	.571	4-2-0	.667	4									

Member of the Skyline Conference (1938-1947) 26-12-4 .667

	Nat'l	Overall				Conference				Nat'l	Overall				Conference		
Year	AP Other	W-L-T	PF	PA	Pct.	W-L-T	Pct.	Rank	Year	AP Other	W-L-T	PF	PA	Pct.	W-L-T	Pct.	Rank
1938		3-4-1	78	78	.438	3-2-1	.583	2	1939		5-3-0	106	110	.625	5-1-0	.833	1
					Frank Potts (1940, 1944-1945) 16-8-1 .660												
1940		5-3-1	182	106	.611	4-1-1	.750	2									
					Jim Yeager (1941-1943, 1946-1947) 24-17-2 .581												
1941		3-4-1	97	161	.438	3-2-1	.583	4	1943		5-2-0	134	47	.714	no conference		
1942		7-2-0	251	73	.778	5-1-0	.833	1									
					Frank Potts (1944-1945)												
1944		6-2-0	201	72	.750	no conference			1945		5-3-0	111	58	.625	no conference		
					Jim Yeager (1946-1947)												
1946		5-4-1	91	147	.550	3-2-1	.583	4	1947		4-5-0	90	162	.444	3-3-0	.500	3

Member of the Big Seven (later Big Eight) (1948-1995) 173-139-7 .553

Dallas Ward (1948-1958) 63-41-6 .600

Year	W-L-T	PF	PA	Pct.	W-L-T	Pct.	Rank	Year	Nat'l AP Other	W-L-T	PF	PA	Pct.	W-L-T	Pct.	Rank
1948	3-6-0	168	164	.333	2-3-0	.400	4	1954		7-2-1	283	91	.750	3-2-1	.583	3
1949	3-7-0	129	184	.300	1-4-0	.200	6	1955		6-4-0	203	149	.600	3-3-0	.500	3
1950	5-4-1	227	172	.550	2-4-0	.333	6	1956	20 18	8-2-1	294	143	.773	4-1-1	.750	2
1951	7-3-0	289	229	.700	5-1-0	.833	2	1957		6-3-1	250	137	.650	3-3-0	.500	3
1952	6-2-2	246	158	.700	2-2-2	.500	4	1958		6-4-0	207	122	.600	4-2-0	.667	3
1953	6-4-0	201	194	.600	2-4-0	.333	4									

Sonny Grandelius (1959-1961) 20-11-0 .645

Year	W-L-T	PF	PA	Pct.	W-L-T	Pct.	Rank	Year	Nat'l AP Other	W-L-T	PF	PA	Pct.	W-L-T	Pct.	Rank
1959	5-5-0	144	177	.500	3-3-0	.500	3	1961	7 7	9-2-0	184	104	.818	7-0-0	1.000	1
1960	6-4-0	140	133	.600	5-2-0	.714	2									

Bud Davis (1962) 2-8-0 .200

Year	W-L-T	PF	PA	Pct.	W-L-T	Pct.	Rank
1962	2-8-0	122	346	.200	1-6-0	.143	7

Eddie Crowder (1963-1973) 67-49-2 .571

Year			W-L-T	PF	PA	Pct	Conf	Pct	Pl
1963			2-8-0	100	245	.200	2-5-0	.286	7
1964			2-8-0	101	156	.200	1-6-0	.143	7
1965	20		6-2-2	163	106	.700	4-2-1	.643	3
1966			7-3-0	191	132	.700	5-2-0	.714	2
1967	13		9-2-0	245	113	.818	5-2-0	.571	2
1968			4-6-0	220	244	.400	3-4-0	.429	4
1969	16		8-3-0	276	227	.727	5-2-0	.714	3
1970		16	6-5-0	309	206	.545	3-4-0	.429	4
1971	3	7	10-2-0	370	220	.833	5-2-0	.714	3
1972	16	14	8-4-0	313	206	.667	4-3-0	.571	3
1973			5-6-0	240	250	.455	2-5-0	.286	6

Bill Mallory (1974-1978) 35-21-1 .623

Year			W-L-T	PF	PA	Pct	Conf	Pct	Pl
1974			5-6-0	226	307	.455	3-4-0	.429	5
1975	16		9-3-0	331	251	.750	5-2-0	.714	3
1976	16	16	8-4-0	305	225	.667	5-2-0	.714	1
1977			7-3-1	266	174	.682	3-3-1	.500	4
1978			6-5-0	230	206	.545	2-5-0	.286	7

Chuck Fairbanks (1979-1981) 7-26-0 .212

Year			W-L-T	PF	PA	Pct	Conf	Pct	Pl
1979			3-8-0	168	274	.273	2-5-0	.286	5
1980			1-10-0	160	451	.091	1-6-0	.143	7
1981			3-8-0	141	322	.273	2-5-0	.286	7

Bill McCartney (1982-1994) 93-55-5 .624

Year			W-L-T	PF	PA	Pct	Conf	Pct	Pl
1982			2-8-1	160	301	.227	1-5-1	.214	6
1983			4-7-0	252	342	.364	2-5-0	.286	6
1984			1-10-0	172	364	.091	1-6-0	.143	7
1985			7-5-0	228	174	.583	4-3-0	.571	3
1986			6-6-0	242	193	.500	6-1-0	.857	2
1987			7-4-0	268	180	.636	4-3-0	.571	4
1988			8-4-0	322	196	.667	4-3-0	.571	4
1989	4	4	11-1-0	458	171	.917	7-0-0	1.000	1
1990	1	2	11-1-1	399	229	.885	7-0-0	1.000	1
1991	20	20	8-3-1	329	180	.708	6-0-1	.929	1
1992	13	13	9-2-1	340	224	.792	5-1-1	.786	2
1993	16	16	8-3-1	368	250	.708	5-1-1	.786	2
1994	3	3	11-1-0	439	235	.917	6-1-0	.857	2

Rick Neuheisel (1995-1998) 33-14-0 .702

Year			W-L-T	PF	PA	Pct	Conf	Pct	Pl
1995	5	4	10-2-0	444	240	.833	5-2-0	.714	2

Member of the Big Twelve Conference (1996-2003) 39-25-0 .609

Year			W-L-T	PF	PA	Pct	Conf	Pct	Pl
1996	8	8	10-2-0	352	220	.833	7-1-0	.875	2
1997			5-6-0	300	295	.455	3-5-0	.375	7
1998			8-4-0	302	253	.667	4-4-0	.500	7

Gary Barnett (1999-2003) 34-28-0 .548

Year			W-L-T	PF	PA	Pct	Conf	Pct	Pl
1999			7-5-0	405	311	.583	5-3-0	.625	5
2000			3-8-0	252	284	.273	3-5-0	.375	7
2001	9	9	10-3-0	412	318	.769	7-1-0	.875	1
2002	20	21	9-5-0	398	325	.643	7-1-0	.875	2
2003			5-7-0	319	398	.417	3-5-0	.375	8

Won-loss records by decades:

Decade	Record	Pct	Decade	Record	Pct	Decade	Record	Pct
1890-99	42-22-0	.656	1930-39	51-26-4	.654	1970-79	67-46-1	.592
1900-09	56-19-6	.728	1940-49	46-38-3	.546	1980-89	50-63-1	.443
1910-19	40-24-3	.619	1950-59	62-33-6	.644	1990-99	87-29-4	.742
1920-29	52-22-6	.688	1960-69	55-46-2	.544	2000-03	27-23-0	.540

Historical record 635-391-36 .615

Post-season won-loss record 12-15-0 .444

1938: Cotton Bowl, Rice 28, Colorado 14
1957: Orange Bowl, Colorado 27, Clemson 21
1962: Orange Bowl, LSU 25, Colorado 7
1967: Bluebonnet Bowl, Colorado 31, Miami (Fl) 21
1969: Liberty Bowl, Colorado 47, Alabama 33
1970: Liberty Bowl, Tulane 17, Colorado 3
1971: Bluebonnet Bowl, Colorado 29, Houston 17
1972: Gator Bowl, Auburn 24, Colorado 3
1975: Bluebonnet Bowl, Texas 38, Colorado 21
1977: Orange Bowl, Ohio State 27, Colorado 10
1985: Freedom Bowl, Washington 20, Colorado 17
1986: Bluebonnet Bowl, Baylor 21, Colorado 9

1988: Freedom Bowl, BYU 20, Colorado 17
1990: Orange Bowl, Notre Dame 21, Colorado 6
1991: Orange Bowl, Colorado 10, Notre Dame 9
1991: Blockbuster Bowl, Alabama 30, Colorado 25
1993: Fiesta Bowl, Syracuse 26, Colorado 22
1993: Aloha Bowl, Colorado 41, Fresno State 30
1995: Fiesta Bowl, Colorado 41, Notre Dame 24
1996: Cotton Bowl, Colorado 38, Oregon 6
1996: Holiday Bowl, Colorado 33, Washington 21
1998: Aloha Bowl, Colorado 51, Oregon 43
1999: Insight.com Bowl, Colorado 62, Boston College 28
2001: Big 12 Championship, Colorado 39, Texas 37
2002: Fiesta Bowl, Oregon 38, Colorado 16
2002: Big 12 Championship, Oklahoma 29, Colorado 7
2002: Alamo Bowl, Wisconsin 31, Colorado 28

College Football Hall of Fame:
Byron White, halfback, 1935-37; Joe Romig, guard, 1959-61; Dick Anderson, safety, 1965-67

Awards: Heisman Trophy: 1994, Rashaan Salaam, halfback; Butkus Award: 1990, Alfred Williams; 1996, Matt Russell; Jim Thorpe Award: 1992, Deon Figures; 1994, Chris Hudson; Doak Walker Award: 1994, Rashaan Salaam; Ray Guy Award: 2002, Mark Mariscal; Mackey Award: 2001, Daniel Graham.

UNIVERSITY OF CONNECTICUT, Storrs, Connecticut; nickname "Huskies"; colors national flag blue and white; Rentschler Field (40,000); I-A Independent. UConn began play in 1896 as a member of the Athletic League of New England State Colleges. In 1923, the Huskies joined the New England Conference. In 1947, UConn became a charter member of the Yankee Conference (name changed to the Atlantic 10 Conference in 1997). UConn left the Atlantic 10 Conference after the 1999 season and began play as a Division I-A independent. UConn is scheduled to join the Big East Conference in 2004.

Early years (1896-1920)

Year	Coach	W-L-T	PF	PA	Pct.	Year	Coach	W-L-T	PF	PA	Pct.
1896	no coach	5-3-0	64	56	.625	1909	S.F.G. McLean	3-5-0	104	191	.375
1897	no coach	5-2-0	92	68	.714	1910	M.F. Claffey	1-5-1	12	117	.214
1898	E. S. Mansfield	0-3-0	0	89	.000	1911	Leo Hafford	0-5-0	6	166	.000
1899	T. D. Knowles	6-2-0	107	62	.750	1912	A. J. Sharadin	3-3-0	41	79	.500
1900	T. D. Knowles	4-3-1	104	45	.562	1913	P. T. Brady	5-3-0	168	122	.625
1901	T. D. Knowles	8-2-0	143	67	.800	1914	Dave Warner	3-0-0	48	9	1.000
1902	E. O. Smith	4-3-0	84	66	.571	1915	John F. Donahue	1-7-0	40	107	.125
1903	E. O. Smith	3-5-0	53	90	.375	1916	John F. Donahue	1-7-0	36	110	.125
1904	E. O. Smith	5-3-1	83	85	.611	1917	no team				
1905	E. O. Smith	2-2-0	27	59	.500	1918	no team				
1906	George Lamson	2-4-0	50	75	.333	1919	Roy F. Guyer	2-6-0	28	174	.250
1907	George Lamson	2-5-0	71	158	.286	1920	Ross Swartz	1-6-1	69	126	.188
1908	W.F. Madden	4-3-1	150	49	.562						

Wilder Tasker (1921-1922) 5-8-4 .412

Year		W-L-T	PF	PA	Pct.	Year		W-L-T	PF	PA	Pct.
1921		3-2-3	115	75	.562	1922		2-6-1	77	108	.278

Sumner A. Dole (1923-1933) 36-39-14 .483

Year	W-L-T	PF	PA	Pct.	Year	W-L-T	PF	PA	Pct.
1923	3-4-1	45	46	.438	1929	4-4-0	92	47	.500
1924	6-0-2	90	13	.875	1930	1-5-1	19	106	.214
1925	3-5-1	39	76	.389	1931	2-3-3	27	84	.438
1926	7-1-0	190	33	.875	1932	0-6-2	27	167	.125
1927	5-4-0	153	100	.556	1933	1-6-1	39	176	.188
1928	4-1-3	96	51	.688					

J. O. Christian (1934-1949) 66-51-4 .562

Year	W-L-T	PF	PA	Pct.	Year	W-L-T	PF	PA	Pct.
1934	1-7-0	19	98	.125	1941	2-6-0	58	82	.250
1935	2-4-1	39	70	.357	1942	6-2-0	141	81	.750
1936	7-2-0	203	48	.778	1943	no team			
1937	6-2-1	187	64	.722	1944	7-1-0	152	13	.875
1938	4-3-0	90	56	.571	1945	7-1-0	265	43	.875
1939	5-3-0	99	97	.625	1946	4-3-1	120	69	.562
1940	4-4-0	67	89	.500					

Member of the Yankee Conference (later renamed the Atlantic 10) (1947-1999) 159-115-9 .578

Year	Overall				Conference		Year	Overall				Conference	
	W-L-T	PF	PA	Pct.	W-L-T	Pct.		W-L-T	PF	PA	Pct.	W-L-T	Pct.
1947	4-4-0	102	85	.500	1-2-0	.333	1949	4-4-1	220	141	.500	2-0-0	1.000
1948	3-5-0	142	147	.375	2-1-0	.667							

Arthur Valpey (1950-1951) 7-9-0 .438

| 1950 | 3-5-0 | 82 | 134 | .375 | 0-3-0 | .000 | 1951 | 4-4-0 | 106 | 102 | .500 | 2-1-0 | .667 |

D. Robert Ingalls (1952-1963) 49-54-3 .477

1952	5-3-0	178	135	.625	3-1-0	.750	1958	7-3-0	281	134	.700	4-0-0	1.000
1953	3-4-1	118	147	.438	2-1-1	.625	1959	6-3-0	197	111	.667	4-0-0	1.000
1954	1-8-0	92	276	.111	0-4-0	.000	1960	5-4-0	179	123	.556	3-1-0	.750
1955	4-4-0	68	105	.500	2-2-0	.500	1961	2-7-0	108	167	.222	2-2-0	.500
1956	6-2-1	240	100	.722	3-0-1	.875	1962	3-6-0	97	139	.333	2-2-0	.500
1957	5-4-1	143	121	.550	3-0-1	.875	1963	2-6-0	91	113	.250	1-3-0	.250

Richard E. Forzano (1964-1965) 7-10-1 .417

| 1964 | 4-4-1 | 99 | 123 | .500 | 2-1-1 | .625 | 1965 | 3-6-0 | 100 | 116 | .333 | 2-2-0 | .500 |

John L. Toner (1966-1970) 20-24-3 .458

1966	2-6-1	92	156	.278	2-2-1	.500	1969	5-4-0	193	187	.556	3-2-0	.600
1967	5-4-0	137	151	.556	4-1-0	.800	1970	4-4-2	240	192	.500	4-0-1	.900
1968	4-6-0	216	191	.400	4-1-0	.800							

Robert F. Casciola (1971-1972) 9-8-1 .531

| 1971 | 5-3-1 | 107 | 145 | .611 | 4-1-1 | .750 | 1972 | 4-5-0 | 143 | 187 | .444 | 4-1-0 | .800 |

Larry L. Naviaux (1973-1976) 18-24-1 .430

| 1973 | 8-2-1 | 208 | 141 | .773 | 5-0-1 | .917 | 1975 | 4-7-0 | 178 | 244 | .364 | 3-2-0 | .600 |
| 1974 | 4-6-0 | 153 | 168 | .400 | 3-3-0 | .500 | 1976 | 2-9-0 | 182 | 246 | .182 | 2-3-0 | .400 |

Walt Nadzak (1977-1982) 24-39-2 .385

1977	1-10-0	84	290	.091	1-4-0	.200	1980	7-3-0	259	191	.700	3-2-0	.600
1978	4-7-0	181	202	.364	3-2-0	.600	1981	4-7-0	291	255	.364	1-4-0	.200
1979	3-6-2	144	173	.364	3-1-1	.700	1982	5-6-0	164	193	.455	3-2-0	.600

Tom Jackson (1983-1993) 62-57-0 .521

Year	Record	PF	PA	Pct	Conf	Pct	Year	Record	PF	PA	Pct	Conf	Pct
1983	5-6-0	164	193	.455	4-1-0	.800	1989	8-3-0	297	252	.727	6-2-0	.750
1984	3-8-0	163	186	.273	1-4-0	.200	1990	6-5-0	308	281	.545	5-3-0	.625
1985	4-5-0	175	181	.444	1-4-0	.200	1991	3-8-0	241	330	.273	2-6-0	.250
1986	8-3-0	249	229	.727	4-2-0	.667	1992	5-6-0	254	239	.455	4-4-0	.500
1987	7-4-0	191	235	.636	6-2-0	.750	1993	6-5-0	261	217	.545	5-3-0	.625
1988	7-4-0	198	180	.636	4-4-0	.500							

Skip Holtz (1994-1998) 34-23-0 .596

Year	Record	PF	PA	Pct	Conf	Pct	Year	Record	PF	PA	Pct	Conf	Pct
1994	4-7-0	240	264	.364	4-4-0	.500	1997	7-4-0	398	246	.636	4-4-0	.500
1995	8-3-0	279	200	.727	5-3-0	.625	1998	10-3-0	461	413	.769	6-2-0	.750
1996	5-6-0	244	191	.455	3-5-0	.375							

Randy Edsall (1999-2003) 24-33-0 .421

1999	4-7-0	255	383	.364	3-5-0	.375

UConn changes to I-A independent status (2000-2003)

Year	Record	PF	PA	Pct		Year	Record	PF	PA	Pct
2000	3-8-0	220	368	.273		2002	6-6-0	373	270	.500
2001	2-9-0	192	370	.182		2003	9-3-0	408	300	.750

Won-loss record

Years	Record	Pct	Years	Record	Pct	Years	Record	Pct
1896-99	16-10-0	.615	1930-39	29-41-9	.424	1970-79	39-59-6	.404
1900-09	37-35-3	.513	1940-49	41-30-2	.575	1980-89	58-49-0	.542
1910-19	16-36-1	.311	1950-59	44-40-3	.523	1990-99	58-54-0	.518
1920-29	38-33-12	.530	1960-69	35-53-2	.400	2000-03	20-26-0	.435

Historic total 431-466-38 .481

Post-season won-loss record: 1-1-0 .500
1998: Division I-AA Playoffs, UConn 42, Hampton 34
1998: Division I-AA Playoffs, Georgia Southern 52, UConn 30

DUKE UNIVERSITY, Durham, North Carolina; nickname "Blue Devils"; colors royal blue and white; Wallace Wade Stadium (33,941); Atlantic Coast Conference. Duke began play in 1888 and then joined the Southern Conference in 1929. Duke played in that conference through the 1952 season and then joined other Southern Conference members in organizing the Atlantic Coast Conference, which began play in the 1953 season.

Early years (1888-1928)

Year	W-L-T	PF	PA	Pct.		Year	W-L-T	PF	PA	Pct.
					John Crowell (1888-1889) 4-1-0 .800					
1888	2-1-0	41	49	.667		1889	2-0-0	9	4	1.000
					No coach (1890-1894)					
1890	0-1-0	4	10	.000		1893	3-1-0	98	40	.750
1891	3-0-0	122	4	1.000		1894	0-1-0	0	28	.000
1892	1-3-0	38	112	.250						
					Football banned on campus (1895-1918)					
					Floyd Egan (1920) 4-0-1 .900					
1920	4-0-1	53	20	.900						
					James Baldwin (1921) 6-1-2 .778					
1921	6-1-2	147	32	.778						
					Herman Steiner (1922) 7-2-1 .750					
1922	7-2-1	156	51	.750						
					S. M. Alexander (1923) 5-4-0 .556					
1923	5-4-0	211	104	.556						
					Howard Jones (1924) 4-5-0 .444					
1924	4-5-0	129	99	.444						
					Pat Herron (1925) 4-5-0 .444					
1925	4-5-0	58	142	.444						
					James DeHart (1926-1930) 24-23-2 .510					
1926	3-6-0	124	106	.333		1928	5-5-0	115	102	.500
1927	4-5-0	215	117	.444						

Member of the Southern Conference (1929-1952) 99-23-5 .799

	Nat'l		Overall				Conference				Nat'l		Overall				Conference		
Year	AP	Other	W-L-T	PF	PA	Pct.	W-L-T	Pct.	Rank	Year	AP	Other	W-L-T	PF	PA	Pct.	W-L-T	Pct.	Rank
1929			4-6-0	153	260	.400	2-1-0	.667	7	1930			8-1-2	147	48	818	4-1-1	.750	4
									Wallace Wade (1931-1941, 1946-1950) 110-36-7 .742										
1931			5-3-2	74	46	.600	3-3-1	.500	8	1937	20		7-2-1	228	56	.750	5-1-0	.833	3
1932			7-3-0	153	40	.700	5-3-0	.625	9	1938	3	2	9-1-0	117	7	.900	5-0-0	1.000	1
1933			9-1-0	181	42	.900	4-0-0	1.000	1	1939	8	8	8-1-0	183	42	.889	5-0-0	1.000	1
1934			7-2-0	185	40	.778	3-1-0	.750	3	1940	18		7-2-0	203	42	.778	4-1-0	.800	2
1935			8-2-0	214	45	.800	5-0-0	1.000	1	1941	2		9-1-0	327	61	.900	5-0-0	1.000	1
1936	11	9	9-1-0	208	28	.900	7-0-0	1.000	1										
									Eddie Cameron (1942-1945) 25-11-1 .689										
1942			5-4-1	211	98	.550	3-1-1	.700	4	1944	11		6-4-0	230	118	.600	4-0-0	1.000	1
1943	7		8-1-0	335	34	.889	4-0-0	1.000	1	1945	13		6-2-0	229	114	.750	4-0-0	1.000	1
									Wallace Wade (1946-1950)										
1946			4-5-0	134	86	.444	3-2-0	.600	5	1949			6-3-0	260	117	.667	4-2-0	.667	4
1947	19		4-3-2	79	90	.556	3-1-1	.700	4	1950			7-3-0	202	108	.700	5-2-0	.714	6
1948			4-3-2	144	92	.556	3-2-1	.583	7										
									Bill Murray (1951-1965) 93-51-9 .637										
1951			5-4-1	201	157	.550	4-2-0	.667	6	1952	16	18	8-2-0	222	72	.800	5-0-0	1.000	1

Member of the Atlantic Coast Conference (1953-2003) 130-194-7 .403

Year	AP	Other	W-L-T	PF	PA	Pct.	W-L-T	Pct.	Rank	Year	AP	Other	W-L-T	PF	PA	Pct.	W-L-T	Pct.	Rank
1953	18	18	7-2-1	227	81	.750	4-0-0	1.000	1	1960	10	11	8-3-0	173	114	.727	5-1-0	.833	1
1954	14	14	8-2-1	270	161	.773	4-0-0	1.000	1	1961	20	14	7-3-0	183	106	.700	5-1-0	.833	1
1955		16	7-2-1	196	95	.750	4-0-0	1.000	1	1962		14	8-2-0	199	105	.800	6-0-0	1.000	1
1956		20	5-4-1	184	100	.550	4-1-0	.800	2	1963			5-4-1	230	198	.550	5-2-0	.714	3
1957	16	14	6-3-2	182	135	.636	5-1-1	.786	2	1964			4-5-1	148	135	.450	3-2-1	.583	2
1958			5-5-0	128	131	.500	3-2-0	.600	3	1965			6-4-0	216	157	.600	4-2-0	.667	1
1959			4-6-0	104	159	.400	2-3-0	.400	6										
									Tom Harp (1966-1970) 22-28-1 .441										
1966			5-5-0	164	237	.500	2-3-0	.400	5	1969			3-6-1	161	224	.350	3-3-1	.500	3
1967			4-6-0	143	153	.400	2-4-0	.333	6	1970			6-5-0	229	252	.545	5-2-0	.714	2
1968			4-6-0	214	287	.400	3-4-0	.429	5										
									Mike McGee (1971-1978) 37-47-4 .443										
1971			6-5-0	170	149	.545	2-3-0	.400	3	1975			4-5-2	197	212	.455	3-0-2	.800	2
1972			5-6-0	132	156	.455	3-3-0	.500	4	1976			5-5-1	234	245	.500	2-3-1	.417	4
1973			2-8-1	132	204	.227	1-4-1	.250	5	1977			5-6-0	231	221	.455	2-4-0	.333	5
1974			6-5-0	201	208	.545	2-4-0	.333	5	1978			4-7-0	108	247	.364	2-4-0	.333	5
									Red Wilson (1979-1982) 16-27-1 .375										
1979			2-8-1	152	264	.227	0-6-0	.000	7	1981			6-5-0	210	230	.545	3-3-0	.500	4
1980			2-9-0	214	296	.182	1-5-0	.167	7	1982			6-5-0	307	290	.545	3-3-0	.500	3

Steve Sloan (1983-1986) 13-31-0 .295

Year	Record	PF	PA	Pct	Conf	Pct	#	Year	Record	PF	PA	Pct	Conf	Pct	#
1983	3-8-0	246	350	.273	3-3-0	.500	4	1985	4-7-0	193	252	.364	2-5-0	.286	6
1984	2-9-0	128	301	.182	1-5-0	.167	6	1986	4-7-0	200	284	.364	2-5-0	.286	6

Steve Spurrier (1987-1989) 20-13-1 .603

Year	Record	PF	PA	Pct	Conf	Pct	#	Year	Record	PF	PA	Pct	Conf	Pct	#
1987	5-6-0	301	243	.455	2-5-0	.286	7	1989	8-4-0	386	286	.667	6-1-0	.857	1
1988	7-3-1	324	324	.682	3-3-1	.500	6								

Barry Wilson (1990-1993) 13-30-1 .307

Year	Record	PF	PA	Pct	Conf	Pct	#	Year	Record	PF	PA	Pct	Conf	Pct	#
1990	4-7-0	240	295	.364	1-6-0	.143	7	1992	2-9-0	265	343	.182	0-8-0	.000	9
1991	4-6-1	231	280	.409	1-6-0	.143	7	1993	3-8-0	214	349	.273	2-6-0	.250	7

Fred Goldsmith (1994-1998) 17-39-0 .304

Year	Record	PF	PA	Pct	Conf	Pct	#	Year	Record	PF	PA	Pct	Conf	Pct	#
1994	8-4-0	360	247	.667	5-3-0	.625	3	1997	2-9-0	223	341	.182	0-8-0	.000	9
1995	3-8-0	282	386	.273	1-7-0	.125	8	1998	4-7-0	229	319	.364	2-6-0	.250	6
1996	0-11-0	162	379	.000	0-8-0	.000	9								

Carl Franks (1999-2003) 7-45-0 .135

Year	Record	PF	PA	Pct	Conf	Pct	#	Year	Record	PF	PA	Pct	Conf	Pct	#
1999	3-8-0	217	363	.273	3-5-0	.375	5	2002	2-10-0	227	353	.167	0-8-0	.000	9
2000	0-11-0	155	430	.000	0-8-0	.000	9	2003*		2-5-0	106	213	.286	0-4-0	.000	8
2001	0-11-0	212	491	.000	0-8-0	.000	9								

Ted Roof (2003*) 2-3-0 .400

Year	Record	PF	PA	Pct	Conf	Pct	#
2003*	2-3-0	105	130	.400	1-3-0	.250	8

*Franks coached the first seven games of 2003, and Roof coached the last five games.

Won-loss record by decades:

1888-89	4- 1-0	.800	1930-39	77-17-5	.803	1970-79	45-60-5	.432
1890-99	7- 6-0	.538	1940-49	59-28-5	.668	1980-89	47-63-1	.428
1900-19	no team		1950-59	62-33-7	.642	1990-99	33-77-1	.302
1920-29	46-39-4	.539	1960-69	54-44-3	.550	2000-03	6-40-0	.130

Historical record (1888-2003) 440-408-31 .518

Post-season won-loss record 3-5-0 .375

1939: Rose Bowl, USC 7, Duke 3
1942: Rose Bowl, Oregon State 20, Duke 16
1945: Sugar Bowl, Duke 29, Alabama 26
1955: Orange Bowl, Duke 34, Nebraska 7

1958: Orange Bowl, Oklahoma 48, Duke 21
1961: Cotton Bowl, Duke 7, Arkansas 6
1989: All American Bowl, Texas Tech 49, Duke 21
1995: Hall of Fame Bowl, Wisconsin 34, Duke 20

College Football Hall of Fame:
Howard Jones, coach, 1924; Fred Crawford, tackle, 1931-33; Wallace Wade, coach, 1931-41, 1946-50; Ace Parker, halfback, 1934-36; Eric Tipton, halfback, 1936-38; Dan Hill, center, 1936-38; George McAfee, halfback, 1937-39; Steve Lach, halfback, 1939-41; Al DeRogatis, center/tackle, 1945-48; Bill Murray, coach, 1951-65; Mike McGee, guard, 1957-59.

Awards: Outland Trophy: 1959, Mike McGee

EAST CAROLINA UNIVERSITY, Greenville, North Carolina; nickname "Pirates"; colors purple and gold; Dowdy-Ficklen Stadium (43,000); Conference USA. East Carolina began play in 1932 as an independent. In 1965, East Carolina joined the Southern Conference and played in that conference through the 1976 season, after which it reverted to independent status. In 1996, East Carolina joined Conference USA.

Year	W-L-T	PF	PA	Pct.

Year W-L-T PF PA Pct.

					Year Nat'l	W-L-T	PF	PA	Pct.

Early years as an independent (1932-1964)
Kenneth Beatty (1932-1933) 1-10-0 .091

| 1932 | 0-5-0 | 0 | 187 | .000 | | 1933 | 1-5-0 | 6 | 98 | .167 |

G. L. Mathis (1934-1935) 4-7-1 .375

| 1934 | 1-4-1 | 18 | 87 | .250 | | 1935 | 3-3-0 | 77 | 32 | .500 |

Bo Farley (1936) 3-2-0 .600

| 1936 | 3-2-0 | 50 | 13 | .500 | | | | | | |

J. D. Alexander (1937-1938) 3-11-1 .233

| 1937 | 2-5-0 | 65 | 78 | .286 | | 1938 | 1-6-1 | 39 | 126 | .188 |

O.A. Hankner (1939) 0-8-0

| 1939 | 0-8-0 | 18 | 168 | .000 | | | | | | |

J. Christenbury (1940-1941) 12-3-0 .800

| 1940 | 5-3-0 | 143 | 70 | .625 | | 1941 | 7-0-0 | 159 | 58 | 1.000 |

1942-1945 no team
Jim Johnson (1946-1948) 8-18-1 .271

| 1946 | 5-3-1 | 158 | 58 | .563 | | 1948 | 0-9-0 | 38 | 206 | .000 |
| 1947 | 3-6-0 | 64 | 142 | .333 | | | | | | |

Bill Dole (1949-1951) 15-14-1 .517

| 1949 | 4-5-1 | 207 | 177 | .450 | | 1951 | 4-6-0 | 184 | 220 | .400 |
| 1950 | 7-3-0 | 252 | 142 | .700 | | | | | | |

Jack Boone (1952-1961) 49-45-5 .521

1952	6-3-2	225	132	.636		1957	1-8-0	73	218	.111
1953	8-2-0	292	81	.800		1958	6-4-0	142	145	.600
1954	5-4-1	144	105	.550		1959	5-6-0	278	271	.455
1955	4-5-0	93	102	.444		1960	7-3-0	144	92	.700
1956	2-6-1	99	249	.278		1961	5-4-1	154	139	.550

C. Stasavich (1962-1969) 50-27-1 .647

| 1962 | 5-4-0 | 215 | 136 | .556 | | 1964 | 9-1-0 | 279 | 99 | .900 |
| 1963 | 9-1-0 | 230 | 54 | .900 | | | | | | |

Member of the Southern Conference (1965-1976) 43-18-1 .702

	Nat'l	Overall				Conference				Nat'l	Overall				Conference		
Year	AP Other	W-L-T	PF	PA	Pct.	W-L-T	Pct.	Rank	Year	AP Other	W-L-T	PF	PA	Pct.	W-L-T	Pct.	Rank
1965		9-1-0	268	83	.900	3-1-0	.750	3	1968		4-6-0	175	244	.400	2-2-0	.500	3
1966		4-5-1	174	175	.450	4-1-1	.750	1	1969		2-7-0	108	204	.222	1-3-0	.250	5
1967		8-2-0	253	178	.800	4-1-0	.800	2									

Mike McGee (1970) 3-8-0 273

| 1970 | | 3-8-0 | 136 | 253 | .273 | 2-2-0 | .500 | 4 | | | | | | | | | |

Sonny Randle (1971-1973) 22-10-0 .688

| 1971 | | 4-6-0 | 181 | 300 | .400 | 3-2-0 | .600 | 4 | 1973 | | 9-2-0 | 352 | 151 | .818 | 7-0-0 | 1.000 | 1 |
| 1972 | | 9-2-0 | 269 | 176 | .818 | 6-0-0 | 1.000 | 1 | | | | | | | | | |

Pat Dye (1974-1979) 48-18-1 .727

| 1974 | | 7-4-0 | 250 | 167 | .636 | 3-3-0 | .500 | 3 | 1976 | | 9-2-0 | 278 | 116 | .818 | 4-1-0 | .800 | 1 |
| 1975 | | 8-3-0 | 269 | 154 | .727 | 4-2-0 | .667 | 2 | | | | | | | | | |

Years as an independent (1977-1996)

| 1977 | 8-3-0 | 268 | 154 | .727 | | 1979 | 7-3-1 | 380 | 193 | .682 |
| 1978 | 9-3-0 | 252 | 123 | .750 | | | | | | |

Ed Emory (1980-1984) 26-29-0 .437

1980	4-7-0	192	312	.364		1983 20	8-3-0	271	180	.727
1981	5-6-0	242	290	.455		1984	2-9-0	210	309	.182
1982	7-4-0	259	228	.636						

Art Baker (1985-1988) 13-31-0 .295

| 1985 | 2-9-0 | 161 | 281 | .182 | | 1987 | 5-6-0 | 229 | 330 | .455 |
| 1986 | 3-8-0 | 187 | 364 | .273 | | 1988 | 3-8-0 | 281 | 325 | .273 |

Bill Lewis (1989-1991) 21-12-1 .632

| 1989 | 5-5-1 | 301 | 286 | .500 | | 1991 9 9 | 11-1-0 | 372 | 243 | .917 |
| 1990 | 5-6-0 | 254 | 267 | .455 | | | | | | |

Steve Logan (1992-2002) 69-58-0 .543

1992	5-6-0	289	367	.455		1995	9-3-0	255	213	.750
1993	2-9-0	175	329	.182		1996	8-3-0	316	214	.727
1994	7-5-0	303	233	.583						

Member of Conference USA (1997-2003) 26-22-0 .542

1997	5-6-0	214	298	.455	4-2-0	.667	3	2000	8-4-0	330	229	.667	5-2-0	.714	2
1998	6-5-0	274	297	.545	3-3-0	.500	4	2001	6-6-0	421	360	.500	5-2-0	.714	2
1999	9-3-0	319	197	.750	4-2-0	.667	2	2002	4-8-0	335	399	.333	4-4-0	.500	5

John Thompson (2003) 1-11-0 .083

2003	1-11-0	217	428	.083	1-7-0	.125	10

Won-loss record by decades:

1932-39	11-38-2	.235	1960-69	62-34-2	.653	1990-99	67-47-0	.588
1940-49	24-26-2	.481	1970-79	73-36-1	.668	2000-03	19-29-0	.396
1950-59	48-47-4	.505	1980-89	44-65-1	.405			

Historical record (1932-2003) 348-322-12 .519

Post-season won-loss record: 7-5-0 .583

1952: Lions Bowl, Clarion College 13, ECU 6
1954: Elks Bowl, Morris-Harvey 12, ECU 0
1963: Eastern Bowl, ECU 27, Northeastern 6
1964: Tangerine Bowl, ECU 14, Massachusetts 13
1965: Tangerine Bowl, ECU 31, Maine 0
1978: Independence Bowl, ECU 35, Louisiana Tech 13

1992: Peach Bowl, ECU 37, NC State 34
1994: St. Jude Liberty Bowl, Illinois 30, ECU 0
1995: St. Jude Liberty Bowl, ECU 19, Stanford 13
1999: Mobile Alabama Bowl, TCU 28, ECU 14
2000: Gallleryfurniture.com Bowl, ECU 40, Texas Tech 27
2001: GMAC Bowl, Marshall 64, ECU 61

EASTERN MICHIGAN UNIVERSITY, Ypsilanti, Michigan; nickname "Eagles"; colors dark green and white; Rynearson Stadium (30,200); Mid-American Conference. Eastern Michigan began play in 1891. It joined the Mid-American Conference in 1976 and has played in that conference since that time.

Early years (1891-1916)

Year	Coach	W-L-T	PF	PA	Pct.	Year	Coach	W-L-T	PF	PA	Pct.
1891	James Swift	0-2-0	4	64	.000	1904	D. Lawrence	6-2-0	121	159	.750
1892	Deane Kelly	2-1-0	36	30	.667	1905	D. Lawrence	4-4-0	81	157	.500
1893	Ernest Goodrich	4-2-0	116	94	.667	1906	Henry Schulte	5-0-1	52	11	.833
1894	Verne Bennett	5-2-0	176	70	.714	1907	Henry Schulte	3-2-0	72	13	.600
1895	A. B. Glaspie	3-3-0	119	554	.400	1908	Henry Schulte	1-4-0	15	40	.200
1896	Fred Green	4-1-0	110	18	.800	1909	Clare Hunter	2-4-0	44	45	.333
1897	A. B. Glaspie	2-3-0	36	62	.400	1910	Curry Hicks	0-5-1	11	68	.083
1898	Enoch Thome	1-5-2	19	100	.250	1911	Dwight Wilson	3-4-0	43	71	.429
1899	Dwight Watson	1-1-1	29	23	.500	1912	Leroy Brown	4-2-1	83	45	.643
1900	Clayton Teetzel	0-4-0	0	81	.000	1913	Leroy Brown	2-3-1	44	72	.417
1901	Clayton Teetzel	3-5-0	58	167	.375	1914	Thomas Ransom	3-2-1	72	46	.573
1902	Clayton Teetzel	1-5-1	43	125	.214	1915	Elmer Mitchell	4-2-1	154	25	.643
1903	Hunter Forest	4-4-0	78	88	.500	1916	Elmer Mitchell	1-2-1	18	33	.375

Elton Rynearson (1917,1919-1920, 1925-1948) 114-58-15 .650

Year	W-L-T	PF	PA	Pct.	Year	W-L-T	PF	PA	Pct.
1917	3-4-0	111	80	.429					

Lynn Bell (1918) 1-2-0 .333

| 1918 | 1-2-0 | 26 | 31 | .333 | | | | | |

Elton Rynearson (1919-1920)

| 1919 | 4-2-1 | 73 | 44 | .643 | 1920 | 6-2-0 | 132 | 86 | .750 |

Joe McCullach (1921-1922) 6-5-2 .538

| 1921 | 3-3-0 | 82 | 50 | .500 | 1922 | 3-2-2 | 31 | 28 | .571 |

James Brown (1923-1924) 4-10-2 .313

| 1923 | 2-5-1 | 55 | 104 | .313 | 1924 | 2-5-1 | 46 | 69 | .313 |

Elton Tynearson (1925-1948)

1925	8-0-0	106	6	1.000	1937	5-2-1	156	59	.688
1926	6-1-0	113	12	.857	1938	6-1-1	166	36	.812
1927	8-0-0	186	13	1.000	1939	3-3-1	68	64	.500
1928	7-1-0	233	43	.875	1940	1-5-1	34	125	.214
1929	5-1-2	156	45	.750	1941	0-5-2	12	65	.143
1930	6-1-0	145	14	.857	1942	3-3-1	64	81	.500
1931	3-2-1	98	54	.583	1943	2-0-0	28	0	1.000
1932	5-2-0	145	31	.571	1944	no team			
1933	6-2-0	115	71	.750	1945	5-0-1	45	13	.917
1934	5-2-0	109	79	.571	1946	3-4-1	65	80	.438
1935	4-2-2	43	41	.625	1947	1-6-0	29	106	.143
1936	6-2-0	76	53	.750	1948	3-5-0	66	114	.375

Harry Ockerman (1949-1951) 7-19-0 .169

| 1949 | 0-8-0 | 67 | 187 | .000 | 1951 | 4-5-0 | 186 | 183 | .444 |
| 1950 | 3-6-0 | 123 | 194 | .333 | | | | | |

Fred Trosko (1952-1964) 50-56-4 .472

1952	5-3-1	154	146	.611	1959	1-7-0	50	217	.125
1953	7-1-1	212	105	.833	1960	0-8-1	38	230	.062
1954	8-1-0	210	67	.889	1961	0-8-1	49	171	.062
1955	7-2-0	138	70	.778	1962	2-5-0	84	104	.286
1956	4-4-0	158	74	.500	1963	2-6-0	96	201	.286
1957	6-3-0	237	127	.667	1964	4-3-0	110	73	.571
1958	4-5-0	108	88	.444					

Jerry Raymond (1965-1966) 8-7-2 .529

| 1965 | 3-4-1 | 125 | 129 | .438 | 1966 | 5-3-1 | 100 | 87 | .611 |

Dan Boisture (1967-1973) 45-20-3 .683

1967	6-3-0	173	77	.667	1971	7-1-2	228	85	.889
1968	8-2-0	248	91	.800	1972	6-4-0	202	162	.600
1969	5-4-0	255	106	.556	1973	6-4-0	265	190	.600
1970	7-2-1	237	109	.750					

George Mans (1974-1975) 8-12-1 .405

| 1974 | 4-6-1 | 143 | 178 | .409 | 1975 | 4-6-0 | 198 | 171 | .400 |

Member of the Mid-American Conference (1976-2003) 74-143-6 .345

	Nat'l		Overall				Conference				Nat'l		Overall				Conference		
Year	AP	Other	W-L-T	PF	PA	Pct.	W-L-T	Pct.	Rank	Year	AP	Other	W-L-T	PF	PA	Pct.	W-L-T	Pct.	Rank

Ed Chlebek (1976-1977) 10-12-0 .478

	Nat'l		Overall				Conference				Nat'l		Overall				Conference		
1976			2-9-0	132	355	.182	1-5-0	.167	9	1977			8-3-0	239	195	.727	4-3-0	.571	4

Mike Stock (1978-1982) 6-38-1 .144

1978			3-7-0	122	238	.300	1-5-0	.167	10	1981			0-11-0	88	338	.000	0-9-0	.000	10
1979			2-8-1	113	236	.227	1-6-1	.188	9	1982 *			0-3-0	19	98	.000	0-1-0	.000	*
1980			1-9-0	81	322	.100	1-7-1	.125	10										

Bob LaPointe (1982) 1-6-1 .188

1982*			1-6-1	66	107	.188	1-6-1	.188	9

*Stock coached the first three games of the 1982 season, and La Pointe coached the last nine games.

Jim Harkema (1983-1992) 41-57-5 .422

1983			1-10-0	134	276	.091	0-9-0	.000	10	1988			6-3-1	173	200	.650	5-2-1	.688	2
1984			2-7-2	151	221	.273	2-5-2	.333	8	1989			7-3-1	252	196	.682	6-2-0	.750	2
1985			4-7-0	188	252	.364	3-6-0	.333	6	1990			2-9-0	179	311	.222	2-6-0	.250	7
1986			6-5-0	222	228	.545	4-4-0	.500	6	1991			3-7-1	144	232	.318	3-4-1	.438	7
1987			10-2-0	343	237	.833	7-1-0	.875	1	1992*			0-4-0	47	127	.000	0-2-0	.000	*

Jan Quarless (1992)* 1-6-0 .143

1992*			1-6-0	70	209	.143	1-5-0	.167	9

*Harkema coached the first four games of the 1992 season, and Quarless finished the season as interim coach.

Ron Cooper (1993-1994) 9-13-0 .409

1993			4-7-0	163	220	.364	3-5-0	.375	7	1994			5-6-0	247	285	.455	5-4-0	.556	7

Rick Rasnick (1995-1999) 20-34-0 .370

1995			6-5-0	363	335	.545	5-3-0	.625	5	1998			3-8-0	216	309	.273	3-5-0	.375	8
1996			3-8-0	210	284	.273	3-5-0	.375	6	1999*			4-6-0	216	308	.400	4-3-0	.571	*
1997			4-7-0	329	352	.364	3-5-0	.375	7										

Tony Lombardi (1999)* 0-1-0 .000

1999*			0-1-0	23	30	.000	0-1-0	.000	8

*Rasnick coached the first ten games of the season, and Lombardi coached the last game as interim coach.

Jeff Woodruff (2000-2003) 8-26-0 .235

2000			3-8-0	209	350	.273	2-5-0	.286	8	2002			3-9-0	286	566	.250	1-7-0	.125	12
2001			2-9-0	197	367	.182	1-6-0	.143	10	2003*			1-8-0	124	306	.111	0-5-0	.000	10

Al Lavan (2003) 2-1-0 .667

2003*			2-1-0	81	65	.667	2-1-0	.667	

*Woodruff coached the first nine games of 2003, and Lavan coached the last three games.

Won-loss record by decades:

1891-99	22-20-3	.522	1930-39	49-19-6	.703	1970-79	49-50-5	.495
1900-09	29-34-2	.462	1940-49	18-36-6	.350	1980-89	38-66-5	.372
1910-19	25-28-7	.4751	1950-59	49-37-2	.568	1990-99	35-74-1	.323
1920-29	50-20-6	.737	1960-69	35-46-4	.435	2000-03	11-35-0	.239

Historical record 410-465-47 .470

Post-season won-loss record: 1-1-0 .500
1971: Pioneer Bowl, Louisiana Tech 14, EMU 3
1987: California Bowl, EMU 30, San Jose State 27

FLORIDA STATE UNIVERSITY, Tallahassee, Florida; nickname "Seminoles"; colors garnet and gold; Doak S. Campbell Stadium (80.000); Atlantic Coast Conference. Florida State began play in 1947 as an independent and joined the Atlantic Coast Conference for the 1992 season.

Year	Nat'l AP	Other	W-L-T	PF	PA	Pct.
1947			0-5-0	18	90	.000
1948			7-1-0	152	64	.875
1949			9-1-0	291	59	.900
1950			8-0-0	219	54	1.000
1953			5-5-0	183	146	.500
1954			8-4-0	277	190	.667
1955			5-5-0	147	186	.500
1959			4-6-0	149	132	.400
1960			3-6-1	111	136	.350
1961			4-5-1	93	128	.450
1962			4-3-3	170	69	.550
1963			4-5-1	167	93	.450
1964	11		9-1-1	263	85	.864
1965			4-5-1	121	119	.450
1971	19		8-4-0	309	174	.667
1972			7-4-0	287	224	.636
1974			1-10-0	130	289	.091
1976			5-6-0	205	258	.455
1977	14	11	10-2-0	314	170	.833
1978			8-3-0	312	208	.727
1979	6	8	11-1-0	326	160	.917
1980	5	5	10-2-0	369	103	.833
1981			6-5-0	240	286	.545
1982	13	10	9-3-0	419	234	.750
1983			8-4-0	381	312	.667

Years as an independent (1947-1991)
Ed Williamson (1947) 0-5-0 .000

Don Veller (1948-1952) 31-12-1 .716

Year	Nat'l AP	Other	W-L-T	PF	PA	Pct.
1951			6-2-0	194	72	.750
1952			1-8-1	101	261	.150

Tom Nugent (1953-1958) 34-28-1 .548

Year	Nat'l AP	Other	W-L-T	PF	PA	Pct.
1956			5-4-1	178	116	.550
1957			4-6-0	136	165	.400
1958			7-4-0	218	124	.636

Perry Moss (1959) 4-6-0 .400

Bill Peterson (1960-1970) 62-42-11 .587

Year	Nat'l AP	Other	W-L-T	PF	PA	Pct.
1966			6-5-0	274	215	.545
1967		15	7-2-2	250	187	.727
1968		14	8-3-0	308	211	.727
1969			6-3-1	220	182	.650
1970			7-4-0	254	195	.636

Larry Jones (1971-1973) 15-19-0 .441

Year	Nat'l AP	Other	W-L-T	PF	PA	Pct.
1973			0-11-0	98	331	.000

Darrell Mudra (1974-1975) 4-18-0 .182

Year	Nat'l AP	Other	W-L-T	PF	PA	Pct.
1975			3-8-0	187	213	.273

Bobby Bowden (1976-2003) 269-67-4 .797

Year	Nat'l AP	Other	W-L-T	PF	PA	Pct.
1984	17	20	7-3-2	406	254	.667
1985	15	13	9-3-0	402	259	.750
1986		20	7-4-1	353	218	.625
1987	2	2	11-1-0	481	163	.917
1988	3	3	11-1-0	455	172	.917
1989	3	2	10-2-0	424	199	.833
1990	4	4	10-2-0	459	206	.833
1991	4	4	11-2-0	449	188	.846

Member of the Atlantic Coast Conference (1992-2003) 90-6-0 .937

Year	Nat'l AP	Other	Overall W-L-T	PF	PA	Pct.	Conference W-L-T	Pct.	Rank
1992	2	2	11-1-0	446	186	.917	8-0-0	1.000	1
1993	1	1	12-1-0	536	129	.923	8-0-0	1.000	1
1994	4	5	10-1-1	428	200	.875	8-0-0	1.000	1
1995	4	5	10-2-0	563	246	.833	7-1-0	.875	1
1996	3	3	11-1-0	446	174	.917	8-0-0	1.000	1
1997	3	3	11-1-0	468	181	.917	8-0-0	1.000	1
1998	3	3	11-2-0	401	161	.846	7-1-0	.875	1
1999	1	1	12-0-0	458	203	1.000	8-0-0	1.000	1
2000	5	4	11-2-0	514	133	.846	8-0-0	1.000	1
2001	15	15	8-4-0	403	304	.667	6-2-0	.750	2
2002	21	23	9-5-0	428	301	.643	7-1-0	.875	1
2003	11	10	10-3-0	419	217	.769	7-1-0	.875	1

Won-loss record by decades:

1947-49	16- 7-0	.696	1970-79	60-49-0	.550	1990-99	109-19-1	.849
1950-59	53-44-2	.545	1980-89	88-28-3	.762	2000-03	38-14-0	.731
1960-69	55-38-11	.582						

Historical record 419-197-17 .672

Post-season won-loss record: 19-12-2 .606

1950: Cigar Bowl, Fla. State 19, Wofford 6
1955: Sun Bowl, Texas Western 47, Fla. State 20
1958: Bluegrass Bowl, Oklahoma State 15, Fla. State 6
1965: Gator Bowl, Fla. State 36, Oklahoma 19
1966: Sun Bowl, Wyoming 28, Fla. State 20
1967: Gator Bowl, Fla. State 17, Penn State 17
1968: Peach Bowl, LSU 31, Fla. State 27
1971: Fiesta Bowl, Arizona State 45, Fla. State 38
1977: Tangerine Bowl, Fla. State 40, Texas Tech 17
1980: Orange Bowl, Oklahoma 24, Fla. State 7
1981: Orange Bowl, Oklahoma 18, Fla. State 17
1982: Gator Bowl, Fla. State 31, West Virginia 12
1983: Peach Bowl, Fla. State 28, North Carolina 3
1984: Citrus Bowl, Fla. State 17, Georgia 17
1985: Gator Bowl, Fla. State 34, Oklahoma State 23
1986: All American Bowl, Fla. State 27, Indiana 13

1988: Fiesta Bowl, Fla. State 31, Nebraska 28
1989: Sugar Bowl, Fla. State 13, Auburn 7
1990: Fiesta Bowl, Fla. State 41, Nebraska 14
1990: Blockbuster Bowl, Fla. State 24, Penn State 17
1992: Cotton Bowl, Fla. State 10, Texas A&M 2
1993: Orange Bowl, Fla. State 27, Nebraska 14
1994: Orange Bowl, Fla. State 18, Nebraska 16
1995: Sugar Bowl, Fla. State 23, Florida 17
1996: Orange Bowl, Fla. State 31, Notre Dame 26
1997: Sugar Bowl, Florida 52, Fla. State 20
1998: Sugar Bowl, Fla. State 31, Ohio State 14
1999: Fiesta Bowl, Tennessee 23, Fla. State 16
2000: Sugar Bowl, Fla. State 46, Virginia Tech 29
2001: Orange Bowl, Oklahoma 13, Fla. State 2
2002: Gator Bowl, Fla. State 30, Virginia Tech 17.
2003: Sugar Bowl, Georgia 26, Fla. State 13
2004: Orange Bowl, Miami 16, Fla. State 14

College Football Hall of Fame: Fred Biletnikoff, wide receiver, 1962-64; Ron Sellers, wide receiver, 1966-68; Darell Mudra, coach, 1974-75.

Awards: Heisman Trophy: 1993, Charlie Ward, quarterback; 2000: Chris Weinke, quarterback; Jim Thorpe Award: 1988: Deion Sanders, cornerback; 1991: Terrell Buckley, cornerback; Butkus Award: 1987: Paul McGowan, linebacker; 1992, Marvin Jones, linebacker; Lou Groza Award: 1998 and 1999, Sebastian Janikowski; Davey O'Brien Award: 1993, Charlie Ward; 2000: Chris Weinke; Maxwell Award: 1993, Charlie Ward; Lombard Award: 1992, Marvin Jones, inside linebacker; 2000: Jamal Reynolds, defensive end; Unitas Award: 1991, Casey Weldon; 1993, Charlie Ward; 2000, Chris Weinke; Camp Award: 1993, Charlie Ward; Baugh Trophy: 1999, Chris Weinke.

UNIVERSITY OF FLORIDA, Gainesville, Florida; nickname "Gators"; colors, orange and blue; Ben Hill Griffin Stadium (83,000); Southeastern Conference. Florida began play in 1906 and joined the Southern Conference as a founding member in 1922. Florida left the SC after the 1932 season to join the newly organized Southeastern Conference and has played in that conference beginning with the 1933 season.

Early years as an independent (1906-1921)

Year	W-L-T	PF	PA	Pct.	Year	W-L-T	PF	PA	Pct.
					Jack Forsythe (1906-1908) 14-6-2 .681				
1906	5-3-0	85	60	.625					
1907	4-1-1	53	10	.750	1908	5-2-1	90	40	.688
					G.E. Pyle (1909-1913) 26-7-3 .763				
1909	6-1-1	117	34	.812	1912	5-2-1	203	55	.688
1910	6-1-0	186	15	.857	1913	4-3-0	228	94	.571
1911	5-0-1	87	14	.917					
					Charles McCoy (1914-1916) 9-10-0 .474				
1914	5-2-0	152	46	.714	1916	0-5-0	3	95	.000
1915	4-3-0	99	67	.571					
					A. L. Busser (1917-1919) 7-8-0 .467				
1917	2-4-0	47	247	.333	1919	5-3-0	174	46	.625
1918	0-1-0	2	14	.000					
					William Kline (1920-1922) 19-8-2 .690				
1920	6-3-0	112	91	.667	1921	6-3-2	134	61	.636

Member of the Southern Conference (1922-1932) 33-22-7 589

	Nat'l		Overall				Conference			Year	Nat'l		Overall				Conference		
Year	AP	Other	W-L-T	PF	PA	Pct.	W-L-T	Pct.	Rank		AP	Other	W-L-T	PF	PA	Pct.	W-L-T	Pct.	Rank
1922			7-2-0	240	39	.778	2-0-0	1.000	2										
							J. A. Van Fleet (1923-1924) 12-3-4 .737												
1923			6-1-2	179	60	.833	1-0-2	.667	3	1924			6-2-2	212	44	.700	2-0-1	.833	2
							H. L. Sebring (1925-1927) 17-11-2 .600												
1925			8-2-0	222	80	.800	3-2-0	.600	8	1927			7-3-0	164	96	.700	5-2-0	.571	6
1926			2-6-2	94	137	.300	1-4-1	.250	18										
							Charles Bachman (1928-1932) 27-18-3 .593												
1928			8-1-0	336	44	.889	6-1-0	.857	3	1931			2-6-2	74	168	.300	2-4-2	.375	15
1929			8-2-0	193	73	.800	6-1-0	.857	4	1932			3-6-0	108	136	.333	1-6-0	.143	20
1930			6-3-1	199	61	.650	4-2-1	.643	7										

Member of the Southeastern Conference (1933-2001) 244-181-14 .572

	Nat'l		Overall				Conference			Year	Nat'l		Overall				Conference		
	AP	Other	W-L-T	PF	PA	Pct.	W-L-T	Pct.	Rank		AP	Other	W-L-T	PF	PA	Pct.	W-L-T	Pct.	Rank
							D. K. Stanley (1933-1935) 14-13-2 .517												
1933			5-3-1	114	53	.611	2-3-0	.400	9	1935			3-7-0	113	154	.300	1-6-0	.143	12
1934			6-3-1	113	110	.650	2-2-1	.500	7										
							Josh Cody (1936-1939) 17-24-2 .418												
1936			4-6-0	99	125	.400	1-5-0	.167	11	1938			4-6-1	112	149	.409	2-2-1	.500	7
1937			4-7-0	86	89	.364	3-4-0	.429	8	1939			5-5-1	78	66	.500	0-3-1	.125	12
							Thomas Lieb (1940-1945) 20-26-1 .436												
1940			5-5-0	136	141	.500	2-3-0	.400	8	1943			no team						
1941			4-6-0	149	97	.400	1-3-0	.250	10	1944			4-3-0	106	136	.571	0-3-0	.000	10
1942			3-7-0	106	185	.300	1-3-0	.250	9	1945			4-5-1	155	100	.450	1-3-1	.300	10
							Raymond Wolf (1946-1949) 13-24-2 .357												
1946			0-9-0	104	264	.000	0-5-0	.000	12	1948			5-5-0	213	206	.500	1-5-0	.167	10
1947			4-5-1	125	156	.450	0-3-1	.125	12	1949			4-5-1	180	218	.450	1-4-1	.250	10
							Bob Woodruff (1950-1959) 53-42-6 .554												
1950			5-5-0	157	181	.500	2-4-0	.333	10	1955			4-6-0	111	126	.400	3-5-0	.375	10
1951			5-5-0	174	131	.500	2-4-0	.333	9	1956			6-3-1	158	98	.650	5-2-0	.714	3
1952	15		8-3-0	304	122	.727	3-3-0	.500	6	1957	17		6-2-1	133	70	.722	4-1-1	.750	3
1953			3-5-2	200	113	.400	1-3-2	.250	9	1958	14		6-4-1	174	100	.591	2-3-1	.417	8
1954			5-5-0	115	128	.500	5-2-0	.714	3	1959	19	20	5-4-1	169	107	.550	2-4-0	.333	9
							Ray Graves (1960-1969) 70-31-4 .686												
1960	18	16	9-2-0	157	86	.818	5-1-0	.833	2	1965		12	7-4-0	239	149	.636	4-2-0	.667	3
1961			4-5-1	97	146	.450	3-3-0	.500	6	1966		11	9-2-0	265	147	.818	5-1-0	.833	3
1962			7-4-0	221	139	.636	4-2-0	.667	5	1967			6-4-0	201	161	.600	4-2-0	.667	3
1963			6-3-1	130	120	.650	3-3-1	.500	7	1968			6-3-1	151	175	.650	3-2-1	.583	6
1964			7-3-0	181	98	.700	4-2-0	.667	2	1969	14	17	9-1-1	329	187	.864	3-1-1	.700	4
							Doug Dickey (1970-1978) 58-43-2 .573												
1970			7-4-0	224	256	.636	3-3-0	.500	5	1975			9-3-0	302	117	.750	5-1-0	.833	4
1971			4-7-0	174	298	.364	1-6-0	.143	8	1976			8-4-0	328	292	.667	4-2-0	.667	4
1972			5-5-1	218	144	.500	3-3-1	.500	6	1977			6-4-1	251	235	.591	3-3-0	.500	5
1973		20	7-5-0	187	189	.583	3-4-0	.429	5	1978			4-7-0	249	223	.364	3-3-0	.500	4
1974	15	12	8-4-0	261	197	.667	3-3-0	.500	4										

Charley Pell (1979-1984) 33-26-3 .549

Year			W-L-T	PF	PA	Pct	Conf	Pct	Fin
1979			0-10-1	106	265	.046	0-6-0	.000	9
1980	19		8-4-0	256	176	.667	4-2-0	.667	4
1981			7-5-0	284	166	.583	3-3-0	.500	4
1982			8-4-0	296	191	.667	3-3-0	.500	6
1983	6	6	9-2-1	304	156	.792	4-2-0	.667	3
1984*			1-1-1	104	74	.500	0-0-1	.500	*

Galen Hall (1984-1989) 40-18-1 .703

Year			W-L-T	PF	PA	Pct	Conf	Pct	Fin
1984*	3	7	8-0-0	237	96	1.000	5-0-0	1.000	*
1985	5		9-1-1	286	162	.864	5-1-0	.833	**
1986			6-5-0	223	173	.545	2-4-0	.333	7
1987			6-6-0	229	178	.600	3-3-0	.500	6
1988			7-5-0	268	185	.583	4-3-0	571	4
1989***			4-1-0	128	57	.800	2-1-0	.667	***

Gary Darnell***(1989) 3-4-0 .429

Year			W-L-T	PF	PA	Pct	Conf	Pct	Fin
1989***			3-4-0	140	145	.429	2-2-0	.500	4

*Pell coached the first three games of the 1984 season, and Hall coached the remaining 8 games. Florida's SEC title was vacated because of NCAA violations.

**Florida was ineligible for the SEC title in 1985.

***Hall coached the first five games of the 1989 season, and Darnell coached the remaining 7 games.

Steve Spurrier (1990-2001) 121-27-1 .815

Year			W-L-T	PF	PA	Pct	Conf	Pct	Fin
1990	13		9-2-0	387	171	.818	6-1-0	.857	*
1991	7	8	10-2-0	389	191	.833	7-0-0	1.000	1
1992	10	11	9-4-0	315	284	.692	6-2-0	.750	2
1993	5	4	11-2-0	513	244	.846	7-1-0	.875	1
1994	7	7	10-2-1	538	228	.808	7-1-0	.875	1
1995	2	3	12-1-0	558	263	.923	8-0-0	1.000	1
1996	1	1	12-1-0	611	221	.923	8-0-0	1.000	1
1997	4	6	10-2-0	430	205	.833	6-2-0	.750	2
1998	5	6	10-2-0	370	165	.833	7-1-0	.875	2
1999	12	14	9-4-0	403	272	.692	7-1-0	.875	2
2000	10	11	10-3-0	468	273	.769	7-1-0	.875	1
2001	3	3	9-2-0	482	155	.818	6-2-0	.750	3

*Florida ineligible for SEC title.

Ron Zook (2002-2003) 16-10-0 .615

Year			W-L-T	PF	PA	Pct	Conf	Pct	Fin
2002	24		8-5-0	336	279	.615	6-2-0	.750	2
2003	24	25	8-5-0	390	271	.615	6-2-0	.750	3

Won-loss record by decades:

1906-09	20- 7-3	.717	1940-49	33-50-3	.401	1980-89	76-38-3	.662
1910-19	36-24-2	.597	1950-59	53-42-6	.554	1990-99	102-22-1	.820
1920-29	64-25-8	.701	1960-69	70-31-4	.686	2000-03	35-15-0	.700
1930-39	42-52-7	.450	1970-79	58-53-3	.522			

Historical record: 589-359-40 .616

Post-season won-loss record 19-18-0 .514

1953: Gator Bowl, Florida 14, Tulsa 13
1958: Gator Bowl, Mississippi 7, Florida 3
1960: Gator Bowl, Florida 13, Baylor 12
1962: Gator Bowl, Florida 17, Penn State 7
1966: Sugar Bowl, Missouri 20, Florida 18
1967: Orange Bowl, Florida 27, Georgia Tech 12
1969: Gator Bowl, Florida 14, Tennessee 13
1973: Tangerine Bowl, Miami (OH) 16, Florida 7`
1974: Sugar Bowl, Nebraska 13, Florida 10
1975: Gator Bowl, Maryland 13, Florida 0
1977: Sun Bowl, Texas A&M 37, Florida 14
1980: Tangerine Bowl, Florida 35, Maryland 20
1981: Peach Bowl, West Virginia 26, Florida 6
1982: Bluebonnet Bowl, Arkansas 28, Florida 24
1983: Gator Bowl, Florida 14, Iowa 6
1987: Aloha Bowl, UCLA 20, Florida 16
1988: All American Bowl, Florida 14, Illinois 10
1989: Freedom Bowl, Washington 34, Florida 7
1992: SEC Championship, Alabama 28, Florida 21
1992: Sugar Bowl, Notre Dame 39, Florida 28
1992: Gator Bowl, Florida 27, NC State 10

1993:SEC Championship, Florida 28, Alabama 13
1994: Sugar Bowl, Florida 41, West Virginia 7
1994: SEC Championship, Florida 24, Alabama 23
1995: Sugar Bowl, Florida State 23, Florida 24
1995: SEC Championship, Florida 35, Arkansas 24
1996: Fiesta Bowl, Nebraska 62, Florida 24
1996: SEC Championship, Florida 45, Alabama 30
1997: Sugar Bowl, Florida 52, Florida State 20
1998: Citrus Bowl, Florida 21, Penn State 6
1999: SEC Championship, Alabama 34, Florida 7
1999: Orange Bowl, Florida 31, Syracuse 10
2000: SEC Championship, Florida 28, Auburj 6
2000: Citrus Bowl, Michigan State 37, Florida 34
2001: Sugar Bowl, Miami 37, Florida 20
2002: Orange Bowl, Florida 56, Maryland 23
2003: Outback Bowl, Michigan 38, Florida 30
2004: Outback Bowl, Iowa 37, Florida 17

College Football Hall of Fame:
Dale Van Sickel, end, 1927-29; Charlie Bachman, coach, 1928-32; Steve Spurrier, quarterback, 1964-66; Jack Youngblood, defensive end, 1968-70; Ray Graves, coach, 1960-69.

Awards: Heisman Trophy: 1966, Steve Spurrier; 1996, Danny Wuerffel; Lou Groza Award: 1993, Judd Davis; Davey O'Brien Award: 1995 and 1996, Danny Wuerffel; Maxwell Award, 1996, Danny Wuerffel; Jim Thorpe Award, 1996, Lawrence Wright: Unitas Award: 1996, Danny Wuerffel; Camp Award: 1996, Danny Wuerffel; Baugh Trophy: 1971, John Reaves; 1995, Danny Wuerffel.

FRESNO STATE UNIVERSITY, Fresno, California; nickname "Bulldogs"; colors Bulldog red and white; Bulldog Stadium (41,041); Western Athletic Conference. Fresno State began play in 1921. In 1969, Fresno State joined the Pacific Coast Athletic Association. The name of this conference was changed to the Big West Conference in 1988. Fresno State left the Big West Conference after the 1991 season and joined the Western Athletic Conference where it has played beginning with the 1992 season.

Early years (1921-1968). Conference data shown only for 1969 on.

Year	W-L-T	PF	PA	Pct.	Year	W-L-T	PF	PA	Pct.
				Arthur Jones (1921-28) 36-26-7 .527					
1921	3-4-0	61	114	.429	1925	2-6-1	123	192	.125
1922	7-1-2	126	29	.800	1926	5-3-1	146	109	.611
1923	7-2-0	211	108	.778	1927	3-3-2	45	79	.500
1924	7-2-0	132	44	.778	1928	2-5-1	56	137	.312
				Stanley Borleske (1929-1932) 16-17-2 .486					
1929	1-7-0	40	250	.125	1931	4-6-0	98	123	.400
1930	8-0-0	154	66	1.000	1932	3-4-2	56	84	.444
				Leo Harris (1933-1935) 18-9-1 .661					
1933	5-4-0	98	71	.556	1935	6-3-0	199	84	.667
1934	7-2-1	225	77	.750					
				James Bradshaw (1936-1942, 1946) 59-18-5 .750					
1936	5-3-1	152	91	.611	1940	9-2-1	132	58	.792
1937	8-1-1	223	75	.850	1941	4-3-2	118	90	.556
1938	7-3-0	227	99	.700	1942	9-1-0	362	45	.900
1939	9-1-0	217	85	.900	1943		no team		
				Earl Wright (1944) 0-6-0 .000					
1944	0-6-0	18	95	.000					
				Pix Pierson (1945, 1949) 7-14-2 .348					
1945	4-6-2	113	112	.417					
				James Bradshw (1946)					
1946	8-4-0	177	129	.667					
				Kenny Gleason (1947-1948) 6-12-3 .357					
1947	3-6-2	133	236	.364	1948	3-6-1	108	267	.350
				Pix Pierson (1949)					
1949	3-8-0	156	344	.273					
				Duke Jacobs (1950-1951) 7-11-1 .395					
1950	2-6-1	131	231	.278	1951	5-5-0	199	189	.500
				Clark Van Galter (1952-1958) 46-22-2					
1952	8-2-0	331	233	.800	1956	8-2-0	249	124	.800
1953	4-4-2	255	188	.500	1957	5-5-0	164	183	.500
1954	7-3-0	245	164	.700	1958	5-5-0	147	206	.500
1955	9-1-0	273	110	.900					
				Cecil Coleman (1959-1963) 37-13-0 .740					
1959	7-3-0	226	146	.700	1962	7-3-0	318	116	.700
1960	9-1-0	298	98	.900	1963	4-6-0	208	242	.400
1961	10-0-0	292	125	1.000					
				Phil Krueger (1964-1965) 10-10-0 .500					
1964	4-6-0	202	204	.400	1965	6-4-0	191	116	.600
				Darryl Rogers (1966-1972) 43-32-1 .573					
1966	7-3-0	158	214	.700	1968	7-4-0	269	197	.636
1967	3-8-0	240	267	.273					

Member of the Pacific Coast Athletic Association (later renamed Big West Conference) (1969-1991) 80-47-1 .629

Year	Nat'l AP Other	Overall W-L-T	PF	PA	Pct.	Conference W-L-T	Pct.	Rank	Year	Nat'l AP Other	Overall W-L-T	PF	PA	Pct.	Conference W-L-T	Pct.	Rank
1969		6-4-0	237	227	.600	1-3-0	.250	4	1971		6-5-0	215	165	.545	3-2-0	.600	3
1970		8-4-0	289	273	.667	4-2-0	.667	3	1972		6-4-1	237	158	.591	1-3-0	.250	3
					J. R. Boone (1973-1975) 10-24-0 .294												
1973		2-9-0	148	283	.182	1-3-0	.250	4	1975		3-8-0	219	274	.274	1-4-0	.200	5
1974		5-7-0	250	206	.417	1-3-0	.250	4									
					Jim Sweeney (1976-1977, 1980-1996) 143-75-3 .654												
1976		5-6-0	237	165	.455	3-1-0	.750	2	1977		9-2-0	354	163	.818	4-0-0	1.000	1
					Bob Padilla (1978-1979) 7-15-0 .318												
1978		3-8-0	247	329	.274	1-4-0	.200	5	1979		4-7-0	245	302	.364	3-2-0	.600	2
					Jim Sweeney (1980-1991)												
1980		5-6-0	192	245	.455	1-4-0	.200	4	1986		9-2-0	302	150	.818	6-1-0	.857	2
1981		5-6-0	264	299	.455	2-3-0	.400	3	1987		6-5-0	260	179	.545	4-3-0	.571	3
1982		11-1-0	381	228	.917	6-0-0	1.000	1	1988		10-2-0	393	169	.833	7-0-0	1.000	1
1983		6-5-0	242	214	.545	2-4-0	.333	5	1989		11-1-0	441	221	.917	7-0-0	1.000	1
1984		6-6-0	293	253	.500	3-4-0	.429	4	1990		8-2-1	346	230	.773	5-1-1	.786	2
1985	16	11-0-1	481	209	.958	7-0-0	1.000	1	1991		10-2-0	507	235	.833	6-1-0	.857	1

Member of the Western Athletic Association (1992-2003) 59-35-1 .626

1992	24	22	9-4-0	510	364	.692	6-2-0	.750	1		1995		5-7-0	371	418	.417	2-6-0	.250	7
1993			8-4-0	461	350	.667	6-2-0	.750	1		1996		4-7-0	267	344	.364	3-5-0	.375	10
1994			5-7-1	376	426	.423	3-4-1	.438	7										

Pat Hill (1997-2003) 55-35-0 .611

1997	6-6-0	318	298	.500	5-3-0	.625	4		2000		7-5-0	319	251	.583	6-2-0	.750	4
1998	5-6-0	265	225	.455	5-3-0	.625	5		2001		11-3-0	560	344	.786	6-2-0	.750	2
1999	8-5-0	413	282	.615	5-2-0	.625	1		2002		9-5-0	348	358	.643	6-2-0	.750	3
									2003		9-5-0	322	317	.643	6-2-0	.750	2

Won-loss record by decades:

1921-29	37-33-7	.526		1950-59	60-36-3	.621		1980-89	80-34-1	.700
1930-39	62-27-5	.686		1960-69	63-39-0	.618		1990-99	68-50-2	.572
1940-49	43-42-8	.505		1970-79	51-60-1	.460		2000-03	36-18-0	.667

Historical record (1921-2003) 500-339-27 .593

Post-season won-lost record 10-8-0 .556

1937: Little All American Bowl, Fresno 27, Arkansas State 26
1940: Pineapple Bowl, Fresno 3, Hawaii 0
1945: Raisin Bowl, Drake 13, Fresno 12
1961: Mercy Bowl, Fresno 36, Bowling Green 6
1968: Camelia Bowl, Humboldt State 29, Fresno 14
1971: Mercy Bowl, C.S. Fullerton 17, Fresno 14
1982: California Bowl, Fresno 29, Bowling Green 28
1985: California Bowl, Fresno 51, Bowling Green 7

1988: California Bowl, Fresno 35, West. Michigan 30
1989: California Bowl, Fresno 27, Ball State 6
1991: California Bowl, Bowling Green 28, Fresno 21
1992: Freedom Bowl, Fresno 24, USC 7
1993: Aloha Bowl, Colorado 41, Fresno 30
1999: Las Vegas Bowl, Utah 17, Fresno 16
2000: Silicon Valley Classic, Air Force 37, Fresno 34
2001: Silicon Valley Classic, Michigan State 44, Fresno 35
2002: Silicon Valley Classic, Fresno 30, Ga. Tech 21
2003: Silicon Valley Classic, Fresno 17, UCLA 9

Awards: Unitas Award: 2001, David Carr; Baugh Trophy: 2001, David Carr.

GEORGIA TECH, Atlanta, Georgia; nickname "Yellow Jackets," "Rambling Wreck"; colors old gold and white; Bobby Dodd Stadium (42,000); Atlantic Coast Conference. Georgia Tech operated as an independent until 1922 when it became a founding member of the Southern Conference. Georgia Tech left that conference after the 1932 season, joining with other Southern Conference teams to organize the Southeastern Conference. Tech played in the Southeastern Conference through the 1963 season and then became an independent from 1964 through 1982. In 1983, Tech joined the Atlantic Coast Conference and has played in that conference since that time.

Early years (1892-1903)

Year	Coach	W-L-T	PF	PA	Pct.	Year	Coach	W-L-T	PF	PA	Pct.
1892	E. E. Wests	0-3-0	16	58	.000	1897	no coach	0-1-0	0	28	.000
1893	F. Spain &					1898	Cow Nalley	0-3-0	6	67	.000
	L. Wood	2-1-1	38	18	.625	1899	Mr. Collier	0-5-0	5	169	.000
1894	F. Spain &					1900	no coach	0-4-0	6	107	.000
	L. Wood	0-3-0	0	136	.000	1901	Cyrus Strickler	4-0-1	97	5	.900
1895	no team					1902	John McKee	0-6-2	23	122	.143
1896	no coach	1-1-1	18	61	.500	1903	no coach	2-5-0	59	148	.286

Year	Nat'l AP Other	W-L-T	PF	PA	Pct.	Year	Nat'l AP Other	W-L-T	PF	PA	Pct.
						John Heisman (1904-1919) 102-29-7 .779					
1904		8-1-1	287	34	.850	1912		5-3-1	100	86	.611
1905		6-0-1	210	35	.929	1913		7-2-0	250	43	.778
1906		5-3-1	73	69	.611	1914		6-2-0	206	40	.750
1907		4-4-0	148	100	.500	1915		7-0-1	233	24	.938
1908		6-3-0	147	74	.667	1916		8-0-1	421	20	.944
1909		7-2-0	217	44	.778	1917	1	9-0-0	491	17	1.000
1910		5-3-0	197	50	.625	1918		6-1-0	466	32	.857
1911		6-2-1	134	21	.722	1919		7-3-0	257	33	.700
						Bill Alexander (1920-1944) 134-95-15 .580					
1920		8-1-0	312	16	.889	1921		8-1-0	360	56	.889

Member of the Southern Conference (1922-1932) 41-23-10 .622

Year	Nat'l AP Other	Overall W-L-T	PF	PA	Pct.	Conference W-L-T	Pct.	Rank	Year	Nat'l AP Other	Overall W-L-T	PF	PA	Pct.	Conference W-L-T	Pct.	Rank
1922		7-2-0	157	59	.778	4-0-0	1.000	2	1928	3	10-0-0	221	47	1.000	7-0-0	1.000	1
1923		3-2-4	75	82	.556	1-0-4	.600	4	1929		3-6-0	105	138	.333	3-5-0	.375	14
1924		5-3-1	82	78	.688	3-2-1	.583	10	1930		2-6-1	79	185	.278	2-4-1	.357	15
1925		6-2-1	102	48	.722	4-1-1	.750	5	1931		2-7-1	98	209	.250	2-4-1	.357	16
1926		4-5-0	87	87	.444	4-3-0	.571	9	1932		4-5-1	111	105	.450	4-4-1	.500	10
1927		8-1-1	125	39	.850	7-0-1	.938	1									

Member of the Southeastern Conference (1933-1963) 115-69-9 .619

Year	Nat'l AP Other	W-L-T	PF	PA	Pct.	Conf W-L-T	Pct.	Rank	Year	Nat'l AP Other	W-L-T	PF	PA	Pct.	Conf W-L-T	Pct.	Rank
1933		5-5-0	117	63	.500	2-5-0	.286	11	1939	16	8-2-0	150	56	.800	6-0-0	1.000	1
1934		1-9-0	56	187	.100	0-6-0	.000	11	1940		3-7-0	139	160	.300	1-5-0	.167	12
1935		5-5-0	162	142	.500	3-4-0	.429	8	1941		3-6-0	82	130	.333	2-4-0	.333	9
1936		5-5-1	251	103	.500	3-3-1	.500	6	1942	5	9-2-0	219	81	.818	4-1-0	.800	2
1937		6-3-1	177	54	.650	3-2-1	.583	6	1943	13	8-3-0	300	142	.727	3-0-0	1.000	1
1938		3-4-3	72	84	.450	2-1-3	.583	5	1944	13	8-3-0	253	101	.727	4-0-0	1.000	1

Bobby Dodd (1945-1966) 165-64-8 .713

Year	Nat'l AP Other	W-L-T	PF	PA	Pct.	Conf W-L-T	Pct.	Rank	Year	Nat'l AP Other	W-L-T	PF	PA	Pct.	Conf W-L-T	Pct.	Rank
1945		4-6-0	157	165	.400	2-2-0	.500	5	1955	7 7	9-1-1	189	46	.864	4-1-1	.750	3
1946	11	9-2-0	284	127	.818	4-2-0	.667	4	1956	4 4	10-1-0	248	47	.909	7-1-0	.875	2
1947	10	10-1-0	240	55	.909	4-1-0	.800	2	1957		4-4-2	75	71	.500	3-4-1	.438	8
1948		7-3-0	226	69	.700	4-3-0	.571	5	1958		5-4-1	93	91	.550	2-3-1	.417	8
1949		7-3-0	197	129	.700	5-2-0	.714	4	1959		6-5-0	136	121	.545	3-3-0	.500	7
1950		5-6-0	182	193	.455	4-2-0	.667	5	1960		5-5-0	118	97	.500	4-4-0	.500	7
1951	5 5	11-0-1	295	90	.917	7-0-0	1.000	1	1961	13 13	7-4-0	177	80	.636	4-3-0	.571	4
1952	2 2	12-0-0	325	59	1.000	6-0-0	1.000	1	1962	11	7-3-1	211	97	.682	5-2-0	.714	4
1953	8 9	9-2-1	288	111	.792	4-1-1	.750	2	1963		7-3-0	173	89	.700	4-3-0	.571	6
1954	11	8-3-0	175	91	.727	6-2-0	.750	2									

Independent (1964-1982)

Year	Nat'l AP Other	W-L-T	PF	PA	Pct.	Year	Nat'l AP Other	W-L-T	PF	PA	Pct.
1964		7-3-0	121	79	.700	1966	8 8	9-2-0	269	108	.818
1965		7-3-1	253	171	.714						
						Bud Carson (1967-1971) 27-27-0 .500					
1967		4-6-0	129	205	.400	1970	13 17	9-3-0	233	165	.750
1968		4-6-0	158	263	.400	1971		6-6-0	207	207	.500
1969		4-6-0	144	183	.400						
						Bill Fulcher (1972-1973) 12-10-1 .543					
1972	20	7-4-1	284	226	.625	1973		5-6-0	192	211	.455

Pepper Rodgers (1974-1979) 34-31-2 .522

Year	Record	PF	PA	Pct				Year			Record	PF	PA	Pct			
1974	6-5-0	238	212	.545				1977			6-5-0	224	221	.545			
1975	7-4-0	270	200	.636				1978			7-5-0	270	253	.583			
1976	4-6-1	221	267	.409				1979			4-6-1	152	190	.409			

Bill Curry (1980-1986) 31-43-4 .423

| 1980 | 1-9-1 | 113 | 260 | .136 | | | | 1982 | | | 6-5-0 | 239 | 286 | .545 | | | |
| 1981 | 1-10-0 | 124 | 309 | .091 | | | | | | | | | | | | | |

Member of the Atlantic Coast Conference (1983-2003) 79-71-2 .526

| 1983 | 3-8-0 | 222 | 313 | .273 | 3-2-0 | .600 | 3 | 1985 | 19 | 18 | 9-2-1 | 252 | 132 | .792 | 5-1-0 | .833 | 2 |
| 1984 | 6-4-1 | 296 | 201 | .591 | 2-2-1 | .500 | 4 | 1986 | | | 5-5-1 | 282 | 211 | .500 | 3-3-0 | .500 | 4 |

Bobby Ross (1987-1991) 31-26-1 .543

1987	2-9-0	199	275	.182	0-6-0	.000	8	1990	2	1	11-0-1	379	186	.958	6-0-1	.929	1
1988	3-8-0	200	194	.273	0-7-0	.000	8	1991			8-5-0	283	214	.615	5-2-0	.714	2
1989	7-4-0	265	213	.636	4-3-0	.571	4										

Bill Lewis (1992-1994) 11-19-0 .367

| 1992 | 5-6-0 | 237 | 286 | .455 | 4-4-0 | .500 | 4 | 1994* | | | 1-7-0 | 152 | 231 | .125 | 0-6-0 | .000 | * |
| 1993 | 5-6-0 | 260 | 286 | .455 | 3-5-0 | .375 | 6 | | | | | | | | | | |

George O'Leary (1995-2001) 53-33-0 .616

1994*	0-3-0	33	88	.000	0-2-0	.000	9	1999	20	21	8-4-0	462	361	.667	5-3-0	.625	2
1995	6-5-0	260	243	.545	5-3-0	.625	4	2000	17	19	9-3-0	386	237	.750	6-2-0	.750	2
1996	5-6-0	220	236	.455	4-4-0	.500	5	2001	24		8-5-0	405	281	.615	4-4-0	.500	4
1997	25	7-5-0	314	294	.583	5-3-0	.625	3									
1998	9	11	10-2-0	426	295	.833	7-1-0	.875	2								

*Lewis coached the first eight games of the 1994 season, and O'Leary coached the remaining three games.

Chan Gailey (2002-2003) 14-12-0 .538

| 2002 | 7-6-0 | 280 | 267 | .538 | 4-4-0 | .500 | 5 | 2003 | | | 7-6-0 | 274 | 266 | .538 | 4-4-0 | .500 | 4 |

Won-loss record by decades:

1892-99	3-17-2	.182	1930-39	41-51-8	.450	1970-79	61-50-3	.548
1900-09	42-28-6	.592	1940-49	68-36-0	.654	1980-89	43-64-4	.405
1910-19	66-16-4	.791	1950-59	79-26-6	.739	1990-99	66-49-1	.573
1920-29	62-23-7	.712	1960-69	61-41-2	.596	2000-03	31-20-0	.608

Historical record: 623-421-43 .594

Post-season won-loss record 21-11-0 .656

1929: Rose Bowl, Georgia Tech 8, California 7
1940: Orange Bowl, Georgia Tech 21, Missouri 7
1943: Cotton Bowl, Texas 14, Georgia Tech 7
1944: Sugar Bowl, Georgia Tech 20, Tulsa 18
1945: Orange Bowl, Tulsa 26, Georgia Tech 12
1947: Oil Bowl, Georgia Tech 41, St. Mary's 19
1948: Orange Bowl, Georgia Tech 20, Kansas 14
1952: Orange Bowl, Georgia Tech 17, Baylor 14
1953: Sugar Bowl, Georgia Tech 24, Mississippi 7
1954: Sugar Bowl, Georgia Tech 42, West Virginia 19
1955: Cotton Bowl, Georgia Tech 14, Arkansas 6
1956: Sugar Bowl, Georgia Tech 7, Pittsburgh 0
1956: Gator Bowl, Georgia Tech 21, Pittsburgh 14
1960: Gator Bowl, Arkansas 14, Georgia Tech 7
1961: Gator Bowl, Penn State 30, Georgia Tech 15
1962: Bluebonnet Bowl, Missouri 14, Georgia Tech 10

1965: Gator Bowl, Georgia Tech 31, Texas Tech 21
1967: Orange Bowl, Florida 27, Georgia Tech 12
1970: Sun Bowl, Georgia Tech 17, Texas Tech 9
1971: Peach Bowl, Mississippi 41, Georgia Tech 18
1972: Liberty Bowl, Georgia Tech 31, Iowa State 30
1978: Peach Bowl, Purdue 41, Georgia Tech 21
1985: All American Bowl, Georgia Tech 17, Michigan State 14
1991: Florida Citrus Bowl, Georgia Tech 45, Nebraska 21
1991: Aloha Bowl, Georgia Tech 18, Stanford 17
1997: Carquest Bowl, Georgia Tech 35, Virginia 30
1999: Toyota Gator Bowl, Georgia Tech 35, Notre Dame 28
2000: Peach Bowl, LSU 28, Georgia Tech 14
2000: Gator Bowl, Miami 28, Georgia Tech 13
2001: Seattle Bowl, Georgia Tech 24, Stanford 14
2002: Silicon Valley Classic, Fresno State 30, Georgia Tech 21
2004: Humanitarian Bowl, Georgia Tec 52, Tulsa 10

College Football Hall of Fame:
John Heisman, coach, 1904-19; Joe Guyon, tackle, 1912-14; Everett Strupper, halfback, 1915-17; Buck Flowers, halfback, 1916-20; Bill Fincher, end/tackle, 1916-20; Bill Alexander, coach, 1920-44; Peter Pund, center, 1926-28; Bobby Davis, tackle, 1944-47; Bobby Dodd, coach, 1945-66; Ray Beck, guard, 1948-51; George Morris, center, 1950-52; Larry Morris, center, 1951-54; Maxie Baughan, center, 1957-59; Randy Rhino, defensive back, 1972-74.

Awards: Davey O'Brien Award, 1999, Joe Hamilton.

UNIVERSITY OF GEORGIA, Athens, Georgia; nickname "Bulldogs"; colors red and black; Sanford Stadium (86,520); Southeastern Conference. Georgia began play in 1892 and joined the Southern Conference when it was organized in 1922. Georgia was in the Southern Conference through the 1932 season. In 1933, the Bulldogs joined the Southeastern Conference.

Year	Coach	W-L-T	PF	PA	Pct.	Year	Coach	W-L-T	PF	PA	Pct.
1892	Charles Herty	1-1-0	50	10	.500	1901	Billy Reynolds	1-5-2	21	171	.250
1893	Ernest Brown	2-2-1	62	71	.500	1902	Billy Reynolds	4-2-1	48	52	.643
1894	Robert Winston	5-1-0	156	20	.833	1903	M.M. Dickinson	3-4-0	65	98	.429
1895	Pop Warner	3-4-0	98	44	.429	1904	Chas. Barnard	1-5-0	68	68	.167
1896	Pop Warner	4-0-0	88	22	1.000	1905	M. M. Dickinson	1-5-0	36	197	.167
1897	Chas. McCarthy	2-1-0	56	17	.667	1906	W. W. Whitney	2-4-1	59	50	.357
1898	Chas. McCarthy	4-2-0	70	70	.667	1907	W. S. Whitney	4-3-1	103	47	.562
1899	Gordon Saussy	2-3-1	44	22	.417	1908	Branch Bocock	5-2-1	71	45	.688
1900	E. E. Jones	2-4-0	28	159	.333	1909	J. Coulter	1-4-2	14	47	.286

W. Cunningham (1910-1919) 43-18-9 .679

Year		W-L-T	PF	PA	Pct.	Year		W-L-T	PF	PA	Pct.
1910		6-2-1	281	52	.722	1915		5-2-2	245	27	.667
1911		7-1-1	147	18	.833	1916		6-3-0	121	58	.667
1912		6-1-1	151	80	.812	1917-1918		no team			
1913		6-2-0	243	55	.750	1919		4-2-3	85	27	.611
1914		3-5-1	120	126	.389						

H. Stegeman (1920-1922) 20-6-3 .741

Year		W-L-T	PF	PA	Pct.	Year		W-L-T	PF	PA	Pct.
1920		8-0-1	250	17	.944	1921		7-2-1	161	31	.750

Member of the Southern Conference (1922-1932) 38-26-4 .588

	Nat'l		Overall				Conference				Nat'l		Overall				Conference		
Year	AP	Other	W-L-T	PF	PA	Pct.	W-L-T	Pct.	Rank	Year	AP	Other	W-L-T	PF	PA	Pct.	W-L-T	Pct.	Rank
1922			5-4-1	178	77	.550	1-3-1	.300	12										

G. Woodruff (1923-1927) 30-16-1 .649

Year	AP	Other	W-L-T	PF	PA	Pct.	W-L-T	Pct.	Rank	Year	AP	Other	W-L-T	PF	PA	Pct.	W-L-T	Pct.	Rank
1923			5-3-1	74	120	.611	3-2-0	.600	10	1926			5-4-0	129	93	.556	4-2-0	.667	4
1924			7-3-0	128	61	.700	5-1-0	.833	2	1927		8	9-1-0	248	35	.900	6-1-0	.857	5
1925			4-5-0	133	91	.444	2-4-0	.333	14										

Harry Mehre (1928-1937) 59-34-6 .639

Year	AP	Other	W-L-T	PF	PA	Pct.	W-L-T	Pct.	Rank	Year	AP	Other	W-L-T	PF	PA	Pct.	W-L-T	Pct.	Rank
1928			4-5-0	122	113	.444	2-4-0	.333	16	1931		6	8-2-0	201	117	.800	6-1-0	.857	4
1929			6-4-0	155	97	.600	4-2-0	.667	7	1932			2-5-2	122	116	.333	2-4-2	.375	15
1930			7-2-1	185	71	.750	3-2-1	.583	10										

Member of the Southeastern Conference (1933-2003) 264-177-13 .596

Year	AP	Other	W-L-T	PF	PA	Pct.	W-L-T	Pct.	Rank	Year	AP	Other	W-L-T	PF	PA	Pct.	W-L-T	Pct.	Rank
1933			8-2-0	148	86	.800	3-1-0	.750	3	1936			5-4-1	115	159	.550	3-3-0	.500	6
1934			7-3-0	141	56	.700	3-2-0	.600	5	1937			6-3-2	151	64	.636	1-2-2	.400	10
1935			6-4-0	169	88	.600	2-4-0	.333	11										

Joel Hunt (1938) 5-4-1 .550

Year	AP	Other	W-L-T	PF	PA	Pct.	W-L-T	Pct.	Rank
1938			5-4-1	145	1443	.550	1-2-1	.375	9

Wallace Butts (1939-1960) 140-86-9 .615

Year	AP	Other	W-L-T	PF	PA	Pct.	W-L-T	Pct.	Rank	Year	AP	Other	W-L-T	PF	PA	Pct.	W-L-T	Pct.	Rank
1939			5-6-0	113	98	.455	1-3-0	.250	9	1950			6-3-3	178	105	.625	3-2-1	.583	6
1940			5-4-1	209	134	.550	2-3-1	.417	7	1951			5-5-0	176	184	.500	2-4-0	.333	9
1941	14		9-1-1	319	85	.864	3-1-1	.700	4	1952			7-4-0	226	208	.636	4-3-0	.571	5
1942	2		11-1-0	376	76	.917	6-1-0	.857	1	1953			3-8-0	155	250	.292	1-5-0	.167	10
1943			6-4-0	264	153	.600	0-3-0	.000	4	1954			6-3-1	89	89	.650	5-3-0	.625	5
1944			7-3-0	269	130	.700	4-2-0	.667	3	1955			4-6-0	173	170	.400	2-5-0	.286	11
1945	18		9-2-0	314	100	.818	4-2-0	.667	4	1956			3-6-1	66	162	.350	1-6-0	.143	12
1946	3		11-0-0	392	110	1.000	5-0-0	1.000	1	1957			3-7-0	93	150	.300	3-4-0	.429	9
1947			7-4-1	212	135	.682	3-3-0	.500	4	1958			4-6-0	196	114	.400	2-4-0	.333	10
1948	8		9-2-0	306	141	.818	6-0-0	1.000	1	1959	5	5	10-1-0	228	89	.909	7-0-0	1.000	1
1949			4-6-1	177	134	.591	1-4-1	.250	10	1960			6-4-0	174	118	.600	4-3-0	.571	5

Johnny Griffith (1961-1963) 10-16-4 .400

Year	AP	Other	W-L-T	PF	PA	Pct.	W-L-T	Pct.	Rank	Year	AP	Other	W-L-T	PF	PA	Pct.	W-L-T	Pct.	Rank
1961			3-7-0	84	177	.300	2-5-0	.286	9	1963			4-5-1	133	151	.450	2-4-0	333	9
1962			3-4-3	109	174	.450	2-3-1	.417	7										

Vince Dooley (1964-1988) 201-77-10 .715

Year	AP	Other	W-L-T	PF	PA	Pct.	W-L-T	Pct.	Rank	Year	AP	Other	W-L-T	PF	PA	Pct.	W-L-T	Pct.	Rank
1964			7-3-1	130	98	.682	4-2-0	.667	2	1977			5-6-0	157	191	.455	2-4-0	.333	7
1965		15	6-4-0	186	158	.600	3-3-0	.500	6	1978	16	15	9-2-1	290	187	.792	5-0-1	.917	2
1966	4	4	10-1-0	235	98	.909	6-0-0	1.000	1	1979			6-5-0	206	189	.545	5-1-0	.833	2
1967		18	7-4-0	257	119	.636	4-2-0	.667	3	1980	1	1	12-0-0	333	137	1.000	6-0-0	1.000	1
1968	8	4	8-1-2	284	114	.818	5-0-1	.917	1	1981	6	5	10-2-0	372	122	.833	6-0-0	1.000	1
1969			5-5-1	218	146	.500	2-3-1	.417	6	1982	4	4	11-1-0	338	160	.917	6-0-0	1.000	1
1970			5-5-0	242	153	.500	3-3-0	.500	5	1983	4	4	10-1-1	274	158	.875	5-1-0	.833	2
1971	7	8	11-1-0	360	115	.917	5-1-0	.833	2	1984			7-4-1	263	230	.682	4-2-0	.667	3
1972			7-4-0	174	163	.636	4-3-0	.571	5	1985			7-3-2	297	171	.667	3-2-1	.583	4
1973			7-4-1	224	166	.682	3-4-0	.429	5	1986			8-4-0	308	233	.667	4-2-0	.667	2
1974			6-6-0	327	285	.500	4-2-0	.667	2	1987	13	14	9-3-0	311	204	.750	4-2-0	.667	3
1975	19	19	9-3-0	299	197	.750	5-1-0	.833	2	1988	15	15	9-3-0	358	212	.750	5-2-0	.714	3
1976	10	10	10-2-0	327	145	.833	5-1-0	.833											

Ray Goff (1989-1995) 46-34-1 .574

Year										Year									
1989			6-6-0	251	198	.500	4-3-0	.571	4	1993			5-6-0	328	289	.455	2-6-0	.250	8
1990			4-7-0	185	293	.364	2-5-0	.286	6	1994			6-4-1	351	283	.591	3-4-1	.438	6
1991	17	19	9-3-0	336	219	.750	4-3-0	.571	4	1995			6-6-0	260	290	.500	3-5-0	.375	6
1992	8	8	10-2-0	373	155	.833	6-2-0	.750	2										

Jim Donnan (1996-2000) 40-19-0 .678

Year										Year									
1996			5-6-0	230	257	.455	3-5-0	.375	7	1999	16	16	8-4-0	367	332	.667	5-3-0	.625	5
1997	10	10	10-2-0	380	204	.833	6-2-0	.750	2	2000	20	17	8-4-0	329	212	.667	5-3-0	.625	3
1998	14	14	9-3-0	327	255	.750	6-2-0	.750	3										

Mark Richt (2001-2003) 32-8-0 .800

Year										Year									
2001	22	25	8-4-0	315	228	.667	5-3-0	.625	3	2003	7	6	11-3-0	371	203	.786	6-2-0	.750	3
2002	3	3	13-1-0	450	212	.929	8-1-0	.889	1										

Won-loss record by decades:

1892-99	23-14-2	.615	1930-39	59-35-7	.619	1970-79	75-38-2	.661	
1900-09	24-38-8	.400	1940-49	78-27-4	.734	1980-89	89-27-4	.758	
1910-19	43-18-9	.679	1950-59	51-49-5	.506	1990-00	72-43-1	.625	
1920-29	60-31-4	.653	1960-69	59-38-8	.600	2000-03	40-12-0	.769	

Historical record: 673-370-54 .638

Post-season won-loss record 22-16-3 .573

1942: Orange Bowl, Georgia 40, TCU 26
1943: Rose Bowl, Georgia 9, UCLA 0
1946: Oil Bowl, Georgia 20, Tulsa 6
1947: Sugar Bowl, Georgia 20, North Carolina 10
1948: Gator Bowl, Georgia 20, Maryland 20
1949: Orange Bowl, Texas 41, Georgia 28
1950: President's Cup, Texas A&M 40, Georgia 20
1960: Orange Bowl, Georgia 14, Missouri 0
1964: Sun Bowl, Georgia 7, Texas Tech 0
1966: Cotton Bowl, Georgia 24, SMU 9
1967: Liberty Bowl, NC State 14, Georgia 7
1969: Sugar Bowl, Arkansas 16, Georgia 2
1969: Sun Bowl, Nebraska 45, Georgia 6
1971: Gator Bowl, Georgia 7, North Carolina 3
1973: Peach Bowl, Georgia 17, Maryland 16
1974: Tangerine Bowl, Miami (OH) 21, Georgia 10
1976: Cotton Bowl, Arkansas 31, Georgia 10
1977: Sugar Bowl, Pittsburgh 27, Georgia 3
1978: Bluebonnet Bowl, Stanford 25, Georgia 22

1981: Sugar Bowl, Georgia 17, Notre Dame 10
1982: Sugar Bowl, Pittsburgh 24, Georgia 20
1983: Sugar Bowl, Penn State 27, Georgia 23
1984: Cotton Bowl, Georgia 10, Texas 9
1984: Citrus Bowl, Georgia 17, Florida State 17
1985: Sun Bowl, Georgia 13, Arizona 13
1986: Hall of Fame Bowl, Boston College 27, Georgia 24
1987: Liberty Bowl, Georgia 20, Arkansas 17
1989: Gator Bowl, Georgia 34, Michigan State 27
1989: Peach Bowl, Syracuse 19, Georgia 18
1991: Independence Bowl, Georgia 24, Arkansas 15
1993: Florida Citrus Bowl, Georgia 21, Ohio State 14
1995: Peach Bowl, Virginia 34, Georgia 27
1998: Outback Bowl, Georgia 33, Wisconsin 6
1998: Peach Bowl, Georgia 35, Virginia 33
2000: Outback Bowl, Georgia 28, Purdue 25
2000: Oahu Bowl, Georgia 37, Virginia 14
2001: Music City Bowl, Boston College 20, Georgia 16
2002: SEC Championship, Georgia 30, Arkansas 3
2003: Sugar Bowl, Georgia 26, Florida State 13
2003: SEC Championship, LSU 34, Georgia 13
2004: Capital One Bowl, Georgia 34, Purdue 27

College Football Hall of Fame:
Pop Warner, coach, 1895-96; Bob McWhorter, halfback, 1910-13; Vernon Smith, end, 1929-31; Bill Hartman, fullback, 1935-37; Wally Butts, coach, 1939-60; Frank Sinkwich, halfback, 1940-42; Charley Trippi, halfback, 1942-46; Fran Tarkenton, quarterback, 1958-60; Vince Dooley, coach, 1964-88; Bill Stanfill, defensive tackle, 1966-68; Herschel Walker, halfback, 1980-82; Terry Hoage, safety, 1980-83; John Rauch, quarterback, 1945-48.

Awards: Heisman Trophy: 1942, Frank Sinkwich; 1982, Herschel Walker; Maxwell Award: 1946, Charlie Trippi; 1982: Herschel Walker; Doak Walker Award: 1992, Garrison Hearst; Outland Trophy: 1968. Bill Stanfill; Nagurski Award: 1998, Champ Bailey; Camp Award: 1982, Herschel Walker.

UNIVERSITY OF HAWAII, Honolulu, Hawaii; nickname "Warriors"; colors green, black, white, and silver; Aloha Stadium (50,000); Western Athletic Conference. Hawaii has had a football team since 1909. In the earliest years, it scheduled mainly local teams along with an occasional West Coast team. In 1946, Hawaii joined the NCAA and in 1979 it joined the Western Athletic Conference. The data below cover only the NCAA period from 1946 on.

NCAA years as an independent (1946-1978)

Year	W-L-T	PF	PA	Pct		Year	W-L-T	PF	PA	Pct.
					Tom Kaulukukui (1946-1950) 34-18-3 .645					
1946	8-2-0	275	93	.800		1949	6-3-0	362	210	.667
1947	8-5-0	294	240	.615		1950	5-4-2	290	256	.545
1948	7-4-1	366	289	.625						
					Archi Kodros (1951) 4-7-0 .364					
1951	4-7-0	226	292	.364						
					Hank Vasconcellos (1952-1960) 43-46-3 .484					
1952	5-5-2	285	280	.500		1957	4-4-1	152	96	.500
1953	5-6-0	189	216	.455		1958	5-7-0	139	260	.417
1954	4-4-0	133	178	.500		1959	3-6-0	100	174	.333
1955	7-4-0	187	166	.636		1960	3-7-0	113	200	.300
1956	7-3-0	291	113	.700		1961	no team			
					Jim Asato (1962-1964) 15-12-0 .556					
1962	6-2-0	112	63	.750		1964	4-5-0	104	131	.444
1963	5-5-0	160	167	.500						
					Clark Shaughnessy (1965) 1-8-1 .150					
1965	1-8-1	85	227	.150						
					Phil Sarboe (1966) 4-6-0 .400					
1966	4-6-0	110	245	.400						
					Don King (1967) 6-4-0 .600					
1967	6-4-0	205	118	.600						
					David Holmes (1968-1973) 46-17-1 .727					
1968	7-3-0	312	199	.700		1971	7-4-0	255	225	.636
1969	6-3-1	313	235	.650		1972	8-3-0	282	214	.727
1970	9-2-0	276	149	.818		1973	9-2-0	205	152	.818
					Larry Price (1974-1976) 15-18-0 .455					
1974	6-5-0	175	211	.545		1976	3-8-0	154	377	.273
1975	6-5-0	180	201	.545						
					Dick Tomey (1977-1986) 63-46-3 .576					
1977	5-6-0	250	233	.455		1978	6-5-0	251	280	.545

Member Western Athletic Conference (1979-2003) 90-101-3 .472

Year	Nat'l AP Other	Overall W-L-T	PF	PA	Pct.	Conference W-L-T	Pct.	Rank	Year	Nat'l AP Other	Overall W-L-T	PF	PA	Pct.	Conference W-L-T	Pct.	Rank
1979		6-5-0	330	213	.545	3-4-0	.429	4	1983		5-5-1	251	236	.500	3-3-1	.500	5
1980		8-3-0	260	212	.727	4-3-0	.571	3	1984		7-4-0	217	181	.636	5-2-0	.714	2
1981		9-2-0	328	130	.818	6-1-0	.857	2	1985		4-6-2	269	262	.417	4-3-1	.563	4
1982		6-5-0	240	230	.545	4-4-0	.500	5	1986		7-5-0	237	235	.583	4-4-0	.500	4
						Bob Wagner (1987-1995) 58-49-3 .541											
1987		5-7-0	337	299	.417	3-5-0	.375	6	1992	20 20	11-2-0	421	317	.846	6-2-0	.750	1
1988		9-3-0	383	283	.750	5-3-0	.625	3	1993		6-6-0	393	357	.500	3-5-0	.375	8
1989		9-3-1	470	281	.731	5-2-1	.688	3	1994		3-8-1	260	273	.292	0-8-0	.000	10
1990		7-5-0	374	257	.583	4-4-0	.500	5	1995		4-8-0	285	401	.333	2-6-0	.250	9
1991		4-7-1	335	388	.375	3-5-0	.375	5									
						Fred Von Appen (1996-1998) 5-31-0 .139											
1996		2-10-0	161	433	.167	1-7-0	.125	7	1998		0-12-0	149	422	.000	0-8-0	.000	15
1997		3-9-0	189	308	.250	1-7-0	.125	8									
						June Jones (1999-2003) 40-25-0 .615											
1999		9-4-0	371	349	.692	5-2-0	.714	1	2001		9-3-0	438	318	.750	5-3-0	.625	4
2000		3-9-0	294	399	.250	2-6-0	.250	6	2002		10-4-0	502	389	.714	7-1-0	.875	2
									2003	·	9-5-0	486	427	.643	5-3-0	.750	2

Won-loss record by decades:

1946-49	29-14-1	.670	1970-79	65-45-0	.591	2000-03	31-21-0	.596
1950-59	49-50-5	.495	1980-89	69-43-4	.612			
1960-69	42-43-2	.494	1990-99	49-71-2	.410			

Historic record 334-287-14 .537
Post-season won-lost record 3-2-0 .600
1989: Aloha Bowl, Michigan State 33, Hawaii 13
1992: Holiday Bowl, Hawaii 27, Illinois 17

1999: Oahu Bowl, Hawaii 23, Oregon State 17.
2002: Oahu Bowl, Tulane 36, Hawaii 28
2003: Hawaii Bowl, Hawaii 54, Houston 48

College Football Hall of Fame: Clark Shaughnessy, coach, 1965

UNIVERSITY OF HOUSTON, Houston, TX; nickname "Cougars"; colors scarlet and white with navy trim; Robertson Stadium (32,000); Conference USA. Houston began play in 1946. In 1976, Houston joined the Southwest Conference and played there until the SWC was disbanded after the 1995 season. In 1996, Houston was one of the founding members of Conference USA.

Early years as an independent (1946-1975)

Jewell Wallace (1946-1947) 7-14-0 .333

Year	Nat'l AP	Nat'l Other	Overall W-L-T	PF	PA	Pct	Conf W-L-T	Conf Pct.	Rank	Year	Nat'l AP	Nat'l Other	Overall W-L-T	PF	PA	Pct.	Conf W-L-T	Conf Pct.	Rank
1946			4-6-0	140	146	.400				1947			3-8-0	96	214	.273			

Clyde Lee (1948-1954) 37-32-2 .535

Year	Nat'l AP	Nat'l Other	Overall W-L-T	PF	PA	Pct	Conf W-L-T	Conf Pct.	Rank	Year	Nat'l AP	Nat'l Other	Overall W-L-T	PF	PA	Pct.	Conf W-L-T	Conf Pct.	Rank
1948			5-6-0	149	182	.455				1950			4-6-0	233	200	.400			
1949			5-4-1	229	169	.550													

Member of the Missouri Valley Conference (1951-1959) 23-10-1 .691

Year	Nat'l AP	Nat'l Other	Overall W-L-T	PF	PA	Pct	Conf W-L-T	Conf Pct.	Rank	Year	Nat'l AP	Nat'l Other	Overall W-L-T	PF	PA	Pct.	Conf W-L-T	Conf Pct.	Rank
1951			6-5-0	221	207	.545	2-2-0	.500	4	1953			4-4-1	189	185	.500	1-2-0	.333	3
1952		19	8-2-0	180	80	.800	3-0-0	1.000	1	1954			5-5-0	125	203	.500	3-1-0	.750	2

Bill Meek (1955-1956) 13-6-1 .675

Year	Nat'l AP	Nat'l Other	Overall W-L-T	PF	PA	Pct	Conf W-L-T	Conf Pct.	Rank	Year	Nat'l AP	Nat'l Other	Overall W-L-T	PF	PA	Pct.	Conf W-L-T	Conf Pct.	Rank
1955			6-4-0	176	139	.600	2-2-0	.500	3	1956			7-2-1	185	90	.750	4-0-0	1.000	1

Harold Lahar (1957-1961) 24-23-2 .510

Year	Nat'l AP	Nat'l Other	Overall W-L-T	PF	PA	Pct	Conf W-L-T	Conf Pct.	Rank	Year	Nat'l AP	Nat'l Other	Overall W-L-T	PF	PA	Pct.	Conf W-L-T	Conf Pct.	Rank
1957			5-4-1	113	141	.550	3-0-1	.875	1	1959			3-7-0	105	170	.300	3-1-0	.750	1
1958			5-4-0	209	152	.556	2-2-0	.500	2										

Houston reverts to independent status

Year	Nat'l AP	Nat'l Other	Overall W-L-T	PF	PA	Pct	Conf W-L-T	Conf Pct.	Rank	Year	Nat'l AP	Nat'l Other	Overall W-L-T	PF	PA	Pct.	Conf W-L-T	Conf Pct.	Rank
1960			6-4-0	141	150	.600				1961			5-4-1	144	138	.550			

Bill Yeoman (1962-1986) 160-108-8 .594

Year	Nat'l AP	Nat'l Other	Overall W-L-T	PF	PA	Pct	Conf W-L-T	Conf Pct.	Rank	Year	Nat'l AP	Nat'l Other	Overall W-L-T	PF	PA	Pct.	Conf W-L-T	Conf Pct.	Rank
1962			7-4-0	198	171	.636				1969	12	16	9-2-0	386	199	.818			
1963			2-8-0	149	208	.200				1970	19	13	8-3-0	295	173	.727			
1964			2-6-1	115	174	.278				1971	17	14	9-3-0	322	170	.750			
1965			4-5-1	159	174	.450				1972			6-4-1	325	202	.591			
1966		17	8-2-0	335	125	.800				1973	9	13	11-1-0	316	135	.917			
1967		19	7-3-0	222	122	.700				1974	19	11	8-3-1	249	154	.708			
1968	18	20	6-2-2	425	154	.700				1975			2-8-0	185	244	.200			

Member of the Southwest Conference (1976-1995) 80-70-4 .532

Year	Nat'l AP	Nat'l Other	Overall W-L-T	PF	PA	Pct.	Conf W-L-T	Conf Pct.	Rank	Year	Nat'l AP	Nat'l Other	Overall W-L-T	PF	PA	Pct.	Conf W-L-T	Conf Pct.	Rank
1976	4	4	10-2-0	313	217	.833	7-1-0	.875	1	1982			5-5-1	215	682	.500	4-3-1	.562	4
1977			6-5-0	282	259	.545	4-4-0	.500	4	1983			4-7-0	225	294	.364	3-5-0	.375	7
1978	10	11	9-3-0	330	178	.750	7-1-0	.875	1	1984			7-5-0	238	222	.583	6-2-0	.750	1
1979	5	5	11-1-0	278	121	.917	7-1-0	.875	1	1985			4-7-0	253	339	.364	3-5-0	.375	5
1980			7-5-0	201	190	.583	5-3-0	.625	2	1986			1-10-0	125	267	.091	0-8-0	.000	7
1981			7-4-1	238	174	.625	5-2-1	.688	3										

Jack Pardee (1987-1989) 22-11-1 .662

Year	Nat'l AP	Nat'l Other	Overall W-L-T	PF	PA	Pct.	Conf W-L-T	Conf Pct.	Rank	Year	Nat'l AP	Nat'l Other	Overall W-L-T	PF	PA	Pct.	Conf W-L-T	Conf Pct.	Rank
1987			4-6-1	284	292	.409	2-4-1	.357	7	1989	14		9-2-0	589	150	.818	5-2-0	.750	*
1988	18		9-3-0	474	209	.750	5-2-0	.750	*										

*Houston ineligible for title due to NCAA infractions.

John Jenkins (1990-1992) 18-15-0 .545

Year	Nat'l AP	Nat'l Other	Overall W-L-T	PF	PA	Pct.	Conf W-L-T	Conf Pct.	Rank	Year	Nat'l AP	Nat'l Other	Overall W-L-T	PF	PA	Pct.	Conf W-L-T	Conf Pct.	Rank
1990	10		10-1-0	511	303	.909	7-1-0	.875	**	1992			4-7-0	378	386	.364	2-5-0	.286	6
1991			4-7-0	353	344	.364	3-5-0	.375	7										

**Houston ineligible for title due to NCAA infractions.

Kim Helton (1993-1999) 24-53-1 .314

Year	Nat'l AP	Nat'l Other	Overall W-L-T	PF	PA	Pct.	Conf W-L-T	Conf Pct.	Rank	Year	Nat'l AP	Nat'l Other	Overall W-L-T	PF	PA	Pct.	Conf W-L-T	Conf Pct.	Rank
1993			1-9-1	171	392	.139	1-5-1	.214	7	1995			2-9-0	188	360	.182	2-5-0	.286	6
1994			1-10-0	115	402	.091	1-6-0	.143	6										

Member of Conference USA (1996-2003) 20-23-0 .465

Year	Nat'l AP	Nat'l Other	Overall W-L-T	PF	PA	Pct.	Conf W-L-T	Conf Pct.	Rank	Year	Nat'l AP	Nat'l Other	Overall W-L-T	PF	PA	Pct.	Conf W-L-T	Conf Pct.	Rank
1996			7-5-0	361	341	.583	4-1-0	.800	1	1998			3-8-0	254	317	.273	2-4-0	.333	5
1997			3-8-0	216	410	.273	2-4-0	.333	4	1999			7-4-0	254	209	.636	3-3-0	.500	6

Dana Dimel (2000-2002) 8-26-0 .235

Year	Nat'l AP	Nat'l Other	Overall W-L-T	PF	PA	Pct.	Conf W-L-T	Conf Pct.	Rank	Year	Nat'l AP	Nat'l Other	Overall W-L-T	PF	PA	Pct.	Conf W-L-T	Conf Pct.	Rank
2000			3-8-0	211	370	.273	2-5-0	.286	7	2002			5-7-0	320	393	.417	3-5-0	.375	8
2001			0-11-0	190	432	.000	0-7-0	.000	10										

Art Briles (2003) 7-6-0 .538

Year	Nat'l AP	Nat'l Other	Overall W-L-T	PF	PA	Pct.	Conf W-L-T	Conf Pct.	Rank
2003			7-6-0	448	468	.538	4-4-0	.500	6

Won-loss record by decades:

1946-49	17-24-1	.417	1970-79	80-33-2	.704	2000-03	15-32-0	.2319
1950-59	53-43-3	.551	1980-89	57-54-3	.513			
1960-69	56-40-5	.579	1990-99	42-68-1	.383			

Historic record: 313-288-14 .520

Post-season won-loss record: 7-7-1 .500

1952: Salad Bowl, Houston 26, Dayton 21
1962: Tangerine Bowl, Houston 49, Miami (OH) 21
1969: Bluebonnet Bowl, Houston 36, Auburn 7
1971: Bluebonnet Bowl, Colorado 29, Houston 17
1973: Bluebonnet Bowl, Houston 47, Tulane 7
1974: Bluebonnet Bowl, Houston 31, NC State 31
1977: Cotton Bowl, Houston 30, Maryland 21

1979: Cotton Bowl, Notre Dame 35, Houston 34
1980: Cotton Bowl, Houston 17, Nebraska 14
1980: Garden State Bowl, Houston 35, Navy 0
1981: Sun Bowl, Oklahoma 40, Houston 14
1985: Cotton Bowl, Boston College 45, Houston 28
1988: Aloha Bowl, Wash. State 24, Houston 22
1996: St. Jude Liberty Bowl, Syracuse 30, Houston 17.
2003: Hawaii Bowl, Hawaii 54, Houston 48

College Football Hall of Fame: Bill Yeoman, coach, 1957-86.

Awards: Heisman Trophy: 1989, Andre Ware; Davey O'Brien Award: 1989, Andre Ware; Lombardi Award: 1976, Wilson Whitley; Baugh Trophy: 1990, David Klinger.

UNIVERSITY OF IDAHO, Moscow, Idaho; nickname "Vandals"; colors silver and gold; Martin Stadium, Pullman, Washington (37,600); Sun Belt Conference. Idaho began play in 1894. In 1922, Idaho joined the Pacific Coast Conference and played in that conference through the 1958 season, after which the PCC disbanded and the AAWU was formed, excluding Idaho, Washington State, Oregon, and Oregon State. Idaho was an independent between 1959 and 1964. In 1965, Idaho joined the Big Sky Conference and played there through the 1995 season. Between 1996 and 2000, Idaho was a member of the Big West Conference. When that conference disbanded after the 2000 season, Idaho joined the newly formed Sun Belt Conference.

Early years as an independent (1894-1897) and as a member of the Northwest Conference (1898-1921)

Year	Coach	W-L-T	PF	PA	Pct.	Year	Coach	W-L-T	PF	PA	Pct.
1894	G. E. Higgins	0-2-0	6	18	.000	1908	J.Middleton	2-2-2	85	42	.500
1895	G. E. Higgins	0-1-0	4	10	.000	1909	John Grogan	3-4-0	86	126	.429
1896	no team					1910	J. G. Griffith	4-2-0	112	69	.667
1897	G. E. Higgins	0-1-0	6	10	.000	1911	J. G. Griffith	4-3-0	98	75	.571
1898	no team					1912	J. G. Griffith	2-2-0	26	33	.500
1899	--- Morse	0-4-0	6	27	.000	1913	J. G. Griffith	2-3-1	93	59	.417
1900	F. D. Herbold	1-0-0	12	6	1.000	1914	J. G. Griffith	2-3-1	12	45	.417
1901	F. D. Herbold	3-2-1	38	25	.583	1915	C. Rademacher	1-4-1	16	118	.250
1902	J. G. Griffith	1-3-1	23	43	.300	1916	W. Bleasmaster	3-5-0	131	159	.375
1903	J. G. Griffith	3-1-0	96	5	.750	1917	W. Bleasmaster	2-3-0	36	62	.400
1904	J. G. Griffith	2-1-0	36	12	.667	1918	no team				
1905	J. G. Griffith	5-0-0	113	2	1.000	1919	R. Hutchinson	2-3-0	26	91	.400
1906	J. G. Griffith	2-4-0	47	49	.333	1920	Thomas Kelley	4-2-0	75	48	.667
1907	J. Middleton	4-1-1	68	25	.750	1921	Thomas Kelley	4-3-1	98	68	.562

Member of Pacific Coast Conference (1922-1958) 31-122-5 .212

Year	Nat'l AP Other	Overall W-L-T	PF	PA	Pct.	Conference W-L-T	Pct.	Rank	Year	Nat'l AP Other	Overall W-L-T	PF	PA	Pct.	Conference W-L-T	Pct.	Rank
							Robert Matthews (1922-1925) 16-14-2 .531										
1922		3-5-0	74	51	.375	0-4-0	.000	8	1924		5-2-1	117	32	.688	4-2-0	.667	4
1923		5-2-1	164	26	.688	2-2-1	.500	3	1925		3-5-0	79	153	.375	2-3-0	.400	6
							Charles Erb (1926-1928) 10-10-4 .500										
1926		3-4-1	75	81	.438	1-4-0	.200	6	1928		3-4-1	93	125	.438	2-3-0	.400	6
1927		4-2-2	120	48	.625	2-0-2	.750	2									
							Leo Calland (1929-1934) 20-30-0 .400										
1929		4-5-0	168	248	.444	1-4-0	.200	7	1932		3-5-0	114	97	.375	1-4-0	.200	8
1930		4-7-0	154	176	.364	0-5-0	.000	10	1933		3-4-0	103	82	.429	1-4-0	.200	9
1931		3-4-0	75	106	.429	1-4-0	.200	8	1934		3-5-0	77	120	.167	1-4-0	.000	8
							Ted Bank (1935-1940) 18-33-3 .361										
1935		2-7-0	52	87	.222	1-5-0	.167	9	1938		6-3-1	133	94	.650	2-3-1	.417	7
1936		3-7-0	69	133	.300	0-4-0	.000	10	1939		2-6-0	45	125	.250	0-3-0	.000	9
1937		4-3-1	35	53	.562	2-2-0	.500	5	1940		1-7-1	30	214	.167	0-4-0	.000	10
							Francis Schmidt (1941-1942) 7-11-1 .395										
1941		4-5-0	123	145	.444	0-4-0	.000	10	1943		no team						
1942		3-6-1	97	181	.350	1-5-0	.167	9	1944		no team						
							J. A. Brown (1945-1946) 2-15-0 .118										
1945		1-7-0	78	175	.125	1-5-0	.167	8	1946		1-8-0	65	247	.111	0-5-0	.000	10
							Dixie Howell (1947-1950) 13-20-1 .397										
1947		4-4-0	92	138	.500	1-4-0	.200	9	1949		3-5-0	220	270	.375	1-4-0	.200	9
1948		3-6-0	154	156	.333	1-5-0	.167	9	1950		3-5-1	180	212	.389	1-1-1	.500	5
							Babe Curfman (1951-1953) 7-19-1 .278										
1951		2-7-0	109	182	.222	0-3-0	.000	9	1953		1-8-0	64	207	.111	0-3-0	.000	9
1952		4-4-1	185	143	.500	1-3-0	.250	8									
							Skip Stahley (1954-1961) 22-51-2 .307										
1954		4-5-0	96	143	.444	1-2-0	.333	7	1957		4-4-1	140	108	.500	0-3-0	.000	9
1955		2-7-0	128	174	.222	0-4-0	.000	9	1958		4-5-0	114	139	.444	0-3-0	.000	9
1956		4-5-0	198	215	.444	0-4-0	.000	9									
							Independent Status (1959-1964)										
1959		1-9-0	79	293	.100				1961		2-7-1	65	351	.100			
1960		1-9-0	104	256	.100												
							Dee Andros (1962-1964) 11-16-1 .411										
1962		2-6-1	108	209	.278				1964		4-6-0	144	143	.400			
1963		5-4-0	186	148	.555												
							Member Big Sky Conference (Division I-AA) (1965-1995) 118-72-3 .619										
							Stephen Musseau (1965-1967) 13-17-0 .433										
1965		5-5-0	201	125	.500	3-1-0	.750	1	1967		4-6-0	156	332	.400	2-2-0	.500	2
1966		4-6-0	182	165	.400	3-1-0	.750	2									
							Y. C. McNease (1968-1969) 7-13-0 .350										
1968		5-5-0	246	301	.500	3-1-0	.750	1	1969		2-8-0	206	346	.200	1-3-0	.250	4
							Don Robbins (1970-1973) 20-24-0 .455										
1970		4-7-0	226	335	.364	2-2-0	.500	3	1972		4-7-0	165	278	.364	2-3-0	.400	5
1971		8-3-0	227	171	.727	4-1-0	.800	1	1973		4-7-0	262	319	.364	3-2-0	.600	2

Ed Troxel (1974-1977) 16-25-3 .398

Year	W-L-T	PF	PA	Pct	Conf	ConfPct	Rk	Year	W-L-T	PF	PA	Pct	Conf	ConfPct	Rk
1974	2-8-1	198	280	.227	2-2-1	.500	3	1976	7-4-0	224	236	.636	5-1-0	.833	2
1975	4-5-2	251	316	.455	2-2-2	.500	4	1977	3-8-0	245	365	.272	2-4-0	.333	5

Jerry Davitch (1978-1981) 15-29-0 .341

1978	2-9-0	162	401	.181	2-5-0	.286	5	1980	6-5-0	266	228	.545	4-3-0	.571	2
1979	4-7-0	210	268	.364	2-5-0	.286	5	1981	3-8-0	310	254	.272	0-7-0	.000	8

Dennis Erickson (1982-1985) 32-15-0 .681

1982	9-4-0	397	299	.692	5-2-0	.714	3	1984	6-5-0	363	283	.545	4-3-0	.571	3
1983	8-3-0	342	257	.727	4-3-0	.571	3	1985	9-3-0	441	247	.750	6-1-0	.857	1

Keith Gilbertson (1986-1988) 28-9-0 .757

1986	8-4-0	307	244	.667	5-2-0	.714	4	1988	11-2-0	392	302	.846	7-1-0	.875	1
1987	9-3-0	358	339	.750	7-1-0	.875	1								

John Smith (1989-1995) 53-21-0 .716

1989	9-3-0	407	314	.750	8-0-0	1.000	1	1992	9-3-0	446	224	.750	6-1-0	.857	1
1990	9-4-0	477	342	.692	6-2-0	.750	2	1993	11-3-0	593	353	.786	5-2-0	.714	2
1991	6-5-0	375	313	.545	4-4-0	.500	4	1994	9-3-0	493	289	.750	5-2-0	.714	2

Chris Tormey (1995-1999) 33-23-0 .589

1995	6-5-0	287	209	.545	4-3-0	.571	2								

Member of the Big West Conference (1996-2000) 16-10-0 .615

1996	6-5-0	374	296	.545	3-2-0	.600	3	1998	9-3-0	392	317	.750	4-1-0	.800	1
1997	5-6-0	302	263	.455	2-3-0	.400	4	1999	7-4-0	304	283	.636	4-2-0	.667	2

Tom Cable (2000-2003) 11-35-0 .239

2000	5-6-0	321	377	.455	3-2-0	.600	3								

Member of the Sun Belt Conference (2001-2003) 5-14-0 .263

2001	1-10-0	313	495	.091	1-5-0	.167	7	2003	3-9-0	248	314	.250	3-4-0	.429	4
2002	2-10-0	285	428	.167	1-5-0	.167	7								

Won-loss record by decades:

1894-99	0- 8-0	.000	1930-39	33-51-3	.397	1970-79	42-65-3	.395
1900-09	26-18-5	.582	1940-49	20-48-2	.300	1980-89	78-40-0	.661
1910-19	22-28-3	.443	1950-59	29-59-3	.335	1990-99	77-41-0	.653
1920-29	38-34-7	.529	1960-69	34-62-2	.357	2000-03	11-35-0	.239

Historical record (1894-2003) 410-489-28 .457

Post-season won-loss record: 7-11-0 .389
1982: IAA Playoffs, Idaho 21, Montana 7
1982: IAA Playoffs, Eastern Kentucky 38, Idaho 30
1985: IAA Playoffs, Eastern Washington 42, Idaho 38
1986: IAA Playoffs, Nevada-Reno 27, Idaho 7
1987: IAA Playoffs, Weber State 59, Idaho 30
1988: IAA Playoffs, Idaho 38, Montana 19
1988: IAA Playoffs, Idaho 38, Northwestern St. 30
1988: IAA Playoffs, Furman 38, Idaho 7
1989: IAA Playoffs, E. Illinois 38, Idaho 21

1990: IAA Playoffs, Idaho 41, SW Missouri St. 35
1990: IAA Playoffs, Ga. Southern 28, Idaho 27
1992: IAA Playoffs, McNeese St. 23, Idaho 20
1993: IAA Playoffs: Idaho 34, NW Louisiana 31
1993: IAA Playoffs, Idaho 21, Boston University 14
1993: IAA Playoffs, Youngstown St. 35, Idaho 16
1994: IAA Playoffs, McNeese St. 38, Idaho 21
1995: IAA Playoffs, McNeese St. 33, Idaho 3
1998: Humanitarian Bowl, Idaho 42, So. Mississippi 35

College Football Hall of Fame:
Francis Schmidt, coach, 1941-42.

UNIVERSITY OF ILLINOIS, Champaign-Urbana, Illinois; nickname "Fighting Illini"; colors orange and blue; Memorial Stadium (70,904); Big Ten Conference. Illinois began play in 1890 and then was one of the founding members of the Big Ten Conference in 1896. Following Big Ten rules, conference won-loss records prior to 1946 ignore ties.

Early years (1890-1895)

Year	W-L-T	PF	PA	Pct.
1890	1-2-0	23	84	.333

Scott Williams (1890) 1-2-0 .333

Robert Lackey (1891) 6-0-0 1.000

Year	W-L-T	PF	PA	Pct.
1891	6-0-0	142	24	1.000

E. K. Hall (1892-1893) 12-5-5 .659

Year	W-L-T	PF	PA	Pct.
1892	9-3-2	240	86	.714
1893	3-2-3	156	106	.562

No coach (1894) 5-3-0 .625

Year	W-L-T	PF	PA	Pct.
1895	5-3-0	182	66	.625

George A. Huff (1895-1899) 21-16-3 .562

Year	W-L-T	PF	PA	Pct.
1895	4-2-1	215	28	.643

Member of the Big Ten Conference (1896-2003) 314-339-32 .482

Year	Nat'l AP	Other	Overall W-L-T	PF	PA	Pct.	Conference W-L-T	Pct.	Rank	Year	Nat'l AP	Other	Overall W-L-T	PF	PA	Pct.	Conference W-L-T	Pct.	Rank
1896			4-2-1	148	36	.643	0-2-1	.000	6	1898			4-5-0	83	78	.444	1-1-0	.500	4
1897			6-2-0	190	45	.750	1-1-0	.500	4	1899			3-5-1	40	96	.438	0-3-0	.000	6

Fred I. Smith (1900) 7-3-2 .667

Year	Overall W-L-T	PF	PA	Pct.	Conf W-L-T	Pct.	Rank
1900	7-3-2	184	67	.667	1-3-2	.250	8

Edgar G. Holt (1901-1902) 18-4-1 .804

Year	Overall W-L-T	PF	PA	Pct.	Conf W-L-T	Pct.	Rank	Year	Overall W-L-T	PF	PA	Pct.	Conf W-L-T	Pct.	Rank
1901	8-2-0	243	39	.800	4-2-0	.667	4	1902	10-2-1	380	44	.808	4-2-0	.667	4

George Woodruff (1903) 8-6-0 .571

Year	Overall W-L-T	PF	PA	Pct.	Conf W-L-T	Pct.	Rank
1903	8-6-0	352	117	.571	1-5-0	.167	7

Student coaches (1904) 9-2-1 .792

Year	Overall W-L-T	PF	PA	Pct.	Conf W-L-T	Pct.	Rank
1904	9-2-1	232	42	.792	3-1-1	.750	4

Fred Lowenthal (1905) 5-4-0 .556

Year	Overall W-L-T	PF	PA	Pct.	Conf W-L-T	Pct.	Rank
1905	5-4-0	84	136	.556	0-3-0	.000	6

Justa Lindgren (1906) 1-3-1 .300

Year	Overall W-L-T	PF	PA	Pct.	Conf W-L-T	Pct.	Rank
1906	1-3-1	20	107	.300	1-3-0	.250	5

Arthur R. Hall (1907-1912) 27-10-3 .712

Year	Overall W-L-T	PF	PA	Pct.	Conf W-L-T	Pct.	Rank	Year	Overall W-L-T	PF	PA	Pct.	Conf W-L-T	Pct.	Rank
1907	3-2-0	64	81	.600	3-2-0	.600	3	1910	7-0-0	89	0	1.000	4-0-0	1.000	1
1908	5-1-1	140	37	.786	4-1-0	.800	2	1911	4-2-1	81	51	.643	2-2-1	.500	4
1909	5-2-0	115	39	.714	3-1-0	.750	3	1912	3-3-1	122	48	.500	1-3-1	.250	6

Bob Zuppke (1913-1941) 131-81-13 .611

Year	Nat'l AP	Other	Overall W-L-T	PF	PA	Pct.	Conf W-L-T	Pct.	Rank	Year	Nat'l AP	Other	Overall W-L-T	PF	PA	Pct.	Conf W-L-T	Pct.	Rank
1913			4-2-1	108	54	.643	2-2-1	.500	5	1928		6	7-1-0	145	16	.875	4-1-0	.800	1
1914			7-0-0	224	22	1.000	6-0-0	1.000	1	1929		5	6-1-1	155	27	.812	3-1-1	.750	2
1915			5-0-2	183	25	.857	3-0-2	1.000	1	1930			3-5-0	78	97	.375	1-4-0	.200	8
1916			3-3-1	74	58	.500	2-2-1	.500	4	1931			2-6-1	58	140	.278	0-6-1	.000	9
1917			5-2-1	134	40	.688	2-2-1	.500	5	1932			5-4-0	96	101	.556	2-4-0	.333	7
1918			5-2-0	86	14	.714	4-0-0	1.000	1	1933			5-3-0	77	32	.625	3-2-0	.600	5
1919			6-1-0	91	48	.857	6-1-0	.857	1	1934		4	7-1-0	103	43	.875	4-1-0	.800	3
1920			5-2-0	97	37	.714	4-2-0	.667	4	1935			3-5-0	59	54	.375	1-4-0	.200	9
1921			3-4-0	88	51	.429	1-4-0	.200	8	1936			4-3-1	57	76	.562	2-2-1	.500	6
1922			2-5-0	26	60	.286	2-4-0	.333	6	1937			3-3-2	59	45	.500	2-3-0	.400	8
1923		1	8-0-0	136	20	1.000	5-0-0	1.000	1	1938			3-5-0	110	88	.375	2-3-0	.400	7
1924		4	6-1-1	204	71	.812	3-1-1	.750	2	1939			3-4-1	75	74	.438	3-3-0	.500	6
1925			5-3-0	98	59	.625	2-2-0	.500	4	1940			1-7-0	71	144	.125	0-5-0	.000	9
1926		10	6-2-0	121	46	.750	2-2-0	.500	6	1941			2-6-0	112	163	.250	0-5-0	.000	9
1927		1	7-0-1	152	24	.938	5-0-0	1.000	1										

Ray Eliot (1942-1959) 83-73-11 .530

Year	Nat'l AP	Other	Overall W-L-T	PF	PA	Pct.	Conf W-L-T	Pct.	Rank	Year	Nat'l AP	Other	Overall W-L-T	PF	PA	Pct.	Conf W-L-T	Pct.	Rank
1942			6-4-0	227	126	.600	3-2-0	.600	3	1951	4	3	9-0-1	220	83	.900	5-0-1	.917	1
1943			3-7-0	154	308	.300	2-4-0	.333	6	1952			4-5-0	194	175	.444	2-5-0	.286	6
1944	15		5-4-1	273	149	.550	3-3-0	.500	6	1953	7	7	7-1-1	228	133	.833	5-1-0	.833	1
1945			2-6-1	93	104	.278	1-4-1	.200	7	1954			1-8-0	103	180	.111	0-6-0	.000	10
1946	5		8-2-0	217	105	.800	6-1-0	.857	1	1955			5-3-1	149	114	.611	3-3-1	.500	5
1947			5-3-1	204	102	.611	3-3-0	.500	3	1956			2-5-2	124	154	.333	1-4-2	.429	7
1948			3-6-0	135	140	.333	2-5-0	.286	8	1957			4-5-0	167	133	.444	3-4-0	.429	7
1949			3-4-2	149	140	.444	3-3-1	.500	5	1958			4-5-0	144	150	.444	4-3-0	.571	6
1950	13	11	7-2-0	137	56	.778	4-2-0	.667	4	1959	13	12	5-3-1	111	93	.611	4-2-1	.643	3

Pete Elliott (1960-1966) 31-34-1 .477

Year	Overall W-L-T	PF	PA	Pct.	Conf W-L-T	Pct.	Rank	Year	Nat'l AP	Overall W-L-T	PF	PA	Pct.	Conf W-L-T	Pct.	Rank
1960	5-4-0	140	117	.556	2-4-0	.333	5	1964	16	6-3-0	142	100	.667	4-3-0	.571	4
1961	0-9-0	53	289	.000	0-7-0	.000	9	1965		6-4-0	235	118	.600	4-3-0	.571	5
1962	2-7-0	75	234	.222	2-5-0	.286	8	1966		4-6-0	173	193	.400	4-3-0	.571	3
1963	3 (Other 4) 8-1-1	170	96	.850	5-1-1	.786	1									

Jim Valek (1967-1970) 8-32-0 .200

Year	Rk	Rk	W-L-T	PF	PA	Pct	Conf	Pct	Rk	Year	Rk	Rk	W-L-T	PF	PA	Pct	Conf	Pct	Rk
1967			4-6-0	143	213	.400	3-4-0	.429	5	1969			0-10-0	106	397	.000	0-7-0	.000	10
1968			1-9-0	107	333	.100	1-6-0	.143	8	1970			3-7-0	165	279	.300	1-6-0	.143	9

Bob Blackman (1971-1976) 29-36-1 .447

Year	Rk	Rk	W-L-T	PF	PA	Pct	Conf	Pct	Rk	Year	Rk	Rk	W-L-T	PF	PA	Pct	Conf	Pct	Rk
1971			5-6-0	163	238	.455	5-3-0	.625	3	1974			6-4-1	210	206	.591	4-3-1	.562	5
1972			3-8-0	197	277	.273	3-5-0	.375	6	1975			5-6-0	229	260	.455	4-4-0	.500	3
1973			5-6-0	164	157	.455	4-4-0	.500	4	1976			5-6-0	235	248	.455	4-4-0	.500	3

Gary Moeller (1977-1979) 6-24-3 .227

Year	Rk	Rk	W-L-T	PF	PA	Pct	Conf	Pct	Rk	Year	Rk	Rk	W-L-T	PF	PA	Pct	Conf	Pct	Rk
1977			3-8-0	141	292	.273	2-6-0	.250	8	1979			2-8-1	156	266	.227	1-6-1	.188	9
1978			1-8-2	103	317	.182	0-6-2	.125	9										

Mike White (1980-1987) 47-41-3 .533

Year	Rk	Rk	W-L-T	PF	PA	Pct	Conf	Pct	Rk	Year	Rk	Rk	W-L-T	PF	PA	Pct	Conf	Pct	Rk
1980			3-7-1	241	326	.318	3-5-0	.375	6	1984			7-4-0	323	209	.636	6-3-0	.667	2
1981			7-4-0	287	288	.636	6-3-0	.667	3	1985			6-5-1	304	334	.542	5-2-1	.688	3
1982			7-5-0	338	229	.583	6-3-0	.667	4	1986			4-7-0	189	299	.364	3-5-0	.375	6
1983	10	10	10-2-0	347	213	.833	9-0-0	1.000	1	1987			3-7-1	153	208	.318	2-5-1	.312	8

John Mackovic (1988-1991) 30-17-1 .635

Year	Rk	Rk	W-L-T	PF	PA	Pct	Conf	Pct	Rk	Year	Rk	Rk	W-L-T	PF	PA	Pct	Conf	Pct	Rk
1988			6-5-1	245	243	.542	5-2-1	.688	3	1990	25	24	8-4-0	293	246	.667	6-2-0	.750	1
1989	10	10	10-2-0	332	182	.833	7-1-0	.875	2	1991			6-6-0	264	188	.500	4-4-0	.500	5

Lou Tepper (1992-1996) 25-30-2 .456

Year	Rk	Rk	W-L-T	PF	PA	Pct	Conf	Pct	Rk	Year	Rk	Rk	W-L-T	PF	PA	Pct	Conf	Pct	Rk
1992			6-5-1	235	228	.542	4-3-1	.562	4	1995			5-5-1	254	229	.500	3-4-1	.438	7
1993			5-6-0	204	210	.455	5-3-0	.625	4	1996			2-9-0	190	372	.182	1-7-0	.125	9
1994			7-5-0	309	210	.583	4-4-0	.500	4										

Ron Turner (1997-2003) 32-48-0 .400

Year	Rk	Rk	W-L-T	PF	PA	Pct	Conf	Pct	Rk	Year	Rk	Rk	W-L-T	PF	PA	Pct	Conf	Pct	Rk
1997			0-11-0	119	368	.000	0-8-0	.000	11	2000			5-6-0	294	286	.455	2-6-0	.250	9
1998			3-8-0	149	216	.273	2-6-0	.250	7	2001	12	12	10-1-0	356	238	.909	7-1-0	.875	1
1999	24	25	8-4-0	388	275	.667	4-4-0	.500	6	2002			5-7-0	346	307	.417	4-4-0	.500	5
										2003			1-11-0	203	398	.083	0-8-0	.000	11

Won-loss record by decades:

1890-99	45-26-8	.620	1930-39	38-39-5	.494	1970-79	38-67-4	.367		
1900-09	61-27-6	.681	1940-49	38-49-5	.440	1980-89	63-48-4	.565		
1910-19	49-15-7	.739	1950-59	48-37-6	.560	1990-99	50-63-2	.443		
1920-29	55-19-3	.734	1960-69	36-59-1	.380	2000-03	21-25-0	.457		

Historic record 542-474-51 .532

Post-season won-loss record: 6-8-0 .429

1947: Rose Bowl, Illinois 45, UCLA 14
1952: Rose Bowl, Illinois 40, Stanford 7
1964: Rose Bowl, Illinois 17, Washington 7
1982: Liberty Bowl, Alabama 21, Illinois 15
1984: Rose Bowl, UCLA 45, Illinois 9
1985: Peach Bowl, Army 31, Illinois 29
1988: All American Bowl, Florida 14, Illinois 10

1990: Citrus Bowl, Illinois 31, Virginia 21
1991: Hall of Fame Bowl, Clemson 30, Illinois 0
1991: John Hancock Bowl, UCLA 6, Illinois 3
1992: Holiday Bowl, Hawaii 27, Illinois 17
1994: Liberty Bowl, Illinois 30, East Carolina 0
1999: Micron.com Bowl, Illinois 63, Virginia 21
2001: Sugar Bowl, LSU 47, Illinois 34

College Football Hall of Fame:
Ed Hall, coach, 1892-93; George Woodruff, coach, 1903; Bob Zuppke, coach, 1913-1941; Bart McComber, halfback, 1914-1916; Chuck Carney, end, 1918-21; Red Grange, halfback, 1923-25; Bernie Shively, guard, 1924-26; Alex Agase, guard, 1941-46; Buddy Young, halfback, 1944-46; Al Brosky, safety, 1950-52; J.C. Caroline, halfback, 1953-54; Dick Butkus, center/linebacker, 1962-64; Jim Grabowski, fullback, 1963-65; Bob Blackman, coach, 1971-76.

Awards: Butkus Award: 1994, Dana Howard; 1995, Kevin Hardy; Baugh Trophy, 1989, Jeff George.

UNIVERSITY OF INDIANA, Bloomington, Indiana; nickname "Hoosiers"; colors cream and crimson; Memorial Stadium (52,354); Big Ten conference. Indiana began play in 1887 and then became a member of the Big Ten Conference in the 1898 season. Following Big Ten rules, conference won-loss percents before 1946 ignore ties.

Early years (1887-1897)

Year	Coach	W-L-T	PF	PA	Pct.	Year	Coach	W-L-T	PF	PA	Pct.
1887	A. B. Woodford	0-1-0	8	10	.000	1893	no coach	1-4-1	54	184	.250
1888	A. B. Woodford	0-0-1	n.a.	n.a.	.500`	1894	Ferbert*	0-4-0	10	124	.000
1889	Evans Wollen	0-1-0	2	40	.000	1895	Dana Osgood**	4-3-1	110	92	.562
1890	no team					1896	M. G. Gonterman	6-2-0	186	60	.750
1891	Billy Herod	1-5-0	46	225	.167	1897	M. G. Gonterman	6-1-1	148	32	.812
1892	no coach	2-2-0	47	102	.500						

*Huddleston also acted as coach during the 1894 season.
**Wren also acted as coach during the 1895 season

James Horne (1898-1904) 33-21-5 .602

Year	Nat'l AP	Other	Overall W-L-T	PF	PA	Pct.	Conference W-L-T	Pct.	Rank	Year	Nat'l AP	Other	Overall W-L-T	PF	PA	Pct.	Conference W-L-T	Pct.	Rank
1898			4-1-2	90	30	.643				1899			6-2-0	134	33	.750			

Member of the Big Ten Conference (1900-2003) 183-404-24 .319

Year	Nat'l AP	Other	Overall W-L-T	PF	PA	Pct.	Conference W-L-T	Pct.	Rank	Year	Nat'l AP	Other	Overall W-L-T	PF	PA	Pct.	Conference W-L-T	Pct.	Rank
1900			4-2-2	110	29	.625	1-2-1	.333	7	1903			4-4-0	148	124	.500	1-2-0	.333	6
1901			6-3-0	214	87	.667	1-2-0	.333	6	1904			6-4-0	73	111	.600	0-3-0	.000	7
1902			3-5-1	94	207	.389	0-4-0	.000	7										

James Sheldon (1905-1913) 34-26-3 .563

Year	Nat'l AP	Other	Overall W-L-T	PF	PA	Pct.	Conference W-L-T	Pct.	Rank	Year	Nat'l AP	Other	Overall W-L-T	PF	PA	Pct.	Conference W-L-T	Pct.	Rank
1905			8-1-1	240	38	.850	0-1-1	.000	6	1910			6-1-0	111	6	.786	3-1-0	.750	3
1906			4-2-0	109	46	.667	0-2-0	.000	6	1911			3-3-1	74	46	.500	0-3-1	.000	7
1907			2-3-1	85	57	.417	0-3-0	.000	5	1912			2-5-0	79	101	.286	0-5-0	.000	8
1908			2-4-0	43	70	.333	1-3-0	.250	4	1913			3-4-0	90	162	.429	2-4-0	.333	6
1909			4-3-0	129	53	.571	1-3-0	.250	5										

Clarence Childs (1914-1915) 6-7-1 .464

Year	Nat'l AP	Other	Overall W-L-T	PF	PA	Pct.	Conference W-L-T	Pct.	Rank	Year	Nat'l AP	Other	Overall W-L-T	PF	PA	Pct.	Conference W-L-T	Pct.	Rank
1914			3-4-0	104	131	.429	1-4-0	.200	8	1915			3-3-1	85	43	.500	1-3-0	.250	8

Ewald Stiehm (1916-1921) 20-18-1 .526

Year	Nat'l AP	Other	Overall W-L-T	PF	PA	Pct.	Conference W-L-T	Pct.	Rank	Year	Nat'l AP	Other	Overall W-L-T	PF	PA	Pct.	Conference W-L-T	Pct.	Rank
1916			2-4-1	51	90	.357	0-3-1	.000	8	1919			3-4-0	70	64	.429	0-2-0	.000	9
1917			5-2-0	225	59	.714	1-2-0	.333	7	1920			5-2-0	129	48	.714	3-1-0	.750	3
1918			2-2-0	64	31	.500	0-0-0			1921			3-4-0	86	94	.429	1-2-0	.333	6

James Herron (1922) 1-4-2 .286

Year	Nat'l AP	Other	Overall W-L-T	PF	PA	Pct.	Conference W-L-T	Pct.	Rank
1922			1-4-2	21	113	.286	0-2-1	.000	9

William Ingram (1923-1925) 10-12-1 .457

Year	Nat'l AP	Other	Overall W-L-T	PF	PA	Pct.	Conference W-L-T	Pct.	Rank	Year	Nat'l AP	Other	Overall W-L-T	PF	PA	Pct.	Conference W-L-T	Pct.	Rank
1923			3-4-0	48	117	.429	2-2-0	.500	5	1925			3-4-1	102	115	.438	0-3-1	.000	9
1924			4-4-0	147	100	.500	1-3-0	.250	7										

Pat Page (1926-1930) 14-24-3 .388

Year	Nat'l AP	Other	Overall W-L-T	PF	PA	Pct.	Conference W-L-T	Pct.	Rank	Year	Nat'l AP	Other	Overall W-L-T	PF	PA	Pct.	Conference W-L-T	Pct.	Rank
1926			3-5-0	80	137	.375	0-4-0	.000	8	1929			2-6-1	58	133	.278	1-3-1	.250	7
1927			3-4-1	104	107	.438	1-2-1	.333	8	1930			2-5-1	28	121	.312	1-3-0	.250	6
1928			4-4-0	55	68	.500	2-4-0	.333	9										

Billy Hayes (1931-1933) 8-14-4 .385

Year	Nat'l AP	Other	Overall W-L-T	PF	PA	Pct.	Conference W-L-T	Pct.	Rank	Year	Nat'l AP	Other	Overall W-L-T	PF	PA	Pct.	Conference W-L-T	Pct.	Rank
1931			4-5-1	57	98	.450	3-4-1	.438	7	1933			1-5-2	25	96	.250	0-3-2	.000	8
1932			3-4-1	65	76	.312	1-4-1	.200	8										

Bo McMillin (1934-1947) 63-48-11 .561

Year	Nat'l AP	Other	Overall W-L-T	PF	PA	Pct.	Conference W-L-T	Pct.	Rank	Year	Nat'l AP	Other	Overall W-L-T	PF	PA	Pct.	Conference W-L-T	Pct.	Rank
1934			3-3-2	67	110	.500	1-3-1	.250	8	1941			2-6-0	101	126	.250	1-3-0	.250	7
1935			4-3-1	70	54	.562	2-2-1	.500	4	1942			7-3-0	256	79	.700	2-2-0	.500	5
1936			5-2-1	123	63	.688	3-1-1	.750	4	1943			4-4-2	193	106	.500	2-3-1	.400	4
1937			5-3-0	72	32	.625	3-2-0	.600	3	1944			7-3-0	292	79	.700	4-3-0	.571	5
1938			1-6-1	21	67	.188	1-4-0	.200	9	1945	4		9-0-1	279	56	.950	5-0-1	1.000	1
1939			2-4-2	70	96	.375	2-3-0	.400	7	1946	20		6-3-0	129	95	.667	4-2-0	.667	3
1940			3-5-0	69	100	.375	2-3-0	.400	6	1947			5-3-1	156	102	.611	2-3-1	.417	6

Clyde Smith (1948-1951) 8-27-1 .236

Year	Nat'l AP	Other	Overall W-L-T	PF	PA	Pct.	Conference W-L-T	Pct.	Rank	Year	Nat'l AP	Other	Overall W-L-T	PF	PA	Pct.	Conference W-L-T	Pct.	Rank
1948			2-7-0	75	217	.222	2-4-0	.333	5	1950			3-5-1	99	155	.389	1-4-0	.200	8
1949			1-8-0	117	254	.111	0-6-0	.000	9	1951			2-7-0	118	191	.222	1-5-0	.167	8

Bernie Crimmins (1952-1956) 13-32-0 .289

Year	Nat'l AP	Other	Overall W-L-T	PF	PA	Pct.	Conference W-L-T	Pct.	Rank	Year	Nat'l AP	Other	Overall W-L-T	PF	PA	Pct.	Conference W-L-T	Pct.	Rank
1952			2-7-0	143	224	.222	1-5-0	.167	9	1955			3-6-0	91	150	.333	1-5-0	.167	9
1953			2-7-0	119	227	.222	1-5-0	.167	9	1956			3-6-0	129	263	.333	1-5-0	.167	10
1954			3-6-0	110	143	.333	2-4-0	.333	7										

Bob Hicks (1957) 1-8-0 .111

Year	Nat'l AP	Other	Overall W-L-T	PF	PA	Pct.	Conference W-L-T	Pct.	Rank
1957			1-8-0	47	307	.111	0-6-0	.000	9

Phil Dickens (1958-1964) 19-42-2 .317

Year	Nat'l AP	Other	Overall W-L-T	PF	PA	Pct.	Conference W-L-T	Pct.	Rank	Year	Nat'l AP	Other	Overall W-L-T	PF	PA	Pct.	Conference W-L-T	Pct.	Rank
1958			5-3-1	81	141	.611	3-2-1	.583	5	1962			3-6-0	126	140	.333	1-5-0	.167	9
1959			4-4-1	142	101	.500	2-4-1	.357	8	1963			3-6-0	151	188	.333	1-5-0	.167	10
1960*			0-9-0	69	243	.000	*	*	*	1964			2-7-0	154	188	.222	1-5-0	.167	9
1961			2-7-0	96	162	.222	0-6-0	.000	9										

*Indiana ineligible for title in 1960 and one conference win in 1960 was later forfeited.

John Pont (1965-1972) 31-51-1 .379

Year			Record	PF	PA	Pct	Conf	Conf%	Fin	Year			Record	PF	PA	Pct	Conf	Conf%	Fin
1965			2-8-0	134	225	.200	1-6-0	.143	9	1969			4-6-0	252	242	.400	3-4-0	.429	5
1966			1-8-1	104	229	.150	1-5-1	.214	9	1970			1-9-0	102	300	.100	1-6-0	.143	9
1967	4	6	9-2-0	197	159	.818	6-1-0	.857	1	1971			3-8-0	152	260	.273	2-6-0	.250	9
1968			6-4-0	250	262	.600	4-3-0	.571	5	1972			5-6-0	204	272	.455	3-5-0	.375	6

Lee Corso (1973-1982) 41-68-2 .375

Year			Record	PF	PA	Pct	Conf	Conf%	Fin	Year			Record	PF	PA	Pct	Conf	Conf%	Fin
1973			2-9-0	151	271	.182	0-8-0	.000	9	1978			4-7-0	228	290	.364	3-5-0	.375	7
1974			1-10-0	166	292	.091	1-7-0	.125	10	1979	19	16	8-4-0	314	252	.667	5-3-0	.625	4
1975			2-8-1	104	254	.227	1-6-1	.188	10	1980			6-5-0	255	235	.545	3-5-0	.375	6
1976			5-6-0	130	254	.455	4-4-0	.500	3	1981			3-8-0	146	293	.273	3-6-0	.333	8
1977			5-5-1	205	228	.500	4-3-0	.563	3	1982			5-6-0	203	250	.455	4-5-0	.444	6

Sam Wyche (1983) 3-8-0 .272

Year			Record	PF	PA	Pct	Conf	Conf%	Fin
1983			3-8-0	201	360	.272	2-7-0	.222	8

Bill Mallory (1984-1996) 69-77-3 .473

Year			Record	PF	PA	Pct	Conf	Conf%	Fin	Year			Record	PF	PA	Pct	Conf	Conf%	Fin
1984			0-11-0	185	338	.000	0-9-0	.000	10	1991			7-4-1	305	224	.625	5-3-0	.625	3
1985			4-7-0	251	340	.364	1-7-0	.125	9	1992			5-6-0	177	197	.455	3-5-0	.375	6
1986			6-6-0	273	227	.500	3-5-0	.375	6	1993			8-4-0	259	187	.667	5-3-0	.625	4
1987		20	8-4-0	283	238	.667	6-2-0	.750	2	1994			7-4-0	296	291	.636	4-4-0	.500	5
1988	20	19	8-3-1	396	235	.708	5-3-0	.625	5	1995			2-9-0	159	326	.182	0-8-0	.000	11
1989			5-6-0	289	262	.455	3-5-0	.375	6	1996			3-8-0	242	291	.273	1-7-0	.125	9
1990			6-5-1	329	238	.542	3-4-1	.438	7										

Cam Cameron (1997-2001) 18-37-0 .327

Year			Record	PF	PA	Pct	Conf	Conf%	Fin	Year			Record	PF	PA	Pct	Conf	Conf%	Fin
1997			2-9-0	120	359	.182	1-7-0	.125	9	2000			3-8-0	337	427	.273	2-6-0	.250	9
1998			4-7-0	245	305	.364	2-6-0	.250	7	2001			5-6-0	305	298	.455	4-4-0	.500	4
1999			4-7-0	291	386	.364	3-5-0	.375	8										

Gerry DiNardo (2002-2003) 5-19-0 .208

Year			Record	PF	PA	Pct	Conf	Conf%	Fin	Year			Record	PF	PA	Pct	Conf	Conf%	Fin
2002			3-9-0	258	445	.250	1-7-0	.125	10	2003			2-10-0	177	388	.167	1-7-0	.125	9

Won-loss record by decades:

1887-89	0- 2-1	.167	1920-29	31-41-5	.435	1960-69	32-63-1	.339
1890-99	30-24-5	.551	1930-39	30-40-12	.439	1970-79	36-72-2	.336
1900-09	43-31-5	.575	1940-49	46-42-4	.522	1980-89	48-64-1	.429
1910-19	32-32-3	.500	1950-59	28-59-3	.328	1990-99	48-63-2	.434
						2000-03	13-33-0	.283

Historic record: 417-566-44 .427

Post-season won-loss record 3-5-0 .375

1968: Rose Bowl, USC 14, Indiana 3	1988: Liberty Bowl, Indiana 34, South Carolina 10
1979: Holiday Bowl, Indiana 38, BYU 37	1990: Peach Bowl, Auburn 27, Indiana 23
1986: All American Bowl, Florida State 27, Indiana 13	1991: Copper Bowl, Indiana 24, Baylor 0
1987: Peach Bowl, Tennessee 27, Indiana 22	1993: Independence Bowl, Va. Tech 45, Indiana 20

College Football Hall of Fame:
Zora Clevenger, halfback, 1900-03; Bill Ingram, coach, 1923-25; John Tavener, center, 1941-44; Pete Pihos, end/fullback, 1942-46; George Taliaferro, halfback, 1945-48.

Awards: Maxwell Award: 1989, Anthony Thompson; Camp Award: 1989, Anthony Thompson.

IOWA STATE UNIVERSITY, Ames, Iowa; nickname "Cyclones"; colors cardinal and gold; Jack Trice Stadium (43,000); Big Twelve Conference. Iowa State began play in 1892 and then joined the Missouri Valley Conference in 1908. Iowa State played in the MVC through the 1927 season and then moved with five other MVC teams into the newly organized Big Six Conference, which evolved into the Big Eight over time. In 1996, the Big Eight became the Big Twelve, with Iowa State a charter member.

Early years as an independent (1892-1907)

Year	Nat'l AP	Other	W-L-T	PF	PA	Pct.		Year	Nat'l AP	Other	W-L-T	PF	PA	Pct.
							Ira Brownlie (1892) 1-0-1 .750							
1892		1-0-1	36	6	.750									
							W. Finney (1893) 0-3-0 .000							
1893		0-3-0	14	56	.000									
							Bert German (1894) 5-1-0 .833							
1894		5-1-0	180	24	.833									
							Pop Warner (1895-1899) 18-8-0 .692							
1895		3-3-0	82	48	.500		1898		3-2-0	49	50	.600	
1896		8-2-0	303	46	.800		1899*		1-0-0	23	0	1.000	
1897		3-1-0	40	22	.750								
							Joe Meyers* (1899) 4-4-1 .500							
1899*		4-4-1	95	38	.500									

*Warner coached the first game of the 1899 season, and Meyers coached the remaining nine games.

C. E. Woodruff (1900) 2-5-1 .312

| 1900 | | 2-5-1 | 38 | 100 | .312 |

Edgar Clinton (1901) 2-6-2 .300

| 1901 | | 2-6-2 | 56 | 127 | .300 |

A. W. Ristine (1902-1906) 36-10-1 .766

1902		6-3-1	246	56	.650		1905		6-3-0	203	93	.667
1903		8-1-0	202	59	.889		1906		9-1-0	268	30	.900
1904		7-2-0	248	48	.778

Clyde Williams (1907-1912) 33-14-2 .694

| 1907 | | 7-1-0 | 142 | 40 | .875 |

Member of the Missouri Valley Conference (1908-1927) 45-33-7 .571

Year	AP	Other	W-L-T	PF	PA	Pct.	W-L-T	Pct.	Rank	Year	AP	Other	W-L-T	PF	PA	Pct.	W-L-T	Pct.	Rank
1908			6-3-0	186	50	.667	2-1-0	.667	2	1911			6-1-1	88	20	.812	2-0-1	.833	1
1909			4-3-1	82	59	.562	0-2-1	.167	6	1912			6-2-0	155	45	.750	2-0-0	1.000	1
1910			4-4-0	37	85	.500	2-2-0	.500	4										

Homer Hubbard (1913-1914) 8-7-0 .533

| 1913 | | | 4-4-0 | 112 | 119 | .500 | 2-2-0 | .500 | 4 | 1914 | | | 4-3-0 | 167 | 78 | .571 | 2-1-0 | .667 | 3 |

Charles Mayser (1915-1919) 21-11-2 .647

1915			6-2-0	129	50	.750	2-1-0	.667	3	1918			0-3-0	0	38	.000	conference inactive		
1916			5-2-1	106	36	.688	2-1-1	.625	3	1919			5-2-1	73	20	.688	3-1-1	.700	2
1917			5-2-0	129	20	.714	3-1-0	.750	2										

Norman Paine (1920) 4-4-0 .500

| 1920 | | | 4-4-0 | 98 | 48 | .500 | 3-2-0 | .600 | 3 |

Maury Kent (1921) 4-4-0 .500

| 1921 | | | 4-4-0 | 87 | 74 | .500 | 3-4-0 | .429 | 6 |

Sam Willaman (1922-1925) 14-15-3 .384

| 1922 | | | 2-6-0 | 51 | 124 | .250 | 2-4-0 | .333 | 5 | 1924 | | | 4-3-1 | 87 | 68 | .562 | 3-2-0 | .600 | 5 |
| 1923 | | | 4-3-1 | 121 | 93 | .562 | 3-2-1 | .583 | 4 | 1925 | | | 4-3-1 | 107 | 94 | .562 | 3-2-1 | .583 | 3 |

Noel Workman (1926-1930) 11-27-3 .305

| 1926 | | | 4-3-1 | 51 | 60 | .562 | 3-3-1 | .500 | 6 | 1927 | | | 4-3-1 | 77 | 78 | .562 | 3-2-0 | .600 | 4 |

Member of the Big Six (later the Big Seven, Big Eight) Conference (1928-1995) 124-277-22 .319

| 1928 | | | 2-5-1 | 39 | 67 | .312 | 2-2-1 | .500 | 4 | 1930 | | | 0-9-0 | 64 | 134 | .000 | 0-5-0 | .000 | 6 |
| 1929 | | | 1-7-0 | 54 | 135 | .125 | 0-5-0 | .000 | 6 | | | | | | | | | | |

George Veenker (1931-1936) 21-22-8 .490

1931			5-3-0	72	74	.625	3-1-0	.750	2	1934			5-3-1	132	66	.611	1-3-1	.300	5
1932			3-4-1	105	101	.438	0-4-1	.100	6	1935			2-4-3	82	101	.389	1-3-1	.300	5
1933			3-5-1	73	120	.389	1-4-0	.200	5	1936			3-3-2	92	112	.500	1-3-1	.300	5

Jim Yeager (1937-1940) 16-19-1 .458

| 1937 | | | 3-6-0 | 50 | 161 | .333 | 1-4-0 | .200 | 5 | 1939 | | | 2-7-0 | 50 | 117 | .222 | 1-4-0 | .200 | 4 |
| 1938 | | | 7-1-1 | 125 | 64 | .833 | 3-1-1 | .700 | 2 | 1940 | | | 4-5-0 | 118 | 132 | .444 | 2-3-0 | .400 | 4 |

Ray Donels (1941-1942) 3-8-1 .292

| 1941 | | | 2-6-1 | 85 | 181 | .278 | 0-4-1 | .100 | 6 | 1942* | | | 1-2-0 | 19 | 60 | .333 | 0-1-0 | .000 | * |

Mike Michalske (1942-1946) 18-18-3 .500

1942*			2-4-0	75	117	.333	1-3-0	.250	5	1945			4-3-1	156	97	.562	2-2-1	.500	3
1943			4-4-0	147	104	.500	3-2-0	.600	2	1946			2-6-1	77	239	.278	1-4-0	.200	5
1944			6-1-1	203	39	.812	3-1-1	.700	2										

*Donels coached the first three games of the 1942 season, and Michalske coached the last six.

Abe Stuber (1947-1953) 24-38-3 .393

Year	W-L-T	PF	PA	Pct	Conf	Conf Pct	Place	Year	Rank	W-L-T	PF	PA	Pct	Conf	Conf Pct	Place
1947	3-6-0	111	141	.333	1-4-0	.200	5	1951		4-4-1	211	216	.500	2-4-0	.333	4
1948	4-6-0	116	197	.400	2-4-0	.333	5	1952		3-6-0	158	189	.333	1-5-0	.167	6
1949	5-3-1	169	134	.611	3-3-0	.500	3	1953		2-7-0	120	211	.222	1-5-0	.167	7
1950	3-6-1	174	200	.350	2-3-1	.417	5									

V. DiFrancesca (1954-1956) 6-21-1 .232

Year	W-L-T	PF	PA	Pct	Conf	Conf Pct	Place	Year	Rank	W-L-T	PF	PA	Pct	Conf	Conf Pct	Place
1954	3-6-0	151	182	.333	1-5-0	.167	6	1956		2-8-0	92	256	.200	0-6-0	.000	7
1955	1-7-1	68	218	.167	1-4-1	.250	5									

J. A. Myers (1957) 4-5-1 .450

Year	W-L-T	PF	PA	Pct	Conf	Conf Pct	Place
1957	4-5-1	142	160	.450	2-4-0	.333	5

Clay Stapleton (1958-1967) 42-53-4 .444

Year	W-L-T	PF	PA	Pct	Conf	Conf Pct	Place	Year	W-L-T	PF	PA	Pct	Conf	Conf Pct	Place
1958	4-6-0	127	88	.400	0-6-0	.000	7	1963	4-5-0	129	143	.444	3-4-0	.429	4
1959	7-3-0	248	80	.700	3-3-0	.500	3	1964	1-8-1	72	155	.150	0-7-0	.000	8
1960	7-3-0	185	139	.700	4-3-0	.571	4	1965	5-4-1	178	147	.550	3-3-1	.500	4
1961	5-5-0	151	133	.500	3-4-0	.429	5	1966	2-6-2	160	207	.300	2-3-2	.429	6
1962	5-5-0	235	235	.500	3-4-0	.429	5	1967	2-8-0	86	275	.200	1-6-0	.143	7

Johnny Majors (1968-1972) 24-30-1 .445

Year	W-L-T	PF	PA	Pct	Conf	Conf Pct	Place	Year	Rank	W-L-T	PF	PA	Pct	Conf	Conf Pct	Place
1968	3-7-0	178	273	.300	1-6-0	.143	8	1971	17	8-4-0	337	250	.667	4-3-0	.571	4
1969	3-7-0	152	231	.300	1-6-0	.143	7	1972		5-6-1	319	218	.458	2-4-1	.357	6
1970	5-6-0	248	284	.455	1-6-0	.143	8									

Earle Bruce (1973-1978) 36-32-0 .529

Year	W-L-T	PF	PA	Pct	Conf	Conf Pct	Place	Year	Rank	W-L-T	PF	PA	Pct	Conf	Conf Pct	Place
1973	4-7-0	245	239	.364	2-5-0	.286	6	1976	19 18	8-3-0	369	216	.727	4-3-0	.571	4
1974	4-7-0	186	198	.364	2-5-0	.286	6	1977		8-4-0	249	178	.667	5-2-0	.714	2
1975	4-7-0	161	265	.364	1-6-0	.143	7	1978		8-4-0	219	188	.667	4-3-0	.571	3

Donnie Duncan (1979-1982) 18-24-2 .432

Year	W-L-T	PF	PA	Pct	Conf	Conf Pct	Place	Year	W-L-T	PF	PA	Pct	Conf	Conf Pct	Place
1979	3-8-0	137	221	.273	2-5-0	.286	5	1981	5-5-1	189	218	.500	2-4-1	.357	6
1980	6-5-0	245	184	.545	2-5-0	.286	6	1982	4-6-1	213	221	.409	1-5-1	.214	6

Jim Criner (1983-1986) 16-24-2 .405

Year	W-L-T	PF	PA	Pct	Conf	Conf Pct	Place	Year	W-L-T	PF	PA	Pct	Conf	Conf Pct	Place
1983	4-7-0	248	385	.364	3-4-0	.429	4	1985	5-6-0	155	318	.455	3-4-0	.429	5
1984	2-7-2	149	263	.273	0-5-2	.143	7	1986*	5-4-0	197	204	.556	2-3-0	.400	5

Chuck Banker (1986) 1-1-0 .500

Year	W-L-T	PF	PA	Pct	Conf	Conf Pct
1986*	1-1-0	60	40	.500	1-1-0	.500

*Criner coached the first nine games of the 1986 season, and Banker coached the last two games.

Jim Walden (1987-1994) 28-57-3 .335

Year	W-L-T	PF	PA	Pct	Conf	Conf Pct	Place	Year	W-L-T	PF	PA	Pct	Conf	Conf Pct	Place
1987	3-8-0	195	417	.273	2-5-0	.286	6	1991	3-7-1	157	266	.318	1-5-1	.214	6
1988	5-6-0	195	258	.455	3-4-0	.429	5	1992	4-7-0	231	244	.364	2-5-0	.286	6
1989	6-5-0	294	305	.545	4-3-0	.571	4	1993	3-8-0	251	324	.273	2-5-0	.286	7
1990	4-6-1	270	307	.409	2-4-1	.357	4	1994	0-10-1	192	363	.045	0-6-1	.071	7

Dan McCarney (1995-2003) 38-67-0 .362

Year	W-L-T	PF	PA	Pct	Conf	Conf Pct	Place
1995	3-8-0	264	409	.273	1-6-0	.143	7

Member of the Big Twelve Conference (1996-2003) 17-47-0 .266

Year	W-L-T	PF	PA	Pct	Conf	Conf Pct	Place	Year	Rank	W-L-T	PF	PA	Pct	Conf	Conf Pct	Place
1996	2-9-0	314	401	.182	1-7-0	.125	11	2000	25 23	9-3-0	345	322	.750	5-3-0	.625	5
1997	1-10-0	214	493	.091	1-7-0	.125	11	2001		7-5-0	309	246	.583	4-4-0	.500	5
1998	3-8-0	221	328	.273	1-7-0	.125	11	2002		7-7-0	404	406	.500	4-4-0	.500	7
1999	4-7-0	247	272	.36t4	1-7-0	.125	11	2003		2-10-0	173	437	.167	0-8-0	.000	12

Won-loss record by decades:

1892-99	28-16-2	.630	1930-39	33-45-9	.431	1970-79	57-56-1	.504	
1900-09	57-28-5	.661	1940-49	37-46-5	.449	1980-89	46-60-4	.436	
1910-19	45-25-3	.637	1950-59	33-58-4	.368	1990-99	27-80-3	.259	
1920-29	33-41-6	.450	1960-69	37-58-4	.394	2000-03	25-25-0	.500	

Historical record: 458-538-46 .462

Post-season won-loss record 1-6-0 .143

1971: Sun Bowl, LSU 33, Iowa State 15
1972: Liberty Bowl, Georgia Tech 31, Iowa State 30
1977: Peach Bowl, NC State 24, Iowa State 14
1978: Hall of Fame Bowl, Texas A&M 28, Iowa State 12
2000: Insight.com Bowl, Iowa State 37, Pittsburgh 29
2001: Independence Bowl, Alabama 14, Iowa State 13
2002: Humanitarian Bowl, Boise State 34, Iowa State 16

College Football Hall of Fame:
Pop Warner, coach, 1896-1899; Ed Bock, guard, 1936-38; Earle Bruce, coach, 1973-79.

UNIVERSITY OF IOWA, Iowa City, Iowa; nickname "Hawkeyes"; colors black and gold; Nike Kinnick Stadium (70,397); Big Ten Conference. Iowa began play in 1889 and then joined the Big Ten for the 1900 season. Iowa was also a member of the Missouri Valley Conference between 1907 and 1910. For its MVC record, see the MVC history in the Conference section. Following Big Ten rules, conference won-loss percents before 1946 ignore ties.

Early years as an independent (1889-1899)

Year	Coach	W-L-T	PF	PA	Pct.	Year	Coach	W-L-T	PF	PA	Pct.
1889	none	0-1-0	0	24	.000	1894	Roger Sherman	4-4-1	146	158	.500
1890	none	1-1-0	97	11	.500	1895	none	2-5-0	42	140	.286
1891	none	3-2-0	112	81	.600	1896	A.E. Bull	7-1-1	132	12	.833
1892	E.A. Dalton	3-2-1	124	68	.583	1897	Otto Wagonhurst	4-4-0	66	104	.500
1893	Ben Donnelly	3-4-0	178	161	.429						

Alden Knipe (1898-1902) 29-11-4 .705

1898		3-4-2	67	95	.444	1899		8-0-1	221	5	.944

Member of the Big Ten (1900-2003) 258-326-23 .444

	Nat'l		Overall				Conference				Nat'l		Overall				Conference		
Year	AP	Other	W-L-T	PF	PA	Pct.	W-L-T	Pct.	Rank	Year	AP	Other	W-L-T	PF	PA	Pct.	W-L-T	Pct.	Rank
1900			7-0-1	311	12	.938	2-0-1	1.000	1	1902			5-4-0	121	238	.556	0-3-0	.000	7
1901			6-3-0	84	115	.667	0-3-0	.000	7										

John Chalmers (1903-1905) 24-8-0 .750

1903			9-2-0	171	102	.818	1-1-0	.500	5	1905			8-2-0	309	86	.800	0-2-0	.000	6
1904			7-4-0	257	109	.636	0-3-0	.000	7										

Mark Catlin (1906-1908) 7-10-0 .412

1906			2-3-0	43	75	.400	0-1-0	.000	6	1908			2-5-0	132	65	.286	0-1-0	.000	6
1907			3-2-0	90	48	.600	1-1-0	.500	4										

John Griffith (1909) 2-4-1 .357

1909			2-4-1	58	97	.357	0-1-0	.000	7

Jess Hawley (1910-1915) 24-18-0 .571

1910			5-2-0	94	15	.714	1-1-0	.500	4	1913			5-2-0	310	51	.714	2-1-0	.667	2
1911			3-4-0	34	53	.429	2-2-0	.500	4	1914			4-3-0	204	36	.571	1-2-0	.333	7
1912			4-3-0	130	138	.571	1-3-0	.250	6	1915			3-4-0	92	149	.429	1-2-0	.333	7

Howard Jones (1916-1923) 42-17-1 .708

1916			4-3-0	121	156	.571	1-2-0	.333	6	1920			5-2-0	142	54	.714	3-2-0	.600	5
1917			3-5-0	91	141	.375	0-2-0	.000	8	1921			7-0-0	185	36	1.000	5-0-0	1.000	1
1918			6-2-1	123	36	.722	2-1-0	.667	4	1922			7-0-0	208	33	1.000	5-0-0	1.000	1
1919			5-2-0	90	44	.714	2-2-0	.500	6	1923			5-3-0	124	55	.625	3-3-0	.500	5

Burt Ingwersen (1924-1931) 33-27-4 .547

1924		6	6-1-1	106	50	.812	3-1-1	.700	2	1928		6	6-2-0	147	42	.750	3-2-0	.600	4
1925			5-3-0	121	74	.625	2-2-0	.500	4	1929			4-2-2	128	28	.625	2-2-2	.500	5
1926			3-5-0	113	117	.375	0-5-0	.000	8	1930			4-4-0	88	74	.500	0-1-0	.000	9
1927			4-4-0	107	83	.500	1-4-0	.200	9	1931			1-6-1	7	131	.188	0-3-1	.000	9

Ossie Solem (1932-1936) 15-21-4 .425

1932			1-7-0	62	171	.125	0-5-0	.000	10	1935			4-2-2	122	39	.625	1-2-2	.333	8
1933			5-3-0	131	56	.625	2-3-0	.400	5	1936			3-4-1	85	103	.438	0-4-1	.000	8
1934			2-5-1	98	153	.312	1-3-1	.250	8										

Ira Tubbs (1937-1938) 2-13-1 .156

1937			1-7-0	36	120	.125	0-5-0	.000	9	1938			1-6-1	46	135	.188	1-3-1	.250	8

Eddie Anderson (1939-1942, 1946-49) 35-33-2 .514

1939	9	11	6-1-1	130	91	.812	4-1-1	.800	2	1941			3-5-0	91	99	.375	2-4-0	.333	6
1940			4-4-0	125	98	.500	2-3-0	.400	6	1942			6-4-0	147	135	.600	3-3-0	.500	5

Slip Madigan (1943-1944) 2-13-1 .156

1943			1-6-1	83	153	.188	0-4-1	.000	9	1944			1-7-0	53	240	.125	0-6-0	.000	8

Clem Crowe (1945) 2-7-0 .222

1945			2-7-0	74	310	.222	1-5-0	.167	8

Eddie Anderson (1946-1949)

1946			5-4-0	129	92	.556	3-3-0	.500	4	1948			4-5-0	127	142	.444	2-4-0	.400	5
1947			3-5-1	145	179	.438	2-3-1	.417	6	1949			4-5-0	184	247	.444	3-3-0	.500	5

Leonard Raffensperger (1950-1951) 5-10-3 .361

1950			3-5-1	121	201	.438	2-4-0	.333	6	1951			2-5-2	160	227	.333	0-5-1	.083	9

Forest Evashevski (1952-1960) 52-27-4 .651

1952			2-7-0	121	220	.222	2-5-0	.286	6	1957	7	5	7-1-1	263	112	.833	4-1-1	.750	3
1953	9	10	5-3-1	187	91	.611	3-0-1	5		1958	2	2	8-1-1	293	146	.850	5-1-0	.833	1
1954			5-4-0	192	141	.556	4-3-0	.571	5	1959			5-4-0	232	100	.556	3-3-0	.500	6
1955			3-5-1	157	173	.389	2-3-1	.417	7	1960	3	2	8-1-0	234	108	.889	5-1-0	.833	1
1956	3	3	9-1-0	219	84	.900	5-1-0	.833	1										

Jerry Burns (1961-1965) 16-27-2 .378

1961			5-4-0	215	162	.556	2-4-0	.333	7	1964			3-6-0	170	209	.333	1-5-0	.167	9
1962			4-5-0	127	166	.444	3-3-0	.500	5	1965			1-9-0	94	192	.100	0-7-0	.000	10
1963			3-3-2	126	112	.500	2-3-1	.417	8										

Ray Nagel (1966-1970) 16-32-2 .340

Year	R1	R2	W-L-T	PF	PA	Pct	Conf	ConfPct	Fin
1966			2-8-0	86	253	.200	1-6-0	.143	10
1967			1-8-1	161	277	.150	0-6-1	.071	9
1968			5-5-0	321	289	.500	4-3-0	.571	5
1969			5-5-0	255	275	.500	3-4-0	.429	5
1970			3-6-1	129	259	.350	3-3-1	.500	4

Frank Lauterbur (1971-1973) 4-28-1 .136

Year	R1	R2	W-L-T	PF	PA	Pct	Conf	ConfPct	Fin
1971			1-10-0	121	390	.091	1-8-0	.111	10
1972			3-7-1	109	208	.318	2-6-1	.278	8
1973			0-11-0	140	402	.000	0-8-0	.000	9

Bob Commings (1974-1978) 18-37-0 .327

Year	R1	R2	W-L-T	PF	PA	Pct	Conf	ConfPct	Fin
1974			3-8-0	141	308	.273	2-6-0	.250	7
1975			3-8-0	182	279	.273	3-5-0	.375	7
1976			5-6-0	161	234	.455	3-5-0	.375	7
1977			5-6-0	165	229	.455	3-5-0	.375	6
1978			2-9-0	125	257	.182	2-6-0	.250	8

Hayden Frye (1979-1998) 143-89-6 .613

Year	R1	R2	W-L-T	PF	PA	Pct	Conf	ConfPct	Fin
1979			5-6-0	239	216	.455	4-4-0	.500	5
1980			4-7-0	154	238	.364	4-4-0	.500	3
1981	18	15	8-4-0	260	157	.667	6-2-0	.750	1
1982			8-4-0	229	230	.667	6-2-0	.750	3
1983	14	14	9-3-0	380	189	.750	7-2-0	.778	3
1984	16	15	8-4-1	359	202	.654	5-3-1	.611	4
1985	10	9	10-2-0	440	187	.833	7-1-0	.875	5
1986	16	15	9-3-0	391	214	.750	5-3-0	.625	3
1987	16	16	10-3-0	390	251	.769	6-2-0	.750	2
1988			6-4-3	337	233	.577	4-1-3	.688	3
1989			5-6-0	197	278	.455	3-5-0	.375	6
1990	18	16	8-4-0	427	312	.667	6-2-0	.750	1
1991	10	10	10-1-1	343	179	875	7-1-0	.875	2
1992			5-7-0	243	278	.417	4-4-0	.500	5
1993			6-6-0	214	293	.500	3-5-0	.375	8
1994			5-5-1	307	324	.500	3-4-1	.438	7
1995	25	22	8-4-0	368	259	.667	4-4-0	.500	6
1996	18	18	9-3-0	339	244	.750	6-2-0	.750	3
1997			7-5-0	412	159	.583	4-4-0	.500	6
1998			3-8-0	172	287	.273	2-6-0	.250	7

Kirk Ferentz (1999-2003) 32-29-0 .525

Year	R1	R2	W-L-T	PF	PA	Pct	Conf	ConfPct	Fin
1999			1-10-0	162	347	.091	0-8-0	.000	11
2000			3-9-0	337	427	.250	3-5-0	.375	8
2001			7-5-0	389	258	.583	4-4-0	.500	4
2002	8	8	11-2-0	484	256	/846	8-0-0	1/000	1
2003	8	8	10-3-0	373	210	.769	5-3-0	/625	5

Won-loss record by decades:

Decade	Record	Pct	Decade	Record	Pct	Decade	Record	Pct
1889-99	38-28-6	.569	1930-39	28-45-7	.394	1970-79	30-77-2	.284
1900-09	51-29-2	.634	1940-49	33-52-2	.391	1980-89	77-40-4	.653
1910-19	42-30-1	.582	1950-59	49-36-7	.571	1990-99	62-53-2	.538
1920-29	52-22-3	.695	1960-69	37-54-3	.410	2000-03	31-19-0	.620

Historic record 530-485-39 .521

Post-season won-loss record: 10-7-1 .583

1957: Rose Bowl, Iowa 35, Oregon State 19
1959: Rose Bowl, Iowa 38, California 12
1982: Rose Bowl, Washington 28, Iowa 0
1982: Peach Bowl, Iowa 28, Tennessee 22
1983: Gator Bowl, Florida 14, Iowa 6
1984: Freedom Bowl, Iowa 55, Texas 17
1986: Rose Bowl, UCLA 45, Iowa 28
1986: Holiday Bowl, Iowa 39, San Diego State 38
1987: Holiday Bowl, Iowa 20, Wyoming 19

1988: Peach Bowl, NC State 28, Iowa 23
1991: Rose Bowl, Washington 46, Iowa 34
1991: Holiday Bowl, Iowa 13, BYU 13
1993: Alamo Bowl, California 27, Iowa 3
1995: Sun Bowl, Iowa 38, Washington 18
1996: Alamo Bowl, Iowa 27, Texas Tech 0
1997: Sun Bowl, Arizona State 17, Iowa 7
2001: Alamo Bowl, Iowa 19, Texas Tech 16
2003: Orange Bowl, USC 38, Iowa 17
2004: Outback Bowl, Iowa 37, Florida 17

College Football Hall of Fame:
Howard Jones, coach, 1916-23; Duke Slater, tackle, 1919-21; Aubrey Devine, quarterback, 1919-21; Gordon Locke, fullback, 1920-22; Ed Bock, guard, 1936-38; Nile Kinnick, halfback, 1937-39; Eddie Anderson, coach, 1939-42, 1946-49; Slip Madigan, coach, 1943-44; Forest Evashevski, coach, 1952-60; Calvin Jones, guard, 1953-55; Alex Karras, tackle, 1955-57; Randy Duncan, quarterback, 1956-58; Hayden Fry, coach, 1979-98; Chuck Long, quarterback, 1981-85.

Awards: Heisman Trophy: 1939, Nile Kinnick; Maxwell Award, 1939, Nile Kinnick; 1985, Chuck Long; Davey O'Brien Award: 1985, Chuck Long, 2002, Brad Banks; Outland Trophy: 1955, Calvin Jones; 1957, Alex Karras; 2003, Robert Gallery; Lou Groza Award: 2002, Nate Kaeding; Tatupu Award: 2001, Kahlil Hill; Mackey Award: 2002, Dallas Clark.

KANSAS STATE UNIVERSITY, Manhattan, Kansas; nickname "Wildcats"; colors purple and white; KSU Stadium (50,000); Big Twelve Conference. K-State began play in 1896 as an independent. In 1913, K-State joined the Missouri Valley Conference playing there through the 1927 season after which it became a founding member of the Big Six (later Big Seven, later Big Eight) Conference. In 1995, the Big Eight Conference, including K-State, took in four members from the disbanded Southwest Conference to form the Big Twelve Conference. In the Missouri Valley Conference records ties are ignored per conference rules at the time.

Early years as an independent (1896-1912)

Year	Coach	W-L-T	PF	PA	Pct.	Year	Coach	W-L-T	PF	PA	Pct.
1896	Ira Pratt	0-1-1	6	20	.250	1901	Wade Moore	3-4-1	65	87	.438
1897	A. W. Ehrsam	1-2-1	4	40	.375	1902	C. E. Dietz	2-6-0	46	121	.250
1898	W. P. Williamson	1-1-2	32	16	.500	1903	G. O. Dietz	3-4-1	56	103	.438
1899	Albert Hanson	2-3-0	23	72	.400	1904	A.A. Booth	1-6-0	48	186	.143
1900	F.G. Mooulton	2-4-0	47	100	.333						

Mike Ahearn (1905-1910) 39-12-0 765

Year	W-L-T	PF	PA	Pct.	Year	W-L-T	PF	PA	Pct.
1905	6-2-0	140	51	.750	1908	6-2-0	182	74	.750
1906	5-2-0	103	37	.714	1909	7-2-0	320	11	.778
1907	5-3-0	135	56	.625	1910	10-1-0	336	23	.909

Guy Lowman (1911-1914) 17-15-3

Year	W-L-T	PF	PA	Pct.	Year	W-L-T	PF	PA	Pct.
1911	5-4-1	47	87	.550	1912	8-2-0	204	103	.800

Member of the Missouri Valley Conference (1913-1927) 20-34-9 .389

Year	Nat'l AP Other	Overall W-L-T	PF	PA	Pct.	Conf. W-L-T	Pct.	Rank	Year	Nat'l AP Other	Overall W-L-T	PF	PA	Pct.	Conf. W-L-T	Pct.	Rank
1913		3-4-1	97	122	.438	0-2-0	.000	6	1914		1-5-1	44	150	.214	0-3-0	.000	5

John R. Bender (1915) 3-4-1 .438

Year	Overall W-L-T	PF	PA	Pct.	Conf. W-L-T	Pct.	Rank
1915	3-4-1	43	84	.438	0-3-0	.000	7

Z.G. Clevenger (1916-1919) 19-9-2 .667

Year	Overall W-L-T	PF	PA	Pct.	Conf. W-L-T	Pct.	Rank	Year	Overall W-L-T	PF	PA	Pct.	Conf. W-L-T	Pct.	Rank
1916	6-1-1	154	36	.812	1-1-1	.500	4	1918	4-1-0	95	29	.800	no conference		
1917	6-2-0	215	25	.750	2-2-0	.500	4	1919	3-5-1	72	109	.389	0-3-1	.000	5

Charles Bachman (1920-1927) 33-23-9 .577

Year	Overall W-L-T	PF	PA	Pct.	Conf. W-L-T	Pct.	Rank	Year	Overall W-L-T	PF	PA	Pct.	Conf. W-L-T	Pct.	Rank
1920	3-3-3	141	48	.500	0-3-1	.000	7	1924	3-4-1	68	79	.438	1-4-1	.200	8
1921	5-3-0	85	64	.625	4-2-0	.667	2	1925	5-2-1	70	43	.688	3-2-1	.600	3
1922	5-1-2	154	61	.750	3-1-2	.750	3	1926	5-3-0	85	42	.625	2-2-0	.500	6
1923	4-2-2	107	72	.625	2-2-2	.500	5	1927	3-5-0	101	146	.375	2-4-0	.333	8

Member of the Big Six (later Big Seven, later Big Eight) (1928-1995) 105-307-11 .261

Bo McMillin (1928-1933) 29-21-1 .578

Year	Overall W-L-T	PF	PA	Pct.	Conf. W-L-T	Pct.	Rank	Year	Overall W-L-T	PF	PA	Pct.	Conf. W-L-T	Pct.	Rank
1928	3-5-0	94	94	.375	0-5-0	.000	6	1931	8-2-0	164	39	.800	3-2-0	.600	3
1929	3-5-0	55	104	.375	3-2-0	.600	3	1932	4-4-0	160	80	.500	2-3-0	.400	4
1930	5-3-0	91	66	.625	3-2-0	.600	3	1933	6-2-1	105	39	.722	4-1-0	.800	2

Lynn Waldorf (1934) 7-2-1 .750

Year	Overall W-L-T	PF	PA	Pct.	Conf. W-L-T	Pct.	Rank
1934	7-2-1	149	81	.750	5-0-0	1.000	1

Wes Fry (1935-1939) 18-21-6 .467

Year	Overall W-L-T	PF	PA	Pct.	Conf. W-L-T	Pct.	Rank	Year	Overall W-L-T	PF	PA	Pct.	Conf. W-L-T	Pct.	Rank
1935	2-4-3	40	49	.389	1-2-2	.400	4	1938	4-4-1	108	134	.500	1-3-1	.300	5
1936	4-3-2	137	89	.556	2-1-2	.600	3	1939	4-5-0	117	108	.444	1-4-0	.200	4
1937	4-5-0	76	84	.444	1-4-0	.200	5								

Hobbs Adams (1940-1941, 1946) 4-21-2 .185

Year	Overall W-L-T	PF	PA	Pct.	Conf. W-L-T	Pct.	Rank	Year	Overall W-L-T	PF	PA	Pct.	Conf. W-L-T	Pct.	Rank
1940	2-7-0	73	145	.222	1-4-0	.200	5	1941	2-5-2	67	168	.333	1-3-1	.300	5

Ward Haylett (1942-1944) 6-20-2 .250

Year	Overall W-L-T	PF	PA	Pct.	Conf. W-L-T	Pct.	Rank	Year	Overall W-L-T	PF	PA	Pct.	Conf. W-L-T	Pct.	Rank
1942	3-8-0	70	334	.273	2-3-0	.400	4	1944	2-5-2	45	215	.333	1-4-0	.200	5
1943	1-7-0	48	209	.125	0-5-0	.000	6								

Lud Fiser (1945) 1-7-0 .125

Year	Overall W-L-T	PF	PA	Pct.	Conf. W-L-T	Pct.	Rank
1945	1-7-0	71	268	.125	0-5-0	.000	6

Hobbs Adams (1946)

Year	Overall W-L-T	PF	PA	Pct.	Conf. W-L-T	Pct.	Rank
1946	0-9-0	41	233	.000	0-5-0	.000	6

Sam Francis (1947) 0-10-0 .000

Year	Overall W-L-T	PF	PA	Pct.	Conf. W-L-T	Pct.	Rank
1947	0-10-0	71	283	.000	0-5-0	.000	6

Ralph Graham (1948-1950) 4-26-1 .145

Year	Overall W-L-T	PF	PA	Pct.	Conf. W-L-T	Pct.	Rank	Year	Overall W-L-T	PF	PA	Pct.	Conf. W-L-T	Pct.	Rank
1948	1-9-0	78	323	.100	0-6-0	.000	7	1950	1-9-1	122	355	.136	0-6-0	.000	7
1949	2-8-0	191	257	.200	1-5-0	.167	7								

Bill Meek (1951-1954) 14-24-1 .372

Year	Overall W-L-T	PF	PA	Pct.	Conf. W-L-T	Pct.	Rank	Year	Overall W-L-T	PF	PA	Pct.	Conf. W-L-T	Pct.	Rank
1951	0-9-0	73	212	.000	0-6-0	.000	7	1953	6-3-1	198	116	.650	4-2-0	.667	2
1952	1-9-0	81	255	.100	0-6-0	.000	7	1954	7-3-0	191	154	.700	3-3-0	.500	5

Bus Mertes (1955-1959) 15-34-1 .310

Year	Overall W-L-T	PF	PA	Pct.	Conf. W-L-T	Pct.	Rank	Year	Overall W-L-T	PF	PA	Pct.	Conf. W-L-T	Pct.	Rank
1955	4-6-0	164	191	.400	3-3-0	.500	3	1958	3-7-0	110	192	.300	2-4-0	.333	5
1956	3-7-0	143	259	.300	2-4-0	.333	5	1959	2-8-0	109	266	.200	1-5-0	.167	7
1957	3-6-1	124	166	.350	2-4-0	.333	5								

Doug Weaver (1960-1966) 8-60-1 .123

Year	Overall W-L-T	PF	PA	Pct.	Conf. W-L-T	Pct.	Rank	Year	Overall W-L-T	PF	PA	Pct.	Conf. W-L-T	Pct.	Rank
1960	1-9-0	78	316	.100	0-7-0	.000	8	1964	3-7-0	64	186	.300	3-4-0	.429	5
1961	2-8-0	58	232	.200	0-7-0	.000	8	1965	0-10-0	43	296	.000	0-7-0	.000	8
1962	0-10-0	39	283	.000	0-7-0	.000	8	1966	0-9-1	66	226	.050	0-6-1	.071	7
1963	2-7-0	91	222	.222	1-5-0	.167	7								

Vince Gibson (1967-1974) 33-52-0 .388

1967			1-9-0	90	263	.100	0-7-0	.000	8	1971			5-6-0	219	296	.455	2-5-0	.286	5
1968			4-6-0	194	247	.400	2-5-0	.286	6	1972			3-8-0	169	377	.273	1-6-0	.143	8
1969			5-5-0	319	233	.500	3-4-0	.429	5	1973			5-6-0	176	260	.455	2-5-0	.286	6
1970			6-5-0	190	218	.545	5-2-0	.714	2	1974			4-7-0	193	283	.364	1-6-0	.143	7

Ellis Rainsberger (1975-1977) 6-27-0 .182

| 1975 | | | 3-8-0 | 89 | 248 | .273 | 0-7-0 | .000 | 8 | 1977 | | | 2-9-0 | 131 | 286 | .182 | 0-7-0 | .000 | 8 |
| 1976 | | | 1-10-0 | 155 | 317 | .091 | 0-7-0 | .000 | 8 | | | | | | | | | | |

Jim Dickey (1978-1985) 25-53-2 .325

1978			4-7-0	201	342	.364	3-4-0	.429	5	1982			6-5-1	230	180	.542	3-3-1	.500	4
1979			3-8-0	154	225	.273	1-6-0	.143	8	1983			3-8-0	186	343	.273	1-6-0	.143	8
1980			4-7-0	129	212	.364	1-6-0	.143	7	1984			3-7-1	185	330	.318	2-4-1	.357	5
1981			2-9-0	164	297	.182	1-6-0	.143	8	1985*			0-2-0	16	26	.000	0-0-0		*

Lee Moon (1985) 1-8-0 .111

| 1985* | | | 1-8-0 | 85 | 269 | .111 | 1-6-0 | .143 | 7 |

*Dickey coached the first two games of the 1985 season, and Moon coached the last nine games.

Stan Parrish (1986-1988) 2-30-1 .076

| 1986 | | | 2-9-0 | 134 | 343 | .182 | 1-6-0 | .143 | 7 | 1988 | | | 0-11-0 | 171 | 448 | .000 | 0-7-0 | .000 | 8 |
| 1987 | | | 0-10-1 | 135 | 421 | .045 | 0-6-1 | .071 | 7 | | | | | | | | | | |

Bill Snyder (1989-2003) 127-55-0 .698

1989			1-10-0	134	349	.091	0-7-0	.000	8	1993	20	18	9-2-1	338	227	.792	4-2-1	.643	3
1990			5-6-0	255	293	.455	2-5-0	.286	5	1994	19	16	9-3-0	312	168	.750	5-2-0	.714	3
1991			7-4-0	263	236	.636	4-3-0	.571	4	1995	7	6	10-2-0	456	166	.833	5-2-0	.714	2
1992			5-6-0	195	228	.455	2-5-0	.286	6										

Member of the Big Twelve Conference (1996-2003) 49-15-0 .766

1996	17	17	9-3-0	325	172	.750	6-2-0	.750	3	2000	9	8	11-3-0	549	261	.786	6-2-0	.750	3
1997	8	7	11-1-0	418	177	.917	7-1-0	.875	2	2001			6-6-0	327	179	.500	3-5-0	.375	8
1998	10	9	11-2-0	610	197	.846	8-0-0	1.000	2	2002	7	6	11-2-0	582	154	.846	6-2-0	.750	2
1999	6	6	11-1-0	457	164	.917	7-1-0	.875	3	2003	14	13	11-4-0	549	244	.733	6-2-0	.750	1

Won-loss record by decades:

1896-99	4- 7-4	.400	1930-39	48-34-8	.578	1970-79	36-74-0	.327
1900-09	40-35-2	.532	1940-49	14-75-4	.172	1980-89	22-86-3	.206
1910-19	49-29-5	.620	1950-59	30-67-3	.315	1990-99	87-30-0	.744
1920-29	39-33-9	.537	1960-69	18-80-1	.187	2000-03	39-15-0	.722

Historic record 426-565-39 .433

Post-season won-loss record: 7-7-0 .500

1993: Insight.com Bowl, K State 52, Wyoming 17
1994: Aloha Bowl, Boston College 12, K State 7
1995: Holiday Bowl, K State 54, Colorado State 21
1996: Cotton Bowl, BYU 19, K State 15
1997: Fiesta Bowl, K State 35, Syracuse 18
1998: Big 12 Championship, Texas A&M 36, K State 33

1998: Alamo Bowl, Purdue 37, K State 34
1999: Holiday Bowl, K State 24, Washington 20
2001: Cotton Bowl, K State 35, Tennessee 21
2000: Big 12 Championship, Oklahoma 27, K State 24
2001: Insight.com Bowl, Syracuse 26, K State 3
2002: Holiday Bowl, K State 34, Arizona State 27
2003: Big 12 Championship, K State 35, Oklahoma 7
2004: Fiesta Bowl, Ohio State 35, K State 28

College Football Hall of Fame:
Charlie Bachman, coach, 1920-27; Pappy Waldorf, coach, 1934; Gary Spani, linebacker, 1974-77.

Player Awards: Jim Thorpe Trophy: 2002, Terrence Newman; Lou Groza Award: 1997, Martin Gramatica

UNIVERSITY OF KANSAS, Lawrence, Kansas; nickname "Jayhawks"; colors crimson and blue; Memorial Stadium (50,250): Big Twelve Conference. KU began play in 1890 and then joined the Missouri Valley Conference in 1907. It played in the MVC through the 1927 season and then left along with five other teams to form the Big Six (later the Big Seven, later the Big Eight Conference). KU began play in the Big Six Conference in 1928 and played in that conference (and its successors) through the 1995 season. In 1995, the Big Eight joined with four teams from the disbanded SWC to form the Big Twelve, and KU has played in the Big Twelve beginning with the 1996 season.

Early years as an independent (1890-1906)

Year	Coach	W-L-T	PF	PA	Pct.	Year	Coach	W-L-T	PF	PA	Pct.
1890	no coach	1-2-0	33	52	.333	1897	Wylie Woodruff	8-2-0	253	16	.800
1891	E.M. Hopkins	7-0-1	160	54	.938	1898	Wylie Woodruff	7-1-0	129	24	.875
1892	A.W. Shepard	7-1-0	144	36	.875	1899	Fielding Yost	10-0-0	280	37	1.000
1893	A.W. Shepard	2-5-0	85	108	.286	1900	Charles Boynton	2-5-2	75	118	.333
1894	Hector Cowan	2-3-1	78	82	.417	1901	John Outland	3-5-2	92	147	.400
1895	Hector Cowan	6-1-0	192	14	.857	1902	Arthur Curtis	6-4-0	108	93	.600
1896	Hector Cowan	7-3-0	136	32	.700	1903	Harrison Weeks	6-3-0	118	42	.667

Bert Kennedy (1904-1910) 53-9-4 .833

1904		8-1-1	179	38	.850	1906		7-2-2	128	51	.727
1905		10-1-0	250	26	.909						

Member of the Missouri Valley Conference (1907-1927) 41-39-10 .511

	Nat'l	Overall				Conference				Nat'l	Overall				Conference		
Year	AP Other	W-L-T	PF	PA	Pct.	W-L-T	Pct.	Rank	Year	AP Other	W-L-T	PF	PA	Pct.	W-L-T	Pct.	Rank
1907		5-3-0	111	57	.625	1-1-0	.500	3	1909		8-1-0	172	22	.889	3-1-0	.750	2
1908		9-0-0	131	20	1.000	4-0-0	1.000	1	1910		6-1-1	75	22	.812	1-1-1	.500	4

Ralph Sherwin (1911) 4-2-2 .625

1911		4-2-2	81	44	.625	1-1-1	.500	4									

Arthur Morse (1912-1913) 9-7-0 .563

1912		4-4-0	128	45	.500	1-2-0	.333	5	1913		5-3-0	127	40	.625	3-2-0	.600	3

H. M. Wheaton (1914) 5-2-1 .688

1914		5-2-1	157	84	.688	2-2-0	.500	4									

Herman Olcott (1915-1917) 16-7-1 .688

1915		6-2-0	153	79	.750	3-1-0	.750	2	1917		6-2-0	126	46	.750	3-1-0	.750	2
1916		4-3-1	68	72	.562	1-2-1	.375	5									

Jay Bond (1918) 2-2-0 .500

1918		2-2-0	33	66	.500	conference inactive											

Leon McCarty (1919) 3-2-3 .562

1919		3-2-3	85	35	.562	KU not in conference											

Phog Allen (1920) 5-2-1 .688

1920		5-2-1	117	60	.688	3-2-0	.600	3									

Potsy Clark (1921-1925) 16-17-6 .487

1921		4-3-0	92	97	.571	3-3-0	.500	4	1924		2-5-1	91	56	.312	2-4-1	.357	7
1922		3-4-1	104	75	.438	1-3-1	.250	7	1925		2-5-1	30	68	.312	2-5-1	.312	8
1923		5-0-3	125	6	.812	3-0-3	.750	2									

Franklin Cappon (1926-1927) 5-10-1 .344

1926		2-6-0	34	135	.250	1-5-0	.167	9	1927		3-4-1	89	146	.438	3-3-1	.500	5

Member of the Big Six (later Big Seven, later Big Eight) (1928-1995) 161-243-19 .394

Bill Hargiss (1928-1932) 18-16-2 .528

1928		2-4-2	34	66	.375	1-3-1	.300	5	1931		5-5-0	112	54	.500	1-3-0	.250	4
1929		4-4-0	97	50	.500	2-3-0	.400	5	1932*		1-1-0	19	33	.500	0-1-0	.000	*
1930		6-2-0	144	50	.750	4-1-0	.800	1									

Ad Lindsey (1932-1938) 23-30-8 .443

1932*		4-2-0	70	44	.667	3-1-0	.750	2	1936		1-6-1	35	153	.188	0-5-0	.000	6
1933		5-4-1	102	51	.550	2-3-0	.400	4	1937		3-4-2	72	74	.444	2-1-2	.600	3
1934		3-4-3	74	48	.450	1-2-2	.400	4	1938		3-6-0	132	169	.333	1-4-0	.200	6
1935		4-4-1	102	118	.500	2-2-1	.500	3									

*Hargiss coached the first three games of the 1932 season, and Lindsey coached the remaining six games.

Gwinn Henry (1939-1942) 9-27-0 .250

1939		2-6-0	47	107	.250	1-4-0	.200	4	1941		3-6-0	74	222	.333	2-3-0	.400	4
1940		2-7-0	75	171	.222	0-5-0	.000	6	1942		2-8-0	77	248	.200	1-4-0	.200	5

Henry Shenk (1943-1945) 11-16-3 .417

1943		4-5-1	96	107	.450	2-3-0	.400	4	1945		4-5-1	139	175	.450	1-3-1	.300	5
1944		3-6-1	128	153	.350	1-4-0	.200	5									

George Sauer (1946-1947) 15-3-3 .786

1946		7-2-1	157	145	.750	4-1-0	.900	1	1947 12		8-1-2	304	102	.818	4-0-1	.900	1

J. V. Sikes (1948-1953) 35-25-0 .583

1948		7-3-0	199	137	.700	4-2-0	.667	3	1951 20		8-2-0	316	208	.800	4-2-0	.667	3
1949		5-5-0	259	183	.500	2-4-0	.333	5	1952		7-3-0	214	110	.700	3-3-0	.500	4
1950		6-4-0	284	188	.600	3-3-0	.500	4	1953		2-8-0	83	179	.200	2-4-0	.333	4

Chuck Mather (1954-1957) 11-26-3 .313

Year			W-L-T	PF	PA	Pct	Conf	Pct		Year			W-L-T	PF	PA	Pct	Conf	Pct	
1954			0-10-0	93	377	.000	0-6-0	.000	7	1956			3-6-1	163	215	.350	2-4-0	.333	5
1955			3-6-1	93	222	.350	1-4-1	.250	5	1957			5-4-1	115	230	.550	4-2-0	.667	2

Jack Mitchell (1958-1966) 42-44-5 .489

Year			W-L-T	PF	PA	Pct	Conf	Pct		Year			W-L-T	PF	PA	Pct	Conf	Pct	
1958			4-5-1	87	175	.450	3-2-1	.583	4	1963			5-5-0	207	122	.500	3-4-0	.429	4
1959			5-5-0	163	134	.500	3-3-0	.500	3	1964			6-4-0	136	146	.600	5-2-0	.714	3
1960*	11	9	5-4-1	219	89	.550	2-4-1	.357	4	1965			2-8-0	119	215	.200	2-5-0	.286	6
1961	15		7-3-1	269	88	.682	5-2-0	.714	2	1966			2-7-1	106	188	.250	0-6-1	.071	7
1962			6-3-1	214	116	.650	4-2-1	.643	4										

*Kansas forfeited two conference games in the 1960 season because of use of an ineligible player.

Pepper Rodgers (1967-1970) 20-22-0 .476

Year			W-L-T	PF	PA	Pct	Conf	Pct		Year			W-L-T	PF	PA	Pct	Conf	Pct	
1967			5-5-0	166	146	.500	5-2-0	.714	3	1969			1-9-0	176	290	.100	0-7-0	.000	8
1968	7	6	9-2-0	394	190	.818	6-1-0	.857	1	1970			5-6-0	270	277	.455	2-5-0	.286	6

Don Fambrough (1971-1974, 1979-1982) 36-49-5 .428

Year			W-L-T	PF	PA	Pct	Conf	Pct		Year			W-L-T	PF	PA	Pct	Conf	Pct	
1971			4-7-0	187	284	.364	2-5-0	.286	5	1973	18	15	7-4-1	253	220	.625	4-2-1	.643	2
1972			4-7-0	208	315	.364	3-4-0	.429	5	1974			4-7-0	157	247	.364	1-6-0	.143	7

Bud Moore (1975-1978) 17-27-1 .389

Year			W-L-T	PF	PA	Pct	Conf	Pct		Year			W-L-T	PF	PA	Pct	Conf	Pct	
1975			7-5-0	262	180	.583	4-3-0	.571	4	1977			3-7-1	131	287	.318	2-4-1	.357	6
1976			6-5-0	260	251	.545	2-5-0	.286	7	1978			1-10-0	124	345	.091	0-7-0	.000	8

Don Fambrough (1979-1982)

Year			W-L-T	PF	PA	Pct	Conf	Pct		Year			W-L-T	PF	PA	Pct	Conf	Pct	
1979			3-8-0	172	346	.273	2-5-0	.286	5	1981			8-4-0	188	195	.667	4-3-0	.571	3
1980			4-5-2	171	180	.455	3-3-1	.500	4	1982			2-7-2	150	270	.273	1-5-1	.214	6

Mike Gottfried (1983-1985) 15-18-1 .441

Year			W-L-T	PF	PA	Pct	Conf	Pct		Year			W-L-T	PF	PA	Pct	Conf	Pct	
1983			4-6-1	296	320	.409	2-5-0	.286	6	1985			6-6-0	263	281	.500	2-5-0	.286	6
1984			5-6-0	218	298	.455	4-3-0	.571	4										

Bob Valesente (1986-1987) 4-17-1 .190

Year			W-L-T	PF	PA	Pct	Conf	Pct		Year			W-L-T	PF	PA	Pct	Conf	Pct	
1986			3-8-0	112	327	.273	0-7-0	.000	8	1987			1-9-1	135	398	.182	0-6-1	.071	7

Glen Mason (1988-1996) 47-54-1 .466

Year			W-L-T	PF	PA	Pct	Conf	Pct		Year			W-L-T	PF	PA	Pct	Conf	Pct	
1988			1-10-0	189	496	.091	1-6-0	.143	7	1992	22	23	8-4-0	380	232	.667	4-3-0	.571	3
1989			4-7-0	248	383	.364	2-5-0	.286	6	1993			5-7-0	242	266	.417	3-4-0	.429	5
1990			3-7-1	213	365	.318	2-4-1	.357	4	1994			6-5-0	324	259	.545	3-4-0	.429	5
1991			6-5-0	303	244	.545	3-4-0	.429	5	1995	9	10	10-2-0	345	261	.833	5-2-0	.714	2

Member of the Big Twelve Conference (1996-2003) 15-49-0 .234

Year			W-L-T	PF	PA	Pct	Conf	Pct		Year			W-L-T	PF	PA	Pct	Conf	Pct	
1996			4-7-0	290	358	.364	2-6-0	.250	9										

Terry Allen (1997-2001) 21-35-0 .375

Year			W-L-T	PF	PA	Pct	Conf	Pct		Year			W-L-T	PF	PA	Pct	Conf	Pct	
1997			5-6-0	187	269	.455	3-5-0	.375	7	2000			4-7-0	261	359	.364	2-6-0	.250	9
1998			4-7-0	280	341	.364	1-7-0	.125	10	2001			3-8-0	182	398	.273	1-7-0	.125	11
1999			5-7-0	294	354	.417	3-5-0	.375	8										

Mark Mangino (2002-2003) 8-17-0 .308

Year			W-L-T	PF	PA	Pct	Conf	Pct		Year			W-L-T	PF	PA	Pct	Conf	Pct	
2002			2-10-0	248	507	.167	0-8-0	.000	12	2003			6-7-0	384	396	.462	3-5-0	.375	8

Won-loss record by decades:

1890-99	57-18-2	.753	1930-39	37-44-8	.461	1970-79	44-66-2	.406	
1900-09	64-25-7	.703	1940-49	45-48-6	.485	1980-89	38-68-6	.366	
1910-19	45-23-8	.645	1950-59	43-53-4	.450	1990-99	56-57-1	.496	
1920-29	32-37-10	.468	1960-69	48-50-4	.490	2000-03	15-32-0	.319	

Historical record: 524-521-58 .501

Post-season won-loss record: 3-6-0 .333

1948: Orange Bowl, Georgia Tech 20, KU 14
1961: Bluebonnet Bowl, KU 33, Rice 7
1969: Orange Bowl, Penn State 15, KU 14
1973: Liberty Bowl, NC State 31, KU 18

1975: Sun Bowl, Pittsburgh 33, KU 19
1981: Hall of Fame Bowl, Mississippi State 10, KU 0
1992: Aloha Bowl, KU 23, BYU 20
1995: Aloha Bowl, KU 51, UCLA 30
2003: Tangerine Bowl, NC State 56, KU 26

College Football Hall of Fame:
Fielding Yost, coach, 1899; Ray Evans, halfback, 19414-42, 1946-47; John Hadl, quarterback/halfback, 1962-64; Gale Sayers, halfback, 1962-64.

KENT STATE UNIVERSITY, Kent, Ohio; nickname "Golden Flashes"; colors navy blue and gold; Dix Stadium (30,250); Mid-American Conference. Kent State began play in 1920, joined the Mid-American Conference in 1951, and has played in the MAC since that time.

Early years (1920-1950)

Year	Nat'l AP	Other	W-L-T	PF	PA	Pct.		Year	Nat'l AP	Other	W-L-T	PF	PA	Pct.
Paul Chandler (1920-1922) 1-11-1 .115														
1920			1-2-0	1	13	.333		1922			0-7-0	0	146	.000
1921			0-2-1	0	20	.167								
Frank Harsh (1923-1924) 0-9-0 .000														
1923			0-5-0	6	260	.000		1924			0-4-0	0	89	.000
Merle Wagoner (1925-1932) 15-33-9 .342														
1925			1-1-3	13	24	.500		1929			1-7-0	20	161	.125
1926			2-6-0	35	176	.250		1930			3-3-1	64	42	.500
1927			1-5-1	25	80	.214		1931			3-4-0	58	80	.429
1928			4-2-2	89	32	.625		1932			0-5-2	0	80	.143
Joe Begala (1933-1934) 4-5-6 .467														
1933			2-2-3	31	31	.500		1934			2-3-3	45	90	.438
G. Donald Starn (1935-1942) 34-28-3 .546														
1935			3-5-0	127	108	.375		1939			3-4-1	66	140	.438
1936			4-4-0	79	59	.500		1940			8-1-0	193	30	.889
1937			3-4-1	79	73	.438		1941			2-5-1	109	100	.312
1938			6-2-0	174	69	.750		1942			5-3-0	114	113	.625
No team (1943-1945)														
Trevor Rees (1946-1963) 92-63-5 .591														
1946			6-2-0	143	47	.750		1949			5-3-0	166	126	.625
1947			4-4-0	89	95	.500		1950			5-4-0	214	120	.556
1948			6-2-1	227	89	.722								

Member of the Mid-American Conference (1951-2003) 120-247-4 .329

Year	Nat'l AP	Other	Overall W-L-T	PF	PA	Pct.	Conference W-L-T	Pct.	Rank		Year	Nat'l AP	Other	Overall W-L-T	PF	PA	Pct.	Conference W-L-T	Pct.	Rank
1951			4-3-2	241	162	.556	2-1-0	.667	3		1958			7-2-0	137	89	.778	5-1-0	.833	2
1952			5-4-0	204	180	.556	2-2-0	.500	4		1959			5-3-0	144	124	.625	3-3-0	.500	4
1953			7-2-0	250	103	.778	3-1-0	.750	3		1960			6-3-0	118	129	.667	4-2-0	.667	3
1954			8-2-0	331	130	.800	4-1-0	.800	2		1961			2-8-0	126	181	.200	1-5-0	.167	7
1955			6-2-1	184	87	.722	4-1-1	.750	2		1962			3-6-0	108	185	.333	2-4-0	.333	5
1956			7-2-0	208	82	.778	4-2-0	.667	3		1963			3-5-1	109	222	.389	1-5-0	.167	6
1957			3-6-0	114	138	.333	1-5-0	.167	7											
Leo Strang (1964-1967) 16-21-2 .436																				
1964			3-5-1	87	121	.389	1-4-1	.250	6		1966			4-6-0	211	161	.400	2-4-0	.333	5
1965			5-4-1	144	114	.550	3-2-1	.583	3		1967			4-6-0	195	144	.400	1-5-0	.167	6
D. Puddington (1968-1970) 9-21-0 .300																				
1968			1-9-0	101	231	.100	1-5-0	.167	6		1970			3-7-0	161	222	.300	1-4-0	.200	5
1969			5-5-0	166	197	.500	1-4-0	.200	5											
Don James (1971-1974) 25-19-1 .567																				
1971			3-8-0	169	304	.272	0-5-0	.000	6		1973			9-2-0	299	131	.818	4-1-0	.800	2
1972			6-5-1	191	196	.542	4-1-0	.800	1		1974			7-4-0	254	161	.636	2-3-0	.400	4
Dennis Fitzgerald (1975-1977) 18-16-0 .529																				
1975			4-7-0	202	289	.364	1-6-0	.143	8		1977			6-5-0	200	241	.545	5-4-0	.556	6
1976			8-4-0	280	216	.667	6-2-0	.750	2											
Ron Blackledge (1978-1980) 8-25-0 .242																				
1978			4-7-0	158	248	.364	2-6-0	.250	8		1980			3-8-0	159	279	.272	3-6-0	.333	8
1979			1-10-0	127	298	.091	1-8-0	.111	10											
Ed Chlebek (1981-1982) 4-18-0 .182																				
1981			4-7-0	144	172	.364	3-6-0	.333	7		1982			0-11-0	114	270	.000	0-9-0	.000	10
Dick Scesniak (1983-1985) 8-25-0 .242																				
1983			1-10-0	157	260	.091	1-8-0	.111	9		1985			3-8-0	212	177	.272	2-6-0	.250	9
1984			4-7-0	135	199	.364	3-6-0	.333	8											
Glen Mason (1986-1987) 12-10-0 .545																				
1986			5-6-0	178	289	.455	5-3-0	.625	2		1987			7-4-0	223	212	.636	5-3-0	.625	2
Dick Crum (1988-1990) 7-26-0 .212																				
1988			5-6-0	256	250	.455	3-5-0	.375	7		1990			2-9-0	177	328	.182	2-6-0	.250	7
1989			0-11-0	179	377	.000	0-8-0	.000	9											
Pete Cordelli (1991-1993) 3-30-0 .091																				
1991			1-10-0	159	307	.091	1-7-0	.125	9		1993			0-11-0	149	357	.000	0-9-0	.000	10
1992			2-9-0	133	301	.222	2-7-0	.222	8											

Jim Corrigall (1994-1997) 8-35-1 .193

Year	Record	PF	PA	Pct	Conf	Conf Pct		Year	Record	PF	PA	Pct	Conf	Conf Pct	
1994	2-9-0	140	293	.182	2-7-0	.222	8	1996	2-9-0	255	492	.182	1-7-0	.125	10
1995	1-9-1	128	390	.136	0-7-1	.062	10	1997	3-8-0	337	490	.272	3-5-0	.375	7

Dean Pees (1998-2003) 17-51-0 .250

Year	Record	PF	PA	Pct	Conf	Conf Pct		Year	Record	PF	PA	Pct	Conf	Conf Pct	
1998	0-11-0	149	454	.000	0-8-0	.000	11	2001	6-5-0	248	281	.545	5-3-0	.625	4
1999	2-9-0	213	376	.182	2-6-0	.250	10	2002	3-9-0	202	424	.250	1-7-0	.125	12
2000	1-10-0	128	359	.091	1-7-0	.125	13	2003	5-7-0	321	396	.417	4-4-0	.500	7

Won-loss record by decades:

1920-29	10-41-7	.233		1950-59	57-30-3	.650	1980-89	32-78-0	.291
1930-39	29-36-11	.454		1960-69	36-57-3	.391	1990-99	15-94-1	.141
1940-49	36-20-2	.638		1970-79	50-59-1	.459	2000-03	15-31-0	.326

Historical record: 280-446-28 .390

Post-season won-loss record: 0-2-0 .000
1954: Refrigerator Bowl, Delaware 19, Kent State 7
1972: Tangerine Bowl, Tampa 21, Kent State 18

College Football Hall of Fame:
Don James, coach, 1971-74.

UNIVERSITY OF KENTUCKY, Lexington, Kentucky; nickname "Wildcats"; colors blue and white; Commonwealth Stadium (67,530); Southeastern Conference. Kentucky began play in 1881 and joined the Southern Conference as a founding member in 1922. Kentucky left the SC after the 1932 season to join the newly organized Southeastern Conference. Kentucky has played in the SEC since, beginning in the 1933 season.

Early years as an independent (1881-1921)

Year	Coach	W-L-T	PF	PA	Pct.	Year	Coach	W-L-T	PF	PA	Pct.
1881	none	1-2-0	10	7	.333	1905	F. E. Schacht	6-3-1	209	171	.650
1882-1890	no team					1906	J. White Guyn	4-3-0	110	67	.571
1891	S. Pottinger &					1907	J. White Guyn	9-1-1	181	42	.864
	J. Selby	1-1-0	8	12	.500	1908	J. White Guyn	4-3-0	87	81	.571
1892	A. Miller &					1909	E. R. Sweetland	9-1-0	261	29	.900
	John Thompson	2-4-1	40	74	.357	1910	E. R. Sweetland	7-2-0	140	29	.778
1893	John Thompson	5-2-1	280	110	.688	1911	P. P. Douglas	7-3-0	97	41	.700
1894	W. P. Finney	5-2-0	218	121	.714	1912	E. R. Sweetland	7-2-0	250	41	.778
1895	Charles Mason	4-5-0	64	94	.444	1913	Alpha Brumage	6-2-0	157	58	.750
1896	Dudley Short	3-6-0	122	134	.333	1914	Alpha Brumage	5-3-0	328	93	.625
1897	Lyman Eaton	2-4-0	28	118	.333	1915	J. J. Tigert	6-1-1	149	38	.812
1898	W. R. Bass	7-0-0	180	0	1.000	1916	J. J. Tigert	4-1-2	152	51	.714
1899	W. R. Bass	5-2-2	98	44	.667	1917	S. A. Boles	3-5-1	104	56	.389
1900	W. H. Kiler	4-6-0	59	64	.400	1918	Andy Gill	2-1-0	45	43	.667
1901	W. H. Kiler	2-6-1	39	87	.278	1919	Andy Gill	3-4-1	31	136	.438
1902	E. N. McLeod	3-5-1	72	83	.389	1920	W. J. Juneau	3-4-1	111	109	.438
1903	C. A. Wright	7-1-0	204	22	.875	1921	W. J. Juneau	4-3-1	187	89	.562
1904	F.E. Schacht	9-1-0	276	15	.900						

Member of the Southern Conference (1922-1932) 26-29-7 .476

Year	Nat'l AP	Other	Overall W-L-T	PF	PA	Pct.	Conference W-L-T	Pct.	Rank	Year	Nat'l AP	Other	Overall W-L-T	PF	PA	Pct.	Conference W-L-T	Pct.	Rank
						W.J. Juneau (1920-1922) 13-10-2 .560													
1922			6-3-0	167	56	.667	1-2-0	.333	11										
							J. J. Winn (1923) 4-3-2 .556												
1923			4-3-2	135	53	.556	0-2-2	.250	17										
							Fred Murphy (1924-1926) 12-14-1 .463												
1924			4-5-0	129	99	.444	2-3-0	.400	14	1926			2-6-1	84	91	.278	1-4-1	.250	18
1925			6-3-0	92	97	.667	4-2-0	.667	7										
							Henry Gamage (1927-1933) 32-25-5 .556												
1927			3-6-1	115	161	.350	1-5-0	.167	21	1930			5-3-0	207	55	.625	4-3-0	.571	11
1928			4-3-1	100	41	.562	2-2-1	.500	9	1931			5-2-2	130	52	.667	4-2-2	.625	6
1929			6-1-1	237	54	.812	3-1-1	.700	5	1932			4-5-0	116	77	.444	4-5-0	.444	12

Member of the Southeastern Conference (1933-2003) 137-298-12 .320

Year	Nat'l AP	Other	Overall W-L-T	PF	PA	Pct.	Conference W-L-T	Pct.	Rank	Year	Nat'l AP	Other	Overall W-L-T	PF	PA	Pct.	Conference W-L-T	Pct.	Rank
1933			5-5-0	91	116	.500	2-3-0	.400	9										
							C.A. Wynne (1934-1937) 20-19-0 .513												
1934			5-5-0	123	86	.500	1-3-0	.250	9	1936			6-4-0	179	84	.600	1-3-0	.250	10
1935			5-4-0	152	88	.556	3-3-0	.500	6	1937			4-6-0	93	130	.400	0-5-0	.000	11
							A. D. Kirwan (1938-1944) 24-28-4 .489												
1938			2-7-0	150	160	.222	0-4-0	.000	12	1942			3-6-1	155	154	.350	0-5-0	.000	11
1939			6-2-1	161	64	.722	2-2-1	.500	5	1943			no team						
1940			5-3-2	190	107	.600	1-2-2	.400	8	1944			3-6-0	125	147	.333	1-5-0	.167	9
1941			5-4-0	151	203	.556	0-4-0	.000	12										
							Bernie Shively (1945) 2-8-0 .200												
1945			2-8-0	96	217	.200	0-5-0	.000	12										
							Bear Bryant (1946-1953) 60-23-5 .710												
1946			7-3-0	233	91	.700	2-3-0	.400	8	1950	7	7	11-1-0	393	69	.917	5-1-0	.833	1
1947			8-3-0	175	73	.727	2-3-0	.400	9	1951	15	17	8-4-0	314	121	.667	3-3-0	.500	5
1948			5-3-2	199	128	.600	1-3-1	.300	9	1952	20	19	5-4-2	161	173	.545	1-3-2	.333	9
1949	11		9-3-0	317	214	.750	4-1-0	.800	2	1953	16	15	7-2-1	201	116	.750	4-1-1	.750	2
							Blanton Collier (1954-1961) 41-36-3 .531												
1954			7-3-0	151	125	.700	5-2-0	.714	3	1958			5-4-1	136	115	.550	3-4-1	.438	6
1955			6-3-1	185	117	.650	3-3-1	.500	6	1959			4-6-0	140	157	.400	1-6-0	.143	10
1956			6-4-0	119	105	.600	4-4-0	.500	6	1960			5-4-1	206	81	.550	2-4-1	.357	9
1957			3-7-0	128	127	.300	1-7-0	.125	12	1961			5-5-0	138	123	.500	2-4-0	.333	8
							Charlie Bradshaw (1962-1968) 25-41-4 .386												
1962			3-5-2	85	101	.400	2-3-1	.417	7	1966			3-6-1	107	196	.350	2-4-0	.333	7
1963			3-6-1	142	168	.350	0-5-1	.083	11	1967			2-8-0	111	230	.200	1-6-0	.143	8
1964			5-5-0	150	194	.500	4-2-0	.667	2	1968			3-7-0	141	206	.300	0-7-0	.000	10
1965	18		6-4-0	202	160	.600	3-3-0	.500	6										
							John Ray (1969-1972) 10-33-0 .233												
1969			2-8-0	104	295	.200	1-6-0	.143	9	1971			3-8-0	144	284	.273	1-6-0	.143	8
1970			2-9-0	131	233	.182	0-7-0	.000	10	1972			3-8-0	131	232	.273	2-5-0	.286	7

			Fran Curci (1973-1981) 47-51-2 .480														
1973			5-6-0	226	196	.455	3-4-0	.429	5	1978	4-6-1	193	189	.409	2-4-0	.333	7
1974			6-5-0	248	194	.545	3-3-0	.500	4	1979	5-6-0	180	143	.455	3-3-0	.500	4
1975			2-8-1	132	183	.227	0-6-0	.000	9	1980	3-8-0	167	280	.273	1-5-0	.167	8
1976	18	19	9-3-0	203	137	.750	5-1-0	.833	1	1981	3-8-0	134	222	.273	2-4-0	.333	6
1977	6		10-1-0	252	111	.909	6-0-0	1.000	2								

			Jerry Claiborne (1982-1989) 41-46-3 .472														
1982			0-10-1	96	287	.046	0-6-0	.000	9	1986	5-5-1	228	187	.500	2-4-0	.333	7
1983			6-5-1	228	237	.542	2-4-0	.333	7	1987	5-6-0	258	187	.455	1-5-0	.167	7
1984	19	19	9-3-0	293	221	.750	3-3-0	.500	5	1988	5-6-0	217	209	.455	2-5-0	.286	8
1985			5-6-0	194	211	.455	1-5-0	.167	8	1989	6-5-0	212	220	.545	2-5-0	.286	7

			Bill Curry (1990-1996) 26-52-0 .333														
1990			4-7-0	228	316	.364	3-4-0	.429	5	1994	1-10-0	149	405	091	0-8-0	.000	11
1991			3-8-0	190	268	.273	0-7-0	.000	10	1995	4-7-0	223	269	.364	2-6-0	.250	8
1992			4-7-0	207	280	.364	2-6-0	.250	9	1996	4-7-0	138	322	.364	3-5-0	.375	7
1993			6-6-0	207	195	.500	4-4-0	.500	3								

			Hal Mumme (1997-2000) 20-26-0 .435														
1997			5-6-0	348	362	.455	2-6-0	.250	8	1999	6-6-0	328	343	.500	4-4-0	.500	6
1998			7-5-0	431	375	.583	4-4-0	.500	6	2000	2-9-0	254	383	.182	0-8-0	.000	12

			Guy Morriss (2001-2002) 9-14-0 .391														
2001			2-9-0	259	367	.182	1-7-0	.125	11	2002	7-5-0	385	301	.583	3-5-0	.375	8

			Rich Brooks (2003) 4-8-0 .333						
2003			4-8-0	328	321	.333	1-7-0	.125	9

Won-loss record by decades:

1881-99	35-28-4	.552	1930-39	47-43-3	.522	1970-79	49-60-2	.450
1900-09	57-30-4	.648	1940-49	47-39-5	.544	1980-89	47-62-3	.433
1910-19	50-24-5	.665	1950-59	62-38-5	.629	1990-99	44-69-0	.389
1920-29	42-37-8	.529	1960-69	37-58-5	.395	2000-03	15-31-0	.326

Historical record: 532-519-44 .506

Post-season won-loss record: 5-5-0 .500

1947: Great Lakes Bowl, Kentucky 24, Villanova 14
1950: Orange Bowl, Santa Clara 21, Kentucky 13
1951: Sugar Bowl, Kentucky 13, Oklahoma 7
1952: Cotton Bowl, Kentucky 20, TCU 7
1976: Peach Bowl, Kentucky 21, North Carolina 0

1983: Hall of Fame Bowl, West Virginia 20, Kentucky 16
1984: Hall of Fame Bowl, Kentucky 20, Wisconsin 19
1994: Peach Bowl, Clemson 14, Kentucky 13
1999: Outback Bowl, Penn State 26, Kentucky 14
1999: Music City Bowl, Syracuse 20, Kentucky 13

College Football Hall of Fame:
Bear Bryant, coach, 1946-53; Bob Gain, guard/tackle, 1947-50; Babe Parilli, quarterback, 1949-51; Lou Michaels, tackle, 1955-57; Jerry Claiborne, coach, 1982-89.

Awards: Davey O'Brien Award: 1998, Tim Couch; Outland Trophy: 1950, Bob Gain; Tatupu Award: 2002, Glenn Pakulak.

UNIVERSITY OF LOUISIANA AT LAFAYETTE, Lafayette, Louisiana; nickname "Ragin' Cajuns"; colors vermilion and white; Cajun Field (31,000); Sun Belt Conference. Formerly known as the University of Southwestern Louisiana. Name changed to University of Louisiana at Lafayette in 1999. Southwest Louisiana was an independent until the 1948 season when it joined the Gulf States Conference. In 1971, the Cajuns moved to the Southland Conference as a Division I-A school. When the Southland Conference opted for Division I-AA status, the Cajuns became an independent Division I-A school. In 1993, the Cajuns joined the Big West conference and then left that conference after the 1995 season. In 2001, ULL became a member of the Sun Belt Conference. Data for conference play are shown only for the Big West and Sun Belt conferences.

Year	W-L-T	PF	PA	Pct.	Year	W-L-T	PF	PA	Pct.
				C. J. McNaspy (1908-1911, 1913, 1917-1918) 34-18-4 .643					
1908	6-0-0	93	16	1.000	1910	6-2-1	110	123	.722
1909	5-5-2	200	60	.500	1911	1-4-1	35	95	.250
				H. L. Prather (1912) 3-4-0 .429					
1912	3-4-0	90	240	.429					
				C. J. McNaspy (1913)					
1913	4-4-0	148	155	.500					
				R. B. Dunbar (1914-1915) 10-5-1 .656					
1914	5-3-0	205	100	.625	1915	5-2-1	127	41	.688
				T.R. Mobley (1916, 1919, 1921-1930) 58-47-7 .549					
1916	7-1-0	238	30	.875					
				C. J. McNaspy (1917-1918)					
1917	8-2-0	336	46	.800	1918	4-1-0	166	100	.800
				T.R. Mobley (1919)					
1919	3-3-2	66	140	.500					
				H. O. Tudor (1920) 2-8-0 .200					
1920	2-8-0	83	232	.200					
				T. R. Mobley (1921-1930)					
1921	9-2-0	218	104	.818	1926	6-3-1	153	98	.650
1922	3-4-2	84	54	.444	1927	2-7-1	30	195	.250
1923	7-3-0	240	107	.700	1928	4-5-0	115	175	.444
1924	6-2-1	214	94	.722	1929	2-7-0	52	203	.222
1925	7-2-0	188	72	.778	1930	2-8-0	52	257	.200
				T. F. Wilbanks (1931-1936) 19-31-3 .387					
1931	1-6-1	29	169	.188	1934	5-4-0	131	60	.556
1932	3-4-0	46	53	.429	1935	2-8-0	48	172	.200
1933	6-3-0	128	33	.667	1936	2-6-2	54	195	.300
				Johnny Cain (1937-1941, 1946) 33-19-5 .623					
1937	4-3-1	59	51	.562	1940	6-3-1	77	74	.650
1938	8-2-1	141	68	.773	1941	6-2-1	124	73	.722
1939	3-5-1	82	60	.389					
				Louis Whitman (1942-1945) 14-14-2 .500					
1942	3-4-0	115	98	.429	1944	5-4-0	124	70	.556
1943	5-0-1	172	70	.917	1945	1-6-1	32	183	.188
				Johnny Cain (1946)					
1946	6-4-0	189	130	.600					
				George Mitchell (1947-1949) 18-8-1 .685					
1947	6-2-0	167	58	.750	1949	6-3-0	174	145	.667
1948	6-3-1	179	134	.650					
				Al Swanson (1950) 5-4-0 .556					
1950	5-4-0	159	100	.556					
				Raymond Didier (1951-1956) 29-27-2 .517					
1951	6-4-0	227	198	.600	1954	5-4-0	222	159	.556
1952	5-2-2	203	131	.667	1955	5-4-0	170	139	.556
1953	4-7-0	168	247	.364	1956	4-6-0	239	299	.400
				John R. Bell (1957) 4-5-1 .450					
1957	4-5-1	99	143	.450					
				Jim Hoggatt (1958-1960) 11-17-0 .393					
1958	1-8-0	67	176	.111	1960	6-4-0	129	108	.600
1959	4-5-0	158	157	.444					
				Russ Faulkinberry (1961-1973) 66-63-2 .511					
1961	2-8-0	99	194	.200	1968	8-2-0	227	153	.800
1962	4-5-1	106	143	.450	1969	5-5-0	179	237	.500
1963	4-5-0	74	150	.444	1970	9-3-0	276	176	.750
1964	5-4-0	140	115	.556	1971	5-4-1	171	162	.550
1965	7-3-0	170	85	.700	1972	5-6-0	160	124	.455
1966	6-4-0	139	103	.600	1973	0-10-0	75	275	.000
1967	6-4-0	142	126	.600					

Augie Tammariello (1974-1979) 30-35-2 .463

Year	W-L-T	PF	PA	Pct.	Year	W-L-T	PF	PA	Pct.
1974	2-9-0	149	287	.182	1977	6-4-2	239	181	.583
1975	6-5-0	259	233	.545	1978	3-8-0	127	229	.273
1976	9-2-0	261	148	.818	1979	4-7-0	147	178	.364

Sam Robertson (1980-1985) 29-34-2 .462

Year	W-L-T	PF	PA	Pct.	Year	W-L-T	PF	PA	Pct.
1980	7-4-0	194	144	.636	1983	4-6-0	194	212	400
1981	1-9-1	135	229	.136	1984	6-5-0	207	198	.545
1982	7-3-1	248	197	.682	1985	4-7-0	162	306	.364

Nelson Stokely (1986-1998) 62-80-1 .437

Year	W-L-T	PF	PA	Pct.	Year	W-L-T	PF	PA	Pct.
1986	6-5-0	242	204	.545	1990	5-6-0	197	242	.455
1987	6-5-0	191	252	.545	1991	2-8-1	148	279	.227
1988	6-5-0	296	224	.545	1992	2-9-0	143	306	.182
1989	7-4-0	241	232	.636					

Member of the Big West Conference (1993-1995) 14-4-0 .778

Year	Nat'l AP Other	Overall W-L-T	PF	PA	Pct.	Conference W-L-T	Pct.	Rank	Year	Nat'l AP Other	Overall W-L-T	PF	PA	Pct.	Conference W-L-T	Pct.	Rank
1993		8-3-0	249	227	.727	5-1-0	.833	1	1995		6-5-0	351	275	.545	4-2-0	.667	2
1994		6-5-0	221	264	.545	5-1-0	.833	1									

Independent (1996-2000)

Year	Overall W-L-T	PF	PA	Pct.	Year	Overall W-L-T	PF	PA	Pct.
1996	5-6-0	304	404	.455	1998	2-9-0	199	453	.182
1997	1-10-0	176	553	.091					

Jerry Baldwin (1999-2001) 6-27-0 .182

Year	Overall W-L-T	PF	PA	Pct.	Year	Overall W-L-T	PF	PA	Pct.
1999	2-9-0	197	408	.182	2000	1-10-0	161	355	.091

Member of the Sun Belt Conference (2001-2003) 8-11-0 .421

Year	Overall W-L-T	PF	PA	Pct.	Conference W-L-T	Pct.	Rank	Year	Overall W-L-T	PF	PA	Pct.	Conference W-L-T	Pct.	Rank
2001	3-8-0	234	365	.272	2-4-0	.333	4								

Rickey Bustle (2002-2003) 7-17-0 .292

Year	Overall W-L-T	PF	PA	Pct.	Conference W-L-T	Pct.	Rank	Year	Overall W-L-T	PF	PA	Pct.	Conference W-L-T	Pct.	Rank
2002	3-9-0	203	352	.250	2-4-0	.333	4	2003	4-8-0	266	415	.333	4-3-0	.571	2

Won-loss record by decades:

1908-09	11- 5-2	.667	1940-49	50-31-5	.610	1980-89	54-53-2	.505
1910-19	46-26-5	.630	1950-59	43-49-3	.468	1990-99	39-70-1	.359
1920-29	48-43-5	.526	1960-69	53-44-1	.546	2000-03	11-35-0	.239
1930-39	36-49-6	.429	1970-79	49-58-3	.496			

Historic record: 440-463-33 .488

Post-season won-loss record: 1-1-0 .500
1943: Oil Bowl, Southwestern Louisiana 24, Arkansas A&M 7
1970: Grantland Rice Bowl, Tennessee State 26, Southwestern Louisiana 25

UNIVERSITY OF LOUISIANA AT MONROE, Monroe, Louisiana; nickname "Indians"; Malone Stadium (30,427); Sun Belt Conference. ULM was a junior college until 1951; data are shown below only for the period from 1951 on. ULM joined the Gulf States conference in 1953 and left the conference in 1971. The team opted for Division I-A status in 1975, but then joined the Division I-AA Southland Conference in 1982. In 1994 the team opted for Division I-A as an independent and in 2001 ULM joined the Sun Belt Conference. Conference data are shown only for the Sun Belt Conference.

Year	W-L-T	PF	PA	Pct.	Year	W-L-T	PF	PA	Pct.
					James Malone (1951-1953) 12-15-0 .444				
1951	6-2-0	253	128	.750	1953	1-9-0	113	284	.100
1952	5-4-0	243	209	.556					
					Devone Payne (1954-1957) 15-22-1 .408				
1954	1-8-1	119	337	.150	1956	8-2-0	220	155	.800
1955	4-6-0	100	206	.400	1957	2-6-0	105	128	.250
					Jack Rowan (1958-1963) 20-37-0 .351				
1958	6-3-0	189	163	.667	1961	3-7-0	145	171	.300
1959	2-8-0	116	216	.200	1962	2-6-0	74	106	.250
1960	3-7-0	91	136	.300	1963	4-6-0	113	141	.400
					Dixie White (1964-1971) 31-45-1 .409				
1964	0-8-0	58	148	.000	1968	6-4-0	170	101	.600
1965	1-8-0	58	194	.111	1969	1-9-0	132	216	.100
1966	7-3-0	181	101	.700	1970	5-4-0	151	146	.556
1967	7-3-0	196	111	.700	1971	4-6-1	122	208	.409
					Ollie Keller (1972-1975) 14-24-3 .378				
1972	3-7-0	125	188	.300	1974	4-6-0	162	190	.400
1973	3-5-2	133	222	.400	1975	4-6-1	252	273	.409
					John David Crow (1976-1980) 20-34-1 .373				
1976	2-9-0	206	321	.182	1979	3-8-0	158	211	.273
1977	2-9-0	122	297	.182	1980	7-4-0	296	267	.636
1978	6-4-1	190	144	.591					
					Pat Collins (1981-1988) 57-35-0 .620				
1981	5-6-0	309	251	.455	1985	6-5-0	227	201	.545
1982	8-3-0	313	216	.727	1986	5-6-0	231	205	.455
1983	8-3-0	198	159	.727	1987	13-2-0	484	343	.867
1984	7-4-0	251	119	.636	1988	5-6-0	160	214	.455
					Dave Roberts (1989-1993) 38-19-2 .661				
1989	5-5-1	201	257	.500	1992	10-3-0	596	284	.769
1990	7-5-0	208	218	.583	1993	9-3-0	462	275	.750
1991	7-3-1	237	175	.682					
					Ed Zaunbrecher (1994-1998) 20-36-0 .351				
1994	3-8-0	242	384	.273	1997	5-7-0	226	319	.417
1995	2-9-0	233	413	.182	1998	5-6-0	227	322	.455
1996	5-6-0	192	353	.455					
					Bobby Keasler (1999-2001) 11-34-0 .244				
1999	5-6-0	186	322	.455	2000	1-10-0	96	415	.091

Member of the Sun Belt Conference (2001-2003) 5-14-0 .263

	Nat'l	Overall				Conference			Nat'l	Overall				Conference		
Year	AP Other	W-L-T	PF	PA	Pct.	W-L-T	Pct.	Rank	Year	AP Other	W-L-T	PF	PA	Pct.	W-L-T	Pct.	Rank
2001		2-9-0	148	351	.182	2-4-0	.333	4	2002		3-9-0	236	451	.250	2-4-0	.333	4
						Charlie Weatherbie (2003) 1-11-0 .083											
2003		1-11-0	239	467	.083	1-6-0	.143	8									

Won-loss record by decades (since 1951):

1951-59	35-48-1	.423	1970-79	36-64-5	.367	1990-99	58-56-1	.509
1960-69	34-61-0	.358	1980-89	69-44-1	.610	2000-03	7-39-0	.152

Historic record (since 1951): 239-312-8 .435

Post-season won-loss record: 5-3-0 .625
1987: Division I-AA Playoffs: ULM 30, North Texas 9
1987: I-AA Playoffs: ULM 33, East Kentucky 32
1987: I-AA Playoffs: ULM 44, Northern Iowa 41
1987: I-AA Championship, ULM 43, Marshall 42
1990: I-AA Playoffs, Nevada 27, ULM 14
1992: I-AA Playoffs, ULM 78, Alcorn State 27
1992: I-AA Playoffs, Delaware 41, ULM 18
1993: I-AA Playoffs, Idaho 34, ULM 31

LOUISIANA STATE UNIVERSITY, Baton Rouge, Louisiana; nickname "Tigers"; colors purple and gold; Tiger Stadium (91,600) Southeastern Conference. LSU began play in 1893 and joined the Southern Conference as a founding member in 1922. LSU left the Southern Conference when the Southeastern Conference was organized after the 1932 season and has been a member of the SEC since that time.

Early years (1893-1921)

Year	Coach	W-L-T	PF	PA	Pct.	Year	Coach	W-L-T	PF	PA	Pct.
1893	Charles Coates	0-1-0	0	34	.000	1908	Edgard Wingard	10-0-0	442	11	1.000
1894	Albert Simmons	2-1-0	62	26	.667	1909	Joe Pritchard &				
1895	Albert Simmons	3-0-0	36	16	1.000		John Mayhew	6-2-0	188	37	.750
1896	Allen Jeardeau	6-0-0	136	4	1.000	1910	John Mayhew	1-5-0	45	119	.167
1897	Allen Jeardeau	1-1-0	28	32	.500	1911	Pat Dwyer	6-3-0	186	34	.667
1898	E. Chavanne	1-0-0	37	0	1.000	1912	Pat Dwyer	4-3-0	165	36	.571
1899	John Gregg	1-4-0	86	126	.200	1913	Pat Dwyer	6-1-2	200	49	.778
1900	E. Chavanne	2-2-0	85	35	.500	1914	E.T. McDonald	4-4-1	163	148	.500
1901	W. Borland	5-1-0	167	28	.833	1915	E.T. McDonald	6-2-0	126	49	.750
1902	W. Borland	6-1-0	80	27	.857	1916	E.T. McDonald	7-1-2	238	45	.800
1903	W. Borland	4-5-0	70	93	.444	1917	Wayne Sutton	3-5-0	112	94	.375
1904	Dan Killian	3-4-0	38	38	.429	1918	no team				
1905	Dan Killian	3-0-0	36	0	1.000	1919	Irving Pray	6-2-0	161	35	.750
1906	Dan Killian	2-2-2	40	36	.500	1920	Branch Bocock	5-3-1	206	63	.611
1907	Edgar Wingard	7-3-0	266	52	.700	1921	Branch Bocock	6-1-1	180	56	.812

Member of the Southern Conference (1922-1932) 19-24-3 .446

Year	Nat'l AP	Other	Overall W-L-T	PF	PA	Pct.	Conference W-L-T	Pct.	Rank	Year	Nat'l AP	Other	Overall W-L-T	PF	PA	Pct.	Conference W-L-T	Pct.	Rank
							Irving Pray (1919,1922) 9-9-0 .500												
1922			3-7-0	72	245	.300	1-2-0	.333	11										
							Mike Donahue (1923-1927) 23-19-3 .544												
1923			3-5-1	103	121	.438	0-3-0	.000	19	1926			6-3-0	128	45	.667	3-3-0	.500	10
1924			5-4-0	124	81	.556	0-3-0	.000	19	1927			4-4-1	128	83	.500	2-3-1	.417	11
1925			5-3-1	90	70	.611	0-2-1	.167	18										
							Russ Cohen (1928-1931) 23-13-1 .635												
1928			6-2-1	180	45	.722	3-1-1	.750	6	1930			6-4-0	296	72	.600	2-3-0	.400	16
1929			6-3-0	246	118	.667	3-2-0	.600	10	1931			5-4-0	137	90	.556	2-2-0	.500	7
							Biff Jones (1931-1934) 20-5-6 .741												
1932			6-3-1	187	31	.650	3-0-0	1.000	3										

Member of the Southeastern Conference (1933-2003) 246-188-20 .564

Year	Nat'l AP	Other	Overall W-L-T	PF	PA	Pct.	Conference W-L-T	Pct.	Rank	Year	Nat'l AP	Other	Overall W-L-T	PF	PA	Pct.	Conference W-L-T	Pct.	Rank
1933			7-0-3	176	27	.850	3-0-2	.800	2	1934			7-2-2	172	77	.727	4-2-0	.667	4
							Bernie Moore (1935-1947) 83-39-6 .671												
1935		4	9-2-0	223	41	.818	5-0-0	1.000	1	1942			7-3-0	192	117	.700	3-2-0	.600	6
1936	2	2	9-1-1	295	54	.864	6-0-0	1.000	1	1943			6-3-0	162	158	.667	2-2-0	.500	2
1937	8	8	9-2-0	234	33	.818	5-1-0	.833	2	1944			2-5-1	92	101	.312	2-3-1	.417	6
1938			6-4-0	160	89	.600	2-4-0	.333	10	1945	15		7-2-0	245	92	.778	5-2-0	.714	3
1939			4-5-0	111	116	.444	1-5-0	.167	10	1946	8		9-1-1	240	123	.864	5-1-0	.833	3
1940			6-4-0	139	112	.600	3-3-0	.500	6	1947			5-3-1	149	161	.611	2-3-1	.417	
1941			4-4-2	119	93	.500	2-2-2	.500	7										
							Gaynell Tinsley (1948-1954) 35-34-6 .507												
1948			3-7-0	99	271	.300	1-5-0	.167	10	1952			3-7-0	148	214	.300	2-5-0	.286	10
1949	9		8-3-0	231	109	.727	4-2-0	.667	5	1953			5-3-3	194	159	.591	2-3-3	.438	8
1950			4-5-2	165	151	.455	2-3-2	.429	7	1954			5-6-0	125	173	.455	2-5-0	.286	9
1951			7-3-1	128	111	.682	4-2-1	.642	3										
							Paul Dietzel (1955-1961) 46-24-3 .651												
1955			3-5-2	139	149	.400	2-3-1	.417	9	1959	3	3	9-2-0	164	50	.818	5-1-0	.833	2
1956			3-7-0	104	197	.300	1-5-0	.167	11	1960			5-4-1	105	50	.550	2-3-1	.417	8
1957			5-5-0	159	110	.500	4-4-0	.500	6	1961	4	3	10-1-0	259	57	.909	6-0-0	1.000	2
1958	1	1	11-0-0	282	53	1.000	6-0-0	1.000	1										
							Charlie McClendon (1962-1979) 137-59-7 .692												
1962	7	8	9-1-1	185	34	.864	5-1-0	.833	3	1971	11	10	9-3-0	353	153	.750	3-2-0	.600	6
1963			7-4-0	142	112	.636	4-2-0	.667	5	1972	11	10	9-2-1	252	145	.792	4-1-1	.750	3
1964	7	7	8-2-1	128	89	.773	4-2-1	.643	5	1973	13	14	9-3-0	267	169	.750	5-1-0	.833	4
1965	8	14	8-3-0	269	164	.727	3-3-0	.500	6	1974			5-5-1	202	168	.500	2-4-0	.333	9
1966			5-4-1	135	124	.550	3-3-0	.500	6	1975			5-6-0	159	202	.455	2-4-0	.333	6
1967			7-3-1	268	127	.682	3-2-1	.583	6	1976			7-3-1	255	149	.682	3-3-0	.500	6
1968	19		8-3-0	221	171	.727	4-2-0	.667	3	1977			8-4-0	389	220	.667	4-2-0	.667	4
1969	10	7	9-1-0	349	91	.900	4-1-0	.800	2	1978			8-4-0	279	193	.667	3-3-0	.500	4
1970	7	6	9-3-0	289	113	.750	5-0-0	1.000	1	1979			7-5-0	275	148	.583	4-2-0	.667	4
							Jerry Stovall (1980-1983) 22-21-4 .511												
1980			7-4-0	213	193	.636	4-2-0	.667	4	1982	11	11	8-3-1	385	191	.708	4-1-1	.750	2
1981			3-7-1	167	281	.318	1-4-1	.250	8	1983			4-7-0	251	253	.364	0-6-0	.000	9

Bill Arnsparger (1984-1986) 26-8-2 .750

1984	15	16	8-3-1	325	226	.708	4-1-1	.750	2	1986	10	11	9-3-0	304	185	.750	5-1-0	.833	1
1985	20	20	9-2-1	227	134	.792	4-1-1	.750	2										

Mike Archer (1987-1990) 27-18-1 .598

1987	5	5	10-1-1	365	184	.875	5-1-0	.833	2	1989	4-7-0	295	252	.364	2-5-0	.286	7
1988	19		8-4-0	249	204	.667	6-1-0	.857	2	1990	5-6-0	183	238	.455	2-5-0	.286	6

Curley Hallman (1991-1994) 16-28-0 .364

1991	5-6-0	248	263	.455	3-40	.429	6	1993	5-6-0	190	308	.455	3-5-0	.375	6
1992	2-9-0	175	261	.182	1-7-0	125	12	1994	4-7-0	269	271	.364	3-5-0	.375	6

Gerry DiNardo (1994-1999) 33-24-1 .578

1995			7-4-1	324	186	.625	4-3-1	.562	5	1998	4-7-0	337	279	.364	2-6-0	.250	11
1996	12	13	10-2-0	335	210	.833	6-2-0	.750	3	1999	3-8-0	223	259	.273	1-7-0	.125	11
1997	13	13	9-3-0	373	188	.750	6-2-0	.750	2								

Nick Saban (2000-2003) 39-13-0 .750

2000	22		8-4-0	320	235	.667	5-3-0	.625	3	2002		8-5-0	323	238	.615	5-3-0	.625	4
2001	7	8	10-3-0	418	302	.769	5-3-0	.625	2	2003	2	1 13-1-0	475	154	.929	7-1-0	.875	1

Won-loss record by decades:

1893-99	14- 7-0	.667		1930-39	68-27-7	.701		1970-79	76-38-3	.662
1900-09	48-20-2	.700		1940-49	57-35-5	.613		1980-89	70-41-5	.625
1910-19	43-26-5	.615		1950-59	55-43-8	.557		1990-99	54-58-1	.482
1920-29	49-35-6	.578		1950-69	76-26-5	.734		2000-03	39-13-0	.750

Historical record: 636-368-47 .627

Post-season won-loss record: 19-17-1 .527

1936: Sugar Bowl, TCU 3, LSU 2
1937: Sugar Bowl, Santa Clara 21, LSU 14
1938: Sugar Bowl, Santa Clara 6, LSU 0
1944: Orange Bowl, LSU 19, Texas A&M 14
1947: Cotton Bowl, LSU 0, Arkansas 0
1950: Sugar Bowl, Oklahoma 35, LSU 0
1959: Sugar Bowl, LSU 7, Clemson 0
1960: Sugar Bowl, Mississippi 21, LSU 0
1962: Orange Bowl, LSU 25, Colorado 7
1963: Cotton Bowl, LSU 13, Texas 0
1963: Bluebonnet Bowl, Baylor 14, LSU 7
1965: Sugar Bowl, LSU 13, Syracuse 10
1966: Cotton Bowl, LSU 14, Arkansas 7
1968: Sugar Bowl, LSU 20, Wyoming 13
1968:Peach Bowl, LSU 31, Florida State 27
1971: Orange Bowl, Nebraska 17, LSU 12
1971: Sun Bowl, LSU 33, Iowa State 16

1972: Bluebonnet Bowl, Tennessee 24, LSU 17
1974: Orange Bowl, Penn State 16, LSU 9
1977. Sun Bowl, Stanford 24, LSU 14
1979: Liberty Bowl, Missouri 20, LSU 15
1978: Tangerine Bowl, LSU 34, Wake Forest 10
1983: Orange Bowl, Nebraska 21, LSU 20
1985: Sugar Bowl, Nebraska 28, LSU 10
1985: Liberty Bowl, Baylor 21, LSU 7
1987: Sugar Bowl, Nebraska 30, LSU 15
1987: Gator Bowl, LSU 30, South Carolina 13
1989: Hall of Fame Bowl, Syracuse 23, LSU 10
1995: Independence Bowl, LSU 45, Michigan State 26
1996: Peach Bowl, LSU 10, Clemson 7
1997: Independence Bowl, LSU 27, Notre Dame 9
2000: Peach Bowl, LSU 28, Georgia Tech 14
2001: SEC Championship, LSU 31, Tennessee 20
2002: Sugar Bowl, LSU 47, Illinois 34
2003: Cotton Bowl, Texas 35, LSU 20
2003: SEC Championship, LSU 34, Georgia 14
2004: Sugar Bowl, LSU 21, Oklahoma 14

College Football Hall of Fame:
Doc Fenton, end/quarterback, 1906-09; Dana Bible, coach, 1916; Mike Donahue, coach, 1923-27; Biff Jones, coach, 1932-34; Abe Mickal, halfback, 1933-35; Gaynell Tinsley, end, 1934-36; Bernie Moore, coach, 1935-47; Ken Kavanaugh, end, 1937-39; Charlie McClendon, coach, 1962-79; Tommy Casanova, cornerback, 1969-71.

Awards: Heisman Trophy: 1959, Billy Cannon; Beletnikoff Award, 2001, Josh Reed.

LOUISIANA TECH, Ruston, Louisiana; nickname "Bulldogs"; Joe Aillet Stadium (30,600); Western Athletic Conference. Tech began play in 1901 as an independent. In 1925, it joined the Southern Intercollegiate Athletic Association (SIAA) where it played through the 1938 season. In 1939, Tech joined the Louisiana Intercollegiate Conference (LIC). It played in that conference through the 1947 season after which it joined the Gulf States Conference. In 1971, Louisiana Tech joined the Southland Conference where it won national championship honors in 1972, 1973, and 1974. In 1987, Tech became a Division I-AA independent and in 1989, this was raised to I-A independent. In 1993, Tech joined the Big West Conference dropping out of that conference after the 1995 season and becoming an independent again. Tech joined the WAC beginning with the 2001 season. Conference data are presented only for the Big West and WAC conferences.

Early years as an independent (1901-1924)

Year	W-L-T	PF	PA	Pct.	Year	W-L-T	PF	PA	Pct.

Record is incomplete for the period (1901-1905). Games reported give records as follows: 1901 0-2-0; 1902 no records; 1903 0-1-0; 1904 1-3-0; 1905 0-1-0. Records are also incomplete for most years up to 1920.

Z. T. Young (1906) 2-1-3 .583

Year	W-L-T	PF	PA	Pct.	Year	W-L-T	PF	PA	Pct.
1906	2-1-3	36	22	.583					

George Watkins (1907) 9-1-0 .900

| 1907 | 9-1-0 | 248 | 37 | .900 | | | | | |

A. J. Cornell (1908) 4-3-1 .562

| 1908 | 4-3-1 | 205 | 91 | .562 | | | | | |

Percy S. Prince (1909-1915. 1918-1919) 24-16-5 .589

1909	4-1-0	136	23	.800	1913	3-4-1	105	72	.438
1910	7-0-0	130	6	1.000	1914	2-4-0	55	161	.333
1911	4-2-1	98	68	.643	1915	3-1-2	110	33	.667
1912	1-2-1	66	56	.375					

A. Flack (1916) 2-4-0 .333

| 1916 | 2-4-0 | 40 | 66 | .333 | | | | | |

V. S. Pugh (1917) 2-3-0 .400

| 1917 | 2-3-0 | 72 | 136 | .400 | | | | | |

Percy S. Prince (1918-1919) 0-2-0

| 1918 | no information available | | | | 1919 | 0-2-0 | 7 | 41 | .000 |

R. F. Clark (1920-1921) 11-1-0 .917

| 1920 | 5-1-0 | 38 | 19 | .833 | 1921 | 6-0-0 | 104 | 20 | 1.000 |

William Dietz (1922-1923) 11-3-1 .767

| 1922 | 5-1-1 | 290 | 63 | .786 | 1923 | 6-2-0 | 194 | 63 | .750 |

Phillip Arbuckle (1924) 1-6-1 .188

| 1924 | 1-6-1 | 42 | 129 | .188 | | | | | |

Member of the SIAA (1925-1938) no conference data

R. C. Kenney (1925) 1-6-2 .222

| 1925 | 1-6-2 | 28 | 176 | .222 | | | | | |

Hugh E. Wilson (1926-1927) 8-7-2 .529

| 1926 | 5-2-2 | 134 | 60 | .667 | 1927 | 3-5-0 | 83 | 118 | .375 |

F. A. Rockwell (1928-1929) 6-11-2 .368

| 1928 | 2-7-0 | 42 | 235 | .222 | 1929 | 4-4-2 | 96 | 137 | .500 |

George Bohler (1930-1933) 15-17-0 .469

| 1930 | 3-6-0 | 39 | 187 | .333 | 1932 | 4-4-0 | 113 | 89 | .500 |
| 1931 | 7-0-0 | 167 | 36 | 1.000 | 1933 | 1-7-0 | 32 | 143 | .125 |

L. P. McLane (1934-1938) 27-19-4 .580

1934	4-6-0	88	116	.400	1937	6-3-2	120	60	.583
1935	8-1-0	253	42	.889	1938	3-7-1	98	163	.318
1936	6-2-1	153	47	.722					

Member of the LIC (1939-1947) No conference data

Ray E. Davis (1939) 5-6-0 .455

| 1939 | 5-6-0 | 125 | 127 | .455 | | | | | |

Joe Aillet (1940-1966) 152-85-8 .637

1940	6-4-0	106	109	.600	1944	3-5-1	120	114	.389
1941	5-4-1	134	112	.550	1945	6-4-0	133	123	.600
1942	6-3-0	252	90	.667	1946	7-3-0	195	87	.700
1943	no team				1947	5-4-0	154	107	.556

Member of the Gulf States Conference (1947-1970) No conference data

1948	7-2-1	183	142	.750	1958	7-3-0	206	104	.700
1949	7-2-0	230	97	.778	1959	9-1-0	191	48	.900
1950	5-4-1	152	165	.550	1960	8-2-0	151	96	.800
1951	5-4-0	156	192	.556	1961	5-4-0	156	109	.556
1952	6-1-2	181	117	.778	1962	4-4-0	125	124	.500
1953	6-3-0	222	119	.667	1963	6-3-0	188	103	.667
1954	6-3-0	189	131	.667	1964	9-1-0	157	64	.900
1955	9-1-0	250	97	.900	1965	4-4-0	161	122	.500
1956	4-3-2	101	68	.556	1966	1-9-0	83	205	.100
1957	6-4-0	165	141	.600					

Maxie Lambright (1967-1978) 95-36-2 .722

Year	W-L-T	PF	PA	Pct.		Year	W-L-T	PF	PA	Pct.
1967	3-7-0	156	242	.300		1969	8-2-0	331	201	.800
1968	9-2-0	337	195	.818		1970	2-8-0	165	175	.200

Member of the Southland Conference (1971-1986) no conference data

Year	W-L-T	PF	PA	Pct.		Year	W-L-T	PF	PA	Pct.
1971	9-2-0	288	175	.818		1975	8-2-0	297	185	.800
1972	12-0-0	333	134	1.000		1976	6-5-0	335	247	.545
1973	12-1-0	355	106	.923		1977	9-1-2	305	147	.833
1974	11-1-0	318	145	.917		1978	6-5-0	228	186	.545

Larry Beightol (1979) 3-8-0 .273

1979	3-8-0	112	222	.273

Billy Brewer (1980-1982) 19-15-1 .557

Year	W-L-T	PF	PA	Pct.		Year	W-L-T	PF	PA	Pct.
1980	5-6-0	193	220	.455		1982	10-3-0	340	177	.769
1981	4-6-1	205	241	.409						

A. L. Williams (1983-1986) 28-19-1 .594

Year	W-L-T	PF	PA	Pct.		Year	W-L-T	PF	PA	Pct.
1983	4-7-0	152	195	.364		1985	8-3-0	259	176	.727
1984	10-5-0	310	204	.667		1986	6-4-1	206	223	.591

Division I-AA independent (1987-1988)
Carl Torbush (1987) 3-8-0 .273

1987	3-8-0	108	197	.273

Joe Peace (1988-1995) 39-46-3 .460

1988	4-7-0	185	352	.364

Division I-A independent (1989-1992)

Year	W-L-T	PF	PA	Pct.		Year	W-L-T	PF	PA	Pct.
1989*	4-6-0	283	265	.400		1991	8-1-2	280	178	.773
1990	8-3-1	365	219	.708		1992	5-6-0	199	167	.455

*One win game forfeited and one tie forfeited. Pre-forfeits, the 1989 record was 5-4-1.

Member of the Big West Conference (1993-1995) 5-13-0 .278

	Nat'l	Overall				Conference				Nat'l	Overall				Conference		
Year	AP Other	W-L-T	PF	PA	Pct.	W-L-T	Pct.	Rank	Year	AP Other	W-L-T	PF	PA	Pct.	W-L-T	Pct.	Rank
1993		2-9-0	143	332	.182	2-4-0	.333	6	1995		5-6-0	320	371	.455	2-4-0	.333	7
1994		3-8-0	164	274	.273	1-5-0	.167	9									

Louisiana Tech reverts to I-A independent status (1996-2000)
Gary Crowton (1996-1998) 21-13-0 .618

Year	W-L-T	PF	PA	Pct.		Year	W-L-T	PF	PA	Pct.
1996	6-5-0	401	292	.545		1998	6-6-0	493	402	.500
1997	9-2-0	364	281	.818						

Jack Bicknell (1999-2003) 27-31-0 .466

Year	W-L-T	PF	PA	Pct.		Year	W-L-T	PF	PA	Pct.
1999	8-3-0	395	313	.727		2000	3-8-0	317	396	.273

Member of the Western Athletic Conference (2001-2003) 13-11-0 .542

Year		Overall				Conference			Year		Overall				Conference		
2001		7-5-0	406	389	.583	7-1-0	.875	1	2003		5-7-0	310	394	.417	3-5-0	.375	7
2002		4-8-0	320	426	.426	3-5-0	.375	6									

Won-loss record by decades:

1901-09	20-13-4	.595	1940-49	52-31-3	.622	1980-89	58-55-2	.513
1910-19	24-22-5	.520	1950-59	63-27-5	.689	1990-99	60-49-3	.549
1920-29	38-34-8	.525	1960-69	57-38-0	.600	2000-03	19-28-0	.404
1930-39	47-42-4	.527	1970-79	78-33-2	.699			

Historic record: 516-372-36 .578

Post-season won-loss record: 12-6-1 .658

1968: Grantland Rice Bowl, La. Tech 33, Akron 13
1969: Grantland Rice Bowl, East Tenn. State 34, La. Tech 14
1971: Pioneer Bowl, La. Tech 14, Eastern Michigan 3
1972: Grantland Rice Bowl, La. Tech 35, Tennessee Tech 0
1973: Division II Playoffs, La. Tech 18, Western Illinois 13
1973: Playoffs, La. Tech 38, Boise State 34
1973: Championship, La. Tech 34, Western Kentucky 0
1974: Division II Playoffs, La. Tech 10, Western Carolina 7
1974: Playoffs, Central Michigan 35, La. Tech 14
1977: Independence Bowl, La. Tech 24, Louisville 14

1978: Independence Bowl, Eastern Carolina 35, La. Tech 13
1982: Division I-AA Playoffs, La. Tech 38, So. Carolina St. 3
1982: Playoffs, Delaware 17, La. Tech 0
1984: I-AA Playoffs, La. Tech 66, Miss. Valley 19
1984: Playoffs, La. Tech 44, Alcorn State 21
1984: Playoffs, La. Tech 21, Middle Tenn. State 13
1984: Championship, Montana State 19, La. Tech 6
1990: Independence Bowl, La. Tech 34, Maryland 34
2001: Humanitarian Bowl, Clemson 48, La. Tech 24

College Football Hall of Fame: Joe Aillet, coach, 1940-66; Terry Bradshaw, quarterback, 1966-69.

Awards: Fred Biletnikoff Award: 1998, Troy Edwards.

UNIVERSITY OF LOUISVILLE, Louisville, Kentucky; nickname "Cardinals"; colors red and black; Papa John's Cardinal Stadium (42,000); Conference USA. Louisville began play in 1912 as an independent. In 1963, Louisville joined the Missouri Valley Conference and played in that conference through the 1974 season. Between 1974 and 1996, Louisville was independent. In the 1996 season, Louisville became one of the founding members of Conference USA.

Year	W-L-T	PF	PA	Pct.		Year	W-L-T	PF	PA	Pct.
					Lester Larson (1912-193) 8-2-0 .800					
1912	3-1-0	128	47	.750		1913	5-1-0	251	20	.833
					Bruce Baker (1914) 1-4-0 .200					
1914	1-4-0	26	135	.200						
					Will Duffy (1915-1916) 3-8-2 .208					
1915	1-5-1	35	119	.214		1916	2-3-1	37	77	.417
					No team (1917-1920)					
					Bill Duncan (1921-1922) 4-9-1 .321					
1921	2-2-1	49	29	.500		1922	2-7-0	79	202	.222
					Fred Enke (1923-1924) 8-8-1 .500					
1923	5-3-0	84	73	.625		1924	3-5-1	43	95	.389
					Tom King (1925-1930) 27-21-0 .563					
1925	8-0-0	133	2	1.000		1928	1-7-0	72	186	.125
1926	6-2-0	226	51	.750		1929	3-5-0	37	101	.375
1927	4-4-0	114	161	.500		1930	5-3-0	134	73	.625
					Jack McGrath (1931) 0-8-0 .000					
1931	0-8-0	18	227	.000						
					C.V. Money (1932) 0-9-0 .000					
1932	0-9-0	18	392	.000						
					Ben Gregor (1933-1935) 4-18-1 .196					
1933	1-7-0	26	214	.125		1935	1-6-1	47	133	.188
1934	2-5-0	40	104	.286						
					Laurie Apitz (1936-1942) 22-29-3 .435					
1936	4-4-0	88	134	.500		1940	3-5-1	91	134	.389
1937	2-5-1	60	114	.312		1941	4-4-0	143	140	.500
1938	2-6-0	40	80	.250		1942	2-3-0	58	95	.400
1939	5-2-1	92	30	.688						
					No team (1943-1945)					
					Frank Camp (1946-68) 118-95-2 .556					
1946	6-2-0	136	62	.750		1955	7-2-0	289	134	.778
1947	7-0-1	193	63	.938		1956	6-3-0	153	111	.667
1948	5-5-0	186	194	.500		1957	9-1-0	350	106	.900
1949	8-3-0	343	143	.727		1958	4-4-0	144	97	.500
1950	3-6-1	239	238	.350		1959	6-4-0	218	132	.600
1951	5-4-0	151	208	.556		1960	7-2-0	196	77	.778
1952	3-5-0	172	224	.375		1961	6-3-0	180	91	.667
1953	1-7-0	70	276	.125		1962	6-4-0	174	173	.600
1954	3-6-0	116	177	.333						

Member of the Missouri Valley Conference (1963-1974) 27-27-0 .500

	Nat'l	Overall				Conference				Nat'l	Overall				Conference		
Year	AP Other	W-L-T	PF	PA	Pct.	W-L-T	Pct.	Rank	Year	AP Other	W-L-T	PF	PA	Pct.	W-L-T	Pct.	Rank
1963		3-7-0	118	213	.300	1-3-0	.250	5	1966		6-4-0	231	159	.600	1-3-0	.250	4
1964		1-9-0	70	217	.100	0-4-0	.000	5	1967		5-5-0	260	162	.500	1-3-0	.250	4
1965		6-4-0	218	164	.600	3-1-0	.750	2	1968		5-5-0	192	233	.500	2-3-0	.400	4

Lee Corso (1969-1972) 28-11-3 .690

1969		5-4-1	206	273	.550	2-3-0	.400	3	1971		6-3-1	190	111	.650	3-2-0	.600	2
1970		8-3-1	252	208	.771	4-0-0	1.000	1	1972	18 16	9-1-0	309	91	.900	4-1-0	.800	1

T. W. Alley (1973-1974) 9-13-0 .409

1973		5-6-0	172	148	.455	3-2-0	.600	3	1974		4-7-0	136	254	.364	3-2-0	.600	2

Louisville reverts to independent status (1975-1995)

Vince Gibson (1975-1979) 25-29-2 .464

1975		2-9-0	108	316	.182				1978		7-4-0	319	202	.636			
1976		5-6-0	177	234	.455				1979		4-6-1	167	202	.409			
1977		7-4-1	291	194	.625												

Bob Weber (1980-1984) 20-35-0 .364

1980		5-6-0	162	203	.455				1983		3-8-0	157	351	.273			
1981		5-6-0	180	212	.455				1984		2-9-0	237	369	.182			
1982		5-6-0	220	355	.455												

Howard Schnellenberger (1985-1994) 54-56-2 .491

1985		2-9-0	199	429	.182				1990	14 12	10-1-1	345	149	.875			
1986		3-8-0	179	276	.273				1991		2-9-0	135	335	.182			
1987		3-7-1	215	348	.318				1992		5-6-0	214	243	.455			
1988		8-3-0	261	245	.727				1993	24 23	9-3-0	350	243	.750			
1989		6-5-0	311	222	.545				1994		6-5-0	255	253	.545			

Ron Cooper (1995-1997) 13-20-0 .394

1995   7-4-0 283 165 .636

Member of Conference USA (1996-2003) 32-21-0 .604

1996   5-6-0 182 205 .455 2-3-0 .400 3 1997   1-10-0 245 407 .091 0-6-0 .000 6

John L. Smith (1998-2002) 41-21-0 .661

1998   7-5-0 473 435 .583 4-2-0 .667 3 2001 17 16 11-2-0 394 223 .846 6-1-0 .857 1

1999   7-5-0 443 365 .583 4-2-0 .667 2 2002   7-6-0 374 319 .538 5-3-0 .625 3

2000   9-3-0 405 268 .750 6-1-0 .857 1

Bob Petrino (2003) 9-4-0 .692

2003   9-4-0 450 361 .692 5-3-0 .625 3

Won-loss record by decades:

1912-19	12-14-2	.464		1950-59	47-42-1	.528	1980-89	42-67-1	.386
1920-29	34-35-2	.493		1960-69	50-47-1	.515	1990-99	58-54-1	.522
1930-39	22-55-3	.294		1970-79	57-49-4	.536	2000-03	36-15-0	.706
1940-49	35-22-2	.610							

Historic record 393-400-17 .496

Post-season won-loss record 4-6-1 .409

1957: Sun Bowl, Louisville 34, Drake 20
1970: Pasadena Bowl, Louisville 24, Long Beach State 24
1977: Independence Bowl, La. Tech 24, Louisville 14
1991: Fiesta Bowl, Louisville 34, Alabama 7
1993: Liberty Bowl, Louisville 18, Michigan State 7

1998: Motor City Bowl, Marshall 48, Louisville 29
1999: Humanitarian Bowl, Boise State 34, Louisville 31
2000: Liberty Bowl, Colorado State 22, Louisville 17
2001: Liberty Bowl, Louisville 28, BYU 10
2002: GMAC Bowl, Marshall 38, Louisville 15
2003: GMAC Bowl, Miami (OH) 49, Louisville 28

Awards: Unitas Award: 1999, Chris Redman.

MARSHALL UNIVERSITY, Huntington, West Virginia; nickname "Thundering Herd"; colors green and white; Marshall University Stadium (38,019); Mid-American Conference. Marshall began play in 1895 as an independent. Marshall was in the Mid-American Conference from 1954 through the 1968 season. Marshall was an independent from 1969 through the 1975 season. In 1976, Marshall joined the Southern Conference and played in that conference through the 1996 season. Marshall rejoined the MAC beginning with the 1997 season. Marshall will join Conference USA in 2004.

Early years (1895-1953)

Year	W-L-T	PF	PA	Pct.	Year	W-L-T	PF	PA	Pct.

No coach (1895-1901)

Year	W-L-T	PF	PA	Pct.	Year	W-L-T	PF	PA	Pct.
1895	0-1-1	0	36	.250	1899	0-0-1	0	0	.500
1896	no team				1900	1-0-2	20	0	.667
1897	0-3-0	16	32	.000	1901	2-0-1	25	0	.833
1898	4-1-0	40	11	.800					

Year	W-L-T	PF	PA	Pct.	Year	W-L-T	PF	PA	Pct.
1902 G. Ford	5-0-2	65	2	.857	1906 P. Rardin	4-0-1	56	5	.900
1903 G. Ford	3-1-1	37	25	.700	1907 No coach	3-2-1	38	34	.583
1904 A.McCrary	1-3-3	16	26	.357	1908 W. Vinal	0-6-0	14	104	.000
1905 A.McCrary	6-2-0	43	98	.760					

Boyd Chambers (1909-1916) 31-25-4 .550

Year	W-L-T	PF	PA	Pct.	Year	W-L-T	PF	PA	Pct.
1909	3-2-1	107	95	.583	1913	3-4-0	39	101	.429
1910	5-1-1	91	14	.786	1914	5-4-0	231	133	.556
1911	4-1-1	122	22	.750	1915	1-7-0	80	244	.125
1912	3-4-0	197	94	.429	1916	7-2-1	267	101	.750

Carl Shipley (1917) 1-7-1 .167

Year	W-L-T	PF	PA	Pct.	Year	W-L-T
1917	1-7-1	7	345	.167	1918	no team

Archer Reilly (1919) 8-0-0 1.000

Year	W-L-T	PF	PA	Pct.
1919	8-0-0	302	13	1.000

Herbert Cramer (1920) 0-8-0 .000

Year	W-L-T	PF	PA	Pct.
1920	0-8-0	0	247	.000

Kemper Shelton (1921-1922) 10-6-1 .618

Year	W-L-T	PF	PA	Pct.	Year	W-L-T	PF	PA	Pct.
1921	5-2-1	78	41	.688	1922	5-4-0	226	100	.556

Harrison Briggs (1923) 1-7-0 .125

Year	W-L-T	PF	PA	Pct.
1923	1-7-0	28	271	.125

Russell Meredith (1924) 4-4-0 .500

Year	W-L-T	PF	PA	Pct.
1924	4-4-0	48	113	.500

Charles Tallman (1925-1928) 22-9-7 .671

Year	W-L-T	PF	PA	Pct.	Year	W-L-T	PF	PA	Pct.
1925	4-1-4	138	29	.667	1927	5-3-1	194	75	.611
1926	5-4-1	150	99	.550	1928	8-1-1	175	33	.850

John Maulbetsch (1929-1930) 8-8-2 .500

Year	W-L-T	PF	PA	Pct.	Year	W-L-T	PF	PA	Pct.
1929	5-3-1	186	79	.611	1930	3-5-1	111	130	.389

Tom Dandelet (1931-1934) 18-16-2 .528

Year	W-L-T	PF	PA	Pct.	Year	W-L-T	PF	PA	Pct.
1931	6-3-0	214	84	.667	1933	3-5-1	109	103	.389
1932	6-2-1	155	58	.722	1934	3-6-0	92	111	.333

Cam Henderson (1935-1949) 68-46-5 .592

Year	W-L-T	PF	PA	Pct.	Year	W-L-T	PF	PA	Pct.
1935	4-6-0	139	117	.401	1942	1-7-1	52	118	.167
1936	6-3-1	314	78	.650	1943-1945 no team				
1937	9-0-1	297	19	.950	1946	2-7-1	145	190	.250
1938	5-4-0	274	67	.556	1947	9-3-0	342	125	.750
1939	9-2-0	286	85	.818	1948	2-7-1	71	243	.250
1940	8-2-0	334	75	.800	1949	6-4-0	168	147	.600
1941	7-1-0	217	47	.875					

Pete Pedersen (1950-1952) 9-19-3 .339

Year	W-L-T	PF	PA	Pct.	Year	W-L-T	PF	PA	Pct.
1950	2-8-0	107	249	.200	1952	2-7-2	193	233	.273
1951	5-4-1	206	176	.550					

Herb Royer (1953-1958) 21-31-2 .407

Year	W-L-T	PF	PA	Pct.
1953	2-5-2	109	180	.333

Member of the Mid-American Conference (1954-1968, 1997-2003) 72-71-1 .504

Year	W-L-T	PF	PA	Pct.	Conf	Pct.	Rk	Year	W-L-T	PF	PA	Pct.	Conf	Pct.	Rk
1954	4-5-0	203	214	.444	2-5-0	.286	7	1957	6-3-0	120	112	.667	4-2-0	.667	2
1955	3-6-0	159	192	.333	1-5-0	.167	6	1958	3-6-0	111	165	.333	1-5-0	.167	7
1956	3-6-0	122	185	.333	2-4-0	.333	4								

Charlie Snyder (1959-1967) 28-58-3 .331

Year	W-L-T	PF	PA	Pct.	Conf	Pct.	Rk	Year	W-L-T	PF	PA	Pct.	Conf	Pct.	Rk
1959	1-8-0	72	343	.111	1-4-0	.200	6	1964	7-3-0	120	93	.700	4-2-0	.667	2
1960	2-7-1	58	160	.250	1-4-0	.200	6	1965	5-5-0	151	168	.500	2-4-0	.333	5
1961	2-7-1	62	183	.250	1-4-0	.200	6	1966	2-8-0	119	210	.200	1-5-0	.167	6
1962	4-6-0	137	237	.400	0-5-0	.000	7	1967	0-10-0	72	311	.000	0-6-0	.000	7
1963	5-4-1	139	139	.550	3-2-1	.583	4								

Perry Moss (1968) 0-9-1 ..050

1968	0-9-1	129	358	.050	0-6-0	.000	7

Marshall reverts to Independent status (1969-1975)

Rick Tolley (1969-1970) 6-13-0 .316

1969	3-7-0	207	281	.300				1970		3-6-0	138	202				

Jack Lengyel (1971-1974) 9-33-0 .21

| 1971 | 2-8-0 | 57 | 299 | .200 | | | | 1973 | | 4-7-0 | 212 | 288 | .364 | | | |
| 1972 | 2-8-0 | 93 | 254 | .200 | | | | 1974 | | 1-10-0 | 111 | 291 | .909 | | | |

Frank Ellwood (1975-1978) 10-34-0 .227

1975	2-9-0	148	296	.182

Member of the Southern Conference (1976-1996) 69-63-2 .522

1976	5-6-0	151	253	.455	0-0-0	-----		1978		1-10-0	113	292	.091	0-5-0	.000	7
1977	2-9-0	234	389	.182	0-5-0	.000	7									

Sonny Randle (1979-1983) 12-42-1 .227

1979	1-10-0	95	309	.091	0-6-0	.000	8	1982		3-8-0	117	279	.273	1-6-0	.143	8
1980	2-8-1	127	245	.227	0-5-1	.083	8	1983		4-7-0	209	212	.364	3-4-0	.429	5
1981	2-9-0	94	284	.182	1-5-0	.167	8									

Stan Parrish (1984-1985) 13-8-1 .614

1984	6-5-0	238	226	.545	2-4-0	.333	6	1985		7-3-1	193	197	.682	3-3-1	.500	4

George Chaump (1986-1989) 33-16-1 .670

1986	6-4-1	287	199	.591	3-3-0	.500	5	1988		11-2-0	370	234	.846	6-1-0	.857	1
1987	10-5-0	498	307	.667	4-2-0	.667	2	1989		6-5-0	298	254	.545	4-3-0	.571	3

Jim Donnan (1990-1995) 64-21-0 .753

1990	6-5-0	310	162	.545	4-3-0	.571	3	1993		11-4-0	414	206	.733	6-2-0	.750	2
1991	11-4-0	506	257	.733	5-2-0	.714	2	1994		12-2-0	560	214	.857	7-1-0	.875	1
1992	12-3-0	604	292	.800	5-2-0	.714	2	1995		12-3-0	492	240	.800	7-1-0	.875	2

Bob Pruett (1996-2003) 88-17-0 .838

1996	15-0-0	658	210	1.000	8-0-0	1.000	1

Marshall returns as Member of the Mid-American Conference (1997-2003)

1997		10-3-0	484	259	.769	7-1-0	.875	1	2000			8-5-0	367	297	.615	5-3-0	.625	3
1998		12-1-0	405	236	.923	7-1-0	.875	1	2001	21		11-2-0	512	369	.846	8-0-0	1.000	1
1999	10	10	13-0-0	463	137	1.000	8-0-0	1.000	1	2002	24	19	11-2-0	457	315	.846	7-1-0	.875	1
										2003			8-4-0	350	278	.667	6-2-0	.750	3

Won-loss record by decades:

1895-99	4- 5-2	.455	1930-39	54-36-5	.595	1970-79	23-83-0	.217
1900-09	28-16-12	.607	1940-49	35-31-3	.529	1980-89	57-56-3	.504
1910-19	37-30-4	.549	1950-59	31-58-5	.356	1990-99	114-25-0	.820
1920-29	42-37-9	.528	1960-69	30-66-4	.320	2000-03	38-13-0	.745

Historic record: 494-456-47 .519

Post-season won-loss record: 33-9-0 .786

1948: Tangerine Bowl, Catawba 7, Marshall 0
1987: I-AA Playoffs, Marshall 41, James Madison 12
1987: I-AA Playoffs, Marshall 51, Weber State 23
1987: I-AA Playoffs, Marshall 24, Appalachian State 10
1987: Championship: NE Louisiana 43, Marshall 42
1988: I-AA Playoffs, Marshall 7, North Texas 0
1988: I-AA Playoffs, Furman 13, Marshall 9
1991: I-AA Playoffs, Marshall 20, W. Illinois 17
1991: I-AA Playoffs, Marshall 41, Northern Iowa 13
1991: I-AA Playoffs, Marshall 14, East Kentucky 7
1991: Championship: Youngstown State 25, Marshall 17
1992: I-AA Playoffs, Marshall 44, East Kentucky 0
1992: I-AA Playoffs, Marshall 35, Middle Tennessee 21
1992: I-AA Playoffs, Marshall 28, Delaware 7
1992: Championship: Marshall 31, Youngstown State 28
1993: I-AA Playoffs, Marshall 28, Howard 14
1993: I-AA Playoffs, Marshall 34, Delaware 31
1993: I-AA Playoffs, Marshall 24, Troy State 21
1993: Championship: Youngstown State 17, Marshall 5
1994: I-AA Playoffs, Marshall 49, Middle Tennessee 14

1994: I-AA Playoffs, Marshall 28, James Madison 21
1994: I-AA Playoffs, Boise State 28, Marshall 24
1995: I-AA Playoffs, Marshall 38, Jackson State 8
1995: I-AA Playoffs, Marshall 41, Northern Iowa 14
1995: I-AA Playoffs, Marshall 25, McNeese State 13
1995: Championship: Montana 22, Marshall 20
1996: I-AA Playoffs, Marshall 59, Delaware 14
1996: I-AA Playoffs, Marshall 54, Furman 0
1996: I-AA Playoffs, Marshall 31, Northern Iowa 14
1996: Championship, Marshall 49, Montana 29
1997: MAC Championship: Marshall 34, Toledo 14
1997: Motor City Bowl, Mississippi 34, Marshall 31
1998: MAC Championship: Marshall 23, Toledo 17
1998: Motor City Bowl, Marshall 48, Louisville 29
1999: MAC Championship: Marshall 34, Western Michigan 30
1999: Motor City Bowl, Marshall 21, BYU 3
2000: MAC Championship: Marshall 19, Western Michigan 14
2000: Motor City Bowl, Marshall 25, Cincinnati 14
2001: MAC Championship: Toledo 41, Marshall 36
2001: GMAC Bowl, Marshall 64, East Carolina 61
2002: MAC Championship: Marshall 49, Toledo 45
2002: GMAC Bowl, Marshall 38, Louisville 15

Awards: Fred Biletnikoff Award, 1997, Randy Moss; Baugh Trophy: 1999, Chad Pennington.

UNIVERSITY OF MARYLAND, College Park, Maryland; nickname "Terrapins"; colors red, white, black, and gold; Byrd Stadium (48,055); Atlantic Coast Conference. Maryland began play in 1892. In 1922, it became one of the founding members of the Southern Conference. Maryland played in that conference through the 1951 season and then left the SC to become an independent for one season. In 1953 it joined with other ex-SC members to form the Atlantic Coast Conference, and it has played in the ACC beginning with the 1953 season.

Early years (1892-1911)

Year	Coach	W-L-T	PF	PA	Pct	Year	Coach	W-L-T	PF	PA	Pct.
1892	Will Skinner	0-3-0	0	128	.000	1903	D. John Markey	7-4-0	104	64	.636
1893	Samuel Harding	6-0-0	104	16	1.000	1904	D. John Markey	2-4-2	33	62	.375
1894	J. G. Bannon	4-3-0	106	76	.571	1905	Fred Neilsen	6-4-0	131	66	.600
1895	no team					1906	Fred Neilsen	5-3-0	98	73	.625
1896	Grenville Lewis	6-2-2	112	34	.700	1907	Charles Melick	3-6-0	44	71	.333
1897	Grenville Lewis	2-4-0	44	68	.333	1908	Bill Lang	3-8-0	27	204	.272
1898	Frank Kenly	2-5-1	80	147	.312	1909	Bill Lang &				
1899	S. M. Cooke	1-4-0	26	157	.200		Edward Larkin	2-5-0	19	103	.286
1900	F. H. Peters	3-4-1	68	67	.438	1910	Royal Alston	4-3-1	78	42	.562
1901	Emmons Dunbar	1-7-0	49	129	.125	1911	Charles Donnelly &				
1902	D. John Markey	3-5-2	28	90	.400		Curley Byrd	4-4-2	37	72	.500

Curley Byrd (1912-1934) 117-82-15 .582

Year		W-L-T	PF	PA	Pct.	Year		W-L-T	PF	PA	Pct.
1912		6-1-1	191	60	.812	1917		4-3-1	89	159	.562
1913		6-3-0	184	139	.667	1918		4-1-1	57	35	.750
1914		5-3-0	72	49	.625	1919		5-4-0	93	74	.556
1915		6-3-0	161	69	.667	1920		7-2-0	149	55	.778
1916		6-2-0	142	52	.750	1921		3-5-1	45	127	.389

Member of the Southern Conference (1922-1951) 64-59-8 .519

	Nat'l		Overall			Conference				Nat'l		Overall				Conference		
Year	AP	Other	W-L-T	PF	PA	Pct.	W-L-T	Pct.	Rank	Year	AP	Other	W-L-T	PF	PA	Pct.	W-L-T	Pct.	Rank
1922			4-5-1	77	137	.450	1-2-0	.333	11	1929			4-4-2	148	133	.500	1-3-1	.300	17
1923			7-2-1	216	56	.750	2-1-0	.667	8	1930			7-5-0	231	142	.583	4-2-0	.667	6
1924			3-3-3	74	78	.500	1-2-1	.375	16	1931			8-1-1	194	98	.850	4-1-1	.750	5
1925			2-5-1	53	82	.312	0-4-0	.000	20	1932			5-6-0	148	158	.455	2-4-0	.333	16
1926			5-4-1	161	93	.550	1-3-1	.400	17	1933			3-7-0	107	149	.300	1-4-0	.200	9
1927			4-7-0	186	44	.364	3-5-0	.375	15	1934			7-3-0	143	49	.700	3-1-0	.750	3
1928			6-3-1	132	70	.650	2-3-1	.417	14										

Jack Faber (1935, 1940-1941) 12-13-4 .483

| 1935 | | | 7-2-2 | 127 | 78 | .727 | 3-1-1 | .700 | 3 | | | | | | | | | | |

Frank Dobson (1936-1939) 18-21-0 .462

| 1936 | | | 6-5-0 | 117 | 59 | .545 | 3-2-0 | .600 | 5 | 1938 | | | 2-7-0 | 86 | 235 | .222 | 1-2-0 | 333 | 12 |
| 1937 | | | 8-2-0 | 127 | 65 | .800 | 2-0-0 | 1.000 | 1 | 1939 | | | 2-7-0 | 64 | 106 | .222 | 0-1-0 | .000 | 14 |

Jack Faber (1940-1941)

| 1940 | | | 2-6-1 | 39 | 171 | .278 | 0-1-1 | .250 | 12 | 1941 | | | 3-5-1 | 49 | 196 | .389 | 1-2-0 | .333 | 11 |

Clark Shaughnessy (1942, 1946) 10-8-0 .556

| 1942 | | | 7-2-0 | 198 | 124 | .778 | 1-2-0 | .333 | 12 | | | | | | | | | | |

Doc Spears (1943-1945) 5-12-1 .306

| 1943 | | | 4-5-0 | 105 | 194 | .444 | 2-0-0 | 1.000 | 2 | 1944 | | | 1-7-1 | 46 | 170 | .167 | 1-1-0 | .500 | 6 |

Bear Bryant (1945) 6-2-1 .722

| 1945 | | | 6-2-1 | 219 | 105 | .722 | 3-2-0 | .600 | 5 | | | | | | | | | | |

Clark Shaughnessy (1946)

| 1946 | | | 3-6-0 | 136 | 193 | .333 | 2-5-0 | .286 | 12 | | | | | | | | | | |

Jim Tatum (1947-1955) 73-15-4 .815

1947			7-2-2	207	121	.727	3-2-1	,583	6	1950			7-2-1	274	120	.750	4-1-1	.750	5
1948			6-4-0	207	132	.600	4-2-0	.667	6	1951	3	4	10-0-0	381	75	1.000	5-0-0	1.000	1
1949	14		9-1-0	266	81	.900	4-0-0	1.000	2										

Independent (1952)

| 1952 | 13 | 13 | 7-2-0 | 218 | 85 | .778 | | | | | | | | | | | | | |

Member of the Atlantic Coast Conference (1953-2003) 180-144-4 .555

| 1953 | 1 | 1 | 10-1-0 | 298 | 38 | .909 | 3-0-0 | 1.000 | 1 | 1955 | 3 | 3 | 10-1-0 | 217 | 77 | .909 | 4-0-0 | 1.000 | 1 |
| 1954 | 8 | 11 | 7-2-1 | 280 | 67 | .750 | 4-0-1 | .900 | 2 | | | | | | | | | | |

Tommy Mont (1956-1958) 11-18-1 .383

| 1956 | | | 2-7-1 | 68 | 168 | 250 | 2-2-1 | .500 | 4 | 1958 | | | 4-6-0 | 132 | 175 | .400 | 3-3-0 | .500 | 5 |
| 1957 | | | 5-5-0 | 119 | 144 | .500 | 4-3-0 | .571 | 3 | | | | | | | | | | |

Tom Nugent (1959-1965) 36-34-0 .514

1959			5-5-0	184	188	.500	4-2-0	.667	3	1963			3-7-0	148	201	.300	2-5-0	.286	5
1960			6-4-0	171	164	.600	5-2-0	.714	3	1964			5-5-0	164	126	.500	4-3-0	.571	3
1961			7-3-0	156	141	.700	3-3-0	.500	3	1965			4-6-0	132	164	.400	3-3-0	.500	5
1962			6-4-0	170	128	.600	5-2-0	.714	3										

Lou Saban (1966) 4-6-0 .400

Year			W-L-T	PF	PA	Pct	Conf	Pct	R	Year			W-L-T	PF	PA	Pct	Conf	Pct	R
1966			4-6-0	180	204	.400	3-3-0	.50	3										

Bob Ward (1967-1968) 2-17-0 .105

Year			W-L-T	PF	PA	Pct	Conf	Pct	R	Year			W-L-T	PF	PA	Pct	Conf	Pct	R
1967			0-9-0	46	231	.000	0-6-0	.000	8	1968			2-8-0	171	299	.200	2-5-0	.286	7

Ray Lester (1969-1971) 7-25-0 .291

Year			W-L-T	PF	PA	Pct	Conf	Pct	R	Year			W-L-T	PF	PA	Pct	Conf	Pct	R
1969			3-7-0	100	249	.300	3-3-0	.500	3	1971			2-9-0	224	283	.182	1-4-0	.200	7
1970			2-9-0	112	241	.182	2-4-0	.333	6										

Jerry Claiborne (1972-1981) 77-37-3 .671

Year			W-L-T	PF	PA	Pct	Conf	Pct	R	Year			W-L-T	PF	PA	Pct	Conf	Pct	R
1972			5-5-1	243	217	.500	3-2-1	.583	3	1977			8-4-0	254	179	.667	4-2-0	.667	3
1973	20	18	8-4-0	335	141	.667	5-1-0	.833	2	1978	20		9-3-0	261	167	.750	5-1-0	.833	2
1974	13	13	8-4-0	317	104	.667	6-0-0	1.000	1	1979			7-4-0	198	135	.636	4-2-0	.667	2
1975	13	11	9-2-1	312	150	.792	5-0-0	1.000	1	1980			8-4-0	211	165	.667	5-1-0	.833	2
1976	8	11	11-1-0	294	115	.917	5-0-0	1.000	1	1981			4-6-1	232	194	.409	4-2-0	.667	3

Bobby Ross (1982-1986) 39-19-1 .669

Year			W-L-T	PF	PA	Pct	Conf	Pct	R	Year			W-L-T	PF	PA	Pct	Conf	Pct	R
1982	20	20	8-4-0	373	220	.667	5-1-0	.833	2	1985	18	19	9-3-0	326	192	.750	6-0-0	1.000	1
1983			8-4-0	316	253	.667	5-0-0	1.000	1	1986			5-5-1	262	211	.500	2-3-1	.417	5
1984	12	11	9-3-0	380	280	.750	5-0-0	1.000	1										

Joe Krivak (1987-1991) 20-34-2 .375

Year			W-L-T	PF	PA	Pct	Conf	Pct	R	Year			W-L-T	PF	PA	Pct	Conf	Pct	R
1987			4-7-0	194	301	.364	3-3-0	.500	5	1990			6-5-1	237	284	.542	4-3-0	.571	4
1988			5-6-0	260	304	.455	4-3-0	.571	4	1991			2-9-0	138	302	.182	2-5-0	.286	6
1989			3-7-1	215	238	.318	2-5-0	.286	6										

Mark Duffner (1992-1996) 20-35-0 .367

Year			W-L-T	PF	PA	Pct	Conf	Pct	R	Year			W-L-T	PF	PA	Pct	Conf	Pct	R
1992`			3-8-0	292	365	.273	2-6-0	.250	7	1995			6-5-0	210	251	.545	4-4-0	.500	5
1993			2-9-0	243	479	.182	2-6-0	.250	7	1996			5-6-0	187	239	.455	3-5-0	.375	6
1994			4-7-0	270	326	.364	2-6-0	.250	7										

R. Vanderlinden (1997-2000) 15-29-0 .341

Year			W-L-T	PF	PA	Pct	Conf	Pct	R	Year			W-L-T	PF	PA	Pct	Conf	Pct	R
1997			2-9-0	161	355	.182	1-7-0	.125	8	1999			5-6-0	292	260	.455	2-6-0	.250	8
1998			3-8-0	202	290	.273	1-7-0	.125	8	2000			5-6-0	247	284	.455	3-5-0	.375	6

Ralph Friedgen (2001-2003) 31-8-0 .795

Year			W-L-T	PF	PA	Pct	Conf	Pct	R	Year			W-L-T	PF	PA	Pct	Conf	Pct	R
2001	11	10	10-2-0	413	266	.833	7-1-0	.875	1	2003	17	20	10-3-0	406	206	.769	6-2-0	.750	2
2002	13	13	11-3-0	41	228	.786	6-2-0	.750	2										

Won-loss record by decades:

1892-99	21-21-3	.500		1930-39	55-45-3	.549	1970-79	69-45-2	.603
1900-09	35-50-5	.417		1940-49	48-40-6	.543	1980-89	63-49-3	.561
1910-19	50-27-6	.639		1950-59	67-31-3	.678	1990-99	38-72-1	.347
1920-29	45-40-11	.526		1960-69	40-59-0	.404	2000-03	36-14-0	.720

Historical record: 567-493-43 .534

Post-season won-loss record: 8-10-2 .450

1948: Gator Bowl, Maryland 20, Georgia 20
1950: Gator Bowl, Maryland 20, Missouri 7
1952: Sugar Bowl, Maryland 28, Tennessee 13
1954: Orange Bowl, Oklahoma 7, Maryland 0
1956: Orange Bowl, Oklahoma 20, Maryland 6
1973: Peach Bowl, Georgia 17, Maryland 16
1974: Liberty Bowl, Tennessee 7, Maryland 3
1975: Gator Bowl, Maryland 13, Florida 0
1977: Cotton Bowl, Houston 30, Maryland 21

1977: Hall of Fame Bowl, Maryland 17, Minnesota 7
1978: Sun Bowl, Texas 42, Maryland 0
1980: Tangerine Bowl, Florida 35, Maryland 20
1982: Aloha Bowl, Washington 21, Maryland 20
1983: Florida Citrus Bowl, Tennessee 30, Maryland 23
1984: Sun Bowl, Maryland 28, Tennessee 27
1985: Cherry Bowl, Maryland 35, Syracuse 18
1990: Independence Bowl, Maryland 34, Louisiana Tech 34
2002: Orange Bowl, Florida 56, Maryland 23
2002: Peach Bowl, Maryland 30, Tennessee 3
2004: Gator Bowl, Maryland 41, West Virginia 7

College Football Hall of Fame:
Clark Shaughnessy, coach, 1942, 1946; Bear Bryant, coach, 1945; Jim Tatum, coach, 1947-55; Bob Ward, guard, 1948-51; Dick Modzelewski, tackle, 1950-52; Jack Scarbath, quarterback, 1950-52; Stan Jones, tackle, 1951-53; Bob Pellegrini, center, 1953-55; Randy White, defensive tackle, 1972-74.

Awards: Lombardi Award, 1974: Randy White; Outland Trophy, 1952, Dick Modzellewski; 1974, Randy White; Chuck Bednarik Award: 2002, E.J. Henderson; Butkus Award: 2002, E.J. Henderson.

UNIVERSITY OF MEMPHIS. Memphis, Tennessee; nickname "Tigers"; colors royal blue and gray; Liberty Bowl Memorial Stadium (62,380); Conference USA. Original name West Tennessee State Normal, name changed in 1925 to West Tennessee State Teachers College, name changed again in 1941 to Memphis State College. Memphis played in the Missouri Valley Conference from the 1968 season through 1973 and played in the Metro Conference in the 1980s; Memphis was an independent Division I-A school in the 1990s before joining Conference USA in 1996. Conference results are shown only for the Conference USA years.

Year	AP	Other	W-L-T	PF	PA	Pct.		Year	AP	Other	W-L-T	PF	PA	Pct.
							Clyde Wilson (1912-1915) 9-12-1			.432				
1912		1-2-1	13	15	.375			1914			3-5-0	65	102	.375
1913		1-2-0	19	86	.333			1915			4-3-0	186	139	.571
							Tom Shea (1916) 2-3-1 .417							
1916		2-3-1	152	90	.417									
							Bic Campbell (1917, 1919) 6-6-0 .500							
1917		3-2-0	48	67	.600									
							John Childerson (1918) 2-4-0 .333							
1918		2-4-0	68	96	.333									
							Bic Campbell (1919)							
1919		3-4-0	91	66	.429									
							Elmore George (1920) 0-5-0 .000							
1920		0-5-0	7	143	.000									
							Rollin Wilson (1921) 4-5-1 .450							
1921		4-5-1	86	206	.450									
							Lester Barnhard (1922-1923) 11-5-3 .658							
1922		5-2-3	174	26	.650			1923			6-3-0	77	55	.667
							Zach Curlin (1924-1936) 43-60-14 .427							
1924		1-7-1	40	239	.167			1931			2-5-2	33	102	.333
1925		0-7-1	44	239	.063			1932			4-5-0	61	54	.444
1926		1-8-0	39	171	.111			1933			7-1-1	147	44	.833
1927		5-3-1	158	116	.611			1934			3-3-2	75	63	.500
1928		5-3-2	157	120	.600			1935			1-6-1	30	209	.188
1929		8-0-2	146	27	.900			1936			0-9-0	7	282	.000
1930		6-3-1	162	92	.650									
							Allyn McKeen (1937-1938) 13-6-0 .684							
1937		3-6-0	124	93	.333			1938			10-0-0	281	41	1.000
							C. Humphreys (1939-1941) 14-15-0 .483							
1939		3-7-0	85	127	.300			1941			6-3-0	172	76	.667
1940		5-5-0	150	172	.500									
							Charlie Jamerson (1942) 2-7-0 .222							
1942		2-7-0	87	255	.222									
							No team (1943-1946)							
							Ralph Hatley (1947-1957) 59-43-5 .575							
1947		6-2-1	238	60	.722			1953			6-4-0	135	140	.600
1948		6-5-0	218	129	.545			1954			3-4-3	166	209	.450
1949		9-1-0	385	73	.900			1955			2-7-0	94	218	.222
1950		9-2-0	374	108	.818			1956			5-4-1	209	152	.550
1951		5-3-0	206	93	.625			1957			6-4-0	195	111	.600
1952		2-7-0	141	263	.222									
							Billy Murphy (1958-1971) 91-44-1 .673							
1958		4-5-0	142	144	.444			1963	14		9-0-1	199	56	.950
1959		6-4-0	142	132	.600			1964			5-4-0	173	103	.556
1960		8-2-0	303	79	.800			1965			5-5-0	215	153	.500
1961		8-2-0	332	75	.800			1966			7-2-0	121	96	.778
1962		8-1-0	261	67	.889			1967			6-3-0	202	152	.667

Member of the Missouri Valley Conference (1968-1972) 19-5-0 .792

	Nat'l	Overall				Conference				Nat'l	Overall				Conference		
Year	AP Other	W-L-T	PF	PA	Pct.	W-L-T	Pct.	Rank	Year	AP Other	W-L-T	PF	PA	Pct.	W-L-T	Pct.	Rank
1968		6-4-0	258	170	.600	5-0-0	1.000	1	1970		6-4-0	227	184	.600	2-2-0	.500	3
1969		8-2-0	328	191	.800	5-0-0	1.000	1	1971		5-6-0	202	152	.455	4-1-0	.800	1

Fred Pancoast (1972-1974) 20-12-1 .621

1972		5-5-1	265	254	.500	3-2-0	.600	4

Memphis reverts to independent status

							1974	7-4-0	225	148	.636

R. Williamson (1975-1980) 31-35-0 .470

1975		7-4-0	180	168	.636		1978			4-7-0	200	297	.364
1976		7-4-0	241	182	.636		1979			5-6-0	166	223	.455
1977		6-5-0	228	194	.545		1980			2-9-0	115	255	.182

Rex Dockery (1981-1983) 8-24-1 .258

Year	W-L-T	PF	PA	Pct.		Year	W-L-T	PF	PA	Pct.
1981	1-10-0	82	209	.091		1983	6-4-1	274	205	.591
1982	1-10-0	129	285	.091						

Rey Dempsey (1984-1985) 7-12-3 .386

| 1984 | 5-5-1 | 201 | 178 | .500 | | 1985 | 2-7-2 | 184 | 248 | .273 |

Charlie Bailey (1986-1988) 12-20-1 .379

| 1986 | 1-10-0 | 104 | 292 | .091 | | 1988 | 6-5-0 | 226 | 205 | .545 |
| 1987 | 5-5-1 | 220 | 210 | .500 | | | | | | |

Chuck Stobart (1989-1994) 29-36-1 .447

1989	2-9-0	174	331	.182		1992	6-5-0	312	181	.545
1990	4-6-1	212	233	.409		1993	6-5-0	268	215	.545
1991	5-6-0	228	229	.455		1994	6-5-0	163	159	.545

Rip Scherer (1995-2000) 22-44-0 .333

1995   3-8-0 150 240 .273

Member of Conference USA (1996-2003) 21-32-0 .396

	Nat'l	Overall				Conference				Nat'l	Overall				Conference		
Year	AP Other	W-L-T	PF	PA	Pct.	W-L-T	Pct.	Rank	Year	AP Other	W-L-T	PF	PA	Pct.	W-L-T	Pct.	Rank
1996		4-7-0	141	219	.364	2-3-0	.400	3	1999		5-6-0	232	182	.455	4-2-0	.667	2
1997		4-7-0	218	243	.364	2-4-0	.333	4	2000		4-7-0	176	199	.364	2-5-0	.286	7
1998		2-9-0	226	340	.182	1-5-0	.167	7									

Tommy West (2001-2002) 8-15-0 .348

| 2001 | | 5-6-0 | 294 | 281 | .455 | 3-4-0 | .429 | 7 | 2003 | | 9-4-0 | 393 | 250 | .692 | 5-3-0 | .625 | 4 |
| 2002 | | 3-9-0 | 303 | 327 | .250 | 2-4-0 | .250 | 9 | | | | | | | | | |

Won-loss record by decades:

1912-19	19-25-2	.435	1950-59	48-44-4	.521	1990-99	45-64-1	.414
1920-29	35-43-11	.455	1960-69	70-25-1	.734	2000-03	21-26-0	.447
1930-39	39-45-7	.467	1970-79	60-48-1	.555			
1940-49	34-23-1	.595	1980-89	31-74-5	.305			

Historic record: 402-417-33 .491

Post-season won-loss record: 3-0-0 1.000
1956: Burley Bowl, Memphis 32, East Tennessee State 12   2003: New Orleans Bowl, Memphis 27, North Texas 17
1971: Pasadena Bowl, Memphis 28, San Jose State 9

College Football Hall of Fame:
Allyn McKeen, coach, 1937-38.

Player Awards: Lou Groza Award: 1992, Joe Allison.

MIAMI UNIVERSITY, Oxford, Ohio; nickname "Red Hawks"; colors red and white; Yager Stadium (30.012); Mid-American Conference. Miami began play in 1888 and was one of the founding members of the Mid-American Conference in 1948. Miami is known for its list of famous coaches who moved on to larger programs and ultimately to the College Football Hall of Fame.

Early years (1888-1911)

Year	Coach	W-L-T	PF	PA	Pct.	Year	Coach	W-L-T	PF	PA	Pct.
1888	none	0-0-1	0	0	.500	1900	Alonzo Branch	0-2-0	12	49	.000
1889	none	4-0-0	100	4	1.000	1901	T. Hazard	1-3-1	23	29	.300
1890	no team					1902	Peter McPherson	5-2-1	86	33	.688
1891	none	1-1-0	38	104	.500	1903	Peter McPherson	1-4-0	27	110	.200
1892	none	2-2-0	42	24	.500	1904	Arthur Smith	1-5-0	12	283	.167
1893	none	3-0-0	58	12	1.000	1905	none	4-3-0	138	76	.571
1894	none	1-2-0	24	34	.333	1906	Arthur Parmalee	1-5-1	16	55	.214
1895	C.K. Fauver	3-0-0	30	4	1.000	1907	Amos Foster	6-1-0	115	37	.857
1896	Ernest Merrill	3-1-0	46	20	.750	1908	Amos Foster	7-0-0	113	10	1.000
1897	H. McIntyre	2-4-1	32	56	.357	1909	Harold Iddings	3-4-0	96	83	.429
1898	none	0-2-0	6	33	.000	1910	Harold Iddings	2-4-1	26	42	.357
1899	none	1-5-0	23	73	.167	1911	Edwin Sweetland	2-4-2	57	45	.375

James Donnelly (1912-1914) 14-8-2 .625

Year		W-L-T	PF	PA	Pct.	Year		W-L-T	PF	PA	Pct.
1912		3-3-2	89	106	.500	1914		5-3-0	131	124	.625
1913		6-2-0	154	68	.750						

C. J. Roberts (1915) 6-2-0 .750

1915		6-2-0	137	87	.750

George Little (1916, 1919-1921) 27-3-2 .875

1916		7-0-1	239	12	.938

George Rider (1917-1918) 11-0-3 .893

1917		6-0-2	202	0	.938	1918		5-0-1	195	13	.917

George Little (1919-1921)

1919		7-1-0	147	32	.875	1921		8-0-0	238	13	1.000
1920		5-2-1	114	38	.688						

Harry Ewing (1922-1923) 7-7-2 .500

1922		4-3-1	61	45	.562	1923		3-4-1	82	81	.438

Chester Pittser (1924-1931) 41-25-2 .618

1924		2-6-0	62	147	.250	1928		6-2-0	140	46	.750
1925		5-3-0	123	55	.625	1929		7-2-0	179	40	.778
1926		5-2-1	112	58	.588	1930		4-4-1	131	82	.500
1927		8-1-0	255	56	.889	1931		4-5-0	161	116	.444

Frank Wilton (1932-1941) 44-39-5 .528

1932		7-1-0	182	56	.875	1937		4-4-1	175	85	.500
1933		7-2-0	223	36	.778	1938		6-3-0	229	100	.667
1934		5-4-0	118	70	.545	1939		1-7-1	21	113	.167
1935		5-3-1	174	80	.611	1940		0-7-1	32	200	.062
1936		7-1-1	84	40	.833	1941		2-7-0	98	176	.222

Stu Holcomb (1942-1943) 10-8-1 .553

1942		3-6-0	154	195	.333	1943		7-2-1	293	91	.750

Sid Gillman (1944-1947) 31-6-1 .829

1944		8-1-0	185	74	.889	1946		7-3-0	220	72	.700
1945		7-2-0	207	75	.778	1947		9-0-1	240	97	.950

Member of the Mid-American Conference (1948-2003) 239-107-11 .666

Year	Nat'l AP	Other	Overall W-L-T	PF	PA	Pct.	Conference W-L-T	Pct.	Rank	Year	Nat'l AP	Other	Overall W-L-T	PF	PA	Pct.	Conference W-L-T	Pct.	Rank

George Backburn (1948) 7-1-1 .833

1948			7-1-1	249	90	.833	4-0-0	1.000	1										

Woody Hayes (1949-1950) 14-5-0 .737

1949			5-4-0	251	263	.545	3-1-0	.750	2	1950			9-1-0	356	100	.900	4-0-0	1.000	1

Ara Parseghian (1951-1955) 39-6-1 .859

1951			7-3-0	225	159	.700	3-1-0	.750	2	1954			8-1-0	294	82	.889	4-0-0	1.000	1
1952			8-1-0	284	108	.889	4-1-0	.800	2	1955	15	20	9-0-0	226	47	1.000	5-0-0	1.000	1
1953			7-1-1	327	52	.833	3-0-1	.875	2										

John Pont (1956-1962) 43-22-2 .657

1956			7-1-1	159	90	.833	4-0-1	.900	2	1960			5-5-0	139	159	.500	2-3-0	.400	4
1957			6-3-0	163	137	.667	5-0-0	1.000	1	1961			6-4-0	153	115	.600	3-2-0	.600	3
1958			6-3-0	193	96	.667	5-0-0	1.000	1	1962			8-2-1	241	175	.773	3-1-1	.700	3
1959			5-4-0	158	94	.556	3-2-0	.600	3										

Bo Schembechler (1963-1968) 40-17-3 .692

1963			5-3-2	208	178	.600	4-1-1	.750	3	1966			9-1-0	229	76	.900	5-1-0	.833	1
1964			6-3-1	209	142	.650	4-2-0	.667	2	1967			6-4-0	181	114	.600	4-2-0	.667	3
1965			7-3-0	247	137	.700	5-1-0	.833	1	1968			7-3-0	240	99	.700	5-1-0	.833	2

Bill Mallory (1969-1973) 39-12-0 .765

Year		Overall	PF	PA	Pct	Conf	Pct	Pl	Year		Overall	PF	PA	Pct	Conf	Pct	Pl
1969		7-3-0	231	139	.700	2-3-0	.400	3	1972		7-3-0	232	116	.700	2-3-0	.400	4
1970		7-3-0	187	112	.700	3-2-0	.600	2	1973	15-17	11-0-0	223	76	1.000	5-0-0	1.000	1
1971		7-3-0	207	117	.700	2-3-0	.400	3									

Dick Crum (1974-1977) 34-10-1 .767

Year		Overall	PF	PA	Pct	Conf	Pct	Pl	Year		Overall	PF	PA	Pct	Conf	Pct	Pl
1974	10-10	10-0-1	303	86	.955	5-0-0	1.000	1	1976		3-8-0	160	208	.273	2-4-0	.333	7
1975	12-16	11-1-0	306	141	.917	6-0-0	1.000	1	1977		10-1-0	262	173	.909	5-0-0	1.000	1

Tom Reed (1978-1982) 34-19-2 .636

Year	Overall	PF	PA	Pct	Conf	Pct	Pl	Year	Overall	PF	PA	Pct	Conf	Pct	Pl
1978	8-2-1	228	161	.773	5-2-0	.714	3	1981	8-2-1	199	154	.773	6-1-1	.813	2
1979	6-5-0	233	142	.545	3-4-0	.429	7	1982	7-4-0	195	121	.636	5-3-0	.625	3
1980	5-6-0	241	192	.455	4-3-0	.571	3								

Tim Rose (1983-1989) 31-44-3 .417

Year	Overall	PF	PA	Pct	Conf	Pct	Pl	Year	Overall	PF	PA	Pct	Conf	Pct	Pl
1983	4-7-0	152	189	.364	3-5-0	.375	7	1987	5-6-0	180	235	.455	5-3-0	.625	2
1984	4-7-0	175	221	.364	3-5-0	.375	6	1988	0-10-1	167	361	.045	0-7-1	.063	9
1985	8-2-1	266	211	.713	7-1-1	.833	2	1989	2-8-1	122	262	.227	2-5-1	.312	7
1986	8-4-0	346	228	.667	6-2-0	.750	1								

Randy Walker (1990-1998) 59-35-5 .621

Year	Overall	PF	PA	Pct	Conf	Pct	Pl	Year	Overall	PF	PA	Pct	Conf	Pct	Pl
1990	5-5-1	200	225	.500	4-3-1	.563	5	1995	8-2-1	326	165	.772	6-1-1	.813	2
1991	6-4-1	214	140	.591	4-3-1	.563	3	1996	6-5-0	278	168	.545	6-2-0	.750	2
1992	6-4-1	210	204	.591	5-3-0	.625	3	1997	8-3-0	412	226	.727	6-2-0	.750	2
1993	4-7-0	186	248	.364	3-6-0	.333	9	1998	10-1-0	317	142	.909	7-1-0	.875	1
1994	6-4-1	262	260	.591	5-3-0	.625	3								

Terry Hoeppner (1999-2003) 40-20-0 .667

Year		Overall	PF	PA	Pct	Conf	Pct	Pl	Year		Overall	PF	PA	Pct	Conf	Pct	Pl
1999		7-4-0	335	264	.636	6-2-0	.750	2	2001		7-5-0	319	309	.583	6-2-0	.750	2
2000		6-5-0	272	284	.545	5-3-0	.625	3	2002		7-5-0	384	325	.583	5-3-0	.625	6
									2003	10 12	13-1-0	602	272	.929	8-0-0	1.000	1

Won-loss record by decades:

1888-99	20-17-2	.538	1930-39	50-34-5	.590	1970-79	80-26-2	.750
1900-09	29-29-3	.500	1940-49	55-33-4	.620	1980-89	51-56-4	.477
1910-19	49-19-9	.695	1950-59	72-18-2	.793	1990-99	66-39-5	.623
1920-29	53-25-4	.671	1960-69	66-31-4	.673	2000-03	33-16-0	.673

Historic record: 624-343-44 .639

Post-season won-loss record: 6-2-0 .750

1948: Sun Bowl, Miami 13, Texas Tech 12	1974: Tangerine Bowl, Miami 21, Georgia 10
1951: Salad Bowl, Miami 34, Arizona State 12	1975: Tangerine Bowl, Miami 20, South Carolina 7
1962: Tangerine Bowl, Houston 49, Miami 21	1986: California Bowl, San Jose State 37, Miami 7
1973: Tangerine Bowl, Miami 16, Florida 7	2003: GMAC Bowl, Miami 49, Louisville 28

College Football Hall of Fame:
George Little, coach, 1916-21; Sid Gillman, coach, 1944-47; Woody Hayes, coach, 1949-50; Ara Parseghian, coach, 1951-55; Bo Schembechler, coach, 1963-68; Bob Babich, linebacker, 1966-68.

UNIVERSITY OF MIAMI (FLORIDA); Coral Gables, Florida; nickname: "Hurricanes"; colors orange, green and white; Orange Bowl (72,319); Big East Conference. Miami began play in 1926 and played as an independent until it joined with seven other Eastern independents to form the Big East Conference, which began play in 1991. After the 2003 season, Miami announced its intention to leave the Big East to join the ACC.

Year	Nat'l AP	Other	W-L-T	PF	PA	Pct.

Howard Buck (1926-1928) 15-10-2 .593

Year	AP	Other	W-L-T	PF	PA	Pct.
1926			8-0-0	122	13	1.000
1927			3-6-1	106	187	.350
1928			4-4-1	163	75	.500

J. Burton Rix (1929) 3-2-0 .600

Year	AP	Other	W-L-T	PF	PA	Pct.
1929			3-2-0	45	26	

Ernest Britt (1930) 3-4-1 .438

Year	AP	Other	W-L-T	PF	PA	Pct.
1930			3-4-1	26	102	.438

Tom McCann (1931-1934) 18-15-4 .541

Year	AP	Other	W-L-T	PF	PA	Pct.
1931			4-8-0	96	170	.333
1932			4-3-1	56	40	.562
1933			5-1-2	197	46	.750
1934			5-3-1	150	92	.611

Irl Tubbs (1935-1936) 11-5-2 .667

Year	AP	Other	W-L-T	PF	PA	Pct.
1935			5-3-0	91	52	.625
1936			6-2-2	129	39	.700

Jack Harding (1937-1942, 1945-1947) 54-32-3 .624

Year	AP	Other	W-L-T	PF	PA	Pct.
1937			4-4-1	118	67	.500
1938			8-2-0	219	52	.800
1939			5-5-0	131	106	.500
1940			3-7-0	131	197	.300
1941			8-2-0	162	54	.800
1942			7-2-0	195	60	.778

Eddie Dunn (1943-1944) 6-8-1 .433

Year	AP	Other	W-L-T	PF	PA	Pct.
1943			5-1-0	124	52	.833
1944			1-7-1	73	274	.167

Jack Harding (1945-1947)

Year	AP	Other	W-L-T	PF	PA	Pct.
1945			9-1-1	211	99	.864
1946			8-2-0	200	147	.800
1947			2-7-1	80	140	.250

Andy Gustafson (1948-1963) 93-65-3 .587

Year	AP	Other	W-L-T	PF	PA	Pct.
1948			4-6-0	154	179	.400
1949			6-3-0	165	96	.667
1950	15	13	9-1-1	251	97	.864
1951			8-3-0	196	126	.727
1952			4-7-0	181	192	.364
1953			4-5-0	155	137	.444
1954	11	9	8-1-0	257	94	.889
1955	14	18	6-3-0	181	81	.667
1956	6	6	8-1-1	161	53	.850
1957			5-4-1	161	103	.550
1958			2-8-0	88	195	.200
1959			6-4-0	140	140	.600
1960			6-4-0	163	143	.600
1961		19	7-4-0	146	85	.636
1962		18	7-4-0	189	217	.636
1963			3-7-0	116	174	.300

Charlie Tate (1964-1970) 34-27-3 .555

Year	AP	Other	W-L-T	PF	PA	Pct.
1964			4-5-1	147	133	,450
1965			5-4-1	199	138	.550
1966	9	10	8-2-1	210	103	.773
1967		16	7-4-0	257	140	.636
1968			5-5-0	161	131	.500
1969			4-6-0	201	216	.400
1970*			1-1-0	57	45	.500

Walt Kichefski (1970) 2-7-0 .222

Year	AP	Other	W-L-T	PF	PA	Pct.
1970*			2-7-0	109	255	.222

*Tate coached the first two games of the 1970 season, and Kichefski the last nine.

Fran Curci (1971-1972) 9-13-0 .409

Year	AP	Other	W-L-T	PF	PA	Pct.
1971			4-7-0	174	221	.364
1972			5-6-0	214	170	.455

Pete Elliott (1973-1974) 11-11-0 .500

Year	AP	Other	W-L-T	PF	PA	Pct.
1973			5-6-0	163	240	.455
1974			6-5-0	167	180	.545

Carl Selmer (1975-1976) 5-16-0 .238

Year	AP	Other	W-L-T	PF	PA	Pct.
1975			2-8-0	157	239	.200
1976			3-8-0	207	213	.273

Lou Saban (1977-1978) 9-13-0 .409

Year	AP	Other	W-L-T	PF	PA	Pct.
1977			3-8-0	125	245	.273
1978			6-5-0	194	193	.545

Howard Schnellenberger (1979-1983) 41-16-0 .719

Year	AP	Other	W-L-T	PF	PA	Pct.
1979			5-6-0	191	236	.455
1980	18	18	9-3-0	278	171	.750
1981	8		9-2-0	245	145	.818
1982			7-4-0	241	153	.636
1983	1	1	11-1-0	333	136	.917

Jimmy Johnson (1984-1988) 52-9-0 .852

Year	AP	Other	W-L-T	PF	PA	Pct.
1984	18		8-5-0	402	314	.615
1985	9	8	10-2-0	406	195	.833
1986	2	2	11-1-0	430	150	.917
1987	1	1	12-0-0	412	125	1.000
1988	2	2	11-1-0	418	116	.917

Dennis Erickson (1989-1994) 63-9-0 .875

Year	AP	Other	W-L-T	PF	PA	Pct.
1989	1	1	11-1-0	426	127	.917
1990	3	3	10-2-0	447	184	.833

Member of the Big East Conference (1991-2003) 72-11-0 .868

Year	Nat'l AP	Other	Overall W-L-T	PF	PA	Pct.	Conference W-L-T	Pct.	Rank
1991	1	2	12-0-0	386	100	1.000	2-0-0	1.000	1
1992	3	3	11-1-0	369	161	.917	4-0-0	1.000	1
1993	15	15	9-3-0	331	167	.750	6-1-0	.857	2
1994	6	6	10-2-0	365	143	.833	7-0-0	1.000	1

Butch Davis (1995-2000) 51-20-0 .718

1995	20		8-3-0	294	201	.727	6-1-0	.857	*	1998	20		9-3-0	448	298	.750	5-2-0	.714	2
1996	14	14	9-3-0	368	210	.750	6-1-0	.857	1	1999	15	15	9-4-0	404	207	.692	6-1-0	.857	2
1997			5-6-0	314	285	.455	3-4-0	.429	5	2000	2		2 11-1-0			.917	7-0-0	1.000	1

Larry Coker (2001-2003) 35-3-0 .921

2001	1	1	12-0-0	482	117	1.000	7-0-0	1.000	1	2003	5	5	11-2-0	361	196	.846	6-1-0	.857	1
2002	2	2	12-1-0	527	248	.923	7-0-0	1.000	1										

Won-loss record by decades:

1926-29	18-12-2	.594		1950-59	60-37-3	.615		1980-89	99-20-0	.832
1930-39	49-35-8	.576		1960-69	56-45-3	.553		1990-99	92-27-0	.773
1940-49	53-38-3	.580		1970-79	41-67-0	.380		2000-03	46- 4-0	.920

Historic record 514-285-19 .637

Post-season won-loss record: 17-13-0 .567

1933: Palm Festival, Miami 7, Manhattan 0
1934: Palm Festival, Duquesne 33, Miami 7
1935: Orange Bowl, Bucknell 26, Miami 0
1946: Orange Bowl, Miami 13, Holy Cross 6
1951: Orange Bowl, Clemson 15, Miami 14
1952: Gator Bowl, Miami 14, Clemson 0
1961: Liberty Bowl, Syracuse 15, Miami 14
1962: Gotham Bowl, Nebraska 36, Miami 34
1966: Liberty Bowl, Miami 14, Virginia Tech 7
1967: Bluebonnet Bowl, Colorado 31, Miami 21
1981: Peach Bowl, Miami 20, Virginia Tech 10
1984: Orange Bowl, Miami 31, Nebraska 30
1985: Fiesta Bowl, UCLA 39, Miami 37
1986: Sugar Bowl, Tennessee 35, Miami 7
1987: Fiesta Bowl, Penn State 14, Miami 10

1988: Orange Bowl, Miami 20, Oklahoma 14
1989: Orange Bowl, Miami 23, Nebraska 3
1990: Sugar Bowl, Miami 33, Alabama 25
1991: Cotton Bowl, Miami 46, Texas 3
1992: Orange Bowl, Miami 22, Nebraska 0
1993: Sugar Bowl, Alabama 34, Miami 13
1994: Fiesta Bowl, Arizona 29, Miami 0
1995: Orange Bowl, Nebraska 24, Miami 17
1996: Carquest Bowl, Miami 31, Virginia 21
1998: Micron PC Bowl, Miami 46, NC State 23
2000: Gator Bowl, Miami 28, Georgia Tech 13
2001: Sugar Bowl, Miami 37, Florida 20
2002: Rose Bowl, Miami 37, Nebraska 14
2003: Fiesta Bowl, Ohio State 31, Miami 24
2004: Orange Bowl, Miami 16, Florida State 14

College Football Hall of Fame:
Jack Harding, coach, 1937-42, 1945-47; Andy Gustafson, coach, 1948-63; Don Bosseler, fullback, 1953-56; Ted Hendricks, defensive end, 1966-69.

Awards: Butkus Award: 2000, Dan Morgan; Davey O'Brien Award: 1986, Vinnie Testaverde; 1992, Gina Toretta; Maxwell Award: 1986, Vinnie Testaverde; 1992, Gina Toretta; 2001, Ken Dorsey; Lombardi Award: 1994, Warren Sapp; Outland Trophy: 1990, Russell Maryland; 2001, Bryant McKinnie; Jim Thorpe Award, 1987, Bennie Blades; Heisman Trophy: 1986, Vinnie Testaverde; 1992, Gina Torreta; Bednarik Award: 1994, Warren Sapp; 2000, Dan Morgan.; Unitas Award: 1990, Craig Erickson; 1992, Gina Torretta; Rimington Trophy: 2002, Brent Romberg; Nagurski Award: 1994, Warren Sapp; 2000, Dan Morgan; Camp Award: 1986, Vinnie Testaverde; 1992, Gina Toretta; Baugh Trophy: 1986, Vinnie Testaverde; 1988, Steve Walsh; Mackey Award: 2003, Kellen Winslow.

MICHIGAN STATE UNIVERSITY, East Lansing, Michigan; nickname "Spartans"; colors green and white; Spartan Stadium (72,027); Big Ten Conference. Michigan State began play in 1896 and continued play as an independent until it joined the Big Ten Conference for the 1953 season.

Years as an independent (1896-1952)

	Nat'l						Nat'l					
Year	AP Other	W-L-T	PF	PA	Pct.	Year	AP Other	W-L-T	PF	PA	Pct.	

No coach (1896)

| 1896 | | 1-2-1 | 26 | 42 | .375 | | | | | | | |

Henry Keep (1897-1898) 8-5-1 .607

| 1897 | | 4-2-1 | 146 | 106 | .643 | 1898 | | 4-3-0 | 142 | 127 | .571 |

Charles O. Benies (1899-1900) 3-7-1 .318

| 1899 | | 2-4-1 | 81 | 101 | .357 | 1900 | | 1-3-0 | 51 | 67 | .250 |

George Denman (1901-1902) 7-9-1 .441

| 1901 | | 3-4-1 | 120 | 94 | .438 | 1902 | | 4-5-0 | 93 | 206 | .444 |

Chester Brewer (1903-1910, 1917, 1919) 58-23-7 .699

1903		6-1-1	178	24	.812	1907		4-2-1	127	60	.714
1904		8-1-0	380	16	.889	1908		6-0-2	205	22	.875
1905		9-2-0	280	75	.818	1909		8-1-0	233	17	.875
1906		7-2-2	195	28	.727	1910		6-1-0	168	8	.857

John F. Macklin (1911-1915) 29-5-0 .853

1911		5-1-0	93	30	.833	1914		5-2-0	197	57	.714
1912		7-1-0	297	98	.875	1915		5-1-0	259	38	.833
1913		7-0-0	180	28	1.000						

Frank Sommers (1916) 4-2-1 .714

| 1916 | | 4-2-1 | 126 | 26 | .714 | | | | | | |

Chester Brewer (1917)

| 1917 | | 0-9-0 | 23 | 179 | .000 | | | | | | |

George Gauthier (1918) 4-3-0 .571

| 1918 | | 4-3-0 | 134 | 68 | .571 | | | | | | |

Chester Brewer (1919)

| 1919 | | 4-4-1 | 132 | 99 | .500 | | | | | | |

Potsy Clark (1920) 4-6-0 .400

| 1920 | | 4-6-0 | 270 | 166 | .400 | | | | | | |

Albert Barron (1921-1922) 6-10-2 .389

| 1921 | | 3-5-0 | 68 | 126 | .375 | 1922 | | 3-5-2 | 111 | 135 | .400 |

Ralph Young (1923-1927) 18-22-1 .451

1923		3-5-0	57	144	.375	1926		3-4-1	97	171	.438
1924		5-3-0	210	48	.625	1927		4-5-0	111	128	.444
1925		3-5-0	105	106	.375						

Harry Kipke (1928) 3-4-1 .438

| 1928 | | 3-4-1 | 153 | 66 | .438 | | | | | | |

Jim Crowley (1929-1932) 22-8-3 .712

| 1929 | | 5-3-0 | 244 | 104 | .625 | 1931 | | 5-3-1 | 291 | 61 | .611 |
| 1930 | | 5-1-2 | 151 | 32 | .750 | 1932 | | 7-1-0 | 220 | 64 | .875 |

Charles Bachman (1933-1946) 70-34-10 .658

1933		4-2-2	73	49	.625	1940		3-4-1	108	76	.438
1934		8-1-0	153	56	.889	1941		5-3-1	150	77	.611
1935		6-2-0	207	57	.750	1942		4-3-2	120	99	.556
1936		6-1-2	143	40	.778	1943		no team				
1937		8-2-0	217	42	.800	1944		6-1-0	167	31	.857
1938		6-3-0	133	59	.667	1945		5-3-1	120	128	.611
1939		4-4-1	102	92	.500	1946		5-5-0	181	202	.500

Biggie Munn (1947-1953) 54-9-2 .846

1947		7-2-0	167	101	.778	1950	8 9	8-1-0	243	107	.889
1948	14	6-2-2	359	130	.700	1951	2 2	9-0-0	270	114	1.000
1949	19	6-3-0	309	107	.667	1952	1 1	9-0-0	312	84	1.000

Member of the Big Ten Conference (1953-2002) 205-168-9 .548

	Nat'l	Overall				Conference			Nat'l	Overall				Conference		
Year	AP Other	W-L-T	PF	PA	Pct.	W-L-T	Pct.	Rank	Year	AP Other	W-L-T	PF	PA	Pct.	W-L-T	Pct. Rank
1953	3 3	9-1-0	240	110	.900	5-1-0	.833	1								

Duffy Daugherty (1954-1972) 109-69-5 .609

Year			W-L-T	PF	PA	Pct	Conf	Pct	Pl	Year			W-L-T	PF	PA	Pct	Conf	Pct	Pl
1954			3-6-0	177	149	.333	1-5-0	.167	8	1964			4-5-0	136	141	.444	3-3-0	.500	6
1955	2	2	9-1-0	253	83	.900	5-1-0	.833	2	1965	2	1	10-1-0	263	76	.909	7-0-0	1.000	1
1956	9	10	7-2-0	237	87	.778	4-2-0	.667	4	1966	2	2	9-0-1	293	99	.950	7-0-0	1.000	1
1957	3	3	8-1-0	264	75	.889	5-1-0	.833	2	1967			3-7-0	173	193	.300	3-4-0	.429	5
1958			3-5-1	117	123	.389	0-5-1	.083	10	1968			5-5-0	202	151	.500	2-5-0	.286	7
1959		16	5-4-0	149	118	.556	4-2-0	.667	2	1969			4-6-0	202	231	.400	2-5-0	.286	9
1960	15	11	6-2-1	193	118	.722	4-2-0	.667	4	1970			4-6-0	190	215	.400	3-4-0	.429	5
1961	8	9	7-2-0	192	50	.778	5-2-0	.714	3	1971			6-5-0	225	169	.545	5-3-0	.625	3
1962			5-4-0	189	96	.556	3-3-0	.500	5	1972			5-5-1	158	156	.500	5-2-1	.688	4
1963	10	10	6-2-1	148	63	.722	4-1-1	.750	2										

Denny Stolz (1973-1975) 19-13-1 .591

Year			W-L-T	PF	PA	Pct	Conf	Pct	Pl	Year	W-L-T	PF	PA	Pct	Conf	Pct	Pl
1973			5-6-0	114	164	.455	4-4-0	.500	4	1975	7-4-0	222	167	.636	4-4-0	.500	3
1974	12	18	7-3-1	270	196	.682	6-1-1	.812	3								

Darryl Rodgers (1976-1979) 24-18-2 .568

Year	W-L-T	PF	PA	Pct	Conf	Pct	Pl	Year		W-L-T	PF	PA	Pct	Conf	Pct	Pl
1976	4-6-1	236	278	.409	3-5-0	.375	7	1978	12	8-3-0	411	170	.727	7-1-0	.875	1
1977	7-3-1	260	162	.682	6-1-1	.812	3	1979		5-6-0	240	253	.455	3-5-0	.375	7

Muddy Waters (1980-1982) 10-23-0 .303

Year	W-L-T	PF	PA	Pct	Conf	Pct	Pl	Year	W-L-T	PF	PA	Pct	Conf	Pct	Pl
1980	3-8-0	221	279	.273	2-6-0	.250	9	1982	2-9-0	202	242	.182	2-7-0	.222	8
1981	5-6-0	263	249	.455	4-5-0	.444	6								

George Perles (1983-1994) 68-67-4 .504

Year			W-L-T	PF	PA	Pct	Conf	Pct	Pl	Year			W-L-T	PF	PA	Pct	Conf	Pct	Pl
1983			4-6-1	162	233	.409	2-6-1	.278	7	1989	16	16	8-4-0	356	163	.667	6-2-0	.750	3
1984			6-6-0	193	203	.500	5-4-0	.556	6	1990	16	14	8-3-1	312	223	.708	6-2-0	.750	1
1985			7-5-0	258	219	.583	5-3-0	.625	4	1991			3-8-0	162	272	.273	3-5-0	.375	6
1986			6-5-0	285	197	.545	4-5-0	.500	5	1992			5-6-0	238	261	.455	5-3-0	.625	3
1987	8	8	9-2-1	261	153	.792	7-0-1	.938	1	1993			6-6-0	277	289	.500	4-4-0	.500	7
1988			6-5-1	269	177	.542	6-1-1	.812	2	1994*			0-11-0	280	267	.000	0-8-0	.000	11

*All five wins in 1994 were forfeited by Michigan State as part of its self-imposed sanctions due to NCAA violations.

Nick Saban (1995-1999) 34-24-1 .585

Year			W-L-T	PF	PA	Pct	Conf	Pct	Pl	Year			W-L-T	PF	PA	Pct	Conf	Pct	Pl
1995			6-5-1	287	338	.542	4-3-1	.562	5	1998			6-6-0	336	294	.500	4-4-0	.500	6
1996			6-6-0	358	302	.500	5-3-0	.625	5	1999 *	7	7	9-2-0	341	211	.818	6-2-0	.750	2
1997			7-5-0	342	237	.583	4-4-0	.500	6										

Bobby Williams (1999-2002) 16-17-0 .485

Year	W-L-T	PF	PA	Pct	Conf	Pct	Pl	Year	W-L-T	PF	PA	Pct	Conf	Pct	Pl
1999*	1-0-0	37	34	1.000	0-0-0			2001	7-5-0	374	311	.583	3-5-0	.375	8
2000	5-6-0			.455	2-6-0	.250	9	2002**	3-6-0	189	271	.333	1-4-0	.200	**

*Saban coached the eleven regular season games, and Williams coached the bowl game in 1999.

Morris Watts (2002) 1-2-0 .333

Year	W-L-T	PF	PA	Pct	Conf	Pct	Pl
2002**	1-2-0	105	127	.333	1-2-0	.333	8

**Williams coached the first nine games of the season, and Watts coached the remaining three

John Smith (2003) 8-5-0 .615

Year	W-L-T	PF	PA	Pct	Conf	Pct	Pl
2003	8-5-0	363	293	.615	5-3-0	.625	4

Won-loss record by decades:

1896-99	11-11-3	.500	1930-39	59-20-8	.724	1970-79	58-47-4	.550
1900-09	56-21-6	.711	1940-49	47-26-7	.631	1980-89	56-56-4	.500
1910-19	47-24-2	.658	1950-59	70-21-1	.766	1990-99	57-58-2	.496
1920-29	36-45-4	.447	1960-69	59-34-3	.630	2000-03	24-24-0	.500

Historic record: 580-387-44 .595

Post-season won-loss record: 7-10-0 .412

1938: Orange Bowl, Auburn 6, Michigan State 0
1954: Rose Bowl, Michigan State 28, UCLA 20
1956: Rose Bowl, Michigan State 17, UCLA 14
1966: Rose Bowl, UCLA 14, Michigan State 12
1984: Cherry Bowl, Army 10, Michigan State 6
1985 All American Bowl, Georgia Tech 17, Michigan State 14
1988: Rose Bowl, Michigan State 20, USC 17
1989: Gator Bowl, Georgia 34, Michigan State 27

1989: Aloha Bowl, Michigan State 33, Hawaii 13
1990: Sun Bowl, Michigan State 17, USC 16
1993: Liberty Bowl, Louisville 18, Michigan State 7
1995: Independence Bowl, LSU 45, Michigan State 26
1996: Sun Bowl, Stanford 38, Michigan State 0
1997: Aloha Bowl, Washington 51, Michigan State 23
2000: Citrus Bowl, Michigan State 37, Florida 34
2001: Silicon Valley Bowl, Michigan State 44, Fresno 35
2003: Alamo Bowl, Nebraska 17, Michigan State 3

College Football Hall of Fame:
Charlie Bachman, coach, 1933-46; Johnny Pingel, halfback, 1936-38; Biggie Munn, coach, 1947-53; Don Coleman, tackle, 1949-51; Duffy Daugherty, coach, 1954-1972; Bubba Smith, defensive end, 1964-66; George Webster, linebacker, 1964-66; Jim Mandich, end, 1967-69; Brad Van Pelt, safety, 1970-72; Muddy Waters, coach, 1980-82.

Awards: Butkus Award: 1989, Percy Snow; Maxwell Award: 1972, Brad Van Pelt; Lombardi Award: 1989, Percy Snow; Outland Trophy: 1949, Ed Bagdon; Fred Biletnikoff Award: 2002, Charles Rogers.

UNIVERSITY OF MICHIGAN, Ann Arbor, Michigan; nickname "Wolverines"; colors blue and gold; Michigan Stadium (107,501); Big Ten Conference. Michigan began play in 1879 and was an independent until the 1896 season when it was a founding member of the Western Conference (later renamed the Big Ten). In 1907, Michigan left the Big Ten in a dispute over conference scheduling rules. Michigan returned to the Big Ten for the 1917 season and has played in the Big Ten since that season. Following Big Ten rules at the time, conference win percents are calculated ignoring ties before the 1946 season.

Early years (1879-1895)

Year	Coach	W-L-T	PF	PA	Pct.	Year	Coach	W-L-T	PF	PA	Pct.
1879	none	1-0-1	1	0	.750	1888	none	4-1-0	130	46	.800
1880	none	1-0-0	13	6	1.000	1889	none	1-2-0	33	80	.333
1881	none	0-3-0	4	28	.000	1890	none	4-1-0	129	36	.800
1882	no team					1891	Mike Murphy &				
1883	none	2-3-0	63	91	.400		Frank Crawford	4-5-0	168	114	.444
1884	none	2-0-0	28	10	1.000	1892	Frank Barbour	7-5-0	298	170	.583
1885	none	3-0-0	82	0	1.000	1893	Frank Barbour	7-3-0	278	102	.700
1886	none	2-0-0	74	0	1.000	1894	William McCauley	9-1-1	244	84	.864
1887	none	3-0-0	66	0	1.000	1895	William McCauley	8-1-0	266	14	.889

Member of the Big Ten Conference (1896-1906, 1917-2002) 436-159-17 .726

Year	Nat'l AP	Other	Overall W-L-T	PF	PA	Pct	Conf. W-L-T	Pct.	Rank	Year	Nat'l AP	Other	Overall W-L-T	PF	PA	Pct	Conf. W-L-T	Pct.	Rank
William Ward (1896) 9-1-0 .900																			
1896			9-1-0	262	11	.900	2-1-0	.667	2										
Gustave Ferbert (1897-1899) 24-3-1 .875																			
1897			6-1-1	166	31	.812	2-1-0	.667	3	1899			8-2-0	176	43	.800	1-1-0	.500	3
1898			10-0-0	205	26	1.000	3-0-0	1.000	1										
Biff Lea (1900) 7-2-1 .750																			
1900			7-2-1	117	55	.750	3-2-0	.600	5										
Fielding Yost (1901-1923,1925-1926) 165-29-10 .833																			
1901	1		11-0-0	550	0	1.000	4-0-0	1.000	1	1904			10-0-0	567	22	1.000	2-0-0	1.000	1
1902	1		11-0-0	644	12	1.000	5-0-0	1.000	1	1905			12-1-0	495	2	.923	2-1-0	.667	2
1903			11-0-1	565	6	.958	3-0-1	1.000	1	1906			4-1-0	72	30	.800	1-0-0	1.000	1
Michigan reverts to independent status (1907-1916)																			
1907			5-1-0	107	6	.833				1912			5-2-0	158	65	.714			
1908			5-2-1	128	81	.688				1913			6-1-0	175	21	.875			
1909			6-1-0	115	34	.857				1914			6-3-0	233	68	.667			
1910			3-0-3	26	9	.750				1915			4-3-1	130	81	.563			
1911			5-1-2	90	38	.750				1916			7-2-0	245	56	.778			
Michigan returns to the Big Ten (1917-2002)																			
1917			8-2-0	304	53	.800	0-1-0	.000	8	1921			5-1-1	187	21	.786	2-1-1	.667	5
1918			5-0-0	96	6	1.000	2-0-0	1.000	1	1922			6-0-1	183	13	.929	4-0-0	1.000	1
1919			3-4-0	93	102	.429	1-4-0	.200	7	1923			8-0-0	150	12	1.000	4-0-0	1.000	1
1920			5-2-0	121	21	.714	2-2-0	.500	6										
George Little (1924) 6-2-0 .750																			
1924			6-2-0	155	54	.750	4-2-0	.667	4										
Fielding Yost (1925-1926)																			
1925	2		7-1-0	227	3	.875	5-1-0	.833	1	1926	3		7-1-0	191	38	.875	5-0-0	1.000	1
Tad Weiman (1927-1928) 9-6-1 .594																			
1927	7		6-2-0	137	39	.750	3-2-0	.600	3	1928			3-4-1	36	62	.438	2-3-0	.400	7
Harry Kipke (1929-1937) 46-26-4 .632																			
1929			5-3-1	109	75	.611	1-3-1	.250	7	1934			1-7-0	21	143	.125	0-6-0	.000	10
1930	5		8-0-1	111	23	.944	5-0-0	1.000	1	1935			4-4-0	68	131	.500	2-3-0	.400	5
1931			8-1-1	181	27	.850	5-1-0	.833	1	1936			1-7-0	36	127	.125	0-5-0	.000	8
1932	1		8-0-0	123	13	1.000	6-0-0	1.000	1	1937			4-4-0	54	110	.500	3-3-0	.500	4
1933	1		7-0-1	131	18	.938	5-0-1	1.000	1										
Fritz Crisler (1938-1947) 71-16-3 .805																			
1938	16	6	6-1-1	131	40	.812	3-1-1	.750	2	1943	3		8-1-0	302	73	.889	6-0-0	1.000	1
1939	20	7	6-2-0	219	94	.750	3-2-0	.600	4	1944	8		8-2-0	204	91	.800	5-2-0	.714	2
1940	3	2	7-1-0	196	34	.875	3-1-0	.750	2	1945	6		7-3-0	187	99	.700	5-1-0	.833	2
1941	5		6-1-1	147	41	.812	3-1-1	.750	2	1946	6		6-2-1	233	73	.722	5-1-1	.786	2
1942	9		7-3-0	221	134	.700	3-2-0	.600	3	1947	2		10-0-0	394	53	1.000	6-0-0	1.000	1
Bennie Oosterbaan (1948-1958) 63-33-4 .650																			
1948	1		9-0-0	252	44	1.000	6-0-0	1.000	1	1954	15	15	6-3-0	139	87	.667	5-2-0	.714	2
1949	7		6-2-1	135	85	.722	4-1-1	.750	1	1955	12	13	7-2-0	179	94	.778	5-2-0	.714	3
1950	9	6	6-3-1	150	114	.650	4-1-1	.750	1	1956	7	7	7-2-0	233	123	.778	5-2-0	.714	2
1951			4-5-0	135	122	444	4-2-0	.667	4	1957			5-3-1	187	147	.611	3-3-1	.500	6
1952			5-4-0	207	134	.556	4-2-0	.667	4	1958			2-6-1	132	211	.278	1-5-1	.214	8
1953	20	19	6-3-0	163	101	.667	3-3-0	.500	5										

Bump Elliott (1959-1968) 51-42-2 .547

Year	AP	UPI	Record	PF	PA	Pct	Conf	Conf Pct	Place
1959			4-5-0	122	161	.444	3-4-0	.429	7
1960			5-4-0	133	84	.556	2-4-0	.333	5
1961			6-3-0	212	163	.667	3-3-0	.500	6
1962			2-7-0	70	214	.222	1-6-0	.143	10
1963			3-4-2	131	127	.444	2-3-2	.429	5
1964	4	4	9-1-0	235	83	.900	6-1-0	.857	1
1965			4-6-0	185	161	.400	2-5-0	.286	7
1966			6-4-0	236	138	.600	4-3-0	.571	3
1967			4-6-0	144	179	.400	3-4-0	.429	5
1968	12	15	8-2-0	277	155	.800	6-1-0	.857	2

Bo Schembechler (1969-1989) 194-48-5 .796

Year	AP	UPI	Record	PF	PA	Pct	Conf	Conf Pct	Place
1969	9	8	8-3-0	352	148	.727	6-1-0	.857	1
1970	9	7	9-1-0	288	90	.900	6-1-0	.857	2
1971	6	4	11-1-0	421	83	.917	8-0-0	1.000	1
1972	6	6	10-1-0	264	57	.909	7-1-0	.875	1
1973	6	6	10-0-1	330	68	.955	7-0-1	.938	1
1974	3	5	10-1-0	324	75	.909	7-1-0	.875	1
1975	8	8	8-2-2	324	130	.750	7-1-0	.875	1
1976	3	3	10-2-0	432	95	.833	7-1-0	.875	1
1977	9	8	10-2-0	353	124	.833	7-1-0	.875	1
1978	5	5	10-2-0	372	105	.833	7-1-0	.875	1
1979	18	19	8-4-0	312	151	.667	6-2-0	.750	3
1980	4	4	10-2-0	322	129	.833	8-0-0	1.000	1
1981	12	10	9-3-0	355	162	.750	6-3-0	.667	3
1982		15	8-4-0	345	204	.667	8-1-0	.889	1
1983	8	9	9-3-0	355	160	.750	8-1-0	.889	2
1984			6-6-0	214	200	.500	5-4-0	.556	6
1985	2	2	10-1-1	342	98	.875	6-1-1	.812	2
1986	8	7	11-2-0	379	203	.846	7-1-0	.875	1
1987	19	18	8-4-0	337	172	.667	5-3-0	.625	4
1988	4	4	9-2-1	361	167	.792	7-0-1	.938	1
1989	7	8	10-2-0	335	184	.833	8-0-0	1.000	1

Gary Moeller (1990-1994) 44-13-3 .758

Year	AP	UPI	Record	PF	PA	Pct	Conf	Conf Pct	Place
1990	7	8	9-3-0	389	198	.750	6-2-0	.750	1
1991	6	6	10-2-0	420	203	.833	8-0-0	1.000	1
1992	5	5	9-0-3	431	171	.875	6-0-2	.875	1
1993	21	19	8-4-0	342	160	.667	5-3-0	.625	4
1994	12	12	8-4-0	330	268	.667	5-3-0	.625	3

Lloyd Carr (1995-2003) 86-26-0 .768

Year	AP	UPI	Record	PF	PA	Pct	Conf	Conf Pct	Place
1995	17	19	9-4-0	338	223	.692	5-3-0	.625	3
1996	20	20	8-4-0	287	184	.667	5-3-0	.625	5
1997	1	2	12-0-0	322	144	1.000	8-0-0	1.000	1
1998	12	12	10-3-0	359	235	.769	7-1-0	.875	1
1999	5	5	10-2-0	361	247	.833	6-2-0	.750	2
2000	11	10	9-3-0	404	229	.750	6-2-0	.750	1
2001	20	20	8-4-0	320	237	.667	6-2-0	.750	2
2002	9	9	10-3-0	361	265	.769	6-2-0	.750	3
2003	6	7	10-3-0	460	219	.769	7-1-0	.875	1

Won-loss record by decades:

Decade	Record	Pct		Decade	Record	Pct		Decade	Record	Pct
1879-89	19- 9-1	.672		1930-39	53-26-4	.663		1970-79	96-16-3	.848
1890-99	72-20-2	.777		1940-49	74-15-3	.821		1980-89	90-29-2	.752
1900-09	82- 8-3	.898		1950-59	52-36-3	.588		1990-99	93-26-3	.775
1910-19	52-18-6	.724		1960-69	55-40-2	.577		2000-03	37-13-0	.740
1920-29	58-16-4	.769								

Historic record: 833-272-36 .746

Post-season won-loss record: 18-17-0 .514

1902: Rose Bowl, Michigan 49, Stanford 0
1948: Rose Bowl, Michigan 49, USC 0
1951: Rose Bowl, Michigan 14, California 6
1965: Rose Bowl, Michigan 34, Oregon State 7
1970: Rose Bowl, USC 10, Michigan 3
1972: Rose Bowl, Stanford 13, Michigan 12
1976: Orange Bowl, Oklahoma 14, Michigan 6
1977: Rose Bowl, USC 14, Michigan 6
1978: Rose Bowl, Washington 27, Michigan 20
1979: Rose Bowl, USC 17, Michigan 10
1979: Gator Bowl, North Carolina 17, Michigan 15
1981: Rose Bowl, Michigan 23, Washington 6
1981: Bluebonnet Bowl, Michigan 33, UCLA 14
1983: Rose Bowl, UCLA 24, Michigan 14
1984: Sugar Bowl, Auburn 9, Michigan 7
1984: Holiday Bowl, BYU 24, Michigan 17
1986: Fiesta Bowl, Michigan 27, Nebraska 23

1987: Rose Bowl, Arizona State 22, Michigan 15
1988: Hall of Fame Bowl, Michigan 28, Alabama 24
1989: Rose Bowl, Michigan 22, USC 14
1990: Rose Bowl, USC 17, Michigan 10
1991: Gator Bowl, Michigan 35, Mississippi 3
1992: Rose Bowl, Washington 34, Michigan 14
1993: Rose Bowl, Michigan 38, Washington 31
1994: Outback Bowl, Michigan 42, NC State 7
1994: Holiday Bowl, Michigan 24, Colorado State 14
1995: Alamo Bowl, Texas A&M 22, Michigan 20
1997: Outback Bowl, Alabama 17, Michigan 14
1998: Rose Bowl, Michigan 21, Wash. State 16
1999: Citrus Bowl, Michigan 45, Arkansas 31
2000: Orange Bowl, Michigan 35, Alabama 34
2001: Citrus Bowl, Michigan 31, Auburn 28
2002: Citrus Bowl, Tennessee 45, Michigan 17
2002: Outback Bowl, Michigan 38, Florida 30
2004: Rose Bowl, USC 28, Michigan 14

College Football Hall of Fame:
Neil Snow, end/fullback, 1898-01; Fielding Yost, coach, 1900-26; Willie Heston, halfback, 1900-04; Germany Schultz, center, 1904-08; Benny Benbrook, guard, 1908-10; Johnny Maulbetsch, fullback, 1911-16; Ernie Vick, center, 1918-21; Harry Kipke, halfback, 1921-23; Benny Friedman, quarterback, 1924-26; George Little, coach, 1924; Tad Wieman, coach, 1927-28; Bennie Oosterbaan, end, 1925-27; Harry Newman, quarterback, 1930-32; Whitey Wistert, tackle, 1931-33; Fritz Crisler, coach ,1938-47; Tom Harmon, halfback, 1938-40; Bob Westfall, fullback, 1939-41; Albert Wistert, tackle, 1940-42; Merv Pregulman, center/tackle, 1941-43; Crazy Legs Hirsch, halfback, 1943; Bob Chappuis, halfback, 1942-47; Bump Elliott, halfback, 1943-47; Pete Elliott, quarterback, 1945-48; Whitely Wistert, tackle, 1946-48; Ron Kramer, end, 1954-56; Ron Johnson, halfback, 1966-68; Dan Dierdorf, tackle, 1968-70; Bo Schembechler, coach, 1969-89; Reggie McKenzie, offensive guard, 1969-71; Anthony Carter, wide receiver, 1979-82.

Awards: Butkus Award: 1991, Erich Anderson; Heisman Trophy: 1940, Tom Harmon; 1991, Desmond Howard; 1997: Charles Woodson; Maxwell Award: 1940, Tom Harmon; 1991, Desmond Howard; Jim Thorpe Award: 1997, Charles Woodson; Bednarik Award: 1997, Charles Wooden.; Nagurski Award, 1997, Charles Wooden; Camp Award: 1991, Desmond Howard; 1997, Charles Wooden; Baugh Trophy: 1992, Elvis Grbac.; Doak Walker Award: 2003, Chris Perry.

MIDDLE TENNESSEE UNIVERSITY, Murfreesboro, Tennessee; nickname "Blue Raiders"; colors royal blue and white; Horace Jones Field (30,788); Sun Belt Conference. Middle Tennessee began play in 1913. After becoming a Division I-A team in the 1990s, Middle Tennessee played as an independent before joining the Sun Belt Conference in 2001.

Year	W-L-T	PF	PA	Pct.	Year	W-L-T	PF	PA	Pct.
					Alfred Miles (1913-1916, 1919-1923) 35-16-4 .673				
1913	5-1-1	164	48	.786	1915	2-3-1	34	92	.417
1914	5-0-1	132	13	.917	1916	5-2-0	111	30	.714
					Red Floyd (1917, 1935-1938) 30-8-1 .782				
1917	7-0-0	201	0	1.000	1918	no team			
					Alfred Miles (1919-1923)				
1919	6-0-0	148	6	1.000	1922	2-6-0	20	175	.250
1920	4-1-0	126	54	.800	1923	3-1-0	109	32	.750
1921	3-2-1	36	74	.583					
					Guy Stephenson (1924-1925) 4-9-2 .333				
1924	1-5-0	14	123	.167	1925	3-4-2	107	128	.444
					F. Faulkinberry (1926-1932) 33-26-4 .555				
1926	4-2-1	102	124	.643	1930	5-5-1	125	98	.500
1927	6-2-0	202	59	.750	1931	6-4-0	167	69	.600
1928	2-4-1	69	84	.357	1932	4-6-0	70	117	.400
1929	6-3-1	85	92	.650					
					E. M. Waller (1933-1934) 4-13-1 .250				
1933	2-6-1	44	187	.278	1934	2-7-0	30	90	.222
					Red Floyd (1935-1938)				
1935	8-0-0	128	25	1.000	1937	6-1-1	142	40	.812
1936	7-1-0	112	65	.875	1938	2-6-0	65	116	.250
					Herc Alley (1939) 2-5-1 .312				
1939	2-5-1	52	112	.312					
					E. W. Midgett (1940-1942, 1946) 17-12-3 .578				
1940	4-4-0	107	78	.500	1943-1945	no team			
1941	4-3-1	120	87	.562	1946	5-3-1	140	75	.611
1942	4-2-1	106	85	.643					
					Charles Murphy (1947-1968) 155-63-8 .704				
1947	9-1-0	224	61	.900	1958	8-2-0	196	77	.800
1948	5-5-0	92	115	.500	1959	10-0-1	324	93	.955
1949	8-0-1	251	79	.944	1960	5-5-0	115	126	.500
1950	9-2-0	303	131	.818	1961	7-4-0	187	128	.636
1951	7-2-2	318	106	.727	1962	6-4-0	161	104	.600
1952	6-5-0	214	194	.545	1963	8-2-0	213	106	.800
1953	7-4-0	186	179	.636	1964	8-2-1	156	65	.773
1954	4-4-2	153	156	.500	1965	10-0-0	286	157	1.000
1955	7-2-1	187	205	.750	1966	7-3-0	160	95	.700
1956	7-3-0	202	132	.700	1967	5-5-0	236	231	.500
1957	10-0-0	241	40	1.000	1968	2-8-0	146	279	.200
					Don Fuos (1969) 1-9-0 .100				
1969	1-9-0	134	216	.100					
					Bill Peck (1970-1974) 27-25-2 .519				
1970	6-3-1	167	105	.650	1973	4-7-0	148	264	.364
1971	7-4-0	196	178	.636	1974	3-8-0	164	254	.273
1972	7-3-1	216	182	.682					
					Ben Hurt (1975-1978) 12-31-1 .273				
1975	4-7-0	189	254	.364	1977	3-8-0	125	283	.273
1976	4-7-0	205	281	.364	1978	1-9-1	95	340	.136
					Boots Donnelly (1979-1998) 140-87-1 .616				
1979	1-9-0	137	333	.100	1989	9-4-0	318	225	.692
1980	2-8-0	85	224	.200	1990	11-2-0	425	128	.846
1981	6-5-0	158	173	.545	1991	9-4-0	345	193	.692
1982	8-3-0-	231	110	.727	1992	10-3-0	417	189	.769
1983	8-2-0	296	111	.800	1993	5-6-0	354	235	.455
1984	11-3-0	374	220	.786	1994	8-3-1	401	229	.708
1985	11-1-0	388	173	.917	1995	7-4-0	303	201	.636
1986	6-5-0	254	155	.545	1996	6-5-0	303	206	.545
1987	6-5-0	248	160	.545	1997	4-6-0	292	244	.400
1988	7-4-0	294	115	.636	1998	5-5-0	250	209	.500

Andy McCollum (1999-2003) 24-32-0 .429

Year	Nat'l AP	Other	Overall W-L-T	PF	PA	Pct.	Conference W-L-T	Pct.	Rank	Year	Nat'l AP	Other	Overall W-L-T	PF	PA	Pct.	Conference W-L-T	Pct.	Rank
1999			3-8-0	272	379	.273				2000			6-5-0	350	316	.545			

Member of the Sun Belt Conference (2001-2003) 11-8-0 .579

Year	Nat'l AP	Other	Overall W-L-T	PF	PA	Pct.	Conference W-L-T	Pct.	Rank	Year	Nat'l AP	Other	Overall W-L-T	PF	PA	Pct.	Conference W-L-T	Pct.	Rank
2001			8-3-0	408	286	.727	5-1-0	.833	1	2003			4-8-0	332	375	.333	4-3-0	.333	2
2002			3-8-0	252	304	.273	2-4-0	.333	4										

Won-loss record by decades:

1913-19	30-6-3	.808	1950-59	75-24-6	.743	1990-99	68-46-1	.596
1920-29	34-30-6	.529	1960-69	59-42-1	.583	2000-03	21-24-0	.467
1930-39	44-41-4	.517	1970-79	40-65-3	.384			
1940-49	39-18-4	.672	1980-89	74-40-0	.659			

Historic record: 484-336-28 .589

Post-season won-loss record: 8-8-0 .500

1956: Refrigerator Bowl, Sam Houston State 27, MTU 13
1959: Tangerine Bowl, MTU 21, Presbyterian 12
1964: Grantland Rice Bowl: MTU 20, Muskingum 0
1984: I-AA Playoffs, MTU 27, Eastern Kentucky 10
1984: I-AA Playoffs, MTU 42, Indiana State 41
1984: I-AA Playoffs, Louisiana Tech 21, MTU 13
1985: I-AA Playoffs, Ga. Southern 28, MTU 21
1989: I-AA Playoffs, MTU 24, Appalachian State 21

1989: I-AA Playoffs, Georgia Southern 45, MTU 3
1990: I-AA Playoffs, MTU 28, Jackson State 7
1990: I-AA Playoffs, Boise State 20, MTU 13
1991: I-AA Playoffs, MTU 20, Sam Houston State 19
1991: I-AA Playoffs, Eastern Kentucky 23, MTU 13
1992: I-AA Playoffs, MTU 35, Appalachian State 10
1992: I-AA Playoffs, Marshall 35, MTU 21
1994: I-AA Playoffs, Marshall 49, MTU 14

UNIVERSITY OF MINNESOTA, Minneapolis, Minnesota; nickname "Golden Gophers"; colors maroon and gold; Humphrey Metrodome (64,172); Big Ten Conference. The Gophers were an independent from 1882 through the 1895 season. In 1896, Minnesota joined with six other teams to form the Western Conference, later renamed the Big Ten. Following Big Ten rules, ties are ignored in calculating the win percent for conference games up to the 1946 season.

Years as an independent (1882-1895)

Year	Coach	W-L-T	PF	PA	Pct.	Year	Coach	W-L-T	PF	PA	Pct.
1882	none	1-1-0	4	2	.500	1889	D.W. McCord*	3-1-0	46	28	.750
1883	Thomas Peebles	1-2-0	9	8	.333	1890	Tom Eck	5-1-1	208	33	.786
1884	no team					1891	Dad Moulton	3-1-1	102	46	.700
1885	no team					1892	none	5-0-0	122	56	1.000
1886	Frederick Jones	0-2-0	13	27	.000	1893	Wallie Winter	6-0-0	148	38	1.000
1887	Frederick Jones	2-0-0	22	0	1.000	1894	Tom Cochran	3-1-0	74	8	.750
1888	Frederick Jones	1-1-0	22	16	.500	1895	Pudge Hefflefinger	7-3-0	136	58	.700

*Also listed as coaches in the 1889 season are Al McCord, Frank Hefflefinger, and Billy Moore.

Member of the Big Ten Conference (1896-2003) 304-320-28 .488

Year	Nat'l AP	Other	Overall W-L-T	PF	PA	Pct.	Conf. W-L-T	Pct.	Rank	Year	Nat'l AP	Other	Overall W-L-T	PF	PA	Pct.	Conf. W-L-T	Pct.	Rank
									Alexande	r Jerrems (1896-1	897) 12	-6-0 .6	67						
1896			8-2-0	168	24	.800	1-2-0	.333	5	1897			4-4-0	112	77	.500	0-3-0	.000	6
									Jac	k Minds (1898) 4-	5-0 .44	4							
1898			4-5-0	92	72	.444	1-2-0	.333	5										
								John Harris	on and William Le	ary (189	9) 6-3-	2 .636						
1899			6-3-2	151	79	.636	0-3-0	.000	6										
								Doc Wil	liams (1900-1921)	134-34-	12 .778							
1900			10-0-2	299	23	.917	3-0-1	1.000	1	1912			4-3-0	87	38	.571	2-2-0	.500	3
1901			9-1-1	183	18	.864	3-1-0	.750	3	1913			5-2-0	116	32	.714	2-1-0	.667	2
1902			9-2-1	335	34	.792	3-1-0	.750	3	1914			6-1-0	123	44	.857	3-1-0	.750	3
1903			14-0-1	618	12	.967	3-0-1	1.000	1	1915			6-0-1	191	35	.929	3-0-1	1.000	1
1904			13-0-0	725	12	1.000	3-0-0	1.000	1	1916			6-1-0	348	28	.857	3-1-0	.750	3
1905			10-1-0	542	22	.909	2-1-0	.667	2	1917			4-1-0	164	25	.800	3-1-0	.750	2
1906			2-2-1	47	29	.500	2-0-0	1.000	1	1918			5-2-1	133	39	.688	2-1-0	.667	3
1907			2-2-1	55	52	.500	0-1-1	.000	5	1919			4-2-1	130	45	.643	3-2-0	.600	4
1908			3-2-1	32	50	.583	0-2-0	.000	7	1920			1-6-0	62	92	.143	0-6-0	.000	9
1909			6-1-0	158	27	.857	3-0-0	1.000	1	1921			3-4-0	60	141	.429	2-4-0	.333	6
1910			6-1-0	179	6	.857	2-0-0	1.000	1										
1911			6-0-1	102	15	.929	3-0-1	1.000	1										
								Bill Spa	ulding (1922-1924	) 11-7-4	.591							
1922			3-3-1	79	65	.500	2-3-1	.400	5	1924			3-3-2	68	63	.500	1-2-1	.375	6
1923			5-1-1	114	60	.786	2-1-1	.667	4										
								Doc S	pears (1925-1929)	28-9-3	.738							
1925			5-2-1	176	91	.688	1-1-1	.500	4	1928			6-2-0	182	36	.750	4-2-0	.667	3
1926			5-3-0	269	64	.625	2-2-0	.500	6	1929			6-2-0	179	55	.750	3-2-0	.600	3
1927		3	6-0-2	209	51	.875	3-0-1	1.000	2										
								Fritz C	risler (1930-1931)	10-7-1	.583							
1930			3-4-1	126	81	.438	1-3-0	.250	6	1931			7-3-0	191	72	.700	3-2-0	.600	4
							Bernie Bi	erman (1932-1941,	1945-50)	93-35-6	.716							
1932			5-3-0	86	42	.625	2-3-0	.400	5	1937	5	11	6-2-0	184	50	.750	5-0-0	1.000	1
1933		3	4-0-4	64	32	.750	2-0-4	1.000	2	1938	10	7	6-2-0	97	38	.750	4-1-0	.800	1
1934		1	8-0-0	270	38	1.000	5-0-0	1.000	1	1939			3-4-1	154	82	.438	2-3-1	.400	7
1935		1	8-0-0	194	46	1.000	5-0-0	1.000	1	1940	1	1	8-0-0	154	71	1.000	6-0-0	1.000	1
1936	1	1	7-1-0	203	32	.875	4-1-0	.800	2	1941	1		8-0-0	186	38	1.000	5-0-0	1.000	1
								Doc H	auser (1942-1944)	15-11-1	.574							
1942	19		5-4-0	152	91	.556	3-3-0	.500	4	1944			5-3-1	225	162	.611	3-2-1	.600	4
1943			5-4-0	170	184	.556	2-3-0	.400	3										
								Bern	ie Bierman (1945-	1950)								
1945			4-5-0	177	155	.444	1-5-0	.167	8	1948	16		7-2-0	203	94	.722	5-2-0	.571	3
1946			5-4-0	130	114	.556	3-4-0	.429	5	1949	8		7-2-0	231	80	.722	4-2-0	.667	3
1947			6-3-0	174	127	.667	3-3-0	.500	3	1950			1-7-1	79	196	.214	1-4-1	.250	7
								Wes F	esler (1951-1953)	10-13-4	.444							
1951			2-6-1	162	258	.278	1-4-1	.250	7	1953			4-4-1	150	160	.500	3-3-1	.500	5
1952			4-3-2	131	171	.556	3-1-2	.667	5										

Murray Warmath (1954-1971) 87-78-7 .526

Year	AP	UPI	W-L-T	PF	PA	Pct	Conf	Conf Pct	Conf Rk
1954	20		7-2-0	195	127	.778	4-2-0	.667	4
1955			3-6-0	110	172	.333	2-5-0	.285	8
1956	12	9	6-1-2	127	87	.778	4-1-2	.714	3
1957			4-5-0	201	188	.444	3-5-0	.375	8
1958			1-8-0	115	157	.111	1-6-0	.143	9
1959			2-7-0	98	159	.222	1-6-0	.143	10
1960	1	1	8-2-0	228	88	.800	5-1-0	.833	1
1961	6	6	8-2-0	161	78	.800	6-1-0	.857	2
1962	10	10	6-2-1	131	61	.722	5-2-0	.714	2
1963			3-6-0	95	117	.333	2-5-0	.286	9
1964			5-4-0	136	131	.556	4-3-0	.571	4
1965			5-4-1	188	160	.550	5-2-0	.714	3
1966			4-5-1	124	160	.450	3-3-1	.500	5
1967	14		8-2-0	163	106	.800	6-1-0	.857	1
1968	18		6-4-0	207	190	.600	5-2-0	.714	3
1969			4-5-1	210	259	.450	4-3-0	.571	4
1970			3-6-1	180	237	.350	2-4-1	.357	7
1971			4-7-0	212	278	.364	3-5-0	.375	6

Cal Stoll (1972-1978) 39-39-0 .500

Year	W-L-T	PF	PA	Pct	Conf	Conf Pct	Conf Rk
1972	4-7-0	185	304	.364	4-4-0	.500	5
1973	7-4-0	260	295	.636	6-2-0	.750	3
1974	4-7-0	161	332	.364	2-6-0	.250	7
1975	6-5-0	236	192	.545	3-5-0	.375	7
1976	6-5-0	201	211	.545	4-4-0	.500	3
1977	7-5-0	171	187	.583	4-4-0	.500	5
1978	5-6-0	210	267	.455	4-4-0	.500	5

Joe Salem (1979-1983) 19-35-1 .355

Year	W-L-T	PF	PA	Pct	Conf	Conf Pct	Conf Rk
1979	4-6-1	264	271	.409	3-5-1	.388	6
1980	5-6-0	210	250	.450	4-5-0	.444	7
1981	6-5-0	274	264	.545	4-5-0	.444	6
1982	3-8-0	247	295	.273	1-8-0	.111	10
1983	1-10-0	181	518	.091	0-9-0	.000	10

Lou Holtz (1984-1985) 10-12-0 .455

Year	W-L-T	PF	PA	Pct	Conf	Conf Pct	Conf Rk
1984	4-7-0	194	316	.364	3-6-0	.333	9
1985*	6-5-0	273	227	.545	4-4-0	.500	6

John Gutekunst (1985-1991) 29-37-2 .441

Year	W-L-T	PF	PA	Pct	Conf	Conf Pct	Conf Rk
1985*	1-0-0	20	13	1.000	0-0-0		
1986	6-6-0	261	316	.500	5-3-0	.625	3
1987	6-5-0	257	262	.545	3-5-0	.375	6
1988	2-7-2	195	246	.273	0-6-2	.125	9
1989	6-5-0	263	283	.545	4-4-0	.500	5
1990	6-5-0	224	281	.545	5-3-0	.625	6
1991	2-9-0	104	302	.182	1-7-0	.125	10

*Holtz coached the first eleven games of the 1985 season, and Gutekunst coached the last (bowl) game of that season.

Jim Wacker (1992-1996) 16-39-0 .291

Year	W-L-T	PF	PA	Pct	Conf	Conf Pct	Conf Rk
1992	2-9-0	200	313	.182	2-6-0	250	10
1993	4-7-0	253	354	.364	3-5-0	.375	8
1994	3-8-0	256	348	.273	1-7-0	.125	11
1995	3-8-0	272	368	.273	1-7-0	.125	10
1996	4-7-0	236	340	.364	1-7-0	.125	9

Glen Mason (1997-2003) 44-40-0 .524

Year	AP	UPI	W-L-T	PF	PA	Pct	Conf	Conf Pct	Conf Rk
1997			3-9-0	238	334	.250	1-7-0	.125	9
1998			5-6-0	229	249	.455	2-6-0	.250	7
1999	18	17	8-4-0	368	196	.667	5-3-0	.625	4
2000			6-6-0	375	318	.500	4-4-0	.500	4
2001			4-7-0	308	299	.364	2-6-0	.250	10
2002			8-5-0	376	319	.615	3-5-0	.375	7
2003	20	17	10-3-0	503	285	.769	5-3-0	.625	4

Won-loss record by decades:

Decade	Record	Pct		Decade	Record	Pct		Decade	Record	Pct
1882-89	8-7-0	.533		1930-39	57-19-6	.732		1970-79	50-58-2	.464
1890-99	51-20-4	.707		1940-49	60-27-1	.688		1980-89	46-64-2	.420
1900-09	80-11-7	.852		1950-59	34-49-7	.417		1990-99	40-72-0	.357
1910-19	52-13-4	.783		1960-69	57-36-4	.593		2000-03	28-21-0	.571
1920-29	43-26-7	.612								

Historic record: 606-423-44 .585

Post-season won-loss record: 4-5-0 .444

1961: Rose Bowl, Washington 17, Minnesota 7
1962: Rose Bowl, Minnesota 21, UCLA 3
1977: Hall of Fame Bowl, Maryland 17, Minnesota 7
1985: Independence Bowl, Minnesota 20, Clemson 13

1986: Liberty Bowl, Tennessee 21, Minnesota 14
1999: Wells Fargo Sun Bowl, Oregon 24, Minnesota 20
2000: Micron.com Bowl, NC State 38, Minnesota 30
2002: Music City Bowl, Minnesota 29, Arkansas 14
2003: Sun Bowl, Minnesota 31, Oregon 30

College Football Hall of Fame:
Ed Rogers, end, 1901-03; Bobby Marshall, 1904-06; Henry Williams, coach, 1900-22; John McGovern, quarterback, 1908-10; Bert Baston, end, 1914-16; Herb Joesting, fullback, 1925-27; Bronko Nagurski, tackle/fullback, 1927-29; Fritz Crisler, coach, 1930-31; Pug Lund, halfback, 1934; Bernie Bierman, coach, 1932-41, 1945-50; Ed Widseth, tackle, 1934-36; George Franck, halfback, 1938-40; Bruce Smith, halfback, 1939-1941; Dick Wildung, tackle, 1940-42; Clayton Tonnemaker, center, 1946-49; Leo Nomellini, tackle/guard, 1946-49; Paul Giel, halfback, 1951-53; Bobby Bell, tackle, 1960-62; Tom Brown, guard, 1958-60.

Awards: Heisman Trophy: 1941, Bruce Smith; Outland Trophy: 1960, Tom Brown; 1962, Bobby Bell; Jim Thorpe Award: 1999, Tyrone Carter.

MISSISSIPPI STATE UNIVERSITY, Starkville, Mississippi; nickname "Bulldogs"; colors maroon and white; Scott Field (52,884); Southeastern Conference. Miss. State began play in 1895 and joined the Southern Conference in 1922. It played in that conference until the Southeastern Conference was formed after the 1932 season, and State has been a member of the SEC since the 1933 season.

Early years (1895-1921)

Year	Nat'l AP	Other	W-L-T	PF	PA	Pct.
W. M. Matthews (1895) 0-2-0 .000						
1895			0-2-0	0	37	000
J. B. Hildebrand (1896) 0-4-0 .000						
1896			0-4-0	0	135	.000
No team (1897-1900)						
L. B. Harvey (1901) 2-2-1 .500						
1901			2-2-1	34	74	.500
L. Gwin (1902) 1-4-1 .250						
1902			1-4-1	43	80	.250
Dan Martin (1903-1906) 10-11-3 .479						
1903			3-0-2	71	6	.800
1904			2-5-0	101	95	.286
1905			3-4-0	98	94	.429
1906			2-2-1	101	45	.500
Fred Furman (1907-1908) 9-7-0 .563						
1907			6-3-0	210	77	.667
1908			3-4-0	108	113	.429
W. D. Chadwick (1909-1913) 29-12-2 .698						
1909			5-4-0	153	44	.556
1910			7-2-0	219	36	.778
1911			7-2-1	206	28	.750
1912			4-3-0	96	75	.571
1913			6-1-1	143	34	.812
E. C. Hayes (1914-1916) 15-8-2 .640						
1914			6-2-0	289	38	.750
1915			5-2-1	110	36	.688
1916			4-4-1	124	60	.500
Sid Robinson (1917-1919) 15-5-0 .750						
1917			6-1-0	163	39	.857
1918			3-2-0	65	13	.600
1919			6-2-0	158	34	.750
Fred Holtkamp (1920-1921) 9-7-1 .559						
1920			5-3-0	112	68	.625
1921			4-4-1	111	125	.500

Member of the Southern Conference (1922-1932) 15-35-2 .308

Year	Nat'l AP	Other	Overall W-L-T	PF	PA	Pct.	Conference W-L-T	Pct.	Rank
Dudy Noble (1922) 3-4-2 .444									
1922			3-4-2	156	184	.444	2-3-0	.400	10
Early Able (1923-1924) 10-6-2 .611									
1923			5-2-2	83	66	.667	2-1-1	.625	9
1924			5-4-0	82	89	.556	3-2-0	.600	6
Bernie Bierman (1925-1926) 8-8-1 .500									
1925			3-4-1	101	60	.438	1-4-0	.200	15
1926			5-4-0	134	98	.556	2-3-0	.400	14
J. W. Hancock (1927-1929) 8-12-4 .417									
1927			5-3-0	93	48	.625	2-3-0	.400	12
1929			1-5-2	51	139	.250	0-3-1	.125	20
1928			2-4-2	70	166	.375	1-4-0	.200	18
Chris Cagle (1930) 2-7-0 .222									
1930			2-7-0	47	170	.222	2-3-0	.400	14
Ray Dauber (1931-1932) 5-11-0 .313									
1931			2-6-0	47	187	.250	0-5-0	.000	23
1932			3-5-0	33	155	.375	0-4-0	.000	21

Member of the Southeastern Conference (1933-2003) 150-299-13 .339

Year	Nat'l AP	Other	Overall W-L-T	PF	PA	Pct.	Conference W-L-T	Pct.	Rank
Ross McKechnie (1933-1934) 7-12-1 .375									
1933			3-6-1	69	149	.350	1-5-1	.214	12
1934			4-6-0	79	126	.400	0-5-0	.000	11
Ralph Sasse (1935-1937) 20-10-2 .656									
1935			8-3-0	190	76	.727	2-3-0	.400	9
1936			7-3-1	220	25	.682	3-2-0	.600	5
1937			5-4-1	119	117	.550	3-2-0	.600	5
Spike Nelson (1938) 4-6-0 .400									
1938			4-6-0	123	131	.400	1-4-0	.200	11
Allyn McKeen (1939-1948) 65-19-3 .764									
1939			8-2-0	216	32	.800	3-2-0	.600	4
1944			6-2-0	219	79	.750	3-2-0	.600	5
1940	9	7	10-0-1	247	58	.955	4-0-1	.800	2
1945			6-3-0	221	108	.667	2-3-0	.400	7
1941	16		8-1-1	191	55	.850	4-0-1	.800	1
1946			8-2-0	271	71	.800	3-2-0	.600	5
1942	18		8-2-0	200	77	.800	5-2-0	.714	4
1947			7-3-0	169	89	.700	2-2-0	.500	4
1943			no team						
1948			4-4-1	103	87	.500	3-3-0	.500	6
Slick Morton (1949-1951) 8-18-1 .315									
1949			0-8-1	38	224	.056	0-6-0	.000	12
1951			4-5-0	82	127	.444	2-5-0	.286	11
1950			4-5-0	169	137	.444	3-4-0	.429	7
Murray Warmath (1952-1953) 10-6-3 .605									
1952			5-4-0	225	186	.556	3-4-0	.429	7
1953			5-2-3	196	119	.650	3-1-3	.653	5

Darrell Royal (1954-1955) 12-8-0 .600

Year	Rk	Rk	Record	PF	PA	Pct	Conf	CPct	Std	Year	Rk	Rk	Record	PF	PA	Pct	Conf	CPct	Std
1954			6-4-0	214	120	.600	3-3-0	.500	5	1955			6-4-0	173	142	.600	4-4-0	.500	6

Wade Walker (1956-1961) 22-32-2 .411

Year	Rk	Rk	Record	PF	PA	Pct	Conf	CPct	Std	Year	Rk	Rk	Record	PF	PA	Pct	Conf	CPct	Std
1956			4-6-0	148	152	.400	2-5-0	.286	8	1959			2-7-0	96	199	.222	0-7-0	.000	12
1957	14		6-2-1	175	100	.722	4-2-1	.643	4	1960			2-6-1	101	119	.278	0-5-1	.083	11
1958			3-6-0	127	129	.333	1-6-0	.143	12	1961			5-5-0	111	135	.500	1-5-0	.167	10

Paul Davis (1962-1966) 20-28-2 .420

Year	Rk	Rk	Record	PF	PA	Pct	Conf	CPct	Std	Year	Rk	Rk	Record	PF	PA	Pct	Conf	CPct	Std
1962			3-6-0	96	132	.333	2-5-0	.286	9	1965			4-6-0	202	172	.400	1-5-0	.167	9
1963	11		7-2-2	185	94	.727	4-1-2	.714	4	1966			2-8-0	75	176	.200	0-6-0	.000	9
1964			4-6-0	155	143	.400	2-5-0	.286	8										

Charley Shira (1967-1972) 16-45-2 .270

Year	Rk	Rk	Record	PF	PA	Pct	Conf	CPct	Std	Year	Rk	Rk	Record	PF	PA	Pct	Conf	CPct	Std
1967			1-9-0	49	259	.100	0-6-0	.000	9	1970			6-5-0	171	264	.545	3-4-0	.429	7
1968			0-8-2	146	260	.100	0-4-2	.167	9	1971			2-9-0	120	312	.182	1-7-0	.125	9
1969			3-7-0	193	385	.300	0-5-0	.000	10	1972			4-7-0	197	254	.364	1-6-0	.143	9

Bob Tyler (1973-1978) 21-44-2 .328

Year	Rk	Rk	Record	PF	PA	Pct	Conf	CPct	Std	Year	Rk	Rk	Record	PF	PA	Pct	Conf	CPct	Std
1973			4-5-2	219	255	.455	2-5-0	.286	8	1976*	20		0-11-0	269	178	.000	0-6-0	.000	9
1974	17	17	9-3-0	327	224	.750	3-3-0	.500	4	1977*			0-11-0	193	227	.000	0-6-0	.000	9
1975*			2-9-0	165	166	.182	0-6-0	.000	9	1978			6-5-0	232	205	.545	2-4-0	.333	7

*All games in 1975-1977 forfeited except for the first two games in the 1975 season.

Emory Bellard (1979-1985) 37-42-0 .468

Year	Rk	Rk	Record	PF	PA	Pct	Conf	CPct	Std	Year	Rk	Rk	Record	PF	PA	Pct	Conf	CPct	Std
1979			3-8-0	162	179	.273	2-4-0	.333	8	1983			3-8-0	196	279	.273	1-5-0	.167	8
1980	19		9-3-0	301	247	.750	5-1-0	.833	2	1984			4-7-0	198	230	.364	1-5-0	.167	9
1981	17		8-4-0	288	137	.667	4-2-0	.667	3	1985			5-6-0	257	288	.455	0-6-0	.000	9
1982			5-6-0	352	244	.455	2-4-0	.333	8										

Rocky Felker (1986-1990) 21-34-0 .382

Year	Rk	Rk	Record	PF	PA	Pct	Conf	CPct	Std	Year	Rk	Rk	Record	PF	PA	Pct	Conf	CPct	Std
1986			6-5-0	195	275	.545	2-4-0	.333	7	1989			5-6-0	205	207	.455	1-6-0	.143	9
1987			4-7-0	169	259	.364	1-5-0	.167	7	1990			5-6-0	207	236	.455	1-6-0	.143	8
1988			1-10-0	172	322	.091	0-7-0	.000	10										

Jackie Sherrill (1991-2003) 75-75-2 .500

Year	Rk	Rk	Record	PF	PA	Pct	Conf	CPct	Std	Year	Rk	Rk	Record	PF	PA	Pct	Conf	CPct	Std
1991			7-5-0	291	194	.583	4-3-0	.571	4	1997			7-4-0	226	215	.636	4-4-0	.500	6
1992	23		7-5-0	252	197	.583	4-4-0	.500	6	1998			8-5-0	371	294	.615	6-2-0	.750	3
1993			4-5-2	241	245	.455	3-4-1	.438	5	1999	13	12	10-2-0	272	163	.833	6-2-0	.750	3
1994	24	25	8-4-0	373	262	.667	5-3-0	.625	3	2000	24	22	8-4-0	390	306	.667	4-4-0	.500	7
1995			3-8-0	261	357	.273	1-7-0	.125	9	2001			3-8-0	196	288	.273	2-6-0	.333	10
1996			5-6-0	249	229	.455	3-5-0	.375	7	2002			3-9-0	227	339	.250	0-8-0	.000	11
										2003			2-10-0	225	471	.167	1-7-0	.125	9

Won-loss record by decades:

Decade	Record	Pct	Decade	Record	Pct	Decade	Record	Pct
1895-99	0- 6-0	.000	1930-39	46-48-3	.490	1970-79	36-73-2	.333
1900-09	27-28-5	.492	1940-49	57-25-4	.686	1980-89	50-62-0	.446
1910-19	54-21-4	.709	1950-59	45-45-4	.500	1990-00	64-50-2	.560
1920-29	38-37-10	.506	1960-69	31-63-5	.338	2000-03	16-31-0	.340

Historical record: 464-489-39 .487

Post-season won-loss record: 6-6-0 .500

1937: Orange Bowl, Duquesne 13, MSU 12
1941: Orange Bowl, MSU 14, Georgetown 7
1963: Liberty Bowl, MSU 16, NC State 12
1974: Sun Bowl, MSU 26, North Carolina 24
1980: Sun Bowl, Nebraska 31, MSU 17
1981: Hall of Fame Bowl, MSU 10, Kansas 0

1991: Liberty Bowl, Air Force 38, MSU 15
1993: Peach Bowl, North Carolina 21, MSU 17
1995: Peach Bowl, NC State 28, MSU 24
1999: Cotton Bowl, Texas 38, MSU 11
1999: Peach Bowl, MSU 17, Clemson 7
2000: Independence Bowl, MSU 43, Texas A&M 41

College Football Hall of Fame:
Bernie Bierman, coach, 1925-26; Allyn McKeen, coach, 1939-48; Jackie Parker, quarterback, 1952-53; Darrell Ryal, coach, 1954-55; D. D. Lewis, linebacker, 1965-67.

UNIVERSITY OF MISSISSIPPI, Oxford, Mississippi; nickname "Ole Miss," "Rebels"; colors cardinal red and navy blue; Vaught-Hemingway Stadium (60,580); Southeastern Conference. Mississippi began play in 1893 and then joined the newly formed Southern Conference as a founding member in 1922. Ole Miss left the SC after the 1932 season to join with other SC members in organizing the Southeastern Conference. Beginning with the 1933 season, Mississippi has played in the SEC.

Early years (1893-1921)

Year	Coach	W-L-T	PF	PA	Pct.	Year	Coach	W-L-T	PF	PA	Pct.
1893	A. L. Bondurant1	4-1-0	120	28	.800	1907	Frank Mason	0-6-0	6	195	.000
1894	C. D. Clark	6-1-0	120	48	.957	1908	Frank Kyle	3-5-0	99	125	.375
1895	H. L. Fairbanks	2-1-0	24	25	.667	1909	Nathan Stauffer	4-3-2	99	49	.556
1896	J. W. Hollister	1-2-0	24	22	.333	1910	Nathan Stauffer	7-1-0	144	9	.875
1897	no team					1911	Nathan Stauffer	6-3-0	184	55	.667
1898	T. G. Scarbrough	1-1-0	18	16	.500	1912	Leo Detray	5-3-0	127	100	.625
1899	W. H. Lyon	3-4-0	44	47	.429	1913	William Driver	6-3-1	140	80	.650
1900	Z. N. Estes	0-3-0	5	30	.000	1914	William Driver	5-4-1	110	125	.550
1901	William Sibley &					1915	Fred Robbins	2-6-0	51	334	.250
	Daniel Martin	2-4-0	34	129	.333	1916	Fred Robbins	3-6-0	128	188	.333
1902	Daniel Martin	4-3-0	121	46	.429	1917	Dudy Noble	1-4-1	49	216	.250
1903	Mike Harvey	2-1-1	34	39	.625	1918	Dudy Noble	1-3-0	39	53	.250
1904	Mike Harvey	4-3-0	185	106	.571	1919	R. L. Sullivan	4-4-0	105	127	.571
1905	no coach	0-2-0	0	29	.000	1920	R.L. Sullivan	4-3-0	217	85	.333
1906	Tom Hammond	4-2-0	71	64	.667	1921	R. L. Sullivan	3-6-0	179	133	.500

Member of the Southern Conference (1922-1932) 12-37-2 .255

Year	Nat'l AP	Other	Overall W-L-T	PF	PA	Pct.	Conference W-L-T	Pct.	Rank	Year	Nat'l AP	Other	Overall W-L-T	PF	PA	Pct.	Conference W-L-T	Pct.	Rank
R. A. Cowell (1922-1923) 8-11-1 .425																			
1922			4-5-1	87	183	.450	0-2-0	.000	18	1923			4-6-0	81	145	.400	0-4-0	.000	19
Chester Barnard (1924) 4-5-0 .444																			
1924			4-5-0	36	142	.444	0-3-0	.000	19										
Homer Hazel (1925-1929) 21-22-3 .489																			
1925			5-5-0	147	87	.500	0-4-0	.000	20	1928			5-4-0	156	121	.556	3-3-0	.500	9
1926			5-4-0	113	110	.556	2-2-0	.500	14	1929			1-6-2	73	222	.222	0-4-2	.167	19
1927			5-3-1	177	80	.625	3-2-0	.600	7										
Ed Walker (1930-1937) 38-38-8 .500																			
1930			3-5-1	128	140	.389	1-5-0	.167	19	1932			5-6-0	148	148	.455	2-3-0	.400	12
1931			2-6-1	73	210	.278	1-5-0	.167	21										

Member of the Southeastern Conference (1932-2001) 226-204-15 .525

Year	Nat'l AP	Other	Overall W-L-T	PF	PA	Pct.	Conference W-L-T	Pct.	Rank	Year	Nat'l AP	Other	Overall W-L-T	PF	PA	Pct.	Conference W-L-T	Pct.	Rank
1933			6-3-2	167	79	.636	2-2-1	.500	6	1936			5-5-2	150	98	.500	0-3-1	.125	12
1934			4-5-1	114	98	.450	2-3-1	.417	8	1937			4-5-1	127	106	.450	0-4-0	.000	11
1935			9-3-0	311	86	.750	3-1-0	.750	3										
Harry Mehre (1938-1945) 39-26-1 .598																			
1938			9-2-0	232	47	.818	3-2-0	.600	4	1942			2-7-0	132	163	.222	0-5-0	.000	11
1939			7-2-0	230	64	.778	2-2-0	.500	5	1943			no team						
1940			9-2-0	251	100	.818	3-1-0	.750	3	1944			2-6-0	77	118	.250	2-3-0	.400	7
1941	17		6-2-1	131	67	.722	2-1-1	.625	5	1945			4-5-0	100	183	.444	3-3-0	.500	5
Red Drew (1946) 2-7-0 .222																			
1946			2-7-0	76	144	.222	1-6-0	.143	11										
Johnny Vaught (1947-1970, 1973) 190-61-12 .745																			
1947	13		9-2-0	269	110	.818	6-1-0	.857	1	1959	2	2	10-1-0	350	21	.909	5-1-0	.833	2
1948	15		8-1-0	226	93	.889	6-1-0	.857	2	1960	2	3	10-0-1	280	70	.955	5-0-1	.917	1
1949			4-5-1	246	243	.450	2-4-0	.333	9	1961	5	5	9-2-0	333	52	.818	5-1-0	.833	3
1950			5-5-0	207	183	.500	1-5-0	.167	11	1962	3	3	10-0-0	247	53	1.000	6-0-0	1.000	1
1951			6-3-1	254	157	.650	4-2-1	.642	3	1963	7	7	7-1-2	214	45	.800	5-0-1	.917	1
1952	7	7	8-1-2	244	120	.818	4-0-2	.833	3	1964		20	5-5-1	217	127	.500	2-4-1	.357	7
1953			7-2-1	236	113	.750	4-1-1	.750	2	1965		17	7-4-0	179	115	.636	5-3-0	.625	5
1954	6	6	9-2-0	283	68	.818	5-1-0	.833	1	1966		12	8-3-0	170	65	.727	5-2-0	.714	4
1955	10	9	10-1-0	265	110	.909	5-1-0	.833	1	1967			6-4-1	181	165	.591	4-2-1	.643	3
1956			7-3-0	207	82	.700	4-2-0	.667	4	1968			7-3-1	212	197	.682	3-2-1	.583	6
1957	7	8	9-1-1	271	59	.864	5-0-1	.917	2	1969	8	13	8-3-0	334	162	.727	4-2-0	.667	5
1958	11	12	9-2-0	222	68	.818	4-2-0	.667	3	1970	20		7-4-0	313	255	.636	4-2-0	.667	4
Billy Kinard (1971-1973) 16-9-0 .640																			
1971	15	20	10-2-0	363	222	.833	4-2-0	.667	4	1973*			1-2-0	37	40	.333	0-0-0		
1972			5-5-0	192	142	.500	2-5-0	.286	7										
Johnny Vaught (1973)																			
1973			5-3-0	165	137	.625	4-3-0	.667	4										

*Kinard coached the first three games of the 1973 season, and Vaught coached the last eight.

Ken Cooper (1974-1977) 21-23-0 .640

| 1974 | 3-8-0 135 241 .273 | 0-6-0 .000 10 | 1976 | 6-5-0 153 180 .545 4-3-0 .571 5 |
| 1975 | 6-5-0 170 162 .545 | 5-1-0 .833 2 | 1977 | 6-5-0 208 196 .545 3-4-0 .429 6 |

Steve Sloan (1978-1982) 20-34-1 .372

1978	5-6-0 181 240 .455	2-4-0 .333 7	1981	4-6-1 167 284 .409 1-4-1 .250 8
1979	4-7-0 251 298 .364	3-3-0 .500 4	1982	4-7-0 208 262 .364 0-6-0 .000 9
1980	3-8-0 263 266 .273	2-4-0 .333 7		

Billy Brewer (1983-1993) 68-55-3 .544

1983	7-5-0 179 234 .636	4-2-0 .667 3	1989	8-4-0 309 314 .667 4-3-0 .571 4
1984	4-6-1 194 203 .409	1-5-0 .167 9	1990 21 23	9-3-0 260 226 .750 5-2-0 .714 2
1985	4-6-1 210 276 .409	2-4-0 .333 6	1991	5-6-0 242 223 .455 1-6-0 .143 9
1986	8-3-1 240 167 .708	4-2-0 .667 2	1992 16 16	9-3-0 243 174 .750 5-3-0 .625 4
1987	3-8-0 223 309 .273	1-5-0 .167 7	1993	6-5-0 242 142 .545 4-4-0 .500 3
1988	5-6-0 221 223 .455	3-4-0 .429 6		

Joe Lee Dunn (1994) 4-7-0 .364

| 1994 | 4-7-0 246 205 .364 | 2-6-0 .250 8 | | |

Tom Tuberville (1995-1998) 25-20-0 .556

| 1995 | 6-5-0 209 208 .545 | 3-5-0 .375 * | 1997 22 22 | 8-4-0 267 240 .667 4-4-0 .500 5 |
| 1996 | 5-6-0 203 270 .455 | 2-6-0 .250 * | 1998** | 6-5-0 245 256 .583 3-5-0 .375 9 |

*Mississippi not eligible for league title.

David Cutliffe (1999-2003) 40-22-0 .645

1998**	1-0-0 35 18 1.000	0-0-0	2001	7-4-0 391 310 .636 4-4-4 .500 7
1999 22 22	8-4-0 296 203 .667	4-4-0 .500 7	2002	7-6-0 324 208 .538 3-5-0 .375 8
2000	7-5-0 314 280 .583	4-4-0 .500 7	2003 13 14	10-3-0 442 285 .769 7-1-0 .875 1

**Tuberville coached the first eleven games in 1998, and Cutliffe coached the last game.

Won-loss record by decades:

1893-99	17-10-0	.630	1930-39	54-42-8	.558	1970-79	58-52-0	.527
1900-09	23-32-3	.422	1940-49	46-37-2	.553	1980-89	50-59-4	.460
1910-19	40-37-3	.519	1950-59	80-21-5	.778	1990-99	67-48-0	.583
1920-29	40-47-4	.462	1960-69	77-25-6	.741	2000-03	31-18-0	.633

Historic record: 583-428-35 .574

Post-season won-loss record: 19-12-0 .613

1936: Orange Bowl, Catholic U. 20, Ole Miss 19
1948: Delta Bowl, Ole Miss 13, TCU 9
1953: Sugar Bowl, Georgia Tech 24, Ole Miss 7
1955: Sugar Bowl, Navy 21, Ole Miss 0
1956: Cotton Bowl, Ole Miss 14, TCU 13
1958: Sugar Bowl, Ole Miss 39, Texas 7
1958: Gator Bowl, Ole Miss 7, Florida 3
1960: Sugar Bowl, Ole Miss 21, LSU 0
1961: Sugar Bowl, Ole Miss 14, Rice 6
1962: Cotton Bowl, Texas 12, Ole Miss 7
1963: Sugar Bowl, Ole Miss 17, Arkansas 13
1964: Sugar Bowl, Alabama 12, Ole Miss 7
1964: Bluebonnet Bowl, Tulsa 14, Ole Miss 7
1965: Liberty Bowl, Ole Miss 13, Auburn 7
1966: Bluebonnet Bowl, Texas 19, Ole Miss 0

1967: Sun Bowl, UTEP 14, Ole Miss 7
1968: Liberty Bowl, Ole Miss 34, Virginia Tech 17
1970: Sugar Bowl, Ole Miss 27, Arkansas 22
1971: Gator Bowl, Auburn 35, Ole Miss 28
1971: Peach Bowl, Ole Miss 41, Ga. Tech 18
1983: Independence Bowl, Air Force 9, Ole Miss 3
1986: Independence Bowl, Ole Miss 20, Texas Tech 17
1989: Liberty Bowl, Ole Miss 42, Air Force 29
1991: Gator Bowl, Michigan 35, Ole Miss 3
1992: Liberty Bowl, Ole Miss 13, Air Force 0
1997: Motor City Bowl, Ole Miss 34, Marshall 31
1998: Independence Bowl, Ole Miss 35, Texas Tech 18
1999: Independence Bowl, Ole Miss 27, Oklahoma 25
2000: Music City Bowl, West Virginia 49, Ole Miss 38
2002: Independence Bowl, Ole Miss 27, Nebraska 23
2004: Cotton Bowl, Ole Miss 31, Oklahoma State 28

College Football Hall of Fame:
Bruiser Kinnard, tackle, 1935-37; Parker Hall, halfback, 1936-38; Charlie Connerly, quarterback, 1942-47; Barney Poole, end, 1946-48; Johnny Vaught, coach, 1947-70, 1973; Charlie Flowers, fullback, 1957-59; Jake Gibbs, quarterback, 1958-60; Archie Manning, quarterback, 1968-70.

Awards: Unitas Award: 2003, Eli Manning; Maxwell Award: 2003, Eli Manning; Groza Award: 2003, Jonathon Nichols.

UNIVERSITY OF MISSOURI, Columbia, Missouri; nickname "Tigers"; colors old gold and black; Memorial Stadium (68,349); Big Twelve Conference. Missouri began play in 1890 and joined the Missouri Valley Conference in 1907. It left the MVC after the 1927 season to join five other MVC teams in forming the Big Six (later renamed the Big Seven, and then the Big Eight). Missouri played in this conference through the 1995 season, after which four members of the disbanded Southwest Conference joined together with the Big Eight to form the Big Twelve. Missouri has played in the Big Twelve beginning with the 1996 season.

Early years (1890-1906)

Year	Coach	W-L-T	PF	PA	Pct.	Year	Coach	W-L-T	PF	PA	Pct.
1890	A.L. McRae	2-1-0	112	34	.667	1898	David Fultz	1-4-1	33	98	.250
1891	Hal Reed	3-1-0	108	28	.750	1899	David Fultz	9-2-0	242	56	.818
1892	E.H. Jones	1-2-0	28	18	.333	1900	Fred Murphy	4-4-1	72	81	.500
1893	H.L. Robinson	4-3-0	148	126	.571	1901	Fred Murphy	2-6-1	30	155	.278
1894	H.L. Robinson	4-3-0	134	109	.571	1902	Pat O'Dea	5-3-0	99	80	.625
1895	Pop Bliss	7-1-0	156	42	.875	1903	John McLean	1-7-1	46	83	.167
1896	Frank Patterson	7-5-0	240	78	.583	1904	John McLean	3-6-0	71	130	.333
1897	Charles Young	5-6-0	112	143	.455	1905	John McLean	5-4-0	94	79	.556

W. J. Monilaw (1906-1908) 18-6-1 .740

Year	Nat'l AP-UP	Overall W-L-T	PF	PA	Pct.	Conference W-L-T	Pct.	Rank	Year	Nat'l AP-UP	Overall W-L-T	PF	PA	Pct.	Conference W-L-T	Pct.	Rank
1906		5-2-1	116	44	.688												

Member of the Missouri Valley Conference (1907-1927) 63-32-9 .649

| 1907 | | 7-2-0 | 278 | 41 | .778 | 1-2-0 | .333 | 4 | 1908 | | 6-2-0 | 196 | 45 | .750 | 3-2-0 | .600 | 4 |

William Roper (1909) 7-0-1 .938

| 1909 | | 7-0-1 | 86 | 36 | .938 | 4-0-1 | .900 | 1 | | | | | | | | | |

W. Hollenbeck (1910) 4-2-2 .625

| 1910 | | 4-2-2 | 77 | 17 | .625 | 2-1-1 | .625 | 3 | | | | | | | | | |

Chester Brewer (1911-1913) 14-8-2 .625

| 1911 | | 2-4-2 | 61 | 67 | .375 | 0-2-2 | .250 | 5 | 1913 | | 7-1-0 | 193 | 67 | .875 | 4-0-0 | 1.000 | 1 |
| 1912 | | 5-3-0 | 135 | 69 | .625 | 2-3-0 | .400 | 4 | | | | | | | | | |

H.F. Schulte (1914-1917) 16-14-2 .531

| 1914 | | 5-3-0 | 128 | 48 | .625 | 4-1-0 | .800 | 2 | 1916 | | 6-1-1 | 112 | 21 | .812 | 3-1-1 | .700 | 2 |
| 1915 | | 2-5-1 | 72 | 102 | .312 | 1-3-1 | .300 | 5 | 1917 | | 3-5-0 | 98 | 124 | .375 | 2-4-0 | .333 | 5 |

No team (1918)

John Miller (1919) 5-1-2 .750

| 1919 | | 5-1-2 | 91 | 42 | .750 | 4-0-1 | .900 | 1 | | | | | | | | | |

John Miller and Jimmy Phelan (1920) 7-1-0 .875

| 1920 | | 7-1-0 | 156 | 61 | .875 | 5-1-0 | .833 | 2 | | | | | | | | | |

Jimmy Phelan (1921) 6-2-0 .750

| 1921 | | 6-2-0 | 136 | 50 | .750 | 4-2-0 | .667 | 2 | | | | | | | | | |

Thomas Kelly (1922) 5-3-0 .625

| 1922 | | 5-3-0 | 98 | 90 | .625 | 4-3-0 | .571 | 4 | | | | | | | | | |

Gwinn Henry (1923-1931) 40-28-9 .578

1923		2-3-3	31	40	.438	1-3-2	.333	7	1926		5-1-2	122	33	.750	4-1-0	.800	3
1924	10	7-2-0	110	41	.778	5-1-0	.833	1	1927		7-2-0	129	90	.778	5-1-0	.833	1
1925	5	6-1-1	110	44	.812	5-1-0	.833	1									

Member of the Big Six (later Big Seven, later Big Eight) (1928-1995) 209-193-22 .521

| 1928 | | 4-4-0 | 138 | 102 | .500 | 3-2-0 | .600 | 2 | 1930 | | 2-5-2 | 41 | 132 | .333 | 1-2-2 | .400 | 5 |
| 1929 | | 5-2-1 | 78 | 28 | .688 | 3-1-1 | .700 | 2 | 1931 | | 2-8-0 | 72 | 183 | .200 | 1-4-0 | .200 | 5 |

Frank Carideo (1932-1934) 2-23-2 .111

| 1932 | | 1-7-1 | 32 | 184 | .167 | 1-3-1 | .300 | 5 | 1934 | | 0-8-1 | 125 | 172 | .056 | 0-5-0 | .000 | 6 |
| 1933 | | 1-8-0 | 58 | 193 | .111 | 0-5-0 | .000 | 6 | | | | | | | | | |

Don Faurot (1935-1942, 1946-1956) 101-79-10 .558

1935		3-3-3	97	77	.500	0-2-3	.300	5	1939	6 9	8-2-0	155	79	.800	5-0-0	1.000	1
1936		6-2-1	107	74	.722	3-1-1	.700	2	1940		6-3-0	213	135	.667	3-2-0	.600	3
1937		3-6-1	42	64	.350	2-2-1	.500	3	1941	7	8-2-0	226	39	.800	5-0-0	1.000	1
1938		6-3-0	111	82	.667	2-3-0	.400	3	1942		8-3-1	288	107	.708	4-0-1	.900	1

Chauncey Simpson (1943-1945) 12-14-2 .464

| 1943 | | 3-5-0 | 170 | 142 | .375 | 3-2-0 | .600 | 2 | 1945 | | 6-4-0 | 170 | 174 | .600 | 5-0-0 | 1.000 | 1 |
| 1944 | | 3-5-2 | 176 | 224 | .400 | 2-1-1 | .600 | 3 | | | | | | | | | |

Don Faurot (1946-1956)

1946		5-4-1	158	166	.550	3-2-0	.600	3	1952		5-5-0	147	159	.500	5-1-0	.833	2
1947		6-4-0	240	116	.600	3-2-0	.600	3	1953		6-4-0	130	116	.600	4-2-0	.667	2
1948		8-3-0	331	161	.727	5-1-0	.833	2	1954		4-5-1	198	261	.450	3-2-1	.583	3
1949	20	7-4-0	264	225	.636	5-1-0	.833	2	1955		1-9-0	92	192	.100	1-5-0	.167	7
1950		4-5-1	166	215	.450	3-2-1	.583	3	1956		4-5-1	200	183	.450	3-2-1	.583	3
1951		3-7-0	169	292	.300	2-4-0	.333	4									

Frank Broyles (1957) 5-4-1 .550

| 1957 | | 5-4-1 | 149 | 157 | .550 | 3-3-0 | .500 | 3 | | | | | | | | | |

Dan Devine (1958-1970) 93-37-7 .704

Year			W-L-T	PF	PA	Pct	Conf	Pct	Pl	Year			W-L-T	PF	PA	Pct	Conf	Pct	Pl
1958			5-4-1	164	141	.550	4-1-1	.750	2	1965	6	6	8-2-1	223	101	.773	6-1-0	.857	2
1959	18	19	6-5-0	125	124	.545	4-2-0	.667	2	1966			6-3-1	121	116	.650	4-2-1	.643	3
1960	5	4	11-0-0	295	93	1.000	7-0-0	1.000	1	1967			7-3-0	134	76	.700	4-3-0	.571	4
1961	11	11	7-2-1	124	57	.750	5-2-0	.714	2	1968	9	17	8-3-0	308	136	.727	5-2-0	.714	3
1962		12	8-1-2	204	62	.818	5-1-1	.786	2	1969	6	6	9-2-0	365	191	.818	6-1-0	.857	1
1963		16	7-3-0	151	86	.700	5-2-0	.714	3	1970			5-6-0	243	223	.455	3-4-0	.429	4
1964		18	6-3-1	142	88	.650	4-2-1	.643	4										

Al Onofrio (1971-1977) 38-41-0 .481

Year			W-L-T	PF	PA	Pct	Conf	Pct	Pl	Year			W-L-T	PF	PA	Pct	Conf	Pct	Pl
1971			1-10-0	93	250	.091	0-7-0	.000	8	1975			6-5-0	282	241	.545	3-4-0	.429	5
1972			6-6-0	219	311	.500	4-3-0	.571	3	1976			6-5-0	246	241	.545	3-4-0	.429	6
1973	17		8-4-0	219	152	.667	3-4-0	.429	5	1977			4-7-0	195	180	.364	3-4-0	.429	5
1974			7-4-0	204	217	.636	5-2-0	.714	2										

Warren Powers (1978-1984) 46-33-3 .580

Year			W-L-T	PF	PA	Pct	Conf	Pct	Pl	Year			W-L-T	PF	PA	Pct	Conf	Pct	Pl
1978	15	14	8-4-0	368	236	.667	4-3-0	.571	3	1982			5-4-2	207	96	.545	2-3-2	.429	5
1979		20	7-5-0	260	166	.583	3-4-0	.429	4	1983			7-5-0	292	202	.583	5-2-0	.714	2
1980			8-4-0	333	175	.667	5-2-0	.714	3	1984			3-7-1	310	301	.318	2-4-1	.357	5
1981	19	20	8-4-0	276	159	.667	3-4-0	.429	5										

Woody Widenhofer (1985-1988) 12-31-1 .284

Year			W-L-T	PF	PA	Pct	Conf	Pct	Pl	Year			W-L-T	PF	PA	Pct	Conf	Pct	Pl
1985			1-10-0	206	342	.091	1-6-0	.143	7	1987			5-6-0	226	209	.455	3-4-0	.429	5
1986			3-8-0	196	314	.273	2-5-0	.286	6	1988			3-7-1	234	330	.318	2-5-0	.429	6

Bob Stull (1989-1993) 15-38-2 .291

Year			W-L-T	PF	PA	Pct	Conf	Pct	Pl	Year			W-L-T	PF	PA	Pct	Conf	Pct	Pl
1989			2-9-0	171	363	.182	1-6-0	.143	7	1992			3-8-0	214	269	.273	2-5-0	.286	6
1990			4-7-0	278	360	.364	2-5-0	.286	5	1993			3-7-1	192	344	.318	2-5-0	.286	6
1991			3-7-1	223	403	.455	1-6-0	.143	7										

Larry Smith (1994-2000) 33-46-1 .413

Year			W-L-T	PF	PA	Pct	Conf	Pct	Pl	Year			W-L-T	PF	PA	Pct	Conf	Pct	Pl
1994			3-8-1	208	323	.292	2-5-0	.286	6	1995			3-8-0	186	311	.273	1-6-0	.143	7

Member of the Big Twelve Conference (1996-2003) 25-39-0 .391

Year			W-L-T	PF	PA	Pct	Conf	Pct	Pl	Year			W-L-T	PF	PA	Pct	Conf	Pct	Pl
1996			5-6-0	278	376	.455	3-5-0	.375	7	1999			4-7-0	224	371	.364	1-7-0	.125	11
1997	23	23	7-5-0	368	332	.583	5-3-0	.625	4	2000			3-8-0	255	348	.273	2-6-0	.250	9
1998	21	25	8-4-0	300	215	.667	5-3-0	.625	5										

Gary Pinkel (2001-2003) 17-19-0 .472

Year			W-L-T	PF	PA	Pct	Conf	Pct	Pl	Year			W-L-T	PF	PA	Pct	Conf	Pct	Pl
2001			4-7-0	240	330	.364	3-5-0	.375	8	2003			8-5-0	399	287	.615	4-4-0	.500	6
2002			5-7-0	360	352	.417	2-6-0	.250	10										

Won-loss record by decades:

1890-99	43-28-1	.604	1930-39	35-52-9	.392	1970-79	58-56-0	.509	
1900-09	45-36-5	.552	1940-49	60-37-4	.614	1980-89	45-64-4	.416	
1910-19	39-25-8	.597	1950-59	43-53-5	.450	1990-99	46-67-3	.409	
1920-29	51-21-7	.690	1960-69	77-22-6	.762	2000-03	20-27-0	.426	

Historic record: 551-483-52 .531

Post-season won-loss record: 9-13-0 .409

1924: Christmas Festival, USC 20, Missouri 9
1940: Orange Bowl, Georgia Tech 21, Missouri 7
1942: Sugar Bowl, Fordham 2, Missouri 0
1946: Cotton Bowl, Texas 40, Missouri 27
1949: Gator Bowl, Clemson 24, Missouri 23
1950: Gator Bowl, Maryland 20, Missouri 7
1960: Orange Bowl, Georgia 14, Missouri 0
1961: Orange Bowl, Missouri 21, Navy 14
1962: Bluebonnet Bowl, Missouri 14, Georgia Tech 10
1966: Sugar Bowl, Missouri 20, Florida 18
1968: Gator Bowl, Missouri 35, Alabama 10

1970: Orange Bowl, Penn State 10, Missouri 3
1972: Fiesta Bowl, Arizona State 49, Missouri 35
1973: Sun Bowl, Missouri 34, Auburn 17
1978: Liberty Bowl, Missouri 20, LSU 15
1979: Hall of Fame Bowl, Missouri 24, South Carolina 14
1980: Liberty Bowl, Purdue 28, Missouri 25
1981: Tangerine Bowl, Missouri 19, Southern Mississippi 17
1983: Holiday Bowl, BYU 21, Missouri 17
1997: Plymouth Holiday Bowl, Colorado State 35, Missouri 24
1999: Insight.com Bowl, Missouri 34, West Virginia 31
2003: Independence Bowl, Arkansas 27, Missouri 24

College Football Hall of Fame:
Ed Travis, tackle, 1916-20; Jimmy Phelan, coach, 1920-21; Don Faurot, coach, 1935-42, 1946-56; Paul Christman, halfback, 1938-40; Darold Jenkins, center, 1939-41; Bob Steuber, tackle, 1940-43; Frank Broyles, coach, 1957; Dan Devine, coach, 1958-70; Kellen Winslow, tight end, 1962-64; Johnny Roland, cornerback, 1962-65; Ron Wehrli, defensive back, 1966-68.

Awards: Tatupu Award: 1997, Brock Olivo.

UNIVERSITY OF NEBRASKA, Lincoln, Nebraska; nickname "Cornhuskers"; colors scarlet and cream; Memorial Stadium (74,031); Big Twelve Conference. Nebraska began play in 1890 as an independent and then joined the Missouri Valley Conference in 1907. Nebraska left the MVC after the 1927 season along with five other MVC members to form the Big Six Conference, which expanded over time into the Big Seven, and then the Big Eight conference. In 1995, after the Southwest Conference disbanded, four members of that conference joined the member of the Big Eight to form the Big Twelve Conference. The MVC ignored ties in calculating the overall and conference win-percents prior to the 1942 season and that rule is followed here.

Early years (1890-1906)

Year	Coach	W-L-T	PF	PA	Pct.	Year	Coach	W-L-T	PF	PA	Pct.
1890	none	2-0-0	28	0	1.000	1899	A. E. Branch	1-7-1	49	164	.167
1891	none	2-2-0	72	40	.500	1900	Walter Booth	6-1-1	112	20	.813
1892	none	2-2-1	21	40	.500	1901	Walter Booth	6-2-0	149	53	.750
1893	Frank Crawford	3-2-1	77	76	.583	1902	Walter Booth	9-0-0	159	0	1.000
1894	Frank Crawford	6-2-0	136	48	.750	1903	Walter Booth	10-0-0	268	11	1.000
1895	Charles Thomas	6-3-0	138	62	.667	1904	Walter Booth	7-3-0	293	52	.700
1896	E. N. Robinson	6-3-1	102	64	.650	1905	Walter Booth	8-2-0	296	83	.800
1897	E. N. Robinson	5-1-0	84	15	.833	1906	Amos Foster	6-4-0	164	73	.600
1898	Fielding Yost	8-3-0	270	78	.727						

Member of the Missouri Valley Conference (1907-1917, 1921-1927) 49-8-5 .831

Year	AP	Other	W-L-T	PF	PA	Pct.	W-L-T	Pct.	Rank	Year	AP	Other	W-L-T	PF	PA	Pct.	W-L-T	Pct.	Rank
	Nat'l		Overall				Conference				Nat'l		Overall				Conference		

W. C. Cole (1907-1910) 25-8-3 .736

| 1907 | | | 8-2-0 | 323 | 69 | .800 | 1-0-0 | 1.000 | 1 | 1909 | | | 3-3-2 | 69 | 52 | .500 | 0-1-1 | .000 | 5 |
| 1908 | | | 7-2-1 | 165 | 93 | .778 | 2-1-0 | .667 | 2 | 1910 | | | 7-1-0 | 260 | 36 | .875 | 2-0-0 | 1.000 | 1 |

E. O. Stiehm (1911-1916) 35-2-3 .913

1911			5-1-2	281	33	.833	2-0-1	1.000	1	1914			7-0-1	174	28	1.000	3-0-0	1.000	1
1912			7-1-0	240	37	.875	2-0-0	1.000	1	1915			8-0-0	282	39	1.000	4-0-0	1.000	1
1913			8-0-0	138	28	1.000	3-0-0	1.000	1										

E. J. Stewart (1916-1917) 11-4-0 .733

| 1916 | | | 6-2-0 | 145 | 51 | .750 | 3-1-0 | .750 | 1 | | | | | | | | | | |
| 1917 | | | 5-2-0 | 228 | 33 | .714 | 2-0-0 | 1.000 | 1 | | | | | | | | | | |

Conference play suspended (1918)
W. G. Kline (1918) 2-3-1 .417

| 1918 | | | 2-3-1 | 53 | 55 | .400 | | | | | | | | | | | | | |

Nebraska reverts to independent status (1919-1920)
Henry F. Schulte (1919-1920) 8-6-3 .559

| 1919 | | | 3-3-2 | 56 | 60 | .500 | | | | 1920 | | | 5-3-1 | 151 | 84 | .611 | | | |

Nebraska rejoins the MVC (1921-1927)
Fred T. Dawson (1921-1924) 23-7-2 .750

| 1921 | | | 7-1-0 | 283 | 17 | .875 | 3-0-0 | 1.000 | 1 | 1923 | | | 4-2-2 | 112 | 71 | .667 | 3-0-2 | 1.000 | 1 |
| 1922 | | | 7-1-0 | 276 | 28 | .875 | 5-0-0 | 1.000 | 1 | 1924 | | | 5-3-0 | 120 | 77 | .625 | 3-1-0 | .750 | 2 |

E. E. Bearg (1925-1928) 23-7-3 .742

| 1925 | | | 4-2-2 | 69 | 27 | .667 | 2-2-1 | .500 | 6 | 1927 | 9 | | 6-2-0 | 211 | 59 | .750 | 4-1-0 | .800 | 2 |
| 1926 | | | 6-2-0 | 123 | 46 | .750 | 5-1-0 | .833 | 2 | | | | | | | | | | |

Member of the Big Six (later Big Seven, later Big Eight) Conference (1928-1995) 304-110-10 .729

| 1928 | | | 7-1-1 | 144 | 31 | .833 | 5-0-0 | 1.000 | 1 | | | | | | | | | | |

Dana X. Bible (1929-1936) 50-15-7 .743

1929	7		4-1-3	93	62	.688	3-0-2	.800	1	1933	2		8-1-0	138	19	.889	5-0-0	1.000	1
1930			4-3-2	119	61	.556	2-2-1	.500	4	1934			6-3-0	106	89	.667	4-1-0	.800	2
1931			8-2-0	136	82	.800	5-0-0	1.000	1	1935			6-2-1	138	71	.722	4-0-1	.900	1
1932			7-1-1	105	52	.833	5-0-0	1.000	1	1936	9	11	7-2-0	185	49	.778	5-0-0	1.000	1

Biff Jones (1937-1941) 28-14-4 .652

1937	11	5	6-1-2	99	42	.778	3-0-2	.800	1	1940	7	10	8-2-0	183	75	.800	5-0-0	1.000	1
1938			3-5-1	68	84	.389	2-3-0	.400	3	1941			4-5-0	93	81	.444	3-2-0	.600	2
1939	18		7-1-1	115	70	.833	4-1-0	.800	2										

Glenn Presnell (1942) 3-7-0 .300

| 1942 | | | 3-7-0 | 55 | 158 | .300 | 3-2-0 | .600 | 3 | | | | | | | | | | |

A. J. Lewandowski (1943-1944) 4-12-0 .250

| 1943 | | | 2-6-0 | 79 | 261 | .250 | 2-3-0 | .400 | 4 | 1944 | | | 2-6-0 | 83 | 210 | .250 | 2-3-0 | .400 | 4 |

George Clark (1945, 1948) 6-13-0 .316

| 1945 | | | 4-5-0 | 145 | 200 | .444 | 2-3-0 | .400 | 4 | | | | | | | | | | |

Bernie Masterson (1946-1947) 5-13-0 .278

| 1946 | | | 3-6-0 | 126 | 161 | .333 | 3-2-0 | .600 | 3 | 1947 | | | 2-7-0 | 73 | 191 | .222 | 2-3-0 | .400 | 4 |

George Clark (1948)

| 1948 | | | 2-8-0 | 137 | 273 | .200 | 2-4-0 | .333 | 5 | | | | | | | | | | |

Bill Glassford (1949-1955) 31-35-3 .471

1949			4-5-0	124	172	.444	3-3-0	.500	3	1953			3-6-1	119	184	.350	2-4-0	.333	4
1950	17	20	6-2-1	267	217	.722	4-2-0	.667	2	1954			6-5-0	233	202	.545	4-2-0	.667	2
1951			2-8-0	116	253	.200	2-4-0	.333	4	1955			5-5-0	127	176	.500	5-1-0	.833	2
1952			5-4-1	173	123	.550	3-2-1	.583	3										

Pete Elliott (1956) 4-6-0 .400

Year	AP	UPI	Record	PF	PA	Pct	Conf	Pct	Place
1956			4-6-0	125	206	.400	3-3-0	.500	4

Bill Jennings (1957-1961) 15-34-1 .310

Year	AP	UPI	Record	PF	PA	Pct	Conf	Pct	Place
1957			1-9-0	67	243	.100	1-5-0	.167	7
1958			3-7-0	71	235	.300	1-5-0	.167	6
1959			4-6-0	108	160	.400	2-4-0	.333	6
1960			4-6-0	95	164	.400	2-5-0	.286	6
1961			3-6-1	119	135	.350	2-5-0	.286	6

Bob Devaney (1962-1972) 101-20-2 .829

Year	AP	UPI	Record	PF	PA	Pct	Conf	Pct	Place
1962			9-2-0	293	161	.818	5-2-0	.714	3
1963	6	5	10-1-0	273	114	.909	7-0-0	1.000	1
1964	6	6	9-2-0	256	85	.818	6-1-0	.857	1
1965	5	3	10-1-0	349	129	.909	7-0-0	1.000	1
1966	6	7	9-2-0	223	118	.818	6-1-0	.857	1
1967			6-4-0	127	83	.600	3-4-0	.429	5
1968			6-4-0	155	161	.600	3-4-0	.429	4
1969	11	12	9-2-0	254	119	.818	6-1-0	.857	1
1970	1	3	11-0-1	426	189	.958	7-0-0	1.000	1
1971	1	1	13-0-0	507	104	1.000	7-0-0	1.000	1
1972	4	9	9-2-1	501	97	.792	5-1-1	.786	1

Tom Osborne (1973-1997) 255-49-3 .836

Year	AP	UPI	Record	PF	PA	Pct	Conf	Pct	Place
1973	7	11	9-2-1	306	163	.792	4-2-1	.643	2
1974	9	8	9-3-0	373	132	.750	5-2-0	.714	2
1975	9	9	10-2-0	367	137	.833	6-1-0	.857	1
1976	9	7	9-3-1	416	181	.731	4-3-0	.571	4
1977	12	10	9-3-0	315	200	.750	5-2-0	.714	2
1978	8	8	9-3-0	444	216	.750	6-1-0	.857	1
1979	9	7	10-2-0	380	131	.833	6-1-0	.857	2
1980	7	7	10-2-0	470	110	.833	6-1-0	.857	2
1981	11	9	9-3-0	364	125	.750	7-0-0	1.000	1
1982	3	3	12-1-0	514	167	.923	7-0-0	1.000	1
1983	2	2	12-1-0	654	217	.923	7-0-0	1.000	1
1984	4	3	10-2-0	387	115	.833	6-1-0	.857	1
1985	11	10	9-3-0	421	163	.750	6-1-0	.857	2
1986	5	4	10-2-0	446	165	.833	5-2-0	.714	3
1987	6	6	10-2-0	451	164	.833	6-1-0	.857	2
1988	10	10	11-2-0	477	205	.846	7-0-0	1.000	1
1989	11	12	10-2-0	509	215	.833	6-1-0	.857	2
1990	24	17	9-3-0	434	192	.750	5-2-0	.714	2
1991	15	16	9-2-1	454	230	.792	6-0-1	.929	1
1992	14	14	9-3-0	441	199	.750	6-1-0	.857	1
1993	3	3	11-1-0	437	194	.917	7-0-0	1.000	1
1994	1	1	13-0-0	459	162	1.000	7-0-0	1.000	1
1995	1	1	12-0-0	638	174	1.000	7-0-0	1.000	1

Member of the Big Twelve Conference (1996-2003) 49-15-0 .766

Year	AP	UPI	Record	PF	PA	Pct	Conf	Pct	Place
1996	6	6	11-2-0	553	174	.846	8-0-0	1.000	2
1997	2	1	13-0-0	607	214	1.000	8-0-0	1.000	1

Frank Solich (1998-2003) 57-19-0 .750

Year	AP	UPI	Record	PF	PA	Pct	Conf	Pct	Place
1998	19	20	9-4-0	403	206	.692	5-3-0	.625	4
1999	3	2	12-1-0	442	171	.923	7-1-0	.875	1
2000	8	7	10-2-0	522	230	.833	6-2-0	.750	3
2001	8	7	11-2-0	449	189	.917	7-1-0	.875	3
2002			7-7-0	383	335	.500	3-5-0	.375	8
2003*	19	18	9-3-0	305	185	.750	5-3-0	.625	4

Bo Pelini (2003) 1-0-0 1.000

Year	AP	UPI	Record	PF	PA	Pct	Conf	Pct	Place
2003*			1-0-0	17	3	1.000	0-0-0		

*Solich coached the first 13 games of the 2003 season, and Pelini coached the last (bowl) game.

Won-loss record by decades:

Decade	Record	Pct	Decade	Record	Pct	Decade	Record	Pct
1890-99	41-25-4	.614	1930-39	62-21-8	.725	1970-79	98-20-4	.820
1900-09	70-19-4	.774	1940-49	34-57-0	.374	1980-89	103-20-0	.837
1910-19	58-13-6	.792	1950-59	39-58-3	.405	1990-99	108-16-1	.864
1920-29	55-18-9	.726	1960-69	75-30-1	.712	2000-03	38-14-0	.731

Historic record 781-311-40 .708

Post-season won-loss record 21-21-0 .500

1941: Rose Bowl, Stanford 21, Nebraska 13
1955: Orange Bowl, Duke 34, Nebraska 7
1962: Gotham Bowl, Nebraska 36, Miami 34
1964: Orange Bowl, Nebraska 13, Auburn 7
1965: Cotton Bowl, Arkansas 10, Nebraska 7
1966: Orange Bowl, Alabama 39, Nebraska 28
1967: Sugar Bowl, Alabama 34, Nebraska 7
1969: Sun Bowl, Nebraska 45, Georgia 6
1971: Orange Bowl, Nebraska 17, LSU 12
1972: Orange Bowl, Nebraska 38, Alabama 6
1973: Orange Bowl, Nebraska 40, Notre Dame 6
1974: Cotton Bowl, Nebraska 19, Texas 3
1974: Sugar Bowl, Nebraska 13, Florida 10
1975: Fiesta Bowl, Arizona State 17, Nebraska 14
1976: Bluebonnet Bowl, Nebraska 27, Texas Tech 24
1977: Liberty Bowl, Nebraska 21, North Carolina 17
1979: Orange Bowl, Oklahoma 31, Nebraska 24
1980: Cotton Bowl, Houston 17, Nebraska 14
1980: Sun Bowl, Nebraska 31, Miss. State 17
1982: Orange Bowl, Clemson 22, Nebraska 15
1983: Orange Bowl, Nebraska 21, LSU 20

1984: Orange Bowl, Miami 31, Nebraska 30
1985: Sugar Bowl, Nebraska 28, LSU 10
1986: Fiesta Bowl, Michigan 27, Nebraska 23
1987: Sugar Bowl, Nebraska 30, LSU 15
1988: Fiesta Bowl, Florida State 31, Nebraska 28
1989: Orange Bowl, Miami 23, Nebraska 3
1990: Fiesta Bowl, Florida State 41, Nebraska 17
1991: Citrus Bowl, Ga. Tech 45, Nebraska 21
1992: Orange Bowl, Miami 22, Nebraska 0
1993: Orange Bowl, Florida State 27, Nebraska 14
1994: Orange Bowl, Florida State 18, Nebraska 16
1995: Orange Bowl, Nebraska 24, Miami 17
1996: Fiesta Bowl, Nebraska 62, Florida 24
1996: Big 12 Championship, Texas 37, Nebraska 27
1996: Orange Bowl, Nebraska 41, Virginia Tech 21
1997: Big 12 Championship, Nebraska 54, Texas A&M 15
1998: Orange Bowl, Nebraska 42, Tennessee 17
1998: Holiday Bowl, Arizona 23, Nebraska 20
1999: Big 12 Championship, Nebraska 22, Texas 6
2000: Fiesta Bowl, Nebraska 31, Tennessee 21
2000: Alamo Bowl, Nebraska 66, Northwestern 17
2002: Rose Bowl, Miami 37, Nebraska 14
2002: Independence Bowl, Ole Miss 27, Nebraska 23
2003: Alamo Bowl, Nebraska 17, Michigan State 3

College Football Hall of Fame:

Edward Robinson, coach, 1896-97; Fielding Yost, coach, 1898; Guy Chamberlin, end/halfback, 1911-15; Clarence Swanson, end, 1918-21; Ed Weir, tackle, 1923-25; Dana X. Bible, coach, 1929-36; George Sauer, fullback, 1931-33; Sam Francis, fullback, 1934-36; Biff Jones, coach, 1937-41; Forrest Behm, tackle, 1938-40; Bobby Reynolds, halfback, 1950-52; Bob Brown, guard, 1961-63; Bob Devaney, coach, 1962-72; Wayne Meylan, middle guard, 1965-67; Rich Glover, middle guard, 1970-72; Johnny Rodgers, wide receiver, 1970-72; Tom Osborne, coach, 1973-97; Dave Rimington, center, 1979-82.

Awards: Butkus Award: 1993, Trev Alberts; Maxwell Award: 1983, Mike Rozier; Lombardi Award: 1972, Rich Glover; 1982, Dave Rimington; 1983, Dean Steinkuhler; 1997, Grant Wistrom; Outland Trophy: 1971: Larry Jacobson; 1972, Rich Glover; 1981, Dave Rimington; 1982, Dave Rimington; 1983, Dean Steinkuhler;; 1992, Will Shields; 1994, Zack Weigert; 1997, Aaron Taylor; Heisman Trophy: 1972, Johnny Rodgers; 1983, Mike Rozier; 2001, Eric Crouch; Davey O'Brien Award: 2001, Eric Crouch; Rimington Trophy: 2000, Dominic Raiola; Camp Award: 1972, Johnny Rogers; 1983, Mike Rozier; 2001, Eric Crouch.

UNIVERSITY OF NEVADA AT LAS VEGAS, Las Vegas, Nevada; nickname "Rebels"; colors scarlet and gray; Sam Boyd Stadium (36,800); Mountain West Conference. UNLV began play in 1968 as an independent. In 1982, UNLV joined the Big West Conference. After the 1995 season, UNLV left the Big West and joined the Western Athletic Conference. UNLV was in that conference for the 1996 through 1998 seasons and then joined with seven other WAC teams to organize the Mountain West Conference.

Early years as an independent (1968-1981)

Year	W-L-T	PF	PA	Pct.		Year	W-L-T	PF	PA	Pct.
					Bill Ireland (1968-1972) 26-23-1 .530					
1968	8-1-0	266	103	.889		1971	5-4-1	254	171	.550
1969	6-4-0	271	255	.600		1972	1-10-0	149	269	.091
1970	6-4-0	313	241	.600						
					Ron Meyer (1973-1975) 27-8-0 .771					
1973	8-3-0	304	151	.727		1975	7-4-0	332	192	.636
1974	12-1-0	444	251	.923						
					Tony Knap (1976-1981) 47-20-2 .695					
1976	9-3-0	296	216	.750		1979	9-1-2	370	300	.833
1977	9-2-0	300	236	.818		1980	7-4-0	384	257	.636
1978	7-4-0	249	182	.636		1981	6-6-0	326	433	.500

Member of the Big West Conference (1982-1995) 34-56-1 .379
Harvey Hyde (1982-1985) 8-37-1* .185

Year	Nat'l AP Other	Overall W-L-T	PF	PA	Pct	Conference W-L-T	Pct.	Rank	Year	Nat'l AP Other	Overall W-L-T	PF	PA	Pct.	Conference W-L-T	Pct.	Rank
1982		3-8-0	246	332	.273	1-4-0	.200	6	1984*		0-13-0	387	255	.000	0-7-0	.000	8
1983*		0-11-0	255	192	.000	0-6-0	.000	7	1985		5-5-1	189	210	.500	4-2-1	.643	3

*UNLV had to forfeit all games in 1983 and 1984 because of the use of an ineligible receiver. Before the forfeits, the overall record of UNLV in 1983 was 7-4-0 and in 1984 was 11-2-0. Hyde's record before forfeits was 26-19-1 .576.

Wayne Nunnely (1986-1989) 19-25-0 .432

1986		6-5-0	286	241	.545	3-4-0	.429	4	1988		4-7-0	176	313	.636	3-4-0	.429	5
1987		5-6-0	244	297	.455	4-3-0	.571	2	1989		4-7-0	233	340	.364	3-4-0	.429	5

Jim Strong (1990-1993) 17-27-0 .386

1990		4-7-0	239	324	.364	3-4-0	.429	5	1992		6-5-0	243	311	.545	3-3-0	.500	4
1991		4-7-0	220	360	.364	2-5-0	.286	5	1993		3-8-0	259	347	.273	2-4-0	.333	6

Jeff Horton (1994-1998) 13-44-0 .228

1994		7-5-0	263	305	.583	5-1-0	.833	1	1995		2-9-0	222	520	.182	1-5-0	.167	10

Member of the Western Athletic Conference (1996-1998) 3-21-0 .125

1996	1-11-0	276	551	.083	1-7-0	.125	14	1998		0-11-0	156	389	.000	0-8-0	.000	15
1997	3-8-0	281	332	.273	2-6-0	.250	13									

Member of the Mountain West Conference (1999-2003) 13-22-0 .371
John Robinson (1999-2003) 26-33-0 .441

1999		3-8-0	160	324	.273	1-6-0	.143	8	2001		4-7-0	284	270	.364	3-4-0	.429	5
2000		8-5-0	385	260	.571	4-3-0	.571	3	2002		5-7-0	292	366	.417	3-4-0	.429	5
									2003		6-6-0	256	272	.500	2-5-0	.286	7

Won-loss record by decades:

1968-69	14-5-0	.737	1980-89*	40-72-1	.358	2000-03	.23-25-0	.479
1970-79	73-36-3	.665	1990-99	33-79-0	.295			

Historic record* 183-217-4 .458

*These figures reflect the forfeiting of all games in 1983 and 1984. Before forfeits, 1980-89 won-loss-tied record is 58-54-1, and the historic record before forfeits would be 195-193-4 .503.

Post-season won-loss record: 2-3-0 .400
1974: Division II playoffs, Delaware 49, UNLV 11
1976: Division II playoffs, Akron 27, UNLV 6
1984: California Bowl, UNLV 30, Toledo 13*
1994: Las Vegas Bowl, UNLV 52, Central Michigan 24
2000: Las Vegas Bowl, UNLV 31, Arkansas 14
*The 1984 bowl game was forfeited later because of ineligible player.

UNIVERSITY OF NEVADA, Reno, Nevada; nickname "Wolf Pack"; colors blue and silver; Mackay Stadium (31,545); Western Athletic Conference. Nevada began play in 1899 as an independent. In 1925, Nevada joined the Far Western Conference and played in that conference through the 1939 season. Nevada was an independent again from 1940 through the 1953 season after which it returned to the Far Western Conference. The Wolf Pack left the Far Western Conference after the 1968 season and was independent until the 1979 season when it joined the Big Sky Conference. In 1992, Nevada left the Big Sky Conference and joined the Big West Conference where it played through the 1999 season. Beginning in 2000, Nevada has been in the Western Athletic Conference.

Early years as an independent (1898-1924)

Year	Coach	W-L-T	PF	PA	Pct.	Year	Coach	W-L-T	PF	PA	Pct.
1898	F. F. Ellis	4-1-0	121	18	.800	1916	Jack Glascock	3-5-0	142	160	.375
1899	A. King Dickson	3-2-0	85	52	.600	1917	Jack Glascock	1-3-0	50	155	.250
1900	James Hopper	4-2-1	78	34	.643	1918	no team				
1901	A. C. Steckle	3-3-0	64	31	.500	1919	R. E. Courtright	8-1-1	450	32	.850
1902	A. C. Steckle	1-2-0	21	40	.333	1920	R. E. Courtright	7-3-1	186	167	.682
1903	A. C. Steckle	2-4-2	56	40	.375	1921	R. E. Courtright	4-3-1	183	113	.562
1904	Bruce Shorts	3-2-0	50	43	.600	1922	R. E. Courtright	5-3-1	166	120	.611
1905	no coach	0-3-1	0	42	.125	1923	R. E. Courtright	2-3-2	97	97	.429
1906-1914	no team, as rugby replaces football					1924	Charlie Erb	3-4-1	100	124	.438
1915	Jack Glascock	0-5-0	22	131	.000						

Member of the Far Western Conference * (1925-1938, 1954-1968) 50-73-6 .411

*Conference ranks not available, 1925-1938.

Year	Nat'l AP Other	Overall W-L-T	PF	PA	Pct.	Conference W-L-T	Pct.	Rank	Year	Nat'l AP Other	Overall W-L-T	PF	PA	Pct.	Conference W-L-T	Pct.	Rank
								Buck Shaw (1925-1928) 10-20-3 .348									
1925		4-3-1	107	115	.562	3-1-0	.750		1927		2-6-1	54	210	.278	1-3-0	.250	
1926		4-4-0	120	119	.500	3-1-0	.750		1928		0-7-1	31	161	.063	0-3-1	.125	
								George Philbrook (1929-1931) 6-14-5 .340									
1929		2-5-1	64	180	.312	2-1-0	.667		1931		2-5-2	76	134	.429	2-1-1	.625	
1930		2-4-2	77	73	.429	2-2-0	.500										
								Brick Mitchell (1932-1935) 10-20-3 .348									
1932		3-3-2	41	99	.500	2-0-1	.833		1934		1-7-1	15	153	.167	0-4-1	.100	
1933		4-4-0	60	144	.500	3-0-0	1.000		1935		2-6-0	57	147	.250	2-3-0	.400	
								Doug Dashiell (1936-1938) 8-13-1 .386									
1936		4-4-0	91	103	.500	2-2-0	.500		1938		2-3-1	65	117	.417	1-2-0	.333	
1937		2-6-0	61	175	.250	1-3-0	.250										
								Jim Aiken (1939-1946) 38-26-4 .588									
1939		5-4-0	49	101	.556	3-0-0	1.000										
								Nevada reverts to independent status (1940-1953)									
1940		4-4-1	261	79	.500				1944		4-4-0	92	93	.500			
1941		3-5-1	101	117	.389				1945		7-3-0	240	147	.700			
1942		4-3-1	81	80	.562				1946		7-2-0	324	82	.778			
1943		4-1-1	114	25	.750												
								Joe Sheeketski (1947-1950) 24-18-0 .571									
1947		9-2-0	316	154	.818				1949		5-5-0	235	212	.500			
1948		9-2-0	480	133	.818				1950		1-9-0	117	363	.100			
								No team (1951)									
								Jake Lawlor (1952-1954) 6-11-0 .353									
1952		2-3-0	111	126	.400				1953		2-3-0	87	116	.400			
								Nevada returns to the Far Western Conference (1954-1968)									
1954		2-5-0	79	212	.286	2-3-0	.400	4									
								Gordon McEachron (1955-1958) 6-23-1 .217									
1955		2-5-0	70	199	.286	1-4-0	.200	5	1957		1-8-0	97	229	.111	1-4-0	.200	5
1956		0-7-1	122	198	.063	0-5-0	.000	6	1958		3-3-0	100	97	.500	2-3-0	.400	4
								Dick Trachok (1959-1968) 40-47-3 .461									
1959		4-3-0	130	91	.571	3-2-0	.600	3	1964		1-9-0	104	263	.100	1-4-0	.200	5
1960		3-6-0	119	153	.333	2-3-0	.400	3	1965		6-4-0	210	162	.600	4-1-0	.800	2
1961		5-4-0	153	179	.556	2-3-0	.400	4	1966		6-3-0	217	153	.667	2-3-0	.400	4
1962		5-2-1	133	68	.688	2-2-1	.500	3	1967		4-4-1	150	159	.500	1-3-1	.300	4
1963		3-6-0	134	182	.333	2-3-0	.400	4	1968		3-6-1	176	183	.350	1-4-0	.200	5
								Nevada reverts to independent status (1969-1978)									
								Jerry Scattini (1969-1975) 37-36-1 .507									
1969		5-5-0	222	225	.500				1973		7-4-0	295	143	.636			
1970		6-3-1	280	220	.650				1974		5-6-0	209	254	.455			
1971		5-5-0	280	220	.500				1975		3-8-0	121	285	.273			
1972		6-5-0	276	218	.545												

Chris Ault (1976-1992, 1994-1995) 163-63-1 .720

Year	Record	PF	PA	Pct	Conf	Pct	Rk		Year	Record	PF	PA	Pct	Conf	Pct	Rk
1976	8-3-0	409	154	.727					1978	11-1-0	413	121	.917			
1977	8-3-0	421	154	.727												

Member of the Big Sky Conference (1979-1991) 68-28-0 .708

1979	8-4-0	325	198	.667	5-2-0	.714	2		1986	13-1-0	531	231	.929	7-0-0	1.000	1
1980	6-4-1	202	113	.591	4-3-0	.571	2		1987	5-6-0	314	300	.455	4-4-0	.500	5
1981	7-4-0	310	194	.636	4-3-0	.571	4		1988	7-4-0	333	242	.636	4-4-0	.500	4
1982	6-5-0	294	228	.545	3-4-0	.429	5		1989	7-4-0	349	256	.636	5-3-0	.625	3
1983	9-5-0	402	244	.643	6-1-0	.857	1		1990	13-2-0	497	321	.867	7-1-0	.875	1
1984	7-4-0	325	298	.636	5-2-0	.714	2		1991	12-1-0	546	245	.923	8-0-0	1.000	1
1985	11-2-0	493	213	.846	6-1-0	.857	2									

Member of the Big West Conference (1992-1999) 33-12-0 .733

1992	7-5-0	318	283	.583	5-1-0	.833	1

Jeff Horton (1993) 7-4-0 .636

1993	7-4-0	419	315	.636	4-2-0	.667	3

Chris Ault (1994-1995)

1994	9-2-0	414	272	.818	5-1-0	.833	1		1995	9-3-0	521	375	.750	6-0-0	1.000	1

Jeff Tisdel (1996-2001) 25-32-0 .439

1996	9-3-0	515	278	.750	4-1-0	.800	1		1998	6-5-0	371	316	.545	3-2-0	.600	2
1997	5-6-0	353	320	.455	4-1-0	.800	1		1999	3-8-0	289	424	.273	2-4-0	.333	6

Member of the Western Athletic Conference (2000-2003) 12-20-0 .375

2000	2-10-0	207	264	.167	1-7-0	.125	9

Chris Tormey (2001-2003) 14-21-0 .400

2001	3-8-0	286	431	.273	3-5-0	.375	7		2003	6-6-0	282	338	.500	4-4-0	.500	6
2002	5-7-0	331	371	.417	4-4-0	.500	4									

Won-loss record by decades:

1898-99	7- 3-0	.700		1930-39	27-46-8	.383	1970-79	67-42-1	.614
1900-09	13-16-4	.455		1940-49	56-31-4	.637	1980-89	80-39-1	.671
1910-19	12-14-1	.463		1950-59	17-46-1	.282	1990-99	80-39-0	.672
1920-29	33-41-10	.452		1960-69	41-49-3	.457	2000-03	16-31-0	.340

Historic record: 449-397-33 .530

Post-season won-loss record 11-10-0 .524
1948: Salad Bowl, Nevada 13, North Texas 6
1949: Harbor Bowl, Villanova 27, Nevada 7
1978: I-AA Playoffs, Massachusetts 44, Nevada 21
1979: I-AA Playoffs: Eastern Kentucky 33, Nevada 30
1983: I-AA Playoffs: Nevada 27, Idaho State 20
1983: I-AA Playoffs: Nevada 20, North Texas 17
1983: I-AA Playoffs: Southern Illinois 23, Nevada 7
1985: I-AA Playoffs: Nevada 24, Arkansas State 23
1985: I-AA Playoffs: Furman 35, Nevada 12
1986: I-AA Playoffs: Nevada 27, Idaho 7
1986: I-AA Playoffs: Nevada 33, Tennessee State 6
1986: I-AA Playoffs: Georgia Southern 48, Nevada 38

1990: I-AA Playoffs, Nevada 27, NE Louisiana 14
1990: I-AA Playoffs, Nevada 42, Furman 35 (3 OT)
1990: I-AA Playoffs, Nevada 59, Boise State 52 (2 OT)
1990: I-AA Playoffs, Georgia Southern 36, Nevada 13
1991: I-AA Playoffs, Nevada 22, McNeese State 16
1991: I-AA Playoffs: Youngstown State 30, Nevada 28
1992: Las Vegas Bowl, Bowling Green 35, Nevada 34
1995: Las Vegas Bowl, Toledo 40, Nevada 37
1996: Las Vegas Bowl, Nevada 18, Ball State 15

College Football Hall of Fame:
Buck Shaw, coach, 1925-28; Chris Ault, coach, 1976-92, 1994-95; Frank Hawkins, halfback, 1977-80.

NEW MEXICO STATE UNIVERSITY, Las Cruces, New Mexico; nickname "Aggies"; colors crimson and white; Aggie Memorial Stadium (30,343); Sun Belt Conference. New Mexico State began play in 1894 and was an independent until 1931 when the team joined the Border Conference. New Mexico State played in the Border Conference until it disbanded after the 1961 season then going independent through the 1970 season. In 1971, New Mexico State joined the Missouri Valley Conference and played there until 1982. After a year of independent status, State moved on to the Pacific Coast Conference (later named the Big West Conference). When that conference disbanded after the 1999 season, New Mexico State moved to the newly formed Sun Belt Conference.

Early years as an independent (1894-1931)

Year	Coach	W-L-T	PF	PA	Pct.	Year	Coach	W-L-T	PF	PA	Pct.
1894	W. H. Clute	0-1-0	6	18	.000	1912	Arthur Badenoch	5-1-0	256	17	.833
1895	Alfred Holt	2-0-0	11	4	1.000	1913	Arthur Badenoch	7-0-1	124	24	.938
1896	no coach	0-2-0	0	16	.000	1914	Clarence Russell	4-2-1	80	29	.643
1897	Charles Barber	1-0-1	10	0	.750	1915	Clarence Russell	3-1-0	82	26	.750
1898	Charles Barber	2-1-0	57	6	.667	1916	Clarence Russell	0-4-0	64	154	.000
1899	John Miller	1-0-0	38	0	1.000	1917	John Griffith	4-2-0	231	75	.667
1900	William Sutherland	3-3-1	49	27	.500	1918	no team				
1901	John Miller	2-1-0	38	6	.667	1919	Anthony Savage	2-3-1	83	69	.417
1902	John Miller	0-1-2	0	6	.333	1920	Arthur Bergman	5-1-1	159	62	.786
1903	John Miller	2-0-1	34	0	.833	1921	Arthur Bergman	2-2-0	126	37	.500
1904	John Miller	1-2-1	42	33	.375	1922	Arthur Bergman	5-2-0	210	53	.714
1905	John Miller	3-0-0	96	0	1.000	1923	Robert Brown	8-0-0	218	17	1.000
1906	John Miller	4-0-0	71	12	1.000	1924	Robert Brown	7-3-0	241	30	.700
1907	John Miller	3-0-0	88	6	1.000	1925	Robert Brown	5-3-1	151	75	.611
1908	W. G. Hummell	4-2-0	179	42	.667	1926	Arthur Burkholder	5-3-1	90	65	.611
1909	J. H. Squires	1-3-1	19	91	.300	1927	Ted Coffman	3-5-0	187	107	.375
1910	Arthur Badenoch	3-2-0	61	23	.600	1928	Ted Coffman	4-5-0	226	139	.444
1911	Arthur Badencoh	7-0-0	192	6	1.000						

Gerald H. Hines (1929-1939) 54-36-10 .594

1929		3-2-3	132	57	.562	1930			5-3-0	115	73	.625

Member of the Border Conference (1931-1961) 34-86-5 .298

	Nat'l	Overall				Conference			Nat'l	Overall				Conference		
Year	AP Other	W-L-T	PF	PA	Pct.	W-L-T	Pct. Rank	Year	AP Other	W-L-T	PF	PA	Pct.	W-L-T	Pct.	Rank
1931		6-4-0	155	90	.600	1-2-0	.333 5	1936		6-4-1	252	118	.591	3-2-0	.600	2
1932		4-5-1	203	81	.450	1-2-1	.375 5	1937		7-2-0	128	60	.778	4-1-0	.800	2
1933		2-6-0	100	72	.250	0-4-0	.000 6	1938		7-2-0	166	75	.778	4-1-0	.800	2
1934		4-1-3	169	25	.688	0-1-3	.375 5	1939		3-6-0	93	141	.333	1-4-0	.200	5
1935		7-1-2	210	42	.750	4-1-0	.800 2									

Julius Johnston (1940-42) 6-21-0 .222

1940		3-6-0	95	200	.333	1-4-0	.200 5	1942		1-8-0	33	223	.111	0-6-0	.000	9
1941		2-7-0	93	228	.222	0-6-0	.000 9									

Maurice Moulder (1943) 4-0-0 1.000

1943		4-0-0	107	20	1.000	no conference										

No team (1944-1945)
Raymond Curfman (1946-1947) 7-11-0 .421

1946		4-5-0	130	147	.444	1-4-0	.200 9	1947		3-6-0	140	169	.333	1-4-0	.200	7

Vaughn Corley (1948-1950) 9-20-0 .310

1948		3-7-0	138	390	.300	0-4-0	.000 9	1950		2-7-0	95	249	.222	1-4-0	.200	8
1949		4-6-0	265	315	.400	1-4-0	.200 7									

Joseph T. Coleman (1951-1952) 3-15-1 .184

1951		1-9-0	115	337	.100	1-5-0	.167 6	1952		2-6-1	118	222	.278	0-2-1	.167	5

James Patton (1953-1954) 2-16-0 .125

1953		2-7-0	56	316	.222	1-4-0	.200 6	1954		0-9-0	87	306	.000	0-4-0	.000	7

Tony Cavallo (1955-1957) 7-23-0 .233

1955		3-7-0	141	226	.300	0-4-0	.000 7	1957		3-7-0	157	205	.300	0-4-0	.000	5
1956		1-9-0	176	231	.100	0-4-0	.000 7									

Warren Woodson (1958-1967) 63-36-3 .626

1958		4-6-0	172	228	.400	1-3-0	.250 4	1960	17 19	11-0-0	394	113	1.000	4-0-0	1.000	1
1959		8-3-0	360	158	.727	2-2-0	.500 3	1961		5-4-1	341	195	.550	2-1-0	.667	2

New Mexico State reverts to independent status (1962-1971)

1962		4-6-0	191	259	.400			1965		8-2-0	236	153	.800			
1963		3-6-1	158	209	.350			1966		7-3-0	321	159	.700			
1964		6-4-0	131	171	.600			1967		7-2-1	346	145	.750			

Jim Wood (1968-1972) 21-30-1 .413

1968		5-5-0	228	244	.500			1970		4-6-0	282	277	.400			
1969		5-5-0	197	235	.500											

Member of the Missouri Valley Conference (1971-1982) 26-32-1 .449

1971		5-5-1	220	208	.500	4-0-0	1.000 *	1972		2-9-0	193	400	.182	1-4-0	.200	7

*New Mexico State not eligible for MVC title, insufficient number of conference games.

Jim Bradley (1973-1977) 23-31-1 .427

Year	Record	PF	PA	Pct	Conf	Conf Pct	Fin	Year	Record	PF	PA	Pct	Conf	Conf Pct	Fin
1973	5-6-0	244	299	.455	3-2-0	.600	3	1976	4-6-1	152	241	.409	2-1-1	.625	1
1974	5-6-0	237	200	.455	2-3-0	.400	5	1977	4-7-0	238	281	.364	3-2-0	.600	3
1975	5-6-0	179	300	.455	2-2-0	.500	2								

Gil Krueger (1978-1982) 17-37-1 .318

Year	Record	PF	PA	Pct	Conf	Conf Pct	Fin	Year	Record	PF	PA	Pct	Conf	Conf Pct	Fin
1978	6-5-0	274	296	.545	5-1-0	.833	1	1981	3-8-0	157	286	.273	1-5-0	.167	7
1979	2-9-0	175	367	.182	1-4-0	.200	4	1982	3-8-0	216	353	.273	1-4-0	.200	6
1980	3-7-1	212	247	.318	1-4-1	.250	6								

New Mexico State reverts to independent status (1983)

Fred Zechman (1983-1985) 8-25-0 .242

Year	Record	PF	PA	Pct
1983	5-6-0	211	292	.455

Member of the Pacific Coast Conference (later named Big West Conference) (1984-2000) 23-82-0 .219

Year	Record	PF	PA	Pct	Conf	Conf Pct	Fin	Year	Record	PF	PA	Pct	Conf	Conf Pct	Fin
1984	2-9-0	185	336	.182	1-6-0	.143	6	1985	1-10-0	190	369	.091	0-7-0	.000	8

Mike Knoll (1986-1989) 4-40-0 .091

Year	Record	PF	PA	Pct	Conf	Conf Pct	Fin	Year	Record	PF	PA	Pct	Conf	Conf Pct	Fin
1986	1-10-0	189	416	.091	1-6-0	.143	8	1988	1-10-0	171	424	.091	0-7-0	.000	8
1987	2-9-0	121	328	.182	0-7-0	.000	8	1989	0-11-0	152	428	.000	0-7-0	.000	8

Jim Hess (1990-1996) 22-55-0 .286

Year	Record	PF	PA	Pct	Conf	Conf Pct	Fin	Year	Record	PF	PA	Pct	Conf	Conf Pct	Fin
1990	1-10-0	200	366	.091	1-6-0	.143	7	1994	3-8-0	235	422	.273	2-4-0	.333	7
1991	2-9-0	224	350	.182	2-5-0	.286	5	1995	4-7-0	349	391	.364	3-3-0	.500	4
1992	6-5-0	286	330	.545	3-3-0	.500	4	1996	1-10-0	166	396	.091	0-5-0	.000	6
1993	5-6-0	231	350	.455	4-2-0	.667	3								

Tony Samuel (1997-2003) 29-51-0 .362

Year	Record	PF	PA	Pct	Conf	Conf Pct	Fin	Year	Record	PF	PA	Pct	Conf	Conf Pct	Fin
1997	2-9-0	221	398	.182	0-5-0	.000	6	1999	6-5-0	311	274	.545	3-3-0	.500	3
1998	3-8-0	331	418	.273	1-4-0	.200	6	2000	3-8-0	295	266	.273	1-4-0	.200	4

Member of the Sun Belt Conference (2001-2003) 11-8-0 .579

Year	Record	PF	PA	Pct	Conf	Conf Pct	Fin	Year	Record	PF	PA	Pct	Conf	Conf Pct	Fin
2001	5-7-0	286	400	.417	4-2-0	.667	3	2003	3-9-0	262	341	.250	2-5-0	.286	7
2002	7-5-0	327	328	.583	5-1-0	.833	2								

Won-loss record by decades:

1894-99	6- 4-1	.591	1930-39	51-34-7	.592	1970-79	43-64-2	.404
1900-09	23-12-6	.634	1940-49	24-45-0	.348	1980-89	21-88-1	.195
1910-19	35-15-3	.689	1950-59	26-70-1	.273	1990-99	33-77-0	.300
1920-29	47-26-6	.633	1960-69	61-37-3	.619	2000-03	18-29-0	.383

Historic record 387-502-30 .437

Post-season won-loss record: 2-0-1 .833
1936: Sun Bowl, New Mexico State 14, Hardin-Simmons 14   1960: Sun Bowl, New Mexico State 20, Utah State 13
1959: Sun Bowl, New Mexico State 28, North Texas State 8

UNIVERSITY OF NEW MEXICO, Albuquerque, New Mexico; nickname "Lobos"; colors cherry and silver; University Stadium (37,370); Mountain West Conference. New Mexico was independent from 1892 through the 1930 season. In 1931, the Lobos were one of the founding members of the Border Conference. New Mexico left the Border Conference after the 1950 season and joined the Mountain States ("Skyline") Conference. This conference disbanded after the 1961 season, and New Mexico joined the newly organized Western Athletic Conference. New Mexico stayed in the WAC through the 1998 season. Then New Mexico joined with several other WAC members to form the Mountain West Conference, which began play in the 1999 season.

Early years as an independent (1892-1930)

Year	W-L-T	PF	PA	Pct.		Year	W-L-T	PF	PA	Pct.
						No coach (1892-1893)				
1892	0-2-0	0	13	.000		1893	3-1-0	39	15	.750
						W. A. Zimmer (1894) 1-1-1 .500				
1894	1-1-1	26	8	.500						
						No team (1895-1898)				
						No coach (1899)				
1899	1-1-0	5	5	.500						
						No team (1900)				
						Joe Napier (1901) 0-3-1 .125				
1901	0-3-1	7	54	.125						
						No team (1902)				
						Walter McEwan (1903-1904) 4-0-1 .900				
1903	3-0-1	30	0	.875		1904	1-0-0	11	0	1.000
						Martin F. Angel (1905-1907) 9-2-1 .792				
1905	5-1-1	90	45	.786		1907	1-0-0	44	0	1.000
1906	3-1-0	59	30	.750						
						H. F. Cornwell (1908) 5-1-0 .833				
1908	5-1-0	107	40	.833						
						C. L. Birnie (1909) 4-2-0 .667				
1909	4-2-0	117	77	.667						
						Carl Hamilton (1910) 0-3-0 .000				
1910	0-3-0	0	90	.000						
						R. F. Hutchinson (1911-1016) 13-13-2 .500				
1911	1-3-1	62	22	.300		1914	3-1-1	83	33	.700
1912	0-4-0	15	76	.000		1915	3-1-0	97	6	.750
1913	3-2-0	84	27	.600		1916	3-2-0	216	70	.600
						Frank E. Worth (1917) 1-2-0 .333				
1917	1-2-0	47	129	.333						
						No team (1918)				
						John McGough (1919) 3-0-2 .800				
1919	3-0-2	136	15	.800						
						Roy Johnson (1920-1930) 41-32-6 .561				
1920	3-3-0	105	91	.500		1926	4-2-1	121	110	.643
1921	2-2-0	41	31	.500		1927	8-0-1	215	28	.944
1922	3-4-0	58	61	.429		1928	5-2-1	172	51	.688
1923	3-5-0	189	98	.375		1929	2-4-2	133	100	.375
1924	5-1-0	103	12	.833		1930	4-5-0	148	133	.444
1925	2-4-1	52	77	.357						

Member of the Border Conference (1931-1950) 39-51-6 .438

	Nat'l	Overall				Conference				Nat'l	Overall				Conference		
Year	AP Other	W-L-T	PF	PA	Pct.	W-L-T	Pct.	Rank	Year	AP Other	W-L-T	PF	PA	Pct.	W-L-T	Pct.	Rank
						Charles Riley (1931-1933) 7-13-3 .350											
1931		3-3-1	80	70	.500	1-0-1	.750	2	1933		3-4-1	92	108	.438	2-2-0	.500	4
1932		1-6-1	31	188	.188	1-3-1	.300	6									
						Gwinn Henry (1934-1936) 16-12-0 .571											
1934		8-1-0	251	73	.889	3-1-0	.750	2	1936		2-7-0	61	95	.222	1-4-0	.200	6
1935		6-4-0	145	102	.600	3-2-0	.600	3									
						Ted Shipkey (1937-1941) 30-17-2 .632											
1937		4-4-1	69	93	.500	2-3-1	.417	5	1940		5-4-0	166	94	.556	3-2-0	.600	4
1938		8-3-0	199	72	.727	4-2-0	.667	3	1941		5-4-1	116	135	.550	3-1-1	.700	5
1939		8-2-0	167	98	.800	4-2-0	.667	2									
						Willis Barnes (1942-1946) 19-20-5 .488											
1942		4-5-2	134	92	.455	3-4-0	.429	6	1945		6-1-1	208	61	.812	no conference		
1943		3-2-0	85	59	.600	no conference			1946		5-5-2	134	216	.500	4-2-1	.653	3
1944		1-7-0	75	248	.125	no conference											
						Berl Huffman (1947-1949) 8-22-1 .267											
1947		4-5-1	171	182	.450	1-5-1	.214	8	1949		2-8-0	98	307	.200	1-6-0	.143	8
1948		2-9-0	146	217	.182	1-6-0	.143	8									

Dudley DeGroot (1950-1952) 13-17-0 .433

Year	Rk	W-L-T	PF	PA	Pct	Conf	Pct	Pl	Year	W-L-T	PF	PA	Pct	Conf	Pct	Pl
1950		2-8-0	160	330	.200	2-5-0	.286	7								

Member of the Skyline Conference (1951-1961) 34-31-1 .523

Year	Rk	W-L-T	PF	PA	Pct	Conf	Pct	Pl	Year	W-L-T	PF	PA	Pct	Conf	Pct	Pl
1951		4-7-0	193	208	.364	2-4-0	.333	7	1952	7-2-0	119	46	.778	5-1-0	.833	2

Bob Titchenal (1953-1955) 12-16-1 .431

Year	Rk	W-L-T	PF	PA	Pct	Conf	Pct	Pl	Year	W-L-T	PF	PA	Pct	Conf	Pct	Pl
1953		5-3-1	154	103	.611	3-2-1	.583	4	1955	2-8-0	61	213	.200	1-5-0	.167	7
1954		5-5-0	152	158	.500	3-3-0	.500	4								

Dick Clausen (1956-1957) 8-12-0 .400

Year	Rk	W-L-T	PF	PA	Pct	Conf	Pct	Pl	Year	W-L-T	PF	PA	Pct	Conf	Pct	Pl
1956		4-6-0	177	205	.400	2-4-0	.333	6	1957	4-6-0	140	144	.400	2-4-0	.333	5

Marv Levy (1958-1959) 14-6-0 .700

Year	Rk	W-L-T	PF	PA	Pct	Conf	Pct	Pl	Year	W-L-T	PF	PA	Pct	Conf	Pct	Pl
1958		7-3-0	204	185	.700	5-1-0	.833	2	1959	7-3-0	260	135	.700	4-2-0	.667	3

Bill Weeks (1960-1967) 40-41-1 .494

Year	Rk	W-L-T	PF	PA	Pct	Conf	Pct	Pl	Year	W-L-T	PF	PA	Pct	Conf	Pct	Pl
1960		5-5-0	234	182	.500	4-2-0	.667	4	1961	7-4-0	215	195	.636	3-3-0	.500	3

Member of the Western Athletic Conference (1962-1998) 91-159-2 .365

Year	Rk	W-L-T	PF	PA	Pct	Conf	Pct	Pl	Year	W-L-T	PF	PA	Pct	Conf	Pct	Pl
1962		7-2-1	210	159	.750	2-1-1	.625	1	1965	3-7-0	127	226	.300	2-3-0	.400	4
1963		6-4-0	177	143	.600	3-1-0	.750	1	1966	2-8-0	101	320	.200	0-5-0	.000	6
1964	16	9-2-0	185	90	.818	3-1-0	.750	1	1967	1-9-0	152	433	.100	0-5-0	.000	6

Rudy Feldman (1968-1973) 24-37-2 .393

Year	Rk	W-L-T	PF	PA	Pct	Conf	Pct	Pl	Year	W-L-T	PF	PA	Pct	Conf	Pct	Pl
1968		0-10-0	120	403	.000	0-7-0	.000	8	1971	6-3-2	341	292	.636	5-1-0	.833	2
1969		4-6-0	158	281	.400	1-5-0	.167	7	1972	3-8-0	208	327	.273	2-4-0	.333	6
1970		7-3-0	291	222	.700	5-1-0	.833	2	1973	4-7-0	257	287	.364	3-4-0	.429	4

Bill Mondt (1974-1979) 32-36-1 .471

Year	Rk	W-L-T	PF	PA	Pct	Conf	Pct	Pl	Year	W-L-T	PF	PA	Pct	Conf	Pct	Pl
1974		4-6-1	192	263	.409	3-4-0	.429	4	1977	5-7-0	273	339	.417	2-5-0	.286	6
1975		6-5-0	291	232	.545	4-3-0	.571	4	1978	7-5-0	283	205	.583	3-3-0	.500	4
1976		4-7-0	229	235	.364	3-4-0	.429	5	1979	6-6-0	211	229	.500	3-4-0	.429	4

Joe Morrison (1980-1982) 18-15-1 .561

Year	Rk	W-L-T	PF	PA	Pct	Conf	Pct	Pl	Year	W-L-T	PF	PA	Pct	Conf	Pct	Pl
1980		4-7-0	246	364	.364	3-4-0	.429	7	1982	10-1-0	374	225	.909	6-1-0	.857	2
1981		4-7-1	225	231	.375	3-4-1	.437	5								

Joe Lee Dunn (1983-1986) 17-30-0 .362

Year	Rk	W-L-T	PF	PA	Pct	Conf	Pct	Pl	Year	W-L-T	PF	PA	Pct	Conf	Pct	Pl
1983		6-6-0	239	233	.500	4-3-0	.571	4	1985	3-8-0	289	415	.273	2-6-0	.250	7
1984		4-8-0	251	359	.333	1-7-0	.125	8	1986	4-8-0	317	338	.333	2-5-0	.286	7

Mike Sheppard (1987-1991) 9-50-0 .153

Year	Rk	W-L-T	PF	PA	Pct	Conf	Pct	Pl	Year	W-L-T	PF	PA	Pct	Conf	Pct	Pl
1987		0-11-0	209	444	.000	0-8-0	.000	9	1990	2-10-0	279	406	.167	1-6-0	.143	8
1988		2-10-0	170	518	.167	1-7-0	.125	8	1991	3-9-0	240	473	.250	2-6-0	.250	8
1989		2-10-0	298	378	.167	0-7-0	.000	9								

Dennis Franchione (1992-1997) 33-36-0 .478

Year	Rk	W-L-T	PF	PA	Pct	Conf	Pct	Pl	Year	W-L-T	PF	PA	Pct	Conf	Pct	Pl
1992		3-8-0	247	287	.273	2-6-0	.250	9	1995	4-7-0	256	303	.364	2-6-0	.250	7
1993		6-5-0	335	256	.545	4-4-0	.500	6	1996	6-5-0	331	280	.545	3-5-0	.375	9
1994		5-7-0	401	386	.417	4-4-0	.500	5	1997	9-4-0	500	256	.692	6-2-0	.750	2

Rocky Long (1998-2003) 33-40-0 .452

Year	Rk	W-L-T	PF	PA	Pct	Conf	Pct	Pl	Year	W-L-T	PF	PA	Pct	Conf	Pct	Pl
1998		3-9-0	294	397	.250	1-7-0	.125	14								

Member of the Mountain West Conference (1999-2003) 20-15-0 .517

Year	Rk	W-L-T	PF	PA	Pct	Conf	Pct	Pl	Year	W-L-T	PF	PA	Pct	Conf	Pct	Pl
1999		4-7-0	240	298	.364	3-4-0	.429	5	2001	6-5-0	304	243	.545	4-3-0	.571	3
2000		5-7-0	229	249	.417	3-4-0	.429	5	2002	7-7-0	341	358	.500	5-2-0	.714	2
									2003	8-5-0	391	290	.615	5-2-0	.714	2

Won-loss record by decades:

1892-99	5-5-1	.500	1930-39	47-39-4	.544	1970-79	52-57-3	.478
1900-09	22-8-3	.712	1940-49	37-50-7	.473	1980-89	39-76-1	.341
1910-19	17-18-4	.487	1950-59	47-51-1	.480	1990-99	45-71-0	.388
1920-29	37-27-6	.571	1960-69	44-57-1	.436	2000-03	26-24-0	.520

Historic record: 418-483-31 .465

Post-season won-loss record 2-5-1 .313

1939: Sun Bowl, Utah 26, New Mexico 0
1944: Sun Bowl, Southwestern 7, New Mexico 0
1946: Sun Bowl, New Mexico 34, Denver 24
1947: Harbor Bowl, New Mexico 13, Montana State 13

1961: Aviation Bowl, New Mexico 28, Western Michigan 12
1997: Insight.com Bowl, Arizona 20, New Mexico 14
2002: Las Vegas Bowl, UCLA 27, New Mexico 13
2003: Las Vegas Bowl, Oregon State 55, New Mexico 14

NORTH CAROLINA STATE UNIVERSITY, Raleigh, North Carolina; nickname "Wolf Pack"; colors red and white; Carter-Finley Stadium (53,000); Atlantic Coast Conference. NC State began play in 1892 and joined the Southern Conference as a founding member in 1922. NC State played in that conference through the 1952 season, after which State joined with other SC members to organize the Atlantic Coast Conference. NC State has played in the ACC beginning with the 1953 season.

Early years (1892-1921)

Year	Coach	W-L-T	PF	PA	Pct.	Year	Coach	W-L-T	PF	PA	Pct.
1892	Perrin Busbee	1-0-0	14	6	1.000	1901	John McGee	1-2-0	27	75	.333
1893	Bart Gatling	2-0-0	25	6	1.000	1902	Arthur Devlin	3-4-2	81	41	.444
1894	Bart Gatling	0-2-0	0	60	.000	1903	Arthur Devlin	4-4-0	142	74	.500
1895	Bart Gatling	1-2-1	50	82	.375	1904	W. S. Kienholz	3-1-2	79	11	.667
1896	Perrin Busbee	1-0-0	6	0	1.000	1905	G. Whitney	4-1-1	66	10	.750
1897	Perrin Busbee	1-2-0	19	58	.333	1906	Willie Heston	3-1-4	100	10	.625
1898	W. C. Riddick	0-1-0	0	34	.000	1907	M. Whitehurst	6-0-1	81	13	.929
1899	W. C. Riddick	1-2-2	29	69	.400	1908	M. Whitehurst	6-1-0	153	11	.857
1900	John McGee	0-4-0	7	64	.000						

Eddie Green (1909-1913) 25-8-2 .743

Year	W-L-T	PF	PA	Pct.	Year	W-L-T	PF	PA	Pct.
1909	6-1-0	110	24	.857	1912	4-3-0	53	104	.571
1910	4-0-2	125	12	.833	1913	6-1-0	155	27	.857
1911	5-3-0	84	34	.625					

Jack Hegarty (1914-1915) 5-6-2 .461

Year	W-L-T	PF	PA	Pct.	Year	W-L-T	PF	PA	Pct.
1914	2-3-1	96	44	.417	1915	3-3-1	71	114	.500

Brit Patterson (1916) 2-5-0 .286

Year	W-L-T	PF	PA	Pct.
1916	2-5-0	24	191	.286

Harry Hartsell (1917. 1921-23) 16-18-4 .474

Year	W-L-T	PF	PA	Pct.
1917	6-2-1	112	70	.722

Tal Stafford (1918) 1-3-0 .250

Year	W-L-T	PF	PA	Pct.
1918	1-3-0	54	174	.250

Bill Fetzer (1919-1920) 14-5-0 .737

Year	W-L-T	PF	PA	Pct.
1919	7-2-0	351	75	.778
1920	7-3-0	284	112	.700

Harry Hartsell (1921-1923)

Year	W-L-T	PF	PA	Pct.
1921	3-3-3	61	98	.500

Member of the Southern Conference (1922-1952) 63-108-14 .378

Year	Nat'l AP UP	Overall W-L-T	PF	PA	Pct	Conference W-L-T	Pct.	Rank	Year	Nat'l AP UP	Overall W-L-T	PF	PA	Pct.	Conference W-L-T	Pct.	Rank
1922		4-6-0	101	92	.400	0-5-0	.000	18	1923		3-7-0	56	134	.300	1-5-0	.167	15

Buck Shaw (1924) 2-6-2 .300

Year	Overall W-L-T	PF	PA	Pct	Conference W-L-T	Pct.	Rank
1924	2-6-2	43	147	.300	1-4-1	.250	18

Gus Tebell (1925-1929) 21-25-2 .479

Year	Overall W-L-T	PF	PA	Pct	Conference W-L-T	Pct.	Rank	Year	Nat'l AP UP	Overall W-L-T	PF	PA	Pct.	Conference W-L-T	Pct.	Rank
1925	3-5-1	57	74	.389	0-4-1	.100	19	1928		4-5-1	157	100	.450	1-3-1	.300	17
1926	4-6-0	66	102	.400	0-4-0	.000	21	1929		1-8-0	44	207	.111	0-5-0	.000	22
1927	9-1-0	216	69	.900	4-0-0	1.000	4									

J. Van Liew (1930) 2-8-0 .200

Year	Overall W-L-T	PF	PA	Pct	Conference W-L-T	Pct.	Rank
1930	2-8-0	57	125	.200	1-5-0	.167	19

Clipper Smith (1931-1933) 10-12-5 .463

Year	Overall W-L-T	PF	PA	Pct	Conference W-L-T	Pct.	Rank	Year	Overall W-L-T	PF	PA	Pct.	Conference W-L-T	Pct.	Rank
1931	3-6-0	60	104	.333	2-4-0	.333	17	1933	1-5-3	23	62	.278	0-4-0	.000	10
1932	6-1-2	90	29	.778	3-1-1	.700	6								

Hunk Anderson (1934-1936) 11-17-1 .396

Year	Overall W-L-T	PF	PA	Pct	Conference W-L-T	Pct.	Rank	Year	Overall W-L-T	PF	PA	Pct.	Conference W-L-T	Pct.	Rank
1934	2-6-1	44	112	.278	1-3-1	.300	8	1936	3-7-0	75	76	.300	2-4-0	.333	10
1935	6-4-0	87	76	.600	2-2-0	.500	5								

Doc Newton (1937-1943) 24-39-6 .391

Year	Overall W-L-T	PF	PA	Pct	Conference W-L-T	Pct.	Rank	Year	Overall W-L-T	PF	PA	Pct.	Conference W-L-T	Pct.	Rank
1937	5-3-1	91	92	.611	4-2-1	.643	6	1941	4-5-2	122	143	.455	3-4-2	.444	8
1938	3-7-1	59	100	.318	3-3-1	.500	6	1942	4-4-2	70	142	.500	3-1-2	.667	6
1939	2-8-0	49	191	.200	2-4-0	.333	9	1943	3-6-0	58	227	.333	1-4-0	.200	9
1940	3-6-0	120	161	.333	3-5-0	.375	11								

Beattie Feathers (1944-1951) 37-38-3 .494

Year	Nat'l AP UP	Overall W-L-T	PF	PA	Pct	Conference W-L-T	Pct.	Rank	Year	Overall W-L-T	PF	PA	Pct.	Conference W-L-T	Pct.	Rank
1944		7-2-0	173	63	.778	3-1-0	.750	3	1948	3-6-1	107	128	.350	1-4-1	.250	14
1945		3-6-0	131	144	.333	2-4-0	.333	8	1949	3-7-0	134	192	.300	3-6-0	.333	13
1946	18	8-3-0	213	67	.727	6-1-0	.857	3	1950	5-4-1	92	119	.550	4-4-1	.500	9
1947	17	5-3-1	92	57	.611	3-2-1	.583	6	1951	3-7-0	141	203	.300	2-6-0	.250	12

Horace Henderson (1952-1953) 4-16-0 .200

Year	Overall W-L-T	PF	PA	Pct	Conference W-L-T	Pct.	Rank
1952	3-7-0	94	169	.300	2-4-0	.333	10

Member of the Atlantic Coast Conference (1953-2003) 174-153-8 .531

Year	Overall W-L-T	PF	PA	Pct	Conference W-L-T	Pct.	Rank
1953	1-9-0	80	265	.100	0-3-0	.000	7

Earle Edwards (1954-1970) 77-88-8 .468

Year	Rank1	Rank2	W-L-T	PF	PA	Pct	Conf	Conf Pct	Conf
1954			2-8-0	104	193	.200	0-4-0	.000	7
1955			4-5-1	206	193	.450	0-2-1	.167	6
1956			3-7-0	94	169	.300	2-4-0	.333	6
1957	15	20	7-1-2	155	67	.889	5-0-1	.917	1
1958			2-7-1	120	160	.250	2-5-0	.286	7
1959			1-9-0	117	201	.100	0-6-0	.000	7
1960			6-3-1	148	133	.650	4-1-1	.750	2
1961			4-6-0	129	149	.400	3-4-0	.429	5
1962			3-6-1	108	139	.350	3-4-0	.429	4
1963			8-3-0	188	107	.727	6-1-0	.857	2
1964			5-5-0	119	194	.500	5-2-0	.714	1
1965			6-4-0	134	110	.600	4-3-0	.571	3
1966			5-5-0	191	168	.500	5-2-0	.714	2
1967	17		9-2-0	214	94	.818	5-1-0	.833	2
1968			6-4-0	134	110	.600	6-1-0	.857	1
1969			3-6-1	183	201	.350	3-2-1	.583	2
1970			3-7-1	90	179	.318	2-3-1	.417	5

Al Michaels (1971) 3-8-0 .273

Year	W-L-T	PF	PA	Pct	Conf	Conf Pct	Conf
1971	3-8-0	137	274	.273	2-4-0	.333	6

Lou Holtz (1972-1975) 33-12-3 .719

Year	Rank1	Rank2	W-L-T	PF	PA	Pct	Conf	Conf Pct	Conf
1972	17		8-3-1	409	240	.708	4-1-1	.750	2
1973	16		9-3-0	396	251	.750	6-0-0	1.000	1
1974	11	9	9-2-1	317	214	.864	4-2-0	.667	2
1975			7-4-1	260	210	.625	2-2-1	.500	3

Bo Rein (1976-1979) 27-18-1 .619

Year	Rank1	Rank2	W-L-T	PF	PA	Pct	Conf	Conf Pct	Conf
1976			3-7-1	205	258	.318	2-3-0	.400	5
1977	19		8-4-0	259	177	.667	4-2-0	.667	3
1978	18	19	9-3-0	280	208	.750	4-2-0	.667	3
1979			7-4-0	258	213	.636	5-1-0	.833	1

Monte Kiffin (1980-1982) 16-17-0 .485

Year	W-L-T	PF	PA	Pct	Conf	Conf Pct	Conf
1980	6-5-0	206	255	.545	3-3-0	.500	3
1981	4-7-0	181	223	.364	2-4-0	.333	5
1982	6-5-0	206	255	.545	3-3-0	.500	3

Tom Reed (1983-1985) 9-24-0 .273

Year	W-L-T	PF	PA	Pct	Conf	Conf Pct	Conf
1983	3-8-0	236	246	.273	1-5-0	.167	6
1984	3-8-0	263	311	.273	1-5-0	.167	6
1985	3-8-0	186	305	.273	2-5-0	.286	6

Dick Sheridan (1986-1992) 52-29-3 .637

Year	Rank1	Rank2	W-L-T	PF	PA	Pct	Conf	Conf Pct	Conf
1986			8-3-1	328	274	.708	5-2-0	.714	2
1987			4-7-0	215	302	.364	4-3-0	.571	3
1988	17		8-3-1	312	165	.708	4-2-1	.643	3
1989			7-5-0	290	230	.583	4-3-0	.571	4
1990			7-5-0	298	189	.583	3-4-0	.429	6
1991	24	25	9-3-0	304	222	.750	5-2-0	.714	2
1992	17	15	9-3-1	335	211	.731	6-2-0	.750	2

Mike O'Cain (1993-1999) 41-40-0 .506

Year	Rank1	Rank2	W-L-T	PF	PA	Pct	Conf	Conf Pct	Conf
1993			7-5-0	278	327	.583	4-4-0	.500	5
1994	17	17	9-3-0	305	272	.750	6-2-0	.750	2
1995			3-8-0	260	354	.273	2-6-0	.250	7
1996			3-8-0	268	401	.273	3-5-0	.375	6
1997			6-5-0	325	268	.545	3-5-0	.375	6
1998			7-5-0	343	302	.583	5-3-0	.625	4
1999			6-6-0	244	302	.500	3-5-0	.375	5

Chuck Amato (2000-2003) 34-17-0 .667

Year	Rank1	Rank2	W-L-T	PF	PA	Pct	Conf	Conf Pct	Conf
2000			8-4-0	341	308	.667	4-4-0	.500	5
2001			7-5-0	319	256	.583	4-4-0	.500	4
2002	12	11	11-3-0	460	238	.786	5-3-0	.625	4
2003			8-5-0	489	385	.615	4-4-0	.500	4

Won-loss record by decades:

Decade	Record	Pct	Decade	Record	Pct	Decade	Record	Pct
1892-99	7-9-3	.447	1930-39	33-55-8	.385	1970-79	66-45-5	.591
1900-09	36-19-10	.631	1940-49	43-48-6	.474	1980-89	52-59-2	.469
1910-19	40-25-5	.607	1950-59	31-64-5	.335	1990-99	66-51-1	.564
1920-29	40-50-7	.448	1960-69	55-44-3	.554	2000-03	34-17-0	.667

Historic record 503-486-55 .508

Post-season won-loss record: 11-10-1 .523

1947: Gator Bowl, Oklahoma 34, NC State 13
1963: Liberty Bowl, Mississippi State 16, NC State 12
1967: Liberty Bowl, NC State 14, Georgia 7
1972: Peach Bowl, NC State 49, West Virginia 13
1973: Liberty Bowl, NC State 31, Kansas 18
1974: Astro Bluebonnet Bowl, NC State 31, Houston 31
1975: Peach Bowl, West Virginia 13, NC State 10
1977: Peach Bowl, NC State 24, Iowa State 14
1978: Tangerine Bowl, NC State 30, Pittsburgh 17
1986: Peach Bowl, Virginia Tech 25, NC State 24
1988: Peach Bowl, NC State 28, Iowa 23

1989: Copper Bowl, Arizona 17, NC State 10
1990: All American Bowl, NC State 31, Southern Miss. 27
1991: Peach Bowl, East Carolina 37, NC State 34
1992: Gator Bowl, Florida 27, NC State 10
1993: Hall of Fame Bowl, Michigan 42, NC State 7
1994: Peach Bowl, NC State 28, Mississippi State 24
1998: Micron PC Bowl: Miami 46, NC State 23
2000: Micronpc.com Bowl, NC State 38, Minnesota 10
2001: Tangerine Bowl, Pittsburgh 34, NC State 19
2003: Gator Bowl, NC State 28, Notre Dame 6
2003: Tangerine Bowl, NC State 56, Kansas 26

College Football Hall of Fame:
Buck Shaw, coach, 1924; Jack McDowall, halfback, 1925-27; Roman Gabriel, quarterback, 1959-61; Jim Richter, center, 1976-79.

Awards: Outland Trophy, 1979, Jim Richter.

UNIVERSITY OF NORTH CAROLINA, Chapel Hill, North Carolina; nickname "Tar Heels"; colors Carolina blue and white; Kenan Memorial Stadium (60,000); Atlantic Coast Conference. North Carolina began play in 1888 and joined the Southern Conference as a founding member in 1922. UNC remained a member of the Southern Conference through the 1952 season. In 1953, North Carolina joined with several other SC members to form the Atlantic Coast Conference. Beginning in the 1953 season, North Carolina has played in the ACC.

Early years (1888-1921)

Year	Coach	W-L-T	PF	PA	Pct.	Year	Coach	W-L-T	PF	PA	Pct.
1888	none	0-2-0	4	22	.000	1905	William Warner	4-3-1	82	90	.562
1889	Hector Cowan	2-2-0	58	43	.500	1906	W. S. Keinholz	1-4-2	18	83	.286
1890	no team					1907	Otis Lamson	4-4-1	93	97	.500
1891	no coach	0-2-0	4	6	.000	1908	Edward Green	3-3-3	62	71	.500
1892	no coach	5-1-0	196	30	.833	1909	A. E. Brides	5-2-0	54	18	.714
1893	no coach	3-4-0	152	66	.429	1910	A. E. Brides	3-6-0	70	67	.333
1894	V. K. Irvine	6-3-0	178	71	.667	1911	Branch Bocock	6-1-1	66	31	.812
1895	T. C. Trenchard	7-1-1	146	17	.833	1912	William Martin	3-4-1	85	168	.438
1896	Gordon Johnson	3-4-1	106	100	.438	1913	T. C. Trenchard	5-4-0	91	76	.556
1897	W. A. Reynolds	7-3-0	150	53	.700	1914	T. C. Trenchard	10-1-0	359	52	.909
1898	W. A. Reynolds	9-0-0	201	8	1.000	1915	T. C. Trenchard	4-3-1	105	98	.562
1899	W. A. Reynolds	7-3-1	173	58	.682	1916	Thomas Campbell	5-4-0	134	93	.556
1900	W.A. Reynolds	4-1-3	162	22	.688	1917	no team				
1901	Charles Jenkins	7-2-0	198	45	.778	1918	no team				
1902	H. B. Olcott	5-1-3	122	34	.722	1919	Thomas Campbell	4-3-1	49	94	.562
1903	H. B. Olcott	6-3-0	137	72	.667	1920	Myron Fuller	2-6-0	16	91	.250
1904	Robert Brown	5-2-2	170	34	.667						

Bob & Bill Fetzer (1921-1925) 30-12-4 .696

Year	Nat'l AP Other	Overall W-L-T	PF	PA	Pct	Conference W-L-T	Pct.	Rank	Year	Nat'l AP Other	Overall W-L-T	PF	PA	Pct.	Conference W-L-T	Pct.	Rank
1921		5-2-2	85	75	.667												

Member of the Southern Conference (1922-1952) 96-53-17 .630

| 1922 | | 9-1-0 | 200 | 72 | .900 | 5-0-0 | 1.000 | 1 | 1924 | | 4-5-0 | 38 | 57 | .444 | 2-3-0 | .400 | 14 |
| 1923 | | 5-3-1 | 77 | 85 | .611 | 2-2-1 | .500 | 12 | 1925 | | 7-1-1 | 123 | 20 | .833 | 4-0-1 | .900 | 2 |

Chuck Collins (1926-1933) 38-31-9 .545

1926		4-5-0	59	74	.444	3-3-0	.500	10	1930		5-3-2	153	103	.600	4-2-2	.625	8
1927		4-6-0	86	107	.400	2-5-0	.286	18	1931		4-3-3	114	92	.550	2-3-3	.438	13
1928		5-3-2	186	115	.600	2-2-2	.500	9	1932		3-5-2	84	142	.400	2-5-1	.312	17
1929		9-1-0	346	60	.900	7-1-0	.875	3	1933		4-5-0	71	90	.444	2-1-0	.667	3

Carl Snavely (1934-1935, 1945-1952) 59-35-5 .621

| 1934 | | 7-1-1 | 125 | 34 | .833 | 2-0-1 | .833 | 2 | 1935 | | 8-1-0 | 270 | 44 | .889 | 4-1-0 | .800 | 2 |

Ray Wolf (1936-1941) 38-17-3 .681

1936		8-2-0	190	100	.800	5-1-0	.833	2	1939		8-1-1	228	52	.850	5-1-0	.833	3
1937	19	7-1-1	173	39	.833	4-0-1	.900	2	1940		6-4-0	159	98	.600	3-2-0	.600	5
1938		6-2-1	117	37	.722	4-1-0	.800	4	1941		3-7-0	130	172	.300	2-4-0	.333	11

Jim Tatum (1942, 1956-1958) 19-17-3 .526

| 1942 | | 5-2-2 | 149 | 102 | .667 | 3-1-1 | .700 | 4 | | | | | | | | | |

Tom Young (1943) 6-3-0 .667

| 1943 | | 6-3-0 | 173 | 93 | .667 | 2-2-0 | .500 | 5 | | | | | | | | | |

Gene McEver (1944) 1-7-1 .167

| 1944 | | 1-7-1 | 33 | 173 | .167 | 0-3-1 | .125 | 9 | | | | | | | | | |

Carl Snavely (1945-1952)

1945		5-5-0	113	149	.500	2-2-0	.500	7	1949	16	7-4-0	190	205	.636	5-0-0	1.000	1
1946	9	8-2-1	271	129	.773	4-0-1	.900	1	1950		3-5-2	101	122	.400	3-2-1	.583	7
1947	9	8-2-0	210	93	.800	4-1-0	.800	2	1951		2-8-0	120	224	.200	2-3-0	.400	10
1948	3	9-1-1	261	94	.864	4-0-1	.900	2	1952		2-6-0	110	206	.250	1-2-0	.333	10

Member of the Atlantic Coast Conference (1953-2003) 180-160-5 .529

George Barclay (1953-1955) 11-18-1 .383

| 1953 | | 4-6-0 | 173 | 187 | .500 | 2-3-0 | .400 | 3 | 1955 | | 3-7-0 | 117 | 218 | .300 | 3-3-0 | .500 | 4 |
| 1954 | | 4-5-1 | 140 | 222 | .450 | 4-2-0 | .667 | 3 | | | | | | | | | |

Jim Tatum (1956-1958)

| 1956 | | 2-7-1 | 99 | 183 | .250 | 2-3-1 | .417 | 5 | 1958 | | 6-4-0 | 195 | 109 | .400 | 4-3-0 | .571 | 4 |
| 1957 | | 6-4-0 | 142 | 129 | .600 | 4-3-0 | .571 | 3 | | | | | | | | | |

Jim Hickey (1959-1966) 36-45-0 .444

1959		5-5-0	198	142	.500	5-2-0	.714	2	1963	19	9-2-0	197	103	.818	6-1-0	.857	1
1960		3-7-0	117	161	.300	2-5-0	.286	6	1964		5-5-0	178	135	.500	4-3-0	.571	3
1961		5-5-0	121	141	.500	4-3-0	.571	2	1965		4-6-0	146	195	.400	3-3-0	.500	5
1962		3-7-0	112	206	.300	3-4-0	.429	4	1966		2-8-0	90	196	.200	1-4-0	.200	8

Bill Dooley (1967-1977) 69-53-2 .565

Year			Record	PF	PA	Pct	Conf	Pct	Fin
1967			2-8-0	104	182	.200	2-5-0	.286	7
1968			3-7-0	178	272	.300	1-6-0	.143	8
1969			5-5-0	200	164	.500	3-3-0	.500	3
1970			8-4-0	372	228	.667	5-2-0	.714	2
1971	18		9-3-0	288	152	.750	6-0-0	1.000	1
1972	12	14	11-1-0	324	210	.917	6-0-0	1.000	1
1973			4-7-0	242	266	.364	1-5-0	.167	6
1974			7-5-0	364	279	.583	4-2-0	.667	2
1975			3-7-1	207	272	.318	1-4-1	.250	6
1976			9-3-0	243	220	.750	4-1-0	.800	2
1977	17	14	8-3-1	251	102	.773	5-0-1	.917	1

Dick Crum (1978-1987) 72-41-3 .634

Year			Record	PF	PA	Pct	Conf	Pct	Fin
1978			5-6-0	199	218	.455	3-3-0	.500	4
1979	15	14	8-3-1	290	167	.708	3-3-0	.500	5
1980	10	9	11-1-0	297	130	.917	6-0-0	1.000	1
1981	9	8	10-2-0	375	150	.833	5-1-0	.833	2
1982	18	13	8-4-0	348	149	.667	3-3-0	.500	3
1983			8-4-0	337	216	.667	4-2-0	.667	2
1984			5-5-1	234	274	.500	3-2-1	.583	3
1985			5-6-0	224	223	.455	3-4-0	.429	5
1986			7-4-1	305	279	.583	5-2-0	.714	2
1987			5-6-0	214	207	.455	3-4-0	.429	6

Mack Brown (1988-1997) 69-46-1 .599

Year			Record	PF	PA	Pct	Conf	Pct	Fin
1988			1-10-0	217	391	.091	1-6-0	.143	7
1989			1-10-0	138	297	.091	0-7-0	.000	8
1990			6-4-1	227	186	.591	3-3-1	.500	5
1991			7-4-0	282	199	.364	3-4-0	.429	5
1992	19	18	9-3-0	289	233	.750	5-3-0	.625	3
1993	19	21	10-3-0	431	253	.769	6-2-0	.750	2
1994		21	8-4-0	374	267	.667	5-3-0	.625	3
1995			7-5-0	284	220	.583	4-4-0	.500	5
1996	10	10	10-2-0	357	123	.833	6-2-0	.750	2
1997*	6	4	10-1-0	306	143	.909	7-1-0	.875	*

Carl Torbush (1997-2000) 17-18-0 .486

Year			Record	PF	PA	Pct	Conf	Pct	Fin
1997*			1-0-0	42	3	1.000	0-0-0		2
1998			7-5-0	288	283	.583	5-3-0	.625	4
1999			3-8-0	186	272	.273	2-6-0	.250	9
2000			6-5-0	269	284	.545	3-5-0	.375	6

*Brown coached the first eleven games of the 1997 season, and Torbush coached the last game.

John Bunting (2001-2003) 13-24-0 .351

Year			Record	PF	PA	Pct	Conf	Pct	Fin
2001			8-5-0	337	271	.615	5-3-0	.625	3
2002			3-9-0	223	421	.250	1-7-0	.125	8
2003			2-10-0	317	459	.167	1-7-0	.125	9

Won-loss record by decades:

Decade	Record	Pct	Decade	Record	Pct	Decade	Record	Pct
1888-89	2-4-0	.333	1930-39	60-24-11	.689	1980-89	61-52-2	.548
1890-99	47-21-3	.683	1940-49	58-37-5	.605	1990-99	78-39-1	.665
1900-09	44-25-15	.613	1950-59	37-57-4	.398	2000-03	19-29-0	.396
1910-19	40-26-4	.600	1960-69	41-60-0	.406			
1920-29	54-33-6	.613	1970-79	72-42-3	.579			

Historic record: 613-449-54 .573

Post-season won-loss record 12-12-0 .500

1947: Sugar Bowl, Georgia 20, UNC 10
1949: Sugar Bowl, Oklahoma 14, UNC 6
1950: Cotton Bowl, Rice 27, UNC 13
1963: Gator Bowl, UNC 35, Air Force 0
1970: Peach Bowl, Arizona State 48, UNC 26
1971: Gator Bowl, Georgia 7, UNC 3
1972: Sun Bowl, UNC 32, Texas Tech 28
1974: Sun Bowl, Mississippi State 26, UNC 24
1976: Peach Bowl, Kentucky 21, UNC 0
1977: Liberty Bowl, Nebraska 21, UNC 17
1979: Gator Bowl, UNC 17, Michigan 15
1980: Bluebonnet Bowl, UNC 16, Texas 7
1981: Gator Bowl, UNC 31, Arkansas 27
1982: Sun Bowl, UNC 26, Texas 10
1983: Peach Bowl, Florida State 28, UNC 3
1986: Aloha Bowl, Arizona 30, UNC 21
1993: Peach Bowl, UNC 21, Mississippi State 17
1993: Gator Bowl, Alabama 24, UNC 10
1994: Sun Bowl, Texas 35, UNC 31
1995: Carquest Bowl, UNC 20, Arkansas 10
1997: Gator Bowl, UNC 20, West Virginia 13
1998: Gator Bowl, UNC 42, Virginia Tech 3
1998: Las Vegas Bowl, UNC 20, San Diego State 13
2001: Peach Bowl, UNC 16, Auburn 10

College Football Hall of Fame:
Hunter Carpenter, halfback, 1900-05; Carl Snavely, coach, 1934-35, 1945-52; Jim Tatum, coach, 1942, 1956-58; Barney Poole, end, 1942-48; Choo Choo Justice, halfback, 1946-49; Art Weiner, end, 1946-49; Don McCauley, halfback, 1968-70.

Awards: Lou Groza Award: 1996, Mark Primanti; Bednarik Award: 2001, Julius Peppers; Lombardi Award: 2001, Julius Peppers.

NORTH TEXAS UNIVERSITY, Denton, Texas; nickname "Eagles" and "Mean Green"; colors green and white; Fouts Field (30,500); Sun Belt Conference. North Texas began play in 1913 as an independent. It joined the TIAA (Texas Intercollegiate Athletic Association) in 1922 and played in that conference until the 1932 season when it moved to the Lone Star Conference. In 1949, North Texas moved to the Gulf Coast Conference where it played through the 1956 season. In 1957, North Texas became a member of the Missouri Valley Conference and played there until the 1975 season, when it opted for independent status once again. In 1983, North Texas joined the Southland Conference, playing there through the 1994 season. In 1995, North Texas left the Southland Conference for Division I-A independent status. In 1996, North Texas began play in the Big West Conference. When that conference disbanded after 2000 season, North Texas moved to the newly organized Sun Belt Conference.

Early years as an independent (1913-1921)

Year	W-L-T	PF	PA	Pct.	Year	W-L-T	PF	PA	Pct.

J. W. Pender (1913-1914) 3-4-0 .429

| 1913 | 0-1-0 | 0 | 40 | .000 | 1914 | 3-3-0 | 56 | 87 | .500 |

J. W. St. Clair (1915-1919) 20-10-2 .656

1915	4-1-0	148	6	.800	1918	1-2-1	39	58	.375
1916	4-3-1	125	74	.562	1919	5-3-0	233	64	.625
1917	6-1-0	146	42	.857					

Theron Fouts (1920-1924) 23-14-2 .615

| 1920 | 7-1-0 | 227 | 44 | .875 | 1921 | 3-3-0 | 135 | 57 | .500 |

Member of the TIAA (1922-1931) 46-38-8 .543

	Nat'; AP Other	Overall W-L-T	PF	PA	Pct.	Conference W-L-T	Pct.	Rank		Nat'l AP Other	Overall W-L-T	PF	PA	Pct.	Conference W-L-T	Pct.	Rank
Year									Year								
1922		5-2-1	85	156	.688	3-0-0	1.000	1	1924		5-3-1	67	64	.611	4-1-1	.750	2
1923		3-5-0	63	136	.375	3-1-0	.750	2									

John Reid (1925-1928) 16-18-3 .473

| 1925 | | 6-4-0 | 111 | 121 | .600 | 4-2-0 | .667 | 4 | 1927 | | 1-6-2 | 31 | 224 | .222 | 0-3-2 | .200 | 8 |
| 1926 | | 5-3-1 | 99 | 104 | .611 | 4-1-0- | .800 | 2 | 1928 | | 4-5-0 | 88 | 139 | .444 | 2-2-0 | .500 | 5 |

Jack Sisco (1929-1941) 74-37-10 .653

| 1929 | | 4-3-2 | 178 | 76 | .556 | 3-0-1 | .875 | 2 | 1931 | | 8-3-0 | 175 | 72 | .727 | 4-0-0 | 1.000 | 1 |
| 1930 | | 5-4-1 | 87 | 136 | .550 | 4-1-0 | .800 | 3 | | | | | | | | | |

Member of the Lone Star Conference (1932-1948) 83-41-8 .659

1932		8-1-1	169	33	.850	5-0-0	1.000	1	1937		4-4-2	74	83	.500	2-1-1	.625	2
1933		3-4-2	49	50	.444	3-1-1	.700	3	1938		7-4-0	190	92	.636	2-2-0	.500	3
1934		5-4-0	50	79	.556	2-2-0	.500	2	1939		6-1-0	116	42	.857	4-0-0	1.000	1
1935		5-3-1	134	93	.611	3-1-0	.750	1	1940		6-3-0	199	79	.667	4-0-0	1.000	1
1936		6-2-1	125	38	.722	4-0-0	1.000	1	1941		7-1-0	165	77	.875	4-0-0	1.000	1

Lloyd Russell (1942) 3-5-0 .375

| 1942 | | 3-5-0 | 123 | 129 | .375 | 1-2-0 | .333 | 3 | | | | | | | | | |

No team (1943-1945)

Odus Mitchell (1946-1966) 122-85-9 .586

| 1946 | | 7-3-1 | 127 | 102 | .682 | 3-1-0 | .750 | 1 | 1948 | | 6-4-0 | 249 | 133 | .600 | 3-2-0 | .600 | 2 |
| 1947 | | 10-2-0 | 256 | 77 | .833 | 6-0-0 | 1.000 | 1 | | | | | | | | | |

Member of the Gulf Coast Conference (1949-1956) 49-31-4 .607

1949		8-4-0	336	192	.667	2-1-0	.667	2	1953		3-6-1	167	167	.350	1-1-0	.500	2
1950		7-2-1	266	173	.750	1-1-1	.500	1	1954		4-6-0	151	176	.400	1-1-0	.500	2
1951		8-4-0	434	132	.667	2-0-0	1.000	1	1955		5-4-1	197	159	.550	2-0-1	.833	1
1952		7-3-0	276	137	.700	2-0-0	1.000	1	1956		7-2-1	188	131	.750	2-0-1	.833	1

Member of the Missouri Valley Conference (1957-1974) 39-33-1 .541

1957		5-5-0	191	150	.500	2-2-0	.500	2	1962		6-4-0	174	182	.600	2-1-0	.667	2
1958		7-2-1	197	93	.750	2-1-1	.625	1	1963		3-6-0	108	195	.333	2-2-0	.500	3
1959		9-2-0	303	103	.818	3-1-0	.750	1	1964		2-7-1	78	172	.250	1-3-0	.250	4
1960		2-6-1	107	208	.278	0-3-0	.000	4	1965		3-7-0	186	312	.300	2-2-0	.500	3
1961		5-4-1	162	206	.550	1-2-0	.333	2	1966		8-2-0	298	120	.800	3-1-0	.750	1

Rod Rust (1967-1972) 29-32-1 .476

1967		7-1-1	278	138	.833	4-0-0	1.000	1	1970		3-8-0	173	227	.273	1-3-0	.250	4
1968		8-2-0	297	184	.800	4-1-0	.800	2	1971		3-8-0	155	321	.273	3-2-0	.600	2
1969		7-3-0	316	174	.700	4-1-0	.800	2	1972		1-10-0	148	354	.091	0-7-0	.000	8

Hayden Fry (1973-1978) 40-23-3 .629

| 1973 | | 5-5-1 | 153 | 243 | .500 | 5-1-0 | .833 | 1 | 1974 | | 2-7-2 | 154 | 239 | .273 | 1-3-2 | .333 | 6 |

North Texas moves to I-A independent status (1975-1982)

| 1975 | | 7-4-0 | 200 | 210 | .636 | | | | 1977 | 16 | 10-1-0 | 320 | 179 | .909 | | | |
| 1976 | | 7-4-0 | 232 | 145 | .636 | | | | 1978 | | 9-2-0 | 277 | 150 | .818 | | | |

Jerry Moore (1979-1980) 11-11-0 .500

| 1979 | | 5-6-0 | 182 | 235 | .455 | | | | 1980 | | 6-5-0 | 268 | 252 | .545 | | | |

Bob Tyler (1981) 2-9-0 .182

| 1981 | | 2-9-0 | 111 | 235 | .182 | | | | | | | | | | | | |

                          Corky Nelson (1982-1990) 48-52-1 .480
```
1982        2-9-0  179 283  .182
                          Member of the Southland Conference (1983-1994) 36-36-2  .500
1983        8-4-0  276 137  .667  5-1-0  .833  1    1987      7-5-0  242 247  .583  5-1-0  .833  2
1984        2-9-0   86 211  .182  1-5-0  .167  6    1988      8-4-0  330 174  .667  4-2-0  .667  3
1985        4-6-1  150 203  .409  2-3-1  .417  5    1989      5-6-0  217 253  .455  2-4-0  .333  5
1986        6-4-0  222 204  .600  3-2-0  .600  2    1990      6-5-0  193 211  .545  2-4-0  .333  6
                          Dennis Parker (1991-1993) 11-21-1  .348
1991        3-7-1  135 327  .318  2-5-0  .286  6    1993      4-7-0  328 365  .364  2-5-0  .286  5
1992        4-7-0  246 254  .364  3-4-0  .429  5
                          Matt Simon (1994-1997) 18-26-1  .411
1994        7-4-1  343 261  .625  5-0-1  .917  1
                  North Texas converts to I-A independent status (1995)
1995        2-9-0  200 424  .182
                  Member of the Big West Conference (1996-2000) 10-16-0  .385
1996        5-6-0  161 293  .455  3-2-0  .600  3    1997      4-7-0  232 331  .364  2-3-0  .400  4
                          Darrell Dickey (1998-2003) 30-40-0  .429
1998        3-8-0  173 297  .273  3-2-0  .600  3    2000      3-8-0  162 300  .273  1-4-0  .200  4
1999        2-9-0  118 291  .182  1-5-0  .167  7
                  Member of the Sun Belt Conference (2001-2003) 18-1-0  .947
2001        5-6-0  255 248  .455  5-1-0  .833  1    2003      9-4-0  358 285  .692  7-0-0  1.000  1
2001        8-5-0  249 192  .615  6-0-0  1.000  1
```

Won-loss record by decades:

1913-19	23-14-2	.615	1950-59	62-36-5	.626	1980-89	50-61-1	.451
1920-29	43-35-7	.547	1960-69	51-42-4	.546	1990-99	40-69-2	.369
1930-39	57-30-8	.642	1970-79	52-55-3	.486	2000-03	25-23-0	.521
1940-49	47-22-1	.679						

Historic record 450-387-33 .536

Post-season won-loss record: 2-8-0 .200

1946: Optimist Bowl, North Texas 14, Pacific 13
1948: Salad Bowl, Nevada 13, North Texas 6
1959: Sun Bowl, New Mexico State 28, North Texas 8
1983: Division I-AA Playoffs, Nevada 20, North Texas 17
1987: I-AA Playoffs, NE Louisiana 30, North Texas 9

1988: I-AA Playoffs, Marshall 7, North Texas 0
1994: I-AA Playoffs, Boise State 24, North Texas 20
2001: New Orleans Bowl, Colorado State 45, North Texas 20
2002: New Orleans Bowl, North Texas 34, Cincinnati 19
2003: New Orleans Bowl, Memphis 27, North Texas 17

College Football Hall of Fame:
Mean Joe Greene, tackle, 1966-68; Hayden Fry, coach, 1973-78.

NORTHERN ILLINOIS UNIVERSITY, DeKalb, Illinois; nickname "Huskies"; colors cardinal and black; Huskies Stadium (31,000); Mid-American Conference. Northern Illinois began play in 1899. It joined the Mid-American Conference in 1975 and played there through the 1986 season. Northern Illinois played as a Division I-A independent from 1987 through the 1992 season. In 1993, Northern Illinois joined the Big West Conference. It left that conference after the 1995 season and operated as an independent for the 1996 season, rejoining the MAC beginning with the 1997 season.

Year	W-L-T	PF	PA	Pct.		Year	W-L-T	PF	PA	Pct
						John Keith (1899-1903) 17-7-5 .672				
1899	1-0-2	21	15	.667		1902	5-1-1	75	16	.786
1900	2-2-2	50	50	.500		1903	3-3-0	44	43	.500
1901	6-1-0	108	18	.857						
						Dixie Fleager (1904) 5-0-0 1.000				
1904	5-0-0	90	17	1.000						
						Harry Sauthoff (1905) 3-1-1 .700				
1905	3-1-1	25	12	.700						
						Nelson Kellogg (1906-1909) 8-17-3 .339				
1906	4-2-1	38	23	.643		1908	1-5-1	31	81	.214
1907	1-4-1	67	63	.250		1909	2-6-0	74	171	.150
						William Wirtz (1910-1916) 33-17-0 .636				
1910	4-2-1	67	39	.643		1914	7-0-1	148	13	.938
1911	8-1-2	196	84	.818		1915	2-5-1	81	210	.312
1912	3-5-0	114	167	.625		1916	6-1-1	105	19	.812
1913	3-3-3	56	236	.500						
						No team (1917-1919)				
						Paul Harrison (1920-1922) 11-14-1 .442				
1920	3-5-0	153	93	.375		1922	5-4-1	138	94	.550
1921	3-5-0	193	168	.375						
						William Muir (1923-1925) 11-9-3 .543				
1923	1-4-3	73	171	.312		1925	6-1-0	52	5	.857
1924	4-4-0	156	85	.500						
						Roland Cowell (1926-1928) 6-11-3 .375				
1926	5-1-1	71	26	.786		1928	0-6-1	12	139	.072
1927	1-4-1	49	92	.250						
						George Evans (1929-1954) 132-70-20 .640				
1929	6-1-1	124	24	.812		1942	4-2-2	75	75	.625
1930	6-2-1	152	60	.722		1943	4-1-1	117	53	.750
1931	5-3-0	76	59	.625		1944	7-0-0	113	48	1.000
1932	4-2-1	76	27	.643		1945	4-3-0	110	70	.571
1933	5-4-0	113	58	.556		1946	9-2-0	207	99	.818
1934	5-1-2	109	42	.750		1947	4-3-3	131	97	.550
1935	7-1-1	201	20	.833		1948	6-4-0	175	147	.600
1936	4-3-1	60	59	.562		1949	7-2-1	273	157	.750
1937	3-2-3	53	40	.562		1950	3-6-0	193	256	.333
1938	6-1-1	133	34	.812		1951	9-0-0	223	101	1.000
1939	5-2-1	96	44	.688		1952	3-6-0	110	194	.333
1940	6-3-0	115	116	.667		1953	1-8-0	74	255	.111
1941	7-1-1	167	45	.833		1954	2-7-0	79	187	.222
						Robert Kahler (1955) 0-8-1 .056				
1955	0-8-1	31	233	.056						
						Howard Fletcher (1956-1968) 74-48-1 .606				
1956	1-8-0	46	188	.111		1963	10-0-0	337	97	1.000
1957	2-7-0	132	268	.222		1964	7-2-0	190	131	.778
1958	4-5-0	184	184	.444		1965	9-1-0	290	147	.900
1959	7-2-0	246	124	.778		1966	8-2-0	293	153	.800
1960	7-2-0	217	126	.778		1967	5-5-0	162	198	.500
1961	4-4-1	159	129	.500		1968	2-8-0	154	258	.200
1962	8-2-0	274	87	.800						
						Richard Urich (1969-1970) 6-14-0 .300				
1969	3-7-0	191	284	.300		1970	3-7-0	168	281	.300
						Jerry Ippoliti (1971-1975) 25-29-1 .464				
1971	5-5-1	202	232	.500		1973	6-5-0	327	270	.545
1972	7-4-0	198	141	.636		1974	4-7-0	186	261	.364

Member of the Mid-American Conference (1975-1986, 1997-2003) 63-71-2 .471

	Nat'l		Overall						Nat'l		Overall					
Year	AP	UP	W-L-T	PF	PA	Pct.	W-L-T	Pct. Rank	Year	AP	UP	W-L-T	PF	PA	Pct.	W-L-T	Pct. Rank
1975			3-8-0	193	230	.273	2-3-0	.400 7									

Pat Culpepper (1976-1979) 14-29-1 .330

Year	Record	PF	PA	Pct	Conf	Pct	Fin	Year	Record	PF	PA	Pct	Conf	Pct	Fin
1976	1-10-0	56	366	.091	0-6-0	.000	10	1978	5-6-0	232	284	.455	2-4-0	.333	7
1977	3-8-0	138	249	.273	2-5-0	.286	8	1979	5-5-1	177	206	.500	3-3-1	.500	4

Bill Mallory (1980-1983) 25-19-0 .568

1980	7-4-0	216	175	.636	4-3-0	.571	3	1982	5-5-0	137	136	.500	5-4-0	.556	5
1981	3-8-0	160	217	.273	2-7-0	.222	9	1983	10-2-0	314	203	.833	8-1-0	.889	1

Lee Corso (1984) 4-6-1 .409

1984	4-6-1	153	188	.409	3-5-1	.389	5

Jerry Pettibone (1985-1990) 33-32-1 .508

1985	4-7-0	174	259	.364	4-4-0	.500	4

Northern Illinois leaves the MAC and operates as an independent (1986-1992)

1986	2-9-0	144	308	.182	1989	9-2-0	344	269	.818
1987	5-5-1	305	262	.500	1990	6-5-0	333	260	.545
1988	7-4-0	155	185	.636					

Charlie Sadler (1991-1995) 18-37-0 .327

1991	2-9-0	143	364	.182	1992	5-6-0	203	193	.455

Member of the Big West Conference (1993-1995) 9-9-0 .500

1993	4-7-0	227	334	.364	3-3-0	.500	5	1995	3-8-0	220	420	.273	3-3-0	.500	4
1994	4-7-0	301	294	.364	3-3-0	.500	5								

Northern Illinois leaves the Big West, and operates as an independent (1996)

Joe Novak (1996-2003) 38-52-0 .422

1996	1-10-0	157	400	.091

Member of the Mid-American Conference (1997-2003) 28-26-0 .519

1997	0-11-0	129	382	.000	0-8-0	.000	12	2000	6-5-0	369	280	.545	4-3-0	.571	7
1998	2-9-0	160	329	.182	2-6-0	.250	10	2001	6-5-0	303	292	.545	4-3-0	.571	6
1999	5-6-0	289	289	.455	5-3-0	.625	4	2002	8-4-0	375	298	.667	7-1-0	.875	2
								2003	10-2-0	386	258	.833	6-2-0	.750	3

Won-loss record by decades:

1899-09	33-25-9	.560	1940-49	58-21-8	.713	1980-89	56-52-2	.518
1910-19	33-17-9	.636	1950-59	32-57-1	.361	1990-99	32-78-0	.291
1920-29	34-35-8	.494	1960-69	63-33-1	.655	2000-03	30-16-0	.652
1930-39	50-21-11	.677	1970-79	42-65-2	.434			

Historic record: 463-420-51 .523

Post-season won-loss record: 2-4-0 .333

1946: Turkey Bowl, Evansville 19, NIU 7
1947: Refrigerator Bowl, Evansville 20, NIU 0
1962: Mineral Water Bowl, Adams State 23, NIU 20

1963: Mineral Water Bowl, NIU 21, SW Missouri State 14
1965: Mineral Water Bowl, North Dakota 37, NIU 20
1983: California Bowl, NIU 20, Cal State Fullerton 13.

College Football Hall of Fame:
George Bork, quarterback, 1960-63.

NORTHWESTERN UNIVERSITY, Evanston, Illinois; nickname "Wildcats"; colors purple and white; Ryan Field (47,130); Big Ten Conference. Northwestern began play in 1882 and was one of the founding members of the Big Ten in 1896. Northwestern dropped out of football in 1906 and 1907, in part because of complaints about the brutality of the game raised by President Theodore Roosevelt, and in part because of economic problems. The Wildcats returned to Big Ten play in 1908. In calculating conference win-percents prior to 1946, ties are ignored as per Big Ten rules for that period.

Early years (1882-1895)

Year	Coach	W-L-T	PF	PA	Pct.	Year	Coach	W-L-T	PF	PA	Pct.
1882	none	1-1-0	not available		.500	1890	none	3-1-1	60	44	.700
1882	no team					1891	Knowlton Ames	1-2-3	38	72	.417
1883-1885	no known results					1892	Knowlton Ames	5-3-2	126	92	.600
1886	none	0-1-0	not available		.000	1893	Paul Noyes	2-5-3	92	176	.350
1887	none	0-0-0	no outside games			1894	A. A. Ewing	1-5-0	18	222	.167
1888	none	2-1-0	32	30	.667	1895	Alvin Culver	7-5-0	214	132	.583
1889	none	2-2-0	42	38	.500						

Member of the Big Ten Conference (1896-2003) 221-429-21 .345

Year	Nat'l AP	Other	W-L-T	PF	PA	Pct.	Conf W-L-T	Conf Pct.	Rank	Year	Nat'l AP	Other	W-L-T	PF	PA	Pct.	Conf W-L-T	Conf Pct.	Rank
Alvin Culver (1895-1896) 13-6-2 .667																			
1896			6-1-2	159	46	.778	2-1-1	.667	2										
Jesse Van Doozer (1897) 4-3-0 .571																			
1897			4-3-0	65	55	.571	0-2-0	.000	7										
W. H. Bannard (1898) 7-4-0 .636																			
1898			7-4-0	202	106	.636	0-4-0	000	6										
C. M. Hollister (1899-1902) 25-16-4 .600																			
1899			6-6-0	120	172	.500	2-2-0	.500	3	1901			8-2-1	153	77	.773	3-2-0	.600	5
1900			6-2-3	94	43	.682	2-1-2	.667	3	1902			5-6-0	72	117	.455	0-4-0	.000	8
Walter Cornack (1903-1905) 25-6-4 .771																			
1903			9-2-3	217	67	.750	1-0-2	1.000	1	1905			8-2-1	214	122	.773	0-2-0	.000	6
1904			8-2-0	312	55	.800	1-2-0	.333	5										
No team (1906-1907)																			
Alton Johnson (1908) 2-2-0 .500																			
1908			2-2-0	72	90	.500	0-2-0	.000	6										
Bill Horr (1909) 1-3-1 .300																			
1909			1-3-1	25	95	.300	1-3-0	.250	5										
Charles Hammett (1910-1912) 6-10-2 .389																			
1910			1-3-1	10	45	.300	1-2-1	.333	5	1912			2-3-1	32	87	.417	2-3-0	.400	5
1911			3-4-0	60	70	.429	1-4-0	.200	7										
Dennis Grady (1913) 1-6-0 .143																			
1913			1-6-0	36	242	.143	0-6-0	.000	9										
Fred J. Murphy (1914-1918) 16-16-1 500																			
1914			1-6-0	13	176	.143	0-6-0	.000	9	1917			5-2-0	145	85	714	3-2-0	.600	3
1915			2-5-0	69	112	.286	0-5-0	.000	9	1918			2-2-1	75	61	.500	1-1-0	.500	6
1916			6-1-0	144	55	.857	4-1-0	.800	2										
Charles Bachman (1919) 2-5-0 .286																			
1919			2-5-0	49	111	.286	1-4-0	.200	7										
Elmer McDevitt (1920-1921) 4-10-0 .286																			
1920			3-4-0	66	90	.429	2-3-0	.400	7	1921			1-6-0	34	120	.143	0-5-0	.000	10
Glenn Thistlewaite (1922-1926) 21-17-1 .551																			
1922			3-3-1	119	92	.500	1-3-1	.250	7	1925			5-3-0	81	69	.625	3-1-0	.750	2
1923			2-6-0	90	112	.250	0-6-0	.000	10	1926			7-1-0	179	22	.875	5-0-0	1.000	1
1924			4-4-0	109	66	.500	1-3-0	.250	7										
Dick Hanley (1927-1934) 36-26-4 .576																			
1927			4-4-0	129	98	.500	2-3-0	.400	6	1931		4	7-1-1	138	40	.833	5-1-0	.833	1
1928			5-3-0	65	43	.625	2-3-0	.400	7	1932			3-4-1	116	76	.438	2-3-1	.400	5
1929			6-3-0	172	95	.667	3-2-0	.600	2	1933			1-5-2	25	42	.250	1-4-1	.200	7
1930		4	7-1-0	182	36	.875	5-0-0	1.000	1	1934			3-5-0	64	120	.375	2-3-0	.400	5
Pappy Waldorf (1935-1946) 49-45-7 .520																			
1935			4-3-1	90	79	.562	2-3-1	.400	5	1941	11		5-3-0	173	67	.625	4-2-0	.667	4
1936	7	6	7-1-0	132	73	.875	6-0-0	1.000	1	1942			1-9-0	96	209	.100	0-6-0	.000	9
1937			4-4-0	68	40	.500	3-3-0	.500	4	1943	9		6-2-0	189	64	.750	5-1-0	.833	3
1938	17		4-2-2	93	32	.625	2-1-2	.667	3	1944			1-7-1	102	160	.167	0-5-1	.000	8
1939			3-4-1	47	67	.438	3-2-1	.600	4	1945			4-4-1	127	148	.500	3-3-1	.500	4
1940	8	11	6-2-0	170	64	.750	4-2-0	.667	3	1946			4-4-1	156	136	.500	2-3-1	.416	6
Bob Voights (1947-1954) 33-39-1 .459																			
1947			3-6-0	129	196	.333	2-4-0	.333	8	1951			5-4-0	112	124	.556	2-4-0	.333	6
1948	7		8-2-0	191	91	.800	5-1-0	.833	2	1952			2-6-1	166	252	.278	2-5-0	.286	6
1949			4-5-0	137	156	.444	3-4-0	.429	7	1953			3-6-0	166	205	.333	0-6-0	.000	10
1950			6-3-0	155	143	.667	3-3-0	.500	5	1954			2-7-0	101	142	.222	1-5-0	.167	8

Lou Sabin (1955) 0-8-1 .055

| 1955 | | 0-8-1 | 66 | 241 | .055 | 0-6-1 | .071 | 10 | | | | | | | | | |

Ara Parseghian (1956-1963) 36-35-1 .507

1956		4-4-1	107	112	.500	3-3-1	.500	6	1960		5-4-0	107	103	.556	2-4-0	.333	5
1957		0-9-0	57	271	.000	0-7-0	.000	9	1961		4-5-0	131	105	.444	2-4-0	.333	7
1958	17	5-4-0	199	148	.556	3-4-0	.429	7	1962	16	7-2-0	237	158	.778	4-2-0	.667	3
1959		6-3-0	174	134	.667	4-3-0	.571	5	1963		5-4-0	162	124	.556	3-4-0	.429	5

Alex Agase (1964-1972) 32-58-1 .357

1964		3-6-0	95	164	.333	2-5-0	.286	7	1969		3-7-0	137	306	.300	3-4-0	.429	5
1965		4-6-0	141	208	.400	3-4-0	.429	6	1970		6-4-0	233	161	.600	6-1-0	.857	2
1966		3-6-1	137	213	.350	2-4-1	.357	7	1971		7-4-0	211	183	.636	6-3-0	.667	2
1967		3-7-0	149	213	.300	2-5-0	.286	8	1972		2-9-0	146	290	.182	1-8-0	.111	10
1968		1-9-0	109	325	.100	1-6-0	.143	8									

John Pont (1973-1977) 12-43-0 .218

1973		4-7-0	188	299	.364	4-4-0	.500	4	1976		1-10-0	134	311	.091	1-7-0	.125	10
1974		3-8-0	140	385	.273	2-6-0	.250	9	1977		1-10-0	102	337	.091	1-8-0	.111	10
1975		3-8-0	149	318	.273	2-6-0	.250	9									

Rick Venturi (1978-1980) 1-31-1 .045

| 1978 | | 0-10-1 | 92 | 440 | .045 | 0-8-1 | .056 | 10 | 1980 | | 0-11-0 | 151 | 444 | .000 | 0-9-0 | .000 | 10 |
| 1979 | | 1-10-0 | 115 | 386 | .091 | 0-9-0 | .000 | 10 | | | | | | | | | |

Dennis Green (1981-1985) 10-45-0 .182

1981		0-11-0	82	505	.000	0-9-0	.000	10	1984		2-9-0	138	349	.182	2-7-0	.222	9
1982		3-8-0	206	379	.273	2-7-0	.222	8	1985		3-8-0	170	332	.273	1-7-0	.125	9
1983		2-9-0	101	398	.182	2-7-0	.222	8									

Francis Peay (1986-1991) 13-51-2 .212

1986		4-7-0	217	251	.364	2-6-0	.250	8	1989		0-11-0	241	497	.000	0-8-0	.000	10
1987		2-8-1	186	328	.227	2-6-0	.250	9	1990		2-9-0	210	370	.182	1-7-0	.125	8
1988		2-8-1	192	350	.227	2-5-1	.313	9	1991		3-8-0	160	306	.273	2-6-0	.250	8

Gary Barnett (1992-1998) 35-45-1 .438

1992		3-8-0	170	373	.273	3-5-0	.375	6	1996	15	16	9-3-0	336	278	.750	7-1-0	.875	1
1993		2-9-0	185	335	.182	0-8-0	.000	10	1997			5-7-0	239	282	.417	3-5-0	.375	8
1994		3-7-1	210	351	.318	3-5-0	.375	9	1998			3-9-0	214	337	.250	0-8-0	.000	11
1995	8	7	10-2-0	311	181	.833	8-0-0	1.000	1									

Randy Walker (1999-2003) 24-35-0 .407

1999		3-8-0	141	302	.273	1-7-0	.125	10	2001		4-7-0	320	378	.364	2-6-0	.250	10
2000		8-4-0	493	350	.667	6-2-0	.750	1	2002		3-9-0	272	493	.250	1-7-0	.125	10
									2003		6-7-0	263	326	.462	4-4-0	.500	7

Won-loss record by decades:

1882-89	5-5-0	.500	1930-39	43-30-8	.580	1970-79	28-80-1	.261
1890-99	42-35-11	.540	1940-49	42-44-3	.489	1980-89	18-90-2	.173
1900-09	47-21-9	.669	1950-59	33-54-3	.383	1990-99	43-70-1	.382
1910-19	25-37-3	.408	1960-69	38-56-1	.405	2000-03	21-27-0	.438
1920-29	40-37-1	.519						

Historic record: 425-586-43 .424

Post-season won-loss record: 1-4-0 .200
1949: Rose Bowl, Northwestern 20, California 14
1996: Rose Bowl, USC 41, Northwestern 32
1997: Citrus Bowl, Tennessee 48, Northwestern 28
2000: Alamo Bowl, Nebraska 66, Northwestern 17
2003: Motor City Bowl, Bowling Green 28, Northwestern 24

College Football Hall of Fame:
Jimmy Johnson, quarterback, 1899-1905; Paddy Driscoll, halfback, 1915-16; Charlie Bachman, coach, 1919; Ralph Baker, halfback, 1924-26; Jack Riley, tackle, 1929-31; Pug Rentner, halfback, 1930-32; Eggs Manske, end, 1931-33; Steve Reid, guard, 1934-36; Pappy Waldorf, coach, 1935-46; Otto Graham, halfback, 1941-43; Alex Sarkisian, center, 1946-48; Ara Parseghian, coach, 1956-63; Ron Burton, halfback, 1957-59; Joe Delaney, halfback, 1977-80; Gary Reasons, linebacker, 1980-83.

Player Awards: Bednarik Award: 1995 and 1996, Pat Fitzgerald; Nagurski Award: 1995 and 1996, Pat Fitzgerald.

UNIVERSITY OF NOTRE DAME, Notre Dame, Indiana; nickname "Fighting Irish"; colors gold and blue; Notre Dame Stadium (80,232); independent. The Notre Dame football team has been an independent over its entire history since it began play in 1887.

Year	AP	Other (Nat'l)	W-L-T	PF	PA	Pct.	Year	AP	Other (Nat'l)	W-L-T	PF	PA	Pct
							No coach (1887-1893)						
1887			0-1-0	0	8	.000	1890-1891			no team			
1888			1-2-0	30	36	.333	1892			1-0-1	66	10	.750
1889			1-0-0	9	0	1.000.	1893			4-1-0	92	24	.800
James Morrison (1894) 3-1-1 .700													
1894			3-1-1	80	31	.700							
H. G. Hadden (1895) 3-1-0 .750													
1895			3-1-0	70	20	.750							
Frank E. Hering (1896-1898) 12-6-1 .658													
1896			4-3-0	182	50	.571	1898			4-2-0	155	34	.667
1897			4-1-1	165	40	.750							
James McWeeney (1899) 6-3-1 .650													
1899			6-3-1	169	55	.650							
Pat O'Dea (1900-1901) 14-4-2 .750													
1900			6-3-1	261	73	.650	1901			8-1-1	145	19	.850
James Faragher (1902-1903) 14-2-2 .833													
1902			6-2-1	203	51	.722	1903			8-0-1	291	0	.944
Red Salmon (1904) 5-3-0 .625													
1903			5-3-0	94	127	.625							
Henry McGlew (1905) 5-4-0 .556													
1905			5-4-0	312	80								
Thomas Barry (1906-1907) 12-1-1 .893													
1906			6-1-0	107	12	.857	1907			6-0-1	137	20	.929
Victor Place (1908) 8-1-0 .889													
1908			8-1-0	326	20	.889							
Frank Longman (1909-1910) 11-1-2 .857													
1909			7-0-1	236	14	.938	1910			4-1-1	192	25	.750
John Marks (1911-1912) 13-0-2) 933													
1911			6-0-2	222	9	.875	1912			7-0-0	389	27	1.000
Jesse Harper (1913-1917) 34-5-1 .863													
1913			7-0-0	268	41	1.000	1916			8-1-0	293	30	.889
1914			6-2-0	286	61	.750	1917			6-1-1	141	9	.812
1915			7-1-0	230	29	.875							
Knute Rockne (1918-1930) 105-12-5 .881													
1918			3-1-2	133	39	.667	1925			7-2-1	200	64	.750
1919			9-0-0	229	47	1.000	1926	3		9-1-0	210	38	.900
1920			9-0-0	250	44	1.000	1927	4		7-1-1	158	57	.833
1921			10-1-0	375	41	.909	1928			5-4-0	99	107	.556
1922			8-1-1	222	27	.850	1929	1		9-0-0	145	38	1.000
1923			9-1-0	275	37	.900	1930	1		10-0-0	265	74	1.000
1924	1		10-0-0	285	54	1.000							
Hunk Anderson (1931-1933) 16-9-2 .630													
1931	11		6-2-1	215	40	.722	1933			3-5-1	32	80	.389
1932	7		7-2-0	255	31	.778							
Elmer Layden (1934-1940) 47-13-3 .770													
1934			6-3-0	108	56	.667	1938	5	1	8-1-0	149	39	.889
1935	9		7-1-1	143	62	.833	1939	13	6	7-2-0	100	73	.778
1936	8	7	6-2-1	128	69	.722	1940			7-2-0	168	67	.778
1937	9	10	6-2-1	77	49	.722							
Frank Leahy (1941-1943, 1946-1953) 87-11-9 .855													
1941	3		8-0-1	189	64	.944	1943	1		9-1-0	340	69	.900
1942	6		7-2-2	184	99	.636							
Ed McKeever (1944) 8-2-0 .800													
1944	9		8-2-0	272	118	.800							
Hugh DeVore (1945, 1963) 9-9-1 .500													
1945	9		7-2-1	255	122	.750							
Frank Leahy (1946-1953)													
1946	1		8-0-1	271	24	.944	1950			4-4-1	139	140	.500
1947	1		9-0-0	291	52	1.000	1951		13	7-2-1	241	122	.750
1948	2		9-0-1	320	93	.950	1952	3	3	7-2-1	183	108	.750
1949	1		10-0-0	360	86	1.000	1953	2	2	9-0-1	317	139	.950

Terry Brennan (1954-1958) 32-18-0 .640

Year			W-L-T	PF	PA	Pct		Year			W-L-T	PF	PA	Pct
1954	4	4	9-1-0	261	115	.900		1957	10	9	7-3-0	200	136	.700
1955	9	10	8-2-0	210	112	.800		1958	17	14	6-4-0	206	173	.600
1956			2-8-0	130	289	.200								

Joe Kuharich (1959-1962) 17-23-0 .425

Year			W-L-T	PF	PA	Pct		Year			W-L-T	PF	PA	Pct
1959	17	18	5-5-0	171	180	.500		1961			5-5-0	175	182	.500
1960			2-8-0	111	188	.200		1962			5-5-0	159	192	.500

Hugh Devore (1963)

Year	W-L-T	PF	PA	Pct
1963	2-7-0	108	159	.222

Ara Parseghian (1964-1974) 95-17-4 .836

Year			W-L-T	PF	PA	Pct		Year			W-L-T	PF	PA	Pct
1964	3	3	9-1-0	287	77	.900		1970	2	5	10-1-0	354	108	.909
1965	9	8	7-2-1	270	73	.750		1971	13	15	8-2-0	225	86	.800
1966	1	1	9-0-1	362	38	.950		1972	14	12	8-3-0	289	192	.727
1967	5	4	8-2-0	337	124	.800		1973	1	4	11-0-0	382	89	1.000
1968	5	8	7-2-1	376	170	.750		1974	5	4	10-2-0	318	147	.833
1969	5	9	8-2-1	351	135	.773								

Dan Devine (1975-1980) 53-16-1 .764

Year			W-L-T	PF	PA	Pct		Year			W-L-T	PF	PA	Pct
1975		17	8-3-0	244	144	.727		1978	7	6	9-3-0	293	197	.750
1976	12	12	9-3-0	294	158	.750		1979			7-4-0	243	197	.636
1977	1	1	11-1-0	420	139	.917		1980	9	10	9-2-1	248	128	.792

Gerry Faust (1981-1985) 30-26-1 .535

Year	W-L-T	PF	PA	Pct		Year	W-L-T	PF	PA	Pct
1981	5-6-0	232	160	.455		1984	7-5-0	299	239	.583
1982	6-4-1	206	174	.591		1985	5-6-0	230	234	.455
1983	7-5-0	316	177	.583						

Lou Holtz (1986-1996) 100-30-2 .765

Year			W-L-T	PF	PA	Pct		Year			W-L-T	PF	PA	Pct
1986			5-6-0	299	219	.455		1992	4	4	10-1-1	437	181	.875
1987	17		8-4-0	339	218	.667		1993	2	2	11-1-0	427	215	.917
1988	1	1	12-0-0	393	156	1.000		1994			6-5-1	342	280	.542
1989	2	3	12-1-0	427	179	.923		1995	11	13	9-3-0	392	247	.750
1990	6	6	9-3-0	359	259	.750		1996	19	21	8-3-0	407	181	.727
1991	13	12	10-3-0	465	289	.769								

Bob Davie (1997-2001) 35-25-0 .583

Year			W-L-T	PF	PA	Pct		Year			W-L-T	PF	PA	Pct
1997			7-6-0	282	265	.538		2000	15	16	9-3-0	353	267	.750
1998	22	22	9-3-0	328	248	.750		2001			5-6-0	214	215	.455
1999			5-7-0	348	331	.417								

Tyrone Willingham (2002-2003) 15-10-0 .600

Year			W-L-T	PF	PA	Pct		Year	W-L-T	PF	PA	Pct
2002	17	17	10-3-0	290	217	.769		2003	5-7-0	243	315	.417

Won-loss record by decades:

Decade	Record	Pct		Decade	Record	Pct		Decade	Record	Pct
1887-89	2-3-0	.400		1930-39	66-20-5	.753		1980-89	76-39-2	.658
1890-99	29-12-4	.689		1940-49	82-9-6	.876		1990-99	84-35-2	.702
1900-09	65-15-6	.791		1950-59	64-31-4	.667		2000-03	29-19-0	.604
1910-19	63-7-6	.868		1960-69	62-34-4	.640				
1920-29	83-11-3	.871		1970-79	91-22-0	.805				

Historic record: (1887-2002) 796-257-42 .746

Post-season won-loss record: 13-12-0 .520

1925: Rose Bowl, Notre Dame 27, Stanford 10
1970: Cotton Bowl, Texas 21, Notre Dame 17
1971: Cotton Bowl, Notre Dame 24, Texas 11
1973: Orange Bowl, Nebraska 40, Notre Dame 6
1973: Sugar Bowl, Notre Dame 24, Alabama 23
1975: Orange Bowl, Notre Dame 13, Alabama 11
1976: Gator Bowl, Notre Dame 20, Penn State 9
1978: Cotton Bowl, Notre Dame 38, Texas 10
1979: Cotton Bowl, Notre Dame 35, Houston 34
1981: Sugar Bowl, Georgia 17, Notre Dame 10
1983: Liberty Bowl, Notre Dame 19, Boston College 18
1984: Aloha Bowl, SMU 27, Notre Dame 20
1988: Cotton Bowl, Texas A&M 35, Notre Dame 10

1989: Fiesta Bowl, Notre Dame 34, West Virginia 21
1990: Orange Bowl, Notre Dame 21, Colorado 6
1991: Orange Bowl, Colorado 10, Notre Dame 9
1992: Sugar Bowl, Notre Dame 39, Florida 28
1993: Cotton Bowl, Notre Dame 28, Texas A&M 3
1994: Cotton Bowl, Notre Dame 24, Texas A&M 21
1995: Fiesta Bowl, Colorado 41, Notre Dame 24
1996: Orange Bowl, Florida State 31, Notre Dame 26
1997: Independence Bowl, LSU 27, Notre Dame 9
1999: Gator Bowl, Georgia Tech 35, Notre Dame 28
2001: Fiesta Bowl, Oregon State 41, Notre Dame 9
2002: Gator Bowl, NC State 28, Notre Dame 6

College Football Hall of Fame:
Red Salmon, fullback, 1900-03; Ray Eichenlaub, fullback, 1911-14; Jesse Harper, coach, 1913-17; George Gipp, halfback, 1917-20; Hunk Anderson, guard, 1918-21; Knute Rockne, coach, 1918-30; Harry Stuhldreher, quarterback, 1922-24; Adam Walsh, center, 1922-24; Elmer Layden, fullback, 1922-24; Don Miller, halfback, 1922-24; Jim Crowley, halfback, 1922-24; Rip Miller, tackle, 1922-24; John Smith, guard, 1925-27; Fred Miller, tackle, 1926-28; Jack Cannon, guard, 1927-29; Tommy Yarr, center, 1929-31; Bert Metzger, guard, 1928-30; Frank Carideo, quarterback, 1928-30; Marchy Schwartz, halfback, 1929-31; Frank Hoffman, guard, 1930-31; Wayne Milner, end, 1933-35; Bill Shakespeare, halfback, 1933-36; Bob Dove, end, 1940-42; Creigton Miller, halfback, 1941-43; Angelo Bertelli, quarterback, 1941-43; George Conner, tackle, 1942-47; Ziggy Czarobski, tackle, 1942-47; Johnny Lujack, quarterback, 1943-47; Jim Martin, end/tackle, 1946-49; Leon Hart, end, 1946-49; Frank Leahy, coach, 1941-43, 1946-53; Bill Fischer, guard/tackle, 1945-48; Red Sitko, fullback/halfback, 1946-49; Jerry Groom, center, 1948-50; Ralph Gglielmi, quarterback, 1951-54; Johnny Lattner, halfback, 1951-53; Paul Hornung, quarterback, 1954-56; Alan Page, defensive end, 1964-66; Ara Parseghian, coach, 1964-74; Jim Lynch, linebacker, 1964-66; Ross Browner, defensive end, 1973-77; Ken McAfee, tight end, 1974-77; Dan Devine, coach, 1975-80; Joe Theismann, quarterback, 1968-70.

Awards: Heisman Trophy: 1943, Angelo Bertelli; 1947, Johnny Lujack; 1949: Leon Hart; 1953: Johnny Lattner; 1956, Paul Hornung; 1964: John Huarte; 1987: Tim Brown; Maxwell Award: 1949, Leon Hart; 1952, Johnny Lattner; 1953, Johnny Lattner; 1966, Jim Lynch; 1977, Ross Browner; Lombardi Award: 1971, Walt Patulski; 1977, Ross Browner; 1990, Chris Zorich; 1993, Aaron Taylor; Outland Trophy: 1946, George Conner, 1948, Bill Fischer; 1976, Ross Browner; Unitas Award: 1989, Tony Rice; Camp Award: 1977, Ken McAfee; 1987, Tim Brown; 1990, Raghib Ismail; Baugh Trophy: 1967, Terry Hanratty.

OHIO STATE UNIVERSITY, Columbus, Ohio; nickname "Buckeyes"; colors scarlet and gray; Ohio Stadium (101,568); Big Ten Conference. Ohio State was the tenth team to join the Western Conference (in 1913). However, because Michigan was out of the league at the time because of disputes about league rules on scheduling non-conference teams, the conference did not become the Big Ten until Michigan returned for the 1917 season. Note that, prior to 1946, conference (but no overall) win-loss percents are calculated by ignoring ties, per Big Ten rules.

Early years (1890-1912)

Year	Coach	W-L-T	PF	PA	Pct	Year	Coach	W-L-T	PF	PA	Pct.
1890	Alexander Lilly	1-3-0	30	110	.750	1902	Perry Hale	6-2-2	172	136	.700
1891	Alexander Lilly	2-2-0	20	80	.500	1903	Perry Hale	8-3-0	265	87	.727
1892	Jack Ryder	5-3-0	260	144	.625	1904	E.R. Sweetland	6-5-0	219	123	.545
1893	Jack Ryder	4-5-0	202	178	.571	1905	E.R. Sweetland	8-2-2	199	63	.750
1894	Jack Ryder	6-5-0	160	114	.545	1906	A.Herrnstein	8-1-0	153	14	.889
1895	Jack Ryder	4-4-2	62	102	.500	1907	A. Herrnstein	7-2-1	160	49	.750
1896	Charles Hickey	5-5-1	122	104	.500	1908	A.Herrnstein	6-4-0	118	92	.600
1897	David Edwards	1-7-1	18	168	.167	1909	A. Herrnstein	7-3-0	219	76	.700
1898	Jack Ryder	3-5-0	80	121	.375	1910	Howard Jones	6-1-3	182	27	.750
1899	John Eckstrom	9-0-1	184	5	.950	1911	Harry Vaughn	5-3-2	47	40	.600
1900	John Eckstrom	8-1-1	213	26	.850	1912	John Richards	6-3-0	246	122	.667
1901	John Eckstrom	5-3-1	94	56	.611						

Member of the Big Ten Conference (1913-2003) 414-157-24 .716

Year	Nat'l AP	Other	Overall W-L-T	PF	PA	Pct.	Conference W-L-T	Pct.	Rank	Year	Nat'l AP	Other	Overall W-L-T	PF	PA	Pct.	Conference W-L-T	Pct.	Rank
John Wilce (1913-1928) 78-33-9 .688																		
1913			4-2-1	154	27	.714	1-2-0	.333	6	1921			5-2-0	110	14	.714	4-1-0	.800	2
1914			5-2-0	108	55	.714	2-2-0	.500	3	1922			3-4-0	43	57	.429	1-4-0	.200	8
1915			5-1-1	105	39	.786	2-1-1	.667	3	1923			3-4-1	124	99	.438	1-4-0	.200	8
1916			7-0-0	258	29	1.000	4-0-0	1.000	1	1924			2-3-3	40	45	.438	1-3-2	.250	7
1917			8-0-1	292	6	.944	4-0-0	1.000	1	1925			4-3-1	55	45	.562	1-3-1	.250	8
1918			3-3-0	134	41	.500	0-3-0	.000	8	1926	8		7-1-0	196	43	.875	3-1-0	.750	3
1919			6-1-0	176	12	.857	3-1-0	.750	2	1927			4-4-0	131	92	.500	2-3-0	.400	6
1920			7-1-0	150	48	.875	5-0-0	1.000	1	1928			5-2-1	135	35	.688	3-2-0	.600	4
Sam Willaman (1929-1933) 26-10-5 .695																		
1929			4-3-1	95	69	.562	2-2-1	.500	5	1932	6		4-1-3	90	41	.688	2-1-2	.667	4
1930			5-2-1	139	48	.688	2-2-1	.500	4	1933	5		7-1-0	161	26	.875	4-1-0	.800	3
1931			6-3-0	194	68	.667	4-2-0	.667	4										
Francis Schmidt (1934-1940) 39-16-1 .705																		
1934	8		7-1-0	267	34	.875	5-1-0	.833	2	1938			4-3-1	119	65	.562	3-2-1	.600	5
1935	7		7-1-0	237	57	.875	5-0-0	1.000	1	1939	15		6-2-0	189	64	.750	5-1-0	.833	1
1936			5-3-0	160	27	.625	4-1-0	.800	2	1940			4-4-0	99	113	.500	3-3-0	.500	4
1937	13		6-2-0	125	23	.750	5-1-0	.833	2										
Paul Brown (1941-1943) 18-8-1 .685																		
1941	13		6-1-1	167	110	.812	3-1-1	.750	2	1943			3-6-0	149	187	.333	1-4-0	.200	7
1942	1		9-1-0	337	114	.900	5-1-0	.833	1										
Carroll Widdoes (1944-1945) 16-2-0 .889																		
1944	2		9-0-0	287	79	1.000	6-0-0	1.000	1	1945	12		7-2-0	194	71	.778	5-2-0	.714	3
Paul Bixler (1946) 4-3-2 .556																		
1946			4-3-2	166	170	.556	2-3-1	.416	6										
Wes Fesler (1947-1950) 21-13-3 .608																		
1947			2-6-1	60	150	.389	1-4-1	.250	9	1949	6		7-1-2	207	136	.800	4-1-1	.750	1
1948			6-3-0	184	94	.667	3-3-0	.500	4	1950	14	10	6-3-0	286	111	.667	5-2-0	.714	2
Woody Hayes (1951-1978) 205-61-10 .755																		
1951			4-3-2	109	104	.556	2-2-2	.500	5	1965		11	7-2-0	156	118	.778	6-1-0	.857	2
1952	17	15	6-3-0	197	119	.667	5-2-0	.714	3	1966			4-5-0	108	123	.444	3-4-0	.429	6
1953		20	6-3-0	182	164	.667	4-3-0	.571	4	1967			6-3-0	145	120	.667	5-2-0	.714	4
1954	1	2	10-0-0	249	75	1.000	7-0-0	1.000	1	1968	1	1	10-0-0	323	150	1.000	7-0-0	1.000	1
1955	5	5	7-2-0	201	97	.778	6-0-0	1.000	1	1969	4	5	8-1-0	383	93	.889	6-1-0	.857	1
1956	15		6-3-0	160	81	.667	4-2-0	.667	4	1970	5	2	9-1-0	290	120	.900	7-0-0	1.000	1
1957	2	1	9-1-0	267	92	.900	7-0-0	1.000	1	1971			6-4-0	224	120	.600	5-3-0	.625	3
1958	8	7	6-1-2	182	132	.778	4-1-2	.714	3	1972	9	3	9-2-0	280	171	.818	7-1-0	.875	1
1959			3-5-1	83	114	.389	2-4-1	.357	9	1973	2	3	10-0-1	413	64	.955	7-0-1	.939	1
1960	8	8	7-2-0	209	90	.778	4-2-0	.600	3	1974	4	3	10-2-0	437	129	.833	7-1-0	.875	1
1961	2	2	8-0-1	221	83	.944	6-0-0	1.000	1	1975	4	4	11-1-0	384	102	.917	8-0-0	1.000	1
1962		13	6-3-0	205	98	.667	4-2-0	.667	3	1976	6	5	9-2-1	305	149	.792	7-1-0	.875	1
1963			5-3-1	110	102	.611	4-1-1	.750	2	1977	11	12	9-3-0	343	120	.750	7-1-0	.875	1
1964	9	9	7-2-0	146	76	.778	5-10	.833	2	1978			7-4-1	339	216	.625	6-2-0	.750	4

                        Earle Bruce (1979-1987) 81-26-1 .755

1979 4   4 11-1-0 390 126 .917 8-0-0 1.000 1   1984 13 12 9-3-0 391 200 .750 7-2-0 .778 1
1980 15 15   9-3-0 387 181 .750 7-1-0 .875 2   1985 14 11 9-3-0 325 212 .750 5-3-0 .600 4
1981 15 12   9-3-0 387 253 .750 6-2-0 .750 1   1986 7   6 10-3-0 347 179 .769 7-1-0 .875 1
1982 12 12   9-3-0 348 208 .750 7-1-0 .875 2   1987   6-4-1 224 181 .591 4-4-0 .500 5
1983 9   8   9-3-0 410 206 .750 6-3-0 .667 4

                        John Cooper (1988-2000) 111-43-4 .715

1988   4-6-1 229 283 .409 2-5-1 .313 7   1995 6   8 11-2-0 475 220 .846 7-1-0 .875 2
1989 24   8-4-0 339 297 .667 6-2-0 .750 3   1996 2   2 11-1-0 455 131 .917 7-1-0 .875 1
1990   7-4-1 349 220 .625 5-2-1 .688 5   1997 12 12 10-3-0 394 170 .769 6-2-0 .750 2
1991   8-4-0 277 187 .667 5-3-0 .625 3   1998 2   2 11-1-0 430 144 .917 7-1-0 .875 1
1992 18 19 8-3-1 271 158 .773 5-2-0 .688 2   1999   6-6-0 285 287 .500 3-5-0 .375 8
1993 11 10 10-1-1 351 193 .875 6-1-1 .813 1   2000   8-4-0 331 222 .667 5-3-0 .625 4
1994 14   9 9-4-0 336 211 .692 6-2-0 .750 2

                        Jim Tressel (2001-2003) 32-7-0 .821

2001   7-5-0 312 244 .583 5-3-0 .625 3   2003 4   4 11-2-0 322 229 .846 6-2-0 .750 2
2002 1   1 14-0-0 410 183 1.000 8-0-0 1.000 1

Won-loss record by decades:

1890-99	40-39-5	.506	1930-39	57-19-5	.735	1970-79	91-20-3	.811
1900-09	69-26-7	.711	1940-49	57-27-6	.667	1980-89	82-35-2	.697
1910-19	55-16-8	.747	1950-59	63-24-5	.712	1990-99	91-29-3	.752
1920-29	44-27-7	.609	1960-69	68-21-2	.758	2000-03	40-11-0	.784

Historic record: 757-294-53 .710

Post-season won-loss record: 16-19-0 .457

1921: Rose Bowl, California 28, OSU 0
1950: Rose Bowl, OSU 17, California 14
1955: Rose Bowl, OSU 20, USC 7
1958: Rose Bowl, OSU 10, Oregon 7
1969: Rose Bowl, OSU 27, USC 16
1971: Rose Bowl, Stanford 27, OSU 17
1973: Rose Bowl, USC 42, OSU 17
1974: Rose Bowl, OSU 42, USC 21
1975: Rose Bowl, USC 18, OSU 17
1976: Rose Bowl, UCLA 23, OSU 10
1977: Orange Bowl, OSU 27, Colorado 10
1978: Sugar Bowl, Alabama 35, OSU 6
1978: Gator Bowl, Clemson 17, OSU 15
1980: Rose Bowl, USC 17, OSU 16
1980: Fiesta Bowl, Penn State 31, OSU 19
1981: Liberty Bowl, OSU 31, Navy 28
1982: Holiday Bowl, OSU 47, BYU 17

1984: Fiesta Bowl, OSU 28, Pittsburgh 23
1985: Rose Bowl, USC 20, OSU 17
1985: Citrus Bowl, OSU 10, BYU 7
1987: Cotton Bowl, OSU 28, Texas A&M 12
1990: Hall of Fame Bowl, Auburn 31, OSU 14
1990: Liberty Bowl, Air Force 23, OSU 11
1992: Hall of Fame Bowl, Syracuse 24, OSU 17
1993: Citrus Bowl, Georgia 21, OSU 14
1993: Holiday Bowl, OSU 28, BYU 21
1995: Citrus Bowl, Alabama 24, OSU 17
1996: Citrus Bowl, Tennessee 20, OSU 14
1997: Rose Bowl, OSU 20, Arizona State 17
1998: Sugar Bowl, Florida State 31, OSU 14
1999: Sugar Bowl, OSU 24, Texas A&M 14
2001: Outback Bowl, South Carolina 24, OSU 7
2001: Outback Bowl, South Carolina 31, OSU 28
2002: Fiesta Bowl, OSU 31, Miami (FL) 24
2004: Fiesta Bowl, OSU 35, Kansas State 28

College Football Hall of Fame:
Howard Jones, coach, 1910; John Wilce, coach, 1913-28; Chic Harley, halfback, 1916-19; Gaylord Stinchcomb, halfback, 1917-20; Wes Fesler, end, 1928-30; Gomer Jones, center, 1933-35; Francis Schmidt, coach, 1934-40; Gust Zarnas, guard, 1935-37; Jim Daniel, tackle, 1939-41; Les Horvath, halfback/quarterback, 1940-44; Bill Willis, tackle, 1942-44; Warren Amling, guard/tackle, 1944-46; Vic Janowicz, halfback, 1949-51; Woody Hayes, coach, 1951-78; Hopalong Cassady, halfback, 1952-55; Jim Parker, guard, 1954-56; Aurealius Thomas, guard, 1968-70; Bob Ferguson, fullback, 1959-61; Jim Stillwagon, middle guard, 1968-70; Jack Tatum, defensive back, 1968-70; John Hicks, tackle, 1970-73; Randy Gradishar, linebacker, 1971-73; Archie Griffin, halfback, 1972-75; Earle Bruce, coach, 1979-87.

Awards:
Heisman Trohy: 1944, Les Horvath; 1950, Vic Janowicz; 1974 and 1975, Archie Griffin; 1995, Eddie George; Butkus Award: 1997, Andy Katzenmoyer; Fred Biletnikoff Award: 1995, Terry Glenn; Maxwell Award: 1955, Hopalong Cassady; 1961, Bob Ferguson; 1975, Archie Griffin; 1995, Eddie George; Lombardi Award: 1970, Jim Stillwagon, 1973, John Hicks; 1987, Chris Spielman, 1995 and 1996, Orlando Pace; Doak Walker Award: 1995: Eddie George; Outland Trophy: 1956, Jim Parker, 1970, Jim Stillwagon, 1973, John Hicks, 1996, Orlando Pace; Jim Thorpe Award, 1998, Antoine Winfield; Rimington Trophy: 2001, LeCharles Bentley; Camp Award: 1974 and 1985, Archie Griffin; 1995, Eddie George; Ray Guy Award: 2003, B. J. Sander.

OHIO UNIVERSITY, Athens, Ohio; nickname "Bobcats"; colors hunter green and white; Peden Stadium (24,000); Mid-American conference. Prior to joining the MAC as one of the founding members in 1947, Ohio U was a member of the Buckeye Athletic Association in the 1930s playing a schedule consisting mainly of colleges from Ohio and the surrounding states, with occasional games with Big Ten teams. Conference data are shown here only for the MAC years.

Early years (1894-1905)

Year	Coach	W-L-T	PF	PA	Pct.	Year	Coach	W-L-T	PF	PA	Pct.
1894	no coach	0-1-0	0	8	.000	1900	Karl Core	3-4-1	84	85	.438
1895	Harvey Deme	2-3-0	78	128	.400	1901	Art Jones	6-1-2	108	43	.778
1896	Frank Remsburg	4-2-1	70	100	.643	1902	H. Monosmith	0-5-1	0	143	.083
1897	Warwick Ford	7-2-0	150	26	.778	1903	Fred Sullivan	2-4-0	38	144	.333
1898	Peter McLaren	1-2-1	23	45	.375	1904	Henry Hart	2-4-1	57	83	.357
1899	Fred Sullivan	2-2-0	78	77	.500	1905	Joseph Railsback	2-5-2	48	141	.333

Arthur McFarland (1906-1908) 13-10-1 .562

| 1906 | | 7-1-0 | 158 | 28 | .875 | 1908 | | 3-5-0 | 103 | 64 | .375 |
| 1907 | | 3-4-1 | 76 | 137 | .438 | | | | | | |

Robert Woods (1909-1910) 2-10-3 .233

| 1909 | | 2-4-2 | 26 | 106 | .375 | 1910 | | 0-6-1 | 0 | 123 | .072 |

Arthur Hinaman (1911-1912) 4-10-3 .323

| 1911 | | 3-3-2 | 38 | 44 | .500 | 1912 | | 1-7-1 | 48 | 168 | .167 |

Mark Banks (1913-1917) 22-17-2 .561

1913		2-5-1	55	159	.312	1916		5-2-1	154	108	.688
1914		4-4-0	119	99	.500	1917		3-5-0	185	107	.375
1915		8-1-0	175	33	.889						

Frank Gullum (1918-1919) 7-5-1 .577

| 1918 | | 4-0-1 | 140 | 19 | .900 | 1919 | | 3-5-0 | 147 | 101 | .375 |

Russ Finsterwald (1920-1922) 13-10-1 .562

| 1920 | | 4-3-0 | 161 | 44 | .571 | 1922 | | 5-3-0 | 100 | 48 | .625 |
| 1921 | | 4-4-1 | 112 | 99 | .500 | | | | | | |

F. B. Heldt (1923) 3-5-1 .389

| 1923 | | 3-5-1 | 65 | 88 | .389 | | | | | | |

Don Peden (1924-1946) 121-46-11 .711

1924		4-4-0	64	59	.500	1936		5-2-1	102	70	.688
1925		6-2-0	95	40	.750	1937		5-3-1	108	52	.611
1926		5-2-1	111	17	.688	1938		7-2-0	161	89	.778
1927		4-2-2	85	69	.625	1939		6-3-0	116	82	.667
1928		6-3-0	256	72	.667	1940		5-2-2	89	32	.667
1929		9-0-0	305	7	1.000	1941		5-2-1	108	42	.688
1930		8-0-1	227	32	.944	1942		5-3-0	144	107	.625
1931		7-1-0	172	14	.875	1943	no team				
1932		7-2-0	172	29	.778	1944	no team				
1933		6-2-1	277	28	.722	1945		3-4-0	100	106	.429
1934		4-4-1	116	67	.500	1946		6-3-0	206	97	.667
1935		8-0-0	170	36	1.000						

Member of the Mid-American Conference (1947-2003) 169-214-11 .445

Year	Nat'l AP Other	Overall W-L-T	PF	PA	Pct.	Conference W-L-T	Pct.	Rank	Year	Nat'l AP Other	Overall W-L-T	PF	PA	Pct.	Conference W-L-T	Pct.	Rank
						Harold Wise (1947-1948) 6-11-1 .361											
1947		3-5-1	80	116	.389	1-3-0	.250	3	1948		3-6-0	98	179	.333	2-3-0	.400	4
						Carroll Widdoes (1949-1957) 42-36-5 .536											
1949		4-4-1	114	120	.500	2-2-0	.500	3	1954		6-3-0	175	158	.667	5-2-0	.714	3
1950		6-4-0	165	161	.600	2-2-0	.500	3	1955		5-4-0	166	134	.556	3-3-0	.500	4
1951		5-4-1	167	141	.550	2-2-0	.500	4	1956		2-7-0	136	211	.222	2-4-0	.333	4
1952		6-2-1	180	133	.722	2-1-0	.714	3	1957		2-6-1	134	156	.278	1-4-1	.250	5
1953		6-2-1	245	86	.722	5-0-1	.917	1									
						Bill Hess (1958-1977) 108-91-4 .542											
1958		5-4-0	159	102	.556	2-4-0	.333	4	1968	20 18	10-1-0	418	228	.909	6-0-0	1.000	1
1959		7-2-0	215	101	.778	4-2-0	.667	2	1969		5-4-1	256	202	.550	2-3-0	.400	3
1960		10-0-0	269	34	1.000	6-0-0	1.000	1	1970		4-5-0	178	261	.444	3-2-0	.600	2
1961		5-3-1	129	116	.611	3-2-1	.583	4	1971		5-5-0	240	173	.500	2-3-0	.400	3
1962		8-3-0	261	112	.727	5-1-0	.833	2	1972		3-8-0	185	321	.273	1-4-0	.200	6
1963		6-4-0	135	103	.600	5-2-0	.833	1	1973		5-5-0	156	231	.500	2-3-0	.400	3
1964		5-4-1	122	99	.550	3-2-1	.583	4	1974		6-5-0	249	211	.545	3-2-0	.600	2
1965		0-10-0	77	210	.000	0-6-0	.000	7	1975		5-5-1	164	143	.500	3-3-1	.500	5
1966		5-5-0	149	183	.500	3-3-0	.500	4	1976		7-4-0	253	175	.636	6-2-0	.750	2
1967		6-4-0	210	152	.600	5-1-0	.833	1	1977		1-10-0	241	371	.091	0-8-0	.000	10

Bob Kappes (1978) 3-8-0 .273

Year	Record	PF	PA	Pct	Conf	Conf Pct	Place
1978	3-8-0	120	246	.273	3-5-0	.375	5

Brian Burke (1979-1984) 31-34-1 .4778

Year	Record	PF	PA	Pct	Conf	Conf Pct	Place
1979	6-5-0	238	174	.545	4-4-0	.500	4
1980	6-5-0	222	196	.545	5-4-0	.556	5
1981	5-6-0	228	257	.455	5-4-0	.556	5
1982	6-5-0	160	259	.545	5-4-0	.556	5
1983	4-7-0	163	270	.364	3-6-0	.333	8
1984	4-6-1	134	262	.409	4-4-1	.500	4

Cleve Bryant (1985-1989) 9-44-2 .182

Year	Record	PF	PA	Pct	Conf	Conf Pct	Place
1985	2-9-0	181	305	.182	2-7-0	.222	10
1986	1-10-0	196	329	.091	0-8-0	.000	10
1987	1-10-0	127	271	.091	0-8-0	.000	10
1988	4-6-1	195	288	.409	4-3-1	.563	5
1989	1-9-1	191	349	.136	1-6-1	.188	7

Tom Lichtenburg (1990-1994) 8-45-2 .145

Year	Record	PF	PA	Pct	Conf	Conf Pct	Place
1990	1-9-1	162	342	.136	0-7-1	.063	9
1991	2-8-1	176	308	.227	1-6-1	.187	8
1992	1-10-0	145	253	.091	1-7-0	.125	9
1993	4-7-0	134	282	.364	4-5-0	.444	6
1994	0-11-0	82	259	.000	0-9-0	.000	10

Jim Grobe (1995-2000) 33-33-1 .500

Year	Record	PF	PA	Pct	Conf	Conf Pct	Place
1995	2-8-1	161	320	.227	1-6-1	.187	9
1996	6-6-0	302	237	.500	5-3-0	.625	4
1997	8-3-0	301	177	.727	6-2-0	.750	3
1998	5-6-0	269	303	.455	5-3-0	.625	4
1999	5-6-0	271	287	.455	5-3-0	.625	4
2000	7-4-0	278	291	.636	5-3-0	.625	3

Brian Knorr (2001-2003) 7-28-0 .200

Year	Record	PF	PA	Pct	Conf	Conf Pct	Place
2001	1-10-0	198	323	.091	1-7-0	.125	12
2002	4-8-0	299	374	.333	4-4-0	.500	7
2003	2-10-0	263	372	.167	1-7-0	.125	12

Won-loss record by decades:

Decade	Record	Pct	Decade	Record	Pct	Decade	Record	Pct
1894-99	16-12-2	.567	1930-39	63-19-5	.753	1970-79	45-60-1	.429
1900-09	30-37-10	.455	1940-49	34-29-5	.537	1980-89	34-73-3	.323
1910-19	33-38-7	.468	1950-59	50-38-4	.565	1990-99	34-74-3	.320
1920-29	50-28-5	.633	1960-69	60-38-3	.609	2000-03	14-32-0	.304

Historic record: 463-478-48 .492

Post-season won-loss record: 0-2-0 .000
1962: Sun Bowl, West Texas State 15, Ohio U 14
1968: Tangerine Bowl, Richmond 49, Ohio U 42

OKLAHOMA STATE UNIVERSITY, Stillwater, Oklahoma; nickname "Cowboys"; colors orange and black; Lewis Field (48,000); Big Twelve Conference. Oklahoma A&M (name later changed to Oklahoma State) started out as an independent and then became one of the founding members of the Southwest Conference in 1915. The Cowboys left the Southwest Conference after the 1924 season to join the Missouri Valley Conference. That conference lost six of its leading members when the Big Six Conference was organized beginning with the 1928 season, but the Cowboys remained in the Missouri Valley Conference until 1957 when the team went independent for three seasons before joining the Big Eight, which became the Big Twelve in 1995 after adding four new members.

Year	Nat'l AP	Other	Overall W-L-T	PF	PA	Pct.	Conf. W-L-T	Pct.	Rank	Year	Nat'l AP	Other	Overall W-L-T	PF	PA	Pct.	Conf. W-L-T	Pct.	Rank
Early years as an independent (1901-1914)																			
No coach (1901-1905)																			
1901			2-3-0	39	29	.400				1904			0-4-1	0	115	.100			
1902			no team							1905			1-3-2	21	29	.333			
1903			0-2-2	6	16	.250													
Boyd Hill (1906) 1-4-2 .286																			
1906			1-4-2	24	92	.286													
Ed Parry (1907-1908) 5-6-1 .458																			
1907			1-3-1	24	95	.300				1908			4-3-0	86	66	.571			
Paul Davis (1909-1914) 29-16-1 .641																			
1909			5-3-0	49	16	.625				1912			6-2-0	335	71	.750			
1910			3-4-0	129	44	.429				1913			4-3-0	165	27	.571			
1911			5-2-0	256	59	.714				1914			6-2-1	327	71	.722			
Member of the Southwest Conference (1915-1924) 6-23-1 .217																			
John Griffith (1915-1916) 8-9-1 .472																			
1915			4-5-1	161	93	.450	0-3-0	.000	6	1916			4-4-0	290	95	.500	0-3-0	.000	5
Earl Pritchard (1917-1918) 8-7-0 .533																			
1917			4-5-0	93	94	.444	1-2-0	.333	5	1918			4-2-0	109	73	.667	0-2-0	.000	6
James Pixlee (1919-1920) 3-10-3 .281																			
1919			3-3-2	126	94	.500	0-2-0	.000	8	1920			0-7-1	35	200	.062	0-3-0	.000	6
John Maulbetsch (1921-1928) 28-37-6 .437																			
1921			5-4-1	135	125	.550	1-1-0	.500	4	1923			2-8-0	40	98	.200	1-3-0	.250	6
1922			5-4-1	131	86	.550	2-3-0	.400	5	1924			6-1-2	117	50	.778	1-1-1	.500	3
Member of the Missouri Valley Conference (1925-1956) 66-39-5 .623																			
1925			2-5-1	41	115	.312	0-3-1	.125	10	1927			4-4-0	110	138	.500	2-1-0	.667	3
1926			3-4-1	79	114	.438	3-0-1	.875	1	1928			1-7-0	25	200	.125	0-1-0	.000	4
Pappy Waldorf (1929-1933) 34-10-7 .735																			
1929			4-3-2	107	79	.556	1-1-0	.500	3	1932			9-1-2	178	48	.833	3-0-0	1.000	1
1930			7-2-1	124	40	.750	2-0-0	1.000	1	1933			6-2-1	132	57	.722	2-0-0	1.000	1
1931			8-2-1	183	61	.773	1-0-0	1.000	1										
Albert Exendine (1934-1935) 7-12-1 .375																			
1934			4-5-1	54	130	.450	1-1-0	.500	3	1935			3-7-0	66	152	.300	0-3-0	.000	7
Ted Cox (1936-1938) 7-23-0 .233																			
1936			1-9-0	43	205	.100	1-2-0	.333	5	1938			2-8-0	75	178	.200	0-4-0	.000	8
1937			4-6-0	101	141	.400	2-2-0	.500	4										
Jim Lookabaugh (1939-1949) 58-41-6 .581																			
1939			5-4-1	128	115	.550	3-1-0	.750	2	1945	5		9-0-0	285	63	1.000	1-0-0	1.000	1
1940			6-3-1	210	137	.650	3-1-0	.750	2	1946			3-7-1	202	264	.318	1-1-0	.500	3
1941			5-4-0	161	123	.556	3-1-0	.750	2	1947			3-7-0	116	134	.300	0-2-0	.000	5
1942			6-3-1	235	116	.650	4-1-0	.800	2	1948			6-4-0	219	127	.600	2-0-0	1.000	1
1943			3-4-0	66	154	.429	0-1-0	.000	2	1949			4-4-2	223	212	.500	1-2-1	.375	3
1944			8-1-0	228	103	.889	1-0-0	1.000	1										
J. B. Whitworth (1950-1954) 22-27-2 .451																			
1950			4-6-1	159	259	.409	1-2-1	.375	4	1953			7-3-0	178	149	.700	3-1-0	.750	1
1951			3-7-0	168	251	.300	3-2-0	.600	3	1954			5-4-1	161	119	.550	2-2-0	.500	3
1952			3-7-0	146	187	.300	2-2-0	.500	3										
Cliff Speegle (1955-1962) 36-42-3 .463																			
1955			2-8-0	88	172	.200	1-3-0	.250	4	1956			3-5-2	131	166	.400	2-1-1	.625	2
Independent (1957-1959)																			
1957			6-3-1	182	129	.650				1959			6-4-0	181	151	.600			
1958	19		8-3-0	201	134	.727													
Member of the Big Eight Conference (1960-1995) 100-142-9 .416																			
1960			3-7-0	102	126	.300	2-5-0	.286	6	1962			4-6-0	138	214	.400	2-5-0	.286	6
1961			4-6-0	154	166	.400	2-5-0	.286	6										
Phil Cutchin (1963-1968) 19-38-2 .339																			
1963			1-8-0	107	260	.111	0-6-0	.000	8	1966			4-5-1	103	138	.450	4-2-1	.643	3
1964			4-6-0	165	192	.400	3-4-0	.429	5	1967			4-5-1	123	140	.450	3-4-0	.429	5
1965			3-7-0	131	173	.300	2-5-0	.286	6	1968			3-7-0	161	288	.300	2-5-0	.286	6

Floyd Gass (1969-1971) 13-18-1 .422

Year			W-L-T	PF	PA	Pct	Conf	Pct	Pl	Year			W-L-T	PF	PA	Pct	Conf	Pct	Pl
1969			5-5-0	197	200	.500	3-4-0	.429	5	1971			4-6-1	184	322	.409	2-5-0	.286	5
1970			4-7-0	213	337	.364	2-5-0	.286	6										

Dave Smith (1972) 6-5-0 .545

Year			W-L-T	PF	PA	Pct	Conf	Pct	Pl
1972			6-5-0	259	203	.545	4-3-0	571	2

Jim Stanley (1973-1978) 35-31-2 .529

Year			W-L-T	PF	PA	Pct	Conf	Pct	Pl	Year			W-L-T	PF	PA	Pct	Conf	Pct	Pl
1973			5-4-2	293	186	.545	2-3-2	.429	4	1976	14	14	9-3-0	329	214	.750	5-2-0	.714	1
1974			7-5-0	262	176	.583	4-3-0	.571	4	1977			4-7-0	235	267	.364	2-5-0	.286	7
1975			7-4-0	285	178	.636	3-4-0	.429	4	1978			3-8-0	167	266	.273	3-4-0	.429	5

Jimmy Johnston (1979-1983) 30-25-2 .529

Year			W-L-T	PF	PA	Pct	Conf	Pct	Pl	Year			W-L-T	PF	PA	Pct	Conf	Pct	Pl
1979			7-4-0	191	212	.636	5-2-0	.714	3	1982			4-5-2	241	267	.455	3-2-2	.571	3
1980			4-7-0	187	268	.364	2-4-0	.333	5	1983		18	8-4-0	271	162	.667	3-4-0	.429	4
1981			7-5-0	197	216	.583	4-3-0	.571	3										

Pat Jones (1984-1994) 62-60-3 .508

Year			W-L-T	PF	PA	Pct	Conf	Pct	Pl	Year			W-L-T	PF	PA	Pct	Conf	Pct	Pl
1984	7	5	10-2-0	312	148	.833	5-2-0	.714	3	1990			4-7-0	233	309	.364	2-5-0	.286	5
1985			8-4-0	255	188	.667	4-3-0	.571	3	1991			0-10-1	106	307	.046	0-6-1	.071	8
1986			6-5-0	181	191	.545	4-3-0	.571	4	1992			4-6-1	161	251	.409	2-4-1	.357	5
1987	11	12	10-2-0	409	242	.833	5-2-0	.714	3	1993			3-8-0	174	236	.273	0-7-0	.000	8
1988	11	11	10-2-0	584	341	.833	5-2-0	.714	3	1994			3-7-1	180	256	.318	0-6-1	.071	7
1989			4-7-0	226	329	.364	3-4-0	.429	5										

Bob Simmons (1995-2000) 30-38-0 .441

Year			W-L-T	PF	PA	Pct	Conf	Pct	Pl
1995			4-8-0	250	345	.333	2-5-0	.286	5

Member of the Big Twelve Conference (1996-2003) 26-38-0 .406

Year			W-L-T	PF	PA	Pct	Conf	Pct	Pl	Year			W-L-T	PF	PA	Pct	Conf	Pct	Pl
1996			5-6-0	243	327	.455	2-6-0	.250	9	1999			5-6-0	304	300	.455	3-5-0	.375	7
1997	24	24	8-4-0	352	229	.667	5-3-0	.625	4	2000			3-8-0	206	303	.273	1-7-0	.125	11
1998			5-6-0	291	272	.455	3-5-0	.375	7										

Les Miles (2001-2003) 21-16-0 .568

Year			W-L-T	PF	PA	Pct	Conf	Pct	Pl	Year			W-L-T	PF	PA	Pct	Conf	Pct	Pl
2001			4-7-0	242	281	.364	2-6-0	.250	10	2003			9-4-0	467	326	.692	5-3-0	.625	4
2002			8-5-0	446	356	.615	5-3-0	.625	5										

Won-loss record by decades:

1901-09	14-25-8	.383	1940-49	53-37-5	.584	1980-89	71-43-2	.621
1910-19	43-32-4	.570	1950-59	47-50-5	.485	1990-99	41-68-3	.379
1920-29	32-47-9	.419	1960-69	35-62-2	.364	2000-03	24-24-0	.500
1930-39	49-46-7	.515	1970-79	56-53-3	.513			

Historic record: 465-487-48 .489

Post-season won-loss record 10-5-0 .667
1945: Cotton Bowl, Oklahoma A&M 34, TCU 0
1946: Sugar Bowl, Oklahoma A&M 33, St. Mary's 13
1949: Delta Bowl, Wm. & Mary 20, Oklahoma A&M 0
1958: Blue Grass Bowl, OSU 15, Florida State 6
1974: Fiesta Bowl, OSU 16, BYU 6
1976: Tangerine Bowl, OSU 49, BYU 21
1981: Independence Bowl, Texas A&M 33, OSU 16

1983: Bluebonnet Bowl, OSU 24, Baylor 14
1984: Gator Bowl, OSU 21, South Carolina 14
1985: Gator Bowl, Florida State 34, OSU 23
1987: John Hancock Bowl, OSU 35, West Virginia 33
1988: Sea World Holiday Bowl, OSU 62, Wyoming 14
1997: Builders Square Alamo Bowl, Purdue 33, OSU 20
2002: Houston Bowl, OSU 33, Southern Mississippi 23
2004: Cotton Bowl, Ole Miss 31, OSU 28

College Football Hall of Fame:
Pappy Waldorf, coach, 1929-33; Bob Fenimore, halfback, 1943-46; Barry Sanders, tailback, 1986-88.

Awards: Heisman Trophy: 1988, Barry Sanders; Maxwell Award: 1988, Barry Sanders; Camp Award: 1988, Barry Sanders.

UNIVERSITY OF OKLAHOMA, Norman, Oklahoma; nickname "Sooners"; colors red and white; Memorial Stadium (72,762). Big Twelve Conference. Oklahoma began play in 1895. Oklahoma began play as an independent. In 1915, Oklahoma joined the Southwest Conference and played there through the 1919 season. In 1920, Oklahoma moved to the Missouri Valley Conference. After the 1927 season, Oklahoma joined with five other MVC members to organize the Big Six Conference (later Big Seven, later Big Eight). After the 1995 season, the Big Eight joined with four members of the disbanded Southwest Conference to establish the Big Twelve Conference.

Early years as an independent (1895-1914)

Year	W-L-T	PF	PA	Pct.	Year	W-L-T	PF	PA	Pct.
					John A. Harts (1895-1896) 2-1-0 .667				
1895	0-1-0	0	34	.000	1896	2-0-0	28	4	1.000
					V. L. Parrington (1897-1900) 9-2-1 .792				
1897	2-0-0	33	8	1.000	1899	2-1-0	61	28	.667
1898	2-0-0	29	0	1.000	1900	3-1-1	118	28	.700
					Fred Roberts (1901) 3-2-0 .600				
1901	3-2-0	93	29	.600					
					Mark McMahon (1902-1903) 11-7-3 .595				
1902	6-3-0	175	60	.667	1903	5-4-3	126	85	.542
					Fred Ewing (1904) 4-3-1 .562				
1904	4-3-1	204	90	.562					
					Bennie Owen (1905-1926) 122-54-16 .677				
1905	7-2-0	229	55	.778	1910	4-2-1	163	31	.643
1906	5-2-2	134	36	.667	1911	8-0-0	282	15	1.000
1907	4-4-0	181	75	.500	1912	5-4-0	197	80	.556
1908	8-1-1	272	35	.850	1913	6-2-0	323	44	.750
1909	6-4-0	202	110	.600	1914	9-1-1	440	96	.864

Member of the Southwest Conference (1915-1919) 10-3-1 .750

Year	Nat'l AP	Other	Overall W-L-T	PF	PA	Pct.	Conference W-L-T	Pct.	Rank	Year	Nat'l AP	Other	Overall W L T	PF	PA	Pct.	Conference W-L-T	Pct.	Rank
1915			10-0-0	370	54	1.000	3-0-0	1.000	1	1918			6-0-0	278	7	1.000	2-0-0	1.000	1
1916			6-5-0	472	115	545	2-1-0	.667	3	1919			5-2-3	275	63	.650	2-1-0	.667	3
1917			6-4-1	451	103	.591	1-1-1	.500	3										

Member of the Missouri Valley Conference (1920-1927) 19-20-6 .489

Year	Nat'l AP	Other	Overall W-L-T	PF	PA	Pct.	Conference W-L-T	Pct.	Rank	Year	Nat'l AP	Other	Overall W L T	PF	PA	Pct.	Conference W-L-T	Pct.	Rank
1920			6-0-1	176	51	.929	4-0-1	.900	1	1924			2-5-1	28	80	.312	2-3-1	.417	6
1921			5-3-0	127	102	.625	2-3-0	.400	7	1925			4-3-1	93	44	.562	3-3-1	.500	5
1922			2-3-3	64	114	.438	1-2-2	.400	6	1926			5-2-1	137	52	.688	3-2-1	.583	5
1923			3-5-0	144	111	.375	2-4-0	.333	6										
							Adrian Lindsey (1927-1931) 19-19-6 .500												
1927			3-3-2	122	101	.500	2-3-0	.400	7										

Member of the Big Eight Conference (1928-1995) 321-86-15 .778

Year	Nat'l AP	Other	Overall W-L-T	PF	PA	Pct.	Conference W-L-T	Pct.	Rank	Year	Nat'l AP	Other	Overall W L T	PF	PA	Pct.	Conference W-L-T	Pct.	Rank
1928			5-3-0	120	88	.625	3-2-0	.600	2	1930			4-3-1	100	57	.562	3-1-1	.700	2
1929			3-3-2	81	81	.500	2-2-1	.500	4	1931			4-7-1	88	108	.375	1-4-0	.200	5
							Lewie Hardage (1932-1934) 11-12-4 .481												
1932			4-4-1	90	81	.500	3-2-0	.600	2	1934			3-4-2	64	43	.444	2-2-1	.500	3
1933			4-4-1	83	70	.500	3-2-0	.600	3										
							Biff Jones (1935-1936) 9-6-3 .583												
1935			6-3-0	99	44	.667	3-2-0	.600	2	1936			3-3-3	84	57	.500	1-2-2	.400	4
							Tom Stidham (1937-1940) 27-8-3 .750												
1937			5-2-2	98	39	.667	3-1-1	.700	2	1939	19		6-2-1	186	62	.722	3-2-0	.600	3
1938	4	5	10-1-0	185	29	.909	5-0-0	1.000	1	1940			6-3-0	121	105	.667	4-1-0	.800	2
							Dewey Luster (1941-1945) 27-18-3 .594												
1941			6-3-0	218	95	.667	3-2-0	.600	2	1944			6-3-1	227	149	.650	4-0-1	.900	1
1942			3-5-2	135	78	.400	3-1-1	.700	2	1945			5-5-0	169	138	.500	4-1-0	.800	2
1943			7-2-0	187	92	.778	5-0-0	1.000	1										
							Jim Tatum (1946) 8-3-0 .727												
1946	14		8-3-0	309	120	.727	4-1-0	.800	1										
							Bud Wilkinson (1947-1963) 145-29-4 .826												
1947	16		7-2-1	194	161	.750	4-0-1	.900	1	1956	1	1	10-0-0	466	51	1.000	6-0-0	1.000	1
1948	5		10-1-0	350	121	.909	5-0-0	1.000	1	1957	4	4	10-1-0	333	99	.909	6-0-0	1.000	1
1949	2		11-0-0	399	88	1.000	5-0-0	1.000	1	1958	5	5	10-1-0	300	55	.909	6-0-0	1.000	1
1950	1	1	10-1-0	352	148	.909	6-0-0	1.000	1	1959	15	17	7-3-0	234	146	.700	5-1-0	.833	1
1951	10	11	8-2-0	321	97	.800	6-0-0	1.000	1	1960			3-6-1	136	158	.350	2-4-1	.357	6
1952	4	4	8-1-1	407	141	.850	5-0-1	.917	1	1961			5-5-0	122	141	.500	4-3-0	.571	4
1953	4	5	9-1-1	293	90	.864	6-0-0	1.000	1	1962	8	7	8-3-0	267	161	.727	7-0-0	1.000	1
1954	3	3	10-0-0	304	60	1.000	6-0-0	1.000	1	1963	9	8	8-2-0	236	137	.800	6-1-0	.857	2
1955	1	1	11-0-0	385	62	1.000	6-0-0	1.000	1										
							Gomer Jones (1964-1965) 9-11-1 .452												
1964			6-4-1	207	170	.591	5-1-1	.786	2	1965			3-7-0	106	150	.300	3-4-0	.429	5

Jim Mackenzie (1966) 6-4-0 .600

Year			Rec	PF	PA	Pct	Conf	Pct	#
1966			6-4-0	192	122	.600	4-3-0	.571	5

Chuck Fairbanks (1967-1972) 49-18-1* .739

Year			Rec	PF	PA	Pct	Conf	Pct	#
1967	3	3	10-1-0	290	92	.909	7-0-0	1.000	1
1968	11	10	7-4-0	343	225	.636	6-1-0	.857	2
1969			6-4-0	285	289	.600	4-3-0	.571	4
1970	20	15	7-4-1	305	239	.625	5-2-0	.714	2
1971	2	3	11-1-0	534	217	.917	6-1-0	.857	2
1972*	2	2	8-4-0	385	74	.667	3-4-0	.429	6

*After the 1972 season, Oklahoma forfeited three conference wins because of use of an ineligible player.

Barry Switzer (1973-1988) 157-29-4 .846

Year			Rec	PF	PA	Pct	Conf	Pct	#
1973	3	2	10-0-1	400	133	.955	7-0-0	1.000	1
1974	1		11-0-0	473	92	1.000	7-0-0	1.000	1
1975	1	1	11-1-0	344	154	.917	6-1-0	.857	1
1976	5	6	9-2-1	326	194	.792	5-2-0	.714	1
1977	7	6	10-2-0	411	217	.833	7-0-0	1.000	1
1978	3	3	11-1-0	440	151	.917	6-1-0	.857	1
1979	3	3	11-1-0	406	145	.917	7-0-0	1.000	1
1980	3	3	10-2-0	396	209	.833	7-0-0	1.000	1
1981	20	14	7-4-1	341	193	.625	4-2-1	.643	2
1982	16	16	8-4-0	317	203	.667	6-1-0	.857	2
1983			8-4-0	312	222	.667	5-2-0	.714	2
1984	6	6	9-2-1	306	164	.792	6-1-0	.857	1
1985	1	1	11-1-0	371	103	.917	7-0-0	1.000	1
1986	3	3	11-1-0	508	81	.917	7-0-0	1.000	1
1987	3	3	11-1-0	493	102	.917	7-0-0	1.000	1
1988	14	14	9-3-0	332	157	.750	6-1-0	.857	2

Gary Gibbs (1989-1994) 44-23-2 .652

Year			Rec	PF	PA	Pct	Conf	Pct	#
1989			7-4-0	380	200	.636	5-2-0	.714	3
1990	17		8-3-0	401	174	.727	5-2-0	.714	2
1991	16	14	9-3-0	383	157	.750	5-2-0	.714	3
1992			5-4-2	271	196	.545	3-2-2	.571	3
1993	17	14	9-3-0	406	145	.750	4-3-0	.571	4
1994			6-6-0	225	238	.500	4-3-0	.571	4

Howard Schnellenberger (1995) 5-5-1 .500

Year			Rec	PF	PA	Pct	Conf	Pct	#
1995			5-5-1	233	275	.500	2-5-0	.286	5

Member of the Big Twelve Conference (1996-2003) 41-23-0 .589

John Blake (1996-1998) 12-22-0 .353

Year			Rec	PF	PA	Pct	Conf	Pct	#
1996			3-8-0	255	392	.273	3-5-0	.375	7
1997			4-8-0	232	379	.333	2-6-0	.250	9
1998			5-6-0	184	229	.455	3-5-0	.375	8

Bob Stoops (1999-2003) 55-11-0 .833

Year			Rec	PF	PA	Pct	Conf	Pct	#
1999			7-5-0	405	202	.583	5-3-0	.625	4
2000	1	1	13-0-0	468	192	1.000	8-0-0	1.000	1
2001	6	6	11-2-0	387	166	.846	6-2-0	.750	4
2002	5	5	12-2-0	541	216	.857	6-2-0	.750	2
2003	3	3	12-2-0	601	214	.857	8-0-0	1.000	2

Won-loss record by decades:

1895-99	8- 2- 0	.800	1930-39	49-33-12	.585	1970-79	99-16-3	.852
1900-09	51-26-8	.647	1940-49	69-27-4	.710	1980-89	91-26-2	.773
1910-19	65-20-6	.747	1950-59	93-10-2	.895	1990-99	61-51-3	.543
1920-29	38-30-11	.551	1960-69	62-40-2	.606	2000-03	48- 6-0	.889

Historic record 734-287-53 .708

Post-season won-loss record 25-14-1 .638

1939: Orange Bowl, Tennessee 17, Oklahoma 0
1947: Gator Bowl, Oklahoma 34, NC State 13
1949: Sugar Bowl, Oklahoma 14, North Carolina 6
1950: Sugar Bowl, Oklahoma 35, LSU 0
1951: Sugar Bowl, Kentucky 13, Oklahoma 7
1954: Orange Bowl, Oklahoma 7, Maryland 0
1956: Orange Bowl, Oklahoma 20, Maryland 6
1958: Orange Bowl, Oklahoma 48, Duke 21
1959: Orange Bowl, Oklahoma 21, Syracuse 6
1963: Orange Bowl, Alabama 17, Oklahoma 0
1965: Gator Bowl, Florida State 36, Oklahoma 19
1968: Orange Bowl, Oklahoma 26, Tennessee 24
1968: Bluebonnet Bowl, SMU 28, Oklahoma 27
1970: Bluebonnet Bowl, Oklahoma 24, Alabama 24
1972: Sugar Bowl, Oklahoma 40, Auburn 22
1973: Sugar Bowl, Oklahoma 14, Penn State 0
1976: Orange Bowl, Oklahoma 14, Michigan 6
1976: Fiesta Bowl, Oklahoma 41, Wyoming 7
1978: Orange Bowl, Arkansas 31, Oklahoma 6
1979: Orange Bowl, Oklahoma 31, Nebraska 24

1980: Orange Bowl, Oklahoma 24, Florida State 7
1981: Orange Bowl, Oklahoma 18, Florida State 17
1981: Sun Bowl, Oklahoma 40, Houston 14
1983: Fiesta Bowl, Arizona State 12, Oklahoma 21
1985: Orange Bowl, Washington 28, Oklahoma 17
1986: Orange Bowl, Oklahoma 25, Penn State 10
1987: Orange Bowl, Oklahoma 42, Arkansas 8
1988: Orange Bowl, Miami (FL) 20, Oklahoma 14
1989: Citrus Bowl, Clemson 13, Oklahoma 6
1991: Gator Bowl, Oklahoma 48, Virginia 14
1993: John Hancock Bowl, Oklahoma 41, Texas Tech 10
1994: Copper Bowl, BYU 31, Oklahoma 6
1999: Independence Bowl, Ole Miss 27, Oklahoma 25
2000: Big 12 Championship: Oklahoma 27, K State 24
2001: Orange Bowl, Oklahoma 13, Florida State 2
2002: Cotton Bowl, Oklahoma 10, Arkansas 3
2002: Big 12 Championship: Oklahoma 29, Colorado 7
2003: Rose Bowl, Oklahoma 34, Washington State 14
2003: Big 12 Championship, K State 35, Oklahoma 7
2004: Sugar Bowl, LSU 21, Oklahoma 14

College Football Hall of Fame:
Bennie Owen, coach, 1905-26; Claude Reeds, fullback, 1910-13; Forest Geyer, fullback, 1913-15; Biff Jones, coach, 1935-36; Waddy Young, end, 1936-38; Jim Tatum, coach, 1946; Jim Owens, end, 1946-49; Bud Wilkinson, coach, 1947-63; Jim Weatherall, tackle, 1948-51; Billy Vessels, halfback, 1950-52; Kurt Burris, center, 1951-54; J.D. Roberts, guard, 1951-53; Jerry Tubbs, center, 1954-56; Tommy McDonald, halfback, 1954-56; Steve Owens, halfback, 1967-69; Greg Pruitt, halfback, 1970-72; Lee Roy Selmon, defensive tackle, 1972-75; Barry Switzer, coach, 1973-88; Billy Sims, halfback, 1975-79; Tony Casilles, middle guard, 1982-85; Keith Jackson, tight end, 1984-87.

Awards:

Heisman Trophy: 1952, Billy Vessels; 1969, Steve Owens; 1978, Billy Sims; 2003, Jason White; Maxwell Award: 1956, Tommy McDonald; Lombardi Award: 1975, Lee Roy Selmon; 1985, Tony Casillas; Outland Trophy: 1951, Jim Weatherall; 1953, J.D. Roberts; 1975, Lee Roy Selmon; 1978, Greg Roberts; Jim Thorpe Award: 1987, Rickey Dixon; 2001, Roy Williams; 2003, Derrick Strait; Butkus Award: 1985 and 1986, Brian Bosworth; 2001, Rocky Calmus; 2003, Teddy Lehman; Tatupu Award: 2000, J.T. Thatcher; Nagurski Award: 2001, Roy Williams; Camp Award: 1969, Steve Owens; 1978, Billy Sims; 2000, Josh Hempel; Davey O'Brien Award: 2003, Jason White; Bednarik Award: 2003, Teddy Lehman.

OREGON STATE UNIVERSITY, Corvallis, Oregon; nickname "Beavers"; colors orange and black; Reser Stadium (40,592); Pac-10 Conference. Oregon State began play in 1893 and then joined the Pacific Coast Conference in 1916. It played in that conference until it was disbanded after the 1958 season. Oregon State played as an independent until the 1964 season when it joined the AAWU, which changed its name a few years later to the Pacific 8; and then to the Pacific-10, after Arizona and Arizona State were admitted for the 1978 season.

Early years as an independent (1893-1915)

Year	Coach	W-L-T	PF	PA	Pct.	Year	Coach	W-L-T	PF	PA	Pct.
1893	Bill Bloss	4-1-0	144	48	.800	1905	Allen Steckle	6-3-0	166	28	.667
1894	Guy Kennedy	2-1-0	52	28	.667	1906	F. S. Norcross	4-1-2	77	4	.714
1895	Paul Downing	0-2-1	6	80	.167	1907	F. S. Norcross	6-0-0	137	0	1.000
1896	Tommy Cade	1-2-0	26	14	.333	1908	F. S. Norcross	4-3-1	83	51	.562
1897	Bill Bloss	2-0-0	42	8	1.000	1909	Sol Metzger	4-2-1	54	41	.714
1898	no coach	1-2-1	36	78	.375	1910	G. Schildmiller	3-2-1	27	43	.583
1899	H. Stickney	3-2-0	75	60	.600	1911	Sam Dolen	5-2-0	119	49	.714
1900, 1901	no team					1912	Sam Dolen	3-4-0	37	40	.429
1902	Frank Herbold	4-1-1	157	16	.750	1913	E. J. Stewart	3-2-3	59	85	.562
1903	----- McFadden	2-4-1	21	32	.357	1914	E. J. Stewart	7-0-2	172	15	.889
1904	Allen Steckle	4-2-0	119	22	.667	1915	E. J. Stewart	5-3-0	166	73	.625

Member of the Pacific Coast Conference (1916-1958, 1964-2002) 188-331-25 .372

Year	Nat'l	Overall W-L-T	PF	PA	Pct.	Conference W-L-T	Pct.	Rank	Year	Nat'l	Overall W-L-T	PF	PA	Pct.	Conference W-L-T	Pct.	Ran
						Joe Pipall (1916-1917) 8-7-1 .531											
1916		4-5-0	92	112	.444	0-2-0	.000	3	1917		4-2-1	73	33	.643	1-2-1	.375	3
						W. G. Hargiss (1918-1919) 6-8-1 .433											
1918		2-4-0	33	46	.333	0-2-0	.000	5	1919		4-4-1	143	64	.500	1-3-0	.250	6
						R. B. Rutherford (1920-1923) 13-14-6 .485											
1920		2-2-2	20	52	.500	1-2-1	.375	5	1922		3-4-0	44	42	.429	1-3-0	.250	5
1921		4-3-2	231	42	.556	1-2-1	.375	4	1923		4-5-2	55	71	.455	1-3-1	.300	6
						Paul Schissler (1924-1932) 48-30-2 .625											
1924		3-5-0	71	85	.375	1-4-0	.200	7	1929		5-4-0	182	106	.556	1-4-0	.200	7
1925		7-2-0	268	81	.778	3-2-0	.600	3	1930		7-3-0	208	60	.700	2-3-0	.400	6
1926		7-1-0	221	30	.875	4-1-0	.800	3	1931		6-3-1	198	62	.650	1-3-1	.300	7
1927		3-3-1	98	78	.500	2-3-0	.400	5	1932		4-6-0	130	109	.400	1-4-0	.200	8
1928		6-3-0	206	53	.667	2-3-0	.400	6									
						Lou Stiner (1933-1948) 74-49-14 .589											
1933		6-2-2	88	48	.700	2-1-1	.625	4	1941	12	8-2-0	143	49	.800	7-2-0	.778	1
1934		3-6-2	104	131	.364	0-5-2	.143	9	1942		4-5-1	157	142	.450	4-4-0	.500	5
1935		6-4-1	175	100	.591	2-3-1	.417	7	1943		no team						
1936		4-6-0	113	151	.400	3-5-0	.375	7	1944		no team						
1937		3-3-3	71	60	.500	2-3-3	.438	6	1945		4-4-1	100	131	.500	4-4-0	.500	4
1938		5-3-1	72	51	.611	4-3-1	.562	3	1946		7-1-1	157	81	.833	6-1-1	.812	2
1939		9-1-1	186	77	.864	6-1-1	.812	3	1947		5-5-0	171	136	.500	3-4-0	.429	6
1940		5-3-1	128	80	.611	4-3-1	.562	3	1948		5-4-3	249	236	.542	2-3-2	.429	6
						Kip Taylor (1949-1954) 20-36-0 .357											
1949		7-3-0	232	188	.700	5-3-0	.625	5	1952		2-7-0	123	267	.222	1-6-0	.143	9
1950		3-6-0	107	183	.333	2-5-0	.286	8	1953		3-6-0	39	187	.333	3-5-0	.375	6
1951		4-6-0	204	180	.400	3-5-0	.375	6	1954		1-8-0	60	296	.111	1-6-0	.143	9
						Tommy Prothro (1955-1964) 63-37-2 .627											
1955		6-3-0	126	120	.667	5-2-0	.714	2	1957	17	8-2-0	203	129	.800	6-2-0	.750	1
1956	10 13	7-3-1	203	201	.682	6-1-1	.812	1	1958		6-4-0	98	118	.600	5-3-0	.625	4

Independent years after PCC disbands (1959-1963)

Year	Nat'l	Overall W-L-T	PF	PA	Pct.	Year	Nat'l	Overall W-L-T	PF	PA	Pct.
1959		3-7-0	166	176	.300	1962	16	9-2-0	273	148	.818
1960		6-3-1	197	145	.650	1963		5-5-0	192	193	.500
1961		5-5-0	165	137	.500						

Member of the AAWU (name changed to the Pac-8, and later Pac-10) (1964-2001)

Year	Nat'l	Overall W-L-T	PF	PA	Pct.	Conference W-L-T	Pct.	Rank	Year	Nat'l	Overall W-L-T	PF	PA	Pct.	Conference W-L-T	Pct.	Ran
1964	8 8	8-3-0	149	124	.727	3-1-0	.750	1									
						Dee Andros (1965-1975) 51-64-1 .444											
1965		5-5-0	125	162	.500	1-3-0	.250	7	1971		5-6-0	268	317	.455	3-3-0	.500	5
1966	19	7-3-0	171	156	.700	3-1-0	.750	2	1972		2-9-0	131	295	.182	1-6-0	.143	8
1967	7 8	7-2-1	187	141	.750	4-1-1	.750	2	1973		2-9-0	166	293	.182	2-5-0	.286	5
1968	15 13	7-3-0	285	177	.700	5-1-0	.833	2	1974		3-8-0	216	285	.273	3-4-0	.429	5
1969		6-4-0	175	148	.600	4-3-0	.571	4	1975		1-10-0	103	264	.091	1-6-0	.143	10
1970		6-5-0	211	239	.545	3-4-0	.429	7									
						Craig Fertig (1976-1979) 8-36-1 .189											
1976		2-10-0	179	325	.167	1-6-0	.144	8	1976		3-7-1	128	266	.318	2-6-0	.250	9
1977		2-9-0	173	303	.182	0-7-0	.000	8	1979		1-10-0	147	396	.091	1-7-0	.125	10

Joe Avezzano (1980-1984) 6-47-2 .127

Year	W-L-T	PF	PA	Pct	Conf	Pct		Year	W-L-T	PF	PA	Pct	Conf	Pct	
1980	0-11-0	108	386	.000	0-8-0	.000	10	1983	2-8-1	171	332	.227	1-6-1	.188	9
1981	1-10-0	145	469	.091	0-7-0	.000	10	1984	2-9-0	158	279	.182	1-7-0	.125	9
1982	1-9-1	134	306	.136	0-7-1	.062	10								

Dave Kragthorpe (1985-1990) 17-48-2 .269

Year	W-L-T	PF	PA	Pct	Conf	Pct		Year	W-L-T	PF	PA	Pct	Conf	Pct	
1985	3-8-0	160	362	.273	2-6-0	.250	9	1988	4-6-1	248	280	.409	2-5-1	312	8
1986	3-8-0	143	270	.273	1-6-0	.143	10	1989	4-7-1	207	357	.375	3-4-1	.438	6
1987	2-9-0	189	433	.187	0-7-0	.000	10	1990	1-10-0	152	371	.091	1-6-0	.143	10

Jerry Pettibone (1991-1996) 13-52-1 .269

Year	W-L-T	PF	PA	Pct	Conf	Pct		Year	W-L-T	PF	PA	Pct	Conf	Pct	
1991	1-10-0	125	365	.091	1-7-0	.125	9	1994	4-7-0	223	239	.364	2-6-0	.333	8
1992	1-9-1	163	363	.136	0-7-1	.062	10	1995	1-10-0	136	237	.091	0-8-0	.000	10
1993	4-7-0	224	294	.364	2-6-0	.333	8	1996	2-9-0	216	388	.187	1-7-0	.125	10

Mike Riley (1997-1998) 8-14-0 .364

Year	W-L-T	PF	PA	Pct	Conf	Pct		Year	W-L-T	PF	PA	Pct	Conf	Pct	
1997	3-8-0	195	285	.273	0-8-0	.000	10	1998	5-6-0	286	291	.455	2-6-0	.333	7

Dennis Erickson (1999-2002) 31-17-0 .646

Year			W-L-T	PF	PA	Pct	Conf	Pct		Year	W-L-T	PF	PA	Pct	Conf	Pct	
1999			7-5-0	347	277	.583	4-4-0	.500	5	2001	5-6-0	287	259	.455	3-5-0	.375	7
2000	4	5	11-1-0	400	212	.917	7-1-0	.875	1	2002	8-5-0	414	267	.615	4-4-0	.500	4

Mike Riley (2003) 8-5-0 .615

Year	W-L-T	PF	PA	Pct	Conf	Pct	
2003	8-5-0	433	301	.615	4-4-0	.500	5

Won-loss record by decades:

1893-99	13-10-2	.560		1930-39	53-37-11	.579		1970-79	27-83-1	.248
1900-09	34-16-6	.661		1940-49	45-27-7	.614		1980-89	22-85-4	.207
1910-19	40-28-8	.579		1950-59	43-52-1	.453		1990-99	29-81-1	.266
1920-29	44-32-7	.572		1960-69	65-35-2	.647		2000-03	32-17-0	.653

Historical record: 447-503-50 .472

Post-season won-loss record: 5-4-0 .556

1940: Pineapple Bowl, OSU 39, Hawaii 6
1942: Rose Bowl, OSU 20, Duke 16
1948: Pineapple Bowl, OSU 47, Hawaii 27
1957: Rose Bowl, Iowa 35, OSU 19
1962: Liberty Bowl, OSU 6, Villanova 0

1965: Rose Bowl, Michigan 34, OSU 7
1999: Oahu Bowl, Hawaii 23, OSU 17
2001: Fiesta Bowl, OSU 41, Notre Dame 9
2002: Insight Bowl, Pittsburgh 38, Oregon State 13
2003: Las Vegas Bowl, Oregon State 55, New Mexico St. 14

College Football Hall of Fame:
Tommy Prothro, coach, 1955-64; Terry Baker, quarterback, 1960-62

Awards: Heisman Trophy: 1962, Terry Baker; Maxwell Award: 1962, Terry Baker

UNIVERSITY OF OREGON, Eugene, Oregon; nickname "Ducks"; colors green and yellow; Autzen Stadium (54,000); Pac-10 Conference. Oregon began play in 1894 and joined the Pacific Coast Conference in 1916. When the PCC was disbanded after the 1958 season and the AAWU was formed, Oregon became an independent and played as an independent from 1959 through 1963. In 1964, Oregon joined the AAWU (name later changed to Pacific-8, and later to the Pacific-10) and has played in the conference since that time.

Early years as an independent (1894-1915)

Year	Coach	W-L-T	PF	PA	Pct.	Year	Coach	W-L-T	PF	PA	Pct.
1894	Cal Young and J. Church	1-2-1	44	30	.375	1905	Bruce Shorts	4-2-2	65	39	.625
1895	Percy Benson	4-0-0	62	10	1.000	1906	Hugo Bezdek	5-0-1	50	10	.917
1896	J. F. Frick	2-1-0	16	16	.667	1907	Gordon Frost	5-1-0	100	14	.833
1897	Joe Smith	1-1-0	10	26	.500	1908	Robert Forbes	5-2-0	74	52	.714
1898	Frank Simpson	3-1-0	167	21	.750	1909	Robert Forbes	3-2-0	69	29	.600
1899	Frank Simpson	3-2-1	102	17	.583	1910	Bill Warner	4-1-0	172	11	.800
1900	L. Kaarsberg	3-3-1	66	44	.500	1911	Bill Warner	3-2-0	59	51	.600
1901	Warren Smith	3-4-1	33	44	.438	1912	Louis Pinkham	3-4-0	39	77	.429
1902	Marion Dolph	3-1-3	87	16	.500	1913	Hugo Bezdek	3-3-1	132	54	.500
1903	Warren Smith	4-2-1	75	18	.643	1914	Hugo Bezdek	4-2-1	113	30	.643
1904	R. S. Smith	5-3-0	64	59	.625	1915	Hugo Bezdek	7-2-0	203	53	.778

Member of the Pacific Coast Conference (1916-1958, 1964-2001) 228-285-18 .446

Hugo Bezdek (1906, 1913-1917) 30-10-4 .727

Year	Nat'l AP	Other	Overall W-L-T	PF	PA	Pct.	Conference W-L-T	Pct.	Rank	Year	Nat'l AP	Other	Overall W-L-T	PF	PA	Pct.	Conference W-L-T	Pct.	Rank
1916			7-0-1	244	14	.875	2-0-1	.833	2	1917			4-3-0	73	74	.571	1-2-0	.333	4

Shy Huntington (1918-1923) 26-12-6 .659

1918			4-2-0	81	35	.667	2-1-0	.667	2	1921			5-1-3	145	75	.722	0-1-2	.333	5
1919			5-2-0	103	40	.714	2-1-0	.667	1	1922			6-1-1	102	26	.813	3-0-1	.875	2
1920			3-2-1	37	38	.583	1-1-1	.500	3	1923			3-4-1	113	66	.438	0-4-1	.100	8

Joe Maddock (1924) 4-3-2 .556

| 1924 | | | 4-3-2 | 94 | 66 | .556 | 2-2-1 | .500 | 6 |

R. S. Smith (1904, 1925) 6-8-1 .433

| 1925 | | | 1-5-1 | 75 | 86 | .214 | 0-5-0 | .000 | 9 |

John McEwan (1926-1929) 20-13-2 .600

| 1926 | | | 2-4-1 | 86 | 88 | .357 | 1-4-0 | .200 | 6 | 1928 | | | 9-2-0 | 234 | 59 | .818 | 4-2-0 | .667 | 4 |
| 1927 | | | 2-4-1 | 45 | 69 | .357 | 0-4-1 | .100 | 8 | 1929 | | | 7-3-0 | 209 | 91 | .700 | 4-1-0 | .800 | 3 |

Doc Spears (1930-1931) 13-4-2 .737

| 1930 | | | 7-2-0 | 131 | 35 | .778 | 3-1-0 | .750 | 4 | 1931 | | | 6-2-2 | 90 | 87 | .700 | 3-1-1 | .700 | 3 |

Prink Callison (1932-1937) 33-23-2 .600

1932			6-3-1	109	64	.650	2-2-1	.500	5	1935			6-3-0	70	57	.667	3-2-0	.600	4
1933	8		9-1-0	165	50	.900	4-1-0	.800	1	1936			2-6-1	34	96	.278	1-6-1	.188	9
1934			6-4-0	108	98	.600	4-2-0	.667	4	1937			4-6-0	114	158	.400	2-5-0	.286	8

Tex Oliver (1938-1941, 1945-1946) 23-28-3 .454

| 1938 | | | 4-5-0 | 60 | 138 | .444 | 4-4-0 | .500 | 5 | 1940 | | | 4-4-1 | 100 | 58 | .500 | 3-4-1 | .438 | 5 |
| 1939 | | | 3-4-1 | 102 | 74 | .438 | 3-3-1 | .500 | 4 | 1941 | | | 5-5-0 | 136 | 184 | .500 | 4-4-0 | .500 | 5 |

John Warren (1942) 2-6-0 .250

| 1942 | | | 2-6-0 | 67 | 138 | .250 | 2-5-0 | .286 | 8 | 1943-1944 No team |

Tex Oliver (1945-1946)

| 1945 | | | 3-6-0 | 116 | 124 | .333 | 3-6-0 | .333 | 6 | 1946 | | | 4-4-1 | 81 | 118 | .500 | 3-4-1 | .438 | 6 |

Jim Aiken (1947-1950) 21-20-0 .512

| 1947 | | | 7-3-0 | 174 | 121 | .700 | 5-1-0 | .833 | 2 | 1949 | | | 4-6-0 | 250 | 219 | .400 | 2-5-0 | .286 | 6 |
| 1948 | 9 | | 9-2-0 | 207 | 103 | .818 | 7-0-0 | 1.000 | 1 | 1950 | | | 1-9-0 | 96 | 214 | .100 | 0-7-0 | .000 | 9 |

Len Casanova (1951-1966) 82-73-8 .528

1951			2-8-0	130	317	.200	1-6-0	.143	8	1955			6-4-0	202	158	.600	4-3-0	.571	4
1952			2-7-1	112	234	.250	2-5-0	.286	6	1956			4-4-2	133	102	.500	3-3-2	.500	4
1953			4-5-1	90	85	.450	2-5-1	.312	8	1957	17		7-4-0	160	97	.636	6-2-0	.750	1
1954			6-4-0	218	159	.600	5-3-0	.625	3	1958			4-6-0	93	103	.400	4-4-0	.500	5

Independent status after PCC disbands (1959-1963)

1959			8-2-0	179	113	.800				1962			6-3-1	229	156	.650			
1960			7-3-1	206	130	.682				1963			8-3-0	274	153	.727			
1961			4-6-0	120	112	.400													

Member of the Pac-8 (later Pac-10) (1964-2001)

| 1964 | | | 7-2-1 | 170 | 94 | .750 | 1-2-1 | .375 | 6 | 1966 | | | 3-7-0 | 113 | 129 | .300 | 1-3-0 | .250 | 6 |
| 1965 | | | 4-5-1 | 165 | 186 | 450 | 0-5-0 | .000 | 8 | | | | | | | | | | |

Jerry Frei (1967-1971) 22-29-2 .434

1967			2-8-0	104	193	.200	1-5-0	.167	7	1970			6-4-1	285	256	.591	4-3-0	.571	2
1968			4-6-0	132	201	.400	2-4-0	.333	5	1971			5-6-0	235	286	.455	2-4-0	.333	6
1969			5-5-1	271	242	.500	2-3-0	.400	5										

Dick Enright (1972-1973) 6-16-0 .273

Year	W-L-T	PF	PA	Pct	Conf	Pct	Fin	Year	W-L-T	PF	PA	Pct	Conf	Pct	Fin
1972	4-7-0	194	285	.364	2-5-0	.286	6	1973	2-9-0	205	230	.182	2-5-0	.286	5

Don Reed (1974-1976) 9-24-0 .273

Year	W-L-T	PF	PA	Pct	Conf	Pct	Fin	Year	W-L-T	PF	PA	Pct	Conf	Pct	Fin
1974	2-9-0	116	230	.182	0-7-0	.000	8	1976	4-7-0	144	271	.364	1-6-0	.143	7
1975	3-8-0	146	266	.273	2-5-0	.286	6								

Rich Brooks (1977-1994) 91-109-4 .456

Year	W-L-T	PF	PA	Pct	Conf	Pct	Fin	Year	W-L-T	PF	PA	Pct	Conf	Pct	Fin
1977	2-9-0	164	367	.182	1-6-0	.143	7	1986	5-6-0	235	338	.455	3-5-0	.374	7
1978	2-9-0	173	212	.182	2-5-0	.286	8	1987	6-5-0	226	228	.545	4-4-0	.500	5
1979	6-5-0	200	212	.545	4-3-0	.571	3	1988	6-6-0	296	247	.500	3-5-0	.375	6
1980	6-3-2	263	193	.636	4-3-1	.562	5	1989	8-4-0	379	251	.667	5-3-0	.625	2
1981	2-9-0	155	247	.182	1-6-0	.143	9	1990	8-4-0	341	221	.667	4-3-0	.571	3
1982	2-8-1	103	223	.227	2-6-0	.250	9	1991	3-8-0	186	248	.273	1-7-0	.125	9
1983	4-6-1	152	224	.409	3-3-1	.500	6	1992	6-6-0	265	222	.500	4-4-0	.500	6
1984	6-5-0	241	247	.545	3-5-0	.375	7	1993	5-6-0	278	276	.455	2-6-0	.250	8
1985	5-6-0	273	300	.455	3-4-0	.429	6	1994 11 11	9-4-0	349	250	.692	7-1-0	.875	1

Mike Bellotti (1995-2003) 75-34-0 .688

Year			W-L-T	PF	PA	Pct	Conf	Pct	Fin	Year			W-L-T	PF	PA	Pct	Conf	Pct	Fin
1995	18	18	9-3-0	326	272	.750	6-2-0	.750	3	1999	19	18	9-3-0	410	284	.750	6-2-0	.750	2
1996			6-5-0	378	356	.545	3-5-0	.375	5	2000	7	9	10-2-0	351	249	.833	7-1-0	.875	1
1997			7-5-0	380	350	.583	3-5-0	.375	7	2001	2	2	11-1-0	412	256	.917	7-1-0	.875	1
1998			8-4-0	473	328	.667	5-3-0	.625	3	2002			7-6-0	417	362	.538	3-5-0	.375	8
										2003			8-5-0	356	348	.615	5-3-0	.625	3

Won-loss record by decades:

1984-99	14- 7-2	.652		1930-39	53-36-5	.590	1970-79	36-73-1	.332
1900-09	40-20-9	.645		1940-49	38-36-2	.513	1980-89	50-58-4	.464
1910-19	44-21-3	.669		1950-59	44-53-4	.455	1990-99	70-48-0	.593
1920-29	42-29-11	.579		1960-69	50-48-5	.510	2000-03	36-14-0	.720
Historic record	517-443-46	.537							

Post-season won-loss record: 7-11-0 .389

1917: Rose Bowl, Oregon 14, Penn 0
1920: Rose Bowl, Harvard 7, Oregon 0
1949: Cotton Bowl, SMU 21, Oregon 13
1958: Rose Bowl, Ohio State 10, Oregon 7
1960: Liberty Bowl, Penn State 41, Oregon 12
1963: Sun Bowl, Oregon 21, SMU 14
1989: Independence Bowl, Oregon 27, Tulsa 24
1990: Freedom Bowl, Colorado State 32, Oregon 31

1992: Independence Bowl, Wake Forest 39, Oregon 35
1995: Rose Bowl, Penn State 38, Oregon 20
1996: Cotton Bowl, Colorado 38, Oregon 6
1997: Las Vegas Bowl, Oregon 41, Air Force 13
1998: Aloha Bowl, Colorado 51, Oregon 43
1999: Sun Bowl, Oregon 24, Minnesota 20
2000: Holiday Bowl, Oregon 35, Texas 30
2002: Fiesta Bowl, Oregon 38, Colorado 16
2002: Seattle Bowl, Wake Forest 38, Oregon 17
2003: Sun Bowl, Minnesota 31, Oregon 30

College Football Hall of Fame:
Hugo Bezdek, coach, 1906, 1913-17; Johnny Beckett, tackle, 1913-16; Johnny Kitzmiller, halfback, 1928-30; Len Casanova, coach, 1946-66; Norm Van Brocklin, quarterback, 1946-48; Mel Renfro, halfback, 1961-63.

PENN STATE, State College, Pennsylvania; nickname "Nittany Lions"; colors blue and white; Beaver Stadium (107,282); Big Ten Conference. Penn State began play in 1887 and played as an independent until the 1993 season when it joined the Big Ten.

	Nat'l							Nat'l					
Year	AP	Other	W-L-T	PF	PA	Pct.	Year	AP	Other	W-L-T	PF	PA	Pct.

No coach (1887-891)

1887			2-0-0	78	0	1.000	1890			2-2-0	91	30	.500
1888			0-2-1	6	52	.167	1891			6-2-0	174	46	.750
1889			2-2-0	32	138	.500							

George Hoskins (1892-1895) 17-4-4 .760

| 1892 | | | 5-1-0 | 108 | 20 | .833 | 1894 | | | 6-0-1 | 179 | 18 | .929 |
| 1893 | | | 4-1-0 | 92 | 36 | .800 | 1895 | | | 2-2-3 | 92 | 60 | .500 |

Samuel Newton (1896-1898) 12-14-0 .462

| 1896 | | | 3-4-0 | 63 | 128 | .429 | 1898 | | | 6-4-0 | 174 | 91 | .600 |
| 1897 | | | 3-6-0 | 69 | 141 | .333 | | | | | | | |

Sam Boyle (1899) 4-6-1 .409

| 1899 | | | 4-6-1 | 104 | 176 | .409 | | | | | | | |

Pops Golden (1900-1902) 16-12-1 .569

| 1900 | | | 4-6-1 | 84 | 144 | .409 | 1902 | | | 7-3-0 | 219 | 34 | .700 |
| 1901 | | | 5-3-0 | 112 | 90 | .625 | | | | | | | |

Dan Reed (1903) 5-3-0 .625

| 1903 | | | 5-3-0 | 182 | 77 | .625 | | | | | | | |

Tom Fennell (1904-1908) 33-17-1 .657

1904			6-4-0	195	72	.600	1907			6-4-0	251	64	.600
1905			8-3-0	195	34	.727	1908			5-5-0	153	51	.500
1906			8-1-1	93	10	.850							

Bill Hollenback (1909, 1911-1914) 28-9-4 .732

| 1909 | | | 5-0-2 | 166 | 11 | .857 | | | | | | | |

Jack Hollenback (1910) 5-2-1 .688

| 1910 | | | 5-2-1 | 243 | 24 | .688 | | | | | | | |

Bill Hollenback (1911-1914)

| 1911 | | | 8-0-1 | 199 | 15 | .944 | 1913 | | | 2-6-0 | 78 | 94 | .250 |
| 1912 | | | 8-0-0 | 285 | 6 | 1.000 | 1914 | | | 5-3-1 | 121 | 52 | .611 |

Dick Harlow (1915-1917) 20-8-0 .714

| 1915 | | | 7-2-0 | 147 | 51 | .778 | 1917 | | | 5-4-0 | 267 | 61 | .556 |
| 1916 | | | 8-2-0 | 348 | 62 | .800 | | | | | | | |

Hugo Bezdek (1918-1929) 65-30-11 .665

1918			1-2-1	22	66	.375	1924			6-3-1	202	65	.650
1919			7-1-0	173	33	.875	1925			4-4-1	67	66	.500
1920			7-0-2	259	35	.889	1926			5-4-0	200	83	.556
1921			8-0-2	251	56	.900	1927			6-2-1	163	81	.722
1922			6-4-1	185	62	.591	1928			3-5-1	93	68	.389
1923			6-2-1	159	46	.722	1929			6-3-0	101	75	.667

Bob Higgins (1930-1948) 91-57-11 .610

1930			3-4-2	142	111	.444	1940	20		6-1-1	135	46	.812
1931			2-8-0	69	167	.200	1941			7-2-0	200	78	.778
1932			2-5-0	82	115	.286	1942			6-1-1	91	70	.812
1933			3-3-1	117	66	.500	1943			5-3-1	124	53	.611
1934			4-4-0	115	58	.500	1944			6-3-0	207	141	.667
1935			4-4-0	76	70	.500	1945			5-3-0	173	89	.625
1936			3-5-0	109	86	.375	1946			6-2-0	192	48	.750
1937			5-3-0	133	114	.625	1947	4		9-0-1	332	25	.950
1938			3-4-1	138	87	.438	1948	18		7-1-1	219	55	.833
1939			5-1-2	114	77	.750							

Joe Bedenk (1949) 5-4-0 .556

| 1949 | | | 5-4-0 | 162 | 175 | .556 | | | | | | | |

Rip Engle (1950-1965) 104-48-4 .679

1950			5-3-1	141	155	.611	1958			6-3-1	237	97	.650
1951			5-4-0	155	161	.566	1959	12	10	9-2-0	262	112	.818
1952			7-2-1	172	149	.750	1960	16		7-3-0	228	113	.700
1953			6-3-0	207	148	.667	1961	17	20	8-3-0	261	143	.727
1954	20	16	7-2-0	206	92	.778	1962	9	9	9-2-0	256	119	.818
1955			5-4-0	163	150	.556	1963		16	7-3-0	165	114	.700
1956			6-2-1	177	60	.722	1964		14	6-4-0	189	111	.600
1957			6-3-0	167	135	.667	1965			5-5-0	202	151	.500

Joe Paterno (1966-2003) 339-109-3 .755

Year	AP	Other	W-L-T	PF	PA	Pct.	Year	AP	Other	W-L-T	PF	PA	Pct.
1966			5-5-0	193	208	.500	1980	8	8	10-2-0	321	158	.833
1967	10	11	8-2-1	299	158	.773	1981	3	3	10-2-0	371	162	.833
1968	2	3	11-0-0	354	120	1.000	1982	1	1	11-1-0	395	196	.917
1969	2	2	11-0-0	322	90	1.000	1983		17	8-4-1	320	312	.654
1970	18	19	7-3-0	303	166	.700	1984			6-5-0	209	230	.545
1971	5	11	11-1-0	484	137	.917	1985	3	3	11-1-0	275	153	.917
1972	10	8	10-2-0	358	189	.833	1986	1	1	12-0-0	340	133	1.000
1973	5	5	12-0-0	447	129	1.000	1987			8-4-0	286	244	.667
1974	7	7	10-2-0	322	142	.833	1988			5-6-0	231	201	.455
1975	10	10	9-3-0	240	123	.750	1989	15	14	8-3-1	259	169	.708
1976			7-5-0	241	173	.583	1990	11	10	9-3-0	297	179	.750
1977	5	4	11-1-0	390	187	.917	1991	3	3	11-2-0	474	194	.846
1978	4	4	11-1-0	333	111	917	1992		24	7-5-0	391	227	.583
1979	20	18	8-4-0	257	178	.667							

Member of the Big Ten Conference (1993-2003) 55-33-0 /629

	Nat'l		Overall				Conference				Nat'l		Overall				Conference		
Year	AP	Other	W-L-T	PF	PA	Pct.	W-L-T	Pct.	Rank	Year	AP	Other	W-L-T	PF	PA	Pct.	W-L-T	Pct.	Rank
1993	8	7	10-2-0	360	215	.833	6-2-0	.750	3	1998	17	15	9-3-0	317	183	.750	5-3-0	.625	5
1994	2	2	12-0-0	557	249	1.000	8-0-0	1.000	1	1999	11	11	10-3-0	417	234	.769	5-3-0	.625	4
1995	13	12	9-3-0	399	265	.750	5-3-0	.625	3	2000			5-7-0	264	293	.417	4-4-0	.500	5
1996	7	7	11-2-0	401	204	.846	6-2-0	.750	3	2001			5-6-0	248	281	.455	4-4-0	.500	4
1997	16	17	9-3-0	366	254	.750	6-2-0	.750	2	2002	16	15	9-4-0	446	227	.692	5-3-0	.625	4
										2003			3-9-0	233	255	.250	1-7-0	.125	9

Won-loss record by decades:

1887-89	4- 4-1	.500	1930-39	34-41-6	.457	1970-79	96-22-0	.814
1890-99	41-28-5	.588	1940-49	62-20-5	.741	1980-89	89-28-2	.756
1900-09	59-32-4	.642	1950-59	62-28-4	.702	1990-99	97-26-4	.780
1910-19	56-22-4	.707	1960-69	77-27-1	.738	2000-03	22-26-0	.458
1920-29	57-27-10	.660						

Historic record: 756-331-42 .688

Post-season won-loss record: 23-12-2

1923: Rose Bowl, USC 14, Penn State 3
1948: Cotton Bowl, Penn State 13, SMU 13
1959: Liberty Bowl, Penn State 7, Alabama 0
1960: Liberty Bowl, Penn State 41, Oregon 12
1961: Gator Bowl, Penn State 30, Georgia Tech 15
1962: Gator Bowl, Florida 17, Penn State 7
1967: Gator Bowl, Penn State 17, Florida State 17
1969: Orange Bowl, Penn State 15, Kansas 14
1970: Orange Bowl, Penn State 10, Missouri 3
1972: Cotton Bowl, Penn State 30, Texas 6
1972: Sugar Bowl, Oklahoma 14, Penn State 0
1974: Orange Bowl, Penn State 16, LSU 9
1975: Cotton Bowl, Penn State 41, Baylor 20
1975: Sugar Bowl, Alabama 13, Penn State 6
1976: Gator Bowl, Notre Dame 20, Penn State 9
1977: Fiesta Bowl, Penn State 42, Arizona State 30
1979: Sugar Bowl, Alabama 14, Penn State 7
1979: Liberty Bowl, Penn State 9, Tulane 6
1980: Fiesta Bowl, Penn State 31, Ohio State 19

1982: Fiesta Bowl, Penn State 26, USC 10
1983: Sugar Bowl, Penn State 27, Georgia 23
1983: Aloha Bowl, Penn State 13, Washington 0
1986: Orange Bowl, Oklahoma 25, Penn State 10
1987: Fiesta Bowl, Penn State 14, Miami (FL) 10
1988: Citrus Bowl, Clemson 35, Penn State 10
1989: Holiday Bowl, Penn State 50, BYU 39
1990: Blockbuster Bowl, Florida State 24, Penn State 17
1992: Fiesta Bowl, Penn State 42, Tennessee 17
1993: Blockbuster Bowl, Stanford 24, Penn State 3
1994: Citrus Bowl, Penn State 31, Tennessee 13
1995: Rose Bowl, Penn State 38, Oregon 20
1996: Outback Bowl, Penn State 43, Auburn 14
1997: Fiesta Bowl, Penn State 38, Texas 15
1998: Citrus Bowl, Florida 21, Penn State 6
1999: Outback Bowl, Penn State 26, Kentucky 14
1999: Alamo Bowl, Penn State 24, Texas A&M 0
2003: Capital One Bowl, Auburn 13, Penn State 9

College Football Hall of Fame:
Dexter Very, end, 1909-12; Pete Mauthe, halfback, 1909-12; Shorty Miller, quarterback, 1910-13; Dick Harlow, coach, 1915-17; Glenn Killinger, quarterback, 1918-21; Hugo Bezdek, coach, 1918-29; Harry Wilson, halfback, 1925-27; Bob Higgins, coach, 1930-48; Steve Suhey, guard, 1942-47; Rip Engle, coach, 1950-66; Richie Lucas, quarterback, 1957-59; Dave Robinson, end, 1960-62; Glenn Ressler, guard, 1962-64; Ted Kawlick, tight end, 1966-68; Mike Reed, defensive tackle, 1966-69; Dennis Onkotz, linebacker, 1967-69; Lyle Mitchell, running back, 1969-71;Jack Ham, linebacker, 1968-70; John Cappelleti, halfback, 1971-73.

Awards: Heisman Trophy: 1973, John Cappelletti,; Fred Biletnikoff Award: 1994, Bobby Engram; Davey O'Brien Award: 1982, Todd Blackledge, 1994, Kerry Collins; Maxwell Award: 1959, Rich Lucas, 1964, Glenn Ressler, 1969, Mike Reid, 1973, John Cappelletti, 1978, Chuck Fusina, 1994, Kerry Collins, 2002, Larry Johnson; Lombardi Award: 1978, Bruce Clark; Outland Trophy, 1969, Mike Reid; Butkus Award: 1999, LaVar Arrington; Doak Walker Award: 2002, Larry Johnson; Bednarik Award: 1999, La Var Arrington; Camp Award: 1973, John Cappelletti; 2002, Larry Johnson; Baugh Trophy: 1994, Kerry Collins.

UNIVERSITY OF PITTSBURGH, Pittsburgh, Pennsylvania; nickname "Panthers"; colors blue and gold; Heinz Field (65,000); Big East Conference. Pittsburgh began play in 1890 and was an independent until joining the Big East Conference as a founding member, beginning in the 1991 season.

Early years (1890-1907)

Year	Coach	W-L-T	PF	PA	Pct.	Year	Coach	W-L-T	PF	PA	Pct.
1890	none	1-2-0	10	74	.333	1899	Fred Robinson	3-1-1	43	23	.700
1891	none	2-5-0	74	98	.286	1900	M. Roy Jackson	5-4-0	40	33	.556
1892	none	4-2-0	38	46	.667	1901	W. Hockensmith	7-2-1	96	53	.750
1893	Anson Harrold	1-4-0	14	70	.200	1902	Fredrick Crolins	5-6-1	128	129	.458
1894	none	1-1-0	6	44	.500	1903	Arthur Mosse	0-8-1	20	262	.056
1895	J. P. Linn	1-6-0	30	136	.143	1904	Arthur Mosse	10-0-0	407	5	1.000
1896	George Hoskins	3-6-0	42	69	.333	1905	Arthur Mosse	10-2-0	406	36	.833
1897	Thomas Trenchard	1-3-0	13	91	.250	1906	E. R. Wingard	6-4-0	229	55	.600
1898	Fred Robinson	5-2-1	74	33	.688	1907	John Moorhead	8-2-0	147	27	.800

Year	AP	Nat'l Other	W-L-T	PF	PA	Pct.	Year	AP	Nat'l Other	W-L-T	PF	PA	Pct.
							Joseph Thompson (1908-1912) 30-14-2 .674						
1908			8-3-0	140	36	.727	1911			4-3-1	72	29	.562
1909			6-2-1	94	26	.722	1912			3-6-0	113	121	.333
1910			9-0-0	282	0	1.000							
							Joseph Duff (1913-1914) 14-3-1 .806						
1913			6-2-1	165	46	722	1914			8-1-0	207	38	.889
							Pop Warner (1915-1923) 60-12-4 .816						
1915			8-0-0	247	26	1.000	1920			6-0-2	146	44	.875
1916	1		8-0-0	255	25	1.000	1921			5-3-1	133	51	.611
1917	1		10-0-0	260	21	1.000	1922			8-2-0	187	43	.800
1918			4-1-0	140	16	.800	1923			5-4-0	83	45	.556
1919			6-2-1	118	66	.722							
							Jock Sutherland (1924-1938) 111-20-12 .818						
1924			5-3-1	98	43	.611	1932		3	8-1-2	182	60	.818
1925	10		8-1-0	151	34	.889	1933		4	8-1-0	147	13	.889
1926			5-2-2	170	73	.667	1934		2	8-1-0	205	44	.889
1927	2		8-1-1	289	27	.850	1935			7-1-2	135	28	.800
1928			6-2-1	177	15	.722	1936	3	3	8-1-1	214	34	.850
1929	3		9-1-0	291	90	.900	1937	1	1	9-0-1	203	34	.950
1930			6-2-1	186	69	.722	1938	8	11	8-2-0	213	59	.800
1931	9		8-1-0	287	37	.889							
							Charles Bowser (1939-1942) 14-20-1 .414						
1939			5-4-0	119	98	.556	1941			3-6-0	82	171	.333
1940			3-4-1	85	102	.438	1942			3-6-0	90	190	.333
							Clark Shaughnessy (1943-1945) 10-17-0 .370						
1943			3-5-0	114	174	.375	1945			3-7-0	87	141	.300
1944			4-5-0	147	293	.444							
							Wes Fesler (1946) 3-5-1 .389						
1946			3-5-1	88	135	.389							
							Walter Milligan (1947-1949) 13-14-0 .481						
1947			1-8-0	26	267	.111	1949			6-3-0	156	154	.667
1948			6-3-0	119	154	.667							
							Len Casanova (1950) 1-8-0 .111						
1950			1-8-0	99	204	.111							
							Tom Hamilton (1951, 1954) 7-9-0 .438						
1951			3-7-0	156	215	.300							
							Red Dawson (1952-1954) 9-11-1 .452						
1952	16		6-3-0	187	156	.667	1954*			0-3-0	83	106	.000
1953			3-5-1	143	138	.389							
							Tom Hamilton (1954)						
1954*			4-2-0	69	82	.667							

*Dawson coached the first three games of the 1954 season, and Hamilton coached the rest of the season.

Year	AP	Other	W-L-T	PF	PA	Pct.	Year	AP	Other	W-L-T	PF	PA	Pct.
							J. Micelosen (1955-1965) 56-49-7						
1955	11	11	7-4-0	181	122	.636	1961			3-7-0	145	209	.300
1956	13	12	7-3-1	156	119	.682	1962			5-5-0	142	185	.500
1957			4-6-0	134	157	.400	1963	4	3	9-1-0	236	130	.900
1958			5-4-1	163	138	.550	1964			3-5-2	152	154	.400
1959	20	19	6-4-0	147	164	.600	1965			3-7-0	173	311	.300
1960			4-3-3	134	77	.550							

David Hart (1966-1968) 3-27-0 .100

Year			W-L-T	PF	PA	Pct		Year			W-L-T	PF	PA	Pct
1966			1-9-0	98	326	.100		1968			1-9-0	99	393	.100
1967			1-9-0	73	295	.100								

Carl DePasqua (1969-1972) 13-29-0 .310

1969			4-6-0	166	287	.400		1971			3-8-0	216	388	.273
1970			5-5-0	179	245	.500		1972			1-10-0	193	350	.091

Johnny Majors (1973-1976, 1992-1996) 45-46-1 .495

1973			6-5-1	225	211	.542		1975	15	13	8-4-0	324	161	.667
1974			7-4-0	227	202	.636		1976	1	1	12-0-0	381	133	1.000

Jackie Sherrill (1977-1981) 50-9-1 .833

1977	8	7	9-2-1	428	134	.792		1980	2	2	11-1-0	380	130	.917
1978			8-4-0	263	187	.667		1981	4	2	11-1-0	385	160	.17
1979	7	6	11-1-0	291	116	.917								

Foge Fazio (1982-1985) 25-18-3 .576

1982	10	9	9-3-0	300	139	.750		1984			3-7-1	178	247	.318
1983	18	19	8-3-1	288	165	.708		1985			5-5-1	202	187	.500

Mike Gottfried (1986-1989) 26-17-2 .578

1986			5-5-1	253	209	.500		1988			6-5-0	300	183	.545
1987			8-4-0	230	146	.667		1989*	17	19	7-3-1	302	240	.682

Paul Hackett (1989-1992) 13-20-1 .382

1989*			1-0-0	31	28	1.000		1990			3-7-1	204	293	.318

Member of the Big East Conference (1991-2003) 35-51-0 .407

	Nat'l		Overall				Conference				Nat'l		Overall				Conference		
Year	AP	Other	W-L-T	PF	PA	Pct	W-L-T	Pct.	Rank	Year	AP	Other	W-L-T	PF	PA	Pct.	W-L-T	Pct.	Rank
1991			6-5-0	244	241	.545	3-2-0	.600	3	1992**			3-8-0	253	406	.273	1-3-0	.250	6

*Gottfried coached the first eleven games of the 1989 season, and Hackett coached the last game of the season.

Johnny Majors (1992-1996)

1992			0-1-0	23	36	.000	0-0-0			1995			2-9-0	217	339	.222	0-7-0	.000	7
1993			3-8-0	168	371	.272	2-5-0	.286	6	1996			4-7-0	214	430	.364	3-4-0	.429	5
1994			3-8-0	246	307	.272	2-5-0	.286	7										

**Hackett coached the first eleven games of the 1992 season, and Majors coached the last game of the season.

Walt Harris (1997-2003) 44-40-0 .524

1997			6-6-0	333	354	.500	4-3-0	.571	3	2000			7-5-0	296	247	.583	4-3-0	.571	3
1998			2-9-0	234	334	.222	0-7-0	.000	8	2001			7-5-0	296	245	.583	4-3-0	.571	3
1999			5-6-0	281	278	.455	2-5-0	.286	6	2002	19	18	9-4-0	331	232	.692	5-2-0	.714	3
										2003			8-5-0	389	311	.615	5-2-0	.714	3

Won-loss record by decades:

1890-99	22-32-2	.411		1930-39	75-14-7	.818		1970-79	70-43-2	.617
1900-09	65-33-4	.657		1940-49	35-52-2	.404		1980-89	74-37-5	.659
1910-19	66-15-3	.804		1950-59	46-49-3	.485		1990-99	37-74-1	.335
1920-29	65-19-8	.750		1960-69	34-61-5	.365		2000-03	31-19-0	.620

Historic record: 620-448-42 .577

Post-season won-loss record: 10-13-0 .435

1928: Rose Bowl, Stanford 7, Pittsburgh 6
1930: Rose Bowl, USC 47, Pittsburgh 14
1933: Rose Bowl, USC 35, Pittsburgh 0
1937: Rose Bowl, Pittsburgh 21, Washington 0
1956: Sugar Bowl, Georgia Tech 7, Pittsburgh 0
1956: Gator Bowl, Georgia Tech 21, Pittsburgh 14
1973: Fiesta Bowl, Arizona State 28, Pittsburgh 7
1975: Sun Bowl, Pittsburgh 33, Kansas 19
1977: Sugar Bowl, Pittsburgh 27, Georgia 3
1977: Gator Bowl, Pittsburgh 34, Clemson 3
1978: Tangerine Bowl, NC State 30, Pittsburgh 17

1979: Fiesta Bowl, Pittsburgh 16, Arizona 10
1980: Gator Bowl, Pittsburgh 37, South Carolina 9
1982: Sugar Bowl, Pittsburgh 24, Georgia 20
1983: Cotton Bowl, SMU 7, Pittsburgh 3
1984: Fiesta Bowl, Ohio State 28, Pittsburgh 23
1987: Bluebonnet Bowl, Texas 32, Pittsburgh 27
1989: John Hancock Bowl, Pittsburgh 31, Texas A&M 28
1997: Liberty Bowl, Southern Mississippi 41, Pittsburgh 7
2000: Insight.com Bowl, Iowa State 37, Pittsburgh 29
2001: Tangerine Bowl, Pittsburgh 34, NC State 19
2002: Insight Bowl, Pittsburgh 38, Oregon State 13
2003: Continental Tire Bowl, Virginia 23, Pittsburgh 16

College Football Hall of Fame:
Joe Thompson, halfback, 1902-06; Hube Wagner, end/halfback, 1910-13; Bob Peck, center, 1913-16; Tank McLaren, fullback, 1915-18; Pop Warner, coach, 1915-23; Tommy Davies, halfback, 1918-21; Herb Stein, center, 1918-21; Jock Sutherland, coach, 1924-38; Joe Donchess, end, 1927-29; Muggsy Skladany, end, 1931-33; Ave Daniell, tackle, 1934-36; Biggie Goldberg, fullback/halfback, 1936-38; Clark Shaughnessy, coach, 1943-45; Len Casanova, coach, 1950; Joe Schmidt, linebacker, 1950-52; Mike Ditka, end, 1958-60; Tony Dorsett, halfback, 1973-76; Hugh Donell Green, defensive end, 1977-80; Dan Marino, quarterback, 1979-82; Bill Fralic, tackle, 1981-84; Jimbo Covert, offensive tackle, 1980-83.

Awards: Heisman Trophy: 1976, Tony Dorsett; Maxwell Award: 1976, Tony Dorsett, 1980, Hugh Green; Lombardi Award: 1980, Hugh Green; Fred Biletnikoff Award: 2000, Antonio Bryant; 2003, Larry Fitzgerald; Outland Trophy: 1980, Mark May; Camp Award: 1976, Tony Dorsett; 1980, Hugh Green; 2003, Larry Fitzgerald.

PURDUE UNIVERSITY, West Lafayette, Indiana; nickname "Boilermakers"; Ross-Ade Stadium (62,000); Big Ten Conference. Purdue began play in 1887 and was a member of the Indiana Intercollegiate Athletic Association in the early 1890s. Purdue then became one of the founding members of the Big Ten in 1896. Conference win-percents prior to 1946 ignore ties, following Big Ten rules at the time.

Early years (1887-1895)

Year	Coach	W-L-T	PF	PA	Pct.	Year	Coach	W-L-T	PF	PA	Pct.
1887	Albert Berg	0-1-0	6	48	.000	1892	Knowlton Ames	8-0-0	320	24	1.000
1888	no team					1893	D. M. Balliet	5-2-1	334	144	.688
1889	G. A. Reisner	2-1-0	52	28	.667	1894	D. M. Balliet	9-1-0	188	36	.900
1890	C. L. Hare	3-3-0	170	56	.500	1895	D. M. Balliet	4-3-0	84	58	.571
1891	Knowlton Ames	4-0-0	192	0	1.000						

Member of the Big Ten Conference (1896-2003) 290-319-30 .477

Year	Nat'l AP	Other	Overall W-L-T	PF	PA	Pct.	Conference W-L-T	Pct.	Rank	Year	Nat'l AP	Other	Overall W-L-T	PF	PA	Pct.	Conference W-L-T	Pct.	Rank
							S.M. Hammond (1896) 4-2-1 .643												
1896			4-2-1	122	60	.643	0-2-1	.000	6										
							W.S. Church (1897) 5-3-1 .611												
1897			5-3-1	106	108	.611	1-2-0	.333	5										
							Alpha P. Jamison (1898-1900) 11-11-1 .500												
1898			3-3-0	34	33	.500	0-1-0	.000	6	1900			4-4-0	172	79	.500	0-4-0	.000	9
1899			4-4-1	100	122	.500	1-2-0	.333	5										
							D. M. Balliet (1893-1895, 1901) 22-10-2 .676												
1901			4-4-1	138	66	.500	0-3-1	.000	7										
							C. M. Best (1902) 7-2-1 .750												
1902			7-2-1	315	68	.750	2-2-0	.500	5										
							Oliver Cutts (1903-1904) 13-5-0 .722												
1903			4-2-0	87	48	.667	0-2-0	.000	8	1904			9-3-0	176	66	.750	1-2-0	.333	8
							A. E. Hernstein (1905) 6-1-1 .812												
1905			6-1-1	177	30	.812	1-1-1	.500	4										
							M. E. Witham (1906) 0-5-0 .000												
1906			0-5-0	5	86	.000	0-3-0	.000	6										
							L.C. Turner (1907) 0-5-0 .000												
1907			0-5-0	10	108	.000	0-3-0	.000	5										
							F. Speik (1908-1909) 6-8-0 .429												
1908			4-3-0	124	78	.571	1-3-0	.250	4	1909			2-5-0	72	147	.286	0-4-0	.000	7
							M. H. Horr (1910-1912) 8-11-1 .425												
1910			1-5-0	19	65	.167	0-4-0	.000	8	1912			4-2-1	176	70	.643	2-2-1	.500	3
1911			3-4-0	58	48	.429	1-3-0	.250	6										
							Andy Smith (1913-1915) 12-6-3 .642												
1913			4-1-2	171	20	.714	2-1-2	.667	2	1915			3-3-1	62	62	.500	2-2-0	.500	5
1914			5-2-0	157	63	.714	2-2-0	.500	4										
							Cleo O'Donnell (1916-1917) 5-8-1 .392												
1916			2-4-1	67	99	.357	0-4-1	.000	8	1917			3-4-0	95	109	.429	0-4-0	.000	8
							A. Butch Scanlon (1918-1920) 7-12-1 .375												
1918			3-3-0	87	78	.500	1-0-0	1.000	1	1920			2-5-0	36	103	.286	0-4-0	.000	9
1919			2-4-1	71	104	.357	0-3-0	.000	9										
							W. H. Dietz (1921) 1-6-0 .143												
1921			1-6-0	9	95	.143	1-4-0	.200	8										
							Jimmy Phelan (1922-1929) 35-22-5 .604												
1922			1-5-1	36	126	.214	0-3-1	.000	9	1926			5-2-1	146	67	.688	2-1-1	.667	4
1923			2-5-1	65	106	.312	1-4-0	.200	8	1927			6-2-0	170	38	.750	2-2-0	.500	4
1924			5-2-0	137	46	.714	2-2-0	.500	5	1928			5-2-1	143	41	.688	2-2-1	.500	6
1925			3-4-1	119	39	.438	0-3-1	.000	9	1929		2	8-0-0	187	44	1.000	5-0-0	1.000	1
							Noble E. Kizer (1930-1936) 42-13-3 .750												
1930			6-2-0	150	41	.750	4-2-0	.667	3	1934			5-3-0	93	75	.625	3-1-0	.750	4
1931	10		9-1-0	192	39	.900	5-1-0	.833	1	1935			4-4-0	65	67	.500	3-3-0	.500	3
1932	4		7-0-1	164	42	.938	5-0-1	1.000	1	1936			5-2-1	157	95	.688	3-1-1	.750	4
1933	10		6-1-1	109	37	.812	3-1-1	.750	4										
							Mal Elward (1937-1941) 16-18-6 .475												
1937			4-3-1	83	69	.562	2-2-1	.500	4	1940			2-6-0	96	106	.250	1-4-0	.200	8
1938			5-1-2	84	38	.750	3-1-1	.750	2	1941			2-5-1	27	62	.312	1-3-0	.250	7
1939			3-3-2	56	53	.500	2-1-2	.667	3										
							Elmer Burnham (1942-1943) 10-8-0 .556												
1942			1-8-0	27	179	.111	1-4-0	.200	8	1943	5		9-0-0	214	55	1.000	6-0-0	1.000	1
							Cecil Isbell (1944-1946) 14-14-1 .500												
1944			5-5-0	207	166	.500	4-2-0	.667	3	1946			2-6-1	97	208	.277	0-5-1	.083	9
1945			7-3-0	198	125	.700	3-3-0	.500	4										

Stu Holcomb (1947-1955) 35-42-4 .457

1947			5-4-0	205	130	.556	3-3-0	.500	3	1952	18		4-3-2	188	151	.556	4-1-1	.750	1
1948			3-6-0	126	175	.333	2-4-0	.333	5	1953			2-7-0	89	167	.222	2-4-0	.333	8
1949			4-5-0	119	135	.444	2-4-0	.333	8	1954			5-3-1	165	134	.611	3-3-0	.500	6
1950			2-7-0	143	200	.222	1-4-0	.200	8	1955			5-3-1	113	103	.611	4-2-1	.643	4
1951	14		5-4-0	153	152	.556	4-1-0	.800	2										

Jack Mollenkopf (1956-1969) 84-39-9 .670

1956			3-4-2	139	122	.444	1-4-2	.286	7	1963			5-4-0	119	149	.556	4-3-0	.571	4
1957			5-4-0	178	114	.556	4-3-0	.571	4	1964			6-3-0	168	146	.667	5-2-0	.714	3
1958	13	11	6-1-2	184	102	.778	3-1-2	.667	4	1965		13	7-2-1	227	127	.750	5-2-0	.714	3
1959			5-2-2	109	81	.667	4-2-1	.643	3	1966	7	6	9-2-0	297	154	.818	6-1-0	.857	2
1960	19	15	4-4-1	212	163	.500	2-4-0	.333	5	1967	9	9	8-2-0	291	154	.800	6-1-0	.857	1
1961	12	11	6-3-0	146	87	.667	4-2-0	.667	4	1968	10	11	8-2-0	291	167	.800	5-2-0	.714	3
1962			4-4-1	141	68	.500	3-3-0	.500	5	1969	18	18	8-2-0	354	264	.800	5-2-0	.714	3

Bob DeMoss (1970-1972) 13-18-0 .419

| 1970 | | | 4-6-0 | 161 | 189 | .400 | 2-5-0 | .286 | 8 | 1972 | | | 6-5-0 | 245 | 135 | .545 | 6-2-0 | .750 | 3 |
| 1971 | | | 3-7-0 | 210 | 228 | .300 | 3-5-0 | .375 | 6 | | | | | | | | | | |

Alex Agase (1973-1976) 18-25-1 .420

| 1973 | | | 5-6-0 | 200 | 213 | .455 | 4-4-0 | .500 | 4 | 1975 | | | 4-7-0 | 128 | 220 | .364 | 4-4-0 | .500 | 3 |
| 1974 | | | 4-6-1 | 223 | 261 | .409 | 3-5-0 | .375 | 6 | 1976 | | | 5-6-0 | 188 | 233 | .455 | 4-4-0 | .500 | 3 |

Jim Young (1977-1981) 38-19-1 .663

1977			5-6-0	231	247	.455	3-5-0	.375	6	1980	17	16	9-3-0	328	233	.750	7-1-0	.875	2
1978	13	13	9-2-1	261	130	.792	6-1-1	.813	3	1981			5-6-0	242	241	.455	3-6-0	.333	8
1979	10	10	10-2-0	287	226	.833	7-1-0	.875	2										

Leon Burtnett (1982-1986) 21-34-1 .384

1982			3-8-0	211	324	.273	3-6-0	.333	7	1985			5-6-0	287	306	.455	3-5-0	.375	7
1983			3-7-1	251	366	.318	3-5-1	.389	6	1986			3-8-0	160	335	.273	2-6-0	.250	8
1984			7-5-0	286	283	.583	6-3-0	.667	2										

Fred Akers (1987-1990) 12-31-1 .284

| 1987 | | | 3-7-1 | 197 | 285 | .318 | 3-5-0 | .375 | 6 | 1989 | | | 3-8-0 | 172 | 281 | .273 | 2-6-0 | .250 | 8 |
| 1988 | | | 4-7-0 | 124 | 303 | .364 | 3-5-0 | .375 | 6 | 1990 | | | 2-9-0 | 177 | 337 | .182 | 1-7-0 | .125 | 8 |

Jim Colletto (1991-1996) 21-42-3 .341

1991			4-7-0	219	272	.364	3-5-0	.375	6	1994			5-4-2	336	346	.545	3-3-2	.500	5
1992			4-7-0	211	267	.364	3-5-0	.375	6	1995			4-6-1	282	269	.409	2-5-1	.313	9
1993			1-10-0	221	326	.091	0-8-0	.000	10	1996			3-8-0	194	324	.273	2-6-0	.250	8

Joe Tiller (1997-2003) 55-32-0 .632

1997	15	15	9-3-0	396	267	.750	6-2-0	.750	2	2000	13	13	8-4-0	381	266	.667	6-2-0	.750	1
1998	24	23	9-4-0	444	276	.692	6-2-0	.750	4	2001			6-6-0	250	278	.500	4-4-0	.500	4
1999	25		7-5-0			.583	4-4-0	.500	6	2002			7-6-0	386	288	.538	4-4-0	.500	5
										2003	18	19	9-4-0	349	226	.692	6-2-0	.750	2

Won-loss record by decades:

1987-99	51-23-4	.679	1930-39	54-20-8	.707	1970-79	55-53-2	.509
1900-09	40-34-3	.539	1940-49	40-48-2	.456	1980-89	45-65-2	.411
1910-19	30-32-6	.485	1950-59	42-38-10	.522	1990-99	48-63-3	.434
1920-29	38-33-5	.533	1960-69	65-28-3	.693	2000-03	30-20-0	.600

Historic record 538-457-48 .539

Post-season won-loss record: 8-5-0 .615

1931: Charity Game, Purdue 7, Northwestern 0
1967: Rose Bowl, Purdue 14, USC 13
1978: Peach Bowl, Purdue 41, Ga. Tech 21
1979: Bluebonnet Bowl, Purdue 27, Tennessee 22
1980: Liberty Bowl, Purdue 28, Missouri 25
1984: Peach Bowl, Virginia 27, Purdue 24

1997: Alamo Bowl, Purdue 33, Oklahoma State 20
1998: Alamo Bowl, Purdue 37, Kansas State 34
2000: Outback Bowl, Georgia 28, Purdue 25
2001: Rose Bowl, Washington 34, Purdue 24
2001: Sun Bowl, Washington State 33, Purdue 27
2002: Sun Bowl, Purdue 34, Washington 24
2004: Capital One Bowl, Georgia 34, Purdue 27

College Football Hall of Fame:
Elmer Oliphant, halfback, 1911-14; Andy Smith, coach, 1913-15; Jimmy Phelan, coach, 1922-29; Cecil Isbell, halfback, 1935-37; Alex Agase, guard, 1943; Bump Elliott, halfback, 1943; Jack Mollenkopf, coach, 1956-69; Bob Griese, quarterback, 1964-66; Leroy Keyes, halfback, 1966-68; Jim Young, coach, 1977-81.

Awards: Ray Guy Award, 2001, Travis Darsch; Maxwell Award: 2000, Drew Brees; Mackey Award: 2000, Tim Stratton; Baugh Trophy: 1966, Bob Griese; 1969, Mike Phipps; 1980: Marc Hermann.

RICE UNIVERSITY, Houston, Texas; nickname "Owls"; colors blue and gray; Rice Stadium (70,000); Western Athletic Conference. Rice was a founding member of the Southwest Conference in 1915, dropped out of the conference in 1916 and 1917, and then returned to the conference in 1918 remaining with the SWC until it disbanded after the 1995 season. Rice joined the Western Athletic Conference in 1996.

Year	AP	Other	W-L-T	PF	PA	Pct.	W-L-T	Pct.	Rank	Year	AP	Other	W-L-T	PF	PA	Pct.	W-L-T	Pct.	Rank
	Nat'l		Overall				Conference				Nat'l		Overall				Conference		
Phil Arbuckle (1912-1917, 1919-1923) 51-24-8 .663																			
1912			3-2-0	49	125	.600				1914			3-2-3	59	113	.562			
1913			4-0-0	81	14	1.000													
Member of the Southwest Conference (1915, 1918-1995) 178-308-12 .369																			
1915			5-3-0	122	143	.625	1-2-0	.333	5	1917			7-1-0	228	42	.875	out of conference		
1916			6-1-2	350	53	.778	out of conference												
John Anderson (1918) 1-5-1 .214																			
1918			1-5-1	13	62	.214	1-1-0	.500	3										
Phil Arbuckle (1919-1923)																			
1919			8-1-0	190	60	.889	3-1-0	.750	2	1922			4-4-0	74	122	.500	1-4-0	.200	7
1920			4-2-2	105	28	.625	2-2-1	.500	4	1923			3-5-0	35	94	.375	1-4-0	.200	7
1921			4-4-1	144	128	.500	1-2-1	.375	6										
John Heisman (1924-1927) 14-18-3 .443																			
1924			4-4-0	85	69	.500	2-2-0	.500	3	1926			4-4-1	84	81	.500	0-4-0	.000	7
1925			4-4-1	85	79	.500	1-2-1	.375	6	1927			2-6-1	64	160	.278	1-3-0	.250	6
Claude Rothgeb (1928) 2-7-0 .222																			
1928			2-7-0	83	174	.222	0-5-0	.000	7										
Jack Meagher (1929-1933) 26-26-0 .500																			
1929			2-7-0	34	203	.222	0-5-0	.000	7	1932			7-3-0	141	77	.700	3-3-0	.500	3
1930			8-4-0	134	91	.667	2-4-0	.333	6	1933			3-8-0	56	137	.273	1-5-0	.167	6
1931			6-4-0	178	66	.600	3-3-0	.500	4										
Jimmy Kitts (1934-1939) 33-29-4 .538																			
1934		5	9-1-1	204	44	.864	5-1-0	.833	1	1937	18		6-3-2	117	94	.636	4-1-1	.750	1
1935			8-3-0	201	95	.727	3-3-0	.500	3	1938			4-6-0	91	133	.400	3-3-0	.500	4
1936			5-7-0	127	108	.417	1-5-0	.167	7	1939			1-9-1	77	143	.136	0-5-1	.083	7
Jess Neely (1940-1966) 144-124-10 .536																			
1940			7-3-0	130	73	.700	4-2-0	.667	3	1954	19	19	7-3-0	205	148	.700	4-2-0	.667	3
1941			6-3-1	167	121	.650	3-2-1	.583	4	1955			2-7-1	110	179	.250	0-6-0	.000	7
1942			7-2-1	177	74	.750	4-1-1	.750	2	1956			4-6-0	160	169	.400	1-5-0	.167	6
1943			3-7-0	60	183	.300	2-3-0	.400	4	1957	8	7	7-4-0	175	121	.636	5-1-0	.833	1
1944			5-6-0	143	163	.455	2-3-0	.400	4	1958			5-5-0	178	155	.500	4-2-0	.667	2
1945			5-6-0	130	153	.455	3-3-0	.500	3	1959			1-7-2	86	197	.200	1-4-1	.250	6
1946	10		9-2-0	245	62	.818	5-1-0	.833	1	1960			7-4-0	174	72	.636	5-2-0	.714	2
1947	18		6-3-1	202	74	.650	4-2-0	.667	3	1961	17		7-4-0	183	158	.636	5-2-0	.714	3
1948			5-4-1	168	119	.550	3-2-1	.583	3	1962			2-6-2	119	173	.300	2-4-1	.357	6
1949	5		10-1-0	273	97	.909	6-0-0	1.000	1	1963			6-4-0	145	114	.600	4-3-0	.571	3
1950			6-4-0	168	196	.600	2-4-0	.333	5	1964			4-5-1	117	111	.450	3-3-1	.500	4
1951			5-5-0	149	144	.500	3-3-0	.500	3	1965			2-8-0	123	248	.200	1-6-0	.143	7
1952			5-5-0	152	175	.500	4-2-0	.667	2	1966			2-8-0	154	211	.200	1-6-0	.143	8
1953	6	6	9-2-0	295	105	.818	5-1-0	.833	1										
Bo Hagan (1967-1970) 12-27-1 .313																			
1967			4-6-0	164	175	.400	2-5-0	.286	7	1969			3-7-0	168	225	.300	2-5-0	.286	6
1968			0-9-1	151	326	.050	0-7-0	.000	8	1970			5-5-0	168	175	.500	3-4-0	.429	5
Bill Peterson (1971) 3-7-1 .318																			
1971			3-7-1	146	209	.318	2-4-1	.357	6										
Al Conover (1972-1975) 14-28-1 .337																			
1972			5-5-1	196	238	.500	3-4-0	.429	6	1974			2-8-1	117	236	.227	2-5-0	.286	7
1973			5-6-0	153	223	.455	4-3-0	.571	3	1975			2-9-0	176	252	.222	1-6-0	.143	7
Homer Rice (1976-1977) 4-18-0 .182																			
1976			3-8-0	236	417	.272	2-6-0	.250	7	1977			1-10-0	151	458	.091	0-8-0	.000	9
Ray Alborn (1978-1983) 13-53-0 .197																			
1978			2-9-0	159	408	.182	2-6-0	.250	8	1981			4-7-0	183	347	.364	3-5-0	.375	6
1979			1-10-0	121	418	.091	0-8-0	.000	9	1982			0-11-0	138	361	.000	0-8-0	.000	9
1980			5-6-0	175	215	.455	4-4-0	.500	4	1983			1-10-0	103	333	.091	0-8-0	.000	9
Watson Brown (1984-1985) 4-18-0 .182																			
1984			1-10-0	213	382	.091	0-8-0	.000	9	1985			3-8-0	233	404	.272	2-6-0	.250	6
Jerry Berndt (1986-1988) 6-27-0 .182																			
1986			4-7-0	185	330	.364	2-6-0	.250	6	1988			0-11-0	165	358	.000	0-7-0	.000	7
1987			2-9-0	237	427	.182	0-7-0	.000	8										

Fred Goldsmith (1989-1993) 23-31-1 .500

Year	W-L-T	PF	PA	Pct	Conf	Pct	Rk	Year	W-L-T	PF	PA	Pct	Conf	Pct	Rk
1989	2-8-1	175	313	.227	2-6-0	.250	6	1992	6-5-0	294	261	.545	4-3-0	.571	2
1990	5-6-0	256	258	.455	3-5-0	.375	4	1993	6-5-0	284	294	.545	3-4-0	.429	4
1991	4-7-0	239	287	.364	2-6-0	.250	8								

Ken Hatfield (1994-2001) 42-46-1 .478

Year	W-L-T	PF	PA	Pct	Conf	Pct	Rk	Year	W-L-T	PF	PA	Pct	Conf	Pct	Rk
1994	5-6-0	206	203	.455	4-3-0	.571	1	1995	2-8-1	215	284	.227	1-6-0	.143	7

Member of the Western Athletic Conference (1996-2003) 35-28-0 .556

Year	W-L-T	PF	PA	Pct	Conf	Pct	Rk	Year	W-L-T	PF	PA	Pct	Conf	Pct	Rk
1996	7-4-0	296	312	.636	6-2-0	.750	3	1999	5-6-0	237	261	.455	4-3-0	.571	4
1997	7-4-0	306	285	.636	5-3-0	.625	4	2000	3-8-0	237	322	.273	2-6-0	.250	8
1998	5-6-0	235	257	.455	5-3-0	.625	5	2001	8-4-0	333	335	.667	5-3-0	.625	4

Ron Ernst (2002-2003) 9-14-0 .391

Year	W-L-T	PF	PA	Pct	Conf	Pct	Rk	Year	W-L-T	PF	PA	Pct	Conf	Pct	Rk
2002	4-7-0	253	296	.364	3-5-0	.375	5	2003	5-7-0	343	378	.417	5-3-0	.625	5

Won-loss record by decades:

1912-19	37-14-6	.702	1950-59	51-48-3	.515	1990-99	52-57-1	.477	
1920-29	33-47-6	.418	1960-69	37-61-4	.382	2000-03	20-26-0	.435	
1930-39	57-48-4	.541	1970-79	29-77-3	.280				
1940-49	63-37-4	.625	1980-89	22-87-1	.205				

Historic record: 401-503-32 .446

Post-season won-loss record: 4-3-0 .571

1938: Cotton Bowl, Rice 28, Colorado 14

1947: Orange Bowl, Rice 8, Tennessee 0

1950: Cotton Bowl, Rice 27, North Carolina 13

1954: Cotton Bowl, Rice 28, Alabama 6

1958: Cotton Bowl, Navy 20, Rice 7

1961: Sugar Bowl, Mississippi 14, Rice 6

1961: Bluebonnet Bowl, Kansas 33, Rice 7

College Football Hall of Fame:

John Heisman, coach, 1924-27; Bill Wallace, halfback, 1932-35; Jess Neely, coach, 1940-66; Weldon Humble, guard, 1941-46; James Williams, end, 1946-49; Dick Maegele, halfback, 1952-54; Buddy Dial, end, 1956-58.

Awards: Doak Walker Award: 1991, Trevor Cobb; Baugh Trophy: 1976, Tommy Kramer.

RUTGERS UNIVERSITY, New Brunswick, New Jersey; nickname "Scarlet Knights"; color scarlet; Rutgers Stadium (41,500); Big East Conference. Rutgers played in the first (American) football game every scheduled in 1869. It continued to play as an independent until 1991 when it became one of the founding members of the Big East Conference.

Early years with no formal coach (1869-1890)

Year	W-L-T	PF	PA	Pct.	Year	W-L-T	PF	PA	Pct.
1869	1-1-0			.500	1880	1-2-0			.333
1870	1-1-0			.500	1881	2-3-1			.417
1871	no information				1882	6-4-0			.600
1872	1-1-1			.500	1883	1-6-0	54	261	.143
1873	1-2-0			.333	1884	3-4-0	137	170	.429
1874	1-3-0			.250	1885	0-1-0	5	10	.000
1875	1-1-1			.500	1886	1-3-0	70	115	.250
1876	1-0-0			1.000	1887	2-6-0	47	187	.250
1877	1-2-0			.333	1888	1-7-1	36	337	.167
1878	1-2-1			.375	1889	1-4-0	22	92	.200
1879	2-1-2			.600	1890	5-5-1	222	177	.500

William Reynolds (1891) 8-6-0 .571

Year	W-L-T	PF	PA	Pct.
1891	8-6-0	265	137	.571

No coach (1892-1894)

1894	4-6-0	63	210	.400
1892	3-5-1	108	160	.389
1893	0-4-0	8	88	.000

H. W. Ambruster (1895) 3-4-0 .429

1895	3-4-0	86	131	.429

John Pendleton (1896-1897) 8-12-0 .400

1897	2-6-0	34	118	.250
1896	6-6-0	74	198	.500

Wm. Van Dyck (1898-1899) 3-15-1 .184

1899	2-9-0	114	245	.182
1898	1-6-1	11	105	.188

Michael Daly (1900) 4-4-0 .500

1900	4-4-0	50	66	.500

Arthur Robinson (1901) 0-7-0 .000

1901	0-7-0	5	133	.000

Harry Van Hovenberg (1902) 3-7-0 .300

1902	3-7-0	42	188	.300

Oliver Mann (1903, 1905) 7-10-1 .417

1903	4-4-1	94	110	.500

A. E. Hitchener (1904) 1-6-2 .222

1904	1-6-2	16	202	.222

Oliver Mann (1905)

1905	3-6-0	44	99	.333

F. H. Gorton (1906-1907) 8-7-3 .528

1907	3-5-1	76	99	.389
1906	5-2-2	122	30	.667

Joseph Smith (1908) 3-5-1 .389

1908	3-5-1	53	104	.389

Herman Pritchard (1909) 3-5-1 .389

1909	3-5-1	62	74	.389

Howard Gargan (1910-1912) 12-10-4 .538

1912	5-4-0	112	102	.556
1910	3-2-3	59	33	.562
1911	4-4-1	25	99	.500

George Sanford (1913-1923) 56-32-5 .731

1913	6-3-0	240	76	.667	1919	5-3-0	115	70	.625
1914	5-3-1	208	73	.611	1920	2-7-0	32	132	.222
1915	7-1-0	351	33	.875	1921	4-5-0	99	168	.444
1916	3-2-2	106	52	.571	1922	5-4-0	134	117	.545
1917	7-1-1	295	28	.833	1923	7-1-1	260	36	.833
1918	5-2-0	192	78	.714					

John Wallon (1924-1926) 12-14-1 .463

1926	3-6-0	49	135	.333
1924	7-1-1	250	48	.833
1925	2-7-0	38	146	.222

Harry Rockafeller (1927-1930, 1942-1945) 33-26-1 .558

1929	5-4-0	109	94	.545
1927	4-4-0	103	179	.500
1928	6-3-0	97	116	.667
1930	4-5-0	159	154	.455

J. Wilder Tasker (1931-1937) 31-27-5 .532

1931	4-3-1	111	100	.562	1935	4-5-0	115	170	.455
1932	6-3-1	159	58	.650	1936	1-6-1	20	133	.188
1933	6-3-1	146	94	.650	1937	5-4-0	128	39	.545
1934	5-3-1	184	68	.611					

Harvey Harman (1938-1941, 1946-1955) 74-44-2 .625

Year	W-L-T	PF	PA	Pct	Year	W-L-T	PF	PA	Pct
1938	7-1-0	118	57	.875	1940	5-3-0	211	56	.625
1939	7-1-1	146	70	.833	1941	7-2-0	174	85	.778

Harry Rockafeller (1942-1945)

Year	W-L-T	PF	PA	Pct	Year	W-L-T	PF	PA	Pct
1942	3-4-1	100	113	.438	1944	3-2-0	58	82	.600
1943	3-2-0	67	21	.600	1945	5-2-0	140	61	.714

Harvey Harman (1946-1955)

Year	W-L-T	PF	PA	Pct	Year	W-L-T	PF	PA	Pct
1946	7-2-0	252	48	.778	1951	4-4-0	184	114	.500
1947	8-1-0	262	99	.889	1952	4-4-1	178	124	.500
1948	7-2-0	224	130	.778	1953	2-6-0	125	216	.250
1949	6-3-0	266	138	.667	1954	3-6-0	140	145	.333
1950	4-4-0	186	154	.500	1955	3-5-0	93	163	.375

John Steigman (1956-1959) 22-15-0 .595

Year		W-L-T	PF	PA	Pct	Year		W-L-T	PF	PA	Pct
1956		3-7-0	117	240	.300	1958	20	8-1-0	301	77	.889
1957		5-4-0	181	133	.545	1959		6-3-0	132	121	.667

John Bateman (1960-1972) 83-51-0 .691

Year		W-L-T	PF	PA	Pct	Year	W-L-T	PF	PA	Pct
1960		8-1-0	225	69	.889	1967	4-5-0	155	170	.444
1961	15	9-0-0	246	102	1.000	1968	8-2-0	276	182	.800
1962		5-5-0	164	169	.500	1969	6-3-0	212	150	.667
1963		3-6-0	145	197	.333	1970	5-5-0	193	218	.500
1964		6-3-0	149	115	.667	1971	4-7-0	193	243	.364
1965		3-6-0	84	152	.333	1972	7-4-0	290	172	.636
1966		5-4-0	184	177	.556					

Frank Burns (1973-1983) 78-43-1 .643

Year			W-L-T	PF	PA	Pct	Year	W-L-T	PF	PA	Pct
1973			6-5-0	245	228	.545	1979	8-3-0	243	174	.727
1974			7-3-1	244	146	.682	1980	7-4-0	279	156	.636
1975			9-2-0	347	91	.818	1981	5-6-0	139	208	.455
1976	17	17	11-0-0	287	81	1.000	1982	5-6-0	180	278	.455
1977			8-3-0	291	181	.727	1983	3-8-0	195	258	.273
1978			9-3-0	284	165	.750					

Dick Anderson (1984-1989) 27-34-4 .446

Year	W-L-T	PF	PA	Pct	Year	W-L-T	PF	PA	Pct
1984	7-3-0	213	155	.700	1987	6-5-0	168	213	.545
1985	2-8-1	149	266	.227	1988	5-6-0	273	255	.455
1986	5-5-1	221	189	.500	1989	2-7-2	245	319	.273

Doug Graber (1990-1995) 29-36-1 .447

Year	W-L-T	PF	PA	Pct
1990	3-8-0	173	302	.273

Member of the Big East Conference (1991-2003) 17-70-1 .199

Year	Nat'l AP Other	Overall W-L-T	PF	PA	Pct	Conference W-L-T	Pct.	Rank	Year	Nat'l AP Other	Overall W-L-T	PF	PA	Pct.	Conference W-L-T	Pct.	Rank
1991		6-5-0	217	217	.545	2-3-0	.400	3	1994		5-5-1	241	261	.500	2-4-1	.357	5
1992		7-4-0	344	245	.636	4-2-0	.667	4	1995		4-7-0	304	412	.364	2-5-0	.286	5
1993		4-7-0	351	334	.364	1-6-0	.143	7									

Terry Shea (1996-2000) 11-44-0 .200

Year	Overall W-L-T	PF	PA	Pct	Conference W-L-T	Pct.	Rank	Year	Overall W-L-T	PF	PA	Pct.	Conference W-L-T	Pct.	Rank
1996	2-9-0	143	380	.182	1-6-0	.143	7	1999	1-10-0	155	427	.091	1-6-0	.143	8
1997	0-11-0	191	496	.000	0-7-0	.000	8	2000	3-8-0	233	399	.273	0-7-0	.000	8
1998	5-6-0	206	376	.455	2-5-0	.286	6								

Greg Schiano (2001-2003) 8-27-0 .229

Year	Overall W-L-T	PF	PA	Pct	Conference W-L-T	Pct.	Rank	Year	Overall W-L-T	PF	PA	Pct.	Conference W-L-T	Pct.	Rank
2001	2-9-0	119	397	.182	0-7-0	.000	8	2003	5-7-0	329	354	.417	2-5-0	.286	7
2002	1-11-0	167	397	.083	0-7-0	.000	8								

Won-loss record by decades:

1869-79	11-14-5	.450	1920-29	45-42-2	.517	1970-79	74-35-1	.677
1880-89	18-40-2	.317	1930-39	49-34-6	.584	1980-89	47-58-4	.450
1890-99	34-57-3	.378	1940-49	54-23-1	.699	1990-99	37-72-1	.341
1900-09	29-51-8	.375	1950-59	42-46-1	.478	2000-03	11-35-0	.239
1910-19	50-25-8	.651	1960-69	57-35-0	.620			

Historic total: 558-567-42 .496

Post-season won-loss record: 0-1-0 .000
1978: Garden State Bowl, Arizona State 34, Rutgers 18

College Football Hall of Fame:
George Sanford, coach, 1913-23; Paul Robeson, end, 1915-18; Homer Hazel, end/fullback, 1916-24; Harvey Harman, coach, 1938-41, 1946-55; Alex Kroll, center, 1956-61.

SAN DIEGO STATE, San Diego, California; nickname "Aztecs"; colors scarlet and black; Qualcomm Stadium (71,400); Mountain West Conference. San Diego State began play in 1921 as a member of the Southern California Intercollegiate Athletic Conference (SCIAC). In 1939, the team became a member of the California Collegiate Athletic Association (CCAA) and played in that conference through the 1967 season. San Diego State played as an independent in 1968. In 1969, San Diego State joined the Pacific Coast Athletic Association (later the Big West Conference) and played in the conference through the 1975 season. State was an independent for two years before joining the Western Athletic Conference in 1978. In 1999, San Diego State joined seven other WAC members to form the Mountain West Conference.

| | Nat'l | | Overall | | | | Conference | | | | Nat'l | | Overall | | | | Conference | | |
Year	AP	Other	W-L-T	PF	PA	Pct.	W-L-T	Pct.	Rank	Year	AP	Other	W-L-T	PF	PA	Pct.	W-L-T	Pct.	Rank
Member of the SCIAC (1921-1924, 1926-1938) 43-34-7 .554																			
C. E. Peterson (1921-1929) 43-31-4 .577																			
1921			4-6-0	60	100	.400	1-3-0	.250	5	1926			3-4-1	78	150	.438	1-3-1	.300	7
1922			6-4-0	191	104	.600	4-0-0	1.000	1	1927			4-3-0	190	79	.571	2-3-0	.400	5
1923			8-2-0	207	82	.800	2-0-0	1.000	1	1928			3-3-0	111	105	.500	2-3-0	.400	5
1924			7-1-2	249	53	.800	3-0-0	1.000	1	1929			3-5-0	81	96	.375	1-5-0	.167	6
1925			5-3-1	108	59	.688	independent												
W. B. Herreid (1930-34) 20-21-5 .489																			
1930			5-4-0	112	71	.556	3-3-0	.500	3	1933			4-4-1	59	72	.500	4-2-1	.643	4
1931			5-3-2	71	45	.600	2-2-1	.500	4	1934			3-5-1	61	106	.389	2-1-1	.700	2
1932			3-5-1	80	72	.388	2-4-1	.357	5										
Leo Calland (1935-1941) 34-22-4 .600																			
1935			3-4-1	55	83	.438	2-2-1	.500	3	1937			7-1-0	90	16	.875	4-1-0	.800	1
1936			6-1-1	118	62	.813	5-0-0	1.000	1	1938			5-2-1	82	69	.688	3-2-1	.583	3
Member of the CCAA (1939-1967) 53-42-5 .555																			
1939			2-7-0	60	148	.222	0-2-0	.000	4	1941			6-4-0	105	87	.600	0-3-0	.000	4
1940			5-3-1	128	87	.611	1-1-1	.500	2										
John Eubank (1942) 0-6-1 .071																			
1942			0-6-1	50	211	.071	no conference												
No team (1943-1944)																			
Bob Breitbard (1945) 2-5-0 .286																			
1945			2-5-0	65	163	.286	no conference												
Bill Terry (1946) 6-4-0 .600																			
1946			6-4-0	152	105	.600	2-3-0	.400	5										
Bill Schutte (1947-1955) 48-36-4 .568																			
1947			7-3-1	191	156	.682	2-2-1	.500	4	1952			4-5-0	238	267	.444	2-2-0	.500	3
1948			4-7-0	158	190	.364	1-4-0	.200	5	1953			5-3-1	230	142	.611	3-1-1	.700	2
1949			6-3-0	195	200	.667	3-1-0	.750	2	1954			5-4-0	177	140	.556	2-2-0	.500	2
1950			5-3-1	212	186	.611	3-0-1	.875	1	1955			2-8-0	65	231	.200	no conference		
1951			10-0-1	386	134	.955	3-0-0	1.000	1										
Paul Governali (1956-1960) 11-27-4 .310																			
1956			4-3-2	149	217	.556	2-1-0	.667	2	1959			1-6-1	74	108	.188	0-5-0	.000	6
1957			2-7-0	77	243	.222	0-1-0	.000	5	1960			1-6-1	53	207	.188	0-5-0	.000	6
1958			3-5-0	84	200	.375	2-3-0	.400	4										
Don Coryell (1961-1972) 104-19-2 .840																			
1961			7-2-1	231	154	.750	2-2-1	.500	4	1965			8-2-0	353	87	.800	3-2-0	.600	3
1962			8-2-0	294	135	.800	5-0-0	1.000	1	1966			11-0-0	317	105	1.000	5-0-0	1.000	1
1963			7-2-0	317	118	.778	3-1-0	.750	1	1967			10-1-0	319	135	.909	5-0-0	1.000	1
1964			8-2-0	423	71	.800	4-1-0	.800	2										
San Diego State is independent (1968)																			
1968			9-0-1	377	155	.950													
Member of the Pacific Coast Athletic Association (1969-1975) 27-6-1 .809																			
1969	18		11-0-0	492	194	1.000	6-0-0	1.000	1	1971			6-5-0	245	230	.545	2-3-0	.400	4
1970			9-2-0	364	123	.818	5-1-0	.833	1	1972		20	10-1-0	266	143	.909	4-0-0	1.000	1
Claude Gilbert (1973-1980) 61-26-2 .697																			
1973	19		9-1-1	321	129	.864	3-0-1	.875	1	1975			8-3-0	320	145	.727	3-2-0	.600	3
1974			8-2-1	291	170	.733	4-0-0	1.000	1										
San Diego State is independent (1976-1977)																			
1976			10-1-0	197	125	.909					1977	16	19	10-1-0	349	165	.909			
Member of the Western Athletic Conference (1978-1998) 88-70-4 556																			
1978			4-7-0	242	257	.364	2-4-0	.333	6	1980			4-8-0	161	294	.333	4-4-0	.500	4
1979			8-3-0	286	276	.727	5-2-0	.714	2										
Doug Scovil (1981-1985) 24-32-3 .432																			
1981			6-5-0	279	227	.556	3-5-0	.375	6	1984			4-7-1	265	250	.375	4-3-1	.562	4
1982			7-5-0	308	320	.583	4-3-0	.571	3	1985			5-6-1	342	317	.458	3-4-1	.438	6
1983			2-9-1	221	352	.208	1-6-1	.188	8										

Denny Stolz (1986-1988) 16-19-0 .457

| 1986 | 8-4-0 | 292 | 279 | .667 | 7-1-0 | .875 | 1 | 1988 | | 3-8-0 | 204 | 384 | .273 | 3-5-0 | .375 | 6 |
| 1987 | 5-7-0 | 357 | 428 | .417 | 4-4-0 | .500 | 5 | | | | | | | | | |

Al Luginbill (1989-1993) 31-25-2 .534

1989	6-5-1	368	372	.542	4-3-0	.571	5	1992		5-5-1	334	338	.500	5-3-0	.625	4
1990	6-5-0	459	386	.545	5-2-0	.714	3	1993		6-6-0	413	392	.500	4-4-0	.500	6
1991	8-4-1	403	337	.654	6-1-1	.812	2									

Ted Tollner (1994-2002) 47-57-0 .452

1994	4-7-0	332	339	.364	2-6-0	.250	8	1997		5-7-0	257	333	.417	4-4-0	.500	4
1995	8-4-0	401	283	.667	5-3-0	.625	5	1998		7-5-0	230	224	.583	7-1-0	.875	1
1996	8-3-0	428	303	.727	6-2-0	.750	3									

Member of the Mountain West Conference (1999-2003) 15-20-0 .429

| 1999 | 5-6-0 | 272 | 226 | .455 | 3-4-0 | .429 | 5 | 2001 | | 3-8-0 | 184 | 290 | 273 | 2-5-0 | .286 | 7 |
| 2000 | 3-8-0 | 170 | 273 | .273 | 3-4-0 | .429 | 5 | | | | | | | | | |

Tom Craft (2002-2003) 10-15-0 .400

| 2002 | 4-9-0 | 309 | 411 | .308 | 4-3-0 | .571 | 3 | 2003 | | 6-6-0 | 256 | 272 | /500 | 2-5-0 | .286 | 4 |

Won-loss record by decades:

1921-29	43-31-4	577	1950-59	41-44-6	.484	1980-89	50-64-4	.441
1930-39	43-36-8	.540	1960-69	80-17-3	.815	1990-99	62-52-2	.543
1940-49	36-35-3	.507	1970-79	82-26-2	.755	2000-03	16-31-0	.340

Historic record: 453-336-32 .570

Post-season record: 3-4-0 .429

1948: Harbor Bowl, Hardin-Simmons 53, San Diego State 0   1986: Holiday Bowl, Iowa 39, San Diego State 38
1966: Camellia Bowl, San Diego State 28, Montana State 7   1991: Freedom Bowl, Tulsa 28, San Diego State 17
1967: Camellia Bowl, San Diego State 28, San Francisco State 6   1998: Las Vegas Bowl, No. Carolina 20, San Diego State 13
1969: Pasadena Bowl, San Diego State 28, Boston U. 7

College Football Hall of Fame: George Brown, guard, 1942-47; Don Coryell, coach, 1961-72; Fred Dryer, end, 1967-68: Baugh Trophy: 1973, Jessee Freitas.

SAN JOSE STATE, San Jose, California; nickname "Spartans"; colors gold, white and blue; Spartan Stadium (30,456); Western Athletic Conference. In 1969, San Jose State was a founding member of the Pacific Coast Athletic Association, later renamed the Big West Conference, and remained a member through the 1995 season. San Jose State has been a member of the WAC since 1996.

Year	Nat'l AP Other	W-L-T	PF	PA	Pct.		Year	Nat'l AP Other	W-L-T	PF	PA	Pct.
						J. E. Addicott (1893, 1895, 1898, 1900) 6-5-3 .536						
1893		0-1-0	0	18	.000							
						No team (1894)						
						J. E. Addicott (1895, 1898, 1900)) 6-4-3 .577						
1895		0-0-1	6	6	.500							
						No team (1896-1897)						
						J. E. Addicott (1898)						
1898		4-1-1	81	22	.750							
						Jess Woods (1899) 5-2-1 .688						
1899		5-2-1	115	68	.688							
						J. E. Addicott (1900)						
1900		2-3-1	11	64	.417							
						Fielding Yost (1900) 1-0-0 1.000						
1900		1-0-0	12	0	1.000							
						No team (1901 – 1920)						
						David Wooster (1921-1922) 3-10-1 .250						
1921		1-5-0	34	134	.167		1922		2-5-1	34	127	.312
						H. C. McDonald (1923) 0-6-0 .000						
1923		0-6-0	3	264	.000							
						E. R. Knollin (1924-1928) 13-21-2 .389						
1924		1-4-0	25	87	.200		1927		4-5-0	121	67	.444
1925		2-5-0	69	158	.286		1928		5-2-1	117	64	.688
1926		1-5-1	26	94	.214							
						Walter Crawford (1929-1931) 6-13-4 .348						
1929		3-3-1	104	78	.500		1931		1-7-0	23	114	.125
1930		2-3-3	50	79	.438							
						Dudley DeGroot (1932-1939) 59-19-8 .733						
1932		7-0-2	116	27	.889		1937		11-2-1	273	79	.821
1933		4-4-0	102	85	.500		1938		11-1-0	322	56	.917
1934		3-3-4	90	126	.500		1939		13-0-0	324	29	1.000
1935		5-5-1	124	93	.500							
1936		5-4-0	136	92	.556							
						Ben Winkleman (1940-1941) 16-4-3 .591						
1940		11-1-0	263	62	.817		1941		5-3-3	149	96	.591
						Glenn Hartranft (1942,1946) 16-3-1 .739						
1942		7-2-0	210	53	.778							
						No team (1943-1945)						
						Glenn Hartrranft (1946)						
1946		9-1-1	227	94	.864							
						Bill Hubbard (1947-1949) 27-10-0 .739						
1947		9-3-0	327	125	.750		1949		9-4-0	477	215	.692
1948		9-3-0	373	168	.750							
						Robert Bronzan (1950-1956) 32-30-5 .515						
1950		6-3-1	201	118	.650		1954		7-3-0	191	141	.700
1951		2-7-1	106	222	.250		1955		5-3-1	159	114	.611
1952		6-3-0	251	164	.667		1956		2-7-1	186	301	.250
1953		4-4-1	156	220	.500							
						Robert Titchenal (1957-1964) 33-45-1 .424						
1957		3-7-0	123	196	.300		1961		6-4-0	183	185	.600
1958		4-5-0	174	106	.444		1962		2-8-1	133	261	.227
1959		4-6-0	190	278	.400		1963		5-5-0	187	194	.500
1960		5-4-0	175	176	.556		1964		4-6-0	151	145	.400
						Harry Anderson (1965-1968) 13-26-0 .333						
1965		5-5-0	184	292	.500		1967		2-7-0	166	286	.222
1966		3-7-0	151	198	.300		1968		3-7-0	248	403	.300

Member of the Pacific Coast Athletic Association (1969-1987) 66-28-4 .694

Year	Nat'l AP Other	Overall W-L-T	PF	PA	Pct.	Conference W-L-T	Pct.	Rank	Year	Nat'l AP Other	Overall W-L-T	PF	PA	Pct.	Conference W-L-T	Pct.	Rank
						Joe McMullen (1969-1970) 3-10-0											
1969		2-8-0	152	346	.200	1-1-0	.500	6	1970*		1-2-0	60	78	.333	1-0-0	1.000	*

Dewey King (1970-1972) 10-20-0 .333

| 1970 * | 1-7-0 | 148 | 215 | .125 | 1-3-0 | .250 | 4 | 1972 | | 4-7-0 | 197 | 287 | .364 | 1-3-0 | .250 | 3 |
| 1971 | 5-6-0 | 249 | 261 | .455 | 4-1-0 | .800 | 2 | | | | | | | | | |

*McMullen coached the first three games of the 1970 season, and King coached the last eight games.

Darrell Rogers (1973-1975) 22-9-3 .691

| 1973 | 5-4-2 | 193 | 173 | .545 | 2-0-2 | .750 | 2 | 1975 | 9-2-0 | 291 | 152 | .818 | 5-0-0 | 1.000 | 1 |
| 1974 | 8-3-1 | 323 | 199 | .708 | 2-2-0 | .500 | 2 | | | | | | | | |

Lynn Stiles (1976-1978) 18-16-0 .529

| 1976 | 7-4-0 | 354 | 213 | .636 | 4-0-0 | 1.000 | 1 | 1978 | 7-5-0 | 259 | 248 | .583 | 4-1-0 | .800 | 2 |
| 1977 | 4-7-0 | 231 | 299 | .364 | 2-2-0 | .500 | 3 | | | | | | | | |

Jack Elway (1979-1983) 32-24-0 .571

1979*	3-8-0	327	301	.591	2-3-0	.400	4	1982	8-3-0	331	199	.727	4-2-0	.667	3
1980	7-4-0	294	249	.636	3-2-0	.600	3	1983	5-6-0	256	253	.455	3-3-0	.500	3
1981	9-3-0	380	254	.750	5-0-0	1.000	1								

*Three wins and 1 tie forfeited in 1979. Record before forfeits was 6-4-1.

Claude Gilbert (1984-1989) 39-29-1 .572

| 1984 | 7-4-0 | 260 | 225 | .636 | 6-1-0 | .857 | 2 | 1986 | 10-2-0 | 397 | 232 | .833 | 7-0-0 | 1.000 | 1 |
| 1985 | 2-8-1 | 212 | 339 | .227 | 2-4-1 | .357 | 6 | 1987 | 10-2-0 | 417 | 223 | .833 | 7-0-0 | 1.000 | 1 |

Member of the Big West Conference (1988-1995) 33-19-0 .635

| 1988 | 4-8-0 | 316 | 334 | .333 | 4-3-0 | .571 | 3 | 1989 | 6-5-0 | 311 | 277 | .545 | 5-2-0 | .714 | 2 |

Terry Shea (1990-1991) 15-6-2 .696

| 1990 | 20 | 9-2-1 | 435 | 228 | .792 | 7-0-0 | 1.000 | 1 | 1991 | 6-4-1 | 372 | 298 | .591 | 6-1-0 | .857 | 2 |

Ron Turner (1992) 7-4-0 .636

| 1992 | 7-4-0 | 330 | 290 | .636 | 4-2-0 | .667 | 2 |

John Ralston (1993-1996) 11-34-0 .244

| 1993 | 2-9-0 | 282 | 337 | .182 | 2-4-0 | .333 | 6 | 1995 | 3-8-0 | 271 | 378 | .273 | 2-4-0 | .333 | 6 |
| 1994 | 3-8-0 | 200 | 377 | .273 | 3-3-0 | .500 | 5 | | | | | | | | |

Member of the Western Athletic Association (1996-2003) 25-37-0 .403

| 1996 | 3-9-0 | 221 | 448 | .250 | 3-5-0 | .375 | 9 |

David Baldwin (1997-2000) 18-27-0

| 1997 | 4-7-0 | 225 | 387 | .364 | 4-4-0 | .500 | 8 | 1999 | 3-7-0 | 258 | 402 | .300 | 1-5-0 | .167 | 7 |
| 1998 | 4-8-0 | 274 | 385 | .333 | 3-5-0 | .375 | 11 | 2000 | 7-5-0 | 374 | 357 | .583 | 5-3-0 | .625 | 7 |

Fritz Hill (2001-2003) 12-24-0 .333

| 2001 | 3-9-0 | 295 | 461 | .250 | 3-5-0 | .375 | 13 | 2003 | 3-8-0 | 259 | 386 | /273 | 2-6-0 | .250 | 8 |
| 2002 | 6-7-0 | 376 | 467 | .462 | 4-4-0 | .500 | 4 | | | | | | | | |

Won-loss record by decades:

1895-99	9- 4-3	.656		1930-39	62-29-11	.662		1970-79*	54-55-4	.496
1900-09	3- 3-1	.500		1940-49	59-17-4	.763		1980-89	68-45-1	.601
1910-19	0- 0-0			1950-59	43-48-5	.474		1990-99	44-66-2	.402
1920-29	19-40-4	.333		1960-69	37-61-1	.379		2000-03	19-29-0	.396

Historic record*: 417-397-36 .512
*3 wins and 1 tie forfeited in 1979 are incorporated into figures.

Post-season won-loss record: 4-3-0 .571

1946: Raisin Bowl, SJ State 20, Utah State 0	1986: California Bowl, SJ State 37, Miami (OH) 7
1949: Raisin Bowl, SJ State 20, Texas Tech 13	1987: California Bowl, Eastern Michigan 30, SJ State 27
1971: Pasadena Bowl, Memphis State 28, SJ State 9	1990: California Raisin Bowl, SJ State 48, Central Michigan 24
1981: California Bowl, Toledo 27, SJ State 25	

College Football Hall of Fame:
Willie Heston, fullback, 1898-1900; John Ralston, coach, 1992-96.

UNIVERSITY OF SOUTH CAROLINA, Columbia, South Carolina; nickname "Gamecocks"; colors garnet and black; Williams-Brice Stadium (80,250); Southeastern Conference. South Carolina began play in 1892. In 1922, it became a founding member of the Southern Conference and played in that conference through the 1952 season. In 1953, South Carolina left the Southern Conference for the newly formed Atlantic Coast Conference and played there through the 1970 season. South Carolina was an independent from 1971 through 1991. In 1992, South Carolina joined the Southeastern Conference.

Early years (1892-1921)

Year	W-L-T	PF	PA	Pct.	Year	W-L-T	PF	PA	Pct.
					No coach (1892-1895)				
1892	0-1-0	0	44	.000	1894	0-2-0	4	56	.000
1893	No team				1895	2-1-0	34	20	.667
					W. H. Whaley (1896) 1-3-0 .250				
1896	1-3-0	20	30	.250					
					W. P. Murphy (1897) 0-3-0 .000				
1897	0-3-0	6	30	.000					
					W. Wertenbaker (1898) 1-2-0 333				
1898	1-2-0	16	35	.333					
					I. O. Hunt (1899-1900) 6-6-0 .500				
1899	2-3-0	23	62	.400	1900	4-3-0	66	66	.571
					R. W. Dickson (1901) 3-4-0 .429				
1901	3-4-0	85	51	.429					
					C. R. Williams (1902-1903) 14-3-0 .823				
1902	6-1-0	195	16	.857	1903	8-2-0	248	35	.800
					Christie Benet (1904-1905, 1908-1909) 13-16-3 .453				
1904	4-3-1	62	43	.562	1905	4-2-1	91	78	.643
					Football banned by trustees (1906)				
					Douglas McKay (1907) 3-0-0 1.000				
1907	3-0-0	30	4	1.000					
					Christie Benet (1908-1909)				
1908	3-5-1	64	103	.389	1909	2-6-0	36	128	.250
					John H. Neff (1910-1911) 5-8-2 .400				
1910	4-4-0	67	109	.500	1911	1-4-2	22	108	.286
					N. B. Edgerton (1912-1915) 19-13-3 .586				
1912	5-2-1	204	47	.688	1914	5-5-1	161	191	.500
1913	4-3-0	95	122	.571	1915	5-3-1	190	93	.611
					Rice Warren (1916) 2-7-0 .222				
1916	2-7-0	85	168	.222					
					Dixon Foster (1917, 1919) 4-12-1 .265				
1917	3-5-0	137	96	.375					
					Frank Dobson (1918) 2-1-1 .625				
1918	2-1-1	33	51	.625					
					Dixon Foster (1919)				
1919	1-7-1	25	105	.167					
					Sal Metzger (1920-1924) 26-18-2 .587				
1920	5-4-0	82	140	.556	1921	5-1-2	116	28	.750

Member of the Southern Conference (1922-1952) 67-84-10 .447

	Nat'l	Overall				Conference				Nat'l	Overall				Conference		
Year	AP Other	W-L-T	PF	PA	Pct.	W-L-T	Pct.	Rank	Year	AP Other	W-L-T	PF	PA	Pct.	W-L-T	Pct.	Rank
1922		5-4-0	92	69	.556	0-2-0	.000	18	1924		7-3-0	120	48	.700	3-2-0	.600	6
1923		4-6-0	104	77	.400	0-4-0	.000	19									
									Branch Bocock (1925-1926) 13-7-0 .650								
1925		7-3-0	150	27	.300	2-2-0	.500	10	1926		6-4-0	159	62	.600	4-2-0	.667	4
									Harry Lightsey (1927) 4-5-0 .444								
1927		4-5-0	46	172	.444	2-4-0	.333	16									
									Billy Laval (1928-1934) 39-26-6 .592								
1928		6-2-2	96	80	.700	2-2-1	.500	9	1932		5-4-2	93	68	.545	2-2-2	.500	10
1929		6-5-0	163	174	.545	2-5-0	.286	15	1933		6-3-1	111	91	.650	3-0-0	1.000	2
1930		6-4-0	108	123	.600	4-3-0	.571	11	1934		5-4-0	96	71	.556	2-3-0	.400	7
1931		5-4-1	146	79	.550	3-3-1	.500	8									
									Dan McCallister (1935-1937) 13-20-1 .397								
1935		3-7-0	73	187	.300	1-4-0	.200	8	1937		5-6-1	191	166	.458	2-2-1	.500	7
1936		5-7-0	100	139	.417	2-5-0	.286	12									
									Rex Enright (1938-1942, 1946-1955) 64-69-5 .482								
1938		6-4-1	169	86	.591	2-2-0	.500	6	1941		4-4-1	100	103	.500	4-0-1	.800	2
1939		3-6-1	41	165	.350	1-3-0	.250	11	1942		1-7-1	46	130	.167	1-4-0	.200	14
1940		3-6-0	107	146	.333	1-3-0	.250	12									
									J. P. Moran (1943) 5-2-0 .714								
1943		5-2-0	118	56	.714	2-1-0	.667	3									

William Newton (1944) 3-4-2 .444

Year			W-L-T	PF	PA	Pct	Conf	Pct						
1944			3-4-2	135	106	.444	1-3-0	.250	7					

Johnny McMillan (1945) 2-4-3 .389

| 1945 | | | 2-4-3 | 113 | 192 | .389 | 0-3-2 | .200 | 10 | | | | | |

Rex Enright (1946-1955)

1946	5-3-0	107	133	.625	4-2-0	.667	4	1950	3-4-2	110	114	.444	2-4-1	.357	12
1947	6-2-1	113	85	.722	4-1-1	.750	3	1951	5-4-0	175	129	.556	5-3-0	.625	7
1948	3-5-0	106	126	.375	1-3-0	.250	13	1952	5-5-0	175	161	.500	2-4-0	.333	10
1949	4-6-0	145	168	.400	3-3-0	.500	7								

Member of the Atlantic Coast Conference (1953-1970) 56-54-4 .510

1953	7-3-0	198	97	.700	2-3-0	.400	3	1955	3-6-0	120	209	.333	1-5-0	.167	6
1954	6-4-0	172	153	.600	3-3-0	.500	4								

Warren Giese (1956-1960) 28-21-1 .570

1956	7-3-0	126	67	.700	5-2-0	.714	3	1959	6-4-0	170	169	.600	4-3-0	.571	4
1957	5-5-0	202	147	.500	2-5-0	.286	7	1960	3-6-1	117	186	.350	3-3-1	.500	5
1958 15	7-3-0	168	116	.700	5-2-0	.714	2								

Marvin Bass (1961-1965) 17-29-4 .380

1961	4-6-0	128	187	.400	3-4-0	.429	5	1964	3-5-2	95	176	.444	2-3-1	.417	6
1962	4-5-1	187	148	.450	3-4-0	.429	4	1965	5-5-0	151	167	.500	4-2-0	.667	1
1963	1-8-1	104	170	.150	1-5-1	.214	6								

Paul Dietzel (1966-1974) 42-53-1 .443

1966	1-9-0	95	216	.100	1-3-0	.250	7	1969	7-4-0	189	195	.636	6-0-0	1.000	1
1967	5-5-0	159	166	.500	4-2-0	.667	3	1970	4-6-1	285	253	.409	3-2-1	.583	4
1968	4-6-0	214	223	.400	4-3-0	.571	4								

South Carolina reverts to independent status (1971-1991)

1971	6-5-0	191	196	.545		1973	7-4-0	347	261	.636
1972	4-7-0	214	232	.364		1974	4-7-0	223	312	.364

Jim Carlen (1975-1981) 45-36-1 .555

1975	7-5-0	328	274	.583		1979	8-4-0	256	205	.667
1976	6-5-0	195	143	.543		1980	8-4-0	348	200	.667
1977	5-7-0	215	202	.417		1981	6-6-0	225	222	.500
1978	5-5-1	238	181	.500						

Richard Bell (1982) 4-7-0 .364

| 1982 | 4-7-0 | 224 | 259 | .364 | | | | | | |

Joe Morrison (1983-1988) 39-28-0 .582

1983		5-6-0	231	237	.455		1986	3-6-2	313	286	.364
1984 11	13	10-2-0	371	258	.833		1987 15	15	8-4-0	341	141	.667
1985		5-6-0	269	290	.455		1988	8-4-0	232	224	.667

Sparky Woods (1989-1993) 24-28-3 .464

1989	6-4-1	228	250	.591		1991	3-6-2	250	268	.364
1990	6-5-0	282	237	.545						

Member of the Southeastern Conference (1992-2003) 34-61-1 .359

1992	5-6-0	160	240	.455	3-5-0	.375	8	1993	4-7-0	188	198	.364	3-5-0	.375	7

Brad Scott (1994-1998) 23-32-1 .420

1994	7-5-0	300	276	.583	4-4-0	.500	5	1997	5-6-0	258	279	.455	3-5-0	.375	8
1995	4-6-1	401	393	.409	2-5-1	.312	7	1998	1-10-0	207	330	.091	0-8-0	.000	12
1996	6-5-0	245	238	.545	4-4-0	.500	5								

Lou Holtz (1999-2003) 27-32-0 .458

1999			0-11-0	90	278	.000	0-8-0	.000	12	2002	5-7-0	225	262	.417	3-5-0	.375	8
2000 19	21		8-4-0			.667	5-3-0	.625	3	2003	5-7-0	268	314	.417	2-6-0	.250	8
2001 13	13		9-3-0	310	236	.750	5-3-0	.625	3								

Won-loss records by decades:

Decade	Record	Pct	Decade	Record	Pct	Decade	Record	Pct
1892-99	6-15-0	.286	1930-39	49-49-7	.500	1970-79	56-55-2	.504
1900-09	37-26-3	.583	1940-49	36-43-8	.460	1980-89	63-49-3	.561
1910-19	32-41-7	.444	1950-59	54-41-2	.567	1990-99	41-67-3	.383
1920-29	55-37-4	.594	1960-69	37-59-5	.391	2000-03	27-21-0	.563

Historic record 493-503-44 .495

Post-season won-loss record: 3-8-0 .273

1946: Gator Bowl, Wake Forest 26, South Carolina 14
1969: Peach Bowl, West Virginia 14, South Carolina 3
1975: Tangerine Bowl, Miami (OH) 20, South Carolina 7
1979: Hall of Fame Bowl, Missouri 24, South Carolina 14
1980: Gator Bowl, Pittsburgh 37, South Carolina 9
1984: Gator Bowl, Oklahoma State 21, South Carolina 14
College Football Hall of Fame: George Rogers, halfback, 1977-80
Awards: Heisman Trophy, 1980, George Rogers.

1987: Gator Bowl, LSU 30, South Carolina 13
1988: Liberty Bowl, Indiana 34, South Carolina 10
1995: Carquest Bowl, South Carolina 24, West Virginia 21
2001: Outback Bowl, South Carolina 24, Ohio State 7
2002: Outback Bowl, South Carolina 31, Ohio State 28

UNIVERSITY OF SOUTH FLORIDA, Tampa, Florida; nickname "Bulls"; colors green and gold; Raymond James Stadium (41,441); Conference USA. USF began play as a I-AA independent in 1997 and advanced to I-A independent status in 2000. It played as an I-A independent through the 2002 season. In 2003, South Florida moved into Conference USA.

Years as independent (1997-2002) 44-22-0 .667
Jim Leavitt (1997-2003) 51-26-0 .662

Year	W-L-T	PF	PA	Pct.
1997	5-6-0	307	181	.455
1998	8-3-0	402	178	.727
1999	7-4-0	246	248	.636

Year	W-L-T	PF	PA	Pct.
2000	7-4-0	347	132	.636
2001	8-3-0	387	231	.727
2002	9-2-0	329	204	.818

Member of Conference USA (2003) 5-3-0 .625

Year	AP	Other	Overall W-L-T	PF	PA	Pct.	Conference W-L-T	Pct.	Rank
2003			7-4-0	276	224	.636	5-3-0	.625	3

Historic record 51-26-0 .662

UNIVERSITY OF SOUTHERN CALIFORNIA, Los Angeles, California; nickname "Trojans"; colors cardinal and gold; Los Angeles Memorial Coliseum (92,000); Pac-10 Conference. USC began play in 1888 as an independent. In 1922, USC joined the Pacific Coast Conference. When that conference was disbanded in 1958, USC joined the newly formed AAWU (Athletic Association of Western Universities) along with four other ex-PCC teams. That conference evolved into the Pac-8 in 1968, after three other ex-PCC teams were added, and into the Pac-10 in 1978 after Arizona and Arizona State were added.

Early years as an independent (1888-1921)

Year	Coach	W-L-T	PF	PA	Pct.	Year	Coach	W-L-T	PF	PA	Pct.
1888	Henry Goddard &					1899	no coach	2-3-1	22	33	.417
	Frank Suffel	2-0-0	20	0	1.000	1900	no coach	1-1-1	5	11	.500
1889	no coach	2-0-0	66	0	1.000	1901	Clair Tappaan	0-1-0	0	6	.000
1890	no team					1902	no coach	2-3-0	29	44	.400
1891	no coach	1-2-0	48	26	.333	1903	John Walker	4-2-0	58	27	.667
1892	no team					1904	Harvey Holmes	6-1-0	199	27	.857
1893	no coach	3-1-0	56	50	.750	1905	Harvey Holmes	6-3-1	211	45	.650
1894	no coach	1-0-0	12	0	1.000	1906	Harvey Holmes	2-0-2	36	0	.750
1895	no coach	0-1-1	4	14	.250	1907	Harvey Holmes	5-1-0	182	20	.833
1896	no coach	0-3-0	0	74	.000	1908	Bill Traeger	3-1-1	63	18	.700
1897	Lewis Freeman	5-1-0	100	18	.833						
1898	no coach	5-1-1	97	28	.786						

Dean Cromwell (1909-1910, 1916-1918) 21-8-6 .686

1909		3-1-2	133	13	.667	1910		7-0-1	189	24	.938

Football replaced by rugby (1911-1913)

Ralph Glaze (1914-1915) 7-7-0 .500

1914		4-3-0	116	68	.571	1915		3-4-0	132	119	.429

Dean Cromwell (1916-1918)

1916		5-3-0	129	80	.625	1918		2-2-2	61	61	.500
1917		4-2-1	127	47	.643						

Elmer Henderson (1919-1924) 45-7-0 .865

1919		4-1-0	87	21	.800	1921		10-1-0	362	52	.909
1920		6-0-0	170	21	1.000						

Member of the Pacific Coast Conference (and successor conferences) (1922-2003) 363-143-28 .706

Year	Nat'l AP	Other	Overall W-L-T	PF	PA	Pct.	Conference W-L-T	Pct.	Rank	Year	Nat'l AP	Other	Overall W-L-T	PF	PA	Pct.	Conference W-L-T	Pct.	Rank
1922			10-1-0	236	31	.909	3-1-0	.750	3	1924	7		9-2-0	269	44	.818	2-1-0	.667	4
1923			6-2-0	173	62	.750	2-2-0	.500	3										

Howard Jones (1925-1940) 121-36-13 .750

Year	Nat'l AP	Other	Overall W-L-T	PF	PA	Pct.	Conference W-L-T	Pct.	Rank	Year	Nat'l AP	Other	Overall W-L-T	PF	PA	Pct.	Conference W-L-T	Pct.	Rank
1925			11-2-0	456	55	.846	3-2-0	.600	3	1933	6		10-1-1	257	30	.875	4-1-1	.750	3
1926	6		8-2-0	317	52	.800	5-1-0	.833	2	1934			4-6-1	120	110	.409	1-4-1	.250	7
1927	10		8-1-1	287	64	.850	4-0-1	.900	1	1935			5-7-0	185	124	.417	2-4-0	.333	8
1928	1		9-0-1	267	59	.950	4-0-1	.900	1	1936			4-2-3	129	65	.611	3-2-2	.571	3
1929	6		10-2-0	492	69	.833	6-1-0	.857	1	1937			4-4-2	136	98	.500	2-3-2	.429	7
1930	6		8-2-0	382	66	.800	5-1-0	.833	2	1938	7	4	9-2-0	172	65	.818	6-1-0	.857	1
1931	1		10-1-0	363	52	.909	7-0-0	1.000	1	1939	3	1	8-0-2	181	33	.900	5-0-2	.857	1
1932	1		10-0-0	201	13	1.000	6-0-0	1.000	1	1940			3-4-2	88	98	.444	2-3-2	.429	7

Sam Barry (1941) 2-6-1 .278

1941			2-6-1	64	134	.278	2-4-1	.357	8										

Jeff Cravath (1942-1950) 54-28-8 .644

Year	Nat'l AP	Other	Overall W-L-T	PF	PA	Pct.	Conference W-L-T	Pct.	Rank	Year	Nat'l AP	Other	Overall W-L-T	PF	PA	Pct.	Conference W-L-T	Pct.	Rank
1942			5-5-1	184	128	.500	4-2-1	.357	8	1947	8		7-2-1	193	114	.750	6-0-0	1.000	1
1943			8-2-0	155	58	.800	5-0-0	1.000	1	1948			6-3-1	142	87	.650	4-2-0	.667	3
1944	7		8-0-2	240	73	.900	3-0-2	.750	1	1949			5-3-1	214	170	.611	4-2-0	.667	3
1945	11		7-4-0	205	150	.636	5-1-0	.833	1	1950			2-5-2	114	182	.333	1-3-2	.333	7
1946			6-4-0	158	106	.600	5-2-0	.714	3										

Jess Hill (1951-1956) 45-17-1 .722

Year	Nat'l AP	Other	Overall W-L-T	PF	PA	Pct.	Conference W-L-T	Pct.	Rank	Year	Nat'l AP	Other	Overall W-L-T	PF	PA	Pct.	Conference W-L-T	Pct.	Rank
1951			7-3-0	224	168	.700	4-2-0	.667	4	1954	17	11	8-4-0	258	159	.667	6-1-0	.857	2
1952	5	4	10-1-0	254	47	.909	6-0-0	1.000	1	1955	13	12	6-4-0	265	158	.600	3-3-0	.500	6
1953			6-3-1	199	161	.650	4-2-1	.643	3	1956	18	15	8-2-0	218	126	.800	5-2-0	.714	2

Don Clark (1957-1959) 13-16-1 .450

Year	Nat'l AP	Other	Overall W-L-T	PF	PA	Pct.	Conference W-L-T	Pct.	Rank	Year	Nat'l AP	Other	Overall W-L-T	PF	PA	Pct.	Conference W-L-T	Pct.	Rank
1957			1-9-0	86	204	.100	1-6-0	.143	7	1959	14	13	8-2-0	195	90	.800	3-1-0	.750	1
1958			4-5-1	151	120	.450	4-2-1	.643	3										

John McKay (1960-1975) 127-40-8 .749

Year	Nat'l AP	Other	Overall W-L-T	PF	PA	Pct.	Conference W-L-T	Pct.	Rank	Year	Nat'l AP	Other	Overall W-L-T	PF	PA	Pct.	Conference W-L-T	Pct.	Rank
1960			4-6-0	95	152	.400	3-1-0	.750	2	1968	4	2	9-1-1	259	168	.864	6-0-0	1.000	1
1961			4-5-1	150	167	.450	2-1-1	.625	2	1969	3	4	10-0-1	261	128	.955	6-0-0	1.000	1
1962	1	1	11-0-0	261	92	1.000	4-0-0	1.000	1	1970	15	19	6-4-1	343	233	.591	3-4-0	.429	6
1963		16	7-3-0	207	114	.700	3-1-0	.750	2	1971	20		6-4-1	229	164	.591	3-2-1	.583	2
1964	10	10	7-3-0	207	130	.700	3-1-0	.750	1	1972	1	1	12-0-0	467	134	1.000	7-0-0	1.000	1
1965	10	9	7-2-1	262	92	.750	4-1-0	.800	2	1973	8	7	9-2-1	322	202	.792	7-0-0	1.000	1
1966	18		7-4-0	199	128	.636	4-1-0	.800	1	1974	2	1	10-1-1	363	142	.875	6-0-1	.929	1
1967	1	1	10-1-0	258	87	.909	6-1-0	.857	1	1975	17	19	8-4-0	247	140	.667	3-4-0	.429	5

John Robinson (1976-1982. 1993-1997) 104-35-4 .741

1976	2	2	11-1-0	386	139	.917	7-0-0	1.000	1	1980	11	12	8-2-1	265	134	.773	4-2-1	.643	3
1977	13	12	8-4-0	357	212	.667	5-2-0	.714	2	1981	14	13	9-3-0	294	170	.750	5-2-0	.714	2
1978	2	1	12-1-0	318	153	.923	6-1-0	.857	1	1982*15			8-3-0	302	143	.727	5-2-0	.714	3
1979	2	2	11-0-1	389	171	.958	6-0-1	.929	1										

*USC banned from post-season play in 1982 season because of NCAA infractions.

Ted Tollner ((1983-1986) 26-20-1 .564

1983			4-6-1	210	238	.409	4-3-0	.571	4	1985			6-6-0	223	187	.500	5-3-0	.625	4
1984	10	9	9-3-0	220	173	.750	7-1-0	.875	1	1986			7-5-0	264	239	.583	5-3-0	.625	4

Larry Smith (1987-1992) 44-25-3 .632

1987	18	17	8-4-0	321	229	.667	7-1-0	.875	1	1990	20	22	8-4-1	348	274	.654	5-2-1	.688	2
1988	7	9	10-2-0	370	184	.833	8-0-0	1.000	1	1991			3-8-0	229	276	.273	2-6-0	.250	8
1989	8	9	9-2-1	336	132	.792	6-0-1	.959	1	1992			6-5-1	264	249	.542	5-3-0	.625	3

John Robinson (1993-1997)

1993		25	8-5-0	340	252	.615	6-2-0	.750	1	1996			6-6-0	325	267	.500	3-5-0	.375	5
1994	13	15	8-3-1	356	243	.708	6-2-0	.750	1	1997			6-5-0	233	233	.545	4-4-0	.500	5
1995	12	11	9-2-1	355	212	.792	6-1-1	.812	1										

Paul Hackett (1998-2000) 19-18-0 .514

1998			8-5-0	346	241	.615	5-3-0	.625	5	2000			5-7-0	309	337	.417	2-6-0	.250	8
1999			6-6-0	348	278	.500	3-5-0	.375	6										

Pete Carroll (2001-2003) 29-9-0 .763

2001			6-6-0	298	221	.500	5-3-0	.625	5	2003	1	2	12-1-0	534	239	.923	7-1-0	.875	1
2002	4	4	11-2-0	465	240	.846	7-1-0	.875	1										

Won-loss record by decades:

1888-99	21-12-3	.625	1930-39	72-25-9	.722	1970-79	93-21-5	.803
1900-09	32-14-7	.670	1940-49	57-33-9	.621	1980-89	78-36-3	.679
1910-19	29-15-4	.646	1950-59	60-38-4	.608	1990-99	68-49-4	.579
1920-29	87-13-2	.863	1960-69	76-25-4	.743	2000-03	34-16-0	.680

Historic record: 707-297-54 .694

Post-season won-loss record: 27-15-0 .643

1923: Rose Bowl, USC 14, Penn State 3	1975: Liberty Bowl, USC 20, Texas A&M 28
1924: Christmas Festival, USC 20, Missouri 7	1977: Rose Bowl, USC 14, Michigan 6
1930: Rose Bowl, USC 47, Pittsburgh 14	1977: Bluebonnet Bowl, USC 47, Texas A&M 28
1932: Rose Bowl, USC 21, Tulane 12	1979: Rose Bowl, USC 17, Michigan 10
1933: Rose Bowl, USC 35, Pittsburgh 0	1980: Rose Bowl, USC 17, Ohio State 16
1939: Rose Bowl, USC 7, Duke 3	1982: Fiesta Bowl, Penn State 26, USC 10
1940: Rose Bowl, USC 14, Tennessee 0	1985: Rose Bowl, USC 20, Ohio State 17
1944: Rose Bowl, USC 29, Washington 0	1985: Aloha Bowl, Alabama 24, USC 3
1945: Rose Bowl, USC 25, Tennessee 0	1987: Citrus Bowl, Auburn 16, USC 7
1946: Rose Bowl, Alabama 34, USC 14	1988: Rose Bowl, Michigan State 20, USC 17
1948: Rose Bowl, Michigan 49, USC 0	1989: Rose Bowl, Michigan 22, USC 14
1953: Rose Bowl, USC 7, Wisconsin 0	1990: Rose Bowl, USC 17, Michigan 10
1955: Rose Bowl, Ohio State 20, USC 7	1990: John Hancock Bowl, Michigan State 17, USC 16
1963: Rose Bowl, USC 42, Wisconsin 37	1992: Freedom Bowl, Fresno State 24, USC 7
1967: Rose Bowl, Purdue 14, USC 13	1993: Freedom Bowl, USC 28, Utah 21
1968: Rose Bowl, USC 14, Indiana 3	1995: Cotton Bowl, USC 55, Texas Tech 14
1969: Rose Bowl, Ohio State 27, USC 16	1996: Rose Bowl, USC 41, Northwestern 32
1970: Rose Bowl, USC 10, Michigan 3	1998: Sun Bowl, TCU 28, USC 19
1973: Rose Bowl, USC 42, Ohio State 17	2001: Las Vegas Bowl, Utah 10, USC 6
1974: Rose Bowl, Ohio State 42, USC 21	2002: Orange Bowl, USC 38, Iowa 17
1975: Rose Bowl, USC 18, Ohio State 17	2004: Rose Bowl, USC 28, Michigan 14

College Football Hall of Fame:
Dan McMillan, tackle, 1917-21; Howard Jones, coach, 1925-40; Mort Kaer, halfback, 1924-26; Morley Drury, quarterback, 1925-27; John Baker, guard, 1930-32; Erny Pinckert, halfback, 1929-31; Tay Brown, tackle, 1930-32; Ernie Smith, tackle, 1930-32; Aaron Rosenberg, guard, 1931-33; Cotton Warburton, quarterback, 1932-34; Harry Smith, guard, 1937-39; John Ferraro, tackle, 1943-47; Paul Cleary, end, 1946-47; Frank Gifford, halfback, 1949-51; Jon Anett, halfback, 1954-56; Mike McKeever, guard, 1958-60; John McKay, coach, 1960-75; Mike Garrett, halfback, 1963-65; Ron Yary, tackle, 1965-67; O.J. Simpson, halfback, 1967-68; Charles Young, 3nd, 1970-72; Lynn Swann, wide receiver, 1971-73; Ricky Bell, running back, 1973-76; Marvin Powell, tackle, 1974-76; Brad Budde, guard, 1976-79; Charlie White, halfback, 1976-79; Ronnie Lott, safety, 1977-80; Marcus Allen, halfback, 1978-81.

Awards: Butkus Award: 1998, Chris Caliborne; Maxwell Award: 1968, O.J. Simpson; 1979, Charles White; 1981, Marcus Allen; Lombardi Award, 1979, Brad Budde; Outland Trophy: 1967, Ron Yary; Jim Thorpe Award: 1989, Mark Carrier; Heisman Trophy: 1965, Mike Garrett; 1968, O.J. Simpson; 1979, Charles White; 2002, Carson Palmer; Unitas Award: 1988, Rodney Peete; 2002: Carson Palmer; Camp Award: 1967 and 1968, O. J. Simpson; 1979, Charles White; 1981, Marcus Allen.

SOUTHERN METHODIST UNIVERSITY, Dallas, Texas; nickname "Mustangs"; colors red and blue; Gerald J. Ford Stadium (32,000); Western Athletic Conference. SMU began play in 1915 and joined the Southwest Conference in 1918 and remained in that conference until it disbanded in 1995, at which time SMU joined the WAC. SMU will be joining Conference USA in 2004.

Year	Nat'l AP	Other	Overall W-L-T	PF	PA	Pct.	Conference W-L-T	Pct.	Rank	Year	Nat'l AP	Other	Overall W-L-T	PF	PA	Pct.	Conference W-L-T	Pct.	Rank
							Ray Morrison (1915-16, 1922-1934) 85-43-22 .640												
1915			2-5-0	20	131	.286				1916			0-8-2	27	455	.100			
							J. Burton Rix (1917-1921) 16-19-7 .464												
1917			3-2-3	74	49	.562													
							Member of the Southwest Conference (1918-1995) 212-240-31 .471												
1918			4-2-0	40	45	.667	1-2-0	.333	5	1920			3-5-2	125	80	.400	0-4-1	.100	6
1919			5-4-1	162	86	.550	0-2-1	.167	6	1921*			1-6-1	15	92	.188	0-4-0	.000	7

*Also coaching during the 1921 season were Bill Cunningham and Choc Kelly.

Year	Nat'l AP	Other	Overall W-L-T	PF	PA	Pct.	Conference W-L-T	Pct.	Rank	Year	Nat'l AP	Other	Overall W-L-T	PF	PA	Pct.	Conference W-L-T	Pct.	Rank
							Ray Morrison (1922-1934)												
1922*			6-3-1	235	69	.650	2-2-0	.500	3	1929		9	6-0-4	172	36	.800	3-0-2	.800	2
1923*			9-0-0	207	9	1.000	5-0-0	1.000	1	1930			6-3-1	187	86	.650	2-2-1	.500	4
1924			5-1-4	92	59	.700	2-0-4	.667	2	1931			9-1-1	160	49	.864	5-0-1	.917	1
1925			5-2-2	148	41	.667	1-1-2	.500	4	1932			3-7-2	82	112	.333	1-4-1	.250	5
1926			8-0-1	229	47	.944	5-0-0	1.000	1	1933**			5-6-1	99	104	.458	3-3-0	.500	5
1927			7-2-0	267	81	.778	4-1-0	.800	2	1934			8-2-2	224	63	.750	3-2-1	.583	3
1928			6-3-1	254	78	.650	2-2-1	.500	5										

*Also coaching during the 1922 and 1923 seasons was E.Y. Freeland.
**Record reflects the forfeit of a game won by Arkansas in the 1933 season.

Year	Nat'l AP	Other	Overall W-L-T	PF	PA	Pct.	Conference W-L-T	Pct.	Rank	Year	Nat'l AP	Other	Overall W-L-T	PF	PA	Pct.	Conference W-L-T	Pct.	Rank
							Matty Bell (1935-1941, 1945-1949) 79-40-6 .656												
1935	1		12-1-0	288	39	.923	6-0-0	1.000	1	1939			6-3-1	118	60	.650	4-2-0	.667	2
1936			5-4-1	118	66	.550	2-3-1	.417	5	1940	16	8	8-1-1	142	75	.850	5-1-0	.833	1
1937			5-6-0	93	80	.455	2-4-0	.333	6	1941			5-5-0	169	106	.500	2-4-0	.333	5
1938			6-4-0	148	125	.600	4-2-0	.667	2										
							James Stewart (1942-1944) 10-18-2 .366												
1942			3-6-2	126	133	.364	1-4-1	.250	6	1944			5-5-0	131	201	.500	2-3-0	.400	4
1943			2-7-0	69	115	.222	2-3-0	.400	3										
							Matty Bell (1945-1949)												
1945			5-6-0	201	110	.455	4-2-0	.667	2	1948	10		9-1-1	250	105	.864	5-0-1	.917	1
1946			4-5-1	114	100	.450	2-4-0	.333	5	1949			5-4-1	215	204	.550	2-3-1	.417	5
1947	3		9-0-2	182	90	.909	5-0-1	.917	1										
							H. N. Russell (1950-1952) 13-15-2 .466												
1950			6-4-0	251	146	.600	2-4-0	333	5	1952			4-5-1	136	163	.450	3-2-1	.583	3
1951			3-6-1	164	144	.350	1-4-1	.250	7										
							Chalmer Woodard (1953-1956) 19-20-1 .487												
1953			5-5-0	128	129	.500	3-3-0	.500	4	1955			4-6-0	118	115	.400	2-4-0	.333	5
1954		17	6-3-1	184	135	.650	4-1-1	.750	2	1956			4-6-0	125	202	.400	2-4-0	.333	5
							Bill Meek (1957-1961) 17-29-4 .388												
1957			4-5-1	127	175	.450	3-3-0	.500	4	1960			0-9-1	31	221	.050	0-6-1	.071	8
1958	18	18	6-4-0	203	134	.600	4-2-0	.667	2	1961			2-7-1	92	191	.250	1-5-1	.214	8
1959			5-4-1	147	133	.550	2-3-1	.417	4										
							Hayden Fry (1962-1972) 49-66-1 .426												
1962			2-8-0	88	130	.200	2-5-0	.286	7	1968	14	16	8-3-0	311	273	.727	5-2-0	.714	3
1963			4-7-0	141	174	.364	2-5-0	.286	6	1969			3-7-0	186	230	.300	3-4-0	.429	5
1964			1-9-0	55	177	.100	0-7-0	.000	8	1970			5-6-0	153	228	.455	3-4-0	.429	4
1965			4-5-1	123	167	.450	3-4-0	.429	4	1971			4-7-0	151	227	.364	3-4-0	.429	5
1966	10	9	8-3-0	210	170	.727	6-1-0	.857	1	1972			7-4-0	269	154	.636	4-3-0	.571	2
1967			3-7-0	135	214	.300	3-4-0	.429	6										
							Dave Smith (1973-1975) 16-15-2 .515												
1973			6-4-1	259	228	.591	3-3-1	.500	4	1975			4-7-0	208	299	.364	2-5-0	.286	5
1974			6-4-1	221	240	.591	3-3-1	.500	4										
							Ron Meyer (1976-1981) 34-32-1 .515												
1976			3-8-0	202	339	.272	2-6-0	.250	7	1979			5-6-0	226	236	.455	3-5-0	.375	6
1977			4-7-0	226	319	.364	3-5-0	.375	6	1980	20	20	8-4-0	324	192	.667	5-3-0	.625	2
1978			4-6-1	300	251	.409	3-5-0	.375	6	1981	5		10-1-0	365	137	.909	7-1-0	.875	1
							Bobby Collins (1982-1986) 43-14-1												
1982	2	2	11-0-1	354	160	.958	7-0-1	.938	1	1985*			6-5-0	280	211	.545	5-3-0	.625	*
1983	12	11	10-2-0	274	137	.833	7-1-0	.875	2	1986*			6-5-0	245	282	.545	5-3-0	.625	*
1984	8	8	10-2-0	328	198	.833	6-2-0	.750	1										

*SMU ineligible for title due to NCAA infractions.
1987 and 1988 seasons canceled.

                    Forrest Gregg (1989-1990) 3-19-0 .136
1989   2-9-0 187 499 .182 0-8-0 .000 8   1990   1-10-0 197 426 .091 0-8-0 .000 8
                    Tom Rossley (1991-1996) 15-48-3 .250
1991   1-10-0 141 359 .091 0-8-0 .000 9   1994   1-9-1 197 343 .136 0-6-1 .072 7
1992   5-6-0 212 276 .455 2-5-0 .286 6   1995   1-10-0 132 352 .091 0-7-0 .000 8
1993   2-7-2 206 277 .272 1-5-1 .214 7
          Member of the Western Athletic Association (1996-2003) 25-37-0 .403
1996   5-6-0 246 267 .455 4-4-0 .500 7
                    Mike Craven (1997-2001) 22-34-0 .393
1997   6-5-0 247 237 .545 5-3-0 .625 4   2000   3-9-0 181 352 .250 2-6-0 .250 6
1998   5-7-0 225 248 .417 4-4-0 .500 9   2001   4-7-0 226 295 .500 4-4-0 .500 6
1999   4-6-0 193 235 .400 3-3-0 .500 5
                    Phil Bennett (2002-2003) 3-21-0 .125
2002   3-9-0 207 378 .250 3-5-0 .375 6   2003   0-12-0 134 386 .000 0-8-0 .000 10

Won-loss record by decades:
1915-19	14-21-6	.415	1950-59	46-48-5	.490	1990-99	31-76-3	.295
1920-29	56-22-16	.681	1960-69	36-65-3	.361	2000-03	10-37-0	.213
1930-39*	65-37-9	.637	1970-79	48-59-3	.446			
1940-49	55-40-8	.573	1980-89	63-28-1	.690			

Historic record*: 424-433-54 .495
*Record includes forfeit of a game by Arkansas in 1933.

Post-season won-loss record 4-5-1 .450
1936: Rose Bowl, Stanford 7, SMU 0
1948: Cotton Bowl, SMU 13, Penn State 13
1949: Cotton Bowl, SMU 21, Oregon 13
1963: Sun Bowl, Oregon 20, SMU 14
1967: Cotton Bowl, Georgia 24, SMU 9
1968: Astro/Bluebonnet Bowl, SMU 28, Oklahoma 27
1980: Holiday Bowl, BYU 46, SMU 45
1983: Cotton Bowl, SMU 7, Pittsburgh 3
1983: Sun Bowl, Alabama 28, SMU 7
1984: Aloha Bowl, SMU 27, Notre Dame 20

College Football Hall of Fame:
Ray Morrison, coach, 1915,16, 1922-34; Gerald Mann, quarterback, 1926-27; Bobby Wilson, halfback, 1933-35; Matty Bell, coach, 1935-41, 1945-49; Doak Walker, halfback, 1945, 1947-49; Kyle Rote, halfback, 1948-49; Don Meredith, quarterback, 1957-59; Jerry Levias, end, 1965-68; Hayden Fry, coach, 1962-72; Ray Guy, punter, 1970-72

Awards: Heisman Trophy: 1948, Doak Walker; Maxwell Award: 1947, Doak Walker; Baugh Trophy: 1968, Chuck Hickson.

UNIVERSITY OF SOUTHERN MISSISSIPPI, Hattiesburg, Mississippi; nickname "Golden Eagles"; colors gold and black; M. M. Roberts Stadium (33,000); Conference USA. Southern Miss played in the college division of the NCAA until being reclassified as a Division I-A independent in 1981. Southern Miss was one of the founding members of Conference USA when it was organized in 1996.

Year	Nat'l AP	Other	W-L-T	PF	PA	Pct.	Year	Nat'l AP	Other	W-L-T	PT	PA	Pct.
— **Ronald Slay (1912) 2-1-0 .667**													
1912			2-1-0	36	6	.667							
Blondie Williams (1913) 1-5-1 .214													
1913			1-5-1	24	82	.214							
A. D. Dillie (1914-1916) 5-8-1 .333													
							1916			0-2-0	0	106	.000
1914			1-2-1	37	63	.375							
1915			4-4-0	114	103	.500							
No team (1917-1918)													
Cephus Anderson (1919) 4-1-2 .714													
1919			4-1-2	100	31	.714							
B. B. O'Mara (1920) 5-2-1 .733													
1920			5-2-1	182	82	.733							
Spout Austin (1921-1923) 8-13-0 .381													
							1923			3-3-0	90	104	.500
1921			3-4-0	183	141	.429							
1922			2-6-0	63	122	.250							
William Bobo (1924-1927) 9-17-4 .367													
							1926			3-4-1	77	129	.438
1924			3-3-2	94	152	.500							
1925			0-6-0	19	195	.000	1927			3-4-1	52	98	.438
William B. Saunders (1928-1929) 6-11-1 .361													
							1929			2-6-1	74	105	.278
1928			4-5-0	62	234	.444							
John Lumpkin (1930) 3-5-1 .389													
1930			3-5-1	162	117	.389							
Pooley Hubert (1931-1936) 26-24-5 .480													
							1934			3-4-2	63	109	.444
1931			2-5-0	67	124	.286							
1932			5-4-0	81	158	.556	1935			6-4-0	101	112	.600
1933			3-5-2	67	180	.400	1936			7-2-1	137	54	.750
Reed Green (1937-1942, 1946-1948) 59-20-4 .735													
1937			7-3-0	223	24	.700	1942			4-0-0	142	7	1.000
1938			7-2-0	203	26	.777	1943-1945 no team						
1939			4-2-3	77	67	.611	1946			7-3-0	243	46	.700
1940			7-4-0	220	80	.636	1947			7-3-0	154	102	.700
1941			9-0-1	246	40	.950	1948			7-3-0	277	127	.700
Thad Vann (1949-1968) 139-59-2 .700													
1949			7-3-0	299	274	.700	1959			6-4-0	171	122	.600
1950			5-5-0	134	233	.500	1960			6-4-0	189	96	.600
1951			6-5-0	306	132	.545	1961			8-2-0	183	68	.800
1952			10-2-0	409	189	.833	1962			9-1-0	258	63	.900
1953			9-2-0	280	122	.818	1963			5-3-1	128	64	.611
1954			6-4-0	172	104	.600	1964			6-3-0	143	144	.667
1955			9-1-0	277	49	.900	1965			7-2-0	127	60	.778
1956			7-2-1	219	92	.750	1966			6-4-0	156	93	.600
1957			8-3-0	152	72	.727	1967			6-3-0	201	114	.667
1958			9-0-0	210	55	1.000	1968			4-6-0	228	232	.400
P. W. Underwood (1969-1974) 31-32-2 .492													
1969			5-5-0	162	307	.500	1972			3-7-1	182	231	.318
1970			5-6-0	228	299	.455	1973			6-4-1	227	166	.591
1971			6-5-0	202	192	.545	1974			6-5-0	160	195	.545
Bobby Collins (1975-1981) 48-30-2 .613													
1975			8-3-0	279	129	.727	1979			6-4-1	228	146	.591
1976			3-8-0	145	296	.273	1980			9-3-0	290	183	.750
1977			6-6-0	215	250	.500	1981	19		9-2-1	305	108	.792
1978			7-40	213	185	.636							
Jim Carmody (1982-1987) 37-29-0 .561													
1982			7-4-0	304	180	.636	1985			7-4-0	255	157	.636
1983			7-4-0	235	128	.636	1986			6-5-0	198	252	.545
1984			4-7-0	188	245	.364	1987			6-5-0	270	296	.545
Curley Hallman (1988-1990) 23-11-0 .676													
1988			10-2-0	353	264	.833	1990*			8-3-0	193	141	.727
1989			5-6-0	240	252	.455							

Jeff Bower (1990-2003) 89-62-1   .589

1990*	0-1-0	27	31	.000		1993	3-7-1	214	311	.318
1991	4-7-0	212	225	.364		1994	6-5-0	278	261	.545
1992	7-4-0	219	195	.636		1995	6-5-0	284	241	.545

*Hallman coached the first eleven games of the 1990 season, and Bower coached the last (bowl) game of the season.

Member of Conference USA (1996-2003) 42-11-0   .792

	Nat'l		Overall				Conference				Nat'l		Overall				Conference		
Year	AP	Other	W-L-T	PF	PA	Pct.	W-L-T	Pct.	Rank	Year	AP	Other	W-L-T	PF	PA	Pct.	W-L-T	Pct.	Rank
1996			8-3-0	287	247	.727	4-1-0	.800	1	2000			8-4-0	314	203	.667	4-3-0	.571	4
1997	19	19	9-3-0	337	200	.750	6-0-0	1.000	1	2001			6-5-0	278	186	.545	4-3-0	.571	5
1998			7-5-0	384	238	.583	5-1-0	.833	2	2002			7-6-0	282	238	.538	5-3-0	.625	3
1999	14	13	9-3-0	333	189	.750	6-0-0	1.000	1	2003			9-4-0	293	226	.692	8-0-0	1.000	1

Won-loss record by decades:

1912-19	12-15-4	.452		1950-59	75-28-1	.726		1990-99	67-46-1	.592
1920-29	28-43-6	.403		1960-69	62-33-1	.651		2000-03	30-19-0	.612
1930-39	47-36-9	.560		1970-79	56-52-3	.518			
1940-49	48-16-1	.746		1980-89	70-42-1	.624			

Historic record: 495-330-27   .597

Post-season won-loss record: 5-9-0   .357

1953: Sun Bowl, Pacific 26, USM 7
1954: Sun Bowl, UTEP 37, USM 14
1957: Tangerine Bowl, West Texas State 20, USM 13
1958: Tangerine Bowl, East Texas State 10, USM 9
1980: Independence Bowl, USM 16, McNeese State 14
1981: Tangerine Bowl, Missouri 19, USM 17
1988: Independence Bowl, USM 38, UTEP 18

1990: All American Bowl, NC State 31, USM 27
1997: Liberty Bowl, USM 41, Pittsburgh 7
1998: Humanitarian Bowl, Idaho 42, USM 35
1999: Liberty Bowl, USM 23, Colorado State 17
2000: GMAC Mobile Alabama Bowl, USM 28, TCU 21
2002: Houston Bowl, Oklahoma State 33, USM 23
2003: Liberty Bowl, Utah 17, USM 0

College Football Hall of Fame: Thad Vann, coach, 1949-74.

STANFORD UNIVERSITY, Stanford, California; nickname "Cardinals"; colors red and white; Stanford Stadium (85,500); Pac-10 Conference. Stanford began play in 1891 and joined the Pacific Coast Conference in 1919. It has played in that conference (and its successor organizations, the AAWU, and the Pac-8 and Pac-10) since that time.

Early years as an independent (1891-1918); football (1891-1905), rugby (1906-1917)

Year	Coach	W-L-T	PF	PA	Pct.	Year	Coach	W-L-T	PF`	PA	Pct.
1891	none	3-1-0	52	26	.750	1905	James Lanagan	8-0-0	138	13	1.000
1892	Walter Camp	2-0-2	58	39	.750	1906	James Lanagan	6-2-1	87	29	.722
1893	Pop Bliss	8-0-1	284	17	.944	1907	James Lanagan	8-4-0	133	93	.667
1894	Walter Camp	6-3-0	100	52	.667	1908	James Lanagan	12-2-0	218	39	.857
1895	Walter Camp	4-0-1	34	8	.900	1909	George Presley	8-1-0	233	22	.889
1896	H. P. Cross	2-1-1	30	4	.625	1910	George Presley	7-1-0	189	25	.875
1897	G. H. Brooke	4-1-0	54	26	.800	1911	George Presley	10-3-0	235	60	.769
1898	H. P. Cross	5-3-1	93	62	.611	1912	George Presley	5-3-1	88	42	.611
1899	B. Chamberlain	2-5-2	61	78	.333	1913	Floyd Brown	8-3-0	214	149	.727
1900	Fielding Yost	7-2-1	154	20	.750	1914	Floyd Brown	10-0-0	228	43	1.000
1901	C. M. Fickert	3-2-2	34	57	.571	1915	Floyd Brown	10-0-1	370	64	.955
1902	C. L. Clemans	6-1-0	111	37	.857	1916	Floyd Brown	9-1-0	256	109	.900
1903	James Lanagan	8-0-3	199	6	.864	1917	Jim Wylie	1-0-0	15	11	1.000
1904	James Lanagan	7-2-1	206	10	.750	1918	no team				

Member of the Pacific Coast Conference (and successor conferences) (1919-2003) 266-247-21 .518

Year	Nat'l AP	Other	Overall W-L-T	PF	PA	Pct.	Conference W-L-T	Pct.	Rank	Year	Nat'l AP	Other	Overall W-L-T	PF	PA	Pct.	Conference W-L-T	Pct.	Rank

Bob Evans (1919) 4-3-0 .571
| 1919 | | | 4-3-0 | 130 | 46 | .571 | 1-1-0 | .500 | 5 | | | | | | | | | | |

Walter Powell (1920) 4-3-0 .571
| 1920 | | | 4-3-0 | 82 | 65 | .571 | 2-1-0 | .667 | 2 | | | | | | | | | | |

C. E. Van Gent (1921) 4-2-2 .611
| 1921 | | | 4-2-2 | 100 | 97 | .611 | 1-1-1 | .500 | 3 | | | | | | | | | | |

Andy Kerr (1922-1923) 11-7-0 .611
| 1922 | | | 4-5-0 | 63 | 96 | .444 | 1-3-0 | .250 | 5 | 1923 | | | 7-2-0 | 284 | 46 | .778 | 2-2-0 | .500 | 4 |

Pop Warner (1924-1932) 71-17-8 .781
1924	5		7-1-1	179	69	.833	3-0-1	.875	1	1929			9-2-0	288	53	.818	5-1-0	.833	2
1925	9		7-2-0	231	71	.788	4-1-0	.899	3	1930		7	9-1-1	252	69	.864	4-1-0	.800	3
1926	1		10-0-1	268	73	.955	4-0-0	1.000	1	1931			7-2-2	160	44	.727	2-2-1	.500	6
1927			8-2-1	162	82	.773	4-0-1	.900	1	1932			6-4-1	171	58	.591	1-3-1	.300	7
1928	4		8-3-1	274	69	.708	4-1-1	.750	3										

Claude Thornhill (1933-1939) 35-25-7 .575
1933	11		8-2-1	131	43	.773	4-1-0	.800	1	1937			4-3-2	68	53	.556	4-2-1	.643	2
1934	10		9-1-1	224	43	.864	5-0-0	1.000	1	1938			3-6-0	67	92	.333	2-5-0	.286	8
1935	5		8-1-0	121	13	.889	4-1-0	.800	1	1939			1-7-1	54	146	.167	0-6-1	.071	9
1936			2-5-2	80	109	.333	2-3-2	.429	6										

Clark Shaughnessy (1940-1941) 16-3-0 .842
| 1940 | 2 | 3 | 10-0-0 | 196 | 85 | 1.000 | 7-0-0 | 1.000 | 1 | 1941 | | | 6-3-0 | 160 | 95 | .667 | 4-3-0 | .571 | 4 |

Marchmont Schwartz (1942, 1946-1950) 28-28-4 .500
1942	12		6-4-0	204	121	.600	5-2-0	.714	3	1948			4-6-0	164	159	.400	3-4-0	.429	5
1943-1945			no team							1949			7-3-1	366	121	.682	4-2-0	.667	3
1946			6-3-1	222	148	.650	3-3-1	.500	5	1950			5-3-2	188	123	.600	2-2-2	.500	4
1947			0-9-0	72	214	.000	0-7-0	.000	10										

Chuck Taylor (1951-1957) 40-29-2 .577
1951	7	7	9-2-0	229	181	.818	6-1-0	.857	1	1955	16	20	6-3-1	198	135	.650	3-2-1	.583	3
1952			5-5-0	187	226	.500	2-5-0	.286	6	1956			4-6-0	218	213	.400	3-4-0	.429	6
1953	19	17	6-3-1	246	148	.650	5-1-1	.786	2	1957			6-4-0	228	158	.600	4-3-0	.571	5
1954			4-6-0	123	229	.400	2-4-0	.333	6										

Jack Curtice (1958-1962) 14-36-0 .280
1958			2-8-0	93	226	.200	2-5-0	.286	7	1961			4-6-0	105	163	.400	1-3-0	.250	4
1959			3-7-0	232	261	.300	0-4-0	.000	5	1962			5-5-0	124	174	.500	2-3-0	.400	4
1960			0-10-0	111	254	.000	0-4-0	.000	5										

John Ralston (1963-1971) 55-36-3 .601
1963			3-7-0	154	199	.300	1-4-0	.200	8	1968		20	6-3-1	268	162	.650	3-3-1	.500	3
1964			5-5-0	150	138	.500	1-4-0	.200	6	1969	19	14	7-2-1	349	172	.750	5-1-1	.786	3
1965			6-3-1	144	149	.650	2-3-0	.400	5	1970	8	10	9-3-0	343	206	.750	6-1-0	.857	1
1966			5-5-0	149	146	.500	1-4-0	.200	8	1971	10	16	9-3-0	261	135	.750	6-1-0	.857	1
1967			5-5-0	157	179	.500	3-4-0	.429	4										

Jack Christiansen (1972-1976) 30-22-2 .573
1972			6-5-0	266	183	.545	2-5-0	.286	7	1975			6-4-1	322	279	.591	5-2-0	.741	3
1973			7-4-0	244	240	.636	5-2-0	.714	3	1976			6-5-0	239	284	.545	5-2-0	.741	3
1974			5-4-2	197	228	.545	5-1-1	.786	2										

Bill Walsh (1977-1978. 1992-1994) 34-24-1 .584

1977	15	15	9-3-0	285	279	.750	5-2-0	.714	2	1978	17	16	8-4-0	326	221	.667	4-3-0	.571	4

Rod Dowhower (1979) 5-5-1 .500

1979	5-5-1	259	239	.500	3-3-1	.500	7

Paul Wiggin (1980-1983) 16-28-0 .364

1980	6-5-0	312	275	.545	3-4-0	.428	6	1982	5-6-0	314	281	.455	3-5-0	.375	5
1981	4-7-0	314	281	.364	4-4-0	.500	6	1983	1-10-0	159	293	.091	1-7-0	.125	10

Jack Elway (1984-1988) 25-29-2 .464

1984	5-6-0	239	279	.455	3-5-0	.375	7	1987	5-6-0	262	268	.455	4-4-0	.500	5
1985	4-7-0	245	313	.364	3-5-0	.375	7	1988	3-6-2	238	216	.364	1-5-2	.250	9
1986	8-4-0	279	191	.667	5-3-0	.625	4								

Dennis Green (1989-1991) 16-18-0 .471

1989	3-8-0	187	258	.273	3-5-0	.375	7	1991	22	22	8-4-0	351	228	.667	6-2-0	.750	3
1990	5-6-0	263	284	.455	4-4-0	.500	6										

Bill Walsh (1992-1994)

1992	9	9	10-3-0	296	193	.769	6-2-0	.750	1	1994	3-7-1	327	359	.318	2-6-0	.250	8
1993			4-7-0	291	389	.364	2-6-0	.250	8								

Tyrone Willingham (1995-2001) 44-36-1 .549

1995	7-4-1	344	311	.625	5-3-0	.625	4	1999	24	8-4-0	418	364	.667	7-1-0	.875	1
1996	7-5-0	209	229	.583	5-3-0	.625	3	2000		5-6-0	261	294	.455	4-4-0	.500	4
1997	5-6-0	276	317	.455	3-5-0	.375	7	2001	16	17	9-3-0	4232	339	750	6-2-0	.750	2
1998	3-8-0	261	365	.273	2-6-0	.250	9									

Buddy Teevens (2002-2003) 6-17-0 .261

2002	2-9-0	225	377	.182	1-7-0	.125	9	2003	4-8-0	193	381	.333	2-6-0	.250	8

Won-loss record by decades:*

1891-99	36-14-8	.670	1930-39	57-32-11	.625	1970-79	70-40-4	.632
1900-09	73-16-8	.794	1940-49	39-28-2	.580	1980-89	44-65-2	.405
1910-19	64-14-2	.813	1950-59	50-47-4	.515	1990-99	60-54-2	.526
1920-29	68-22-6	.719	1960-69	46-51-3	.475	2000-03	20-26-0	.435

Historical record (1891-2001)* 627-409-52 .600
* Totals include rugby years (1906-1917): 94-20-3; excluding rugby years, historical record is 533-389-49 .574

Post-season won-loss record 9-10-1 .475

1902: Rose Bowl, Michigan 49, Stanford 0
1925: Rose Bowl, Notre Dame 27, Stanford 10
1927: Rose Bowl, Stanford 7, Alabama 7
1928: Rose Bowl, Stanford 7, Pittsburgh 6
1934: Rose Bowl, Columbia 7, Stanford 0
1935: Rose Bowl, Alabama 29, Stanford 13
1936: Rose Bowl, Stanford 7, SMU 0
1941: Rose Bowl, Stanford 21, Nebraska 13
1952: Rose Bowl, Illinois 40, Stanford 7
1971: Rose Bowl, Stanford 27, Ohio State 17

1972: Rose Bowl, Stanford 13, Michigan 12
1977: Sun Bowl, Stanford 24, LSU 14
1978: Bluebonnet Bowl, Stanford 25, Georgia 22
1986: Gator Bowl, Clemson 27, Stanford 21
1991: Aloha Bowl, Georgia Tech 18, Stanford 17
1993: Blockbuster Bowl, Stanford 24, Penn State 3
1995: Liberty Bowl, East Carolina 19, Stanford 13
1996: Sun Bowl, Stanford 38, Michigan State 0
2000: Rose Bowl, Wisconsin 17, Stanford 9
2001: Seattle Bowl, Georgia Tech 24, Stanford 14

College Football Hall of Fame:
Walter Camp coach, 1892, 1894-95; Fielding Yost, coach, 1900; Andy Kerr, coach, 1922-24; Ernie Nevers, fullback, 1923-25; Pop Warner, coach, 1924-32; Bill Corbus, guard, 1931-33; Bobby Grayson, fullback, 1923-25; Bones Hamilton, halfback, 1933-35; Monk Moscrip, halfback, 1933-35; Bob Reynolds, tackle, 1933-35; Hugh Gallerlneau, fullback, 1938-41; Frankie Albert, quarterback, 1939-41; Clark Shaughnessy, coach, 1940-41; Chuck Taylor, guard, 1940-42; Bill McColl, end, 1949-51; Chuck Taylor, coach, 1951-57; John Brodie, quarterback, 1954-56; Chris Buford, end, 1956-59; John Ralston, coach, 1963-71; Jim Plunkett, quarterback, 1968-70; John Elway, quarterback, 1980-83.

Awards: Heisman Trophy: 1970, Jim Plunkett; Maxwell Trophy: 1970, Jim Plunkett; Belitnikoff Award; 1999: Troy Walters; Baugh Trophy: 1959, Dick Norman; 1977, Guy Benjamin; 1978, Steve Dils; 1981, John Elway.

SYRACUSE UNIVERSITY, Syracuse, New York; nickname "Orangemen"; color orange; The Carrier Dome (49,550); Big East Conference. Syracuse played as an independent from 1889 through 1990. In 1991 Syracuse was one of the founding teams of the Big East Conference and has been a member since that time.

Early years (1889-1905)

Year	Coach	W-L-T	PF	PA	Pct.	Year	Coach	W-L-T	PF	PA	Pct.
1889	no coach	0-1-0	0	36	.000	1898	Frank Wade	8-2-1	192	69	.773
1890	Bobby Winston	7-4-0	128	95	.636	1899	Frank Wade	4-4-0	63	63	.500
1891	William Galbraith	4-6-0	110	229	.400	1900	Edwin Sweetland	7-2-1	208	60	.750
1892	Jordan Wells	0-8-1	4	218	.056	1901	Edwin Sweetland	7-1-0	185	27	.875
1893	no coach	4-9-1	124	318	.321	1902	Edwin Sweetland	6-2-1	159	93	.722
1894	George Bond	6-5-0	188	157	.545	1903	Jason Parish	5-4-0	159	69	.556
1895	George Redington	6-2-2	154	46	.700	1904	Charles Hutchins	6-3-0	405	57	.667
1896	George Redington	5-3-2	194	78	.600	1905	Charles Hutchins	8-3-0	225	69	.727
1897	Frank Wade	5-3-1	160	48	.611						

Frank O'Neill (1906-1907, 1913-1915, 1917-1919) 52-19-6 .714

Year	W-L-T	PF	PA	Pct.	Year	W-L-T	PF	PA	Pct.
1906	6-3-0	169	75	.667	1907	5-3-1	133	64	.611

Howard Jones (1908) 6-3-1 .650

Year	W-L-T	PF	PA	Pct.
1908	6-3-1	171	38	.650

T.A.D. Jones (1909-1910) 9-9-2 .500

Year	W-L-T	PF	PA	Pct.	Year	W-L-T	PF	PA	Pct.
1909	4-5-1	110	100	.450	1910	5-4-1	53	42	.550

C. Deforest Cummings (1911-1912) 9-8-2 .526

Year	W-L-T	PF	PA	Pct.	Year	W-L-T	PF	PA	Pct.
1911	5-3-2	63	59	.600	1912	4-5-0	95	160	.444

Frank O'Neill (1913-1915)

Year	W-L-T	PF	PA	Pct.	Year	W-L-T	PF	PA	Pct.
1913	6-4-0	271	126	.600	1915	9-1-2	331	16	.833
1914	5-3-2	204	95	.600					

William Hollenback (1916) 5-4-0 .556

Year	W-L-T	PF	PA	Pct.
1916	5-4-0	275	87	.556

Frank O'Neill (1917-1919)

Year	W-L-T	PF	PA	Pct.	Year	W-L-T	PF	PA	Pct.
1917	8-1-1	197	67	.850	1919	8-3-0	131	47	.727
1918	5-1-0	141	21	.833					

John Meehan (1920-1924) 35-8-4 .787

Year	W-L-T	PF	PA	Pct.	Year	W-L-T	PF	PA	Pct.
1920	6-2-1	201	27	.722	1923	8-1-0	237	19	.889
1921	7-2-0	194	54	.778	1924	8-2-1	154	58	.773
1922	6-1-2	176	41	.778					

C.W. P. Reynolds (1925-1926) 15-3-2 .800

Year	W-L-T	PF	PA	Pct.	Year	W-L-T	PF	PA	Pct.
1925	8-1-1	202	27	.850	1926	7-2-1	225	59	.750

Lewis Andreas (1927-1929) 15-10-3 .589

Year	W-L-T	PF	PA	Pct.	Year	W-L-T	PF	PA	Pct.
1927	5-3-2	116	81	.600	1929	6-3-0	259	46	.667
1928	4-4-1	136	79	.500					

Victor Hanson (1930-1936) 33-21-5 .602

Year	W-L-T	PF	PA	Pct.	Year	W-L-T	PF	PA	Pct.
1930	5-2-2	207	79	.667	1934	6-2-0	141	42	.750
1931	7-1-1	238	56	.833	1935	6-1-1	112	56	.812
1932	4-4-1	138	96	.500	1936	1-7-0	45	116	.125
1933	4-4-0	131	79	.500					

Ossie Solem (1937-1945) 30-27-6 .524

Year	W-L-T	PF	PA	Pct.	Year	W-L-T	PF	PA	Pct.
1937	5-2-1	132	57	.688	1942	6-3-0	152	61	.667
1938	5-3-0	137	85	.625	1943	no team			
1939	3-3-2	63	92	.500	1944	2-4-1	102	152	.357
1940	3-4-1	114	134	.438	1945	1-6-0	38	106	.143
1941	5-2-1	190	86	.688					

Biggie Munn (1946) 4-5-0 .444

Year	W-L-T	PF	PA	Pct.
1946	4-5-0	146	158	.444

Reeves Maysinger (1947-1948) 4-14-0 .222

Year	W-L-T	PF	PA	Pct.	Year	W-L-T	PF	PA	Pct.
1947	3-6-0	77	167	.333	1948	1-8-0	89	244	.111

Ben Schwartzwalder (1949-1973) 153-91-3 .626

Year			W-L-T	PF	PA	Pct.	Year		W-L-T	PF	PA	Pct.
1949			4-5-0	207	215	.444	1962		5-5-0	159	110	.500
1950			5-5-0	199	139	.500	1963	12	8-2-0	255	101	.800
1951			5-4-0	180	147	.556	1964	12	7-4-0	264	157	.626
1952	14		7-3-0	197	141	.700	1965	19	7-3-0	237	146	.700
1953			5-3-1	197	99	.611	1966	16	8-3-0	266	156	.727
1954			4-4-0	135	147	.500	1967	12	8-2-0	210	127	.800
1955			5-3-0	180	130	.625	1968		6-4-0	252	154	.600
1956	8	8	7-2-0	203	90	.778	1969		5-5-0	169	126	.500
1957			5-3-1	183	97	.611	1970		6-4-0	248	208	.600
1958	9	10	8-2-0	264	59	.800	1971		5-5-1	197	179	.500
1959	1	1	11-0-0	390	59	1.000	1972		5-6-0	141	229	.455
1960	19		7-2-0	203	74	.778	1973		2-9-0	129	288	.182
1961	14	16	8-3-0	268	131	.727						

Frank Maloney (1974-1980) 32-46-0 .410

Year	W-L-T	PF	PA	Pct.	Year	AP	Other	W-L-T	PF	PA	Pct.
1974	2-9-0	121	271	.182	1978			3-8-0	192	295	.273
1975	6-5-0	174	182	.545	1979			7-5-0	324	293	.583
1976	3-8-0	154	263	.273	1980			5-6-0	207	222	.455
1977	6-5-0	218	234	.545							

Dick MacPherson (1981-1990) 66-46-4 .586

Year	W-L-T	PF	PA	Pct.	Year	AP	Other	W-L-T	PF	PA	Pct.
1981	4-6-1	248	265	.409	1986			5-6-0	241	195	.455
1982	2-9-0	159	244	.182	1987	4		4 11-0-1	379	169	.958
1983	6-5-0	178	200	.545	1988	13		12 10-2-0	341	189	.833
1984	6-5-0	151	151	.545	1989			8-4-0	286	242	.667
1985	7-5-0	284	195	.583	1990		21	7-4-2	341	213	.615

Paul Pasqualoni (1991-2003) 101-53-1 .655

Member of the Big East Conference (1991-2003) 58-31-0 .683

Year	Nat'l AP	Other	Overall W-L-T	PF	PA	Pct.	Conference W-L-T	Pct.	Rank	Year	Nat'l AP	Other	Overall W-L-T	PF	PA	Pct.	Conference W-L-T	Pct.	Rank
1991	11	11	10-2-0	321	200	.833	5-0-0	1.000	2	1997	21	20	9-4-0	441	226	.692	6-1-0	.857	1
1992	6	7	10-2-0	340	205	.833	6-1-0	.857	2	1998	25	24	8-4-0	478	287	.667	6-1-0	.857	1
1993			6-4-1	281	288	.591	3-4-0	.429	5	1999			7-5-0	300	256	.583	3-4-0	.429	4
1994			7-4-0	256	259	.636	4-3-0	.571	3	2000			6-5-0	294	212	.545	4-3-0	.571	3
1995	19	16	9-3-0	375	203	.750	5-2-0	.714	2	2001	14	14	10-3-0	334	247	.769	6-1-0	.857	2
1996	21	19	9-3-0	437	208	.750	6-1-0	.857	1	2002			4-8-0	347	406	.333	2-5-0	.286	6
										2003			6-6-0	320	301	.500	2-5-0	.286	6

Won-loss record by decades:

Decade	Record	Pct.	Decade	Record	Pct.	Decade	Record	Pct.
1889-99	49-47-8	.510	1930-39	46-29-8	.602	1970-79	45-64-1	.414
1900-09	60-29-5	.665	1940-49	29-43-3	.407	1980-89	64-48-2	.570
1910-19	60-29-8	.660	1950-59	62-29-2	.677	1990-99	82-35-3	.696
1920-29	65-21-9	.736	1960-69	69-33-0	.676	2000-03	26-22-0	.542

Historic record: 657-429-49 .600

Post-season won-loss record: 13-8-0 .619

1953: Orange Bowl, Alabama 61, Syracuse 6
1957: Cotton Bowl, TCU 28, Syracuse 27
1959: Orange Bowl, Oklahoma 21, Syracuse 6
1960: Cotton Bowl, Syracuse 23, Texas 14
1961: Liberty Bowl, Syracuse 15, Miami (FL) 14
1965: Sugar Bowl, LSU 13, Syracuse 10
1966: Gator Bowl, Tennessee 18, Syracuse 12
1979: Independence Bowl, Syracuse 31, McNeese State 7
1985: Cherry Bowl, Maryland 35, Syracuse 18
1988: Sugar Bowl, Syracuse 16, Auburn 14
1989: Hall of Fame Bowl, Syracuse 23, LSU 10

1989: Peach Bowl, Syracuse 19, Georgia 18
1990: Aloha Bowl, Syracuse 28, Arizona 0
1992: Hall of Fame Bowl, Syracuse 24, Ohio State 17
1993: Fiesta Bowl, Syracuse 26, Colorado 22
1996: Gator Bowl, Syracuse 41, Clemson 0
1996: Liberty Bowl, Syracuse 30, Houston 17
1997: Fiesta Bowl, Kansas State 35, Syracuse 18
1999: Orange Bowl, Florida 31, Syracuse 10
1999: Music City Bowl, Syracuse 20, Kentucky 13
2001: Insight.com Bowl, Syracuse 26, Kansas State 3

College Football Hall of Fame:
Buck O'Neill, coach, 1906-07, 1913-15, 1917-19; Howard Jones, coach, 1908; Tad Jones, coach, 1909-10; Joe Alexander, center/guard 1916-20; Vic Hanson, end, 1924-26; Ben Schwarzwalder, coach, 1949-73; Jim Brown, halfback, 1954-56; Ernie Davis, halfback, 1959-61; Tim Green, defensive tackle, 1962-65; Floyd Little, halfback, 1964-66; Larry Czonka, fullback, 1965-67.

Awards: Heisman Trophy: 1962, Ernie Davis; Davey O'Brien Award, 1987: Don McPherson; Maxwell Award: 1987, Don McPherson; Unitas Award: 1987, Don McPherson; Baugh Trophy, 1987, Don McPherson.

TEMPLE UNIVERSITY, Philadelphia, Pennsylvania; nickname "Owls"; colors cherry and white; Veterans' Stadium (66,592) or Franklin Field (52,593); Big East Conference. Temple was an independent from 1894 through the 1959 season. In 1960, Temple joined the Middle Atlantic Conference and played in that conference for nine years. Temple was then an independent for 21 years, joining the Big East Conference when it was organized in 1991.

Years as an independent (1894-1959)

Year	W-L-T	PF	PA	Pct.	Year	W-L-T	PF	PA	Pct.
Charles M. Williams (1894-1898) 13-15-1 .466									
1894	4-1-0	70	32	.800	1897	3-3-0	100	85	.500
1895	1-4-1	30	89	.250	1898	2-5-0	32	133	.286
1896	3-2-0	50	32	.600					
John Rogers (1899-1900) 4-8-2 .357									
1899	1-4-1	27	126	.250	1900	3-4-1	95	69	.438
H. S. Wingert (1901-1905) 13-9-2 .583									
1901	3-2-0	37	65	.600	1904	3-2-0	51	23	..600
1902	1-4-1	29	62	.250	1905	2-0-1	48	12	..833
1903	4-1-0	56	18	.800					
No team (1906)									
H. Butterworth (1907) 4-0-2 .833									
1907	4-0-2	82	40	.833					
Frank White (1908) 3-2-1 .583									
1908	3-2-1	55	73	.583					
William Schatz (1909-1913) 13-13-3 .500									
1909	0-4-1	0	99	.100	1912	3-2-0	38	47	.600
1910	3-3-0	64	123	.500	1913	1-3-2	31	81	.333
1911	6-1-0	90	54	.857					
William Nicholai (1914-1916) 9-5-3 .618									
1914	3-3-0	69	80	.500	1916	3-1-2	61	14	.667
1915	3-1-1	32	40	.700					
Elwood Geiges (1917) 0-6-1 .072									
1917	0-6-1	6	6	.072					
No team (1918-1921)									
Francoois D'Eliscu (1922-1923) 1-9-1 .136									
1922	1-4-1	26	122	.250	1923	0-5-0	13	101	.000
Albert Barron (1924) 1-4-0									
1924	1-4-0	15	106	.200					
Henry Miller (1925-1932) 50-15-8 .740									
1925	5-2-2	104	39	.667	1929	6-3-1	133	65	.650
1926	5-3-0	88	93	.625	1930	7-3-0	224	110	.700
1927	7-1-0	351	60	.875	1931	8-1-1	158	42	.850
1928	7-1-2	224	23	.800	1932	5-1-2	105	53	.750
Pop Warner (1933-1938) 31-18-9 .612									
1933	5-3-0	110	96	.625	1936	6-3-2	117	66	.636
1934	7-1-2	181	68	.800	1937	3-2-4	38	97	.556
1935	7-3-0	181	68	.700	1938	3-6-1	97	170	.350
Fred Swan (1939) 2-7-0 .222									
1939	2-7-0	51	96	.222					
Ray Morrison (1940-1948) 31-38-9 .455									
1940	4-4-1	155	113	.500	1945	7-1-0	198	51	.875
1941	7-2-0	176	146	.778	1946	2-4-2	61	114	.375
1942	2-5-3	48	135	.350	1947	3-6-0	91	128	.333
1943	2-6-0	65	163	.250	1948	2-6-1	95	182	.278
1944	2-4-2	93	96	.375					
Albert Kawal (1949-1954) 24-28-3 .464									
1949	5-4-0	156	225	.556	1952	2-7-1	128	221	.250
1950	4-4-1	173	132	.500	1953	4-4-1	134	157	.500
1951	6-4-0	168	176	.600	1954	3-5-0	95	148	.375
Josh Cody (1955) 0-8-0 .000									
1955	0-8-0	49	223	.000					
Peter Stevens (1956-1959) 4-28-0 .125									
1956	3-5-0	94	126	.375	1958	0-8-0	56	251	.000
1957	1-6-0	62	210	.143	1959	0-9-0	73	270	.000

Member of the Middle Atlantic Conference (1960-1969) 20-21-3

Year	Nat'l AP	Other	Overall W-L-T	PF	PA	Pct.	Conf. W-L-T	Pct.	Rank	Year	Nat'l AP	Other	Overall W-L-T	PF	PA	Pct.	Conf. W-L-T	Pct.	Rank
George Makris (1960-1969) 45-44-4 .505																			
1960			2-7-0	113	137	.222	0-5-0	.000	7	1965			5-5-0	203	210	.500	3-2-0	.600	3
1961			2-5-2	86	129	.333	1-2-2	.400	6	1966			6-3-0	266	196	.667	2-2-0	.500	3
1962			3-6-0	133	115	.333	2-3-0	.400	4	1967			7-2-0	201	224	.778	4-0-0	1.000	1
1963			5-3-1	209	130	.611	1-2-0	.333	4	1968			4-6-0	240	241	.400	2-2-0	.500	5
1964			7-2-0	247	128	.778	4-1-0	.800	2	1969			4-5-1	180	144	.450	1-2-1	.375	5
Temple reverts to independent status (1970-1990)																			
Wayne Hardin (1970-1982) 80-52-3 .604																			
1970			7-3-0	190	151	.700				1977			5-5-1	229	286	.500			
1971			6-2-1	210	136	.722				1978			7-3-1	280	203	.682			
1972			5-4-0	164	176	.556				1979	17	17	10-2-0	399	198	.833			
1973			9-1-0	353	167	.900				1980			4-7-0	170	262	.364			
1974			8-2-0	335	142	.800				1981			5-5-0	181	195	.500			
1975			6-5-0	289	225	.545				1982			4-7-0	230	206	.364			
1976			4-6-0	196	216	.400													
Bruce Ariens (1983-1988) 22-44-0 .333																			
1983			4-7-0	171	241	.364				1986*			0-11-0	308	271	.000			
1984			6-5-0	226	180	.545				1987			4-7-0	154	251	.364			
1985			4-7-0	233	223	.364				1988			4-7-0	207	318	.364			

*Temple forfeited six games in the 1886 season because of an ineligible player.

Year	Nat'l AP	Other	Overall W-L-T	PF	PA	Pct.	Conf. W-L-T	Pct.	Rank	Year	Nat'l AP	Other	Overall W-L-T	PF	PA	Pct.	Conf. W-L-T	Pct.	Rank
Jerry Berndt (1989-1992) 11-33-0 .250																			
1989			1-10-0	141	387	.091				1990			7-4-0	261	269	.364			
Member of the Big East Conference (1991-2003) 13-75-0 .148																			
1991			2-9-0	138	290	.182	0-5-0	.000	8	1992			1-10-0	132	383	.091	0-6-0	.000	7
Ron Dickerson (1993-1997) 8-47-0 .145																			
1993			1-10-0	115	517	.091	0-7-0	.000	8	1996			1-10-0	218	386	.091	0-7-0	.000	8
1994			2-9-0	244	417	.182	0-7-0	.000	8	1997			3-8-0	212	317	.273	3-4-0	.429	5
1995			1-10-0	187	538	.182	1-6-0	.143	7										
Bobby Wallace (1998-2003) 17-51-0 .250																			
1998			2-9-0	198	360	.182	2-5-0	.286	6	2001			4-7-0	198	311	.364	2-5-0	.286	6
1999			2-9-0	153	366	.182	2-5-0	.286	6	2002			4-8-0	242	351	.333	2-5-0	.286	6
2000			4-7-0	224	269	.364	1-6-0	.143	7	2003			1-11-0	235	393	.083	0-7-0	.000	8

Won-loss record by decades:

1894-99	14-19-2	.492	1930-39	53-30-12	.621	1970-79	67-33-3	.665
1900-09	23-19-7	.541	1940-49	36-42-9	.466	1980-89	36-73-0	.330
1910-19	22-20-6	.521	1950-59	23-60-3	.285	1990-99	22-88-0	.200
1920-29	32-23-6	.574	1960-69	45-44-4	.505	2000-03	13-33-0	.283

Historic record: 386-484-52 .447

Post-season won-loss record: 2-2-0 .500
1935: Sugar Bowl, Tulane 20, Temple 14
1977: Mirage Bowl, Grambling 35, Temple 32
1978: Mirage Bowl, Temple 28, Boston College 24
1979: Garden State Bowl, Temple 28, California 17

College Football Hall of Fame: Pop Warner, coach, 1933-38

Awards: Maxwell Award; 1974, Steve Joachim

UNIVERSITY OF TENNESSEE, Knoxville, Tennessee; nickname "Volunteers"; colors orange and white; Neyland Stadium (104.079); Southeastern Conference. Tennessee began play in 1891 and joined the Southern Intercollegiate Athletic Association in 1896. Tennessee played in the SIAA through the 1920 season, but conference records are not available. In 1922, Tennessee joined the new Southern Conference. In 1933, Tennessee joined twelve other departing Southern Conference teams in forming the Southeastern Conference.

Early years (1891-1910)

Year	Coach	W-L-T	PF	PA	Pct.	Year	Coach	W-L-T	PF	PA	Pct.
1891	no coach	0-1-0	0	24	.000						
1892	no coach	2-5-0	51	51	.286	1902	H. F. Fisher	6-2-0	88	39	.750
1893	no coach	2-4-0	44	256	.333	1903	H. F. Fisher	4-5-0	76	110	.444
1894-1895	no team					1904	S. D. Crawford	3-5-1	45	77	.389
1896	no coach	4-0-0	50	10	1.000	1905	J. D.Depree	3-5-1	162	151	.389
1897	no coach	4-1-0	64	16	.800	1906	J. D.Depree	1-6-2	15	127	.222
1898	no team					1907	George Levene	7-2-1	169	17	.750
1899	J.A. Pierce	5-2-0	80	61	.714	1908	George Levene	7-2-0	124	41	.778
1900	J.A. Pierce	3-2-1	67	51	.583	1909	George Levene	1-6-2	11	113	.222
1901	George Kelley	3-3-2	42	56	.500	1910	Andrew Stone	3-5-1	50	143	.389

Z. G. Clevenger (1911-1915) 26-15-2 .628

Year	W-L-T	PF	PA	Pct.	Year	W-L-T	PF	PA	Pct.
1911	3-4-2	82	93	.444	1914	9-0-0	374	37	1.000
1912	4-4-0	294	80	.500	1915	4-4-0	303	58	.500
1913	6-3-0	283	37	.667					

John Bender (1916-1920) 18-5-4 .741

Year	W-L-T	PF	PA	Pct.	Year	W-L-T	PF	PA	Pct.
1916	8-0-1	168	19	.944	1919	3-3-3	103	62	.500
1917-1918	no team				1920	7-2-0	243	40	.778

M. B. Banks (1921-1925) 27-15-3 .633

Year	W-L-T	PF	PA	Pct.
1921	6-2-1	102	35	.722

Member of the Southern Conference (1922-1932) 50-13-6 .768

	Nat'l		Overall				Conference				Nat'l		Overall					Conference	
Year	AP	Other	W-L-T	PF	PA	Pct	W-L-T	Pct.	Rank	Year	AP	Other	W-L-T	PF	PA	Pct.	W-L-T	Pct.	Rank
1922			8-2-0	239	45	.800	3-2-0	.600	7	1924			3-5-0	83	135	.375	0-4-0	.000	19
1923			5-4-1	82	167	.550	4-3-0	.571	11	1925			5-2-1	129	73	.688	2-2-1	.500	10

R. R. Neyland (1926-1934, 1936-1940, 1946-1952) 173-31-12 .829

Year	AP	Other	W-L-T	PF	PA	Pct	W-L-T	Pct.	Rank	Year	AP	Other	W-L-T	PF	PA	Pct.	W-L-T	Pct.	Rank
1926			8-1-0	151	34	.889	5-1-0	.833	2	1930		10	9-1-0	209	31	.900	6-1-0	.857	2
1927			8-0-1	245	26	.944	5-0-1	.917	3	1931		3	9-0-1	243	15	.950	6-0-1	.929	2
1928			9-0-1	249	51	.950	6-0-1	.929	2	1932		9	9-0-1	238	36	.950	7-0-1	.938	1
1929			9-0-1	330	19	.950	6-0-1	.929	2										

Member of the Southeastern Conference (1932-2003) 289-142-18 .664

Year	AP	Other	W-L-T	PF	PA	Pct	W-L-T	Pct.	Rank	Year	AP	Other	W-L-T	PF	PA	Pct.	W-L-T	Pct.	Rank
1933			7-3-0	176	47	.700	5-2-0	.714	4	1934			8-2-0	175	58	.800	5-1-0	.833	3

W. H. Britton (1935) 4-5-0 .444

Year	AP	Other	W-L-T	PF	PA	Pct	W-L-T	Pct.	Rank
1935			4-5-0	98	155	.444	2-3-0	.400	9

R. R. Neyland (1936-1940)

Year	AP	Other	W-L-T	PF	PA	Pct	W-L-T	Pct.	Rank	Year	AP	Other	W-L-T	PF	PA	Pct.	W-L-T	Pct.	Rank
1936	17		6-2-2	147	52	.750	3-1-2	.667	4	1939	2	5	10-1-0	212	14	.909	6-0-0	1.000	1
1937			6-3-1	189	47	.650	4-3-0	.571	7	1940	4	4	10-1-0	332	45	.909	5-0-0	1.000	1
1938	2	3	11-0-0	283	16	1.000	7-0-0	1.000	1										

John Barnhill (1941-1945) 32-5-2 .846

Year	AP	Other	W-L-T	PF	PA	Pct	W-L-T	Pct.	Rank	Year	AP	Other	W-L-T	PF	PA	Pct.	W-L-T	Pct.	Rank
1941	18		8-2-0	182	73	.800	3-1-0	.750	2	1944	12		7-1-1	173	73	.833	5-0-1	.917	2
1942	7		9-1-1	259	61	.864	4-1-0	.800	2	1945	14		8-1-0	238	52	.889	3-1-0	.750	2
1943			no team																

R. R. Neyland (1946-1952)

Year	AP	Other	W-L-T	PF	PA	Pct	W-L-T	Pct.	Rank	Year	AP	Other	W-L-T	PF	PA	Pct.	W-L-T	Pct.	Rank
1946	7		9-2-0	175	97	.818	5-0-0	1.000	1	1950	4	3	11-1-0	335	71	.917	4-1-0	.800	2
1947			5-5-0	164	152	.500	2-3-0	.400	9	1951	1	1	10-1-0	385	116	.909	5-0-0	1.000	2
1948			4-4-2	140	98	.500	2-3-1	.417	8	1952	8	8	8-2-1	259	79	.773	5-0-1	.917	2
1949	17		7-2-1	214	104	.750	4-1-1	.750	3										

Harvey Robinson (1953-1954) 10-10-1 .500

Year	AP	Other	W-L-T	PF	PA	Pct	W-L-T	Pct.	Rank	Year	AP	Other	W-L-T	PF	PA	Pct.	W-L-T	Pct.	Rank
1953			6-4-1	240	153	.591	3-2-1	.583	7	1954			4-6-0	105	164	.400	1-5-0	.167	11

Bowden Wyatt (1955-1962) 49-29-4 .622

Year	AP	Other	W-L-T	PF	PA	Pct	W-L-T	Pct.	Rank	Year	AP	Other	W-L-T	PF	PA	Pct.	W-L-T	Pct.	Rank
1955			6-3-1	188	92	.650	3-2-1	.583	4	1959			5-4-1	112	118	.550	3-4-1	.438	8
1956	2	2	10-1-0	275	88	.909	6-0-0	1.000	1	1960		20	6-2-2	209	79	.700	3-2-2	.571	5
1957	13	16	8-3-0	164	75	.727	4-3-0	.571	5	1961			6-4-0	221	149	.600	4-3-0	.571	4
1958			4-6-0	77	122	.400	4-3-0	.571	5	1962			4-6-0	179	134	.400	2-6-0	.250	10

Jim McDonald (1963) 5-5-0 .500

Year	AP	Other	W-L-T	PF	PA	Pct	W-L-T	Pct.	Rank
1963			5-5-0	168	121	.500	3-5-0	.375	8

Doug Dickey (1964-1969) 46-15-4 .739

Year	AP	Other	W-L-T	PF	PA	Pct	W-L-T	Pct.	Rank	Year	AP	Other	W-L-T	PF	PA	Pct.	W-L-T	Pct.	Rank
1964			4-5-1	80	121	.450	1-5-1	.214	10	1967	2	2	9-2-0	283	141	.818	6-0-0	1.000	1
1965	7	7	8-1-2	220	98	.818	3-1-2	.667	3	1968	13	7	8-2-1	261	146	.773	4-1-1	.750	2
1966			8-3-0	240	99	.727	4-2-0	.667	5	1969	15	11	9-2-0	328	179	.818	5-1-0	.833	1

1970	4	4	11-1-0	370	116	.917	4-1-0	.800	2	1974	20	15	7-3-2	211	181	.667	2-3-1	.417	7
1971	9	9	10-2-0	270	119	.833	4-2-0	.667	4	1975			7-5-0	253	193	.583	3-3-0	.500	5
1972	8	11	10-2-0	297	100	.833	4-2-0	.667	4	1976			6-5-0	237	162	.545	2-4-0	.333	8
1973	19		8-4-0	291	247	.667	3-3-0	.500	4										

Johnny Majors (1977-1992) 116-62-8 .645

1977			4-7-0	229	229	.364	1-5-0	.167	8	1985	4	4	9-1-2	325	140	.833	5-1-0	.833	1
1978			5-5-1	251	209	.500	3-3-0	500	4	1986			7-5-0	293	249	.583	3-3-0	.500	6
1979			7-5-0	311	235	.583	3-3-0	.500	4	1987	14	13	10-2-1	422	246	.808	4-1-1	.750	3
1980			5-6-0	256	189	.455	3-3-0	.500	6	1988			5-6-0	212	286	.455	3-4-0	.429	8
1981			8-4-0	244	265	.667	3-3-0	.500	4	1989	5	5	11-1-0	346	217	.917	6-1-0	.857	1
1982			6-5-1	281	239	.542	3-2-1	.583	5	1990	8	7	9-2-2	465	220	.769	5-1-1	.786	1
1983			9-3-0	282	165	.750	4-2-0	.667	3	1991	14	15	9-3-0	352	263	.750	5-2-0	.714	3
1984			7-4-1	327	276	.625	3-3-0	.500	5	1992*12		12	5-3--0	206	125	.625	3-3-0	.500	4

Phillip Fulmer (1993-2003) 113-28-0 .801

1992*			4-0-0	141	71	1.000	2-0-0		*										
1993	12	11	10-2-0	484	175	.833	7-1-0	.875	1	1998	1	1	13-0-0	431	189	1.000	8-0-0	1.000	1
1994	22	18	8-4-0	363	208	.667	5-3-0	.625	3	1999	9	9	9-3-0	348	163	.750	6-2-0	.750	3
1995	3	2	11-1-0	431	228	.917	7-1-0	.875	2	2000		25	8-4-0	380	247	.667	5-3-0	.625	3
1996	9	9	10-2-0	389	157	.833	7-1-0	.875	2	2001	4	4	11-2-0	400	251	.846	7-1-0	.875	1
1997	7	8	11-2-0	428	286	.846	7-1-0	.875	1	2002			8-5-0	296	227	.615	5-3-0	.625	4
										2003	15	16	10-3-0	365	239	.769	6-2-0	.750	3

*The first three games of the 1992 season plus the bowl game were coached by Fulmer, with the other eight games coached by Majors.

Won-loss record by decades:

1891-99	17-13-0	.567	1930-39	79-17-5	.807	1970-79	75-39-3	.654
1900-09	38-38-10	.500	1940-49	67-19-5	.764	1980-89	77-37-5	.668
1910-19	40-23-7	.621	1950-59	72-31-4	.692	1990-99	99-22-2	.813
1920-29	68-18-6	.772	1960-69	67-32-6	.667	2000-03	37-14-0	.725

Historic record: 736-303-53 .698

Post-season won-loss record: 26-22-0 .542

1931: New York Charity Game, Tennessee 13, NYU 0
1939: Orange Bowl, Tennessee 17, Oklahoma 0
1940: Rose Bowl, USC 14, Tennessee 0
1941: Sugar Bowl, Boston College 19, Tennessee 13
1943: Sugar Bowl, Tennessee 14, Tulsa 7
1945: Rose Bowl, USC 25, Tennessee 0
1947: Orange Bowl, Rice 8, Tennessee 0
1951: Cotton Bowl, Tennessee 20, Texas 14
1952: Sugar Bowl, Maryland 28, Tennessee 13
1953: Cotton Bowl, Texas 16, Tennessee 0
1957: Sugar Bowl, Baylor 13, Tennessee 7
1957: Gator Bowl, Tennessee 3, Texas A&M 0
1965: Bluebonnet Bowl, Tennessee 27, Tulsa 6
1966: Gator Bowl, Tennessee 18, Syracuse 12
1968: Orange Bowl, Oklahoma 26, Tennessee 24
1969: Cotton Bowl, Texas 36, Tennessee 13
1969: Gator Bowl, Florida 14, Tennessee 13
1971: Sugar Bowl, Tennessee 34, Air Force 13
1971: Liberty Bowl, Tennessee 14, Arkansas 13
1972: Bluebonnet Bowl, Tennessee 24, USC 17
1973: Gator Bowl, Texas Tech 28, Tennessee 19
1974: Liberty Bowl, Tennessee 7, Maryland 3

1979: Bluebonnet Bowl, Purdue 27, Tennessee 22
1981: Garden State Bowl, Tennessee 28, Wisconsin 21
1982: Peach Bowl, Iowa 28, Tennessee 22
1983: Florida Citrus Bowl, Tennessee 30, Maryland 23
1984: Sun Bowl, Maryland 28, Tennessee 27
1986: Sugar Bowl, Tennessee 35, Miami (FL) 7
1986: Liberty Bowl, Tennessee 21, Minnesota 14
1988: Peach Bowl, Tennessee 27, Indiana 22
1990: Cotton Bowl, Tennessee 31, Arkansas 27
1991: Sugar Bowl, Tennessee 23, Virginia 22
1992: Fiesta Bowl, Penn State 42, Tennessee 17
1993: Hall of Fame Bowl, Tennessee 38, Boston College 23
1994: Citrus Bowl, Penn State 31, Tennessee 13
1994: Gator Bowl, Tennessee 45, Virginia Tech 23
1996: Citrus Bowl, Tennessee 20, Ohio State 14
1997: SEC Championship, Tennessee 30, Auburn 29
1997: Citrus Bowl, Tennessee 48, Northwestern 28
1998: SEC Championship, Tennessee 24, Mississippi St. 14
1998: Orange Bowl, Nebraska 42, Tennessee 17
1999: Fiesta Bowl, Tennessee 23, Florida State 16
2000: Fiesta Bowl, Nebraska 31, Tennessee 21
2001: Cotton Bowl, Kansas State 35, Tennessee 21
2001: SEC Championship, LSU 31, Tennessee 20
2002: Citrus Bowl, Tennessee 45, Michigan 17
2002: Peach Bowl, Maryland 30, Tennessee 3
2004: Peach Bowl, Clemson 27, Tennessee 14

College Football Hall of Fame:
Nathan Dougherty, guard, 1906-9; Bob Neyland, coach, 1926-34, 1936-40, 1946-52; Gene McEver halfback, 1928-31; Herman Hickman, guard, 1929-31; Beattie Feathers, halfback, 1931-33; George Cafego, halfback, 1937-39; Ed Moliniski, guard, 1938-40; Bob Suffridge, guard, 1938-40; Bobby Dodd, quarterback, 1945-48; Joe Steffy, guard, 1945-47; Hank Lauricella, halfback, 1948-51; John Michels, guard, 1950-52; Doug Atkins, defensive end, 1950-52; Johnny Majors, halfback, 1954-56; Bowden Wyatt, coach, 1955-62; Steve DeLong, middle guard, 1962-64; Bob Johnson, center, 1965-67; Steve Kiner, linebacker, 1967-69; Jim Lee Youngblood, linebacker, 1969-72; Doug Dickey, coach, 1964-69; Reggie White, defensive tackle, 1980-83.

Awards: Davey O'Brien Award: 1997, Peyton Manning; Maxwell Award: 1997, Peyton Manning; Outland Trophy: 1964, Steve DeLong, 2000, John Henderson; Unitas Award: 1998, Peyton Manning.

TEXAS A&M, College Station, Texas; nickname "Aggies"; colors maroon and white; Kyle Field (82,600); Big Twelve Conference. Texas A&M was an independent from 1894 through the 1914 season. In 1915, A&M became one of the founding members of the Southwest Conference and played in the conference until it disbanded after the 1995 season. In 1996, A&M joined the newly formed Big Twelve Conference.

Early years as an independent (1894-1914)

Year	W-L-T	PF	PA	Pct.		Year	W-L-T	PF	PA	Pct
					J. Perkins (1894) 1-1-0 .500					
1894	1-1-0	14	44	.500						
					No team (1895)					
					A. Soule and H. South (1896) 2-0-1 .833					
1896	2-0-1	50	4	.833						
					C. W. Taylor (1897) 1-2-0 .333					
1897	1-2-0	10	40	.333						
					H. Williams (1898) 4-2-0 .667					
1898	4-2-0	117	60	.667						
					W. Murray (1899-1901) 7-8-1 .469					
1899	4-2-0	150	16	.667		1901	1-4-0	12	112	.200
1900	2-2-1	61	22	.500						
					J. Platt (1902-1904) 18-5-3 .750					
1902	7-0-2	128	11	.889		1904	4-2-0	104	51	.667
1903	7-3-1	92	59	.682						
					W. Bachman (1905-1906) 13-3-0 .813					
1905	7-2-0	180	83	.778		1906	6-1-0	170	42	.857
					L. Larson (1907) 6-1-1 .813					
1907	6-1-1	125	27	.813						
					N. Merriam (1908) 3-5-0 .375					
1908	3-5-0	76	117	.375						
					C. B. Moran (1909-1914) 38-8-4 .800					
1909	7-0-1	130	14	.938		1912	8-1-0	366	26	.889
1910	8-1-0	203	24	.889		1913	3-4-2	53	76	.444
1911	6-1-0	134	17	.857		1914	6-1-1	205	33	.812

Member of the Southwest Conference (1915-1995) 252-220-30 .532

Year	Nat'l AP	Other	Overall W-L-T	PF	PA	Pct.	Conf. W-L-T	Pct.	Rank	Year	Nat'l AP	Other	Overall W-L-T	PF	PA	Pct.	Conf. W-L-T	Pct.	Rank
E. Harlan (1915-1916) 12-5-0 .706																			
1915			6-2-0	182	34	.750	1-1-0	.500	2	1916			6-3-0	188	66	.667	2-1-0	.667	3
Dana Bible (1917, 1919-1928) 72-19-9 .765																			
1917			8-0-0	270	0	1.000	2-0-0	1.000	1										
D. Graves (1918) 6-1-0 .857																			
1918			6-1-0	123	19	.857	1-1-0	.500	3										
Dana Bible (1919-1928)																			
1919			10-0-0	275	0	1.000	4-0-0	1.000	1	1924			7-2-1	229	35	.750	2-2-1	.500	3
1920			6-1-1	229	7	.812	5-1-0	.833	2	1925			7-1-1	191	25	.833	4-1-0	.800	1
1921			6-1-2	110	57	.778	3-0-2	.800	1	1926			5-3-1	184	59	.688	1-3-1	.300	6
1922			5-4-0	166	69	.556	2-2-0	.500	3	1927		11	8-0-1	262	32	.944	4-0-1	.900	1
1923			5-3-1	135	23	.688	0-3-1	.125	8	1928			5-4-1	205	77	.550	1-3-1	.300	6
Matty Bell (1929-1933) 24-21-3 .531																			
1929			5-4-0	203	65	.556	2-3-0	.400	6	1932			4-4-2	75	78	.500	1-2-2	.400	4
1930			2-7-0	66	100	.222	0-5-0	.000	7	1933			6-3-1	160	80	.650	2-2-1	.500	3
1931			7-3-0	137	34	.700	3-2-0	.600	3										
Homer Norton (1934-1947) 82-53-9 .601																			
1934			2-7-2	84	186	.273	1-4-1	.250	6	1941	9		9-2-0	281	75	.818	5-1-0	.833	1
1935			3-7-0	125	121	.300	1-5-0	.167	6	1942			4-5-1	130	79	.450	2-3-1	.417	5
1936			8-3-1	156	74	.708	3-2-1	.583	3	1943			7-2-1	184	65	.750	4-1-0	.800	2
1937			5-2-2	117	59	.667	2-2-2	.500	4	1944			7-4-0	289	87	.636	2-3-0	.400	4
1938			4-4-1	137	71	.500	2-3-1	.417	5	1945			6-4-0	179	103	.600	3-3-0	.500	3
1939	1	2	11-0-0	212	31	1.000	6-0-0	1.000	1	1946			4-6-0	125	107	.400	3-3-0	.500	4
1940	6	5	9-1-0	183	46	.900	5-1-0	.833	1	1947			3-6-1	169	185	.350	1-4-1	.250	5
Harry Stiteler (1948-1950) 8-21-2 .290																			
1948			0-9-1	123	247	.050	0-5-1	.083	7	1950			7-4-0	344	206	.636	3-3-0	.500	3
1949			1-8-1	92	267	.150	0-5-1	.083	7										
Ray George (1951-1953) 12-14-4 .467																			
1951			5-3-2	213	179	.600	1-3-2	.333	5	1953			4-5-1	128	186	.450	1-5-0	.167	6
1952			3-6-1	137	187	.350	1-4-1	.250	6										
Bear Bryant (1954-1957) 25-14-2 .634																			
1954			1-9-0	97	177	.100	0-6-0	.000	7	1956	5	5	9-0-1	223	81	.950	6-0-0	1.000	1
1955	17	14	7-2-1	160	89	.750	4-1-1	.750	2	1957	9	10	8-3-0	158	50	.636	4-2-0	.667	3

Jim Myers (1958-1961) 12-24-4 .350

1958			4-6-0	124	217	.400	2-4-0	.333	5	1960			1-6-3	73	117	.250	0-4-3	.214	6
1959			3-7-0	101	141	.300	0-6-0	.000	7	1961			4-5-1	184	118	.450	3-4-0	.429	4

Hank Folberg (1962-1964) 6-23-1 .217

| 1962 | | | 3-7-0 | 61 | 155 | .300 | 3-4-0 | .429 | 4 | 1964 | | | 1-9-0 | 88 | 162 | .100 | 1-6-0 | .143 | 7 |
| 1963 | | | 2-7-1 | 90 | 153 | .250 | 1-5-1 | .214 | 8 |

Gene Stallings (1965-1971) 27-45-1 .377

1965			3-7-0	80	170	.300	1-6-0	.143	7	1969			3-7-0	116	192	.300	2-5-0	.286	6
1966			4-5-1	145	183	.450	4-3-0	.571	4	1970			2-9-0	170	304	.182	0-7-0	.000	8
1967			7-4-0	211	154	.636	6-1-0	.857	1	1971			5-6-0	144	212	.455	4-3-0	.571	4
1968			3-7-0	196	184	.300	2-5-0	.286	6

Emory Bellard (1972-1978) 48-27-0 .640

1972			3-8-0	165	243	.273	2-5-0	.286	7	1976	7	8	10-2-0	364	140	.833	6-2-0	.750	2
1973			5-6-0	292	231	.455	3-4-0	.429	6	1977			8-4-0	350	304	.667	6-2-0	.750	3
1974	16	15	8-3-0	222	131	.727	5-2-0	.714	2	1978	*19	18	4-2-0	176	78	.667	1-2-0	.333	*
1975	11	12	10-2-0	265	124	.833	6-1-0	.857	1

Tom Wilson (1978-1981) 21-19-0 .525

| 1978* | | | 4-2-0 | 115 | 105 | .667 | 3-2-0 | .600 | 5 | 1980 | | | 4-7-0 | 160 | 259 | .364 | 3-5-0 | .375 | 6 |
| 1979 | | | 6-5-0 | 243 | 159 | .545 | 4-4-0 | .500 | 5 | 1981 | | | 7-5-0 | 280 | 203 | .583 | 4-4-0 | .500 | 5 |

*Bellard coached the first six games of the 1978 season, and Wilson coached the last six games.

Jackie Sherrill (1982-1988) 52-28-1 .648

1982			5-6-0	286	314	.455	3-5-0	.375	6	1986	13	12	9-3-0	372	215	.750	7-1-0	.875	1
1983			5-5-1	218	174	.500	4-3-1	.562	3	1987	10	9	10-2-0	313	168	.833	6-1-0	.857	1
1984			6-5-0	245	217	.545	3-5-0	.375	7	1988			7-5-0	293	253	.583	6-1-0	.857	**
1985	6	7	10-2-0	375	196	.833	7-1-0	.875	1

**Texas A&M ineligible for conference title due to NCAA violations.

R. C. Slocum (1989-2002) 123-47-2 .721

1989	20		8-4-0	343	192	.667	6-2-0	.750	2	1993	9	8	10-2-0	425	143	.833	7-0-0	1.000	1
1990	15	13	9-3-1	465	232	.731	5-2-1	.688	2	1994	8		10-0-1	319	147	.955	6-0-1	.929	***
1991	12	13	10-2-0	404	154	.833	8-0-0	1.000	1	1995	15	15	9-3-0	327	168	.750	5-2-0	.714	2
1992	7	6	12-1-0	352	196	.923	7-0-0	1.000	1

***Texas A&M ineligible for conference title due to NCAA violations.

Member of the Big Twelve Conference (1996-2003) 37-27-0 .578

1996			6-6-0	351	206	.500	4-4-0	.500	6	2000			7-5-0	348	239	.583	5-3-0	.625	5
1997	20	21	9-4-0	422	207	.692	6-2-0	.750	3	2001			8-4-0	248	213	.667	4-4-0	.500	5
1998	11	13	11-3-0	321	190	.786	8-0-0	1.000	1	2002			6-6-0	345	280	.500	3-5-0	.375	8
1999	21	20	8-4-0	318	232	.667	5-3-0	.625	4

Dennis Franchione (2003) 4-8-0 .333

| 2003 | | | 4-8-0 | 304 | 465 | .333 | 2-6-0 | .250 | 10 |

Won-loss record by decades:

1894-99	12-7-1	.625		1930-39	52-40-9	.559		1970-79	65-49-0	.570
1900-09	50-20-6	.697		1940-49	50-47-5	.515		1980-89	71-44-1	.616
1910-19	67-14-3	.815		1950-59	51-45-6	.529		1990-99	94-28-2	.766
1920-29	59-23-9	.698		1960-69	31-64-6	.337		2000-03	25-23-0	.521

Historic record: 627-404-48 .603

Post-season won-loss record: 14-15-0 .483

1922: Dixie Classic, A&M 22, Centre College 14	1987: Cotton Bowl, Ohio State 28, A&M 12
1940: Sugar Bowl, A&M 14, Tulane 13	1988: Cotton Bowl, A&M 35, Notre Dame 10
1941: Cotton Bowl, A&M 13, Fordham 12	1989: John Hancock Bowl, Pittsburgh 31, A&M 28
1942: Cotton Bowl, Alabama 29, A&M 21	1990: Holiday Bowl, A&M 65, BYU 14
1944: Orange Bowl, LSU 19, A&M 14	1992: Cotton Bowl, Florida State 10, A&M 2
1950: Presidential Cup, A&M 40, Georgia 20	1993: Cotton Bowl, Notre Dame 28, A&M 3
1957: Gator Bowl, Tennessee 3, A&M 0	1994: Cotton Bowl, Notre Dame 24, A&M 21
1968: Cotton Bowl, A&M 20, Alabama 16	1995: Alamo Bowl, A&M 22, Michigan 20
1975: Liberty Bowl, USC 20, A&M 0	1997: Big 12 Championship, Nebraska 54, A&M 15
1977: Sun Bowl, A&M 37, Florida 14	1998: Cotton Bowl, UCLA 29, A&M 23
1977: Bluebonnet Bowl, USC 47, A&M 28	1998: Big 12 Championship, A&M 36, Kansas State 33
1978: Hall of Fame Bowl, A&M 28, Iowa State 12	1999: Sugar Bowl, Ohio State 24, A&M 14
1981: Independence Bowl, A&M 33, Oklahoma State 16	1999: Alamo Bowl, Penn State 24, A&M 0
1986: Cotton Bowl, A&M 36, Auburn 16	2000: Independence Bowl, Miss. State 43, A&M 41
	2001: Gallleryfurniture.com Bowl, A&M 28, TCU 9

College Football Hall of Fame:
Joe Utay, halfback, 1905-07; Dana X. Bible, coach, 1917, 1919-28; Joel Hunt, quarterback, 1935-37; Matty Bell, coach, 1929-33; Homer Norton, coach, 1934-47; Joe Routt, guard, 1935-37; John Kimbrough, fullback, 1938-40; Bear Bryant, coach, 1954-57; Jack Pardee, fullback, 1954-56; John David Crow, halfback, 1955-57; Charlie Krueger, tackle, 1955-57; Dave Elmendorf, safety, 1968-70.
Awards: Heisman Trophy: 1957, John David Crow; Lombardi Award: 1998, Dat Nguyen; Benarik Award: 1999, Dat Nguyen.

UNIVERSITY OF TEXAS AT EL PASO (UTEP), El Paso, Texas; nickname "Miners"; colors dark blue, orange, silver accent; Sun Bowl (52,000); Western Athletic Conference. UTEP has gone through a series of name changes, beginning as the Texas College of the Mines, becoming Texas Western in 1950, and then UTEP in 1966. UTEP began play in 1914 as an independent. In 1935, the team moved to the Border Conference and played there until the conference was disbanded in 1961. The team reverted to independent status between 1962 and 1967. Beginning with the 1968 season, UTEP has been a member of the WAC.

Early years as an independent (1914-1934)

Year	W-L-T	PF	PA	Pct.	Year	W-L-T	PF	PA	Pct.
Tommy Dwyer (1914-1919) 5-11-2 .333									
1914	2-3-0	34	64	.400	1917	0-0-1	0	0	.500
1915	0-1-1	10	43	.250	1918	no team			
1916	1-4-0	28	216	.200	1919	2-3-0	65	122	.400
H.E. Van Surdam (1920) 2-4-0 .333									
1920	2-4-0	45	180	.333					
Thomas C. Holiday (1921) 0-5-0 .000									
1921	0-5-0	14	149	.000					
Jack C. Vowell (1922-1923) 8-8-0 .500									
1922	5-4-0	157	102	.556	1923	3-4-0	106	65	.429
George B. Powell (1924-1926) 11-7-2 .600									
1924	3-2-1	68	51	.583	1926	3-4-0	106	92	.429
1925	5-1-1	114	57	.786					
E.J. Stewart (1927-1928) 5-6-3 .464									
1927	2-2-2	69	70	.500	1928	3-4-1	100	103	.438
Mack Saxon (1929-1941) 66-44-8 .593									
1929	6-1-2	154	46	.778	1932	7-3-0	205	108	.700
1930	7-1-1	183	60	.833	1933	3-6-0	65	85	.333
1931	7-1-0	147	83	.788	1934	4-4-0	131	101	.500

Member of the Border Conference (1935-1961) 62-57-7 .520

Year	Nat'l AP	Other	Overall W-L-T	PF	PA	Pct.	Conf. W-L-T	Pct.	Rank	Year	Nat'l AP	Other	Overall W-L-T	PF	PA	Pct.	Conf. W-L-T	Pct.	Rank
1935			1-8-0	23	178	.111	0-3-0	.000	6	1939			5-4-0	113	71	.556	3-2-0	.600	4
1936			5-3-1	92	86	.611	2-1-1	.625	2	1940			4-4-1	129	121	.500	3-1-1	.700	3
1937			7-1-2	215	91	.800	2-1-1	.625	4	1941			3-5-1	177	172	.389	2-4-0	.333	6
1938			6-3-0	153	72	.600	3-2-0	.600	4										
Walter Miller (1942) 5-4-0 .556																			
1942			5-4-0	155	102	.556	4-3-0	.571	5										
No team (1943-1945)																			
Jack Curtice (1946-1949) 24-13-3 .638																			
1946			3-6-0	136	150	.333	2-4-0	.333	7	1948			8-2-1	361	182	.773	4-1-1	.750	2
1947			5-3-1	159	79	.611	2-3-1	.417	5	1949			8-2-1	292	113	.773	4-2-0	.667	3
Mike Brumbelow (1950-1956) 46-24-3 .651																			
1950			7-3-0	272	232	.700	4-2-0	.667	3	1954			8-3-0	290	197	.727	4-2-0	.667	3
1951			3-7-0	152	241	.300	2-4-0	.333	5	1955			6-2-2	227	114	.700	3-2-1	.583	4
1952			5-5-1	204	231	.500	2-3-1	.417	6	1956			9-2-0	305	78	.818	6-0-0	1.000	1
1953			8-2-0	257	144	.800	4-2-0	.667	3										
Ben Collins (1957-1961) 18-29-1 .385																			
1957			6-3-0	202	168	.667	3-2-0	.600	3	1960			4-5-1	167	176	.450	2-3-0	.400	4
1958			2-7-0	92	179	.222	1-4-0	.200	5	1961			3-7-0	176	283	.300	1-3-0	.250	4
1959			3-7-0	163	191	.300	2-3-0	.400	5										
UTEP reverts to independent status (1962-1967)																			
Bum Phillips (1962) 4-5-0 .444																			
1962			4-5-0	84	144	.444													
Warren Harper (1963-1964) 3-15-2 .200																			
1963			3-7-0	98	142	.300				1964			0-8-2	64	217	.100			
Bobby Dodds (1965-1972) 42-38-2 .524																			
1965			8-3-0	317	206	.727				1967			7-2-1	337	145	.750			
1966			6-4-0	293	187	.600													
Member of the Western Athletic Conference (1968-2003) 59-208-2 .223																			
1968			4-5-1	232	225	.450	3-3-0	.500	4	1971			5-6-0	166	217	.455	1-6-0	.143	8
1969			4-6-0	158	242	.400	2-5-0	.286	6	1972			2-8-0	172	344	.200	1-6-0	.143	8
1970			6-4-0	258	236	.600	4-3-0	.571	4										
Tommy Hudspeth (1973) 0-11-0 .000																			
1973			0-11-0	142	544	.000	0-7-0	.000	8										
Gil Bartosh (1974-1976) 6-28-0 .176																			
1974			4-7-0	246	298	.364	3-4-0	.429	4	1976			1-11-0	172	356	.083	0-7-0	.000	8
1975			1-10-0	109	281	.091	0-6-0	.000	8										

Bill Michael (1977-1981) 5-43-0 .104

1977	1-10-0	151	460	.091	0-7-0	.000	8	1980		1-11-0	143	424	.083	1-6-0	.143	8
1978	1-11-0	138	427	.083	1-5-0	.167	8	1981*		0-2-0	22	51	.000	0-0-0		
1979	2-9-0	106	266	.182	0-7-0	.000	8									

Bill Alton (1981) 1-8-0 .111

| 1981* | 1-8-0 | 124 | 390 | .111 | 1-6-0 | .143 | 8 |

*Michael coached the first two games of the 1981 season, and Alton coached the remaining nine games.

Bill Yung (1982-1985) 7-39-0 .152

| 1982 | 2-10-0 | 177 | 417 | .167 | 1-6-0 | .143 | 9 | 1984 | | 2-9-0 | 180 | 374 | .182 | 1-7-0 | .125 | 8 |
| 1983 | 2-10-0 | 210 | 359 | .167 | 0-8-0 | .000 | 9 | 1985 | | 1-10-0 | 196 | 376 | .091 | 1-7-0 | .125 | 9 |

Bob Stull (1986-1988) 21-15-0 .583

| 1986 | 4-8-0 | 309 | 392 | .333 | 2-6-0 | .250 | 8 | 1988 | | 10-3-0 | 445 | 275 | .769 | 6-2-0 | .750 | 2 |
| 1987 | 7-4-0 | 307 | 234 | .636 | 5-3-0 | .625 | 4 | | | | | | | | | |

David Lee (1989-1993) 11-41-1 .217

1989	2-10-0	240	412	.167	1-7-0	.125	8	1992		1-10-0	254	386	.091	1-7-0	.125	10
1990	3-8-0	191	342	.273	1-7-0	.125	8	1993*		1-6-0	156	254	.143	0-3-0	.000	*
1991	4-7-1	254	252	.375	2-5-1	.313	6									

Charlie Bailey (1993-1999) 19-53-1 .267

1993*	0-5-0	67	195	.000	0-5-0	.000	10	1997		4-7-0	162	311	.364	3-5-0	.375	13
1994	3-7-1	217	359	.318	1-6-1	.188	9	1998		3-8-0	226	305	.273	3-5-0	.375	11
1995	2-10-0	263	486	.833	1-7-0	.125	10	1999		5-7-0	306	389	.417	3-4-0	.429	6
1996	2-9-0	183	314	.182	0-8-0	.000	15									

Gary Nord (2000-03) 14-34-0 .292

| 2000 | 8-4-0 | | | .667 | 7-1-0 | .875 | 2 | 2002 | | 2-10-0 | 220 | 511 | .167 | 1-7-0 | .125 | 9 |
| 2001 | 2-9-0 | 235 | 414 | .182 | 1-7-0 | .125 | 9 | 2003 | | 2-11-0 | 288 | 498 | .154 | 1-7-0 | .125 | 9 |

Won-loss record by decades:

1914-19	5-11-2	.333		1950-59	57-41-3	579		1980-89	32-85-0	.274
1920-29	32-31-7	.507		1960-69	43-52-5	.455		1990-99	28-84-1	.252
1930-39	52-34-4	.600		1970-79	23-86-0	.211		2000-03	14-34-0	.292
1940-49	36-26-5	.558								

Historic record 322-484-27 .403

Post-season won-loss record: 5-5-0

1937: Sun Bowl, Hardin-Simmons 34, UTEP 6
1949: Sun Bowl, West Virginia 21, UTEP 12
1950: Sun Bowl, UTEP 33, Georgetown 20
1954: Sun Bowl, UTEP 37, Southern Mississippi 14
1955: Sun Bowl, UTEP 47, Florida State 20

1957: Sun Bowl, George Washington 13, UTEP 0
1965: Sun Bowl, UTEP 13, TCU 12
1967: Sun Bowl, UTEP 14, Mississippi 7
1988: Independence Bowl, Southern Miss. 38, UTEP 18
2000: Humanitarian Bowl, Boise State 38, UTEP 23

TEXAS CHRISTIAN UNIVERSITY, Fort Worth, Texas; nickname "Horned Frogs"; colors purple and white; Amos G. Carter Stadium (44,008); Conference USA. TCU began play in 1896 as an independent. In 1909, TCU became a member of the Texas Intercollegiate Athletic Association and played in that association until 1923 when TCU joined the Southwestern Conference, which had been in existence since 1915. TCU played in the Southwestern Conference until it disbanded after the 1995 season. TCU moved into the Western Athletic Conference where it played through the 2000 season. In 2001, TCU moved into Conference USA. Conference standings are not available for the TIAA years (1909-1922).

Early years (1896-1922)

Year	Coach	W-L-T	PF	PA	Pct.	Year	Coach	W-L-T	PF	PA	Pct.
1896	none	1-1-1	8	28	.500	1910	Kemp Lewis	2-6-1	45	187	.278
1897	Joe Field	3-1-0	78	24	.750	1911	Henry Lever	4-5-0	114	106	.444
1898	James Morrison	1-3-1	41	60	.300	1912	W. Stewart	8-1-0	230	53	.889
1899	none	0-0-1	0	60	.500	1913	Fred Cahoon	3-1-2	44	6	.667
1900	no team					1914	S. Boles	4-4-2	117	118	.500
1901	none	1-2-1	5	78	.375	1915	E.Freeland	4-5-0	130	182	.444
1902	H. Hildebrand	0-5-1	0	93	.084	1916	Milton Daniel	6-2-1	217	85	.722
1903	none	0-7-0	11	100	.000	1917	Milton Daniel	8-2-0	201	59	.800
1904	C.Cronk	1-4-1	5	90	.250	1918	E. Tipton	4-3-0	96	40	.571
1905	E.Hyde	4-4-0	77	65	.500	1919	T. Hackney	2-6-0	28	111	.250
1906	E.Hyde	2-5-0	26	108	.286	1920	W. Driver	9-1-0	170	109	.900
1907	E. Hyde	4-2-2	90	69	.625	1921	W. Driver	6-3-1	132	75	.650
1908	J. Langley	6-3-0	155	68	.667	1922	John McKnight	2-5-3	91	167	.350
1909	J. Langley	5-2-1	95	33	.688						

Member of the Southwest Conference (1923-1995) 195-259-22 .433

Year	Nat'l AP	Other	Overall W-L-T	PF	PA	Pct.	Conference W-L-T	Pct.	Rank	Year	Nat'l AP	Other	Overall W-L-T	PF	PA	Pct.	Conference W-L-T	Pct.	Rank
							Matty Bell (1923-1928) 33-17-5 .645												
1923			4-5-0	93	137	.444	2-1-0	.667	3	1926			6-1-2	110	74	.778	1-1-2	.500	6
1924			4-5-0	83	96	.444	1-5-0	.167	8	1927			4-3-2	89	64	.556	1-2-2	.400	5
1925			7-1-1	133	54	.833	2-1-1	.625	2	1928			8-2-0	142	28	.800	3-2-0	.600	3
							Francis Schmidt (1929-1933) 47-5-5 .868												
1929	8		9-0-1	249	33	.950	4-0-1	.900	1	1932	10		10-0-1	283	23	.955	6-0-0	1.000	1
1930			9-2-1	298	49	.792	4-2-0	.667	3	1933*			10-1-1	208	49	.875	5-1-0	.833	1
1931			9-2-1	149	41	.792	4-1-1	.750	2										

*Includes a forfeit win in a game that Arkansas originally won, 13-0.

Year	Nat'l AP	Other	Overall W-L-T	PF	PA	Pct.	Conference W-L-T	Pct.	Rank	Year	Nat'l AP	Other	Overall W-L-T	PF	PA	Pct.	Conference W-L-T	Pct.	Rank
							Dutch Meyer (1934-1952) 109-79-13 .575												
1934			8-4-0	173	116	.667	3-3-0	.500	4	1944			7-3-1	134	109	.682	3-1-1	700	1
1935		8	12-1-0	265	73	.923	5-1-0	.833	2	1945			5-5-0	91	156	.500	3-3-0	.500	3
1936	16		9-2-2	164	58	.769	4-1-1	.750	2	1946			2-7-1	90	148	.250	2-4-0	.333	5
1937	16		4-4-2	73	66	.500	3-1-2	.667	2	1947			4-5-2	114	105	.455	2-3-1	.417	4
1938	1	8	11-0-0	269	60	1.000	6-0-0	1.000	1	1948			4-5-1	125	143	.450	1-4-1	.250	6
1939			3-7-0	116	119	.300	1-5-0	.167	6	1949			6-3-1	205	185	.650	3-3-0	.500	3
1940			3-7-0	116	121	.300	2-4-0	.333	5	1950			5-5-0	157	166	.500	3-3-0	.500	3
1941			7-3-1	162	135	.682	4-1-1	.750	2	1951	11	10	6-5-0	206	183	.545	5-1-0	.833	1
1942			7-3-0	129	82	.700	4-2-0	.667	3	1952			4-4-2	141	103	.500	2-2-2	.500	4
1943			2-6-0	71	146	.250	1-4-0	.200	5										
							Abe Martin (1953-1966) 74-64-7 548												
1953			3-7-0	116	150	.300	1-5-0	167	6	1960			4-4-2	85	94	.500	3-3-1	.500	5
1954			4-6-0	164	142	.400	1-5-0	.167	6	1961			3-5-2	113	194	.400	2-4-1	.357	5
1955	6	6	9-2-0	306	105	.818	5-1-0	.833	1	1962			6-4-0	167	154	.600	5-2-0	.714	3
1956	14	14	8-3-0	231	110	818	5-1-0	.833	2	1963			4-5-1	131	194	.450	2-4-1	.357	5
1957			5-4-1	134	101	.550	2-4-0	.333	5	1964			4-6-0	94	169	.400	3-4-0	.429	6
1958	10	9	8-2-1	218	78	.773	5-1-0	.833	1	1965			6-5-0	170	156	.545	5-2-0	.714	2
1959	7	8	8-3-0	169	75	.727	5-1-0	.833	1	1966			2-8-0	55	149	.200	2-5-0	.286	6
							Fred Taylor (1967-1970) 15-25-1 .383												
1967			4-6-0	115	185	.400	4-3-0	.571	3	1969			4-6-0	177	293	.400	4-3-0	.571	3
1968			3-7-0	176	215	.300	2-5-0	.286	6	1970			4-6-1	189	265	.409	3-4-0	.429	4
							Jim Pittman (1971) 3-3-1 .500												
1971*			3-3-1	159	203	.500	3-1-0	.750	*										
							Billy Tohill (1971-1973) 11-15-0 .423												
1971*			3-1-0	55	72	.750	2-1-0	.667	3	1973			3-8-0	189	290	.273	1-6-0	.143	7
1972			5-6-0	213	245	.455	2-5-0	.286	7										

*Pittman coached the first seven games of the 1971 season, and Tohill coached the last four.

Year	Nat'l AP	Other	Overall W-L-T	PF	PA	Pct.	Conference W-L-T	Pct.	Rank	Year	Nat'l AP	Other	Overall W-L-T	PF	PA	Pct.	Conference W-L-T	Pct.	Rank
							Jim Shofner (1974-1976) 2-31-0 .061												
1974			1-10-0	79	345	.091	0-7-0	.000	8	1976			0-11-0	128	430	.000	0-8-0	.000	9
1975			1-10-0	103	325	.091	1-6-0	.143	7										

1977	2-9-0	184	434	.182	1-7-0	.125	8	1980		1-10-0	143	292	.091	1-7-0	.125	9
1978	2-9-0	109	357	.182	0-8-0	.000	9	1981		2-7-2	230	266	.273	1-6-1	.188	8
1979	2-8-1	127	226	.227	1-6-1	.188	8	1982		3-8-0	203	266	.273	2-6-0	.250	8

Jim Wacker (1983-1991) 40-58-2 .414

1983	1-8-2	174	252	.182	1-6-1	.188	8	1988	4-7-0	206	286	.364	2-5-0	.286	4
1984	8-4-0	376	280	.667	5-3-0	.625	3	1989	4-7-0	183	301	.364	2-6-0	.250	6
1985	3-8-0	150	383	.273	0-8-0	.000	8	1990	5-6-0	292	353	.455	3-5-0	.375	4
1986	3-8-0	259	376	.273	1-7-0	.125	**	1991	7-4-0	278	267	.636	4-4-0	.500	5
1987	5-6-0	261	226	.455	3-4-0	.429	5								

**TCU ineligible for conference title due to NCAA violations.

Pat Sullivan (1992-1997) 24-42-1 .366

1992	2-8-1	195	319	.227	1-6-0	.143	8	1994	7-5-0	302	303	.583	4-3-0	.571	1
1993	4-7-0	211	313	.364	2-5-0	.286	6	1995	6-5-0	217	246	.545	3-4-0	.429	5

Member of the Western Athletic Conference (1996-2000) 20-19-1 .513

1996	4-7-0	211	302	.364	3-5-0	.375	9	1997		1-10-0	172	325	.091	1-7-0	.125	15

Dennis Franchione (1998-1999) 25-10-0 .714

1998	7-5-0	267	235	.583	4-4-0	.500	9	2000*	21	18	10-1-0	410	106	.909	7-1-0	.875	1
1999	8-4-0	327	213	.667	5-2-0	.714	1										

Gary Patterson (2000-2003) 27-11-0 .711

2000*	0-1-0	21	28	.000	0-0-0

*Franchione coached the first eleven games of the 2000 season, and Patterson coached the last (bowl) game.

Member of Conference USA (2001-2003) 17-6-0 .739

2001		6-6-0	289	285	.500	4-3-0	.571	5	2003	25	24	11-2-0	380	276	.846	7-1-0	.875	2
2002	23	22	10-2-0	361	222	.833	6-2-0	.750	1										

Won-loss record by decades:

1896-99	5-5-3	.500	1930-39	85-23-8	.767	1970-79	26-81-3	.250
1900-09	23-34-6	.413	1940-49	47-47-7	.500	1980-89	34-73-4	.330
1910-19	45-35-6	.558	1950-59	60-41-4	.590	1990-99	51-61-1	.456
1920-29	59-26-10	.674	1960-69	40-56-5	.421	2000-03	37-12-0	.755

Historic record: 512-494-57 .508

Post-season won-loss record: 7-12-1 .375

1936: Sugar Bowl, TCU 3, LSU 2
1937: Cotton Bowl, TCU 16, Marquette 6
1939: Sugar Bowl, TCU 15, Carnegie Tech 7
1942: Orange Bowl, Georgia 40, TCU 26
1945: Cotton Bowl, Oklahoma A&M 34, TCU 0
1948: Delta Bowl, Mississippi 13, TCU 9
1952: Cotton Bowl, Kentucky 20, TCU 7
1956: Cotton Bowl, Mississippi 14, TCU 13
1957: Cotton Bowl, TCU 28, Syracuse 27

1959: Cotton Bowl, TCU 0, Air Force 0
1959: Bluebonnet Bowl, Clemson 23, TCU 7
1965: Sun Bowl, Texas Western 13, TCU 12
!984: Bluebonnet Bowl, West Virginia 31, TCU 14
1994: Independence Bowl, Virginia 20, TCU 10
1998: Norwest Sun Bowl, TCU 28, USC 19
1999: Mobile Alabama Bowl, TCU 28, East Carolina 14
2000: Mobile Alabama Bowl, Southern Mississippi 28, TCU 21
2001: Galleryfurniture.com Bowl, Texas A&M 28, TCU 9
2002: Liberty Bowl, TCU 17, Colorado State 3
2003: Fort Worth Bowl, Boise State 34, TCU 31

College Football Hall of Fame:
Matty Bell, coach, 1923-29; Rags Mathews, end, 1925-27; Francis Schmidt, coach, 1930-33; Darrell Lester, center, 1933-35; Dutch Meyer, coach, 1934-52; Sammy Baugh, halfback, 1934-36; Ki Aldrich, center, 1936-38; Davey O'Brien, quarterback, 1936-38; Jim Swink, halfback, 1954-56; Bob Lilly, tackle, 1958-60.

Awards: Heisman Trophy: 1938, Davey O'Brien; Maxwell Award: 1938, Davey O'Brien.

TEXAS TECH UNIVERSITY, Lubbock, Texas; nickname "Red Raiders"; colors scarlet and black; Jones SBC Stadium (62,000); Big Twelve Conference. Texas Tech began play in 1925 as an independent. In 1932, Tech joined the Border Conference and played in that conference through the 1956 season. The team was independent again for three years before joining the Southwest Conference, beginning with the 1960 season. When that conference disbanded after the 1995 season, Tech, along with three other SWC members, joined the members of the Big Eight Conference to form the Big Twelve Conference.

Year	Nat'l AP	Other	Overall W-L-T	PF	PA	Pct.	Conf W-L-T	Pct.	Rank	Year	Nat'l AP	Other	Overall W-L-T	PF	PA	Pct.	Conf W-L-T	Pct.	Rank

Early years as an independent (1925-1931)
E. Y. Freeland (1925-1928) 21-10-6 .649

Year	Nat'l AP	Other	Overall W-L-T	PF	PA	Pct.	Conf W-L-T	Pct.	Rank	Year	Nat'l AP	Other	Overall W-L-T	PF	PA	Pct.	Conf W-L-T	Pct.	Rank
1925			6-1-2	210	65	.778				1927			5-4-0	134	100	.556			
1926			6-1-3	106	49	.750				1928			4-4-1	47	79	.500			

Grady Higgenbotham (1929) 1-7-2 .200

| 1929 | | | 1-7-2 | 31 | 141 | .200 | | | | | | | | | | | | | |

Pete Cawthon (1930-1940) 76-32-6 .693

| 1930 | | | 3-6-0 | 90 | 123 | .333 | | | | 1931 | | | 6-3-0 | 150 | 66 | .667 | | | |

Member of the Border Conference (1932-1956) 55-9-3 .838

Year	AP	Other	W-L-T	PF	PA	Pct.	W-L-T	Pct.	Rank	Year	AP	Other	W-L-T	PF	PA	Pct.	W-L-T	Pct.	Rank
1932			10-2-0	382	35	.833	2-0-0	1.000	1	1937			8-4-0	163	93	.667	3-0-0	1.000	1
1933			8-1-0	144	30	.889	1-0-0	1.000	1	1938	11		10-1-0	287	55	.909	2-0-0	1.000	1
1934			7-2-1	193	84	.750	1-0-0	1.000	1	1939			5-5-1	150	74	.500	2-1-0	.667	3
1935			5-3-2	110	55	.600	0-1-0	.000	6	1940			9-1-1	241	131	.864	0-1-0	.000	6
1936			5-4-1	121	85	.550	0-0-1	.500	5										

Dell Morgan (1941-1950) 55-49-3 .528

1941			9-2-0	226	36	.818	2-0-0	1.000	2	1946			8-3-0	148	116	.727	3-1-0	.750	2
1942			4-5-1	111	87	.450	3-0-1	.875	1	1947			6-5-0	184	228	.545	4-0-0	1.000	1
1943			4-6-0	128	177	.400	no conference			1948			7-3-0	212	135	.700	5-0-0	1.000	1
1944			4-7-0	134	170	.364	no conference			1949			7-5-0	187	184	.583	5-0-0	1.000	1
1945			3-5-2	63	145	.400	no conference			1950			3-8-0	222	241	.273	3-2-0	.600	4

Dewitt Weaver (1951-1960) 49-51-5 .490

1951			7-4-0	301	169	.636	4-0-0	1.000	1	1954			7-2-1	367	157	.750	4-0-0	1.000	1
1952			3-7-1	233	239	.318	2-1-1	.625	2	1955			7-3-1	202	166	.682	3-0-1	.875	1
1953	12	12	11-1-0	463	166	.917	5-0-0	1.000	1	1956			2-7-1	117	216	.250	1-3-0	.250	5

Texas Tech reverts to independent status (1957-1959)

| 1957 | | | 2-8-0 | 120 | 190 | .200 | | | | 1959 | | | 4-6-0 | 139 | 158 | .400 | | | |
| 1958 | | | 3-7-0 | 126 | 163 | .300 | | | | | | | | | | | | | |

Member of the Southwest Conference (1960-1995) 125-135-6 .481

| 1960 | | | 3-6-1 | 148 | 182 | .350 | 1-5-1 | .214 | 6 | | | | | | | | | | |

J. T. King (1961-1969) 44-45-3 .495

1961			4-6-0	94	201	.400	2-5-0	.286	6	1966			4-6-0	181	216	.400	2-5-0	.286	6
1962			1-9-0	83	250	.100	0-7-0	.000	8	1967			6-4-0	217	165	.600	5-2-0	.714	2
1963			5-5-0	147	178	.500	2-5-0	.286	6	1968			5-3-2	255	241	.600	4-3-0	.571	4
1964			6-4-1	172	120	.591	3-3-1	.500	4	1969			5-5-0	212	240	.500	4-3-0	.571	3
1965		10	8-3-0	278	222	.727	5-2-0	.714	2										

Jim Carlen (1970-1974) 37-20-2 .657

1970			8-4-0	222	165	.667	5-2-0	.714	3	1973	11	11	11-1-0	342	187	.917	6-1-0	.857	2
1971			4-7-0	131	134	.364	2-5-0	.286	7	1974			6-4-2	193	158	.583	3-4-0	.429	6
1972			8-4-0	282	188	.667	4-3-0	.571	2										

Steve Sloan (1975-1977) 23-12-0 .657

| 1975 | | | 6-5-0 | 272 | 251 | .545 | 4-3-0 | .571 | 4 | 1977 | | | 7-5-0 | 299 | 256 | .583 | 4-4-0 | .500 | 4 |
| 1976 | 13 | 13 | 10-2-0 | 336 | 206 | .833 | 7-1-0 | .875 | 1 | | | | | | | | | | |

Rex Dockery (1978-1980) 15-16-2 .484

| 1978 | | | 7-4-0 | 246 | 268 | .636 | 5-3-0 | .625 | 4 | 1980 | | | 5-6-0 | 178 | 188 | .455 | 3-5-0 | .375 | 6 |
| 1979 | | | 3-6-2 | 141 | 182 | .364 | 2-5-1 | .312 | 7 | | | | | | | | | | |

Jerry Moore (1981-1985) 16-37-2 .302

1981			1-9-1	198	298	.136	0-7-1	.062	9	1984			4-7-0	200	212	.364	2-6-0	.250	8
1982			4-7-0	157	234	.364	3-5-0	.375	6	1985			4-7-0	249	220	.364	1-7-0	.125	7
1983			3-7-1	160	252	.318	3-4-1	.436	6										

Dave McWilliams (1986) 7-4-0 .636

| 1986* | | | 7-4-0 | 254 | 248 | .636 | 5-3-0 | .625 | 4 | | | | | | | | | | |

Spike Dykes (1986-1999) 85-65-1 .566

Year			W-L-T	PF	PA	Pct	Conf	Pct	Bowl
1986*			0-1-0	17	20	.000			
1987			6-4-1	315	266	.591	3-3-1	.500	4
1988			5-6-0	328	332	.455	4-3-0	.571	4
1989	19	16	9-3-0	360	281	.750	5-3-0	.625	3
1990			7-5-0	320	356	.583	3-5-0	.375	4
1991			6-5-0	315	272	.545	5-3-0	.625	2
1992			5-6-0	287	332	.455	4-3-0	.571	2
1993			6-6-0	419	335	.500	5-2-0	.714	2
1994			6-6-0	316	246	.500	4-3-0	.571	1
1995	23	20	9-3-0	385	247	.750	5-2-0	.714	2

*McWilliams coached the first eleven games of the 1986 season, and Dykes coached the last (bowl) game.

Member of the Big Twelve Conference (1996-2003) 37-27-0 .578

Year	W-L-T	PF	PA	Pct	Conf	Pct	Bowl
1996	7-5-0	323	232	.583	5-3-0	.625	5
1997	6-5-0	221	241	.545	5-3-0	.625	4
1998	7-5-0	315	255	.583	4-4-0	.500	6
1999	6-5-0	253	282	.545	5-3-0	.625	5

Mike Leach (2000-2003) 31-21-0 .596

Year	W-L-T	PF	PA	Pct	Conf	Pct	Bowl
2000	7-6-0	330	279	.538	3-5-0	.625	5
2001	7-5-0	386	362	.583	4-4-0	.500	5
2002	9-5-0	537	439	.643	5-3-0	.625	5
2003	8-5-0	52	442	.615	4-4-0	.500	6

Won-loss record by decades:

Decade	Record	Pct	Decade	Record	Pct	Decade	Record	Pct
1925-29	22-17-8	.553	1950-59	49-53-4	.481	1980-89	48-61-3	.442
1930-39	67-31-5	.675	1960-69	47-51-4	.480	1990-99	62-53-0	.539
1940-49	61-42-4	.589	1970-79	70-42-4	.621	2000-03	31-21-0	.596

Historic record: 457-371-32 .550

Post-season won-loss record: 7-19-1 .278

1938: Sun Bowl, West Virginia 7, Texas Tech 6
1939: Cotton Bowl, St. Mary's (CA) 20, Texas Tech 13
1942: Sun Bowl, Tulsa 6, Texas Tech 0
1948: Sun Bowl, Miami (OH) 13, Texas Tech 12
1949: Raisin Bowl, San Jose State 20, Texas Tech 13
1952: Sun Bowl, Texas Tech 25, Pacific 14
1954: Gator Bowl, Texas Tech 35, Auburn 14
1956: Sun Bowl, Wyoming 21, Texas Tech 14
1964: Sun Bowl, Georgia 7, Texas Tech 0
1965: Gator Bowl, Georgia Tech 31, Texas Tech 21
1970: Sun Bowl, Georgia Tech 17, Texas Tech 9
1972: Sun Bowl, North Carolina 32, Texas Tech 28
1973: Gator Bowl, Texas Tech 28, Tennessee 19

1974: Peach Bowl, Texas Tech 6, Vanderbilt 6
1976: Bluebonnet Bowl, Nebraska 27, Texas Tech 24
1977: Tangerine Bowl, Florida State 40, Texas Tech 17
1986: Independence Bowl, Mississippi 20, Texas Tech 17
1989: All American Bowl, Texas Tech 49, Duke 21
1993: John Hancock Bowl, Oklahoma 41, Texas Tech 14
1995: Cotton Bowl, USC 55, Texas Tech 14
1995: Copper Bowl, Texas Tech 55, Air Force 41
1996: Alamo Bowl, Iowa 27, Texas Tech 0
1998: Independence Bowl, Mississippi 35, Texas Tech 18
2000: Galleryfurniture.com Bowl, East Carolina 40, Texas Tech 27
2001: Alamo Bowl, Iowa 19, Texas Tech 16
2002: Tangerine Bowl, Texas Tech 55, Clemson 15
2003: Houston Bowl, Texas Tech 38, Navy 14

College Football Hall of Fame:
Hub Bechtol, tackle, 1943-46; E. J. Holub, center, 1958-60; Donny Anderson, halfback, 1963-65.

Player Awards: Doak Walker Award: 1993, Byron Morris; 1996, Bryon Hanspard; Baugh Trophy: 2002, Kliff Kingsbury.

UNIVERSITY OF TEXAS, Austin, Texas; nickname "Longhorns"; colors red and white; Royal-Texas Memorial Stadium (80,082); Big Twelve Conference. Texas began play in 1893 as an independent and then joined the Southwest Conference as a founding member in 1915. Texas played in that conference until it was disbanded after the 1995 season. Beginning in 1996, Texas has played as a member of the Big Twelve Conference.

Early years as an independent (1893-1914)

Year	Coach	W-L-T	PF	PA	Pct.	Year	Coach	W-L-T	PF	PA	Pct.
1893	no coach	4-0-0	98	16	1.000	1904	Ralph Hutchinson	6-2-0	219	88	.750
1894	R. D. Wentworth	6-1-0	191	28	.857	1905	Ralph Hutchinson	5-4-0	90	68	.556
1895	Frank Crawford	5-0-0	96	0	1.000	1906	H. R. Schenker	9-1-0	201	60	.900
1896	Harry Robinson	4-2-1	88	36	.643	1907	W. E. Metzenthin	6-1-1	154	53	.812
1897	W. F. Kelly	6-2-0	144	60	.750	1908	W. E. Metzenthin	5-4-0	135	135	.556
1898	D. F. Edwards	5-1-0	136	4	.833	1909	Dexter Draper	4-3-1	105	50	.562
1899	M. G. Clarke	6-2-0	117	24	.750	1910	W. S. Wasmund	6-2-0	157	26	.750
1900	S. H. Thompson	6-0-0	113	13	1.000	1911	Dave Allerdice	5-2-0	66	19	.714
1901	S. H. Thompson	8-2-1	165	71	.773	1912	Dave Allerdice	7-1-0	201	62	.875
1902	J. B. Hart	6-3-1	87	40	.650	1913	Dave Allerdice	7-1-0	250	56	.875
1903	Ralph Hutchinson	5-1-2	131	28	.750	1914	Dave Allerdice	8-0-0	358	21	1.000

Member of the Southwest Conference (1915-1995) 346-149-14 .694

Year	Nat'l AP	Other	Overall W-L-T	PF	PA	Pct.	Conference W-L-T	Pct.	Rank	Year	Nat'l AP	Other	Overall W-L-T	PF	PA	Pct.	Conference W-L-T	Pct.	Rank

Dave Allerldice (1911-1915) 33-7-0 .825

| 1915 | | | 6-3-0 | 335 | 69 | .667 | 2-2-0 | .500 | 2 |

Eugene Van Gent (1916) 7-2-0 .778

| 1916 | | | 7-2-0 | 218 | 36 | .778 | 5-1-0 | .833 | 1 |

Bill Juneau (1917-1919) 19-7-0 .731

| 1917 | | | 4-4-0 | 89 | 40 | .500 | 2-3-0 | .400 | 4 | 1919 | | | 6-3-0 | 181 | 63 | .667 | 3-2-0 | .600 | 4 |
| 1918 | | | 9-0-0 | 194 | 14 | 1.000 | 4-0-0 | 1.000 | 1 |

Barry Whitaker (1920-1922) 22-3-1 .865

| 1920 | | | 9-0-0 | 282 | 13 | 1.000 | 5-0-0 | 1.000 | 1 | 1922 | | | 7-2-0 | 202 | 58 | .778 | 2-1-0 | .667 | 2 |
| 1921 | | | 6-1-1 | 268 | 27 | .812 | 1-0-1 | .750 | 2 |

E. J. Stewart (1923-1926) 24-9-3 .708

| 1923 | | | 8-0-1 | 241 | 21 | .944 | 2-0-1 | ..833 | 2 | 1925 | | | 6-2-1 | 157 | 51 | .722 | 2-1-1 | .625 | 2 |
| 1924 | | | 5-3-1 | 109 | 64 | .611 | 2-3-0 | .400 | 6 | 1926 | | | 5-4-0 | 146 | 69 | .556 | 2-2-0 | .500 | 3 |

Clyde Littlefield (1927-1933) 45-17-6 .706

1927			6-2-1	164	73	.722	2-2-1	.500	4	1931			6-4-0	131	58	.600	2-3-0	.400	5
1928			7-2-0	122	32	.778	5-1-0	.833	1	1932			8-2-0	220	49	.800	5-1-0	.833	2
1929			5-2-2	132	28	.667	2-2-2	.500	4	1933*			5-4-2	112	104	.545	3-2-1	.583	3
1930			8-1-0	179	20	.850	4-1-0	.800	1

*Record reflects the forfeit of a game won by Arkansas in 1933.

Jack Chevigny (1934-1936) 13-14-2 .483

| 1934 | | | 7-2-1 | 137 | 85 | .750 | 4-1-1 | .750 | 2 | 1936 | | | 2-6-1 | 69 | 128 | .278 | 1-5-0 | .167 | 6 |
| 1935 | | | 4-6-0 | 138 | 174 | .400 | 1-5-0 | .167 | 6 |

Dana X. Bible (1937-1946) 63-31-3 .665

1937			2-6-1	60	103	.278	1-5-0	.167	7	1942	11		9-2-0	244	49	.818	5-1-0	.833	1
1938			1-8-0	52	162	.111	1-5-0	.167	6	1943	14		7-1-1	277	54	.833	5-0-0	1.000	1
1939			5-4-0	106	125	.556	3-3-0	.500	4	1944			5-4-0	119	76	.556	3-2-0	.600	2
1940		9	8-2-0	172	77	.800	4-2-0	.667	3	1945	10		10-1-0	257	86	.909	5-1-0	.833	1
1941	4		8-1-1	338	55	.850	4-1-1	.750	2	1946	15		8-2-0	290	68	.800	4-2-0	.667	3

Blair Cherry (1947-1950) 32-10-1 756

| 1947 | 5 | | 10-1-0 | 292 | 74 | .909 | 5-1-0 | .833 | 2 | 1949 | | | 6-4-0 | 290 | 93 | .600 | 3-3-0 | .500 | 3 |
| 1948 | | | 7-3-1 | 223 | 147 | .682 | 4-1-1 | .750 | 2 | 1950 | 3 | 2 | 9-2-0 | 252 | 148 | .818 | 6-0-0 | 1.000 | 1 |

Ed Price (1951-1956) 33-27-1 .549

1951			7-3-0	182	129	.700	3-3-0	.500	3	1954			4-5-1	158	161	.450	2-3-1	.417	5
1952	10	11	9-2-0	278	164	.818	6-0-0	1/000	1	1955			5-5-0	189	212	.500	4-2-0	.667	3
1953	11	8	7-3-0	190	125	.700	5-1-0	.833	1	1956			1-9-0	101	272	.100	0-6-0	.000	7

Darrell Royal (1957-1976) 167-47-5 .774

1957	11	11	6-4-1	159	149	.591	4-1-1	.750	2	1967			6-4-0	186	123	.600	4-3-0	.571	3
1958			7-3-0	157	152	.700	3-3-0	.500	4	1968	3	5	9-1-1	379	198	.864	6-1-0	.857	1
1959	4	4	9-2-0	216	96	.818	5-1-0	.833	1	1969	1	1	11-0-0	435	119	1.000	7-0-0	1.000	1
1960		17	7-3-1	167	78	.682	5-2-0	.714	2	1970	3	1	10-1-0	423	149	.909	7-0-0	1.000	1
1961	3	4	10-1-0	303	66	.909	6-1-0	.857	1	1971	18	12	8-3-0	281	168	.727	6-1-0	.857	1
1962	4	4	9-1-1	184	72	.864	6-0-1	.929	1	1972	3	5	10-1-0	271	121	.909	7-0-0	1.000	1
1963	1	1	11-0-0	243	71	1.000	7-0-0	1.000	1	1973	14	8	8-3-0	367	197	.727	7-0-0	1.000	1
1964	5	5	10-1-0	220	81	.909	6-1-0	.857	2	1974	17		8-4-0	367	201	.667	5-2-0	.714	2
1965			6-4-0	231	153	.600	3-4-0	.429	4	1975	6	7	10-2-0	401	181	.909	6-1-0	.857	1
1966			7-4-0	194	111	.636	5-2-0	.714	2	1976			5-5-1	195	188	.500	4-4-0	.500	5

Fred Akers (1977-1986) 86-31-2 .731

Year			W-L-T	PF	PA	Pct			
1977	4	5	11-1-0	441	152	.917	8-0-0	1.000	1
1978	9	9	9-3-0	287	136	.750	6-2-0	.750	2
1979	12	13	9-3-0	221	104	.750	6-2-0	.750	3
1980			7-5-0	267	214	.583	4-4-0	.500	4
1981	2	4	10-1-1	262	158	.875	6-1-1	.812	2
1982	17	18	9-3-0	357	170	.750	7-1-0	.875	2
1983	5	5	11-1-0	289	114	.917	8-0-0	1.000	1
1984			7-4-1	264	261	.625	5-3-0	.625	3
1985			8-4-0	270	259	.667	6-2-0	.750	2
1986			5-6-0	229	245	.455	4-4-0	.500	5

Dave McWilliams (1987-1991) 31-26-0 .544

Year			W-L-T	PF	PA	Pct			
1987	19		7-5-0	335	324	.583	5-2-0	.714	2
1988			4-7-0	252	304	.364	2-5-0	.286	4
1989			5-6-0	220	289	.455	4-4-0	.500	4
1990	12	11	10-2-0	358	227	.833	8-0-0	1.000	1
1991			5-6-0	195	144	.455	4-4-0	.500	5

John Mackovic (1992-1997) 41-28-2 .592

Year			W-L-T	PF	PA	Pct			
1992			6-5-0	292	282	.545	4-30	.571	2
1993			5-5-1	281	269	.500	5-2-0	.714	2
1994	25		8-4-0	366	291	.667	4-3-0	.571	1
1995	14	14	10-2-1	390	255	.808	7-0-0	1.000	1

Member of the Big Twelve Conference (1996-2002) 47-17-0 .734

Year			W-L-T	PF	PA	Pct			
1996	23	23	8-5-0	504	305	.614	6-2-0	.750	1
1997			4-7-0	283	306	.364	2-6-0	.250	9

Mack Brown (1998-2003) 59-18-0 .766

Year			W-L-T	PF	PA	Pct			
1998	15	16	9-3-0	437	337	.750	6-2-0	.750	3
1999	23	23	9-5-0	450	295	.643	6-2-0	.750	3
2000	12	12	9-3-0	455	192	.846	7-1-0	.875	2
2001	5	5	11-2-0	517	207	.846	7-1-0	.875	2
2002	6	7	11-2-0	404	192	..846	6-2-0	.750	2
2003	12	13	10-3-0	533	280	.769	7-1-0	.875	3

Won-loss record by decades:

1893-99	36-8-1	.811	1930-39	48-43-6	.526	1970-79	88-26-1	.770
1900-09	60-21-6	.724	1940-49	78-21-3	.779	1980-89	73-42-2	.632
1910-19	65-18-0	.783	1950-59	64-38-2	.625	1990-99	74-44-2	.625
1920-29	64-18-7	.758	1960-69	85-19-3	.808	2000-03	41-10-0	.804

Historic record 766-306-33 .709

Post-season won-loss record: 21-22-2 .489

1943: Cotton Bowl, Texas 14, Ga. Tech 7
1944: Cotton Bowl, Texas 7, Randolph Field 7
1946: Cotton Bowl, Texas 40, Missouri 27
1948: Sugar Bowl, Texas 27, Alabama 7
1949: Orange Bowl, Texas 41, Georgia 28
1951: Cotton Bowl, Tennessee 20, Texas 14
1953: Cotton Bowl, Texas 16, Tennessee 0
1958: Sugar Bowl, Mississippi 39, Texas 7
1960 Cotton Bowl, Syracuse 23, Texas 14
1960: Bluebonnet Bowl, Texas 3, Alabama 3
1962: Cotton Bowl, Texas 12, Mississippi 7
1963: Cotton Bowl, LSU 13, Texas 0
1964: Cotton Bowl, Texas 28, Navy 6
1965: Orange Bowl, Texas 21, Alabama 7
1966: Bluebonnet Bowl, Texas 19, Mississippi 0
1969: Cotton Bowl, Texas 36, Tennessee 13
1970: Cotton Bowl, Texas 21, Notre Dame 17
1971: Cotton Bowl, Notre Dame 24, Texas 11
1972: Cotton Bowl, Penn State 30, Texas 6
1973: Cotton Bowl, Texas 17, Alabama 13
1974: Cotton Bowl, Nebraska 19, Texas 3
1974: Gator Bowl, Auburn 27, Texas 3

1975: Bluebonnet Bowl, Texas 38, Colorado 21
1978: Cotton Bowl, Notre Dame 38, Texas 10
1978: Sun Bowl, Texas 42, Maryland 0
1979: Sun Bowl, Washington 14, Texas 7
1980: Bluebonnet Bowl, No. Carolina 16, Texas 7
1982: Cotton Bowl, Texas 14, Alabama 12
1982: Sun Bowl, No. Carolina 26, Texas 10
1984: Cotton Bowl, Georgia 10, Texas 9
1984: Freedom Bowl, Iowa 55, Texas 17
1985: Bluebonnet Bowl, Air Force 24, Texas 16
1987: Bluebonnet Bowl, Texas 32, Pittsburgh 27
1991: Cotton Bowl, Miami 46, Texas 3
1994: Sun Bowl, Texas 35, No. Carolina 31
1995: Sugar Bowl, Va. Tech 28, Texas 10
1996: Big 12 Championship, Texas 37, Nebraska 27
1997: Fiesta Bowl, Penn State 38, Texas 15
1999: Cotton Bowl, Texas 38, Miss. State 11
1999: Big 12 Championship, Nebraska 22, Texas 6
2000: Cotton Bowl, Arkansas 27, Texas 6
2000: Holiday Bowl, Oregon 35, Texas 30
2001: Holiday Bowl, Texas 47, Washington 43
2003: Cotton Bowl, Texas 35, LSU 20
2003: Holiday Bowl, Wash. State 28, Texas 20

College Football Hall of Fame:
Bud Sprague, tackle, 1922-24; Harrison Stafford, halfback, 1930-32; Dana Bible, coach, 1932-46; Mal Kutner, end, 1939-41; Hub Bechtol, end, 1943-46; Bobby Layne, quarterback, 1944-47; Bud McFadin, guard/tackle, 1948-50; Harley Sewell, guard, 1950-52; Darrell Royal, coach, 1957-1976; Jim Saxton, halfback, 1959-61; Tommy Nobis, guard/linebacker, 1963-65; Chris Gilbert, halfback, 1966-68; Jerry Sizemore, offensive tackle, 19970-72; Earl Campbell, halfback, 1974-77.

Awards:
Maxwell Award: 1965, Tommy Nobis; 1998, Ricky Williams; Lombardi Award: 1981, Kenneth Sims; 1984, Tony Degrate; Doak Walker Award: 1997, Ricky Williams; 1998, Ricky Williams; Outland Trophy: 1963, Scott Appleton; 1965, Tommy Nobis; 1977, Brad Shearer; Heisman Trophy: 1977, Earl Campbell; 1998, Ricky Williams: Camp Award: 1998, Ricky Williams.

UNIVERSITY OF TOLEDO, Toledo, Ohio; nickname "Rockets"; colors midnight blue and gold; Glass Bowl (26,248); Mid-American Conference. Toledo began play in 1917 and was a member of the Northwest Ohio Conference during the 1920s and 1930s. In 1951, Toledo joined the MAC competing for the conference title for the first time in 1952. Toledo has played in the MAC since 1952.

Early years (1917-1951)

Year	W-L-T	PF	PA	Pct.		Year	W-L-T	PF	PA	Pct.
					John Brandeberry (1917) 0-3-0 .000					
1917	0-3-0	0	262	.000						
					James Baxter (1918) 1-1-0 .500					
1918	1-1-0	37	43	.500						
					Walt Hobt (1919-1920) 2-7-0 .222					
1919	2-4-0	31	73	.333		1920	0-3-0	7	67	.000
					Joseph Dwyer (1921-1922) 5-7-3 .433					
1921	3-5-0	94	54	.375		1922	2-2-3	17	19	.500
					James Dwyer (1923-25) 12-15-0 .444					
1923	6-4-0	257	105	.600		1925	1-8-0	28	173	.111
1924	5-3-0	84	127	.625						
					Boni Petcoff (1926-1929) 13-15-1 .466					
1926	3-5-0	81	153	.375		1928	1-6-0	46	130	.143
1927	5-2-0	88	62	.714		1929	4-2-1	68	70	.643
					Jim Nicholson (1930-1935) 20-16-4 .550					
1930	2-5-1	50	138	.312		1933	4-2-2	99	66	.625
1931	no team					1934	5-3-0	123	55	.625
1932	3-4-0	42	40	.429		1935	6-2-1	185	32	.722
					Doc Spears (1936-1942) 38-26-2 .591					
1936	2-6-0	94	58	.250		1940	6-3-0	146	78	.667
1937	6-3-0	128	95	.667		1941	7-4-0	195	122	.636
1938	6-3-1	156	83	.650		1942	4-4-1	91	114	.500
1939	7-3-0	180	59	.700						
					No team (1943-1945)					
					Bill Orwig (1946-1947) 15-4-2 .762					
1946	6-2-2	200	138	.700		1947	9-2-0	255	115	.818
					J. N. Stahley (1948-1949) 11-10-0 .524					
1948	5-6-0	206	225	.455		1949	6-4-0	318	210	.600
					Robert Snyder (1950) 4-5-0 .444					
1950	4-5-0	200	234	.444						
					Don Greenwood (1951) 4-3-0 .571					
1951*	4-3-0	203	127	.444						
					Clair Dunn (1951-1953) 9-12-0 .429					
1951*	2-1-0	57	56	.667						

*Greenwood coached the first seven games of the 1951 season, and Dun coached the last three games.

Member of the Mid-American Conference (1952-2003) 196-164-6 .544

	Nat'l		Overall				Conference				Nat'l		Overall				Conference		
Year	AP	Other	W-L-T	PF	PA	Pct.	W-L-T	Pct.	Rank	Year	AP	Other	W-L-T	PF	PA	Pct.	W-L-T	Pct.	Rank
1952			4-5-0	132	151	.444	1-4-0	.200	6	1953			3-6-0	113	305	.333	2-3-0	.400	4
							Forrest England (1954-1955) 9-7-2 .556												
1954			6-2-1	205	113	.722	3-2-0	.600	4	1955			3-5-1	77	206	.389	2-4-0	.333	5
							Jack Morton (1956) 1-7-1 .167												
1956			1-7-1	118	250	.167	1-5-0	.167	7										
							Harry Larche (1957-1959) 11-15-1 .426												
1957			5-4-0	136	147	.556	3-2-0	.600	4	1959			2-6-1	123	200	.277	0-6-0	.000	7
1958			4-5-0	122	168	.444	1-4-0	.200	6										
							Clive Rush (1960-1962) 8-20-0 .286												
1960			2-7-0	126	192	.222	0-6-0	.000	7	1962			3-6-0	133	176	.333	1-5-0	.167	6
1961			3-7-0	146	170	.300	2-4-0	.333	5										
							Frank Lauterbur (1963-1970) 48-32-2 .598												
1963			2-7-0	118	176	.222	1-5-0	.167	6	1967			9-1-0	266	83	.900	5-1-0	.833	1
1964			2-8-0	127	218	.200	1-5-0	.167	7	1968			5-4-1	230	156	.550	3-2-1	.583	3
1965			5-5-0	104	96	.500	2-4-0	.333	5	1969			11-0-0	385	160	1.000	5-0-0	1.000	1
1966			2-7-1	137	162	.250	1-5-0	.167	6	1970	12	17	12-0-0	374	88	1.000	5-0-0	1.000	1
							John Murphy (1971-1976) 35-32-0 .522												
1971	14	13	12-0-0	383	96	1.000	5-0-0	1.000	1	1974			6-5-0	262	270	.545	3-2-0	.600	2
1972			6-5-0	196	210	.545	2-3-0	.400	4	1975			5-6-0	244	277	.455	4-4-0	.500	5
1973			3-8-0	229	288	.273	1-4-0	.200	5	1976			3-8-0	185	232	.273	2-6-0	.250	8

Chuck Stobart (1977-1981) 24-31-1 .438

Year			W-L-T	PF	PA	Pct	Conf	Pct	Rk	Year	W-L-T	PF	PA	Pct	Conf	Pct	Rk
1977			2-9-0	112	287	.182	2-7-0	.222	9	1980	4-7-0	187	190	.364	3-6-0	.333	8
1978			2-9-0	144	256	.182	2-7-0	.222	9	1981	9-3-0	270	170	.750	8-1-0	.889	1
1979			7-3-1	213	189	.682	7-1-1	.833	2								

Dan Simrell (1982-1989) 50-37-2 .567

Year			W-L-T	PF	PA	Pct	Conf	Pct	Rk	Year	W-L-T	PF	PA	Pct	Conf	Pct	Rk
1982			6-5-0	184	162	.545	5-4-0	.556	5	1986	7-4-0	216	197	.636	5-3-0	.625	2
1983			9-2-0	278	157	.818	7-2-0	.778	2	1987	3-7-1	165	245	.318	3-4-1	.438	6
1984			9-2-1	187	164	.792	7-1-1	.833	1	1988	6-5-0	244	221	.545	4-4-0	.500	6
1985			4-7-0	135	187	.364	3-6-0	.333	6	1989	6-5-0	254	272	.545	6-2-0	.750	2

Nick Saban (1990) 9-2-0 .818

Year			W-L-T	PF	PA	Pct	Conf	Pct	Rk
1990			9-2-0	284	178	.818	7-1-0	.875	1

Gary Pinkel (1991-2000) 73-38-3 .654

Year			W-L-T	PF	PA	Pct	Conf	Pct	Rk	Year	W-L-T	PF	PA	Pct	Conf	Pct	Rk
1991			5-5-1	187	209	.500	4-3-1	.563	3	1996	7-4-0	210	259	.636	6-2-0	.750	2
1992			8-3-0	269	153	.273	5-3-0	.625	3	1997	9-3-0	356	268	.750	7-1-0	.875	1
1993			4-7-0	252	270	.364	3-5-0	.375	7	1998	7-5-0	229	216	.583	6-2-0	.750	3
1994			6-4-1	352	324	.591	4-3-1	.563	6	1999	6-5-0	293	231	.545	5-3-0	.625	4
1995	24	24	11-0-1	411	260	.958	7-0-1	.938	1	2000	10-1-0	400	125	.909	6-1-0	.857	2

Tom Amstutz (2001-2003) 27-11-0 .711

Year			W-L-T	PF	PA	Pct	Conf	Pct	Rk	Year	W-L-T	PF	PA	Pct	Conf	Pct	Rk
2001	23	22	10-2-0	407	297	.833	5-2-0	.714	3	2003	8-4-0	389	285	.667	6-2-0	.750	3
2002			9-5-0	495	378	.643	7-2-0	.778	3								

Won-loss record by decades:

1917-19	3- 8-0	.273	1950-59	38-49-4	.440	1980-89	63-47-2	.571
1920-29	30-40-4	.432	1960-69	44-52-2	.459	1990-99	72-38-3	.650
1930-39	41-31-5	.565	1970-79	58-53-1	.522	2000-03	37-12-0	.755
1940-49	43-25-3	.627						

Historic record: 429-355-24 .546

Post-season won-loss record: 10-5-0 .667

1946: Glass Bowl, Toledo 21, Bates 12
1947: Glass Bowl, Toledo 20, New Hampshire 14
1948: Glass Bowl, Toledo 27, Oklahoma City 14
1949: Glass Bowl, Cincinnati 33, Toledo 13
1969: Tangerine Bowl, Toledo 56, Davidson 33
1970: Tangerine Bowl, Toledo 40, Wm. & Mary 12
1971: Tangerine Bowl, Toledo 28, Richmond 3
1981: California Bowl, Toledo 27, San Jose State 25

1984: California Bowl, Toledo 1, UNLV 0 (forfeit win after UNLV had used ineligibile player in a win, 30-13)
1995: Las Vegas Bowl, Toledo 40, Nevada 37
1997: MAC Championship, Marshall 34, Toledo 14
1998: MAC Championship, Marshall 23, Toledo 17
2001: MAC Championship, Toledo 41, Marshall 36
2001: Motor City Bowl, Toledo 23, Cincinnati 16
2002: MAC Championship, Marshall 49, Toledo 45
2002: Motor City Bowl, Boston College 51, Toledo 25

College Football Hall of Fame:
Merle Gulick, quarterback, 1924-29; Mel Long, defensive tackle, 1969-71.

Awards: Baugh Trophy: 1975, Gene Swick.

TROY STATE UNIVERSITY, Troy, Alabama; nickname "Trojans"; colors cardinal, silver, and black; Richard M. Scrushy Field (17,500); independent. Troy State began football in 1905, and was an independent from 1905 through 1937. In 1938, Troy State joined the Alabama Intercollegiate Conference and played in the AIC through the 1970 season. In 1971, Troy State moved up to Division II, joining the Gulf South Conference. In 1992, Troy State became an independent Division I-AA team. In 1996, Troy State joined the Southland Football League and played in that league through the 2000 season. The 2001 season was the first year that Troy State was a Division I-A team, as an independent. Troy State joins the Sunbelt Conference for the 2004 season.

Early years as an independent (1909-1937)

Year	W-L-T	PF	PA	Pct.	Year	W-L-T	PF	PA	Pct.
					V. P. McKinley (1909) 1-0-2 .667				
1909	1-0-2	6	0	.667					
					Dan Herren (1910) 1-1-2 .500				
1910	1-1-2	11	16	.500					
					George Penton (1911-1912) 7-1-1 .833				
1911	4-1-1	49	20	.750	1912	3-0-0	61	10	1.000
					No team (1913-1920)				
					Professor Campbell (1921-1923) 12-13-1 .481				
1921	1-7-0	19	284	.125	1923	5-2-0	96	55	.714
1922	6-4-1	177	92	.591					
					Ross Ford (1924) 2-1-4 .571				
1924	2-1-4	59	20	.571					
					Otis Bynum (1925-1926) 12-4-1 .735				
1925	5-3-0	76	120	.625	1926	7-1-1	147	21	.833
					Gladwin Gaumer (1927-1928) 6-7-0 .462				
1927	4-3-0	138	66	.571	1928	2-4-0	20	155	.333
					No team (1928)				
					No coach (1929-1930)				
1929	1-2-0	7	73	.333	1930	1-2-0	7	73	.333
					Albert Elmore (1931-1937) 33-25-3 .566				
1931	6-3-0	136	87	.667	1935	5-5-0	169	181	.500
1932	6-4-0	135	70	.600	1936	3-4-0	39	130	.429
1933	5-1-0	93	26	.833	1937	2-6-2	43	114	.300
1934	6-2-1	170	51	.722					

Member of the Alabama Intercollegiate Conference (1938-1970)

Year	W-L-T	PF	PA	Pct.	Year	W-L-T	PF	PA	Pct.
					Albert Choate (1938-1942, 1946) 26-25-0 .510				
1938	4-4-1	85	94	.500	1942	4-3-0	129	135	.571
1939	7-4-0	121	71	.636	1943-1945	no team			
1940	3-6-0	60	119	.333	1946	3-4-0	57	117	.429
1941	5-4-0	102	126	.556					
					Buddy McCollum (1947-1950) 20-18-3 .524				
1947	5-4-1	183	109	.550	1949	6-3-1	160	105	.650
1948	6-5-0	170	121	.545	1950	3-6-1	122	150	.350
					Jim Grantham (1951-1954) 11-23-1 .329				
1951	2-7-0	80	277	.222	1953	3-5-0	66	86	.375
1952	4-6-0	161	233	.400	1954	2-5-1	98	156	.312
					William Clipson (1955-1965) 26-68-0 .277				
1955	2-6-0	65	161	.250	1961	1-8-0	56	273	.111
1956	3-5-0	107	147	.375	1962	2-6-0	83	177	.250
1957	2-6-0	60	181	.250	1963	2-7-0	64	124	.222
1958	3-6-0	129	150	.250	1964	6-3-0	126	122	.667
1959	3-5-0	98	170	.375	1965	1-8-0	63	236	.111
1960	1-8-0	82	236	.111					
					Billy Atkins (1966-1971) 44-16-2 .726				
1966	5-5-0	229	186	.500	1969	8-1-1	283	110	.850
1967	8-2-0	287	100	.800	1970	6-4-1	259	198	.591
1968	11-1-0	519	158	.917					

Member of the Division II Gulf South Conference (1971-1991)

Year	W-L-T	PF	PA	Pct.	Year	W-L-T	PF	PA	Pct.
1971	6-3-0	178	146	.667					
					Tom Jones (1972-1973) 11-7-2 .600				
1972	4-5-1	176	143	.450	1972	7-2-1	208	111	.750
					Byrd Whigham (1974-1975) 12-8-0 .600				
1974	6-4-0	264	218	.600	1985	6-4-0	194	161	.600
					Charles Bradshaw (1976-1982) 41-27-2 .600				
1976	8-1-1	206	119	.850	1980	8-2-0	282	105	.800
1977	6-4-0	214	194	.600	1981	3-7-0	182	192	.300
1978	8-2-0	229	144	.800	1982	2-8-0	177	210	.200
1979	6-3-1	234	116	.650					

Chan Gailey (1983-1984) 19-5-0 .792

1983	7-4-0	263	226	.636		1984	12-1-0	372	185	.923

Rick Rhoades (1985-1987) 28-7-1 .792

1985	6-4-0	256	157	.600		1987	12-1-1	467	166	.893
1986	10-2-0	403	239	.833						

Robert Maddox (1988-1990) 13-17-0 .433

1988	4-6-0	215	184	.400		1990	5-5-0	228	209	.500
1989	4-6-0	160	230	.400						

Larry Blakeney (1991-2001) 103-41-1 .714

1991	5-6-0	230	200	.455

Troy State becomes an independent Divison I-AA team.

1992	10-1-0	295	122	.909		1994	8-4-0	430	326	.667
1993	12-1-1	505	227	.893		1995	11-1-0	447	168	.917

Member of the Division I-AA Southland Football League (1996-2000)

1996	12-2-0	434	252	.857		1999	11-2-0	362	224	.846
1997	5-6-0	217	157	.455		2000	10-2-0	330	202	.833
1998	8-4-0	235	203	.667						

Troy State becomes an independent Division I-A team.

2001	7-4-0	246	269	.636		2003	6-6-0	185	272	.500
2002	4-8-0	218	252	.333						

Won-loss record by decades:

1909	1-0-2		.667		1940-49	32-29-2	524		1980-89	68-41-1	.623
1910-19	8-2-3		.731		1950-59	27-57-2	.326		1990-99	87-32-1	.729
1920-29	32-27-6		.538		1960-69	45-49-1	.479		2000-03	27-20-0	.574
1930-39	45-35-4		.560		1970-79	63-28-5	.682				

Historic record: 435-320-27 .574

Record by Division: NAIA: 252-219-21 .534; Division II: 144-82-5 .634; Division I-AA: 77-22-1 .778; Division I-A: 11-12-0 .478.

Post-season won-loss record: 14-8-0 .636, with three national championships: 1 NAIA, 2 NCAA Division II.

1948: Paper Bowl, Jacksonville State 19, TSU 9
1968: NAIA Playoffs: TSU 63, Williamette 10
   Championship: TSU 43, Texas A&I 35
1984: Division II Playoffs, TSU 31, Central State 21
   TSU 45, Towson State 3
   Championship TSU 18, North Dakota State 17
1986: Division II Playoffs: TSU 31, Virginia Union 7
   South Dakota 42, TSU 28
1987: Division II Playoffs: TSU 45, Winston Salem 14
   TSU 31, Central Florida 10
   Championship: TSU 31, Portland State 17
1993: Division I-AA Playoffs: TSU 42, Stephen Austin 20
   TSU 35, McNeese State 28
   Championship: Marshall 24, TSU 21

1994: I-AA Playoffs: James Madison 45, TSU 26
1995: I-AA Playoffs: Georgia Southern 24, TSU 21
1996: I-AA Playoffs: TSU 29, Florida A&M 25
   TSU 31, Murray State 3
   Championship: Montana 70, TSU 7
1998: I-AA Playoffs: Florida A&M 27, TSU 17
1999: I-AA Playoffs: TSU 27, James Madison 7
   Florida A&M 17, TSU 10
2000: I-AA Playoffs: Appalachian State 33, TSU 30

TULANE UNIVERSITY, New Orleans, Louisiana; nickname "Green Wave"; colors olive green and sky blue; Louisiana Superdome (69,767); Conference USA. Tulane was an independent from 1893 through 1921 and then was one of the founding members of the Southern Conference in 1922. Tulane left the Southern Conference after the 1932 season to join 12 other members of the conference in organizing the Southeastern Conference. Tulane left the SEC after the 1965 season and operated as an independent for thirty years. In 1996, Tulane became one of the founders of Conference USA.

Early years (1893-1921)

Year	Coach	W-L-T	PF	PA	Pct.	Year	Coach	W-L-T	PF	PA	Pct.
1893	T. L. Bayne	1-2-0	38	24	.333	1904	T. Berry/J. Janvier	5-2-0	58	24	.714
1894	Fred Sweet	0-4-0	14	50	.000	1905	J. Tobin/H. Ludlow	0-1-0	0	5	.000
1895	T.L. Bayne	3-2-0	66	28	.600	1906	John Russ	0-4-1	0	92	.100
1896	H. Baum	3-2-0	74	18	.600	1907	John Lombard	3-2-0	71	44	.600
1897	no team					1908	John Lombard	7-1-0	103	23	.875
1898	John Lombard	1-1-0	14	46	.500	1909	Buster Brown	4-3-2	40	50	.556
1899	H.H. Collier	0-6-1	0	141	.072	1910	A.A. Mason	0-7-0	6	126	.000
1900	H.T. Summersgill	5-0-0	105	0	1.000	1911	A.A. Mason	5-3-1	106	46	.611
1901	H.T. Summersgill	5-1-0	109	19	.833	1912	A.A. Mason	5-3-0	216	99	.625
1902	Virginius Dabney	1-4-2	47	67	.286	1913	A.C. Hoffman	3-5-0	59	159	.375
1903	Charles Eshleman	2-2-1	64	56	.500	1914	E.R.Sweetland	3-3-1	145	146	.500

Clark Shaughnessy (1915-1920, 1922-1926) 59-28-7 .665

Year	W-L-T	PF	PA	Pct.	Year	W-L-T	PF	PA	Pct.
1915	4-4-0	118	78	.500	1918	4-1-1	133	16	.750
1916	4-3-1	126	149	.562	1919	6-2-1	224	55	.722
1917	5-3-0	159	163	.625	1920	6-2-1	181	28	.722

Myron Fuller (1921) 4-6-0 .400

Year	W-L-T	PF	PA	Pct.
1921	4-6-0	84	96	.400

Member of the Southern Conference (1922-1932) 43-21-4 .662

Year	Nat'l AP	Other	Overall W-L-T	PF	PA	Pct.	Conference W-L-T	Pct.	Rank	Year	Nat'l AP	Other	Overall W-L-T	PF	PA	Pct.	Conference W-L-T	Pct.	Rank

Clark Shaughnessy (1922-1926)

Year	Nat'l AP	Other	Overall W-L-T	PF	PA	Pct.	Conf W-L-T	Pct.	Rank	Year	Nat'l AP	Other	Overall W-L-T	PF	PA	Pct.	Conf W-L-T	Pct.	Rank
1922			4-4-0	136	100	.500	1-4-0	.200	17	1925		6	9-0-1	246	32	.950	5-0-0	1.000	2
1923			6-3-1	117	89	.650	2-2-1	.500	12	1926			3-5-1	71	60	.389	2-4-0	.333	15
1924			8-1-0	201	59	.889	4-1-0	.800	4										

Bernie Bierman (1927-1931) 36-10-2 .771

Year	Nat'l AP	Other	Overall W-L-T	PF	PA	Pct.	Conf W-L-T	Pct.	Rank	Year	Nat'l AP	Other	Overall W-L-T	PF	PA	Pct.	Conf W-L-T	Pct.	Rank
1927			2-5-1	56	120	.312	2-5-1	.312	18	1930		11	8-1-0	263	30	.889	5-0-0	1.000	2
1928			6-3-1	264	76	.650	3-3-1	.500	9	1931		2	11-1-0	350	49	.917	8-0-0	1.000	1
1929	10		9-0-0	279	45	1.000	6-0-0	1.000	1										

Ted Cox (1932-1935) 28-10-2 .725

Year	Overall W-L-T	PF	PA	Pct.	Conf W-L-T	Pct.	Rank
1932	6-2-1	131	104	.722	5-2-1	.688	8

Member of the Southeastern Conference (1933-1965) 69-114-13 .385

Year	Nat'l AP	Other	Overall W-L-T	PF	PA	Pct.	Conf W-L-T	Pct.	Rank	Year	Nat'l AP	Other	Overall W-L-T	PF	PA	Pct.	Conf W-L-T	Pct.	Rank
1933			6-3-1	160	68	.650	4-2-1	.643	5	1935			6-4-0	159	123	.600	3-3-0	.500	6
1934	11		10-1-0	215	83	.909	8-0-0	1.000	1										

Red Dawson (1936-1941) 36-19-4 .644

Year	Nat'l AP	Other	Overall W-L-T	PF	PA	Pct.	Conf W-L-T	Pct.	Rank	Year	Nat'l AP	Other	Overall W-L-T	PF	PA	Pct.	Conf W-L-T	Pct.	Rank
1936			6-3-1	163	117	.650	2-3-1	.417	8	1939	5	4	8-1-1	194	60	.850	5-0-0	1.000	3
1937			5-4-1	164	69	.550	2-3-1	.417	9	1940			5-5-0	144	126	500	1-3-0	.250	10
1938	19		7-2-1	211	53	.750	4-1-1	.750	2	1941			5-4-0	220	95	.556	2-3-0	.400	8

Monk Simons (1942-1945) 13-17-1 .435

Year	Overall W-L-T	PF	PA	Pct.	Conf W-L-T	Pct.	Rank	Year	Overall W-L-T	PF	PA	Pct.	Conf W-L-T	Pct.	Rank
1942	4-5-0	121	154	.444	1-4-0	.200	10	1944	4-3-0	113	125	.571	1-2-0	.333	8
1943	3-3-0	92	94	.500	1-1-0	.500	2	1945	2-6-1	93	212	.278	1-3-1	.300	10

Henry Frnka (1946-1951) 31-23-4 .569

Year	Nat'l AP	Other	Overall W-L-T	PF	PA	Pct.	Conf W-L-T	Pct.	Rank	Year	Nat'l AP	Other	Overall W-L-T	PF	PA	Pct.	Conf W-L-T	Pct.	Rank
1946			3-7-0	179	209	.300	2-4-0	.333	9	1949			7-2-1	251	142	.750	5-1-0	.833	1
1947			2-5-2	94	192	.333	2-3-2	.429	7	1950	20		6-2-1	260	97	.722	3-1-1	.700	4
1948	13		9-1-0	207	60	.900	5-1-0	.833	3	1951			4-6-0	143	172	.400	1-5-0	.167	12

Raymond Wolf (1952-1953) 6-13-1 .325

Year	Overall W-L-T	PF	PA	Pct.	Conf W-L-T	Pct.	Rank	Year	Overall W-L-T	PF	PA	Pct.	Conf W-L-T	Pct.	Rank
1952	5-5-0	188	146	.500	3-5-0	375	8	1953	1-8-1	129	228	.150	0-7-0	.000	12

Andy Pilney (1954-1961) 25-49-6 .350

Year	Nat'l AP	Other	Overall W-L-T	PF	PA	Pct.	Conf W-L-T	Pct.	Rank	Year	Overall W-L-T	PF	PA	Pct.	Conf W-L-T	Pct.	Rank
1954			1-6-3	46	144	.250	1-6-1	.188	10	1958	3-7-0	105	189	.300	1-5-0	.167	11
1955			5-4-1	163	136	.550	3-3-1	.500	6	1959	3-6-1	94	176	.350	0-5-1	.083	11
1956			6-4-0	124	123	.600	3-3-0	.500	6	1960	3-6-1	139	140	.350	1-4-1	.250	10
1957			2-8-0	94	195	.200	1-5-0	.167	10	1961	2-8-0	60	225	.200	1-5-0	.167	10

Tommy O' Boyle (1962-1965) 6-33-1 .163

Year	Overall W-L-T	PF	PA	Pct.	Conf W-L-T	Pct.	Rank	Year	Overall W-L-T	PF	PA	Pct.	Conf W-L-T	Pct.	Rank
1962	0-10-0	76	293	.000	0-7-0	.000	12	1964	3-7-0	79	147	.300	1-5-0	.167	11
1963	1-8-1	43	191	.150	0-6-1	.072	12	1965	2-8-0	71	268	.200	1-5-0	.167	9

Tulane becomes independent (1966-1995)
Jim Pittman (1966-1970) 21-30-0 .396

Year	Nat'l AP	Other	Overall W-L-T	PF	PA	Pct.	Year	Nat'l AP	Other	Overall W-L-T	PF	PA	Pct.
1966			5-4-1	153	182	.550	1969			3-7-0	152	235	.300
1967			3-7-0	164	223	300	1970		17	8-4-0	196	160	.667
1968			2-8-0	163	300	.200							

Bennie Ellender (1971-1975) 27-29-0 .482

1971		3-8-0	152	215	.273			1974		5-6-0	176	214	.455
1972		6-5-0	212	165	.545			1975		4-7-0	123	192	.364
1973	20	15	9-3-0	228	194	.750							

Larry Smith (1976-1979) 18-27-0 .400

| 1976 | 2-9-0 | 149 | 228 | .182 | | 1978 | 4-7-0 | 183 | 211 | .364 |
| 1977 | 3-8-0 | 181 | 289 | .273 | | 1979 | 9-3-0 | 320 | 179 | .750 |

Vince Gibson (1980-1982) 17-17-0 .500

| 1980 | 7-5-0 | 279 | 243 | .583 | | 1982 | 4-7-0 | 201 | 271 | .364 |
| 1981 | 6-5-0 | 213 | 144 | .545 | | | | | | |

Wally English (1983-1984) 5-17-0 .227

| 1983 | 2-9-0 | 192 | 241 | .182 | | 1984 | 3-8-0 | 177 | 275 | .273 |

Mack Brown (1985-1987) 11-23-0 .324

| 1985 | 1-10-0 | 166 | 334 | .909 | | 1987 | 6-6-0 | 370 | 376 | .500 |
| 1986 | 4-7-0 | 265 | 334 | .364 | | | | | | |

Greg Davis (1988-1991) 14-31-0 .311

| 1988 | 5-6-0 | 251 | 334 | .455 | | 1990 | 4-7-0 | 237 | 253 | .364 |
| 1989 | 4-8-0 | 247 | 337 | .333 | | 1991 | 1-10-0 | 146 | 384 | .091 |

Buddy Teevens (1992-1996) 11-45-0 .196

| 1992 | 2-9-0 | 146 | 349 | .182 | | 1994 | 1-10-0 | 135 | 358 | .091 |
| 1993 | 4-8-0 | 154 | 355 | .333 | | 1995 | 2-9-0 | 187 | 303 | .182 |

Member of Conference USA (1996-2003) 24-29-0 .453

| 1996 | 2-9-0 | 213 | 268 | .182 | 1-4-0 | .200 | 6 | | | | | | | | | |

Tommy Bowden (1997-1998) 18-4-0 .818

| 1997 | 7-4-0 | 375 | 225 | .636 | 5-1-0 | .833 | 2 | 1998* | 7 | 7 | 11-0-0 | 499 | 268 | 1.000 | 6-0-0 | 1.000 | 1 |

Chris Scelfo (1998-2003) 26-34-0 .433

1998*	1-0-0	41	27	1.000	0-0-0			2001	3-9-0	344	495	.250	1-6-0	.143	9
1999	3-8-0	279	399	.273	1-5-0	.167	7	2002	8-5-0	361	282	.615	4-4-0	.500	5
2000	6-5-0	329	346	.556	3-4-0	.429	5	2003	5-7-0	337	424	.417	3-5-0	.375	8

*Bowden coached the first eleven games, and Scelfo coached the bowl game.

Won-loss record by decades:

1893-99	8-17-1	.327		1930-39	73-22-6	.752		1970-79	53-60-0	.469
1900-09	32-20-6	.603		1940-49	44-41-4	.517		1980-89	42-71-0	.372
1910-19	39-34-5	.532		1950-59	36-56-7	.399		1990-99	38-74-0	.339
1920-29	57-29-6	.652		1960-69	24-73-3	.255		2000-03	22-26-0	.458

Historic record: 468-535-38 .468

Post-season won-loss record: 4-6-0 .400

1932: Rose Bowl, USC 21, Tulane 12
1935: Sugar Bowl, Tulane 20, Temple 14
1940: Sugar Bowl, Texas A&M 14, Tulane 13
1970: Liberty Bowl, Tulane 17, Colorado 3
1973: Astro-Bluebonnet Bowl, Houston 47, Tulane 7

1979: Liberty Bowl, Penn State 9, Tulane 6
1980: Hall of Fame Bowl, Arkansas 34, Tulane 15
1987: Independence Bowl, Washington 24, Tulane 12
1998: Liberty Bowl, Tulane 41, BYU 27
2002: Hawaii Bowl, Tulane 36, Hawaii 28

College Football Hall of Fame:
Clark Shaughnessy, coach, 1915-20, 1922-26; Les Lautenschlaeger, quarterback, 1922-25; Bernie Bierman, coach, 1927-31; Bill Banker, halfback, 1927-29; Jerry Dalrymple, end, 1929-31; Monk Simons, halfback, 1932-34; Jack Green, guard, 1942-45; Eddie Price, fullback, 1946-49.

Awards: Groza Award: 2001, Seth Marler.

UNIVERSITY OF TULSA, Tulsa, Oklahoma; nickname "Golden Hurricanes"; colors old gold, royal blue, crimson; Skelly Stadium (40,385); Western Athletic Conference. Tulsa was an independent from 1895 through the 1913 season. In 1914, Tulsa became a member of the Oklahoma Collegiate Conference and played in it until 1929 when Tulsa joined the Big Four Conference. In 1933, Tulsa went independent. Three years later, in 1935, Tulsa joined the Missouri Valley Conference and played in it for fifty-one years, through the 1985 season. The MVC dropped out of football after the 1985 season, and Tulsa was independent for ten years. In 1996, Tulsa joined the Western Athletic Conference.

Early years as an independent (1895-1913)

Year	W-L-T	PF	PA	Pct.	Year	W-L-T	PF	PA	Pct.
1895* Norman Leard	1-0-0			1.000	1903 – 1904 no team				
1896* Norman Leard	2-1-0			.667	1905 Unknown	1-2-0	10	24	.333
1897* Norman Leard	2-1-0			667	1906-1907 no team				
1898* Fred Taylor	1-0-0			1.000	1908 Sam McBirney	2-3-0	80	43	.400
1899 Fred Taylor	0-1-1	0	11	.250	1909 Unknown	4-2-0	23	33	.667
1900 Unknown	2-1-0	43	23	.667	1910 Unknown	2-1-0	9	11	.667
1901 Unknown	0-1-0	0	48	.000	1911 no team				
1902 Unknown	0-1-0	0	33	.000	1912 Harvey Allen	1-3-0	75	103	.250
					1913 George Evans	5-2-0	271	59	.714

*No data available on points for or gains.

Member of the Oklahoma Collegiate Conference (1914-1928) 46-7-4 .842

Year	Nat'l AP	Other	Overall W-L-T	PF	PA	Pct.	Conf. W-L-T	Pct.	Rank	Year	Nat'l AP	Other	Overall W-L-T	PF	PA	Pct.	Conf. W-L-T	Pct.	Rank
Sam McBirney (1908, 1914-1916) 25-6-1 .806																			
1914			6-2-0	261	48	.750	3-2-0	.600	3	1916			10-0-0	566	40	1.000	4-0-0	1.000	1
1915			6-1-1	257	33	.812	4-1-1	.750	2										
Hal Medford (1917) 0-8-1 .056																			
1917			0-8-1	66	221	.056	no conference												
Arthur Smith (1918) 1-2-0 .333																			
1917			1-2-0	9	56	.333	no conference												
Francis Schmidt (1919-1921) 24-3-2 .889																			
1919			8-0-1	594	27	.944	5-0-1	.917	1	1921			6-3-0	257	95	.667	5-1-0	.833	1
1920			10-0-1	621	21	.955	6-0-1	.929	1										
Howard Acher (1922-1924) 12-11-2 .522																			
1922			9-0-0	157	60	1.000	4-0-0	1.000	1	1924			1-6-1	17	133	.188	0-0-0		
1923			2-5-1	107	165	.312	0-0-0												
Elmer Henderson (1925-1935) 70-25-5 .737																			
1925			6-2-0	128	91	.750	4-0-0	1.000	1	1927			8-1-0	201	84	.889	3-1-1	.700	2
1926			7-2-0	169	56	.778	5-1-0	.833	2	1928			7-2-1	273	73	.750	3-1-1	.700	2
Member of the Big Four Conference (1929-1932) 12-1-1 .893																			
1929			6-3-1	107	81	.650	4-0-1	.900	1	1931			8-3-0	255	55	.727	2-1-0	.667	2
1930			7-2-0	171	79	.778	3-0-0	1.000	1	1932			7-1-1	175	36	.833	3-0-0	1.000	1
Tulsa reverts to independent status (1933-1934)																			
1933			6-1-0	93	19	.857				1934			5-2-1	106	39	.688			
Member of the Missouri Valley Conference (1935-1985) 141-54-6 .716																			
1935			3-6-1	58	94	.350	3-0-0	1.000	1										
Vic Hurt (1936-1938) 15-9-5 .625																			
1936			5-2-2	154	56	.667	3-0-0	1.000	1	1938			4-5-1	115	148	.450	3-1-0	.750	1
1937			6-2-2	195	90	.700	3-0-0	1.000	1										
Chet Benefiel (1939-1940) 11-8-1 .589																			
1939			4-5-1	94	104	.450	2-1-1	.625	3	1940			7-3-0	166	112	.700	4-0-0	1.000	1
Henry Frnka (1941-1945) 40-9-1 .816																			
1941			8-2-0	194	65	.800	4 0 0	1.000	1	1944			8-2-0	380	128	.800	0-1-0	.000	2
1942	4		10-1-0	434	46	.909	5-0-0	1.000	1	1945	17		8-3-0	275	84	.727	2-1-0	.667	2
1943	15		6-1-1	269	52	.812	1-0-0	1.000	1										
J. O. Brothers (1946-1952) 45-25-4 .635																			
1946	17		9-1-0	295	83	.900	3-0-0	1.000	1	1950	19		9-1-1	339	124	.864	3-0-1	.875	1
1947			5-5-0	143	128	.500	3-0-0	1.000	1	1951			9-2-0	371	200	.818	4-0-0	1.000	1
1948			0-9-1	135	330	.050	0-1-1	.250	4	1952	12		8-2-1	341	197	.773	3-1-0	.750	2
1949			5-5-1	223	233	.500	1-2-1	.375	5										
Bernie Witucki (1953-1954) 3-18-0 .143																			
1953			3-7-0	117	258	.300	1-3-0	.250	5	1954			0-11-0	118	333	.000	0-4-0	.000	5
Bobby Dodds (1955-1960) 30-28-2 .517																			
1955			2-7-1	124	232	.250	1-3-0	.250	4	1958			7-3-0	216	100	.700	2-2-0	.500	3
1956			7-2-1	169	67	.750	2-1-1	.625	2	1959			5-5-0	137	164	.500	2-2-0	.500	3
1957			4-6-0	110	145	.400	2-3-0	.400	3	1960			5-5-0	159	230	.500	2-1-0	.667	2

Glenn Dobbs (1961-1968) 45-37-0 .549

1961		2-8-0	91	205	.200	1-2-0	.333	2	1965	16	8-3-0	321	171	.727	4-0-0	1.000	1
1962		5-5-0	219	181	.500	3-0-0	1.000	1	1966		6-4-0	220	203	.600	3-1-0	.750	1
1963		5-5-0	214	241	.500	2-2-0	.500	3	1967		7-3-0	304	155	.700	3-1-0	.750	2
1964	18	9-2-0	398	140	.818	3-1-0	.750	2	1968		3-7-0	149	314	.300	2-3-0	.400	5

Vince Carillot (1969) 1-9-0 .100

1969	1-9-0	183	377	.100	1-4-0	.200	5

Claude Gibson (1970-1972) 11-16-0 .407

1970	6-4-0	187	178	.600	3-1-0	.750	2	1972*	1-5-0	70	142	.167	1-0-0	1.000	*
1971	4-7-0	173	297	.364	3-2-0	.600	2								

F. A. Dry (1972-1976) 31-18-1 .633

1972*	3-2-0	125	127	.600	2-1-0	.667	4	1975	7-4-0	368	181	.636	4-0-0	1.000	1
1973	6-5-0	258	193	.545	5-1-0	.833	1	1976	7-4-1	253	208	.625	2-1-1	.625	1
1974	19 8-3-0	285	204	.727	6-0-0	1.000	1								

*Gibson coached the first six games of the 1972 season, and Dry the last five games.

John Cooper (1977-1984) 57-31-0 .648

1977	3-8-0	192	398	.273	2-3-0	.400	4	1981	7-4-0	304	196	.636	5-1-0	.833	1
1978	9-2-0	289	203	.818	4-1-0	.800	2	1982	10-1-0	312	196	.909	6-0-0	1.000	1
1979	6-5-0	195	221	.545	2-0-0	1.000	**	1983	8-3-0	297	185	.727	5-0-0	1.000	1
1980	8-3-0	243	196	.727	4-1-0	.800	1	1984	6-5-0	261	206	.545	5-0-0	1.000	1

**Insufficient number of games to qualify for league title.

Don Morton (1985-1986) 13-9-0 .591

1985	6-5-0	274	328	.545	5-0-0	1.000	1

Tulsa reverts to independent status (1986-1995)

1986	7-4-0	293	186	.636

George Henshaw (1987) 3-8-0 .273

1987	3-8-0	175	371	.273

David Rader (1988-1999) 49-80-1 .376

1988	4-7-0	254	318	.364	1992	4-7-0	240	303	.364
1989	6-6-0	302	271	.500	1993	4-6-1	262	259	.409
1990	3-8-0	183	281	.273	1994	3-8-0	244	384	.273
1991 21	21 10-2-0	305	208	.833	1995	4-7-0	233	300	.364

Member of the Western Athletic Association (1996-2003) 18-45-0 .286

1996	4-7-0	245	333	.364	2-6-0	.250	13	1998	4-7-0	222	258	.364	2-6-0	.250	13
1997	2-9-0	258	426	.182	2-6-0	.250	14	1999*	1-6-0	125	274	.143	0-4-0	.000	*

Pat Henderson (1999) 1-3-0 .250

1999*	1-3-0	105	112	.250	1-2-0	.333	8

*Rader coached the first seven games of the 1999 season, and Henderson coached the last four.

Keith Burns (2000-2002) 7-28-0 .200

2000	5-7-0	240	283	.417	4-4-0	.500	5	2002	1-11-0	233	417	.083	1-7-0	.125	10
2001	1-10-0	191	387	.091	0-8-0	.000	10								

Steve Kragthorpe (2003) 8-5-0 .615

2003	8-5-0	400	361	.615	6-2-0	.750	2

Won-loss record by decades:

1895-99	6-3-1	.650	1930-39	55-29-9	.640	1970-79	60-49-1	.550
1900-09	7-9-0	.438	1940-49	66-32-3	.668	1980-89	65-46-0	.586
191019	39-19-3	.664	1950-59	54-46-4	.538	1990-99	40-70-1	.365
1920-29	62-24-5	.709	1960-69	51-51-0	.500	2000-03	15-33-0	.312

Historic record 520-411-27 .557

Post-season won-loss record: 4-8-0 .333

1942: Sun Bowl, Tulsa 6, Texas Tech 0
1943: Sugar Bowl, Tennessee 14, Tulsa 7
1944: Sugar Bowl, Georgia Tech 20, Tulsa 18
1945: Orange Bowl, Tulsa 26, Georgia Tech 12
1946: Oil Bowl, Georgia 20, Tulsa 6
1953: Gator Bowl, Florida 14, Tulsa 13

1964: Bluebonnet Bowl, Tulsa 14, Mississippi 7
1965: Bluebonnet Bowl, Tennessee 27, Tulsa 6
1976: Independence Bowl, McNeese State 20, Tulsa 16
1989: Independence Bowl, Oregon 27, Tulsa 24
1991: Freedom Bowl, Tulsa 28, San Diego State 17
2004: Humanitarian Bowl, Georgia Tech 52, Tulsa 10

College Football Hall of Fame:
Francis Schmidt, coach, 1919-21; Glenn Dobbs, halfback, 1940-42; Jerry Rhome, quarterback, 1961-64; Howard Twilley, wide receiver, 1963-65.

Awards: Baugh Trophy: 1964, Jerry Rhome.

UCLA, Los Angeles, California; nickname "Bruins"; colors blue and gold; Rose Bowl (91,500); Pac-10 Conference. UCLA began play in 1919 and joined the Pacific Coast Conference in 1928. It has been a member of that conference, including its successor conferences, since that time.

Year	Nat'l AP	Other	Overall W-L-T	PF	PA	Pct.	Conf. W-L-T	Pct.	Rank	Year	Nat'l AP	Other	Overall W-L-T	PF	PA	Pct.	Conf. W-L-T	Pct.	Rank

Early years as an independent (1919-1927)

Fred Cozens (1919) 2-6-0 .250

Year	AP	Other	W-L-T	PF	PA	Pct.	W-L-T	Pct.	Rank	Year	AP	Other	W-L-T	PF	PA	Pct.	W-L-T	Pct.	Rank
1919			2-6-0	52	193	.250													

Harry Trotter (1920-1922) 2-13-1 .156

1920			0-5-0	21	224	.000				1922			2-3-1	83	62	.417			
1921			0-5-0	14	214	.000													

James Cline (1923-1924) 2-10-3 .233

1923			2-5-0	54	132	.280				1924			0-5-3	40	109	.188			

Bill Spaulding (1925-1938) 72-51-8 .573

1925			5-3-1	91	130	.611				1927			6-2-1	144	54	.722			
1926			5-3-0	153	67	.625													

Member of the Pacific Coast Conference (and successor conferences) (1928-2003) 293-187-20 .606

1928			4-4-1	171	136	.500	0-4-0	.000	9	1934			7-3-0	146	69	.700	2-3-0	.400	6
1929			4-4-0	121	190	.500	1-3-0	.259	5	1935		10	8-2-0	160	79	.800	4-1-0	.800	1
1930			3-5-0	77	125	.375	1-4-0	.200	8	1936			6-3-1	143	91	.650	4-3-1	.562	5
1931			3-4-1	83	57	.438	0-3-0	.000	9	1937			2-6-1	93	133	.278	1-5-1	.214	9
1932			6-4-0	149	61	.600	4-2-0	.667	3	1938			7-4-1	217	106	.625	4-3-1	.562	3
1933			6-4-1	124	62	591	1-3-1	.300	6										

Edwin Horrell (1939-1944) 24-31-6 .443

1939	7	10	6-0-4	127	62	.800	5-0-3	.812	2	1942	13		7-4-0	175	98	.636	6-1-0	.857	1
1940			1-9-0	79	174	.174	1-6-0	.143	9	1943			1-8-0	59	199	.111	0-4-0	.000	3
1941			5-5-1	128	178	.500	3-4-1	.438	6	1944			4-5-1	189	149	.450	1-2-1	.375	3

Bert LaBrucherie (1945-1948) 23-16-0 .590

1945			5-4-0	135	79	.555	2-3-0	.400	5	1947			5-4-0	172	80	.555	4-2-0	.667	4
1946	4		10-1-0	327	117	.909	7-0-0	1.000	1	1948			3-7-0	156	235	.300	2-6-0	.250	8

Red Sanders (1949-1957) 66-19-1 .773

1949			6-3-0	227	188	.667	5-2-0	.714	2	1954	2	1	9-0-0	367	40	1.000	6-0-0	1.000	1
1950			6-3-0	196	96	.667	5-2-0	.714	3	1955	4	4	9-2-0	299	74	.818	6-0-0	1.000	1
1951	17	17	5-3-1	188	120	.611	4-1-1	.750	2	1956			7-3-0	148	122	.700	5-2-0	.714	2
1952	6	6	8-1-0	220	55	.889	5-1-0	.833	2	1957		18	8-2-0	190	90	.800	5-2-0	.714	3
1953	5	4	8-2-0	224	76	.800	6-1-0	.857	1										

George Dickerson (1958) 1-2-0 .333

1958			1-2-0	24	55	.333	0-1-0	.000	*										

Bill Barnes (1958-1964) 31-34-3 .463

1958*			2-4-1	112	118	.357	2-3-1	.357*	6	1962			4-6-0	118	139	.400	1-3-0	.250	5
1959			5-4-1	169	150	.550	3-1-0	.750	1	1963			2-8-0	96	219	.200	2-2-0	.500	3
1960			7-2-1	175	84	.750	2-2-0	.500	3	1964			4-6-0	145	236	.400	2-2-0	.500	4
1961	16		7-4-0	185	142	.636	3-1-0	.750	1										

*Dickerson coached the first three games of the 1958 season, and Barnes coached the last seven games.

Tommy Prothro (1965-1970) 41-18-3 .686

1965	4	5	8-2-1	257	168	.773	4-0-0	1.000	1	1968			3-7-0	197	246	.300	2-4-0	.333	5
1966	5	5	9-1-0	281	127	.900	3-1-0	.750	2	1969	13	10	8-1-1	329	103	.850	5-1-1	.944	2
1967		10	7-2-1	284	161	.750	4-1-1	.750	2	1970			6-5-0	274	240	.545	4-3-0	.571	2

Pepper Rogers (1971-1973) 19-12-1 .609

1971			2-7-1	166	243	.250	1-4-1	.250	8	1973	12	9	9-2-0	470	199	.818	6-1-0	.857	2
1972	15	17	8-3-0	351	239	.727	5-2-0	.714	2										

Dick Vermeil (1974-1975) 15-5-3 .717

1974			6-3-2	240	174	.636	4-2-1	.643	3	1975	5	5	9-2-1	349	243	.792	6-1-0	.857	1

Terry Donahue (1976-1995) 151-74-8 .665

1976	15	15	9-2-1	391	173	.792	6-1-0	.857	2	1986	14	14	8-3-1	385	222	.708	5-2-1	.688	2
1977			7-4-0	269	196	.636	5-2-0	.714	2	1987	9	11	10-2-0	426	195	.833	7-1-0	.875	1
1978	14	12	8-3-1	261	172	.708	6-2-0	.750	2	1988	6	6	10-2-0	392	190	.833	6-2-0	.750	2
1979			5-6-0	257	256	.455	3-4-0	.429	7	1989			3-7-1	209	246	.318	2-5-1	.312	8
1980	13	14	9-2-0	306	135	.818	5-2-0	.714	2	1990			5-6-0	305	332	.455	4-4-0	.500	6
1981			7-4-1	302	197	.625	5-2-1	.688	2	1991	19	18	9-3-0	323	190	.750	6-2-0	.750	2
1982	5	5	10-1-1	399	197	.625	5-1-1	.786	1	1992			6-5-0	201	228	.545	3-5-0	.375	8
1983	17	13	7-4-1	309	265	.625	6-1-1	.812	1	1993	18	17	8-4-0	368	230	.667	6-2-0	.750	1
1984	9	10	9-3-0	275	248	.750	5-2-0	.714	3	1994			5-6-0	239	295	.455	3-5-0	.375	6
1985	7	6	9-2-1	363	214	.792	6-2-0	.750	1	1995			7-5-0	338	300	.583	4-4-0	.500	5

Bob Toledo (1996-2002) 50-32-0 .610

1996			5-6-0	330	318	.455	4-4-0	.500	4	2000	6-6-0	353	368	.500	3-5-0	.375	5
1997	5	5	10-2-0	477	247	.833	7-1-0	.875	1	2001	7-4-0	317	225	.636	4-4-0	.500	6
1998	8	8	10-2-0	476	340	.833	8-0-0	1.000	1	2002	8-5-0	387	326	.615	4-4-0	.500	4
1999			4-7-0	230	311	.364	2-6-0	.250	9								

Karl Dorrell (2003) 6-7-0 .462

2003   6-7-0 248 305 .462 4-4-0 .500 5

Won-loss record by decades:

1919-29	30-45-7	.409	1950-59	68-26-3	.716	1980-89	82-30-6	.720
1930-39	54-35-9	.597	1960-69	59-39-4	.598	1990-99	69-46-0	.600
1940-49	47-50-2	.485	1970-79	69-37-6	.637	2000-03	27-22-0	.551

Historical record: 505-330-37 .600

Post-season won-loss record: 12-12-1 .500

1943: Rose Bowl, Georgia 9, UCLA 0
1947: Rose Bowl, Illinois 45, UCLA 14
1954: Rose Bowl, Michigan State 28, UCLA 20
1956: Rose Bowl, Michigan State 17, UCLA 14
1962: Rose Bowl, Minnesota 21, UCLA 3
1966: Rose Bowl, UCLA 14, Michigan State 12
1976: Rose Bowl, UCLA 23, Ohio State 10
1976: Liberty Bowl, Alabama 36, UCLA 6
1978: Fiesta Bowl, UCLA 10, Arkansas 10
1981: Bluebonnet Bowl, Michigan 33, UCLA 14
1983: Rose Bowl, UCLA 24, Michigan 14
1984: Rose Bowl, UCLA 45, Illinois 9

1985: Fiesta Bowl, UCLA 39, Miami (FL) 37
1986: Rose Bowl, UCLA 45, Iowa 28
1987: Freedom Bowl, UCLA 31, BYU 10
1987: Aloha Bowl, UCLA 20, Florida 16
1989: Cotton Bowl, UCLA 17, Arkansas 3
1991: Hancock Bowl, UCLA 6, Illinois 3
1994: Rose Bowl, Wisconsin 21, UCLA 16
1995: Aloha Bowl, Kansas 51, UCLA 30
1998: Cotton Bowl, UCLA 29, Texas A&M 23
1999: Rose Bowl, Wisconsin 38, UCLA 31
2000: Sun Bowl, Wisconsin 21, UCLA 20
2002: Las Vegas Bowl, UCLA 27, New Mexico 13
2003: Silicon Valley Bowl, Fresno State 19, UCLA 9

College Football Hall of Fame:
Kenny Washington, halfback, 1937-39; Al Sparlis, guard, 1941-45; Tom Fears, end, 1942-47; Red Sanders, coach, 1949-57; Don Moomaw, center, 1950; Billy Kilmer, halfback, 1958-60; Tommy Prothro, coach, 1965-70; Gary Beban, quarterback, 1965-67; Jerry Robinson, linebacker, 1975-78; Terry Donahue, coach, 1976-95; Kenny Easley, safety, 1977-80.

Awards: Heisman Trophy: 1967, Gary Beban; Maxwell Trophy: 1967, Gary Beban; Davey O'Brien Award: 1988, Troy Aikman; Outland Trophy: 1995, Jonathon Ogden; 1998, Kris Farris; Doak Walker Award: 2000, La Daiman Tomlinson; Unitas Award, Cade McNown; Nagurski Award: 2003, Dave Ball.

UNITED STATES AIR FORCE ACADEMY, United States Air Force Academy, Colorado; nickname "Falcons"; colors blue and silver; Falcon Stadium (52,480); Mountain West Conference. Air Force began play in 1955 as an independent. In 1980, Air Force joined the Western Athletic Conference and played in that conference through the 1998 season. In 1999, Air Force joined with seven other WAC teams to form a new conference, the Mountain West Conference.

	Nat'l								Nat'l					
Year	AP	Other	W-L-T	PF	PA	Pct		Year	AP	Other	W-L-T	PF	PA	Pct.

Early years as an independent (1955-1970)
Robert Whitlow (1955) 4-4-0 .500

1955			4-4-0	101	175	.500

Buck Shaw (1956-1957) 9-8-2 .526

1956			6-2-1	293	101	.722		1957			3-6-1	125	184	350

Ben Martin (1958-1977) 96-103-9 .483

Year	AP	Other	W-L-T	PF	PA	Pct		Year	AP	Other	W-L-T	PF	PA	Pct.
1958	6	8	9-0-2	247	102	.909		1968			7-3-0	251	155	.700
1959			5-4-1	160	124	.550		1969			6-4-0	267	177	.600
1960			4-6-0	147	178	.400		1970	16	11	9-3-0	366	239	.750
1961			3-7-0	87	173	.300		1971			6-4-0	187	187	.600
1962			5-5-0	173	171	.400		1972			6-4-0	304	183	.600
1963			7-4-0	249	150	.636		1973			6-4-0	223	239	.600
1964			4-5-1	106	146	.450		1974			2-9-0	178	215	.182
1965			3-6-1	166	156	.350		1975			2-8-1	156	265	.227
1966			4-6-0	154	161	.400		1976			4-7-0	180	273	.364
1967			2-6-2	86	173	.300		1977			2-8-1	114	286	.227

Bill Parcells (1978) 3-8-0 .273

1978			3-8-0	215	328	.273

Ken Hatfield (1979-1983) 26-32-1 .449

1979			2-9-0	127	253	.182

Member of the Western Athletic Association (1980-1998) 86-57-1 .597

	Nat'l		Overall				Conference				Nat'l		Overall				Conference		
Year	AP	Other	W-L-T	PF	PA	Pct.	W-L-T	Pct.	Rank	Year	AP	Other	W-L-T	PF	PA	Pct.	W-L-T	Pct.	Rank
1980			2-9-1	161	290	.208	1-6-0	.143	8	1982			8-5-0	359	339	.617	4-3-0	.571	2
1981			4-7-0	171	252	.364	2-5-0	.286	7	1983	13	15	10-2-0	367	221	.833	5-2-0	.714	2

Fisher DeBerry (1984-2003) 156-88-1 .639

1984			8-4-0	369	198	.667	4-3-0	.571	3	1992			7-5-0	229	238	.583	4-4-0	.500	5
1985	8	5	12-1-0	469	179	.923	7-1-0	.875	1	1993			4-8-0	296	291	.333	1-7-0	.125	7
1986			6-5-0	229	215	.545	5-2-0	.714	3	1994			8-4-0	371	285	.667	6-2-0	.750	2
1987			9-4-0	405	269	.692	6-2-0	.750	3	1995			8-5-0	401	341	.615	6-2-0	.750	1
1988			5-7-0	422	392	.417	3-5-0	.375	6	1996			6-5-0	360	231	.545	5-3-0	.625	7
1989			8-4-1	475	358	.654	5-1-1	.786	2	1997		25	10-3-0	279	192	.769	6-2-0	.750	2
1990			7-5-0	262	283	.583	3-4-0	.429	6	1998	13	10	12-1-0	468	185	.923	7-1-0	.875	1
1991	25	24	10-3-0	382	263	.769	6-2-0	.750	3										

Member of the Mountain West Conference (1999-2003) 17-18-0 .486

1999			6-5-0	264	218	.545	2-5-0	.286	7	2001			6-6-0	337	386	.500	3-4-0	.429	5
2000			9-3-0	422	301	.750	5-2-0	.714	2	2002			8-5-0	440	303	.615	4-3-0	.241	3
										2003			7-5-0	322	242	.583	3-4-0	.429	4

Won-loss record by decades:

1955-59	27-16-5	.615		1970-79	42-64-2	.398		1990-99	78-44-0	.639
1960-69	45-52-4	.465		1980-89	72-48-2	.598		2000-03	30-19-0	.612

Historic record: 294-243-13 .546

Post-season won-loss record: 9-8-1 .528

1959: Cotton Bowl, Air Force 0, TCU 0
1963: Gator Bowl, North Carolina 35, Air Force 0
1971: Sugar Bowl, Tennessee 34, Air Force 13
1982: Hall of Fame Bowl, Air Force 36, Vanderbilt 28
1983: Independence Bowl, Air Force 9, Mississippi 3
1984: Independence Bowl, Air Force 23, Virginia Tech 7
1985: Bluebonnet Bowl, Air Force 24, Texas 16
1987: Freedom Bowl, Arizona State 33, Air Force 28
1989: Liberty Bowl, Mississippi 42, Air Force 29

1990: Liberty Bowl, Air Force 23, Ohio State 11
1991: Liberty Bowl, Air Force 38, Mississippi State 15
1992: Liberty Bowl, Mississippi 13, Air Force 0
1995: Copper Bowl, Texas Tech 55, Air Force 41
1997: Las Vegas Bowl, Oregon 41, Air Force 13
1998: WAC Championship, Air Force 20, BYU 13
1998: Oahu Bowl, Air Force 45, Washington 25
2000: Silicon Valley Bowl, Air Force 37, Fresno State 34
2002: San Francisco Bowl, Virginia Tech 20, Air Force 13

College Football Hall of Fame:
Brock Strom, tackle, 1956-58; Buck Shaw, coach, 1956-57.

Awards: Outland Trophy: 1987, Chad Hennings.

UNITED STATES MILITARY ACADEMY, West Point, New York; nickname "Army", "Cadets", "Black Knights of the Hudson"; colors black, gold, and gray; Michie Stadium (41, 684); Conference USA. Army was an independent for its entire history until joining Conference USA for the 1998 season. After the 2003 season, Army announced its plans to return to independent status.

Early years (1890-1912)

Year	Coach	W-L-T	PF	PA	Pct.	Year	Coach	W-L-T	PF	PA	Pct.
1890	Dennis Michie	0-1-0	0	24	.000	1902	Dennis Nolan	6-1-1	180	28	.812
1891	Henry Williams	4-1-1	80	73	.750	1903	Edward King	6-2-1	164	33	.722
1892	Dennis Michie	3-1-1	90	18	.700	1904	Robert Boyers	7-2-0	136	27	.778
1893	Laurie Bliss	4-5-0	84	109	.444	1905	Robert Boyers	4-4-1	104	60	.500
1894	Harmon Graves	3-2-0	95	22	.600	1906	Henry Smither*	3-5-1	59	37	.389
1895	Harmon Graves	5-2-0	139	32	.714	1907	Henry Smither	6-2-1	125	24	.722
1896	George Dyer	3-2-1	93	45	.583	1908	Harry Nelly	6-1-2	87	21	.778
1897	Herman Koehler	6-1-1	194	41	.812	1909	Harry Nelly	3-2-0	57	32	.600
1898	Herman Koehler	3-2-1	90	51	.583	1910	Harry Nelly	6-2-0	96	12	.750
1899	Herman Koehler	4-5-0	57	100	.444	1911	Joseph Beacham	6-1-1	88	11	.812
1900	Heman Koehler	7-3-1	109	68	.682	1912	Ernest Graves	5-3-0	108	59	.625
1901	Leon Kromer	5-1-2	98	22	.667						

*Ernest Graves is also listed as a coach for the 1905 season.

Year	Nat'l AP	Other	W-L-T	PF	PA	Pct.	Year	Nat'l AP	Other	W-L-T	PF	PA	Pct.
					Charles Daly (1913-1916, 1919-1922) 58-13-3	.804							
1913			8-1-0	253	57	.889	1915			5-3-1	114	57	.611
1914	1		9-0-0	219	20	1.000	1916			9-0-0	235	36	1.000
					Geoffrey Keyes (1917) 7-1-0	.875							
1917			7-1-0	202	24	.875							
					Hugh Mitchell (1918) 1-0-0	1.000							
1918			1-0-0	20	0	1.000							
					Charles Daly (1919-1922)								
1919			6-3-0	140	389	.667	1921			6-4-0	217	65	.600
1920			7-2-0	318	47	.778	1922			8-0-2	228	27	.900
					John McEwan (1923-1925) 18-5-3	.750							
1923			6-2-1	237	56	.722	1925			7-2-0	185	71	.778
1924			5-1-2	111	41	.667							
					Biff Jones (1926-1929) 30-8-2	.775							
1926	9		7-1-1	240	71	.833	1928		9	8-2-0	215	79	.800
1927	6		9-1-0	197	37	.900	1929			6-4-1	276	132	.591
					Ralph Sasse (1930-1932) 25-5-2	.813							
1930	9		9-1-1	268	22	.864	1932		8	8-2-0	261	38	.800
1931			8-2-1	296	72	.773							
					Gar Davidson (1933-1937) 35-11-1	.755							
1933	9		9-1-0	27	26	.900	1936			6-3-0	238	71	.667
1934			7-3-0	215	40	.700	1937			7-2-0	176	72	.778
1935			6-2-1	178	62	.722							
					William Wood (1938-1940) 12-13-3	.482							
1938			8-2-0	243	95	.800	1940			1-7-1	54	197	.167
1939			3-4-2	106	105	.444							
					Earl Blaik (1941-1958) 121-33-10	.768							
1941			5-3-1	105	87	.611	1950	2	5	8-1-0	267	40	.889
1942			6-3-0	149	74	.667	1951			2-7-0	116	183	.222
1943	11		7-2-1	299	66	.750	1952			4-4-1	155	151	.500
1944	1		9-0-0	504	35	1.000	1953	14	16	7-1-1	210	81	.833
1945	1		9-0-0	412	46	1.000	1954	7	7	7-2-0	325	121	.778
1946	2		9-0-1	263	80	.950	1955	20	15	6-3-0	256	72	.667
1947	11		5-2-2	220	68	.667	1956			5-3-1	223	153	.611
1948	6		8-0-1	294	89	.944	1957	18	13	7-2-0	251	129	.778
1949	4		9-0-0	354	68	1.000	1958	3	3	8-0-1	264	49	.944
					Dale Hall (1959-1961) 16-11-2	.586							
1959			4-4-1	174	141	.500	1961			6-4-0	224	118	.600
1960			6-3-1	222	95	.650							
					Paul Dietzel (1962-1965) 21-18-1	.538							
1962			6-4-0	152	104	.600	1964			4-6-0	118	43	.400
1963			7-3-0	177	97	.700	1965			4-5-1	119	32	.450
					Tom Cahill (1966-1973) 40-39-2	.506							
1966			8-2-0	141	105	800	1970			1-9-1	151	291	.136
1967			8-2-0	183	94	.800	1971			6-4-0	146	206	.600
1968			7-3-0	270	137	.700	1972			6-4-0	160	282	.600
1969			4-5-1	161	160	.450	1973			0-10-0	67	382	.000

Homer Smith (1974-1978) 21-33-1 .391

Year	W-L-T	PF	PA	Pct.	Year	W-L-T	PF	PA	Pct.
1974	3-8-0	156	306	.273	1977	7-4-0	287	245	.636
1975	2-9-0	165	337	.182	1978	4-6-1	184	255	.409
1976	5-6-0	201	267	.455					

Lou Saban (1979) 2-8-1 .227

Year	W-L-T	PF	PA	Pct.
1979	2-8-1	93	308	.227

Ed Cavanaugh (1980-1982) 10-21-2 .333

Year	W-L-T	PF	PA	Pct.	Year	W-L-T	PF	PA	Pct.
1980	3-7-1	204	295	.318	1982	4-7-0	164	271	.364
1981	3-7-1	126	212	.318					

Jim Young (1983-1990) 51-39-1 .566

Year	W-L-T	PF	PA	Pct.	Year	W-L-T	PF	PA	Pct.
1983	2-9-0	140	304	.182	1987	5-6-0	277	223	.455
1984	8-3-1	310	212	.708	1988	9-3-0	308	197	.750
1985	9-3-0	35	203	.750	1989	6-5-0	316	212	.545
1986	6-5-0	276	292	.545	1990	6-5-0	295	264	.545

Bob Sutton (1991-1999) 44-55-1 .445

Year			W-L-T	PF	PA	Pct.	Year	AP	Other	W-L-T	PF	PA	Pct.
1991			4-7-0	196	226	.364	1995			5-5-1	325	211	.500
1992			5-6-0	225	251	.455	1996	25	24	10-2-0	350	192	.833
1993			6-5-0	289	243	.545	1997			4-7-0	221	311	.364
1994			4-7-0	215	252	.364							

Member of Conference USA (1998-2003) 7-35-0 .167

	Nat'l		Overall				Conference				Nat'l		Overall				Conference		
Year	AP	Other	W-L-T	PF	PA	Pct.	W-L-T	Pct.	Rank	Year	AP	Other	W-L-T	PF	PA	Pct.	W-L-T	Pct.	Rank
1998			3-8-0	257	325	.273	2-4-0	.333	5	1999			3-8-0	225	317	.273	1-5-0	.167	7

Todd Berry (2000-2003) 5-34-0 .128

Year	AP	Other	W-L-T	PF	PA	Pct.	W-L-T	Pct.	Rank	Year	AP	Other	W-L-T	PF	PA	Pct.	W-L-T	Pct.	Rank
2000			1-10-0	224	372	.091	1-6-0	.143	7	2002			1-11-0	226	491	.083	1-7-0	.125	10
2001			3-8-0	229	365	.273	2-5-0	.286	8	2003*			0-6-0	85	223	.000	0-4-0	.000	11

John Mumford (2003*) 0-7-0 .000

Year	AP	Other	W-L-T	PF	PA	Pct.	W-L-T	Pct.	Rank
2003*			0-7-0	121	253	.000	0-4-0	.000	

*Berry coached the first six games of the 2003 season, and Mumford coached the last seven.

Won-loss record by decades:

1890-99	35-22-5	.605	1930-39	71-22-5	.750	1970-79	36-68-3	.387
1900-09	53-23-10	.674	1940-49	68-17-7	.777	1980-89	55-55-3	.500
1910-19	62-14-2	.808	1950-59	58-27-5	.672	1990-99	50-60-1	.455
1920-29	69-19-7	.763	1960-69	60-37-3	.615	2000-03	5-42-0	.106

Historic record: 622-406-51 .600

Post-season won-loss record: 2-2-0 .500

1984: Cherry Bowl, Army 10, Michigan State 6   1988: John Hancock Bowl, Alabama 29, Army 28
1985: Peach Bowl, Army 31, Illinois 29   1996: Independence Bowl, Auburn 32, Army 29

College Football Hall of Fame:
Henry Williams, coach, 1891; Paul Bunker, halfback/tackle, 1899-1902; Charlie Daly, quarterback, 1900-02; Alex Weyand, tackle, 1911-15; Elmer Oliphant, halfback, 1914-17; John McEwan, center, 1913-16; Edgar Garbisch, center/guard, 1917-21; Harry Wilson, halfback, 1921-24; Bud Sprague, tackle, 1922-25; Biff Jones, coach, 1926-29; Chris Cagle, halfback, 1926-29; Harvey Jablonski, guard, 1927-30; Earl Blaik, coach, 1941-58; Robin Olds, tackle, 1941-42; Frank Merritt, tackle, 1942-43; Doug Kenna, quarterback, 1942-44; Barney Poole, end, 1942-45; John Green, guard, 1943-45; Glenn Davis, halfback, 1943-46; Doc Blanchard, fullback, 1944-46; Joe Steffy, guard, 1944-45; Arnold Galiffa, quarterback, 1946-49; Bob Anderson, running back, 1957-59; Don Hollender, end/quarterback, 1953-55; Pete Dawkins, halfback, 1956-58; Bill Carpenter, end, 1957-59; Jim Young, coach, 1983-90.

Awards: Heisman Trophy: 1945, Doc Blanchard; 1946, Glenn Davis; 1958, Pete Dawkins; Maxwell Award: 1944, Glenn Davis; 1945, Doc Blanchard; 1958, Pete Dawkins; Outland Trophy: 1947, Joe Steffy.

UNITED STATES NAVAL ACADEMY, Annapolis, Maryland; nickname "Navy", "Middies"; colors navy blue and gold; Navy-Marine Corps Memorial Stadium (35,000); independent. Navy has been independent over its entire football history.

Early years (1879-1910)

Year	Coach	W-L-T	PF	PA	Pct.	Year	Coach	W-L-T	PF	PA	Pct.
1879	none	0-0-1	0	0	.500	1896	Johnny Poe	5-3-0	180	53	.625
1880-1881	no team					1897	Bill Armstrong	8-1-0	147	34	.889
1882	Vauix Carter	1-0-0	8	0	1.000	1898	Bill Armstrong	7-1-0	130	56	.875
1883	none	0-1-0	0	2	.000	1899	Bill Armstrong	5-3-0	94	27	.625
1884	none	1-0-0	9	6	1.000	1900	Garrett Cochran	6-3-0	106	51	.667
1885	none	1-2-0	54	32	.333	1901	Doc Hillebrand	6-4-1	113	81	.591
1886	none	3-3-0	33	64	.500	1902	Doc Hillebrand	2-7-1	35	99	.250
1887	none	3-1-0	41	22	.750	1903	Burr Chamberlain	4-7-1	77	130	.375
1888	none	1-4-0	35	73	.200	1904	Paul Dashiell	7-2-1	149	38	.750
1889	none	4-1-1	112	42	.750	1905	Paul Dashiell	10-1-1	243	23	.875
1890	none	5-1-1	205	40	.786	1906	Paul Dashiell	8-2-2	149	14	.750
1891	Edgar Poe	5-2-0	121	62	.714	1907	Joe Reeves	9-2-1	218	38	.792
1892	Ben Crosby	5-2-0	146	64	.714	1908	Frank Berrien	9-2-1	118	34	.792
1893	Josh Hartwell	5-3-0	122	78	.625	1909	Frank Berrien	4-3-1	99	42	.562
1894	Bill Wurtenburg	4-1-2	72	30	.714	1910	Frank Berrien	8-0-1	99	0	.944
1895	Matt McClung	5-2-0	153	16	.714						

Year	AP	Other	W-L-T	PF	PA	Pct.	Year	AP	Other	W-L-T	PF	PA	Pct.
							Doug Howard (1911-1914) 25—7-4 .750						
1911			6-0-3	116	11	.833	1913			7-1-1	304	29	.833
1912			6-3-0	125	61	.667	1914			6-3-0	174	83	.667
							Jonas Ingram (1915-1916) 9-8-2 .526						
1915			3-5-1	99	118	.389	1916			6-3-1	199	76	.650
							Gil Dobie (1917-1919) 17-3-0 .850						
1917			7-1-0	443	23	.875	1919			6-1-0	283	18	.857
1918			4-1-0	283	20	.800							
							Bob Folwell (1920-1924) 24-12-3 .654						
1920			6-2-0	164	43	.750	1923			5-1-3	168	62	.722
1921			6-1-0	147	13	.857	1924			2-6-0	91	79	.250
1922			5-2-0	185	37	.714							
							Jack Owsley (1925) 5-2-1 .688						
1925			5-2-1	134	81	.688							
							Bill Ingram (1926-1930) 32-13-4 .694						
1926		2	9-0-1	236	88	.950	1929			6-2-2	233	59	.700
1927			6-3-0	192	84	.667	1930			6-5-0	148	117	.545
1928			5-3-1	121	21	.611							
							Rip Miller (1931-1933) 12-15-2 .448						
1931			5-5-1	78	95	.500	1933			5-4-0	90	86	.556
1932			2-6-1	67	80	.278							
							Tom Hamilton (1934-1936, 1946-1947) 21-23-1 .478						
1934		3	8-1-0	138	70	.889	1936	18		6-3-0	115	74	.667
1935			5-4-0	136	86	.556							
							Hank Hardwick (1937-1938) 8-7-3 .528						
1937			4-4-1	150	74	.500	1938			4-3-2	126	60	.556
							Swede Larson (1939-1941) 16-8-3 .648						
1939			3-5-1	88	107	.389	1941	10		7-1-1	192	34	.833
1940			6-2-1	106	46	.722							
							Billick Wheichel (1942-1943) 13-5-0 .722						
1942			5-4-0	82	58	.556	1943	4		8-1-0	237	80	.889
							Oscar Hagberg (1944-1945) 13-4-1 .750						
1944	4		6-3-0	236	88	.667	1945	3		7-1-1	220	65	.833
							Tom Hamilton (1946-1947)						
1946			1-8-0	105	186	.111	1947			1-7-1	86	165	.167
							George Sauer (1948-1949) 3-13-2 .222						
1948			0-8-1	77	227	.056	1949			3-5-1	150	238	.389
							Eddie Erdelatz (1950-1958) 50-26-8 .643						
1950			3-6-0	122	176	.333	1955	18	20	6-2-1	188	56	.722
1951			2-6-1	132	155	.277	1956	16	19	6-1-2	207	76	.778
1952		17	6-2-1	147	82	.722	1957	5	6	9-1-1	281	71	.864
1953			4-3-2	186	99	.556	1958			6-3-0	212	134	.667
1954	5	5	8-2-0	304	73	.800							

Wayne Hardin (1959-1964) 38-22-2 .629

Year			W-L-T	PF	PA	Pct	Year			W-L-T	PF	PA	Pct
1959			5-4-1	199	166	.550	1962			5-5-0	184	174	.500
1960	4	6	9-2-0	262	103	.818	1963	2	2	9-2-0	320	165	.818
1961			7-3-0	201	136	.700	1964			3-6-1	140	185	.350

Bill Elias (1965-1968) 15-22-3 .413

Year	W-L-T	PF	PA	Pct	Year	W-L-T	PF	PA	Pct
1965	4-4-2	128	129	.500	1967	5-4-1	205	253	.550
1966	4-6-0	147	152	.400	1968	2-8-0	136	303	.200

Rick Forzano (1969-1972) 10-33-0 .233

Year	W-L-T	PF	PA	Pct	Year	W-L-T	PF	PA	Pct
1969	1-9-0	98	307	.100	1971	3-8-0	146	321	.273
1970	2-9-0	131	327	.182	1972	4-7-0	191	232	.364

George Welsh (1973-1981) 55-46-1

Year		W-L-T	PF	PA	Pct	Year		W-L-T	PF	PA	Pct
1973		4-7-0	131	237	.364	1978	17	9-3-0	260	136	.750
1974		4-7-0	122	229	.364	1979		7-4-0	180	154	.636
1975		7-4-0	227	125	.636	1980		8-4-0	226	146	.667
1976		4-7-0	187	257	.364	1981		7-4-1	244	183	.625
1977		5-6-0	229	230	.455						

Gary Tranquill (1982-1986) 20-34-1 .373

Year	W-L-T	PF	PA	Pct	Year	W-L-T	PF	PA	Pct
1982	6-5-0	220	196	.545	1985	4-7-0	243	239	.364
1983	3-8-0	202	272	.273	1986	3-8-0	238	306	.273
1984	4-6-1	240	254	.409					

Elliot Uzelac (1987-1989) 8-25-0 .242

Year	W-L-T	PF	PA	Pct	Year	W-L-T	PF	PA	Pct
1987	2-9-0	160	317	.182	1989	3-8-0	145	272	.273
1988	3-8-0	221	274	.273					

George Chaump (1990-1994) 14-41-0 .255

Year	W-L-T	PF	PA	Pct	Year	W-L-T	PF	PA	Pct
1990	5-6-0	209	294	.455	1993	4-7-0	203	307	.364
1991	1-10-0	160	321	.091	1994	3-8-0	188	399	.273
1992	1-10-0	131	338	.091					

Charlie Weatherbie (1995-2001) 30-48-0 .385

Year	W-L-T	PF	PA	Pct	Year	W-L-T	PF	PA	Pct
1995	5-6-0	222	189	.455	1999	5-7-0	328	332	.417
1996	9-3-0	392	309	.750	2000	1-10-0	182	389	.091
1997	7-4-0	398	209	.636	2001	0-10-0	183	344	.000
1998	3-8-0	273	361	.273					

Paul Johnson (2002-2003) 10-14-0 .417

Year	W-L-T	PF	PA	Pct	Year	W-L-T	PF	PA	Pct
2002	2-10-0	290	436	.167	2003	8-4-0	379	262	.667

Won-loss record by decades:

Decade	Record	Pct	Decade	Record	Pct	Decade	Record	Pct
1879-89	14-12-2	.536	1920-29	55-22-8	.694	1960-69	49-49-4	.500
1890-99	54-19-3	.730	1930-39	48-40-6	.574	1970-79	49-62-0	.441
1900-09	65-33-10	.642	1940-49	44-40-6	.522	1980-89	43-67-2	.393
1910-19	59-18-7	.744	1950-59	55-30-9	.633	1990-99	43-69-0	.384
						2000-03	11-34-0	.244

Historic record: 589-495-57 .541

Post-season won-loss record: 4-5-1 .450

1924: Rose Bowl, Navy 14, Washington 14	1978: Holiday Bowl, Navy 23, BYU 16
1955: Sugar Bowl, Navy 21, Mississippi 0	1980: Garden State Bowl, Houston 35, Navy 0
1958: Cotton Bowl, Navy 20, Rice 7	1981: Liberty Bowl, Ohio State 31, Navy 28
1961: Orange Bowl, Missouri 21, Navy 14	1996: Aloha Bowl, Navy 42, California 38
1964: Cotton Bowl, Texas 28, Navy 6	2003: Houston Bowl, Texas Tech 38, Navy 14

College Football Hall of Fame:
Jonas Ingram, fullback, 1904-06; Jack Dalton, halfback, 1908-11; John Brown, guard/tackle, 1910-13; Gil Dobie, coach, 1917-19; Tom Hamilton, halfback, 1924-26; Frank Wickhorst, tackle, 1924-26; Bill Ingram, coach, 1926-30; Slade Cutter, tackle, 1932-34; Buzz Borries, halfback, 1932-34; Don Whitmire, tackle, 1941-42; George Brown, guard, 1945-47; Dick Duden, end, 1943-45; Clyde Scott, halfback, 1944-48; Skip Minisi, halfback, 1944-47; Dick Scott, center, 1945-47; Steve Eisenhauer, guard/tackle, 1951-53; Ron Beagle, end, 1953-55; Bob Reifsnyder, tackle, 1956-58; Joe Bellino, halfback, 1958-60; Roger Staubach, quarterback, 1962-64; George Welch, coach, 1973-81; Napoleon McCallum, back, 1983-85.

Awards: Heisman Trophy: 1960, Joe Bellino, 1963, Roger Staubach; Maxwell Award: 1954, Ron Beale, 1957, Bob Reifsnyder, 1960, Joe Bellino, 1963, Roger Staubach.

UTAH STATE UNIVERSITY, Logan, Utah; nickname "Aggies"; colors blue and white; Romney Stadium (30,257); Sun Belt Conference. Utah State was an independent from 1892 through 1937. In 1938, Utah State became one of the founding members of the Mountain States ("Skyline") Conference. The Skyline Conference disbanded after the 1961 season, and Utah State reverted to independent status from 1962 through 1977. In 1978, Utah State joined the Big West Conference, and remained in that conference until it also disbanded, after the 2000 season. Utah State reverted to independent status in 2001 and 2002 and then joined the Sun Belt Conference for the 2003 season.

Early years as an independent (1892-1937)

Year	W-L-T	PF	PA	Pct.	Year	W-L-T	PF	PA	Pct.
				No coach (1892)					
1892	1-0-0	12	0	1.000					
				No team (1893-1895)					
				Professor Major (1896) 0-1-0 .000					
1896	0-1-0	0	6	.000					
				No team (1897)					
				Lieutenant Dunning (1898) 0-1-0 .000					
1898	0-1-0	5	12	.000					
				Willard Langton (1899-1900) 1-1-0 .500					
1899	1-0-0	10	6	1.000	1900	0-1-0	0	21	.000
				Dick Richards (1901) 3-2-1 .583					
1901	3-2-1	41	40	.583					
				George Campbell (1902-1906) 10-14-1 .420					
1902	0-4-0	10	73	.000	1905	2-2-1	31	33	.500
1903	3-0-0	78	0	1.000	1906	3-1-0	38	51	.750
1904	2-7-0	26	229	.222					
				Fred Walker (1907-1908) 11-2-0 .846					
1907	7-0-0	207	25	1.000	1908	4-2-0	142	39	.667
				Clayton Teetzel (1909-1915) 24-18-2 .568					
1909	2-2-1	34	55	.500	1913	3-3-0	97	69	.500
1910	5-2-0	104	33	.714	1914	2-5-0	56	208	.286
1911	5-0-0	164	0	1.000	1915	3-4-0	56	99	.529
1912	4-2-1	154	40	.643					
				Jack Watson (1916-1917) 8-5-2 .600					
1916	1-5-1	69	1778	.214	1917	7-0-1	267	26	.938
				No team (1918)					
				E.L. Romney (1919-1948) 128-91-16 .579					
1919	5-2-0	234	44	.714	1929	3-4-0	50	60	.429
1920	4-2-1	84	48	.643	1930	3-5-1	73	205	.389
1921	7-1-0	151	82	.875	1931	6-2-0	147	72	.750
1922	5-4-0	132	83	.556	1932	4-4-0	123	105	.500
1923	5-2-0	147	59	.714	1933	4-4-0	115	61	.500
1924	4-2-1	127	52	.643	1934	5-1-1	131	42	.786
1925	6-1-0	111	39	.857	1935	5-2-1	165	73	.688
1926	5-1-2	93	43	.750	1936	7-0-1	99	13	.938
1927	3-4-1	129	53	.438	1937	2-4-2	47	152	.375
1928	5-3-1	182	87	.611					

Member of the Mountain States ("Skyline") Conference (1938-1961) 56-68-6 .454

	Nat'l		Overall			Conference				Nat'l		Overall			Conference		
Year	AP	Other	W-L-T	PF	PA	Pct	W-L-T	Pct. Rank	Year	AP	Other	W-L-T	PF	PA	Pct.	W-L-T	Pct. Rank
1938			4-4-0	85	87	.500	3-3-0	.500 5	1944			3-3-0	88	109	.500	no conference	
1939			3-4-1	76	81	.438	2-3-1	.417 5	1945			4-3-0	173	92	.571		
1940			2-5-1	48	104	.312	2-4-0	.333 5	1946			7-2-1	220	75	.750	4-1-1	.750 1
1941			0-8-0	46	153	.000	0-6-0	.000 7	1947			6-5-0	228	203	.545	3-3-0	.500 3
1942			6-3-1	202	137	.650	2-3-1	.417 4	1948			5-6-0	196	238	.455	2-3-0	.400 4
1943			no team														
						George Melinkovich (1949-1950) 5-16-0 .238											
1949			3-7-0	105	211	.300	1-3-0	.250 5	1950			2-9-0	107	374	.182	0-5-0	.000 6
						John Roning (1951-1954) 18-21-2 .463											
1951			3-5-1	161	183	.389	2-4-1	.357 6	1953			8-3-0	207	139	.727	5-2-0	.714 2
1952			3-7-1	121	209	.318	3-4-0	.429 5	1954			4-6-0	158	187	.400	4-3-0	.571 3
						Ev Faunce (1955-1958) 15-24-1 .388											
1955			4-6-0	179	173	.400	3-4-0	.429 5	1957			2-7-1	153	255	.250	1-5-1	.214 8
1956			6-4-0	221	199	.600	4-3-0	.571 3	1958			3-7-0	123	188	.300	1-5-0	.143 6
						John Ralston (1959-1962) 31-11-1 .733											
1959			5-6-0	181	185	.455	2-5-0	.286 5	1961	10	10	9-1-1	396	102	.864	5-0-1	.917 1
1960			9-2-0	274	85	.818	6-1-0	.857 1									

Utah State reverts to independent status (1962-1977)

Year	W-L-T	PF	PA	Pct.
1962	8-2-0	273	139	.800

Coach / Year	W-L-T	PF	PA	Pct	Conf	Pct	Rk
Tony Knap (1963-1966) 25-14-1 .638							
1963	8-2-0	317	99	.800			
1964	5-4-1	294	136	.550			
1965	8-2-0	271	136	.800			
1966	4-6-0	181	163	.400			
Chuck Mills (1967-1972) 38-23-1 .621							
1967	7-2-1	205	143	.750			
1968	7-3-0	247	142	.700			
1969	3-7-0	134	250	.300			
1970	5-5-0	217	225	.500			
1971	8-3-0	339	195	.727			
1972 (19)	8-3-0	329	230	.727			
Phil Krueger (1973-1975) 21-12-0 .636							
1973	7-4-0	230	202	.636			
1974	8-3-0	189	199	.727			
1975	6-5-0	193	240	.545			
Bruce Snyder (1976-1982) 37-38-2 .494							
1976	3-8-0	170	263	.273			
1977	4-7-0	117	249	.364			
Member of the Big West Conference (1978-2000) 85-51-1 .624							
1978	7-4-0	269	214	.636	4-1-0	.800	1
1979	7-3-1	347	270	.682	5-0-0	1.000	1
1980	6-5-0	290	255	.545	4-1-0	.800	2
1981	5-5-1	204	210	.500	4-1-0	.800	2
1982	5-6-0	191	262	.455	2-3-0	.400	4
Chris Pella (1983-1985) 9-24-0 .273							
1983	5-6-0	193	214	.455	4-2-0	.667	2
1984	1-10-0	196	390	.091	1-6-0	.143	7
1985	3-8-0	177	319	.273	3-4-0	.429	5
Chuck Shelton (1986-1991) 26-39-1 .402							
1986	3-8-0	134	243	.273	3-4-0	.429	4
1987	5-6-0	205	306	.455	4-3-0	.571	2
1988	4-7-0	213	262	.364	4-3-0	.571	3
1989	4-7-0	191	355	.364	4-3-0	.571	4
1990	5-5-1	287	310	.500	5-1-1	.786	2
1991	5-6-0	219	265	.455	5-2-0	.714	3
Charles Weatherbie (1992-1994) 15-19-0 .441							
1992	5-6-0	300	320	.455	4-2-0	.667	2
1993	7-5-0	363	354	.583	5-1-0	.833	1
1994	3-8-0	209	313	.273	2-4-0	.333	7
John Smith (1995-1997) 16-18-0 .471							
1995	4-7-0	293	297	.364	4-2-0	.667	2
1996	6-5-0	330	339	.545	4-1-0	.800	1
1997	6-6-0	389	296	.500	4-1-0	.800	1
Dave Arsanian (1998-1999) 7-15-0 .318							
1998	3-8-0	237	309	.273	2-3-0	.400	4
1999	4-7-0	234	301	.364	3-3-0	.500	4
Mike Dennehy (2000-2003) 16-29-0 .356							
2000	5-6-0	293	356	.455	4-1-0	.800	2
Utah State reverts to independent status (2001-2002)							
2001	4-7-0	316	421	.364			
2002	4-7-0	305	432	.364			
Member of the Sun Belt Conference (2003) 3-4-0 .429							
2003	3-9-0	264	315	.250	3-4-0	.429	4

Won-loss records by decades:

1892-99	2- 2-0	.500		1930-39	43-30-7	.581	1970-79	63-45-1	.583
1900-09	26-21-3	.550		1940-49	36-42-3	.463	1980-89	41-68-1	.377
1910-19	35-23-3	.598		1950-59	40-60-3	.403	1990-99	48-63-1	.433
1920-29	47-24-6	.649		1960-69	68-31-3	.681	2000-03	16-29-0	.356

Historic record: 465-438-31 .514

Post-season won-loss record: 1-5-0 .167
1946: Raisin Bowl, San Jose State 20, Utah State 0
1947: Grape Bowl, Pacific 35, Utah State 21
1960: Sun Bowl, New Mexico State 20, Utah State 13
1961: Gotham Bowl, Baylor 24, Utah State 9
1993: Las Vegas Bowl, Utah State 42, Ball State 33
1997: Humanitarian Bowl, Cincinnati 35, Utah State 19

College Football Hall of Fame:
Dick Romney, coach, 1919-48; Merlin Olsen, tackle, 1959-61; John Ralston, coach, 1959-62.

Awards: Outland Trophy: 1961, Merlin Olsen

UNIVERSITY OF UTAH, Salt Lake City, Utah; nickname "Utes"; colors crimson and white; Rice-Eccles Stadium (45,634); Mountain West Conference. Utah was an independent from 1892 to 1909, following which the Utes joined the Rocky Mountain Conference. In 1938, Utah became a founding member of the Big Seven Conference later known as the Mountain States Conference or the Skyline Conference. Both the Border Conference and the Skyline Conference disbanded after the 1961 season, with the leading teams from both conferences (including Utah) joining together to organize the Western Athletic Conference. Utah played in the WAC until the 1999 season when it joined seven other members of the WAC in forming the Mountain West Conference. (Conference rank not available for Rocky Mountain Conference period.)

Early years (1892-1909)

Year	Coach	W-L-T	PF	PA	Pct.	Year	Coach	W-L-T	PF	PA	Pct.
1892	Unknown	0-1-0	0	12	.000	1901	Harvey Holmes	3-1-0	47	6	.750
1893	no team					1902	Harvey Holmes	5-2-1	139	51	.688
1894	Unknown	1-2-0	18	40	.333	1903	Harvey Holmes	3-4-0	125	65	.429
1895	Unknown	0-1-0	0	20	.000	1904	Joseph Maddock	7-1-0	301	38	.875
1896	C.B. Ferris	3-2-0	30	20	.600	1905	Joseph Maddock	6-2-0	260	74	.750
1897	Mr. Cummings	1-5-0	12	66	.167	1906	Joseph Maddock	4-1-0	111	6	.800
1898	Mr. Wilson	2-1-0	5	6	.667	1907	Joseph Maddock	4-2-0	78	59	.667
1899	Unknown	2-1-0	23	24	.667	1908	Joseph Maddock	3-2-1	126	49	.583
1900	Harvey Holmes	2-2-0	57	34	.500	1909	Joseph Maddock	4-1-0	125	19	.800

Member of the Rocky Mountain Conference (1910-1937) 102-34-7 .738

Year	Nat'l AP Other	Overall W-L-T	PF	PA	Pct.	Conference W-L-T	Pct.	Rank	Year	Nat'l AP Other	Overall W-L-T	PF	PA	Pct.	Conference W-L-T	Pct.	Rank

Fred Bennion (1910-1913) 16-8-3 .648

| 1910 | | 4-2-0 | 70 | 44 | .667 | 2-2-0 | .500 | | 1912 | | 5-1-1 | 153 | 16 | .786 | 4-1-0 | .800 | |
| 1911 | | 5-1-1 | 200 | 15 | .786 | 3-1-1 | .700 | | 1913 | | 2-4-1 | 129 | 103 | .357 | 1-2-0 | .333 | |

Nelson Norgren (1914-1917) 13-11-0 .542

| 1914 | | 3-3-0 | 96 | 108 | .500 | 2-3-0 | .400 | | 1916 | | 3-2-0 | 113 | 45 | .600 | 2-2-0 | .500 | |
| 1915 | | 5-2-0 | 162 | 71 | .714 | 4-2-0 | .667 | | 1917 | | 2-4-0 | 48 | 116 | .333 | 2-3-0 | .400 | |

No team (1918)

Tom Fitzpatrick (1919-1924) 23-17-3 .570

1919		5-2-0	151	54	.714	4-1-0	.800		1922		7-1-0	153	41	.875	5-0-0	1.000	
1920		1-5-1	19	116	.214	1-2-1	.375		1923		4-3-0	241	48	.571	2-3-0	.400	
1921		3-2-1	55	55	.583	2-1-1	.625		1924		3-4-1	116	95	.438	2-2-1	.500	

Ike Armstrong (1925-1949) 141-55-15 .702

1925		6-2-0	110	51	.750	5-1-0	.833		1932		6-1-1	162	47	.812	6-0-0	1.000	
1926		7-0-0	164	23	1.000	5-0-0	1.000		1933		5-3-0	129	78	.625	5-1-0	.833	
1927		3-3-1	93	60	.500	4-0-1	.900		1934		5-3-0	150	42	.625	4-2-0	.667	
1928		5-0-2	117	41	.857	4-0-1	.900		1935		4-3-1	166	69	.562	4-1-1	.750	
1929		7-0-0	219	23	1.000	6-0-0	1.000		1936		6-3-0	142	75	.667	5-2-0	.714	
1930		8-0-0	340	20	1.000	7-0-0	1.000		1937		5-3-0	133	52	.625	5-2-0	.714	
1931		7-2-0	301	31	.778	6-0-0	1.000										

Member of the Skyline Conference (1938-1961) 85-26-7 .750

1938		7-1-2	187	36	.800	4-0-2	.833	1	1944		5-2-1	161	86	.688	1-2-1	*	
1939		6-1-2	261	74	.778	4-1-1	.750	2	1945		4-4-0	146	165	.500	3-2-0	*	
1940		7-2-0	169	87	.778	5-1-0	.833	1	1946		8-3-0	257	104	.727	4-2-0	.667	3
1941		6-0-2	209	65	.875	4-0-2	.833	1	1947		8-1-1	207	74	.850	6-0-0	1.000	1
1942		6-3-0	155	84	.667	5-1-0	.833	1	1948		8-1-1	221	96	.850	5-0-0	1.000	1
1943		0-7-0	38	297	.000	0-2-0	*		1949		2-7-1	141	166	.250	2-3-0	.400	4

*Conference inactive from 1943 through 1945.

Jack Curtice (1950-1957) 45-32-4 .580

1950		3-4-3	240	254	.450	1-2-2	.400	4	1954		4-7-0	172	212	.364	3-3-0	.500	4
1951		7-4-0	236	247	.636	4-1-0	.800	1	1955		6-3-0	182	136	.667	4-1-0	.800	2
1952		6-3-1	188	128	.650	5-0-0	1.000	1	1956		5-5-0	227	177	.500	5-1-0	.833	2
1953		8-2-0	264	150	.800	5-0-0	1.000	1	1957		6-4-0	262	136	.600	5-1-0	.833	1

Ray Nagel (1958-1965) 42-39-1 .518

| 1958 | | 4-7-0 | 161 | 187 | .364 | 3-3-0 | .500 | 5 | 1960 | | 7-3-0 | 194 | 90 | .700 | 5-1-0 | .833 | 3 |
| 1959 | | 5-5-0 | 224 | 195 | .500 | 3-2-0 | .600 | 4 | 1961 | | 6-4-0 | 176 | 134 | .600 | 3-3-0 | .500 | 3 |

Member of the Western Athletic Conference (1962-1998) 125-118-4 .514

| 1962 | | 4-5-1 | 169 | 196 | .450 | 1-2-1 | .375 | 5 | 1964 | 14 | 9-2-0 | 234 | 68 | .818 | 3-1-0 | .750 | 1 |
| 1963 | | 4-6-0 | 204 | 187 | .400 | 2-2-0 | .500 | 2 | 1965 | | 3-7-0 | 177 | 164 | .300 | 1-3-0 | .250 | 5 |

Mike Giddings (1966-1967) 9-12-0 .429

| 1966 | | 5-5-0 | 176 | 203 | .500 | 3-2-0 | .600 | 2 | 1967 | | 4-7-0 | 204 | 252 | .364 | 2-3-0 | .400 | 4 |

Bill Meek (1968-1973) 33-31-0 .516

1968		3-7-0	162	234	.300	2-3-0	.400	5	1971		3-8-0	244	315	.273	3-4-0	.429	4
1969		8-2-0	231	107	.800	5-1-0	.833	2	1972		6-5-0	354	346	.545	5-2-0	.714	2
1970		6-4-0	208	176	.600	4-2-0	.667	3	1973		7-5-0	385	344	.583	4-2-0	.667	3

Tom Lovat (1974-1976) 5-28-0 .152

| 1974 | | 1-10-0 | 115 | 341 | .091 | 1-5-0 | .167 | 7 | 1976 | | 3-8-0 | 245 | 361 | .273 | 3-3-0 | .500 | 4 |
| 1975 | | 1-10-0 | 132 | 332 | .091 | 1-4-0 | .200 | 6 | | | | | | | | | |

Wayne Howard (1977-1981) 30-24-2 .554

Year	W-L-T	PF	PA	Pct	Conf	Pct	Pl		Year	W-L-T	PF	PA	Pct	Conf	Pct	Pl
1977	3-8-0	212	379	.273	2-5-0	.286	6		1980	5-5-1	259	315	.500	2-3-1	.417	7
1978	8-3-0	291	182	.727	4-2-0	.667	2		1981	8-2-1	321	205	.773	5-1-1	.786	3
1979	6-6-0	267	296	.500	5-2-0	.714	2									

Chuck Stobart (1982-1984) 16-17-1 .485

Year	W-L-T	PF	PA	Pct	Conf	Pct	Pl		Year	W-L-T	PF	PA	Pct	Conf	Pct	Pl
1982	5-6-0	247	188	.455	2-4-0	.333	6		1984	6-5-1	347	253	.542	4-3-1	.562	4
1983	5-6-0	296	289	.455	4-4-0	.500	5									

Jim Fassel (1985-1989) 25-33-0 .431

Year	W-L-T	PF	PA	Pct	Conf	Pct	Pl		Year	W-L-T	PF	PA	Pct	Conf	Pct	Pl
1985	8-4-0	405	339	.667	5-3-0	.625	3		1988	6-5-0	399	357	.545	4-4-0	.500	5
1986	2-9-0	278	444	.182	1-7-0	.125	9		1989	4-8-0	365	524	.333	2-6-0	.250	7
1987	5-7-0	321	362	.417	2-6-0	.250	7									

Ron McBride (1990-2001) 88-63-0 .591

Year			W-L-T	PF	PA	Pct	Conf	Pct	Pl		Year	W-L-T	PF	PA	Pct	Conf	Pct	Pl
1990			4-7-0	214	342	.364	2-6-0	.250	7		1995	7-4-0	296	230	.636	6-2-0	.750	1
1991			7-5-0	276	277	.583	4-4-0	.500	4		1996	8-4-0	313	309	.667	6-2-0	.750	3
1992			6-6-0	320	289	.500	4-4-0	.500	5		1997	6-5-0	253	200	.545	5-3-0	.625	4
1993			7-6-0	390	396	.538	5-3-0	.625	4		1998	7-4-0	339	229	.636	5-3-0	.625	5
1994	10	8	10-2-0	426	210	.833	6-2-0	.750	2									

Member of the Mountain West Conference (1999-2003) 21-14-0 .600

Year	W-L-T	PF	PA	Pct	Conf	Pct	Pl		Year	W-L-T	PF	PA	Pct	Conf	Pct	Pl
1999	9-3-0	380	210	.750	5-2-0	.714	1		2001	8-4-0	329	210	.667	4-3-0	.571	3
2000	4-7-0	238	207	.364	3-4-0	.429	5		2002	5-6-0	249	226	.455	3-4-0	.429	5

Urban Meyer (2003) 10-2-0 .833

Year			W-L-T	PF	PA	Pct	Conf	Pct	Pl
2003	21	21	10-2-0	344	229	.833	6-1-0	.857	1

Won-loss record by decades:

1892-99	9-13-0	.409	1930-39	59-20-6	.729	1970-79	44-67-0	.396
1900-09	40-18-2	.683	1940-49	54-30-5	.635	1980-89	54-57-3	.487
1910-19	34-21-3	.612	1950-59	54-44-5	.549	1990-99	71-46-0	.607
1920-29	46-20-6	.681	1960-69	53-48-1	.525	2000-03	27-19-0	.587

Historic record: 545-403-31 573

Post-season won-loss record: 6-4-0 .600

1939: Sun Bowl, Utah 26, New Mexico 0
1946: Pineapple Bowl, Hawaii 19, Utah 16
1964: Liberty Bowl, Utah 32, West Virginia 6
1992: Copper Bowl, Washington State 31, Utah 28
1993: Freedom Bowl, USC 28, Utah 21

1994: Freedom Bowl, Utah 16, Arizona 13
1996: Copper Bowl, Wisconsin 38, Utah 10
1999: Las Vegas Bowl, Utah 17, Fresno State 16
2001: Las Vegas Bowl, Utah 10, USC 6
2003: Liberty Bowl, Utah 17, Southern Miss 0

College Football Hall of Fame: Ike Armstrong, coach, 1925-1949.

VANDERBILT UNIVERSITY, Nashville, Tennessee; nickname "Commodores"; colors black and gold; Vanderbilt Stadium (41,600); Southeastern Conference. Vanderbilt began play in 1890 and was an independent until 1922 when it was one of the original members of the newly formed Southern Conference. Vanderbilt played in that conference through the 1932 season, after which it joined twelve other members of the SC to form a new conference, the Southeastern Conference, in which the Commodores still play.

Early years (1890-1903)

Year	Coach	W-L-T	PF	PA	Pct.	Year	Coach	W-L-T	PF	PA	Pct.
1890	Elliott Jones	1-0-0	40	0	1.000	1897	R.G. Acton	6-0-1	141	0	.929
1891	Elliott Jones	3-1-0	58	28	.750	1898	R. G.Acton	1-5-0	9	61	.167
1892	Elliott Jones	4-4-0	114	102	.500	1899	J. L. Crane	7-2-0	109	42	.778
1893	W. J. Keller	6-1-0	181	50	.857	1900	J. L. Crane	4-4-1	90	92	.500
1894	Henry Thornton	7-1-0	246	20	.875	1901	W. H. Watkins	6-1-1	181	12	.812
1895	C. L. Upton	5-3-1	67	50	.611	1902	W. H. Watkins	8-1-0	214	60	.889
1896	R.G. Acton	3-2-2	58	76	.571	1903	J. H. Henry	6-1-1	192	16	.812

Dan McGugin (1904-1917, 1919-1934) 197-55-19 .762

Year	W-L-T	PF	PA	Pct.	Year	W-L-T	PF	PA	Pct.
1904	9-0-0	474	4	1.000	1911	8-1-0	259	9	.889
1905	7-1-0	372	22	.875	1912	8-1-1	391	19	.850
1906	8-1-0	278	16	.889	1913	5-3-0	218	100	.625
1907	5-1-1	242	36	.786	1914	2-6-0	147	95	.250
1908	7-2-1	207	61	.750	1915	9-1-0	513	38	.900
1909	7-3-0	210	32	.700	1916	7-1-1	328	25	.833
1910	8-0-1	166	8	.944	1917	5-3-0	142	170	.625

Ray Morrison (1918. 1935-1939) 29-22-2 .566

Year	W-L-T	PF	PA	Pct.
1918	4-2-0	176	31	.667

Dan McGugin (1919-1934)

Year	W-L-T	PF	PA	Pct.	Year	W-L-T	PF	PA	Pct.
1919	5-1-2	110	68	.750	1921	7-0-1	161	21	.938
1920	5-3-1	169	124	.611					

Member of the Southern Conference (1922-1932) 42-17-5 .695

	Nat'l	Overall				Conference			Nat'l	Overall				Conference		
Year	AP Other	W-L-T	PF	PA	Pct	W-L-T	Pct.	Rank	Year	AP Other	W-L-T	PF	PA	Pct.	W-L-T	Pct.	Rank
1922		8-0-1	177	16	.944	3-0-0	1.000	2	1928		8-2-0	152	57	.800	4-2-0	.667	7
1923		5-2-1	207	33	.688	3-0-1	.875	2	1929		7-2-0	187	56	.778	5-1-0	.833	5
1924		6-3-1	240	53	.650	3-3-0	.500	11	1930		8-2-0	225	45	.800	5-2-0	.714	5
1925		6-3-0	158	63	.667	3-3-0	.500	10	1931		5-4-0	192	103	.556	3-4-0	.529	12
1926		8-1-0	241	42	.889	4-1-0	.800	3	1932		6-1-2	128	46	.778	4-1-2	.714	5
1927		8-1-2	295	93	.818	5-0-2	.857	2									

Member of the Southeastern Conference (1933-2003) 107-332-18 .254

	Nat'l	Overall				Conference			Nat'l	Overall				Conference		
1933		4-3-3	126	107	.550	2-2-2	.500	6	1934		6-3-0	105	100	.667	4-3-0	.571	6

Ray Morrison (1935-1939)

1935		7-3-0	179	68	.700	5-1-0	.833	2	1938		6-3-0	86	49	.667	4-3-0	.571	6
1936		3-5-1	115	87	.389	1-3-1	.300	9	1939		2-7-1	96	165	.250	1-6-0	.143	11
1937		7-2-0	121	42	.778	4-2-0	.667	4									

Red Sanders (1940-1942, 1946-1948) 36-22-2 .617

1940		3-6-1	101	98	.350	1-5-1	.214	11	1942		6-4-0	232	113	.600	2-4-0	.333	8
1941		8-2-0	260	89	.800	3-2-0	.600	6									

E. H. Alley (1943) 5-0-0 1.000

1943		5-0-0	155	33	1.000	0-0-0	*										

Doby Bartling (1944-1945) 6-6-1 .500

1944		3-0-1	67	23	.875	0-0-0	*		1945		3-6-0	71	215	.333	2-4-0	.333	9

*Because of disruptions caused by the war, Vanderbilt did not schedule any SEC games in 1943 and 1944.

Red Sanders (1946-1948)

1946		5-4-0	108	43	.556	3-4-0	.429	8	1948	12	8-2-1	328	73	.773	4-2-1	.643	4
1947		6-4-0	182	85	.600	3-3-0	.500	4									

Bill Edwards (1949-1952) 21-19-2 .524

1949		5-5-0	177	183	.500	4-4-0	.500	7	1951		6-5-0	201	195	.545	3-5-0	.375	7
1950		7-4-0	252	216	.636	3-4-0	.429	7	1952		3-5-2	151	199	.400	1-4-1	.250	11

Art Guepe (1953-1962) 39-54-7 .425

1953		3-7-0	131	258	.300	1-5-0	.167	10	1958		5-2-3	131	71	.650	2-1-3	.583	4
1954		2-7-0	134	169	.222	1-5-0	.167	11	1959		5-3-2	138	106	.600	3-2-2	.571	5
1955		8-3-0	240	86	.727	4-3-0	.571	5	1960		3-7-0	74	193	.300	0-7-0	.000	12
1956		5-5-0	147	113	.500	3-3-0	.286	8	1961		2-8-0	95	220	.200	1-6-0	.143	12
1957		5-3-2	113	118	.600	3-3-1	.500	6	1962		1-9-0	62	215	.100	1-6-0	.143	11

Jack Green (1963-1966) 7-29-4 .225

1963		1-7-2	73	146	.200	0-5-2	.143	10	1965		2-7-1	165	241	.250	1-5-0	.167	9
1964		3-6-1	79	122	.350	1-4-1	.250	9	1966		1-9-0	72	237	.100	0-6-0	.000	9

Bill Pace (1967-1972) 22-38-3 .373

Year	Record	PF	PA	Pct	Conf	Conf Pct	#	Year	Record	PF	PA	Pct	Conf	Conf Pct	#
1967	2-7-1	164	241	.250	0-6-0	.000	9	1970	4-7-0	201	213	.364	1-5-0	.167	9
1968	5-4-1	163	147	.550	2-3-1	.417	8	1971	4-6-1	137	208	.409	1-5-0	.167	7
1969	4-6-0	242	264	.400	2-3-0	.400	7	1972	3-8-0	139	243	.273	0-6-0	.000	10

Steve Sloan (1973-1974) 12-9-2 .565

Year	Record	PF	PA	Pct	Conf	Conf Pct	#	Year	Record	PF	PA	Pct	Conf	Conf Pct	#
1973	5-6-0	181	262	.455	1-5-0	.167	10	1974	7-3-2	313	199	.682	2-3-1	.417	7

Fred Pancoast (1975-1978) 13-31-0 .295

Year	Record	PF	PA	Pct	Conf	Conf Pct	#	Year	Record	PF	PA	Pct	Conf	Conf Pct	#
1975	7-4-0	119	200	.636	2-4-0	.333	6	1977	2-9-0	141	276	.182	0-6-0	.000	9
1976	2-9-0	131	282	.182	0-6-0	.000	9	1978	2-9-0	164	418	.182	0-6-0	.000	10

George MacIntyre (1979-1985) 25-52-1 .327

Year	Record	PF	PA	Pct	Conf	Conf Pct	#	Year	Record	PF	PA	Pct	Conf	Conf Pct	#
1979	1-10-0	179	418	.091	0-6-0	.000	9	1983	2-9-0	183	274	.182	0-6-0	.000	9
1980	2-9-0	140	352	.182	0-6-0	.000	9	1984	5-6-0	276	277	.455	2-4-0	.333	7
1981	4-7-0	211	281	.364	1-5-0	.167	10	1985	3-7-1	166	308	.318	1-4-1	.250	7
1982	8-4-0	293	242	.667	4-2-0	.667	3								

Watson Brown (1986-1990) 10-45-0 .182

Year	Record	PF	PA	Pct	Conf	Conf Pct	#	Year	Record	PF	PA	Pct	Conf	Conf Pct	#
1986	1-10-0	193	347	.091	0-6-0	.000	10	1989	1-10-0	162	265	.091	0-7-0	.000	10
1987	4-7-0	286	355	.364	1-5-0	.167	7	1990	1-10-0	227	457	.091	1-6-0	.143	8
1988	3-8-0	202	277	.273	2-5-0	.286	8								

Gerry DiNardo (1991-1994) 19-25-0 .432

Year	Record	PF	PA	Pct	Conf	Conf Pct	#	Year	Record	PF	PA	Pct	Conf	Conf Pct	#
1991	5-6-0	205	267	.455	3-4-0	.429	6	1993	5-6-0	137	290	.455	2-6-0	.250	9
1992	4-7-0	224	277	.364	2-6-0	.250	10	1994	5-6-0	203	277	.455	2-6-0	.250	8

Rod Dowhower (1995-1996) 4-18-0 .182

Year	Record	PF	PA	Pct	Conf	Conf Pct	#	Year	Record	PF	PA	Pct	Conf	Conf Pct	#
1995	2-9-0	122	281	.182	1-7-0	.125	9	1996	2-9-0	122	234	.182	0-8-0	.000	12

Woody Widenhofer (1997-2001) 15-40-0 .273

Year	Record	PF	PA	Pct	Conf	Conf Pct	#	Year	Record	PF	PA	Pct	Conf	Conf Pct	#
1997	3-8-0	138	204	.273	0-8-0	.000	12	2000	3-8-0	193	273	.273	1-7-0	.125	11
1998	2-9-0	142	369	.182	1-7-0	.125	10	2001	2-9-0	226	402	.182	0-8-0	.000	12
1999	5-6-0	252	256	.455	2-6-0	.333	9								

Bobby Johnson (2002-2003) 4-20-0 .167

Year	Record	PF	PA	Pct	Conf	Conf Pct	#	Year	Record	PF	PA	Pct	Conf	Conf Pct	#
2002	2-10-0	221	368	.167	0-8-0	.000	12	2003	2-10-0	235	358	.167	1-7-0	.125	9

Won-loss record by decades:

Decade	Record	Pct		Decade	Record	Pct		Decade	Record	Pct
1890-99	43-19-4	.682		1930-39	54-33-7	.612		1970-79	37-71-3	.377
1900-09	67-15-5	.799		1940-49	52-33-3	.608		1980-89	33-77-1	.302
1910-19	61-19-5	.747		1950-59	49-44-9	.525		1990-99	34-76-0	.309
1920-29	68-17-7	.777		1960-69	24-70-6	.270		2000-03	9-37-0	.196

Historic record: 531-511-50 .509

Post-season won-loss record: 1-1-1 .500

1955: Gator Bowl, Vanderbilt 25, Auburn 13
1974: Peach Bowl, Vanderbilt 6, Texas Tech 6

1982: Hall of Fame Bowl, Air Force 36, Vanderbilt 28

College Football Hall of Fame:
John Tigert, halfback, 1901-03; Dan McGugin, coach, 1904-17, 1919-34; Josh Cody, tackle, 1914-19; Ray Morrison, coach, 1918, 1935-39; Lynn Bomar, end, 1921-24; Bill Spears, quarterback, 1925-27; Carl Hinkle, center, 1935-37; Red Sanders, coach, 1940-42; Bill Edwards, coach, 1949-52.

VIRGINIA TECH, Blacksburg, Virginia; nickname "Hokies"; colors Chicago maroon and burnt orange; Lane Stadium (65,115); Big East Conference. Tech began play in 1892 and soon after joined the South Atlantic Conference. In 1922, Tech became one of the founding members of the Southern Conference and played in that conference through the 1964 season. In 1965, Tech became an independent and played as an independent until 1991 when Tech joined the newly formed Big East Conference. Conference standings are shown only for the Southern Conference and the Big East.

Early years (1892-1920)

Year	Coach	W-L-T	PF	PA	Pct.	Year	Coach	W-L-T	PF	PA	Pct.
1892	E. A. Smyth	1-1-0	14	20	.500	1907	C. R. Williams	7-2-0	157	30	.778
1893	E. A. Smyth	0-2-0	6	40	.000	1908	R. M. Brown	5-4-0	104	41	.556
1894	Joseph Massie	4-1-0	112	10	.800	1909	Branch Bocock	6-1-0	148	27	.857
1895	A. C. Jones	4-2-0	69	76	.667	1910	Branch Bocock	6-2-0	109	19	.750
1896	A. C. Jones	5-2-1	158	50	.688	1911	Charles Reiss	6-1-2	176	52	.778
1897	Charles Firth	5-2-0	149	36	.714	1912	Branch Bocock	5-4-0	202	92	.556
1898	J. L. Ingles	3-2-0	110	51	.600	1913	Branch Bocock	7-1-1	175	59	.833
1899	James Morrison	4-1-0	106	28	.800	1914	Branch Bocock	6-2-1	143	33	.722
1900	Dr. Davis	3-3-1	65	42	.500	1915	Branch Bocock	4-4-0	91	109	.500
1901	A. B. Morrison	6-1-0	115	33	.857	1916	Jack Ingersoll	7-2-0	193	60	.778
1902	R. R. Brown	3-2-1	89	23	.583	1917	Charles Bernier	6-2-1	220	75	.722
1903	C. A. Lueder	5-1-0	108	21	.833	1918	Charles Bernier	7-0-0	152	13	1.000
1904	John O'Connor	5-3-0	121	27	.625	1919	Charles Bernier	5-4-0	186	52	.556
1905	C. P. Miles	9-1-0	305	24	.900	1920	Stanley Sutton	4-6-0	171	111	.400
1906	C. P. Miles	5-2-2	74	15	.667						

B. C. Cubbage (1921-1925) 30-12-6 .688

| 1921 | | 7-3-0 | 191 | 50 | .700 | | | | | | |

Member of the Southern Conference (1922-1964) 107-112-4 .489

	Nat'l	Overall				Conference				Nat'l	Overall				Conference		
Year	AP Other	W-L-T	PF	PA	Pct.	W-L-T	Pct.	Rank	Year	AP Other	W-L-T	PF	PA	Pct.	W-L-T	Pct.	Rank
1922		8-1-1	262	32	.850	3-0-0	1.000	2	1924		4-2-3	103	18	.688	2-2-3	.500	11
1923		6-3-0	116	55	.667	4-2-0	.667	7	1925		5-3-2	39	52	.600	3-3-1	.500	10

A. F. Gustafson (1926-1929) 22-13-1 .625

| 1926 | | 5-3-1 | 134 | 81 | .611 | 3-2-1 | .583 | 7 | 1928 | | 7-2-0 | 198 | 92 | .778 | 4-1-0 | .800 | 4 |
| 1927 | | 5-4-0 | 125 | 48 | .556 | 2-3-0 | .400 | 12 | 1929 | | 5-4-0 | 170 | 128 | .556 | 2-3-0 | .400 | 12 |

O. E. Neale (1930-1931) 8-7-3 .528

| 1930 | | 5-3-1 | 122 | 130 | .611 | 2-3-1 | .417 | 13 | 1931 | | 3-4-2 | 76 | 104 | .444 | 1-4-1 | .250 | 19 |

Henry Redd (1932-1940) 43-37-8 .534

1932		8-1-0	153	28	.889	6-1-0	.857	4	1937		5-5-0	117	116	.500	2-4-0	.333	12
1933		4-3-3	54	86	.550	1-1-3	.500	5	1938		3-5-2	75	86	.400	2-3-2	.400	10
1934		5-5-0	95	113	.500	3-3-0	.500	6	1939		4-5-1	106	84	.450	1-4-1	.250	11
1935		4-3-2	68	47	.556	3-3-1	.500	5	1940		5-5-0	140	145	.500	2-3-0	.400	10
1936		5-5-0	63	100	.500	3-5-0	.375	11									

James Kitts (1941, 1946-1947) 13-13-3 .500

| 1941 | | 6-4-0 | 112 | 120 | .600 | 4-2-0 | .667 | 5 | | | | | | | | | |

H. M. McEver (1942, 1945) 9-8-1 .528

| 1942* | | 7-2-1 | 161 | 114 | .750 | 5-1-0 | .833 | 2 | 1945 | | 2-6-0 | 78 | 150 | .250 | 2-5-0 | .286 | 9 |
| 1943-1944 | no team | | | | | | | | | | | | | | | | |

*S. Tilson listed as co-coach with McEver in 1942.

James Kitts (1946-1947)

| 1946 | | 3-4-3 | 102 | 149 | .450 | 3-3-3 | .500 | 7 | 1947 | | 4-5-0 | 162 | 191 | .444 | 4-3-0 | .571 | 8 |

Robert McNeish (1948-1950) 1-25-3 .086

| 1948 | | 0-8-1 | 28 | 209 | .055 | 0-6-1 | .072 | 15 | 1950* | | 0-10-0 | 72 | 430 | .000 | 0-8-0 | .000 | 17 |
| 1949 | | 1-7-2 | 130 | 172 | .200 | 1-5-2 | .250 | 14 | | | | | | | | | |

*Allan Learned listed as co-coach with McNeish in 1950.

Frank Mosley (1951-1960) 54-42-4 .560

1951		2-8-0	105	311	.200	1-7-0	.125	17	1956		7-2-1	264	98	.750	3-0-0	1.000	2
1952		5-6-0	155	221	.455	4-4-0	.500	6	1957		4-6-0	114	148	.400	1-3-0	.250	7
1953		5-5-0	142	124	.500	3-3-0	.500	5	1958		5-4-1	165	196	.550	3-1-0	.750	2
1954	16	8-0-1	198	75	.944	3-0-1	.833	3	1959		6-4-0	222	178	.600	3-1-0	.750	3
1955		6-3-1	191	133	.650	2-1-1	.625	2	1960		6-4-0	173	103	.600	4-2-0	.667	2

Jerry Claiborne (1961-1970) 61-39-2 .608

| 1961 | | 4-5-0 | 93 | 112 | .444 | 2-3-0 | .400 | 7 | 1963 | | 8-2-0 | 216 | 126 | .800 | 5-0-0 | 1.000 | 1 |
| 1962 | | 5-5-0 | 137 | 137 | .500 | 2-3-0 | .400 | 5 | 1964 | | 6-4-0 | 224 | 178 | .600 | 3-1-0 | .750 | 2 |

Virginia Tech becomes an independent (1965-1990)

1965		7-3-0	188	134	.700				1968		7-4-0	240	165	.636			
1966	20	8-2-1	245	104	.773				1969		4-5-1	234	110	.450			
1967		7-3-0	183	112	.700				1970		5-6-0	199	228	.455			

Charlie Coffey (1971-1973) 12-20-1 .379

| 1971 | | 4-7-0 | 249 | 272 | .364 | | | | 1973 | | 2-9-0 | 223 | 380 | .182 | | | |
| 1972 | | 6-4-1 | 307 | 253 | .591 | | | | | | | | | | | | |

Jimmy Sharpe (1974-1977) 21-22-1 .489

Year	Record	PF	PA	Pct	Year	Record	PF	PA	Pct
1974	4-7-0	278	261	.364	1976	6-5-0	223	176	.545
1975	8-3-0	238	151	.727	1977	3-7-1	174	210	.318

Bill Dooley (1978-1986) 64-37-1 .632

Year	Record	PF	PA	Pct	Year	Rank	Record	PF	PA	Pct
1978	4-7-0	162	225	.364	1983		9-2-0	301	91	.818
1979	5-6-0	224	222	.455	1984		8-4-0	253	150	.667
1980	8-4-0	249	129	.667	1985		6-5-0	253	150	.545
1981	7-4-0	232	128	.636	1986	20	10-1-1	286	208	.875
1982	7-4-0	211	141	.636						

Frank Beamer (1987-2003) 125-74-2 .627

Year	Record	PF	PA	Pct	Year	Record	PF	PA	Pct
1987	2-9-0	203	300	.182	1989	6-4-1	203	180	.591
1988	3-8-0	176	264	.273	1990	6-5-0	245	227	.545

Member of the Big East Conference (1991-2003) 57-26-0 .687

Year	Rank	Rank	Record	PF	PA	Pct	Conf	Pct	Pos	Year	Rank	Rank	Record	PF	PA	Pct	Conf	Pct	Pos
1991			5-6-0	275	229	.455	1-0-0	1.000	6	1997			7-5-0	324	227	.583	5-2-0	.714	2
1992			2-8-1	270	282	.227	1-4-0	.200	7	1998	23	19	9-3-0	381	149	.750	5-2-0	.714	2
1993	22	20	9-3-0	445	270	.750	4-3-0	.571	4	1999	2	3	11-1-0	474	162	.917	7-0-0	1.000	1
1994		24	8-4-0	327	247	.667	5-2-0	.714	2	2000	6	6	11-1-0	484	269	.917	6-1-0	.857	2
1995	10	9	10-2-0	349	165	.833	6-1-0	.857	1	2001	18	18	8-4-0	376	177	.667	4-3-0	.571	3
1996	13	12	10-2-0	370	209	.833	6-1-0	.857	1	2002	18	14	10-4-0	429	263	.714	3-4-0	.429	4
										2003			8-5-0	460	299	.615	4-3-0	.571	4

Won-loss record by decades:

Decade	Record	Pct	Decade	Record	Pct	Decade	Record	Pct
1892-99	26-15-1	.631	1930-39	46-39-11	.536	1970-79	47-61-2	.436
1900-09	54-20-4	.718	1940-49	28-41-7	.414	1980-89	66-45-2	.593
1910-19	59-20-5	.732	1950-59	48-48-4	.500	1990-99	77-39-1	.662
1920-29	56-31-7	.633	1960-69	62-37-2	.624	2000-03	37-14-0	.725

Historic record: 606-410-46 .592

Post-season won-loss record: 6-11-0 .353

1947: Sun Bowl, Cincinnati 18, Virginia Tech 6
1966: Liberty Bowl, Miami (FL) 14, Virginia Tech 7
1968: Liberty Bowl, Mississippi 34, Virginia Tech 17
1981: Peach Bowl, Miami (FL) 20, Virginia Tech 10
1984: Independence Bowl, Air Force 23, Virginia Tech 7
1986: Peach Bowl, Virginia Tech 25, NC State 24
1993: Independence Bowl, Virginia Tech 45, Indiana 20
1994: Gator Bowl, Tennessee 45, Virginia Tech 23

1995: Sugar Bowl, Virginia Tech 28, Texas 10
1996: Orange Bowl, Nebraska 41, Virginia Tech 21
1998: Gator Bowl, North Carolina 42, Virginia Tech 3
1998: Music City Bowl, Virginia Tech 38, Alabama 7
2000: Sugar Bowl, Florida State 46, Virginia Tech 29
2001: Gator Bowl, Virginia Tech 41, Clemson 20
2002: Gator Bowl, Florida State 30, Virginia Tech 17
2002: San Francisco Bowl, Virginia Tech 20, Air Force 13
2003: Insight.com Bowl, California 52, Virginia Tech 49

College Football Hall of Fame:
Hunter Carpenter, halfback, 1900-05; Andy Gustafson, coach, 1926-29; Carroll Dale, end, 1956-59; Jerry Claiborne, coach, 1961-70; Frank Loria, safety, 1965-67.

Awards: Lombardi Award: 1999, Corey Moore; Outland Trophy: 1984, Bruce Smith; Nagurski Award: 1999, Corey Moore; Baugh Trophy: 1972, Don Strock; Rimington Trophy: 2003, Jake Grove.

UNIVERSITY OF VIRGINIA, Charlottesville, Virginia; nickname "Cavaliers"; colors orange and blue; Scott Stadium (61,500); Atlantic Coast Conference. Virginia began football in 1888 as an independent. In 1894, Virginia joined the Southern Intercollegiate Athletic Association and played in that conference until after World War I. In 1920, Virginia joined the Southern Intercollegiate Conference, which evolved into the Southern Conference in 1922. Virginia withdrew from the Southern Conference in 1935 and reverted to independent status. It played as an independent until the 1953 season when it joined the newly organized Atlantic Coast Conference and has played in that conference since that time. Conference data are available only for the Southern Conference and Atlantic Coast conference years.

Early years (1888-1921)

Year	Coach	W-L-T	PF	PA	Pct.	Year	Coach	W-L-T	PF	PA	Pct.
1888	unknown coach	2-1-0	36	26	.667	1905	William Cole	5-4-0	169	78	.556
1889	unknown coach	4-2-0	204	50	.667	1906	William Cole	7-2-2	159	41	.727
1890	unknown coach	5-2-0	224	197	.714	1907	Edward Johnson	6-3-1	169	64	.650
1891	unknown coach	2-1-2	68	42	.600	1908	M.T. Cooke	7-0-1	106	9	.938
1892	unknown coach	3-2-1	110	84	.783	1909	John Neff	7-1-0	155	11	.875
1893	John Poe	8-3-0	244	78	.727	1910	Charles Crawford	6-2-0	117	37	.750
1894	John Poe	8-2-0	414	30	.800	1911	Kemper Yancey	8-2-0	262	30	.800
1895	Henry Mackey	9-2-0	206	104	.818	1912	Speed Elliott	6-3-0	220	48	.667
1896	Martin Bergen	7-2-2	238	86	.727	1913	Rice Warren	7-1-0	265	28	.875
1897	Martin Bergen	6-2-1	111	54	.722	1914	Joseph Wood	8-1-0	353	38	.889
1898	Joseph Massie	6-5-0	117	70	.545	1915	Harry Varner	8-1-0	219	26	.889
1899	Archie Hoxton	4-3-2	92	88	.556	1916	Peyton Evans	4-5-0	106	172	.444
1900	Archie Hoxton	7-2-1	186	37	.750	1917	no team				
1901	Wesley Abbot	8-2-0	270	48	.800	1918	no team				
1902	John De Saulles	8-1-1	157	51	.850	1919	Harris Coleman	2-5-2	39	134	.333
1903	Gresham Poe	7-2-1	177	34	.750	1920	Rice Warren	5-2-2	140	53	.667
1904	Foster Sanford	6-3-0	78	54	.667	1921	Rice Warren	5-4-0	101	83	.556

Member of the Southern Conference (1922-1935) 24-46-10 .362

Year	Nat'l AP	Other	Overall W-L-T	PF	PA	Pct.	Conference W-L-T	Pct.	Rank	Year	Nat'l AP	Other	Overall W-L-T	PF	PA	Pct.	Conference W-L-T	Pct.	Rank

Thomas Campbell (1922) 4-4-1 .500

| 1922 | | | 4-4-1 | 102 | 60 | .500 | 1-1-1 | .500 | 9 | | | | | | | | | | |

Earle Neale (1923-1928) 28-22-5 .555

1923			3-5-1	87	81	.389	0-4-1	.100	18	1926			6-2-2	161	53	.700	4-2-1	.643	6
1924			5-4-0	72	83	.556	3-2-0	.600	6	1927			5-4-0	117	122	.556	4-4-0	.500	8
1925			7-1-1	144	31	.833	4-1-1	.750	5	1928			2-6-1	121	142	.278	1-6-0	.143	19

Earl Abel (1929-1930) 8-9-2 .474

| 1929 | | | 4-3-2 | 129 | 139 | .556 | 1-3-2 | .333 | 16 | 1930 | | | 4-6-0 | 144 | 212 | .400 | 2-5-0 | .286 | 17 |

Fred Dawson (1931-1933) 8-17-4 .345

| 1931 | | | 1-7-2 | 40 | 112 | .200 | 0-5-1 | .083 | 22 | 1933 | | | 2-6-2 | 83 | 149 | .300 | 1-3-1 | .300 | 8 |
| 1932 | | | 5-4-0 | 95 | 67 | .556 | 2-3-0 | .400 | 13 | | | | | | | | | | |

Gus Tebell (1934-1936) 6-18-4 .286

| 1934 | | | 3-6-0 | 70 | 151 | .333 | 1-4-0 | .200 | 9 | 1935 | | | 1-5-4 | 39 | 133 | .300 | 0-3-2 | .200 | 8 |

Virginia reverts to independent status (1936-1952)

| 1936 | | | 2-7-0 | 73 | 222 | .222 | | | | | | | | | | | | | |

Frank Murray (1937-1945) 41-34-5 .544

1937			2-7-0	52	169	.222				1942			2-6-1	123	181	.278			
1938			4-4-1	113	169	.500				1943			3-4-1	106	133	.438			
1939			5-4-0	143	75	.556				1944			6-1-2	197	52	.778			
1940			4-5-0	117	103	.444				1945			7-2-0	265	79	.778			
1941			8-1-0	279	42	.889													

Art Gueppe (1946-1952) 47-17-2 .727

1946			4-4-1	180	170	.500				1950			8-2-0	260	151	.800			
1947			7-3-0	244	99	.700				1951	13		8-1-0	278	104	.889			
1948			5-3-1	175	157	.611				1952			8-2-0	297	90	.800			
1949			7-2-0	199	121	.778													

Member of the Atlantic Coast Conference (1953-2003) 131-183-4 .418

Ned McDonald (1953-1955) 5-23-0 .179

| 1953 | | | 1-8-0 | 75 | 242 | .111 | * | | | 1955 | | | 1-9-0 | 96 | 201 | .100 | 0-4-0 | .000 | 8 |
| 1954 | | | 3-6-0 | 113 | 162 | .333 | 0-2-0 | .000 | 7 | | | | | | | | | | |

*Virginia ineligible for league title because of too few league games.

Ben Martin (1956-1957) 7-12-1 .375

| 1956 | | | 4-6-0 | 92 | 167 | .400 | 1-4-0 | .200 | 8 | 1957 | | | 3-6-1 | 117 | 164 | .350 | 2-4-0 | .333 | 6 |

Richard Voris (1958-1960) 1-29-0 .022

| 1958 | | | 1-9-0 | 89 | 301 | .100 | 1-5-0 | .167 | 8 | 1960 | | | 0-10-0 | 103 | 332 | .000 | 0-6-0 | .000 | 8 |
| 1959 | | | 0-10-0 | 80 | 392 | .000 | 0-5-0 | .000 | 7 | | | | | | | | | | |

Year			W-L-T	PF	PA	Pct	Conf	Pct	R	Year			W-L-T	PF	PA	Pct	Conf	Pct	R
1961			4-6-0	123	190	.400	2-4-0	.333	8	1963			2-7-1	76	169	.250	0-5-1	.083	8
1962			5-5-0	194	167	.500	1-4-0	.200	7	1964			5-5-0	163	214	.500	1-5-0	.167	8

George Blackburn (1965-1970) 29-32-0 .475

Year			W-L-T	PF	PA	Pct	Conf	Pct	R	Year			W-L-T	PF	PA	Pct	Conf	Pct	R
1965			5-5-0	170	189	.500	2-4-0	.333	7	1968			7-3-0	329	222	.700	3-2-0	.600	3
1966			4-6-0	214	235	.400	3-3-0	.500	3	1969			3-7-0	115	270	.300	1-5-0	.167	8
1967			5-5-0	172	169	.500	3-3-0	.500	4	1970			5-6-0	240	187	.455	0-6-0	.000	8

Don Lawrence (1971-1973) 11-22-0 .333

Year			W-L-T	PF	PA	Pct	Conf	Pct	R	Year			W-L-T	PF	PA	Pct	Conf	Pct	R
1971			3-8-0	134	272	.273	2-3-0	.400	3	1973			4-7-0	199	300	.364	3-3-0	.500	4
1972			4-7-0	199	276	.364	1-5-0	.167	6										

Sonny Randle (1974-1975) 5-17-0 .227

Year			W-L-T	PF	PA	Pct	Conf	Pct	R	Year			W-L-T	PF	PA	Pct	Conf	Pct	R
1974			4-7-0	207	239	.364	1-5-0	.167	6	1975			1-10-0	175	428	.091	0-5-0	.000	8

Dick Bestwick (1976-1981) 16-49-1 .246

Year			W-L-T	PF	PA	Pct	Conf	Pct	R	Year			W-L-T	PF	PA	Pct	Conf	Pct	R
1976			2-9-0	106	266	.182	1-4-0	.200	6	1979			6-5-0	258	134	.545	2-4-0	.333	6
1977			1-9-1	56	280	.136	1-5-0	.167	6	1980			4-7-0	144	259	.364	2-4-0	.333	4
1978			2-9-0	139	236	.182	0-6-0	.000	7	1981			1-10-0	127	261	.091	0-6-0	.000	6

George Welsh (1982-2000) 134-86-3 .608

Year			W-L-T	PF	PA	Pct	Conf	Pct	R	Year			W-L-T	PF	PA	Pct	Conf	Pct	R
1982			2-9-0	208	320	.182	1-5-0	.167	6	1992			7-4-0	341	229	.636	4-4-0	.500	4
1983			6-5-0	252	280	.545	3-3-0	.500	4	1993			7-5-0	317	217	.583	5-3-0	.625	3
1984	20	17	8-2-2	337	216	.750	3-1-2	.667	2	1994	15	13	9-3-0	370	195	.750	5-3-0	.625	3
1985			6-5-0	262	217	.545	4-3-0	.571	3	1995	16	17	9-4-0	378	270	.692	7-1-0	.875	1
1986			3-8-0	198	315	.273	2-5-0	.286	6	1996			7-5-0	341	203	.583	5-3-0	.625	4
1987			8-4-0	292	276	.667	5-2-0	.714	2	1997			7-4-0	277	242	.636	5-3-0	.625	3
1988			7-4-0	251	244	.636	5-2-0	.714	2	1998	18	18	9-3-0	358	247	.750	6-2-0	.750	3
1989	18	15	10-3-0	371	272	.769	6-1-0	.857	1	1999			7-5-0	345	365	.583	5-3-0	.625	2
1990	23	15	8-4-0	464	227	.667	5-2-0	.714	2	2000			6-6-0	242	292	.500	5-3-0	.625	4
1991			8-3-1	327	167	.708	4-2-1	.643	4										

Al Groh (2001-2003) 22-17-0 .564

Year			W-L-T	PF	PA	Pct	Conf	Pct	R	Year			W-L-T	PF	PA	Pct	Conf	Pct	R
2001			5-7-0	249	331	.417	3-5-0	.375	8	2003			8-5-0	36	265	.615	4-4-0	.500	4
2002	22	25	9-5-0	402	348	.643	6-2-0	.750	2										

Won-loss record by decades:

1888-99	64-27-8	.687		1930-39	29-56-9	.356	1970-79	32-77-1	.295
1900-09	68-20-7	.753		1940-49	53-31-6	.622	1980-89	55-57-2	.491
1910-19	49-20-2	.704		1950-59	37-59-1	.387	1990-99	78-40-1	.660
1920-29	46-35-10	.560		1960-69	40-59-1	.405	2000-03	28-23-0	.549

Historic record: 579-504-48 .533

Post-season won-loss record: 6-8-0 .429

1984: Peach Bowl, Virginia 27, Purdue 24
1987: All American Bowl, Virginia 22, BYU 16
1990: Florida Citrus Bowl, Illinois 31, Virginia 21
1991: USF&G Sugar Bowl, Tennessee 23, Virginia 22
1991: Gator Bowl, Oklahoma 48, Virginia 14
1994: Carquest Bowl: Boston College 31, Virginia 13
1994: Independence Bowl, Virginia 20, TCU 10

1995: Peach Bowl, Virginia 34, Georgia 27
1996: Carquest Bowl, Miami (FL) 31, Virginia 21
1998: Chick-fil-A Peach Bowl, Georgia 35, Virginia 33
1999: Micronpc.com Bowl, Illinois 63, Virginia 21
2000: Jeep Oahu Bowl, Georgia 37, Virginia 14
2002: Continental Tire Bowl, Virginia 48, West Va. 22
2003: Continental Tire Bowl, Virginia 23, Pittsburgh 16

College Football Hall of Fame:
Bill Dudley, halfback, 1939-41; Joe Palumbo, guard, 1949-51; Tom Scott, end, 1950-52; Frank Murray, coach, 1937-45; George Welch, 1982-2000.

Awards: Maxwell Award: 1941, Bill Dudley.

WAKE FOREST UNIVERSITY, Winston-Salem, North Carolina; nickname "Demon Deacons"; colors old gold and black; Groves Stadium (31,500); Atlantic Coast Conference. Wake Forest was an independent from 1888 until 1936, when it joined the Southern Conference. Following the 1952 season, Wake Forest joined with five other SC members plus Maryland and Virginia to form the Atlantic Coast Conference.

Early years as an independent (1888-1935)

Year	Coach	W-L-T	PF	PA	Pct.	Year	Coach	W-L-T	PF	PA	Pct.
1888	W. C. Dowd	1-0-0	6	4	1.000	1911	Frank Thompson	3-5-0	160	81	.375
1889	W. C. Riddick	3-3-0	90	99	.500	1912	Frank Thompson	2-6-0	108	87	.250
1890	no team					1913	Frank Thompson	0-8-0	30	220	.000
1891	W. E. Sikes	1-0-0	1	0	1.000	1914	W. C. Smith	3-6-0	86	221	.333
1892	W. E. Sikes	4-0-1	94	18	.900	1915	W. C. Smith	3-4-0	161	90	.429
1893	W. E. Sikes	1-2-0	70	52	.333	1916	G. M. Billings	3-3-0	107	85	.500
1894	no team					1917	E. T. MacDonald	1-6-1	59	215	.188
1895	unknown coach	0-0-1	4	4	.000	1918	Harry Rabenhorst	1-2-0	28	47	.333
1896-1907	no team					1919	Harry Rabenhorst	2-6-0	118	144	.250
1908	A. P. Hall	1-4-0	25	149	.200	1920	J. L. White	2-7-0	98	196	.222
1909	A. T. Myers	2-4-0	11	45	.333	1921	J. L. White	2-8-0	66	222	.200
1910	Reddy Rowe	2-7-0	53	154	.222	1922	George Levene	3-5-2	66	144	.444

	Nat'l							Nat'l				
Year	AP	Other	W-L-T	PF	PA	Pct.	Year	AP	Other	W-L-T	PF	PA	Pct.
					Hank Garrity (1923-1925) 19-7-1 .722							
1923			6-3-0	125	64	.667	1925			6-2-1	185	40	.722
1924			7-2-0	207	62	.778							
					James Baldwin (1926-1927) 7-10-3 .425							
1926			5-4-1	86	46	.550	1927			2-6-2	65	223	.300
					Stanley Cofall (1928) 2-6-2 .300							
1928			2-6-2	64	203	.300							
					F. S. Miller (1929-1932) 18-15-4 .540							
1929			6-5-1	107	155	.542	1931			4-4-0	45	138	.500
1930			5-3-1	125	77	.611	1932			3-3-2	39	36	.500
					Jim Weaver (1933-1936) 10-23-1 .309							
1933			0-5-1	13	93	.084	1935			2-7-0	52	106	.222
1934			3-7-0	118	141	.300							

Member of the Southern Conference (1936-1952) 65-40-5 .614

	Nat'l		Overall				Conference				Nat'l		Overall				Conference		
Year	AP	Other	W-L-T	PF	PA	Pct.	W-L-T	Pct.	Rank	Year	AP	Other	W-L-T	PF	PA	Pct.	W-L-T	Pct.	Rank
1936			5-4-0	110	72	.556	2-3-0	.400	9										
					D.C. Walker (1937-1950) 77-51-6 .597														
1937			3-6-0	68	220	.333	1-4-0	.200	14	1944			8-1-0	178	82	.889	6-1-0	.857	2
1938			4-5-1	161	98	.450	3-4-1	.438	9	1945	19		5-3-1	163	160	.611	4-1-1	.750	2
1939			7-3-0	257	89	.700	3-3-0	.500	6	1946			6-3-0	156	92	.667	2-3-0	.400	10
1940			7-3-0	193	113	.700	4-2-0	.667	3	1947			6-4-0	133	101	.600	3-4-0	.429	10
1941			5-5-1	218	158	.500	4-2-1	.643	7	1948	20		6-4-0	224	168	.600	5-2-0	.714	5
1942			6-2-1	134	66	.722	6-1-1	.812	3	1949			4-6-0	207	183	.400	3-3-0	.500	7
1943			4-5-0	165	101	.444	3-2-0	600	4	1950			6-1-2	168	54	.778	6-1-1	.812	4
					Tom Rogers (1951-1955) 21-25-4 .460														
1951			6-4-0	200	142	.600	5-3-0	.625	7	1952			5-4-1	162	133	.550	5-1-0	.833	2

Member of the Atlantic Coast Conference (1953-2003) 97-243-5 .288

Year	AP	Other	W-L-T	PF	PA	Pct.	W-L-T	Pct.	Rank	Year	AP	Other	W-L-T	PF	PA	Pct.	W-L-T	Pct.	Rank
1953			3-6-1	114	157	.350	2-3-0	.400	3	1955			5-4-1	131	153	.550	3-3-1	.500	4
1954			2-7-1	129	165	.250	1-4-1	.250	6										
					Paul Amen (1956-1959) 11-26-3 .313														
1956			2-5-3	91	102	.350	1-5-1	.214	7	1958			3-7-0	124	163	.300	2-4-0	.333	6
1957			0-10-0	64	225	.000	0-7-0	.000	8	1959			6-4-0	218	178	.600	4-3-0	.571	4
					Billy Hildebrand (1960-1963) 7-33-0 .175														
1960			2-8-0	119	211	.200	2-5-0	.286	6	1962			0-10-0	66	278	.000	0-7-0	.000	8
1961			4-6-0	103	159	.400	3-4-0	.429	5	1963			1-9-0	37	318	.100	1-5-0	.167	7
					Bill Tate (1964-1968) 17-32-1 .17-32-1 .209														
1964			5-5-0	172	178	.500	4-3-0	.571	3	1967			4-6-0	175	256	.400	3-4-0	.429	5
1965			3-7-0	88	204	.300	1-5-0	.167	8	1968			2-7-1	212	228	.250	2-3-1	.417	6
1966			3-7-0	90	162	.300	2-4-0	.333	6										
					Cal Stoll (1969-1971) 15-17-0 .469														
1969			3-7-0	125	279	.300	2-5-0	.286	7	1971			6-5-0	218	178	.545	2-3-0	400	3
1970			6-5-0	191	241	.545	5-1-0	.833	1										
					Tom Harper (1972) 2-9-0 .182														
1972			2-9-0	88	339	.182	1-5-0	.167	6										

Chuck Mills (1973-1977) 11-43-1 .209

Year	W-L-T	PF	PA	Pct	Conf	Pct		Year		W-L-T	PF	PA	Pct	Conf	Pct	
1973	1-9-1	73	326	.136	0-5-1	.083	7	1976		5-6-0	177	206	.455	3-3-0	.500	3
1974	1-10-0	74	348	.091	0-6-0	.000	7	1977		1-10-0	113	270	.091	0-6-0	.000	7
1975	3-8-0	221	264	.273	3-3-0	.500	3									

John Mackovic (1978-1980) 14-20-0 .412

1978	1-10-0	104	274	.091	1-5-0	.167	6	1980		5-6-0	251	213	.455	2-4-0	.333	4
1979	8-4-0	240	283	.667	4-2-0	.667	2									

Al Groh (1981-1986) 26-40-0 .394

1981	4-7-0	217	365	.364	1-5-0	.167	6	1984		6-5-0	205	232	.545	3-3-0	.500	4
1982	3-8-0	200	322	.273	0-6-0	.000	7	1985		4-7-0	212	249	.364	1-6-0	.143	8
1983	4-7-0	257	281	.364	1-5-0	.167	6	1986		5-6-0	325	295	.455	2-5-0	.286	4

Bill Dooley (1987-1992) 29-36-2 .448

1987	7-4-0	201	185	.636	4-3-0	.571	3	1990		3-8-0	247	351	.273	0-7-0	.000	7
1988	6-4-1	282	238	.591	4-3-0	.571	3	1991		3-8-0	195	300	.273	1-6-0	.143	7
1989	2-8-1	194	319	.227	1-6-0	.143	7	1992	25 25	8-4-0	266	260	.667	4-4-0	.500	4

Jim Caldwell (1993-2000) 26-63-0 .292

1993	2-9-0	199	318	.182	1-7-0	.125	9	1997		5-6-0	245	288	.455	3-5-0	.375	6
1994	3-8-0	143	373	.273	1-7-0	.125	8	1998		3-8-0	235	335	.273	2-6-0	.250	6
1995	1-10-0	190	360	.091	0-8-0	.000	9	1999		7-5-0	266	209	.583	3-5-0	.375	5
1996	3-8-0	144	305	.273	1-7-0	.125	8	2000		2-9-0	181	372	.182	1-7-0	.125	8

Jim Grobe (2001-2003) 18-18-0 .500

2001	6-5-0	292	311	.545	3-5-0	.375	7	2003		5-7-0	335	347	.417	3-5-0	.375	6
2001	7-6-0	356	327	.538	3-5-0	.375	7									

Won-loss record by decades:

Decade	Record	Pct	Decade	Record	Pct	Decade	Record	Pct
1888-89	4-3-0	.571	1930-39	36-47-5	.438	1970-79	34-76-1	.311
1890-99	6-2-2	.700	1940-49	57-36-3	.609	1980-89	46-62-2	.427
1900-09	3-8-0	.273	1950-59	38-52-9	.429	1990-99	38-74-0	.339
1910-19	20-53-1	.277	1960-69	27-72-1	.275	2000-03	20-27-0	.426
1920-29	41-48-9	.464						

Historic record: 370-560-33 .401

Post-season won-loss record: 4-2-0 .667

1946: Gator Bowl, Wake Forest 26, South Carolina 14
1949: Dixie Bowl, Baylor 20, Wake Forest 7
1979: Tangerine Bowl, LSU 34, Wake Forest 10

1992: Independence Bowl, Wake Forest 39, Oregon 35
1999: Jeep Aloha Bowl, Wake Forest 23, Arizona State 3
2002: Seattle Bowl, Wake Forest 38, Oregon 17

WASHINGTON STATE UNIVERSITY, Pullman, Washington; nickname "Cougars"; colors crimson and gray; Martin Stadium (37,600); Pac-10 Conference. WSU began play in 1894 and then became a member of the Pacific Coast Conference, beginning play in 1916. When the PCC disbanded after the 1958 season, with four ex-PCC members forming the AAWU, Washington State became an independent, until it joined the AAWU for the 1962 season. Washington State has played in the AAWU and successor conferences (Pac-8, Pac-10) since that time.

Early years (1894-1915)

Year	Coach	W-L-T	PF	PA	Pct.	Year	Coach	W-L-T	PF	PA	Pct.
1894	W. Goodyear	1-1-0	10	18	.500	1905	Everett Sweeley	4-4-0	175	61	.500
1895	W.W. Waite	2-0-0	36	8	1.000	1906	John Bender	6-0-0	44	0	1.000
1896	D.A. Brodie	2-0-1	56	6	.833	1907	John Bender	7-1-0	282	18	.875
1897	Robert Galley	2-0-0	32	12	1.000	1908	W. Rheinschild	4-0-2	164	10	.833
1898	Frank Snively	0-0-1	0	0	.500	1909	W. Klenholz	4-1-0	159	17	.800
1899	Frank Snively	1-1-0	21	11	.500	1910	Oscar Osthoff	2-3-0	25	34	.400
1900	William Allen	4-0-1	39	5	.900	1911	Oscar Osthoff	3-3-0	92	42	.500
1901	William Namack	4-1-0	47	7	.800	1912	John Bender	2-3-0	25	34	.400
1902	William Allen	2-3-0	28	39	.400	1913	John Bender	4-4-0	111	61	.500
1903	James Ashmore	3-3-2	92	54	.500	1914	John Bender	2-4-0	10	75	.333
1904	Everett Sweeley	2-2-0	46	26	.500	1915	William Dietz	7-0-0	204	10	1.000

Member of the Pacific Coast Conference (1916-1958, 1962-2003) 233-291-26 .447

William Dietz (1915-1917) 17-2-1 .875

Year	Nat'l AP Other	Overall W-L-T	PF	PA	Pct.	Conference W-L-T	Pct.	Rank	Year	Nat'l AP Other	Overall W-L-T	PF	PA	Pct.	Conference W-L-T	Pct.	Rank
1916		4-2-0	135	25	.667	no games			1917		6-0-1	112	3	.929	3-0-0	1.000	1

Emory Avord (1918) 1-1-0 .500

| 1918 | | 1-1-0 | 26 | 13 | .500 | no games | | | | | | | | | | | |

Gus Welch (1919-1922) 16-10-1 .611

| 1919 | | 5-2-0 | 156 | 33 | .714 | 2-2-0 | .500 | 3 | 1921 | | 4-2-1 | 109 | 62 | .642 | 2-1-1 | .625 | 2 |
| 1920 | | 5-1-0 | 129 | 76 | .833 | 1-1-0 | .500 | 4 | 1922 | | 2-5-0 | 44 | 163 | .286 | 1-5-0 | .167 | 7 |

A.A. Exendine (1923-1925) 6-13-4 .348

| 1923 | | 2-4-1 | 56 | 84 | .357 | 1-3-1 | .300 | 6 | 1925 | | 3-4-1 | 67 | 104 | .438 | 2-3-0 | .400 | 6 |
| 1924 | | 1-5-2 | 107 | 74 | .250 | 0-4-1 | .100 | 8 | | | | | | | | | |

Babe Hollingbery (1926-1942) 93-53-14 .625

1926		6-1-0	85	28	.857	4-1-0	.800	3	1935		5-3-1	136	81	.611	3-2-0	.600	5
1927		3-3-2	120	67	.500	1-3-1	.300	7	1936		6-3-1	108	102	.650	6-2-1	.722	2
1928		7-3-0	202	65	.700	4-3-0	.571	5	1937		3-3-3	36	67	.500	3-3-2	.500	4
1929		10-2-0	301	70	.833	4-2-0	.667	5	1938		2-8-0	44	159	.200	1-7-0	.125	9
1930	2	9-1-0	218	56	.900	6-0-0	1.000	1	1939		4-5-0	67	134	.444	3-5-0	.375	6
1931		6-4-0	123	111	.600	4-3-0	.571	4	1940		4-4-2	131	147	.500	3-4-2	.444	4
1932		7-1-1	130	28	.833	5-1-1	.786	2	1941	19	6-4-0	157	63	.600	5-3-0	.675	2
1933		5-3-1	122	67	.611	3-3-1	.500	4	1942	17	6-2-2	157	95	.700	5-1-1	.786	2
1934		4-3-1	108	28	.562	4-0-1	.900	2	1943, 1944	no team							

Phil Sarboe (1945-1949) 17-26-3 .402

1945		6-2-1	157	70	.722	6-2-1	.722	2	1948		4-5-1	164	219	.450	4-3-1	.562	4
1946		1-6-1	118	147	.188	1-5-1	.214	8	1949		3-6-0	149	205	.333	2-6-0	.250	8
1947		3-7-0	93	148	.300	2-5-0	.286	7									

Forest Evashevski (1950-1951) 11-6-2 .632

| 1950 | | 4-3-2 | 168 | 182 | .556 | 2-3-2 | .429 | 6 | 1951 | 18   14 | 7-3-0 | 280 | 187 | .700 | 4-3-0 | .571 | 6 |

Al Kircher (1952-1955) 13-25-2 .350

| 1952 | | 4-6-0 | 171 | 215 | .400 | 3-4-0 | .429 | 5 | 1954 | | 4-6-0 | 149 | 225 | .400 | 3-4-0 | .429 | 5 |
| 1953 | | 4-6-0 | 146 | 256 | .400 | 3-4-0 | .429 | 5 | 1955 | | 1-7-2 | 67 | 357 | .200 | 1-5-1 | .214 | 8 |

Jim Sutherland (1956-1963) 37-39-4 .488

| 1956 | | 3-6-1 | 163 | 247 | .350 | 2-5-1 | .312 | 7 | 1958 | | 7-3-0 | 199 | 117 | .700 | 6-2-0 | .750 | 2 |
| 1957 | | 6-4-0 | 193 | 161 | .600 | 5-3-0 | .625 | 4 | | | | | | | | | |

PCC is dissolved, years as an independent (1959-1961)

| 1959 | | 6-4-0 | 177 | 121 | .600 | | | | 1961 | | 3-7-0 | 162 | 213 | .300 | | | |
| 1960 | | 4-5-1 | 210 | 161 | .450 | | | | | | | | | | | | |

Member of the AAWU Conference (1962-1967)

| 1962 | | 5-4-1 | 213 | 167 | .550 | 1-1-0 | .500 | 3 | 1963 | | 3-6-1 | 95 | 160 | .350 | 1-1-0 | .500 | 4 |

Bert Clark (1964-1967) 15-24-1 .388

| 1964 | | 3-6-1 | 165 | 208 | .350 | 1-2-1 | .375 | 6 | 1966 | | 3-7-0 | 132 | 211 | .300 | 1-3-0 | .250 | 7 |
| 1965 | | 7-3-0 | 139 | 103 | .700 | 2-1-0 | .667 | 3 | 1967 | | 2-8-0 | 141 | 266 | .200 | 1-5-0 | .167 | 8 |

Member of the Pac-8 (later Pac-10) Conference (1968-2001)

Jim Sweeney (1968-1975) 26-59-1 .308

1968		3-6-1	189	188	.350	1-3-1	.300	8	1972	19 17	7-4-0	274	241	.636	4-3-0	.571	3
1969		1-9-0	143	339	.100	0-7-0	.000	8	1973		5-6-0	250	290	.455	4-3-0	.571	4
1970		1-10-0	231	460	.091	0-7-0	.000	8	1974		2-9-0	162	272	.182	1-6-0	.143	7
1971		4-7-0	245	286	.364	2-5-0	.286	7	1975		3-8-0	262	295	.273	0-7-0	.000	8

Jackie Sherrill (1976) 3-8-0 .273

Year			Record	PF	PA	Pct	Conf	Pct	Pl
1976			3-8-0	240	331	.273	2-5-0	.286	6

Warren Powers (1977) 7-4-0 .636

Year			Record	PF	PA	Pct	Conf	Pct	Pl
1977			7-4-0	263	236	.636	3-4-0	.429	5

Jim Walden (1978-1986) 44-52-4 .460

Year			Record	PF	PA	Pct	Conf	Pct	Pl	Year			Record	PF	PA	Pct	Conf	Pct	Pl
1978			4-6-1	276	296	.409	2-6-0	.250	9	1983			7-4-0	237	211	.636	5-3-0	.625	3
1979			5-6-0	241	367	.455	4-4-0	.500	6	1984			6-5-0	317	319	.545	4-3-0	.571	5
1980			4-7-0	287	271	.364	3-4-0	.429	6	1985			4-7-0	313	282	.364	3-5-0	.375	7
1981			8-3-1	297	197	.708	5-2-1	.688	4	1986			3-7-1	221	312	.318	2-6-1	.278	8
1982			3-7-1	170	255	.318	2-4-1	.357	8										

Dennis Erickson (1987-1988) 12-10-1 .543

Year			Record	PF	PA	Pct	Conf	Pct	Pl	Year	R1	R2	Record	PF	PA	Pct	Conf	Pct	Pl
1987			3-7-1	238	356	.318	1-5-1	.214	9	1988	16	16	9-3-0	415	303	.455	5-3-0	.625	3

Mike Price (1989-2002) 83-78-0 .516

Year	R1	R2	Record	PF	PA	Pct	Conf	Pct	Pl	Year	R1	R2	Record	PF	PA	Pct	Conf	Pct	Pl
1989			6-5-0	351	268	.545	3-5-0	.375	7	1996			5-6-0	314	317	.455	3-5-0	.375	5
1990			3-8-0	286	381	.273	2-6-0	.250	9	1997	9	9	10-2-0	483	296	.833	7-1-0	.875	1
1991			4-7-0	280	340	.364	3-5-0	.375	6	1998			3-8-0	223	349	.273	0-8-0	.000	10
1992	15	17	9-3-0	337	281	.750	5-3-0	.625	3	1999			3-9-0	248	327	.250	1-7-0	.125	10
1993			5-6-0	271	248	.455	3-5-0	.375	7	2000			4-7-0	281	354	.364	2-6-0	.250	8
1994	21	19	8-4-0	191	136	.667	5-3-0	.625	4	2001	10	11	10-2-0	420	269	.833	6-2-0	.750	2
1995			3-8-0	236	274	.273	2-6-0	.200	8	2002	10	10	10-3-0	431	296	.769	7-1-0	.875	1

Bill Doba (2003) 10-3-0 .769

Year	R1	R2	Record	PF	PA	Pct	Conf	Pct	Pl
2003	9	9	10-3-0	394	257	.769	6-2-0	.750	2

Won-loss record by decades:

1894-99	8- 2-2	.750	1930-39	51-34-8	.597	1970-79	41-68-1	.377	
1900-09	40-15-5	.708	1940-49	33-36-7	.480	1980-89	55-55-4	.491	
1910-19	36-22-1	.619	1950-59	46-48-5	.490	1990-99	53-61-0	.465	
1920-29	43-3-0-7	.581	1960-69	34-61-5	.365	2000-03	34-15-0	.694	

Historic record: 474-447-45 .514

Post-season won-loss record: 6-4-0 .600

1916: Rose Bowl, WSU 14, Brown 0
1931: Rose Bowl, Alabama 24, WSU 0
1981: Holiday Bowl, BYU 38, WSU 36
1988: Eagle Aloha Bowl, WSU 24, Houston 22
1992: Weiser Lock Copper Bowl, WSU 31, Utah 28

1994: Builder Square Alamo Bowl, WSU 10, Baylor 3
1998: Rose Bowl, Michigan 21, WSU 16
2001: Sun Bowl, WSU 33, Purdue 27
2003: Rose Bowl, Oklahoma 34, WSU 14
2003: Holiday Bowl, WSU 28, Texas 20

College Football Hall of Fame:
Babe Hollingberry, coach, 1926-42; Mel Hein, center, 1928-30; Turk Edwards, tackle, 1929-31; Forest Evashevski, coach, 1950-51

Player Awards: Outland Trophy: 2002, Rien Long; Baugh Trophy: 1997, Ryan Leaf.

UNIVERSITY OF WASHINGTON, Seattle, Washington; nickname "Huskies" or "U Dub"; colors purple and gold; Husky Stadium (72,500); Pac-10 Conference. Washington began play in 1889 and joined the Pacific Coast Conference as a founding member in 1916. It has played in the PCC (and successor conferences – the AAWU, the Pac-8, and the Pac-10) since that time.

Early years as an independent (1889-1915)

Year	Coach	W-L-T	PF	PA	Pct.	Year	Coach	W-L-T	PF	PA	Pct.
1889	no coach	0-1-0	0	20	.000	1899	A. S. Jeffs	4-1-1	71	21	.750
1890	no coach	0-0-1	0	0	.500	1900	J. Dodge	1-2-2	27	71	.400
1891	no team					1901	J. Wright	3-3-0	43	42	.500
1892	W. Goodwin	1-1-0	14	28	.500	1902	J. Knight	5-1-0	65	18	.833
1893	W. Goodwin	1-3-1	18	86	.300	1903	J. Knight	6-1-0	63	11	.857
1894	C. Cobb	1-1-1	60	38	.500	1904	J. Knight	4-2-1	116	65	.643
1895	R. Nichols	4-0-1	98	8	.900	1905	O. Cutts	4-2-2	79	52	.625
1896	R. Nichols	2-3-0	20	40	.400	1906	V. Place	4-1-4	49	35	.667
1897	C. Clemans	1-2-0	16	26	.333	1907	V. Place	4-4-2	95	48	.500
1898	R. Nichols	1-1-0	24	18	.500						

Gil Dobie (1908-1916) 58-0-3 .975

Year		W-L-T	PF	PA	Pct.	Year		W-L-T	PF	PA	Pct.
1908		6-0-1	128	15	.929	1912		6-0-0	190	17	1.000
1909		7-0-0	214	6	1.000	1913		7-0-0	266	20	1.000
1910		6-0-0	150	8	1.000	1914		6-0-1	243	13	.929
1911		7-0-0	277	9	1.000	1915		7-0-0	274	18	1.000

Member of the Pacific Coast Conference (1916-2003) 337-231-27 .589

Year	Nat'l AP	Other	Overall W-L-T	PF	PA	Pct.	Conference W-L-T	Pct.	Rank	Year	Nat'l AP	Other	Overall W-L-T	PF	PA	Pct.	Conference W-L-T	Pct.	Rank
1916			6-0-1	189	16	.929	3-0-1	.875	1										

Claude Hunt (1917, 1919) 6-3-1 .650

| 1917 | | | 1-2-1 | 14 | 47 | .375 | 0-2-1 | .166 | 5 | | | | | | | | | | |

Tony Savage (1918) 1-1-0 .500

| 1918 | | | 1-1-0 | 6 | 7 | .500 | 1-1-0 | .500 | 3 | | | | | | | | | | |

Claude Hunt (1919)

| 1919 | | | 5-1-0 | 202 | 31 | .833 | 2-1-0 | .667 | 1 | | | | | | | | | | |

Leonard Allison (1920) 1-5-0 .167

| 1920 | | | 1-5-0 | 54 | 83 | .167 | 0-3-0 | .000 | 6 | | | | | | | | | | |

Enoch Bagshaw (1921-1929) 64-21-6 .736

1921			3-4-1	69	145	.429	0-3-1	.125	6	1926			8-2-0	213	60	.800	3-2-0	.600	5
1922			6-1-1	129	72	.813	4-1-1	.750	3	1927			9-2-0	287	59	.818	4-2-0	.667	4
1923			10-1-1	300	58	.875	4-1-0	.800	2	1928			7-4-0	188	74	.636	2-4-0	.333	8
1924			8-1-1	355	24	.850	3-1-1	.700	3	1929			2-6-1	145	127	.278	0-5-1	.083	10
1925	7		11-0-1	480	59	.958	5-0-0	1.000	1										

Jimmy Phelan (1930-1941) 65-37-8 .616

1930			5-4-0	182	67	.556	3-4-0	.429	5	1936	5	4	7-2-1	148	56	.750	7-0-1	.938	1
1931			5-3-1	166	83	.611	3-3-1	.500	5	1937			7-2-2	187	52	.727	4-2-2	.556	3
1932			6-2-2	193	56	.700	3-2-2	.571	4	1938			3-5-1	68	83	.389	3-4-1	.438	6
1933			5-4-0	88	81	.556	3-4-0	.429	7	1939			4-5-0	77	93	.444	4-4-0	.500	4
1934			6-1-1	104	51	.812	5-1-1	.786	3	1940	10		7-2-0	169	54	.778	7-1-0	.875	2
1935			5-3-0	93	42	.625	4-3-0	.571	6	1941			5-4-0	120	94	.556	5-3-0	.625	2

Ralph Welch (1942-1947) 27-20-3 .480

1942			4-3-3	113	60	.550	3-3-2	.500	6	1945			6-3-0	91	54	.667	6-3-0	.667	3
1943	12		4-1-0	150	61	.800	0-1-0	.000	3	1946			5-4-0	144	140	.556	5-3-0	.625	4
1944			5-3-0	293	132	.625	1-1-0	.500	2	1947			3-6-0	98	99	.333	2-5-0	.286	7

Howard Odell (1948-1952) 23-25-2 .480

1948			2-7-1	89	189	.250	2-5-1	.312	7	1951			3-6-1	275	218	.350	1-5-1	.214	7
1949			3-7-0	167	285	.300	2-5-0	.286	7	1952			7-3-0	248	208	.700	6-2-0	.750	3
1950	11	15	8-2-0	265	133	.800	6-1-0	.857	2										

John Cherberg (1953-1955) 10-18-2 .344

| 1953 | | | 3-6-1 | 154 | 217 | .350 | 2-4-1 | .357 | 7 | 1955 | | | 5-4-1 | 141 | 93 | .550 | 4-3-1 | .562 | |
| 1954 | | | 2-8-0 | 78 | 215 | .200 | 1-6-0 | .143 | 8 | | | | | | | | | | |

Darrell Royal (1956) 5-5-0 .500

| 1956 | | | 5-5-0 | 232 | 206 | .500 | 4-4-0 | .500 | 5 | | | | | | | | | | |

Jim Owens (1957-1974) 98-82-6 .545

1957			3-6-1	120	212	.350	3-4-0	.429	6	1966			6-4-0	171	141	.600	4-3-0	.571	4
1958			3-7-0	102	146	.300	1-6-0	.143	8	1967			5-5-0	136	130	.500	3-4-0	.429	4
1959	8	7	10-1-0	253	73	.909	3-1-0	.750	1	1968			3-5-2	154	177	.400	1-5-1	.214	8
1960	6	5	10-1-0	272	107	.909	4-0-0	1.000	1	1969			1-9-0	116	304	.100	1-6-0	.143	7
1961			5-4-1	119	98	.550	2-1-1	.625	2	1970			6-4-0	334	216	.600	4-3-0	.571	2
1962		14	7-1-2	208	83	.800	4-1-0	.800	2	1971	19		8-3-0	357	188	.727	4-3-0	.571	3
1963		15	6-5-0	183	141	.545	4-1-0	.800	1	1972			8-3-0	208	204	.727	4-3-0	.571	3
1964			6-4-0	139	110	.600	5-2-0	.714	3	1973			2-9-0	218	376	.182	0-7-0	.000	8
1965			5-5-0	205	185	.500	4-3-0	.571	4	1974			5-6-0	272	285	.455	3-4-0	.428	5

Don James (1975-1992) 153-57-2 .726

Year	AP	UPI	W-L-T	PF	PA	Pct	Conf	Conf Pct	Fin
1975			6-5-0	196	250	.545	5-2-0	.714	3
1976			5-6-0	237	207	.455	3-4-0	.429	4
1977	10	9	10-2-0	344	174	.833	6-1-0	.857	1
1978			7-4-0	270	155	.636	6-2-0	.750	2
1979	11	11	10-2-0	321	154	.833	5-2-0	.714	2
1980	16	17	9-3-0	333	198	.750	6-1-0	.857	1
1981	10	7	10-2-0	281	171	.833	6-2-0	.750	1
1982	7	7	10-2-0	354	193	.822	6-2-0	.750	2
1983			8-4-0	285	178	.667	5-2-0	.714	2
1984	2	2	11-1-0	412	145	.916	6-1-0	.857	2
1985			7-5-0	238	225	.583	5-3-0	.625	4
1986	18	17	8-3-1	378	197	.708	5-2-1	.688	2
1987			7-4-1	295	254	.625	4-3-1	.562	3
1988			6-5-0	254	223	.545	3-5-0	.375	6
1989	23	20	8-4-0	299	218	.667	5-3-0	.625	2
1990	5	5	10-2-0	411	184	.833	7-1-0	.875	1
1991	2	1	12-0-0	505	114	1.000	8-0-0	1.000	1
1992	11	10	9-3-0	340	186	.750	6-2-0	.750	1

Jim Lambright (1993-1998) 44-25-1 .664

Year	AP	UPI	W-L-T	PF	PA	Pct	Conf	Conf Pct	Fin
1993			7-4-0	288	198	.636	5-3-0	.625	4
1994			7-4-0	295	253	.636	4-4-0	.500	5
1995			7-4-1	312	280	.625	6-1-1	.812	1
1996	16	15	9-3-0	391	242	.750	7-1-0	.875	2
1997	18	18	8-4-0	420	259	.667	5-3-0	.625	5
1998			6-6-0	303	323	.500	4-4-0	.500	5

Rick Neuheisel (1999-2002) 33-16-0 .673

Year	AP	UPI	W-L-T	PF	PA	Pct	Conf	Conf Pct	Fin
1999			7-5-0	331	302	.583	6-2-0	.750	2
2000	3	3	11-1-0	387	270	.917	7-1-0	.875	1
2001	19	19	8-4-0	353	370	.667	6-2-0	.750	2
2002			7-6-0	398	342	.538	4-4-0	.500	4

Keith Gilbertson (2003) 6-6-0 .500

Year	AP	UPI	W-L-T	PF	PA	Pct	Conf	Conf Pct	Fin
2003			6-6-0	312	316	.500	4-4-0	.500	6

Won-loss record by decades:

1889-99	15-13-5	.530	1930-39	53-31-8	.620	1970-79	67-44-0	.604	
1900-09	44-16-12	.694	1940-49	44-40-4	.523	1980-89	84-33-2	.714	
1910-19	52-4-3	.907	1950-59	49-48-4	.505	1990-99	82-35-1	.699	
1920-29	65-26-6	.701	1960-69	54-43-5	.554	2000-03	32-17-0	.653	

Historic record: 641-350-50 .640

Post-season won-loss record: 17-14-1 .547

1924: Rose Bowl, UW 14, Navy 14
1926: Rose Bowl, Alabama 20, UW 19
1937: Rose Bowl, Pitt 21, UW 0
1938: Pineapple Bowl, UW 53, Hawaii 13
1944: Rose Bowl, USC 29, UW 0
1960: Rose Bowl, UW 44, Wisconsin 8
1961: Rose Bowl, UW 17, Minnesota 7
1964: Rose Bowl, Illinois 17, UW 7
1978: Rose Bowl, UW 27, Michigan 20
1979: Sun Bowl, UW 14, Texas 7
1981: Rose Bowl, Michigan 23, UW 6
1982: Rose Bowl, UW 28, Iowa 0
1982: Aloha Bowl, UW 21, Maryland 20
1983: Aloha Bowl, Penn State 13, UW 10
1985: Orange Bowl, UW 28, Oklahoma 17

1985: Freedom Bowl, UW 20, Colorado 17
1986: Sun Bowl, Alabama 28, UW 6
1987: Independence Bowl, UW 24, Tulane 12
1989: Freedom Bowl, UW 34, Florida 7
1991: Rose Bowl, UW 46, Iowa 34
1992: Rose Bowl, UW 34, Michigan 14
1993: Rose Bowl, Michigan 38, UW 31
1995: Sun Bowl, Iowa 38, UW 18
1996: Holiday Bowl, Colorado 33, UW 21
1997: Jeep Aloha Bowl, UW 51, Michigan State 23
1998: Jeep Aloha Bowl, Air Force 45, UW 25
1999: Culligan Holiday Bowl, Kansas State 24, UW 20
2001: Rose Bowl, UW 34, Purdue 24
2001: Holiday Bowl, Texas 47, UW 43
2002: Sun Bowl, Purdue 34, UW 24

College Football Hall of Fame:
Gil Dobie, coach, 1908-16; George Wilson, halfback, 1923-25; Chuck Carroll, halfback, 1926-28; Paul Schwegler, tackle, 1929-31; Jimmy Phelan, coach, 1930-41; Max Starcevich, guard, 1934-36; Vic Markov, tackle, 1937-39; High McElhenny, halfback, 1949-51; Don Heinrich, quarterback, 1949-50, 1952; Darrell Royal, coach, 1956; Jim Owens, coach, 1957-74; Bob Schlordedt, quarterback, 1958-60; Rick Redman, guard, 1962-64; Don James, coach, 1975-92.

Awards: Lombardi Award: 1990, Steve Emtman; Outland Trophy: 1991, Steve Emtman; Doak Walker Award: 1990: Greg Lewis.

WEST VIRGINIA UNIVERSITY, Morgantown, West Virginia; nickname "Mountaineers"; colors old gold and blue; Mountaineer Field (63,500); Big East Conference. West Virginia began play in 1891. The team joined the Southern Conference in 1950. West Virginia left the Southern Conference after the 1967 season and reverted to independent status until the 1991 season when it began play as one of the founding members of the Big East Conference.

Early years (1891-1915)

Year	Coach	W-L-T	PF	PA	Pct.	Year	Coach	W-L-T	PF	PA	Pct.
1891	F. L. Emory	0-1-0	0	72	.000	1904	Anthony Chez	6-3-0	99	233	.667
1892	no team					1905	Carl Forkum	8-1-0	204	22	.889
1893	F. W. Rane	2-1-0	24	60	.667	1906	Carl Forkum	5-5-0	192	74	.500
1894	F. W. Rane	2-2-0	28	52	.500	1907	Clarence Russell	6-4-0	236	38	.600
1895	Harry McCrory	5-1-0	58	10	.833	1908	C. A. Leuder	5-3-0	101	29	.625
1896	T. G. Trenchard	3-7-2	14	101	.333	1909	C. A. Leuder	4-3-2	113	81	.556
1897	George Krebs	5-4-1	92	45	.550	1910	C. A. Leuder	2-4-1	20	95	.357
1898	Harry Anderson	6-1-0	64	23	.857	1911	C. A. Leuder	6-3-0	91	67	.667
1899	Louis Yeager	2-3-0	28	78	.400	1912	W. P. Edmunds	6-3-0	131	106	.667
1900	John Hill	4-3-0	53	104	.571	1913	E. R. Sweetland	3-4-2	109	137	.444
1901	Louis Yeager	3-2-0	73	34	.600	1914	Sol Metzger	5-4-0	159	96	.556
1902	Louis Yeager	7-4-0	219	87	.636	1915	Sol Metzger	5-2-1	208	20	.688
1903	H. E. Trout	7-1-0	146	45	.875						

Mount McIntire (1916-1917, 1919-1920) 24-11-4 .667

Year	W-L-T	PF	PA	Pct.	Year	W-L-T	PF	PA	Pct.
1916	5-2-2	198	38	.667	1919	8-2-0	326	47	.800
1917	6-3-1	161	50	.650	1920	5-4-1	169	113	.550
1918	no team								

Doc Spears (1921-1924) 30-6-3 .808

Year	W-L-T	PF	PA	Pct.	Year	W-L-T	PF	PA	Pct.
1921	5-4-1	158	82	.550	1923	7-1-1	297	41	.833
1922	10-0-1	267	34	.955	1924	8-1-0	282	18	.889

Ira Rodgers (1925-1930, 1943-1945) 44-31-8 .578

Year	W-L-T	PF	PA	Pct.	Year	W-L-T	PF	PA	Pct.
1925	8-1-0	175	18	.889	1928	8-2-0	152	38	.800
1926	6-4-0	141	93	.600	1929	4-3-3	77	95	.550
1927	2-4-3	68	129	.389	1930	5-5-0	111	103	.500

Earle Neale (1931-1933) 12-16-3 .435

Year	W-L-T	PF	PA	Pct.	Year	W-L-T	PF	PA	Pct.
1931	4-6-0	91	122	.400	1933	3-5-3	87	145	.409
1932	5-5-0	137	115	.500					

Charles Tallman (1934-1936) 15-12-2 .552

Year	W-L-T	PF	PA	Pct.	Year	W-L-T	PF	PA	Pct.
1934	6-4-0	117	113	.600	1936	6-4-0	151	122	.600
1935	3-4-2	129	96	.444					

Marshall Glenn (1937-1939) 14-12-3 .534

Year	W-L-T	PF	PA	Pct.	Year	W-L-T	PF	PA	Pct.
1937	8-1-1	183	39	.850	1939	2-6-1	70	94	.278
1938	4-5-1	98	117	.450					

William Kern (1940-1942, 1946-1947) 24-23-1 .510

Year	W-L-T	PF	PA	Pct.	Year	W-L-T	PF	PA	Pct.
1940	4-4-1	127	94	.500	1942	5-4-0	119	91	.556
1941	4-6-0	85	126	.400					

Ira Rodgers (1943-1945)

Year	W-L-T	PF	PA	Pct.	Year	W-L-T	PF	PA	Pct.
1943	4-3-0	124	79	.571	1944	2-6-1	122	126	.278
1944	5-3-1	191	130	.611					

William Kern (1946-1947)

Year	W-L-T	PF	PA	Pct.	Year	W-L-T	PF	PA	Pct.
1946	5-5-0	120	99	.500	1947	6-4-0	252	84	.600

Dudley DeGroot (1948-1949) 13-9-1 .587

Year	W-L-T	PF	PA	Pct.	Year	W-L-T	PF	PA	Pct.
1948	9-3-0	257	140	.750	1949	4-6-1	227	275	.409

Member of the Southern Conference (1950-1967) 58-14-3 .793

Year	Nat'l AP	Other	Overall W-L-T	PF	PA	Pct.	Conference W-L-T	Pct.	Rank	Year	Nat'l AP	Other	Overall W-L-T	PF	PA	Pct.	Conference W-L-T	Pct.	Rank

Art Lewis (1950-1959) 58-38-2 .602

1950			2-8-0	163	259	.200	1-3-0	.250		1955	19	17	8-2-0	285	104	.800	4-0-0	1.000	
1951			5-5-0	225	190	.500	2-3-0	.400		1956			6-4-0	130	106	.600	5-0-0	1.000	
1952			7-2-0	234	116	.778	5-1-0	.833		1957			7-2-1	179	118	.750	3-0-0	1.000	
1953	10	13	8-2-0	309	154	.800	4-0-0	1.000		1958			4-5-1	268	200	.450	4-0-0	1.000	
1954	12		8-1-0	209	74	.889	3-0-0	1.000		1959			3-7-0	74	204	.300	2-2-0	.500	

Gene Corum (1960-1965) 29-30-2 .492

1960			0-8-2	40	259	.100	0-2-1	.167		1963			4-6-0	154	201	.400	3-1-0	.750	
1961			4-6-0	134	145	.400	2-1-0	.333		1964			7-4-0	162	211	.636	5-0-0	1.000	
1962			8-2-0	211	137	.800	4-0-0	1.000		1965			6-4-0	279	264	.600	4-0-0	1.000	

Jim Carlen (1966-1969) 25-13-3 .622

| 1966 | | | 3-5-2 | 158 | 197 | .444 | 3-1-1 | .700 | | 1967 | | | 5-4-1 | 188 | 117 | .550 | 4-0-1 | .900 | |

West Virginia reverts to independent status (1968-1990)

| 1968 | | | 7-3-0 | 207 | 141 | .700 | | | | 1969 | 17 | 18 | 10-1-0 | 302 | 113 | .909 | | | |

— 250 —

Bobby Bowden (1970-1975) 42-26-0 .618

1970			8-3-0	311	200	.727	1973			6-5-0	212	266	.545
1971			7-4-0	280	220	.636	1974			4-7-0	210	227	.364
1972			8-4-0	415	289	.667	1975	20	17	9-3-0	283	192	.750

Frank Cigneti (1976-1979) 17-27-0 .386

1976			5-6-0	184	202	.455	1978			2-9-0	167	364	.182
1977			5-6-0	244	264	.455	1979			5-6-0	185	279	.455

Don Nehlen (1980-2000) 149-93-4 .614

1980			6-6-0	305	299	.500	1986			4-7-0	210	286	.364
1981	17	18	9-3-0	284	155	.750	1987			6-6-0	330	212	.500
1982	19	19	9-3-0	272	151	.750	1988	5	5	11-1-0	493	208	.917
1983	16	16	9-3-0	322	189	.750	1989	21		8-3-1	339	221	.708
1984	18		8-4-0	259	170	.667	1990			4-7-0	217	238	.364
1985			7-3-1	189	158	.682							

Member of the Big East Conference (1991-2003) 52-37-1 .583

1991			6-5-0	187	224	.545	3-4-0	.429	3	1996	8-4-0	271	156	.667	4-3-0	.571	4
1992			5-4-2	286	238	.545	2-3-1	.417	5	1997	7-5-0	360	280	.583	4-3-0	.571	3
1993	7	6	11-1-0	408	212	.917	7-0-0	1.000	1	1998	8-4-0	410	265	.667	5-2-0	.714	2
1994			7-6-0	296	286	.538	4-3-0	.571	3	1999	4-7-0	292	289	.364	3-4-0	.429	4
1995			5-6-0	253	210	.455	4-3-0	.571	3	2000	7-5-0	356	363	.583	3-4-0	.429	5

Rich Rodriguez (2001-2003) 20-17-0 .541

2001			3-8-0	235	268	.273	1-6-0	.143	7	2003	8-5-0	376	297	.615	6-1-0	.857	1
2002	25	20	9-4-0	396	302	.692	6-1-0	.857	2								

Won-loss record by decades:

1890-99	25-20-3	.552	1930-39	46-45-8	.505	1970-79	59-53-0	527
1900-09	55-29-2	.651	1940-49	48-44-4	.521	1980-89	77-39-2	.661
1910-19	46-27-7	.619	1950-59	58-38-2	.602	1990-99	65-49-2	.569
1920-29	63-24-10	.701	1960-69	54-43-5	.554	2000-03	27-22-0	.551

Historic record: 623-433-45 .586

Post-season won-loss record: 9-14-0 .391

1922: East-West Bowl, WVA 21, Gonzaga 13
1938: Sun Bowl, WVA 7, Texas Tech 6
1949: Sun Bowl, WVA 21, Texas Western 12
1954: Sugar Bowl, Georgia Tech 42, WVA 19
1964: Liberty Bowl, Utah 32, WVA 6
1969: Peach Bowl, WVA 14, South Carolina 3
1972: Peach Bowl, NC State 49, WVA 13
1975: Peach Bowl, WVA 13, NC State 10
1981: Peach Bowl, WVA 26, Florida 6
1982: Gator Bowl, Florida State 21, WVA 12
1983: Hall of Fame Bowl, WVA 20, Kentucky 16

1984: Bluebonnet Bowl, WVA 31, TCU 14
1987: Sun Bowl, Oklahoma State 35, WVA 33
1989: Sunkist Fiesta Bowl, Notre Dame 34, WVA 21
1989: Mazda Gator Bowl, Clemson 27, WVA 7
1994: Sugar Bowl, Florida 41, WVA 7
1995: Carquest Bowl, South Carolina 24, WVA 21
1997: Toyota Gator Bowl, North Carolina 20, WVA 13
1997: Carquest Bowl, Georgia Tech 35, WVA 30
1998: Insight.com Bowl, Missouri 34, WVA 31
2000: Music City Bowl, WVA 49, Mississippi 38
2002: Continental Tire Bowl, Virginia 48, WVA 22
2003: Gator Bowl, Maryland 41, WVA 7

College Football Hall of Fame:
Ira Rodgers, fullback, 1915-19; Cliff Battles, halfback, 1928-31; Greasy Neale, coach, 1931-33; Joe Stydahar, tackle, 1933-35; Bruce Bosley, tackle, 1952-55; Sam Huff, guard/tackle, 1952-55.

WESTERN MICHIGAN UNIVERSITY, Kalamazoo, Michigan; nickname "Broncos"; colors brown and gold; Waldo Stadium (30,200); Mid American Conference. WMU began play in 1906 and then joined the MAC in 1948. Western Michigan has played in the MAC since that time.

Early years (1906-1947)

Melvin Myers (1906) 1-2-0 .333

Year	W-L-T	PF	PA	Pct.
1906	1-2-0	26	28	.333

Bill Spaulding (1907-1921) 62-25-3 .713

Year	W-L-T	PF	PA	Pct.	Year	W-L-T	PF	PA	Pct.
1907	3-2-1	42	8	.583	1915	5-1-0	291	43	.833
1908	3-3-0	33	98	.500	1916	5-1-0	389	38	.833
1909	7-0-0	194	8	1.000	1917	4-3-0	203	105	.571
1910	4-1-1	75	20	.750	1918	3-2-0	223	30	.600
1911	2-3-0	110	59	.400	1919	4-1-0	156	91	.800
1912	3-2-1	86	49	.583	1920	3-4-0	119	131	.429
1913	4-0-0	59	15	1.000	1921	6-2-0	262	40	.750
1914	6-0-0	180	7	1.000					

Milton Olander (1922-1923) 12-1-1 .893

Year	W-L-T	PF	PA	Pct.	Year	W-L-T	PF	PA	Pct.
1922	6-0-0	160	0	1.000	1923	6-1-1	160	21	.812

Earl Martinueau (1924-1928) 26-10-2 .722

Year	W-L-T	PF	PA	Pct.	Year	W-L-T	PF	PA	Pct.
1924	5-1-1	101	46	.786	1927	3-4-0	100	72	.429
1925	6-2-1	125	47	.722	1928	5-2-0	119	32	.714
1926	7-1-0	132	20	.875					

Mike Gary (1929-1941) 59-34-5 .627

Year	W-L-T	PF	PA	Pct.	Year	W-L-T	PF	PA	Pct.
1929	5-2-1	161	44	.688	1936	2-5-0	60	91	.286
1930	5-1-1	192	25	.786	1937	5-3-0	92	65	.625
1931	5-2-0	86	51	.714	1938	4-3-0	102	26	.571
1932	6-0-1	174	6	.929	1939	2-6-1	51	85	.278
1933	3-3-1	66	64	.500	1940	2-5-0	77	117	.286
1934	7-1-0	104	52	.875	1941	8-0-0	183	27	1.000
1935	5-3-0	78	91	.625					

John Gill (1942-1952) 50-34-1 .594

Year	W-L-T	PF	PA	Pct.	Year	W-L-T	PF	PA	Pct.
1942	5-1-0	66	37	.833	1945	4-3-0	147	105	.571
1943	4-2-0	151	89	.667	1946	5-2-1	158	100	.688
1944	4-3-0	162	123	.571	1947	5-4-0	139	147	.556

Member of the Mid-American Conference (1948-2003) 184-195-9 .486

Year	Nat'l AP Other	Overall W-L-T	PF	PA	Pct.	Conference W-L-T	Pct.	Rank	Year	Nat'l AP Other	Overall W-L-T	PF	PA	Pct.	Conference W-L-T	Pct.	Rank
1948		6-3-0	199	106	.667	3-1-0	.750	2	1951		4-4-0	164	160	.500	1-4-0	.200	6
1949		4-4-0	148	123	.500	2-3-0	.400	4	1952		4-4-0	154	159	.500	1-4-0	.200	6
1950		5-4-0	188	163	.556	0-4-0	.000	5									

Jack Petoskey (1953-1956) 8-25-2 .257

Year	Nat'l AP Other	Overall W-L-T	PF	PA	Pct.	Conference W-L-T	Pct.	Rank	Year	Nat'l AP Other	Overall W-L-T	PF	PA	Pct.	Conference W-L-T	Pct.	Rank
1953		1-6-1	66	238	.188	0-4-1	.100	6	1955		1-7-1	80	200	.167	0-5-0	.000	7
1954		4-5-0	136	186	.444	3-4-0	.429	5	1956		2-7-0	114	168	.222	1-4-0	.200	6

Merle Schlosser (1957-1963) 28-33-3 .459

Year	Nat'l AP Other	Overall W-L-T	PF	PA	Pct.	Conference W-L-T	Pct.	Rank	Year	Nat'l AP Other	Overall W-L-T	PF	PA	Pct.	Conference W-L-T	Pct.	Rank
1957		4-4-1	150	126	.500	1-4-1	.250	5	1961		5-4-1	143	179	.550	4-1-1	.750	2
1958		4-5-0	188	200	.444	2-4-0	.333	5	1962		5-4-0	158	112	.556	3-3-0	.500	4
1959		4-5-0	185	116	.444	3-3-0	.500	5	1963		2-7-0	111	201	.222	2-4-0	.333	5
1960		4-4-1	173	106	.500	2-4-0	.333	5									

Bill Doolittle (1964-1974) 58-49-2 .542

Year	Nat'l AP Other	Overall W-L-T	PF	PA	Pct.	Conference W-L-T	Pct.	Rank	Year	Nat'l AP Other	Overall W-L-T	PF	PA	Pct.	Conference W-L-T	Pct.	Rank
1964		3-6-0	77	185	.333	2-4-0	.333	5	1970		7-3-0	277	132	.700	2-3-0	.400	4
1965		6-2-1	128	127	.722	3-2-1	.583	3	1971		7-3-0	228	124	.700	2-3-0	.400	4
1966		7-3-0	175	194	.700	5-1-0	.833	1	1972		7-3-1	229	201	.682	2-2-1	.500	3
1967		5-4-0	156	164	.556	4-2-0	.667	3	1973		6-5-0	190	218	.545	1-4-0	.200	5
1968		3-6-0	160	191	.333	2-4-0	.333	5	1974		3-8-0	187	269	.273	0-5-0	.000	6
1969		4-6-0	216	103	.400	1-4-0	.200	5									

Elliot Uzelac (1975-1981) 38-39-0 .494

Year	Nat'l AP Other	Overall W-L-T	PF	PA	Pct.	Conference W-L-T	Pct.	Rank	Year	Nat'l AP Other	Overall W-L-T	PF	PA	Pct.	Conference W-L-T	Pct.	Rank
1975		1-10-0	119	297	.091	0-7-0	.000	9	1979		6-5-0	196	120	.545	5-4-0	.545	3
1976		7-4-0	270	202	.636	6-3-0	.667	4	1980		7-4-0	233	179	.636	6-3-0	.667	2
1977		4-7-0	261	231	.364	3-5-0	.375	7	1981		6-5-0	206	170	.545	5-4-0	.556	5
1978		7-4-0	220	152	.636	5-4-0	.556	4									

Jack Harbaugh (1982-1986) 25-27-3 .482

Year	Nat'l AP Other	Overall W-L-T	PF	PA	Pct.	Conference W-L-T	Pct.	Rank	Year	Nat'l AP Other	Overall W-L-T	PF	PA	Pct.	Conference W-L-T	Pct.	Rank
1982		7-2-2	186	78	.727	5-2-2	.667	2	1985		4-6-1	182	212	.409	4-4-1	.500	4
1983		6-5-0	179	208	.545	4-5-0	.444	6	1986		3-8-0	183	257	.273	3-5-0	.375	8
1984		5-6-0	234	213	.455	3-6-0	.333	8									

1987	5-6-0	218	240	.455	4-4-0	.500	5	1992		7-3-1	197	177	.682	6-3-0	.667	2
1988	9-3-0	354	237	.750	7-1-0	.875	1	1993		7-3-1	236	187	.682	6-1-1	.812	2
1989	5-6-0	210	210	.455	3-5-0	.375	6	1994		7-4-0	274	189	.636	5-3-0	.625	3
1990	7-4-0	249	218	.636	5-3-0	.625	3	1995		7-4-0	253	190	.636	6-2-0	.750	3
1991	6-5-0	218	253	.545	4-4-0	.500	5	1996		2-9-0	208	304	.182	2-6-0	.200	9

Gary Darnell (1997-2003) 45-36-0 .556

1997	8-3-0	301	265	.727	6-2-0	.750	2	2000		9-3-0	359	139	.750	7-1-0	.875	1
1998	7-4-0	360	312	.636	5-3-0	.625	3	2001		5-6-0	277	126	.455	4-4-0	.500	8
1999	7-5-0	373	342	.583	6-2-0	.750	1	2002		4-8-0	303	330	.333	3-5-0	.375	9
								2003		5-7-0	331	370	.417	4-4-0	.500	7

Won-loss record by decades:

1906-09	14-7-1	.659	1940-49	47-27-1	.633	1980-89	57-51-3	.527
1910-19	40-14-2	.732	1950-59	33-51-3	.397	1990-99	65-44-2	.595
1920-29	52-19-4	.720	1960-69	44-46-3	.489	2000-03	23-24-0	.489
1930-39	44-27-4	.613	1970-79	55-52-1	.514			

Historic record: 474-362-24 .565

Post-season won-loss record: 0-2-0 .000
1961: Aviation Bowl, New Mexico 28, Western Michigan 12
1988: California Raisin Bowl, Fresno State 35, Western Michigan 30

TEXAS CHRISTIAN UNIVERSITY, Fort Worth, Texas; nickname "Horned Frogs"; colors purple and white; Amos G. Carter Stadium (44,008); Conference USA. TCU began play in 1896 as an independent. In 1909, TCU became a member of the Texas Intercollegiate Athletic Association and played in that association until 1923 when TCU joined the Southwestern Conference, which had been in existence since 1915. TCU played in the Southwestern Conference until it disbanded after the 1995 season. TCU moved into the Western Athletic Conference where it played through the 2000 season. In 2001, TCU moved into Conference USA. Conference standings are not available for the TIAA years (1909-1922).

Early years (1896-1922)

Year	Coach	W-L-T	PF	PA	Pct.	Year	Coach	W-L-T	PF	PA	Pct.
1896	none	1-1-1	8	28	.500	1910	Kemp Lewis	2-6-1	45	187	.278
1897	Joe Field	3-1-0	78	24	.750	1911	Henry Lever	4-5-0	114	106	.444
1898	James Morrison	1-3-1	41	60	.300	1912	W. Stewart	8-1-0	230	53	.889
1899	none	0-0-1	0	60	.500	1913	Fred Cahoon	3-1-2	44	6	.667
1900	no team					1914	S. Boles	4-4-2	117	118	.500
1901	none	1-2-1	5	78	.375	1915	E.Freeland	4-5-0	130	182	.444
1902	H. Hildebrand	0-5-1	0	93	.084	1916	Milton Daniel	6-2-1	217	85	.722
1903	none	0-7-0	11	100	.000	1917	Milton Daniel	8-2-0	201	59	.800
1904	C.Cronk	1-4-1	5	90	.250	1918	E. Tipton	4-3-0	96	40	.571
1905	E. Hyde	4-4-0	77	65	.500	1919	T. Hackney	2-6-0	28	111	.250
1906	E. Hyde	2-5-0	26	108	.286	1920	W. Driver	9-1-0	170	109	.900
1907	E. Hyde	4-2-2	90	69	.625	1921	W. Driver	6-3-1	132	75	.650
1908	J. Langley	6-3-0	155	68	.667	1922	John McKnight	2-5-3	91	167	.350
1909	J. Langley	5-2-1	95	33	.688						

Member of the Southwest Conference (1923-1995) 195-259-22 .433

Year	Nat'l AP	Other	Overall W-L-T	PF	PA	Pct.	Conference W-L-T	Pct.	Rank	Year	Nat'l AP	Other	Overall W-L-T	PF	PA	Pct.	Conference W-L-T	Pct.	Rank

Matty Bell (1923-1928) 33-17-5 .645

1923			4-5-0	93	137	.444	2-1-0	.667	3	1926			6-1-2	110	74	.778	1-1-2	.500	6
1924			4-5-0	83	96	.444	1-5-0	.167	8	1927			4-3-2	89	64	.556	1-2-2	.400	5
1925			7-1-1	133	54	.833	2-1-1	.625	2	1928			8-2-0	142	28	.800	3-2-0	.600	3

Francis Schmidt (1929-1933) 47-5-5 .868

1929		8	9-0-1	249	33	.950	4-0-1	.900	1	1932		10	10-0-1	283	23	.955	6-0-0	1.000	1
1930			9-2-1	298	49	.792	4-2-0	.667	3	1933*			10-1-1	208	49	.875	5-1-0	.833	1
1931			9-2-1	149	41	.792	4-1-1	.750	2										

*Includes a forfeit win in a game that Arkansas originally won , 13-0.

Dutch Meyer (1934-1952) 109-79-13 .575

1934			8-4-0	173	116	.667	3-3-0	.500	4	1944			7-3-1	134	109	.682	3-1-1	700	1
1935		8	12-1-0	265	73	.923	5-1-0	.833	2	1945			5-5-0	91	156	.500	3-3-0	.500	3
1936	16		9-2-2	164	58	.769	4-1-1	.750	2	1946			2-7-1	90	148	.250	2-4-0	.333	5
1937	16		4-4-2	73	66	.500	3-1-2	.667	2	1947			4-5-2	114	105	.455	2-3-1	.417	4
1938	1	8	11-0-0	269	60	1.000	6-0-0	1.000	1	1948			4-5-1	125	143	.450	1-4-1	.250	6
1939			3-7-0	116	119	.300	1-5-0	.167	6	1949			6-3-1	205	185	.650	3-3-0	.500	3
1940			3-7-0	116	121	.300	2-4-0	.333	5	1950			5-5-0	157	166	.500	3-3-0	.500	3
1941			7-3-1	162	135	.682	4-1-1	.750	2	1951	11	10	6-5-0	206	183	.545	5-1-0	.833	1
1942			7-3-0	129	82	.700	4-2-0	.667	3	1952			4-4-2	141	103	.500	2-2-2	.500	4
1943			2-6-0	71	146	.250	1-4-0	.200	5										

Abe Martin (1953-1966) 74-64-7 548

1953			3-7-0	116	150	.300	1-5-0	167	6	1960			4-4-2	85	94	.500	3-3-1	.500	5
1954			4-6-0	164	142	.400	1-5-0	.167	6	1961			3-5-2	113	194	.400	2-4-1	.357	5
1955	6	6	9-2-0	306	105	.818	5-1-0	.833	1	1962			6-4-0	167	154	.600	5-2-0	.714	3
1956	14	14	8-3-0	231	110	818	5-1-0	.833	2	1963			4-5-1	131	194	.450	2-4-1	.357	5
1957			5-4-1	134	101	.550	2-4-0	.333	5	1964			4-6-0	94	169	.400	3-4-0	.429	6
1958	10	9	8-2-1	218	78	.773	5-1-0	.833	1	1965			6-5-0	170	156	.545	5-2-0	.714	2
1959	7	8	8-3-0	169	75	.727	5-1-0	.833	1	1966			2-8-0	55	149	.200	2-5-0	.286	6

Fred Taylor (1967-1970) 15-25-1 .383

| 1967 | | | 4-6-0 | 115 | 185 | .400 | 4-3-0 | .571 | 3 | 1969 | | | 4-6-0 | 177 | 293 | .400 | 4-3-0 | .571 | 3 |
| 1968 | | | 3-7-0 | 176 | 215 | .300 | 2-5-0 | .286 | 6 | 1970 | | | 4-6-1 | 189 | 265 | .409 | 3-4-0 | .429 | 4 |

Jim Pittman (1971) 3-3-1 .500

| 1971* | | | 3-3-1 | 159 | 203 | .500 | 3-1-0 | .750 | * | | | | | | | | | | |

Billy Tohill (1971-1973) 11-15-0 .423

| 1971* | | | 3-1-0 | 55 | 72 | .750 | 2-1-0 | .667 | 3 | 1973 | | | 3-8-0 | 189 | 290 | .273 | 1-6-0 | .143 | 7 |
| 1972 | | | 5-6-0 | 213 | 245 | .455 | 2-5-0 | .286 | 7 | | | | | | | | | | |

*Pittman coached the first seven games of the 1971 season, and Tohill coached the last four.

Jim Shofner (1974-1976) 2-31-0 .061

| 1974 | | | 1-10-0 | 79 | 345 | .091 | 0-7-0 | .000 | 8 | 1976 | | | 0-11-0 | 128 | 430 | .000 | 0-8-0 | .000 | 9 |
| 1975 | | | 1-10-0 | 103 | 325 | .091 | 1-6-0 | .143 | 7 | | | | | | | | | | |

F. A. Dry (1977-1982) 12-51-3 .201

Year									Year									
1977	2-9-0	184	434	.182	1-7-0	.125	8		1980		1-10-0	143	292	.091	1-7-0	.125	9
1978	2-9-0	109	357	.182	0-8-0	.000	9		1981		2-7-2	230	266	.273	1-6-1	.188	8
1979	2-8-1	127	226	.227	1-6-1	.188	8		1982		3-8-0	203	266	.273	2-6-0	.250	8

Jim Wacker (1983-1991) 40-58-2 .414

1983	1-8-2	174	252	.182	1-6-1	.188	8		1988		4-7-0	206	286	.364	2-5-0	.286	4
1984	8-4-0	376	280	.667	5-3-0	.625	3		1989		4-7-0	183	301	.364	2-6-0	.250	6
1985	3-8-0	150	383	.273	0-8-0	.000	8		1990		5-6-0	292	353	.455	3-5-0	.375	4
1986	3-8-0	259	376	.273	1-7-0	.125	**		1991		7-4-0	278	267	.636	4-4-0	.500	5
1987	5-6-0	261	226	.455	3-4-0	.429	5										

**TCU ineligible for conference title due to NCAA violations.

Pat Sullivan (1992-1997) 24-42-1 .366

1992	2-8-1	195	319	.227	1-6-0	.143	8		1994		7-5-0	302	303	.583	4-3-0	.571	1
1993	4-7-0	211	313	.364	2-5-0	.286	6		1995		6-5-0	217	246	.545	3-4-0	.429	5

Member of the Western Athletic Conference (1996-2000) 20-19-1 .513

1996	4-7-0	211	302	.364	3-5-0	.375	9		1997		1-10-0	172	325	.091	1-7-0	.125	15

Dennis Franchione (1998-1999) 25-10-0 .714

1998	7-5-0	267	235	.583	4-4-0	.500	9		2000* 21	18	10-1-0	410	106	.909	7-1-0	.875	1
1999	8-4-0	327	213	.667	5-2-0	.714	1										

Gary Patterson (2000-2003) 27-11-0 .711

2000* 0-1-0 21 28 .000 0-0-0

*Franchione coached the first eleven games of the 2000 season, and Patterson coached the last (bowl) game.

Member of Conference USA (2001-2003) 17-6-0 .739

2001	6-6-0	289	285	.500	4-3-0	.571	5		2003 25	24	11-2-0	380	276	.846	7-1-0	.875	2
2002 23	22	10-2-0	361	222	.833	6-2-0	.750	1									

Won-loss record by decades:

1896-99	5- 5-3	.500		1930-39	85-23-8	.767		1970-79	26-81-3	.250
1900-09	23-34-6	.413		1940-49	47-47-7	.500		1980-89	34-73-4	.330
1910-19	45-35-6	.558		1950-59	60-41-4	.590		1990-99	51-61-1	.456
1920-29	59-26-10	.674		1960-69	40-56-5	.421		2000-03	37-12-0	.755

Historic record: 512-494-57 .508

Post-season won-loss record: 7-12-1 .375

1936: Sugar Bowl, TCU 3, LSU 2
1937: Cotton Bowl, TCU 16, Marquette 6
1939: Sugar Bowl, TCU 15, Carnegie Tech 7
1942: Orange Bowl, Georgia 40, TCU 26
1945: Cotton Bowl, Oklahoma A&M 34, TCU 0
1948: Delta Bowl, Mississippi 13, TCU 9
1952: Cotton Bowl, Kentucky 20, TCU 7
1956: Cotton Bowl, Mississippi 14, TCU 13
1957: Cotton Bowl, TCU 28, Syracuse 27

1959: Cotton Bowl, TCU 0, Air Force 0
1959: Bluebonnet Bowl, Clemson 23, TCU 7
1965: Sun Bowl, Texas Western 13, TCU 12
!984: Bluebonnet Bowl, West Virginia 31, TCU 14
1994: Independence Bowl, Virginia 20, TCU 10
1998: Norwest Sun Bowl, TCU 28, USC 19
1999: Mobile Alabama Bowl, TCU 28, East Carolina 14
2000: Mobile Alabama Bowl, Southern Mississippi 28, TCU 21
2001: Galleryfurniture.com Bowl, Texas A&M 28, TCU 9
2002: Liberty Bowl, TCU 17, Colorado State 3
2003: Fort Worth Bowl, Boise State 34, TCU 31

College Football Hall of Fame:
Matty Bell, coach, 1923-29; Rags Mathews, end, 1925-27; Francis Schmidt, coach, 1930-33; Darrell Lester, center, 1933-35; Dutch Meyer, coach, 1934-52; Sammy Baugh, halfback, 1934-36; Ki Aldrich, center, 1936-38; Davey O'Brien, quarterback, 1936-38; Jim Swink, halfback, 1954-56; Bob Lilly, tackle, 1958-60.

Awards: Heisman Trophy: 1938, Davey O'Brien; Maxwell Award: 1938, Davey O'Brien.

UNIVERSITY OF WISC0NSIN, Madison, Wisconsin; nickname "Badgers"; colors red and white; Camp Randall Stadium (76,643); Big Ten Conference. Wisconsin was one of the founding members of the Big Ten, which began play in 1896. The conference win percent before 1946 is calculated ignoring ties, which was the conference rule up to that season.

Early years as an Independent (1889-1895)

Year	W-L-T	PF	PA	Pct.		Year	W-L-T	PF	PA	Pct.
					Alvin Kletsch (1889) 0-2-0 .000					
1889	0-2-0	0	31	.000						
					Ted Mestre (1890) 1-3-0 .250					
1890	1-3-0	122	101	.250						
					Herb Alward (1891) 3-1-1 .700					
1891	3-1-1	98	34	.700						
					Frank Crawford (1892) 4-3-0 .571					
1892	4-3-0	102	96	.571						
					Parke Davis (1893) 4-2-0 .667					
1893	4-2-0	112	110	.667						
					H. O. Stickney (1894-1895) 10-4-1 .700					
1894	5-2-0	152	20	.714		1895	5-2-1	144	71	.688

Member of the Big Ten Conference (1896-2003) 290-341-40 .462

Year	Nat'l AP	Other	Overall W-L-T	PF	PA	Pct.	Conf W-L-T	Conf Pct.	Rank	Year	Nat'l AP	Other	Overall W-L-T	PF	PA	Pct.	Conf W-L-T	Conf Pct.	Rank
Phil King (1896-1902, 1905) 65-11-1 .851																			
1896			7-1-1	206	30	.833	2-0-1	1.000	1	1900			8-1-0	300	11	.889	2-1-0	.667	3
1897			9-1-0	212	14	.900	3-0-0	1.000	1	1901			9-0-0	317	5	1.000	2-0-0	1.000	2
1898			9-1-0	298	17	.900	2-1-0	.667	3	1902			6-3-0	228	39	.667	1-3-0	.250	6
1899			9-2-0	270	33	.818	4-1-0	.800	2										
Art Curtis (1903-1904) 11-6-1 .639																			
1903			6-3-1	305	67	.650	0-3-1	.000	8	1904			5-3-0	265	74	.625	0-3-0	.000	7
Phil King (1905)																			
1905			8-2-0	226	28	.800	2-2-0	.500	5										
C. P. Hutchins (1906-1907) 8-1-1 .850																			
1906			5-0-0	78	15	1.000	3-0-0	1.000	1	1907			3-1-1	50	51	.700	3-1-1	.750	2
J. A. Barry (1908-1910) 9-4-3 .656																			
1908			5-1-0	101	39	.833	2-1-0	.667	3	1910			1-2-2	19	46	.400	1-2-1	.333	6
1909			3-1-1	61	54	.700	2-1-1	.667	4										
J. R. Richards (1911, 1917, 1919-1922) 29-9-4 .738																			
1911			5-1-1	111	14	.786	2-2-2	.667	3										
William Juneau (1912-1915) 18-8-2 .679																			
1912			7-0-0	246	29	1.000	5-0-0	1.000	1	1914			4-2-1	102	51	.643	2-2-1	.500	4
1913			3-3-1	100	66	.500	1-2-1	.333	6	1915			4-3-0	235	54	.571	2-3-0	.400	6
Paul Withington (1916) 4-2-1 .643																			
1916			4-2-1	104	78	.643	1-2-1	.333	6										
J. R. Richards (1917)																			
1917			4-2-1	85	30	.643	3-2-0	.600	3										
Guy Lowman (1918) 3-3-0 .500																			
1918			3-3-0	42	44	.500	1-2-0	.333	7										
J. R. Richards (1919-1922)																			
1919			5-2-0	91	41	.714	3-2-0	.600	4	1921			5-1-1	141	13	.786	3-1-1	.750	4
1920			6-1-0	141	29	.857	4-1-0	.800	2	1922			4-2-1	101	22	.643	2-2-1	.500	4
Jack Ryan (1923-1924) 5-6-4 .467																			
1923			3-3-1	89	32	.500	1-3-1	.250	7	1924			2-3-3	66	94	.438	0-2-2	.000	10
George Little (1925-1926) 11-3-2 .750																			
1925	8		6-1-1	131	50	.812	3-1-1	.750	2	1926			5-2-1	122	72	.688	3-2-1	.600	5
Glenn Thistlewaite (1927-1931) 26-16-3 .611																			
1927			4-4-0	96	69	.500	1-4-0	.200	9	1930			6-2-1	227	40	.722	2-2-1	.500	4
1928		4	7-1-1	163	38	.812	3-1-1	.750	2	1931			5-4-1	105	110	.550	3-3-1	.500	6
1929			4-5-0	88	78	.444	1-4-0	.200	10										
Doc Spears (1932-1935) 13-17-2 .438																			
1932	11		6-1-1	151	48	.812	4-1-1	.800	3	1934			4-4-0	48	84	.500	2-3-0	.400	5
1933			2-5-1	54	79	.312	0-5-1	.000	9	1935			1-7-0	53	171	.125	1-4-0	.200	9
Harry Stuhldreher (1936-1948) 45-62-6 .425																			
1936			2-6-0	95	144	.250	0-4-0	.000	8	1943			1-9-0	41	282	.100	1-6-0	.143	8
1937			4-3-1	103	61	.562	2-2-1	.500	6	1944			3-6-0	112	180	.333	2-4-0	.333	7
1938			5-3-0	111	93	.625	3-2-0	.600	5	1945			3-4-2	128	128	.444	2-3-1	.400	6
1939			1-6-1	54	113	.188	0-5-1	.000	9	1946			4-5-0	140	144	.444	2-5-0	.286	8
1940			4-4-0	125	134	.500	3-3-0	.500	4	1947			5-3-1	153	156	.611	3-2-1	.583	2
1941			3-5-0	144	208	.375	3-3-0	.500	5	1948			2-7-0	88	193	.222	1-5-0	.167	9
1942	3		8-1-1	149	68	.850	4-1-0	.800	2										

Ivy Williamson (1949-1955) 41-19-4 .672

Year			W-L-T	PF	PA	Pct	Conf	Conf Pct	Pl	Year			W-L-T	PF	PA	Pct	Conf	Conf Pct	Pl
1949			5-3-1	207	129	.611	3-2-1	.583	4	1953	15	14	6-2-1	179	110	.722	4-1-1	.750	3
1950	20		6-3-0	127	97	.667	5-2-0	.714	2	1954	9	10	7-2-0	199	98	.778	5-2-0	.714	2
1951	8	8	7-1-1	196	59	.833	5-1-1	.786	3	1955			4-5-0	172	166	.444	3-4-0	.429	6
1952	11	10	6-3-1	182	150	.650	4-1-1	.750	1										

Milt Bruhn (1956-1966) 52-45-6 .534

Year			W-L-T	PF	PA	Pct	Conf	Conf Pct	Pl	Year			W-L-T	PF	PA	Pct	Conf	Conf Pct	Pl
1956			1-5-3	93	129	.278	0-4-3	.214	9	1962	2	2	8-2-0	322	130	.800	6-1-0	.857	1
1957	19	14	6-3-0	234	122	.667	4-3-0	.571	4	1963			5-4-0	150	124	.556	3-4-0	.429	5
1958	7	6	7-1-1	201	77	.859	5-1-0	.833	1	1964			3-6-0	98	229	.333	2-5-0	.286	7
1959	6	6	7-3-0	165	149	.700	5-2-0	.714	1	1965			2-7-1	81	291	.250	2-5-0	.286	7
1960			4-5-0	148	183	.444	2-5-0	.286	9	1966			3-6-1	87	212	.350	2-4-1	.357	7
1961	18		6-3-0	179	158	.667	4-3-0	.571	5										

John Coata (1967-1969) 3-26-1 .117

Year			W-L-T	PF	PA	Pct	Conf	Conf Pct	Pl	Year			W-L-T	PF	PA	Pct	Conf	Conf Pct	Pl
1967			0-9-1	120	334	.050	0-6-1	.071	9	1969			3-7-0	196	349	.300	3-4-0	.429	5
1968			0-10-0	86	310	.000	0-7-0	.000	10										

John Jardine (1970-1977) 37-47-3 .443

Year			W-L-T	PF	PA	Pct	Conf	Conf Pct	Pl	Year			W-L-T	PF	PA	Pct	Conf	Conf Pct	Pl
1970			4-5-1	198	195	.450	3-4-0	.429	5	1974			7-4-0	341	243	.636	5-3-0	.625	4
1971			4-6-1	240	258	.409	3-5-0	.375	6	1975			4-6-1	174	269	.409	3-4-1	.438	6
1972			4-7-0	152	229	.364	2-6-0	.250	9	1976			5-6-0	298	266	.545	3-5-0	.375	7
1973			4-7-0	216	237	.364	3-5-0	.375	8	1977			5-6-0	133	200	.545	3-6-0	.333	8

Dave McClain (1978-1985) 46-42-3 .522

Year			W-L-T	PF	PA	Pct	Conf	Conf Pct	Pl	Year			W-L-T	PF	PA	Pct	Conf	Conf Pct	Pl
1978			5-4-2	223	277	.545	3-4-2	.444	6	1982			7-5-0	341	243	.636	5-4-0	.556	5
1979			4-7-0	208	311	.364	3-5-0	.375	7	1983			7-4-0	359	242	.636	5-4-0	.556	5
1980			4-7-0	138	211	.364	3-5-0	.375	6	1984			7-4-1	242	206	.625	5-3-1	.611	4
1981			7-5-0	268	220	.583	6-3-0	.667	3	1985			5-6-0	231	263	.455	2-6-0	.250	8

Jim Hilles (1986) 3-9-0 .250

Year			W-L-T	PF	PA	Pct	Conf	Conf Pct	Pl
1986			3-9-0	201	266	.250	2-6-0	.250	8

Don Morton (1987-1989) 6-27-0 .188

Year			W-L-T	PF	PA	Pct	Conf	Conf Pct	Pl	Year			W-L-T	PF	PA	Pct	Conf	Conf Pct	Pl
1987			3-8-0	202	299	.273	1-7-0	.125	10	1989			2-9-0	172	341	.182	1-7-0	.143	9
1988			1-10-0	106	314	.091	1-7-0	.125	10										

Barry Alvarez (1990-2003) 99-67-4 .606

Year			W-L-T	PF	PA	Pct	Conf	Conf Pct	Pl	Year			W-L-T	PF	PA	Pct	Conf	Conf Pct	Pl
1990			1-10-0	133	285	.091	0-8-0	.000	10	1997			8-5-0	291	306	.615	5-3-0	.625	5
1991			5-6-0	172	194	.455	2-6-0	.250	8	1998	6	5	11-1-0	382	143	.917	7-1-0	.875	1
1992			5-6-0	212	199	.455	3-5-0	.375	6	1999	4	4	10-2-0	409	154	.833	7-1-0	.875	1
1993	6	5	10-1-1	354	195	.875	6-1-1	.813	1	2000	23	24	9-4-0	328	265	.692	4-4-0	.500	5
1994			8-3-1	357	248	.625	5-2-1	.688	4	2001			5-7-0	313	346	.417	3-5-0	.374	8
1995			4-5-2	235	253	455	3-4-1	.438	7	2002			8-6-0	372	322	.571	2-6-0	.250	8
1996			8-5-0	377	243	.615	3-5-0	.375	7	2003			7-6-0	355	306	.538	4-4-0	.500	7

Won-loss record by decades:

1889-99	56-20-3	.728	1930-39	36-41-6	.470	1970-79	46-58-5	.445	
1900-09	58-15-3	.783	1940-49	38-47-5	.450	1980-89	46-67-1	.408	
1910-19	40-20-7	.649	1950-59	57-28-7	.658	1990-99	70-44-4	.610	
1920-29	46-23-9	.647	1960-69	34-59-3	.370	2000-03	29-23-0	.558	

Historic record: 556-445-53 .553

Post-season won-loss record: 8-7-0 .533

1953: Rose Bowl, USC 7, Wisconsin 0
1960: Rose Bowl, Washington 44, Wisconsin 8
1963: Rose Bowl, USC 42, Wisconsin 37
1981: Garden State Bowl, Tennessee 28, Wisconsin 21
1982: Independence Bowl, Wisconsin 14, Kansas State 3
1984: Hall of Fame Bowl, Kentucky 20, Wisconsin 19
1994: Rose Bowl, Wisconsin 21, UCLA 16

1995: Hall of Fame Bowl, Wisconsin 34, Duke 20\
1996: Copper Bowl, Wisconsin 38, Utah 10
1998: Outback Bowl, Georgia 33, Wisconsin 6
1999: Rose Bowl, Wisconsin 38, UCLA 31
2000: Rose Bowl, Wisconsin 17, Stanford 9
2000: Sun Bowl, Wisconsin 21, UCLA 10
2002: Alamo Bowl, Wisconsin 31, Colorado 28
2003: Music City Bowl, Auburn 28, Wisconsin 14

College Football Hall of Fame:
Pat O' Dea, Fullback, 1896-99; Bob Butler, tackle, 1911-13; Marty Below, tackle, 1918-23; Dave Schreiner, end, 1940-42; Pat Harder, fullback, 1941-42; Elroy "Crazy Legs" Hirsch, halfback, 1942-43; Alan "The Horse" Ameche, fullback, 1951-54; Pat Richter, end, 1960-62.

Awards: Heisman Trophy: 1999, Ron Dayne; Doak Walker Award: 1999, Ron Dayne; Jim Thorpe Award: 2000, James Fletcher; Maxwell Award: 1999, Ron Dayne; Ray Guy Award: 2000, Kevin Stemke; Camp Award: 1999, Ron Dayne; Baugh Trophy: 1961, Ron Miller.

UNIVERSITY OF WYOMING, Laramie, Wyoming; nickname "Cowboys"; War Memorial Stadium (33,500); Mountain West Conference. Wyoming began play in 1893. In 1938 Wyoming joined the newly formed Skyline Conference. When the Skyline Conference disbanded after the 1961 season, Wyoming was a founding member of the Western Athletic Conference. Wyoming left the WAC after the 1998 season joining with other ex-WAC members to form the Mountain West Conference.

Early years (1893-1937)

Year	W-L-T	PF	PA	Pct.		Year	W-L-T	PF	PA	Pct.
						Fred Hess (1893-1894, 1898) 4-4-0 .500				
1893	1-0-0	14	0	1.000		1894*	3-0-0	46	6	1.000

*Also coaching with Hess was J. F. Soule.

						J. F. Soule (1895-1897, 1899) 5-1-1 .786				
1895	1-0-0	34	0	1.000						
1896	2-0-0	28	20	1.000		1897	2-0-0	20	0	1.000
						Fred Hess (1898)				
1898	0-4-0	8	95	.000						
						J. F. Soule (1899)				
1899	0-1-1	5	17	.250						
						William McMurray (1900-1906) 16-11-1 .589				
1900	3-3-0	105	59	.500		1904	4-1-1	97	35	.750
1901	1-0-0	38	0	1.000		1905	3-4-0	63	162	.429
1902	1-0-0	18	0	1.000		1906	1-1-0	12	35	.500
1903	3-2-0	32	63	.600						
						Robert Ehlman (1907-1908) 3-3-0 .500				
1907	2-1-0	68	79	.667		1908	1-2-0	66	95	.333
						H. I. Dean (1909-1911) 11-12-1 .479				
1909	3-5-0	93	170	.375		1911	4-3-1	139	53	.562
1910	4-4-0	107	75	.500						
						L. C. Excelby (1912) 2-7-0 .222				
1912	2-7-0	64	291	.222						
						R. W. Thatcher (1913-1914) 1-10-0 .091				
1913	0-5-0	0	183	.000		1914	1-5-0	31	158	.167
						John Corbett (1915-1923) 15-44-3 .266				
1915	2-6-0	46	212	.250		1920	4-5-1	58	106	.450
1916	1-4-0	50	115	.200		1921	1-4-2	39	82	.286
1917	3-4-0	24	140	.429		1922	1-8-0	13	255	.111
1918	no team					1923	0-8-0	16	265	.000
1919	3-5-0	68	115	.625						
						W. H. Dietz (1924-1927) 14-18-2 .441				
1924	2-6-0	59	140	.250		1926	2-4-2	152	90	.365
1925	6-3-0	147	83	.667		1927	4-5-0	122	105	.444
						George McLaren (1928-1929) 3-14-0 .176				
1928	2-7-0	95	230	.222		1929	1-7-0	33	160	.125
						John Rhodes (1930-1932) 10-15-2 .407				
1930	2-5-1	86	161	.312		1932	2-6-1	53	137	.278
1931	6-4-0	172	75	.600						
						Willard Witte (1933-1938) 16-30-3 .357				
1933	2-6-1	51	111	.278		1936	2-5-1	74	159	.312
1934	3-5-0	77	109	.375		1937	3-5-0	86	92	.375
1935	4-4-0	76	57	.500						

Member of the Mountain States ("Skyline") Conference (1938-1961) 72-52-8 .576

Year	Nat'l AP Other	Overall W-L-T	PF	PA	Pct.	Conference W-L-T	Pct.	Rank	Year	Nat'l AP Other	Overall W-L-T	PF	PA	Pct.	Conference W-L-T	Pct.	Rank
1938		2-5-1	66	142	.312	1-4-1	.250	6									
						Joel Hunt (1939) 0-7-1 .062											
1939		0-7-1	47	241	.071	0-5-1	.083	7									
						Okie Blanchard (1940) 1-7-1 .167											
1940		1-7-1	32	190	.167	0-5-1	.083	7									
						Bunny Oakes (1941-1946) 6-20-2 .250											
1941		2-7-1	44	233	.250	1-5-0	.167	6	1943-1945		no team						
1942		3-5-0	106	115	.375	1-5-0	.167	7	1946		1-8-1	44	192	.150	0-6-0	.000	7
						Bowden Wyatt (1947-1952) 39-17-1 .693											
1947		4-5-0	175	168	.444	2-4-0	.333	6	1950	12 14	10-0-0	363	59	1.000	5-0-0	1.000	1
1948		4-5-0	270	145	.444	0-5-0	.000	6	1951		7-2-1	220	82	.750	5-1-1	.786	2
1949		9-1-0	375	65	.900	5-0-0	1.000	1	1952		5-4-0	114	102	.556	4-3-0	.571	4
						Phil Dickens (1953-1956) 29-11-1 .738											
1953		5-4-1	195	110	.550	4-2-1	.643	3	1955		8-3-0	225	137	.727	5-2-0	.714	3
1954		6-4-0	215	171	.600	5-1-0	.833	2	1956	16	10-0-0	252	112	1.000	7-0-0	1.000	1

Bob Devaney (1957-1961) 35-10-5 .750

Year	Rank	Record	PF	PA	Pct	Conf	Conf Pct	Place
1957		4-3-3	139	135	.550	3-2-2	.571	4
1958		8-3-0	205	136	.727	6-1-0	.857	1
1959	16	9-1-0	287	62	.900	7-0-0	1.000	1
1960		8-2-0	212	71	.800	6-1-0	.857	1
1961	17	6-1-2	171	74	.778	5-0-1	.833	1

Member of the Western Athletic Conference (1962-1998) 146-116-1 .557

Lloyd Eaton (1962-1970) 57-33-2 .630

Year	Rank	Record	PF	PA	Pct	Conf	Conf Pct	Place
1962		5-5-0	165	143	.500	2-2-0	.500	2
1963		6-4-0	191	152	.600	2-3-0	.400	4
1964		6-2-2	181	117	.700	2-2-0	.500	4
1965		6-4-0	201	182	.600	3-2-0	.600	3
1966	15	10-1-0	355	89	.909	5-0-0	1.000	1
1967	6 5	10-1-0	289	119	.909	5-0-0	1.000	1
1968		7-3-0	242	118	.700	6-1-0	.857	1
1969		6-4-0	232	187	.600	4-3-0	.571	3
1970		1-9-0	110	314	.100	1-6-0	.143	7

Fritz Shurmur (1971-1974) 15-29-0 .341

Year	Rank	Record	PF	PA	Pct	Conf	Conf Pct	Place
1971		5-6-0	222	264	.455	3-4-0	.429	4
1972		4-7-0	223	309	.364	3-4-0	.429	5
1973		4-7-0	248	290	.364	3-4-0	.429	4
1974		2-9-0	150	283	.182	1-6-0	.143	8

Fred Akers (1975-1976) 10-13-0 .435

Year	Rank	Record	PF	PA	Pct	Conf	Conf Pct	Place
1975		2-9-0	170	220	.182	1-6-0	.143	7
1976		8-4-0	278	250	.667	6-1-0	.857	1

Bill Lewis (1977-1979) 14-20-1 .414

Year	Rank	Record	PF	PA	Pct	Conf	Conf Pct	Place
1977		4-6-1	166	273	.409	4-3-0	.571	4
1978		5-7-0	253	245	.417	4-2-0	.667	2
1979		5-7-0	186	278	.417	2-5-0	.286	7

Pat Dye (1980) 6-5-0 .545

Year	Rank	Record	PF	PA	Pct	Conf	Conf Pct	Place
1980		6-5-0	316	243	.545	4-4-0	.500	4

Al Kincaid (1981-1985) 29-29-0 .500

Year	Rank	Record	PF	PA	Pct	Conf	Conf Pct	Place
1981		8-3-0	344	203	.727	6-2-0	.750	4
1982		5-7-0	267	280	.417	2-6-0	.250	8
1983		7-5-0	330	327	.583	5-3-0	.625	3
1984		6-6-0	334	342	.500	4-4-0	.500	6
1985		3-8-0	210	371	.273	2-6-0	.250	7

Dennis Erickson (1986) 6-6-0 .500

Year	Rank	Record	PF	PA	Pct	Conf	Conf Pct	Place
1986		6-6-0	299	272	.500	4-4-0	.500	4

Paul Roach (1987-1990) 35-15-0 .700

Year	Rank	Record	PF	PA	Pct	Conf	Conf Pct	Place
1987		10-3-0	426	261	.769	8-0-0	1.000	1
1988	20	11-2-0	511	280	.846	8-0-0	1.000	1
1989		5-6-0	281	299	.455	5-3-0	.625	4
1990		9-4-0	327	298	.692	5-3-0	.625	4

Joe Tiller (1991-1996) 39-30-1 .564

Year	Rank	Record	PF	PA	Pct	Conf	Conf Pct	Place
1991		4-6-1	305	357	.409	2-5-1	.313	6
1992		5-7-0	302	341	.417	3-5-0	375	7
1993		8-4-0	357	329	.667	6-2-0	.750	1
1994		6-6-0	319	341	.500	4-4-0	.500	5
1995		6-5-0	322	264	.545	4-4-0	.500	6
1996	22 22	10-2-0	464	284	.833	7-1-0	.875	2

Dana Dimel (1997-1999) 23-12-0 .657

Year	Rank	Record	PF	PA	Pct	Conf	Conf Pct	Place
1997		8-5-0	322	215	.615	4-4-0	.500	8
1998		8-3-0	222	215	.727	6-2-0	.750	4

Member of the Mountain West Conference (1999-2003) 7-28-0 .200

Year	Rank	Record	PF	PA	Pct	Conf	Conf Pct	Place
1999		7-4-0	302	270	.626	4-3-0	.571	4

Vic Koenning (2000-2002) 5-29-0 .147

Year	Rank	Record	PF	PA	Pct	Conf	Conf Pct	Place
2000		1-10-0	170	393	.091	0-7-0	.000	8
2001		2-9-0	229	368	.182	0-7-0	.000	8
2002		2-10-0	288	432	.167	1-6-0	.143	8

Joe Glenn (2003) 4-8-0 .333

Year	Rank	Record	PF	PA	Pct	Conf	Conf Pct	Place
2003		4-8-0	286	360	.333	2-5-0	.286	7

Won-loss record by decades:

1893-99	9-5-1	.633	1930-39	26-52-6	.345	1970-79	40-71-1	.362
1900-09	22-19-1	.536	1940-49	24-38-3	.392	1980-89	67-51-0	.568
1910-19	20-43-1	.320	1950-59	72-24-5	.748	1990-99	71-46-1	.606
1920-29	23-57-5	.300	1960-69	70-27-4	.692	2000-03	9-37-0	.196

Historic record: 453-470-28 .491

Post-season won-loss record: 4-7-0 .364

1951: Gator Bowl, Wyoming 20, Wash. & Lee 7
1956: Sun Bowl, Wyoming 21, Texas Tech 14
1958: Sun Bowl, Wyoming 14, Hardin Simmons 6
1966: Sun Bowl, Wyoming 28, Florida State 20
1968: Sugar Bowl, LSU 20, Wyoming 13
1976: Fiesta Bowl, Oklahoma 41, Wyoming 7

1987: Holiday Bowl, Iowa 20, Wyoming 19
1988: Holiday Bowl, Oklahoma State 62, Wyoming 14
1990: Copper Bowl, California 17, Wyoming 15
1993: Copper Bowl, Kansas State 52, Wyoming 17
1996: WAC Championship: BYU 28, Wyoming 25 (OT)

College Football Hall of Fame:
Bowden Wyatt, coach, 1947-52; Eddie Talboom, halfback, 1948-50; Bob Devaney, coach, 1957-1961.

Awards: Fred Biletnikoff Award: 1996, Marcus Harris.

PART III

Records of Other Major Football Teams

BROWN UNIVERSITY, Providence, Rhode Island; nickname "Bears"; colors seal brown, cardinal red, and white; Brown Stadium (20,000); Ivy League. Brown began play in 1878 and played as an independent until the Ivy League was formally organized beginning with the 1956 season.

Early years (1878-1897)

Year	Coach	W-L-T	PF	PA	Pct.	Year	Coach	W-L-T	PF	PA	Pct.
1878	none	0-1-0			.000	1891	J. H. Lindsey	4-6-0	76	120	.400
1879	no team					1892	Mr. Howland	4-5-1	60	86	.450
1880	none	0-1-0			.000	1893	William Odlin	6-3-0	168	94	.667
1881-1885	no team					1894	Mr. Norton	10-5-0	262	102	.667
1886	none	1-1-0	76	10	.500	1895	Wallace Moyle	7-6-1	150	109	.537
1887-1888	no team					1896	Wallace Moyle	4-5-1	126	100	.450
1889	J. E. Walker	2-2-0	30	64	.500	1897	Wallace Moyle	7-4-0	180	152	.636
1890	J. H. Lindsey	2-4-1	78	104	.357						

E. N. Robinson (1898-1901, 1904-1907, 1910-1925) 140-82-12 .624

Year	Nat'l AP Other	W-L-T	PF	PA	Pct.	Year	Nat'l AP Other	W-L-T	PF	PA	Pct.
1898		6-4-0	135	96	.600	1900		7-3-1	145	67	.682
1899		7-3-1	175	57	.682	1901		4-7-1	70	212	.375

J. A. Gammons (1902, 1908-1909) 17-10-2 .621

| 1902 | | 5-4-1 | 115 | 52 | .550 | | | | | | |

D. S. Fultz (1903) 5-4-1 .550

| 1903 | | 5-4-1 | 98 | 161 | .550 | | | | | | |

E. N. Robinson (1904-1907)

| 1904 | | 6-5-0 | 181 | 51 | .545 | 1906 | | 6-3-0 | 112 | 32 | .667 |
| 1905 | | 7-4-0 | 281 | 58 | .636 | 1907 | | 7-3-0 | 168 | 50 | .700 |

J. A. Gammons (1908-1909)

| 1908 | | 5-3-1 | 117 | 40 | .611 | 1909 | | 7-3-0 | 102 | 58 | .700 |

E. N. Robinson (1910-1925)

1910		7-2-1	198	47	.750	1918		2-3-0	48	98	.400
1911		7-3-1	187	53	.682	1919		5-4-1	74	61	.550
1912		6-4-0	117	107	.600	1920		6-3-0	149	61	.667
1913		4-5-0	70	111	.444	1921		5-3-1	107	89	.611
1914		5-2-2	105	65	.556	1922		6-2-1	92	47	.722
1915		5-4-1	166	46	.550	1923		6-4-0	159	71	.600
1916		8-1-0	254	37	.889	1924		5-4-0	154	65	.556
1917		8-2-0	160	62	.800	1925		5-4-1	215	80	.550

Tuss McLaughry (1926-1940) 76-58-5 .565

1926	10	9-0-1	223	36	.950	1934		3-6-0	64	169	.333
1927		3-6-1	109	103	.350	1935		1-8-0	21	197	.111
1928		8-1-0	167	72	.889	1936		3-7-0	76	234	.300
1929		5-5-0	140	124	.500	1937		5-4-0	73	119	.556
1930		6-3-1	135	78	.650	1938		5-3-0	203	129	.625
1931		7-3-0	184	100	.700	1939		5-3-1	188	91	.611
1932		7-1-0	81	42	.875	1940		6-3-1	124	94	.650
1933		3-5-0	68	116	.375						

J. N. Stanley (1941-1943) 14-11-0 .560

| 1941 | | 5-4-0 | 102 | 81 | .556 | 1943 | | 5-3-0 | 194 | 180 | .625 |
| 1942 | | 4-4-0 | 96 | 114 | .500 | | | | | | |

Rip Engle (1944-1949) 28-20-4 .576

1944		3-4-1	132	150	.438	1947		4-4-1	185	139	.500
1945		3-4-1	123	141	.438	1948		7-2-0	242	103	.778
1946		3-5-1	122	184	.389	1949		8-1-0	263	94	.889

G. G. Zitrides (1950) 1-8-0 .111

| 1950 | | 1-8-0 | 147 | 271 | .111 | | | | | | |

A. E. Kelley (1951-1958) 31-39-2 .444

1951		2-7-0	124	222	.222	1954		6-2-1	225	120	.722
1952		2-7-0	89	220	.222	1955		2-7-0	86	139	.222
1953		3-5-1	134	127	.389						

Member of the Ivy League (1956-2003) 134-195-7 .409

Year	Nat'l AP Other	Overall W-L-T	PF	PA	Pct.	Conference W-L-T	Pct.	Rank	Year	Nat'l AP Other	Overall W-L-T	PF	PA	Pct.	Conference W-L-T	Pct.	Rank
1956		5-4-0	124	94	.556	3-4-0	.429	5	1958		6-3-0	211	140	.667	4-3-0	.571	4
1957		5-4-0	154	125	.556	3-4-0	.429	4									

John McLaughry (1959-1966) 17-51-3 .260

1959		2-6-1	51	139	.278	1-5-1	.214	7	1963		3-5-0	157	168	.375	2-5-0	.286	7
1960		3-6-0	100	212	.333	1-6-0	.143	7	1964		5-4-0	119	117	.556	3-4-0	.429	5
1961		0-9-0	24	245	.000	0-7-0	.000	8	1965		2-7-0	128	169	.222	1-6-0	.143	7
1962		1-6-2	116	188	.222	0-6-1	.071	8	1966		1-8-0	137	266	.111	0-7-0	.000	8

Len Jardine (1967-1972) 9-44-1 .173

Year	W-L-T	PF	PA	Pct	Conf	Conf Pct	Place
1967	2-6-1	77	206	.278	1-5-1	.214	7
1968	2-7-0	97	286	.222	0-7-0	.000	8
1969	2-7-0	95	190	.222	1-6-0	.143	7
1970	2-7-0	112	217	.222	1-6-0	.143	7
1971	0-9-0	139	238	.000	0-7-0	.000	8
1972	1-8-0	172	301	.111	1-6-0	.143	8

John Anderson (1973-1983) 60-39-3 .603

Year	W-L-T	PF	PA	Pct	Conf	Conf Pct	Place
1973	4-3-1	183	163	.562	4-3-0	.571	5
1974	5-4-0	141	152	.556	4-3-0	.571	4
1975	6-2-1	258	168	.722	5-1-1	.786	2
1976	8-1-0	171	102	.889	6-1-0	.857	1
1977	7-2-0	173	96	.778	5-2-0	.714	2
1978	6-3-0	189	165	.667	5-2-0	.714	2
1979	6-3-0	197	129	.667	5-2-0	.714	2
1980	6-4-0	240	195	.600	4-3-0	.571	3
1981	3-7-0	153	250	.300	2-5-0	.286	4
1982	5-5-0	214	228	.500	3-4-0	.429	4
1983	4-5-1	204	237	.450	4-2-1	.643	3

John Rosebenberg (1984-1989) 23-33-3 .426

Year	W-L-T	PF	PA	Pct	Conf	Conf Pct	Place
1984	4-5-0	165	231	.444	4-3-0	.571	4
1985	5-4-1	200	128	.550	4-3-0	.571	4
1986	5-4-1	188	181	.550	4-2-1	.643	3
1987	7-3-0	144	160	.700	5-2-0	.714	2
1988	0-9-1	125	285	.050	0-6-1	.071	8
1989	2-8-0	170	265	.200	2-5-0	.296	5

Mickey Kwiatkowski (1990-1993) 7-33-0 .175

Year	W-L-T	PF	PA	Pct	Conf	Conf Pct	Place
1990	2-8-0	160	299	.200	2-5-0	.286	6
1991	1-9-0	227	372	.100	1-6-0	.143	7
1992	0-10-0	156	333	.000	0-7-0	.000	8
1993	4-6-0	190	267	.400	3-4-0	.429	4

Mark Whipple (1994-1997) 24-16-0 .600

Year	W-L-T	PF	PA	Pct	Conf	Conf Pct	Place
1994	7-3-0	229	197	.700	4-3-0	.571	2
1995	5-5-0	282	239	.500	2-5-0	.286	6
1996	5-5-0	238	246	.500	4-3-0	.571	3
1997	7-3-0	274	194	.700	4-3-0	.571	3

Phil Estes (1998-2003) 31-18-0 .633

Year	W-L-T	PF	PA	Pct	Conf	Conf Pct	Place
1998	7-3-0	265	241	.700	5-2-0	.571	2
1999	9-1-0	324	239	.900	6-1-0	.857	1
2000	7-3-0	375	301	.700	4-3-0	.571	*
2001	6-3-0	319	235	.667	5-2-0	.714	3
2002	2-8-0	223	279	.200	2-5-0	.286	6
2003	5-5-0	244	246	.500	4-3-0	.571	2

*Ineligible for conference title.

Won-loss record by decades:

1878-89	3-5-0	.375	1930-39	45-43-2	.511	1970-79	45-42-2	.517	
1890-99	57-45-5	.556	1940-49	48-34-5	.580	1980-89	41-54-4	.402	
1900-09	59-39-5	.598	1950-59	34-53-3	.394	1990-99	47-53-0	.470	
1910-19	57-30-6	.645	1960-69	21-65-3	.253	2000-03	20-19-0	.513	
1920-29	58-32-5	.637							

Historic record: 535-514-40 .510

Post-season won-loss record: 0-1-0 .000
1916: Rose Bowl, Washington State 14, Brown 0

College Football Hall of Fame:
Edward Robinson, coach, 1898-1901, 1904-07, 1910-25; Bill Sprackling, quarterback, 1908-11; Fritz Pollard, halfback, 1915-16; Tuss McLaughry, coach, 1926-40; Rip Engle, coach, 1944-49.

CARLISLE INSTITUTE, Carlisle, PA: nickname "Indians." Carlisle began play in 1893 and played as an independent until it discontinued football after the 1917 season.

Early years (1893-1898)

Year	Coach	W-L-T	PF	PA	Pct.	Year	Coach	W-L-T	PF	PA	Pct.
1893	W. G. Thompson	2-0-0	60	0	1.000	1896	William Hickok	6-4-0	170	90	.600
1894	Vance McCormick	1-6-2	62	108	.222	1897	William T. Bull	6-4-0	232	98	.600
1895	Vance McCormick	4-4-0	88	114	.500	1898	John A. Hall	5-4-0	188	93	.556

Pop Warner (1899-1903, 1906-1914) 122-42-8 .733

Year		W-L-T	PF	PA	Pct.	Year		W-L-T	PF	PA	Pct.
1899		9-2-0	383	44	.818	1902		8-3-0	251	51	.727
1900		6-4-1	211	92	.591	1903		11-2-1	275	46	.800
1901		5-7-1	135	168	.423						

Ed Rogers (1904) 9-2-0 .818

Year		W-L-T	PF	PA	Pct.
1904		9-2-0	335	44	.818

George Woodruff (1905) 10-4-0 .714

Year		W-L-T	PF	PA	Pct.
1905		10-4-0	354	55	.714

Pop Warner (1906-1914)

Year		W-L-T	PF	PA	Pct.	Year		W-L-T	PF	PA	Pct.
1906		9-2-0	244	36	.818	1911		11-1-0	298	49	.917
1907		10-1-0	267	62	.909	1912		12-1-1	504	114	.893
1908		10-2-1	212	55	.808	1913		10-1-1	295	63	.875
1909		8-3-1	243	94	.708	1914		5-8-1	125	167	.393
1910		8-6-0	235	68	.571						

Victor Kelly (1915) 3-6-2 .364

Year		W-L-T	PF	PA	Pct.
1915		3-6-2	84	196	.364

M. L. Clevett (1916) 1-3-1 .300

Year		W-L-T	PF	PA	Pct.
1916		1-3-1	55	65	.300

George Tibbetts (1917) 2-7-0 .222

Year		W-L-T	PF	PA	Pct.
1917		2-7-0	129	264	.222

Carlisle abandoned football after the 1917 season.

Won-loss record by decades:

1893-99	33-24-2	.576	1910-17	52-33-6	.604
1900-09	86-30-5	.731			

Historic record: 171-87-13 .655

(Source: John S. Steckbeck, Fabulous Redmen: The Carlisle Indians and Their Famous Football Teams, Harrisburg, PA: J. Horace McFarland Co., 1951)

College Football Hall of Fame:
Pop Warner, coach, 1899-1903, 1906-14; George Woodruff, coach 1905; Ed Rogers, end, 1896-99; Jimmy Johnson, quarterback, 1899-1905; Albert Exendine, end, 1905-07; Jim Thorpe, halfback, 1907-12; Gus Welch, quarterback, 1910-14; Joe Guyon, halfback/tackle, 1912-14.

CARNEGIE TECH (later Carnegie Mellon University), Pittsburgh, Pennsylvania; nickname "Tartans"; colors cardinal and grey. Carnegie Tech played a major college schedule as an independent in the 1920s and 1930s, including long series of games against Notre Dame and Pittsburgh, but Carnegie went to a small school schedule after World War II and currently plays in a Division III conference.

Year	Nat'l AP	Other	W-L-T	PF	PA	Pct.	Year	Nat'l AP	Other	W-L-T	PF	PA	Pct.
						Early years with unknown coaches (1906-1914)							
1906			1-4-2	10	122	.286	1910			1-6-1	8	172	.188
1907			1-8-0	17	105	.111	1911			4-5-0	45	60	.444
1908			3-7-0	29	167	.300	1912			3-4-1	53	151	.438
1909			5-3-1	74	76	.611	1913			2-4-1	31	106	.357
						Walter Steffen (1914-1932) 88-53-8 .617							
1914			4-4-0	181	99	.500	1924			5-4-0	149	78	.556
1915			7-1-0	317	60	.875	1925			5-2-1	161	47	.688
1916			4-3-0	198	61	.571	1926			7-2-0	207	23	.778
1917			2-3-1	31	76	.417	1927			5-4-1	221	95	.550
1918			no team				1928		6	7-1-0	214	54	.875
1919			3-4-0	65	73	.429	1929			5-3-1	145	92	.611
1920			5-3-0	121	95	.625	1930			6-3-0	275	77	.667
1921			7-2-0	238	54	.778	1931			3-5-0	82	76	.375
1922			5-3-1	182	55	.611	1932			4-3-2	111	74	.556
1923			4-3-1	103	68	.562							
						Howard Harpster (1933-1936) 12-19-3 .397							
1933			4-3-2	61	40	.556	1935			2-5-1	22	69	.312
1934			4-5-0	35	107	.444	1936			2-6-0	48	92	.250
						William Kern (1937-1939) 12-12-1 .500							
1937			2-5-1	49	77	.312	1939			3-5-0	75	62	.375
1938	6	10	7-2-0	177	64	.778							
						Edward Baker (1940-1942) 7-15-0 .318							
1940			3-5-0	66	112	.375	1942			3-3-0	84	89	.500
1941			1-7-0	37	148	.125							
						Unknown coach (1943) 0-4-1 .100							
1943			0-4-1	19	129	.100	1944, 1945			no team			

Won-loss record by decades (pre-1944)

1906-09	10-22-3	.329	1920-29	55-27-5	.661	1940-43	7-19-1	.278	
1910-19	30-34-4	.471	1930-39	37-42-6	.471				

Historical record: (1906-1943) 139-144-19 .492

Post-season won-loss record: 0-1-0 .000
1938: Sugar Bowl, TCU 15, Carnegie Tech 7. (In 1938, Carnegie Tech was voted the champion of the East.)

College Football Hall of Fame:
Lloyd Yoder, tackle, 1923-26; Howard Harpster, quarterback, 1926-1928.

Carnegie-Notre Dame series:

1923: Notre Dame 26, Carnegie 0	1933: Carnegie 7, Notre Dame 0
1924: Notre Dame 40, Carnegie 19	1934: Notre Dame 13, Carnegie 0
1925: Notre Dame 26, Carnegie 0	1935: Notre Dame 14, Carnegie 3
1926: Carnegie 19, Notre Dame 0	1936: Notre Dame 21, Carnegie 7
1928: Carnegie 27, Notre Dame 7	1937: Carnegie 9, Notre Dame 7
1929: Notre Dame 7, Carnegie 0	1938: Notre Dame 7, Carnegie 0
1930: Notre Dame 20, Carnegie 6	1939: Notre Dame 7, Carnegie 6
1931: Notre Dame 19, Carnegie 0	1940: Notre Dame 61, Carnegie 0
1932: Notre Dame 42, Carnegie 0	1941: Notre Dame 16, Carnegie 0

UNIVERSITY OF CHICAGO, Chicago, Ill.; nickname "Maroons"; Big Ten; discontinued intercollegiate football after the 1939 season.

Amos Alonzo Stagg (1892-1932) 224-113-27 .653
Early years as an independent (1892-1895)

Year	W-L-T	PF	PA	Pct.		Year	W-L-T	PF	PA	Pct.
1892	1-4-2	54	112	.286		1894	11-7-1	308	140	.605.
1893	6-4-2	148	129	.583		1895	7-3-0	166	60	.700

Member of the Big Ten (1896-1939) 120-100-14 .543

Year	Nat'l AP	Other	Overall W-L-T	PF	PA	Pct.	Conference W-L-T	Pct.	Rank	Year	Nat'l AP	Other	Overall W-L-T	PF	PA	Pct.	Conference W-L-T	Pct.	Rank
1896			11-2-1	303	82	.846	3-2-0	.600	4	1915			5-2-0	83	50	.714	4-2-0	.667	3
1897			8-1-0	277	68	.889	3-1-0	.750	2	1916			3-4-0	65	110	.429	3-3-0	.500	4
1898			9-2-0	214	40	.818	3-1-0	.750	2	1917			3-2-1	82	51	.583	2-2-1	.500	5
1899			12-0-2	407	28	.929	4-0-0	1.000	1	1918			0-5-0	9	77	.000	0-5-0	.000	8
1900			7-5-1	181	135	.577	2-3-1	.417	6	1919			5-2-0	205	26	.714	4-2-0	.667	3
1901			5-5-2	128	120	.500	0-4-1	.000	7	1920			3-4-0	77	27	.429	2-4-0	.333	8
1902			11-1-0	249	27	.917	5-1-0	.833	2	1921			6-1-0	111	13	.857	4-1-0	.800	2
1903			10-2-1	340	61	.808	4-1-1	.750	4	1922			5-1-1	88	37	.786	4-0-1	1.000	1
1904			8-1-1	320	44	.850	5-1-1	.786	3	1923			7-1-0	134	22	.875	5-1-0	.833	3
1905	1		10-0-0	245	5	1.000	7-0-0	1.000	1	1924		11	4-1-3	88	40	.688	3-0-3	1.000	1
1906			4-1-0	175	17	.800	3-1-0	.750	4	1925			3-5-1	44	76	.389	2-2-1	.500	4
1907			4-1-0	147	42	.800	4-0-0	1.000	1	1926			2-6-0	47	116	.250	0-5-0	.000	8
1908			5-0-1	132	30	1.000	5-0-0	1.000	1	1927			4-5-0	65	68	.444	3-3-0	.500	4
1909			4-1-2	127	40	.714	4-1-1	.750	2	1928			2-7-0	70	177	.222	0-5-0	.000	10
1910			2-5-0	24	66	.286	2-4-0	.333	5	1929			7-3-0	130	92	.700	1-3-0	.250	7
1911			6-1-0	79	42	.857	5-1-0	.833	2	1930			2-5-2	33	131	.286	0-4-0	.000	9
1912			6-1-0	86	44	.857	6-1-0	.857	2	1931			2-6-1	64	124	.278	1-4-0	.200	7
1913			7-0-0	124	27	1.000	7-0-0	1.000	1	1932			3-4-1	95	94	.438	1-4-0	.200	8
1914			4-2-1	104	34	.643	4-2-1	.643	3										

Clark Shaughnessy (1933-1939) 17-34-4 .345

Year	W-L-T	PF	PA	Pct.	Conf W-L-T	Pct.	Rank	Year	W-L-T	PF	PA	Pct.	Conf W-L-T	Pct.	Rank
1933	3-3-2	118	56	.500	0-3-2	.000	8	1937	1-6-0	45	143	.143	0-4-0	.000	9
1934	4-4-0	113	106	.500	2-4-0	.333	7	1938	1-6-1	75	241	.188	0-4-0	.000	10
1935	4-4-0	102	110	.500	2-3-0	.400	5	1939	2-6-0	37	308	.250	0-3-0	.000	9
1936	2-5-1	68	166	.312	1-4-0	.200	7								

Chicago discontinues college football after the 1939 season.

Won-loss record by decades:

1892-99	65-23-8	.719		1910-19	41-24-2	.627		1930-39	24-49-8	.346
1900-09	68-17-7	.777		1920-29	43-34-5	.555				

Historic record: 241-147-30 .612

College Football Hall of Fame:
Amos Alonzo Stagg, coach, 1892-1933; Andy Wyant, center/guard, 1887-94; Clarence Herschberger, fullback, 1895-98; Bob Maxwell, guard, 1902-05; Walter Eckersall, quarterback, 1903-06; Walter Steffen, quarterback, 1906-08; Paul Des Jardien, center, 1912-14; Jay Berwanger, halfback, 1933-35; Clark Shaughnessy, coach, 1934-39.

Awards: Heisman Trophy: 1935, Jay Berwanger

See Robin Lester, Stagg's University, University of Illinois Press, Champaign-Urbana, Illinois, for details of the Stagg years at Chicago.

COLGATE UNIVERSITY, Hamilton, New York; nickname "Red Raiders"; colors maroon, gray, and white; Andy Kerr Stadium (10,221); Patriot League. Until the 1970s, Colgate played a college schedule that included regular games against major Eastern colleges. In 1982, Colgate opted to continue to play in the Patriot League as a Division I-AA team. Data shown here are for the period 1890-1981. Conference data are not shown.

Year	Nat'l AP	Other	W-L-T	PF	PA	Pct	Year	Nat'l AP	Other	W-L-T	PF	PA	Pct.
						Samuel Colgate (1890-1891) 5-2-0 .714							
1890			1-1-0	28	38	.714	1891			4-1-0	80	50	.800
						No coach (1892-1895)							
1892			3-0-0	50	10	1.000	1894			2-1-1	112	26	.625
1893			3-0-1	86	12	.875	1895			4-2-0	118	38	.667
						Joseph Conon (1896) 3-4-1 .437							
1896			3-4-1	52	30	.437							
						Charles Mason (1897-1898. 1901) 9-12-1 .432							
1897			5-2-1	66	26	.688	1898			2-5-0	23	78	.286
						Joseph Stannard (1899) 3-5-0 .375							
1899			3-5-0	47	133	.375							
						Joseph Short (1900) 3-7-0 .300							
1900			3-7-0	41	82	.300							
						Charles Mason (1901)							
1901			2-5-0	29	106	.286							
						Frank O'Neill (1902.,1904-1905) 18-8-2 .678							
1902			5-3-1	177	55	.611							
						J. A. Hatch (1903) 4-2-1 .642							
1903			4-2-1	89	28	.642							
						Frank O'Neill (1904-1905)							
1904			8-1-1	268	30	.850	1905			5-4-0	217	83	.556
						William Warner (1906-1907) 8-6-3 .558							
1906			4-2-2	102	56	.625	1907			4-4-1	108	71	.500
						Edwin Sweetland (1908) 4-3-0 .571							
1906			4-3-0	78	25	.571							
						Gus Brown (1909) 5-2-1 .687							
1909			5-2-1	171	61	.687							
						Laurence Bankart (1910, 1913-1916) 28-7-3 .776							
1910			4-2-1	146	53	.642							
						Jack Ingersoll (1911) 3-6-0 .333							
1911			3-6-0	61	103	.333							
						Frank Sommer (1912) 5-2-0 .714							
1912			5-2-0	90	47	.714							
						Laurence Bankart (1913-1916)							
1913			6-1-1	157	26	.812	1915			5-1-0	223	38	.833
1914			5-2-1	146	73	.687	1916			8-1-0	218	30	.889
						Harold McDevitt (1917) 4-2-0 .667							
1917			4-2-0	118	40	.667	1918		no team				
						Ellery Huntingdon (1919-1921) 10-10-5 .500							
1919			5-1-1	111	27	.786	1921			4-4-2	118	105	.500
1920			1-5-2	114	119	.250							
						Dick Harlow (1922-1925) 24-9-3 .708							
1922			6-3-0	297	62	.667	1924			5-4-0	218	94	.556
1923			6-2-1	233	73	.722	1925		4	7-0-2	219	34	.889
						George Hauser (1926-1927) 9-4-5 .638							
1926			5-2-2	218	58	.667	1927			4-2-3	99	33	.611
						Earl Abell (1928) 6-3-0 .667							
1928			6-3-0	175	107	.667							
						Andy Kerr (1929-1946) 95-50-7 .648							
1929			8-1-0	315	19	.889	1938			2-5-0	39	63	.286
1930			9-1-0	383	27	.900	1939			2-5-1	66	92	.312
1931			8-1-0	227	34	.889	1940			5-3-0	125	76	.625
1932	5		9-0-0	264	0	1.000	1941			3-3-2	150	112	.500
1933			6-1-1	189	12	.812	1942			6-2-1	172	104	.722
1934	9		7-1-0	188	38	.875	1943			5-3-1	128	91	.611
1935			7-3-0	224	29	.700	1944			2-5-0	79	127	.286
1936			6-3-0	199	67	.667	1945			3-4-1	128	111	.438
1937			3-5-0	89	86	.375	1946			4-4-0	154	95	.500
						Paul Bixler (1947-1951) 14-27-2 .348							
1947			1-5-2	87	139	.250	1950			5-3-0	184	193	.625
1948			3-6-0	133	196	.333	1951			4-5-0	184	187	.444
1949			1-8-0	186	291	.111							

Harold Lahar (1952-1956, 1962-1967) 53-40-8 .564

Year	Record				Year	Record			
1952	6-3-0	195	107	.667	1955	6-3-0	164	107	.667
1953	3-4-2	147	161	.444	1956	4-5-0	201	214	.444
1954	5-2-2	141	117	.667					

Fred Rice (1957-1958) 4-14-0 .222

1957	3-6-0	84	251	.333	1958	1-8-0	46	251	.111

Alva Kelley (1959-1961) 9-18-0 .333

1959	2-7-0	115	268	.222	1961	5-4-0	116	145	.545
1960	2-7-0	158	267	.222					

Harold Lahar (1962-1967)

1962	3-5-1	97	134	.389	1965	6-3-1	128	109	.650
1963	3-4-1	75	147	.438	1966	8-1-1	242	67	.850
1964	7-2-0	135	52	.778	1967	2-8-0	121	181	.200

Neil Wheelwright (1968-1975) 41-37-2 .525

1968	5-5-0	208	220	.500	1972	5-4-1	219	269	.550
1969	5-3-1	172	197	.611	1973	5-5-0	295	264	.500
1970	5-6-0	198	288	.455	1974	4-6-0	220	318	.400
1971	6-4-0	287	262	.600	1975	6-4-0	205	218	.600

Fredrick Dunlap (1976-1981)* 38-22-2 .542

1976	8-2-0	173	134	.800	1979	5-4-1	149	163	.550
1977	10-1-0	380	217	.909	1980	5-4-1	243	207	.550
1978	3-8-0	149	226	.273	1981	7-3-0	238	151	.700

*Dunlap's career record at Colgate (1976-1987) is 77-49-3 .608.

Won-loss record by decades:

Decade	Record	Pct.	Decade	Record	Pct.	Decade	Record	Pct.
1890-99	30-21-4	.582	1930-39	59-25-2	.698	1970-79	57-44-2	.573
1900-09	44-33-7	.565	1940-49	33-43-7	.440	1980-821	12-7-1	.625
1910-19	45-18-4	.701	1950-59	39-46-4	.461			
1920-29	52-26-12	.644	1960-69	46-42-5	.584			

Historical record (1890-1981) 417-305-48 .573

College Football Hall of Fame:
Frank O'Neill, coach, 1902, 1904-05; Ellery Huntingdon, quarterback, 1910-13: Earl Abell, tackle, 1912-15; Belford West, tackle, 1914-19; Dick Harlow, coach, 1922-25; Ed Tryon, halfback, 1922-25; Andy Kerr, coach, 1929-46; John Orsi, end, 1929-31; Danny Fortmann, tackle, 1933-35; Kenny Gamble, running back, 1984-87.

COLUMBIA UNIVERSITY, New York, New York; nickname "Lions"; colors Blue and White; Wien Stadium; Ivy League. Columbia played as an independent until the Ivy League was formally organized for play in the 1956 season. Columbia has been a member of the Ivy League since that time.

Early Years with no coach (1870-1897)

Year	Coach	W-L-T	PF	PA	Pct.	Year	Coach	W-L-T	PF	PA	Pct.
1870		0-1-0	3	6	.000	1880		1-2-0			.333
1871	no games played					1881		3-3-1			.500
1872		1-2-1	11	10	.375	1882		0-5-0			.000
1873		2-1-0	10	9	.667	1883		1-3-0	13	147	.250
1874		1-5-0	9	28	.167	1884		1-1-0	21	35	.500
1875		4-1-1	19	10	.750	1885-1888	no games played				
1876		1-3-0	7	10	.250	1889		2-7-2	54	298	.273
1877		2-2-0	9	25	.500	1890		1-5-1	46	178	.214
1878		0-0-1	0	0	.500	1891		1-5-0	32	220	.167
1879		0-3-2			.200	1892-98	no games played				

Year	Nat'l AP	Other	W-L-T	PF	PA	Pct.
1899			8-3-0	194	85	.727
1900			7-3-1	124	77	.682
George Sanford (1899-1901) 23-11-1 .671						
1901			8-5-0	157	91	.615
William Morely (1902-1905) 26-11-3 .688						
1902			6-4-1	163	101	.591
1903			9-1-0	148	43	.900
1904			7-3-0	120	68	.700
1905			4-3-2	77	109	.556
Football banned at Columbia (1906-1914)						
T. N. Metcalf (1915-1917) 8-9-2 .474						
1915			5-0-0	126	28	1.000
1916			1-5-2	13	81	.375
1917			2-4-0	110	38	.333
Fred Dawson (1918-1919) 7-5-3 .567						
1918			5-1-0	87	27	.833
1919			2-4-3	48	107	.389
Frank O'Neill (1920-1922) 11-14-0 .440						
1920			4-4-0	96	120	.500
1921			2-6-0	89	148	.200
1922			5-4-0	147	183	.556
Percy Haughton (1923-1924) 8-5-1 .615						
1923			4-4-1	68	107	.500
1924*			4-1-0	150	16	.800
Paul Withington (1924) 1-2-1 .375						
1924*			1-2-1	60	37	.375

*Haughton died after the fifth game of the 1924 season, and Withington coached the last four games of that season.

Year	Nat'l AP	Other	W-L-T	PF	PA	Pct.
Charles Crowley (1925-1929) 26-16-4 .619						
1925			6-3-1	288	55	.650
1926			6-3-0	144	73	.667
1927			5-2-2	135	54	.667
1928			5-3-1	132	95	.611
1929			4-5-0	160	111	.444
Lou Little (1930-1956) 110-116-11 .487						
1930			5-4-0	141	138	.556
1931			7-1-1	223	26	.833
1932			7-1-1	199	32	.833
1933			8-1-0	179	45	.889
1934	7		7-1-1	140	49	.833
1935			4-4-1	86	115	.500
1936			5-3-0	145	73	.625
1937			2-5-2	102	100	.333
1938			3-6-0	154	144	.333
1939			2-4-2	72	88	.375
1940			5-2-2	81	72	.667
1941			3-5-0	81	103	.375
1942			3-6-0	174	193	.333
1943			0-8-0	33	313	.000
1944			2-6-0	71	125	.250
1945		20	8-1-0	251	105	.889
1946			6-3-0	222	176	.667
1947		20	7-2-0	170	113	.778
1948			4-5-0	194	177	.444
1949			2-7-0	82	276	.222
1950			4-5-0	151	169	.444
1951			5-3-0	149	103	.625
1952			2-6-1	117	184	.278
1953			4-5-0	126	153	.444
1954			1-8-0	71	306	.111
1955			1-8-0	74	251	.111

Member of the Ivy League (1956-2003) 80-251-5 .246

Year	Nat'l AP	Other	Overall W-L-T	PF	PA	Pct.	Conference W-L-T	Pct.	Rank
1956			3-6-0	94	237	.333	2-5-0	.286	6
Aldo Donelli (1957-1967) 30-67-2 .309									
1957			1-8-0	54	214	.111	1-6-0	.143	8
1958			1-8-0	35	291	.111	1-6-0	.143	7
1959			2-7-0	82	210	.222	1-6-0	.143	8
1960			3-6-0	126	191	.333	3-4-0	.429	5
1961			6-3-0	240	117	.667	6-1-0	.857	1
1962			5-4-0	124	206	.556	4-3-0	.571	3
1963			4-4-1	171	165	.500	2-4-1	.357	6
1964			2-6-1	145	194	.278	1-5-1	.214	7
1965			2-7-0	83	229	.222	1-6-0	.143	7
1966			2-7-0	156	306	.222	2-5-0	.286	6
1967			2-7-0	109	205	.222	0-7-0	.000	8

Frank Novarro (1968-1973) 16-36-2 .315

Year	Record	PF	PA	Pct	Conf	C.Pct	Rk		Year	Record	PF	PA	Pct	Conf	C.Pct	Rk
1968	2-7-0	174	247	.222	2-5-0	.286	6		1971	6-3-0	168	136	.667	5-2-0	.714	3
1969	1-8-0	84	237	.111	1-6-0	.143	8		1972	3-5-1	143	124	.389	2-4-1	.357	6
1970	3-6-0	164	224	.333	1-6-0	.143	7		1973	1-7-1	58	274	.167	1-6-0	.143	7

Bill Campbell (1974-1979) 12-41-1 .231

Year	Record	PF	PA	Pct	Conf	C.Pct	Rk		Year	Record	PF	PA	Pct	Conf	C.Pct	Rk
1974	1-8-0	81	258	.111	0-7-0	.000	8		1977	2-7-0	149	222	.222	1-6-0	.143	7
1975	2-7-0	151	261	.222	2-5-0	.286	6		1978	3-5-1	111	228	.389	2-4-1	.357	5
1976	3-6-0	137	247	.333	2-5-0	.286	5		1979	1-8-0	68	215	.111	1-6-0	.143	7

Bob Naso (1980-1984) 4-43-2 .102

Year	Record	PF	PA	Pct	Conf	C.Pct	Rk		Year	Record	PF	PA	Pct	Conf	C.Pct	Rk
1980	1-9-0	89	275	.111	0-7-0	.000	8		1983	1-7-2	218	363	.200	1-5-1	.214	7
1981	1-9-0	116	243	.111	1-6-0	.143	7		1984	0-9-0	117	282	.000	0-7-0	.000	8
1982	1-9-0	236	390	.111	1-6-0	.143	8									

Jim Garrett (1985) 0-10-0 .000

Year	Record	PF	PA	Pct	Conf	C.Pct	Rk
1985	0-10-0	75	331	.000	0-7-0	.000	8

Larry McElreavy (1986-1988) 2-28-0 .067

Year	Record	PF	PA	Pct	Conf	C.Pct	Rk		Year	Record	PF	PA	Pct	Conf	C.Pct	Rk
1986	0-10-0	91	379	.000	0-7-0	.000	8		1988	2-8-0	140	303	.200	2-5-0	.286	6
1987	0-10-0	104	311	.000	0-7-0	.000	8									

Ray Tellier (1989-2003) 46-102-2 .313

Year	Record	PF	PA	Pct	Conf	C.Pct	Rk		Year	Record	PF	PA	Pct	Conf	C.Pct	Rk
1989	1-9-0	130	287	.100	1-6-0	.143	8		1996	8-2-0	181	159	.800	5-2-0	.714	2
1990	1-9-0	115	292	.100	1-6-0	.143	8		1997	4-6-0	134	235	.400	3-4-0	.429	5
1991	1-9-0	154	249	.100	1-6-0	.143	7		1998	4-6-0	129	189	.400	3-4-0	.429	5
1992	3-7-0	205	286	.300	2-5-0	.286	6		1999	3-7-0	175	301	.300	1-6-0	.143	7
1993	2-8-0	155	294	.200	1-6-0	.143	7		2000	3-7-0	256	306	.300	1-6-0	.143	6
1994	5-4-1	240	230	.550	3-4-0	.429	4		2001	3-7-0	206	326	.300	3-4-0	.429	4
1995	3-6-1	201	281	.350	3-4-0	.429	5		2002	1-9-0	161	295	.100	0-7-0	.000	8
									2003	4-6-0	211	283	.400	3-4-0	.429	6

Won-lost record by decades:

Decade	Record	Pct	Decade	Record	Pct	Decade	Record	Pct
1870-79	11-18-5	.397	1920-29	46-37-6	.551	1970-79	25-62-3	.294
1880-89	8-21-3	.297	1930 39	50-30-8	.614	1980-89	7-90-2	.081
1890-99	10-13-1	.438	1940-49	40-45-2	.471	1990-99	34-64-2	.350
1900-09	41-19-4	.672	1950-59	24-64-1	.275	2000-03	11-29-0	.275
1910-19	15-14-5	.515	1960-69	29-59-2	.333			

Historical record (1870-2002) 351-566-44 .390

Won-loss record in post-season games: 1-0-0 1.000
1933: Rose Bowl, Columbia 7, Stanford 0

College Football Hall of Fame: George Sanford, coach, 1899-1901; Bill Morely, halfback, 1899-01; Harold Weekes, halfback, 1899-02; Buck O'Neill, coach, 1920-22; Walter Koppisch, halfback, 1921-24; Percy Haughton, coach, 1923-24; Lou Little, coach, 1930-56; Cliff Montgomery, quarterback, 1931-33; Sid Luckman, halfback, 1936-38; Paul Governali, halfback, 1940-42; Bill Swiacki, end, 1942-43.

Awards: Maxwell Award: 1942, Paul Governali

CORNELL UNIVERSITY, Ithaca, New York; nickname "Big Red"; colors carnelian and white; Schoellkopf Field (25,597); Ivy League. Cornell was an independent until 1956 when the Ivy League was formally organized.

Early years with no regular coach (1887-1893)

Year	Nat'l AP	Other	W-L-T	PF	PA	Pct.		Year	Nat'l AP	Other	W-L-T	PF	PA	Pct.
1887			0-2-0	20	62	.000		1891			7-3-0	298	34	.500
1888			4-2-0	96	20	.667		1892			10-1-0	434	54	.909
1889			7-2-0	354	130	.778		1893			2-5-1	44	166	.389
1890			7-4-0	260	130	.636								

Marshall Newell (1894-1895) 9-8-2 .473

| 1894 | | | 6-4-1 | 174 | 58 | .591 | | 1895 | | | 3-4-1 | 28 | 91 | .438 |

Joseph Beacham (1896) 5-3-1 .611

| 1896 | | | 5-3-1 | 162 | 82 | .611 | | | | | | | | |

Pop Warner (1897-1898, 1904-1906) 36-13-3 .721

| 1897 | | | 5-3-1 | 133 | 42 | .611 | | 1898 | | | 10-2-0 | 296 | 29 | .833 |

Percy Houghton (1899-1900) 17-5-0 .772

| 1899 | | | 7-3-0 | 134 | 52 | .700 | | 1900 | | | 10-2-0 | 167 | 55 | .833 |

Raymond Starbuck (1901-1902) 19-4-0 .826

| 1901 | | | 11-1-0 | 333 | 14 | .917 | | 1902 | | | 8-3-0 | 324 | 38 | .727 |

William Warner (1903) 6-3-1 .650

| 1903 | | | 6-3-1 | 120 | 103 | .650 | | | | | | | | |

Pop Warner (1904-1906)

| 1904 | | | 7-3-0 | 226 | 92 | .700 | | 1906 | | | 8-1-2 | 237 | 37 | .818 |
| 1905 | | | 6-4-0 | 173 | 59 | .600 | | | | | | | | |

Henry Schoellkopf (1907-1908) 15-3-1 .816

| 1907 | | | 8-2-0 | 176 | 45 | .800 | | 1908 | | | 7-1-1 | 96 | 43 | .833 |

George Walder (1909) 3-4-1 .438

| 1909 | | | 3-4-1 | 66 | 65 | .438 | | | | | | | | |

Daniel Reed (1910-1911) 12-5-1 .694

| 1910 | | | 5-2-1 | 165 | 44 | .688 | | 1911 | | | 7-3-0 | 101 | 52 | .700 |

Al Sharpe (1912-1917) 34-21-1 .523

1912			3-7-0	63	136	.300		1915	1		9-0-0	287	50	1.000
1913			5-4-1	132	89	.550		1916			6-2-0	165	73	.750
1914			8-2-0	257	54	.800		1917			3-6-0	78	146	.333

No team (1918)

John Rush (1919) 3-5-0 .375

| 1919 | | | 3-5-0 | 34 | 95 | .375 | | | | | | | | |

Gil Dobie (1920-1935) 82-36-7 .684

1920			6-2-0	231	68	.750		1928			3-3-2	72	86	.500
1921		1	8-0-0	392	21	1.000		1929			6-2-0	204	60	.750
1922		1	8-0-0	339	27	1.000		1930			6-2-0	273	63	.750
1923			8-0-0	320	33	1.000		1931			7-1-0	239	20	.875
1924			4-4-0	209	71	.500		1932			5-2-1	174	39	.688
1925			6-2-0	258	83	.750		1933			4-3-0	116	89	.571
1926			6-1-1	191	64	.812		1934			2-5-0	55	114	.286
1927			3-3-2	136	121	.500		1935			0-6-1	59	201	.072

Carl Snavely (1936-1944) 46-26-3 .633

1936			3-5-0	145	132	.375		1941			5-3-0	88	65	.675
1937			5-2-1	146	82	.688		1942			3-5-1	95	148	.389
1938	12		5-1-1	110	45	.786		1943			6-4-0	158	138	.600
1939	4	3	8-0-0	197	52	1.000		1944			5-4-0	131	130	.556
1940	15		6-2-0	201	38	.750								

Ed McKeever (1945-1946) 10-7-1 .583

| 1945 | | | 5-4-0 | 169 | 166 | .556 | | 1946 | | | 5-3-1 | 135 | 115 | .611 |

George James (1947-1960) 66-58-2 .532

1947			4-5-0	126	161	.444		1952			2-7-0	68	195	.222
1948	19		8-1-0	224	112	.889		1953			4-3-2	128	152	.556
1949	12		8-1-0	284	111	.889		1954			5-4-0	194	153	.556
1950	20		7-2-0	170	85	.778		1955			5-4-0	159	134	.556
1951			6-3-0	207	139	.667								

Member of the Ivy League (1956-2003) 153-178-5 .466

Year	Nat'l AP	Other	Overall W-L-T	PF	PA	Pct.	Conference W-L-T	Pct.	Rank	Year	Nat'l AP	Other	Overall W-L-T	PF	PA	Pct.	Conference W-L-T	Pct.	Rank
1956			1-8-0	100	209	.111	1-6-0	.143	8	1959			5-4-0	110	136	.556	3-4-0	.429	5
1957			3-6-0	100	159	.333	3-4-0	.429	4	1960			2-7-0	78	167	.222	1-6-0	.143	7
1958			6-3-0	147	135	.667	5-2-0	.714	2										

Tom Harp (1961-1965) 19-23-3 .456

Year	W-L-T	PF	PA	Pct	Conf	Pct	Pl	Year	W-L-T	PF	PA	Pct	Conf	Pct	Pl
1961	3-6-0	143	137	.333	2-5-0	.286	6	1964	3-5-1	196	139	.389	3-4-0	.429	5
1962	4-5-0	168	237	.444	4-3-0	.571	3	1965	4-3-2	192	137	.556	3-3-1	.500	4
1963	5-4-0	152	165	.556	4-3-0	.571	4								

Jack Musick (1966-1974) 45-33-3 .574

Year	W-L-T	PF	PA	Pct	Conf	Pct	Pl	Year	W-L-T	PF	PA	Pct	Conf	Pct	Pl
1966	6-3-0	181	157	.667	4-3-0	.571	4	1971	8-1-0	240	136	.889	6-1-0	.857	1
1967	6-2-1	210	145	.722	4-2-1	.643	3	1972	6-3-0	228	183	.667	4-3-0	.571	3
1968	3-6-0	130	163	.333	1-6-0	.167	7	1973	3-5-1	170	154	.389	2-5-0	.286	6
1969	4-5-0	148	162	.444	4-3-0	.571	4	1974	3-5-1	183	193	.389	1-5-1	.214	7
1970	6-3-0	193	185	.667	4-3-0	.571	4								

George Seifert (1975-1976) 3-15-0 .167

Year	W-L-T	PF	PA	Pct	Conf	Pct	Pl	Year	W-L-T	PF	PA	Pct	Conf	Pct	Pl
1975	1-8-0	151	247	.111	0-7-0	.000	8	1976	2-7-0	109	177	.222	2-5-0	.286	5

Bob Blackman (1977-1982) 23-33-1 .412

Year	W-L-T	PF	PA	Pct	Conf	Pct	Pl	Year	W-L-T	PF	PA	Pct	Conf	Pct	Pl
1977	1-8-0	86	199	.111	1-6-0	.143	7	1980	5-5-0	179	192	.500	5-2-0	.714	2
1978	5-3-1	188	154	.611	3-3-1	.500	4	1981	3-7-0	148	256	.300	2-5-0	.286	5
1979	5-4-0	215	152	.556	4-3-0	.571	4	1982	4-6-0	211	202	.400	3-4-0	.429	4

Maxie Baughan (1983-1988) 28-29-2 .492

Year	W-L-T	PF	PA	Pct	Conf	Pct	Pl	Year	W-L-T	PF	PA	Pct	Conf	Pct	Pl
1983	3-6-1	161	268	.350	3-3-1	.500	5	1986	8-2-0	202	103	.800	6-1-0	.857	2
1984	2-7-0	96	161	.222	2-5-0	.286	6	1987	5-5-0	154	197	.500	4-3-0	.571	4
1985	3-7-0	157	178	.300	2-5-0	.286	7	1988	7-2-1	234	137	.750	6-1-0	.857	1

Jack Fouts (1989) 4-6-0 .400

Year	W-L-T	PF	PA	Pct	Conf	Pct	Pl
1989	4-6-0	158	194	.400	2-5-0	.286	5

Jim Hofher (1990-1997) 45-35-0 562

Year	W-L-T	PF	PA	Pct	Conf	Pct	Pl	Year	W-L-T	PF	PA	Pct	Conf	Pct	Pl
1990	7-3-0	263	212	.700	6-1-0	.857	1	1994	6-4-0	193	190	.600	3-4-0	.429	4
1991	5-5-0	181	218	.500	4-3-0	.571	4	1995	6-4-0	261	222	.600	5-2-0	.714	2
1992	7-3-0	263	183	.700	4-3-0	.571	4	1996	4-6-0	221	280	.400	4-3-0	.571	3
1993	4-6-0	213	158	.400	3-4-0	.429	4	1997	6-4-0	269	251	.600	4-3-0	.571	3

Pete Mangurian (1998-2000) 16-14-0 .533

Year	W-L-T	PF	PA	Pct	Conf	Pct	Pl	Year	W-L-T	PF	PA	Pct	Conf	Pct	Pl
1998	4-6-0	159	200	.400	1-6-0	.143	7	2000	5-5-0	264	334	.500	5-2-0	.714	2
1999	7-3-0	254	135	.700	5-2-0	.714	3								

Tim Pendergast (2001-2003) 10-18-0 .357

Year	W-L-T	PF	PA	Pct	Conf	Pct	Pl	Year	W-L-T	PF	PA	Pct	Conf	Pct	Pl
2001	3-7-0	187	292	.300	2-5-0	.286	6	2003	1-9-0	130	304	.100	0-7-0	.000	8
2002	4-6-0	169	292	.400	3-4-0	.429	5								

Won-loss record by decades:

1887-89	11- 6-0	.647	1930-39	45-27-4	.618	1970-79	40-47-3	.461	
1890-99	62-32-5	.651	1940-49	55-32-2	.629	1980-89	44-53-2	.455	
1900-09	74-24-5	.743	1950-59	44-44-2	.500	1990-99	56-44-0	.560	
1910-19	49-31-2	.610	1960-69	40-46-4	.467	2000-03	13-27-0	.325	
1920-29	58-17-5	.756							

Historic record: 592-430-34 .577

Members of the College Football Hall of Fame:
Clinton Wycoff, quarterback, 1893-95; Marshall Newell, coach, 1894-95; Pop Warner, coach, 1897-98, 1904-06; William Warner, guard, 1899-1902; Percy Haughton, coach, 1899-1900; John O'Hearn, end, 1912-14; Murray Shelton, end, 1913-15; Charles Barrett, quarterback, 1913-15; Eddie Kaw, halfback, 1920-22; Gil Dobie, coach, 1920-35; George Pfann, quarterback, 1921-23; Frank Sunstrom, tackle, 1921-23; Carl Snavely, coach, 1936-44; Brud Holland, end, 1936-38; Nick Drahos, tackle, 1938-40; Ed Marinaro, tailback, 1969-71; Bob Blackman, coach, 1977-82; Maxie Baughan, coach, 1983-88.

Awards: Maxwell Award: 1971, Ed Marinaro.

DARTMOUTH COLLEGE, Hanover, New Hampshire; nickname "The Green"; Memorial Field (21,416). Ivy League. Dartmouth began play in 1881 as an independent and continued as an independent until 1956, when Dartmouth became one of the founding members of the formalized Ivy League.

Early years with no regular coach (1881-1892)

	Nat'l								Nat'l				
Year	AP	Other	W-L-T	PF	PA	Pct.	Year	AP	Other	W-L-T	PF	PA	Pct.
1881			1-0-1	1	0	.750	1887			3-1-1	189	28	.700
1882			1-1-0	5	53	.500	1888			3-4-0	120	136	.429
1883			0-1-0	3	5	.000	1889			7-1-0	239	72	.875
1884			1-2-1	30	152	.375	1890			4-4-0	133	122	.500
1885			no team				1891			2-2-1	60	62	.500
1886			2-2-0	113	94	.500	1892			5-3-0	102	146	.825

Wallace S. Moyle (1893-1894) 9-7-0 .562

Year	AP	Other	W-L-T	PF	PA	Pct.	Year	AP	Other	W-L-T	PF	PA	Pct.
1893			4-3-0	84	90	.571	1894			5-4-0	112	80	.556

William Wurtenberg (1895-1899) 23-23-2 .500

Year	AP	Other	W-L-T	PF	PA	Pct.	Year	AP	Other	W-L-T	PF	PA	Pct.
1895			7-5-1	184	99	.577	1898			5-6-0	205	136	.455
1896			5-2-1	122	84	.688	1899			2-7-0	70	99	.222
1897			4-3-0	164	77	.571							

Frederick Jennings (1900) 2-4-2 .375

Year	AP	Other	W-L-T	PF	PA	Pct.
1900			2-4-2	38	68	.375

Walter McCornack (1901-1902) 15-3-1 .816

Year	AP	Other	W-L-T	PF	PA	Pct.	Year	AP	Other	W-L-T	PF	PA	Pct.
1901			9-1-0	267	53	.900	1902			6-2-1	105	39	.722

Fred Folsom (1903-1906) 29-5-4 .816

Year	AP	Other	W-L-T	PF	PA	Pct.	Year	AP	Other	W-L-T	PF	PA	Pct.
1903			9-1-0	242	23	.900	1905			7-1-2	150	34	.800
1904			7-0-1	143	13	.938	1906			6-3-1	72	87	.650

John O'Connor (1907-1908) 14-1-2 .882

Year	AP	Other	W-L-T	PF	PA	Pct.	Year	AP	Other	W-L-T	PF	PA	Pct.
1907			8-0-1	150	10	.944	1908			6-1-1	97	17	.812

Walter Lillard (1909) 5-1-2 .750

Year	AP	Other	W-L-T	PF	PA	Pct.
1909			5-1-2	89	18	.750

William Randall (1910) 5-2-0 .714

Year	AP	Other	W-L-T	PF	PA	Pct.
1910			5-2-0	111	27	.714

Frank Cavanaugh (1911-1916) 42-9-3 .806

Year	AP	Other	W-L-T	PF	PA	Pct.	Year	AP	Other	W-L-T	PF	PA	Pct.
1911			8-2-0	137	22	.800	1914			8-1-0	359	25	.889
1912			7-2-0	281	34	.778	1915			7-1-1	194	40	.833
1913			7-1-0	218	79	.875	1916			5-2-2	206	47	.667

Doc Spears (1917-1920) 21-9-1 .681

Year	AP	Other	W-L-T	PF	PA	Pct.	Year	AP	Other	W-L-T	PF	PA	Pct.
1917			5-3-0	83	68	.625	1919			6-1-1	141	53	.812
1918			3-3-0	78	83	.500	1920			7-2-0	198	68	.778

Jackson Cannell (1921-1922, 1929-1933) 39-19-4 .661

Year	AP	Other	W-L-T	PF	PA	Pct.	Year	AP	Other	W-L-T	PF	PA	Pct.
1921			6-2-1	166	103	.722	1922			6-3-0	111	55	.667

Jesse Hawley (1923-1928) 39-10-1 .790

Year	AP	Other	W-L-T	PF	PA	Pct.	Year	AP	Other	W-L-T	PF	PA	Pct.
1923			8-1-0	202	54	.889	1926			4-4-0	203	64	.500
1924		9	7-0-1	225	31	.938	1927			7-1-0	280	53	.875
1925		1	8-0-0	340	29	1.000	1928			5-4-0	182	103	.556

Jackson Cannell (1929-1933)

Year	AP	Other	W-L-T	PF	PA	Pct.	Year	AP	Other	W-L-T	PF	PA	Pct.
1929			7-2-0	305	56	.778	1932			4-4-0	156	51	.500
1930		8	7-1-1	301	43	.833	1933			4-4-1	128	87	.500
1931			5-3-1	216	110	.611							

Earl Blaik (1934-1940) 45-15-4 .734

Year	AP	Other	W-L-T	PF	PA	Pct.	Year	AP	Other	W-L-T	PF	PA	Pct.
1934			6-3-0	177	73	.667	1938			7-2-0	254	69	.778
1935			8-2-0	302	57	.800	1939			5-3-1	154	73	.611
1936	13		7-1-1	238	53	.833	1940			5-4-0	135	82	.556
1937	7	3	7-0-2	248	33	.889							

Tuss McLaughry (1941-1942, 1945-1954) 44-58-3 .425

Year	AP	Other	W-L-T	PF	PA	Pct.	Year	AP	Other	W-L-T	PF	PA	Pct.
1941			5-4-0	146	104	.556	1942			5-4-0	193	135	.556

Earl Brown (1943-1944) 8-6-1 .567

Year	AP	Other	W-L-T	PF	PA	Pct.	Year	AP	Other	W-L-T	PF	PA	Pct.
1943	16		6-1-0	185	39	.857	1944			2-5-1	57	142	.312

Tuss McLaughry (1945-1954)

Year	AP	Other	W-L-T	PF	PA	Pct.	Year	AP	Other	W-L-T	PF	PA	Pct.
1945			1-6-1	40	119	.188	1950			3-5-1	123	157	.389
1946			3-6-0	91	194	.667	1951			4-5-0	121	152	.444
1947			4-4-1	102	127	.500	1952			2-7-0	116	198	.222
1948			6-2-0	213	130	.750	1953			2-7-0	152	219	.222
1949			6-2-0	183	107	.750	1954			3-6-0	121	250	.333

Bob Blackman (1955-1970) 104-37-3 .726

Year	W-L-T	PF	PA	Pct.
1955	3-6-0	92	120	.333

Member of the Ivy League (1956-2003) 210-118-9 .63

Year	Nat'l AP	Other	Overall W-L-T	PF	PA	Pct.	Conf. W-L-T	Pct.	Rank	Year	Nat'l AP	Other	Overall W-L-T	PF	PA	Pct.	Conf. W-L-T	Pct.	Rank
1956			5-3-1	122	89	.611	4-3-0	.571	3	1964			6-3-0	235	135	.667	4-3-0	.571	4
1957			7-1-1	163	77	.833	5-1-1	.786	2	1965			9-0-0	271	71	1.000	7-0-0	1.000	1
1958			7-2-0	182	83	.778	6-1-0	.857	1	1966			7-2-0	273	131	.778	6-1-0	.857	1
1959			5-3-1	96	106	.611	5-1-1	.786	2	1967			7-2-0	205	146	.778	5-2-0	.714	2
1960			5-4-0	98	66	.556	4-3-0	.571	3	1968			4-5-0	206	183	.444	3-4-0	.429	5
1961			6-3-0	197	104	.667	5-2-0	.714	3	1969			8-1-0	282	99	.889	6-1-0	.857	1
1962			9-0-0	231	57	1.000	7-0-0	1.000	1	1970	14	13	9-0-0	311	42	1.000	7-0-0	1.000	1
1963			7-2-0	175	94	.778	5-2-0	.714	1										

Jake Crouthamel (1971-1977) 41-20-2 .667

Year	Nat'l AP	Other	Overall W-L-T	PF	PA	Pct.	Conf. W-L-T	Pct.	Rank	Year	Nat'l AP	Other	Overall W-L-T	PF	PA	Pct.	Conf. W-L-T	Pct.	Rank
1971			8-1-0	207	106	.889	6-1-0	.857	1	1975			5-3-1	160	121	.611	4-2-1	.642	4
1972			7-1-1	260	168	.833	5-1-1	.786	1	1976			6-3-0	236	111	.667	4-3-0	.571	3
1973			6-3-0	184	119	.667	6-1-0	.857	1	1977			6-3-0	141	96	.667	4-3-0	.571	3
1974			3-6-0	103	115	.333	3-4-0	.429	5										

Joseph Yukica (1978-1986) 36-47-4 .437

Year	Nat'l AP	Other	Overall W-L-T	PF	PA	Pct.	Conf. W-L-T	Pct.	Rank	Year	Nat'l AP	Other	Overall W-L-T	PF	PA	Pct.	Conf. W-L-T	Pct.	Rank
1978			6-3-0	187	159	.667	6-1-0	.857	1	1983			4-5-1	185	208	.450	4-2-1	.643	3
1979			4-4-1	98	86	.500	4-3-0	.571	4	1984			2-7-0	174	226	.222	2-5-0	.286	6
1980			4-6-0	207	170	.400	4-3-0	.571	3	1985			2-7-1	144	199	.250	2-4-1	.357	6
1981			6-4-0	208	137	.600	6-1-0	.857	1	1986			3-6-1	188	272	.350	3-3-1	.500	4
1982			5-5-0	219	235	.500	5-2-0	.714	1										

Buddy Tevens (1987-1991) 26-22-2 .540

Year	Nat'l AP	Other	Overall W-L-T	PF	PA	Pct.	Conf. W-L-T	Pct.	Rank	Year	Nat'l AP	Other	Overall W-L-T	PF	PA	Pct.	Conf. W-L-T	Pct.	Rank
1987			2-8-0	110	302	.200	1-6-0	.143	7	1990			7-2-1	211	121	.750	6-1-0	.857	1
1988			5-5-0	209	190	.500	4-3-0	.571	3	1991			7-2-1	283	209	.750	6-0-1	.929	1
1989			5-5-0	170	178	.500	4-3-0	.571	4										

John Lyons (1992-2002) 59-59-1 .500

Year	Nat'l AP	Other	Overall W-L-T	PF	PA	Pct.	Conf. W-L-T	Pct.	Rank	Year	Nat'l AP	Other	Overall W-L-T	PF	PA	Pct.	Conf. W-L-T	Pct.	Rank
1992			8-2-0	364	203	.800	6-1-0	.857	1	1998			2-8-0	142	226	.200	1-6-0	.143	7
1993			7-3-0	258	168	.700	6-1-0	.857	2	1999			2-8-0	138	300	.200	2-5-0	.286	6
1994			4-6-0	166	187	.400	2-5-0	.286	7	2000			2-8-0	231	388	.200	1-6-0	.143	6
1995			7-2-1	221	137	.750	4-2-1	.643	4	2001			1-8-0	203	301	.111	1-6-0	.143	7
1996			10-0-0	275	104	1.000	7-0-0	1.000	1	2002			3-7-0	247	295	.300	2-5-0	.286	6
1997			8-2-0	208	165	.800	6-1-0	.857	2	2003			5-5-0	211	261	.500	4-2-0	.571	2

Won-loss record by decades:

Decade	Record	Pct.	Decade	Record	Pct.	Decade	Record	Pct.
1881-89	18-12-3	.591	1930-39	60-23-7	.706	1970-79	60-27-3	.672
1890-99	43-39-3	.524	1940-49	43-38-3	.530	1980-89	38-58-3	.399
1900-09	65-14-11	.783	1950-59	41-45-4	.478	1990-99	62-35-3	.635
1910-19	61-18-4	.759	1960-69	68-22-0	.756	2000-03	11-28-0	.282
1920-29	65-19-2	.767						
Historic record	635-378-46	.621						

College Football Hall of Fame:
Frank Cavanaugh, coach, 1911-16; Doc Spears, guard, 1912-15; Ed Healey, tackle, 1914-19; Swede Oberlander, halfback/tackle, 1923-25; Myles Lane, halfback, 1925-27; Bill Morton, quarterback, 1929-31; Earl Blaik, coach, 1934-40; Bob MacLeod, halfback, 1936-38; Tuss McLaughry, coach, 1941-42, 1945-54; Bob Blackman, coach, 1955-70, Murray Bowden, defensive back, 1967-70.

UNIVERSITY OF DENVER, Denver, Colorado; nickname "Pioneers," "Hilltoppers"; colors crimson and gold. Denver began play in 1885. In 1938, Denver became a founding member of the new Mountain States (Skyline) Conference. Denver played in the Skyline Conference through the 1960 season, leaving one year before the Conference disbanded. Denver dropped intercollegiate football after the 1960 season.

Early years with no formal coach (1885-1900)

Year	W-L-T	PF	PA	Pct.	Year	W-L-T	PF	PA	Pct.
1885	0-1-0	0	12	.000	1894	1-3-0	12	99	.250
1886-1887	no team				1895	0-3-2	12	64	.200
1888	0-1-0	0	20	.000	1896	2-4-0	16	34	.333
1889	0-1-0	0	10	.000	1897	0-3-2	4	20	.200
1890	no team				1898	6-4-1	78	121	.591
1891	0-4-1	12	60	.100	1899	0-0-1	0	0	.500
1892	0-4-0	0	136	.000	1900	1-1-0	5	21	.500
1893	1-2-0	30	16	.333					

----- Leland (1901) 2-3-0 .400

Year	W-L-T	PF	PA	Pct.
1901	2-3-0	74	54	.400

Ben Griffith (1902-1903) 9-11-1 .452

1902	3-4-1	34	60	.438
1903	6-7-0	164	111	.462

Ora Smith Fowler (1904-1905) 5-10-2 .353

1904	2-5-0	44	105	.286
1905	3-5-2	61	103	.400

John Koehler (1906-1910) 22-15-1 .592

1906	2-3-0	17	47	.400
1907	2-6-0	30	179	.250
1908	7-1-0	152	37	.875
1909	7-2-0	177	31	.778
1910	4-3-1	72	65	.562

Tom Berry (1911) 5-2-1 .688

1911	5-2-1	81	22	.688

Clem Crowley (1912) 2-6-1 .278

1912	2-6-1	87	130	.278

Charles Wingerider (1913) 2-5-0 .286

1913	2-5-0	47	140	.286

Henry Buckingham (1914) 5-4-0 .556

1914	5-4-0	166	115	.556

John Filke (1915-1918) 20-7-1 .732

1915	4-3-0	103	83	.571
1916	4-2-1	91	79	.643
1917	9-0-0	226	45	1.000
1918	3-2-0	49	74	.600

George Koonsman (1919) 1-5-1 .214

1919	1-5-1	23	191	.214

Fred Murphy (1920-1922) 13-7-2 .636

1920	3-4-0	46	82	.429
1921	4-2-1	133	77	.643
1922	6-1-1	106	48	.812

Elmer McDevitt (1923-1924) 10-5-2 .647

1923	6-3-0	117	99	.667
1924	4-2-2	36	55	.625

Fred Dawson (1925-1928) 14-16-1 .468

1925	1-6-0	27	152	.143
1926	4-4-0	106	72	.500
1927	5-2-0	120	51	.714
1928	4-4-1	128	96	.500

Jeff Cravath (1929-1931) 14-11-1 .558

1929	5-1-1	92	33	.786
1930	5-4-0	140	148	.556
1931	4-6-0	104	143	.400

Percy Lacey (1932-1935) 20-14-3 .581

1932	4-3-1	60	74	.561
1933	5-3-1	107	46	.611
1934	5-5-1	122	91	.500
1935	6-3-0	109	101	.667

Bill Saunders (1936-1938) 17-8-2 .667

1936	7-1-1	141	88	.833
1937	6-3-0	122	61	.667

Member of the Skyline Conference (1938-1960) 59-56-10 .512

Year	Nat'l AP Other	Overall W-L-T	PF	PA	Pct.	Conference W-L-T	Pct.	Rank
1938		4-4-1	65	86	.500	3-2-1	.583	2

Clyde Hubbard (1939-1941, 1945-1947) 30-22-7 .568

Year	Nat'l AP Other	Overall W-L-T	PF	PA	Pct.	Conference W-L-T	Pct.	Rank
1939		5-3-1	129	75	.611	3-2-1	.583	3
1940		7-2-1	162	93	.750	4-1-1	.750	2
1941		4-3-2	141	46	.556	3-1-2	.667	2

Ellison Ketchum (1942) 6-3-1 .650

1942		6-3-1	182	98	.650	3-2-1	.583	3

Mark Duncan (1943) 2-5-0 .286

1943		2-5-0	70	186	.286	no conference		

Adam Esslinger and Clyde Hubbard (1944) 4-3-2 .556

1944		4-3-2	193	120	.556	no conference		

Clyde Hubbard (1945-1947)

| 1945 | 4-5-1 | 201 | 182 | .450 | no conference | | | 1947 | | 5-4-1 | 153 | 138 | .550 | 3-2-1 | .583 | 2 |
| 1946 | 5-5-1 | 179 | 182 | .500 | 4-1-1 | .750 | 1 | | | | | | | | | |

John Baker (1948-1952) 20-30-2 .404

1948	4-5-1	166	174	.450	2-2-0	.500	3	1951		6-4-0	283	133	.600	4-3-0	.571	3
1949	4-6-0	192	214	.400	2-2-0	.500	3	1952		3-7-0	143	190	.300	0-7-0	.000	8
1950	3-8-1	266	261	.292	2-2-1	.500	3									

Bob Blackman (1953-1954) 12-6-2 .650

| 1953 | 3-5-2 | 159 | 195 | .400 | 1-5-1 | .214 | 7 | 1954 | 18 | 9-1-0 | 298 | 96 | .900 | 6-1-0 | .857 | 1 |

John Roning (1955-1959) 27-33-0 .450

1955	8-2-0	310	89	.800	5-2-0	.714	3	1958		2-8-0	135	163	.200	2-5-0	.286	5
1956	6-4-0	250	206	.600	4-3-0	.571	3	1959		2-8-0	104	230	.200	2-5-0	.286	5
1957	6-4-0	150	155	.600	5-2-0	.714	3	1960		3-7-0	n.a.	n.a.	.300	1-6-0	.143	7

Won-loss record by decades:

1885-89	0- 3-0	.000	1910-19	39-32-5	.546	1940-49	45-41-10	.521
1890-99	10-27-7	.307	1920-29	42-29-6	.584	1950-60	51-58-3	.469
1900-09	35-37-3	.487	1930-39	51-35-6	.587			

Historic record: 273-262-40 .510

Post-season record: 0-3-0 .000

| 1945: Sun Bowl, New Mexico 34, Denver 24 | 1950: Pineapple Bowl, Hawaii 28, Denver 27 |
| 1947: Alamo Bowl, Hardin-Simmons 20, Denver 0 | |

College Football Hall of Fame:
Bob Blackman, coach, 1953-54.

DRAKE UNIVERSITY; Des Moines, Iowa: nickname "Bulldogs"; colors Bulldog blue and white; Drake Stadium (18,000); Pioneer Football League (Division I-AA). Drake began play in 1893 and was an independent until it joined the Missouri Valley Conference for the 1908 season. Drake left the MVC after the 1951 season following the Johnny Bright incident. Drake rejoined the MVC for the 1971 season and played in that conference until it dropped football after the 1985 season, later joining the Pioneer League. Drake played a major college schedule in the pre-World War II years. Data are shown here through the 1951 season. MVC rules ignored ties in calculating win percents through the 1945 season.

Early years (1893-1907)

Year	Coach	W-L-T	PF	PA	Pct.	Year	Coach	W-L-T	PF	PA	Pct.
1893	None	0-2-1	0	68	.167	1901	Charles Best	4-4-0	113	34	.500
1894	W. W. Wharton	2-2-0	34	48	.500	1902	G. O. Dietz	5-2-1	127	23	.688
1895	Hermon Williams	1-4-0	22	48	.200	1903	W. J. Monilaw	5-3-0	170	93	.625
1896	Fred Rogers	2-3-0	28	98	.400	1904	W. J. Monilaw	5-4-0	213	164	.556
1897	A. B. Potter	2-3-0	34	66	.400	1905	Willie Heston	4-4-0	151	141	.500
1898	A. B. Potter	4-2-0	102	45	.667	1906	Charles Pell	2-4-1	41	62	.357
1899	A. B. Potter	5-2-0	94	57	.714	1907	Charles Pell	3-4-1	61	74	.438
1900	Charles Best	6-3-0	129	45	.667						

Member of the Missouri Valley Conference (1908-1952, 1971-1985) 106-87-10 .541

Year	Nat'l AP Other	Overall W-L-T	PF	PA	Pct.	Conference W-L-T	Pct.	Rank	Year	Nat'l AP Other	Overall W-L-T	PF	PA	Pct.	Conference W-L-T	Pct.	Rank
						John L. Griffith (1908-1915) 36-25-3 .586											
1908		6-2-0	108	29	.667	1-2-0	.333	5	1912		5-3-0	201	73	.625	2-2-0	.500	3
1909		7-1-0	138	36	.875	2-1-0	.667	3	1913		4-3-1	104	64	.571	1-3-0	.250	5
1910		3-5-0	43	67	.375	0-3-0	.000	6	1914		4-3-1	124	133	.571	0-3-0	.000	5
1911		5-2-1	165	29	.688	0-2-1	.000	4	1915		2-6-0	131	240	.250	1-4-0	.200	9
						Ralph Glaze (1916-1917) 3-10-2 .267											
1916		3-5-0	72	163	.375	1-3-0	.250	6	1917		0-5-2	24	167	.143	0-3-0	.000	7
						M. B. Banks (1918-1920) 11-10-1 .523											
1918		3-2-0	83	117	.600	no conference			1920		4-5-1	170	128	.450	1-3-1	.250	5
1919		4-3-0	68	46	.571	2-2-0	.500	3									
						Ossie Solem (1921-1931) 44-35-2 556											
1921		5-2-0	149	40	.714	2-2-0	.500	4	1927		3-6-0	89	151	.333	1-2-0	.333	8
1922		7-0-0	155	26	1.000	4-0-0	1.000	1	1928		7-1-0	141	52	.875	3-0-0	1.000	1
1923		5-2-0	168	49	.714	3-1-0	.750	3	1929		5-3-1	145	79	.611	3-0-1	1.000	1
1924		5-2-1	106	56	.714	3-1-1	.750	2	1930		5-4-0	59	135	.556	3-0-0	1.000	1
1925		5-3-0	66	41	.625	5-2-0	.714	2	1931		5-6-0	130	226	.455	3-0-0	1.000	1
1926		2-6-0	60	118	.250	1-4-0	.200	8									
						E. O. Williams (1932) 2-6-1 .250											
1932		2-6-1	57	196	.250	1-3-1	.250	4									
						Vee Green (1933-1946) 66-59-7 .528											
1933		6-3-1	105	74	.667	4-1-0	.800	2	1940		4-5-0	127	108	.444	2-2-0	.500	3
1934		3-6-1	59	135	.333	2-2-0	.500	3	1941		4-5-1	83	134	.444	0-3-1	.000	6
1935		4-4-2	141	204	.500	1-2-1	.333	4	1942		3-7-0	115	225	.300	1-4-0	.200	5
1936		6-4-0	238	153	.600	3-2-0	.600	3	1943		4-2-0	110	64	.667	0-0-0	......	
1937		8-2-0	235	73	.800	4-1-0	.800	2	1944		7-2-0	221	57	.778	0-0-0	......	
1938		5-4-1	115	225	.556	2-1-1	.667	2	1945		5-4-1	217	115	.550	1-2-0	.333	4
1939		5-5-0	89	104	.500	2-3-0	.400	4	1946		2-6-1	78	247	.277	0-4-0	.000	5
						Al Kawai (1947-1948) 8-10-1 .447											
1947		1-7-1	97	191	.167	1-3-0	.250	4	1948		7-3-0	199	105	.700	1-1-0	.500	3
						Warren Gaer (1949-1958) 43-43-2 .500											
1949		6-2-1	202	95	.722	3-1-0	.750	2	1951		7-2-0	187	107	.778	3-1-0	.750	2
1950		6-2-1	247	117	.722	1-2-1	.375	4									

Win-percent by decades (1893-1951):

1893-99	16-18-1	.471	1920-29	48-30-3	.611	1940-49	43-43-5	.500	
1900-09	47-31-3	.599	1930-39	49-44-6	.525	1950-51	13-4-1	.750	
1910-19	33-37-5	.473							

Historic record (1893-1951) 249-207-24 .544

College Football Hall of Fame: Johnny Bright, halfback, 1949-51

DUQUESNE UNIVERSITY, Pittsburgh, Pennsylvania; nickname "Dukes"; colors red and blue; Arthur Rooney Athletic Field (4,500); Metro Atlantic Athletic Conference. Duquesne played a major college schedule between 1930 and 1950. Following the 1950 season, Duquesne dropped football until 1969 when it began fielding a club team. It moved to Division III in 1979 and to Division I-AA non-scholarship in 1993. Data are shown through the 1950 season.

Year	AP	Nat'l Other	W-L-T	PF	PA	Pct.
1894			9-3-0	216	52	.750
1896			12-1-0	268	66	.923
1897			1-2-1*	19	50	.333
1898			5-4-1*	101	94	.550
1899			2-0-2*	23	12	.750

*Incomplete records

Year	AP	Nat'l Other	W-L-T	PF	PA	Pct.
1902			1-6-0	45	150	.143
1903			3-5-0	17	115	.375
1913			3-5-1	81	118	.389
1920			3-3-1	88	73	.500
1922			0-8-0	6	125	.000
1924			2-4-2	26	106	.375
1925			0-7-0	9	165	.000
1927			4-4-1	82	78	.500
1928			8-1-0	118	32	.889
1929			9-0-1	156	53	.900
1930			7-3-0	131	56	.700
1934			8-2-0	322	22	.800
1935			6-3-0	99	63	.667
1936	14		8-2-0	140	28	.800
1937			6-4-0	151	52	.600
1939	10		8-0-1	152	43	.944
1940			7-1-0	118	64	.875
1947			2-8-0	45	262	.200
1949			3-6-0	160	226	.333
1950			2-6-1	169	265	.278

Year	AP	Nat'l Other	W-L-T	PF	PA	Pct.
Team exists, but no records (1891-1893)						
Unknown coach (1894) 9-3-0 .750						
1895 no team						
Mr. Brown (1896) 12-1-0 .923						
J. Wolfe (1897) 1-2-1* .333						
J. Van Cleve (1898) 5-4-1* .550						
Mr. Walker (1899) 2-0-2 * .750						
1900-1901 team exists, but no records						
Mr. Hickson (1902) 1-6-0 .43						
T. A. Giblin (1903) 3-5-0 .375						
1904-1912 no team						
Dr. Budd (1913-1914) 4-10-1 .300						
1914		1-5-0		70	135	.167
1915-1919 no team						
Jake Stahl (1920-1921) 3-7-2 .333						
1921		0-4-1		7	100	.100
Hal Ballin (1922-1923) 4-12-0 .250						
1923		4-4-0		65	82	.500
Mike Shortley (1924) 2-4-2 .375						
Frank McDermott (1925-1926) 2-12-1 .167						
1926		2-5-1		53	109	.312
Elmer Layden (1927-1933) 48-16-6 .729						
1931		3-5-3		56	85	.409
1932		7-2-1		132	58	.750
1933		10-1-0		206	33	.909
Joe Bach (1934) 8-2-0 .800						
Christy Flanagan (1935) 6-3-0 .667						
Clipper Smith (1936-1938) 18-12-0 .667						
1938		4-6-0		96	114	.400
Buff Donelli (1939-1942) 29-4-2 .857						
1941	8	8-0-0		143	21	1.000
1942		6-3-1		143	58	.650
1943-1946 no team						
Kass Kovalcheck (1947-1948) 4-15-0 .211						
1948		2-7-0		102	240	.222
Phil Ahwesh (1949) 3-6-0 .333						
Doc Skender (1950) 2-6-1 .278						

Won-loss record by decades:

1894-99	29-10-4	.721	1910-19	4-10-1	.300	1930-39	67-28-5	.695
1900-09	4-11-0	.267	1920-29	32-40-7	.449	1940-50	30-31-2	.492

Historical record: (1894-1950) 166-130-19 .560

Post-season won-loss record as a major college team: 2-0-1 .833
1931: Relief Fund Charity Game, Duquesne 0, Central Michigan 0
1934: Festival of Palms Bowl, Duquesne 33, Miami (FL) 7
1937: Orange Bowl, Duquesne 13, Mississippi State 12

FORDHAM UNIVERSITY, Bronx, New York; nickname "Rams"; colors maroon and white; Jack Coffey Stadium (7,000); Patriot League. While Fordham fielded a football team beginning in 1882, most of the teams scheduled were local club teams prior to World War I. Fordham played a major college schedule as a leading East Coast independent from around 1920 through 1954. Football was dropped because of financial reasons in 1954. Football was reinstated at the club level in 1964, upgraded to the Division III level in 1970, and to the Division I-AA level in 1989. Data are shown here beginning with the 1916 season, the first year that Frank Gargan coached the team, and through the 1954 season.

Year	Nat'l AP	Other	W-L-T	PF	PA	Pct.	Year	Nat'l AP	Other	W-L-T	PF	PA	Pct.
							Frank Gargan * (1916–1917, 1919, 1922-1926) 79-29-4 .723						
1916			25-1-1	346	32	.912	1917			18-3-0	290	74	.857
*Frank McCaffrey also is listed as coach for the 1916 season.													
							Edward Siskind (1918) 13-2-1 .844						
1918			13-2-1	187	62	.844							
							Frank Gargan (1919)						
1919			9-6-0	36	65	.600							
							Joseph DuMoe* (1920-1921) 10-6-1 .618						
1920*			5-3-0	154	105	.625	1921			5-3-1	191	107	.611
*Charles Brickley also is listed as coach for the 1920 season.													
							Frank Gargan (1922-1926)						
1922			3-5-2	93	146	.300	1925			9-1-0	311	55	.900
1923			3-7-0	107	139	.300	1926			3-4-1	119	131	.438
1924			9-2-0	225	71	.818							
							Frank Cavanaugh (1927-1932) 34-14-4 .692						
1927			3-5-0	82	139	.375	1930			8-1-0	215	29	.889
1928			4-5-0	121	130	.444	1931			6-1-2	205	36	.778
1929			7-0-2	176	19	.778	1932			6-2-0	193	28	.750
							Jim Crowley (1933-1941) 56-13-7 .783						
1933			6-2-0	195	40	.750	1938	15		6-1-2	186	30	.778
1934			5-3-0	165	92	.625	1939	17		6-2-0	124	41	.750
1935	11		6-1-2	132	41	.778	1940	12		7-2-0	162	62	.778
1936	15		5-1-2	128	33	.750	1941	6		8-1-0	182	67	.889
1937	3	2	7-0-1	182	16	.938							
							Earl Walsh (1942) 5-3-1 .611						
1942			5-3-1	103	155	.611	1943–1945 no team						
							Ed Danowski (1946-1954) 29-44-3 .401						
1946			0-7-0	43	228	.000	1951			5-4-0	232	183	.556
1947			1-6-1	44	245	.188	1952			2-5-1	151	119	.312
1948			3-6-0	182	192	.333	1953			4-5-0	176	128	.444
1949			5-3-0	226	139	.625	1954			1-7-1	96	292	.167
1950			8-1-0	174	123	.889							

Won-loss record by decades (as a major college team):

1916-19	65-12-2	.835	1930-39	61-14-9	.780	1950-54	20-22-2	.477
1920-29	51-35-6	.587	1940-49	29-28-2	.508			

Historical record: 226-111-19 662

Post-season won-loss record (as a major college): 1-1-0 .500
1941: Cotton Bowl, Texas A&M 13, Fordham 12
1942: Sugar Bowl, Fordham 2, Missouri 0

College Football Hall of Fame:
Frank Cavanaugh, coach, 1927-32; Ed Franco, tackle, 1935-37; Alex Wojciechowicz, center, 1935-37.

GEORGETOWN UNIVERSITY, Washington, D.C.; nickname "Hoyas." Georgetown played as an independent until intercollegiate football was dropped after the 1950 season. Georgetown restored football, and became a Division III school in 1970 moving up to a Division I-AA status in 1993. Data are shown here only for the period up to 1950.

Early Years (1887-1903)

Year	Coach	W-L-T	PF	PA	Pct.	Year	Coach	W-L-T	PF	PA	Pct.
1887	none	2-1-0	66	36	.667	1895-97	no team				
1888	none	4-2-0	31	34	.667	1898	B. Donovan	7-3-0	143	44	.700
1889	none	5-1-0	70	30	.833	1899	Bill Church	5-2-1	60	33	.688
1890	none	3-3-1	37	128	.500	1900	A.E. Bull	5-1-3	161	42	.722
1891	Tom Dowd	2-2-0	62	44	.500	1901	Bill Church	3-3-2	56	84	.500
1892	Tom Dowd	4-2-1	160	55	.643	1902	H. Sutter	7-3-0	137	88	.700
1893	Dick Harley	4-4-0	110	174	.500	1903	Phil King	7-3-0	195	50	.700
1894	B. Carmody	4-5-0	102	122	.444						

Years as a Major Eastern Independent (1904-1950)

Year	Nat'l AP	Other	W-L-T	PF	PA	Pct.	Year	Nat'l AP	Other	W-L-T	PF	PA	Pct.
							Joe Reilly (1904-1908) 19-17-2 .526						
1904			7-1-0	193	14	,875	1907			2-4-1	26	94	.357
1905			2-7-0	22	231	.222	1908			2-4-1	54	55	.357
1906			6-1-0	92	23	.857							
							Bill Newman (1909) 3-2-1 .583						
1909			3-2-1	59	31	.583							
							Fred Neilson (1910-1911) 14-2-2 .833						
1910			7-1-1	181	26	.833	1911			7-1-1	257	31	.833
							Frank Gargan (1912-1913) 12-5-0 .706						
1912			8-1-0	315	60	.888	1913			4-4-0	95	99	.500
							Albert Exendine (1914-1922) 55-21-3 .715						
1914			2-4-2	52	76	.375	1919			7-3-0	251	79	.700
1915			7-2-0	317	30	.777	1920			6-4-0	235	138	.600
1916			9-1-0	474	33	.900	1921			8-1-0	245	51	.888
1917			7-1-0	170	53	.875	1922			6-3-1	175	77	.650
1918			3-2-0	188	48	.600							
							Jackie Maloney (1923) 3-6-0 .333						
1923			3-6-0	79	100	.333							
							Lou Little (1924-1929) 41-12-3 .759						
1924			4-4-0	84	39	.500	1927			8-1-0	377	21	.889
1925			9-1-0	281	19	.900	1928			8-2-0	306	62	.800
1926			7-2-1	308	56	.750	1929			5-2-2	112	21	.667
							Tommy Mills (1930-1932) 11-13-1 .460						
1930			5-5-0	138	107	.500	1932*			2-3-0	46	70	.400
1931			4-5-1	78	86	.450							
							Jack Hagerty (1932-1948) 61-42-9 .585						
1932*			0-3-1	6	90	.125	1940	13		8-2-0	280	55	.800
1933			1-6-1	56	130	.188	1941			5-4-0	113	61	.555
1934			4-3-1	65	33	.562	1942			5-3-1	92	115	.611
1935			4-4-0	71	40	.500	1943-1945			no team			
1936			6-2-1	160	36	.722	1946			5-3-0	114	97	.625
1937			2-4-2	70	71	.375	1947			3-4-1	95	70	.438
1938			8-0-0	185	26	1.000	1948			3-4-1	99	105	.438
1939			7-0-1	109	22	.938							

*Mills coached the first five games of the 1932 season, and Hagerty coached the remaining four games.

							Bob Margarita (1949-1950) 7-12-0 .368						
1949			5-5-0	139	210	.500	1950			2-7-0	116	187	.222

Intercollegiate football discontinued after 1950 season.

Won-loss record by decades:

1887-89	11-4-0	.733	1910-19	61-20-4	.741	1940-49	34-25-3	.573
1890-99	29-21-3	.575	1920-29	64-26-4	.702	1950	2-7-0	.222
1900-09	44-29-8	.593	1930-39	43-35-8	.547			

Historical record: (1887-1950) 288-167-30 .625

Post-season record: 0-2-0 .000
1941 Orange Bowl, Mississippi State 14, Georgetown 7
1950: Sun Bowl, UTEP 33, Georgetown 20

College Football Hall of Fame: Lou Little, coach, 1924-29; Augie Lio, guard, 1938-40; Al Blozis, tackle, 1939-41.

HARDIN-SIMMONS UNIVERSITY, Abilene, TX; nickname: "Cowboys"; colors: purple and gold; Abilene Public Schools Stadium (15,046). Hardin-Simmons began play in 1897. The Cowboys joined the Border Conference in 1941 and played in the conference until it disbanded in 1961. Hardin-Simmons left major college football after 1962 season and the records shown here end in 1962.

Early years (1897-1940)

Year	Nat'l AP	Other	W-L-T	PF	PA	Pct.	Year	Nat'l AP	Other	W-L-T	PF	PA	Pct.
Carl A. Krause (1897-1898, 1904) 1-3-0 .250													
1897			1-0-0	12	0	1.000	1899-1903 no team						
1898			0-2-0	14	36	.000	1904			0-1-0	0	18	.000
Dallas Scarborough (1905-1907) 5-3-4 .583													
1905			1-2-1	28	33	.375	1907			2-1-2	32	22	.600
1906			2-0-1	17	5	.833							
George W. Mullins (1908-1909) 12-3-0 .800													
1908			5-2-0	74	53	.714	1909			7-1-0	158	31	.875
No team (1910-1916)													
H. D. Martin (1917-1918) 0-8-0 .000													
1917			0-6-0	15	197	.000	1918			0-2-0	19	59	.000
R. A. Easterday (1919-1920) 7-9-2 .444													
1919			5-3-1	265	64	.611	1920			2-6-1	82	162	.278
A. B. Hayes (1921-1923) 14-12-4 .533													
1921			6-4-0	110	93	.600	1923			3-5-3	78	55	.409
1922			5-3-1	122	88	.611							
Pete Shotwell (1924-1925) 11-8-0 .579													
1924			2-6-0	70	92	.250	1925			9-2-0	232	74	.818
Vic Payne (1926) 6-1-3 .750													
1926			6-1-3	85	44	.750							
Fred Bridges (1927-1929) 17-12-4 .576													
1927			5-3-2	92	75	.600	1929			6-3-1	78	65	.650
1928			6-6-1	152	116	.500							
Leslie Cranfill (1930-1934) 22-21-7 .510													
1930			6-1-2	144	45	.778	1933			3-6-1	46	83	.350
1931			6-4-1	193	86	.591	1934			3-5-2	98	73	.400
1932			4-5-1	51	101	.450							
Frank Kimbrough (1935-1940) 47-8-3 .836													
1935			6-3-1	182	64	.650	1938			8-2-0	195	66	.800
1936			9-2-0	302	41	.818	1939			7-1-1	137	54	.833
1937			8-0-1	247	46	.944	1940	17		9-0-0	229	76	.889

Member of the Border Conference (1941-1961) 53-33-3 .612

Year	Nat'l AP	Other	Overall W-L-T	PF	PA	Pct.	Conference W-LT	Pct.	Rank	Year	Nat'l AP	Other	Overall W-L-T	PF	PA	Pct.	Conference W-L-T	Pct.	Rank
Warren Woodson (1941-1951) 58-24-7 .691																			
1941			7-3-1	178	88	.682	3-1-0	.750	4	1948			6-2-3	345	212	.682	3-2-1	.583	5
1942			9-1-1	234	71	.864	3-0-1	.875	1	1949			6-4-1	318	189	.591	4-2-0	.667	3
1943-45	no team									1950			5-5-0	278	180	.500	3-3-0	.500	5
1946			11-0-0	322	48	1.000	6-0-0	1.000	1	1951			6-6-1	275	216	.500	4-1-0	.800	2
1947			8-3-0	278	81	.700	5-1-0	.833	2										
Murray Evans (1952-1954) 15-14-2 .516																			
1952			5-3-2	221	189	.600	2-2-1	.500	4	1954			4-6-0	153	204	.400	2-3-0	.400	5
1953			6-5-0	199	211	.545	4-1-0	.800	2										
Sammy Baugh (1955-1959) 22-29-0 .431																			
1955			5-5-0	223	256	.500	3-2-0	.600	3	1958			5-6-0	141	176	.545	4-0-0	1.000	1
1956			4-6-0	164	217	.400	2-3-0	.400	4	1959			3-7-0	154	244	.300	2-2-0	.500	3
1957			5-5-0	203	240	.500	3-2-0	.600	3										
Howard McChesney (1960) 0-10-0 .000																			
1960			0-10-0	68	308	.000	0-4-0	.000	6										
Floyd Huggins (1961) 1-9-0 .100																			
1961			1-9-0	na	na	.100	0-4-0	.000	6										

Border Conference disbands after 1961 season. 1962 season played as an independent.

Unknown coach (1962) 1-9-0 .100

Year			W-L-T	PF	PA	Pct.
1962			1-9-0	na	na	.100

Won-loss record by decades:

1897-99	1-2-0	.333	1920-29	50-39-12	.554	1950-59	48-54-3	.471
1900-09	17-7-4	.679	1930-39	60-29-10	.657	1960-62	2-28-0	.067
1910-19	5-11-1	.324	1940-49	56-13-6	.787			

Historic record: 239-183-36 .561

Post-season record: 5-2-2 .667

1935: Sun Bowl, Hardin-Simmons 14, New Mexico State 14
1936: Sun Bowl, Hardin-Simmons 34, Texas Western 6
1943: Sun Bowl, Second Air Force 13, Hardin-Simmons 7
1947: Alamo Bowl, Hardin-Simmons 20, Denver University 0
1948: Harbor Bowl, Hardin-Simmons 53, San Diego State 0

1948: Grape Bowl, Hardin-Simmons 35, Pacific 35
1948: Shrine Bowl, Hardin-Simmons 40, Ouachita College 12
1949: Camelia Bowl, Hardin-Simmons 49, Wichita 12
1958: Sun Bowl, Wyoming 14, Hardin-Simmons 6

College Football Hall of Fame: Bulldog Turner, center, 1937-39; Warren Woodson, coach, 1941-51.

Awards: Sammy Baugh Trophy: 1960, Hayseed Stephens.

HARVARD UNIVERSITY, Cambridge, Massachusetts; nickname "Crimson"; colors crimson and white; Harvard Stadium (30,898); Ivy League. Harvard began play in 1874 as an independent and continued as an independent until the Ivy League was organized in 1956.

Early years (1974-1907)

Year	Coach	W-L-T	PF	PA	Pct.	Year	Coach	W-L-T	PF	PA	Pct.
1874	none	1-0-1	3	0	.750	1891	George Stewart	13-1-0	588	26	.929
1874-1875	none	1-1-0	0	1	.500	1892	George Stewart	10-1-0	365	42	.909
1875-1876	none	4-0-0	7	0	1.000	1893	George Stewart	12-1-0	418	15	.923
1876-1877	none	3-1-0	4	1	.750	1894	Wm. Brooks	11-2-0	334	46	.846
1877	none	3-1-0	12	1	.750	1895	Robert Emmons	8-2-1	179	35	.773
1878	none	1-2-0	3	1	.333	1896	Bertram Waters	7-4-0	132	40	.636
1879	none	2-1-2	3	1	.600	1897	W. C. Forbes	10-1-1	233	20	.875
1880	none	2-2-2	6	4	.500	1898	W. C. Forbes	11-0-0*	254	20	1.000
1881	Lucius Littauer	6-1-1	20	1	.812	1899	Benjamin Dibblee	10-0-1*	210	10	.954
1882	none	7-1-0	19	2	.875	1900	Benjamin Dibblee	10-1-0	205	44	.909
1883	none	8-2-0	135	63	.800	1901	William Reid	12-0-0	254	24	1.000
1884	none	7-4-0	281	119	.636	1902	John Farley	11-1-0	184	45	.917
1885	no team					1903	John Cranston	9-3-0	150	59	.750
1886	Frank Mason	12-2-0	765	41	.857	1904	E. Wrightington	7-2-1	119	28	.750
1887	none	10-1-0	660	23	.909	1905	William Reid	8-2-1	147	41	.773
1888	none	12-1-0	635	32	.923	1906	William Reid	10-1-0	167	26	.909
1889	none	9-2-0	419	53	.818	1907	Joshua Crane	7-3-0	122	71	.700
1890	George Stewart	11-0-0*	555	12	1.000						

*Mythical national champion in 1890, 1898, and 1899. It should be noted that between 1890 and 1892, George Adams was also listed as a coach, and Everett Lake was also listed as a coach in 1893.

Year	Nat'l AP	Other	W-L-T	PF	PA	Pct.	Year	Nat'l AP	Other	W-L-T	PF	PA	Pct.
							Percy Haughton (1908-1916) 71-7-5 .886						
1908			9-0-1	132	8	.950	1913	1		9-0-0	225	28	1.000
1909			8-1-0	103	17	.889	1914			7-0-2	187	28	.889
1910	1		8-0-1	155	5	.944	1915			8-1-0	164	36	.889
1911			6-2-1	98	35	.722	1916			7-3-0	187	34	.700
1912	1		9-0-0	176	22	1.000							
							Wingate Rollins (1917) 3-1-3 .643						
1917			3-1-3	75	14	.643							
							Pooch Donovan (1918) 2-1-0 .667						
1918			2-1-0	24	12	.667							
							Robert Fisher (1919-1925) 43-14-5 .734						
1919	1		9-0-1	229	19	.950	1923			4-3-1	75	55	.562
1920			8-0-1	208	28	.944	1924			4-4-0	61	78	.500
1921			7-2-1	101	54	.750	1925			4-3-1	118	88	.562
1922			7-2-0	128	29	.778							
							Arnold Horween (1926-1930) 21-17-3 .549						
1926			3-5-0	140	105	.375	1929			5-2-1	158	80	.688
1927			4-4-0	85	108	.500	1930			4-4-1	126	59	.500
1928			5-2-1	125	29	.688							
							Edward Casey (1931-1934) 20-11-1 .641						
1931	7		7-1-0	149	29	.875	1933			5-2-1	139	56	.688
1932			5-3-0	169	99	.625	1934			3-5-0	84	99	.375
							Dick Harlow (1935-1942, 1945-1947) 45-39-7 .533						
1935			3-5-0	107	89	.375	1939			4-4-0	162	67	.500
1936			3-4-1	178	112	.438	1940			3-2-3	77	49	.562
1937			5-2-1	158	46	.688	1941			5-2-1	70	43	.688
1938			4-4-0	157	106	.500	1942			2-6-1	52	123	.278
							Henry Lamar (1943-1944) 7-3-1 .682						
1943			2-2-1	34	39	.500	1944			5-1-0	100	37	.833
							Dick Harlow (1945-1947)						
1945			5-3-0	161	80	.625	1947			4-5-0	139	177	.444
1946			7-2-0	214	65	.778							
							Arthur Valpey (1948-1949) 5-12-0 .294						
1948			4-4-0	130	184	.500	1949			1-8-0	103	276	.111

Lloyd Jordan (1950-1956) 24-31-3 .440

Year	W-L-T	PF	PA	Pct.		Year	W-L-T	PF	PA	Pct.
1950	1-7-0	74	248	.125		1953	6-2-0	146	78	.750
1951	3-5-1	143	266	.389		1954	4-3-1	108	97	.562
1952	5-4-0	214	198	.556		1955	3-4-1	143	114	.438

Member of the Ivy League (1956-2003) 192-135-9 .585

	Nat'l		Overall				Conference				Nat'l		Overall				Conference		
Year	AP	Other	W-L-T	PF	PA	Pct.	W-L-T	Pct.	Rank	Year	AP	Other	W-L-T	PF	PA	Pct.	W-L-T	Pct.	Rank
1956			2-6-0	153	199	.250	2-5-0	.286	6										

John Yovicsin (1957-1970) 78-42-5 .644

Year	AP	Other	W-L-T	PF	PA	Pct.	W-L-T	Pct.	Rank	Year	AP	Other	W-L-T	PF	PA	Pct.	W-L-T	Pct.	Rank
1957			3-5-0	78	180	.375	2-5-0	.286	7	1964			6-3-0	131	123	.667	5-2-0	.714	2
1958			4-5-0	149	99	.444	3-4-0	.429	6	1965			5-2-2	120	62	.667	3-2-2	.571	3
1959			6-3-0	177	101	.667	4-3-0	.571	3	1966			8-1-0	231	60	.889	6-1-0	.857	1
1960			5-4-0	90	119	.556	4-3-0	.571	3	1967			6-3-0	256	144	.667	4-3-0	.571	4
1961			6-3-0	160	97	.667	6-1-0	.857	1	1968			8-0-1	236	90	.944	6-0-1	.929	1
1962			6-3-0	202	118	.667	5-2-0	.714	2	1969			3-6-0	165	166	.333	2-5-0	.286	5
1963			5-2-2	122	76	.667	4-2-1	.643	3	1970			7-2-0	227	157	.778	5-2-0	.714	2

Joe Restic (1971-1993) 117-97-6 .545

Year	AP	Other	W-L-T	PF	PA	Pct.	W-L-T	Pct.	Rank	Year	AP	Other	W-L-T	PF	PA	Pct.	W-L-T	Pct.	Rank
1971			5-4-0	180	167	.556	4-3-0	.571	4	1983			6-2-2	188	140	.700	5-1-1	.786	1
1972			4-4-1	198	186	.500	3-3-1	.500	5	1984			5-4-0	182	196	.556	5-2-0	.714	2
1973			7-2-0	224	157	.778	5-2-0	.714	2	1985			7-3-0	192	136	.700	5-2-0	.714	2
1974			7-2-0	236	129	.778	6-1-0	.857	1	1986			3-7-0	139	190	.300	3-4-0	.429	5
1975			7-2-0	216	133	.778	6-1-0	.857	1	1987			8-2-0	243	163	.800	6-1-0	.857	1
1976			6-3-0	176	115	.667	4-3-0	.571	3	1988			2-8-0	202	272	.200	2-5-0	.286	6
1977			4-5-0	153	173	.444	4-3-0	.571	3	1989			5-5-0	207	257	.500	5-2-0	.714	3
1978			4-4-1	196	189	.500	2-4-1	.357	5	1990			5-5-0	199	206	.500	3-4-0	.429	4
1979			3-6-0	148	157	.333	3-4-0	.429	6	1991			4-5-1	203	223	.450	4-2-1	.643	3
1980			7-3-0	159	138	.700	4-3-0	.571	3	1992			3-7-0	167	240	.300	3-4-0	.429	5
1981			5-4-1	218	173	.550	4-2-1	.643	4	1993			3-7-0	233	279	.300	1-6-0	.143	7
1982			7-3-0	259	136	.700	5-2-0	.714	1										

Tim Murphy (1994-2003) 49-40-0 .551

Year	AP	Other	W-L-T	PF	PA	Pct.	W-L-T	Pct.	Rank	Year	AP	Other	W-L-T	PF	PA	Pct.	W-L-T	Pct.	Rank
1994			4-6-0	209	254	.400	2-5-0	.286	7	1998			4-6-0	136	211	.400	3-4-0	.429	5
1995			2-8-0	183	258	.200	1-6-0	.143	8	1999			5-5-0	254	191	.500	3-4-0	.429	5
1996			4-6-0	163	164	.400	2-5-0	.286	6	2000			5-5-0	327	255	.500	4-3-0	.571	3
1997			9-1-0	301	123	.900	7-0-0	1.000	1	2001			9-0-0	293	184	1.000	7-0-0	1.000	1
										2002			7-3-0	267	230	.700	6-1-0	.857	2
										2003			7-3-0	317	221	.700	4-3-0	.571	2

Won-loss record by decades:

1874-79	15- 6-3	.688		1920-29	51-27-6	.643	1970-79	54-34-2	.611
1889-89	73-16-3	.810		1930-39	43-34-4	.556	1980-89	55-41-3	.571
1890-99	103-12-3	.886		1940-49	38-35-6	519	1990-99	43-56-1	.435
1900-09	91-14-3	.856		1950-59	37-44-3	.458	2000-03	27-11-0	.711
1910-19	68- 8-8	.857		1960-69	58-27-5	.672			

Historical record: 757-365-50 .667

Post-season won-loss record: 1-0-0 1.000
1920: Rose Bowl, Harvard 7, Oregon 6

College football Hall of Fame:
Marshall Newell, tackle, 1890-93; Charlie Brewer, fullback, 1892-95; Bill Reid, fullback, 1897-99; Charlie Daly, quarterback, 1898-1902; Dave Campbell, end, 1899-1901; Hamilton Fish, tackle, 1907-09; Percy Haughton, coach, 1908-16; Bob Fisher, guard, 1909-11; Percy Wendell, halfback, 1910-12; Huntington Hardwick, end/halfback, 1912-14; Stan Pennock, guard, 1912-14; Eddie Mahan, fullback, 1913-15; Eddie Casey, halfback, 1916-19; George Owen, halfback, 1920-22; Ben Ticknor, center, 1928-30; Barry Wood, quarterback, 1929-31; Dick Harlow, coach, 1935-42, 1945-47; Endicott Peabody, guard, 1939-41; Lloyd Jordan, coach, 1950-56.

COLLEGE OF THE HOLY CROSS, Worcester, Massachusetts; nickname "Crusaders"; color royal purple; Filton Field (23,500); Patriot League. Holy Cross began play as an independent in 1896, and, within a few years, was playing the leading teams in the East. Between 1937 and 1951. Holy Cross was nationally ranked in five years. In 1981, Holy Cross opted for Division I-AA status. The record shown below covers the history of Holy Cross up to the 1981 season.

Year	Nat'l AP	Other	W-L-T	PF	PA	Pct.	Year	Nat'l AP	Other	W-L-T	PF	PA	Pct.
							Dr. A.C.N. Peterson (1896-1897) 6-5-3 .536						
1896			2-2-2	22	20	.500	1897			4-3-1	50	36	.562
							John J. Corbett (1898) 1-0-0 1.000						
1898*			1-0-0	23	0	1.000							
							Maurice Connor (1898-1902) 27-15-4 .630						
1898*			4-4-1	80	60	.500	1901			7-1-1	126	43	.833
1899			5-5-0	135	81	.500	1902			6-2-1	83	45	.722
1900			5-3-1	55	61	.611							

*Corbett coached the first game of the 1898 season, and Conner coached the remaining ten games.

Year	Nat'l AP	Other	W-L-T	PF	PA	Pct.	Year	Nat'l AP	Other	W-L-T	PF	PA	Pct.
							Frank Cavanaugh (1903-05) 16-10-2 .586						
1903			8-2-0	174	69	.800	1905			6-3-0	119	73	.667
1904			2-5-2	64	135	.333							
							George W. King (1906) 4-3-1 .562						
1906			4-3-1	64	64	.562							
							Timothy Larkin (1907-1912) 18-26-7 .422						
1907			1-7-2	31	212	.200	1910			3-3-2	54	35	.500
1908			4-4-0	44	74	.500	1911			4-5-0	78	77	.444
1909			2-4-2	41	43	.375	1912			4-3-1	77	53	.562
							Harry Van Kersberg (1913) 3-6-0 .333						
1913			3-6-0	128	158	.333							
							Luke L. Kelly (1914-1917) 12-17-3 .422						
1914			2-5-1	20	118	.312	1916			4-5-0	58	119	.444
1915			3-3-2	84	60	.500	1917			3-4-0	79	114	.429
							Bart F. Sullivan (1918) 2-0-0 1.000						
1918			2-0-0	49	14	1.000							
							Cleo A. O'Donnell (1919-1929) 69-27-6 .706						
1919			5-3-0	174	48	.625	1925			8-2-0	209	63	.800
1920			5-3-0	177	44	.625	1926			7-1-2	180	51	.800
1921			5-3-0	153	44	.625	1927			6-3-0	125	42	.667
1922			7-2-1	147	53	.750	1928			5-3-2	180	50	.600
1923			8-2-0	272	29	.800	1929			6-4-0	147	73	.600
1924			7-1-1	192	36	.833							
							John J. McEwen (1930-1932) 21-5-1 .796						
1930			8-2-0	195	45	.800	1932*			6-1-0	101	35	.857
1931			7-2-1	166	53	.750							
							Arthur Corcoran (1932) 0-1-2 .500						
1932*			0-1-2	0	7	.500							

*McEwen coached the first seven games of the 1932 season, and then was fired for fighting with ex-coach Bart Sullivan on the sidelines of a game. Corcoran finished out the season.

Year	Nat'l AP	Other	W-L-T	PF	PA	Pct.	Year	Nat'l AP	Other	W-L-T	PF	PA	Pct.
							Dr. Eddie Anderson (1933-1938, 1950-1964) 129-67-8 .652						
1933			7-2-0	172	70	.778	1936			7-2-1	157	42	.750
1934			8-2-0	187	61	.800	1937	14		8-0-2	107	19	.900
1935			9-0-1	260	19	.950	1938	9		8-1-0	225	51	.889
							Joseph L. Sheeketski (1939-1941) 15-11-3 .569						
1939			7-2-0	176	47	.778	1941			4-4-2	103	104	.500
1940			4-5-1	116	125	.450							
							Anthony Scanlon (1942-1944) 16-8-3 .648						
1942	19		5-4-1	210	99	.550	1944			5-2-2	173	90	.667
1943			6-2-0	168	43	.750							
							John DaGrosa (1945-1947) 17-10-2 .621						
1945	16		8-2-0	223	52	.800	1947			4-4-2	144	75	.500
1946			5-4-0	114	103	.556							
							Dr. Bill Osmanski (1948-1949) 6-14-0 .300						
1948			5-5-0	151	128	.500	1949			1-9-0	116	325	.100

Dr. Eddie Anderson (1950-1964)

Year			Record	PF	PA	Pct.		Year	Record	PF	PA	Pct.
1950			4-5-1	247	209	.450		1958	6-3-0	112	104	.667
1951	19	17	8-2-0	362	117	.800		1959	6-4-0	142	160	.600
1952			8-2-0	226	77	.800		1960	6-4-0	172	119	.600
1953			5-5-0	134	89	.500		1961	7-3-0	207	152	.700
1954			3-7-0	180	243	.300		1962	6-4-0	214	206	.600
1955			6-4-0	148	160	.600		1963	2-6-1	77	154	.278
1956			5-3-1	142	123	.611		1964	5-5-0	146	153	.500
1957			5-3-1	191	130	.611						

Mel Massucco (1965-1966) 8-10-2 .450

1965	2-7-1	71	173	.250		1966	6-3-1	135	163	.650

Tom Boisture (1967-1968) 8-11-1 .425

1967	5-5-0	158	170	.500		1968	3-6-1	179	247	.350

Bill Whitton (1969-1970) 0-12-1 .038

1969*	0-2-0	6	51	.000		1970	0-10-1	117	343	.045

*Final 8 games of 1969 season cancelled because of an outbreak of hepatitis.

Ed Doherty (1971-1975) 20-31-2 .396

1971	4-6-0	188	239	.400		1974	5-5-1	182	219	.500
1972	5-4-1	187	182	.550		1975	1-10-0	119	274	.091
1973	5-6-0	221	221	.455						

Neil Wheelwright (1976-1980) 20-35-0 .364

1976	3-8-0	204	330	.273		1979	5-6-0	174	179	.455
1977	2-9-0	130	270	.182		1980	3-8-0	163	228	.273
1978	7-4-0	258	201	.636						

Holy Cross opts for Division I-AA status

Won-loss record by decades:

1896-99	16-14-4	.529		1920-29	64-24-6	.713		1950-59	56-38-3	.593
1900-09	45-34-9	.562		1930-39	75-15-7	.809		1960-69	42-45-4	.484
1910-19	33-37-6	.474		1940-49	47-41-8	.531		1970-80	40-76-3	.355

Historic record (1896-1980) 418-324-50 .559

Post-season won-loss record (1896-1980) 0-1-0
1946: Orange Bowl, Miami (FL) 13, Holy Cross 6

College Football Hall of Fame:
Frank Cavanaugh, coach, 1903-05; Ed Healey, tackle, 1914-19; Eddie Anderson, coach, 1933-38, 1950-64; Bill Osmanski, fullback, 1936-38; George Connor, tackle, 1942-47; Bill Swiacki, end, 1942-47; Gordie Lockbaum, halfback, 1984-87

LAFAYETTE COLLEGE, Easton, Pennsylvania; nickname "Leopards"; colors maroon and white; Fisher Field (13,750); Patriot League. Lafayette began play in 1882 and has played a major Eastern college schedule, featuring Ivy League teams, Syracuse, and Rutgers, among other teams, since that time. The data below cover the history of Lafayette up to 1981, when Lafayette opted for Division I-AA status in the NCAA.

Early years (1882-1918)

Year	Coach	W-L-T	PF	PA	Pct.	Year	Coach	W-L-T	PF	PA	Pct.
1882	no coach	0-2-0			.000	1900	S. B. Newton	9-2-0	214	25	.818
1883	no coach	2-4-0	112	119	.333	1901	S. B. Newton	9-3-0	230	94	.750
1884	no coach	2-5-0	88	250	.286	1902	David Futz	8-3-0	203	56	.727
1885	no coach	3-2-1	83	120	.583	1903	Alfred Bull	7-3-0	187	69	.700
1886	no coach	10-2-0	213	75	.857	1904	Alfred Bull	8-2-0	251	33	.800
1887	no coach	7-2-0	141	67	.778	1905	Alfred Bull	7-2-1	313	55	.750
1888	no coach	6-3-0	126	78	.667	1906	Alfred Bull	8-1-1	223	30	.850
1889	no coach	3-4-2	78	88	.444	1907	Alfred Bull	7-2-1	198	50	.750
1890	no coach	2-5-1	110	160	.312	1908	George Barclay	6-2-2	102	57	.700
1891	W. S. Moyle	2-9-1	86	161	.208	1909	Bob Folwell	7-0-1	176	6	.938
1892	W. S. Moyle	5-7-0	126	139	.417	1910	Bob Folwell	7-2-0	135	21	.778
1893	P. Haskell &					1911	Folwell & Newton	8-2-0	143	47	.800
	H. Vincent	3-6-0	24	186	.333	1912	George McCaa	4-5-1	71	118	.450
1894	Hugh Janeway	5-6-0	190	201	.455	1913	George McCaa	4-5-1	83	76	.450
1895	Parke Davis	6-2-0	162	62	.750	1914	Wilmer Crowell	5-3-2	191	76	.600
1896	Parke Davis	11-0-1	240	10	.958	1915	Wilmer Crowell	8-3-0	206	112	.727
1897	Parke Davis	9-2-1	256	113	.792	1916	Wilmer Crowell	2-6-1	65	138	.278
1898	S. B. Newton	3-8-0	39	191	.273	1917	Punk Berryman	3-5-0	81	206	.375
1899	S. B. Newton	12-1-0	253	23	.923	1918	L. A. Cobbett	3-4-0	48	92	.429

Year	AP	Other	W-L-T	PF	PA	Pct.	Year	AP	Other	W-L-T	PF	PA	Pct.

Jock Sutherland (1919-1923) 33-8-2 .791

1919			6-2-0	174	40	.750	1922			7-2-0	199	40	.778
1920			5-3-0	182	47	.625	1923			6-1-2	152	28	.778
1921			9-0-0	274	26	1.000							

G. Herbert McCracken (1924-1935) 59-40-6 .590

1924			7-2-0	158	58	.778	1930			5-3-1	141	123	.611
1925	11		7-1-1	208	43	.833	1931			7-2-0	188	26	.778
1926	5		9-0-0	327	37	1.000	1932			3-5-0	94	75	.375
1927			5-3-1	264	114	.611	1933			3-5-1	124	128	.389
1928			6-1-2	236	44	.778	1934			2-6-0	71	131	.250
1929			3-5-0	84	64	.375	1935			2-7-0	39	297	.222

Ernie Nevers (1936) 1-8-0 .111

| 1936 | | | 1-8-0 | 26 | 220 | .111 | | | | | | | |

Hook Mylin (1937-1942, 1946) 36-24-1 .598

1937			8-0-0	103	6	1.000	1940	19		9-0-0	237	33	1.000
1938			5-3-0	92	66	.625	1941			5-4-0	154	98	.556
1939			4-5-0	127	67	.444	1942			3-5-1	75	104	.389

Ben Wolfson (1943-1945) 11-9-1 .548

| 1943 | | | 4-1-0 | 118 | 22 | .800 | 1945 | | | 1-7-1 | 58 | 210 | .167 |
| 1944 | | | 6-1-0 | 246 | 59 | .857 | | | | | | | |

Hook Mylin (1946)

| 1946 | | | 2-7-0 | 56 | 286 | .222 | | | | | | | |

Ivy Williamson (1947-1948) 13-5-0 .722

| 1947 | | | 6-3-0 | 89 | 156 | .667 | 1948 | | | 7-2-0 | 277 | 171 | .778 |

Clipper Smith (1949-1951) 4-21-0 .160

| 1949 | | | 2-6-0 | 104 | 128 | .250 | 1951 | | | 1-7-0 | 67 | 269 | .125 |
| 1950 | | | 1-8-0 | 48 | 230 | .111 | | | | | | | |

Steve Hokuf (1952-1957) 25-27-0 .481

1952			0-9-0	51	267	.000	1955			6-2-0	174	82	.750
1953			5-4-0	171	106	.556	1956			6-3-0	197	94	.667
1954			4-5-0	146	111	.444	1957			4-4-0	173	104	.500

James McConlogue (1958-1962) 20-23-2 .466

1958			5-3-1	144	107	.611	1961			2-6-1	80	193	.278
1959			5-4-0	159	132	.556	1962			3-6-0	77	157	.333
1960			5-4-0	89	160	.556							

Kenneth Bunn (1963-1966) 7-28-2 .216

| 1963 | | | 1-8-0 | 52 | 271 | .111 | 1965 | | | 3-7-0 | 121 | 253 | .300 |
| 1964 | | | 0-7-2 | 67 | 236 | .111 | 1966 | | | 3-6-0 | 164 | 140 | .333 |

Harry Gamble (1967-1970) 21-19-0 .525

| 1967 | | | 4-5-0 | 102 | 177 | .444 | 1969 | | | 4-6-0 | 227 | 227 | .400 |
| 1968 | | | 7-3-0 | 178 | 102 | .700 | 1970 | | | 6-5-0 | 275 | 281 | .545 |

Neil Putnam (1971-1980) 44-55-3 .446

1971	5-5-0	114	248	.500	1976	5-5-0	214	171	.500
1972	3-7-0	127	230	.300	1977	5-6-0	212	247	.455
1973	6-3-1	168	191	.650	1978	4-7-0	165	186	.364
1974	3-7-0	104	204	.300	1979	5-3-2	162	110	.600
1975	5-5-0	126	216	.500	1980	3-7-0	73	192	.300

Lafayette opts for Division I-AA status in 1981

Won-loss record by decades (1882-1980)

1882-89	33-24-3	.575	1920-29	64-18-6	.761	1950-59	37-49-1	.431
1890-99	58-46-4	.556	1930-39	40-44-2	.477	1960-69	32-58-3	.360
1900-09	76-20-6	.775	1940-49	45-36-2	.554	1970-80	50-60-3	.456
1910-19	50-37-5	.571						

Historic record (1882-1980) 485-392-35 .551

College Football Hall of Fame:
Babe Rinehart, guard, 1893-97; Dutch Schwab, guard, 1919-22; Jock Sutherland, coach, 1919-23; Charlie Berry, end, 1921-24; Herb McCracken, coach, 1924-35; George Wilson, halfback, 1926-28; Hook Mylin, coach, 1937-42, 1946.

MARQUETTE UNIVERSITY, Milwaukee, WI; nickname in football playing day, "Hoyas"; independent. Marquette began play in 1892 and remained an independent over its history as a major college team. Marquette dropped intercollegiate football in 1960.

Early years (1892-1917)
No coach (1892-1901) 18-13-3 .573

Year	Coach	W-L-T	PF	PA	Pct.	Year	Coach	W-L-T	PF	PA	Pct.
1892	no coach	1-2-0	10	30	.333	1897	no coach	1-1-0	20	12	.500
1893	no coach	3-1-0	42	27	.750	1898	no coach	2-3-1	33	60	.417
1894	no coach	2-1-0	46	17	.667	1899	no football team				
1895	no coach	4-0-0	74	34	1.000	1900	no coach	1-2-1	11	28	.375
1896	no coach	0-3-0	12	86	.000	1901	no coach	4-0-1	53	0	.900

Early Coaches (1902-1916)

1902	M. Erickson	6-1-1	213	22	.812	1910	Bill Juneau	6-1-2	267	11	.778
1903	Jerry Riordan	6-1-0	131	17	.857	1911	Bill Juneau	7-0-2	169	31	.889
1904	Tom Skelly	5-2-0	93	45	.714	1912	C. J. Kenny	3-4-0	73	121	.429
1905	John Ford	2-3-1	28	70	.417	1913	Lee Foley	4-3-1	125	56	.562
1906	John Ford	1-4-2	8	74	.286	1914	John P. Koehler	2-7-0	26	151	.222
1907	M. Clark	6-0-0	123	4	1.000	1915	John P. Koehler	4-2-2	107	167	.625
1908	Bill Juneau	4-2-1	182	21	.643	1916	John McAuliffe	4-3-1	167	73	.562
1909	Bill Juneau	2-2-1	38	16	.500						

Year	Nat'l AP	Other	W-L-T	PF	PA	Pct.	Year	Nat'l AP	Other	W-L-T	PF	PA	Pct.
							Jack Ryan (1917-1921) 28-5-5 .803						
1917			8-0-1	348	7	.944	1920			7-2-0	211	64	.778
1918			2-0-1	14	6	.833	1921			6-2-1	137	29	.722
1919			5-1-2	131	19	.667							
							Frank Murray (1922-1936, 1946-49) 104-54-6 .652						
1922			8-0-1	213	3	.944	1930			8-0-1	155	7	.944
1923			8-0-0	161	12	1.000	1931			8-1-0	172	25	.889
1924			5-2-0	158	68	.714	1932			4-3-1	98	48	.562
1925			7-2-0	108	21	.778	1933			3-4-1	62	82	.438
1926			6-3-0	146	64	.667	1934			4-5-0	129	104	.444
1927			6-3-0	153	49	.667	1935			7-1-0	173	65	.875
1928			5-3-1	121	68	.611	1936	20		7-1-0	136	60	.875
1929			4-3-1	118	53	.562							
							Paddy Driscoll (1937-1940) 10-23-1 .309						
1937			3-6-0	48	124	.333	1939			4-4-0	99	95	.500
1938			1-7-0	35	122	.125	1940			2-6-1	162	206	.278
							Tom Stidham (1941-1945) 20-22-2 .477						
1941			4-5-0	170	151	.444	1944			1-7-0	73	191	.125
1942			7-2-0	193	90	.778	1945			5-4-1	238	156	.550
1943			3-4-1	143	153	.438							
							Frank Murray (1946-1949) 14-23-0 .378						
1946			4-5-0	139	148	.444	1948			2-8-0	127	212	.200
1947			4-5-0	185	223	.444	1949			4-5-0	257	209	.444
							Lisle Blackbourn (1950-1953, 1959-1960) 24-30-4 .431						
1950			5-3-1	204	146	.611	1952			3-5-1	181	214	.389
1951			4-6-1	223	209	.409	1953			6-3-1	196	108	.650
							F. L. Ferzacca (1954-1955) 5-11-2 .353						
1954			3-5-1	136	216	.389	1955			2-6-1	77	194	.278
							John Druze (1956-1958) 2-26-1 .086						
1956			0-9-0	72	303	.000	1958			2-7-1	106	257	.250
1957			0-10-0	68	237	.000							
							Lisle Blackbourn (1959-1960) 6-13-0 .316						
1959			3-7-0	172	214	.300	1960			3-6-0	101	202	.333

Won-loss record by decades:

1892-99	13-11-1	.540	1910-19	45-21-12	.646	1930-39	49-32-3	.601	1950-59	28-61-7	.328
1900-09	37-17-8	.661	1920-29	62-20-4	.744	1940-49	36-51-3	.417	1960	3-6-0	.333

Historical total (1892-1960): 273-219-38 .551

Post-season won-lost record: 0-1-0 .000
1937: Cotton Bowl, TCU 16, Marquette 6.

College Football Hall of Fame: Frank Murray, coach, 1922-36, 1946-49.

UNIVERSITY OF MONTANA, Missoula, Montana; nickname "Grizzlies"; colors copper, silver and gold; Washington Grizzly Stadium (19.005); Big Sky Conference. Montana began play in 1897. In 1924, Montana joined the Pacific Coast Conference and played in that conference through the 1949 season. After leaving the PCC, Montana played one year as an independent and then joined the Mountain States (Skyline) Conference for the 1951 season and played in that conference until it disbanded after the 1961 season. Montana played as an independent for one year again and then joined the Big Sky Conference for the 1963 season and has played in that conference since that time. The data below cover only the early years of Montana together with the team's years in the PCC and the Skyline conferences. For the record, it should be noted that Montana has been a power in Division I-AA, going to the playoffs ten years in a row and winning two I-AA championships (1995 and 2001).

Early years (1897-1923)

Year	Coach	W-L-T	PF	PA	Pct.	Year	Coach	W-L-T	PF	PA	Pct.
1897	Fred Smith	1-2-3	32	56	.417	1911	Robert Cary	2-1-0	40	14	.667
1898	F. B. Searight	3-2-0	32	24	.600	1912	W. C. Philoon	4-2-0	95	36	.667
1899	Guy Cleveland	1-2-0	12	48	.333	1913	A. G. Heilman	2-4-0	50	94	.333
1900	Frank Bean	0-1-0	11	12	.000	1914	A. G. Heilman	6-0-1	187	9	.929
1901	*Frank Bean	2-3-0	26	31	.400	1915	Jerry Nissen	2-2-2	95	56	.500
1902	Dewitt Peck	0-2-0	0	54	.000	1916	Jerry Nissen	4-1-1	74	46	.750
1903	H. B. Conibear	2-5-0	49	46	.286	1917	Jerry Nissen	1-4-0	21	84	.200
1904	H. B. Conibear	3-2-0	99	23	.600	1918	no football				
1905	F. W. Schule	2-3-0	117	75	.400	1919	Bernie Bierman	2-3-2	80	121	.429
1906	F. W. Schule	2-4-0	49	75	.333	1920	Bernie Bierman	4-3-0	227	92	.571
1907	Albion Findlay	4-1-1	114	38	.750	1921	Bernie Bierman	3-3-1	66	90	.500
1908	Roy White	1-2-1	12	15	.375	1922	J. W. Stewart	3-4-0	91	107	.429
1909	Roy White	6-0-1	169	5	.929	1923	J. W. Stewart	4-4-0	108	117	.500
1910	Robert Cary	3-2-1	29	22	.583						

*No scores available for three 1901 games

Member of the Pacific Coast Conference (1924-1949) 9-79-3 .115

	Nat'l	Overall				Conference				Nat'l	Overall				Conference		
Year	AP Other	W-L-T	PF	PA	Pct.	W-L-T	Pct.	Rank	Year	AP Other	W-L-T	PF	PA	Pct.	W-L-T	Pct.	Rank

Earl Clark (1924-1925) 7-8-1 .469

| 1924 | | 4-4-0 | 264 | 174 | .500 | 0-3-0 | .000 | 9 | 1925 | | 3-4-1 | 144 | 128 | .438 | 1-4-0 | .200 | 8 |

Frank Milburn (1926-1930) 18-22-3 .453

1926		3-5-0	128	168	.375	0-4-0	.000	8	1929		3-5-1	118	121	.389	0-4-1	.100	9
1927		3-4-1	52	142	.438	0-4-0	.000	9	1930		5-3-0	122	175	.625	1-3-0	.250	7
1928		4-5-1	72	147	.450	0-5-0	.000	9									

Bernard Oakes (1931-1934) 8-22-1 .274

| 1931 | | 1-6-0 | 56 | 155 | .143 | 0-5-0 | .000 | 9 | 1933 | | 3-4-0 | 91 | 85 | .429 | 0-4-0 | .000 | 10 |
| 1932 | | 2-7-0 | 84 | 226 | .222 | 0-5-0 | .000 | 10 | 1934 | | 2-5-1 | 90 | 82 | .312 | 0-4-1 | .100 | 10 |

Doug Fessenden (1935-1941, 1946-1948) 46-39-4 .539

1935		1-5-2	48	108	.250	0-5-1	.083	10	1939		3-5-0	34	64	.375	1-2-0	.333	7
1936		6-3-0	138	89	.667	1-3-0	.250	8	1940		4-4-1	95	149	.500	1-2-0	.333	8
1937		7-1-0	143	28	.875	0-1-0	.000	10	1941		6-3-0	119	94	.667	1-3-0	.250	9
1938		5-3-1	82	51	.556	0-1-0	.000	10									

Clyde Carpenter (1942) 0-8-0 .000

| 1942 | | 0-8-0 | 35 | 239 | .000 | 0-6-0 | .000 | 10 | | | | | | | | | |

No football team (1943-1944)

Jiggs Dahlberg (1945) 1-4-0 .200

| 1945 | | 1-4-0 | 75 | 127 | .200 | 0-1-0 | .000 | 9 | | | | | | | | | |

Doug Fessenden (1946-1948)

| 1946 | | 4-4-0 | 103 | 156 | .500 | 1-3-0 | .250 | 7 | 1948 | | 3-7-0 | 143 | 221 | .300 | 0-3-0 | .000 | 10 |
| 1947 | | 7-4-0 | 199 | 171 | .636 | 2-1-0 | .667 | 4 | | | | | | | | | |

Ted Shipkey (1949-1951) 12-16-0 .429

| 1949 | | 5-4-0 | 181 | 226 | .556 | 0-3-0 | .000 | 10 | | | | | | | | | |

Montana reverts to independent status (1950)

| 1950 | | 5-5-0 | 235 | 147 | .500 | | | | | | | | | | | | |

Member of the Skyline Conference (1951-1961) 15-54-0 .217

| 1951 | | 2-7-0 | 108 | 266 | .222 | 1-4-0 | .200 | 8 | | | | | | | | | |

Ed Chinske (1952-1954) 8-18-0 .308

| 1952 | | 2-7-1 | 99 | 201 | .250 | 1-5-0 | .167 | 7 | 1954 | | 3-6-0 | 170 | 225 | .333 | 1-5-0 | .167 | 7 |
| 1953 | | 3-5-0 | 145 | 205 | .375 | 2-4-0 | .333 | 6 | | | | | | | | | |

Jerry Williams (1955-1957) 6-23-0 .207

| 1955 | | 3-7-0 | 103 | 281 | .300 | 2-4-0 | .333 | 6 | 1957 | | 2-7-0 | 129 | 201 | .222 | 2-5-0 | .286 | 6 |
| 1956 | | 1-9-0 | 144 | 244 | .100 | 1-6-0 | .143 | 8 | | | | | | | | | |

Ray Jenkins (1958-1963) 14-43-0 .246

| 1958 | | 0-10-0 | 93 | 297 | .000 | 0-7-0 | .000 | 8 | 1960 | | 5-5-0 | 131 | 135 | .500 | 2-5-0 | .286 | 5 |
| 1959 | | 1-8-0 | 85 | 270 | .111 | 1-5-0 | .167 | 8 | 1961 | | 2-6-0 | 109 | 167 | .250 | 2-4-0 | .333 | 5 |

Montana reverts to independent status (1962) and then joins the Big Sky Conference (1963-2002).

Won-loss record by decades (1897-1961)

1897-99	5- 6-3	.464	1920-29	34-41-5	.456	1950-59	22-71-1	.239
1900-09	22-23-3	.490	1930-39	35-42-4	.457	1960-61	7-11-0	.389
1910-19	26-19-7	.567	1940-49	30-38-1	.442			

Historic record (1897-1961) 181-251-24 .423

College Football Hall of Fame:
Bernie Bierman, coach, 1919-21; Wild Bill Kelly, quarterback, 1924-26.

NEW YORK UNIVERSITY, New York; nickname "Violets"; color violet. NYU began play in 1873 and played as an independent until it dropped intercollegiate football after the 1952 season.

Early years with no coach* (1873-1897)

Year	W-L-T	PF	PA	Pct.	Year	W-L-T	PF	PA	Pct.
1873	0-1-0			.000	1890	2-3-0	54	94	.400
1874	0-1-0			.000	1891	0-3-1	10	134	.125
1875	0-1-0			.000	1892	0-1-0	0	26	.000
1876	0-1-0			.000	1893	no records			
1877-1881	no records				1894*	0-2-0	0	34	.000
1882	0-1-0			.000	1895	0-4-0	12	104	.000
1883-1888	no records				1896	7-2-0	162	62	.778
1889	0-3-0	6	66	.000	1897	3-3-0	46	88	.500

Note: scoring under modern rules only introduced after 1882.
*Coach Hartwell is listed as coach for 1894.

Year	AP	Other	W-L-T	PF	PA	Pct.	Year	AP	Other	W-L-T	PF	PA	Pct.
							Frank H. Cann (1898) 1-3-0 .250						
1898			1-3-0	15	68	.250							
							Coach Ogilvie (1899) 2-6-0 .250						
1899			2-6-0	29	191	.250							
							Nelson B. Hatch (1900) 3-6-1 .350						
1900			3-6-1	85	106	.350							
							W. H. Rorke (1901-1902) 9-6-1 .594						
1901			4-3-1	134	66	.562	1902			5-3-0	91	78	.625
							Robert P. Wilson (1903) 2-5-0 .286						
1903			2-5-0	97	54	.286							
							David L. Fultz (1904) 3-6-0 .333						
1904			3-6-0	99	152	.333							
							Marshall Mills (1905) 3-3-1 .500						
1905			3-3-1	39	74	.500							
							Douglas J. Church (1906) 0-4-0 .000						
1906			0-4-0	11	115	.000							
							Herman P. Olcott (1907-1912) 18-18-7 .500						
1907			5-2-0	69	69	.500	1910			2-4-1	47	59	.357
1908			2-3-2	27	45	.429	1911			1-3-3	16	42	.357
1909			6-0-1	141	18	.929	1912			2-6-0	32	175	.250
							Jake High (1913) 0-8-0 .000						
1913			0-8-0	0	241	.000							
							Thomas T. Reilley (1914-1915) 9-8-1 .528						
1914			5-4-0	130	103	.556	1915			4-4-1	96	160	.500
							Richard E. Eustis (1916) 4-3-1 .562						
1916			4-3-1	68	34	.562							
							Francis P. Wall (1917) 2-2-3 .500						
1917			2-2-3	33	32	.500							
							Appleton A. Masin (1918) 0-4-0 .000						
1918			0-4-0	4	38	.000							
							John P. Longwell (1919) 4-4-0 .500						
1919			4-4-0	95	63	.500							
							Francis J. Gargan (1920-1921) 4-8-4 .375						
1920			2-5-1	149	112	.312	1921			2-3-3	82	74	.438
							Thomas J. Thorp (1922-1924) 14-9-2 .600						
1922			5-4-0	88	116	.556	1924			3-3-1	47	114	.500
1923			6-2-1	98	34	.722							
							John F. Meehan (1925-1931) 49-15-4 .750						
1925			6-2-1	168	45	.722	1929			7-3-0	184	92	.700
1926			8-1-0	172	25	.889	1930			7-3-0	201	40	.700
1927			7-1-2	345	65	.750	1931			6-3-1	212	47	.650
1928	10		8-2-0	316	71	.800							
							Howard G. Cann (1932-1933) 7-7-1 .500						
1932			5-3-0	128	68	.625	1933			2-4-1	38	73	.357
							Marvin A. Stevens (1934-1941) 33-34-2 .493						
1934			3-4-1	105	108	.438	1938			4-4-0	108	84	.500
1935			7-1-0	206	47	.875	1939			5-4-0	105	85	.556
1936			5-3-1	176	108	.611	1940			2-7-0	71	185	.222
1937			5-4-0	154	85	.556	1941			2-7-0	47	243	.222

No football team (1942-1943)

                    J. J. Weinheimer (1944-1946) 10-12-0 .455
1944   2-5-0   71 160   .286   1946   5-3-0   101 163   .625
1945   3-4-0   89 125   .429
                    Edward E. Mylin (1947-1949) 8-17-1 .327
1947   2-5-1   65 194   .312   1949   3-6-0   146 181   .333
1948   3-6-0   96 190   .333
                    Hugh Devore (1950-1952) 4-17-2 .217
1950   1-5-1   88 157   .214   1952   2-5-1   n.a. n.a.   .357
1951   1-7-0   79 327   .125
                    NYU drops football after 1952 season.

Won-loss record by decades:
1873-79   0- 4-0   .000   1900-09   33-35-6   .486   1930-39   49-33-4   .593
1880-89   0- 4-0   .000   1910-19   24-42-9   .380   1940-49   22-43-1   .341
1890-99   15-27-1   .360   1920-29   54-26-9   .657   1950-52   4-17-2   .217
Historic record: 201-231-32   .469

College Football Hall of Fame:
Ken Strong, fullback, 1926-28; Edward "Hook" Mylin, coach, 1947-49

UNIVERSITY OF THE PACIFIC, Stockton, California; nickname "Tigers"; colors orange and blue; no football program since 1995. Pacific began play in 1919 as an independent and then joined the Far West Conference in 1925. During World War II, Pacific was independent again and the then joined the California Collegiate Athletic Association for three years (1945-1948). The team was independent from 1949 through 1968 and then joined the Pacific Coast Athletic Association in 1969 (name changed later to the Big West Conference). Pacific played in this conference until 1995 when it dropped intercollegiate football.

Year	Nat'l AP	Other	W-L-T	PF	PA	Pct.	W-L-T	Pct.	Rank	Year	AP	Other	W-L-T	PF	PA	Pct.	W-L-T	Pct.	Rank

Early years as an independent (1919-1924)
George Sperry (1919) 1-4-0 .200

| 1919 | | | 1-4-0 | 27 | 285 | .200 | | | | | | | | | | | | | |

Paul McCoy (1920) 1-2-1 .375

| 1920 | | | 1-2-1 | 28 | 55 | .375 | | | | | | | | | | | | | |

Swede Richter (1921-1932) 54-34-4 .619

| 1921 | | | 3-1-0 | 103 | 49 | .750 | | | | 1923 | | | 7-0-0 | 171 | 6 | 1.000 | | | |
| 1922 | | | 6-1-0 | 105 | 12 | .857 | | | | 1924 | | | 6-3-0 | 152 | 115 | .667 | | | |

Member of the Far West Conference (1925-1942) 40-24-4 .618

1925			5-2-0	71	46	.714	1-2-0	.333	4	1929			3-4-1	67	89	.438	1-3-1	.300	4
1926			5-3-1	105	112	.611	1-2-1	.375	3	1930			3-6-0	101	104	.333	2-2-0	.500	3
1927			2-6-0	61	148	.250	1-4-0	.200	6	1931			5-2-2	110	52	.667	2-1-2	.600	3
1928			5-2-0	95	64	.714	2-1-0	.667	4	1932			4-4-0	125	73	.500	2-2-0	.500	4

Amos Alonzo Stagg (1933-1946) 59-77-7 .437

1933			5-5-0	71	59	.500	3-2-0	.600	3	1938			7-3-0	203	103	.700	4-0-0	1.000	1
1934			4-5-0	67	76	.444	2-2-0	.500	4	1939			6-6-1	145	116	.500	2-1-0	.667	2
1935			5-4-1	106	124	.550	3-1-0	.750	2	1940			4-5-0	81	94	.444	2-0-0	1.000	1
1936			5-4-1	107	63	.550	4-0-0	1.000	1	1941			4-7-0	72	100	.364	3-0-0	1.000	1
1937			3-5-2	58	122	.400	3-1-0	.750	2	1942			2-6-1	58	141	.278	2-0-0	1.000	1

Independent years (1943-1945)

| 1943 | 19 | | 7-2-0 | 146 | 66 | .778 | | | | 1945 | | | 0-10-1 | 33 | 318 | .091 | | | |
| 1944 | | | 3-8-0 | 80 | 149 | .272 | | | | | | | | | | | | | |

Member of the California Collegiate Athletic Association (1946-1948) 9-3-0 .750

| 1946 | | | 4-7-0 | 184 | 177 | .364 | 2-2-0 | .500 | 2 | | | | | | | | | | |

Larry Siemering (1947-1950) 35-5-3 .875

| 1947 | | | 10-1-0 | 373 | 111 | .909 | 5-0-0 | 1.000 | 1 | 1948 | | | 7-1-2 | 356 | 147 | .800 | 4-1-0 | .800 | 2 |

Independent years (1949-1968)

| 1949 | 10 | | 11-0-0 | 575 | 66 | 1.000 | | | | 1950 | | | 7-3-1 | 348 | 130 | .682 | | | |

Ernie Jorge (1951-1952) 13-8-1 .542

| 1951 | | | 6-5-0 | 275 | 216 | .545 | | | | 1952 | | | 7-3-1 | 310 | 166 | .682 | | | |

Moose Myers (1953-1960) 39-33-5 .542

1953			4-4-2	191	172	.500				1957			5-3-2	145	127	.611			
1954			4-5-0	99	118	.444				1958			6-4-0	266	179	.600			
1955			5-4-0	132	121	.556				1959			5-4-0	132	117	.556			
1956			6-3-1	241	148	.650				1960			5-6-0	140	278	.400			

John Rohde (1961-1963) 12-17-0 .414

| 1961 | | | 5-4-0 | 200 | 187 | .556 | | | | 1963 | | | 2-8-0 | 99 | 275 | .200 | | | |
| 1962 | | | 5-5-0 | 180 | 187 | .500 | | | | | | | | | | | | | |

Don Campora (1964-1965) 2-17-0 .105

| 1964 | | | 1-9-0 | 68 | 304 | .100 | | | | 1965 | | | 1-8-0 | 81 | 250 | .111 | | | |

Doug Scovill (1966-1969) 21-19-0 .525

| 1966 | | | 4-7-0 | 211 | 303 | .364 | | | | 1968 | | | 6-4-0 | 179 | 158 | .600 | | | |
| 1967 | | | 4-5-0 | 201 | 158 | .444 | | | | | | | | | | | | | |

Member of the Pacific Coast Athletic Association (later Big West Conference) (1969-1995) 57-93-1 .372

| 1969 | | | 7-3-0 | 284 | 146 | .700 | 2-2-0 | .500 | 3 | | | | | | | | | | |

Homer Smith (1970-1971) 8-14-0 .364

| 1970 | | | 5-6-0 | 166 | 231 | .455 | 2-3-0 | .400 | 4 | 1971 | | | 3-8-0 | 176 | 198 | .273 | 1-4-0 | .200 | 6 |

Chester Caddas (1972-1978) 38-38-2 .500

1972			8-3-0	232	176	.727	3-1-0	.750	2	1976			2-9-0	190	301	.182	0-4-0	.000	5
1973			7-2-1	279	110	.750	2-1-1	.625	3	1977			6-5-0	230	161	.545	3-1-0	.750	2
1974			6-5-0	238	248	.545	2-2-0	.500	2	1978			4-8-0	222	306	.333	3-2-0	.600	3
1975			5-6-1	231	276	.458	2-3-0	.400	4										

Bob Toledo (1979-1982) 14-30-0 .318

| 1979 | | | 3-7-0 | 162 | 193 | .300 | 0-5-0 | .000 | 6 | 1981 | | | 5-6-0 | 170 | 253 | .455 | 2-3-0 | .400 | 3 |
| 1980 | | | 4-8-0 | 212 | 329 | .333 | 1-4-0 | .200 | 4 | 1982 | | | 2-9-0 | 200 | 330 | .182 | 2-4-0 | .333 | 4 |

Bob Cope (1983-1988) 22-46-0 .324

1983			3-9-0	211	346	.250	1-5-0	.167	6	1986			4-7-0	271	269	.364	2-5-0	.286	6
1984			4-7-0	209	280	.364	2-5-0	.286	6	1987			4-7-0	174	252	.364	3-4-0	.429	6
1985			5-7-0	292	301	.417	2-5-0	.286	7	1988			2-9-0	174	324	.182	2-5-0	.286	7

Walt Harris (1989-1991) 11-24-0 .314

1989	2-10-0	177	406	.167	2-5-0	.286	7	1991	5-7-0	435	481	.417	4-3-0	.571	4
1990	4-7-0	353	411	.364	2-5-0	.286	6								

Chuck Shelton (1992-1995) 15-29-0 .341

1992	3-8-0	253	287	.273	2-4-0	.333	6	1994	6-5-0	252	275	.545	4-2-0	.667	4
1993	3-8-0	184	260	.273	2-4-0	.333	6	1995	3-8-0			.273	2-4-0	.333	7

Won-loss record by decades:

1919-29	44-28-3	.607	1950-59	55-38-7	.617	1980-89	35-79-0	.307
1930-39	47-44-7	.515	1960-69	40-59-0	.404	1990-95	24-43-0	.358
1940-49	52-47-4	.524	1970-79	49-59-2	.455			

Historical record (1919-1994) 346-397-23 .468

Post-season won-loss record 3-2-1 .583

1946: Optimist Bowl, North Texas State 14, Pacific 13
1947: Grape Bowl, Pacific 35, Utah State 21
1947: Raisin Bowl, Pacific 26, Wichita State 14
1948: Grape Bowl, Pacific 35, Hardin-Simmons 35
1951: Sun Bowl, Texas Tech 25, Pacific 14
1952: Sun Bowl, Pacific 27, So. Mississippi 7

College Football Hall of Fame:
Amos Alonzo Stagg, coach, 1933-46; Eddie LeBaron, quarterback, 1946-49.

UNIVERSITY OF PENNSYLVANIA, Philadelphia, Pennsylvania; nickname "Quakers"; colors red and blue; Franklin Field (52,958); Ivy League. Penn was an Eastern independent until the Ivy League was formed in 1956. Penn has played in the Ivy League since that time.

Early years with no regular coach (1876-1884)

Year	W-L-T	PF	PA	Pct.	Year	W-L-T	PF	PA	Pct.
1876	1-2-0			.333	1881	0-5-0			.000
1877	no team				1882	2-4-0			.333
1878	1-2-1			.375	1883	6-2-1	203	68	.722
1879	2-2-0			.500	1884	5-1-1	118	59	.786
1880	2-2-0			.500					

(Points scored not available for seasons prior to 1883.)

Frank Dole (1885-1887) 23-19-1 .547

Year	Nat'l AP	Other	W-L-T	PF	PA	Pct.	Year	Nat'l AP	Other	W-L-T	PF	PA	Pct.
1885			8-5-0	354	333	.615	1887			6-7-0	137	341	.462
1886			9-7-1	344	286	.559							

E.O. Wagenhurst (1888-1891) 38-18-0 .679

Year	W-L-T	PF	PA	Pct.	Year	W-L-T	PF	PA	Pct.
1888	9-7-0	278	294	.562	1890	11-3-0	252	132	.786
1889	7-6-0	198	165	.538	1891	11-2-0	267	109	.846

George Woodruff (1892-1901) 124-15-2 .887

Year	AP	Other	W-L-T	PF	PA	Pct.	Year	AP	Other	W-L-T	PF	PA	Pct.
1892			15-1-0	405	52	.938	1897		1	15-0-0	443	20	1.000
1893			12-3-0	484	62	.800	1898			12-1-0	392	32	.923
1894			12-0-0	366	20	1.000	1899			8-3-2	268	81	.692
1895	1		14-0-0	480	24	1.000	1900			12-1-0	335	46	.923
1896			14-1-0	326	24	.933	1901			10-5-0	203	121	.667

Carl Williams (1902-1907) 60-10-4 .838

Year	W-L-T	PF	PA	Pct.	Year	W-L-T	PF	PA	Pct.
1902	9-4-0	157	68	.692	1905	12-0-1	259	33	.962
1903	9-3-0	370	57	.750	1906	7-2-3	186	58	.708
1904	1 12-0-0	272	4	1.000	1907	11-1-0	256	40	.917

Sol Metzger (1908) 11-0-1 .958

Year	AP	W-L-T	PF	PA	Pct.
1908	1	11-0-1	215	28	.958

Andrew Smith (1909-1912) 30-10-3 .733

Year	W-L-T	PF	PA	Pct.	Year	W-L-T	PF	PA	Pct.
1909	7-1-2	146	38	.800	1911	7-4-0	131	83	.636
1910	9-1-1	184	19	.864	1912	7-4-0	191	106	.636

George Brooke (1913-1915) 13-12-4 .517

Year	W-L-T	PF	PA	Pct.	Year	W-L-T	PF	PA	Pct.
1913	6-3-1	164	81	.650	1915	3-5-2	109	88	.400
1914	4-4-1	89	121	.500					

Bob Folwell (1916-1919) 27-10-2 .692

Year	W-L-T	PF	PA	Pct.	Year	W-L-T	PF	PA	Pct.
1916	7-3-1	120	57	.682	1918	5-3-0	119	71	.625
1917	9-2-0	245	71	.818	1919	6-2-1	283	40	.722

John Heisman (1920-1922) 16-10-2 .607

Year	W-L-T	PF	PA	Pct.	Year	W-L-T	PF	PA	Pct.
1920	6-4-0	167	133	.600	1922	6-3-0	100	44	.667
1921	4-3-2	164	135	.556					

Louis Young (1923-1929) 49-15-2 .758

Year	AP	W-L-T	PF	PA	Pct.	Year	AP	W-L-T	PF	PA	Pct.
1923		5-4-0	95	63	.556	1927		6-4-0	167	78	.600
1924	8	9-1-1	203	31	.864	1928	11	8-1-0	271	26	.889
1925		7-2-0	165	64	.778	1929	11	7-2-0	116	68	.778
1926	10	7-1-1	204	20	.833						

Ludlow Wray (1930) 5-4-0 .556

Year	W-L-T	PF	PA	Pct.
1930	5-4-0	225	145	.556

Harvey Harman (1931-1937) 31-23-2 .571

Year	AP	W-L-T	PF	PA	Pct.	Year	AP	Other	W-L-T	PF	PA	Pct.
1931		6-3-0	121	94	.667	1935			4-4-0	199	80	.500
1932		6-2-0	178	58	.750	1936	10	10	7-1-0	166	44	.875
1933		2-4-1	57	80	.357	1937			2-5-1	75	129	.312
1934		4-4-0	118	83	.500							

George Munger (1938-1953) 82-42-10 .649

Year	AP	Other	W-L-T	PF	PA	Pct.	Year	AP	W-L-T	PF	PA	Pct.
1938			3-2-3	91	58	.562	1946	13	6-2-0	265	112	.750
1939			4-4-0	70	98	.500	1947	7	7-0-1	219	35	.938
1940	14	6	6-1-1	247	79	.812	1948		5-3-0	169	117	.625
1941	15		7-1-0	180	55	.875	1949		4-4-0	159	118	.500
1942			5-3-1	168	72	.611	1950		6-3-0	223	95	.667
1943	20		6-2-1	248	88	.722	1951		5-4-0	121	117	.556
1944			5-3-0	165	149	.625	1952		4-3-2	122	107	.556
1945	8		6-2-0	237	88	.750	1953		3-5-1	96	152	.389

Steve Sebo (1954-1959) 18-35-1 .343

Year	W-L-T	PF	PA	Pct.	Year	W-L-T	PF	PA	Pct.
1954	0-9-0	73	308	.000	1955	0-9-0	34	270	.000

Member of the Ivy League (1956-2003) 171-161-4 .515

Year	W-L-T	PF	PA	Pct.				Year	W-L-T	PF	PA	Pct.			
1956	4-5-0	106	218	.444	4-3-0	.571	3	1958	4-5-0	153	177	.444	4-3-0	.571	4
1957	3-6-0	121	140	.333	3-4-0	.429	4	1959	7-1-1	195	74	.833	6-1-0	.857	1

John Stiegman (1960-1964) 12-33-0 .267

Year	Record	PF	PA	Pct	Ivy	Ivy Pct	Rk	Year	Record	PF	PA	Pct	Ivy	Ivy Pct	Rk
1960	3-6-0	104	149	.333	2-5-0	.286	6	1963	3-6-0	97	189	.333	1-6-0	.143	8
1961	2-7-0	42	194	.222	1-6-0	.143	7	1964	1-8-0	48	222	.111	0-7-0	.000	8
1962	3-6-0	89	174	.333	2-5-0	.286	6								

Bob Odell (1965-1970) 24-29-1 .454

Year	Record	PF	PA	Pct	Ivy	Ivy Pct	Rk	Year	Record	PF	PA	Pct	Ivy	Ivy Pct	Rk
1965	4-4-1	136	192	.500	2-4-1	.357	6	1968	7-2-0	165	131	.778	5-2-0	.714	3
1966	2-7-0	176	237	.222	1-6-0	.143	7	1969	4-5-0	104	185	.444	2-5-0	.286	5
1967	3-6-0	173	237	.333	2-5-0	.286	6	1970	4-5-0	185	195	.444	2-5-0	.286	6

Harry Gamble (1971-1980) 34-55-2 .385

Year	Record	PF	PA	Pct	Ivy	Ivy Pct	Rk	Year	Record	PF	PA	Pct	Ivy	Ivy Pct	Rk
1971	2-7-0	120	207	.222	1-6-0	.143	7	1976	3-6-0	90	159	.333	2-5-0	.286	5
1972	6-3-0	263	203	.667	4-3-0	.571	3	1977	5-4-0	162	144	.556	4-3-0	.571	3
1973	6-3-0	239	160	.667	5-2-0	.714	2	1978	2-6-1	139	187	.278	1-5-1	.214	8
1974	6-2-1	187	179	.722	4-2-1	.643	3	1979	0-9-0	100	251	.000	0-7-0	.000	8
1975	3-6-0	151	184	.333	2-5-0	.286	6	1980	1-9-0	109	262	.100	1-6-0	.143	7

Jerry Berndt (1981-1985) 29-18-2 .612

Year	Record	PF	PA	Pct	Ivy	Ivy Pct	Rk	Year	Record	PF	PA	Pct	Ivy	Ivy Pct	Rk
1981	1-9-0	133	324	.100	1-6-0	.143	8	1984	8-1-0	286	152	.889	7-0-0	1.000	1
1982	7-3-0	221	192	.700	5-2-0	.714	1	1985	7-2-1	197	161	.750	6-1-0	.857	1
1983	6-3-1	225	204	.650	5-1-1	.786	1								

Ed Zubrow (1986-1988) 22-8-0 .733

Year	Record	PF	PA	Pct	Ivy	Ivy Pct	Rk	Year	Record	PF	PA	Pct	Ivy	Ivy Pct	Rk
1986	10-0-0	274	108	1.000	7-0-0	1.000	1	1988	8-2-0	239	170	.818	6-1-0	.857	1
1987	4-6-0	241	201	.400	3-4-0	.429	6								

Gary Steele (1989-1991) 9-21-0 .300

Year	Record	PF	PA	Pct	Ivy	Ivy Pct	Rk	Year	Record	PF	PA	Pct	Ivy	Ivy Pct	Rk
1989	4-6-0	171	229	.400	2-5-0	.286	5	1991	2-8-0	142	236	.200	2-5-0	.286	4
1990	3-7-0	155	197	.300	3-4-0	.429	4								

Al Bagnoli (1992-2003) 86-32-0 .729

Year	Record	PF	PA	Pct	Ivy	Ivy Pct	Rk	Year	Record	PF	PA	Pct	Ivy	Ivy Pct	Rk
1992	7-3-0	207	144	.700	5-2-0	.714	3	1998	8-2-0	297	212	.800	6-1-0	.857	1
1993	10-0-0	308	131	1.000	7-0-0	1.000	1	1999	5-5-0	245	216	.500	4-3-0	.514	4
1994	9-0-0	233	68	1.000	7-0-0	1.000	1	2000	7-3-0	349	257	.700	6-1-0	.857	1
1995	7-3-0	274	199	.700	5-2-0	.714	2	2001	8-1-0	264	103	.889	6-1-0	.857	2
1996	5-5-0	222	172	.500	3-4-0	.429	5	2002	9-1-0	363	132	.900	7-0-0	1.000	1
1997 *	1-9-0	198	175	.100	0-7-0	.000	8	2003	10-0-0	346	164	1.000	7-0-0	1.000	1

*All Ivy League games forfeited in 1997 because of use of an ineligible player.

Won-loss record by decades:

1876-79	4- 6-1	.409	1920-29	65-25-4	.713	1970-79	37-51-2	.422	
1880-89	54-46-3	.539	1930-39	43-33-5	.562	1980-89	56-41-2	.575	
1890-99	124-14-2	.893	1940-49	57-21-4	.720	1990-99	57-42-0	.576	
1900-09	100-17-7	.835	1950-59	36-50-4	.422	2000-03	34- 5-0	.872	
1910-19	63-31-7	.658	1960-69	32-57-1	.361				

Historic record 762-439-42 .630

Post-season record: 0-1-0 .000

1917: Rose Bowl, Oregon 14, Penn 0

Members of the College Football Hall of Fame:
Win Osgood, halfback, 1888-1894; George Brooke, fullback, 1889-1895; George Woodruff, coach, 1892-1901; Buck Wharton, guard, 1893-1896; Charlie Gelbert, end/guard, 1893-1896; Jack Minds, fullback, 1894-1897; John Outland, tackle, 1895-1899; Trux Hare, guard, 1897-1900; Bob Torrey, center/tackle, 1902-05; Steve Stevenson, quarterback, 1904-05; Big Bill Hollenback, halfback, 1904-08; Hunter Scarlett, end, 1905-08; Andy Smith, coach, 1909-12; Roy Mercer, fullback, 1910-12; John Heisman, coach, 1920-22; Ed McGinley, tackle, 1923-24; Harvey Harman, coach, 1931-37; George Munger, coach, 1938-1953; Bob Odell, halfback, 1941-43; George Savitsky, tackle, 1944-47; Skip Minisi, halfback, 1944-47; Chuck Bednarik, center, 1945-48; Reds Bagnell, halfback, 1948-50.

PRINCETON UNIVERSITY, Princeton, New Jersey; nickname "Tigers"; colors orange and black; Princeton Stadium (27,800); Ivy League. The Ivy League was only an informal organization until 1956 so that no league records are given here before 1956. Points scored are not available until 1883.

Early years with no team coach (1869-1900)

	Nat'l							Nat'l					
Year	AP	Other	W-L-T	PF	PA	Pct.	Year	AP	Other	W-L-T	PF	PA	Pct.
1869			1-1-0			.500	1885		1	9-0-0	539	25	1.000
1870			1-0-0			1.000	1886			7-0-1	320	27	.938
1871		no team					1887			7-2-0	390	24	.778
1872			1-0-0			1.000	1888			11-1-0	609	16	.917
1873			1-0-0			1.000	1889		1	10-0-0	484	29	1.000
1874			2-0-0			1.000	1890			11-1-1	478	58	.885
1875			2-0-0			1.000	1891			12-1-0	391	19	.923
1876			3-1-0			.750	1892			12-2-0	433	18	.857
1877			2-1-1			.625	1893		1	11-0-0	270	14	1.000
1878			6-0-0			1.000	1894			8-2-0	208	44	.800
1879			4-0-1			.900	1895			10-1-1	224	28	.875
1880			4-0-1			.900	1896		1	10-0-1	299	12	.955
1881			7-0-2			.889	1897			10-1-0	339	6	.909
1882			7-2-0			.778	1898			11-0-1	266	5	.958
1883			7-1-0	239	31	.875	1899			12-1-0	185	11	.923
1884			9-0-1	404	13	.950	1900			8-3-0	164	57	.727

Langdon Lea (1901) 9-1-1 .864

| 1901 | | | 9-1-1 | 247 | 24 | .864 |

Garrett Cochran (1902) 8-1-0 .889

| 1902 | | | 8-1-0 | 165 | 17 | .889 |

A.R.T. Hillenbrand (1903-1905) 27-4-0 .871

| 1903 | 1 | | 11-0-0 | 259 | 6 | 1.000 | 1905 | | | 8-2-0 | 229 | 45 | .800 |
| 1904 | | | 8-2-0 | 181 | 34 | .800 |

Bill Roper (1906-1908, 1910-1911, 1919-1930) 89-28-16 .729

| 1906 | 1 | | 9-0-1 | 205 | 9 | .950 | 1908 | | | 5-2-3 | 84 | 25 | .650 |
| 1907 | | | 7-2-0 | 282 | 23 | .778 |

James McCormick (1909) 6-2-1 .722

| 1909 | | | 6-2-1 | 101 | 50 | .722 |

Bill Roper (1910-1911)

| 1910 | | | 7-1-0 | 101 | 5 | .875 | 1911 | | 1 | 8-0-2 | 179 | 15 | .900 |

Logan Cunningham (1912) 7-1-1 .833

| 1912 | | | 7-1-1 | 322 | 35 | .833 |

W. G. Andrews (1913) 5-2-1 .688

| 1913 | | | 5-2-1 | 181 | 21 | .688 |

Wilder Penfied (1914) 5-2-1 .688

| 1914 | | | 5-2-1 | 87 | 65 | .688 |

John Rush (1915-1916) 12-4-0 .750

| 1915 | | | 6-2-0 | 136 | 33 | .750 | 1916 | | | 6-2-0 | 135 | 16 | .750 |

No coach (1917-1918) 5-0-0 1.000

| 1917 | | | 2-0-0 | 50 | 0 | 1.000 | 1918 | | | 3-0-0 | 61 | 7 | 1.000 |

Bill Roper (1919-1930)

1919			4-2-1	94	54	.643	1925			5-1-1	125	44	.786
1920			6-0-1	144	23	.929	1926			5-1-1	90	54	.786
1921			4-3-0	91	45	.571	1927			6-1-0	151	31	.857
1922			8-0-0	127	34	1.000	1928			5-1-2	143	29	.750
1923			3-3-1	73	73	.500	1929			2-4-1	66	67	.357
1924			4-2-1	112	48	.643	1930			1-5-1	46	73	.214

Al Witmer (1931) 1-7-0 .125

| 1931 | | | 1-7-0 | 55 | 164 | .125 |

Fritz Crisler (1932-1937) 35-9-5 .765

1932			2-2-3	96	41	.500	1935	3		9-0-0	256	32	1.000
1933	7		9-0-0	217	8	1.000	1936			4-2-2	145	80	.625
1934			7-1-0	280	8	.875	1937			4-4-0	96	126	.500

Tad Wieman (1938-1942) 20-18-3 .524

1938			3-4-1	117	107	.438	1941			2-6-0	64	152	.240
1939			7-1-0	132	65	.875	1942			3-5-1	109	135	.389
1940			5-2-1	119	112	.688

Harry Mahnken (1943-1944) 2-8-0 .200

| 1943 | | | 1-6-0 | 96 | 226 | .143 | 1944 | | | 1-2-0 | 22 | 40 | .333 |

Charlie Caldwell (1945-1956) 70-30-3 .694

Year	Nat'l AP	Other	W-L-T	PF	PA	Pct		Year	Nat'l AP	Other	W-L-T	PF	PA	Pct
1945			2-3-2	69	112	.429		1951	6	6	9-0-0	310	82	1.000
1946			3-5-0	104	130	.375		1952	19	14	8-1-0	297	74	.889
1947			5-3-0	140	100	.625		1953			5-4-0	144	204	.556
1948			4-4-0	184	156	.500		1954			5-3-1	182	124	.611
1949	18		6-3-0	192	137	.667		1955			7-2-0	139	66	.778
1950	6	8	9-0-0	349	94	1.000								

Member of the Ivy League (1956-2003)) 184-147-5 .555

Year	Nat'l AP	Other	Overall W-L-T	PF	PA	Pct	Conference W-L-T	Pct.	Rank	Year	Nat'l AP	Other	Overall W-L-T	PF	PA	Pct.	Conference W-L-T	Pct.	Rank
1956			7-2-0	278	94	.778	5-2-0	.714	2										

Dick Colman (1957-1968) 75-33-0 .694

1957			7-2-0	206	95	.778	6-1-0	.857	1	1963			7-2-0	247	83	.778	5-2-0	.714	1
1958			6-3-0	217	164	.667	5-2-0	.714	2	1964		13	9-0-0	216	53	1.000	7-0-0	1.000	1
1959			4-5-0	124	97	.444	3-4-0	.429	5	1965			8-1-0	281	100	.889	6-1-0	.857	2
1960			7-2-0	232	133	.778	6-1-0	.857	2	1966			7-2-0	135	103	.778	6-1-0	.857	1
1961			5-4-0	173	128	.556	5-2-0	.857	3	1967			6-3-0	233	162	.667	4-3-0	.571	4
1962			5-4-0	187	146	.556	4-3-0	.571	3	1968			4-5-0	228	149	.444	4-3-0	.571	4

Jake McCandless (1969-1972) 18-17-1 .514

| 1969 | | | 6-3-0 | 248 | 138 | .667 | 6-1-0 | .857 | 1 | 1971 | | | 4-5-0 | 195 | 160 | .444 | 3-4-0 | .429 | 6 |
| 1970 | | | 5-4-0 | 196 | 180 | .556 | 3-4-0 | .429 | 5 | 1972 | | | 3-5-1 | 118 | 161 | .389 | 2-4-1 | .357 | 6 |

Bob Casciola (1973-1977) 14-30-1 .322

1973			1-8-0	127	233	.111	0-7-0	.000	8	1976			2-7-0	63	152	.222	2-5-0	.286	5
1974			4-4-1	188	160	.500	3-4-0	.429	5	1977			3-6-0	137	144	.333	3-4-0	.429	6
1975			4-5-0	163	157	.444	3-4-0	.429	5										

Frank Navarro (1978-1984) 29-35-3 .455

1978			2-5-2	126	183	.333	1-4-2	.286	7	1982			3-7-0	229	317	.300	3-4-0	.429	4
1979			5-4-0	166	152	.556	5-2-0	.714	2	1983			4-6-0	285	277	.400	2-5-0	.286	6
1980			6-4-0	175	198	.600	4-3-0	.571	3	1984			4-5-0	185	192	.444	3-4-0	.429	5
1981			5-4-1	233	323	.550	5-1-1	.786	3										

Ron Rogerson (1985-1986) 7-13-0 .350

| 1985 | | | 5-5-0 | 212 | 212 | .500 | 5-2-0 | .714 | 2 | 1986 | | | 2-8-0 | 123 | 262 | .200 | 2-5-0 | .286 | 6 |

Steve Tosches (1987-1999) 78-50-2 .608

1987			6-4-0	230	155	.600	4-3-0	571	4	1994			7-3-0	181	149	.700	4-3-0	.571	2
1988			6-4-0	269	208	.600	4-3-0	.571	3	1995			8-1-1	243	124	.850	5-1-1	.786	1
1989			7-2-1	237	177	.750	6-1-0	.857	1	1996			3-7-0	144	202	.300	2-5-0	.286	6
1990			3-7-0	168	224	.300	2-5-0	.286	6	1997			6-4-0	148	132	.600	3-4-0	.429	5
1991			8-2-0	253	171	.800	5-2-0	.714	2	1998			5-5-0	229	165	.500	4-3-0	.571	4
1992			8-2-0	264	175	.800	6-1-0	.857	1	1999			3-7-0	184	225	.300	1-6-0	.143	7
1993			8-2-0	241	136	.800	5-2-0	.714	3										

Roger Hughes (2000-2003) 14-25-0 .359

| 2000 | | | 3-7-0 | 248 | 286 | .300 | 3-4-0 | .429 | 5 | 2002 | | | 6-4-0 | 226 | 236 | .600 | 4-3-0 | .571 | 3 |
| 2001 | | | 3-6-0 | 200 | 202 | .333 | 3-4-0 | .429 | 4 | 2003 | | | 2-8-0 | 204 | 267 | .200 | 2-5-0 | .286 | 7 |

Won-loss record by decades:

1869	1- 1-0	.500	1910-19	53-12-6	.789	1960-69	64-26-0	.711
1870-79	22- 2-2	.885	1920-29	48-16-8	.694	1970-79	35-53-4	.389
1880-89	78- 6-5	.904	1930-39	47-26-7	.631	1980-89	48-49-2	.495
1890-99	107- 9-4	.908	1940-49	32-39-4	.453	1990-99	59-40-1	.595
1900-09	79-15-6	.820	1950-59	67-22-1	.750	2000-03	14-25-0	.359

Historic record: 752-341-50 .680

College Foorball Hall of Fame:
Alex Moffat, halfback, 1881-83; Hector Cowan, tackle, 1885-89; Knowlton Ames, fullback, 1886-89; Phil King, quarterback, 1890-93; Landon Lea, end/tackle, 1892-95; Art Wheeler, guard, 1892-94; Gary Cochran, end, 1894-97; Bill Edwards, guard, 1896-99; Art Hillelblrand, tackle, 1896-99; Art Poe, end, 196-99; John De Witt, guard, 1901-02; Bill Roper, coach, 1906-08, 1910-11, 1919-30; Jim McCormick, fullback, 1904-07; Ed Hart, tackle, 1908-11; Hobey Baker, quarterback, 1911-13; Harold Ballin, tackle, 1912-14; Stan keck, guard/tackle, 1915-21; Don Lourie, quarterback, 1919-21; Fritz Crisler, coach, 1932-37; John Weller, guard, 1933-35; Tad Wieman, coach, 1938-42; Charley Caldwell, coach, 1945-56; Dick Kazmaier, halfback, 1949-51; Hollie Donan, tackle, 1948-50; Dick Colman, coach, 1957-68; Cosmo Iacavazzi, back, 1962-64.

Awards: Heisman Trophy: 1951, Dick Kazmaier; Maxwell Award: 1951, Dick Kazmaier.

UNIVERSITY OF SAN FRANCISCO, San Francisco, California; nickname "Dons"; colors green and gold; when a major college, played in Kezar Stadium (50,000) and as an independent. San Francisco began play in 1924 and played a major college schedule through the 1930s and 1940s. The 1951 season was the last season that USF played major college football. Following the 1951 season, USF dropped intercollegiate football. Football was reinstated beginning in 1960 at a small college level. Data are shown here through the 1951 season.

Year	AP	Other	W-L-T	PF	PA	Pct.	Year	AP	Other	W-L-T	PF	PA	Pct.
							James R. Needles (1924-1931) 25-31-8 .453						
1924			0-5-0	19	83	.000	1928			4-4-0	63	99	.500
1925			2-4-1	45	59	.357	1929			4-3-1	62	79	.562
1926			2-3-3	32	98	.438	1930			6-3-0	113	86	.667
1927			3-5-1	83	126	.389	1931			4-4-2	155	87	.500
							Spud Lewis (1932-1935) 11-18-2 .387						
1932			2-6-0	77	90	.250	1934			3-3-1	47	16	.500
1933			1-6-1	42	74	.188	1935			5-3-0	104	55	.625
							Duke Malley (1936-1940) 18-20-8 .478						
1936			4-4-2	104	114	.500	1939			4-3-3	92	91	.550
1937			4-5-1	48	85	.450	1940			1-6-1	73	125	.188
1938			5-2-1	93	26	.688							
							Jeff Cravath (1941) 6-4-0 .600						
1941			6-4-0	193	206	.600							
							Albert A. Tassi (1942-1943) 7-11-0 .389						
1942			6-4-0	221	106	.600	1943			1-7-0	13	109	.125
							No team (1944-1945)						
							Clipper Smith (1946) 3-6-0 .333						
1946			3-6-0	162	172	.333							
							Ed McKeever (1947) 7-3-0 .700						
1947			7-3-0	275	113	.700							
							Joe Kuharich (1949-1951) 25-14-0 .641						
1948			2-7-0	123	216	.222	1950			7-4-0			.636
1949			7-3-0	260	144	.700	1951	14	14	9-0-0			1.000

Won-loss record by decades:

1924-1929	15-24-6	.400	1940-1949	33-40-1	.453
1930-1939	38-39-11	.494	1950-1951	16- 4-0	.800
Historic total (1924-1951) 102-107-18 .489					

College Football Hall of Fame:
Ollie Matson, fullback, 1949-51.

SANTA CLARA UNIVERSITY, Santa Clara, California; nickname "Broncos"; colors red and white. Santa Clara played a major college schedule from 1923 through 1952 as an independent. The football team was disbanded after the 1952 season. Santa Clara resumed football in the 1959 season, as a Division II level, later raised to a Division I-AA level. The football program was disbanded again after the 1991 season. Data are shown below only for the period from 1902 through 1952.

Year	Nat'l AP	Other	W-L-T	PF	PA	Pct	Year	Nat'l AP	Other	W-L-T	PF	PA	Pct.
							Gene Sheehy (1902-1905) 7-5-4 .576						
1902			2-1-2	17	6	.600	1904			3-0-1	46	0	.875
1903			1-3-0	39	22	.250	1905			1-1-1	28	10	.500
							No football team in 1906 or 1907						
							William H. Howard (1908) 1-3-1 .300						
1908			1-3-1	13	66	.300							
							Harry Renwick (1909) 4-3-1 .563						
1909			4-3-1	49	43	.563							
							No coach (1910-1911) 9-5-3 .618						
1910			4-3-1	81	42	.563	1911			5-2-2	95	58	.667
							Pat Higgins (1912-1914) 18-6-0 .750						
1912			9-2-0	155	58	.818	1914			4-1-0	56	29	.800
1913			5-3-0	112	86	.625	1915			no team			
							Charles Austin (1916) 9-0-0 1.000						
1916			9-0-0	294	8	1.000							
							Austin Mandershed (1917) 9-1-0 .900						
1917			9-1-0	334	18	.900	1918			no record available			
							Robert Harmon (1919-1920) 7-5-0 .583						
1919			2-4-0	130	79	.333	1920			5-1-0	151	55	.833
							H. O. Buckingham (1921-1922) 10-3-1						
1921			6-0-0	240	9	1.000	1922			4-3-1	156	84	.562
							Eddie Kienholz (1923-1924) 7-9-1 .441						
1923			3-4-1	43	165	.438	1924			4-5-0	58	86	.444
							Adam Walsh (1925-1928) 20-16-2 .553						
1925			5-4-0	147	126	.556	1927			5-4-2	137	143	.545
1926			5-4-0	147	101	.556	1928			5-4-0	179	106	.556
							Clipper Smith (1929-1935) 37-23-4 .609						
1929			5-3-0	123	67	.625	1933			6-2-1	102	39	.722
1930			5-3-1	151	54	.611	1934			7-2-1	133	35	.750
1931			5-4-1	94	53	.550	1935			3-6-0	82	69	.333
1932			6-3-0	121	41	.667							
							Buck Shaw (1936-1942) 48-9-4 .820						
1936	6	8	9-0-0	139	36	1.000	1940	11		6-1-1	154	46	.812
1937	9	9	9-0-0	163	9	1.000	1941			6-3-0	170	103	.667
1938			6-2-0	97	26	.750	1942	15		7-2-0	101	52	.778
1939	14		5-1-3	117	40	.722	1943,1944, 1945			no team			
							Len Casanova (1946-1949) 20-14-2 .583						
1946			1-6-1	112	181	.188	1948			7-2-1	228	153	.750
1947			4-4-0	109	158	.500	1949	15		8-2-0	222	114	.800
							Richard Gallagher (1950-1952) 9-18-2 .345						
1950			4-6-0	165	198	.400	1952			2-7-1	78	182	.250
1951			3-5-1	133	208	.389							

Won-loss record by decades:

1902-09	12-11-6	.517	1930-39	61-23-7	.709	
1910-19	47-16-3	.735	1940-49	39-20-4	.651	
1920-29	47-32-4	.590	1950-52	9-18-2	.345	

Historical record: (1902-1952) 215-120-26 .632

Post-season won-loss record: 3-0-0 1.000
1936: Sugar Bowl, Santa Clara 21, LSU 14   1949: Orange Bowl, Santa Clara 21, Kentucky 13
1937: Sugar Bowl, Santa Clara 6, LSU 0

College Football Hall of Fame:
Nello Falaschi, quarterback, 1934-36; Buck Shaw, coach, 1936-1942; Tom Fears, end, 1942-47; Len Casanova, coach, 1946-49; Brent Jones, tight end, 1982-85.

ST. MARY'S COLLEGE, Moraga, California: nickname "Gaels"; colors blue and white; St. Mary's Stadium (8,000); West Coast Conference (Division I-AA). Data are shown only for the period when St. Mary's played a major college schedule (1915-1950), as an independent. Between 1951 and 1966, the school had no football team. In 1967, a club football team was organized. St. Mary's moved to Division III in 1970, then to Division II in the mid-1970s, and became a Division I-AA team in 1993.

Year	Nat'l AP	Other	W-L-T	PF	PA	Pct.	Year	Nat'l AP	Other	W-L-T	PF	PA	Pct.
					David McAndrews (1915-1916) 10-8-1 .553								
1915			4-5-0	82	155	.444	1916			6-3-1	76	100	.650
					Russell Wilson (197-1919) 11-10-2 .522								
1917			8-1-1	199	46	.850	1919			3-3-1	109	80	.500
1918			0-6-0	41	138	.000							
					Bill Hollander (1920) 0-3-0 .000								
1920			0-3-0	6	228	.000							
					Slip Madigan (1921-1939) 117-45-12 .707								
1921			4-3-0	155	70	.571	1931	5		8-2-0	119	65	.800
1922			3-6-0	67	161	.333	1932			6-2-1	118	59	.722
1923			5-3-1	212	111	.611	1933			6-3-1	161	72	.650
1924			9-1-0	226	50	.900	1934			7-2-0	125	40	.778
1925			8-2-0	313	72	.800	1935			5-2-2	115	37	.667
1926			9-0-1	242	27	.950	1936			6-3-1	137	80	.650
1927			7-2-1	168	28	.750	1937			4-3-2	73	52	.556
1928			5-4-0	105	59	.556	1938			6-2-0	106	41	.750
1929			8-0-1	198	6	.944	1939			3-4-1	84	57	.438
1930			8-1-0	168	31	.889							
					Red Strader (1940-1941) 10-7-0 .588								
1940			5-3-0	100	68	.625	1941			5-4-0	132	123	.556
					Jimmy Phelan (1942-1947) 24-25-1 .490								
1942			6-3-1	132	47	.650	1945	7		7-2-0	282	65	.778
1943			2-5-0	92	126	.286	1946			6-3-0	229	160	.667
1944			0-5-0	14	159	.000	1947			3-7-0	178	246	.300
					Joe Verducci (1948-1949) 7-12-1 .375								
1948			4-6-0	150	161	.400	1949			3-6-1	168	243	.350
					Joe Ruetz (1950) 2-7-1 .250								
1950			2-7-1	95	235	.250							

Won-loss record by decades:
1915-19   21-18-3   .536   1930-39   59-24-8   .692
1920-29   58-24-4   .698   1940-50   43-51-3   .459
Historical record (1915-1950): 181-117-18 .601

Post-season won-loss record: 1-2-0 .333
1939: Cotton Bowl, St. Mary's 20, Texas Tech 13   1947: Oil Bowl, Georgia Tech 41, St. Mary's 19
1946: Sugar Bowl, Oklahoma A&M 33, St. Mary's 13

College Football Hall of Fame:
Slip Madigan, coach, 1921-39; Larry Bettencourt, center, 1924-27; Jimmy Phelan, coach, 1942-46; Herrman Wedemeyer, halfback, 1943-47.

During the 1930's and early 1940's, St. Mary's became well known because of its cross-country rivalry with Fordham. Scores of the series are the following:

	St. Mary's	Fordham		St. Mary's	Fordham
1930	20	12	1938	0	3
1932	0	14	1939	0	13
1933	13	6	1940	9	6
1934	14	9	1941	7	35
1935	7	7	1942	0	7
1936	6	7	1946	33	2
1937	0	8			

There were 13 games in the series, with St. Mary's winning 5, Fordham 6, and with two ties.

VILLANOVA UNIVERSITY, Villanova, PA; nickname "Wildcats"; colors blue and white; Villanova Stadium (12,000); Atlantic 10. Beginning about 1904, Villanova was one of the leading independent teams in the country and played a major college schedule through the 1980 season. Villanova discontinued major college football after the 1980 season. In 1985, Villanova returned to football as a Division I-AA team.

Early years (1894-1903)

Year	Coach	W-L-T	PF	PA	Pct.	Year	Coach	W-L-T	PF	PA	Pct.
1894	M. Murphy	1-0-0	24	0	1.000	1900	J. Powers &				
1895	J. McDonald	4-2-0	54	40	.667		John Egan	5-1-3	92	6	.722
1896	J. McDonald	10-4-0	161	96	.714	1901	John Egan	2-3-0	22	69	.400
1897	John Bagley	3-5-1	101	122	.389	1902	R.Kelly &				
1898	John Bagley	2-4-1	42	50	.357		T. O'Rourke	4-3-0	64	128	.571
1899	Richard Nallin	7-2-1	62	46	.750	1903	Martin Caine	2-2-0	6	110	.500

Years playing major college football (1904-1980)

Frederick Crollius (1904-1911) 15-38-5 .302

Year	AP	Nat'l Other	W-L-T	PF	PA	Pct.	Year	AP	Nat'l Other	W-L-T	PF	PA	Pct.
1904			4-2-1	101	66	.643	1908			1-6-0	51	84	.167
1905			3-7-0	70	185	.300	1909			3-2-0	80	27	.600
1906			3-7-0	91	97	.300	1910			0-4-2	6	70	.167
1907			1-5-1	42	157	.214	1911			0-5-1	6	94	.167

Charles McGeehan (1912) 3-3-0 .500

| 1912 | | | 3-3-0 | 62 | 170 | .500 | | | | | | | |

Thomas St.Germaine (1913) 4-2-1 .643

| 1913 | | | 4-2-1 | 110 | 69 | 643 | | | | | | | |

Frank A. Sommer (1914-1915) 10-4-1 .700

| 1914 | | | 4-3-1 | 30 | 71 | .562 | 1915 | | | 6-1-0 | 101 | 29 | .857 |

Edward M. Bennis (1916) 1-8-0 .111

| 1916 | | | 1-8-0 | 44 | 253 | .111 | | | | | | | |

Thomas M. Reap (1917-1920) 9-12-5 .442

| 1917 | | | 0-3-2 | 17 | 124 | .200 | 1919 | | | 5-3-1 | 85 | 142 | .611 |
| 1918 | | | 3-2-0 | 56 | 67 | .600 | 1920 | | | 1-4-2 | 39 | 106 | .286 |

Allie C. Miller (1921-22) 11-4-3 .694

| 1921 | | | 6-1-2 | 113 | 93 | .778 | 1922 | | | 5-3-1 | 67 | 56 | .611 |

Hugh McGeehan (1923) 0-7-1 .062

| 1923 | | | 0-7-1 | 0 | 171 | .062 | | | | | | | |

Frank A. Sommer (1924) 2-5-1 .312

| 1924 | | | 2-5-1 | 70 | 109 | .312 | | | | | | | |

Harry Stuhldreher (1925-35) 65-25-9 .702

1925			6-2-1	116	40	.722	1931			4-3-2	131	62	.556
1926			6-2-1	219	73	.722	1932			7-2-0	192	53	.778
1927			6-1-0	181	56	.857	1933			7-2-1	234	54	.750
1928			7-0-1	133	34	.938	1934			3-4-2	100	54	.444
1929			7-2-1	187	73	.750	1935			7-2-0	199	67	.778
1930			5-5-0	86	81	.500							

Maurice J. Smith (1936-1942) 41-17-3 .697

1936			7-2-1	129	39	.750	1940			4-5-0	147	99	.444
1937	6		8-0-1	185	7	.944	1941			4-4-0	84	58	.500
1938	18		8-0-1	242	50	.944	1942			4-4-0	116	66	.500
1939			6-2-0	109	55	.750							

Jordan Oliver (1943-1948) 33-20-2 .618

1943			5-3-0	167	119	.625	1946			6-4-0	182	142	.600
1944			4-4-0	53	180	.500	1947			6-3-1	168	106	.650
1945			4-4-0	89	169	.500	1948			8-2-1	282	125	.773

James Leonard (1949-1950) 12-6-0 .667

| 1949 | 13 | | 8-1-0 | 265 | 103 | .889 | 1950 | | | 4-5-0 | 141 | 166 | .444 |

Arthur Raimo (1951-1953) 16-10-1 .611

| 1951 | | | 5-3-0 | 174 | 173 | .625 | 1953 | | | 4-6-0 | 132 | 215 | .400 |
| 1952 | | | 7-1-1 | 219 | 115 | .833 | | | | | | | |

Francis X. Reagan (1954-1959) 16-36-0 .308

1954			1-9-0	95	297	.100	1957			3-6-0	109	96	.333
1955			1-9-0	86	204	.100	1958			6-4-0	113	151	.600
1956			5-4-0	152	92	.556	1959*			0-4-0	33	120	.000

Joseph P. Rogers (1959) 1-5-0 .167

| 1959* | | | 1-5-0 | 54 | 129 | .167 | | | | | | | |

*Reagan coached the first four games of the 1959 season, and Rogers coached the remaining six games.

Alexander Bell (1960-1966) 35-30-0 .538

Year	Record	PF	PA	Pct	Year	Record	PF	PA	Pct
1960	2-8-0	82	225	.200	1964	6-2-0	193	47	.750
1961	8-2-0	239	89	.800	1965	1-8-0	102	206	.111
1962	7-3-0	208	95	.700	1966	6-3-0	134	115	.667
1963	5-4-0	110	155	.556					

John Gregory (1967-1969) 16-13-0 .551

Year	Record	PF	PA	Pct	Year	Record	PF	PA	Pct
1967	4-6-0	165	205	.400	1969	6-3-0	280	185	.667
1968	6-4-0	242	182	.600					

Louis Ferry (1970-1973) 20-26-1 .436

Year	Record	PF	PA	Pct	Year	Record	PF	PA	Pct
1970	9-2-0	288	190	.818	1973	3-8-0	153	212	.273
1971	6-4-1	211	154	.591	1974*	0-3-0	13	68	.000
1972	2-9-0	140	217	.182					

James Weaver (1974) 3-5-0 .375

Year	Record	PF	PA	Pct
1974*	3-5-0	74	220	.375

*Weaver coached the first eight games of the 1974 season, and Ferry coached the last three games of the season.

Richard Bedesen (1975-1980) 30-35-1 .462

Year	Record	PF	PA	Pct	Year	Record	PF	PA	Pct
1975	4-7-0	123	242	.364	1978	5-6-0	206	242	.455
1976	6-4-1	254	200	.591	1979	5-6-0	221	230	.455
1977	4-7-0	231	238	.364	1980	6-5-0	206	137	.545

Villanova dropped football after the 1980 season, resumed play in 1985 as a Division I-AA school.

Won-loss record by decades:

1894-99	27-17-3	.606	1930-39	62-22-8	.717	1970-79	47-61-2	.436	
1900-09	28-38-5	.430	1940-49	53-34-2	.607	1980	6- 5-0	.545	
1910-19	26-34-8	.441	1950-59	37-56-1	.399				
1920-29	46-30-11	.592	1960-69	51-43-0	.543				

Historical record: (1894-1980) 383-340-40 .528

Post-season won-loss record (1894-1980): 2-2-1 .500

1936: Bacardi Bowl, Villanova 7, Auburn 7
1947: Great Lakes Bowl, Kentucky 24, Villanova 14
1949: Harbor Bowl, Villanova 27, Nevada 7

1961: Sun Bowl, Villanova 17, Wichita 9
1962: Liberty Bowl, Oregon 6, Villanova 0

VIRGINIA MILITARY INSTITUTE, Lexington, Virginia; nickname "Keydets"; Alumni Memorial Field (10,000); Southern Conference. VMI began play in 1891 and joined the Southern Conference in 1923. It has played in the Southern Conference since 1923. The data below cover the history of VMI from 1891 through the 1981 season. Beginning with the 1982 season, the Southern Conference opted for Division I-AA status in the NCAA.

Early years (1891-1919)

Year	Coach	W-L-T	PF	PA	Pct.	Year	Coach	W-L-T	PF	PA	Pct.
1891	Walter Taylor	3-0-1	52	12	.875	1906	I. B. Johnson	4-4-0	68	49	.500
1892	no coach	4-0-1	128	18	.900	1907	C. S. Roller	5-3-0	282	50	.625
1893	no coach	3-1-0	72	26	.750	1908	C. S. Roller	3-2-0	120	20	.600
1894	no coach	6-0-0	138	6	1.000	1909	W. C. Gloth	4-3-0	59	51	.571
1895	G. W. Bryant	5-1-0	164	12	.833	1910	W. C. Gloth	3-3-1	69	48	.500
1896	G. W. Bryant	3-4-0	68	98	.429	1911	Alpha Brummage	7-1-0	203	27	.875
1897	R. N. Groner	3-2-0	76	26	.600	1912	Alpha Brummage	7-1-0	163	36	.875
1898	S. A. Boyle	4-2-0	110	41	.667	1913	Henry G. Poque	7-1-2	197	54	.800
1899	S. A. Boyle	1-0-0	39	0	1.000	1914	Frank Gorton	4-4-0	110	95	.500
1900	Sam Walker	4-1-2	86	16	.714	1915	Frank Gorton	6-2-1	103	102	.722
1901	Sam Walker	4-3-0	199	61	.571	1916	Frank Gorton	4-5-0	233	119	.444
1902	Sam Walker	3-3-1	99	90	.500	1917	Earl Abell	4-4-1	162	111	.500
1903	W. W. Roper	2-1-0	36	28	.667	1918	Abell & Mose Goodman	1-3-0	25	60	.250
1904	W. W. Roper	3-5-0	70	70	.375	1919	Red Fleming	6-2-0	121	45	.750
1905	I. B. Johnson	2-5-1	40	103	.312						

B. B. Clarkson (1920-1926) 45-20-2 .687

Year	Nat'l AP Other	Overall W-L-T	PF	PA	Pct.	Conf. W-L-T	Pct.	Rank
1920		9-0-0	431	20	1.000			
1921		3-5-1	107	102	.388			
1922		7-2-0	291	23	.778			

Member of the Southern Conference (1923-1981) 153-156-20 .495

Year	Nat'l AP Other	Overall W-L-T	PF	PA	Pct.	Conf. W-L-T	Pct.	Rank
1923		9-1-0	224	23	.900	5-1-0	.833	5
1924		6-3-1	152	29	.650	2-3-1	.417	13
1925		6-4-0	169	108	.600	2-4-0	.333	17
1926		5-5-0	80	98	.500	2-4-0	.333	15

W. C. Rafferty (1927-1936) 38-55-5 .413

Year	Nat'l AP Other	Overall W-L-T	PF	PA	Pct.	Conf. W-L-T	Pct.	Rank
1927		6-4-0	144	64	.600	2-4-0	.333	16
1928		5-3-2	95	75	.600	2-3-1	.417	14
1929		8-2-0	155	61	.800	4-2-0	.667	7
1930		3-6-0	30	122	.333	0-5-0	.000	23
1931		3-6-1	82	123	.350	2-4-0	.333	17
1932		2-8-0	44	166	.200	1-4-0	.200	18
1933		2-7-1	44	170	.250	2-1-1	.625	4
1934		1-8-0	51	190	.111	0-5-0	.000	10
1935		2-7-1	63	157	.250	0-3-1	.125	10
1936		6-4-0	122	140	.600	4-2-0	.667	4

Allison Hubert (1937-1946) 43-45-8 .490

Year	Nat'l AP Other	Overall W-L-T	PF	PA	Pct.	Conf. W-L-T	Pct.	Rank
1937		5-5-0	134	94	.500	4-2-0	.667	5
1938		6-1-4	159	86	.727	4-0-3	.786	3
1939		6-3-1	125	100	.650	3-1-1	.700	4
1940		7-2-1	127	62	.750	3-2-1	.583	7
1941		4-6-0	134	173	.400	4-2-0	.667	5
1942		3-5-1	111	130	.389	2-4-1	.357	10
1943		2-6-0	46	183	.250	2-3-0	.400	7
1944		1-8-0	65	231	.111	1-5-0	.167	8
1945		5-4-0	155	138	.556	3-2-0	.600	5
1946		4-5-1	122	188	.450	2-3-1	.417	8

A. W. Morton (1947-1948) 9-8-1 .528

Year	Nat'l AP Other	Overall W-L-T	PF	PA	Pct.	Conf. W-L-T	Pct.	Rank
1947		3-5-1	120	152	.389	2-3-1	.417	11
1948		6-3-0	183	116	.667	5-1-0	.833	3

Thomas Nugent (1949-1952) 19-18-2 .513

Year	Nat'l AP Other	Overall W-L-T	PF	PA	Pct.	Conf. W-L-T	Pct.	Rank
1949		3-5-1	157	207	.389	3-2-1	.583	6
1950		6-4-0	189	166	.600	5-1-0	.833	3
1951		7-3-0	227	162	.700	5-0-0	1.000	1
1952		3-6-1	165	279	.350	2-3-1	.417	9

John McKenna (1953-1965) 62-60-8 .508

Year	Nat'l AP Other	Overall W-L-T	PF	PA	Pct.	Conf. W-L-T	Pct.	Rank
1953		5-5-0	174	196	.500	3-3-0	.500	5
1954		4-6-0	132	223	.400	4-3-0	.571	5
1955		1-9-0	85	259	.111	1-6-0	.143	9
1956		3-6-1	167	220	.350	2-3-1	.417	6
1957	20	9-0-1	201	101	.950	6-0-0	1.000	1
1958		6-2-2	214	99	.700	2-2-1	500	4
1959		8-1-1	243	93	.850	5-0-1	.917	1
1960		7-2-1	218	135	.750	4-1-0	.800	1
1961		6-4-0	134	105	.600	4-2-0	.667	3
1962		6-4-0	119	119	.600	6-0-0	1.000	1
1963		3-5-2	140	134	.400	3-1-2	.667	3
1964		1-9-0	123	200	.111	1-4-0	.200	8
1965		3-7-0	121	200	.300	3-2-0	.600	4

Vito Ragazzo (1966-1970) 10-41-0 .196

Year	Nat'l AP Other	Overall W-L-T	PF	PA	Pct.	Conf. W-L-T	Pct.	Rank
1966		2-8-0	129	305	.200	1-4-0	.200	8
1967		6-4-0	205	195	.600	2-3-0	.400	5
1968		1-9-0	90	290	.100	1-3-0	.250	6
1969		0-10-0	78	409	.000	0-4-0	.000	6
1970		1-10-0	120	451	.091	1-4-0	.200	7

Bob Thalman (1971-1981) 46-70-3 .399

Year	Nat'l AP Other	Overall W-L-T	PF	PA	Pct.	Conf. W-L-T	Pct.	Rank
1971		1-10-0	78	257	.091	1-4-0	.200	6
1972		2-9-0	150	299	.182	1-5-0	.167	6
1973		3-8-0	118	316	.273	2-4-0	.333	6
1974		7-4-0	212	175	.636	5-1-0	.833	1
1975		3-8-0	162	187	.273	2-4-0	.333	6
1976		5-5-0	138	206	.500	2-3-0	.400	5
1977		7-4-0	223	155	.636	4-1-0	.800	1
1978		3-8-0	114	227	.273	1-4-0	.200	6
1979		6-4-1	158	210	.591	4-1-0	.800	2
1980		3-7-1	142	242	.318	1-4-1	.250	6
1981		6-3-1	165	156	.650	3-1-1	.700	2

Won-loss record by decades (1891-1981:

1891-99	32-10-2	.750	1930-39	36-55-8	.404	1960-69	35-62-3	.365
1900-09	34-30-4	.529	1940-49	38-49-5	.440	1970-79	38-70-1	.353
1910-19	49-26-5	.644	1950-59	52-42-6	.550	1980-81	9-10-2	.476
1920-29	64-29-4	.680						

Historic record (1891-1981) 387-383-40 .502

WASHINGTON AND LEE, Lexington, VA; nickname "Generals"; colors blue and white; Wilson Field (7,000). Washington and Lee began play in 1873, but records are lacking concerning the team before 1897. W & L was a founding member of the Southern Conference in 1922. It left the Southern Conference after the 1957 season and joined the College Division of the NCAA, becoming a Division III school in 1974. Washington & Lee was a founding member of the Old Dominion Athletic Conference in 1974. No point totals available.

Early Years (1897-1921)

Year	Coach	W-L-T	Pct.	Year	Coach	W-L-T	Pct.
1897	no coach	3-1-0	.750	1910	T. N. Pfeiffer	4-3-0	.571
1898	no coach	2-4-0	.333	1911	J. W. H. Pollard	4-1-1	.750
1899	T. G. Trenchard	1-5-2	.188	1912	J. Reilly	8-1-0	.889
1900	W. Wertenbacker	0-5-0	.000	1913	H. L Dowd	8-1-0	.889
1901	W. Wertenbacker	3-4-0	.429	1914	W. B. Elcock	9-0-0	1.000
1902	T. G. Trenchard	4-3-0	.571	1915	W. B. Elcock	7-1-1	.833
1903	unknown	3-1-0	.750	1916	W. B. Elcoci	5-2-2	.667
1904	A. J. Byles	3-4-0	.429	1917	W. C. Raftery	4-3-0	.571
1905	D. W. Baillet	6-2-0	.750	1918	J. J. Fitzpatrick	1-2-0	.333
1906	unknwon	4-1-1	.750	1919	W. C. Raftery	6-1-0	.857
1907	R. R. Brown	3-2-1	.583	1920	W. C. Raftery	5-3-0	.625
1908	R. R. Brown	4-2-1	.653	1921	W. C. Raftery	6-3-0	.667
1909	R. R. Brown	4-3-0	.571				

Member of Southern Conference (1922-1957) 64-70-11 .479

Year	Nat'l AP	Other	Overall W-L-T	Pct.	Conference W-L-T	Pct.	Rank	Year	Nat'l AP	Other	Overall W-L-T	Pct	Conference W-L-T	Pct.	Rank
James DeHart (1922-1925) 22-14-3 .603																
1922			5-3-1	.611	1-2-0	.333	11	1924			6-3-1	.650	4-1-1	.750	5
1923			6-3-1	.650	4-0-1	.900	1	1925			5-5-0	.500	5-1-0	.333	4
Pat Herron (1926-1928) 10-15-3 .411																
1926			4-3-2	.556	3-2-1	.583	7	1928			2-8-0	.200	1-6-0	.167	20
1927			4-4-1	.500	2-3-0	.400	12								
Eugene Oberst (1929-1930) 6-11-2 .368																
1929			3-5-1	.389	1-4-1	.250	18	1930			3-6-1	.350	0-4-1	.100	22
James DeHart (1931-1932) 5-14-1 .275																
1931			4-5-1	.450	2-3-0	.400	14	1932			1-9-0	.100	1-4-0	.200	18
W. E. Tilson (1933-1940) 31-37-6 .459																
1933			4-4-2	.500	1-1-1	.500	5	1937			4-5-0	.444	2-3-0	.400	8
1934			7-3-0	.700	4-0-0	1.000	1	1938			4-4-1	.500	2-2-0	.500	6
1935			3-4-1	.438	1-3-1	.300	7	1939			3-4-1	.438	1-2-0	.333	10
1936			4-6-0	.400	2-2-0	.500	8	1940			2-7-1	.250	1-1-1	.500	9
Riley Smith (1941) 1-6-2 .222																
1941			1-6-2	.222	1-2-2	.400	10								
P. A. Holstein (1942) 1-8-0 .111																
1942			1-8-0	.111	0-4-0	.000	16								
No Team (1943-1945)																
Art Lewis (1946-1948) 11-17-0 .393																
1946			2-6-0	.250	1-4-0	.200	13	1948			4-6-0	.400	2-2-0	.500	9
1947			5-5-0	.500	3-2-0	.600	5								
George Barclay (1949-1951) 17-12-1 .583																
1949			3-5-1	.389	3-1-1	.700	3	1951			6-4-0	.600	5-1-0	.833	3
1950	18	18	8-3-0	.727	6-0-0	1.000	1								
Carl Wise (1952-1953) 7-13-0 .350																
1952			3-7-0	.300	3-4-0	.429	8	1954			no team				
1953			4-6-0	.400	2-4-0	.333	8								
W. Chipley (1955-1956) 1-14-0 ..067																
1955			0-7-0	.000	0-1-0	.000	10	1956			1-7-0	.125	0-1-0	.000	9
L. McLaughlin (1957) 0-8-0 .000																
1957			0-8-0	.000	0-0-0										

Washington & Lee left the Southern Conference after the 1957 season.

Won-loss record by decades:

1897-99	6-10-2	.389	1910-19	56-15-4	.773	1930-39	37-50-7	.431	1950-57 22-42-0
1900-09	34-27-3	.555	1920-29	46-40-7	.532	1940-49	18-43-4	.308	

Historic record as a major team (1897-1957) 219-227-2 .491

Post-season record: 0-1-0
1951: Gator Bowl, Wyoming 20, Washington and Lee 7.

College Football Hall of Fame: Harry "Cy" Young, back, 1913-16.

WASHINGTON UNIVERSITY, St. Louis; nickname "Bears"; colors red and green; Francis Field (4,000); University Athletic Association. Wash U began play in 1890 and was a founding member of the Missouri Valley Conference in 1907. During the pre-World War II years, Wash U played a major college schedule. The school dropped football between 1943 and 1946 and left the MVC after the 1945 season. Data are shown here only for the period through 1942, the last year that Wash U. played MVC football. Under MVC rules, ties were ignored in calculating conference win percent before the 1946 season.

Early years (1890-1906)

Year	Coach	W-L-T	PF	PA	Pct.	Year	Coach	W-L-T	PF	PA	Pct.
1890	Unknown	1-0-0	28	0	1.000	1899	Arthur Sager	3-1-0	34	48	.750
1891	Unknown	3-1-1	96	16	.700	1900	Unknown	2-2-1	61	23	.500
1892	Unknown	1-2-0	14	59	.333	1901	Gordon Clark	5-1-0	68	37	.833
1893	no team					1902	Wayne Smith	2-5-1	84	192	.312
1894	Unknown	2-1-0	34	50	.667	1903	L. W. Boynton	4-4-1	109	103	.500
1895-96	no team					1904	L. W. Boynton	4-7-0	84	157	.364
1897	Unknown	0-1-1	6	14	.250	1905	C. A. Fairweather	6-3-1	159	88	.650
1898	Arthur Sager	5-0-0	112	24	1.000	1906	J. M. Blanchard	2-1-0	30	21	.667

Member of the Missouri Valley Conference (1907-1941) 33-81-8 .303

Year	Nat'l AP	Other	Overall W-L-T	PF	PA	Pct.	Conf. W-L-T	Pct.	Rank	Year	Nat'l AP	Other	Overall W-L-T	PF	PA	Pct.	Conf. W-L-T	Pct.	Rank
J. M. Blanchard (1906-1907) 3-6-0 .333																			
1907			1-5-0	47	129	.167	0-1-0	.000	5										
Francis Cayou (1908-1912) 18-18-3 .500																			
1908			4-4-1	61	108	.500	0-2-0	.000	6	1911			4-2-2	107	38	.667	0-0-2	.000	4
1909			3-4-0	52	87	.429	0-2-0	.000	5	1912			4-4-0	162	117	.500	0-2-0	.000	6
1910			3-4-0	75	138	.429	0-2-0	.000	5										
W. P. Edmunds (1913-1916) 10-13-2 .440																			
1913			1-5-0	64	164	.167	0-4-0	.000	6	1915			3-2-0	83	46	.600	1-1-0	.500	4
1914			3-3-1	170	87	.500	0-1-1	.000	5	1916			3-3-1	44	105	.500	0-2-0	.000	7
R. B. Rutherford (1917-1919) 15-5-0 .750																			
1917			4-3-0	77	109	.571	1-2-0	.333	5	1919			5-2-0	127	30	.714	1-2-0	.333	4
1918			6-0-0	163	27	1.000	no conference												
George Rider (1920-1922) 9-12-2 .478																			
1920			4-4-0	134	50	.500	1-4-0	.200	6	1922			1-5-1	35	115	.286	0-5-1	.000	9
1921			4-3-1	54	82	.562	2-3-0	.400	7										
Byron Wimberly (1923-1924) 7-9-0) .438																			
1923			3-5-0	50	241	.375	1-4-0	.200	9	1924			4-4-0	42	107	.500	0-4-0	.000	9
Bob Higgins (1925-1927) 8-14-3 .380																			
1925			2-5-1	29	96	.286	1-4-1	.200	9	1927			5-2-2	98	75	.714	2-2-1	.500	5
1926			1-7-0	40	151	.125	0-6-0	.000	10										
Al Sharpe (1928-1931) 11-18-4 .394																			
1928			2-5-1	35	60	.286	0-2-0	.000	4	1930			4-2-2	88	47	.667	2-2-0	.500	3
1929			3-4-1	74	65	.429	0-1-1	.000	4	1931			2-7-0	26	194	.222	0-3-0	.000	5
Jimmy Conzelman (1932-1939) 40-35-2 .532																			
1932			4-4-0	80	92	.500	1-2-0	.333	3	1936			3-7-0	151	123	.300	1-1-0	.500	4
1933			4-5-0	116	124	.444	1-2-0	.333	4	1937			4-6-0	104	164	.400	2-2-0	.500	4
1934			7-3-0	212	59	.700	1-0-0	1.000	1	1938			6-3-1	242	94	.667	2-1-1	.667	2
1935			6-4-0	185	149	.600	3-0-0	1.000	1	1939			6-3-1	172	103	.667	4-1-0	.800	1
Frank Loebs (1940-1941) 7-11-0 .389																			
1940			3-6-0	126	141	.333	1-3-0	.250	6	1941			4-5-0	159	165	.444	1-3-0	.250	4

Won-loss percent by decades (1890-1941):

1890-99	15-6-2	.696	1910-19	36-28-4	559	1930-39	46-44-4	.511
1900-09	33-36-5	.480	1920-29	29-44-7	.406	1940-41	7-11-0	.389

Historic record (1890-1941): 166-169-22 .496

THE COLLEGE OF WILLIAM AND MARY, Williamsburg, Virginia; nickname "The Tribe"; colors green, gold, and silver; Cary Field (13,100); Atlantic 10 Conference. William and Mary began play in 1893 and joined the Southern Conference for the 1936 season. The Tribe played in the SC through the 1976 season and then joined the Atlantic 10. Data are shown here through the 1976 season.

Early years (1893-1935)

Year	Coach	W-L-T	PF	PA	Pct.	Year	Coach	W-L-T	PF	PA	Pct.
1893	no coach	2-1-0	26	24	.667	1915	D. W. Draper	0-9-1	20	306	.050
1894	no coach	0-1-0	0	28	.000	1916	S. H. Hubbard	2-5-2	34	191	.333
1895	no team					1917	H. J. Young	3-5-0	41	159	.375
1896	R. Armstrong	0-2-0	0	14	.000	1918	V. M. Geddy	0-2-0	0	20	.000
1897	W. J. King	0-1-0	0	26	.000	1919	J. G. Driver	2-6-1	28	80	.278
1898	W. J. King	1-1-0	5	15	.500	1920	J. G. Driver	4-5-0	125	163	.444
1899	W. H. Burke	2-3-0	47	31	.400	1921	W. E. Fincher	4-3-1	171	79	.562
1900	W. J. King	1-2-0	5	28	.333	1922	Bill Ingram	6-3-0	171	80	.667
1901	no coach	2-1-1	28	33	.625	1923	J. W. Tasker	6-3-0	224	115	.667
1902	no coach	1-1-1	6	42	.500	1924	J. W. Tasker	5-2-1	170	61	.688
1903	H. J. Duvall	1-3-0	15	86	.250	1925	J. W. Tasker	6-4-0	230	86	.600
1904	J. M. Blanchard	3-3-0	69	48	.500	1926	J. W. Tasker	7-3-0	169	87	.700
1905	J. M. Blanchard	2-4-1	15	90	.357	1927	J. W. Tasker	4-5-1	111	118	.450
1906	H. M. Withers	2-6-0	30	160	.250	1928	Branch Bocock	6-3-2	218	54	.636
1907	James H. Barry	6-3-0	70	143	.667	1929	Branch Bocock	8-2-0	250	77	.800
1908	G. E. O'Hearne	4-6-1	49	110	.409	1930	Branch Bocock	7-2-1	247	39	.750
1909	G. E. O'Hearne	6-4-0	65	81	.600	1931	John Kellison	5-2-2	187	33	.667
1910	J. M. Blanchard	1-7-1	40	115	.167	1932	John Kellison	8-4-0	221	96	.667
1911	W. V. Young	1-5-2	14	186	.200	1933	John Kellison	6-5-0	108	88	.545
1912	W. V. Young	0-7-0	0	226	.000	1934	John Kellison	2-6-0	48	69	.250
1913	D. W. Draper	0-5-1	51	157	.083	1935	Tommy Dowler	3-4-3	86	110	.450
1914	D. W. Draper	1-7-0	22	220	.125						

Member of the Southern Conference (1936-1976) 113-90-11 .554

Year	Nat'l AP	Other	Overall W-L-T	PF	PA	Pct.	Conf W-L-T	Conf Pct.	Rank	Year	Nat'l AP	Other	Overall W-L-T	PF	PA	Pct.	Conf W-L-T	Conf Pct.	Rank
Branch Bocock (1928-1930, 1936-1938) 28-27-3 .509																			
1936			1-8-0	51	112	.111	0-4-0	.000	14	1938			2-7-0	78	154	.222	0-4-0	.000	15
1937			4-5-0	129	103	.444	1-3-0	.250	13										
Carl M. Voyes (1939-1942) 29-7-3 .782																			
1939			6-2-1	158	95	.722	1-1-1	.500	6	1941			8-2-0	259	64	.800	4-1-0	.800	4
1940			6-2-1	185	60	.722	2-1-1	.625	4	1942	14		9-1-1	245	55	.864	4-0-0	1.000	1
No football team (1943)																			
Rube McCray (1944-1950) 45-22-3 .664																			
1944			5-2-1	191	65	.688	2-1-1	.625	5	1948	17		7-2-2	163	67	.727	5-1-1	.917	4
1945			6-3-0	180	110	.667	4-2-0	.667	3	1949			6-4-0	256	169	.600	4-2-0	.667	4
1946			8-2-0	347	71	.800	7-1-0	.875	2	1950			4-7-0	210	230	.364	3-3-0	.500	9
1947	14		9-2-0	320	87	.818	7-1-0	.875	1										
Marvin Bass (1951) 7-3-0 .700																			
1951			7-3-0	172	220	.700	5-1-0	.833	3										
Jack Freeman (1952-1956) 14-29-5 .344																			
1952			4-5-0	236	177	.444	4-1-0	.800	4	1955			1-7-1	81	183	.167	1-3-1	.300	8
1953			5-4-1	122	191	.550	3-2-0	.600	4	1956			0-9-1	84	246	.050	0-5-0	.000	9
1954			4-4-2	82	137	.500	1-2-2	.400	6										
Milt Drewer (1957-1963) 21-46-2 .319																			
1957			4-6-0	111	138	.400	2-4-0	.333	5	1961			1-9-0	125	279	.100	1-6-0	.143	9
1958			2-6-1	72	179	.278	1-4-1	.250	9	1962			4-5-1	109	131	.450	4-3-1	.562	4
1959			4-6-0	140	155	.400	2-5-0	.286	7	1963			4-6-0	153	171	.400	4-4-0	.500	5
1960			2-8-0	120	232	.200	1-5-0	.167	8										
Marv Levy (1964-1968) 23-25-2 .480																			
1964			4-6-0	138	194	.400	4-3-0	.571	4	1967			5-4-1	196	177	.550	2-2-1	.500	4
1965			6-4-0	197	163	.600	5-1-0	.833	2	1968			3-7-0	97	195	.300	2-2-0	..500	3
1966			5-4-1	176	144	.550	4-1-1	.750	1										
Lou Holtz (1969-1971) 13-20-0 .394																			
1969			3-7-0	146	250	.300	2-2-0	.500	4	1971			5-6-0	278	241	.455	4-1-0	.800	2
1970			5-7-0	218	335	.417	3-1-0	.750	1										
Jim Root (1972-1976)* 29-31-0 .483																			
1972			5-6-0	261	191	.455	4-2-0	.667	3	1975			2-9-0	95	261	.182	2-3-0	.400	5
1973			6-5-0	278	288	.545	3-2-0	.600	3	1976			7-4-0	210	149	.636	3-2-0	.600	2
1974			4-7-0	211	269	.364	2-3-0	.400	6										

*Root record at Wm & Mary over his career is (1972-1979) 39-48-1 .449

William and Mary leaves the Southern Conference.

Won-Loss record by decade (1893-1976):

1893-99	5- 9-0	.357	1920-29	56-33-5	.622	1950-59	35-57-6	.388
1900-09	28-33-4	.492	1930-39	44-45-7	.495	1960-69	37-60-3	.385
1910-19	10-58-8	.184	1940-49	64-20-5	.747	1970-76	34-44-0	.436

Historic record as a major college (1893-1976) 313-359-38 .468

Post-season record (1893-1976): 2-2-0 .500

1926: Southern Title, Wm. & Mary 9, Chattanooga 6

1947: Dixie Bowl, Arkansas 21, Wm. & Mary 19

1949: Delta Bowl, Wm. & Mary 20, Oklahoma A&M 0

1970: Tangerine Bowl, Toledo 40, Wm. & Mary 12

YALE UNIVERSITY, New Haven, Connecticut; nickname "Bulldogs"; colors Yale blue and white; Yale Bowl (64,269); Ivy League. Yale began play in 1872 and remained an independent until the formation of the formal Ivy League, beginning the 1956 season. Yale has played in the Ivy League since that time.

Early years (1972-1919)

No coach (1872-1887)

Year	Nat'l AP	Other	W-L-T	PF	PA	Pct.	Year	Nat'l AP	Other	W-L-T	PF	PA	Pct.
1872			!-0-0	3	0	1.000	1880			4-0-1	30	0	.900
1873			2-1-0	5	5	.667	1881			5-0-1	9	0	.917
1874			3-0-0	17	2	1.000	1882			8-0-0	52	1	1.000
1875			2-2-0	12	8	.500	1883	1		8-0-0	486	2	1.000
1876			3-0-0	5	0	1.000	1884	1		8-0-1	495	10	.944
1877			3-0-1	21	0	.875	1885			7-0-1	366	11	.938
1878			4-1-1	8	1	.750	1886	1		9-0-1	687	4	.950
1879			3-0-2	10	0	.800	1887	1		9-0-0	515	12	1.000

Walter Camp (1888-1892) 67-2-0 .971

Year	Nat'l AP	Other	W-L-T	PF	PA	Pct.	Year	Nat'l AP	Other	W-L-T	PF	PA	Pct.
1888	1		13-0-0	698	0	1.000	1891	1		13-0-0	488	0	1.000
1889			15-1-0	665	31	.938	1892	1		13-0-0	435	0	1.000
1890			13-1-0	486	18	.929							

William Rhodes (1893-1894) 26-1-0 .963

Year	Nat'l AP	Other	W-L-T	PF	PA	Pct.	Year	Nat'l AP	Other	W-L-T	PF	PA	Pct.
1893			10-1-0	330	12	.909	1894		1	16-0-0	485	13	1.000

Other short-term tenured coaches (1895-1919)

Year	Nat'l AP	Other	Coach	W-L-T	PF	PA	Pct.	Year	Nat'l AP	Other	Coach	W-L-T	PF	PA	Pct.
1895			John Hartwell	13-0-2	316	38	.933	1908			L. Bigelow	7-1-1	153	20	.833
1896			Samuel Thorn	13-1-0	218	44	.929	1909	1		Howard Jones	10-0-0	209	0	1.000
1897			J.O. Rodgers	9-0-2	170	35	.909	1910			Edward Coy	6-2-2	90	39	.700
1898			F. Butterworth	9-2-0	146	34	.818	1911			John Field	7-2-1	161	15	.750
1899			J.O. Rodgers	7-2-1	191	16	.750	1912			Arthur Howe	7-1-1	89	32	.833
1900		1	M. McBride	12-0-0	336	10	1.000	1913			Howard Jones	5-2-3	126	34	.650
1901			G. Stillman	11-1-1	251	37	.885	1914			Frank Hinkey	7-2-0	178	79	.778
1902			J. Swan	11-0-1	286	22	.958	1915			Frank Hinkey	4-5-0	83	98	.444
1903			G. Chadwick	11-1-0	312	26	.917	1916			Tad Jones	8-1-0	182	44	.889
1904			C.Rafferty	10-1-0	220	20	.909	1917			Tad Jones	3-0-0	47	0	1.000
1905			J. Oswsley	10-0-0	227	4	1.000	1918			no team				
1906			F. Rockwell	9-0-1	144	6	.950	1919			Albert Sharp	5-3-0	148	35	.625
1907		1	Wm. Knox	9-0-1	206	10	.950								

Modern era (1920-2002)

Tad Jones (1916-1917, 1920-1927) 60-15-4 .785

Year	Nat'l AP	Other	W-L-T	PF	PA	Pct.	Year	Nat'l AP	Other	W-L-T	PF	PA	Pct.
1920			5-3-0	137	67	.625	1924		3	6-0-2	144	36	.875
1921			8-1-0	202	31	.889	1925			5-2-1	204	76	.688
1922			6-3-1	192	29	.650	1926			4-4-0	103	79	.500
1923			8-0-0	230	38	1.000	1927		5	7-1-0	157	32	.875

Marvin Stevens (1928-1932) 21-11-8 .625

Year	Nat'l AP	Other	W-L-T	PF	PA	Pct.	Year	Nat'l AP	Other	W-L-T	PF	PA	Pct.
1928			4-4-0	106	73	.500	1931		8	5-1-2	204	79	.750
1929			5-2-1	172	69	.688	1932			2-2-3	41	41	.500
1930			5-2-2	196	58	.667							

Reginald Root (1933) 4-4-0 .500

Year	Nat'l AP	Other	W-L-T	PF	PA	Pct.
1933			4-4-0	64	100	.500

Ducky Pond (1934-1940) 30-25-2 .544

Year	Nat'l AP	Other	W-L-T	PF	PA	Pct.	Year	Nat'l AP	Other	W-L-T	PF	PA	Pct.
1934			5-3-0	104	54	.625	1938			2-6-0	69	135	.250
1935			6-3-0	182	99	.667	1939			3-4-1	78	122	.438
1936	12		7-1-0	131	60	.875	1940			1-7-0	43	162	.125
1937	12	6	6-1-1	137	36	.812							

Emerson Nelson (1941) 1-7-0 .125

Year	Nat'l AP	Other	W-L-T	PF	PA	Pct.
1941			1-7-0	54	136	.125

Howard Odell (1942-1947) 35-15-2 .692

Year	Nat'l AP	Other	W-L-T	PF	PA	Pct.	Year	Nat'l AP	Other	W-L-T	PF	PA	Pct.
1942			5-3-0	116	83	.625	1945			6-3-0	160	102	.667
1943			4-5-0	132	166	.444	1946	12		7-1-1	272	72	.833
1944			7-0-1	120	32	.938	1947			6-3-0	182	101	.667

Herman Hickman (1948-1951) 16-17-2 .486

Year	Nat'l AP	Other	W-L-T	PF	PA	Pct.	Year	Nat'l AP	Other	W-L-T	PF	PA	Pct.
1948			4-5-0	167	170	.444	1950			6-3-0	142	120	.667
1949			4-4-0	142	137	.500	1951			2-5-2	126	131	.333

Jordan Oliver (1952-1962) 61-32-7 .645

Year	W-L-T	PF	PA	Pct.		Year	W-L-T	PF	PA	Pct.
1952	7-2-0	240	120	.778		1954	5-3-1	169	154	.611
1953	5-2-2	123	89	.667		1955	7-2-0	176	79	.778

Member of the Ivy League (1956-2002) 190-132-7 .588

Year	Nat'l AP	Other	Overall W-L-T	PF	PA	Pct.	Conference W-L-T	Pct.	Rank	Year	Nat'l AP	Other	Overall W-L-T	PF	PA	Pct.	Conference W-L-T	Pct.	Rank
1956	17		8-1-1	246	97	.889	7-0-0	1.000	1	1960	14	18	9-0-0	253	73	1.000	7-0-0	1.000	1
1957			6-2-1	212	88	.722	4-2-1	.643	3	1961			4-5-0	99	105	.444	3-4-0	.429	5
1958			2-7-0	92	203	.222	0-7-0	.000	8	1962			2-5-2	102	108	.333	1-5-1	.214	7
1959			6-3-0	159	95	.667	4-3-0	.571	3										

John Pont (1963-1964) 12-5-1 .694

Year	Nat'l AP	Other	Overall W-L-T	PF	PA	Pct.	Conference W-L-T	Pct.	Rank	Year	Nat'l AP	Other	Overall W-L-T	PF	PA	Pct.	Conference W-L-T	Pct.	Rank
1963			6-3-0	135	78	.667	4-3-0	.571	4	1964			6-2-1	195	120	.722	4-2-1	.643	3

Carmen Cozza (1965-1996) 179-120-5 .597

Year	Nat'l AP	Other	Overall W-L-T	PF	PA	Pct.	Conference W-L-T	Pct.	Rank	Year	Nat'l AP	Other	Overall W-L-T	PF	PA	Pct.	Conference W-L-T	Pct.	Rank
1965			3-6-0	84	138	.333	3-4-0	.429	5	1981			9-1-0	285	147	.900	6-1-0	.857	1
1966			4-5-0	149	128	.444	3-4-0	.429	5	1982			4-6-0	197	227	.400	3-4-0	.429	4
1967			8-1-0	278	110	.889	7-0-0	1.000	1	1983			1-9-0	138	272	.100	1-6-0	.143	8
1968			8-0-1	317	147	.944	6-0-1	.929	1	1984			6-3-0	219	185	.667	5-2-0	.714	2
1969			7-2-0	206	127	.778	6-1-0	.857	1	1985			4-4-1	140	182	.500	3-3-1	.500	5
1970			7-2-0	218	97	.778	5-2-0	.714	2	1986			3-7-0	168	217	.300	2-5-0	.286	6
1971			4-5-0	150	156	.444	3-4-0	.429	5	1987			7-3-0	197	205	.700	5-2-0	.714	2
1972			7-2-0	283	157	.778	5-2-0	.714	2	1988			3-6-1	131	239	.350	3-3-1	.500	5
1973			6-3-0	213	140	.667	5-2-0	.714	2	1989			8-2-0	239	170	.800	6-1-0	.857	1
1974			8-1-0	229	67	.889	6-1-0	.857	1	1990			6-4-0	233	223	600	5-2-0	.714	3
1975			7-3-0	196	123	.700	5-2-0	.714	3	1991			6-4-0	241	190	.600	4-3-0	.571	4
1976			8-1-0	198	77	.889	6-1-0	.857	1	1992			4-6-0	161	209	.400	2-5-0	.286	6
1977			7-2-0	212	108	.778	6-1-0	.857	1	1993			3-7-0	172	293	.300	2-5-0	.286	6
1978			5-2-2	192	114	.667	4-1-2	.714	2	1994			5-5-0	224	195	.500	3-4-0	.429	4
1979			8-1-0	193	94	.889	6-1-0	.857	1	1995			3-7-0	172	247	.300	2-5-0	.286	6
1980			8-2-0	209	124	.800	6-1-0	.857	1	1996			2-8-0	145	246	.200	1-6-0	.143	8

Jack Siedlecki (1997-2003) 39-30-0 .565

Year	Nat'l AP	Other	Overall W-L-T	PF	PA	Pct.	Conference W-L-T	Pct.	Rank	Year	Nat'l AP	Other	Overall W-L-T	PF	PA	Pct.	Conference W-L-T	Pct.	Rank
1997			2-8-0	113	250	.200	1-6-0	.143	7	2000			7-3-0	276	183	.700	4-3-0	.571	3
1998			6-4-0	237	259	.600	5-2-0	.714	2	2001			3-6-0	214	250	.333	1-6-0	.143	7
1999			9-1-0	315	159	.900	6-1-0	.857	1	2002			6-4-0	226	236	.600	4-3-0	.571	3
										2003			6-4-0	257	188	.600	4-3-0	.571	3

Won-loss record by decades:

1872-79	21- 4-4	.793		1920-29	58-20-5	.729	1970-79	67-22-2	.747
1880-89	86- 1-5	.962		1930-39	45-24-4	.644	1980-89	53-43-2	.551
1890-99	116- 7-5	.926		1940-49	45-38-2	.541	1990-99	46-54-0	.460
1900-09	100- 4-5	.940		1950-59	54-30-7	.632	2000-03	22-17-0	.564
1910-19	52-18-7	.721		1960-69	57-29-4	.636			

Historic record: 822-312-58 .715

College Football Hall of Fame:
Pat Corbin, center, 1886-88; Walter Camp, coach, 1888-92; Pudge Hefflefinger, guard, 1888-91; Lee McClung, halfback, 1888-91; Amos Alonzo Stagg, end, 1888-91; Frank Hinkey, end, 1891-94; Bill Hickock, guard, 1892-94; Sam Thorne, halfback, 1893-95; Gordon Brown, guard, 1897-1900; James Hogan, tackle, 1901-04; Tom Shevlin, end, 1902-05; Ted Coy, fullback, 1907-09; John Reed Kilpatrick, end, 1908-10; Howard Jones, coach, 1909, 1913; Art Howe, quarterback, 1909-11; Doug Bomeisler, end, 1910-12; Henry Ketcham, center/guard, 1911-13; Tad Jones, coach, 1916-17, 1920-27; Mal Alrdrich, halfback, 1919-21; Mal Stevens, halfback/quarterback, 1919-23; Century Milstead, tackle, 1920-23; Bill Mallory, fullback, 1921-23; Herbert Surhahn, guard, 1924-26; Albie Booth, halfback, 1929-31; Larry Kelley, end, 1934-36; Clint Frank, halfback, 1935-37; Alex Kroll, center, 1956-61; Carmen Cozza, coach, 1965-96.

PART IV

Records of Service Teams During World War II

RECORDS OF SERVICE TEAMS DURING WORLD WAR II

1942 Season

Alameda Coast Guard
Alameda, CA
(1-7-1) J. J. Verdacci

6	San Franc. Packers	7
0	California Ramblers	0
0	St. Mary's Pre-Flt.	40
6	Loyola (CA)	38
0	Mather Field	27
0	San Jose State	9
13	Pacific	7
6	San. Franc. University	44
0	St. Mary's College	26
31	Total	198

Albuquerque Air Base
Albuquerque, NM
(4-3-0)

6	New Mexico	7
12	Lubbock Army Base	0
13	West Texas State	18
13	New Mex. A&M	0
13	Arizona State	0
0	San. Franc. University	28
40	Coll. Spgs. Air Base	6
97	Total	59

California Pre-Flt.*
St. Mary's College, CA
(6-3-1) G. A. Oliver

38	Pacific	9
10	Oregon	9
18	UCLA	7
40	Alameda Coast Guard	0
59	Santa Ana Air Base	0
0	Washington	0
13	Santa Clara	6
13	Stanford	28
6	California	12
13	USC	21
210	Total	92

*Also known as St. Mary's P-F

Camp Davis
Wilmington, No. Carolina
(4-3-2) H. A. Johnson

0	The Citadel	32
13	Appalachian	13
14	Catawba	21
20	High Point	0
2	No. Carol. Navy Base	0
0	Presbyterian	26
37	Cherry Point	0
21	Daniel Field	7
6	No. Carol. Navy Base	6
113	Total	105

Camp Grant
Camp Grant, Illinois
(6-6-0) Glen Rose

6	Chicago Bears	32
22	Milwaukee Falks	0
0	Wisconsin	7
20	Milwaukee Falks	0
43	DeKalb Teachers	0
16	Iowa	33

Camp Grant *(cont'd)*

26	Bradley Tech	7
20	Fort Knox	0
0	Great Lakes	33
40	St. Norbert's	6
0	Marquette	34
0	Illinois	20
193	Total	172

Camp Pickett
Blackstone, Virginia
(1-6-0)

0	Richmond	27
2	Newport News	20
0	Hampton Institute	13
2	Randolph-Macon	13
6	Howard University	0
6	Virginia State	9
6	Virginia State	13
22	Total	95

Carlisle Barracks
Medical Field, PA.
(3-3-1) E.P. Quarantillo

0	Harrisburg	12
6	Indiantown Gap	6
13	Indiantown Gap	0
0	Shippensburg	13
13	Lancaster	0
27	Baltimore Fire Dept.	6
0	Quantico Marines	20
59	Total	57

Colorado Springs Air Base
Colorado Springs, CO.
(1-6-0) K. L. Ormiston

0	Greeley State	33
0	Creighton	20
7	Aero Parts	33
7	Colorado College	6
6	Regis	7
6	Albuquerque Air Base	40
13	Greeley State	42
39	Total	181

Corpus Christi Naval Air Station
Corpus Christi, TX
(4-3-1) M. G. Karow

0	Texas	40
7	Rice	18
18	Texas A&M	7
6	SMU	21
74	Ellington Field	0
18	Pensacola NAS	6
52	Randolph Field	0
7	Pensacola NAS	7
182	Total	99

Curtis Bay Coast Guard
Curtis Bay, Maryland
(3-2-1) Andy Jakomas

0	Western Maryland	28
6	Arcadia Club	6
21	Arcadia Club	0
6	Viking Club	13

Curtis Bay *(cont'd)*

7	Camp Somerset	2
28	Camp Somerset	0
68	Total	49

Daniel Field Air Base
Augusta, Georgia
(4-6-0) H. H. Stovall

0	So. Carolina Frosh	46
21	Spence Field	0
14	Benning Infantry	21
21	Benning Armor	6
6	Clemson Frosh	7
0	Jacksonville NAS	55
7	Camp Davis	21
14	Presbyterian	21
21	Benning Engineers	0
28	Benning Infantry	0
132	Total	177

Fort Benning
Fort Benning, Georgia
(0-5-0)

0	Chattanooga	20
0	Auburn B team	20
7	Pensacola NAS	36
7	Wooford	46
0	Tampa	30
14	Total	152

Fort Douglas Military Police
Fort Douglas, Utah
(5-3-0) F. W. Goates

45	Weber College	0
12	Logan Marines	7
0	Second Air Force	37
24	BYU	13
7	Utah State	40
6	Denver	44
26	Hill Field	7
39	Idaho Southern	17
159	Total	165

Fort Hamilton
Brooklyn, New York
(0-6-0)

0	Franklin & Marshall	59
0	St. Vincent	39
0	Moravian	26
0	Brooklyn College	39
7	Canisius	47
14	Fort Totten	39
14	Total	249

Fort Knox
Fort Knox, Kentucky
(2-7-0) Joe Bach

7	Iowa Pre Flight	13
0	Ohio State	59
2	Xavier	12
0	Detroit	16
20	Marshall	6
0	Camp Grant	0
0	Pittsburgh Steelers	28
7	Youngstown	0

Fort Knox *(cont'd)*

0	Indiana	51
36	Total	185

Fort Monmouth
Red Bank, New Jersey
(5-2-2) August Bossu

0	Columbia	39
13	Scranton	0
3	Lafayette	7
14	Manhattan Coast Guard	14
13	Army Plebes	2
13	Camp Upston	0
39	Lancaster	0
0	Rutgers	0
6	Fort Totten	0
121	Total	62

Fort Riley
Fort Riley, Kansas
(6-3-0) C. Ned Vaughan

0	Missouri	31
39	Emporia Teachers	14
21	Kansas State	7
7	Creighton	34
13	Missouri B team	6
6	Wichita	0
13	Washburn	0
6	Second Air Force	54
39	Kansas Wesleyan	6
144	Total	152

Fort Totten
Fort Totten, New York
(3-5-1)

6	Harwich	6
27	Brooklyan	7
0	Holy Cross	60
0	St. Bonaventure	7
7	Canisius	14
51	CCNY	0
6	Scranton	13
39	Fort Hamilton	7
0	Fort Monmouth	6
136	Total	120

Georgia Navy Pre-Flight
Athens, Georgia
(7-1-1) R. B. Wolf

14	Pennsylvania	6
14	North Carolina Navy	14
26	Duke	12
26	Pensacola NAS	0
0	LSU	34
20	Jacksonville NAS	6
41	Auburn	14
7	Tulane	0
35	Alabama	19
183	Total	105

Great Lakes Naval Training Station
Great Lakes, Illinois
(8-3-1) Tony Hinkle

0	Michigan	9
25	Iowa	0
7	Wisconsin	13
0	Michigan State	14

Great Lakes *(cont'd)*

7	Pittsburgh	6
17	Missouri	0
42	Purdue	0
33	Camp Grant	0
24	Marquette	0
6	Illinois	0
48	Northwestern	0
13	Notre Dame	13
222	Total	55

Grosse Ile NAS
(4-4-0) R. B. Clogston

0	Hillsdale	19
20	Grand Rapids University	0
37	Wyandotte	6
14	Otterbein	0
7	Wayne University	3
2	Western Michigan	13
0	Baldwin-Wallace	54
7	Bowling Green	19
87	Total	114

Hill Field
Ogden, Utah
(0-5-0) A. A. Dominique

0	Weber J. C.	19
6	Logan Navy	13
7	Fort Doublans	26
7	Logan Navy	8
13	Carlon J. C.	27
33	Total	93

Indiantown Military Reservation
Indiantown Gap, PA
(0-5-1) Joseph M. Hill

0	Allbright	47
0	Lock Haven Teachers	27
6	Carlisle Barracks	6
0	Lock Haven	6
0	Carlisle Barracks	13
0	Kutztown Teachers	18
6	Total	117

Iowa Navy Pre-Flight
Iowa City, IA
(7-3-1) Bernie Bierman

61	Kansas	0
26	Northwestern	12
7	Minnesota	6
26	Michigan	28
0	Notre Dame	28
13	Fort Knox	7
26	Indiana	6
46	Nebraska	0
12	Ohio State	41
0	Missouri	7
217	Total	121

Iowa Navy P-F B Team
(3-3-0)

0	Case Institute	6
0	Carleton	6
14	Grinnell	13
0	Wisconsin B team	6
12	Parsons College	0

Iowa Navy B Team *(cont'd)*

18	Wisconsin B Team	18
44	Total	49

Jacksonville Naval Air Station
Jacksonville, FL
(9-3-0) John Adams

20	Florida	7
0	Georgia	14
14	Miami (FL)	0
33	Spence Field AB	0
55	Daniel Field AB	0
26	Tampa	0
6	Georgia Navy P-F	20
6	Rollins	13
24	Clemson	6
16	Pensacola NAS	10
13	Duke	0
19	Spence Field AB	6
232	Total	76

Lakehurst Naval Air Station
Lakehurst, New Jersey
(4-4-1) M. Elward

6	Princeton	20
0	Maryland	14
7	Delaware	20
14	Allbright	0
20	Penn. Military College	7
14	Lafayette	0
27	Muhlenburg	7
0	Duquesne	13
14	Scranton	14
102	Total	95

Manhattan Beach Coast Guard
Brooklyn, NY
(6-0-1) Gar Griffith

30	Brooklyn	0
31	CCNY	0
20	Villanova	13
14	Fort Monmouth	14
26	Toledo	0
14	Springfield	13
27	Scranton	0
162	Total	40

Mather Field
Mills, CA
(3-2-0)

19	Montana	13
0	Santa Ana Air Base	7
27	Alameda Coast Guard	0
20	McClellan Field	6
0	St. Mary's College	33
66	Total	59

March Field Flyers
Riverside, CA
(11-2-0) P. J. Schissler

18	Bombers	0
25	Redlands	14
0	Fresno	20
30	San Diego State	6
47	Los Angeles	6
21	Mather Field	3

March Field *(cont'd)*

26	San Diego NAS	0
16	Santa Ana AB	7
33	San Diego Bombers	12
19	Hollywood Bears	6
13	Second Air Force	26
14	All Stars	12
28	San Diego Bombers	14
290	Total	126

McClellan Field
McClellan Field, CA
(5-2-0) Ray Riegals

6	Stockton Military	0
26	San Francisco State	6
7	Sacramento J. C.	6
31	Muroc Air Base	2
13	California Ramblers	7
6	Mather Field	20
7	San Jose State	27
96	Total	68

Minter Field
Bakersfield, CA
(6-2-0) Lee Frankovich

17	Stockton Military	6
32	Porterville	0
21	Visalia J.C.	0
7	San Francisco B team	6
7	California Frosh	20
38	Muroc Air Base	0
20	Commandos	0
7	Bakersfield	13
149	Total	45

North Carolina Navy Pre-Flight
Chapel Hill, North Carolina
(8-2-1) Jim Crowley

13	Catawba	2
13	Harvard	0
14	Georgia Navy P-F	14
19	NC State	7
6	Boston College	7
34	Temple	0
9	Syracuse	0
23	Georgetown	7
17	Manhattan College	0
14	Wm. & Mary	0
0	Fordham	6
162	Total	43

Patterson Field
Fairfield, Ohio
(3-6-1)

14	Miami (OH) NT	7
0	Muskingum	6
6	Denison	0
6	Miami (OH) NT	20
6	Findlay College	9
0	Kent State	24
6	West Liberty	25
0	John Carroll	0
12	Wittenberg	0
13	Wooster	24
63	Total	115

Pensacola Naval Air Station
Pensacola, FL
(3-5-1) George Clark

13	SE Louisiana	0
75	Spence Field	0
0	Alabama	27
0	Georgia Navy P-F	26
0	TCU	21
36	Fort Benning	7
6	Corpus Christi NAS	18
7	Corpus Christi NAS	7
10	Jacksonville NAS	16
147	Total	122

Quantico Marines
Quantico, VA.
(4-0-0) Francis Reagan

21	Geo. Washington Frosh	6
14	Maryland J.V.	6
29	Christie Barracks	0
38	Baltimore Firemen	0
102	Total	12

Santa Ana Army Air Base
Goleta, CA
(5-4-0)

26	Hollywood Pros	34
19	Los Angeles Pros	7
14	Compton	0
27	Whittier	13
7	Mather Field	0
0	Nevada	3
42	Arizona State	0
0	California Navy P-F	59
0	Loyola (CA)	12
135	Total	128

Second Air Force
(10-0-1) William Reese

21	St. Martin's	0
19	Eastern Washington	7
14	Idaho	0
37	Fort Douglas	0
20	Portland University	13
75	College of Idaho	0
47	Kansas Wesleyan	0
54	Fort Riley	6
6	Washington State	6
27	Arizona	13
SUN BOWL		
13	Hardin-Simmons	7
359	Total	65

Wahpeton Naval Training Station
Wahpeton, North Dakota
(0-4-1) Bernard Dyke

6	North Dakota State	6
0	Concordia	46
6	Carleton	34
6	Winnipeg	30
7	Moorhead Teachers	10
25	Total	126

Will Rogers Field
Oklahoma City, OK
(4-4-0) E. W. Gentry

13	E. Central Okla. St.	19
0	Oklahoma Frosh	7
7	Central Oklahoma St.	27
12	Fort Sill	7
21	E. Central Okla. St.	20
6	Fort Sill	0
12	Oklahoma Frosh	6
7	Central Oklahoma St.	27
78	Total	113

Yuma Army Air Fiele
Yuma, Arizona
(2-0-0) C. L. Swagerty

18	Yuma H.S. Alumni	14
31	Sixth Division	0
49	Total	14

Abilene Army Air Base
Abilene, TX
(1-2-0) Donald Beeler

0	Forty First Cavalry	12
18	778th Tank Battalion	6
6	Southwestern	45
24	Total	63

Alameda Coast Guard
Alameda, CA
(4-2-1) J. J. Verducci

7	Pacific	14
7	Del Monte Pre Flight	34
26	San Francisco U.	0
21	St. Mary's	7
46	Pleasanton Navy	6
13	St. Mary's Pre Flight	13
7	California	0
127	Total	74

Bainbridge Naval Training Station
Bainbridge, MD.
(7-0-0) Joe Maniaci

9	Camp Lejeunne	0
57	Fort Monroe	0
26	Curtis Bay Coast Guard	7
49	Camp Lee	0
72	Yellowjackets	0
54	Curtis Bay Coast Guard	0
46	Maryland	0
313	Total	7

Bunker Hill Naval Air Station
Bunker Hill, Indiana
(6-0-0) H. B. Kisssell

9	Patterson Field	6
42	Notre Dame V-12	6
13	Bowling Green	12
32	Alma	0
19	Ottumwa NAS	13
56	Fort Sheridan	0
171	Total	37

Camp Davis
Holly Ridge, NC
(8-2-0) H. A. Johnson

24	Wake Forest	20
25	Charleston Coast Guard	0
27	NC State	0
18	North Carolina P-F	23
27	Davidson	0
0	Camp Lejeunne	14
31	Fort Monroe	6
32	Presbyterian	0
41	Daniel Field	0
42	Fort Bragg	0
267	Total	63

Camp Edwards
Camp Edwards, MA
(4-5-0) Clell Barton

0	Harvard	7
7	Batesq	13
30	Milford	0
7	Tufts	18
6	Worcester Tech	21
7	Harvard	14

Camp Edwards *(cont'd)*

35	New Bedford	0
34	Murphy Club	0
20	Fall River	18
146	Total	91

Camp Grant
Rockford, Illinois
(2-6-2) Charles Bachman

23	Illinois	0
0	Michigan	26
10	Wisconsin	7
7	Marquette	7
0	Purdue	19
7	Minnesota	13
13	Fort Riley	13
0	Great Lakes NTS	12
13	Iowa Pre Flight	28
6	Fort Riley	10
79	Total	135

Camp Kearns
Camp Kearns, UT
(5-2-0) James O"Brien

4	Salt Lake Air Base	0
0	Fort Douglas	6
20	Logan NTS	0
25	Bushnell Hospital	0
19	Pocatello Air Base	0
0	Salt Lake Air Base	10
46	Fort Douglas	6
116	Total	42

Camp Lee
Camp Lee, VA
(5-5-0) Warren Casey

6	Brooklyn Dodgers	28
0	New York Giants	21
40	Norfolk Marines	0
20	Cherry Point	0
0	Bainbridge NTS	49
6	Curtis Bay Coast Guard	7
0	Richmond Air Base	6
33	Curtis Bay Coast Guard	0
6	Fort Monroe	0
6	Richmond Air Base	0
117	Total	111

Camp Lejeune
New River, NC
(6-2-1) M. Bell & Jack Chevigny

0	Duke	40
0	Bainbridge NTS	9
26	North Carolina B team	0
51	Fort Monroe	0
20	Jacksonville NAS	7
14	Camp Davis	0
55	Norfolk Marines	6
14	North Carolina P F	14
13	Jacksonville NAS	6
193	Total	82

Charleston Coast Guard
Charleston, SC
(6-3-0) Mark Brashares

53	Fort Jackson	0
0	Camp Davis	25
36	Davidson	0
0	South Carolina	20
0	Miami	13
21	Newberry	0
25	Camp Gordon	6
20	Augusta Training Station	7
20	Richmond	6
181	Total	77

Cherry Point Marines
Cherry Point, NC
(4-2-0) Bill Hopp

0	Camp Lee	20
39	Wilmington Coast Gd.	0
68	Wake Forest Army	6
20	Richmond Army AB	0
40	Camp Butner	9
0	Greensboro BTC	19
167	Total	54

Curtis Bay Coast Guard
Curtis Bay, MD
(4-5-0)

13	Maryland	7
2	Richmond	13
7	Navy J.V.	22
7	Bainbridge NTS	54
40	Camp Lee	33
20	York Vikings	0
13	Fort Monroe	6
7	Camp Lee	6
0	Bainbridge NTS	54
109	Total	167

Daniel Field Air Base
(2-7-0) H. L. Stovall

13	Georgia Pre Fliight	19
0	Fort Benning 300th	39
18	Georgia	7
40	Presbyterian	14
7	Fort Benning 300th	48
7	Fort Benning 176th	47
0	Jacksonville NAS	44
0	Camp Davis	0
13	Camp Gordon 10th	14
104	Total	232

Del Monte Pre Flight
Del Monte, CA
(7-1-0) W. F. Kern

34	Alameda Coast Guard	7
33	St. Mary's	7
34	Pleasanton Navy	6
7	Pacific	16
34	San Francisco U.	0
26	UCLA	7
37	St. Mary's Pre Flight	14
47	California	8
252	Total	65

1943 Season (cont'd)

Fort Crook
Fort Crook, Nebraska
(2-4-0) Earl Shuette

0	Peru Teachers	64
0	Ottumwa NAS	29
2	Doane NAS	54
6	Central	0
19	Wentworth Military	0
12	Kearney Air Base	20
39	Total	167

Fort Jackson
Fort Jackson, SC
(0-3-0)
J. E. Williams

0	Presbyterian	41
0	Newberry	52
0	Charleston Coast Gd.	54
0	Total	147

Fort Knox
Fort Knox, KY
(4-2-0) E. L. Bruner

13	Bowman Field	0
0	Arkansas A&M	33
19	Camp Campbell	0
19	Bowman Field	0
0	DePauw	42
14	Camp Campbell	13
65	Total	88

Fort Sheridan
Fort Sheridan, Illinois
(4-3-0) John C. Phipps

14	Gardiner Hospital	0
0	Patterson Field	7
13	Wilson	0
0	Falk Corp	19
7	Maitowoc Gaiels	0
0	Bunker Hill NAS	56
26	Camp McCoy	0
60	Total	82

Fort Frances E. Warren
Cheyenne, WY
(4-3-0) Willis M. Smith

0	Lowry Field	7
0	Colorado	38
60	Utah	0
26	Kearney Air Base	6
33	Kearney Air Base	6
10	Salt Lake Air Base	0
7	Fort Riley	14
136	Total	71

Georgia Pre Flight
Athens, GA
(5-1-0) R. E. Enright

19	Daniel Field	13
7	Georgia Tech	35
53	Newberry	0
20	North Carolina P F	7
14	Tulane	6
32	Clemson	6
145	Total	74

Great Lakes NTS
Great Lakes, IL
(10-2-0) Tony Hinkle

20	Fort Riley	19
13	Purdue	23
21	Iowa	7
40	Pittsburgh	0
13	Ohio State	6
0	Northwestern	13
41	Marquette	7
32	Western Michigan	6
12	Camp Grant	0
21	Indiana	7
25	Marquette	6
19	Notre Dame	14
257	Total	108

Greensboro Army Air Base
Greensboro, NC
(4-0-0) R. W. Erickson

56	Camp Butner	0
59	Wake Forest Army	0
14	Wake Forest	0
19	Cherry Point	0
148	Total	0

Iowa Pre Flight
Iowa City, IA.
(9-1-0) Don Faurot

32	Illinois	18
29	Ohio State	13
33	Iowa State	12
25	Iowa	0
21	Missouri	6
19	Fort Riley	2
49	Drake	0
28	Camp Grant	13
13	Notre Dame	14
32	Minnesota	0
281	Total	78

Jackson Barracks
New Orleans, LA
(2-4-0) Herman Mopsick

7	LaGarde	0
6	Gulfport Seabees	7
0	Huma Air Base	29
8	LaGarde	30
7	Gulfport Sea Bees	6
0	Houma Air Base	10
28	Total	73

Kessler Field
Biloxi, MS
(3-1-0) G.B. Huffman

56	Camp Gordon	0
51	Gulfport Sea Bees	0
7	Arkansas A&M	19
47	Houma Air Base	0

Kirtland Field
Albuquerque, NM
(1-2-0) Ted E. Shipkey

13	New Mexico	19
0	Colorado College	20
18	Lubbock Army A.B.	0
31	Total	39

Lakehurst Naval Air Station
Lakehurst, NJ
(2-4-0) A. H. Elward

0	Muhlenberg	13
6	Army Plebes	0
6	Pennsylvania	74
14	Villanova	27
0	Bucknell	13
26	Camp Kilmer	12
52	Total	139

Lubbock Army Air Base
Lubbock, TX
(5-1-0) A. Wirz & G. B. Morris

14	Texas Tech	26
28	South Plains AAF	12
47	Fort Bliss	7
10	Texas Tech	7
12	Oklahoma NAS	0
46	Camp Berkeley	6
157	Total	58

March Field
March Field, CA
(9-1-0) P. J. Schissler

45	Pacific All Stars	13
40	Redlands	0
47	UCLA	7
7	San Diego NTS	0
7	Washington	27
7	St. Mary's Pre Flight	6
72	Pomona Ordinance	0
35	USC	0
13	San Diego NTS	2
19	Pacific	0
292	Total	55

North Carolina Pre Flight
Chapel Hill, North Carolina
(2-4-1)

0	Navy	31
0	Duke	42
23	Camp Davis	18
7	Georgia Pre Flight	20
12	Wake Forest	20
14	Camp Lejeune	14
21	NC State	7
77	Total	152

Oklahoma Naval Air Station
Norman, Oklahoma
(4-3-0) Lou Zarza

6	Oklahoma	22
40	Forty Ninth Army	0
0	Fort Riley	33
20	Oklahoma A&M	0
19	Oklahoma J.V.	0
0	Lubbocvk AAB	13
33	Will Rogers AAB	6
118	Total	74

Ottumwa Naval Air Station
Ottumwa, IA
(5-1-0) J. B. Kitts

54	Iowa State Prison	0
14	Iowa Pre Flight B team	6
9	Fort Crock	0
13	Iowa Pre Flight B team	0
13	Iowa State	12
13	Bunker Hill NAS	19
136	Total	37

Patterson Field
Fairfield, Ohio
(2-3-1) C. O. Stipes

6	Bunker Hill NAS	9
10	Bowman Field	6
7	Fort Sheridan	0
3	Wooster	21
0	Wright Field	0
0	Ohio Wesleyan	49
26	Total	85

Pleasanton Navy
Shoemaker, CA
(1-4-0) James Banach

13	San Francisco U.	0
0	St. Mary's Pre Flight	48
6	Del Monte Pre Flight	34
6	Alameda Coast Guard	46
6	Modesto J.C.	8
31	Total	136

Pomona Ordnance Base
Pomona, CA
(2-6-0) Don Stone

16	Calif. Inst. For Men	0
0	Redlands	19
7	San Diego Bombers	20
2	San Diego NAS	48
14	Yuma Army Air Base	20
0	March Field	72
14	Pasadena J.C.	6
0	USC J.V.	30
53	Total	215

Randolph Field
San Antonio, TX
(10-1-0) Frank Tritico

30	Bryan Army Air Force	0
6	Rice	0
47	Bryan AAF	0
39	Ward Island	9
26	Blackland Field	7
53	Ward Island	14
26	North Texas Aggies	13
0	SW Louisiana	6
7	Blackland Field	0
34	Mexico City	0
COTTON BOWL		
7	Texas	7
275	Total	7

Reno Army Base
Reno, Nevada
(2-1-1) Jim Akien & Dayton Docker

0	Los Angeles Mustangs	34
25	Tonopah Air Base	0
34	Utah	28
0	Salt Lake Air Base	0
58	Total	62

Richmond Army Air Base
Richmond, VA
(4-5-1) John Anderson & Steve Alcorn

0	Richmond	45
7	Virginia	7
6	Fort Monroe	0
6	Maryland	10
20	Norfolk Marines	0
40	Norfolk Marines	0
15	Fort Monroe	18
6	Camp Lee	0
6	William & Mary	14
0	Camp Lee	6
106	Total	109

St. Mary's Pre Flight
St. Mary's College, CA
(4-4-1) E. W. Nelson

7	Pacific	13
48	Pleasonton Navy	0
0	USC	13
39	California	0
6	March Field	7
13	Alameda Coast Guard	13
41	San Francisco U.	0
14	Del Monte Pre Flight	37
19	Modesto J.C.	6
187	Total	89

Sampson Naval Training Station
Sampson, New York
(7-2-0) M. A. Stevens

13	Cornell	27
47	Yellow Jackets	7
17	Vallanova	7
47	Rome Army Air Base	0
7	RPI	0
48	Rome Army Air Base	7
55	York Vikings	0
28	Muhlenberg	7
7	Army	16
269	Total	71

San Diego Naval Training Station
San Diego, CA
(7-2-0) Bob Molenda

20	Redlands	0
59	Fort Ord	0
48	Pomoan Ordnance	2
0	March Field	7
35	Compton	0
28	UCLA	0
10	USC	7
58	San Pedro A.S.	7
2	March Field	13
260	Total	36

Spokane Air Base
Spokane, WA
(2-2-0) Izzy Weinstock

12	Washington	47
12	Whitman	0
7	Washington	41
35	Whitman	13
66	Total	107

Will Rogers Field
Oklahoma City, OK
(2-1-1) H. Davidson & A. Exendine

26	Borden Hospital	0
0	Tulsa Bombers	0
26	49th General Hospital	0
7	Oklahoma NAS	33
59	Total	33

Wright Field
Dayton, Ohio
(1-0-1) O. E. Mohler

0	Patterson Field	0
13	Bowman Field	9
13	Total	9

1944 Season

Alameda Coast Guard
Alameda, CA
(4-2-2) J. J. Verducci

7	Fleet City	7
35	Nevada	0
18	St. Mary's	0
20	March Field	20
19	Pacific	0
13	UCLA	26
12	California	6
13	St. Mary's Pre Flight	32

Atlantic City Naval Air Station
Atlantic City, NJ
(5-2-0) L. H. Elverson & J. Morgan

3	Swarthmore	0
45	Ursilnus	7
21	Scranton	7
7	Muhlenberg	14
2	Army B team	12
25	Villanova	6
31	Princeton	6
134	Total	52

Bainbridge Naval Training Station
Bainbridge, MD
(10-0-0) Joe Maniaci

43	Camp Lee	0
53	Camp Lejeune	7
47	Camden Pros	7
7	Camp Peary	0
15	Maxwell Field	7
49	North Carolina P F	20
50	Cherry Point	7
33	Camp Lejeune	6
21	Camp Peary	13
13	Maxwell Field	3
331	Total	70

Bryan Army Air Force
Bryan, TX
(1-7-0) Roy C. Johnson

0	Texas A&M	39
0	Blackland AAF	27
0	Ellington AAF	6
0	Galveston AAF	19
6	Eagle Mount. Lake	0
0	Blackland AAF	41
0	Ellington AAF	7
6	Hondo AAF	13
12	Total	152

Camp Beale
Camp Beale, CA
(6-4-0) Kenneth Hayden

6	McClellan Field	20
0	Klamath Falls	8
14	California Ramblers	27
6	Coast Guard Pilots	25
32	McClelland Field	0
32	Grant-Union Teachers	12
12	Fairfield-Suisun	0
39	Coast Guard Stevedores	6
6	Pacific	2
19	California Ramblers	0
166	Total	98

Camp Campbell
Camp Campbell, KY
(6-0-0) B. J. Milroy

47	Twentieth Ferry Group	0
19	Fort Knox	7
20	Fort Knox	0
48	Nashville	0
52	Fort Knox	0
19	Bowman Field	0
205	Total	7

Camp Lee
Camp Lee, Virginia
(4-5-0) Ray Bedard

47	Indiantown Gap	0
0	Bainbridge NTS	43
0	Camp Perry	38
18	Richmond AAB	0
0	Cherry Point	6
0	Camp Peary	41
35	Richmond AAB	0
26	Fort Monroe	13
0	Cherry Point	13
126	Total	154

Camp Lejeune
New River, NC
(6-2-0) Frank Knox

6	Duke J.V.	0
7	Bainbridge NTS	53
33	Camp Detrick	0
33	Kinston Marines	0
41	Bogue Field	0
26	Fort Monroe	0
6	Bainbridge NTS	33
52	Camp Markall	6
204	Total	92

Camp Lockett
Camp Lockett, CA
(1-4-1) W.C. Downing

13	Grossmontt H.S.	0
0	Brown Military Academy	33
6	Brown Military Academy	13
0	El Centro J. C.	0
0	Grossmont H.S.	50
6	El Centro J.C.	13
25	Total	109

Camp Peary Naval Training Station
Camp Peary, VA
(5-2-0) N. Strader

33	Washington Redskins	27
20	Cherry Point	0
38	Camp Lee	0
0	Bainbridge NTS	7
41	Camp Lee	0
19	North Carolina P F	7
13	Bainbridge NTS	21
164	Total	62

Chatham Field
Chatham Field, GA
(2-8-1) A.P. White

12	Newberry College	6
0	Fort Benning Fourth	0

Chatham Field *(cont'd)*

0	Morris Field	45
0	Charleston Coast Gd.	14
0	Fort Pierce Amphibs	74
0	Pittsburgh	26
7	TCU	19
0	Cherry Point	35
25	Havana University	7
0	Mayport NAB	26
44	Total	252

Cherry Point Marines
Cherry Point, NC
(3-7-0) James McMurdo

14	North Carolina P F	27
0	Camp Peary	20
0	Georgia Pre Flight	33
14	North Carolina	20
7	Morris Field	29
6	Camp Lee	0
0	Jacksonville NAS	33
7	Bainbridge NTS	50
35	Chatham Field	0
13	Camp Lee	0
96	Total	212

Ellington Army Air Field
Ellington Field, TX
(6-3-2) J. L. McCullough

7	Rice B team	0
6	Bryan AAF	0
0	Galveston AAF	0
0	Blackland AAF	19
7	Bryan AAF	0
0	Hondo AAF	7
0	Blackland AAF	0
20	Bergstrom AAF	13
7	Hondo AAF	13
6	Eagle Mountain Lake	0
33	Eagle Mountain Lake	0
86		52

Fairfield-Suisun AAF
Fairfield-Suisun Field, CA
(1-7-1) E. Davidson & J. Giannoni

0	Pacific	25
0	California Ramblers	0
13	C. Park Seabees	0
7	Coast Guard Pilots	40
0	El Toro Marines	56
12	Klamath Falls	14
7	Tonopah AAB	20
0	Tonopah AAB	9
0	Camp Beale	12
39	Total	176

Fleet City
Shoemaker, CA
(6-4-1) J.J. Malevich

7	Pacific	6
7	El Toro Marines	13
7	Alameda Coast Guard	7
12	St. Mary's P F	0
0	March Field	38
19	California	2

1944 Season *(cont'd)*

Fleet City *(cont'd)*

27	Coast Guard Pilots	6
0	El Toro Marines	14
26	St. Mary's	0
19	Nevada	2
0	St. Mary's Pre Flight	3
124	Total	92

Fort Benning Third Infantry
Fort Benning, GA
(4-5-0) Charles A. Zioga

26	Maxwell Field	0
0	Morris Field	22
6	Fort Benning Fourth	14
41	Miami NTC	7
19	Fort Knox	0
13	Jacksonville NAS	35
7	Miami NTC	6
7	Fort Benning Fourth	9
0	Kessler Field	19
119	Total	112

Fort Knox
Fort Knox, KY
(4-6-0) E. L. Bruner

0	Indiana	72
13	Bowman Field	7
7	Camp Campbell	19
0	Camp Campbell	20
52	Nashville Air Base	0
14	George Field	0
0	Fort Benning Third	9
7	Bowman Field	14
0	Camp Campbell	52
14	Nashville Air Base	0
107	Total	203

Fort MacArthur
San Pedro, CA
(7-1-1) Glen Clark

41	1005th Engineers	0
21	Compton	18
18	Santa Ana College	13
19	Redlands	13
0	San Diego Navy	69
13	USC J.V.	0
6	UCLA J.V.	6
14	Pasadena City College	0
25	Pasadena City College	12
157	Total	131

Fort Monroe
Fort Monroe, VA
(5-5-0) Joe Murray

7	Richmond Army AB	6
0	William & Mary	46
13	Richmond AAB	0
6	Portsmouth Fleet	7
0	Catawba College	26
26	Indiantown Gap	6
0	Camp Lejeune	26
13	Camp Lee	26
19	Camp Detrick	6
13	Camp Detrick	12
97	Total	161

Fort Pierce Amphibs
Fort Pierce, FL
(9-0-0) Hampton Pool

40	Miami NTC	7
74	Chatham Field	0
38	Miami (FL)	0
53	Mayport NSB	0
70	Miami NTC	0
48	Mayport NSB	2
21	Jacksonville NAS	0
7	Morris Field	6
34	Kessler Field	7
385	Total	22

Fort Sheridan
Fort Sheridan, IL
(0-2-0)

6	Western Michigan	67
0	Great Lakes	62
6	Total	129

Fort Frances Warren
Cheyenne, WY
(5-4-1) Willis M. Smith

21	Brooklyn Tigers	20
7	Colorado	6
5	Lincoln AAB	14
33	Colorado College	13
66	Idaho Southern	0
0	Iowa Pre Flight	30
19	Lincoln AAB	6
0	Second Air Force	20
7	Great Lakes	28
21	San Francisco Clippers	21
179	Total	158

Fourth Air Force
March Field, CA
(7-1-2) John Baker

56	San Diego Bombers	7
39	Fleet City	0
20	Alameda Coast Guard	20
21	El Toro Marines	14
7	St. Mary's Pre Flight	0
35	UCLA	13
28	Washington	0
7	San Diego NTS	0
0	Second Air Force	0
7	Randolph Field	20
220	Total	74

Galveston Army Air Field
Galveston, TX
(5-3-2) Jocko Lyons & Bill Loungo

6	Southwestern	32
0	Rice	57
0	Ellington AAF	0
19	Bryan AAF	0
0	Selman Field	0
40	John Tarleton	0
14	Texas A&M B team	2
19	Hondo AAF	14
20	Lake Charles AAF	0
14	Selman Field	20
132	Total	125

Georgia Pre Flight
Athens, GA
(4-5-0) Raymond W. Pond

20	South Carolina	14
33	Cherry Point	0
7	Morris Field	19
0	North Carolina P F	3
7	Georgia Tech	13
12	Third Air Force	34
19	North Carolina P F	33
30	Daniel Field	0
53	Daniel Field	12
181	Total	128

Great Lakes Naval Training Station
Great Lakes, IL
(9-2-1) Paul Brown

62	Fort Sheridan	0
27	Purdue	18
26	Illinois	26
25	Northwestern	0
38	Western Michigan	0
6	Ohio State	26
40	Wisconsin	12
45	Marquette	7
12	Morris Field	10
32	Marquette	0
28	Fort Warren	7
7	Notre Dame	28
348	Total	134

Gulfport Army Air Field
Gulfport, MS
(5-3-0) John Walsh

30	Algiers Navy	0
34	Gulfport Navy	0
6	Jackson AAB	12
27	Marine TO	0
0	Kessler Field	20
12	Gulfport Navy	6
0	Kessler Field	39
13	Algiers Navy	12
122	Total	89

Iowa Pre Flight
Iowa City, IA
(10-1-0) Jack Meagher

7	Michigan	12
19	Minnesota	13
45	Olathe NAS	12
12	Second Air Force	6
13	Purdue	6
30	Fort Warren	0
26	Marquette	0
47	Tulsa	27
33	Bunker Hill	7
51	Missouri	7
30	Iowa	6
313	Total	96

Jacksonville Naval Air Station
Jacksonville, FL
(4-3-0) Don Faurot

20	Florida	27
35	Miami NTC	0
13	North Carolina P F	14
33	Cherry Point	0
35	Fort Benning Third	13
26	Fort Benning Fourth	19
0	Fort Pierce Amphibs	21
162	Total	94

Kearney Army Air Field
Kearney, Nebraska
(5-3-0) Marty Slovak

6	Peru Teachers	0
38	McCook AAF	7
21	Doane College	22
0	Lincoln AAF	20
0	McCook AAF	8
7	McCook AAF	0
19	Fort Riley	7
16	Fort Riley	0
107	Total	64

Kessler Field
Biloxi, MS
(8-1-2) G. B. Huffman

41	Algiers Navy	0
13	Southwest	0
62	Flora Ordnance	0
19	Selman Field	19
20	Gulfport AAF	0
7	Fort Benning Fourth	7
20	Selman Field	0
39	Gulfport AAF	0
33	Algiers Navy	0
19	Fort Benning Third	0
7	Fort Pierece Amphibs	34
280	Total	60

Kinston Marines
Kinston, NC
(2-2-1) Chris Iverson

7	North Carolina P F JV	0
8	Bogue Field	0
0	Maxwell Fiedl	62
0	Norfolk Navy	0
0	Camp Lejeune	33
15	Total	95

Klamath Falls Marines
Klamath Falls, Oregon
(2-2-1) Clyde C. Roberts

14	Willamette	33
0	California Ramblers	13
14	Fairfield-Suisun	12
8	Camp Beale	0
6	Coast Guard Rec. Sta.	0
42	Total	58

Lubbock Army Air Field
Lubbock, TX
(5-4-0) G. B. Morris & A. Wirz

27	Texas Tech	13
0	Amarillo AAF	19
0	Amarillo AAF	31
19	Beaumont Hospital	6
46	South Plains AAF	14
13	Fort Bliss	0
12	West Texas Teachers	14
0	Norman Navy Base	42
62	John Tarleton	0
184	Total	139

Maxwell Field
Maxwell Field, Alabama
(5-5-0) J. H. Yarborough

0	Fort Benning Infantry	26
62	Kinston Marines	0
40	Chatham Field	0
7	Bainbridge NTS	15
25	Fort Benning Fourth	7
0	Randolph Field	25
7	Third Air Force	41
26	Fort Benning Fourth	7
13	Miami NTS	0
3	Bainbridge NTS	13
183	Total	134

Mayport NAAS
Mayport, FL
(4-5-0) M.P. Merritt

6	Florida	36
0	Daniel Field	13
0	Fort Pierce	53
6	Jacksonville NATTC	0
7	Daniel Field	15
2	Fort Pierce	15
25	Jacksonville NATTC	6
26	Chatham Field	0
19	Charleston Coast Guard	6
91	Total	177

Morris Field (Third Air Force)
Charlotte, NC
(8-3-0) James Q. Decker

31	Charleston Coast Guard	0
45	Chatham Field	0
22	Fort Benning Third	0
19	Georgia Pre Flight	7
29	Cherry Point	7
0	Randolph Field	19
34	Georgia Pre Flight	12
10	Great Lakes	12
41	Maxwell Field	7
6	Fort Pierce	7
14	Second Air Force	7
251	Total	78

North Carolina Pre Flight
Chapel Hill, NC
(8-2-1) W. Killinger

27	Cherry Point	14
21	Navy	14
13	Duke	6
13	Virginia	13

North Carolina Pre Flight *(cont'd)*

3	Georgia Pre Flight	0
14	Jacksonville NAS	13
20	Bainbridge NTS	49
33	Georgia Pre Flight	18
7	Camp Peary	19
151	Total	146

Olathe NAS
Olathe, KS
(4-2-2) Paul Holstein

6	Pittsburgh Teachers	0
12	Iowa Pre Flight	45
13	Wichita	0
20	Fort Riley	0
6	Fort Riley	6
14	Kansas	33
13	Warrensburg Teaches	12
0	Kansas State	0
84	Total	96

Randolph Field
San Antonio, TX
(11-0-0) Frank Tritico

59	Rice	0
42	Texas	6
41	SMU	0
67	Camp Polk	0
19	Morris Field	0
68	North Texas Aggies	0
25	Maxwell Field	0
54	Southwestern	0
33	Amarillo AF	0
20	March Field	7
13	Second Air Force	6
441	Total	19

Richmond AAB
Richmond, VA
(0-9-1) G. C. Philbrick

0	Hampton-Sydney	0
6	Fort Monroe	7
0	Richmond	34
0	Camp Lee	18
0	Fort Monroe	13
0	Catawba College	33
2	Norfolk Fleet	13
0	Camp Lee	35
0	Navy Plebes	58
0	William & Mary	39
8	Total	253

St. Mary's Pre Flight
St. Mary's College, CA
(4-4-0) Jules Sikes

6	Pacific	14
0	Fleet City	12
0	USC	6
21	UCLA	12
0	March Field	7
32	Alameda Coast Guard	13
3	Fleet City	0
33	California	6
95	Total	70

1944 Season *(cont'd)*

Sampson Naval Training Station
(2-6-0) Jim Crowley

0	Boston Yanks	14
14	Green Bay Packers	25
0	New York Giants	13
12	Cleveland Rams	26
6	Villanova	7
60	Rochester Shipbuilding	0
6	Cornell	7
39	Scranton	0
137	Total	92

San Diego Naval Training Center
San Diego, CA
(4-3-1) J. N. Stabley

65	1005th Engineers	0
95	Compton College	0
14	UCLA	12
69	Fort MacArthur	0
0	Corondao Amphibs	0
0	El Toro Marines	6
21	USC	28
0	March Field	7
234	Total	53

Second Air Force
Colorado Springs, CO
(10-4-1) William B. Reese

38	Peru V-12	0
24	Colorado College	0
45	Idaho Southern	0
78	Whitman	0
33	Colorado	6
6	Iowa Pre-Flight	12
89	New Mexico	6
68	North Texas Aggies	0
6	Norman Navy	13
46	Amarillo Air Field	6
20	Fort Warren	0
47	Washington University	6
0	March Field	0
7	Third Air Force	14
6	Randolph Field	13
513	Total	76

Selman Field
Monroe, LA
(4-2-2) R. Funderburk

0	Arkansas A&M	20
13	Louisiana Tech	6
20	Louisiana Normal	6
19	Kessler Field	19
0	Galveston AAB	0
12	Algiers Navy	0
0	Kessler Field	20
20	Galveston AAB	14
84	Total	83

Thomasville AAF
Thomasville, GA
(3-1-1) F. McCormick

6	Georgia Mil. College	6
2	Waycross AAB	0
7	Georgia Mil. Academy	14
6	Thomasville Reds	0
14	Georgia Mil. College	6
35	Total	26

Tonopah Fourth AAF
Tonopah, Nevada
(5-2-0) George Solari

0	Nevada	20
0	Arizona State Navy	13
7	Nevada	6
40	Compton College	7
20	Fairfield-Suison	7
9	Fairfield-Suison	0
7	Fresno State	6
83	Total	59

1945 Season

Aberdeen Proving Ground
Aberdeen, MD
(5-3-1)

7	Howard University	0
15	Lincoln University	0
13	Edgewood Arsenal	0
6	Harrisburg	14
6	Perth Amboy	0
7	Camp Detrick	13
0	Pittsburgh Bears	0
7	Bainbridge NTS	59
31	Camp Detrick	25
92	Total	118

Air Training Command
Fort Worth, TX
(8-2-1) Douglas Fessenden

29	Kessler Field	0
27	Fort Benning	0
19	Fort Pierce	7
14	Air Tspt. Command	0
19	Fourth Air Force	7
0	El Toro Marines	7
6	First Air Force	24
7	Third Air Force	7
45	Maxwell Field	7
37	Second Air Force	7
14	Per. Dis. C.ommand	0
217	Total	66

Air Training Command
Nashville, TN
(6-2-3)

13	Fort Pierce	10
7	First Air Force	7
14	Fourth Air Force	21
15	Per. Dis. Command	8
0	Air Training Command	14
7	First Air Force	7
27	Cherry Point	0
24	Bainbridge	6
15	Second Air Force	0
23	Fort Benning	7
6	Third Air Force	15
151	Total	95

Albany Navy Landing Field
Albany, CA
(4-3-1)

26	San Francisco JC	6
6	California Ramblers	0
12	Santa Barbara Marines	20
13	Camp Cooke	14
20	Stockton Air Base	20
7	Camp Beale	24
14	Modesto JC	6
18	Pacific	13
116	Total	103

Amarillo Army Air Field
Amarillo, TX
(3-1-0)

26	Lubbock AAF	0
20	West Texas	12
6	Ellington Field	19
36	Dalhart	0
88	Total	11

Amphibious Training Base
Little Creek, VA
(7-2-0)

0	Camp Peary	6
27	Fort Bragg	0
21	Camp Lee	7
14	Navy Plebes	7
7	Bainbridge	0
27	Fort Pierce	7
12	Florida	0
6	Camp Lee	12
20	Fort Pierce	0
134	Total	39

Atlantic City Navy
Atlantic City, NJ
(4-2-1)

6	Bainbridge	14
6	Brooklyn College	6
0	Scranton	14
24	Lock Haven	0
42	CCNY	6
12	Lafayette	7
33	Swarthmore	6
123	Total	53

Bainbridge Naval Air Station
Bainbridge, MD
(5-4-0) Paul Pierce

14	Atlantic City	0
59	Aberdeen Proving Ground	7
27	Camp Lee	0
40	Camp Detrick	0
6	Air Transport	24
0	Amphib.Training Base	7
0	Camp Lee	26
14	Fort Bragg	50
53	Oceana NAS	14
213	Total	128

Barksdale Field
Shreveport, LA
(4-7-0)

0	Maxwell Field	13
6	Arkansas	12
8	Army JV	13
19	NW Louisiana	6
13	Lake Charles	9
0	Selman Field	13
46	Camp Swift	0
12	Louisiana Tech	7
0	Maxwell Field	29
0	Selman Field	29
6	Corpus Christi	21
110	Total	133

Bergstrom Field
Austin, TX
(3-5-1)

6	Southwestern	6
7	Texas	13
13	Iowa	14
15	Hondo AAF	13
0	Corpus Christi	34
0	PDC	26

Bergstrom Field (cont'd)

18	Camp Hood	13
12	Camp Grant	0
0	Camp Cooke	14
75	Total	133

Camp Beale
Marysville, CA
(5-2-1) George Hurley

0	Stockton AB	0
14	Oregon State	14
13	Pacific	7
0	Fleet City	88
21	Williams Field	0
55	San Joaquin	0
24	Albany Field	7
21	Fresno State	13
148	Total	129

Camp Cooke
Camp Cooke, CA
(4-0-0)

46	Cal Poly	0
14	Albany Navy	13
44	California Ramblers	0
14	Bergstrom Field	0
118	Total	13

Camp Detrick
Frederick, MD
(4-4-0)

7	Fort Monroe	0
6	Camp Lee	33
0	Bulls School	7
0	Bainbridge	40
13	Edgewood Arsenal	7
21	Aberdeen Proving Grd.	0
21	Fort Monroe	0
25	Aberdeen Proving Grd.	31
93	Total	118

Camp Gordon Johnson
Tallahassee,FL
(1-2-1)

12	Torpedo Boat Base	0
0	Miami NAS	33
0	Fort McClellan	39
0	Jacksonville NTS	0
12	Total	72

Camp Grant
Camp Grant, IL
(1-3-0)

8	Loras	20
15	Granville D.B.	0
13	Ripon	33
0	Bergstrom	12
36	Total	65

Camp Hood - North
Gatesville, TX
(7-1-0)

21	South Camp Hood	6
12	Allen Academy	0
12	John Tarleton	0
6	Ellington Field	0
34	North Texas Aggies	7

Camp Hood – North *(cont'd)*

13	Fort Sill	0
18	SW Univ. of Texas	13
7	Hutchinson NAS	46
123	Total	72

Camp Hood – South
Gatesville, TX
(4-3-0)

6	North Camp Hood	21
20	John Tarleton	0
24	Fort Sill	0
13	Transport Carrier	18
21	Camp Swift	6
33	Fort Sill	0
0	Williams Field	2
117	Total	47

Camp Lee
Camp Lee, VA
(7-4-0) Ray Bedard

0	North Carolina	6
0	New York Giants	21
33	Camp Detrick	6
0	Bainbridge	27
7	Amphib. Training Base	21
27	Fort Bragg	18
27	Cherry Point	7
26	Bainbridge	0
7	Camp Peary	6
12	Amphib. Training Base	6
13	Camp Peary	0
152	Total	118

Camp Peary
Williamsburg, VA
(3-4-0)

6	Amphib Training Base	0
0	Camp Lee	13
40	Fort Monroe	0
12	Fort Bragg	0
0	Cherry Point	7
6	Camp Lee	7
14	Per. Dis. Command	21
78	Total	48

Cherry Point Marines
Cherry Point, NC
(3-7-0)

0	Jacksonville NAS	26
6	Oak Grove Marines	0
29	Camp Mackall	0
0	Third Air Force	20
14	North Carolina	20
0	Air Training Command	27
0	Camp Peary	27
7	Camp Lee	27
7	Camp Peary	0
0	Kessler Field	41
63	Total	188

Corpus Christi NAS
Corpus Christi, TX
(7-1-0) Moon Mullins

26	Rice	12
22	SMU	7
7	Jacksonville NAS	35

Corpus Christi NAS *(cont'd)*

34	Bergstrom Field	0
30	Pensacola NAS	0
26	Pensacola NAS	6
14	Jacksonville NAS	13
21	Barksdale AF	6
180	Total	80

Eastern Flying Training Command
Maxwell Field, Alabama
(6-4-1)

13	Barksdale Field	0
40	Gulfport Army AF	0
7	Auburn	0
7	Army JV	6
6	Mississippi State	16
19	Pensacola NAS	6
29	Barksdale Field	0
7	Kessler Field	14
7	Air Training Command	45
0	First Air Force	7
7	Pensacola NAS	7
142	Total	101

El Toro Marines
El Toro, CA
(8-2-0) R.E. Hanley

13	Hollywood Ramblers	12
68	Los Angeles Rangers	0
7	Fleet City	21
61	Camp Pendleton	0
20	Second Air Force	9
7	Air Training Command	0
20	San Diego NTS	0
7	St. Mary's Pre Flight	0
40	Fort Warren	7
25	Fleet City	48
268	Total	97

Ellington Field
Houston, TX
(1-4-1) L.A. Gray

7	Hondo Air Field	7
0	Texas A&M	13
0	Selman Field	13
0	North Camp Hood	6
19	Amarillo	6
6	Hondo Air Field	7
32	Total	52

Farragut Navy
Farragut, ID
(6-2-0)

36	Idaho Marines	0
18	Idaho	7
21	Montana	13
0	Fort Warren	27
14	Idaho	6
33	Bremerton Naval Base	0
7	Fort Lewis	13
18	Montana	13
147	Total	79

First Air Force
Mitchell Field, NY
(4-2-3) Jess Yarborough

7	Air Training Command	7
19	Fort Pierce	7
0	Third Air Force	10
0	Per. Dis. Command	7
7	Air Transport Command	7
6	Fourth Air Force	6
24	Air Training Command	6
15	Second Air Force	0
7	Eastern Flight Training	0
85	Total	50

Fleet City
Shoemaker, CA
(11-0-1) Bill Reinhart

48	El Toro Marines	25
77	San Joaquin	0
7	Second Air Force	0
21	El Toro Marines	7
88	Camp Beale	0
16	Hollywood Ramblers	0
21	Fort Warren	9
13	St. Mary's Pre Flight	13
41	Los Angeles Broncos	6
26	San Jose State	0
20	Fourth Air Force	10
23	P. H. All Stars	7
401	Total	75

Fletcher General Hospital
Cambridge, Ohio
(3-4-0)

0	Ohio Wesleyan	31
14	Rio Grande	0
0	Ohio State B team	21
25	Washington-Jefferson	0
14	Washington-Jefferson	0
0	Wright Field	31
0	Muskingum	6
53	Total	108

Fort Benning Rec. Center
Fort Benning, GA
(3-1-0)

26	Tuskegee Air Field	0
7	Tuskegee Air Field	18
26	Fort McClellan	0
21	Fort McClellan	6
80	Total	24

Fort Benning Infantry
Fort Benning, GA
(4-4-1)

0	Air Training Command	27
21	Great Lakes	12
26	Kessler Field	7
0	Kessler Field	0
7	Jacksonville NAS	33
13	Fort Pierce	14
7	Air Transport Command	23
14	Jacksonville NAS	7
40	Fort Pierce	6
128	Total	129

Fort Bragg
Mendocino, CA
(3-3-0)

27	Camp Lee	18
0	Amphib Training Base	27
0	Camp Peary	12
18	Camp Lee	27
37	Newberry	0
20	Bainbridge	14
102	Total	98

Fort McClellan
Anniston, Alabama
(4-3-0)

7	Georgia Tech JV	0
0	Fort Benning Rec.	26
6	Alabama B team	7
14	Alabama B team	6
39	Camp Gordon Johnson	0
10	Miami NAS	7
6	Fort Benning Rec.	21
82	Total	67

Fort Monroe
Fort Monroe, VA
(0-6-0) Joe Murray

0	Catawba	34
7	Kinston Marines	13
0	Camp Detrick	7
0	Camp Peary	40
0	Oak Grove Marines	7
0	Camp Detrick	21
7	Total	122

Fort Pierce
Fort Pierce, FL
(3-9-0) Hampton Pool

10	Air Training Command	13
7	First Air Force	19
7	Air Training Command	19
6	Jacksonville NAS	13
26	Third Air Force	12
7	Jacksonville NAS	35
7	Pers. Dis. Command	16
14	Fort Benning	13
7	Amphib Training Base	27
21	Kessler Field	7
6	Fort Benning	40
0	Amphib. Training Base	20
118	Total	234

Fort Riley
Fort Riley, KS
(1-6-0)

0	Kearney Air Field	20
0	Washburn	19
0	Kansas B team	12
13	Wichita	38
0	Hutchinson	39
18	Kearney Air Field	13
7	St. Louis University	14
38	Total	155

Fort Sill
Fort Sill, OK
(0-5-1)

0	Ada	26
6	Ada	6
0	South Camp Hood	24
0	North Camp Hood	13
0	Hutchinson NAS	39
0	South Camp Hood	33
6	Total	141

Fort Warren
Cheyenne, WY
(4-6-0) Willis Smith

6	Colorado	0
0	Fourth Air Force	25
0	Second Air Force	19
61	Colorado State	6
0	Minnesota	14
28	Hondo Air Field	26
9	Fleet City	21
27	Farragut	0
14	Great Lakes	47
7	El Toro	40
152	Total	198

Fourth Air Force
Riverside, CA
(5-3-1) John Baker

25	Fort Warren	0
17	Second Air Force	14
21	Air Training Command	14
20	St. Mary's Pre Flight	7
7	Air Transport Command	19
6	First Air Force	6
7	Pers. Dis. Command	9
10	Fleet City	20
20	Third Air Force	7
123	Total	96

Goldman Field
Goldman Field, KY
(7-1-0)

12	Camp Lejeune	0
39	Lincoln	7
62	Bluefield	7
7	Wilberforce	3
28	Fort Wood	0
24	Tennessee State	45
33	Southern	21
238	Total	83

Great Bend Field
Great Bend, KS
(3-4-0) William Jacobs

6	Hutchinson NAS	20
0	Hondo AAF	27
45	Fort Riley	6
12	Kearney Air Field	0
33	Ada	6
13	Nevada	26
7	Camp Hood	21
116	Total	106

Goldman Field
Great Lakes
Great Lakes, IL

2	Michigan	27
0	Wisconsin	0
6	Purdue	20
12	Fort Benning	21
37	Marquette	20
39	Western Michigan	0
12	Illinois	6
27	Michigan State	7
47	Fort Warren	14
39	Notre Dame	2
221	Total	129

Gulfport Army Air Field
Gulfport, MS
(2-5-0)

7	Pensacola	20
13	Selman Field	7
32	Homestead Field	0
0	Eastern Fly. Command	40
31	Selman Field	46
0	Kessler Field	14
7	Pensacola	26
90	Total	153

Homestead Field
(1-3-0)

0	Camp Blanding	26
0	Miami NTS	53
13	Miami AAF	0
0	Gulfport Field	32

Hondo Army Air Field
Hondo, TX
(6-4-1) Bob Coe

7	Ellington Field	7
6	Oklahoma	21
13	Bergstrom	15
27	Great Bend	0
26	Fort Warren	28
7	Ellington Field	6
18	Camp Swift	0
13	S.B. Marines	7
12	North Texas	0
19	Southwestern	7
18	Tulsa	20
166	Total	111

Hutchinson Naval Air Station
Hutchinson, KS
(8-0-0) Kenneth Gleason

33	Missouri B team	7
20	Great Bend	6
15	Olathe NAS	0
54	Sterling	0
39	Fort Riley	0
39	Fort Sill	0
39	Pittsburgh	0
46	North Camp Hood	7
285	Total	20

Jacksonville Naval Training Station
Jacksonville, FL
(9-2-1) Jim Tatum

35	Miami NTC	6
26	Cherry Point Marines	0
35	Corpus Christi	7
13	Fort Pierce	6
61	Miami NAS	0
35	Fort Pierce	7
33	Fort Benning	7
13	Corpus Christi	14
48	Pensacola NAS	0
7	Fort Benning	14
48	Pensacola NAS	0
0	Camp Johnson	0
354	Total	61

Kearney Army Air Field
Kearney, Nebraska
(3-4-0) John Nucatola

19	Herrington	6
13	Drake	40
20	Fort Riley	0
24	Dalhart AAF	8
0	Great Bend AAF	12
13	Fort Riley	18
6	Wichita	34
95	Total	118

Kessler Field
Biloxi, MS
(3-7-1) James Coffis

0	Air Training Command	29
0	Alabama	21
13	Second Air Force	28
7	Missouri	41
7	Fort Benning	26
0	Fort Benning	0
14	Gulfport	0
0	Third Air Force	42
14	Maxwell Field	7
7	Fort Pierce	21
41	Cherry Point	0
103	Total	215

Kinston Marines
Kinston, NC
(1-3-0)

13	Fort Monroe	7
0	Catawba	21
6	Oak Grove Marines	10
6	North Carolina JV	9
25	Total	47

Lake Charles Army Air Field
Lake Charles, LA
(1-4-0)

2	Louisiana Tech	7
21	St. Ives	7
0	NW Louisiana	7
7	Selman Field	18
9	Barksdale	13
39	Total	52

Las Vegas Army Air Field
Las Vegas, Nevada
(1-4-0) L.A. Anton

0	Modesto JC	20
8	San Jose State	13
19	San Joaquin State	0
7	Williams AAF	19
0	Nevada	40
34	Total	92

Miami Naval Air Station
Miami, FL
(1-30)

0	Jacksonville NAS	61
33	Camp Johnson	0
6	PDC	45
7	Fort McClellan	10
46	Total	116

Minter Field
Bakersfield, CA
(2-1-1)

0	Fresno State	0
12	Stockton Air Base	0
6	California Rams	13
19	Cal Poly	0
37	Total	13

Oak Grove Marines
(3-3-1)

0	Catawba	20
0	Bogue Field	6
0	Cherry Point	6
10	Kinston Marines	6
7	Fort Monroe	0
0	Oceana NAS	0
20	Camp Mackall	6
37	Total	44

Oak Ridge Military
Oak Ridge, TN
(4-1-0)

27	Appalachian	7
12	Tennessee Tech	6
52	Camp Campbell	0
13	Milligan	6
6	Camp Campbell	32
110	Total	51

Oceana NAS
Richmond, VA
(0-3-1)

0	Oak Grove Marines	0
12	Richmond	28
0	Virginia	40
14	Bainbridge	53
26	Total	121

Olathe Naval Air Station
Olathe, KS
(3-3-0) Roy Engle

19	Washburn	0
32	Kansas State	14
0	Hutchinson	15

Olathe NAS *(cont'd)*

13	St. Louis U.	19
26	Loras	18
7	Missouri B team	25
97	Total	91

Pensacola Air Base
Pensacola, FL
(2-7-1)

30	Gulfport AAF	7
6	Clemson	7
6	Corpus Christi	30
6	Corpus Christi	26
26	Gulfport AAF	7
6	Maxwell Field	19
0	Jacksonville NAS	48
6	Alabama	55
0	Jacksonville NAS	48
7	Eastern Fly. Training	7
83	Total	254

Personnel District Command
Louisville, KY
(7-4-0) Wally Marks

27	Third Air Force	9
0	Army	32
8	Air Transport Command	15
7	First Air Force	0
0	Second Air Force	13
26	Troop C. Command	0
16	Fort Pierce	7
9	Fourth Air Force	7
45	Miami NAS	0
21	Camp Peary	14
0	Air Training Command	14
159	Total	111

St. Mary's Pre Flight
St. Mary's, CA
(2-4-1) Bernie Masterson

69	Pacific	0
14	USC	26
7	Fourth Air Force	20
13	UCLA	6
13	Fleet City	13
0	El Toro Marines	7
0	California	6
116	Total	78

San Diego Naval Training Center
San Diego, CA
(4-2-0) J.N. Stahley

14	UCLA	20
33	USC	6
61	Compton	0
0	El Toro Marines	30
34	Goleta Marines	0
19	San Diego Bombers	0
161	Total	56

1945 Season *(cont'd)*

Santa Barbara Marines
Santa Barbara, CA
(5-2-1) Joe Reiner

7	Pacific	7
25	Minter Field	0
20	Albany Naval Yard	12
14	Nevada	19
6	Fresno State	0
42	Caltech	0
40	Compton	7
6	Hondo AAF	13
160	Total	58

Second Air Force
Colorado Springs, CO
(3-7-0) Ed Walker

14	Fourth Air Force	17
0	Fleet City	7
19	Fort Warren	0
28	Kessler Field	13
9	El Toro Marines	20
13	Pers. Dis. Command	0
0	Third Air Force	33
0	Air Transport Command	15
0	First Air Force	15
7	Air Training Command	37
90	Total	157

Selman Field
Monroe, LA
(7-1-0) B.E. Wilson

12	NW Louisiana	9
13	Ellington Field	0
18	Lake Charles	7
7	Gulfport AB	13
13	Barksdale Field	0
46	Gulfport AB	31
13	NW Louisiana	0
10	Barksdale	0
132	Total	60

Stockton Army Air Base
Stockton, CA
(2-4-2)

12	Pacific	0
0	Camp Beale	0
0	St. Mary's	26
27	McClellan Field	9
0	Minter Field	12
20	Albany Navy	20
7	Compton JC	19
19	Stanford	13
85	Total	99

Third Air Force
Tampa, FL
(7-2-1) Quinn Decker

27	Pers. Dis. Command	9
39	Miami NAS	0
19	First Air Force	0
20	Cherry Point	0
12	Fort Pierce	26
33	Second Air Force	0
42	Kessler Field	0

Third Air Force *(cont'd)*

7	Air Training Command	7
15	Air Transport Command	6
7	Fourth Air Force	10
221	Total	58

Tuskegee Air Field
Tuskegee, Alabama
(4-2-0)

26	Camp Lejeune	0
6	Fort Benning	26
18	Fort Benning	7
0	Macdill Field	6
14	North Carolina College	0
14	US Sub Base	7
72	Total	46

U.S. Sub Base
New London, CT
(4-4-0)

13	Quincy Pros	0
26	New Bedford Pros	0
32	Worcester	0
0	Cornell	39
7	Melville P. T. Base	32
18	Harvard	7
6	Holy Cross	20
7	Tuskegee Air Base	14
109	Total	112

Williams Field
Williams, AZ
(2-3-0)

31	Hondo Air Base	6
6	USC JV	26
0	Camp Beale	21
6	Arizona	30
2	Camp Hood	0
45	Total	83

Winnipeg Bombers
Winnipeg, Ontario
(4-1-0)

13	Minot	19
27	North Dakota State	0
21	North Dakota State	16
40	Bemidji	7
28	Concordia College	7
129	Total	49

Wright Field
Dayton, OH
(3-2-0)

0	Miami (OH)	14
0	Ohio State B team	18
6	Duke B team	0
25	Purdue B team	7
31	Fletcher GH	0
62	Total	39

PART V

Major College Football Conferences

ATLANTIC COAST CONFERENCE (1953–2003). The ACC was organized in 1953 by six members of the Southern Conference who banded together with Maryland and Virginia to form the new conference. In 2003, the ACC announced the addition of three more teams: Virginia Tech, Miami (FL), and Boston College, all from the Big East joining the ACC beginning with the 2004 and 2005 seasons.

1953		Conference		Overall	
1.	Maryland	3-0-0	1.000	10-1-0	.909
1.	Duke	4-0-0	1.000	7-2-1	.750
3.	S. Carolina	2-3-0	.400	7-3-0	.700
3.	N. Carolina	2-3-0	.400	4-6-0	.400
3.	Wake Forest	2-3-0	.400	3-6-1	.350
6.	Clemson	1-2-0	.333	3-5-1	.389
7.	NC State	0-3-0	.000	1-9-0	.100
	Virginia	----------------		1-8-0	.111

Virginia not eligible for title in 1953.
Non-conference record 21-18-3 .536

1954					
1.	Duke	4-0-0	1.000	8-2-1	.773
2.	Maryland	4-0-1	.900	7-2-1	.750
3.	N. Carolina	4-2-0	.667	4-5-1	.450
4.	S. Carolina	3-3-0	.500	6-4-0	.600
5.	Clemson	1-2-0	.333	5-5-0	.500
6.	Wake Forest	1-4-1	.250	2-7-1	.250
7.	Virginia	0-2-0	.000	3-6-0	.333
7.	NC State	0-4-0	.000	2-8-0	.200

Non-conference record 20-22-2 .477

1955					
1.	Maryland	4-0-0	1.000	10-1-0	.909
1.	Duke	4-0-0	1.000	7-2-1	.750
3.	Clemson	3-1-0	.750	7-3-0	.700
4.	N. Carolina	3-3-0	.500	3-7-0	.300
4.	Wake Forest	3-3-1	.500	5-4-1	.550
6.	S. Carolina	1-5-0	.167	3-6-0	.333
6.	NC State	0-2-1	.167	4-5-1	.450
8.	Virginia	0-4-0	.000	1-9-0	.100

Non-conference record 22-19-1 .536

1956					
1.	Clemson	4-0-1	.900	7-2-2	.727
2.	Duke	4-1-0	.800	5-4-1	.545
3.	S. Carolina	5-2-0	.714	7-3-0	.700
4.	Maryland	2-2-1	.500	2-7-1	.250
5.	N. Carolina	2-3-1	.417	2-7-1	.250
6.	NC State	2-4-0	.333	3-7-0	.300
7.	Wake Forest	1-5-1	.214	2-5-3	.350
8.	Virginia	1-4-0	.200	3-7-0	.300

Non-conference record 10-21-4 .343

1957					
1.	NC State	5-0-1	.917	7-1-2	.800
2.	Duke	5-1-1	.786	6-3-2	.636
3.	Clemson	4-3-0	.571	7-3-0	.700
3.	N. Carolina	4-3-0	.571	6-4-0	.600
3.	Maryland	4-3-0	.571	5-5-0	.500
6.	Virginia	2-4-0	.333	3-6-1	.350
7.	S. Carolina	2-5-0	.286	5-5-0	.500
8.	Wake Forest	0-7-0	.000	0-10-0	.000

Non-conference record 13-11-3 .537

1958					
1.	Clemson	5-1-0	.833	8-3-0	.727
2.	S. Carolina	5-2-0	.714	7-3-0	.700
3.	Duke	3-2-0	.600	5-5-0	.500
4.	N. Carolina	4-3-0	.571	6-4-0	.600
5.	Maryland	3-3-0	.500	4-6-0	.400
6.	Wake Forest	2-4-0	.333	3-7-0	.300
7.	NC State	2-5-0	.286	2-7-1	.250
8.	Virginia	1-5-0	.167	1-9-0	.100

Non-conference record 11-19-1 .371

1959					
1.	Clemson	6-1-0	.857	9-2-0	.818
2.	N. Carolina	5-2-0	.714	5-5-0	.500
3.	Maryland	4-2-0	.667	5-5-0	.500
4.	Wake Forest	4-3-0	.571	6-4-0	.600
4.	S. Carolina	4-3-0	.571	6-4-0	.600
6.	Duke	2-3-0	.400	4-6-0	.400
7.	NC State	0-6-0	.000	1-9-0	.100
7.	Virginia	0-5-0	.000	0-10-0	.000

Non-conference record 11-20-0 .355

1960					
1.	Duke	5-1-0	.833	8-3-0	.727
2.	NC State	4-1-1	.750	6-3-1	.650
3.	Maryland	5-2-0	.714	6-4-0	.600
4.	Clemson	4-2-0	.667	6-4-0	.600
5.	S. Carolina	3-3-1	.500	3-6-1	.350
6.	N. Carolina	2-5-0	.286	3-7-0	.300
6.	Wake Forest	2-5-0	.286	2-8-0	.200
8.	Virginia	0-6-0	.000	0-10-0	.000

Non-conference record 9-20-0 .310

1961					
1.	Duke	5-1-0	.833	7-3-0	.700
2.	N. Carolina	4-3-0	.571	5 5 0	.500
3.	Maryland	3-3-0	.500	7-3-0	.700
3.	Clemson	3-3-0	.500	5-5-0	.500
5.	NC State	3-4-0	.429	4-6-0	.400
5.	S. Carolina	3-4-0	.429	4-6-0	.400
5.	Wake Forest	3-4-0	.429	4-6-0	.400
8.	Virginia	2-4-0	.333	4-6-0	.400

Non-conference record 14-14-0 .500

1962					
1.	Duke	6-0-0	1.000	8-2-0	.800
2.	Clemson	5-1-0	.833	6-4-0	.600
3.	Maryland	5-2-0	.714	6-4-0	.600
4.	S. Carolina	3-4-0	.429	4-5-1	.450
4.	NC State	3-4-0	.429	3-6-1	.350
4.	N. Carolina	3-4-0	.429	3-7-0	.300
7.	Virginia	1-4-0	.200	5-5-0	.500
8.	Wake Forest	0-7-0	.000	0-10-0	.000

Non-conference record 9-17-2 .358

1963					
1.	N. Carolina	6-1-0	.857	9-2-0	.818
1.	NC State	6-1-0	.857	8-3-0	.727
3.	Duke	5-2-0	.714	5-4-1	.550
3.	Clemson	5-2-0	.714	5-4-1	.550
5.	Maryland	2-5-0	.286	3-7-0	.300
6.	S. Carolina	1-5-1	.214	1-8-1	.150
7.	Wake Forest	1-5-0	.167	1-9-0	.100
8.	Virginia	0-5-1	.083	2-7-1	.250

Non-conference record 8-18-2 .321

1964					
1.	NC State	5-2-0	.714	5-5-0	.500
2.	Duke	3-2-1	.583	4-5-1	.450
3.	Maryland	4-3-0	.571	5-5-0	.500
3	N. Carolina	4-3-0	.571	5-5-0	.500
3.	Wake Forest	4-3-0	.571	5-5-0	.500
6.	S. Carolina	2-3-1	.417	3-5-2	.400
7.	Clemson	2-4-0	.333	3-7-0	.300
8.	Virginia	1-5-0	.167	5-5-0	.500

Non-conference record 10-17-1 .375

1965		Conference		Overall	
1.	Duke	4-2-0	.667	6-4-0	.600
1.	S. Carolina	4-2-0	.667	5-5-0	.500
3.	NC State	4-3-0	.571	6-4-0	.600
3.	Clemson	4-3-0	.571	5-5-0	.500
5.	N. Carolina	3-3-0	.500	4-6-0	.400
5.	Maryland	3-3-0	.500	4-6-0	.400
7.	Virginia1	2-4-0	.333	4-6-0	.400
8.	Wake Forest	1-5-0	.167	3-7-0	.300

Non-conference record 12-18-0 .400

1966					
1.	Clemson	6-1-0	.857	6-4-0	.600
2.	NC State	5-2-0	.714	5-5-0	.500
3.	Virginia	3-3-0	.500	4-6-0	.400
3.	Maryland	3-3-0	.500	4-6-0	.400
5.	Duke	2-3-0	.400	5-5-0	.500
6.	Wake Forest	2-4-0	.333	3-7-0	.300
7.	S. Carolina	1-3-0	.250	1-9-0	.100
8.	N. Carolina	1-4-0	.200	2-8-0	.200

Non-conference record 7-27-0 .206

1967					
1.	Clemson	6-0-0	1.000	6-4-0	.600
2.	NC State	5-1-0	.833	9-2-0	.818
3.	S. Carolina	4-2-0	.667	5-5-0	.500
4.	Virginia	3-3-0	.500	5-5-0	.500
5.	Wake Forest	3-4-0	.429	4-6-0	.400
6.	Duke	2-4-0	.333	4-6-0	.400
7.	N. Carolina	2-5-0	.286	2-8-0	.200
8.	Maryland	0-6-0	.000	0-9-0	.000

Non-conference record 10-20-0 .333

1968					
1.	NC State	6-1-0	.857	6-4-0	.600
2.	Clemson	4-1-1	.750	4-5-1	.450
3.	Virginia	3-2-0	.600	7-3-0	.700
4.	S. Carolina	4-3-0	.571	4-6-0	.400
5.	Duke	3-4-0	.429	4-6-0	.400
6.	Wake Forest	2-3-1	.417	2-7-1	.250
7.	Maryland	2-5-0	.286	2-8-0	.200
8.	N. Carolina	1-6-0	.143	3-7-0	.300

Non-conference record 7-21-0 .250

1969					
1.	S. Carolina	6-0-0	1.000	7-4-0	.636
2.	NC State	3-2-1	.583	3-6-1	.350
3.	Clemson	3-3-0	.500	4-6-0	.400
3.	Duke	3-3-1	.500	3-6-1	.350
3.	Maryland	3-3-0	.500	3-7-0	.300
3.	N. Carolina	3-3-0	.500	5-5-0	.500
7.	Wake Forest	2-5-0	.286	3-7-0	.300
8.	Virginia	1-5-0	.167	3-7-0	.300

Non-conference record 7-24-0 .226

1970					
1.	Wake Forest	5-1-0	.833	6-5-0	.545
2.	Duke	5-2-0	.714	6-5-0	.545
2.	N. Carolina	5-2-0	.714	8-4-0	.667
4.	S. Carolina	3-2-1	.583	4-6-1	.409
5.	NC State	2-3-1	.417	3-7-1	.318
6.	Clemson	2-4-0	.333	3-8-0	.273
6.	Maryland	2-4-0	.333	2-9-0	.182
8.	Virginia	0-6-0	.000	5-6-0	.455

Non-conference record 13-26-0 .333

South Carolina leaves the ACC after the 1970 season.

1971		Conference		Overall	
1.	N. Carolina	6-0-0	1.000	9-3-0	.750
2.	Clemson	4-2-0	.667	5-6-0	.455
3.	Duke	2-3-0	.400	6-5-0	.545
3.	Virginia	2-3-0	.400	3-8-0	.273
3.	Wake Forest	2-3-0	.400	6-5-0	.545
6.	NC State	2-4-0	.333	3-8-0	.273
7.	Maryland	1-4-0	.200	2-9-0	.182

Non-conference record 15-25-0 .375

1972					
1.	N. Carolina	6-0-0	1.000	11-1-0	.917
2.	NC State	4-1-1	.750	8-3-1	.708
3.	Maryland	3-2-1	.583	5-5-1	.500
4.	Duke	3-3-0	.500	5-6-0	.455
5.	Clemson	2-4-0	.333	4-7-0	.364
6.	Virginia	1-5-0	.167	4-7-0	.364
6.	Wake Forest	1-5-0	.167	2-9-0	.182

Non-conference record 19-18-0 .514

1973					
1.	NC State	6-0-0	1.000	9-3-0	.750
2.	Maryland	5-1-0	.833	8-4-0	.667
3.	Clemson	4-2-0	.667	5-6-0	.455
4.	Virginia	3-3-0	.500	4-7-0	.364
5.	Duke	1-4-1	.250	2-8-1	.227
6.	N. Carolina	1-5-0	.167	4-7-0	.364
7.	Wake Forest	0-5-1	.083	1-9-1	.136

Non-conference record 13-24-0 .351

1974					
1.	Maryland	6-0-0	1.000	8-4-0	.667
2.	NC State	4-2-0	.667	9-2-1	.864
2.	Clemson	4-2-0	.667	7-4-0	.636
2.	N. Carolina	4-2-0	.667	7-5-0	.583
5.	Duke	2-4-0	.333	6-5-0	.545
6.	Virginia	1-5-0	.167	4-7-0	.364
7.	Wake Forest	0-6-0	.000	1-10-0	.091

Non-conference record 21-16-1 .566

1975					
1.	Maryland	5-0-0	1.000	9-2-1	.917
2.	Duke	3-0-2	.800	4-5-2	.455
3.	NC State	2-2-1	.500	7-4-1	.625
3.	Wake Forest	3-3-0	.500	3-8-0	.273
5.	Clemson	2-3-0	.400	2-9-0	.182
6.	N. Carolina	1-4-1	.250	3-7-1	.318
7.	Virginia	0-5-0-	.000	1-10-0	.091

Non-conference record 13-28-1 .321

1976					
1.	Maryland	5-0-0	1.000	11-1-0	.917
2.	N. Carolina	4-1-0	.800	9-3-0	.750
3.	Wake Forest	3-3-0	.500	5-6-0	.455
4.	Duke	2-3-1	.417	5-5-1	.500
5.	NC State	2-3-0	.400	3-7-1	.318
6.	Virginia	1-4-0	.200	2-9-0	.182
7.	Clemson	0-4-1	.100	3-6-2	.364

Non-conference record 21-19-2 .524

1977					
1.	N. Carolina	5-0-1	.917	8-3-1	.773
2.	Clemson	4-1-1	.750	8-3-1	.773
3.	NC State	4-2-0	.667	8-4-0	.667
3.	Maryland	4-2-0	.667	8-4-0	.667
5.	Duke	2-4-0	.667	5-6-0	.455
6.	Virginia	1-5-0	.167	1-9-1	.136
7.	Wake Forest	0-6-0	.000	1-10-0	.091

Non-conference record 19-19-1 .500

— 336 —

1978

		Conference		Overall	
1.	Clemson	6-0-0	1.000	11-1-0	.917
2.	Maryland	5-1-0	.833	9-3-0	.750
3.	NC State	4-2-0	.667	9-3-0	.750
4.	N. Carolina	3-3-0	.500	5-6-0	.455
5.	Duke	2-4-0	.333	4-7-0	.364
6.	Wake Forest	1-5-0	.167	1-10-0	.091
7.	Virginia	0-6-0	.000	2-9-0	.182

Non-conference record 20-18-0 .526

1979

		Conference		Overall	
1.	NC State	5-1-0	.833	7-4-0	.636
2.	Clemson	4-2-0	.667	8-4-0	.667
2.	Maryland	4-2-0	.667	7-4-0	.636
2.	Wake Forest	4-2-0	.667	8-4-0	.667
5.	N. Carolina	3-3-0	.500	8-3-1	.708
6.	Virginia	2-4-0	.333	2-8-1	.227
7.	Duke	0-6-0	.000	2-8-1	.227
	Ga. Tech	-----------------		4-6-1	.409

Ga. Tech joins the ACC; not eligible for title until 1983.
Non-conference record 20-15-3 .565

1980

		Conference		Overall	
1.	N. Carolina	6-0-0	1.000	11-1-0	.917
2.	Maryland	5-1-0	.833	8-4-0	.667
3.	NC State	3-3-0	.500	6-5-0	.545
4.	Clemson	2-4-0	.333	6-5-0	.545
4.	Virginia	2-4-0	.333	4-7-0	.364
4.	Wake Forest	2-4-0	.333	5-6-0	.455
7.	Duke	1-5-0	.167	2-9-0	.182
	Ga. Tech	-----------------		1-9-1	.136

Non-conference record 21-16-0 .568

1981

		Conference		Overall	
1.	Clemson	6-0-0	1.000	12-0-0	1.000
2.	N. Carolina	5-1-0	.833	10-2-0	.833
3.	Maryland	4-2-0	.667	4-6-1	.409
4.	Duke	3-3-0	.500	6-5-0	.545
5.	NC State	2-4-0	.333	4-7-0	.364
6.	Wake Forest	1-5-0	.167	4-7-0	.364
7.	Virginia	0-6-0	.000	1-10-0	.091
	Ga. Tech	-----------------		1-10-0	.091

Non-conference record 20-16-1 .554

1982

		Conference		Overall	
1.	Clemson	6-0-0	1.000	9-1-1	.864
2.	Maryland	5-1-0	.833	8-4-0	.667
3.	N. Carolina	3-3-0	.500	8-4-0	.667
3.	Duke	3-3-0	.500	6-5-0	.545
3.	NC State	3-3-0	.500	6-5-0	.545
6.	Virginia	1-5-0	.167	2-9-0	.182
7.	Wake Forest	0-6-0	.000	3-8-0	.273
	Ga. Tech	-----------------		6-5-0	.545

Non-conference record 21-15-1 .581

1983

		Conference		Overall	
1.	Maryland	5-0-0	1.000	8-4-0	.667
2.	N. Carolina	4-2-0	.667	8-4-0	.667
3.	Ga. Tech	3-2-0	.600	3-8-0	.273
4.	Duke	3-3-0	.500	3-8-0	.273
4.	Virginia	3-3-0	.500	6-5-0	.545
6.	NC State	1-5-0	.167	3-8-0	.273
6.	Wake Forest	1-5-0	.167	4-7-0	.364
	Clemson*	-----------------		9-1-1	.864

*Clemson on NCAA suspension.
Non-conference record 15-24-0 .385

1984

		Conference		Overall	
1.	Maryland	5-0-0	1.000	9-3-0	.750
2.	Virginia	3-1-2	.667	8-2-2	.750
3.	N. Carolina	3-2-1	.583	5-5-1	.500
4.	Wake Forest	3-3-0	.500	6-5-0	.545
4.	Ga. Tech	2-2-1	.500	6-4-1	.591
6.	Duke	1-5-0	.167	2-9-0	.182
6.	NC State	1-5-0	.167	3-8-0	.273
	Clemson*	-----------------		7-4-0	.636

*Clemson on NCAA suspension.
Non-conference record 21-18-0 .538

1985

		Conference		Overall	
1.	Maryland	6-0-0	1.000	9-3-0	.750
2.	Ga. Tech	5-1-0	.833	9-2-1	.792
3.	Clemson	4-3-0	.571	6-6-0	.500
3.	Virginia	4-3-0	.571	6-5-0	.545
5.	N. Carolina	3-4-0	.429	5-6-0	.455
6.	Duke	2-5-0	.286	4-7-0	.364
6.	NC State	2-5-0	.286	3-8-0	.273
8.	Wake Forest	1-6-0	.143	4-7-0	.364

Non-conference record 19-17-1 .527

1986

		Conference		Overall	
1.	Clemson	5-1-1	.786	8-2-2	.750
2.	N. Carolina	5-2-0	.714	7-5-0	.583
2.	NC State	5-2-0	.714	8-3-1	.708
4.	Ga. Tech	3-3-0	.500	5-5-1	.500
5.	Maryland	2-3-1	.417	5-5-1	.500
6.	Duke	2-5-0	.286	4-7-0	.364
6.	Virginia	2-5-0	.286	3-8-0	.273
6.	Wake Forest	2-5-0	.286	5-6-0	.455

Non-conference record 19-15-3 .554

1987

		Conference		Overall	
1.	Clemson	6-1-0	.857	10-2-0	.833
2.	Virginia	5-2-0	.714	8-4-0	.667
3.	Wake Forest	4-3-0	.571	7-4-0	.636
3.	NC State	4-3-0	.571	4-7-0	.364
5.	Maryland	3-3-0	.500	4-7-0	.364
6.	N. Carolina	3-4-0	.429	5-6-0	.455
7.	Duke	2-5-0	.286	5-6-0	.455
8.	Ga. Tech	0-6-0	.000	2-9-0	.182

Non-conference record 18-18-0 .500

1988

		Conference		Overall	
1.	Clemson	6-1-0	.857	10-2-0	.833
2.	Virginia	5-2-0	.714	7-4-1	.625
3.	NC State	4-2-1	.643	8-3-1	.708
4.	Wake Forest	4-3-0	.571	6-4-1	.591
4.	Maryland	4-3-0	.571	5-6-0	.455
6.	Duke	3-3-1	.500	7-3-1	.682
7.	N. Carolina	1-6-0	.143	1-10-0	.091
8.	Ga. Tech	0-7-0	.000	3-8-0	.273

Non-conference record 20-13-2 .600

1989

		Conference		Overall	
1.	Virginia	6-1-0	.857	10-3-0	.769
1.	Duke	6-1-0	.857	8-4-0	.667
3.	Clemson	5-2-0	.714	10-2-0	.833
4.	Ga. Tech	4-3-0	.571	7-4-0	.636
4.	NC State	4-3-0	.571	7-5-0	.583
6.	Maryland	2-5-0	.286	3-7-1	.318
7.	Wake Forest	1-6-0	.143	2-8-1	.227
8.	N. Carolina	0-7-0	.000	1-10-0	.091

Non-conference record 20-15-2 .568

1990		Conference		Overall	
1.	Ga. Tech	6-0-1	.929	11-0-1	.958
2.	Clemson	5-2-0	.714	10-2-0	.833
2.	Virginia	5-2-0	.714	8-4-0	.667
4.	Maryland	4-3-0	.571	6-5-1	.542
5.	N. Carolina	3-3-1	.500	6-4-1	.591
6.	NC State	3-4-0	.429	7-5-0	.583
7.	Duke	1-6-0	.143	4-7-0	.364
8.	Wake Forest	0-7-0	.000	3-8-0	.273

Non-conference record 28-8-1 .770

1991					
1.	Clemson	6-0-1	.929	9-2-1	.792
2.	NC State	5-2-0	.714	9-3-0	.750
2.	Ga. Tech	5-2-0	.714	8-5-0	.615
4.	Virginia	4-2-1	.643	8-3-1	.708
5.	N. Carolina	3-4-0	.429	7-4-0	.636
6.	Maryland	2-5-0	.286	2-9-0	.182
7.	Wake Forest	1-6-0	.143	3-8-0	.273
7.	Duke	1-6-0	.143	4-6-1	.409
	Florida State	----------------		11-2-0	.846

Florida State joins the ACC, eligible for title in 1992.
Non-conference record 23-13-1 .635

1992					
1.	Florida State	8-0-0	1.000	11-1-0	.917
2.	NC State	6-2-0	.750	9-3-1	.731
3.	N. Carolina	5-3-0	.625	9-3-0	.750
4.	Wake Forest	4-4-0	.500	8-4-0	.667
4.	Virginia	4-4-0	.500	7-4-0	.636
4.	Ga. Tech	4-4-0	.500	5-6-0	.455
7.	Clemson	3-5-0	.375	5-6-0	.455
8.	Maryland	2-6-0	.250	3-8-0	.273
9.	Duke	0-8-0	.000	2-9-0	.182

Non-conference record 23-8-1 .734

1993					
1.	Florida State	8-0-0	1.000	12-1-0	.923
2.	N. Carolina	6-2-0	.750	10-3-0	.769
3.	Clemson	5-3-0	.625	9-3-0	.750
3.	Virginia	5-3-0	.625	7-5-0	.583
5.	NC State	4-4-0	.500	7-5-0	.583
6.	Ga. Tech	3-5-0	.375	5-6-0	.455
7.	Duke	2-6-0	.250	3-8-0	.273
7.	Maryland	2-6-0	.250	2-9-0	.182
9.	Wake Forest	1-7-0	.125	2-9-0	.182

Non-conference record 21-13-0 .618

1994					
1.	Florida State	8-0-0	1.000	10-1-1	.875
2.	NC State	6-2-0	.750	9-3-0	.750
3.	Virginia	5-3-0	.625	9-3-0	.750
3.	N. Carolina	5-3-0	.625	8-4-0	.667
3.	Duke	5-3-0	.625	8-4-0	.667
6.	Clemson	4-4-0	.500	5-6-0	.455
7.	Maryland	2-6-0	.250	4-7-0	.364
8.	Wake Forest	1-7-0	.125	3-8-0	.273
9.	Ga. Tech	0-8-0	.000	1-10-0	.091

Non-conference record 21-10-1 .672

1995		Conference		Overall	
1.	Florida State	7-1-0	.875	10-2-0	.833
1.	Virginia	7-1-0	.875	9-4-0	.692
3.	Clemson	6-2-0	.750	8-4-0	.667
4.	Ga. Tech	5-3-0	.625	6-5-0	.545
5.	N. Carolina	4-4-0	.500	7-5-0	.583
5.	Maryland	4-4-0	.500	6-5-0	.545
7.	NC State	2-6-0	.250	3-8-0	.273
8.	Duke	1-7-0	.125	3-8-0	.273
9.	Wake Forest	0-8-0	.000	1-10-0	.091

Non-conference record 17-15-0 .531

1996					
1.	Florida State	8-0-0	1.000	11-1-0	.917
2.	N. Carolina	6-2-0	.750	10-2-0	.833
2.	Clemson	6-2-0	.750	7-5-0	.583
4.	Virginia	5-3-0	.625	7-5-0	.583
5.	Ga. Tech	4-4-0	.500	5-6-0	.455
6.	Maryland	3-5-0	.375	5-6-0	.455
6.	NC State	3-5-0	.375	3-8-0	.273
8.	Wake Forest	1-7-0	.125	3-8-0	.273
9.	Duke	0-8-0	.000	0-11-0	.000

Non-conference record 15-16-0 .484

1997					
1.	Florida State	8-0-0	1.000	11-1-0	.917
2.	N. Carolina	7-1-0	.875	11-1-0	.917
3.	Virginia	5-3-0	.625	7-4-0	.636
3.	Ga. Tech	5-3-0	.625	7-5-0	.583
5.	Clemson	4-4-0	.500	7-5-0	.583
6.	NC State	3-5-0	.375	6-5-0	.545
6.	Wake Forest	3-5-0	.375	5-6-0	.455
8.	Maryland	1-7-0	.125	2-9-0	.182
9.	Duke	0-8-0	.000	2-9-0	.182

Non-conference record 22-9-0 .710

1998					
1.	Florida State	7-1-0	.875	11-2-0	.846
1.	Ga. Tech	7-1-0	.875	10-2-0	.833
3.	Virginia	6-2-0	.750	9-3-0	.750
4.	NC State	5-3-0	.625	7-5-0	.583
4.	N. Carolina	5-3-0	.625	7-5-0	.583
6.	Wake Forest	2-6-0	.250	3-8-0	.273
6.	Duke	2-6-0	.250	4-7-0	.364
8.	Clemson	1-7-0	.125	3-8-0	.273
8.	Maryland	1-7-0	.125	3-8-0	.273

Non-conference record 21-12-0 .636

1999					
1.	Florida State	8-0-0	1.000	12-0-0	1.000
2.	Ga. Tech	5-3-0	.625	8-4-0	.667
2.	Virginia	5-3-0	.625	7-5-0	.583
2.	Clemson	5-3-0	.625	6-6-0	.500
5.	Wake Forest	3-5-0	.375	7-5-0	.583
5.	NC State	3-5-0	.375	6-6-0	.500
5.	Duke	3-5-0	.375	3-8-0	.273
8.	Maryland	2-6-0	.250	5-6-0	.455
9.	N. Carolina	2-6-0	.250	3-8-0	.273

Non-conference record 21-12-0 .636

2000

		Conference		Overall	
1.	Florida State	8-0-0	1.000	11-2-0	.846
2.	Ga. Tech	6-2-0	.750	9-3-0	.750
2.	Clemson	6-2-0	.750	9-3-0	.750
4.	Virginia	5-3-0	.625	6-6-0	.500
5.	NC State	4-4-0	.500	8-4-0	.667
6.	N. Carolina	3-5-0	.375	6-5-0	.545
6.	Maryland	3-5-0	.375	5-6-0	.455
8.	Wake Forest	1-7-0	.125	2-9-0	.182
9.	Duke	0-8-0	.000	0-11-0	.000

Non-conference record 20-13-0 .606

2001

1.	Maryland	7-1-0	.875	10-2-0	.833
2.	Florida State	6-2-0	.750	8-4-0	.667
3.	N. Carolina	5-3-0	.625	8-5-0	.615
4.	NC State	4-4-0	.500	7-5-0	.583
4.	Ga. Tech	4-4-0	.500	8-5-0	.615
4.	Clemson	4-4-0	.500	7-5-0	.583
7.	Wake Forest	3-5-0	.375	6-5-0	.545
7.	Virginia	3-5-0	.375	5-7-0	.417
9.	Duke	0-8-0	.000	0-11-0	.000

Non-conference record 23-13-0 .639

2002

1.	Florida State	7-1-0	.875	9-5-0	.643
2.	Maryland	6-2-0	.750	11-3-0	.786
2.	Virginia	6-2-0	.750	9-5-0	.643
4.	NC State	5-3-0	.625	11-3-0	.786
5.	Clemson	4-4-0	.500	7-6-0	.538
5.	Georgia Tech	4-4-0	.500	7-6-0	.538
7.	Wake Forest	3-5-0	.375	7-6-0	.538
8.	N. Carolina	1-7-0	.125	3-9-0	.250
9.	Duke	0-8-0	.000	2-10-0	.167

Non-conference record 30-17-0 .638

2003

1.	Florida State	7-1-0	.875	10-3-0	.769
2.	Maryland	6-2-0	.750	10-3-0	.769
3.	Clemson	5-3-0	.625	9-4-0	.692
4.	NC State	4-4-0	.500	8-5-0	.615
4.	Virginia	4-4-0	.500	8-5-0	.615
4.	Georgia Tech	4-4-0	.500	7-6-0	.538
7.	Wake Forest	3-5-0	.375	5-7-0	.417
8.	Duke	2-6-0	.250	4-8-0	.333
9.	N. Carolina	1-7-0	.125	2-10-0	.167

Non-conference record: 27-15-0 .643

BIG EAST CONFERENCE (1991-2003). The Big East was organized in 1991, bringing together eight Eastern teams that had previously played as independents. By agreement among the teams, conference standings in 1991 and 1992 were based on the overall won-loss record; from 1993 on, conference standings are based on the conference won-loss record. In 2003, the Big East announced the loss of Virginia Tech, Miami, and Boston College to the ACC, and added Louisville, Cincinnati, and South Florida from Conference USA.

1991

Rank	School	Big East W-L-T	Pct.	Overall W-L-T	Pct.
1.	Miami	2-0-0	1.000	12-0-0	1.000
2.	Syracuse	5-0-0	1.000	10-2-0	.833
3.	Pittsburgh	3-2-0	.600	6-5-0	.545
3.	West Virginia	3-4-0	.429	6-5-0	.545
3.	Rutgers	2-3-0	.400	6-5-0	.545
6.	Virginia Tech	1-0-0	1.000	5-6-0	.455
7.	Boston College	2-4-0	.333	4-7-0	.364
8.	Temple	0-5-0	.000	2-9-0	.182

Non-conference record: 33-21-0 .611

1992

Rank	School	Big East W-L-T	Pct.	Overall W-L-T	Pct.
1.	Miami	4-0-0	1.000	11-1-0	.917
2.	Syracuse	6-1-0	.857	10-2-0	.833
3.	Boston College	2-1-1	.625	8-3-1	.708
4.	Rutgers	4-2-0	.667	7-4-0	.636
5.	West Virginia	2-3-1	.417	5-4-2	.545
6.	Pittsburgh	1-3-0	.250	3-9-0	.250
7.	Virginia Tech	1-4-0	.200	2-8-1	.227
8.	Temple	0-6-0	.000	1-10-0	.091

Non-conference record: 27-21-2 .560

1993

Rank	School	Big East W-L-T	Pct.	Overall W-L-T	Pct.
1.	West Virginia	7-0-0	1.000	11-1-0	.917
2.	Miami	6-1-0	.857	9-3-0	.750
3.	Boston College	5-2-0	.714	9-3-0	.750
4.	Virginia Tech	4-3-0	.571	9-3-0	.750
5.	Syracuse	3-4-0	.429	6-4-1	.591
6.	Pittsburgh	2-5-0	.286	3-8-0	.273
7.	Rutgers	1-6-0	.167	4-7-0	.364
8.	Temple	0-7-0	.000	1-10-0	.091

Non-conference record: 24-11-1 .686

1994

Rank	School	Big East W-L-T	Pct.	Overall W-L-T	Pct.
1.	Miami	7-0-0	1.000	10-2-0	.833
2.	Virginia Tech	5-2-0	.714	8-4-0	.667
3.	Syracuse	4-3-0	.571	7-4-0	.636
3.	West Virginia	4-3-0	.571	7-6-0	.538
5.	Boston College	3-3-1	.500	7-4-1	.625
6.	Rutgers	2-4-1	.357	5-5-1	.500
7.	Pittsburgh	2-5-0	.286	3-8-0	.273
8.	Temple	0-7-0	.000	2-9-0	.182

Non-conference record: 22-15-0 .595

1995

Rank	School	Big East W-L-T	Pct.	Overall W-L-T	Pct.
1.	Virginia Tech	6-1-0	.857	10-2-0	.833
2.	Syracuse	5-2-0	.714	9-3-0	.750
3.	West Virginia	4-3-0	.571	5-6-0	.455
3.	Boston College	4-3-0	.571	4-8-0	.333
5.	Rutgers	2-5-0	.286	4-7-0	.364
6.	Temple	1-6-0	.143	1-10-0	.091
7.	Pittsburgh	0-7-0	.000	2-9-0	.182
	Miami*	6-1-0	.857	8-3-0	.727

*Miami ineligible for title.
Non-conference record: 15-20-0 .428

1996

Rank	School	Big East W-L-T	Pct.	Overall W-L-T	Pct.
1.	Virginia Tech	6-1-0	.857	10-2-0	.833
1.	Miami	6-1-0	.857	9-3-0	.750
1.	Syracuse	6-1-0	.857	9-3-0	.750
4.	West Virginia	4-3-0	.571	8-4-0	.667
5.	Pittsburgh	3-4-0	.429	4-7-0	.364
6.	Boston College	2-5-0	.286	5-7-0	.417
7.	Rutgers	1-6-0	.143	2-9-0	.182
8.	Temple	0-7-0	.000	1-10-0	.091

Non-conference record: 20-17-0 .541

1997

Rank	School	Big East W-L-T	Pct.	Overall W-L-T	Pct.
1.	Syracuse	6-1-0	.857	9-4-0	.692
2.	Virginia Tech	5-2-0	.714	7-5-0	.583
3.	West Virginia	4-3-0	.571	6-6-0	.500
3.	Pittsburgh	4-3-0	.571	6-6-0	.500
5.	Miami	3-4-0	.429	5-6-0	.455
5.	Boston College	3-4-0	.429	4-7-0	.364
5.	Temple	3-4-0	.429	3-8-0	.273
8.	Rutgers	0-7-0	.000	0-11-0	.000

Non-conference record: 13-24-0 .351

1998

Rank	School	Big East W-L-T	Pct.	Overall W-L-T	Pct.
1.	Syracuse	6-1-0	.857	8-4-0	.667
2.	Miami	5-2-0	.714	9-3-0	.750
2.	Virginia Tech	5-2-0	.714	9-3-0	.750
2.	West Virginia	5-2-0	.714	8-4-0	.667
5.	Boston College	3-4-0	.429	4-7-0	.364
6.	Rutgers	2-5-0	.286	5-6-0	.455
6.	Temple	2-5-0	.286	2-9-0	.182
8.	Pittsburgh	0-7-0	.000	2-9-0	.182

Non-conference record: 19-17-0 .529

1999

Rank	School	Big East W-L-T	Pct.	Overall W-L-T	Pct.
1.	Virginia Tech	7-0-0	1.000	11-1-0	.917
2.	Miami	6-1-0	.857	9-4-0	.692
3.	Boston College	4-3-0	.571	8-4-0	.667
4.	Syracuse	3-4-0	.429	7-5-0	.583
4.	West Virginia	3-4-0	.429	4-7-0	.364
6.	Pittsburgh	2-5-0	.286	5-6-0	.455
6.	Temple	2-5-0	.286	2-9-0	.182
8.	Rutgers	1-6-0	.143	1-10-0	.091

Non-conference record: 19-18-0 .514

2000

Rank	School	Big East W-L-T	Pct.	Overall W-L-T	Pct.
1.	Miami	7-0-0	1.000	11-1-0	.917
2.	Virginia Tech	6-1-0	.857	11-1-0	.917
3.	Pittsburgh	4-3-0	.571	7-5-0	.583
3.	Syracuse	4-3-0	.571	6-5-0	.545
5.	Boston College	3-4-0	.429	7-5-0	.583
5.	West Virginia	3-4-0	.429	7-5-0	.583
7.	Temple	1-6-0	.143	4-7-0	.364
8.	Rutgers	0-7-0	.000	3-8-0	.273

Non-conference record: 28-9-0 .757

2001
1.	Miami	7-0-0	1.000	12-0-0	1.000
2.	Syracuse	6-1-0	.857	10-3-0	.769
3.	Virginia Tech	4-3-0	.571	8-4-0	.667
3.	Boston College	4-3-0	.571	8-4-0	.667
3.	Pittsburgh	4-3-0	.571	7-5-0	.583
6.	Temple	2-5-0	.286	4-7-0	.364
7.	West Virginia	1-6-0	.143	3-8-0	.273
8.	Rutgers	0-7-0	.000	2-9-0	.182

Non-conference: 26-12-0 .684

2002
1.	Miami	7-0-0	1.000	12-1-0	.923
2.	West Virginia	6-1-0	.857	9-4-0	.692
3.	Pittsburgh	5-2-0	.714	9-4-0	.692
4.	Virginia Tech	3-4-0	.429	10-4-0	.714
4.	Boston College	3-4-0	.429	9-4-0	.692
6.	Syracuse	2-5-0	.286	4-8-0	.333
6.	Temple	2-5-0	.286	4-8-0	.333
8.	Rutgers	0-7-0	.000	1-11-0	.083

Non-conference record: 30-16-0 .652

2003
1.	Miami	6-1-0	.857	11-2-0	.846
1.	West Virginia	6-1-0	.857	8-5-0	.615
3.	Pittsburgh	5-2-0	.714	8-5-0	.615
4.	Virginia Tech	4-3-0	.571	8-5-0	.615
5.	Boston College	3-4-0	.429	8-5-0	.615
6.	Syracuse	2-5-0	.286	6-6-0	.500
6.	Rutgers	2-5-0	.286	5-7-0	.417
8.	Temple	0-7-0	.000	1-11-0	.083

Non-conference record: 27-18-0 .600

BIG EAST W-L-T RECORDS BY DECADES

Decade	BC	Miami	Pitt	Rutgers	Syracuse	Temple	Va. Tech	W.Va.
1991-99	28-29-2	45-10-0	17-41-0	15-44-1	44-17-0	8-52-0	40-15-0	36-25-1
2000-03	13-15-0	27- 1-0	18-10 -0	2-26-0	14-14-0	5-23-0	17-11-0	16-12-0
Total	41-44-2	72-11-0	35-51-0	17-70-1	58-31-0	13-75-0	57-26-0	52-37-1
Pct.	.483	.867	407	.199	.652	.148	.687	.583
Titles		7.5			2		2.5	1

BIG EIGHT CONFERENCE (1928-1995) The Big Eight (earlier the Big Six, and then the Big Seven) was formed by Nebraska, Missouri, Oklahoma, Iowa State, Kansas and Kansas State, when all of these teams left the Missouri Valley Conference following the 1927 season. The Big Eight evolved into the Big Twelve after the 1995 season when Baylor, Texas, Texas A&M, and Texas Tech of the just-disbanded Southwest Conference joined with the Big Eight teams to form this expanded conference.

1928

		Conference		Overall	
1.	Nebraska	5-0-0	1.0-00	7-1-1	.822
2.	Missouri	3-2-0	.600	4-4-0	.500
2.	Oklahoma	3-2-0	.600	5-3-0	.625
4.	Iowa State	2-2-1	.500	2-5-1	.312
5.	Kansas	1-3-1	.300	2-4-2	.375
6.	Kansas State	0-5-0	.000	3-5-0	.375

Non-conference record: 9-8-2 .526

1929

		Conference		Overall	
1.	Nebraska	3-0-2	.800	4-1-3	.688
2.	Missouri	3-1-1	.700	5-2-1	.688
3.	Kansas State	3-2-0	.600	3-5-0	.375
4.	Oklahoma	2-2-1	.500	3-3-2	.500
5.	Kansas	2-3-0	.400	4-4-0	.500
6.	Iowa State	0-5-0	.000	1-7-0	.125

Non-conference record: 7-9-2 .444

1930

		Conference		Overall	
1.	Kansas	4-1-0	.800	6-2-0	.750
2.	Oklahoma	3-1-1	.700	4-3-1	.562
3.	Kansas State	3-2-0	.600	5-3-0	.625
4.	Nebraska	2-2-1	.500	4-3-2	.625
5.	Missouri	1-2-2	.400	2-5-2	.333
6.	Iowa State	0-5-0	.000	0-9-0	.000

Non-conference record: 8-12-1 .405

1931

		Conference		Overall	
1.	Nebraska	5-0-0	1.000	8-2-0	.800
2.	Iowa State	3-1-0	.750	5-3-0	.625
3.	Kansas State	3-2-0	.600	8-2-0	.800
4.	Kansas	1-3-0	.250	5-5-0	.500
5.	Missouri	1-4-0	.200	2-8-0	.200
5.	Oklahoma	1-4-0	.200	4-7-1	.375

Non-conference record: 18-13-1 .578

1932

		Conference		Overall	
1.	Nebraska	5-0-0	1.000	7-1-1	.833
2.	Kansas	3-2-0	.600	5-3-0	.625
2.	Oklahoma	3-2-0	.600	4-4-1	.500
4.	Kansas State	2-3-0	.400	4-4-0	.500
5.	Missouri	1-3-1	.300	1-7-1	.167
6.	Iowa State	0-4-1	.100	3-4-1	.438

Non-conference record: 10-9-2 .524

1933

		Conference		Overall	
1.	Nebraska	5-0-0	1.000	8-1-0	.889
2.	Kansas State	4-1-0	.800	6-2-1	.722
3.	Oklahoma	3-2-0	.600	4-4-1	.500
4.	Kansas	2-3-0	.400	5-4-1	.550
5.	Iowa State	1-4-0	.200	3-5-1	.389
6.	Missouri	0-5-0	.000	1-8-0	.111

Non-conference record: 12-9-4 .560

1934

		Conference		Overall	
1.	Kansas State	5-0-0	1.000	7-2-1	.750
2.	Nebraska	4-1-0	.800	6-3-0	.667
3.	Oklahoma	2-2-1	.500	3-4-2	.444
4.	Kansas	1-2-2	.400	3-4-3	.450
5.	Iowa State	1-3-1	.300	5-3-1	.611
6.	Missouri	0-5-0	.000	0-8-1	.056

Non-conference record: 11-11-4 .500

1935

		Conference		Overall	
1.	Nebraska	4-0-1	.900	6-2-1	.722
2.	Oklahoma	3-2-0	.600	6-3-0	.667
3.	Kansas	2-2-1	.500	4-4-1	.500
4.	Kansas State	1-2-2	.400	2-4-3	.389
5.	Iowa State	1-3-1	.300	2-4-3	.389
5.	Missouri	0-2-3	.300	3-3-3	.500

Non-conference record: 12-9-3 .562

1936

		Conference		Overall	
1.	Nebraska	5-0-0	1.000	7-2-0	.778
2.	Missouri	3-1-1	.700	6-2-1	.722
3.	Kansas State	2-1-2	.600	4-3-2	.556
4.	Oklahoma	1-2-2	.400	3-3-3	.500
5.	Iowa State	1-3-1	.300	3-3-2	.500
6.	Kansas	0-5-0	.000	1-6-1	.188

Non-conference record: 12-7-3 .614

1937

		Conference		Overall	
1.	Nebraska	3-0-2	.800	6-1-2	.778
2.	Oklahoma	3-1-1	.700	5-2-2	.667
3.	Kansas	2-1-2	.600	3-4-2	.444
4.	Missouri	2-2-1	.500	3-6-1	.350
5.	Iowa State	1-4-0	.200	3-6-0	.333
5.	Kansas State	1-4-0	.200	4-5-0	.444

Non-conference record: 12-12-1 .500

1938

		Conference		Overall	
1.	Oklahoma	5-0-0	1.000	10-1-0	.909
2.	Iowa State	3-1-1	.700	7-1-1	.833
3.	Missouri	2-3-0	.400	6-3-0	.667
3.	Nebraska	2-3-0	.400	3-5-1	.389
5.	Kansas State	1-3-1	.300	4-4-1	.500
6.	Kansas	1-4-0	.200	3-6-0	.333

Non-conference record: 19-6-1 .750

1939

		Conference		Overall	
1.	Missouri	5-0-0	1.000	8-2-0	.800
2.	Nebraska	4-1-0	.800	7-1-1	.833
3.	Oklahoma	3-2-0	.600	6-2-1	.722
4.	Kansas	1-4-0	.200	2-6-0	.250
4.	Iowa State	1-4-0	.200	2-7-0	.222
4.	Kansas State	1-4-0	.200	4-5-0	.444

Non-conference record: 14-8-2 .625

1940

		Conference		Overall	
1.	Nebraska	5-0-0	1.000	8-2-0	.800
2.	Oklahoma	4-1-0	.800	6-3-0	.667
3.	Missouri	3-2-0	.600	6-3-0	.667
4.	Iowa State	2-3-0	.400	4-5-0	.444
5.	Kansas State	1-4-0	.200	2-7-0	.222
6.	Kansas	0-5-0	.000	2-7-0	.222

Non-conference record: 13-12-0 .520

1941

		Conference		Overall	
1.	Missouri	5-0-0	1.000	8-2-0	.800
2.	Nebraska	3-2-0	.600	4-5-0	.444
2.	Oklahoma	3-2-0	.600	6-3-0	.667
4.	Kansas	2-3-0	.400	3-6-0	.333
5.	Kansas State	1-3-1	.300	2-5-2	.333
6.	Iowa State	0-4-1	.100	2-6-1	.278

Non-conference record: 11-13-1 .460

1942		Conference		Overall	
1.	Missouri	4-0-1	.900	8-3-1	.708
2.	Oklahoma	3-1-1	.700	3-5-2	.400
3.	Nebraska	3-2-0	.600	3-7-0	.300
4.	Kansas State	2-3-0	.400	3-6-0	.333
5.	Iowa State	1-4-0	.200	3-6-0	.333
5.	Kansas	1-4-0	.200	2-8-0	.200

Non-conference record: 8-21-1 .283

1943					
1.	Oklahoma	5-0-0	1.000	7-2-0	.778
2.	Missouri	3-2-0	.600	3-5-0	.375
2.	Iowa State	3-2-0	.600	4-4-0	.500
4.	Kansas	2-3-0	.400	4-5-1	.450
4.	Nebraska	2-3-0	.400	2-6-0	.250
6.	Kansas State	0-5-0	.000	1-7-0	.125

Non-conference record: 6-14-1 .310

1944					
1.	Oklahoma	4-0-1	.900	6-3-1	.650
2.	Iowa State	3-1-1	.700	6-1-1	.812
3.	Missouri	2-1-2	.600	3-5-2	.400
4.	Nebraska	2-3-0	.400	2-6-0	.250
5.	Kansas	1-4-0	.200	3-6-1	.350
5.	Kansas State	1-4-0	.200	2-5-2	.333

Non-conference record: 9-13-3 .420

1945					
1.	Missouri	5-0-0	1.000	6-4-0	.600
2.	Oklahoma	4-1-0	.800	5-5-0	.500
3.	Iowa State	2-2-1	.500	4-3-1	.562
4.	Nebraska	2-3-0	.400	4-5-0	.444
5.	Kansas	1-3-1	.300	4-5-1	.450
6.	Kansas State	0-5-0	.000	1-7-0	.125

Non-conference record: 10-15-0 .400

1946					
1.	Kansas	4-1-0	.800	7-2-1	.750
1.	Oklahoma	4-1-0	.800	8-3-0	.727
3.	Missouri	3-2-0	.600	4-5-1	.450
3.	Nebraska	3-2-0	.600	3-6-0	.333
5.	Iowa State	1-4-0	.200	2-6-1	.278
6.	Kansas State	0-5-0	.000	0-9-0	.000

Non-conference record: 9-16-3 .375

1947					
1.	Kansas	4-0-1	.900	8-1-2	.818
1.	Oklahoma	4-0-1	.900	7-2-1	.750
3.	Missouri	3-2-0	.600	6-4-0	.600
4.	Nebraska	2-3-0	.400	2-7-0	.222
5.	Iowa State	1-4-0	.200	3-6-0	.333
6.	Kansas State	0-5-0	.000	0-10-0	.000

Non-conference record: 12-16-1 .431

1948					
1.	Oklahoma	5-0-0	1.000	10-1-0	.909
2.	Missouri	5-1-0	.833	8-3-0	.727
3.	Kansas	4-2-0	.667	7-3-0	.700
4.	Colorado	2-3-0	.400	3-6-0	.333
5.	Iowa State	2-4-0	.333	4-6-0	.400
5.	Nebraska	2-4-0	.333	2-8-0	.200
7.	Kansas State	0-6-0	.000	1-9-0	.100

Colorado joins the Big Six beginning with the 1948 season, to form the Big Seven.
Non-conference record: 15-16-0 .484

1949		Conference		Overall	
1.	Oklahoma	5-0-0	1.000	11-0-0	1.000
2.	Missouri	5-1-0	.833	7-4-0	.636
3.	Iowa State	3-3-0	.500	5-3-1	.611
3.	Nebraska	3-3-0	.500	4-5-0	.444
5.	Kansas	2-4-0	.333	5-5-0	.500
6.	Colorado	1-4-0	.200	3-7-0	.300
7.	Kansas State	1-5-0	.167	2-8-0	.200

Non-conference record: 17-12-1 .583

1950					
1.	Oklahoma	6-0-0	1.000	10-1-0	.909
2.	Nebraska	4-2-0	.667	6-2-1	.722
3.	Missouri	3-2-1	.583	4-5-1	.450
4.	Kansas	3-3-0	.500	6-4-0	.600
5.	Iowa State	2-3-1	.417	3-6-1	.350
6.	Colorado	2-4-0	.333	5-4-1	.550
7.	Kansas State	0-6-0	.000	1-9-1	.136

Non-conference record: 15-11-3 .569

1951					
1.	Oklahoma	6-0-0	1.000	8-2-0	.800
2.	Colorado	5-1-0	.833	7-3-0	.700
3.	Kansas	4-2-0	.667	8-2-0	.800
4.	Iowa State	2-4-0	.333	4-4-1	.500
4.	Nebraska	2-4-0	.333	2-8-0	.200
4.	Missouri	2-4-0	.333	3-7-0	.300
7.	Kansas State	0-6-0	.000	0-9-0	.000

Non-conference record: 11-14-1 .442

1952					
1.	Oklahoma	5-0-1	917	8-1-1	.850
2.	Missouri	5-1-0	.833	5-5-0	.500
3.	Nebraska	3-2-1	.583	5-4-1	.550
4.	Colorado	2-2-2	.500	6-2-2	.700
4.	Kansas	3-3-0	.500	7-3-0	.700
6.	Iowa State	1-5-0	.167	3-6-0	.333
7.	Kansas State	0-6-0	.000	1-9-0	.100

Non-conference record: 16-11-0 .593

1953					
1.	Oklahoma	6-0-0	1.000	9-1-1	.864
2.	Kansas State	4-2-0	.667	6-3-1	.650
2.	Missouri	4-2-0	.667	6-4-0	.600
4.	Kansas	2-4-0	.333	2-8-0	.200
4.	Colorado	2-4-0	.333	6-4-0	.600
4.	Nebraska	2-4-0	.333	3-6-1	350
7.	Iowa State	1-5-0	.167	2-7-0	.222

Non-conference record: 13-12-3 .518

1954					
1.	Oklahoma	6-0-0	1.000	10-0-0	1.000
2.	Nebraska	4-2-0	.667	6-5-0	.545
3.	Colorado	3-2-1	.583	7-2-1	.750
3.	Missouri	3-2-1	.583	4-5-1	.450
5.	Kansas State	3-3-0	.500	7-3-0	.700
6.	Iowa State	1-5-0	.167	3-6-0	.333
7.	Kansas	0-6-0	.000	1-10-0	.091

Non-conference record: 18-11-0 .621

1955		Conference		Overall	
1.	Oklahoma	6-0-0	1.000	11-0-0	1.000
2.	Nebraska	5-1-0	.833	5-5-0	.500
3.	Colorado	3-3-0	.500	6-4-0	.600
3.	Kansas State	3-3-0	.500	4-6-0	.400
5.	Kansas	1-4-1	.250	3-6-1	.350
5.	Iowa State	1-4-1	.250	1-7-1	.167
7.	Missouri	1-5-0	.167	1-9-0	.100

Non-conference record: 11-17-0 .393

1956					
1.	Oklahoma	6-0-0	1.000	10-0-0	1.000
2.	Colorado	4-1-1	.750	8-2-1	.773
3.	Missouri	3-2-1	.583	4-5-1	.450
4.	Nebraska	3-3-0	.500	4-6-0	.400
5.	Kansas	2-4-0	.333	3-6-1	.350
5.	Kansas State	2-4-0	.333	3-7-0	.300
7.	Iowa State	0-6-0	.000	2-8-0	.200

Non-conference record: 14-14-1 .500

1957					
1.	Oklahoma	6-0-0	1.000	10-1-0	.909
2.	Kansas	4-2-0	.667	5-4-1	.550
3.	Colorado	3-3-0	.500	6-3-1	.650
3.	Missouri	3-3-0	.500	5-4-1	.550
5.	Iowa State	2-4-0	.333	4-5-1	.450
5.	Kansas State	2-4-0	.333	3-6-1	.350
7.	Nebraska	1-5-0	.167	1-9-0	.100

Non-conference record: 13-11-5 .534

1958					
1.	Oklahoma	6-0-0	1.000	10-1-0	.909
2.	Missouri	4-1-1	.750	5-4-1	.550
3.	Colorado	4-2-0	.667	6-4-0	.600
4.	Kansas	3-2-1	.583	4-5-1	.450
5.	Kansas State	2-4-0	.333	3-7-0	.300
6.	Nebraska	1-5-0	.167	3-7-0	.300
7.	Iowa State	0-6-0	.000	4-6-0	.400

Non-conference record: 15-14-0 .517

1959					
1.	Oklahoma	5-1-0	.833	7-3-0	.700
2.	Missouri	4-2-0	.667	6-5-0	.545
3.	Kansas	3-3-0	.500	5-5-0	.500
3.	Iowa State	3-3-0	.500	7-3-0	.700
3.	Colorado	3-3-0	.500	5-5-0	.500
6.	Nebraska	2-4-0	.333	4-6-0	.400
7.	Kansas State	1-5-0	.167	2-8-0	.200

Non-conference record: 15-14-0 .517

1960					
1.	Missouri	7-0-0	1.000	11-0-0	1.000
2.	Colorado	6-1-0	.857	7-3-0	.700
3.	Kansas*	4-2-1	.643	5-4-1	.550
4.	Iowa State	4-3-0	.571	7-3-0	.700
5.	Oklahoma	2-4-1	.357	3-6-1	.350
6.	Oklahoma State	2-5-0	.286	3-7-0	.300
6.	Nebraska	2-5-0	.286	4-6-0	.400
8.	Kansas State	0-7-0	.000	1-9-0	.100

Oklahoma State joins the Big Seven. * Data above reflect the two games forfeited by Kansas due to ineligible player.
Non-conference record; 14-11-0 .560

1961		Conference		Overall	
1.	Colorado	7-0-0	1.000	9-2-0	.818
2.	Kansas	5-2-0	.714	7-3-1	.682
2.	Missouri	5-2-0	.714	7-2-1	.750
4.	Oklahoma	4-3-0	.571	5-5-0	.500
5	Iowa State	3-4-0	.429	5-5-0	.500
6.	Nebraska	2-5-0	.286	3-6-1	.350
6.	Okla. State	2-5-0	.286	4-6-0	.400
8.	Kansas State	0-7-0	.000	2-8-0	.200

Non-conference record: 14-9-2 .600

1962					
1.	Oklahoma	7-0-0	1.000	8-3-0	.727
2.	Missouri	5-1-1	.786	8-1-2	.818
3.	Nebraska	5-2-0	.714	9-2-0	.818
4.	Kansas	4-2-1	.643	6-3-1	.650
5.	Iowa State	3-4-0	.429	5-5-0	.500
6.	Okla. State	2-5-0	.286	4-6-0	.400
7.	Colorado	1-6-0	.143	2-8-0	.200
8.	Kansas State	0-7-0	.000	0-10-0	.000

Non-conference record: 15-11-1 .574

1963					
1.	Nebraska	7-0-0	1.000	10-1-0	.909
2.	Oklahoma	6-1-0	.857	8-2-0	.800
3.	Missouri	5-2-0	.714	7-3-0	.700
4.	Kansas	3-4-0	.429	5-5-0	.500
4.	Iowa State	3-4-0	.429	4-5-0	.444
6.	Colorado	2-5-0	.286	2-8-0	.200
7.	Kansas State	1-5-0	.167	2-7-0	.222
8.	Okla. State	0-6-0	.000	1-8-0	.111

Non-conference record: 12-12-0 .500

1964					
1.	Nebraska	6-1-0	.857	9-2-0	.818
2.	Oklahoma	5-1-1	.786	6-5-1	.591
3.	Kansas	5-2-0	.714	6-4-0	.600
4.	Missouri	4-2-1	.643	6-3-1	.650
5.	Kansas State	3-4-0	.429	3-7-0	.300
5.	Okla. State	3-4-0	.429	4-6-0	.400
7.	Colorado	1-6-0	.143	2-8-0	.200
8.	Iowa State	0-7-0	.000	1-8-1	.150

Non-conference record: 10-15-1 404

1965					
1.	Nebraska	7-0-0	1.000	10-1-0	.909
2.	Missouri	6-1-0	.857	8-2-1	.773
3.	Colorado	4-2-1	.643	6-2-2	.700
4.	Iowa State	3-3-1	.500	5-4-1	.550
5.	Oklahoma	3-4-0	.429	3-7-0	.300
6.	Okla. State	2-5-0	.286	3-7-0	.300
6.	Kansas	2-5-0	.286	2-8-0	.200
8.	Kansas State	0-7-0	.000	0-10-0	.000

Non-conference record: 10-14-2 .423

1966		Conference		Overall	
1.	Nebraska	6-1-0	.857	9-2-0	.818
2.	Colorado	5-2-0	.714	7-3-0	.700
3.	Okla. State	4-2-1	.643	4-5-1	.450
3.	Missouri	4-2-1	.643	6-3-1	.650
5.	Oklahoma	4-3-0	.571	6-4-0	.600
6.	Iowa State	2-3-2	.429	2-6-2	.300
7.	Kansas State	0-6-1	.071	0-9-1	.050
7.	Kansas	0-6-1	.071	2-7-1	.250

Non-conference record: 11-14-0 .440

1967					
1.	Oklahoma	7-0-0	1.000	10-1-0	.909
2.	Colorado	5-2-0	.714	9-2-0	.818
3.	Kansas	5-2-0	.714	5-5-0	.500
4.	Missouri	4-3-0	.571	7-3-0	.700
5.	Okla. State	3-4-0	.429	4-5-1	.450
5.	Nebraska	3-4-0	.429	6-4-0	.600
7.	Iowa State	1-6-0	.143	2-8-0	.200
8.	Kansas State	0-7-0	.000	1-9-0	.100

Non-conference record: 16-9-1 .635

1968					
1.	Kansas	6-1-0	.857	9-2-0	.818
1.	Oklahoma	6-1-0	.857	7-4-0	.636
3.	Missouri	5-2-0	.714	8-3-0	.727
4.	Colorado	3-4-0	.429	4-6-0	.400
4.	Nebraska	3-4-0	.429	6-4-0	.600
6.	Kansas State	2-5-0	.286	4-6-0	.400
6.	Okla. State	2-5-0	.286	3-7-0	.300
8.	Iowa State	1-6-0	.143	3-7-0	.300

Non-conference record: 16-11-0 593

1969					
1.	Missouri	6-1-0	.857	9-2-0	.818
1.	Nebraska	6-1-0	.857	9-2-0	.818
3.	Colorado	5-2-0	.714	8-3-0	.727
4.	Oklahoma	4-3-0	.571	6-4-0	.600
5.	Kansas State	3-4-0	.429	5-5-0	.500
5.	Okla. State	3-4-0	.429	5-5-0	.500
7.	Iowa State	1-6-0	.143	3-7-0	.300
8.	Kansas	0-7-0	.000	1-9-0	.100

Non-conference record: 18-9-0 .667

1970					
1.	Nebraska	7-0-0	1.000	11-0-1	.958
2.	Kansas State	5-2-0	.714	6-5-0	.545
2.	Oklahoma	5-2-0	.714	7-4-1	.625
4.	Colorado	3-4-0	.429	6-5-0	.545
4.	Missouri	3-4-0	.429	5-6-0	.455
6.	Okla. State	2-5-0	.286	4-7-0	.364
6.	Kansas	2-5-0	.286	5-6-0	.455
8.	Iowa State	1-6-0	.143	5-6-0	.455

Non-conference record: 21-11-2 .647

1971					
1.	Nebraska	7-0-0	1.000	13-0-0	1.000
2.	Oklahoma	6-1-0	.856	11-1-0	.917
3.	Colorado	5-2-0	.714	10-2-0	.833
4.	Iowa State	4-3-0	.571	8-4-0	.667
5.	Kansas State	2-5-0	.286	5-6-0	.455
5.	Okla. State	2-5-0	.286	4-6-1	.409
5.	Kansas	2-5-0	.286	4-7-0	.364
8.	Missouri	0-7-0	.000	1-10-0	.091

Non-conference record: 28-8-1 .770

1972		Conference		Overall	
1.	Nebraska	5-1-1	.786	10-1-1	.875
2.	Okla. State	5-2-0	.714	7-4-0	.636
3.	Colorado	4-3-0	.571	8-4-0	.667
3.	Missouri	4-3-0	.571	6-6-0	.500
5.	Kansas	3-4-0	.429	5-6-0	.455
5.	Oklahoma*	3-4-0	.429	8-4-0	.667
7.	Iowa State	2-4-1	.357	5-6-1	.458
8.	Kansas State	1-6-0	.143	3-8-0	.273

*Oklahoma forfeited three games due to ineligible player.
Non-conference record: 25-12-0 .676

1973					
1.	Oklahoma	7-0-0	1.000	10-0-1	.955
2.	Kansas	4-2-1	.643	7-4-1	.625
2.	Nebraska	4-2-1	.643	9-2-1	.792
4.	Okla. State	2-3-2	.429	5-4-2	.545
5.	Missouri	3-4-0	.429	8-4-0	.667
6.	Iowa State	2-5-0	.286	4-7-0	.364
6.	Kansas State	2-5-0	.286	4-7-0	.364
6.	Colorado	2-5-0	.286	5-6-0	.455

Non-conference record: 26-8-1 .757

1974					
1.	Oklahoma	7-0-0	1.000	11-0-0	1.000
2.	Missouri	5-2-0	.714	7-4-0	.636
2.	Nebraska	5-2-0	.714	9-3-0	.750
4.	Okla. State	4-3-0	.571	7-5-0	.583
5.	Colorado	3-4-0	.429	5-6-0	.455
6.	Iowa State	2-5-0	.286	4-7-0	.364
7.	Kansas State	1-6-0	.143	4-7-0	.364
7.	Kansas	1-6-0	.143	4-7-0	.364

Non-conference record: 23-11-0 .676

1975					
1.	Nebraska	6-1-0	.857	10-2-0	.833
1.	Oklahoma	6-1-0	.857	11-1-0	.917
3.	Colorado	5-2-0	.714	9-3-0	.750
4.	Kansas	4-3-0	.571	7-5-0	.583
5.	Okla. State	3-4-0	.429	7-4-0	.646
5.	Missouri	3-4-0	.429	6-5-0	.545
7.	Iowa State	1-6-0	.143	6-6-0	.500
8.	Kansas State	0-7-0	.000	4-7-0	.364

Non-conference record: 32-5-0 865

1976					
1.	Okla. State	5-2-0	.714	9-3-0	.750
1.	Colorado	5-2-0	.714	8-4-0	.667
1.	Oklahoma	5-2-0	.714	9-2-1	.792
4.	Iowa State	4-3-0	.571	8-3-0	.727
4.	Nebraska	4-3-0	.571	9-3-1	.731
6.	Missouri	3-4-0	.429	6-5-0	.545
7.	Kansas	2-5-0	.286	6-5-0	.545
8.	Kansas State	0-7-0	.000	1-10-0	.091

Non-conference record: 28-7-2 .784

1977					
1.	Oklahoma	7-0-0	1.000	10-2-0	.833
2.	Iowa State	5-2-0	.714	8-4-0	.667
2.	Nebraska	5-2-0	.714	9-3-0	.750
4.	Colorado	3-3-1	.500	7-3-1	.682
5.	Missouri	3-4-0	.429	4-7-0	.364
6.	Kansas	2-4-1	.357	3-7-1	.318
7.	Okla. State	2-5-0	.286	4-7-0	.364
8.	Kansas State	0-7-0	.000	1-10-0	.091

Non-conference record: 19-16-0 .543

1978		Conference		Overall	
1.	Oklahoma	6-1-0	.857	11-1-0	.917
1.	Nebraska	6-1-0	.857	9-3-0	.750
3.	Iowa State	4-3-0	.571	8-4-0	.667
3.	Missouri	4-3-0	.571	8-4-0	.667
5.	Kansas State	3-4-0	.429	4-7-0	.364
5.	Okla. State	3-4-0	.429	3-8-0	.273
7.	Colorado	2-5-0	.286	6-5-0	.545
8.	Kansas	0-7-0	.000	1-10-0	.091

Non-conference record: 22-14-0 611

1979		Conference		Overall	
1.	Oklahoma	7-0-0	1.000	11-1-0	.917
2.	Nebraska	6-1-0	.857	10-2-0	.833
3.	Okla. State	5-2-0	.714	7-4-0	.636
4.	Missouri	3-4-0	.429	7-5-0	.583
5.	Iowa State	2-5-0	.286	3-8-0	.273
5.	Colorado	2-5-0	.286	3-8-0	.273
5.	Kansas	2-5-0	.286	3-8-0	.273
8.	Kansas State	1-6-0	.143	3-8-0	.273

Non-conference record: 19-16-0 .543

1980		Conference		Overall	
1.	Oklahoma	7-0-0	1.000	10-2-0	.833
2.	Nebraska	6-1-0	.857	10-2-0	.833
3.	Missouri	5-2-0	.714	8-4-0	.667
4.	Kansas	3-3-1	.500	4-5-2	.455
5.	Okla. State	2-4-0	.333	4-7-0	.364
6.	Iowa State	2-5-0	.286	6-5-0	.545
7.	Kansas State	1-6-0	.143	3-8-0	.273
7.	Colorado	1-6-0	.143	1-10-0	.091

Non-conference record: 19-16-1 .542

1981		Conference		Overall	
1.	Nebraska	7-0-0	1.000	9-3-0	.750
2.	Oklahoma	4-2-1	.643	7-4-1	.625
3.	Okla. State	4-3-0	.571	7-5-0	.583
3.	Kansas	4-3-0	.571	8-4-0	.667
5.	Missouri	3-4-0	.429	8-4-0	.667
6.	Iowa State	2-4-1	.357	5-5-1	.500
7.	Colorado	2-5-0	.286	3-8-0	.273
8.	Kansas State	1-6-0	.143	2-9-0	.182

Non-conference record: 22-15-0 .595

1982		Conference		Overall	
1.	Nebraska	7-0-0	1.000	12-1-0	.923
2.	Oklahoma	6-1-0	.857	8-4-0	.667
3.	Okla. State	3-2-2	.571	4-5-2	.455
4.	Kansas State	3-3-1	.500	6-5-1	.542
5.	Missouri	2-3-2	.429	5-4-2	.545
6.	Iowa State	1-5-1	.214	4-6-1	.409
6.	Kansas	1-5-1	.214	2-7-2	.273
6.	Colorado	1-5-1	.214	2-8-1	.227

Non-conference record: 19-16-1 .542

1983		Conference		Overall	
1.	Nebraska	7-0-0	1.000	12-1-0	.923
2.	Missouri	5-2-0	.714	7-5-0	.583
2.	Oklahoma	5-2-0	.714	8-4-0	.667
4.	Okla. State	3-4-0	.429	8-4-0	.667
4.	Iowa State	3-4-0	.429	4-7-0	.364
6.	Colorado	2-5-0	.286	4-7-0	.364
6.	Kansas	2-5-0	.286	4-6-1	.409
8.	Kansas State	1-6-0	.143	3-8-0	.273

Non-conference record: 22-14-1 .608

1984		Conference		Overall	
1.	Nebraska	6-1-0	.857	10-2-0	.833
1.	Oklahoma	6-1-0	.857	9-2-1	.792
3.	Okla. State	5-2-0	.714	10-2-0	.833
4.	Kansas	4-3-0	.571	5-6-0	.455
5.	Kansas State	2-4-1	.357	3-7-1	.318
5.	Missouri	2-4-1	.357	3-7-1	.318
7.	Colorado	1-6-0	.143	1-10-0	.091
7.	Iowa State	0-5-2	.143	2-7-2	.273

Non-conference record: 17-17-1 .500

1985		Conference		Overall	
1.	Oklahoma	7-0-0	1.000	10-1-0	.909
2.	Nebraska	6-1-0	.857	9-2-0	.818
3.	Okla. State	4-3-0	.571	8-3-0	.727
3.	Colorado	4-3-0	.571	7-5-0	.583
5.	Iowa State	3-4-0	.429	5-6-0	.455
6.	Kansas	2-5-0	.286	6-6-0	.500
7.	Kansas State	1-6-0	.143	1-10-0	.091
7.	Missouri	1-6-0	.143	1-10-0	.091

Non-conference record: 19-15-0 .559

1986		Conference		Overall	
1.	Oklahoma	7-0-0	1.000	11-1-0	.917
2.	Colorado	6-1-0	.857	6-6-0	.500
3.	Nebraska	5-2-0	.714	10-2-0	.833
4.	Okla. State	4-3-0	.571	6-5-0	.545
5.	Iowa State	3-4-0	.429	6-5-0	.545
6.	Missouri	2-5-0	.286	3-8-0	.273
7.	Kansas State	1-6-0	.143	2-9-0	.182
8.	Kansas	0-7-0	.000	3-8-0	.273

Non-conference record: 19-16-0 543

1987		Conference		Overall	
1.	Oklahoma	7-0-0	1.000	11-1-0	.917
2.	Nebraska	6-1-0	.857	10-2-0	.833
3.	Okla. State	5-2-0	.714	10-2-0	.833
4.	Colorado	4-3-0	.571	7-4-0	.636
5.	Missouri	3-4-0	.429	5-6-0	.455
6.	Iowa State	2-5-0	.286	3-8-0	.273
7.	Kansas	0-6-1	.071	1-9-1	.136
7.	Kansas State	0-6-1	.071	0-10-1	.045

Non-conference record: 20-15-0 .571

1988		Conference		Overall	
1.	Nebraska	7-0-0	1.000	11-2-0	.846
2.	Oklahoma	6-1-0	.857	9-3-0	.750
3.	Okla. State	5-2-0	.714	10-2-0	.833
4.	Colorado	4-3-0	.571	8-4-0	.667
5.	Iowa State	3-4-0	.429	5-6-0	.455
6.	Missouri	2-5-0	.286	3-7-1	.318
7.	Kansas	1-6-0	.143	1-10-0	.091
8.	Kansas State	0-7-0	.000	0-11-0	.000

Non-conference record: 19-17-1 .527

1989		Conference		Overall	
1.	Colorado	7-0-0	1.000	11-1-0	.917
2.	Nebraska	6-1-0	.857	10-1-0	.909
3.	Oklahoma	5-2-0	.714	7-4-0	.636
4.	Iowa State	4-3-0	.571	6-5-0	.545
5.	Okla. State	3-4-0	.429	4-7-0	.364
6.	Kansas	2-5-0	.286	4-7-0	.364
7.	Missouri	1-6-0	.143	2-9-0	.182
8.	Kansas State	0-7-0	.000	1-10-0	.091

Non-conference record: 17-16-0 .515

1990		Conference		Overall	
1.	Colorado	7-0-0	1.000	11-1-1	.885
2.	Nebraska	5-2-0	.714	9-3-0	.750
2.	Oklahoma	5-2-0	.714	8-3-0	.727
4.	Iowa State	2-4-1	.357	4-6-1	.409
4.	Kansas	2-4-1	.357	3-7-1	.318
5.	Kansas State	2-5-0	.286	5-6-0	.455
5.	Okla. State	2-5-0	.286	4-7-0	.264
5.	Missouri	2-5-0	.286	4-7-0	.264

Non-conference record: 21-13-1 .614

1991					
1.	Nebraska	6-0-1	.929	9-2-1	.792
1.	Colorado	6-0-1	.929	8-3-1	.708
3.	Oklahoma	5-2-0	.714	9-3-0	.750
4.	Kansas State	4-3-0	.571	7-4-0	.736
5.	Kansas	3-4-0	.429	6-5-0	.545
6.	Iowa State	1-5-1	.214	3-7-1	.318
7.	Missouri	1-6-0	.143	3-6-2	.455
8.	Okla. State	0-6-1	.071	0-10-1	.045

Non-conference record: 19-14-2 .571

1992					
1.	Nebraska	6-1-0	.857	9-3-0	.750
2.	Colorado	5-1-1	.786	9-2-1	.792
3.	Kansas	4-3-0	.571	8-4-0	.667
3.	Oklahoma	3-2-2	.571	5-4-2	.545
5.	Okla. State	2-4-1	.357	4-6-1	.409
6.	Kansas State	2-5-0	.286	5-6-0	.455
6.	Iowa State	2-5-0	.286	4-7-0	.364
6.	Missouri	2-5-0	.286	3-8-0	.273

Non-conference record: 21-14-0 .600

1993					
1.	Nebraska	7-0-0	1.000	11-1-0	.917
2.	Colorado	5-1-1	.786	8-3-1	.708
3.	Kansas State	4-2-1	.643	9-2-1	.792
4.	Oklahoma	4-3-0	.571	9-3-0	.750
5.	Kansas	3-4-0	.429	5-7-0	.417
6.	Missouri	2-5-0	.286	3-7-1	.318
7.	Iowa State	2-5-0	.286	3-8-0	.273
8.	Okla. State	0-7-0	.000	3-8-0	.273

Non-conference record: 24-12-1 .662

1994					
1.	Nebraska	7-0-0	1.000	13-0-0	1.000
2.	Colorado	6-1-0	.857	11-1-0	.917
3.	Kansas State	5-2-0	.714	9-3-0	.750
4.	Oklahoma	4-3-0	.571	6-6-0	.500
5.	Kansas	3-4-0	.429	6-5-0	.545
6.	Missouri	2-5-0	.286	3-8-1	.292
7.	Okla. State	0-6-1	.071	3-7-1	.318
7.	Iowa State	0-6-1	.071	0-10-1	.045

Non-conference record: 24-13-1 .645

1995					
1.	Nebraska	7-0-0	1.000	12-0-0	1.000
2.	Colorado	5-2-0	.714	10-2-0	.833
2.	Kansas State	5-2-0	.714	10-2-0	.833
2.	Kansas	5-2-0	.714	10-2-0	.833
5.	Oklahoma	2-5-0	.286	5-5-1	.500
5	Okla. State	2-5-0	.286	4-8-0	.333
7.	Missouri	1-6-0	.143	3-8-0	.273
7.	Iowa State	1-6-0	.143	3-8-0	.273

Non-conference record: 29-7-1 .797

BIG EIGHT W-L-T RECORDS BY DECADES (1928-1995)

Decade	Iowa St.	Kansas	K. State	Missouri	Nebraska	Oklahoma	Colorado	Okla. State
1928-29	2-7-1	3-6-1	3-7-0	6-3-1	8-0-2	5-4-1		
1930-39	12-32-5	17-27-5	23-22-5	15-27-8	39-7-4	27-18-5		
1940-49	18-31-3	21-29-2	6-45-1	38-11-3	27-25-0	41-6-3	3-7-0	
1950-59	13-45-2	25-33-2	17-43-0	32-24-4	27-32-1	58-1-1	31-25-4	
1960-69	21-46-3	34-33-3	9-59-1	51-16-3	47-23-0	48-20-2	39-30-1	23-45-1
1970-79	27-42-1	22-46-2	15-55-0	31-39-0	55-13-2	59-11-0	34-35-1	33-35-2
1980-89	23-43-4	19-48-3	10-57-3	26-41-3	63-7-0	60-9-1	32-37-1	38-29-3
1990-95	8-31-3	20-21-1	22-19-1	10-32-0	38-3-1	23-17-2	34-5-3	6-33-3

BIG EIGHT W-L-T Records (1928-1995)

Iowa State	124-277-22	.319		Nebraska	304-110-10	.729
Kansas	161-243-19	.394		Oklahoma	321- 86-15	.778
K. State	105-307-11	.261		Colorado	173-139- 7	.553
Missouri	209-193-22	.519		Okla. State	100-142- 9	.416

BIG EIGHT TITLES BY DECADES (1928-1995)

Decade	Iowa St.	Kansas	K. State	Missouri	Nebraska	Oklahoma	Colorado	Okla. State
1928-29					2			
1930-39		1	1	1	6	1		
1940-49		1		3	1	5		
1950-59						10		
1960-69		.5		1.5	4.5	2.5	1	
1970-79					4	5.33	.33	.33
1980-89					4.5	4.5	1	
1990-95					4.5	1.5		
Totals		2.5	1	5.5	26.5	29.83	2.33	.33

BIG TEN (1896-2003) The Big Ten, originally named the Western Conference, was the first major college conference organized. Until 1946, the Big Ten did not include ties in calculating a school's final standing in the league. The conference win percents reflect this ruling, prior to 1946. However, to provide comparability with other teams and other conferences, the "overall" win percents for all years are calculated using the "half a win, half a loss" interpretation of a tie.

1896		Conference		Overall	
1.	Wisconsin	2-0-1	1.000	6-1-1	.857
2.	Northwestern	2-1-1	.667	6-1-2	.778
2.	Michigan	2-1-0	.667	9-1-0	.900
4.	Chicago	3-2-0	.600	11-2-1	.846
5.	Minnesota	1-2-0	.333	8-2-0	.800
6.	Illinois	0-2-1	.000	4-2-1	.643
6.	Purdue	0-2-1	.000	4-2-1	.643

Non-conference record: 38-1-2 .951

1897					
1.	Wisconsin	3-0-0	1.000	9-1-0	.900
2.	Chicago	3-1-0	.750	8-1-0	.889
3.	Michigan	2-1-0	.667	6-1-1	.813
4.	Illinois	1-1-0	.500	5-2-0	.714
5.	Purdue	1-2-0	.333	5-3-1	.611
6.	Minnesota	0-3-0	.000	4-4-0	.500
6.	Northwestern	0-2-0	.000	4-3-0	.571

Non-conference record: 31-5-2 .842

1898					
1.	Michigan	3-0-0	1.000	10-0-0	1.000
2.	Chicago	3-1-0	.750	9-2-0	.818
3.	Wisconsin	2-1-0	.667	9-1-0	.900
4.	Illinois	1-1-0	.500	4-5-0	.444
5.	Minnesota	1-2-0	.333	4-5-0	.444
6.	Northwestern	0-4-0	.000	7-4-0	.636
6.	Purdue	0-1-0	.000	3-3-0	.500

Non-conference record: 36-10-0 .783

1899					
1.	Chicago	4-0-0	1.000	12-0-2	.929
2.	Wisconsin	4-1-0	.800	9-2-0	.818
3.	Northwestern	2-2-0	.500	6-6-0	.500
3.	Michigan	1-1-0	.500	8-2-0	.800
5.	Purdue	1-2-0	.333	4-4-1	.500
6.	Illinois	0-3-0	.000	3-5-1	.438
6.	Minnesota	0-3-0	.000	6-3-2	.636

Non-conference record: 36-10-6 .750

1900					
1.	Minnesota	3-0-1	1.000	10-0-2	.917
1.	Iowa	2-0-1	1.000	7-0-1	.938
3.	Northwestern	2-1-2	.667	6-2-3	.682
3.	Wisconsin	2-1-0	.667	8-1-0	.944
5.	Michigan	3-2-0	.600	7-2-1	.750
6.	Chicago	2-3-1	.400	7-5-1	.577
7.	Indiana	1-2-1	.333	4-2-2	.625
8.	Illinois	1-3-2	.250	7-3-2	.667
9.	Purdue	0-4-0	.000	4-4-0	.500

Non-conference record 44-3-4 .902
Iowa and Indiana join the conference in the 1900 season.

1901					
1.	Michigan	4-0-0	1.000	11-0-0	1.000
1.	Wisconsin	2-0-0	1.000	9-0-0	1.000
3.	Minnesota	3-1-0	.750	9-1-1	.864
4.	Illinois	4-2-0	.667	8-2-0	.800
5.	Northwestern	3-2-0	.600	8-2-1	.773
6.	Indiana	1-2-0	.333	6-3-0	.667
7.	Purdue	0-3-1	.000	4-4-1	.500
7.	Iowa	0-3-0	.000	5-3-0	.625
7.	Chicago	0-4-1	.000	5-5-2	.500

Non-conference record: 48-3-3 .917

1902		Conference		Overall	
1.	Michigan	5-0-0	1.000	11-0-0	1.000
2.	Chicago	5-1-0	.833	11-1-0	.917
3.	Minnesota	3-1-0	.750	9-2-1	.792
4.	Illinois	4-2-0	.667	10-2-1	.833
5.	Purdue	2-2-0	.500	7-2-1	.750
6.	Wisconsin	1-3-0	.250	6-3-0	.667
7.	Iowa	0-3-0	.000	5-3-0	.625
7.	Indiana	0-4-0	.000	3-5-1	.389
7.	Northwestern	0-4-0	.000	5-6-0	.455

Non-conference record: 47-4-4 .891

1903					
1.	Michigan	3-0-1	1.000	11-0-1	.958
1.	Minnesota	3-0-1	1.000	14-0-1	.967
1.	Northwestern	1-0-2	1.000	9-2-3	.750
4.	Chicago	4-1-1	.800	10-2-1	.808
·5.	Iowa	1-1-0	.500	9-2-0	.818
6.	Indiana	1-2-0	.333	4-4-0	.500
7.	Illinois	1-5-0	.167	8-6-0	.571
8.	Purdue	0-2-0	.000	4-2-0	.667
8.	Wisconsin	0-3-1	.000	6-3-1	.650

Non-conference record: 61-7-1 .891

1904					
1.	Minnesota	3-0-0	1.000	13-0-0	1.000
1.	Michigan	2-0-0	1.000	10-0-0	1.000
3.	Chicago	5-1-1	.833	8-1-1	.850
4.	Illinois	3-1-1	.750	9-2-1	.792
5.	Northwestern	1-2-0	.333	8-2-0	.800
5.	Purdue	1-2-0	.333	8-3-0	.727
7.	Wisconsin	0-3-0	.000	5-3-0	.625
7.	Indiana	0-3-0	.000	6-4-0	.600
7.	Iowa	0-3-0	.000	7-4-0	.636

Non-conference record: 59-4-0 .937

1905					
1.	Chicago	7-0-0	1.000	10-0-0	1.000
2.	Michigan	2-1-0	.667	12-1-0	.923
2.	Minnesota	2-1-0	.667	10-1-0	.909
4.	Purdue	1-1-1	.500	6-1-1	.812
5.	Wisconsin	1-2-0	.333	7-3-0	.700
6.	Indiana	0-1-1	.000	8-1-1	.850
6.	Iowa	0-2-0	.000	8-3-0	.727
6.	Northwestern	0-2-0	.000	8-2-1	.773
6.	Illinois	0-3-0	.000	5-4-0	.556

Non-conference record 61-3-1 .946

1906					
1.	Wisconsin	3-0-0	1.000	5-0-0	1.000
1.	Minnesota	2-0-0	1.000	2-2-1	.500
1.	Michigan	1-0-0	1.000	4-1-0	.800
4.	Chicago	3-1-0	.750	4-1-0	.800
5.	Illinois	1-3-0	.250	1-3-1	.300
6.	Iowa	0-1-0	.000	3-3-0	.500
6.	Indiana	0-2-0	.000	4-2-0	.000
6.	Purdue	0-3-0	.000	0-5-0	.000

Non-conference record: 13-7-2 .636
Northwestern drops football for 1906 and 1907.

— 350 —

1907		Conference		Overall	
1.	Chicago	4-0-0	1.000	4-1-0	.800
2.	Wisconsin	3-1-1	.750	3-1-1	.750
3.	Illinois	3-2-0	.600	3-2-0	.600
4.	Iowa	1-1-0	.500	3-2-0	.600
5.	Minnesota	0-1-1	.000	2-2-1	.500
5.	Indiana	0-3-0	.000	2-3-1	.417
5.	Purdue	0-3-0	.000	0-5-0	.000

Non-conference record: 6-5-1 .542
Michigan drops out of the Big Ten.

1908					
1.	Chicago	5-0-0	1.000	5-0-0	1.000
2.	Illinois	4-1-0	.800	5-1-1	.786
3.	Wisconsin	2-1-0	.667	5-1-0	.833
4.	Indiana	1-3-0	.250	2-4-0	.333
4.	Purdue	1-3-0	.250	4-3-0	.571
6.	Iowa	0-1-0	.000	2-5-0	.286
6.	Minnesota	0-2-0	.000	3-2-1	.583
6.	Northwestern	0-2-0	.000	2-2-0	.500

Non-conference record: 15-5-2 .727

1909					
1.	Minnesota	3-0-0	1.000	6-1-0	.857
2.	Chicago	4-1-1	.800	4-1-2	.714
3.	Illinois	3-1-0	.750	5-2-0	.714
4.	Wisconsin	2-1-1	.667	3-1-1	.700
5.	Indiana	1-3-0	.250	4-3-0	.571
5.	Northwestern	1-3-0	.250	1-3-1	.300
7.	Iowa	0-1-0	.000	2-4-1	.357
7.	Purdue	0-4-0	.000	2-5-0	.286

Non-conference record: 13-6-3 .659

1910					
1.	Illinois	4-0-0	1.000	7-0-0	1.000
1.	Minnesota	2-0-0	1.000	6-1-0	.857
3.	Indiana	3-1-0	.750	5-1-1	.786
4.	Iowa	1-1-0	.500	5-2-0	.714
5.	Chicago	2-4-0	.333	2-5-0	.286
5.	Wisconsin	1-2-1	.333	1-2-2	.400
5.	Northwestern	1-2-1	.333	1-3-1	.300
8.	Purdue	0-4-0	.000	1-5-0	.167

Non-conference record: 14-5-2 .714

1911					
1.	Minnesota	3-0-1	1.000	6-0-1	.929
2.	Chicago	5-1-0	.833	6-1-0	.857
3.	Wisconsin	2-1-1	.667	5-1-1	.786
4.	Illinois	2-2-1	.500	3-3-1	.500
4.	Iowa	2-2-0	.500	3-4-0	.429
6.	Purdue	1-3-0	.250	3-4-0	.429
7.	Northwestern	1-4-0	.200	3-4-0	.429
7.	Indiana	0-3-1	.000	3-3-1	.500

Non-conference record: 16-4-0 .800

1912					
1.	Wisconsin	5-0-0	1.000	7-0-0	1.000
2.	Chicago	6-1-0	.857	6-1-0	.857
3.	Minnesota	2-2-0	.500	4-3-0	.571
3.	Purdue	2-2-1	.500	4-2-1	.643
5.	Northwestern	2-3-0	.400	2-3-1	.417
6.	Illinois	1-3-1	.250	3-3-1	.500
6.	Iowa	1-3-0	.250	4-3-0	.571
8.	Indiana	0-5-0	.000	2-5-0	.286
---	Ohio State	------------------		6-3-0	.667

Non-conference record: 13-1-1 .900
Ohio State joins conference, qualifies for title in 1913.

1913		Conference		Overall	
1.	Chicago	7-0-0	1.000	7-0-0	1.000
2.	Iowa	2-1-0	.667	5-2-0	.714
2.	Minnesota	2-1-0	.667	5-2-0	.714
2.	Purdue	2-1-2	.667	4-1-2	.714
5.	Illinois	2-2-1	.500	4-2-1	.643
6.	Indiana	2-4-0	.333	3-4-0	.429
6.	Ohio State	1-2-0	.333	4-2-1	.714
6.	Wisconsin	1-2-1	.333	3-3-1	.500
9.	Northwestern	0-6-0	.000	1-6-0	.143

Non-conference record: 17-3-1 .833

1914					
1.	Illinois	6-0-0	1.000	7-0-0	1.000
2.	Minnesota	3-1-0	.750	6-1-0	.857
3.	Chicago	4-2-1	.667	4-2-1	.643
4.	Ohio State	2-2-0	.500	5-2-0	.714
4.	Purdue	2-2-0	.500	5-2-0	.714
4.	Wisconsin	2-2-1	.500	4-2-1	.643
7.	Iowa	1-2-0	.333	4-3-0	.571
8.	Indiana	1-4-0	.200	3-4-0	.429
9.	Northwestern	0-6-0	.000	1-6-0	.143

Non-conference record: 18-1-0 .947

1915					
1.	Minnesota	3-0-1	1.000	6-0-1	.929
1.	Illinois	3-0-2	1.000	5-0-2	.857
3.	Chicago	4-2-0	.667	5-2-0	.714
3.	Ohio State	2-1-1	.667	5-1-1	.786
5.	Purdue	2-2-0	.500	3-3-1	.500
6.	Wisconsin	2-3-0	.400	4-3-0	.571
7.	Iowa	1-2-0	.333	3-4-0	.429
8.	Indiana	1-3-0	.250	3-3-1	.500
9.	Northwestern	0-5-0	.000	2-5-0	.286

Non-conference record: 18-3-2 .826

1916					
1.	Ohio State	4-0-0	1.000	7-0-0	1.000
2.	Northwestern	4-1-0	.800	6-1-0	.857
3.	Minnesota	3-1-0	.750	6-1-0	.857
4.	Chicago	3-3-0	.500	3-4-0	.429
4.	Illinois	2-2-1	.500	3-3-1	.500
6.	Wisconsin	1-2-1	.333	4-2-1	.643
6.	Iowa	1-2-0	.333	4-3-0	.571
8.	Indiana	0-3-1	.000	2-4-1	.357
8.	Purdue	0-4-1	.000	2-4-1	.357

Non-conference record: 19-4-0 .826

1917					
1.	Ohio State	4-0-0	1.000	8-0-1	.944
2.	Minnesota	3-1-0	.750	4-1-0	.800
3.	Northwestern	3-2-0	.600	5-2-0	.714
3.	Wisconsin	3-2-0	.600	4-2-1	.643
5.	Illinois	2-2-1	.500	5-2-1	.688
5.	Chicago	2-2-1	.500	3-2-1	.583
7.	Indiana	1-2-0	.333	5-2-0	.714
8.	Iowa	0-2-0	.000	2-4-0	.333
8.	Purdue	0-4-0	.000	2-4-0	.333
8.	Michigan	0-1-0	.000	8-2-0	.800

Non-conference record: 28-3-2 .879
Michigan rejoins the Big Ten.

1918

		Conference		Overall	
1.	Illinois	4-0-0	1.000	5-2-0	.714
1.	Michigan	2-0-0	1.000	5-0-0	1.000
1.	Purdue	1-0-0	1.000	3-3-0	.500
4.	Iowa	2-1-0	.667	6-2-1	.722
4.	Minnesota	2-1-0	.667	5-2-1	.688
6.	Northwestern	1-1-0	.500	2-2-1	.500
7.	Wisconsin	1-2-0	.333	3-3-0	.500
8.	Ohio State	0-3-0	.000	3-3-0	.500
8.	Chicago	0-5-0	.000	0-5-0	.000
	Indiana	0-0-0	-----	2-2-0	.500

Non-conference record: 21-11-3 .643

1919

		Conference		Overall	
1.	Illinois	6-1-0	.857	6-1-0	.857
2.	Ohio State	3-1-0	.750	6-1-0	.857
3.	Chicago	4-2-0	.667	5-2-0	.714
4.	Wisconsin	3-2-0	.600	5-2-0	.714
4.	Minnesota	3-2-0	.600	4-2-1	.643
6.	Iowa	2-2-0	.500	5-2-0	.714
7.	Michigan	1-4-0	.200	3-4-0	.429
7.	Northwestern	1-4-0	.200	2-5-0	.286
9.	Indiana	0-2-0	.000	3-4-0	.429
9.	Purdue	0-3-0	.000	2-4-1	.357

Non-conference record: 18-4-2 .792

1920

		Conference		Overall	
1.	Ohio State	5-0-0	1.000	7-1-0	.875
2.	Wisconsin	4-1-0	.800	6-1-0	.857
3.	Indiana	3-1-0	.750	5-2-0	.714
4.	Illinois	4-2-0	.667	5-2-0	.714
5.	Iowa	3-2-0	.600	5-2-0	.714
6.	Michigan	2-2-0	.500	5-2-0	.714
7.	Northwestern	2-3-0	.400	3-4-0	.429
8.	Chicago	2-4-0	.333	3-4-0	.429
9.	Purdue	0-4-0	.000	2-5-0	.286
9.	Minnesota	0-6-0	.000	1-6-0	.167

Non-conference record: 17-4-0 .810

1921

		Conference		Overall	
1.	Iowa	5-0-0	1.000	7-0-0	1.000
2.	Chicago	4-1-0	.800	6-1-0	.857
2.	Ohio State	4-1-0	.800	5-2-0	.714
4.	Wisconsin	3-1-1	.750	5-1-1	.786
5.	Michigan	2-1-1	.667	5-1-1	.786
6.	Minnesota	2-4-0	.333	3-4-0	.429
6.	Indiana	1-2-0	.333	3-4-0	.429
8.	Illinois	1-4-0	.200	3-4-0	.429
8.	Purdue	1-4-0	.200	1-7-0	.125
10.	Northwestern	0-5-0	.000	1-6-0	.167

Non-conference record: 16-7-0 .696

1922

		Conference		Overall	
1.	Iowa	5-0-0	1.000	7-0-0	1.000
1.	Michigan	4-0-0	1.000	6-0-1	.929
2.	Chicago	4-0-0	1.000	5-1-1	.786
4.	Wisconsin	2-2-1	.500	4-2-1	.643
5.	Minnesota	2-3-1	.400	3-3-1	.500
6.	Illinois	2-4-0	.333	2-5-0	.286
7.	Northwestern	1-3-1	.250	3-3-1	.500
8.	Ohio State	1-4-0	.200	3-4-0	.429
9.	Indiana	0-2-1	.000	1-4-2	.286
9.	Purdue	0-3-1	.000	1-5-1	.214

Non-conference record: 14-6-3 .674

1923

		Conference		Overall	
1.	Illinois	5-0-0	1.000	8-0-0	1.000
1.	Michigan	4-0-0	1.000	8-0-0	1.000
3.	Chicago	5-1-0	.833	7-1-0	.875
4.	Minnesota	2-1-1	.667	5-1-1	.786
5.	Iowa	3-3-0	.500	5-3-0	.625
5.	Indiana	2-2-0	.500	3-4-0	.429
7.	Wisconsin	1-3-1	.250	3-3-1	.500
8.	Ohio State	1-4-0	.200	3-4-1	.438
8.	Purdue	1-4-0	.200	2-5-1	.312
10.	Northwestern	0-6-0	.000	2-6-0	.250

Non-conference record: 22-3-2 .852

1924

		Conference		Overall	
1.	Chicago	3-0-3	.750	4-1-3	.688
2.	Illinois	3-1-1	.750	6-1-1	.812
2.	Iowa	3-1-1	.750	6-1-1	.812
4.	Michigan	4-2-0	.667	6-2-0	.750
5.	Purdue	2-2-0	.500	5-2-0	.714
6.	Minnesota	1-2-1	.333	3-3-2	.500
7.	Northwestern	1-3-0	.250	4-4-0	.500
7.	Indiana	1-3-0	.250	4-4-0	.500
7.	Ohio State	1-3-2	.250	2-3-3	.438
10.	Wisconsin	0-2-2	.000	2-3-3	.438

Non-conference record: 23-5-3 .855

1925

		Conference		Overall	
1.	Michigan	5-1-0	.833	7-1-0	.875
2.	Northwestern	3-1-0	.750	5-3-0	.625
2.	Wisconsin	3-1-1	.750	6-1-1	.812
4.	Illinois	2-2-0	.500	5-3-1	.611
4.	Chicago	2-2-1	.500	3-5-1	.389
4.	Iowa	2-2-0	.500	5-3-0	.625
4.	Minnesota	1-1-1	.500	5-2-1	.688
8.	Ohio State	1-3-1	.250	4-3-1	.562
9.	Indiana	0-3-1	.000	3-4-1	.438
9.	Purdue	0-3-1	.000	3-4-1	.438

Non-conference record: 27-10-1 .724

1926

		Conference		Overall	
1.	Michigan	5-0-0	1.000	7-1-0	.875
1.	Northwestern	5-0-0	1.000	7-1-0	.875
3.	Ohio State	3-1-0	.750	7-1-0	.875
4.	Purdue	2-1-1	.667	5-2-1	.688
5.	Wisconsin	3-2-1	.600	5-2-1	.688
6.	Illinois	2-2-0	.500	6-2-0	.750
6.	Minnesota	2-2-0	.500	5-3-0	.625
8.	Indiana	0-4-0	.000	3-5-0	.375
8.	Iowa	0-5-0	.000	3-5-0	.375
8.	Chicago	0-5-0	.000	2-6-0	.250

Non-conference record: 28-6-0 .824

1927

		Conference		Overall	
1.	Illinois	5-0-0	1.000	7-0-1	.938
1.	Minnesota	3-0-1	1.000	6-0-2	.875
3.	Michigan	3-2-0	.600	6-2-0	.750
4.	Chicago	3-3-0	.500	4-5-0	.444
4.	Purdue	2-2-0	.500	6-2-0	.750
6.	Ohio State	2-3-0	.400	4-4-0	.500
6.	Northwestern	2-3-0	.400	4-4-0	.500
8.	Indiana	1-2-1	.333	3-4-1	.438
9.	Iowa	1-4-0	.200	4-4-0	.500
9.	Wisconsin	1-4-0	.200	4-4-0	.500

Non-conference record: 25-6-2 .788

1928		Conference		Overall	
1.	Illinois	4-1-0	.800	7-1-0	.875
2.	Wisconsin	3-1-1	.750	6-1-1	.812
3.	Minnesota	4-2-0	.667	6-2-0	.750
4.	Iowa	3-2-0	.600	6-2-0	.750
4.	Ohio State	3-2-0	.600	5-2-1	.688
6.	Purdue	2-2-1	.500	5-2-1	.688
7.	Northwestern	2-3-0	.400	5-3-0	.625
7.	Michigan	2-3-0	.400	3-4-1	.438
9.	Indiana	2-4-0	.333	4-4-0	.500
10.	Chicago	0-5-0	.000	2-7-0	.222

Non-conference record: 24-3-2 .862

1929					
1.	Purdue	5-0-0	1.000	8-0-0	1.000
2.	Illinois	3-1-1	.750	6-1-1	.812
3.	Minnesota	3-2-0	.600	6-2-0	.750
3.	Northwestern	3-2-0	.600	6-3-0	.667
5.	Iowa	2-2-0	.500	4-2-2	.625
5.	Ohio State	2-2-1	.500	4-3-1	.562
7.	Chicago	1-3-0	.250	7-3-0	.700
7.	Michigan	1-3-1	.250	5-3-1	.611
7.	Indiana	1-3-1	.250	2-6-1	.278
10.	Wisconsin	1-4-0	.200	4-5-0	.444

Non-conference record: 30-6-2 .816

1930					
1.	Michigan	5-0-0	1.000	8-0-1	.944
1.	Northwestern	5-0-0	1.000	7-1-0	.875
3.	Purdue	4-2-0	.667	6-2-0	.750
4.	Wisconsin	2-2-1	.500	6-2-1	.722
4.	Ohio State	2-2-1	.500	5-2-1	.688
6.	Minnesota	1-3-0	.250	3-4-1	.438
6.	Indiana	1-3-0	.250	2-5-1	.312
8.	Illinois	1-4-0	.200	3-5-0	.375
9.	Iowa	0-1-0	.000	4-4-0	.500
9.	Chicago	0-4-0	.000	2-5-2	.333

Non-conference record: 25-9-5 .705

1931					
1.	Purdue	5-1-0	.833	9-1-0	.900
1.	Michigan	5-1-0	.833	8-1-1	.850
1.	Northwestern	5-1-0	.833	7-1-1	.833
4.	Ohio State	4-2-0	.667	6-3-0	.667
5.	Minnesota	3-2-0	.600	7-3-0	.700
6.	Wisconsin	3-3-0	.500	5-4-1	.550
7.	Indiana*	1-4-1	.200	4-5-1	.450
7.	Chicago	1-4-0	.200	2-6-1	.278
9.	Illinois	0-6-0	.000	2-6-0	.333
9.	Iowa	0-3-1	.000	1-6-1	.188

Non-conference record: 19-4-3 .788
*Five post-season charity games between Big Ten teams not included in conference standings.

1932					
1.	Michigan	6-0-0	1.000	8-0-0	1.000
1.	Purdue	5-0-1	1.000	7-0-1	.938
3.	Wisconsin	4-1-1	.800	6-1-1	.812
4.	Ohio State	2-1-2	.500	4-1-3	.688
5.	Minnesota	2-3-0	.400	5-3-0	.625
5.	Northwestern	2-3-1	.400	3-4-1	.438
6.	Illinois	2-4-0	.333	5-4-0	.556
8.	Chicago	1-4-0	.200	3-4-1	.438
8.	Indiana	1-4-1	.200	2-5-1	.450
10.	Iowa	0-5-0	.000	1-7-0	.125

Non-conference record: 19-4-2 .800

1933		Conference		Overall	
1.	Michigan	5-0-1	1/000	7-0-1	.938
1.	Minnesota	2-0-4	1.000	4-0-4	.750
3.	Ohio State	4-1-0	.800	7-1-0	.875
4.	Purdue	3-1-1	.750	6-1-1	.812
5.	Iowa	3-2-0	.600	5-3-0	.625
5.	Illinois	3-2-0	.600	5-3-0	.625
7.	Northwestern	1-4-1	.200	1-5-2	.250
8.	Chicago	0-3-2	.000	3-3-2	.500
8.	Indiana	0-3-2	.000	1-5-2	.250
8.	Wisconsin	0-5-1	.000	2-5-1	.312

Non-conference record: 20-5-1 .788

1934					
1.	Minnesota	5-0-0	1.000	8-0-0	1.000
2.	Ohio State	5-1-0	.833	7-1-0	.875
3.	Illinois	4-1-0	.800	7-1-0	.875
4.	Purdue	3-1-0	.750	5-3-0	.625
5.	Wisconsin	2-3-0	.400	4-4-0	.500
5.	Northwestern	2-3-0	.400	3-5-0	.375
7.	Chicago	2-4-0	.333	4-4-0	.500
8.	Indiana	1-3-1	.250	3-3-2	.500
8.	Iowa	1-3-1	.250	2-5-1	.312
10.	Michigan	0-6-0	.000	1-7-0	.125

Non-conference record: 19-8-1 .696

1935					
1.	Minnesota	5-0-0	1.000	8-0-0	1.000
1.	Ohio State	5-0-0	1.000	7-1-0	.875
3.	Purdue	3-3-0	.500	4-4-0	.500
3.	Indiana	2-2-1	.500	4-3-1	.562
5.	Michigan	2-3-0	.400	4-4-0	.500
5.	Chicago	2-3-0	.400	4-4-0	.500
5.	Northwestern	2-3-1	.400	4-3-1	.562
8.	Iowa	1-2-2	.333	4-2-2	.625
9.	Illinois	1-4-0	.200	3-5-0	.375
9.	Wisconsin	1-4-0	.200	1-7-0	.125

Non-conference record: 19-9-0 .679

1936					
1.	Northwestern	6-0-0	1.000	7-1-0	.875
2.	Minnesota	4-1-0	.800	7-1-0	.875
2.	Ohio State	4-1-0	.800	5-3-0	.625
4.	Indiana	3-1-1	.750	5-2-1	.688
4.	Purdue	3-1-1	.750	5-2-1	.688
6.	Illinois	2-2-1	.500	4-3-1	.562
7.	Chicago	1-4-0	.200	2-5-1	.312
8.	Iowa	0-4-1	.000	3-4-1	.438
8.	Wisconsin	0-4-0	.000	2-6-0	.250
8.	Michigan	0-5-0	.000	1-7-0	.125

Non-conference record: 18-11-1 .617

1937					
1.	Minnesota	5-0-0	1.000	6-2-0	.750
2.	Ohio State	5-1-0	.833	6-2-0	.750
3.	Indiana	3-2-0	.600	5-3-0	.625
4.	Northwestern	3-3-0	.500	4-4-0	.500
4.	Michigan	3-3-0	.500	4-4-0	.500
4.	Purdue	2-2-1	.500	4-3-1	.562
4.	Wisconsin	2-2-1	.500	4-3-1	.562
8.	Illinois	2-3-0	.400	3-3-2	.500
9.	Chicago	0-4-0	.000	1-6-0	.143
9.	Iowa	0-5-0	.000	1-7-0	.125

Non-conference record: 13-12-2 .51

1938		Conference		Overall	
1.	Minnesota	4-1-0	.800	6-2-0	.750
2.	Michigan	3-1-1	.750	5-1-1	.786
2.	Purdue	3-1-1	.750	5-1-2	.750
4.	Northwestern	2-1-2	.667	4-2-2	.625
5.	Ohio State	3-2-1	.600	4-3-1	.562
5.	Wisconsin	3-2-0	.600	5-3-0	.625
7.	Illinois	2-3-0	.400	3-5-0	.375
8.	Iowa	1-3-1	.250	1-6-1	.188
9.	Indiana	1-4-0	.200	1-6-1	.188
10.	Chicago	0-4-0	.000	1-6-1	.188

Non-conference record: 13-13-3 .500

1939					
1.	Ohio State	5-1-0	.833	6-2-0	.750
2.	Iowa	4-1-1	.800	6-1-1	.812
3.	Purdue	2-1-2	.667	3-3-2	.500
4.	Michigan	3-2-0	.600	6-2-0	.750
4.	Northwestern	3-2-1	.600	3-4-1	.438
6.	Illinois	3-3-0	.500	3-4-1	.438
7.	Minnesota	2-3-1	.400	3-4-1	.438
7	Indiana	2-3-0	.400	2-4-2	.375
9.	Chicago	0-3-0	.000	2-6-0	.250
9.	Wisconsin	0-5-1	.000	1-6-1	.188

Non-conference record: 11-12-3 .481

1940					
1.	Minnesota	6-0-0	1.000	8-0-0	1.000
2.	Michigan	3-1-0	.750	7-1-0	.875
3.	Northwestern	4-2-0	.667	6-2-0	.750
4.	Wisconsin	3-3-0	.500	4-4-0	.500
4.	Ohio State	3-3-0	.500	4-4-0	.500
6.	Iowa	2-3-0	.400	4-4-0	.500
6.	Indiana	2-3-0	.400	3-5-0	.375
8.	Purdue	1-4-0	.200	2-6-0	.250
9.	Illinois	0-5-0	.000	1-7-0	.125

Non-conference record: 15-9-0 .625
Chicago drops football.

1941					
1.	Minnesota	5-0-0	1.000	8-0-0	1.000
2.	Michigan	3-1-1	.750	6-1-1	.812
2.	Ohio State	3-1-1	.750	6-1-1	.812
4.	Northwestern	4-2-0	.667	5-3-0	.625
5.	Wisconsin	3-3-0	.500	3-5-0	.375
6.	Iowa	2-4-0	.333	3-5-0	.375
7.	Purdue	1-3-0	.250	2-5-1	.312
7.	Indiana	1-3-0	.250	2-6-0	.250
9.	Illinois	0-5-0	.000	2-6-0	.250

Non-conference record: 15-10-1 .596

1942					
1.	Ohio State	5-1-0	.833	9-1-0	.900
2.	Wisconsin	4-1-0	.800	8-1-1	.850
3.	Illinois	3-2-0	.600	6-4-0	.600
3.	Michigan	3-2-0	.600	7-3-0	.700
5.	Indiana	2-2-0	.500	7-3-0	.700
5.	Iowa	3-3-0	.500	6-4-0	.600
5.	Minnesota	3-3-0	.500	5-4-0	.556
8.	Purdue	1-4-0	.200	1-8-0	.111
9.	Northwestern	0-6-0	.000	1-9-0	.100

Non-conference record: 26-13-1 .662

1943		Conference		Overall	
1.	Purdue	6-0-0	1.000	9-0-0	1.000
1.	Michigan	6-0-0	1.000	8-1-0	.889
3.	Northwestern	5-1-0	.883	6-2-0	.750
4.	Indiana	2-3-1	.400	4-4-2	.500
4.	Minnesota	2-3-0	.400	5-4-0	.556
6.	Illinois	2-4-0	.333	3-7-0	.300
7.	Ohio State	1-4-0	.200	3-5-0	.375
8.	Wisconsin	1-6-0	.143	1-9-0	.100
9.	Iowa	0-4-1	.000	1-6-1	.188

Non-conference record: 15-13-1 .534

1944					
1.	Ohio State	6-0-0	1.000	9-0-0	1.000
2.	Michigan	5-2-0	.714	8-2-0	.800
3.	Purdue	4-2-0	.667	5-5-0	.500
4.	Minnesota	3-2-1	.600	5-3-1	.611
5.	Indiana	4-3-0	.571	7-3-0	.700
6.	Illinois	3-3-0	.500	5-4-1	.550
7.	Wisconsin	2-4-0	.333	3-6-0	.333
8.	Northwestern	0-5-1	.000	1-7-1	.167
8.	Iowa	0-6-0	.000	1-7-0	.125

Non-conference record: 17-10-1 .625

1945					
1.	Indiana	5-0-1	1.000	9-0-1	.950
2.	Michigan	5-1-0	.833	7-3-0	.700
3.	Ohio State	5-2-0	.714	7-2-0	.778
4.	Northwestern	3-3-1	.500	4-4-1	.500
4.	Purdue	3-3-0	.500	7-3-0	.700
6.	Wisconsin	2-3-1	.400	3-4-2	.444
7	Illinois	1-4-1	.200	2-6-1	.278
8.	Minnesota	1-5-0	.167	4-5-0	.444
8.	Iowa	1-5-0	.167	2-7-0	.222

Non-conference record: 19-8-1 .696

1946					
1.	Illinois	6-1-0	.857	8-2-0	.800
2.	Michigan	5-1-1	.785	6-2-1	.722
3.	Indiana	4-2-0	.667	6-3-0	.667
4.	Iowa	3-3-0	.500	5-4-0	.556
5.	Minnesota	3-4-0	.429	5-4-0	.556
6.	Northwestern	2-3-1	.416	4-4-1	.500
6.	Ohio State	2-3-1	.416	4-3-2	.555
8.	Wisconsin	2-5-0	.286	4-5-0	.444
9.	Purdue	0-5-1	.083	2-6-1	.277

Non-conference record: 17-6-1 .729

1947					
1.	Michigan	6-0-0	1.000	10-0-0	1.000
2.	Wisconsin	3-2-1	.583	5-3-1	.611
3.	Illinois	3-3-0	.500	5-3-1	.611
3.	Minnesota	3-3-0	.500	6-3-0	.667
3.	Purdue	3-3-0	.500	5-4-0	.556
6.	Iowa	2-3-1	.417	3-5-1	.367
6.	Indiana	2-3-1	.417	5-3-1	.611
8.	Northwestern	2-4-0	.333	3-6-0	.333
9.	Ohio State	1-4-1	.250	2-6-1	.278

Non-conference record: 19-8-1 .696

<table>
<tr><td colspan="6">

1948   Conference   Overall

</td></tr>
</table>

1948		Conference		Overall	
1.	Michigan	6-0-0	1.000	9-0-0	1.000
2.	Northwestern	5-1-0	.833	8-2-0	.800
3.	Minnesota	5-2-0	.714	7-2-0	.788
4.	Ohio State	3-3-0	.500	6-3-0	.667
5.	Indiana	2-4-0	.333	2-7-0	.222
5.	Iowa	2-4-0	.333	4-5-0	.444
5.	Purdue	2-4-0	.333	3-6-0	.333
8.	Illinois	2-5-0	.286	2-6-0	.333
9.	Wisconsin	1-5-0	.167	2-7-0	.222

Non-conference record: 15-10-0 .600

1949		Conference		Overall	
1.	Ohio State	4-1-1	.750	7-1-2	.800
2.	Michigan	4-1-1	.750	6-2-1	.722
3.	Minnesota	4-2-0	.667	7-2-0	.778
4.	Wisconsin	3-2-1	.583	5-3-1	.611
5.	Illinois	3-3-1	.500	3-4-2	.444
5.	Iowa	3-3-0	.500	4-5-0	.444
7.	Northwestern	3-4-0	.429	4-5-0	.444
8.	Purdue	2-4-0	.333	4-5-0	.444
9.	Indiana	0-6-0	.000	1-8-0	.111

Non-conference record: 13-9-2 .583

1950		Conference		Overall	
1.	Michigan	4-1-1	.750	6-3-1	.650
2.	Ohio State	5-2-0	.714	6-3-0	.667
2.	Wisconsin	5-2-0	.714	6-3-0	.667
4.	Illinois	4-2-0	.667	7-2-0	.778
5.	Northwestern	3-3-0	.500	6-3-0	.667
6.	Iowa	2-4-0	.333	3-5-1	.389
7.	Minnesota	1-4-1	.250	1-7-1	.167
8.	Indiana	1-4-0	.200	3-5-1	.389
8.	Purdue	1-4-0	.200	2-7-0	.222
	Michigan State	-------	------	8-1-0	.889

Non-conference record: 14-12-2 .536*
Michigan State joins the Big Ten, eligible for title in 1953.

1951		Conference		Overall	
1.	Illinois	5-0-1	.917	9-0-1	.950
2.	Purdue	4-1-0	.800	5-4-0	.554
3.	Wisconsin	5-1-1	.786	7-1-1	.833
4.	Michigan	4-2-0	.667	4-5-0	.444
5.	Ohio State	2-2-2	.500	4-3-2	.564
6.	Northwestern	2-4-0	.333	5-4-0	.554
7.	Minnesota	1-4-1	.250	2-6-1	.278
8.	Indiana	1-5-0	.167	2-7-0	.222
9.	Iowa	0-5-1	.083	2-5-2	.333
	Michigan State	-------	-----	9-0-0	1.000

Non-conference record: 16-11-1 .589*

1952		Conference		Overall	
1.	Wisconsin	4-1-1	.750	6-3-1	.650
1.	Purdue	4-1-1	.750	4-3-2	.555
3.	Ohio State	5-2-0	.714	6-3-0	.667
4.	Michigan	4-2-0	.667	5-4-0	.555
4.	Minnesota	3-1-2	.667	4-3-2	.555
6.	Illinois	2-5-0	.286	4-5-0	.444
6.	Northwestern	2-5-0	.286	2-6-1	.278
6.	Iowa	2-5-0	.286	2-7-0	.222
9.	Indiana	1-5-0	.167	2-7-0	.222
	Michigan State	-------	-----	9-0-0	1.000

Non-conference record: 8-14-2 .375 *
*Games against Michigan State are treated as non-conference. games.

1953		Conference		Overall	
1.	Michigan State	5-1-0	.833	9-1-0	.900
1.	Illinois	5-1-0	.833	7-1-1	.833
3.	Wisconsin	4-1-1	.750	6-2-1	.722
4.	Ohio State	4-3-0	.571	6-3-0	.667
5.	Minnesota	3-3-1	.500	4-4-1	.500
5.	Iowa	3-3-0	.500	5-3-1	.611
5.	Michigan	3-3-0	.500	6-3-0	.667
8.	Purdue	2-4-0	.333	2-7-0	.222
9.	Indiana	1-5-0	.167	2-7-0	.222
10.	Northwestern	0-6-0	.000	3-6-0	.333

Non-conference record: 20-7-2 .724

1954		Conference		Overall	
1.	Ohio State	7-0-0	1.000	10-0-0	1.000
2.	Wisconsin	5-2-0	.714	7-2-0	.778
2.	Michigan	5-2-0	.714	6-3-0	.667
4.	Minnesota	4-2-0	.667	7-2-0	.778
5.	Iowa	4-3-0	.571	5-4-0	.555
6.	Purdue	3-3-0	.500	5-3-1	.611
7.	Indiana	2-4-0	.333	3-6-0	.333
8.	Michigan State	1-5-0	.167	3-6-0	.333
8.	Northwestern	1-5-0	.167	2-7-0	.222
10.	Illinois	0-6-0	.000	1-8-0	.111

Non-conference record: 17-9-1 .648

1955		Conference		Overall	
1.	Ohio State	6-0-0	1.000	7-2-0	.778
2.	Michigan State	5-1-0	.833	9-1-0	.900
3.	Michigan	5-2-0	.714	7-2-0	778
4.	Purdue	4-2-1	.643	5-3-1	611
5.	Illinois	3-3-1	.500	5-3-1	.611
6.	Wisconsin	3-4-0	.429	4-5-0	.444
7.	Iowa	2-3-1	.417	3-5-1	.389
8.	Minnesota	2-5-0	.286	3-6-0	.333
9.	Indiana	1-5-0	.167	3-6-0	.333
10.	Northwestern	0-6-1	.071	0-8-1	.056

Non-conference record: 15-10-0 .600

1956		Conference		Overall	
1.	Iowa	5-1-0	.833	9-1-0	.900
2.	Michigan	5-2-0	.714	7-2-0	.778
2.	Minnesota	4-1-2	.714	6-1-2	.778
4.	Michigan State	4-2-0	.667	7-2-0	.778
4.	Ohio State	4-2-0	.667	6-3-0	.667
6.	Northwestern	3-3-1	.500	4-4-1	.500
7.	Purdue	1-4-2	.286	3-4-2	.444
7.	Illinois	1-4-2	.286	2-5-2	.333
9.	Wisconsin	0-4-3	.214	1-5-3	.278
10.	Indiana	1-5-0	.167	3-6-0	.333

Non-conference record: 20-5-0 .800

1957		Conference		Overall	
1.	Ohio State	7-0-0	1.000	9-1-0	.900
2.	Michigan State	5-1-0	.833	8-1-0	.889
3.	Iowa	4-1-1	.750	7-1-1	.833
4.	Purdue	4-3-0	.571	5-4-0	.556
4.	Wisconsin	4-3-0	.571	6-3-0	.667
6.	Michigan	3-3-1	.500	5-3-1	.611
7.	Illinois	3-4-0	.427	4-5-0	.444
8.	Minnesota	3-5-0	.375	4-5-0	.444
9.	Indiana	0-6-0	.000	1-8-0	.111
9.	Northwestern	0-7-0	.000	0-9-0	.000

Non-conference record: 16-7-0 .696

1958		Conference		Overall	
1.	Iowa	5-1-0	.833	8-1-1	.859
1.	Wisconsin	5-1-0	.833	7-1-1	.833
3.	Ohio State	4-1-2	.714	6-1-2	.778
4.	Purdue	3-1-2	.667	6-1-2	.778
5.	Indiana	3-2-1	.583	5-3-1	.611
6.	Illinois	4-3-0	.571	4-5-0	.444
7.	Northwestern	3-4-0	.429	5-4-0	.556
8.	Michigan	1-5-1	.214	2-6-1	.278
9.	Minnesota	1-6-0	.142	1-8-0	.111
10.	Michigan State	0-5-1	.083	3-5-1	.389

Non-conference record: 18-6-2 .731

1959					
1.	Wisconsin	5-2-0	.714	7-3-0	.700
2.	Michigan State	4-2-0	.667	5-4-0	.556
3.	Purdue	4-2-1	.643	5-2-2	.667
3.	Illinois	4-2-1	.643	5-3-1	.611
5.	Northwestern	4-3-0	.571	6-3-0	.667
6.	Iowa	3-3-0	.500	5-4-0	.556
7.	Michigan	3-4-0	.429	4-5-0	.444
8.	Indiana	2-4-1	.357	4-4-1	.500
8.	Ohio State	2-4-1	.357	3-5-1	.389
10.	Minnesota	1-6-0	.143	2-7-0	.222

Non-conference record: 14-8-1 .630

1960					
1.	Minnesota	5-1-0	.833	8-2-0	.800
2.	Iowa	5-1-0	.833	8-1-0	.889
3.	Ohio State	4-2-0	.667	7-2-0	.778
4	Michigan State	3-2-0	.600	6-2-1	.722
5.	Illinois	2-4-0	.333	5-4-0	.556
5.	Michigan	2-4-0	.333	5-4-0	.556
5.	Northwestern	2-4-0	.333	5-4-0	.556
5.	Purdue	2-4-0	.333	4-4-1	.500
9.	Wisconsin	2-5-0	.286	4-5-0	.444
	Indiana *	-----------------		1-8-0	.111

Non-conference record (excl. Indiana) 18-2-2 .864
*Indiana not eligible for title.

1961					
1.	Ohio State	6-0-0	1.000	8-0-1	.944
2.	Minnesota	6-1-0	.875	8-2-0	.800
3.	Michigan State	5-2-0	.714	7-2-0	.778
4.	Purdue	4-2-0	.667	6-3-0	.667
5.	Wisconsin	4-3-0	.571	6-3-0	.667
6.	Michigan	3-3-0	.500	6-3-0	.667
7.	Iowa	2-4-0	.333	4-5-0	.444
7.	Northwestern	2-4-0	.333	4-5-0	.444
9.	Indiana	0-6-0	.000	2-7-0	.222
10.	Illinois	0-7-0	.000	0-9-0	.000

Non-conference record: 19-7-1 .722

1962					
1.	Wisconsin	6-1-0	.857	8-2-0	.800
2.	Minnesota	5-2-0	.714	6-2-1	.722
3.	Northwestern	4-2-0	.667	7-2-0	.778
3.	Ohio State	4-2-0	.667	6-3-0	.667
5.	Michigan State	3-3-0	.500	5-4-0	.556
5.	Purdue	3-3-0	.500	4-4-1	.500
5.	Iowa	3-3-0	.500	4-5-0	.444
8.	Illinois	2-5-0	.286	2-7-0	.222
9.	Indiana	1-5-0	.167	3-6-0	.333
10.	Michigan	1-6-0	.143	2-7-0	.222

Non-conference record: 15-10-2 .593

1963		Conference		Overall	
1.	Illinois	5-1-1	.786	8-1-1	.850
2.	Michigan State	4-1-1	.750	6-2-1	.722
2.	Ohio State	4-1-1	.750	5-3-1	.611
4.	Purdue	4-3-0	.571	5-4-0	.536
5.	Northwestern	3-4-0	.429	5-4-0	.556
5.	Wisconsin	3-4-0	.429	5-4-0	.556
7.	Michigan	2-3-2	.429	3-4-2	.444
8.	Iowa	2-3-1	.417	3-3-2	.500
9.	Minnesota	2-5-0	.286	3-6-0	.333
10.	Indiana	1-5-0	.167	3-6-0	.333

Non-conference record: 16-7-1 .611

1964					
1.	Michigan	6-1-0	.857	9-1-0	.900
2.	Ohio State	5-1-0	.833	7-2-0	.778
3.	Purdue	5-2-0	.714	6-3-0	.667
4.	Illinois	4-3-0	.571	6-3-0	.667
4.	Minnesota	4-3-0	.571	5-4-0	.556
6.	Michigan State	3-3-0	.500	4-5-0	.444
7.	Northwestern	2-5-0	.286	3-6-0	.333
7.	Wisconsin	2-5-0	.286	3-6-0	.333
9.	Iowa	1-5-0	.167	3-6-0	.333
9.	Indiana	1-5-0	.167	2-7-0	.222

Non-conference record: 15-10-0 .600

1965					
1.	Michigan State	7-0-0	1.000	10-1-0	.902.
2.	Ohio State	6-1-0	.857	7-2-0	.778
3.	Purdue	5-2-0	.714	7-2-1	.750
3.	Minnesota	5-2-0	.714	5-4-1	.550
5.	Illinois	4-3-0	.571	6-4-0	.600
6.	Northwestern	3-4-0	.429	4-6-0	.400
7.	Michigan	2-5-0	.286	4-6-0	.400
7.	Wisconsin	2-5-0	.286	2-7-1	.250
9.	Indiana	1-6-0	.143	2-8-0	.200
10.	Iowa	0-7-0	.000	1-9-0	.100

Non-conference record: 13-14-3 .483

1966					
1.	Michigan State	7-0-0	1.000	9-0-1	.950
2.	Purdue	6-1-0	.857	9-2-0	.818
3.	Michigan	4-3-0	.571	6-4-0	.600
3.	Illinois	4-3-0	.571	4-6-0	.400
5.	Minnesota	3-3-1	.500	4-5-1	.450
6.	Ohio State	3-4-0	.429	4-5-0	.444
7.	Northwestern	2-4-1	.357	3-6-1	.350
7.	Wisconsin	2-4-1	.357	3-6-1	.350
9.	Indiana	1-5-1	.214	1-8-1	.150
10.	Iowa	1-6-0	.143	2-8-0	.200

Non-conference record: 12-17-1 .417

1967					
1.	Indiana	6-1-0	.857	9-2-0	.818
1.	Minnesota	6-1-0	.857	8-2-0	.800
1.	Purdue	6-1-0	.857	8-2-0	.800
4.	Ohio State	5-2-0	.714	6-3-0	.667
5.	Illinois	3-4-0	.429	4-6-0	.400
5.	Michigan	3-4-0	.429	4-6-0	.400
5.	Michigan State	3-4-0	.429	3-7-0	.300
8.	Northwestern	2-5-0	.286	3-7-0	.300
9.	Iowa	0-6-1	.071	1-8-1	.150
9.	Wisconsin	0-6-1	.071	0-9-1	.050

Non-conference record: 12-18-0 .400

1968

		Conference		Overall	
1.	Ohio State	7-0-0	1.000	10-0-0	1.000
2.	Michigan	6-1-0	.857	8-2-0	.800
3.	Purdue	5-2-0	.714	8-2-0	.800
3.	Minnesota	5-2-0	.714	6-4-0	.600
5.	Indiana	4-3-0	.571	6-4-0	.600
5.	Iowa	4-3-0	.571	5-5-0	.500
7.	Michigan State	2-5-0	.286	5-5-0	.500
8.	Illinois	1-6-0	.143	1-9-0	.100
8.	Northwestern	1-6-0	.143	1-9-0	.100
10.	Wisconsin	0-7-0	.000	0-10-0	.000

Non-conference record: 15-15-0 .500

1969

1.	Ohio State	6-1-0	.857	8-1-0	.889
1.	Michigan	6-1-0	.857	8-3-0	.727
3.	Purdue	5-2-0	.714	8-2-0	.800
4.	Minnesota	4-3-0	.571	4-5-1	.450
5.	Indiana	3-4-0	.429	4-6-0	.400
5.	Iowa	3-4-0	.429	5-5-0	.500
5.	Northwestern	3-4-0	.429	3-7-0	.300
5.	Wisconsin	3-4-0	.429	3-7-0	.300
9.	Michigan State	2-5-0	.286	4-6-0	.400
10.	Illinois	0-7-0	.000	0-10-0	.000

Non-conference record: 12-17-1 .417

1970

1.	Ohio State	7-0-0	1.000	9-1-0	.900
2.	Michigan	6-1-0	.857	9-1-0	.900
2.	Northwestern	6-1-0	.857	6-4-0	.600
4.	Iowa	3-3-1	.500	3-6-1	.350
5.	Wisconsin	3-4-0	.429	4-5-1	.450
5.	Michigan State	3-4-0	.429	4-6-0	.400
7.	Minnesota	2-4-1	.357	3-6-1	.350
8.	Purdue	2-5-0	.286	4-6-0	.400
9.	Illinois	1-6-0	.143	3-7-0	.300
9.	Indiana	1-6-0	.143	1-9-0	.100

Non-conference record: 12-17-1 .417

1971

1.	Michigan	8-0-0	1.000	11-1-0	.917
2.	Northwestern	6-3-0	.667	7-4-0	.636
3.	Ohio State	5-3-0	.625	6-4-0	.600
3.	Illinois	5-3-0	.625	5-6-0	.455
3.	Michigan State	5-3-0	.625	6-5-0	.545
6.	Wisconsin	3-5-0	.375	4-6-1	.405
6.	Minnesota	3-5-0	.375	4-7-0	.364
6.	Purdue	3-5-0	.375	3-7-0	.300
9.	Indiana	2-6-0	.250	3-8-0	.273
10.	Iowa	1-8-0	.111	1-10-0	.091

Non-conference record: 9-17-1 .352

1972

1.	Michigan	7-1-0	.875	10-1-0	.909
1.	Ohio State	7-1-0	.875	9-2-0	.818
3.	Purdue	6-2-0	.750	6-5-0	.545
4.	Michigan State	5-2-1	.688	5-5-1	.500
5.	Minnesota	4-4-0	.500	4-7-0	.364
6.	Indiana	3-5-0	.375	5-6-0	.455
6.	Illinois	3-5-0	.375	3-8-0	.273
8.	Iowa	2-6-1	.278	3-7-1	.318
9.	Wisconsin	2-6-0	.250	4-7-0	.364
10.	Northwestern	1-8-0	.111	2-9-0	.182

Non-conference record: 11-17-0 .393

1973

		Conference		Overall	
1.	Michigan	7-0-1	.939	10-0-1	.954
1.	Ohio State	7-0-1	.939	10-0-1	.954
3.	Minnesota	6-2-0	.750	7-4-0	.636
4.	Illinois	4-4-0	.500	5-6-0	.454
4.	Michigan State	4-4-0	.500	5-6-0	.454
4.	Purdue	4-4-0	.500	5-6-0	.454
4.	Northwestern	4-4-0	.500	4-7-0	.363
8.	Wisconsin	3-5-0	.375	4-7-0	.363
9.	Indiana	0-8-0	.000	2-9-0	.182
9.	Iowa	0-8-0	.000	0-11-0	.000

Non-conference record: 13-17-0 .433

1974

1.	Michigan	7-1-0	.875	10-1-0	.909
1.	Ohio State	7-1-0	.875	10-2-0	.833
3.	Michigan State	6-1-1	.813	7-3-1	.682
4.	Wisconsin	5-3-0	.625	7-4-0	.636
5.	Illinois	4-3-1	.563	6-4-1	.590
6.	Purdue	3-5-0	.375	4-6-1	.410
7.	Minnesota	2-6-0	.250	4-7-0	.364
7.	Iowa	2-6-0	.250	3-8-0	.273
7.	Northwestern	2-6-0	.250	3-8-0	.273
10.	Indiana	1-7-0	.125	1-10-0	.091

Non-conference record: 16-14-1 .532

1975

1.	Ohio State	8-0-0	1.000	11-1-0	.917
2.	Michigan	7-1-0	.875	8-2-2	.750
3.	Michigan State	4-4-0	.500	7-4-0	.636
3.	Illinois	4-4-0	.500	5-6-0	.455
3.	Purdue	4-4-0	.500	4-7-0	.363
6.	Wisconsin	3-4-1	.438	4-6-1	.409
7.	Minnesota	3-5-0	.375	6-5-0	.545
7.	Iowa	3-5-0	.375	3-8-0	.273
9.	Northwestern	2-6-0	.250	3-8-0	.273
10.	Indiana	1-6-1	.188	2-8-1	.227

Non-conference record: 14-16-2 .469

1976

1.	Michigan	7-1-0	.875	10-2-0	.833
1.	Ohio State	7-1-0	.875	9-2-1	.792
3.	Minnesota	4-4-0	.500	6-5-0	.545
3.	Purdue	4-4-0	.500	5-6-0	.455
3.	Illinois	4-4-0	.500	5-6-0	.455
3.	Indiana	4-4-0	.500	5-6-0	.455
7.	Iowa	3-5-0	.375	5-6-0	.455
7.	Wisconsin	3-5-0	.375	5-6-0	.455
7.	Michigan State	3-5-0	.375	4-6-1	.409
10.	Northwestern	1-7-0	.125	1-10-0	.091

Non-conference record: 15-15-2 .500

1977

1.	Michigan	7-1-0	.875	10-2-0	.833
1.	Ohio State	7-1-0	.875	9-3-0	.750
3.	Michigan State	6-1-1	.813	7-3-1	.682
4.	Indiana	4-3-1	.563	5-5-1	.500
5.	Minnesota	4-4-0	.500	7-5-0	.583
6.	Purdue	3-5-0	.375	5-6-0	.456
6.	Iowa	3-5-0	.375	4-7-0	.364
8.	Wisconsin	3-6-0	.333	5-6-0	.456
9.	Illinois	2-6-0	.250	3-8-0	.273
10.	Northwestern	1-8-0	.111	1-10-0	.091

Non-conference record: 16-15-1 .516

1978		Conference		Overall	
1.	Michigan	7-1-0	.875	10-2-0	.833
1.	Michigan State	7-1-0	.875	8-3-0	.727
3.	Purdue	6-1-1	.813	9-2-1	.792
4.	Ohio State	6-2-0	.750	7-4-1	.625
5.	Minnesota	4-4-0	.500	5-6-0	.455
6.	Wisconsin	3-4-2	.444	5-4-2	.545
7.	Indiana	3-5-0	.375	4-7-0	.364
8.	Iowa	2-6-0	.250	2-9-0	.182
9.	Illinois	0-6-2	.125	1-8-2	.182
10.	Northwestern	0-8-1	.056	0-10-1	.046

Non-conference record: 13-17-1 .435

1979					
1.	Ohio State	8-0-0	1.000	11-1-0	.917
2.	Purdue	7-1-0	.875	10-2-0	.833
3.	Michigan	6-2-0	.750	8-4-0	.667
4.	Indiana	5-3-0	.625	8-4-0	.667
5.	Iowa	4-4-0	.500	5-6-0	.454
6.	Minnesota	3-5-1	.389	4-6-1	.409
7.	Michigan State	3-5-0	.375	5-6-0	.454
7.	Wisconsin	3-5-0	.375	4-7-0	.373
9.	Illinois	1-6-1	.188	2-8-1	.227
10.	Northwestern	0-9-0	.000	1-10-0	.091

Non-conference record: 18-14-0 .562

1980					
1.	Michigan	8-0-0	1.000	10-2-0	.833
2.	Ohio State	7-1-0	.875	9-3-0	.750
2.	Purdue	7-1-0	.875	9-3-0	.750
3.	Iowa	4-4-0	.500	4-7-0	.364
5.	Minnesota	4-5-0	.444	5-6-0	.454
6.	Indiana	3-5-0	.375	6-5-0	.545
6.	Wisconsin	3-5-0	.375	4-7-0	.364
6.	Illinois	3-5-0	.375	3-7-1	.318
9.	Michigan State	2-6-0	.250	3-8-0	.273
10.	Northwestern	0-9-0	.000	0-11-0	.000

Non-conference record: 12-18-1 .403

1981					
1.	Ohio State	6-2-0	.750	9-3-0	.750
1.	Iowa	6-2-0	.750	8-4-0	.667
3.	Michigan	6-3-0	.667	9-3-0	.750
3.	Illinois	6-3-0	.667	7-4-0	.636
3.	Wisconsin	6-3-0	.667	7-5-0	.583
6.	Minnesota	4-5-0	.444	6-5-0	.545
6.	Michigan State	4-5-0	.444	5-6-0	.454
8.	Purdue	3-6-0	.333	5-6-0	.454
8.	Indiana	3-6-0	.333	3-8-0	.272
10.	Northwestern	0-9-0	.000	0-11-0	.000

Non-conference record: 15-11-0 .577

1982					
1.	Michigan	8-1-0	.889	8-4-0	.667
2.	Ohio State	7-1-0	.875	9-3-0	.750
3.	Iowa	6-2-0	.750	8-4-0	.667
4.	Illinois	6-3-0	.667	7-5-0	.583
5.	Wisconsin	5-4-0	.556	7-5-0	.583
6.	Indiana	4-5-0	.444	5-6-0	.455
7.	Purdue	3-6-0	.333	3-8-0	.273
8.	Northwestern	2-7-0	.222	3-8-0	.273
8.	Michigan State	2-7-0	.222	2-9-0	.181
10.	Minnesota	1-8-0	.111	3-8-0	.273

Non-conference record: 11-16-0 .407

1983		Conference		Overall	
1.	Illinois	9-0-0	1.000	10-2-0	.833
2.	Michigan	8-1-0	.889	9-3-0	.750
3.	Iowa	7-2-0	.778	9-3-0	.750
4.	Ohio State	6-3-0	.667	9-3-0	.750
5.	Wisconsin	5-4-0	.556	7-4-0	.636
6.	Purdue	3-5-1	.389	3-7-1	.358
7.	Michigan State	2-6-1	.278	4-6-1	.409
8.	Indiana	2-7-0	.222	3-8-0	.272
8.	Northwestern	2-7-0	.222	2-9-0	.181
10.	Minnesota	0-9-0	.000	1-10-0	.090

Non-conference record: 13-11-0 .542

1984					
1.	Ohio State	7-2-0	.778	9-3-0	.750
2.	Illinois	6-3-0	.667	7-4-0	.636
2.	Purdue	6-3-0	.667	7-5-0	.583
4.	Iowa	5-3-1	.611	8-4-1	.654
4.	Wisconsin	5-3-1	.611	7-4-1	.625
6.	Michigan	5-4-0	.556	6-6-0	.500
6.	Michigan State	5-4-0	.556	6-6-0	.500
8.	Minnesota	3-6-0	.333	4-7-0	.364
9.	Northwestern	2-7-0	.222	2-9-0	.182
10.	Indiana	0-9-0	.000	0-11-0	.000

Non-conference record: 12-15-0 .444

1985					
1.	Iowa	7-1-0	.875	10-2-0	.833
2.	Michigan	6-1-1	.813	10-1-1	.875
3.	Illinois	5-2-1	.688	6-5-1	.542
4.	Ohio State	5-3-0	.625	9-3-0	.750
4.	Michigan State	5-3-0	.625	7-5-0	.583
6.	Minnesota	4-4-0	.500	7-5-0	.583
7.	Purdue	3-5-0	.375	5-6-0	.455
8.	Wisconsin	2-6-0	.250	5-6-0	.455
9.	Indiana	1-7-0	.125	4-7-0	.364
9.	Northwestern	1-7-0	.125	3-8-0	.273

Non-conference record: 27-9-0 .750

1986					
1.	Michigan	7-1-0	.875	11-2-0	.846
1.	Ohio State	7-1-0	.875	10-3-0	.769
3.	Iowa	5-3-0	.625	9-3-0	.750
3.	Minnesota	5-3-0	.625	6-6-0	.500
5.	Michigan State	4-4-0	.500	6-5-0	.545
6.	Indiana	3-5-0	.375	6-6-0	.500
6.	Illinois	3-5-0	.375	4-7-0	.364
8.	Northwestern	2-6-0	.250	4-7-0	.364
8.	Purdue	2-6-0	.250	3-8-0	.273
8.	Wisconsin	2-6-0	.250	3-9-0	.250

Non-conference record: 22-16-0 .578

1987					
1.	Michigan State	7-0-1	.938	9-2-1	.792
2.	Iowa	6-2-0	.750	10-3-0	.769
2.	Indiana	6-2-0	.750	8-4-0	.667
4.	Michigan	5-3-0	.625	8-4-0	.667
5.	Ohio State	4-4-0	.500	6-4-1	.591
6.	Minnesota	3-5-0	.375	6-5-0	.545
6.	Purdue	3-5-0	.375	3-7-1	.318
8.	Illinois	2-5-1	.313	3-7-1	.318
9.	Northwestern	2-6-0	.250	2-8-1	.227
10.	Wisconsin	1-7-0	.125	3-8-0	.272

Non-conference record: 19-13-3 .586

1988		Conference		Overall	
1.	Michigan	7-0-1	.938	9-2-1	.792
2.	Michigan State	6-1-1	.813	6-5-1	.542
3.	Iowa	4-1-3	.688	6-4-3	.577
3.	Illinois	5-2-1	.688	6-5-1	.542
5.	Indiana	5-3-0	.625	8-3-1	.708
6.	Purdue	3-5-0	.375	4-7-0	.364
7.	Ohio State	2-5-1	.313	4-6-1	409
8.	Northwestern	2-5-1	.313	2-8-1	.227
9.	Minnesota	0-6-2	.125	2-7-2	.227
9.	Wisconsin	1-7-0	.125	1-10-0	.091

Non-conference record: 13-22-1 .375

1989					
1.	Michigan	8-0-0	1.000	10-2-0	.833
2.	Illinois	7-1-0	.875	10-2-0	.833
3.	Michigan State	6-2-0	.750	8-4-0	.667
3.	Ohio State	6-2-0	.750	8-4-0	.667
5.	Minnesota	4-4-0	.500	6-5-0	.545
6.	Indiana	3-5-0	.375	5-6-0	.455
6.	Iowa	3-5-0	.375	5-6-0	.455
8.	Purdue	2-6-0	.250	3-8-0	.272
9.	Wisconsin	1-7-0	.125	2-9-0	.182
10.	Northwestern	0-8-0	.000	0-11-0	.000

Non-conference record: 17-17-0 .500

1990					
1.	Michigan	6-2-0	.750	9-3-0	.750
1.	Michigan State	6-2-0	.750	8-3-1	.708
1.	Illinois	6-2-0	.750	8-4-0	.667
1.	Iowa	6-2-0	.750	8-4-0	.667
5.	Ohio State	5-2-1	.688	7-4-1	.625
6.	Minnesota	5-3-0	.625	6-5-0	.545
7.	Indiana	3-4-1	.438	6-5-1	.542
8.	Northwestern	1-7-0	.125	2-9-0	.182
8.	Purdue	1-7-0	.125	2-9-0	.182
10.	Wisconsin	0-8-0	.000	1-10-0	.090
	Penn State	-----------------		9-3-0	.750

Non-conference record*: 18-17-1 .514
(excludes Penn State games)
Penn State joins Big Ten, eligible for title in 1993.

1991					
1.	Michigan	8-0-0	1.000	10-2-0	.833
2.	Iowa	7-1-0	.875	10-1-1	.875
3.	Ohio State	5-3-0	.625	8-4-0	.667
3.	Indiana	5-3-0	.625	7-4-1	.625
5.	Illinois	4-4-0	.500	6-6-0	.500
6.	Purdue	3-5-0	.375	4-7-0	.364
6.	Michigan State	3-5-0	.375	3-8-0	.273
8.	Wisconsin	2-6-0	.250	5-6-0	.455
8.	Northwestern	2-6-0	.250	3-8-0	.273
10.	Minnesota	1-7-0	.125	2-9-0	.182
	Penn State	-----------------		11-2-0	.846

Non-conference record*: 18-15-2 .543
*excludes Penn State

1992		Conference		Overall	
1.	Michigan	6-0-2	.778	8-0-3	.864
2.	Ohio State	5-2-1	.688	8-2-1	.773
3.	Michigan State	5-3-0	.625	5-6-0	.455
4.	Illinois	4-3-1	.563	6-5-1	.591
5.	Iowa	4-4-0	.500	5-7-0	.417
6.	Indiana	3-5-0	.375	5-6-0	.455
6.	Wisconsin	3-5-0	.375	5-6-0	.455
6.	Purdue	3-5-0	.375	4-7-0	.364
6.	Northwestern	3-5-0	.375	3-8-0	.273
10.	Minnesota	2-6-0	.250	2-9-0	.182
	Penn State	-----------------		7-5-0	.583

Non-conference record*: 13-18-1 .422

1993					
1.	Ohio State	6-1-1	.813	10-1-1	.875
1.	Wisconsin	6-1-1	.813	10-1-1	.875
3.	Penn State	6-2-0	.750	10-2-0	.833
4.	Indiana	5-3-0	.625	8-4-0	.667
4.	Michigan	5-3-0	.625	8-4-0	.667
4.	Illinois	5-3-0	.625	5-6-0	.455
7.	Michigan State	4-4-0	.500	6-6-0	.500
8.	Iowa	3-5-0	.375	6-6-0	.500
8.	Minnesota	3-5-0	.375	4-7-0	.364
10.	Northwestern	0-8-0	.000	2-9-0	.182
10.	Purdue	0-8-0	.000	1-10-0	.091

Non-conference record: 27-13-0 .675

1994					
1.	Penn State	8-0-0	1.000	12-0-0	1.000
2.	Ohio State	6-2-0	.750	9-4-0	.692
3.	Michigan	5-3-0	.625	8-4-0	.667
4.	Wisconsin	5-2-1	.688	8-3-1	.708
5.	Illinois	4-4-0	.500	7-5-0	.583
5.	Purdue	3-3-2	.500	5-4-2	.545
5.	Indiana	4-4-0	.500	7-4-0	.636
8.	Iowa	3-4-1	.438	5-5-1	.500
9.	Northwestern	3-5-0	.375	4-6-1	.409
10.	Minnesota	1-7-0	.125	3-8-0	.273
11.	Michigan State*	0-8-0	.000	0-11-0	.000

Non-conference record: 26-10-3 .705 *Records reflect that Michigan State forfeited five games due to ineligible player.

1995					
1.	Northwestern	8-0-0	1.000	10-2-0	.833
2.	Ohio State	7-1-0	.875	11-2-1	.846
3.	Michigan	5-3-0	.625	9-4-0	.692
3.	Penn State	5-3-0	.625	9-3-0	.750
5.	Michigan State	4-3-1	.563	6-5-1	.542
6.	Iowa	4-4-0	.500	8-4-0	.667
7.	Illinois	3-4-1	.438	5-5-1	.500
7.	Wisconsin	3-4-1	.4438	4-5-2	.455
9.	Purdue	2-5-1	.313	4-6-1	.409
10.	Minnesota	1-7-0	.125	3-8-0	.273
11.	Indiana	0-8-0	.000	2-9-0	.182

Non-conference record: 29-11-2 .714

1996		Conference		Overall	
1.	Ohio State	7-1-0	.875	11-1-0	.917
1.	Northwestern	7-1-0	.875	9-3-0	.750
3.	Penn State	6-2-0	.750	11-2-0	.846
3.	Iowa	6-2-0	.750	9-3-0	.750
5.	Michigan	5-3-0	.625	8-4-0	.667
5.	Michigan State	5-3-0	.625	6-6-0	.500
7.	Wisconsin	3-5-0	.375	8-5-0	.615
8.	Purdue	2-6-0	.250	3-8-0	.273
9.	Minnesota	1-7-0	.125	4-7-0	.364
9.	Indiana	1-7-0	.125	3-8-0	.273
9.	Illinois	1-7-0	.125	2-9-0	.182

Non-conference record: 30-12-0 .714

1997					
1	Michigan	8-0-0	1.000	12-0-0	1.000
2.	Ohio State	6-2-0	.750	10-3-0	.769
2.	Penn State	6-2-0	.750	9-3-0	.750
2.	Purdue	6-2-0	.750	9-3-0	.750
5.	Wisconsin	5-3-0	.625	8-5-0	.615
6.	Iowa	4-4-0	.500	7-5-0	.583
6.	Michigan State	4-4-0	.500	7-5-0	.583
8.	Northwestern	3-5-0	.375	5-7-0	.416
9.	Minnesota	1-7-0	.125	3-9-0	.250
9.	Indiana	1-7-0	.125	2-9-0	.250
11.	Illinois	0-8-0	.000	0-11-0	.000

Non-conference record: 28-16-0 .636

1998					
1.	Ohio State	7-1-0	.875	11-1-0	.917
1.	Wisconsin	7-1-0	.875	11-1-0	.917
1.	Michigan	7-1-0	.875	10-3-0	.769
4.	Purdue	6-2-0	.750	9-4-0	.692
5.	Penn State	5-3-0	.625	9-3-0	.750
6.	Michigan State	4-4-0	.500	6-6-0	.500
7.	Minnesota	2-6-0	.250	5-6-0	.455
7.	Indiana	2-6-0	.250	4-7-0	.364
7.	Illinois	2-6-0	.250	3-8-0	.273
7.	Iowa	2-6-0	.250	3-8-0	.273
11.	Northwestern	0-8-0	.000	3-9-0	.250

Non-conference record: 30-12-0 .714

1999					
1.	Wisconsin	7-1-0	.875	10-2-0	.833
2.	Michigan	6-2-0	.750	10-2-0	.833
2.	Michigan State	6-2-0	.750	10-2-0	.833
4.	Minnesota	5-3-0	.625	8-4-0	.667
4.	Penn State	5-3-0	.625	10-3-0	.769
6.	Illinois	4-4-0	.500	8-4-0	.667
6.	Purdue	4-4-0	.500	7-5-0	.583
8.	Ohio State	3-5-0	.375	6-6-0	.500
8.	Indiana	3-5-0	.375	4-7-0	.363
10.	Northwestern	1-7-0	.125	3-8-0	.273
11.	Iowa	0-8-0	.000	1-10-0	.090

Non-conference record: 33-9-0 .786

2000		Conference		Overall	
1.	Michigan	6-2-0	.750	9-3-0	.750
1.	Northwestern	6-2-0	.750	8-4-0	.667
1.	Purdue	6-2-0	.750	8-4-0	.667
4.	Ohio State	5-3-0	.625	8-4-0	.667
5.	Wisconsin	4-4-0	.500	9-4-0	.692
5.	Minnesota	4-4-0	.500	6-6-0	.500
5.	Penn State	4-4-0	.500	5-7-0	.417
8.	Iowa	3-5-0	.375	3-9-0	.250
9.	Illinois	2-6-0	.250	5-6-0	.455
9.	Michigan State	2-6-0	.250	5-6-0	.455
9.	Indiana	2-6-0	.250	3-8-0	.273

Non-conference record: 25-17-0 .595

2001					
1.	Illinois	7-1-0	.875	10-2-0	.833
2.	Michigan	6-2-0	.750	8-4-0	.667
3.	Ohio State	5-3-0	.625	7-5-0	.583
4.	Iowa	4-4-0	.500	7-5-0	.583
4.	Purdue	4-4-0	.500	6-6-0	.500
4.	Indiana	4-4-0	.500	5-6-0	.455
7.	Penn State	4-4-0	.500	5-6-0	.455
8.	Michigan State	3-5-0	.375	7-5-0	.583
8.	Wisconsin	3-5-0	.375	5-7-0	.417
10.	Minnesota	2-6-0	.250	4-7-0	.364
10.	Northwestern	2-6-0	.250	4-7-0	.364

Non-conference record: 24-16-0 .600

2002					
1.	Ohio State	8-0-0	1.000	14-0-0	1.000
1.	Iowa	8-0-0	1.000	11-2-0	.846
3.	Michigan	6-2-0	.750	10-3-0	.769
4.	Penn State	5-3-0	.625	9-4-0	.692
5.	Purdue	4-4-0	.500	7-6-0	.538
5.	Illinois	4-4-0	.500	5-7-0	.417
7.	Minnesota	3-5-0	.375	8-5-0	.615
8.	Wisconsin	2-6-0	.333	8-6-0	.571
8.	Michigan State	2-6-0	.333	4-8-0	.333
10.	Indiana	1-7-0	.125	3-9-0	.250
10.	Northwestern	1-7-0	.125	3-9-0	.250

Non-conference record: 38-15-0 .717

2003					
1.	Michigan	7-1-0	.875	10-3-0	.769
2.	Ohio State	6-2-0	.750	11-2-0	.846
2.	Purdue	6-2-0	.750	9-4-0	.692
4.	Iowa	5-3-0	.625	10-3-0	.769
4.	Minnesota	5-3-0	.625	10-3-0	.769
4.	Michigan State	5-3-0	.625	8-5-0	.615
7.	Wisconsin	4-4-0	.500	7-6-0	.538
7.	Northwestern	4-4-0	.500	6-7-0	.462
9.	Penn State	1-7-0	.125	3-9-0	.250
10.	Indiana	1-7-0	.125	2-10-0	.167
11.	Illinois	0-8-0	.000	1-11-0	.083

Non-conference record: 33-19-0 .635

BIG TEN W-L-T RECORDS BY DECADES (1896-2003)

Decade	Chicago	Illinois	Michigan	Minn.	NW	Purdue	Wis.	Indiana	Iowa	Ohio State	Mich. St.
1896-99	13-4-0	2-7-2	8-3-0	2-10-0	4-9-1	2-7-1	11-2-1				
1900-09	39-13-5	24-23-3	20-3-1	22-6-3	8-16-4	5-27-2	16-15-3	5-25-2	4-16-1		
1910-19	37-22-2	32-12-7	3-5-0	26-9-2	13-34-1	10-25-4	21-19-5	8-27-2	13-18-0	16-9-1	
1920-29	24-24-4	31-17-2	32-14-2	20-23-5	19-29-1	15-25-4	21-21-8	11-26-4	27-21-1	23-23-4	
1930-39	7-37-2	20-32-1	32-21-2	33-13-5	31-20-6	33-13-7	17-31-5	15-29-7	10-29-7	39-12-4	
1940-49		23-35-2	46-9-3	35-24-1	28-31-3	23-32-1	24-34-3	24-29-3	18-38-2	33-22-4	
1950-59		31-30-5	37-26-2	23-37-7	18-46-2	30-25-7	40-21-6	13-45-2	30-29-3	46-16-5	24-17-1
1960-69		25-43-1	35-31-2	44-23-1	24-42-1	45-22-0	24-44-2	18-40-1	21-42-2	50-14-1	39-25-1
1970-79		28-47-4	69-9-1	34-43-2	23-60-1	42-36-1	31-47-3	24-53-2	23-56-2	69-9-1	46-30-3
1980-89		52-29-3	68-14-2	28-55-2	13-71-1	35-48-1	31-52-1	30-54-0	53-25-4	57-24-1	43-38-3
1990-99		33-45-2	61-17-2	22-58-0	27-52-0	30-47-3	41-36-3	27-52-1	39-40-1	57-20-3	41-38-1
2000-03		13-19-0	25- 7-0	14-18-0	13-19-0	20-12--0	13-19-0	8-24-0	20-12-0	24-8-0	12-20-0

	Penn St.
1990-99	41-15-0
2000-02	14- 18-0

BIG TEN WIN PERCENTS (1896-2003)

Chicago	120-100-14	.543		Indiana	183-404-24	319
Illinois	314-339-32	.482		Iowa	258-326-23	.444
Michigan	436-159-17	.738		Ohio State	414-157-24	.716
Minnesota	304-320-28	.488		Mich. State	205-168- 9	.548
N.W.	221-429-21	.345		Penn State	55- 33 - 0	.625
Purdue	290-319-30	.477				
Wisconsin	290-341-40	.462				

BIG TEN TITLES BY DECADES (1896-2002)

Decade	Chicago	Illinois	Mich.	Minn.	NW	Purdue	Wis.	Indiana	Iowa	Ohio State	Mich. St.
1896-99	1		1				2				
1900-09	3		2.5	3.5			1				
1910-19	1	4.5		1.5			1			2	
1920-29	1	3	1.5		.5	1			2	1	
1930-39			3.33	3.5	1.83	.33				1	
1940-49		1	3	2		.5		1		2.5	
1950-59		1.5	1			.5	2		1.5	3	.5
1960-69		1	1.5	.83		.33	1	.33	.5	2.5	2
1970-79			4							5.5	.5
1980-89		1	4.5						1.5	2	1
1990-99		.25	3.58		1.5		1.83		.25	1.33	.25
2000-03		1	1.33		.33	.33			.5	.5	
Totals	6	13.25	27.25	11.33	4.16	3	8.83	1.33	6.25	21.33	3.25

	Penn State
1990-99	1
2000-01	
Totals	1

BIG TWELVE CONFERENCE (1996-2003) After the 1995 season, the Southwest Conference was disbanded, and four SWC members – Texas, Texas Tech, Texas A&M, and Baylor – joined with the members of the Big Eight to form the Big Twelve Conference. The conference was organized into a North Division and a South Division with the conference champion to be determined by a championship game held after the season. The result of the conference championship is included in the overall won-loss figures but not in the conference won-loss figures.

1996

		Conference		Overall	
	NORTH DIVISION				
1.	Nebraska	8-0-0	1.000	11-2-0	.846
2.	Colorado	7-1-0	.875	10-2-0	.833
3.	Kansas State	6-2-0	.750	9-3-0	.750
4.	Missouri	3-5-0	.375	5-6-0	.455
5.	Kansas	2-6-0	.250	4-7-0	.364
6.	Iowa State	1-7-0	.125	2-9-0	.182
	SOUTH DIVISION				
1.	Texas	6-2-0	.750	8-5-0	.614
2.	Texas Tech	5-3-0	.625	7-5-0	.583
3.	Texas A&M	4-4-0	.500	6-6-0	.500
4.	Oklahoma	3-5-0	.375	3-8-0	.273
5.	Okla. State	2-6-0	.250	5-6-0	.455
6.	Baylor	1-7-0	.125	4-7-0	.364

Championship: Texas 37, Nebraska 27
Non-conference record: 25-15-0 .625

1997

		Conference		Overall	
	NORTH DIVISION				
1.	Nebraska	8-0-0	1.000	13-0-0	1.000
2.	Kansas State	7-1-0	.875	11-1-0	.917
3.	Missouri	5-3-0	.625	7-5-0	.583
4.	Colorado	3-5-0	.375	5-6-0	.455
4.	Kansas	3-5-0	.375	5-6-0	.455
6.	Iowa State	1-7-0	.125	1-10-0	.091
	SOUTH DIVISION				
1.	Texas A&M	6-2-0	.750	9-4-0	.692
2.	Texas Tech	5-3-0	.625	6-5-0	.545
2.	Okla. State	5-3-0	.625	8-4-0	.667
4.	Texas	2-6-0	.250	4-7-0	.364
4.	Oklahoma	2-6-0	.250	4-8-0	.333
6.	Baylor	1-7-0	.125	2-9-0	.182

Championship: Nebraska 54, Texas A&M 15
Non-conference record: 25-16-0 .5610

1998

		Conference		Overall	
	NORTH DIVISION				
1.	Kansas State	8-0-0	1.000	11-2-0	.846
2.	Nebraska	5-3-0	.625	9-4-0	.692
2.	Missouri	5-3-0	.625	8-4-0	.667
4.	Colorado	4-4-0	.500	8-4-0	.667
5.	Kansas	1-7-0	.125	4-7-0	.364
5.	Iowa State	1-7-0	.125	3-8-0	.273
	SOUTH DIVISION				
1.	Texas A&M	7-1-0	.875	11-3-0	.786
2.	Texas	6-2-0	.750	9-3-0	.750
3.	Texas Tech	4-4-0	.500	7-5-0	.583
4.	Oklahoma State	3-5-0	.375	5-6-0	.455
4.	Oklahoma	3-5-0	.375	5-6-0	.455
6.	Baylor	1-7-0	.125	2-9-0	.182

Championship: Texas A&M 36, Kansas State 33
Non-conference record 33-12-0 .733

1999

		Conference		Overall	
	NORTH DIVISION				
1.	Nebraska	7-1-0	.875	12-1-0	.923
2.	Kansas State	7-1-0	.875	11-1-0	.917
3.	Colorado	5-3-0	.625	7-5-0	.583
4.	Kansas	3-5-0	.375	5-7-0	.417
5.	Missouri	1-7-0	.125	4-7-0	.364
5.	Iowa State	1-7-0	.125	4-7-0	.364
	SOUTH DIVISION				
1.	Texas	6-2-0	.750	9-5-0	.643
2.	Texas Tech	5-3-0	.625	6-5-0	.545
2.	Texas A&M	5-3-0	.625	8-4-0	.667
2.	Oklahoma	5-3-0	.625	7-5-0	.583
5.	Oklahoma State	3-5-0	.375	5-6-0	.455
6.	Baylor	0-8-0	.000	1-10-0	.091

Championship: Nebraska 22, Texas 6
Non-conference record: 30-14-0 .682

2000

		Conference		Overall	
	NORTH DIVISION				
1.	Kansas State	6-2-0	.750	11-3-0	.786
1.	Nebraska	6-2-0	.750	10-2-0	.833
3.	Iowa State	5-3-0	.625	9-3-0	.750
4.	Colorado	3-5-0	.375	3-8-0	.273
5.	Kansas	2-6-0	.250	4-7-0	.364
5.	Missouri	2-6-0	.250	3-8-0	.273
	SOUTH DIVISION				
1.	Oklahoma	8-0-0	1.000	13-0-0	1.000
2.	Texas	7-1-0	.875	9-3-0	.750
3.	Texas A&M	5-3-0	.625	7-5-0	.583
4.	Texas Tech	3-5-0	.375	7-6-0	.538
5.	Okla. State	1-7-0	.125	3-8-0	.273
6.	Baylor	0-8-0	.000	2-9-0	.182

Championship: Oklahoma 27, Kansas State 24
Non-conference record: 33-13-0 .717

2001

		Conference		Overall	
	NORTH DIVISION				
1.	Nebraska	7-1-0	.875	11-2-0	.846
1.	Colorado	7-1-0	.875	10-3-0	.769
3.	Iowa State	4-4-0	.500	7-5-0	.583
4.	Kansas State	3-5-0	.375	6-6-0	.500
5.	Missouri	3-5-0	.375	4-7-0	.364
6.	Kansas	1-7-0	.125	3-8-0	.273
	SOUTH DIVISION				
1.	Texas	7-1-0	.875	11-2-0	.846
2.	Oklahoma	6-2-0	.750	11-2-0	.846
3.	Texas A&M	4-4-0	.500	8-4-0	.667
3.	Texas Tech	4-4-0	.500	7-5-0	.583
5.	Okla. State	2-6-0	.250	4-7-0	.364
6.	Baylor	0-8-0	.000	3-8-0	.273

Championship: Colorado 39, Texas 37
Non-conference record 36-8-0 .818

2002		Conference		Overall	
		NORTH DIVISION			
1	Colorado	7-1-0	.875	9-5-0	.643
2.	Kansas State	6-2-0	.750	11-2-0	.846
3	Iowa State	4-4-0	.500	7-7-0	.500
4.	Nebraska	3-5-0	.375	7-7-0	.500
5.	Missouri	2-6-0	.250	5-7-0	.417
6.	Kansas	0-8-0	.000	2-10-0	.167
		SOUTH DIVISION			
1.	Oklahoma	6-2-0	.750	12-2-0	.857
1.	Texas	6-2-0	.750	11-2-0	.846
3.	Texas Tech	5-3-0	.625	9-5-0	.643
3.	Oklahoma State	5-3-0	.625	8-5-0	.615
5.	Texas A&M	3-5-0	.375	6-6-0	.500
6.	Baylor	1-7-0	.125	3-9-0	.250

Championship: Oklahoma 29, Colorado 7

Non-conference record: 41-18-0 .695

2003		Conference		Overall	
		NORTH DIVISION			
1.	Kansas State	6-2-0	.750	11-4-0	.733
2.	Nebraska	5-3-0	.625	10-3-0	.769
3.	Missouri	4-4-0	.500	8-5-0	.615
4.	Kansas	3-5-0	.375	6-7-0	.462
5.	Colorado	3-5-0	.375	5-7-0	.417
6.	Iowa State	0-8-0	.000	2-10-0	.167
		SOUTH DIVISION			
1.	Oklahoma	8-0-0	1.000	12-2-0	.857
2.	Texas	7-1-0	.875	10-3-0	.769
3.	Oklahoma State	5-3-0	.625	9-4-0	.692
4.	Texas Tech	4-4-0	.500	8-5-0	.615
5.	Texas A&M	2-6-0	.250	4-8-0	.333
6.	Baylor	1-7-0	.125	3-9-0	.250

Championship: Kansas State 35, Oklahoma 7

Non-conference record: 40-19-0 .678

BIG TWELVE W-L-T RECORDS (1996-2003)

NORTH DIVISION				SOUTH DIVISION		
Nebraska	49-15-0	.766		Texas	47-17-0	.734
Kansas State	49-15-0	.766		Texas A&M	37-27-0	.578
Colorado	39-25-0	.609		Oklahoma	41-23-0	.641
Missouri	25-39-0	.391		Texas Tech	37-27-0	.578
Iowa State	17-47-0	.266		Oklahoma State	26-38-0	.406
Kansas	15-49-0	.235		Baylor	5-59-0	.078

BIG TWELVE CHAMPIONSHIPS (1996-2003)

Nebraska	2
Oklahoma	2
Texas	1
Texas A&M	1
Colorado	1
Kansas State	1

BIG WEST CONFERENCE (1969-2000) Organized as the Southern California Intercollegiate Athletic Association in 1921, name changed to the California Collegiate Athletic Association in 1939, and to the Pacific Coast Athletic Association in 1969. The name was changed to the Big West Conference in 1988. The Big West was disbanded after the 2000 season with a number of the teams transferring to the newly organized Sun Belt Conference.

1969		Conference		Overall	
1.	San Diego State	6-0-0	1.000	11-0-0	1.000
2.	Long Beach State	3-1-0	.750	8-3-0	.727
3.	Pacific	2-2-0	.500	7-3-0	.700
4.	Fresno State	1-3-0	.250	6-4-0	.600
4.	UC S. Barbara	1-3-0	.250	6-4-0	.600
6.	San Jose State	1-1-0	.500	2-8-0	.200
7.	Cal State LA	0-4-0	.000	0-9-0	.000

Non-conference record: 26-17-0 .605

1970					
1.	Long Beach State	5-1-0	.833	9-2-1	.792
1.	San Diego State	5-1-0	.833	9-2-0	.818
3.	Fresno State	4-2-0	.667	8-4-0	.667
4.	Pacific	2-3-0	.400	5-6-0	.455
4.	San Jose State	2-3-0	.400	2-9-0	.182
6.	UC S. Barbara	1-5-0	.167	2-9-0	.182
7.	Cal State LA	0-4-0	.000	1-9-0	.091

Non-conference record: 17-22-1 .438

1971					
1.	Long Beach State	5-1-0	.833	8-4-0	.667
2.	San Jose State	4-1-0	.800	5-6-1	.4585.
3	Fresno State	3-2-0	.600	6-5-0	.545
4.	San Diego State	2-3-0	.400	6-5-0	.545
4.	UC S. Barbara	2-3-0	.400	3-8-0	.273
6.	Pacific	1-4-0	.200	3-8-0	.273
7.	Cal State LA	0-3-0	.000	2-8-0	.200

Non-conference record: 16-27-1 .375

1972					
1.	San Diego State	4-0-0	1.000	10-1-0	.909
2.	Pacific	3-1-0	.750	8-3-0	.727
3.	Fresno State	1-3-0	.250	6-4-1	.591
3.	Long Beach State	1-3-0	.250	5-6-0	.455
3.	San Jose State	1-3-0	.250	4-7-0	.364

UC Santa Barbara and Cal State LA leave the BWC.
Non-conference record: 23-11-1 .671

1973					
1.	San Diego State	3-0-1	.875	9-1-1	.864
2.	San Jose State	2-0-2	.750	5-4-2	.545
3.	Pacific	2-1-1	.625	7-2-1	.750
4.	Fresno State	1-3-0	.250	2-9-0	.818
5.	Long Beach State	0-4-0	.000	1-9-1	.136

Non-conference record: 16-17-1 .485

1974					
1.	San Diego State	4-0-0	1.000	8-2-1	.773
2.	San Jose State	2-2-0	.500	8-3-1	.792
2.	Pacific	2-2-0	.500	6-5-0	.545
4.	Long Beach State	1-3-0	.250	6-5-0	.545
4.	Fresno State	1-3-0	.250	5-7-0	.417

Non-conference record: 23-12-2 .649

1975					
1.	San Jose State	5-0-0	1.000	9-2-0	.818
2.	Long Beach State	4-1-0	.800	9-2-0	.818
3.	San Diego State	3-2-0	.600	8-3-0	.727
4.	Pacific	2-3-0	.400	5-6-1	.458
5.	Fresno State	1-4-0	.200	3-8-0	.273
6.	CS Fullerton	0-5-0	.000	2-9-0	.182

Cal State Fullerton joins the BWC.
Non-conference record: 21-15-1 .581

1976		Conference		Overall	
1.	San Jose State	4-0-0	1.000	7-4-0	.636
2.	Fresno State	3-1-0	.750	6-5-0	.545
3.	Long Beach State	2-2-0	.500	8-3-0	.727
4.	CS Fullerton	1-3-0	.250	3-7-1	.318
5.	Pacific	0-4-0	.000	2-9-0	.182

San Diego State leaves the BWC.
Non-conference record: 16-18-1 .471

1977					
1.	Fresno State	4-0-0	1.000	9-2-0	.818
2.	Pacific	3-1-0	.750	6-5-0	.545
3.	San Jose State	2-2-0	.500	4-7-0	.364
4.	Long Beach State	1-3-0	.250	4-6-0	.400
5.	CS Fullerton	0-4-0	.000	4-7-0	.364

Non-conference record: 17-17-0 .500

1978					
1.	Utah State	4-1-0	.800	7-4-0	.636
1.	San Jose State	4-1-0	.800	7-5-0	.583
3.	Pacific	3-2-0	.600	4-8-0	.333
4.	CS Fullerton	2-3-0	.400	5-7-0	.417
5.	Long Beach State	1-4-0	.200	5-6-0	.455
5.	Fresno State	1-4-0	.200	3-8-0	.273

Utah State joins the conference, with Utah State over Wyoming and UNLV over CS Fullerton included as conference games.
Non-conference record: 16-23-0 .410

1979					
1.	Utah State	5-0-0	1.000	7-3-1	.682
2.	CS Fullerton	3-2-0	.600	5-6-0	.455
2.	Long Beach State	3-2-0	.600	7-4-0	.636
4.	San Jose State	2-3-0	.400	3-8-0	.273
4.	Fresno State	2-3-0	.400	4-7-0	.364
6.	Pacific	0-5-0	.000	3-7-0	.300

Won-loss records are those after all forfeits.
Non-conference record: 14-20-1 .414

1980					
1.	Long Beach State	5-0-0	1.000	8-3-0	.727
2.	Utah State	4-1-0	.800	6-5-0	.545
3.	San Jose State	3-2-0	.600	7-4-0	.636
4.	Fresno State	1-4-0	.200	5-6-0	.455
4.	CS Fullerton	1-4-0	.200	4-7-0	.364
4.	Pacific	1-4-0	.200	4-8-0	.333

Non-conference record: 19-18-0 .514

1981					
1.	San Jose State	5-0-0	1.000	9-3-0	.750
2.	Utah State	4-1-0	.800	5-5-1	.500
3.	Fresno State	2-3-0	.400	5-6-0	.455
3.	Pacific	2-3-0	.400	5-6-0	.455
5.	CS Fullerton	1-4-0	.200	3-8-0	.273
5.	Long Beach State	1-4-0	.200	2-8-0	.200

Non-conference record: 14-21-1 .403

1982					
1.	Fresno State	6-0-0	1.000	11-1-0	.917
2.	Long Beach State	5-1-0	.833	6-5-0	.545
3.	San Jose State	4-2-0	.667	8-3-0	.727
4.	Utah State	2-3-0	.400	5-6-0	.455
4.	Pacific	2-4-0	.333	2-9-0	.182
6.	UNLV	1-4-0	.200	3-8-0	.273
7.	CS Fullerton	0-6-0	.000	3-9-0	.250

UNLV joins the BWC.
Non-conference record: 18-21-0 .462

1983

		Conference		Overall	
1.	CS Fullerton	6-0-0	1.000	8-4-0	.667
2.	Utah State	4-2-0	.667	5-6-0	.545
3.	Long Beach State	3-3-0	.500	8-4-0	.667
3.	San Jose State	3-3-0	.500	5-6-0	.455
3.	Fresno State	3-3-0	.500	7-4-0	.636
6.	Pacific	2-4-0	.333	4-8-0	.333
7.	UNLV	0-6-0	.000	0-11-0	.000

Standings reflect the fact that UNLV had to forfeit all games.
Non-conference record: 16-22-0 .421

1984

		Conference		Overall	
1.	CS Fullerton	7-0-0	1.000	12-0-0	1.000
2.	San Jose State	6-1-0	.857	7-4-0	.636
3.	Fresno State	4-3-0	.571	7-5-0	.583
3.	Long Beach State	4-3-0	.571	5-6-0	.455
5.	Pacific	3-4-0	.429	5-6-0	.455
6.	New Mexico State	2-5-0	.286	3-8-0	.273
7.	Utah State	2-5-0	.286	2-9-0	.182
8.	UNLV	0-7-0	.000	0-12-0	.000

New Mexico State joins the BWC.
UNLV again had to forfeit all of its games because of the
same ineligible player.
Non-conference record: 13-22-0 .371

1985

		Conference		Overall	
1.	Fresno State	7-0-0	1.000	11-0-1	.958
2.	CS Fullerton	5-2-0	.714	6-5-0	.545
3.	UNLV	4-2-1	.643	5-5-1	.500
4.	Long Beach State	4-3-0	.571	6-6-0	.500
5.	Utah State	3-4-0	.429	3-8-0	.273
6.	San Jose State	2-4-1	.357	2-8-1	.227
7.	Pacific	2-5-0	.286	5-7-0	.417
8.	New Mexico State	0-7-0	.000	1-10-0	.091

Non-conference record: 12-22-1 .357

1986

		Conference		Overall	
1.	San Jose State	7-0-0	1.000	10-2-0	.833
2.	Fresno State	6-1-0	.833	9-2-0	.818
3.	Long Beach State	4-3-0	.571	6-5-0	.545
4.	UNLV	3-4-0	.429	6-5-0	.545
4.	Utah State	3-4-0	.429	3-8-0	.273
6.	Pacific	2-5-0	.286	4-7-0	.364
6.	CS Fullerton	2-5-0	.286	3-9-0	.333
8.	New Mexico State	1-6-0	.143	1-10-0	.091

Non-conference record: 14-20-0 .412

1987

		Conference		Overall	
1.	San Jose State	7-0-0	1.000	10-2-0	.833
2.	Fresno State	4-3-0	.571	6-5-0	.545
2.	CS Fullerton	4-3-0	.571	6-6-0	.500
2.	UNLV	4-3-0	.571	5-6-0	.455
2.	Utah State	4-3-0	.571	5-6-0	.455
6.	Pacific	3-4-0	.429	4-7-0	.364
7.	Long Beach State	2-5-0	.286	4-7-0	.364
8.	New Mexico State	0-7-0	.000	2-9-0	.182

Non-conference record: 14-20-0 .412

1988

		Conference		Overall	
1.	Fresno State	7-0-0	1.000	10-2-0	.833
2.	CS Fullerton	5-2-0	.714	5-6-0	.455
3.	Utah State	4-3-0	.571	4-7-0	.364
3.	San Jose State	4-3-0	.571	4-8-0	.333
5.	UNLV	3-4-0	.429	4-7-0	.364
5.	Long Beach State	3-4-0	.429	3-9-0	.250
7.	Pacific	2-5-0	.286	2-9-0	.182
8.	New Mexico State	0-7-0	.000	1-10-0	.091

Non-conference record: 5-30-0 .143

1989

		Conference		Overall	
1.	Fresno State	7-0-0	1.000	11-1-0	.917
2.	CS Fullerton	5-2-0	.714	6-4-1	.591
2.	San Jose State	5-2-0	.714	6-5-0	.545
4.	Utah State	4-3-0	.571	4-7-0	.364
5.	UNLV	3-4-0	.429	4-7-0	.364
6.	Long Beach State	2-5-0	.286	4-8-0	.333
7.	Pacific	2-5-0	.286	2-10-0	.167
8.	New Mexico State	0-7-0	.000	0-11-0	.000

Non-conference record: 9-25-1 .271

1990

		Conference		Overall	
1.	San Jose State	7-0-0	1.000	9-2-1	.792
2.	Fresno State	5-1-1	.786	8-2-1	.773
2.	Utah State	5-1-1	.786	5-5-1	.500
4.	Long Beach State	4-3-0	.571	6-5-0	.545
5.	UNLV	3-4-0	.429	4-7-0	.364
6.	Pacific	2-5-0	.286	4-7-0	.364
7.	New Mexico State	1-6-0	.143	1-10-0	.091
8.	CS Fullerton	0-7-0	.000	1-11-0	.083

Non-conference record: 11-21-1 .348

1991

		Conference		Overall	
1.	Fresno State	6-1-0	.857	10-2-0	.833
1.	San Jose State	6-1-0	.857	6-4-1	.591
3.	Utah State	5-2-0	.714	5-6-0	.455
4.	Pacific	4-3-0	.571	5-7-0	.417
5.	UNLV	2-5-0	.286	4-7-0	.364
5.	New Mexico State	2-5-0	.286	2-9-0	.182
5.	Long Beach State	2-5-0	.286	2-9-0	.182
8.	CS Fullerton	1-6-0	.143	2-9-0	.182

Non-conference record: 8-25-1 .250

1992

		Conference		Overall	
1.	Nevada	5-1-0	.833	7-5-0	.583
2.	San Jose State	4-2-0	.667	7-4-0	.636
2.	Utah State	4-2-0	.667	5-6-0	.455
4.	New Mexico State	3-3-0	.500	6-5-0	.545
4.	UNLV	3-3-0	.500	6-5-0	.545
6.	Pacific	2-4-0	.333	3-8-0	.273
7.	CS Fullerton	0-6-0	.000	2-9-0	.182

Fresno State and Long Beach State leave the BWC, while
Nevada (Reno) joins the BWC.
Non-conference record: 15-21-0 .417

1993

		Conference		Overall	
1.	Utah State	5-1-0	.833	7-5-0	.583
1.	SW Louisiana	5-1-0	.833	8-3-0	.727
3.	Nevada	4-2-0	.667	7-4-0	.636
3.	New Mexico State	4-2-0	.667	5-6-0	.455
5.	Northern Illinois	3-3-0	.500	4-7-0	.364
6.	UNLV	2-4-0	.333	3-8-0	.273
6.	Pacific	2-4-0	.333	3-8-0	.273
6.	San Jose State	2-4-0	.333	2-9-0	.182
6.	La. Tech	2-4-0	.333	2-9-0	.182
10.	Arkansas State	1-5-0	.167	2-8-1	.227

Southwest Louisiana, Northern Illinois, Louisiana Tech, and
Arkansas State join the BWC, and Cal State Fullerton leaves.
Non-conference record: 13-37-1 .270

1994		Conference		Overall	
1.	UNLV	5-1-0	.833	7-5-0	.583
1.	Nevada	5-1-0	.833	9-2-0	.818
1.	SW Louisiana	5-1-0	.833	6-5-0	.545
4.	Pacific	4-2-0	.667	6-5-0	.545
5.	N. Illinois	3-3-0	.500	4-7-0	.364
5.	San Jose State	3-3-0	.500	3-8-0	.273
7.	Utah State	2-4-0	.333	3-8-0	.273
7.	New Mexico State	2-4-0	.333	3-8-0	.273
9.	La. Tech	1-5-0	.167	3-8-0	.273
10.	Arkansas State	0-6-0	.000	1-10-0	.091

Non-conference record: 15-36-0 .294

1995		Conference		Overall	
1.	Nevada	6-0-0	1.000	9-3-0	.750
2.	SW Louisiana	4-2-0	.667	6-5-0	.545
2.	Utah State	4-2-0	.667	4-7-0	.364
4.	Arkansas State	3-3-0	.500	6-5-0	.545
4.	New Mexico State	3-3-0	.500	4-7-0	.364
4.	Northern Illinois	3-3-0	.500	3-8-0	.273
7.	Louisiana Tech	2-4-0	.333	5-6-0	.455
7.	Pacific	2-4-0	.333	3-8-0	.273
7.	San Jose State	2-4-0	.333	3-8-0	.273
10.	UNLV	1-5-0	.167	2-9-0	.182

Non-conference record: 15-36-0 .294

1996		Conference		Overall	
1.	Nevada	4-1-0	.800	9-3-0	.750
1.	Utah State	4-1-0	.800	6-5-0	.545
3.	Idaho	3-2-0	.600	6-5-0	.545
3.	North Texas	3-2-0	.600	5-6-0	.455
5.	Boise State	1-4-0	.200	2-10-0	.167
6.	New Mexico State	0-5-0	.000	1-10-0	.091

SW Louisiana, Arkansas State, Northern Illinois, Louisiana Tech, Pacific, San Jose State, and UNLV leave the BWC.
North Texas and Boise State join the BWC.
Non-conference record: 14-24-0 .368

1997		Conference		Overall	
1.	Nevada	4-1-0	.800	5-6-0	.455
1.	Utah State	4-1-0	.800	6-6-0	.500
3.	Boise State	3-2-0	.600	4-7-0	.364
4.	Idaho	2-3-0	.400	5-6-0	.455
4.	North Texas	2-3-0	.400	4-7-0	.364
6.	New Mexico State	0-5-0	.000	2-9-0	.182

Non-conference record: 11-26-0 .297

1998		Conference		Overall	
1.	Idaho	4-1-0	.800	9-3-0	.750
2.	Nevada	3-2-0	.600	6-5-0	.545
2.	North Texas	3-2-0	.600	3-8-0	.273
4.	Boise State	2-3-0	.400	7-5-0	.583
4.	Utah State	2-3-0	.400	3-8-0	.273
6.	New Mexico State	1-4-0	.200	3-8-0	.273

Non-conference record: 16-22-0 .421

1999		Conference		Overall	
1.	Boise State	5-1-0	.833	10-3-0	.769
2.	Idaho	4-2-0	.667	7-4-0	.636
3.	New Mexico State	3-2-0	.600	6-5-0	.545
4.	Utah State	3-3-0	.500	4-7-0	.364
5.	Arkansas State	2-3-0	.400	4-7-0	.364
6.	Nevada	2-4-0	.333	3-8-0	.273
7.	North Texas	1-5-0	.167	2-9-0	.182

Arkansas State rejoins BWC.
Non-conference record: 16-23-0 .410

2000		Conference		Overall	
1.	Boise State	5-0-0	1.000	10-2-0	.833
2.	Utah State	4-1-0	.800	5-6-0	.455
3.	Idaho	3-2-0	.600	5-6-0	.455
4.	New Mexico State	1-4-0	.200	3-8-0	.273
4.	North Texas	1-4-0	.200	3-8-0	.273
4.	Arkansas State	1-4-0	.200	1-10-0	.091

Nevada leaves the BWC.
Non-conference record: 12-25-0 .324
Big West Conference drops football, and North Texas, New Mexico State, Arkansas State, and Idaho join with Middle Tennessee, UL Lafayette, and UL Monroe to form the Sun Belt Football Conference.

BIG WEST W-L-T RECORDS BY DECADES (1969-2000)

Decade	S.D.State	LB State	Pacific	Fresno St.	UCSB	S.J. State	CalStLA	Fullerton	Utah St.	UNLV
1969-79	27- 6-1	26-25-0	20-28-1	22-28-0	4-11-0	29-16-2	0-11-0	6-17-0	9- 1-0	
1980-89		33-31-0	21-43-0	47-17-0		46-17-1		36-28-0	34-29-0	18-34-1
1990-00		6- 8-0	16-22-0	11-2-1		24-14-0		1-19-0	42-21-1	16-22-0

Decade	N.MexSt.	Nevada	SW La.	No. Ill.	La.Tech	Ark. St.	Idaho	No.Texas	Boise St.
1969-79									
1980-89	3-39-0								
1990-00	20-43-0	33-12-0	14- 4-0	9- 9-0	5-13-0	7-21-0	16-10-0	10-16-0	16-10-0

BIG WEST W-L-T RECORDS (1969-2000)

Team	W-L-T	Pct.	Team	W-L-T	Pct.	Team	W-L-T	Pct.
San Diego State	27- 6-1	.809	Cal State Fullerton	43-64-0	.402	No. Illinois	9- 9-0	.500
Long Beach State	65-64-0	.504	Utah State	85-51-1	.624	Louisiana Tec	5-13-0	.278
Pacific	57-93-1	.372	UNLV	34-56-1	.379	Arkansas State	7-21-0	.250
Fresno State	80-47-1	.629	New Mexico State	23-82-0	.219	Idaho	16-10-0	.615
UC Santa Barbara	4-11-0	.267	Nevada	33-12-0	.733	North Texas	10-16-0	.385
San Jose State	99-47-3	.674	SW Louisiana	14- 4-0	.778	Boise State	16-10-0	.615
Cal State LA	0-11-0	.000						

BIG WEST TITLES BY DECADE

Decade	S.D. State	LB State	Fresno St.	S.J. State	Fullerton	Utah St.	UNLV	Nevada	SW La	Idaho	Boise St.
1969-79	4.5	1.5	1	2.5		1.5					
1980-89		1	4	3	2						
1990-00			.5	1.5		1.5	.33	3.33	.83	1	2
Totals	4.5	2.5	5.5	7.0	2	3	.33	3.33	.83	1	2

BORDER CONFERENCE (1931-1961) The names of several of the Border Conference teams changed since the 1931-61 period. Tempe State became Arizona State; New Mexico A&M became New Mexico State; Flagstaff State became Northern Arizona; Texas Mines became Texas Western, and then UTEP. In what follows, we will use the current names of the teams.

1931		Conference		Overall	
1.	Arizona State	3-1-0	.750	6-2-0	.750
2.	New Mexico	1-0-1	.750	3-3-1	.500
3.	Arizona	1-1-1	.500	3-5-1	.389
4.	No. Arizona	2-3-0	.400		
5.	N.M. State	1-2-0	.333	6-4-0	.600

1932					
1.	Texas Tech	2-0-0	1.000	10-2-0	.833
2.	Arizona	3-2-0	.600	4-5-0	.444
3.	No. Arizona	2-2-0	.500		
3.	Arizona State	2-2-0	.500	3-3-1	.500
5.	N.M. State	1-2-1	.375	4-5-1	.450
6.	New Mexico	1-3-1	.300	1-6-1	.188

Texas Tech joins the Border Conference.

1933					
1.	Texas Tech	1-0-0	1.000	8-1-0	.889
2.	No. Arizona	3-1-0	.750		
3.	Arizona	3-2-0	.600	5-3-0	.625
4.	Arizona State	2-2-0	.500	3-5-0	.375
4.	New Mexico	2-2-0	.500	3-4-1	.438
6.	N.M. State	0-4-0	.000	2-6-0	.250

1934					
1.	Texas Tech	1-0-0	1.000	7-2-1	.750
2.	New Mexico	3-1-0	.750	8-1-0	.889
3.	Arizona	2-1-1	.625	7-2-1	.750
4.	Arizona State	1-2-1	.375	4-3-1	.562
5.	N.M. State	0-1-3	.375	4-1-3	.688
6.	No. Arizona	0-2-1	.167		

1935					
1.	Arizona	4-0-0	1.000	7-2-0	.778
2.	N.M. State	4-1-0	.800	7-1-2	.800
3.	New Mexico	3-2-0	.600	6-4-0	.600
4.	Arizona State	2-3-1	.417	2-5-1	.312
5.	No. Arizona	0-3-1	.125		
6.	Texas Tech	0-1-0	.000	5-3-2	.600
6.	UTEP	0-3-0	.000		

Texas Mines (UTEP) joins the Border Conference.

1936					
1.	Arizona	3-0-1	.875	5-2-3	.650
2.	N.M. State	3-2-0	.600	6-4-1	.591
3.	No. Arizona	2-1-1	.625		
3.	UTEP	2-1-1	.625		
5.	Arizona State	2-5-0	.286	4-5-0	.444
6.	New Mexico	1-4-0	.200	2-7-0	.222
7.	Texas Tech	0-0-1	.000	5-4-1	.550

1937					
1.	Texas Tech	3-0-0	1.000	8-4-0	.667
2.	N.M. State	4-1-0	.800	7-2-0	.778
3.	Arizona	3-1-0	.750	8-2-0	.800
4.	UTEP	2-1-1	.625		
5.	New Mexico	2-3-1	.417	4-4-1	.500
6.	No. Arizona	1-4-0	.200		
7.	Arizona State	0-5-0	.000	0-8-1	.055

1938		Conference		Overall	
1.	Texas Tech	2-0-0	1.000	10-1-0	.909
2.	N.M. State	4-1-0	.800	7-2-0	.778
3.	New Mexico	4-2-0	.667	8-3-0	.727
4.	UTEP	3-2-0	.600		
5.	No. Arizona	1-2-0	.333		
6.	Arizona	0-3-0	.000	3-6-0	.333
6.	Arizona State	0-4-0	.000	3-6-0	.333

1939					
1.	Arizona State	4-0-0	1.000	8-2-1	.773
2.	New Mexico	4-2-0	.667	8-2-0	.800
3.	UTEP	2-2-0	.500		
4.	Arizona	1-2-0	.333	6-4-0	.600
5.	N.M. State	1-4-0	.200	3-6-0	.333
6.	No. Arizona	0-3-0	.000		

Texas Tech out of the Border Conference.

1940					
1.	Arizona State	3-0-1	.875	7-2-2	.727
2.	Arizona	3-1-0	.750	7-2-0	.778
3.	UTEP	3-1-1	.700		
4.	New Mexico	3-2-0	.600	5-4-0	.556
5.	N.M. State	1-4-0	.200	3-6-0	.333
6.	No. Arizona	0-5-0	.000		

1941					
1.	Arizona	5-0-0	1.000	7-3-0	.700
2.	Texas Tech	2-0-0	1.000	9-2-0	.818
3.	West Texas	4-1-0	.800		
4.	Hard. Simmons	3-1-0	.750	7-3-1	.682
5.	New Mexico	3-1-1	.700	5-4-1	.550
6.	UTEP	3-4-0	.429		
7.	Arizona State	2-4-1	.357	5-5-1	.500
8.	No. Arizona	1-4-0	.200		
9.	N.M. State	0-6-0	.000	2-7-0	.222

Texas Tech returns to the Border Conference, and West Texas and Hardin-Simmons join the BC.

1942					
1.	Hard.-Simmons	3-0-1	.875	9-1-1	.864
1.	Texas Tech	3-0-1	.875	4-5-1	.450
3.	West Texas	5-2-0	.714		
4.	Arizona	4-2-0	.667	6-4-0	.600
5.	UTEP	4-3-0	.571		
6.	New Mexico	3-4-0	.429	4-5-2	.455
7.	Arizona State	2-4-0	.333	2-8-0	.200
8.	No. Arizona	1-4-0	.200		
9.	N.M. State	0-6-0	.000	1-8-0	.111

1943-1945: No league standings due to WW II.

1946					
1.	Hard-Simmons	6-0-0	1.000	11-0-0	1.000
2.	Texas Tech	3-1-0	.750	8-3-0	.727
3.	New Mexico	4-2-1	.653	5-5-2	.500
4.	Arizona	2-2-1	.500	4-4-2	.500
5.	West Texas	3-4-0	.429		
6.	UTEP	2-4-0	.333		
7.	No. Arizona	1-2-1	.375		
8.	Arizona State	1-4-1	.250	2-7-2	.273
9.	N.M. State	1-4-0	.200	4-5-0	.444

1947		Conference		Overall	
1.	Texas Tech	4-0-0	1.000	6-5-0	.545
2.	Hard-Simmons	5-1-0	.833	7-3-0	.700
3.	West Texas	5-2-0	.714	7-4-0	.636
4.	Arizona	3-2-0	.600	5-4-1	.550
5.	UTEP	3-3-1	.500	5-3-1	.611
6.	Arizona State	3-4-0	.429	4-7-0	.364
7.	N.M. State	1-4-0	.200	3-6-0	.333
8.	New Mexico	1-5-1	.214	4-5-1	.450
9.	No. Arizona	0-4-0	.000	1-7-0	.125

1948					
1.	Texas Tech	5-0-0	1.000	7-3-0	.700
2.	UTEP	4-1-1	.750	8-2-1	.773
3.	Arizona	3-2-0	.600	6-5-0	.545
3.	Arizona State	3-2-0	.600	5-5-0	.500
5.	Hard-Simmons	3-2-1	.583	6-2-3	.682
6	West Texas	2-3-0	.400	6-5-0	.545
7.	No. Arizona	1-2-0	.333	4-5-0	.444
8.	New Mexico	1-6-0	.143	2-9-0	.182
9.	N.M. State	0-4-0	.000	3-7-0	.300

1949					
1.	Texas Tech	5-0-0	1.000	7-5-0	.583
2.	Arizona State	4-1-0	.800	7-3-0	.700
3.	Hard-Simmons	4-2-0	.667	6-4-1	.591
3.	UTEP	4-2-0	.667	8-2-1	.773
5.	West Texas	3-2-0	.600	5-4-0	.556
6.	Arizona	2-4-0	.333	2-7-1	.250
7.	N.M. State	1-4-0	.200	4-6-0	.400
8.	New Mexico	1-6-0	.143	2-8-0	.200
9.	No. Arizona	0-3-0	.000	1-6-1	.188

1950					
1.	West Texas	6-0-0	1.000	10-1-0	.909
2.	Arizona State	4-1-0	.800	9-2-0	.818
3.	UTEP	4-2-0	.667	7-3-0	.700
4.	Texas Tech	3-2-0	.600	3-8-0	.273
5.	Hard-Simmons	3-3-0	.500	5-5-0	.500
6.	Arizona	2-4-0	.333	4-6-0	.400
7.	New Mexico	2-5-0	.286	2-8-0	.200
8.	N.M. State	1-4-0	.200	2-7-0	.222
9.	No. Arizona	0-4-0	.000	2-7-0	.222

1951					
1.	Texas Tech	4-0-0	1.000	7-4-0	.636
2.	Arizona State	4-1-0	.800	6-3-1	.650
2.	Hard-Simmons	4-1-0	.800	6-6-0	.500
4.	Arizona	3-3-0	.500	6-5-0	.545
5.	UTEP	2-4-0	.333	3-7-0	.300
6.	N.M. State	1-4-0	.200	1-9-0	.100
7.	West Texas	1-5-0	.167	2-7-0	.222
8.	No. Arizona	0-1-0	.000	1-7-0	.125

New Mexico leaves conference after 1950 season

1952					
1.	Arizona State	4-0-0	1.000	6-3-0	.667
2.	Texas Tech	2-1-1	.625	3-7-1	.318
3.	Arizona	3-2-0	.600	6-4-0	.600
4.	Hard-Simmons	2-2-1	.500	5-3-2	.600
5.	UTEP	1-3-1	.500	5-5-1	.500
6.	N.M. State	0-2-0	.000	2-6-1	.278
6.	West Texas	0-3-1	.000	3-6-0	.333

No. Arizona leaves conference after 1951 season.

1953		Conference		Overall	
1.	Texas Tech	5-0-0	1.000	11-1-0	.917
2.	Hard-Simmons	4-1-0	.800	6-5-0	.545
3.	UTEP	4-2-0	.667	8-2-0	.800
4.	Arizona	3-2-0	.600	4-5-1	.450
5.	Arizona State	1-3-0	.250	4-5-1	.450
6.	N.M. State	1-4-0	.200	2-7-0	.222
7.	West Texas	0-6-0	.000	1-8-1	.150

1954					
1.	Texas Tech	4-0-0	1.000	7-2-1	.750
2.	Arizona State	3-1-0	.750	5-5-0	.500
3.	UTEP	4-2-0	.667	8-3-0	.727
4.	Arizona	3-2-0	.600	7-3-0	.700
5.	Hard-Simmons	2-3-0	.400	4-6-0	.400
6.	West Texas	1-5-0	.167	1-8-0	.111
7.	N.M. State	0-4-0	.000	0-9-0	.000

1955					
1.	Texas Tech	3-0-1	.875	7-3-1	.682
2.	Arizona State	4-1-0	.800	8-2-1	.773
3.	Hard-Simmons	3-2-0	.600	5-5-0	.500
4.	UTEP	3-2-1	.583	6-2-2	.700
5.	Arizona	1-2-1	.375	4-4-1	.500
6.	West Texas	1-4-1	.250	4-4-1	.500
7.	N.M. State	0-4-0	.000	3-7-0	.300

1956					
1.	UTEP	6-0-0	1.000	9-2-0	.818
2.	Arizona State	3-1-0	.750	9-1-0	.900
3.	West Texas	3-2-0	.600	8-2-0	.800
4.	Hard-Simmons	2-3-0	.400	4-6-0	.400
5.	Arizona	1-3-0	.250	4-6-0	.600
5.	Texas Tech	1-3-0	.250	2-7-1	.250
7.	N.M. State	0-4-0	.000	1-9-0	.100

1957					
1.	Arizona State	4-0-0	1.000	10-0-0	1.000
2.	West Texas	3-1-0	.750	7-3-0	.700
3.	UTEP	3-2-0	.600	6-3-0	.667
3.	Hard-Simmons	3-2-0	.600	5-5-0	.500
5.	N.M. State	0-4-0	.000	3-7-0	.300
5.	Arizona	0-4-0	.000	1-8-1	.150

Texas Tech leaves conference after 1956 season.

1958					
1.	Hard-Simmons	4-0-0	1.000	5-6-0	.455
2.	Arizona State	4-1-0	.800	7-3-0	.700
3.	Arizona	2-1-0	.667	3-7-0	.300
4.	N.M. State	1-3-0	.250	4-6-0	.400
5.	UTEP	1-4-0	.200	2-7-0	.222
5.	West Texas	1-4-0	.200	1-9-0	.100

1959					
1.	Arizona State	5-0-0	1.000	10-1-0	.909
2.	Arizona	2-1-0	.667	4-6-0	.400
3.	N.M. State	2-2-0	.500	8-3-0	.727
4.	Hard-Simmons	2-2-0	.500	3-7-0	.300
5.	UTEP	2-3-0	.400	3-7-0	.300
6.	West Texas	0-5-0	.000	1-9-0	.100

1960					
1.	N.M. State	4-0-0	1.000	11-0-0	1.000
2.	Arizona	3-0-0	1.000	7-3-0	.700
3.	Arizona State	3-2-0	.600	7-3-0	.700
4.	UTEP	2-3-0	.400	4-5-1	.450
5.	West Texas	1-4-0	.200	3-7-0	.300
6.	Hard-Simmons	0-4-0	.000	0-10-0	.000

1961		Conference		Overall	
1.	Arizona State	3-0-0	1.000	7-3-0	.700
2.	West Texas	3-1-0	.750	6-4-0	.600
3.	N.M. State	2-1-0	.667	5-4-1	.550
4.	UTEP	1-3-0	.250	3-7-0	.300
5.	Hard-Simmons	0-4-0	.000	1-9-0	.100

Arizona leaves the conference after the 1960 season. The Border Conference disbands after the 1961 season. Hardin-Simmons drops major college football after the 1962 season.

Source: Harold Claassen and Steve Boda, The Encyclopedia of Football, 3rd edition, New York: Ronald Press, 1963, with several corrections.

BORDER CONFERENCE W-L-T RECORDS BY DECADES (1931-1961)

Decade	Arizona	Az. State	New Mex.	NM State`	No. Ariz	Tex Tech	UTEP	W. Texas	H-Simmons
1931-39	20-12-3	16-24-2	21-20-3	18-18-4	11-21-3	11- 2-1	9- 9-2		
1940-49	22-13-1	18-19-3	16-26-3	4-32-0	4-24-1	22- 1-1	19-18-3	22-14-0	24- 6-2
1950-59	20-23-1	36- 9-0	2- 5-0	7-35-1	0- 5-0	22-6-2	31-24-2	16-33-1	29-19-1
1960-61	3- 0-0	6- 2-0		6- 1-0			3- 6-0	4- 5-0	0- 8-0

BORDER CONFERENCE WIN PERCENTS (1931-1961)

Arizona	65-48-5	.572	Texas Tech	55- 9-4	.838
Az. State	76-54-5	.581	UTEP	62-57-7	.520
New Mexico	39-51-6	.438	West Texas	42-52-1	.447
N. M. State	35-86-5	.298	Hardin-Simmons	53-33-3	.612
No. Arizona	15-50-4	.246			

BORDER CONFERENCE TITLES BY DECADE (1931-1961)

Decade	Arizona	Az. State	New Mex.	NM State	No. Ariz.	Tex. Tech	UTEP	W. Texas	H. Simmons
1931-39	2	2				5			
1940-49	1	1				3.5			1.5
1950-59		3				4	1	1	1
1960-61		1		1					
Totals	3	7		1		12.5	1	1	2.5

CONFERENCE USA (1996-2003) After the 2003 season, Conference USA announced the loss of Louisville, Cincinnati, and South Florida to the Big East Conference. It then added Rice, SMU, and Tulsa from the WAC, and Marshall and UCF from the MAC, to form a 12-team conference, after Army had announced prospective plans to go independent after its contractual obligations to Conference USA were satisfied.

1996		Conference		Overall	
1.	Houston	4-1-0	.800	7-5-0	.583
1.	Southern Miss.	4-1-0	.800	8-3-0	.727
3.	Cincinnati	2-3-0	.400	6-5-0	.545
3.	Louisville	2-3-0	.400	5-6-0	.455
3.	Memphis	2-3-0	.400	4-7-0	.364
6.	Tulane	1-4-0	.200	2-9-0	.182

Non-conference record 17-20-0 .459

1997					
1.	Southern Miss.	6-0-0	1.000	9-3-0	.750
2.	Tulane	5-1-0	.833	7-4-0	.636
3.	East Carolina	4-2-0	.667	5-6-0	.455
4.	Cincinnati	2-4-0	.333	8-4-0	.667
4.	Memphis	2-4-0	.333	4-7-0	.364
4.	Houston	2-4-0	.333	3-8-0	.273
7.	Louisville	0-6-0	.000	1-10-0	.091

E. Carolina joins the conference.
Non-conference record 16-21-0 .432

1998					
1.	Tulane	6-0-0	1.000	12-0-0	1.000
2.	Southern Miss.	5-1-0	.833	7-5-0	.583
3.	Louisville	4-2-0	.667	7-5-0	.583
4.	East Carolina	3-3-0	.500	6-5-0	.545
5.	Army	2-4-0	.333	3-8-0	.273
5.	Houston	2-4-0	.333	3-8-0	.273
7.	Memphis	1-5-0	.167	2-9-0	.182
7.	Cincinnati	1-5-0	.167	2-9-0	.182

Army joins the conference.
Non-conference record 18-25-0 .419

1999					
1.	Southern Miss.	6-0-0	1.000	9-3-0	.750
2.	East Carolina	4-2-0	.667	9-3-0	.750
2.	Louisville	4-2-0	.667	7-5-0	.583
2.	Memphis	4-2-0	.667	5-6-0	.455
2.	UAB	4-2-0	.667	5-6-0	.455
6.	Houston	3-3-0	.500	7-4-0	.636
7.	Tulane	1-5-0	.167	3-8-0	.273
7.	Army	1-5-0	.167	3-8-0	.273
9.	Cincinnati	0-6-0	.000	3-8-0	.273

University of Alabama at Birmingham joins the conference.
Non-conference record 24-24-0 .500

2000					
1.	Louisville	6-1-0	.857	9-3-0	.750
2.	Cincinnati	5-2-0	.714	7-5-0	.583
2.	East Carolina	5-2-0	.714	8-4-0	.667
4.	Southern Miss.	4-3-0	.571	8-4-0	.667
5.	UAB	3-4-0	.429	7-4-0	.636
5.	Tulane	3-4-0	.429	6-5-0	.545
7.	Memphis	2-5-0	.286	4-7-0	.364
7.	Houston	2-5-0	.286	3-8-0	.273
9.	Army	1-6-0	.143	1-10-0	.091

Non-conference record 22-18-0 .550

2001		Conference		Overall	
1.	Louisville	6-1-0	.857	11-2-0	.846
2.	Cincinnati	5-2-0	.714	7-5-0	.583
2.	East Carolina	5-2-0	.714	6-6-0	.500
2.	UAB	5-2-0	.714	6-5-0	.545
5.	Southern Miss.	4-3-0	.571	6-5-0	.545
5.	TCU	4-3-0	.571	6-6-0	.500
7.	Memphis	3-4-0	.429	5-6-0	.455
8.	Army	2-5-0	.286	3-8-0	.273
9.	Tulane	1-6-0	.143	3-9-0	.250
10.	Houston	0-7-0	.000	0-11-0	.000

Texas Christian joins the conference.
Non-conference record 18-28-0 .391

2002					
1.	TCU	6-2-0	.750	10-2-0	.833
1.	Cincinnati	6-2-0	.750	7-7-0	.500
3.	Louisville	5-3-0	.625	7-6-0	.538
3.	Southern Miss.	5-3-0	.625	7-6-0	.538
5.	Tulane	4-4-0	.500	8-5-0	.615
5.	UAB	4-4-0	.500	5-7-0	.417
7.	East Carolina	4-4-0	.500	4-8-0	.333
8.	Houston	3-5-0	.375	5-7-0	.417
9.	Memphis	2-6-0	.250	3-9-0	.250
10.	Army	1-7-0	.125	1-11-0	.083

Non-conference record 17-28-0 .378

2003					
1.	Southern Miss	8-0-0	1.000	9-4-0	.692
2.	TCU	7-1-0	.875	11-2-0	.846
3.	Louisville	5-3-0	.625	9-4-0	.692
3.	Memphis	5-3-0	.625	9-4-0	.692
3.	South Florida	5-3-0	.625	7-4-0	.636
6.	Houston	4-4-0	.500	7-6-0	.538
6.	UAB	4-4-0	.500	5-7-0	.417
8.	Tulane	3-5-0	.375	5-7-0	.417
9.	Cincinnati	2-6-0	.250	5-7-0	.417
10.	E. Carolina	1-7-0	.125	1-11-0	.083
11.	Army	0-8-0	.000	0-13-0	.000

Non-conference record: 24-25-0 .490

CONFERENCE USA W-L-T RECORDS BY DECADES (1996-2002)

Decade	Army	Cincinn.	E. Carolina	Houston	Louisville	Memphis	So. Miss.	TCU	Tulane	UAB	USF
1996-99	3- 9-0	5-18-0	11- 7-0	11- 2-0	10-13-0	9-14-0	21- 2-0		13-10-0	4- 2-0	
2000-03	4-26-0	18-12-0	15-15-0	9-21-0	22- 8-0	12-18-0	21- 9-0	17- 6-0	11-19-0	16- 14-0	5-3-0

CONFERENCE USA WIN PERCENTAGES (1996-2003)

Army	7-35-0	.167	Southern Mississippi	42-11-0	.792
Cincinnati	23-30-0	.434	Texas Christian University	17-6-0	.739
East Carolina	26-22-0	.542	Tulane	24-29-0	.453
Houston	20-23-0	.465	UAB	20-16-0	.556
Louisville	32-21-0	.604	USF	5- 3-0	.625
Memphis	21-32-0	.396			

CONFERENCE USA TITLES BY DECADE (1996-2003)

Decade	Houston	Louisville	So. Miss.	Tulane	TCU	Cincinnati
1996-99	.5		1.5	1		
2000-02		2	1		.5	.5
Totals	.5	2	2.5	1	.5	.5

IVY LEAGUE (1956–2003) The Ivy League was only an informal organization until 1956. Conference standings are shown from 1956 on.

1956		Conference		Overall	
1.	Yale	7-0-0	1.000	8-1-0	.889
2.	Princeton	5-2-0	.714	7-2-0	.778
3.	Dartmouth	4-3-0	.571	5-3-1	.611
3.	Penn	4-3-0	.571	4-5-0	.444
5.	Brown	3-4-0	.429	5-4-0	.556
6.	Columbia	2-5-0	.286	3-6-0	.333
6.	Harvard	2-5-0	.286	2-6-0	.250
8.	Cornell	1-6-0	.143	1-8-0	.111
Non-conference record 7-7-1		.500			

1957					
1.	Princeton	6-1-0	.857	7-2-0	.778
2.	Dartmouth	5-1-1	.786	7-1-1	.833
3.	Yale	4-2-1	.643	6-2-1	.722
4.	Brown	3-4-0	.429	5-4-0	.556
4.	Cornell	3-4-0	.429	3-6-0	.333
4.	Penn	3-4-0	.429	3-6-0	.333
7.	Harvard	2-5-0	.286	3-5-0	.375
8.	Columbia	1-6-0	.143	1-8-0	.111
Non-conference record 8-7-0		.533			

1958					
1.	Dartmouth	6-1-0	.857	7-2-0	.778
2.	Cornell	5-2-0	.714	6-3-0	.667
2	Princeton	5-2-0	.714	6-3-0	.667
4.	Brown	4-3-0	.571	6-3-0	.667
4.	Penn	4-3-0	.571	4-5-0	.444
6.	Harvard	3-4-0	.429	4-5-0	.444
7.	Columbia	1-6-0	.143	1-8-0	.111
8.	Yale	0-7-0	.000	2-7-0	.222
Non-conference record 8-8-0		.500			

1959					
1.	Penn	6-1-0	.857	7-1-1	.833
2.	Dartmouth	5-1-1	.786	5-3-1	.611
3.	Harvard	4-3-0	.571	6-3-0	.667
3.	Yale	4-3-0	.571	6-3-0	.667
5.	Cornell	3-4-0	.429	5-4-0	.556
5.	Princeton	3-4-0	.429	4-5-0	.444
7.	Brown	1-5-1	.214	2-6-1	.278
8.	Columbia`	1-6-0	.143	2-7-0	.222
Non-conference record 10-5-0		.667			

1960					
1.	Yale	7-0-0	1.000	9-0-0	1.000
2.	Princeton	6-1-0	.857	7-2-0	.778
3.	Dartmouth	4-3-0	.571	5-4-0	.556
3.	Harvard	4-3-0	.571	5-4-0	.556
5.	Columbia	3-4-0	.429	3-6-0	.333
6.	Penn	2-5-0	.286	3-6-0	.333
7.	Brown	1-6-0	.143	3-6-0	.333
7.	Cornell	1-6-0	.143	2-7-0	.222
Non-conference record 9-7-0		.562			

1961					
1.	Columbia	6-1-0	.857	6-3-0	.667
1.	Harvard	6-1-0	.857	6-3-0	.667
3.	Dartmouth	5-2-0	.714	6-3-0	.667
3.	Princeton	5-2-0	.714	5-4-0	.556
5.	Yale	3-4-0	.429	4-5-0	.444
6.	Cornell	2-5-0	.286	3-6-0	.333
7.	Penn	1-6-0	.143	2-7-0	.222
8.	Brown	0-7-0	.000	0-9-0	.000
Non-conference record 4-12-0		.250			

1962		Conference		Overall	
1.	Dartmouth	7-0-0	1.000	9-0-0	1.000
2.	Harvard	5-2-0	.714	6-3-0	.667
3.	Columbia	4-3-0	.571	5-4-0	.556
3.	Princeton	4-3-0	.571	5-4-0	.556
3.	Cornell	4-3-0	.571	4-5-0	.444
6.	Penn	2-5-0	.286	3-6-0	.333
7.	Yale	1-5-1	.214	2-5-2	.333
8.	Brown	0-6-1	.071	1-6-2	.222
Non-conference record 8-6-2 .562					

1963					
1.	Dartmouth	5-2-0	.714	7-2-0	.222
1.	Princeton	5-2-0	.714	7-2-0	.222
3.	Harvard	4-2-1	.643	5-2-2	.667
4.	Yale	4-3-0	.571	6-3-0	.667
4.	Cornell	4-3-0	.571	5-4-0	.556
6.	Columbia	2-4-1	.357	4-4-1	.500
7.	Brown	2-5-0	.286	3-5-0	.375
8.	Penn	1-6-0	.143	3-6-0	.333
Non-conference record 13-1-0 .929					

1964					
1.	Princeton	7-0-0	1.000	9-0-0	1.000
2.	Harvard	5-2-0	.714	6-3-0	.667
3.	Yale	4-2-1	.643	6-2-1	.722
4.	Dartmouth	4-3-0	.571	6-3-0	.667
5.	Cornell	3-4-0	.429	3-5-1	.389
5.	Brown	3-4-0	.429	5-4-0	.556
7.	Columbia	1-5-1	.214	2-6-1	.278
8.	Penn	0-7-0	.000	1-8-0	.111
Non-conference record 11-4-1 .719					

1965					
1.	Dartmouth	7-0-0	1.000	9-0-0	1.000
2.	Princeton	6-1-0	.857	8-1-0	.889
3.	Harvard	3-2-2	.571	5-2-2	.667
4.	Cornell	3-3-1	.500	4-3-2	.556
5.	Yale	3-4-0	.429	3-6-0	.333
6.	Penn	2-4-1	.357	4-4-1	.500
7.	Brown	1-6-0	.143	2-7-0	.222
7.	Columbia	1-6-0	.143	2-7-0	.222
Non-conference record 11-4-1 .719					

1966					
1.	Dartmouth	6-1-0	.857	7-2-0	.778
1.	Harvard	6-1-0	.857	8-1-0	.889
1.	Princeton	6-1-0	.857	7-2-0	.778
4.	Cornell	4-3-0	.571	6-3-0	.667
5.	Yale	3-4-0	.429	4-5-0	.444
6.	Columbia	2-5-0	.286	2-7-0	.222
7.	Penn	1-6-0	.143	2-7-0	.222
8.	Brown	0-7-0	.000	1-8-0	.111
Non-conference record 9-7-0 .562					

1967					
1.	Yale	7-0-0	1.000	8-1-0	.889
2.	Dartmouth	5-2-0	.714	7-2-0	.778
3.	Cornell	4-2-1	.643	6-2-1	.722
4.	Harvard	4-3-0	.571	6-3-0	.667
4.	Princeton	4-3-0	.571	6-3-0	.667
6.	Penn	2-5-0	.286	3-6-0	.333
7.	Brown	1-5-1	.214	2-6-1	.278
8.	Columbia	0-7-0	.000	2-7-0	.222
Non-conference record 13-3-0 .812					

1968		Conference		Overall	
1.	Yale	6-0-1	.929	8-0-1	.944
1.	Harvard	6-0-1	.929	8-0-1	.944
3.	Penn	5-2-0	.714	7-2-0	.778
4.	Princeton	4-3-0	.571	4-5-0	.444
5.	Dartmouth	3-4-0	.429	4-5-0	.444
6.	Columbia	2-5-0	.286	2-7-0	.222
7.	Cornell	1-6-0	.143	3-6-0	.333
8.	Brown	0-7-0	.000	2-7-0	.222

Non-conference record 11-5-0 .688

1969					
1.	Dartmouth	6-1-0	.857	8-1-0	.889
1.	Yale	6-1-0	.857	7-2-0	.778
1.	Princeton	6-1-0	.857	6-3-0	.667
4.	Cornell	4-3-0	.571	4-5-0	.444
5.	Penn	2-5-0	.286	4-5-0	.444
5.	Harvard	2-5-0	.286	3-6-0	.333
7.	Brown	1-6-0	.143	2-7-0	.222
8.	Columbia	1-6-0	.143	1-8-0	.111

Non-conference record 7-9-0 .438

1970					
1.	Dartmouth	7-0-0	1.000	9-0-0	1.000
2.	Harvard	5-2-0	.714	7-2-0	.778
2.	Yale	5-2-0	.714	7-2-0	.778
4.	Cornell	4-3-0	.571	6-3-0	.667
5.	Princeton	3-4-0	.429	5-4-0	.556
6.	Penn	2-5-0	.286	4-5-0	.444
7.	Columbia	1-6-0	.143	3-6-0	.333
7.	Brown	1-6-0	.143	2-7-0	.222

Non-conference record 15-1-0 .938

1971					
1.	Cornell	6-1-0	.857	8-1-0	.889
1.	Dartmouth	6-1-0	.857	8-1-0	.889
3.	Columbia	5-2-0	.714	6-3-0	.667
4.	Harvard	4-3-0	.571	5-4-0	.556
5.	Princeton	3-4-0	.429	4-5-0	.444
5.	Yale	3-4-0	.429	4-5-0	.444
7.	Penn	1-6-0	.143	2-7-0	.222
8.	Brown	0-7-0	.000	0-9-0	.000

Non-conference record 9-7-0 .562

1972					
1.	Dartmouth	5-1-1	.786	7-1-1	.833
2.	Yale	5-2-0	.714	7-2-0	.778
3.	Penn	4-3-0	.571	6-3-0	.667
3.	Cornell	4-3-0	.571	6-3-0	.667
5.	Harvard	3-3-1	.500	4-4-1	.500
6.	Princeton	2-4-1	.357	3-5-1	389
6.	Columbia	2-4-1	.357	3-5-1	.389
8.	Brown	1-6-0	.143	1-8-0	.111

Non-conference record 11-5-0 .688

1973					
1.	Dartmouth	6-1-0	.857	6-3-0	.667
2.	Harvard	5-2-0	.714	7-2-0	.778
2.	Penn	5-2-0	.714	6-3-0	.667
2.	Yale	5-2-0	.714	6-3-0	.667
5.	Brown	4-3-0	.571	4-3-1	.562
6.	Cornell	2-5-0	.286	3-5-1	.389
7.	Columbia	1-6-0	.143	1-7-1	.167
8.	Princeton	0-7-0	.000	1-8-0	.111

Non-conference record 6-6-3 .500

1974		Conference		Overall	
1.	Harvard	6-1-0	.857	7-2-0	.778
1.	Yale	6-1-0	.857	8-1-0	.889
3.	Penn	4-2-1	.643	6-2-1	.722
4.	Brown	4-3-0	.571	5-4-0	.556
5.	Dartmouth	3-4-0	.429	3-6-0	.333
5.	Princeton	3-4-0	.429	4-4-1	.500
7.	Cornell	1-5-1	.214	3-5-1	.389
8.	Columbia	0-7-0	.000	1-8-0	.111

Non-conference record 10-5-1 .656

1975					
1.	Harvard	6-1-0	.857	7-2-0	.778
2.	Brown	5-1-1	.786	6-2-1	.722
3.	Yale	5-2-0	.714	7-3-0	.700
4.	Dartmouth	4-2-1	.643	5-3-1	.611
5.	Princeton	3-4-0	.429	4-5-0	.444
6.	Penn	2-5-0	.286	3-6-0	.333
6.	Columbia	2-5-0	.286	2-7-0	.222
8.	Cornell	0-7-0	.000	1-8-0	.111

Non-conference record 8-9-0 .471

1976					
1.	Brown	6-1-0	.857	8-1-0	.889
1.	Yale	6-1-0	.857	8-1-0	.889
3.	Dartmouth	4-3-0	.571	6-3-0	.667
3.	Harvard	4-3-0	.571	6-3-0	.667
5	Columbia	2-5-0	.286	3-6-0	.333
5.	Penn	2-5-0	.286	3-6-0	.333
5.	Princeton	2-5-0	.286	2-7-0	.222
5.	Cornell	2-5-0	.286	2-7-0	.222

Non-conference record 10-6-0 .625

1977					
1.	Yale	6-1-0	.857	7-2-0	.778
2.	Brown	5-2-0	.714	7-2-0	.778
3.	Dartmouth	4-3-0	.571	6-3-0	.667
3.	Penn	4-3-0	.571	5-4-0	.556
3.	Harvard	4-3-0	.571	4-5-0	.444
6.	Princeton	3-4-0	.429	3-6-0	.333
7.	Columbia	1-6-0	.143	2-7-0	.222
7.	Cornell	1-6-0	.143	1-8-0	.111

Non-conference record 7-9-0 .438

1978					
1.	Dartmouth	6-1-0	.857	6-3-0	.667
2.	Brown	5-2-0	.714	6-3-0	.667
2.	Yale	4-1-2	.714	5-2-2	.667
4.	Cornell	3-3-1	.500	5-3-1	.611
5.	Harvard	2-4-1	.357	4-4-1	.500
5.	Columbia	2-4-1	.357	3-5-1	.389
7.	Princeton	1-4-2	.286	2-5-2	.333
8.	Penn	1-5-1	.214	2-6-1	.278

Non-conference record 9-7-0 .562

1979					
1.	Yale	6-1-0	.857	8-1-0	.889
2.	Brown	5-2-0	.714	6-3-0	.667
2.	Princeton	5-2-0	.714	5-4-0	.556
4.	Cornell	4-3-0	.571	5-4-0	.556
4.	Dartmouth	4-3-0	.571	4-4-1	.500
6.	Harvard	3-4-0	.429	3-6-0	.333
7.	Columbia	1-6-0	.143	1-8-0	.111
8.	Penn	0-7-0	.000	0-9-0	.000

Non-conference record 4-11-1 .281

1980		Conference		Overall	
1.	Yale	6-1-0	.857	8-2-0	.800
2.	Cornell	5-2-0	.714	5-5-0	.500
3.	Harvard	4-3-0	.571	7-3-0	.700
3.	Princeton	4-3-0	.571	6-4-0	.600
3.	Brown	4-3-0	.571	6-4-0	.600
3.	Dartmouth	4-3-0	.571	4-6-0	.400
7.	Penn	1-6-0	.143	1-9-0	.100
8.	Columbia	0-7-0	.000	1-9-0	.100

Non-conference record 10-14-0 .417

1981		Conference		Overall	
1.	Yale	6-1-0	.857	9-1-0	.900
1.	Dartmouth	6-1-0	.857	6-4-0	.600
3.	Princeton	5-1-1	.786	5-4-1	.550
4.	Harvard	4-2-1	.643	5-4-1	.550
5.	Brown	2-5-0	.286	3-7-0	.300
5.	Cornell	2-5-0	.286	3-7-0	.300
7.	Columbia	1-6-0	.143	1-9-0	.100
7.	Penn	1-6-0	.143	1-9-0	.100

Non-conference record 6-18-0 .250

1982		Conference		Overall	
1.	Harvard	5-2-0	.714	7-3-0	.700
1.	Penn	5-2-0	.714	7-3-0	.700
1.	Dartmouth	5-2-0	.714	5-5-0	.500
4.	Brown	3-4-0	.429	5-5-0	.500
4.	Cornell	3-4-0	.429	4-6-0	.400
4.	Yale	3-4-0	.429	4-6-0	.400
4.	Princeton	3-4-0	.429	3-7-0	.300
8.	Columbia	1-6-0	.143	1-9-0	.100

Non-conference record 8-16-0 .250

1983		Conference		Overall	
1.	Harvard	5-1-1	.786	6-2-2	.700
1.	Penn	5-1-1	.786	6-3-1	.650
3.	Brown	4-2-1	.643	4-5-1	.450
3.	Dartmouth	4-2-1	.643	4-5-1	.450
5.	Cornell	3-3-1	.500	3-6-1	.350
6.	Princeton	2-5-0	.286	4-6-0	.400
7.	Columbia	1-5-1	.214	1-7-2	.200
8.	Yale	1-6-0	.143	1-9-0	.100

Non-conference record 4-18-2 .208

1984		Conference		Overall	
1.	Penn	7-0-0	1.000	8-1-0	.889
2.	Harvard	5-2-0	.714	5-4-0	.556
2.	Yale	5-2-0	.714	6-3-0	.666
4.	Brown	4-3-0	.571	4-5-0	.444
5.	Princeton	3-4-0	.429	4-5-0	.444
6.	Cornell	2-5-0	.286	2-7-0	.222
6.	Dartmouth	2-5-0	.286	2-7-0	.222
8.	Columbia	0-7-0	.000	0-9-0	.000

Non-conference record 3-13-0 .188

1985		Conference		Overall	
1.	Penn	6-1-0	.857	7-2-1	.750
2.	Harvard	5-2-0	.714	7-3-0	.700
2.	Princeton	5-2-0	.714	5-5-0	.500
4.	Brown	4-3-0	.571	5-4-1	.550
5.	Yale	3-3-1	.500	4-4-1	.500
6.	Dartmouth	2-4-1	.357	2-7-1	.250
7.	Cornell	2-5-0	.286	3-7-0	.300
8.	Columbia	0-7-0	.000	0-10-0	.000

Non-conference record 6-15-2 .304

1986		Conference		Overall	
1.	Penn	7-0-0	1.000	10-0-0	1.000
2.	Cornell	6-1-0	.857	8-2-0	.800
3.	Brown	4-2-1	.643	5-4-1	.550
4.	Dartmouth	3-3-1	.500	3-6-1	.350
5.	Harvard	3-4-0	.429	3-7-0	.300
6.	Yale	2-5-0	.286	3-7-0	.300
6.	Princeton	2-5-0	.286	2-8-0	.200
8.	Columbia	0-7-0	.000	0-10-0	.000

Non-conference record 7-17-0 .292

1987		Conference		Overall	
1.	Harvard	6-1-0	.857	8-2-0	.800
2.	Brown	5-2-0	.714	7-3-0	.700
2.	Yale	5-2-0	.714	7-3-0	.700
4.	Princeton	4-3-0	.571	6-4-0	.600
4.	Cornell	4-3-0	.571	5-5-0	.500
6.	Penn	3-4-0	.429	4-6-0	.400
7.	Dartmouth	1-6-0	.143	2-8-0	.200
8.	Columbia	0-7-0	.000	0-10-0	.000

Non-conference record 11-13-0 .458

1988		Conference		Overall	
1.	Penn	6-1-0	.857	8-2-0	.800
1.	Cornell	6-1-0	.857	7-2-1	.750
3.	Princeton	4-3-0	.571	6-4-0	.600
3.	Dartmouth	4-3-0	.571	5-5-0	.500
5.	Yale	3-3-1	.500	3-6-1	.350
6.	Columbia	2-5-0	.286	2-8-0	.200
6.	Harvard	2-5-0	.286	2-8-0	.200
8.	Brown	0-6-1	.071	0-9-1	.050

Non-conference record 6-17-1 .271

1989		Conference		Overall	
1.	Yale	6-1-0	.857	8-2-0	.800
1.	Princeton	6-1-0	.857	7-2-1	.750
3.	Harvard	5-2-0	.714	5-5-0	.500
4.	Dartmouth	4-3-0	.571	5-5-0	.500
5.	Cornell	2-5-0	.286	4-6-0	.400
5.	Penn	2-5-0	.286	4-6-0	.400
5.	Brown	2-5-0	.286	2-8-0	.200
8.	Columbia	1-6-0	.143	1-9-0	.100

Non-conference record 8-15-1 .354

1990		Conference		Overall	
1.	Dartmouth	6-1-0	.857	7-2-1	.750
1.	Cornell	6-1-0	.857	7-3-0	.700
3.	Yale	5-2-0	.714	6-4-0	.600
4.	Harvard	3-4-0	.429	5-5-0	.500
4.	Penn	3-4-0	.429	3-7-0	.300
6.	Princeton	2-5-0	.286	3-7-0	.300
6.	Brown	2-5-0	.286	2-8-0	.200
8.	Columbia	1-6-0	.143	1-9-0	.100

Non-conference record 6-17-0 .261

1991		Conference		Overall	
1.	Dartmouth	6-0-1	.929	7-2-1	.750
2.	Princeton	5-2-0	.714	8-2-0	.800
3.	Harvard	4-2-1	.643	4-5-1	.450
4.	Yale	4-3-0	.571	6-4-0	.600
4.	Cornell	4-3-0	.571	5-5-0	.500
6.	Penn	2-5-0	.286	2-8-0	.200
7.	Brown	1-6-0	.143	1-9-0	.100
7.	Columbia	1-6-0	.143	1-9-0	.100

Non-conference record 7-17-0 .292

1992		Conference		Overall	
1.	Dartmouth	6-1-0	.857	8-2-0	.800
1.	Princeton	6-1-0	.857	8-2-0	.800
3.	Penn	5-2-0	.714	7-3-0	.700
4.	Cornell	4-3-0	.571	7-3-0	.700
5.	Harvard	3-4-0	.429	3-7-0	.300
6.	Yale	2-5-0	.286	4-6-0	.400
6.	Columbia	2-5-0	.286	3-7-0	.300
8	Brown	0-7-0	.000	0-10-0	.000

Non-conference record 12-12-0 .500

1993					
1.	Penn	7-0-0	1.000	10-0-0	1.000
2.	Dartmouth	6-1-0	.857	7-3-0	.700
3.	Princeton	5-2-0	.714	8-2-0	.800
4.	Brown	3-4-0	.429	4-6-0	.400
4.	Cornell	3-4-0	.429	4-6-0	.400
6.	Yale	2-5-0	.286	3-7-0	.300
7.	Harvard	1-6-0	.143	3-7-0	.300
7.	Columbia	1-6-0	.143	2-8-0	.200

Non-conference record 13-11-0 .542

1994					
1.	Penn	7-0-0	1.000	9-0-0	1.000
2.	Brown	4-3-0	.571	7-3-0	.700
2.	Princeton	4-3-0	.571	7-3-0	.700
4.	Cornell	3-4-0	.429	6-4-0	.600
4.	Columbia	3-4-0	.429	5-4-1	.550
4.	Yale	3-4-0	.429	5-5-0	.500
7.	Harvard	2-5-0	.285	4-6-0	.400
7.	Dartmouth	2-5-0	.286	4-6-0	.400

Non-conference record 19-3-1 .848

1995					
1.	Princeton	5-1-1	.786	8-1-1	.850
2.	Penn	5-2-0	.714	7-3-0	.700
2.	Cornell	5-2-0	.714	6-4-0	.600
4.	Dartmouth	4-2-1	.643	7-2-1	.750
5.	Columbia	3-4-0	.429	3-6-1	.350
6.	Brown	2-5-0	.286	5-5-0	.500
6.	Yale	2-5-0	.286	3-7-0	.300
8.	Harvard	1-6-0	.143	2-8-0	.200

Non-conference record 14-9-1 .604

1996					
1.	Dartmouth	7-0-0	1.000	10-0-0	1.000
2.	Columbia	5-2-0	.714	8-2-0	.800
3.	Brown	4-3-0	.571	5-5-0	.500
3.	Cornell	4-3-0	.571	4-6-0	.400
5.	Penn	3-4-0	.429	5-5-0	.500
6.	Harvard	2-5-0	.286	4-6-0	.400
6.	Princeton	2-5-0	.286	3-7-0	.300
8.	Yale	1-6-0	.143	2-8-0	.200

Non-conference record 13-11-0 .542

1997					
1.	Harvard	7-0-0	1.000	9-1-0	.900
2.	Dartmouth	6-1-0	.857	8-2-0	.800
3.	Brown	4-3-0	.571	7-3-0	.700
3.	Cornell	4-3-0	.571	6-4-0	.600
5.	Princeton	3-4-0	.429	6-4-0	.600
5.	Columbia	3-4-0	.429	4-6-0	.400
7.	Yale	1-6-0	.143	2-8-0	.200
8.	Penn	0-7-0	.000	1-9-0	.100

Non-conference record 15-9-0 .625

1998		Conference		Overall	
1.	Penn	6-1-0	.857	8-2-0	.800
2.	Brown	5-2-0	.714	7-3-0	.700
2.	Yale	5-2-0	.714	6-4-0	.600
4.	Princeton	4-3-0	.571	5-5-0	.500
5.	Columbia	3-4-0	.429	4-6-0	.400
5.	Harvard	3-4-0	.429	4-6-0	.400
7.	Cornell	1-6-0-	.143	4-6-0	.400
7.	Dartmouth	1-6-0	.143	2-8-0	.200

Non-conference record 12-12-0 .500

1999					
1.	Yale	6-1-0	.857	9-1-0	.900
1.	Brown	6-1-0	.857	9-1-0	.900
3.	Cornell	5-2-0	.714	7-3-0	.700
4.	Penn	4-3-0	.571	5-5-0	.500
5.	Harvard	3-4-0	.429	5-5-0	.500
6.	Dartmouth	2-5-0	.286	2-8-0	.200
7.	Columbia	1-6-0	.143	3-7-0	.300
7.	Princeton	1-6-0	.143	3-7-0	.300

Non-conference record 15-9-0 .625

2000					
1.	Penn	6-1-0	.857	7-3-0	.700
2.	Cornell	5-2-0	.714	5-5-0	.500
3.	Yale	4-3-0	.571	7-3-0	.700
3.	Harvard	4-3-0	.571	5-5-0	.500
5.	Princeton	3-4-0	.429	3-7-0	.300
6.	Columbia	1-6-0	.143	3-7-0	.300
6.	Dartmouth	1-6-0	.143	2-8-0	.200
8.	Brown*	4-3-0	.571	7-3-0	.300

*Ineligible for title

Non-conference record 11-13-0 .458

2001					
1.	Harvard	7-0-0	1.000	9-0-0	1.000
2.	Penn	6-1-0	.857	8-1-0	.889
3.	Brown	5-2-0	.714	6-3-0	.667
4.	Princeton	3-4-0	.429	3-6-0	.333
4.	Columbia	3-4-0	.429	3-7-0	.300
6.	Cornell	2-5-0	.286	2-7-0	.222
7.	Yale	1-6-0	.143	3-6-0	.333
7.	Dartmouth	1-6-0	.143	1-8-0	.111

Non-conference record 7-10-0 .412

2002					
1.	Penn	7-0-0	1.000	9-1-0	.900
2.	Harvard	6-1-0	.857	7-3-0	.700
3.	Princeton	4-3-0	.571	6-4-0	.600
3.	Yale	4-3-0	.571	6-4-0	.600
5.	Cornell	3-4-0	.429	4-6-0	.400
6.	Dartmouth	2-5-0	.286	3-7-0	.300
6.	Brown	2-5-0	.286	2-8-0	.200
8.	Columbia	0-7-0	.000	1-9-0	.100

Non-conference record 10-14-0 .417

2003					
1.	Penn	7-0-0	1.000	10-0-0	1.000
2.	Harvard	4-3-0	.571	7-3-0	.700
2.	Yale	4-3-0	.571	6-4-0	.600
2.	Brown	4-3-0	.571	5-5-0	.500
2.	Dartmouth	4-3-0	.571	5-5-0	.500
6.	Columbia	3-4-0	.429	5-6-0	.400
7.	Princeton	2-5-0	.286	2-8-0	.200
8.	Cornell	0-7-0	.000	1-9-0	.100

Non-conference record: 13-12-0 .520

IVY LEAGUE W-L-T RECORDS BY DECADES (1956-2003)

Decade	Brown	Columbia	Cornell	Dartmouth	Harvard	Penn	Princeton	Yale
1956-59	11-16-1	5-23-0	12-16-0	20- 6-2	11-17-0	17-11-0	19- 9-0	15-12-1
1960-69	9-59-2	22-46-2	30-38-2	52-18-0	45-21-4	18-51-1	53-17-0	44-23-3
1970-79	36-33-1	17-51-2	27-41-2	49-19-2	42-26-2	25-43-2	25-42-3	51-17-2
1980-89	32-35-3	6-63-1	35-34-1	35-32-3	44-24-2	43-26-1	38-31-1	40-28-1
1990-99	31-39-0	23-47-0	39-31-0	46-23-2	29-40-1	42-28-0	37-32-1	31-39-0
2000-03	15- 13-0	7-21-0	10-18-0	8-20-0	21- 7-0	26- 2-0	12-16- 0	13-15-0

IVY LEAGUE W-L-T PERCENTAGES (1956-2003)

Brown	134-195-7	.409	Harvard	192-135-9	.585
Columbia	80-251-5	.246	Penn	171-161-4	.515
Cornell	153-178-5	.466	Princeton	184-147-5	.555
Dartmouth	210-118-9	.636	Yale	194-134-7	.590

IVY LEAGUE CHAMPIONSHIPS BY DECADES (1956-2003)

Decade	Brown	Columbia	Cornell	Dartmouth	Harvard	Penn	Princeton	Yale
1956-59				1		1	1	1
1960-69		.5		3.16	1.33		2.16	2.83
1970-79	.5		.5	4.5	1.5			3
1980-89			.5	.83	1.83	4.33	.5	2
1990-99	.5		.5	3	1	3	1.5	.5
2000-03					1	3		
Totals	1	.5	1.5	12.5	5.66	11.33	4.16	9.33

MID-AMERICAN CONFERENCE (MAC) (1947–2003) Following the 2003 season, the MAC announced the loss of Marshall and Central Florida to Conference USA.

1947		Conference		Overall	
1.	Cincinnati	3-1-0	.750	7-3-0	.700
2.	West. Reserve	2-1-0	.667	4-5-0	.444
3.	Butler	1-3-0	.250	5-3-1	.611
3.	Ohio	1-3-0	.250	3-5-1	.389
Miami*		------------------		9-0-1	.950
West. Michigan*		------------------		5-4-0	.556

*did not compete for conference title.
Non-conference record 12-8-2 .591

1948					
1.	Miami	4-0-0	1.000	7-1-1	.833
2.	West. Michigan	3-1-0	.750	6-3-0	.667
2.	Cincinnati	3-1-0	.750	3-6-1	.350
4.	Ohio	2-3-0	.400	3-6-0	.333
5.	West. Reserve	1-4-0	.200	1-8-1	.150
6.	Butler	0-4-0	.000	3-5-0	.375

Butler joins the MAC.
Non-conference record 10-16-3 .397

1949					
1.	Cincinnati	4-0-0	1.000	7-4-0	.636
2.	Miami	3-1-0	.750	5-4-0	.556
3.	Ohio	2-2-0	.500	4-4-1	.500
4.	West. Michigan	2-3-0	.400	4-4-0	.500
5.	West. Reserve	1-3-1	.300	4-5-1	.450
6.	Butler	0-3-0	.000	2-6-0	.250

Non-conference record 14-15-1 .483

1950					
1.	Miami	4-0-0	1.000	9-1-0	.900
2.	Cincinnati	3-1-0	.750	8-4-0	.667
3.	Ohio	2-2-0	.500	6-4-0	.600
4.	West. Reserve	1-3-0	.250	2-8-0	.200
5.	West. Michigan	0-4-0	.000	5-4-0	.556

Butler leaves the MAC.
Non-conference record 20-11-0 .645

1951					
1.	Cincinnati	3-0-0	1.000	10-1-0	.909
2.	Miami	3-1-0	.750	7-3-0	.700
3.	Kent	2-1-0	.667	4-3-2	.556
4.	Ohio	2-2-0	.500	5-4-1	.550
5.	West. Reserve	1-3-0	.250	2-6-1	.278
6.	West. Michigan	1-4-0	.200	4-4-0	.500
Toledo*		------------------		6-4-0	.600

Kent State and Toledo join the MAC.
*Did not compete for title.
Non-conference record 20-10-4 ..647

1952					
1.	Cincinnati	3-0-0	1.000	8-1-1	.850
2.	Miami	4-1-0	.800	8-1-0	.889
3.	Ohio	5-2-0	.714	6-2-1	.722
4.	Bowling Green	2-2-0	.500	7-2-0	.778
4.	Kent	2-2-0	.500	5-4-0	.556
6.	West. Michigan	1-4-0	.250	4-4-0	.500
6.	West. Reserve	1-4-0	.250	5-4-0	.556
6.	Toledo	1-4-0	.250	4-5-0	.444

Bowling Green joins the MAC.
Non-conference record 28-4-2 .853

1953		Conference		Overall	
1.	Ohio	5-0-1	.917	6-2-1	.722
2.	Miami	3-0-1	.875	7-1-1	.833
3.	Kent	3-1-0	.750	7-2-0	.778
4.	Toledo	2-3-0	.400	3-6-0	.333
5.	West. Reserve	1-2-1	.375	5-3-1	.611
6.	West. Michigan	0-4-1	.100	1-6-1	.188
7.	Bowling Green	0-4-0	.000	1-8-0	.111

Cincinnati leaves the MAC.
Non-conference record 16-14-0 .533

1954					
1.	Miami	4-0-0	1.000	8-1-0	.889
2.	Kent	4-1-0	.800	8-2-0	.800
3.	Ohio	5-2-0	.714	6-3-0	.667
4.	Toledo	3-2-0	.600	6-2-1	.722
5.	West. Michigan	3-4-0	.428	4-5-0	.444
6.	West. Reserve	2-3-0	.400	3-4-1	.438
7.	Marshall	2-5-0	.286	4-5-0	.444
8.	Bowling Green	0-6-0	.000	2-7-0	.222

Marshall joins the MAC.
Non-conference record 18-6-2 .731

1955					
1.	Miami	5-0-0	1.000	9-0-0	1.000
2.	Bowling Green	4-1-1	.750	7-1-1	.833
2.	Kent	4-1-1	.750	6-2-1	.722
4.	Ohio	3-3-0	.500	5-4-0	.556
5.	Toledo	2-4-0	.333	3-5-1	.389
6.	Marshall	1-5-0	.167	3-6-0	.333
7.	West. Michigan	0-5-0	.000	1-7-1	.167

Western Reserve leaves the MAC.
Non-conference record 15-6-2 .696

1956					
1.	Bowling Green	5-0-1	.917	8-0-1	.944
2.	Miami	4-0-1	.900	7-1-1	.833
3.	Kent	4-2-0	.667	7-2-0	.778
4.	Marshall	2-4-0	.333	3-6-0	.333
4.	Ohio	2-4-0	.333	2-7-0	.222
6.	West. Michigan	1-4-0	.200	2-7-0	.222
7.	Toledo	1-5-0	.167	1-7-1	.167

Non-conference record 11-11-0 .500

1957					
1.	Miami	5-0-0	1.000	6-3-0	.667
2.	Bowling Green	3-1-2	.667	6-1-2	.778
2.	Marshall	4-2-0	.667	6-3-0	.667
4.	Toledo	3-2-0	.600	5-4-0	.556
5.	West. Michigan	1-4-1	.250	4-4-1	.500
5.	Ohio	1-4-1	.250	2-6-1	.278
7.	Kent	1-5-0	.167	3-6-0	.333

Non-conference record 14-9-0 .609

1958					
1.	Miami	5-0-0	1.000	6-3-0	.667
2.	Kent	5-1-0	.833	7-2-0	.778
3.	Bowling Green	4-2-0	.667	7-2-0	.778
4.	Ohio	2-4-0	.333	5-4-0	.556
4.	West. Michigan	2-4-0	.333	4-5-0	.444
6.	Toledo	1-4-0	.200	4-5-0	.444
7.	Marshall	1-5-0	.167	3-6-0	.333

Non-conference record 16-7-0 .696

1959		Conference		Overall	
1.	Bowling Green	6-0-0	1.000	9-0-0	1.000
2.	Ohio	4-2-0	.667	7-2-0	.778
3.	Miami	3-2-0	.600	5-4-0	.556
4.	Kent	3-3-0	500	5-3-0	.625
4.	West. Michigan	3-3-0	.500	4-5-0	.444
6.	Marshall	1-4-0	.200	1-8-0	.111
7.	Toledo	0-6-0	.000	2-6-1	.277

Non-conference record 13-8-1 .614

1960					
1.	Ohio	6-0-0	1.000	10-0-0	1.000
2.	Bowling Green	5-1-0	.833	8-1-0	.889
3.	Kent	4-2-0	.667	6-3-0	.667
4.	Miami	2-3-0	.400	5-5-0	.500
5.	West. Michigan	2-4-0	.333	4-4-1	.500
6.	Marshall	1-4-0	.200	2-7-1	.250
7.	Toledo	0-6-0	.000	2-7-0	.222

Non-conference record 17-7-2 .692

1961					
1.	Bowling Green	5-1-0	.833	8-2-0	.800
2.	West. Michigan	4-1-1	.750	5-4-1	.550
3.	Miami	3-2-0	.600	6-4-0	.600
4.	Ohio	3-2-1	.583	5-3-1	.611
5.	Toledo	2-4-0	.333	3-7-0	.300
6.	Marshall	1-4-0	.200	2-7-1	.250
7.	Kent	1-5-0	.167	2-8-0	.200

Non-conference record 12-16-1 .431

1962					
1.	Bowling Green	5-0-1	.917	7-1-1	.833
2.	Ohio	5-1-0	.833	8-3-0	.727
3.	Miami	3-1-1	.700	8-2-1	.773
4.	West. Michigan	3-3-0	.500	5-4-0	.556
5.	Kent	2-4-0	.333	3-6-0	.333
6.	Toledo	1-5-0	.167	3-6-0	.333
7.	Marshall	0-5-0	.000	4-6-0	.400

Non-conference record 19-9-0 .679

1963					
1.	Ohio	5-1-0	.833	6-5-0	.545
2.	Miami	4-1-1	.750	5-3-2	.600
3.	Bowling Green	4-2-0	.600	8-2-0	.800
4.	Marshall	3-2-1	.583	5-4-1	.550
5.	West. Michigan	2-4-0	.333	2-7-0	.222
6.	Kent	1-5-0	.167	3-5-1	.389
6.	Toledo	1-5-0	.167	2-7-0	.222

Non-conference record 11-13-2 .462

1964					
1.	Bowling Green	5-1-0	.833	9-1-0	.900
2.	Marshall	4-2-0	.667	7-3-0	.700
2.	Miami	4-2-0	.667	6-3-1	.650
4.	Ohio	3-2-1	.583	5-4-1	.550
5.	West. Michigan	2-4-0	.333	3-6-0	.333
6.	Kent	1-4-1	.250	3-5-1	.389
7.	Toledo	1-5-0	.167	2-8-0	.200

Non-conference record 15-10-1 .596

1965					
1.	Bowling Green	5-1-0	.833	7-2-0	.778
1.	Miami	5-1-0	.833	7-3-0	.700
3.	West. Michigan	3-2-1	.583	6-2-1	.722
3.	Kent	3-2-1	.583	5-4-1	.550
5.	Toledo	2-4-0	.333	5-5-0	.500
5.	Marshall	2-4-0	.333	5-5-0	.500
7.	Ohio	0-6-0	.000	0-10-0	.000

Non-conference record 15-11-0 .577

1966		Conference		Overall	
1.	Miami	5-1-0	.833	9-1-0	.900
1.	West. Michigan	5-1-0	.833	7-3-0	.700
3.	Bowling Green	4-2-0	.667	6-3-0	.667
4.	Ohio	3-3-0	.500	5-5-0	.500
5.	Kent	2-4-0	.333	4-6-0	.400
6.	Toledo	1-5-0	.167	2-7-1	.250
6.	Marshall	1-5-0	.167	2-8-0	.200

Non-conference record 14-12-1 .537

1967					
1.	Toledo	5-1-0	.833	9-1-0	.900
1.	Ohio	5-1-0	.833	6-4-0	.600
3.	Miami	4-2-0	.667	6-4-0	.600
3.	West. Michigan	4-2-0	.667	5-4-0	.556
5.	Bowling Green	2-4-0	.333	6-4-0	.600
6	Kent	1-5-0	.167	4-6-0	.400
7.	Marshall	0-6-0	.000	0-10-0	.000

Non-conference record 15-12-0 .556

1968					
1.	Ohio	6-0-0	1.000	10-1-0	.909
2.	Miami	5-1-0	.833	7-3-0	.700
3.	Bowling Green	3-2-1	.583	6-3-1	.650
3.	Toledo	3-2-1	.583	5-4-1	.550
5.	West. Michigan	2-4-0	.333	3-6-0	.333
6.	Kent	1-5-0	.167	1-9-0	.100
7.	Marshall	0-6-0	.000	0-9-1	.050

Non-conference record 12-15-1 .446

1969					
1.	Toledo	5-0-0	1.000	11-0-0	1.000
2.	Bowling Green	4-1-0	.800	6-4-0	.600
3.	Miami	2-3-0	.400	7-3-0	.700
3.	Ohio	2-3-0	.400	5-4-1	.550
5.	Kent	1-4-0	.200	5-5-0	.500
5.	West. Michigan	1-4-0	.200	4-6-0	.400

Marshall leaves the MAC.
Non-conference record 23-7-1 .758

1970					
1.	Toledo	5-0-0	1.000	12-0-0	1.000
2.	Miami	3-2-0	.600	7-3-0	.700
2.	Ohio	3-2-0	.600	4-5-0	.444
4.	West. Michigan	2-3-0	.400	7-3-0	.700
5.	Kent	1-4-0	.200	3-7-0	.300
5.	Bowling Green	1-4-0	.200	2-6-1	.278

Non-conference record 20-9-1 683

1971					
1.	Toledo	5-0-0	1.000	12-0-0	1.000
2.	Bowling Green	4-1-0	.800	6-4-0	.600
3.	Miami	2-3-0	.400	7-3-0	.700
3.	West. Michigan	2-3-0	.400	7-3-0	.700
3.	Ohio	2-3-0	.400	5-5-0	.500
6.	Kent	0-5-0	.000	3-8-0	.272

Non-conference record 25-8-0 .756

1972					
1.	Kent	4-1-0	.800	6-5-1	.542
2.	Bowling Green	3-1-1	.700	6-3-1	.650
3.	West. Michigan	2-2-1	.500	7-3-1	.682
4.	Miami	2-3-0	.400	7-3-0	.700
4.	Toledo	2-3-0	.400	6-5-0	.545
6.	Ohio	1-4-0	.200	3-8-0	.273

Non-conference record 21-13-1 .614

1973		Conference		Overall	
1.	Miami	5-0-0	1.000	11-0-0	1.000
2.	Kent	4-1-0	.800	9-2-0	.818
3.	Bowling Green	2-3-0	.400	7-3-0	.700
3.	Ohio	2-3-0	.400	5-5-0	.500
5.	West. Michigan	1-4-0	.200	6-5-0	.545
5.	Toledo	1-4-0	.200	3-8-0	.273

Non-conference record 26-8-0 .765

1974					
1.	Miami	5-0-0	1.000	10-0-1	.955
2.	Toledo	3-2-0	.600	6-5-0	.545
2.	Ohio	3-2-0	.600	6-5-0	.545
4.	Kent	2-3-0	.400	7-4-0	.636
4.	Bowling Green	2-3-0	.400	6-4-1	.591
6.	West. Michigan	0-5-0	.000	3-8-0	.273

Non-conference record 23-11-2 .667

1975					
1.	Miami	6-0-0	1.000	11-1-0	.917
2.	Cent. Michigan	4-1-1	.750	8-2-1	.773
3.	Ball State	4-2-0	.667	9-2-0	.818
3.	Bowling Green	4-2-0	.667	8-3-0	.727
5.	Toledo	4-4-0	.500	5-6-0	.455
5.	Ohio	3-3-1	.500	5-5-1	.500
7.	No. Illinois	2-3-0	.400	3-8-0	.273
8.	Kent	1-6-0	.143	4-7-0	.364
9.	West. Michigan	0-7-0	.000	1-10-0	.091

Central Michigan, Ball State, and Northern Illinois
join the MAC.
Non-conference record 26-16-0 .619

1976					
1.	Ball State	4-1-0	.800	8-3-0	.727
2.	Ohio	6-2-0	.750	7-4-0	.636
2.	Kent	6-2-0	.750	8-4-0	.667
4.	West. Michigan	6-3-0	.667	7-4-0	.636
5.	Cent. Michigan	4-3-0	.571	7-4-0	.636
5.	Bowling Green	4-3-0	.571	6-5-0	.545
7.	Miami	2-4-0	.333	3-8-0	.273
8.	Toledo	2-6-0	.250	3-8-0	.273
9.	East. Michigan	1-5-0	.167	2-9-0	.189
10.	No. Illinois	0-6-0	.000	1-10-0	.091

Eastern Michigan joins the MAC.
Non-conference record 17-24-0 .415

1977					
1.	Miami	5-0-0	1.000	10-1-0	.909
2.	Cent. Michigan	7-1-0	.875	10-1-0	.909
3.	Ball State	5-1-0	.833	9-2-0	.818
4.	East. Michigan	4-3-0	.571	8-3-0	.757
4.	Bowling Green	4-3-0	.571	5-7-0	.417
6.	Kent	5-4-0	.556	6-5-0	.545
7.	West. Michigan	3-5-0	.375	5-6-0	.455
8.	No. Illinois	2-5-0	.286	3-8-0	.273
9.	Toledo	2-7-0	.222	2-9-0	.182
10.	Ohio	0-8-0	.000	1-10-0	.091

Non-conference record 22-15-0 .595

1978		Conference		Overall	
1.	Ball State	8-0-0	1.000	10-1-0	.909
2	Cent. Michigan	8-1-0	.889	9-2-0	.818
3.	Miami	5-2-0	.714	8-2-1	.773
4.	West. Michigan	5-4-0	.556	7-4-0	.636
5.	Bowling Green	3-5-0	.375	4-7-0	.364
5.	Ohio	3-5-0	.375	3-8-0	.273
7.	No. Illinois	2-4-0	.333	5-6-0	.455
8.	Kent	2-6-0	.250	4-7-0	.364
9.	Toledo	2-7-0	.222	2-9-0	.182
10.	East. Michigan	1-5-0	.167	3-7-0	.300

Non-conference record 16-14-1 .532

1979					
1.	Cent. Michigan	8-0-1	.944	10-0-1	.955
2.	Toledo	7-1-1	.833	7-3-1	.682
3.	West. Michigan	5-4-0	.556	6-5-0	.545
4.	Ohio	4-4-0	.500	6-5-0	.545
4.	Ball State	4-4-0	.500	6-5-0	.545
4	No. Illinois	3-3-1	.500	5-5-1	.500
7.	Miami	3-4-0	.429	6-5-0	.545
8.	Bowling Green	3-5-0	.375	4-7-0	.364
9.	East. Michigan	1-6-1	.188	2-8-1	.227
10.	Kent	1-8-0	.111	1-10-0	.091

Non-conference record 14-14-0 .500

1980					
1.	Cent. Michigan	7-2-0	.778	9-2-0	.818
2.	West. Michigan	6-3-0	.667	7-4-0	.636
3.	No. Illinois	4-3-0	.571	7-4-0	.636
3.	Miami	4-3-0	.571	5-6-0	.455
5.	Ball State	5-4-0	.556	6-5-0	.545
5.	Ohio	5-4-0	.556	6-5-0	.545
7.	Bowling Green	4-4-0	.500	4-7-0	.364
8.	Toledo	3-6-0	.333	4-7-0	.364
8.	Kent	3-6-0	.333	3-8-0	.273
10.	East. Michigan	1-7-0	.125	1-9-0	.100

Non-conference record 10-15-0 .400

1981					
1.	Toledo	8-1-0	.889	9-3-0	.750
2.	Miami	6-1-1	.813	8-2-1	.773
3.	Cent. Michigan	7-2-0	.778	7-4-0	.636
4.	Bowling Green	5-3-1	.611	5-5-1	.500
5.	West. Michigan	5-4-0	.556	6-5-0	.545
5.	Ohio	5-4-0	.556	5-6-0	.455
7.	Kent	3-6-0	.333	4-7-0	.364
8.	Ball State	2-6-0	.250	4-7-0	.364
9.	No. Illinois	2-7-0	.222	3-8-0	.273
10.	East. Michigan	0-9-0	.000	0-11-0	.000

Non-conference record 8-15-0 .348

1982					
1.	Bowling Green	7-2-0	.778	7-5-0	.583
2.	West. Michigan	5-2-2	.667	7-2-2	.727
3.	Miami	5-3-0	.625	7-4-0	.636
4.	Cent. Michigan	5-3-1	.611	6-4-1	.591
5.	Ohio	5-4-0	.556	6-5-0	.545
5.	Toledo	5-4-0	.556	6-5-0	.545
5.	No. Illinois	5-4-0	.556	5-5-0	.500
8.	Ball State	4-4-0	.500	5-6-0	.455
9.	East. Michigan	1-7-1	.167	1-9-1	.136
10.	Kent	0-9-0	.000	0-11-0	.000

Non-conference record 8-14-0 .364

1983		Conference		Overall	
1.	No. Illinois	8-1-0	.889	10-2-0	.833
2.	Toledo	7-2-0	.778	9-2-0	.818
2.	Cent. Michigan	7-2-0	.778	8-3-0	.727
2.	Bowling Green	7-2-0	.778	8-3-0	.727
5.	Ball State	4-4-0	.500	6-5-0	.545
6.	West. Michigan	4-5-0	.444	6-5-0	.545
7.	Miami	3-5-0	.375	4-7-0	.364
8.	Ohio	3-6-0	.333	4-7-0	.364
9.	Kent	1-8-0	.111	1-10-0	.091
10.	East. Michigan	0-9-0	.000	1-10-0	.091

Non-conference record 13-10-0 .565

1984		Conference		Overall	
1.	Toledo	7-1-1	.833	9-2-1	.792
2.	Bowling Green	7-2-0	.778	8-3-0	.727
3.	Cent. Michigan	6-2-1	.722	8-2-1	.773
4.	Ohio	4-4-1	.500	4-6-1	.409
5.	No. Illinois	3-5-1	.389	4-6-1	.409
6.	Miami	3-5-0	.375	4-7-0	.364
6.	Ball State	3-5-0	.375	3-8-0	.273
8.	West. Michigan	3-6-0	.333	5-6-0	.455
8.	Kent	3-6-0	.333	4-7-0	.364
8.	East. Michigan	2-5-2	333	2-7-2	.273

Non-conference record 10-13-0 .434

1985		Conference		Overall	
1.	Bowling Green	9-0-0	1.000	11-1-0	.917
2.	Miami	7-1-1	.833	8-2-1	.713
3.	Cent. Michigan	6-3-0	.667	7-3-0	.700
4.	West. Michigan	4-4-1	.500	4-6-1	.409
4.	No. Illinois	4-4-0	.500	4-7-0	.364
6.	East. Michigan	3-6-0	.333	4-7-0	.364
6.	Ball State	3-6-0	.333	4-7-0	.364
6.	Toledo	3-6-0	.333	4-7-0	.364
9.	Kent	2-6-0	.250	3-8-0	.273
10.	Ohio	2-7-0	.222	2-9-0	.182

Non-conference record 8-14-0 .364

1986		Conference		Overall	
1.	Miami	6-2-0	.750	8-4-0	.667
2.	Toledo	5-3-0	.625	7-4-0	.636
2.	Kent	5-3-0	.625	5-6-0	.455
2.	Bowling Green	5-3-0	.625	5-6-0	.455
5.	Ball State	4-4-0	.500	6-5-0	.545
5.	East. Michigan	4-4-0	.500	6-5-0	.545
5.	Cent. Michigan	4-4-0	.500	5-5-0	.500
8.	West. Michigan	3-5-0	.375	3-8-0	.273
9.	Ohio	0-8-0	.000	1-10-0	.091

No. Illinois leaves the MAC.
Non-conference record 10-17-0 .370

1987		Conference		Overall	
1.	East. Michigan	7-1-0	.875	10-2-0	.833
2.	Kent	5-3-0	.625	7-4-0	.636
2.	Miami	5-3-0	.625	5-6-0	.455
2.	Bowling Green	5-3-0	.625	5-6-0	.455
5.	West. Michigan	4-4-0	.500	5-6-0	.455
6.	Cent. Michigan	3-4-1	.438	5-5-1	.500
6.	Toledo	3-4-1	.438	3-7-1	.318
8.	Ball State	3-5-0	.375	4-7-0	.364
9.	Ohio	0-8-0	.000	1-10-0	.091

Non-conference record 10-18-0 .357

1988		Conference		Overall	
1.	West. Michigan	7-1-0	.875	9-3-0	.750
2.	East. Michigan	5-2-1	.688	6-3-1	.650
3.	Ball State	5-3-0	.625	8-3-0	.727
3.	Cent. Michigan	5-3-0	.625	7-4-0	.636
5.	Ohio	4-3-1	.563	4-6-1	.409
6.	Toledo	4-4-0	.500	6-5-0	.545
7.	Kent	3-5-0	.375	5-6-0	.455
8.	Bowling Green	1-6-1	.188	2-8-1	.227
9.	Miami	0-7-1	.063	0-10-1	.045

Non-conference record 13-14-0 .481

1989		Conference		Overall	
1.	Ball State	6-1-1	.813	7-3-2	.667
2.	East. Michigan	6-2-0	.750	7-3-1	.682
2.	Toledo	6-2-0	.750	6-5-0	.545
4.	Cent. Michigan	5-2-1	.688	5-5-1	.500
5.	Bowling Green	5-3-0	.625	5-6-0	.455
6.	West. Michigan	3-5-0	.375	5-6-0	.455
7.	Miami	2-5-1	.312	2-8-1	.227
7.	Ohio	1-6-1	.188	1-9-1	.136
9.	Kent	0-8-0	.000	0-11-0	.000

Non-conference record 4-22-0 .154

1990		Conference		Overall	
1.	Cent. Michigan	7-1-0	.875	8-3-1	.708
1.	Toledo	7-1-0	.875	9-2-0	.828
3.	Ball State	5-3-0	.625	7-4-0	.636
3.	West. Michigan	5-3-0	.625	7-4-0	.636
5.	Miami	4-3-1	.563	5-5-1	.500
6.	Bowling Green	2-4-2	.375	3-5-2	.400
7.	Kent	2-6-0	.250	2-9-0	.182
7.	East. Michigan	2-6-0	.250	2-9-0	.182
9.	Ohio	0-7-1	.063	1-9-1	.136

Non-conference record 10-16-1 .389

1991		Conference		Overall	
1.	Bowling Green	8-0-0	1.000	11-1-0	.916
2.	Cent. Michigan	3-1-4	.625	6-1-4	.727
3.	Toledo	4-3-1	.563	5-5-1	.500
3.	Miami	4-3-1	.563	6-4-1	.591
5.	West. Michigan	4-4-0	.500	6-5-0	.545
5.	Ball State	4-4-0	.500	6-5-0	.545
7.	East. Michigan	3-4-1	.438	3-7-1	.318
8.	Ohio	1-6-1	.187	2-8-1	.227
9.	Kent	1-7-0	.125	1-10-0	.091

Non-conference record 14-14-0 .500

1992		Conference		Overall	
1.	Bowling Green	8-0-0	1.000	10-2-0	.833
2.	West. Michigan	6-3-0	.667	7-3-1	.682
3.	Miami	5-3-0	.667	6-4-1	.591
4.	Toledo	5-3-0	.625	8-3-0	.727
4.	Akron	5-3-0	.625	7-3-1	.682
6.	Ball State	5-4-0	.556	5-6-0	.455
7.	Cent. Michigan	4-5-0	.444	5-6-0	.455
8.	Kent	2-7-0	.222	2-9-0	.182
9.	East. Michigan	1-7-0	.125	1-10-0	.091
9.	Ohio	1-7-0	.125	1-10-0	.091

Akron joins the MAC.
Non-conference record 11-15-3 .431

1993		Conference		Overall	
1.	Ball State	7-0-1	.938	8-3-1	.708
2.	West. Michigan	6-1-1	.813	7-3-1	.682
3.	Bowling Green	5-1-2	.750	6-3-2	.636
4.	Cent. Michigan	5-4-0	.556	5-6-0	.455
5.	Akron	4-4-0	.500	5-6-0	.455
6.	Ohio	4-5-0	.444	4-7-0	364
7.	Toledo	3-5-0	.375	4-7-0	.364
7.	East. Michigan	3-5-0	.375	4-7-0	.364
9.	Miami	3-6-0	.333	4-7-0	.364
10.	Kent	0-9-0	.000	0-11-0	.000

Non-conference record 7-20-0 .259

1994					
1.	Cent. Michigan	8-1-0	.889	9-3-0	.750
2.	Bowling Green	7-1-0	.875	9-2-0	.818
3.	West. Michigan	5-3-0	.625	7-4-0	.636
3.	Miami	5-3-0	.625	6-4-1	.591
5.	Ball State	5-3-1	.611	5-5-1	.500
6.	Toledo	4-3-1	.563	6-4-1	.591
7.	East. Michigan	5-4-0	.556	5-6-0	.455
8.	Kent	2-7-0	.222	2-9-0	.182
9.	Akron	1-8-0	.111	1-10-0	.091
10.	Ohio	0-9-0	.000	0-11-0	.000

Non-conference record 8-16-2 .346

1995					
1.	Toledo	7-0-1	.938	11-0-1	.958
2.	Miami	6-1-1	.813	8-2-1	.772
3.	Ball State	6-2-0	.750	7-4-0	.636
3.	West. Michigan	6-2-0	.750	7-4-0	.636
5.	East. Michigan	5-3-0	.625	6-5-0	.545
6.	Bowling Green	3-5-0	.375	5-6-0	.455
7.	Cent. Michigan	2-6-0	.250	4-7-0	.363
7.	Akron	2-6-0	.250	2-9-0	.181
9.	Ohio	1-6-1	187	2-8-1	.227
10.	Kent	0-7-1	.062	1-9-1	.136

Non-conference record 15-16-0 .484

1996					
1.	Ball State	7-1-0	.875	8-4-0	.667
2.	Miami	6-2-0	.750	6-5-0	.545
2.	Toledo	6-2-0	.750	7-4-0	.636
4.	Ohio	5-3-0	.625	6-6-0	.500
5.	Cent. Michigan	4-4-0	.500	5-6-0	.455
6.	Bowling Green	3-5-0	.375	4-7-0	.363
6.	Akron	3-5-0	.375	4-7-0	.363
6.	East Michigan	3-5-0	.375	3-8-0	.273
9.	West. Michigan	2-6-0	.250	2-9-0	.182
10.	Kent	1-7-0	.125	2-9-0	.182

Non-conference record 7-23-0 .233

1997		Conference		Overall	
East Division					
1.	Marshall	7-1-0	.875	10-3-0	.769
2.	Miami	6-2-0	.750	8-3-0	.727
2.	Ohio	6-2-0	.750	8-3-0	.727
4.	Kent	3-5-0	.375	3-8-0	.273
4.	Bowling Green	3-5-0	.375	3-8-0	.273
6.	Akron	2-6-0	.250	2-9-0	.182
West Division					
1.	Toledo	7-1-0	.875	9-3-0	.750
2.	West. Michigan	6-2-0	.750	8-3-0	.727
3.	Ball State	4-4-0	.500	5-6-0	.455
4.	East. Michigan	3-5-0	.375	4-7-0	.364
5.	Cent. Michigan	1-7-0	.125	2-9-0	.182
6.	No. Illinois	0-8-0	.000	0-11-0	.000

Marshall and No. Illinois join the MAC, which goes to a two-divisional setup.
Championship Game: Marshall 34, Toledo 14
Non-conference record 13-24-0 .351

1998					
East Division					
1.	Marshall	7-1-0	.875	12-1-0	.923
1.	Miami	7-1-0	.875	10-1-0	.909
3.	Bowling Green	5-3-0	.625	5-6-0	.455
3.	Ohio	5-3-0	.625	5-6-0	.455
5.	Akron	2-6-0	.250	4-7-0	.364
6.	Kent	0-8-0	.000	0-11-0	.000
West Division					
1.	Toledo	6-2-0	.750	7-5-0	.583
2.	West. Michigan	5-3-0	.625	7-4-0	.636
2.	Cent. Michigan	5-3-0	.625	6-5-0	.545
4.	East. Michigan	3-5-0	.375	3-8-0	.273
5.	No. Illinois	2-6-0	.250	2-9-0	.182
6.	Ball State	1-7-0	.125	1-10-0	.091

Championship Game: Marshall 23, Toledo 17
Non-conference record 13-24-0 .351

1999					
East Division					
1.	Marshall	8-0-0	1.000	13-0-0	1.000
2.	Miami	6-2-0	.750	7-4-0	.636
3.	Akron	5-3-0	.625	7-4-0	.636
3.	Ohio	5-3-0	.625	5-6-0	.455
5.	Bowling Green	3-5-0	.375	5-6-0	.455
6.	Kent	2-6-0	.250	2-9-0	.182
7.	Buffalo	0-8-0	.000	0-11-0	.000
West Division					
1.	West. Michigan	6-2-0	.750	7-5-0	.583
2.	Toledo	5-3-0	.625	6-5-0	.545
2.	No. Illinois	5-3-0	.625	5-6-0	.455
4.	East. Michigan	4-4-0	.500	4-7-0	.364
5.	Cent. Michigan	3-5-0	.375	4-7-0	.364
6.	Ball State	0-8-0	.000	0-11-0	.000

Buffalo joins the MAC.
Marshall 34, Western Michigan 30
Non-conference record 12-28-0 .300

2000		Conference		Overall	
East Division					
1.	Marshall	5-3-0	.625	8-5-0	.615
1.	Akron	5-3-0	.625	6-5-0	.545
1.	Miami	5-3-0	.625	6-5-0	.545
1.	Ohio	5-3-0	.625	7-4-0	.636
5.	Buffalo`	2-6-0	.250	2-9-0	.182
5.	Bowling Green	2-6-0	.250	2-9-0	.182
7.	Kent	1-7-0	.25	1-10-0	.091
West Division					
1.	West. Michigan	7-1-0	.875	9-3-0	.750
2.	Toledo	6-1-0	.857	10-1-0	.909
3.	Ball State	4-3-0	.571	5-6-0	.455
3.	No. Illinois	4-3-0	.571	6-5-0	.545
5.	East. Michigan	2-5-0	.286	3-8-0	.273
6.	Cent. Michigan	2-6-0	.250	2-9-0	.182

Championship Game: Marshall 19, West. Michigan 14
Non-conference record: 15-26-0 .366

2001 East Division					
1.	Marshall	8-0-0	1.000	11-2-0	.846
2.	Miami	6-2-0	.750	7-5-0	.583
3.	Bowling Green	5-3-0	.625	8-3-0	.727
3.	Kent	5-3-0	.625	6-5-0	.545
5.	Akron	4-4-0	.500	4-7-0	.364
6.	Buffalo	1-7-0	.125	3-8-0	.273
6.	Ohio	1-7-0	.125	1-10-0	.091
West Division					
1.	Toledo	5-2-0	.714	10-2-0	.833
2.	No. Illinois	4-3-0	.571	6-5-0	.545
2.	Ball State	4-3-0	.571	5-6-0	.455
4.	West. Michigan	4-4-0	.500	5-6-0	.455
5.	Cent. Michigan	2-6-0	.250	3-8-0	.273
6.	East. Michigan	1-6-0	.143	2-9-0	.182

Championship Game: Toledo 41, Marshall 36
Non-conference record: 28-25-0 .528

2002		Conference		Overall	
East Division					
1.	Marshall	7-1-0	.875	11-2-0	.846
2.	UCF	6-2-0	.750	7-5-0	.583
3.	Miami	5-3-0	.625	7-5-0	.583
4.	Ohio	4-4-0	.500	4-8-0	.333
5.	Akron	3-5-0	.325	4-8-0	.333
6.	Kent	1-7-0	.125	3-9-0	.250
7	Buffalo	0-8-0	.000	1-11-0	.083
West Division					
1.	No. Illinois	7-1-0	.875	8-4-0	.667
2.	Toledo	7-1-0	.875	9-5-0	.692
3.	Bowling Green	6-2-0	.750	9-3-0	.750
4.	Ball State	4-4-0	.500	6-6-0	.500
5.	West. Michigan	3-5-0	.375	4-8-0	.333
6.	Cent. Michigan	2-6-0	.250	4-8-0	.333
7.	East. Michigan	1-7-0	.125	3-9-0	.250

University of Central Florida joins the MAC.
Championship game: Marshall 49, Toledo 45
Non-conference record: 22-33-0 .400

2003 East Division					
1.	Miami	8-0-0	1.000	13-1-0	.929
2	Marshall	6-2-0	.750	8-4-0	.667
3.	Akron	5-3-0	.625	7-5-0	.583
4.	Kent State	4-4-0	.500	7-5-0	.583
5	UCF	2-6-0	.250	3-9-0	.250
6.	Ohio U.	1-7-0	.125	2-10-0	.167
6.	Buffalo	1-7-0	.125	1-11-0	.083
West Division					
1.	Bowling Green	7-1-0	.875	11-3-0	.786
2.	No. Illinois	6-2-0	.750	10-2-0	.833
2.	Toledo	6-2-0	.750	8-4-0	.667
4.	West. Michigan	4-4-0	.500	5-7-0	.417
5.	Ball State	3-5-0	.375	4-8-0	.333
6.	East. Michigan	2-6-0	.250	3-9-0	.250
7.	Cent. Michigan	1-7-0	.125	3-9-0	.250

Championship Game: Miami 49, Bowling Green 27

Non-conference record: 15-15-0 .500

MAC W-L-T RECORDS BY DECADES (1947-2003)

Decade	Cincinnat	W. Reserve	Butler	Ohio	Miami	W.Mich.	Kent	B. Green	Toledo	Marshall
1947-49	10- 2-0	4- 8-1	1-10-0	5- 8-0	7- 1-0	5- 4-0				
1950-59	9- 1-0	6-15-1		31-25-2	40- 4-2	12-40-2	28-17-1	24-16-4	13-30-0	11-25-0
1960-69				38-19-2	37-17-2	28-29-2	17-40-2	42-15-2	21-37-1	12-38-1
1970-79				27-36-1	38-18-0	26-40-1	26-40-0	31-29-1	33-34-1	
1980-89				29-54-3	40-36-4	44-39-3	25-60-0	55-28-2	51-33-2	
1990-99				28-51-3	53-23-3	51-29-1	13-69-1	47-29-4	54-23-2	22- 2-0
2000-03				11-21-0	24- 8-0	18-14-0	11-21-0	20-12-0	24- 7-0	27- 6-0

Decade	C. Mich.	Ball St.	No. Ill.	E. Mich.	Akron	Buffalo	UCF
1970-79	31- 6-2	25- 9-0	9-21-1	7-19-1			
1980-89	55-27-4	39-42-1	26-24-1	29-52-4			
1990-99	42-37-4	44-36-2	7-17-0	32-48-1	24-41-0	0- 8-0	
2000-03	7-25-0	15- 15-0	21- 9-0	6-24-0	17-15-0	4-28-0	8- 8-0

MAC W-L-T PERCENTAGES (1947-2003)

Cincinnati	19- 3- 0	.864		Toledo	196-164- 6	.529
Western Reserve	10- 23- 1	.309		Marshall	72- 71- 1	.503
Butler	1- 10- 0	.091		Central Michigan	135- 95-10	.583
Ohio	169-214-11	.443		Ball State	123-102- 3	.546
Miami	239-107-11	.666		Northern Illinois	63- 71- 2	.471
Western Michigan	184-195- 9	.486		Eastern Michigan	74-143- 6	.345
Kent State	120-247- 4	.329		Akron	41- 56- 0	.423
Bowling Green	219-129-13	.625		Buffalo	4- 36- 0	.100
				UCF	8- 8- 0	.500

MAC TITLES BY DECADE (1947-2003)

In the years preceding divisional play (1947-1996), the MAC title is the team with the highest win percent. In the divisional play years, the MAC title is awarded to the team winning the post-season championship game.

Decade	Cincinnati	W. Reserve	Butler	Ohio	Miami	W.Mich.	Kent	B. Green	Toledo	Marshall	
1947-49	2				1						
1950-59	2			1	5			2			
1960-69				3.5	.5	.5		4	1.5		
1970-79					4		1		2		
1980-89					1	1		2	2		
1990-99								2	1.5	3	
2000-03					1					1	2
Totals	4			4.5	12.5	1.5	1	10	8	5	

Decade	Cent. Mich.	Ball St.	No. Ill.	E. Mich.	Akron	Buffalo
1970-79	1	2				
1980-89	1	1	1	1		
1990-99	1.5	2				
2000-01						
Totals	3.5	5	1	1		

MISSOURI VALLEY CONFERENCE (1907-1985). The MVC football conference was organized in 1907. In 1927, the six leading members of the conference left to form the Big Six Conference. Several of the remaining teams in the MVC were and have remained small college teams, but a number of the later MVC members have become Division 1-A teams. The MVC dropped football as a sponsored sport after the 1985 season. Until 1942, the MVC ignored ties in calculating win percents, conference and overall. From 1942 on, ties were treated as half a win and half a loss. There is some ambiguity about the period 1917-1922. The MVC records show a gap for this period, but *Claassen's Encyclopedia of Football* shows conference data for this period. We follow the MVC records in what follows, except that, for completeness, the Claassen data for 1917-1922 are shown at the end of the table.

1907		Conference		Overall	
1.	Iowa	1-0-0	1.000	3-2-0	.600
1.	Nebraska	1-0-0	1.000	8-2-0	.800
3.	Kansas	1-1-0	.500	5-3-0	.625
4.	Missouri	1-2-0	.333	7-2-0	.778
5.	Washington	0-1-0	.000	1-5-0	.167

Non-conference record: 20-10-0 .667

1908					
1.	Kansas	4-0-0	1.000	9-0-0	1.000
2.	Iowa State	2-1-0	.667	6-3-0	.667
2.	Nebraska	2-1-0	.667	7-2-1	.778
4.	Missouri	3-2-0	.600	6-2-0	.750
5.	Drake	1-2-0	.333	5-2-0	.714
6.	Washington	0-2-0	.000	4-4-1	.500
6.	Iowa	0-4-0	.000	2-5-0	.286

Non-conference record: 27-6-2 .778
Iowa State and Drake join the conference

1909					
1.	Missouri	4-0-1	1.000	7-0-1	1.000
2	Kansas	3-1-0	.750	8-1-0	.889
3.	Drake	2-1-0	.667	6-1-0	.857
4.	Iowa	1-3-1	.250	2-4-1	.333
5.	Nebraska	0-1-1	.000	3-3-2	.500
5.	Iowa State	0-2-1	.000	4-3-1	.571
5.	Washington	0-2-0	.000	3-4-0	.429

Non-conference record: 23-6-1 .783

1910					
1.	Nebraska	2-0-0	1.000	7-1-0	.875
2.	Iowa	3-1-0	.750	5-2-0	.714
3.	Missouri	2-1-1	.667	4-2-2	.667
4.	Iowa State	2-2-0	.500	4-4-0	.500
4.	Kansas	1-1-1	.500	6-1-1	.857
6.	Washington	0-2-0	.000	3-4-0	.429
6.	Drake	0-3-0	.000	2-5-0	.286

Non-conference record: 21-9-0 .700

1911					
1.	Iowa State	2-0-1	1.000	6-1-1	.857
1.	Nebraska	2-0-1	1.000	5-1-2	.833
3.	Kansas	1-1-1	.500	4-2-2	.667
4.	Washington	0-0-2	.000	4-2-2	.667
4.	Missouri	0-2-2	.000	2-4-2	.333
4.	Drake	0-2-0	.000	5-2-1	.714

Non-conference record: 21-7-2 .733
Iowa leaves the MVC after the 1910 season.

1912					
1.	Iowa State	2-0-0	1.000	6-2-0	.750
1.	Nebraska	2-0-0	1.000	8-1-0	.889
3.	Drake	2-2-0	.500	4-3-0	.571
4.	Missouri	2-3-0	.400	5-3-0	.625
5.	Kansas	1-2-0	.333	4-4-0	.500
6.	Washington	0-2-0	.000	4-4-0	.500

Non-conference record: 22-8-0 .733

1913					
1.	Missouri	4-0-0	1.000	7-1-0	.857
1.	Nebraska	3-0-0	1.000	8-0-0	1.000
3.	Kansas	3-2-0	.600	5-3-0	.625
4.	Iowa State	2-2-0	.500	4-4-0	.500

1913 (cont'd)		Conference		Overall	
5.	Drake	1-3-0	.250	4-3-1	.571
6.	Kansas State	0-2-0	.000	3-4-1	.429
6.	Washington	0-4-0	.000	1-5-0	.167

Non-conference record: 19-7-2 .741
Kansas State joins the MVC.

1914					
1.	Nebraska	3-0-0	1.000	7-0-1	1.000
2.	Missouri	4-1-0	.800	5-3-0	.625
3.	Iowa State	2-1-0	.667	4-3-0	.571
4.	Kansas	2-2-0	.500	5-2-1	.714
5.	Washington	0-1-1	.000	3-3-1	.500
5.	Drake	0-3-0	.000	4-3-1	.571
5.	Kansas State	0-3-0	.000	1-5-1	.167

Non-conference record: 18-8-4 .667

1915					
1.	Nebraska	4-0-0	1.000	8-0-0	1.000
2.	Kansas	3-1-0	.750	6-2-0	.750
3.	Iowa State	2-1-0	.667	6-2-0	.750
4.	Washington	1-1-0	.500	3-2-0	.600
5.	Missouri	1-3-1	.250	2-5-1	.286
6.	Drake	1-4-0	.200	2-6-0	.250
7.	Kansas State	0-3-0	.000	3-4-1	.429

Non-conference record: 18-8-1 .685

1916					
1.	Nebraska	3-1-0	.750	6-2-0	.750
1.	Missouri	3-1-1	.750	6-1-1	.857
3.	Iowa State	2-1-1	.667	5-2-1	.714
4.	Kansas State	1-1-1	.500	6-1-1	.857
5.	Kansas	1-2-1	.333	4-3-1	.571
6.	Drake	1-3-0	.250	3-5-0	.375
7.	Washington	0-2-0	.000	3-3-1	.500

Non-conference record: 22-6-1 .776

1917 - 1922   No conference records.

1923					
1.	Nebraska	3-0-2	1.000	4-2-2	.667
1.	Kansas	3-0-3	1.000	5-0-3	1.000
3.	Drake	3-1-0	.750	5-2-0	.714
4.	Iowa State	3-2-1	.600	4-3-1	.571
5.	Kansas State	2-2-2	.500	4-2-2	.667
6.	Oklahoma	2-4-0	.667	3-5-0	.375
7.	Grinnell	1-3-0	.250	2-6-0	.250
7.	Missouri	1-3-2	.250	2-3-3	.400
9.	Washington	1-4-0	.200	3-5-0	.375

Non-conference record: 13-9-1 .587
Oklahoma and Grinnell join the MVC.

1924					
1.	Missouri	5-1-0	.833	7-2-0	.778
2.	Nebraska	3-1-0	.750	5-3-0	.625
2.	Drake	3-1-1	.750	5-2-1	.714
4.	Grinnell	2-1-0	.667	3-3-0	.500
5.	Iowa State	3-2-0	.600	4-3-1	.571
6.	Oklahoma	2-3-1	.400	2-5-1	.286
7.	Kansas	2-4-1	.333	2-5-1	.286
8.	Kansas State	1-4-1	.200	3-4-1	.429
9.	Washington	0-4-0	.000	4-4-0	.500

Non-conference record: 14-10-1 .580

1925		Conference		Overall	
1.	Missouri	5-1-0	.833	6-1-1	.857
2.	Drake	5-2-0	.714	5-3-0	.625
3.	Kansas State	3-2-1	.600	5-2-1	.714
3.	Iowa State	3-2-1	.600	4-3-1	.571
5.	Oklahoma	3-3-1	.500	4-3-1	.571
6.	Nebraska	2-2-1	.500	4-2-2	.667
6.	Grinnell	2-2-1	.500	3-3-2	.500
8.	Kansas	2-5-1	.286	2-5-1	.286
9.	Washington	1-4-1	.200	2-5-1	.286
10.	Okla. A&M	0-3-1	.000	2-5-1	.286

Non-conference record: 11-6-3 .625
Oklahoma A&M (later Oklahoma State) joins the MVC.

1926					
1.	Okla. A&M	3-0-1	1.000	3-4-1	.429
2.	Nebraska	5-1-0	.833	6-2-0	.750
3.	Missouri	4-1-0	.800	5-1-2	.833
4.	Grinnell	3-1-1	.750	6-1-1	.857
5.	Oklahoma	3-2-1	.600	5-2-1	.714
6.	Kansas State	2-2-0	.500	5-3-0	.625
6.	Iowa State	3-3-1	.500	4-3-1	.571
8.	Drake	1-4-0	.200	2-6-0	.250
9.	Kansas	1-5-0	.167	2-6-0	.250
10.	Washington	0-6-0	.000	1-7-0	.125

Non-conference record: 14-10-2 .600

1927					
1.	Missouri	5-1-0	.833	7-2-0	.778
2	Nebraska	4-1-0	.800	6-2-0	.750
3.	Okla. A&M	2-1-0	.667	4-4-0	.500
4.	Iowa State	3-2-0	.600	4-3-1	.571
5.	Kansas	3-3-1	.500	3-4-1	.429
5.	Washington	2-2-1	.500	5-2-2	.714
7.	Oklahoma	2-3-0	.400	3-3-2	.500
8.	Kansas State	2-4-0	.333	3-5-0	.375
8.	Drake	1-2-0	.333	3-6-0	.333
10.	Grinnell	0-5-0	.000	0-7-1	.000

Non-conference record: 14-14-5 .500

1928					
1.	Drake	3-0-0	1.000	7-1-0	.875
2.	Creighton	2-1-0	.667	3-5-1	.375
3.	Grinnell	1-2-0	.333	4-3-1	.571
4.	Washington	0-2-0	.000	2-5-1	.286
5.	Okla. A&M	0-1-0	.000	1-7-0	.125

Non-conference record: 11-15-3 .431
Missouri, Nebraska, Iowa State, Kansas, Oklahoma and Kansas State leaves the MVC, and Creighton joins.

1929					
1.	Drake	3-0-1	1.000	5-3-1	.611
1.	Grinnell	1-0-2	1.000	5-1-2	.833
3.	Okla. A&M	1-1-0	.500	4-3-2	.571
4.	Washington	0-1-1	.000	3-4-1	.429
4.	Creighton	0-3-0	.000	2-6-0	.250

Non-conference record: 14-12-2 .536

1930					
1.	Drake	3-0-0	1.000	5-4-0	.556
1.	Okla. A&M	2-0-0	1.000	7-2-1	.778
3.	Washington	2-2-0	.500	4-2-2	.667
4.	Grinnell	1-2-0	.333	5-4-0	.556
5.	Creighton	0-4-0	.000	1-7-0	.125

Non-conference record: 14-11-3 .554

1931		Conference		Overall	
1.	Drake	3-0-0	1.000	5-6-0	.455
1.	Okla. A&M	1-0-0	1.000	8-2-1	.800
3.	Creighton	2-2-0	.500	4-5-0	.444
4.	Grinnell	1-2-0	.333	5-3-0	.625
5.	Washington	0-3-0	.000	2-7-0	.222

Non-conference record: 17-16-1 .515

1932					
1.	Okla. A&M	3-0-0	1.000	9-1-2	.900
2.	Creighton	3-1-0	.750	5-2-1	.714
3.	Washington	1-2-0	.333	4-4-0	.500
4.	Grinnell	1-3-0	.250	3-4-1	.429
4.	Drake	1-3-1	.250	2-6-1	.250
6.	Butler	0-0-1	.000	2-4-1	.357

Non-conference record: 16-12-4 .562
Butler joins the MVC.

1933					
1.	Okla. A&M	2-0-0	1.000	6-2-1	.750
2.	Drake	4-1-0	.800	6-3-1	.667
3.	Creighton	2-2-0	.500	3-4-1	.429
4.	Washington	1-2-0	.333	4-5-0	.444
5.	Butler	0-2-0	.000	2-6-0	.250
5.	Grinnell	0-2-0	.000	0-8-1	.000

Non-conference record: 12-19-4 .400

1934					
1.	Washington	1-0-0	1.000	7-3-0	.700
2.	Creighton	2-1-0	.667	2-7-0	.222
3.	Drake	2-2-0	.500	3-6-1	.333
4.	Okla. A&M	1-1-0	.500	4-5-1	.444
5.	Grinnell	0-2-0	.000	2-7-0	.222

Non-conference record: 12-22-2 .361
Butler leaves the MVC.

1935					
1.	Tulsa	3-0-0	1.000	3-6-1	.333
1.	Washington	3-0-0	1.000	6-4-0	.600
3.	Creighton	2-2-1	.500	3-5-1	.375
4.	Drake	1-2-1	.333	4-4-2	.500
4.	Grinnell	1-2-0	.333	3-5-1	.375
4.	Washburn	1-2-0	.333	4-6-0	.400
7.	Okla. A&M	0-3-0	.000	3-7-0	.300

Non-conference record: 15-26-3 .375
Tulsa and Washburn join the MVC.

1936					
1.	Creighton	3-0-0	1.000	4-4-0	.500
1.	Tulsa	3-0-0	1.000	5-2-2	.714
3.	Drake	3-2-0	.600	6-4-0	.600
4.	Washington	1-1-0	.500	3-7-0	.300
5.	Okla. A&M	1-2-0	.333	1-9-0	.100
6.	Washburn	1-4-0	.200	2-6-1	.250
7.	Grinnell	0-3-0	.000	0-10-0	.000

Non-conference record: 9-30-3 .250

1937					
1.	Tulsa	3-0-0	1.000	6-2-2	.750
2.	Drake	4-1-0	.800	8-2-0	.800
3.	St. Louis	2-1-0	.667	7-2-1	.750
4.	Okla. A&M	2-2-0	.500	4-6-0	.400
4.	Washington	2-2-0	.500	4-6-0	.400
5.	Creighton	1-3-0	.250	2-7-0	.222
5.	Grinnell	1-3-0	.250	2-6-1	.250
7.	Washburn	0-3-0	.000	0-10-0	.000

Non-conference record: 18-26-4 .417
St. Louis University joins the conference.

1938		Conference		Overall	
1. Tulsa	3-1-0	.750	4-5-1	.444
2. Drake	2-1-1	.667	5-4-1	.556
2. Washington	2-1-1	.667	6-3-1	.667
4. Okla. A&M	0-4-0	.000	2-8-0	.200

Teams lacking required minimum of 4 MVC games:

Washburn	2-0-0	1.000	6-3-0	.667
Creighton	1-0-1	1.000	6-1-1	.857
St. Louis	1-1-1	.500	3-5-2	.400
Grinnell	0-3-0	.000	3-5-0	.375

Non-conference record: 24-23-1 .510

1939					
1. Washington	4-1-0	.800	6-3-1	.667
2. Okla. A&M	3-1-0	.750	5-4-1	.556
3. Tulsa	2-1-1	.667	4-5-1	.444
4. Drake	2-3-0	.400	5-5-0	.500
5. St. Louis	1-2-1	.333	5-3-2	.600
5. Creighton	2-4-0	.333	4-5-0	.444
7. Washburn	1-3-0	.250	6-4-0	.600

Non-conference record: 20-14-3 .581
Grinnell leaves the conference

1940					
1. Tulsa	4-0-0	1.000	7-3-0	.700
2. Okla. A&M	4-1-0	.800	6-3-1	.667
3. Creighton	2-2-0	.500	6-2-2	.750
3. Drake	2-2-0	.500	4-5-0	.444
5. St. Louis	2-3-0	.400	3-6-1	.350
6. Washington	1-3-0	.250	3-6-0	.333
7. Washburn	0-4-0	.000	4-6-0	.400

Non-conference record: 18-16-4 .526

1941					
1. Tulsa	4-0-0	1.000	8-2-0	.800
2. Okla. A&M	3-1-0	.750	5-4-0	.555
3. Creighton	3-2-0	.600	5-5-0	.500
4. St. Louis	1-3-1	.250	4-5-1	.450
4. Washington	1-3-0	.250	4-5-0	.444
6. Drake	0-3-1	.000	4-5-1	.444

Non-conference record: 18-14-0 .556
Washburn leaves the MVC.

1942					
1. Tulsa	5-0-0	1.000	10-1-0	.091
2. Okla. A&M	4-1-0	.800	6-3-1	.650
3. St. Louis	2-3-0	.400	4-5-0	.444
3. Washington	2-3-0	.400	5-5-0	.500
5. Drake	1-4-0	.200	3-7-0	.300
5. Creighton	1-4-0	.200	5-4-0	.556

Non-conference record: 18-10-1 .638

1943					
1. Tulsa	1-0-0	1.000	6-1-1	.813
2. Okla. A&M	0-1-0	.000	3-4-0	.429
Drake	0-0-0	------	4-2-0	.667

(Only three MVC teams fielded a team in 1943 -44.)
Non-conference record: 12-6-1 .658

1944					
1. Okla. A&M	1-0-0	1.000	8-1-0	.889
2. Tulsa	0-1-0	.000	3-4-0	.429
Drake	0-0-0	------	7-2-0	.778

Non-conference record: 17-6-0 .739

1945		Conference		Overall	
1. Okla. A&M	1-0-0	1.000	9-0-0	1.000
2. Tulsa	2-1-0	.667	8-3-0	.727
3. Wichita	1-1-0	.500	6-4-0	.600
4. Drake	1-2-0	.333	5-4-1	.550
5. St. Louis	0-1-0	.000	5-4-0	.556

Non-conference record: 28-10-1 .731
Creighton and Washington leave the MVC, and Wichita joins the conference.

1946					
1. Tulsa	3-0-0	1.000	9-1-0	.900
2. Wichita	2-1-0	.667	5-5-0	.500
3. St. Louis	1-1-0	.500	4-6-0	.400
3. Okla. A&M	1-1-0	.500	3-7-1	.318
5. Drake	0-4-0	.000	2-6-1	.277

Non-conference record: 16-18-2 .472

1947					
1. Tulsa	3-0-0	1.000	5-5-0	.500
2. Wichita	2-1-0	.667	7-4-0	.636
3. St. Louis	1-1-0	.500	4-6-0	.400
4. Drake	1-3-0	.250	1-7-1	.167
5. Okla. A&M	0-2-0	.000	3-7-0	.300

Non-conference record: 13-22-1 .375

1948					
1. Okla. A&M	2-0-0	1.000	6-4-0	.600
2. Wichita	2-1-1	.625	5-4-1	.550
3. Drake	1-1-0	.500	7-3-0	.700
4. Tulsa	0-1-1	.250	0-9-1	.050
5. St. Louis	0-2-0	.000	4-7-0	.364

Non-conference record: 17-22-0 .436

1949					
1. Detroit	4-0-0	1.000	5-4-0	.556
2. Drake	3-1-0	.750	6-2-1	.722
3. Okla. A&M	2-1-1	.625	4-4-2	.500
4. Wichita	2-3-1	.416	3-6-1	.350
5. Tulsa	1-2-1	.375	5-5-1	.500
6. Bradley	1-3-0	.250	5-5-0	.500
7. St. Louis	0-3-1	.125	2-6-1	.278

Non-conference record: 17-19-2 .474
Detroit and Bradley join the MVC.

1950					
1. Tulsa	3-0-1	.875	9-1-1	.866
2. Detroit	2-1-1	.625	6-3-1	.650
3. Wichita	3-2-0	.600	5-4-1	.550
4. Okla. A&M	1-2-1	.375	4-6-1	.409
4. Drake	1-2-1	.375	6-2-1	.722
6. Bradley	0-3-0	.000	5-5-0	.500

Non-conference record: 25-11-1 .689
St. Louis leaves the MVC, and drops football.

1951					
1. Tulsa	4-0-0	1.000	9-2-0	.818
2. Drake	3-1-0	.750	7-2-0	.778
3. Okla. A&M	3-2-0	.600	3-7-0	.300
4. Houston	2-2-0	.500	6-5-0	.545
5. Detroit	2-4-0	.333	4-7-0	.364
5. Wichita	2-4-0	.333	2-7-0	.222
7. Bradley	0-3-0	.000	4-5-0	.444

Non-conference record: 19-19-0 .500
Houston joins the MVC.

1952		Conference		Overall	
1.	Houston	3-0-0	1.000	8-2-0	.800
2.	Tulsa	3-1-0	.750	8-2-1	.771
3.	Okla. A&M	2-2-0	.500	3-7-0	.300
4.	Detroit	1-3-0	.250	2-7-0	.222
5.	Wichita	0-3-0	.000	3-6-1	.350

Non-conference record: 15-15-2 .500
Drake and Bradley leave the MVC.

1953					
1.	Okla. A&M	3-1-0	.750	7-3-0	.700
1.	Detroit	3-1-0	.750	5-4-0	.556
3.	Wichita	1-2-0	.333	4-4-1	.500
3.	Houston	1-2-0	.333	4-4-1	.500
5.	Tulsa	1-3-0	.250	3-7-0	.300

Non-conference record: 14-13-2 .517

1954					
1.	Wichita	4-0-0	1.000	9-1-0	.900
2.	Houston	3-1-0	.750	5-5-0	.500
3.	Okla. A&M	2-2-0	.500	5-4-1	.550
4.	Detroit	1-3-0	.250	2-6-1	.277
5.	Tulsa	0-4-0	.000	0-11-0	.000

Non-conference record: 11-17-2 .400

1955					
1.	Detroit	3-1-0	.750	5-3-1	.611
1.	Wichita	3-1-0	.750	7-2-1	.750
3.	Houston	2-2-0	.500	6-4-0	.600
4.	Okla. A&M	1-3-0	.250	2-8-0	.200
4.	Tulsa	1-3-0	.250	2-7-1	.250

Non-conference record: 12-14-3 .466

1956					
1.	Houston	4-0-0	1.000	7-2-1	.750
2.	Tulsa	2-1-1	.625	7-2-1	.750
2.	Okla. A&M	2-1-1	.625	3-5-2	.400
4.	Wichita	1-3-0	.250	4-6-0	.400
5.	Detroit	0-4-0	.000	2-8-0	.200

Non-conference record: 14-14-2 .500

1957					
1.	Houston	3-0-1	.875	5-4-1	.550
2.	N. Texas St.	2-2-0	.500	5-5-0	.500
3.	Tulsa	2-3-0	.400	4-6-0	.400
4.	Cincinnati	1-3-0	.250	5-4-1	.550
5.	Wichita	1-4-0	.200	1-9-0	.100

Non-conference record: 11-16-1 .411
North Texas State and Cincinnati join the MVC, and
Oklahoma A&M and Detroit leave the MVC.

1958					
1.	N. Texas State	2-1-1	.625	7-2-1	.750
2.	Cincinnati	1-1-2	.500	6-2-2	.700
2.	Houston	2-2-0	.500	5-4-0	.556
2.	Tulsa	2-2-0	.500	7-3-0	.700
5.	Wichita	1-2-1	.375	4-5-1	.450

Non-conference record: 21-8-0 .724

1959					
1.	N. Texas State	3-1-0	.750	9-2-0	.818
1.	Houston	3-1-0	.750	3-7-0	.300
3.	Tulsa	2-2-0	.500	5-5-0	.500
4.	Wichita	1-2-1	.375	5-4-1	.550
5.	Cincinnati	0-3-1	.125	5-4-1	.550

Non-conference record: 18-13-0 .581

1960					
1.	Wichita	3-0-0	1.000	8-2-0	.800
2.	Tulsa	2-1-0	.667	5-4-1	.550

1960 (cont'd)		Conference		Overall	
3.	Cincinnati	1-2-0	.333	3-7-0	.300
4.	N. Texas State	0-3-0	.000	2-6-1	.277

Non-conference record: 12-13-2 .481
Houston leaves the MVC.

1961					
1.	Wichita	3-0-0	1.000	8-2-0	.800
2.	N. Texas State	1-2-0	.333	5-4-1	.550
2.	Cincinnati	1-2-0	.333	3-7-0	.300
2.	Tulsa	1-2-0	.333	2-8-0	.200

Non-conference record: 12-15-1 .446

1962					
1.	Tulsa	3-0-0	1.000	5-5-0	.500
2.	N. Texas State	2-1-0	.667	6-4-0	.600
3.	Cincinnati	1-2-0	.333	2-8-0	.200
4.	Wichita	0-3-0	.000	3-7-0	.300

Non-conference record: 10-18-0 .357

1963					
1.	Wichita	3-1-0	.750	7-2-0	.778
1.	Cincinnati	3-1-0	.750	6-4-0	.600
3.	N. Texas State	2-2-0	.500	3-6-0	.333
3.	Tulsa	2-2-0	.500	5-5-0	.500
5.	Louisville	1-3-0	.250	3-7-0	.300

Non-conference record: 13-15-0 .464
Louisville joins the MVC.

1964					
1.	Cincinnati	4-0-0	1.000	8-2-0	.800
2.	Tulsa	3-1-0	.750	9-2-0	.818
3.	Wichita	2-2-0	.500	4-6-0	.400
4.	N. Texas State	1-3-0	.250	2-7-1	.250
5.	Louisville	0-4-0	.000	1-9-0	.100

Non-conference record: 14-16-1 .468

1965					
1.	Tulsa	4-0-0	1.000	8-3-0	.727
2.	Louisville	3-1-0	.750	6-4-0	.600
3.	Cincinnati	2-2-0	.500	5-5-0	.500
3.	N. Texas State	2-2-0	.500	3-7-0	.300
5.	Wichita	0-4-0	.000	2-7-0	.222

Non-conference record: 13-17-0 .433

1966					
1.	N. Texas State	3-1-0	.750	8-2-0	.800
1.	Tulsa	3-1-0	.750	6-4-0	.600
3.	Cincinnati	2-2-0	.500	3-7-0	.300
4.	Louisville	1-3-0	.250	6-4-0	.600
5.	Wichita	1-3-0	.250	2-8-0	.200

Non-conference record: 15-15-0 .500

1967					
1.	N. Texas State	4-0-0	1.000	7-1-1	.833
2.	Tulsa	3-1-0	.750	7-3-0	.700
3.	Cincinnati	2-2-0	.500	3-6-0	.333
4.	Louisville	1-3-0	.250	5-5-0	.500
5.	Wichita	0-4-0	.000	2-7-1	.250

Non-conference record: 14-12-2 .536

1968					
1.	Memphis State	5-0-0	1.000	6-4-0	.600
2.	N. Texas State	4-1-0	.800	8-2-0	.800
3.	Cincinnati	3-2-0	.600	5-4-1	.550
4.	Louisville	2-3-0	.400	5-5-0	.500
5.	Tulsa	2-3-0	.400	3-7-0	.300
6.	Wichita	0-5-0	.000	0-10-0	.000

Non-conference record: 11-18-1 .383
Memphis State joins the MVC.

1969

		Conference		Overall	
1.	Memphis State	5-0-0	1.000	8-2-0	.800
2.	N. Texas State	4-1-0	.800	7-3-0	.700
3.	Louisville	2-3-0	.400	5-4-1	.500
3.	Cincinnati	2-3-0	.400	4-6-0	.400
5.	Wichita	1-4-0	.200	2-8-0	.200
5.	Tulsa	1-4-0	.200	1-9-0	.100

Non-conference record: 12-17-1 .417

1970

		Conference		Overall	
1.	Louisville	4-0-0	1.000	8-3-1	.771
2.	Tulsa	3-1-0	.750	6-4-0	.600
3.	Memphis State	2-2-0	.500	6-4-0	.600
4.	N. Texas State	1-3-0	.250	3-8-0	.273
5.	Wichita	0-4-0	.000	0-9-0	.000

Non-conference record: 13-18-1 .422

1971

		Conference		Overall	
1.	Memphis State	4-1-0	.800	5-5-0	.500
2.	Louisville	3-2-0	.600	6-3-1	.650
2.	Tulsa	3-2-0	.600	4-7-0	.364
2.	N. Texas State	3-2-0	.600	3-8-0	.273
5.	Drake	2-3-0	.400	7-4-0	.636
6.	W. Texas State	1-4-0	.200	2-9-0	.182
7.	Wichita	0-5-0	.000	3-8-0	.273

Non-conference record: 14-25-1 .362
Drake and West Texas State join the MVC.

1972

		Conference		Overall	
1.	Louisville	4-1-0	.800	9-1-0	.900
1.	Drake	4-1-0	.800	7-5-0	.583
1.	W. Texas	4-1-0	.800	5-5-0	.500
4.	Memphis State	3-2-0	.600	5-5-0	.500
4.	Tulsa	3-2-0	.600	4-7-0	.364
6.	Wichita	2-4-0	.333	6-5-0	.545
7.	New Mex. St.	1-4-0	.200	2-9-0	.182
8.	N. Texas	0-7-0	.000	1-10-0	.091

Non-conference record: 18-25-0 .419
New Mexico State joins the MVC.

1973

		Conference		Overall	
1.	North Texas	5-1-0	.833	5-5-1	.500
1.	Tulsa	5-1-0	.833	6-5-0	.545
3.	New Mex. State	3-2-0	.600	5-6-0	.455
3.	Louisville	3-2-0	.600	5-6-0	.455
5.	Wichita State	2-4-0	.333	4-7-0	.364
6.	W. Texas	1-5-0	.167	2-9-0	.182
7.	Drake	1-5-0	.167	2-9-0	.182

Non-conference record: 9-27-1 .257
Memphis State leaves the MVC.

1974

		Conference		Overall	
1.	Tulsa	6-0-0	1.000	8-3-0	.727
2.	Louisville	3-2-0	.600	4-7-0	.364
3.	W. Texas St.	3-3-0	.500	6-5-0	.545
4.	Drake	2-3-1	.417	3-7-1	.318
5.	New Mex. St.	2-3-0	.400	5-6-0	.455
6.	Wichita	1-4-1	.250	1-9-1	.136

Non-conference record: 10-22-0 .312
North Texas leaves the MVC. Southern Illinois joins,
But does not compete for title until 1977.

1975

		Conference		Overall	
1.	Tulsa	4-0-0	1.000	7-4-0	.636
2.	W. Texas St.	2-2-0	.500	5-6-0	.455
3.	New Mex. St.	2-2-0	.500	5-6-0	.455
4.	Drake	1-3-0	.250	3-8-0	.273
5.	Wichita	1-3-0	.250	3-8-0	.273

Non-conference record: 13-22-0 .371
Louisville leaves the MVC.

1976

		Conference		Overall	
1.	Tulsa	2-1-1	.625	7-4-1	.625
1.	New Mex. St.	2-1-1	.625	4-6-1	.409
3.	Wichita	2-2-0	.500	4-7-0	.364
3.	W. Texas St.	1-1-2	.500	4-5-2	.454
5.	Drake	1-3-0	.250	1-10-0	.091

Non-conference record: 12-24-0 .333
Indiana State joins the MVC, does not compete for title
Until 1977.

1977

		Conference		Overall	
1.	W. Texas St.	5-1-0	.833	6-4-1	.591
2.	Wichita	4-1-0	.800	5-6-0	.455
3.	New Mex. St.	3-2-0	.600	4-7-0	.364
4.	Indiana St.	2-3-0	.400	3-7-0	.300
4.	Tulsa	2-3-0	.400	3-8-0	.273
6.	Drake	1-5-0	.167	2-9-0	.182
7.	So. Illinois	0-5-0	.000	3-8-0	.273

Non-conference record: 9-29-1 .244

1978

		Conference		Overall	
1.	New Mex. St.	5-1-0	.833	6-5-0	.545
2.	Tulsa	4-1-0	.800	9-2-0	.818
3.	So. Illinois	3-2-0	.600	7-4-0	.636
4.	Drake	3-3-0	.500	4-7-0	.364
5.	Indiana State	2-3-0	.400	3-8-0	.273
6.	Wichita	2-4-0	.333	4-7-0	.364
7.	W. Texas St.	1-5-0	.167	3-8-0	.273

Non-conference record: 16-22-0 .421

1979

		Conference		Overall	
1.	W. Texas St.	5-0-0	1.000	5-5-1	.500
2.	So. Illinois	4-1-0	.800	8-3-0	.727
3.	Indiana St.	3-2-0	.600	8-3-0	.727
4.	Drake	1-4-0	.200	3-8-0	.273
4.	New Mex. St.	1-4-0	.200	2-9-0	.182
4.	Wichita	1-4-0	.200	1-10-0	.091
7.	Tulsa *			6-5-0	.545

* Ineligible for conference title.
Non-conference record: 12-23-1 .347

1980

		Conference		Overall	
1.	Tulsa	4-1-0	.800	8-3-0	.727
2.	Wichita	4-1-1	.750	5-5-1	.500
3.	Indiana St.	4-2-0	.667	6-5-0	.545
4.	Drake	3-2-0	.600	8-3-0	.727
5.	W. Texas St.	2-4-0	.333	5-6-0	.455
6.	New Mex. St.	1-4-1	.250	3-7-1	.318
7	So. Illinois	1-5-0	.167	3-8-0	.273

Non-conference record: 19-18-0 .514

1981

		Conference		Overall	
1.	Drake	5-1-0	.833	10-1-0	.909
1	Tulsa	5-1-0	.833	6-5-0	.545
3.	So. Illinois	5-2-0	.714	7-4-0	.636
4.	W. Texas St.	3-3-0	.500	7-4-0	.636
4.	Wichita	3-3-1	.500	4-6-1	.409
6.	Indiana St.	2-4-1	.357	5-5-1	.500
7.	New Mex. St.	1-5-0	.167	3-8-0	.273
8.	Illinois St.	0-5-0	.000	3-7-0	.300

Non-conference record: 21-16-0 .568
Illinois State joins the MVC.

1982

		Conference		Overall	
1.	Tulsa	6-0-0	1.000	10-1-0	.909
2.	Wichita St.	4-1-0	.800	8-3-0	.727
2.	So. Illinois	4-1-0	.800	6-5-0	.545
4.	Indiana St.	3-2-0	.600	5-6-0	.455
5.	Drake	2-4-0	.333	4-7-0	.364
6.	New Mex. St.	1-4-0	.200	3-8-0	.273

1982 (cont'd)

		Conference		Overall	
6.	W. Texas St.	1-4-0	.200	3-8-0	.273
7.	Illinois St.	0-5-0	.000	2-9-0	.182

Non-conference record; 20-26 .435

1983

		Conference		Overall	
1.	Tulsa	5-0-0	1.000	8-3-0	.727
2.	So. Illinois	4-1-0	.800	13-1-0	.929
3.	Indiana St.	3-2-0	.600	9-4-0	.692
4.	Illinois St.	2-2-1	.500	6-4-1	.591
4.	Wichita St.	3-3-0	.500	3-8-0	.273
6.	Drake	1-6-0	.143	1-10-0	.091
7.	W. Texas St.	0-5-1	.083	0-10-1	.045

Non-conference record: 22-21-0 .512

1984

		Conference		Overall	
1.	Tulsa	5-0-0	1.000	6-5-0	.545
2.	Indiana St.	4-1-0	.800	9-2-0	.818
3.	Illinois St.	3-2-0	.600	5-6-0	.455
4.	Drake	2-3-0	.400	4-7-0	.364
4.	W. Texas St.	2-3-0	.400	3-8-0	.273
4.	Wichita St.	2-3-0	.400	2-9-0	.182
7.	So. Illinois	0-5-0	.000	3-8-0	.273

Non-conference record: 14-28-0 .333

1985

		Conference		Overall	
1.	Tulsa	3-0-0	1.000	6-5-0	.545
2.	W. Texas St.	3-1-1	.700	6-3-1	.650
2.	Illinois St.	3-1-1	.700	6-3-2	.636
4.	Indiana St.	2-2-0	.500	4-6-0	.400
5.	Wichita St.	2-3-0	.400	3-8-0	.273
6.	Drake	1-4-0	.200	4-7-0	.364
7.	So. Illinois	1-4-0	.200	4-7-0	.364

Non-conference record: 18-24-0 .429
The MVC dropped football after the 1985 season.

Addendum: Claassen records for 1917-1923

1917

		Conference		Overall	
1.	Nebraska	2-0-0	1.000	5-2-0	.714
2.	Kansas	3-1-0	.750	6-2-0	.750
2.	Iowa State	3-1-0	.750	5-2-0	.714
4.	Kansas State	2-2-0	.500	6-2-0	.750
5.	Missouri	2-4-0	.333	3-5-0	.375
5.	Washington	1-2-0	.333	4-3-0	.571
7.	Drake	0-3-0	.000	0-5-2	.143

Non-conference record: 16-8-2 .654

1918: no conference

1919

		Conference		Overall	
1.	Missouri	4-0-1	.800	5-1-2	.750
2.	Iowa State	3-1-1	.750	5-2-1	.714
3.	Drake	2-2-0	.500	4-3-0	.571
4	Washington	1-2-0	.333	5-2-0	.714
5.	Kansas State	0-3-1	.000	3-5-1	.375
5.	Grinnell	0-2-0	.000	1-4-1	.250

Non-conference record: 13-7-2 .636
Nebraska is independent, and Grinnell joins the MVC.

1920

		Conference		Overall	
1.	Oklahoma	4-0-1	1.000	6-0-1	1.000
2.	Missouri	5-1-0	.833	7-1-0	.875
3.	Kansas	3-2-0	.600	5-2-1	.714
3.	Iowa State	3-2-0	.600	4-4-0	.500
5.	Drake	1-3-1	.250	4-5-1	.444
6.	Washington	1-4-0	.200	4-4-0	.714
7.	Grinnell	0-2-1	.000	3-3-1	.500
7.	Kansas State	0-3-1	.000	3-3-3	.500

Non-conference record: 19-5-3 .759
Oklahoma joins the MVC, and Kansas returns.

1921

		Conference		Overall	
1.	Nebraska	3-0-0	1.000	7-1-0	.875
2.	Kansas State	4-2-0	.667	5-3-0	.625
2.	Missouri	4-2-0	.667	6-2-0	.750
4.	Drake	2-2-0	.500	5-2-0	.714
4.	Kansas	3-3-0	.500	4-3-0	.571
6.	Iowa State	3-4-0	.429	4-4-0	.500
7.	Oklahoma	2-3-0	.400	5-3-0	.625
7.	Washington	2-3-0	.400	4-3-1	.562
9.	Grinnell	0-4-0	.000	2-5-0	.286

Non-conference record: 19-3-1 .847
Nebraska returns to the MVC.

1922

		Conference		Overall	
1.	Nebraska	5-0-0	1.000	7-1-0	.875
1.	Drake	4-0-0	1.000	7-0-0	1.000
3.	Kansas State	3-1-2	.750	5-1-2	.833
4.	Missouri	4-3-0	.571	5-3-0	.625
5.	Iowa State	2-4-0	.333	2-6-0	.250
6.	Oklahoma	1-2-2	.300	2-3-3	.400
7.	Grinnell	1-3-0	.250	3-4-0	.429
7.	Kansas	1-3-1	.250	3-4-1	.429
9.	Washington	0-5-1	.083	2-5-1	.286

Non-conference record: 15-6-1 .705

MISSOURI VALLEY CONFERENCE W-L-T RECORDS BY DECADES (1907-27)

Decade	Iowa	Nebraska	Kansas	Missouri	Wash.	Iowa St.	Drake	K. State	Grinnell	Okla.	Okla.A&M
1907-09	2- 7-1	3- 2-1	8- 2- 0	8- 4-0	0- 5-0	2- 3-1	3- 3-0				
1910-19	3- 1-0	21- 1-1	15-12-3	23-15-5	3-16-3	20- 9-3	7-25-2	3-14-2	0- 2-1		
1920-27		25- 5-3	18-25-7	33-13-2	7-32-3	23-21-3	20-15-2	17-20-7	9-21-3	19-20-4	5-4-2

MVC W-L-T PERCENTAGES (1907-1927)

Iowa	5- 8-1	.393	Iowa State	45-33-7	.571
Nebraska	49- 8-5	.831	Drake	30-43-4	.416
Kansas	41-39-10	.511	Kansas State	20-34-9	.389
Missouri	64-32-7	.655	Grinnell	9-23-4	.306
Washington (St.L)	10-53-6	.188	Oklahoma	19-20-4	.488
			Oklahoma A&M	5- 4-2	.545

MVC TITLES BY DECADES (1907-1927)

Decade	Iowa	Nebraska	Kansas	Missouri	Wash.	Iowa St.	Drake	K. State	Grinnell	Okla.	Okla. A&M
1907-09	.5	.5	1	1							
1910-19		6		2		2					
1920-27		3		3							1
Totals	.5	9.5	1	6		2					1

1938		Conference		Overall	
1.	Utah	4-0-2	.833	7-1-2	.800
2.	Colorado	3-2-1	.583	3-4-1	.438
2.	BYU	3-2-1	.583	4-3-1	.562
2.	Denver	3-2-1	.583	4-4-1	.500
5.	Utah State	3-3-0	.500	4-4-0	.500
6.	Wyoming	1-4-1	.250	2-5-1	.312
7.	Colo. State	0-4-2	.167	1-5-2	.250

1939					
1.	Colorado	5-1-0	.833	5-3-0	.625
2.	Utah	4-1-1	.750	6-1-2	.778
3.	Denver	3-2-1	.583	5-3-1	.611
4.	BYU	2-2-2	.500	5-2-2	.600
5.	Utah State	2-3-1	.417	3-4-1	.438
6.	Colo. State	2-4-0	.333	2-7-0	.222
7.	Wyoming	0-5-1	.083	0-7-1	.062

1940					
1.	Utah	5-1-0	.833	7-2-0	.778
2.	Colorado	4-1-1	.750	5-3-1	.611
2.	Denver	4-1-1	.750	7-2-1	.750
4.	BYU	2-3-1	.417	2-4-2	.375
5.	Utah State	2-4-0	.333	2-5-1	.312
6.	Colo. State	1-3-2	.250	3-5-2	.400
7.	Wyoming	0-5-1	.083	1-7-1	.167

1941					
1.	Utah	4-0-2	.833	6-0-2	.875
2.	Denver	3-1-2	.667	4-3-2	.556
2.	BYU	3-1-2	.667	4-3-2	.556
4.	Colo. State	3-2-1	.583	4-2-1	.643
4.	Colorado	3-2-1	.583	3-4-1	.438
6.	Wyoming	1-5-0	.167	2-7-1	.250
7.	Utah State	0-6-0	.000	0-8-0	.000

1942					
1.	Colorado	5-1-0	.833	7-2-0	.778
1	Utah	5-1-0	.833	6-3-0	.667
3.	Denver	3-2-1	.583	6-3-1	.650
4.	Utah State	2-3-1	.417	6-3-1	.650
5.	Colo. State	2-3-0	.400	4-3-0	.571
6.	BYU	1-4-0	.200	2-5-0	.286
7.	Wyoming	1-5-0	.167	3-5-0	.375

1943-1945: No league standings

1946					
1.	Utah State	4-1-1	.750	7-2-1	.750
1.	Denver	4-1-1	.750	5-5-1	.500
3.	Utah	4-2-0	.667	8-3-0	.727
4.	Colorado	3-2-1	.583	5-4-1	.550
4.	BYU	3-2-1	.583	5-4-1	.550
6.	Colo. State	1-5-0	.167	2-7-0	.222
7.	Wyoming	0-6-0	.000	1-8-1	.150

1947		Conference		Overall	
1.	Utah	6-0-0	1.000	8-1-0	.889
2.	Denver	3-2-1	.583	5-4-1	.550
3.	Utah State	3-3-0	.500	6-5-0	.545
3.	Colorado	3-3-0	.500	4-5-0	.444
5.	Colo. State	2-3-1	.417	5-4-1	.550
6.	Wyoming	2-4-0	.333	4-5-0	.444
7.	BYU	1-5-0	.167	3-7-0	.300

1948					
1.	Utah	5-0-0	1.000	8-1-1	.850
2.	Colo. State	4-1-0	.800	8-3-0	.727
3.	Denver	2-2-0	.500	4-5-1	.450
4.	Utah State	2-3-0	.400	5-6-0	.455
5.	BYU	1-3-0	.250	5-6-0	.455
6.	Wyoming	0-5-0	.000	4-5-0	.444

Colorado leaves the conference to join the Big Eight.

1949					
1.	Wyoming	5-0-0	1.000	9-1-0	.900
2.	Colo. State	4-1-0	.800	9-1-0	.900
3.	Denver	2-2-0	.500	4-6-0	.400
4.	Utah	2-3-0	.400	2-7-1	.250
5.	Utah State	1-3-0	.250	3-7-0	.300
6.	BYU	0-5-0	.000	0-11-0	.000

1950					
1.	Wyoming	5-0-0	1.000	10-0-0	1.000
2.	Colo. State	4-1-0	.800	6-3-0	.667
3.	Denver	2-2-1	.500	3-8-1	.292
4.	Utah	1-2-2	.400	3-4-3	.450
5.	BYU	1-3-1	.300	4-5-1	.450
6.	Utah State	0-5-0	.000	2-9-0	.182

1951					
1.	Utah	4-1-0	.800	7-4-0	.636
2.	Wyoming	5-1-1	.786	7-2-1	.750
3.	Denver	4-3-0	.571	6-4-0	.600
4.	Colo. State	3-3-1	.500	5-4-1	.550
5.	BYU	2-3-1	.417	6-3-1	.650
6.	Utah State	2-4-1	.357	3-5-1	.389
7.	New Mexico	2-4-0	.333	4-7-0	.364
8.	Montana	1-4-0	.200	2-7-0	.222

Montana and New Mexico join the conference

1952					
1.	Utah	5-0-0	1.000	6-3-1	.650
2.	New Mexico	5-1-0	.833	7-2-0	.778
3.	Colo. State	5-2-0	.714	6-4-0	.600
4.	Wyoming	4-3-0	.571	5-4-0	.556
5.	BYU	3-4-0	.429	4-6-0	.400
5.	Utah State	3-4-0	.429	3-7-1	.318
7.	Montana	1-5-0	.167	2-7-1	.250
8.	Denver	0-7-0	.000	3-7-0	.300

1953

		Conference		Overall	
1.	Utah	5-0-0	1.000	8-2-0	.800
2.	Utah State	5-2-0	.714	8-3-0	.727
3.	Wyoming	4-2-1	.643	5-4-1	.550
4.	New Mexico	3-2-1	.583	5-3-1	.611
5.	Colo. State	3-4-0	.429	4-5-0	.444
6.	Montana	2-4-0	.333	3-5-0	.375
7.	Denver	1-5-1	.214	3-5-2	.400
7.	BYU	1-5-1	.214	2-7-1	.250

1954

1.	Denver	6-1-0	.857	9-1-0	.900
2.	Wyoming	5-1-0	.833	6-4-0	.600
3.	Utah State	4-3-0	.571	4-6-0	.400
4.	New Mexico	3-3-0	.500	5-5-0	.500
4.	Utah	3-3-0	.500	4-7-0	.364
6.	Colo. State	3-4-0	.429	3-7-0	.300
7.	Montana	1-5-0	.167	3-6-0	.333
8.	BYU	1-6-0	.143	1-8-0	.111

1955

1.	Colo. State	6-1-1	.857	8-2-0	.800
2.	Utah	4-1-0	.800	6-3-0	.667
3.	Denver	5-2-0	.714	8-2-0	.800
3.	Wyoming	5-2-0	.714	8-3-0	.727
5.	Utah State	3-4-0	.429	4-6-0	.400
6.	Montana	2-4-0	.333	3-7-0	.300
7.	New Mexico	1-5-0	.167	2-8-0	.200
8.	BYU	0-7-0	.000	1-9-0	.100

1956

1.	Wyoming	7-0-0	1.000	10-0-0	1.000
2.	Utah	5-1-0	.833	5-5-1	.500
3.	Denver	4-3-0	.571	6-4-0	.600
3.	Utah State	4-3-0	.571	6-4-0	.600
5.	Colo. State	2-4-1	.357	2-7-1	.250
6.	New Mexico	2-4-0	.333	4-6-0	.400
7.	BYU	1-5-1	.214	2-7-1	.250
8.	Montana	1-6-0	.143	1-9-0	.100

1957

1.	Utah	5-1-0	.833	6-4-0	.600
2.	BYU	5-1-1	.786	5-3-2	.600
3.	Denver	5-2-0	.714	6-4-0	.600
4.	Wyoming	3-2-2	.571	4-3-3	.550
5.	New Mexico	2-4-0	.333	4-6-0	.400
6.	Colo. State	2-5-0	.286	3-7-0	.300
6.	Montana	2-5-0	.286	2-7-0	.222
8.	Utah State	1-5-1	.214	2-7-1	.250

1958

1.	Wyoming	6-1-0	.857	8-3-0	.727
2.	New Mexico	5-1-0	.833	7-3-0	.700
3.	BYU	5-2-0	.714	6-4-0	.600
4.	Colo. State	4-3-0	.571	6-4-0	.600
5.	Utah	3-3-0	.500	4-7-0	.364
6.	Utah State	2-5-0	.286	3-7-0	.300
6.	Denver	2-5-0	.286	2-8-0	.200
8.	Montana	0-7-0	.000	0-10-0	.000

1959

		Conference		Overall	
1.	Wyoming	6-1-0	.857	9-1-0	.900
2.	Colo. State	5-2-0	.714	6-4-0	.600
3.	New Mexico	4-2-0	.667	7-3-0	.700
4.	Utah	3-2-0	.600	5-5-0	.500
5.	Denver	2-5-0	.286	2-8-0	.200
5.	Utah State	2-5-0	.286	5-6-0	.455
5.	BYU	2-5-0	.286	3-7-0	.300
8.	Montana	1-5-0	.167	1-8-0	.111

1960

1.	Utah State	6-1-0	.857	9-2-0	.818
1.	Wyoming	6-1-0	.857	8-2-0	.800
3.	Utah	5-1-0	.833	7-3-0	.700
4.	New Mexico	4-2-0	.667	5-5-0	.500
5.	BYU	2-5-0	.286	3-8-0	.273
5.	Montana	2-5-00	.286	5-5-0	.500
7.	Denver	1-6-0	.143		
7.	Colo. State	1-6-0	.143	2-8-0	.200

1961

1.	Utah State	5-0-1	.917	9-1-1	.864
1.	Wyoming	5-0-1	.917	6-1-2	.778
3.	Utah	3-3-0	.500	6-4-0	.600
3.	New Mexico	3-3-0	.500	7-4-0	.636
5.	Montana	2-4-0	.333	2-6-0	.250
5.	BYU	2-4-0	.333	2-8-0	.200
7.	Colo. State	0-6-0	.000	0-10-0	.000

Denver left the conference after the 1960 season, and the MSC disbanded after the 1961 season.

MOUNTAIN STATES ("SKYLINE") CONFERENCE W-L-T RECORDS BY DECADES (1938-1961)

Decade	Utah	Colo.	BYU	Denver	Utah St.	Wyoming	Colo. St.	N. Mexico	Montana
1938-39	8- 1-3	8- 3-1	5- 4-3	6- 4-2	5- 6-1	1- 9-2	2- 8-2		
1940-49	31- 7-2	18- 9-3	11-23 5	21-11-6	14-23-2	9-30-1	17-18-4		
1950-59	38-14-2		21-41-5	31-35-2	26-40-2	51-12-4	37-29-2	27-26-1	11-45-0
1960-61	8- 4-0		4- 9-0	1- 6-0	11- 1-1	11- 1-1	1-12-0	7- 5-0	4- 9-0

MOUNTAIN STATES W-L-T PERCENTAGES (1938-1961)

Utah	85-26-7	.750	Denver	59-56-10	.512	Colo. State	57-67-8	.462
Colorado	26-12-4	.667	Utah State	56-68-6	.454	New Mexico	34-31-1	.523
BYU	41-79-13	.357	Wyoming	72-52-8	.576	Montana	15-54-0	.217

MOUNTAIN STATES TITLES BY DECADES (1938-1961)

Decade	Utah	Colo.	Denver	Utah St.	Wyoming	Colo.St.
1938-39	1	1				
1940-49	4.5	.5	.5	.5	1	
1950-59	4			1	4	1
1960-61				1	1	
Total	9.5	1.5	.5	2.5	6	1

MOUNTAIN WEST CONFERENCE (1999- 2003) Organized in 1999 by eight teams that left the WAC to form this conference.

1999		Conference		Overall	
Rank	School	W-L-T	Pct.	W-L-T	Pct.
1.	Utah	5-2-0	.714	9-3-0	.750
1.	Colorado State	5-2-0	.714	8-4-0	.667
1.	BYU	5-2-0	.714	8-4-0	.667
4.	Wyoming	4-3-0	.571	7-4-0	.636
5.	San Diego State	3-4-0	.429	5-6-0	.455
5.	New Mexico	3-4-0	.429	4-7-0	.364
7.	Air Force	2-5-0	.286	6-5-0	.545
8.	UNLV	1-6-0	.143	3-8-0	.273

Non-conference record: 22-13-0 .629

2000					
1.	Colorado State	6-1-0	.857	10-2-0	.833
2.	Air Force	5-2-0	.714	9-3-0	.750
3.	UNLV	4-3-0	.571	8-5-0	.615
3.	BYU	4-3-0	.571	6-6-0	.500
5.	New Mexico	3-4-0	.428	5-7-0	.416
5.	Utah	3-4-0	.428	4-7-0	.362
5.	San Diego State	3-4-0	.428	3-8-0	.272
8.	Wyoming	0-7-0	.000	1-10-0	.091

Non-conference record: 18-20-0 .474

2001		Conference		Overall	
Rank	School	W-L-T	Pct.	W-L-T	Pct.
1.	BYU	7-0-0	1.000	12-1-0	.923
2.	Colorado State	5-2-0	.714	6-5-0	.545
3.	Utah	4-3-0	.571	8-4-0	.667
3.	New Mexico	4-3-0	.571	6-5-0	.545
5.	Air Force	3-4-0	.429	6-6-0	.500
5.	UNLV	3-4-0	.429	4-7-0	.362
7.	San Diego State	2-5-0	.286	3-8-0	.272
8.	Wyoming	0-7-0	.000	2-9-0	.182

Non-conference record: 19-17-0 .527

2002					
1.	Colorado State	6-1-0	.857	10-4-0	.714
2.	New Mexico	5-2-0	.714	7-7-0	.500
3.	Air Force	4-3-0	.571	8-5-0	.615
3.	San Diego State	4-3-0	.571	4-9-0	.308
5.	Utah	3-4-0	.429	5-6-0	.455
5.	UNLV	3-4-0	.429	5-7-0	.417
7.	BYU	2-5-0	.286	5-7-0	.417
8.	Wyoming	1-6-0	.143	2-10-0	.167

Non-conference record: 18-27-0 .400

2003					
1.	Utah	6-1-0	.857	10-2-0	.833
2.	New Mexico	5-2-0	.714	8-5-0	.615
3.	Colorado State	4-3-0	.571	7-6-0	.538
4.	Air Force	3-4-0	.429	7-5-0	.583
4.	San Diego State	3-4-0	.429	6-6-0	.500
4.	BYU	3-4-0	.429	4-8-0	.333
7.	UNLV	2-5-0	.286	6-6-0	.500
7.	Wyoming	2-5-0	.286	4-8-0	.333

Non-conference record: 24-18-0 .571

MOUNTAIN WEST WIN PERCENTAGES (1999-2003)

Air Force	17-18-0	.486	San Diego State	15-20-0	.429
BYU	21-14-0	.600	UNLV	13-22-0	.371
Colorado State	26- 9-0	.743	Utah	21-14-0	.600
New Mexico	20-15-0	.571	Wyoming	7-28-0	.200

MOUNTAIN WEST TITLES (1999-2003)

BYU	1.33
Colorado State	2.33
Utah	1.33

PACIFIC-10 CONFERENCE (1916-2003). Between 1916 and 1958, the conference was known as the Pacific Coast Conference. In 1958, the PCC was disbanded and replaced by the Athletic Association of Western Universities, a five-team conference (Washington, UCLA, USC, Berkeley, and Stanford). Over the next five years, Washington State, Oregon State, and Oregon were added to the AAWU, which was renamed the Pacific 8 in 1968. With the addition of Arizona and Arizona State in 1978, the Pac-8 became the Pac-10.

1916		Conference		Overall	
1.	Washington	3-0-1	.875	6-0-1	.929
2.	Oregon	2-0-1	.833	7-0-1	.938
3.	Oregon State	0-2-0	.000	4-5-0	.444
4.	California	0-3-0	.000	6-4-1	.591

Non-conference record: 18-4-1 .804

1917					
1.	Wash. State	3-0-0	1.000	6-0-0	1.000
2.	California	2-1-0	.667	5-5-1	.500
3.	Oregon State	1-2-1	.375	4-2-1	.643
4.	Oregon	1-2-0	.333	4-3-0	.571
5.	Washington	0-2-1	.167	1-2-1	.375

Washington State joins the PCC.
Non-conference record: 13-5-1 .711

1918					
1.	California	2-0-0	1.000	7-2-0	.778
2.	Oregon	2-1-0	.667	4-2-0	.667
3.	Washington	1-1-0	.500	1-1-0	.500
4.	Stanford	0-1-0	.000	0-1-0	.000
5.	Oregon State	0-2-0	.000	2-4-0	.333

Stanford joins the PCC; Washington State out for 1918.
Non-conference record: 9-5-0 .643

1919					
1.	Oregon	2-1-0	.667	5-2-0	.714
1.	Washington	2-1-0	.667	5-1-0	.833
3.	California	2-2-0	.500	6-2-1	.722
3.	Wash. State	2-2-0	.500	5-2-0	.714
3.	Stanford	1-1-0	.500	4-3-0	.571
6.	Oregon State	1-3-0	.250	4-4-1	.500

Washington State back in PCC.
Non-conference record: 19-4-2 .800

1920					
1.	California	3-0-0	1.000	9-0-0	1.000
2.	Stanford	2-1-0	.667	4-3-0	.571
3.	Oregon	1-1-1	.500	3-2-1	.583
3.	Wash. State	1-1-0	.500	5-1-0	.833
5.	Oregon State	1-2-1	.375	2-2-2	.500
6.	Washington	0-3-0	.000	1-5-0	.167

Non-conference record: 16-5-1 .750

1921					
1.	California	4-0-0	1.000	9-0-1	.950
2.	Wash. State	2-1-1	.625	4-2-1	.643
3.	Stanford	1-1-1	.500	4-2-2	.625
4.	Oregon State	1-2-1	.375	4-3-2	.556
5.	Oregon	0-1-2	.333	5-1-3	.722
6.	Washington	0-3-1	.125	3-4-1	.438

Non-conference record: 21-4-4 .793

1922					
1.	California	4-0-0	1.000	9-0-0	1.000
2.	Oregon	3-0-1	.875	6-1-1	.812
3.	Washington	4-1-1	.750	6-1-1	.812
3.	USC	3-1-0	.750	10-1-0	.909
5.	Oregon State	1-3-0	.250	3-4-0	.429
5.	Stanford	1-3-0	.250	4-5-0	.444
7.	Wash. State	1-5-0	.167	2-5-0	.286
8.	Idaho	0-4-0	.000	3-5-0	.375

USC and Idaho join the PCC.
Non-conference record: 26-5-0 .839

1923		Conference		Overall	
1.	California	5-0-0	1.000	9-0-1	.950
2.	Washington	4-1-0	.800	10-1-1	.875
3.	Idaho	2-2-1	.500	5-2-1	.688
3.	Stanford	2-2-0	.500	7-2-0	.778
3.	USC	2-2-0	.500	6-2-0	.750
6.	Wash. State	1-3-1	.300	2-4-1	.357
6.	Oregon State	1-3-1	.300	4-5-2	.455
8.	Oregon	0-4-1	.100	3-4-1	.438

Non-conference record: 29-3-3 .871

1924					
1.	Stanford	3-0-1	.875	7-1-1	.833
2.	California	2-0-2	.750	8-0-2	.900
3.	Washington	3-1-1	.700	8-1-1	.850
4.	Idaho	4-2-0	.667	5-2-0	.714
4.	USC	2-1-0	.667	9-2-0	.818
6.	Oregon	2-2-1	.500	4-2-3	.611
7.	Oregon State	1-4-0	.200	3-5-0	.375
8.	Wash. State	0-4-1	.100	1-5-2	.250
9.	Montana	0-3-0	.000	4-4-0	.500

Montana joins the PCC.
Non-conference record: 32-5-3 .838

1925					
1.	Washington	5-0-0	1.000	10-1-1	.875
2.	Stanford	4-1-0	.800	7-2-0	.778
3.	USC	3-2-0	.600	11-2-0	.846
3.	Oregon State	3-2-0	.600	7-2-0	.778
5.	California	2-2-0	.500	6-3-0	.667
6.	Idaho	2-3-0	.400	3-5-0	.375
6.	Wash. State	2-3-0	.400	3-4-1	.438
8.	Montana	1-4-0	.200	3-4-1	.438
9.	Oregon	0-5-0	.000	1-5-1	.214

Non-conference record: 30-6-4 .800

1926					
1.	Stanford	4-0-0	1.000	10-0-1	.955
2.	USC	5-1-0	.833	8-2-0	.800
3.	Oregon State	4-1-0	.800	7-1-0	.875
3.	Wash. State	4-1-0	.800	6-1-0	.857
5.	Washington	3-2-0	.600	8-2-0	.800
6.	Oregon	1-4-0	.200	2-4-1	.357
6.	Idaho	1-4-0	.200	3-4-1	.438
8.	Montana	0-4-0	.000	3-5-0	.375
8.	California	0-5-0	.000	3-6-0	.333

Non-conference record: 28-3-3 .868

1927					
1.	USC	4-0-1	.900	8-1-1	.850
1.	Stanford	4-0-1	.900	8-2-1	.773
2.	Idaho	2-0-2	.500	4-1-3	.611
4.	Washington	4-2-0	.667	9-2-0	.818
5.	Oregon State	2-3-0	.400	3-3-1	.500
5.	California	2-3-0	.400	7-3-0	.700
7.	Wash. State	1-3-1	.300	3-3-2	.500
8.	Oregon	0-4-1	.100	2-4-1	.357
9.	Montana	0-4-0	.000	3-4-1	.438

Non-conference record: 28-4-4 .833

1928		Conference		Overall	
1.	USC	4-0-1	.900	9-0-1	.950
2.	California	3-0-2	.800	6-2-2	.700
3.	Stanford	4-1-1	750	8-3-1	.708
4.	Oregon	4-2-0	.667	9-2-0	.818
5.	Wash. State	4-3-0	.571	7-3-0	.700
6.	Oregon State	2-3-0	.400	6-3-0	.667
6.	Idaho	2-3-0	.400	3-4-1	.438
8.	Washington	2-4-0	.333	7-4-0	.636
9.	UCLA	0-4-0	.000	4-4-1	.500
9.	Montana	0-5-0	.000	4-5-1	.450

UCLA joins the PCC.
Non-conference record: 39-5-3 .862

1929					
1.	USC	6-1-0	.875	10-2-0	.833
2.	Stanford	5-1-0	.833	9-2-0	.818
3.	Oregon	4-1-0	.800	7-3-0	.700
3.	California	4-1-0	.800	7-1-1	.833
5.	Wash. State	4-2-0	.667	10-2-0	.833
6.	UCLA	1-3-0	.250	4-4-0	.500
7.	Oregon State	1-4-0	.200	5-4-0	.556
7.	Idaho	1-4-0	.200	4-5-0	.454
9.	Montana	0-4-1	.100	3-5-1	.389
10.	Washington	0-5-1	.083	2-6-1	.278

Non-conference record: 35-8-1 .807

1930					
1.	Wash. State	6-0-0	1.000	9-1-0	.900
2.	USC	5-1-0	.833	8-2-0	.800
3.	Stanford	4-1-0	.800	9-1-1	.864
4.	Oregon	3-1-0	.750	7-2-0	.778
5.	Washington	3-4-0	.429	5-4-0	.556
6.	Oregon State	2-3-0	.400	7-3-0	.700
7.	Montana	1-3-0	.250	5-3-0	.625
8.	California	1-4-0	.200	4-5-0	.444
8.	UCLA	1-4-0	.200	3-5-0	.375
10.	Idaho	0-5-0	.000	4-7-0	.364

Non-conference record: 35-7-1 .826

1931					
1.	USC	7-0-0	1.000	10-1-0	.909
2.	California	4-1-0	.800	8-2-0	.800
3.	Oregon	3-1-1	.700	6-2-2	.700
4.	Wash. State	4-3-0	.571	6-4-0	.600
5.	Washington	3-3-1	.500	5-3-1	.611
6.	Stanford	2-2-1	.500	7-2-2	.727
7.	Oregon State	1-3-1	.300	6-3-1	.650
8.	Idaho	1-4-0	.200	3-4-0	.429
9.	UCLA	0-3-0	.000	3-4-1	.438
9.	Montana	0-5-0	.000	1-6-0	.143

Non-conference record: 30-6-3 .808

1932					
1.	USC	6-0-0	1.000	10-0-0	1.000
2.	Wash. State	5-1-1	.786	7-1-1	.833
3.	UCLA	4-2-0	.667	6-4-0	1.000
4.	Washington	3-2-2	.571	6-2-2	.700
5.	Oregon	2-2-1	.500	6-3-1	.650
5.	California	2-2-1	.500	7-3-2	.667
7.	Stanford	1-3-1	.300	6-4-1	.591
8.	Oregon State	1-4-0	.200	4-6-0	.400
8.	Idaho	1-4-0	.200	3-5-0	.375
10.	Montana	0-5-0	.000	2-7-0	.222

Non-conference record: 32-10-1 .756

1933		Conference		Overall	
1.	Stanford	4-1-0	.800	8-2-1	.773
1.	Oregon	4-1-0	.800	9-1-0	.900
3.	USC	4-1-1	.750	10-1-1	.875
4.	Oregon State	2-1-1	.625	6-2-2	.700
5.	Wash. State	3-3-1	.500	5-3-1	.611
5.	California	2-2-2	.500	6-3-2	.636
7.	Washington	3-4-0	.429	5-4-0	.556
8.	UCLA	1-3-1	.300	6-4-1	.591
9.	Idaho	1-4-0	.200	4-4-0	.500
10.	Montana	0-4-0	.000	3-4-0	.429

Non-conference record: 38-4-2 .886

1934					
1.	Stanford	5-0-0	1.000	9-1-1	.864
2.	Wash. State	4-0-1	.900	4-3-1	.562
3.	Washington	5-1-1	.786	6-1-1	.812
4.	Oregon	4-2-0	.667	6-4-0	.600
5.	California	3-2-0	.600	6-6-0	.500
6.	UCLA	2-3-0	.400	7-3-0	.700
7.	USC	1-4-1	.250	4-6-1	.409
8.	Idaho	1-4-0	.200	3-5-0	.375
9.	Oregon State	0-5-2	.143	3-6-2	.364
10.	Montana	0-4-1	.100	2-5-1	.312

Non-conference record: 25-15-1 .622

1935					
1.	UCLA	4-1-0	.800	8-2-0	.800
1.	Stanford	4-1-0	.800	8-1-0	.889
1.	California	4-1-0	.800	9-1-0	.900
4.	Wash. State	3-2-0	.600	5-3-1	.611
4.	Oregon	3-2-0	.600	6-3-0	.667
6.	Washington	4-3-0	.571	5-3-0	.625
7.	Oregon State	2-3-1	.417	6-4-1	.591
8.	USC	2-4-0	.333	5-7-0	.417
9.	Idaho	1-5-0	.167	2-7-0	.222
10.	Montana	0-5-1	.083	1-5-2	.250

Non-conference record: 28-9-2 .744

1936					
1.	Washington	7-0-1	.938	7-2-1	.750
2.	Wash. State	6-2-1	.722	6-3-1	.650
3.	USC	3-2-2	.571	4-2-3	.611
3.	California	4-3-0	.571	6-5-0	.545
5.	UCLA	4-3-1	.563	6-3-1	.650
6.	Stanford	2-3-2	.429	2-5-2	.333
7.	Oregon State	3-5-0	.375	4-6-0	.400
8.	Montana	1-3-0	.250	6-3-0	.667
9.	Oregon	1-6-1	.188	2-6-1	.278
10.	Idaho	0-4-0	.000	3-7-0	.300

Non-conference record: 15-11-1 .574

1937					
1.	California	6-0-1	.929	10-0-1	.955
2.	Stanford	4-2-1	.643	4-3-2	.556
3.	Washington	4-2-2	.625	7-2-2	.727
4.	Wash. State	3-3-2	.500	3-3-3	.500
4.	Idaho	2-2-0	.500	4-3-1	.562
6.	Oregon State	2-3-3	.438	3-3-3	.500
7.	USC	2-3-2	.429	4-4-2	.500
8.	Oregon	2-5-0	.286	4-6-0	.400
9.	UCLA	1-5-1	.214	2-6-1	.278
10.	Montana	0-1-0	.000	7-1-0	.875

Non-conference record: 22-5-3 .783

1938		Conference		Overall	
1.	USC	6-1-0	.857	9-2-0	.818
1.	California	6-1-0	.857	10-1-0	.909
3.	UCLA	4-3-1	.562	7-4-1	.625
3.	Oregon State	4-3-1	.562	5-3-1	.611
5.	Oregon	4-4-0	.500	4-5-0	.444
6.	Washington	3-4-1	.438	3-5-1	.389
7.	Idaho	2-3-1	.417	6-3-1	.650
8.	Stanford	2-5-0	.286	3-6-0	.333
9.	Wash. State	1-7-0	.125	2-8-0	.200
10.	Montana	0-1-0	.000	5-3-1	.556

Non-conference record: 22-8-1 .726

1939					
1.	USC	5-0-2	.857	8-0-2	.900
2.	UCLA	5-0-3	.812	6-0-4	.800
3.	Oregon State	6-1-1	.812	9-1-1	.864
4.	Washington	4-4-0	.500	4-5-1	.450
4.	Oregon	3-3-1	.500	3-4-1	.438
6.	Wash. State	3-5-0	.375	4-5-0	.444
7.	Montana	1-2-0	.333	3-5-0	.375
8.	California	2-5-0	.286	3-7-0	.300
9.	Stanford	0-6-1	.072	1-7-1	.167
10.	Idaho	0-3-0	.000	2-6-0	.333

Non-conference record: 14-11-2 .556

1940					
1.	Stanford	7-0-0	1.000	10-0-0	1.000
2.	Washington	7-1-0	.875	7-2-0	.778
3.	Oregon State	4-3-1	.562	5-3-1	.611
4.	Wash. State	3-4-2	.444	4-4-2	.500
5.	Oregon	3-4-1	.438	4-4-1	.500
6.	California	3-4-0	.429	4-6-0	.400
7.	USC	2-3-2	.429	3-4-2	.444
8.	Montana	1-2-0	.333	4-4-1	.500
9.	UCLA	1-6-0	.143	1-9-0	.100
10.	Idaho	0-4-0	.000	1-7-1	.167

Non-conference record: 12-12-2 .500

1941					
1.	Oregon State	7-2-0	.778	8-2-0	.800
2.	Washington	5-3-0	.625	5-4-0	.556
2.	Wash. State	5-3-0	.625	6-4-0	.600
4.	Stanford	4-3-0	.571	6-3-0	.667
5.	Oregon	4-4-0	.500	5-5-0	.500
6.	UCLA	3-4-1	.438	5-5-1	.500
7.	California	3-4-0	.429	4-5-0	.444
8.	USC	2-4-1	.357	2-6-1	.278
9.	Montana	1-3-0	.250	6-3-0	.667
10.	Idaho	0-4-0	.000	4-5-0	.444

Non-conference record: 17-8-0 .680

1942					
1.	UCLA	6-1-0	.857	7-4-0	.636
2.	Wash. State	5-1-1	.786	6-2-2	.700
3.	Stanford	5-2-0	.714	6-4-0	.600
4.	USC	4-2-1	.643	5-5-1	.500
5.	Oregon State	4-4-0	.500	4-5-1	.450
5.	Washington	3-3-2	.500	4-3-3	.550
7.	California	3-4-0	.429	5-5-0	.500
8.	Oregon	2-5-0	.286	2-6-0	.250
9.	Idaho	1-5-0	.167	3-7-0	.300
10.	Montana	0-6-0	.000	0-8-0	.000

Non-conference record: 8-16-3 .352

1943		Conference		Overall	
1.	USC	5-0-0	1.000	8-2-0	.800
2.	California	2-2-0	.500	4-6-0	.400
3.	Washington	0-1-0	.000	4-1-0	.800
3.	UCLA	0-4-0	.000	1-8-0	.111

Other conference schools drop football in 1943 and 1944.
Non-conference record 10-10-0 .500

1944					
1.	USC	3-0-2	.800	8-0-2	.800
2.	Washington	1-1-0	.500	5-3-0	.625
3.	UCLA	1-2-1	.375	4-5-1	.450
4.	California	1-3-1	.300	3-6-1	.350

Non-conference record: 14-8-0 .636

1945					
1.	USC	5-1-0	.833	7-4-0	.636
2.	Wash. State	6-2-1	.722	6-2-1	.722
3.	Washington	6-3-0	.667	6-3-0	.667
4.	Oregon State	4-4-0	.500	4-4-1	.500
5.	UCLA	2-3-0	.400	5-4-0	.556
6.	California	2-4-1	.357	4-5-1	.450
7.	Oregon	3-6-0	.333	3-6-0	.333
8.	Idaho	1-5-0	.167	1-7-0	.125
9.	Montana	0-1-0	.000	1-4-0	.200

Stanford drops football in 1945.
Non-conference record: 8-10-1 .447

1946					
1.	UCLA	7-0-0	1.000	10-1-0	.909
2.	Oregon State	6-1-1	.812	7-1-1	.833
3.	USC	5-2-0	.714	6-4-0	.600
4.	Washington	5-3-0	.625	5-4-0	.556
5.	Stanford	3-3-1	.500	6-3-1	.650
6.	Oregon	3-4-1	.438	4-4-1	.500
7.	Montana	1-3-0	.250	4-4-0	.500
8.	Wash. State	1-5-1	.214	1-6-1	.188
9.	California	1-6-0	.143	2-7-0	.222
10.	Idaho	0-5-0	.000	1-8-0	.111

Non-conference record: 14-10-0 .583

1947					
1.	USC	6-0-0	1.000	7-2-1	.750
2.	California	5-1-0	.833	9-1-0	.900
2.	Oregon	5-1-0	.833	7-3-0	.700
4.	UCLA	4-2-0	.667	5-4-0	.556
4.	Montana	2-1-0	.667	7-4-0	.636
6.	Oregon State	3-4-0	.429	5-5-0	.500
7.	Washington	2-5-0	.286	3-6-0	.333
7.	Wash. State	2-5-0	.286	3-7-0	.300
9.	Idaho	1-4-0	.200	4-4-0	.500
10.	Stanford	0-7-0	.000	0-9-0	.000

Non-conference record: 20-15-1 .569

1948					
1.	Oregon	7-0-0	1.000	9-2-0	.818
1.	California	6-0-0	1.000	10-1-0	.909
3.	USC	4-2-0	.667	6-3-1	.650
4.	Wash. State	4-3-1	.562	4-5-1	.450
5.	Stanford	3-4-0	.429	4-6-0	.400
6.	Oregon State	2-3-2	.429	5-4-3	.542
7.	Washington	2-5-1	.312	2-7-1	.250
8.	UCLA	2-6-0	.250	3-7-0	.300
9.	Idaho	1-5-0	.167	3-6-0	.333
10.	Montana	0-3-0	.000	3-7-0	.300

Non-conference record: 18-17-2 .514

1949		Conference		Overall	
1.	California	7-0-0	1.000	10-1-0	.909
2.	UCLA	5-2-0	.714	6-3-0	.667
3.	Stanford	4-2-0	.667	7-3-1	.682
3.	USC	4-2-0	.667	5-3-1	.611
5.	Oregon State	5-3-0	.625	7-3-0	.700
6.	Oregon	2-5-0	.286	4-6-0	.400
6.	Washington	2-5-0	.286	3-7-0	.300
8.	Wash. State	2-6-0	.250	3-6-0	.333
9.	Idaho	1-4-0	.200	3-5-0	.375
10.	Montana	0-3-0	.000	5-4-0	.556

Non-conference record: 21-9-2 .688

1950					
1.	California	5-0-1	.917	9-1-1	.864
2.	Washington	6-1-0	.857	8-2-0	.800
3.	UCLA	5-2-0	.714	6-3-0	.667
4.	Stanford	2-2-2	.500	5-3-2	.600
4.	Idaho	1-1-1	.500	3-5-1	.389
6.	Wash. State	2-3-2	.429	4-3-2	.556
7.	USC	1-3-2	.333	2-5-2	.333
8.	Oregon State	2-5-0	.286	3-6-0	.333
9.	Oregon	0-7-0	.000	1-9-0	.100

Montana leaves the PCC.
Non-conference record: 17-13-0 .567

1951					
1.	Stanford	6-1-0	.857	9-2-0	.818
2.	UCLA	4-1-1	.750	5-3-1	.611
3.	California	5-2-0	.714	8-2-0	.800
4.	USC	4-2-0	.667	7-3-0	.700
5.	Wash. State	4-3-0	.571	7-3-0	.700
6.	Oregon State	3-5-0	.375	4-6-0	.400
7.	Washington	1-5-1	.214	3-6-1	.350
8.	Oregon	1-6-0	.143	2-8-0	.200
9.	Idaho	0-3-0	.000	2-7-0	.222

Non-conference record: 19-12-0 .613

1952					
1.	USC	6-0-0	1.000	10-1-0	.909
2.	UCLA	5-1-0	.833	8-1-0	.889
3.	Washington	6-2-0	.750	7-3-0	.700
4.	California	3-3-0	.500	7-3-0	.700
5.	Wash. State	3-4-0	.429	4-6-0	.400
6.	Stanford	2-5-0	.286	5-5-0	.500
6.	Oregon	2-5-0	.286	2-7-1	.250
8.	Idaho	1-3-0	.250	4-4-1	.500
9.	Oregon State	1-6-0	.143	2-7-0	.222

Non-conference record: 20-8-2 .700

1953					
1.	UCLA	6-1-0	.857	8-2-0	.800
2.	Stanford	5-1-1	.786	6-3-1	.650
3.	USC	4-2-1	.643	6-3-1	.650
4.	California	2-2-2	.500	4-4-2	.500
5.	Wash. State	3-4-0	.429	4-6-0	.400
6.	Oregon State	3-5-0	.375	3-6-0	.333
7.	Washington	2-4-1	.357	3-6-1	.350
8.	Oregon	2-5-1	.312	4-5-1	.450
9.	Idaho	0-3-0	.000	1-8-0	.111

Non-conference record: 12-16-0 .429

1954					
1.	UCLA	6-0-0	1.000	9-0-0	1.000
2.	USC	6-1-0	.857	8-4-0	.667
3.	Oregon	5-3-0	.625	6-4-0	.600
4.	California	4-3-0	.571	5-5-0	.500
5.	Wash. State	3-4-0	.429	4-6-0	.400
6.	Stanford	2-4-0	.333	4-6-0	.400

1954 *(cont'd)*		Conference		Overall	
6.	Idaho	1-2-0	.333	4-5-0	.444
8.	Washington	1-6-0	.143	2-8-0	.200
8.	Oregon State	1-6-0	.143	1-8-0	.111

Non-conference record: 14-17-0 .452

1955					
1.	UCLA	6-0-0	1.000	9-2-0	.818
2.	Oregon State	5-2-0	.714	6-3-0	.667
3.	Stanford	3-2-1	.583	6-3-1	.650
4.	Oregon	4-3-0	.571	6-4-0	.600
5.	Washington	4-3-1	.562	5-4-1	.550
6.	USC	3-3-0	.500	6-4-0	.600
7.	California	1-5-1	.214	2-7-1	.250
7.	Wash. State	1-5-1	.214	1-7-2	.200
9.	Idaho	0-4-0	.000	2-7-0	.222

Non-conference record: 16-14-1 .532

1956					
1.	Oregon State	6-1-1	.812	7-3-1	.682
2.	USC	5-2-0	.714	8-2-0	.800
2.	UCLA	5-2-0	.714	7-3-0	.700
4.	Washington	4-4-0	.500	5-5-0	.500
4.	Oregon	3-3-2	.500	4-4-2	.500
6.	Stanford	3-4-0	.429	4-6-0	.400
7.	Wash. State	2-5-1	.312	3-6-1	.350
8.	California	2-5-0	.286	3-7-0	.300
9.	Idaho	0-4-0	.000	2-7-0	.222

Non-conference record: 13-13-0 .500

1957					
1.	Oregon State	6-2-0	.750	8-2-0	.800
1.	Oregon	6-2-0	.750	7-4-0	.636
3.	UCLA	5-2-0	.714	8-2-0	.800
4.	Wash. State	5-3-0	.625	6-4-0	.600
5.	Stanford	4-3-0	.571	6-4-0	.600
6.	Washington	3-4-0	.429	3-6-1	.350
7.	California	1-6-0	.143	1-9-0	.100
7.	USC	1-6-0	.143	1-9-0	.100
9.	Idaho	0-3-0	.000	4-4-1	.500

Non-conference record: 13-13-2 .500

1958					
1.	California	6-1-0	.857	7-4-0	.636
2.	Wash. State	6-2-0	.750	7-3-0	.700
3.	USC	4-2-1	.643	4-5-1	.450
4.	Oregon State	5-3-0	.625	6-4-0	.600
5.	Oregon	4-4-0	.500	4-6-0	.400
6.	UCLA	2-4-1	.357	3-6-1	.350
7.	Stanford	2-5-0	.286	2-8-0	.200
8.	Washington	1-6-0	.143	1-7-0	.125
9.	Idaho	0-3-0	.000	4-5-0	.444

Non-conference record: 8-18-0 .308

1959					
1.	Washington	3-1-0	.750	10-1-0	.909
1.	USC	3-1-0	.750	8-2-0	.800
1.	UCLA	3-1-0	.750	5-4-1	.550
4.	California	1-3-0	.250	2-8-0	.200
5.	Stanford	0-4-0	.000	3-7-0	.300

PCC disbanded, AAWU formed, dropping Wash. State, Oregon, Oregon State, and Idaho.
Non-conference record: 18-12-1 .597

1960		Conference		Overall	
1.	Washington	4-0-0	1.000	10-1-0	.909
2.	USC	3-1-0	.750	4-6-0	.400
3.	UCLA	2-2-0	.500	7-2-1	.750
4.	California	1-3-0	.250	2-7-1	.250
5.	Stanford	0-4-0	.000	0-10-0	.000

Non-conference record: 13-16-2 .452

1961					
1.	UCLA	3-1-0	.750	7-4-0	.636
2.	USC	2-1-1	.625	4-5-1	.450
2.	Washington	2-1-1	.625	5-4-1	.550
4.	Stanford	1-3-0	.250	4-6-0	.400
4.	California	1-3-0	.250	1-8-0	.111

Non-conference record: 12-18-0 .400

1962					
1.	USC	4-0-0	1.000	11-0-0	1.000
2.	Washington	4-1-0	.800	7-1-2	.800
3.	Wash. State	1-1-0	.500	5-4-1	.550
4.	Stanford	2-3-0	.400	5-5-0	.500
5.	UCLA	1-3-0	.250	4-6-0	.400
6.	California	0-4-0	.000	1-9-0	.100

Wash. State joins the AAWU.
Non-conference record: 21-13-2 .611

1963					
1.	Washington	4-1-0	.800	6-5-0	.545
2.	USC	3-1-0	.750	7-3-0	.700
3.	UCLA	2-2-0	.500	2-8-0	.200
3.	Wash. State	1-1-0	.500	3-6-1	.350
5.	California	1-3-0	.250	4-5-1	.450
6.	Stanford	1-4-0	.200	3-7-0	.300

Non-conference record: 13-22-2 .378

1964					
1.	Oregon State	3-1-0	.750	8-3-0	.727
1.	USC	3-1-0	.750	7-3-0	.700
3.	Washington	5-2-0	.714	6-4-0	.600
4.	UCLA	2-2-0	.500	4-6-0	.400
5.	Stanford	3-4-0	.429	5-5-0	.500
6.	Oregon	1-2-1	.375	7-2-1	.750
6.	Wash. State	1-2-1	.375	3-6-1	.350
8.	California	0-4-0	.000	3-7-0	.300

Oregon and Oregon State join the AAWU.
Non-conference record: 25-18-0 .581

1965					
1.	UCLA	4-0-0	1.000	8-2-1	.773
2.	USC	4-1-0	.800	7-2-1	.750
3.	Wash. State	2-1-0	.667	7-3-0	.700
4.	Washington	4-3-0	.571	5-5-0	.500
5.	Stanford	2-3-0	.400	6-3-1	.650
5.	California	2-3-0	.400	5-5-0	.500
7.	Oregon State	1-3-0	.250	5-5-0	.500
8.	Oregon	0-5-0	.000	4-5-1	.450

Non-conference record: 28-11-4 .698

1966					
1.	USC	4-1-0	.800	7-4-0	.636
2.	UCLA	3-1-0	.750	9-1-0	.900
2.	Oregon State	3-1-0	.750	7-3-0	.700
4.	Washington	4-3-0	.571	6-4-0	.600
5.	California	2-3-0	.400	3-7-0	.300
6.	Oregon	1-3-0	.250	3-7-0	.300
6.	Wash. State	1-3-0	.250	3-7-0	.300
8.	Stanford	1-4-0	.200	5-5-0	.500

Non-conference record: 24-19-0 .558

1967		Conference		Overall	
1.	USC	6-1-0	.857	10-1-0	.909
2.	UCLA	4-1-1	.750	7-2-1	.750
2.	Oregon State	4-1-1	.750	7-2-1	.750
4.	Washington	3-4-0	.429	5-5-0	.500
4.	Stanford	3-4-0	.429	5-5-0	.500
6.	California	2-3-0	.400	5-5-0	.500
7.	Oregon	1-5-0	.167	2-8-0	.200
7.	Wash. State	1-5-0	.167	2-8-0	.200

Non-conference record: 19-12-0 .613

1968					
1.	USC	6-0-0	1.000	9-1-1	.864
2.	Oregon State	5-1-0	.833	7-3-0	.700
3.	Stanford	3-3-1	.500	6-3-1	.650
3.	California	2-2-1	.500	7-3-1	.682
5.	Oregon	2-4-0	.333	4-6-0	.400
5.	UCLA	2-4-0	.333	3-7-0	.300
7.	Wash. State	1-3-1	.300	3-6-1	.350
8.	Washington	1-5-1	.214	3-5-2	.400

Conference renamed the Pacific-8.
Non-conference record: 20-12-2 .618

1969					
1.	USC	6-0-0	1.000	10-0-1	.955
2.	UCLA	5-1-1	.786	8-1-1	.850
2.	Stanford	5-1-1	.786	7-2-1	.750
4.	Oregon State	4-3-0	.571	6-4-0	.600
5.	Oregon	2-3-0	.400	5-5-1	.500
6.	California	2-4-0	.333	5-5-0	.500
7.	Washington	1-6-0	.167	1-9-0	.100
8.	Wash. State	0-7-0	.000	1-9-0	.100

Non-conference record: 18-10-2 .633

1970					
1.	Stanford	6-1-0	.857	9-3-0	.750
2.	Washington	4-3-0	.571	6-4-0	.600
2.	Oregon	4-3-0	.571	6-4-1	.591
2.	UCLA	4-3-0	.571	6-5-0	.545
2.	California	4-3-0	.571	6-5-0	.545
6.	USC	3-4-0	.429	6-4-1	.591
6.	Oregon State	3-4-0	.429	6-5-0	.545
8.	Wash. State	0-7-0	.000	1-10-0	.091

Non-conference record: 18-12-2 .594

1971					
1.	Stanford	6-1-0	.857	9-3-0	.750
2.	USC	3-2-1	.583	6-4-1	.591
3.	Washington	4-3-0	.571	8-3-0	.727
3.	California	4-3-0	.571	6-5-0	.545
5.	Oregon State	3-3-0	.500	5-6-0	.455
6.	Oregon	2-4-0	.333	5-6-0	.455
7.	Wash. State	2-5-0	.286	4-7-0	.364
8.	UCLA	1-4-1	.250	2-7-1	.250

Non-conference record: 20-18-0 .526

1972					
1.	USC	7-0-0	1.000	12-0-0	1.000
2.	UCLA	5-2-0	.714	8-3-0	.727
3.	Wash. State	4-3-0	.571	7-4-0	.636
3.	Washington	4-3-0	.571	8-3-0	.727
5.	California	3-4-0	.429	3-8-0	.273
6.	Oregon	2-5-0	.286	4-7-0	.364
6.	Stanford	2-5-0	.286	6-5-0	.545
8.	Oregon State	1-6-0	.143	2-9-0	.182

Non-conference record: 22-11-0 .667

1973		Conference		Overall	
1.	USC	7-0-0	1.000	9-2-1	.792
2.	UCLA	6-1-0	.857	9-2-0	.818
3.	Stanford	5-2-0	.714	7-4-0	.636
4.	Wash. State	4-3-0	.571	5-6-0	.455
5.	California	2-5-0	.286	4-7-0	.364
5.	Oregon	2-5-0	.286	2-9-0	.182
5.	Oregon State	2-5-0	.286	2-9-0	.182
8.	Washington	0-7-0	.000	2-9-0	.182

Non-conference record: 12-20-1 .379

1974					
1.	USC	6-0-1	.929	10-1-1	.875
2.	Stanford	5-1-1	.786	5-4-2	.545
3.	California	4-2-1	.643	7-3-1	.682
3.	UCLA	4-2-1	.643	6-3-2	.636
5.	Washington	3-4-0	.429	5-6-0	.455
5.	Oregon State	3-4-0	.429	3-8-0	.273
7.	Wash. State	1-6-0	.143	2-9-0	.182
8.	Oregon	0-7-0	.000	2-9-0	.182

Non-conference record: 13-17-2 .438

1975					
1.	UCLA	6-1-0	.857	9-2-1	.792
1.	California	6-1-0	.857	8-3-0	.727
3.	Washington	5-2-0	.714	6-5-0	.545
3.	Stanford	5-2-0	.714	6-4-1	.591
5.	USC	3-4-0	.429	8-4-0	.667
6.	Oregon	2-5-0	.286	3-8-0	.273
7.	Oregon State	1-6-0	.143	1-10-0	.091
8.	Wash. State	0-7-0	.000	3-8-0	.273

Non-conference record: 16-16-2 .500

1976					
1.	USC	7-0-0	1.000	11-1-0	.917
2.	UCLA	6-1-0	.857	9-2-1	.792
3.	Stanford	5-2-0	.714	6-5-0	.545
4.	California	3-4-0	.429	5-6-0	.455
4.	Washington	3-4-0	.429	5-6-0	.455
6.	Wash. State	2-5-0	.286	3-8-0	.273
7.	Oregon	1-6-0	.143	4-7-0	.364
8.	Oregon State	1-6-0	.143	2-10-0	.167

Non-conference record: 17-17-1 .500

1977					
1.	Washington	6-1-0	.857	8-4-0	.667
2.	Stanford	5-2-0	.714	9-3-0	.750
2.	USC	5-2-0	.714	8-4-0	.667
2.	UCLA	5-2-0	.714	7-4-0	.636
5.	California	3-4-0	.429	7-4-0	.636
5.	Wash. State	3-4-0	.429	6-5-0	.545
7.	Oregon	1-6-0	.143	2-9-0	.182
8	Oregon State	0-7-0	.000	2-9-0	.182

Non-conference record: 21-14-0 .600

1978					
1.	USC	6-1-0	.857	12-1-0	.923
2.	UCLA	6-2-0	.750	8-3-1	.708
2.	Washington	6-2-0	.750	7-4-0	.636
4.	Ariz. State	4-3-0	.571	9-3-0	.750
4.	Stanford	4-3-0	.571	8-4-0	.667
6.	California	3-4-0	.429	6-5-0	.545
6.	Arizona	3-4-0	.429	5-6-0	.455
8.	Oregon	2-5-0	.286	2-9-0	.182
9.	Oregon State	2-6-0	.250	3-7-1	.292
9.	Wash. State	2-6-0	.250	3-7-1	.292

Arizona and Arizona State join the conference;
Name changed to Pacific-10.
Non-conference record: 25-13-3 .646

		Conference		Overall	
1979					
1.	USC	6-0-1	.929	11-0-1	.958
2.	Washington	6-1-0	.857	10-2-0	.833
3.	Arizona	4-3-0	.571	6-5-1	.542
3.	Oregon	4-3-0	.571	6-5-0	.545
5.	California	5-4-0	.556	6-6-0	.500
6.	Stanford	3-3-1	.500	5-5-1	.500
7.	UCLA	3-4-0	.429	5-6-0	.455
8.	Wash. State	3-5-0	.375	5-6-0	.455
9.	Oregon State	2-6-0	.250	2-9-0	.182
10.	Ariz. State	1-6-0	.143	1-10-0	.091

Non-conference record: 19-20-2 .488
Records are after forfeits of five games by Ariz. State.

1980					
1.	Washington	6-1-0	.857	9-3-0	.750
2.	UCLA	5-2-0	.714	9-2-0	.818
3.	USC	4-2-1	.643	8-2-1	.773
4.	Ariz. State	5-3-0	.625	7-4-0	.636
5.	Oregon	4-3-1	.562	6-3-2	.636
6.	Stanford	3-4-0	.429	6-5-0	.545
6.	Arizona	3-4-0	.429	5-6-0	.455
6.	Wash. State	3-4-0	.429	4-7-0	.364
9.	California	3-5-0	.375	3-8-0	.273
10.	Oregon State	0-8-0	.000	0-11-0	.000

Non-conference record: 21-15-1 .581

1981					
1.	Washington	6-2-0	.750	10-2-0	.833
2.	Ariz. State	5-2-0	.714	9-2-0	.818
2.	USC	5-2-0	.714	9-3-0	.750
4.	Wash. State	5-2-1	.688	8-3-1	.708
4.	UCLA	5-2-1	.688	7-4-1	.625
6.	Arizona	4-4-0	.500	6-5-0	.545
6.	Stanford	4-4-0	.500	4-7-0	.364
8.	California	2-6-0	.250	2-9-0	.182
9.	Oregon	1-6-0	.143	2-9-0	.182
10.	Oregon State	0-7-0	.000	1-10-0	.091

Non-conference record: 21-17-0 .553

1982					
1.	UCLA	5-1-1	.786	10-1-1	.875
2.	Washington	6-2-0	.750	10-2-0	.833
3.	Ariz. State	5-2-0	.714	10-2-0	.833
3.	USC	5-2-0	.714	8-3-0	.727
5.	Arizona	4-3-1	.562	6-4-1	.591
6.	California	4-4-0	.500	7-4-0	.636
7.	Stanford	3-5-0	.375	5-6-0	.455
8.	Wash. State	2-4-1	.357	3-7-1	.318
9.	Oregon	2-6-0	.250	2-8-1	.227
10.	Oregon State	0-7-1	.062	1-9-1	.136

Non-conference record: 26-10-1 .716

1983					
1.	UCLA	6-1-1	.812	7-4-1	.625
2.	Washington	5-2-0	.714	8-4-0	.667
3.	Wash. State	5-3-0	.625	7-4-0	.636
4.	USC	4-3-0	.571	4-6-1	.409
5.	Arizona	4-3-1	.562	7-3-1	.682
6.	Ariz. State	3-3-1	.500	6-4-1	.591
6.	Oregon	3-3-1	.500	4-6-1	.409
8.	California	3-4-1	.438	5-5-1	.500
9.	Oregon State	1-6-1	.188	2-8-1	.227
10.	Stanford	1-7-0	.125	1-10-0	.091

Non-conference record: 16-19-1 .458

1984		Conference		Overall	
1.	USC	7-1-0	.875	9-3-0	.750
2.	Washington	6-1-0	.857	11-1-0	.917
3.	UCLA	5-2-0	.714	9-3-0	.750
3.	Arizona	5-2-0	.714	7-4-0	.636
5.	Wash. State	4-3-0	.571	6-5-0	.545
6.	Ariz. State	3-4-0	.429	5-6-0	.455
7.	Oregon	3-5-0	.375	6-5-0	.545
7.	Stanford	3-5-0	.375	5-6-0	.455
9.	Oregon State	1-7-0	.125	2-9-0	.182
10.	California	1-8-0	.111	2-9-0	.182

Non-conference record: 24-13-0 .649

1985					
1.	UCLA	6-2-0	.750	9-2-1	.792
2.	Arizona	5-2-0	.714	8-3-1	.708
2.	Ariz. State	5-2-0	.714	8-4-0	.667
4.	Washington	5-3-0	.625	7-5-0	.583
4.	USC	5-3-0	.625	6-6-0	.500
6.	Oregon	3-4-0	.429	5-6-0	.455
7.	Wash. State	3-5-0	.375	4-7-0	.364
7.	Stanford	3-5-0	.375	4-7-0	.364
9.	Oregon State	2-6-0	.250	3-8-0	.273
10.	California	2-7-0	.222	4-7-0	.364

Non-conference record: 19-16-2 .541

1986					
1.	Ariz. State	5-1-1	.786	10-1-1	.875
2.	UCLA	5-2-1	.688	8-3-1	.708
2.	Washington	5-2-1	.688	8-3-1	.708
4.	Arizona	5-3-0	.625	9-3-0	.750
4.	Stanford	5-3-0	.625	8-4-0	.667
4.	USC	5-3-0	.625	7-5-0	.583
7.	Oregon	3-5-0	.375	5-6-0	.455
8.	Wash. State	2-6-1	.278	3-7-1	.318
9.	California	2-7-0	.222	2-9-0	.182
10.	Oregon State	1-6-0	.143	3-8-0	.273

Non-conference record: 25-11-0 .694

1987					
1.	USC	7-1-0	.875	8-4-0	.667
1.	UCLA	7-1-0	.875	10-2-0	.833
3.	Washington	4-3-1	.562	7-4-1	.625
4.	Ariz. State	3-3-1	.500	7-4-1	.625
5.	Oregon	4-4-0	.500	6-5-0	.545
5.	Stanford	4-4-0	.500	5-6-0	.455
7.	Arizona	2-3-3	.438	4-4-3	.500
8.	California	2-3-2	.429	6-3-2	.636
9.	Wash. State	1-5-1	.214	3-7-1	.318
10.	Oregon State	0-7-0	.000	2-9-0	.182

Non-conference record: 24-14-0 .632

1988					
1.	USC	8-0-0	1.000	10-2-0	.833
2.	UCLA	6-2-0	.750	10-2-0	.833
3.	Wash. State	5-3-0	.625	9-3-0	.750
3.	Arizona	5-3-0	.625	7-4-0	.636
5.	Ariz. State	3-4-0	.429	6-5-0	.545
6.	Washington	3-5-0	.375	6-5-0	.545
6.	Oregon	3-5-0	.375	6-6-0	.500
8.	Oregon State	2-5-1	.312	4-6-1	.409
9.	Stanford	1-5-2	.250	3-6-2	.364
10.	California	1-5-1	.214	5-5-1	.500

Non-conference record: 29-7-0 .806

1989		Conference		Overall	
1.	USC	6-0-1	.959	9-2-1	.792
2.	Washington	5-3-0	.625	8-4-0	.667
2.	Oregon	5-3-0	.625	8-4-0	.667
2.	Arizona	5-3-0	.625	8-4-0	.667
5.	Ariz. State	3-3-1	.500	6-4-1	.591
6.	Oregon State	3-4-1	.438	4-7-1	.375
7.	Wash. State	3-5-0	.375	6-5-0	.545
7.	Stanford	3-5-0	.375	3-8-0	.273
9.	UCLA	2-5-1	.312	3-7-1	.318
10.	California	2-6-0	.250	4-7-0	.364

Non-conference record: 22-15-0 .595

1990					
1.	Washington	7-1-0	.875	10-2-0	.833
2.	USC	5-2-1	.688	8-4-1	.654
3.	Oregon	4-3-0	.571	8-4-0	.667
4.	California	4-3-1	.562	7-4-1	.625
5.	Arizona	5-4-0	.556	7-5-0	.583
6.	UCLA	4-4-0	.500	5-6-0	.455
6.	Stanford	4-4-0	.500	5-6-0	.455
8.	Ariz. State	2-5-0	.286	4-7-0	.364
9.	Wash. State	2-6-0	.250	3-8-0	.273
10.	Oregon State	1-6-0	.143	1-10-0	.091

Non-conference record: 20-18-0 .526

1991					
1.	Washington	8-0-0	1.000	12-0-0	1.000
2.	California	6-2-0	.750	10-2-0	.833
2.	UCLA	6-2-0	.750	9-3-0	.750
2.	Stanford	6-2-0	.750	8-4-0	.667
5.	Ariz. State	4-4-0	.500	6-5-0	.545
6.	Wash. State	3-5-0	.375	4-7-0	.364
6.	Arizona	3-5-0	.375	4-7-0	.364
8.	USC	2-6-0	.250	3-8-0	.273
9.	Oregon	1-7-0	.125	3-8-0	.273
9.	Oregon State	1-7-0	.125	1-10-0	.091

Non-conference record: 20-14-0 .588

1992					
1.	Washington	6-2-0	.750	9-3-0	.750
1.	Stanford	6-2-0	.750	10-3-0	.769
3.	Wash. State	5-3-0	.625	9-3-0	.750
3.	USC	5-3-0	.625	6-5-1	.542
5.	Arizona	4-3-1	.562	6-5-1	.542
6.	Ariz. State	4-4-0	.500	6-5-0	.545
6.	Oregon	4-4-0	.500	6-6-0	.500
8.	UCLA	3-5-0	.375	6-5-0	.545
9.	California	2-6-0	.250	4-7-0	.364
10.	Oregon State	0-7-1	.063	1-9-1	.136

Non-conference record: 24-12-1 .662

1993					
1.	UCLA	6-2-0	.750	8-4-0	.667
1.	Arizona	6-2-0	.750	10-2-0	.833
1.	USC	6-2-0	.750	8-5-0	.615
4.	Washington	5-3-0	.675	7-4-0	.636
5.	California	4-4-0	.500	9-4-0	.692
5.	Ariz. State	4-4-0	.500	6-5-0	.545
7.	Wash. State	3-5-0	.375	5-6-0	.455
8.	Oregon	2-6-0	.250	5-6-0	.455
8.	Stanford	2-6-0	.250	4-7-0	.364
8.	Oregon State	2-6-0	.250	4-7-0	.364

Non-conference record: 26-10-0 .722

1994

		Conference		Overall	
1.	Oregon	7-1-0	.875	9-4-0	.692
2.	USC	6-2-0	.750	8-3-1	.708
2.	Arizona	6-2-0	.750	8-4-0	.667
4.	Wash. State	5-3-0	.625	8-4-0	.667
5.	Washington	4-4-0	.500	7-4-0	.636
6.	UCLA	3-5-0	.375	5-6-0	.455
6.	California	3-5-0	.375	4-7-0	.364
8.	Oregon State	2-6-0	.250	4-7-0	.364
8.	Stanford	2-6-0	.250	3-7-1	.318
8.	Ariz. State	2-6-0	.250	3-8-0	.273

Non-conference record: 19-14-2 .571

1995

		Conference		Overall	
1.	USC	6-1-1	.812	9-2-1	.792
1.	Washington	6-1-1	.812	7-4-1	.625
3.	Oregon	6-2-0	.750	9-3-0	.750
4.	Stanford	5-3-0	.625	7-4-1	.625
5.	UCLA	4-4-0	.500	7-5-0	.583
5.	Arizona	4-4-0	.500	6-5-0	.545
5.	Ariz. State	4-4-0	.500	6-5-0	.545
8.	California	2-6-0	.250	3-8-0	.273
8.	Wash. State	2-6-0	.250	3-8-0	.273
10.	Oregon State	0-8-0	.000	1-10-0	.091

Non-conference record: 19-15-1 .557

1996

		Conference		Overall	
1.	Ariz. State	8-0-0	1.000	11-1-0	.917
2.	Washington	7-1-0	.875	9-3-0	.750
3.	Stanford	5-3-0	.625	7-5-0	.583
4.	UCLA	4-4-0	.500	5-6-0	.455
5.	Oregon	3-5-0	.375	6-5-0	.545
5.	California	3-5-0	.375	6-6-0	.500
5.	USC	3-5-0	.375	6-6-0	.500
5.	Arizona	3-5-0	.375	5-6-0	.455
5.	Wash. State	3-5-0	.375	5-6-0	.455
10.	Oregon State	1-7-0	.125	2-9-0	.182

Non-conference record: 22-13-0 .629

1997

		Conference		Overall	
1.	Wash. State	7-1-0	.875	10-2-0	.833
1.	UCLA	7-1-0	.875	10-2-0	.833
3.	Ariz. State	6-2-0	.750	9-3-0	.750
4.	Washington	5-3-0	.625	8-4-0	.727
5.	Arizona	4-4-0	.500	7-5-0	.583
5.	USC	4-4-0	.500	6-5-0	.545
7.	Oregon	3-5-0	.375	7-5-0	.583
7.	Stanford	3-5-0	.375	5-6-0	.455
9.	California	1-7-0	.125	3-8-0	.273
10.	Oregon State	0-8-0	.000	3-8-0	.273

Non-conference record: 28-8-0 .778

1998

		Conference		Overall	
1.	UCLA	8-0-0	1.000	10-2-0	.833
2.	Arizona	7-1-0	.875	12-1-0	.923
3.	Oregon	5-3-0	.625	8-4-0	.667
3.	USC	5-3-0	.625	8-5-0	.615
5.	Washington	4-4-0	.500	6-6-0	.500
5.	Ariz. State	4-4-0	.500	5-6-0	.455
7.	California	3-5-0	.375	5-6-0	.455
8.	Oregon State	2-6-0	.250	5-6-0	.455
8.	Stanford	2-6-0	.250	3-8-0	.273
10.	Wash. State	0-8-0	.000	3-8-0	.273

Non-conference record: 25-12-0 676

1999

		Conference		Overall	
1.	Stanford	7-1-0	.875	8-4-0	.667
2.	Oregon	6-2-0	.750	9-3-0	.750
2.	Washington	6-2-0	.750	7-5-0	.583
4.	Ariz. State	5-3-0	.625	6-6-0	.500
5.	Oregon State	4-4-0	.500	7-5-0	.583
6.	Arizona	3-5-0	.375	6-6-0	.500
6.	USC	3-5-0	.375	6-6-0	.500
6.	California	3-5-0	.375	4-7-0	.364
9.	UCLA	2-6-0	.250	4-7-0	.364
10.	Wash. State	1-7-0	.125	3-9-0	.250

Non-conference record: 20-18-0 .526

2000

		Conference		Overall	
1.	Washington	7-1-0	.875	11-1-0	.917
1.	Oregon State	7-1-0	.875	11-1-0	.917
1.	Oregon	7-1-0	.875	10-2-0	.833
4.	Stanford	4-4-0	.500	5-6-0	.455
5.	UCLA	3-5-0	.375	6-6-0	.500
5.	Ariz. State	3-5-0	.375	6-6-0	.500
5.	Arizona	3-5-0	.375	5-6-0	.455
8.	USC	2-6-0	.250	5-7-0	.417
8.	Wash. State	2-6-0	.250	4-7-0	.364
8.	California	2-6-0	.250	3-8-0	.273

Non-conference record: 26-10-0 .722

2001

		Conference		Overall	
1.	Oregon	7-1-0	.875	11-1-0	.917
2.	Stanford	6-2-0	.750	9-3-0	.750
2.	Wash. State	6-2-0	.750	10-2-0	.833
2.	Washington	6-2-0	.750	8-4-0	.667
5.	USC	5-3-0	.625	6-6-0	.500
6.	UCLA	4-4-0	.500	7-4-0	.636
7.	Oregon State	3-5-0	.375	5-6-0	.455
8.	Arizona	2-6-0	.250	5-6-0	.455
9.	Ariz. State	1-7-0	.125	4-7-0	.364
10.	California`	0-8-0	.000	1-10-0	.091

Non-conference record: 26-9-0 .743

2002

		Conference		Overall	
1.	Wash. State	7-1-0	.875	10-3-0	.769
1.	USC	7-1-0	.875	11-2-0	.846
3.	Ariz. State	5-3-0	.625	8-6-0	.571
4.	Oregon State	4-4-0	.500	8-5-0	.615
4.	California	4-4-0	.500	7-5-0	.583
4.	UCLA	4-4-0	.500	8-5-0	.615
4.	Washington	4-4-0	.500	7-6-0	.538
8.	Oregon	3-5-0	.375	7-6-0	.538
9.	Arizona	1-7-0	.125	4-8-0	.333
9.	Stanford	1-7-0	.125	2-9-0	.182

Non-conference record: 32-15-0 .681

2003

		Conference		Overall	
1.	USC	7-1-0	.875	12-1-0	.923
2.	Wash. State	6-2-0	.750	10-3-0	.769
3.	Oregon	5-3-0	.625	8-5-0	.615
3.	California	5-3-0	.625	8-6-0	.571
5.	Oregon State	4-4-0	.500	8-5-0	.615
5.	Washington	4-4-0	.500	6-6-0	.500
5.	UCLA	4-4-0	.500	6-7-0	.462
8.	Ariz. State	2-6-0	.250	5-7-0	.417
8	Stanford	2-6-0	.250	4-7-0	.364
10.	Arizona	1-7-0	.125	2-10-0	.167

Non-conference record: 29-17-0 .630

Decade	Wash.	Cal.	Oregon	Ore. St.	Wash. St.	Stanford	USC	Idaho	Montana	UCLA
1916-19	6- 4-2	6- 6-0	7- 4-1	2- 9-1	5- 2-0	1- 2-0				
1920-29	25-22-4	29-11-4	15-24-7	17-27-3	20-26-4	30-10-4	29- 8-2	14-22-3	1-24-1	1- 7-0
1930-39	39-27-8	34-21-4	29-27-4	23-31-10	38-26-6	28-24-6	41-16-8	9-38-1	3-33-2	26-27-7
1940-49	33-30-3	33-28-3	29-29-2	35-24-4	28-29-6	26-21-1	40-16-6	5-36-0	5-22-0	31-30-2
1950-59	31-36-3	30-30-4	27-38-3	32-35-1	29-33-4	29-31-4	37-22-4	3-26-1		47-14-2
1960-69	32-26-2	13-32-1	7-22-1	20-10-1	8-23-2	21-33-2	41- 7-1			28-17-2
1970-79	41-30-0	37-34-1	20-49-0	18-53-0	20-52-0	46-22-2	53-13-3			46-22-2
1980-89	51-24-2	22-55-4	31-44-2	10-63-4	33-40-4	30-47-2	56-17-2			52-20-5
1990-99	58-21-1	31-48-1	41-38-0	13-65-1	31-49-0	42-38-0	45-33-2			47-33-0
2000-03	21-11-0	11-21-0	22-10-0	18-14-0	21-11-0	13-19-0	21-11-0			15-17-0

Decade	Ariz.	Ariz. St.
1970-79	7- 7-0	4-10-0
1980-89	42-30-5	40-27-4
1990-99	45-35-1	43-36-0
2000-03	7-25-0	11-21-0

PAC-10 W-L-T PERCENTAGE (1916-2003)

Washington	337-231-27	.589	Southern California	363-143-28	.706
California	246-286-22	.464	Idaho	31-122-5	.212
Oregon	228-285-18	.451	Montana	9- 79-3	.115
Oregon State	188-331-25	.369	UCLA	293-187-20	.606
Washington State	233-291-26	.447	Arizona	101- 97-6	.510
Stanford	266-247-21	.518	Arizona State	98- 94-4	.510

PAC-10 TITLES BY DECADES (1916-2203)

Decade	Wash.	Cal.	Oregon	Ore. St.	Wash. St.	Stanford	USC	Idaho	Montana	UCLA
1916-19	1.5	1	.5		1					
1920-29	1	4				2.5	2.5			
1930-39	1	1.83	.5		1	1.83	3.5			.33
1940-49		1	1	1		1	4			2
1950-59	.33	2	.5	1.5		1	1.33			3.33
1960-69	2			.5			5.5			2
1970-79	1	.5				2	6			.5
1980-89	2						3.5			3.5
1990-99	3		1		.5	1.5	.83			1.83
2000-01	.33		1.33	.33	.5		1.5			
Totals	12.16	10.33	4.83	3.33	3.0	9.83	28.66			13.5

Decade	Arizona	Ariz. St.
1970-79		
1980-89		1
1990-99	.33	1
2000-01		
Totals	.33	2

SOUTHEASTERN CONFERENCE (1933 –2003). The SEC was formed by thirteen Southern Conference members who left the SC after the 1932 season to form the SEC.

1933

		Conference		Overall	
1.	Alabama	5-0-1	.917	7-1-1	.833
2.	LSU	3-0-2	.800	7-0-3	.850
3.	Georgia	3-1-0	.750	8-2-0	.800
4.	Tennessee	5-2-0	.714	7-3-0	.700
5.	Tulane	4-2-1	.643	6-3-1	.650
6.	Auburn	2-2-0	.500	5-5-0	.500
6.	Ole Miss	2-2-1	.500	6-3-2	.636
6.	Vanderbilt	2-2-2	.500	4-3-3	.550
9.	Florida	2-3-0	.400	5-3-1	.611
9.	Kentucky	2-3-0	.400	5-5-0	.500
11.	Ga. Tech	2-5-0	.286	5-5-0	.500
12	Miss. State	1-5-1	.214	3-6-1	.350
13.	Sewanee	0-6-0	.000	3-6-0	.333

Non-conference record: 38-12-4 .741

1934

		Conference		Overall	
1.	Tulane	8-0-0	1.000	10-1-0	.909
2.	Alabama	7-0-0	1.000	10-0-0	1.000
3.	Tennessee	5-1-0	.833	8-2-0	.800
4.	LSU	4-2-0	.667	7-2-2	.727
5.	Georgia	3-2-0	.600	7-3-0	.700
6.	Vanderbilt	4-3-0	.571	6-3-0	.667
7.	Florida	2-2-1	.500	6-3-1	.650
8.	Ole Miss	2-3-1	.417	4-5-1	.450
9.	Kentucky	1-3-0	.250	5-5-0	.500
10.	Auburn	1-6-0	.143	2-8-0	.200
11.	Sewanee	0-4-0	.000	2-7-0	.222
11.	Miss. State	0-5-0	.000	4-6-0	.400
11.	Ga. Tech	0-6-0	.000	1-9-0	.100

Non-conference record: 35-17-2 .667

1935

1.	LSU	5-0-0	1.000	9-2-0	.818
2.	Vanderbilt	5-1-0	.833	7-3-0	.700
3.	Ole Miss	3-1-0	.750	9-3-0	.750
4.	Auburn	5-2-0	.714	8-2-0	.800
5.	Alabama	4-2-0	.667	6-2-1	.722
6.	Tulane	3-3-0	.500	6-4-0	.600
6.	Kentucky	3-3-0	.500	5-4-0	.556
8.	Ga. Tech	3-4-0	.429	5-5-0	.500
9.	Miss. State	2-3-0	.400	8-3-0	.727
9.	Tennessee	2-3-0	.400	4-5-0	.444
11.	Georgia	2-4-0	.333	6-4-0	.600
12.	Florida	1-6-0	.143	3-7-0	.300
13.	Sewanee	0-6-0	.000	2-7-0	.222

Non-conference record: 40-13-1 .750

1936

1.	LSU	6-0-0	1.000	9-1-1	.864
2.	Alabama	5-0-1	.917	8-0-1	.944
3.	Auburn	4-1-1	.750	7-2-2	.727
4.	Tennessee	3-1-2	.667	6-2-2	.700
5.	Miss. State	3-2-0	.600	7-3-1	.682
6.	Georgia	3-3-0	.500	5-4-1	.550
6.	Ga. Tech	3-3-1	.500	5-5-1	.500
8.	Tulane	2-3-1	.417	6-3-1	.650
9.	Vanderbilt	1-3-1	.300	3-5-1	.389
10.	Kentucky	1-3-0	.250	6-4-0	.600
11.	Florida	1-5-0	.167	4-6-0	.400
12.	Ole Miss	0-3-1	.125	5-5-2	.500
13.	Sewanee	0-5-0	.000	0-6-1	.072

Non-conference record: 39-14-6 .686

1937

		Conference		Overall	
1.	Alabama	6-0-0	1.000	9-1-0	.900
2.	LSU	5-1-0	.833	9-2-0	.818
3.	Auburn	4-1-2	.714	6-2-3	.682
4.	Vanderbilt	4-2-0	.667	7-2-0	.778
5.	Miss. State	3-2-0	.600	5-4-1	.550
6.	Ga. Tech	3-2-1	.583	6-3-1	.650
7.	Tennessee	4-3-0	.571	6-3-1	.650
8.	Florida	3-4-0	.429	4-7-0	.364
9.	Tulane	2-3-1	.417	5-4-1	.550
10.	Georgia	1-2-2	.400	6-3-2	.636
11.	Ole Miss	0-4-0	.000	4-5-1	.450
11.	Kentucky	0-5-0	.000	4-6-0	.400
11.	Sewanee	0-6-0	.000	2.-7-0	.222

Non-conference record: 38-14-4 .714

1938

1.	Tennessee	7-0-0	1.000	11-0-0	1.000
2.	Alabama	4-1-1	.750	7-1-1	.833
2.	Tulane	4-1-1	.750	7-2-1	.750
4.	Ole Miss	3-2-0	.600	9-2-0	.818
5.	Ga. Tech	2-1-3	.583	3-4-3	.450
6.	Vanderbilt	4-3-0	.571	6-3-0	.667
7.	Florida	2-2-1	.500	4-6-1	.409
7.	Auburn	3-3-1	.500	4-5-1	.450
9.	Georgia	1-2-1	.375	5-4-1	.550
10.	LSU	2-4-0	.333	6-4-0	.600
11.	Miss. State	1-4-0	.200	4-6-0	.400
12.	Kentucky	0-4-0	.000	2-7-0	.222
12.	Sewanee	0-6-0	.000	1-8-0	.111

Non-conference record: 36-19-0 .655

1939

1.	Tennessee	6-0-0	1.000	10-1-0	.909
1.	Ga. Tech	6-0-0	1.000	8-2-0	.800
3.	Tulane	5-0-0	1.000	8-1-1	.850
4.	Miss. State	3-2-0	.600	8-2-0	.800
5.	Ole Misss	2-2-0	.500	7-2-0	.778
5.	Kentucky	2-2-1	.500	6-2-1	.722
5.	Auburn	3-3-1	.500	5-5-1	.500
8.	Alabama	2-3-1	.417	5-3-1	.611
9.	Georgia	1-3-0	.250	5-6-0	.455
10.	LSU	1-5-0	.167	4-5-0	.444
11.	Vanderbilt	1-6-0	.143	2-7-1	.250
12.	Florida	0-3-1	.125	5-5-1	.500
13.	Sewanee	0-3-0	.000	3-5-0	.375

Non-conference record: 44-14-2 .750

1940

1.	Tennessee	5-0-0	1.000	10-1-0	.909
2.	Miss. State	4-0-1	.900	10-0-1	.955
3.	Ole Miss	3-1-0	.750	9-2-0	.818
4.	Alabama	4-2-0	.667	7-2-0	.778
5.	Auburn	3-2-1	.583	6-4-1	.591
6.	LSU	3-3-0	.500	6-4-0	.600
7.	Georgia	2-3-1	.417	5-4-1	.550
8.	Florida	2-3-0	.400	5-5-0	.500
8.	Kentucky	1-2-2	.400	5-3-2	.600
10.	Tulane	1-3-0	.250	5-5-0	.500
11.	Vanderbilt	1-5-1	.214	3-6-1	.350
12.	Ga. Tech	1-5-0	.167	3-7-0	.300
13.	Sewanee	0-1-0	.000	3-5-0	.375

Non-conference record: 47-18-0 .723

1941		Conference		Overall	
1.	Miss. State	4-0-1	.900	8-1-1	.850
2.	Tennessee	3-1-0	.750	8-2-0	.800
3.	Alabama	5-2-0	.714	9-2-0	.818
4.	Georgia	3-1-1	.700	9-1-1	.864
5.	Ole Miss	2-1-1	.625	6-2-1	.722
6.	Vanderbilt	3-2-0	.600	8-2-0	.800
7.	LSU	2-2-2	.500	4-4-2	.500
8.	Tulane	2-3-0	.400	5-4-0	.556
9.	Ga. Tech	2-4-0	.333	3-6-0	.333
10.	Florida	1-3-0	.250	4-6-0	.400
11.	Auburn	0-4-1	.100	4-5-1	.450
12.	Kentucky	0-4-0	.000	5-4-0	.556

Sewanee leaves SEC after 1940 season.
Non-conference record: 46-12-0 .793

1942					
1.	Georgia	6-1-0	.857	11-1-0	.917
2.	Ga. Tech	4-1-0	.800	9-2-0	.818
2.	Tennessee	4-1-0	.800	9-1-1	.864
4.	Miss. State	5-2-0	.714	8-2-0	.800
5.	Alabama	4-2-0	.667	8-3-0	.727
6.	LSU	3-2-0	.600	7-3-0	.700
7.	Auburn	3-3-0	.500	6-4-1	.591
8.	Vanderbilt	2-4-0	.333	6-4-0	.600
9.	Florida	1-3-0	.250	3-7-0	.300
10.	Tulane	1-4-0	.200	4-5-0	.444
11	Kentucky	0-5-0	.000	3-6-1	.350
11.	Ole Miss	0-5-0	.000	2-7-0	.222

Non-conference record: 43-12-3 .767

1943					
1.	Ga. Tech	3-0-0	1.000	8-3-0	.727
2.	Tulane	1-1-0	.500	3-3-0	.500
2.	LSU	2-2-0	.500	6-3-0	.667
4.	Georgia	0-3-0	.000	6-4-0	.600
	Vanderbilt	0-0-0	-----	5-0-0	1.000

The other eight SEC members dropped football for
the 1943 season.
Non-conference record: 22-7-0 .759

1944					
1.	Ga. Tech	4-0-0	1.000	8-3-0	.727
2.	Tennessee	5-0-1	.917	7-1-1	.833
3.	Georgia	4-2-0	.667	7-3-0	.700
3.	Alabama	3-1-2	.667	5-2-2	.667
5.	Miss. State	3-2-0	.600	6-2-0	.750
6.	LSU	2-3-1	.417	2-5-1	.312
7.	Ole Miss	2-3-0	.400	2-6-0	.250
8.	Tulane	1-2-0	.333	4-3-0	.571
9.	Kentucky	1-5-0	.167	3-6-0	.333
10.	Florida	0-3-0	.000	4-3-0	.571
10.	Auburn	0-4-0	.000	4-4-0	.500
	Vanderbilt	0-0-0	-----	3-0-1	.875

Non-conference record: 30-13-1 .693

1945					
1.	Alabama	6-0-0	1.000	10-0-0	1.000
2.	Tennessee	3-1-0	.750	8-1-0	.889
3.	LSU	5-2-0	.714	7-2-0	.778
4.	Georgia	4-2-0	.667	9-2-0	.818
5.	Ole Miss	3-3-0	.500	4-5-0	.444
5.	Ga. Tech	2-2-0	.500	4-6-0	.400
7.	Miss. State	2-3-0	.400	6-3-0	.667
7.	Auburn	2-3-0	.400	5-5-0	.500
9.	Vanderbilt	2-4-0	.333	3-6-0	.333
10.	Florida	1-3-1	.300	4-5-1	.450
10.	Tulane	1-3-1	.300	2-6-1	.278
12.	Kentucky	0-5-0	.000	2-8-0	.200

Non-conference record: 33-18-0 .647

1946		Conference		Overall	
1.	Georgia	5-0-0	1.000	11-0-0	1.000
1.	Tennessee	5-0-0	1.000	9-2-0	.818
3.	LSU	5-1-0	.833	9-1-1	.864
4.	Ga. Tech	4-2-0	.667	9-2-0	.818
5.	Miss. State	3-2-0	.600	8-2-0	.800
6.	Alabama	4-3-0	.571	7-4-0	.636
7.	Vanderbilt	3-4-0	.429	5-4-0	.556
8.	Kentucky	2-3-0	.400	7-3-0	.700
9.	Tulane	2-4-0	.333	3-7-0	.300
10.	Auburn	1-5-0	.167	4-6-0	.400
11.	Ole Miss	1-6-0	.143	2-7-0	.222
12.	Florida	0-5-0	.000	0-9-0	.000

Non-conference record: 39-11-1 .775

1947					
1.	Ole Miss	6-1-0	.857	9-2-0	.818
2.	Ga. Tech	4-1-0	.800	10-1-0	.909
3.	Alabama	5-2-0	.714	8-3-0	.727
4.	Miss. State	2-2-0	.500	7-3-0	.700
4.	Georgia	3-3-0	.500	7-4-1	.625
4.	Vanderbilt	3-3-0	.500	6-4-0	.600
7.	Tulane	2-3-2	.429	2-5-2	.333
8.	LSU	2-3-1	.417	5-3-1	.611
9.	Kentucky	2-3-0	.400	8-3-0	.727
9.	Tennessee	2-3-0	.400	5-5-0	.500
11.	Auburn	1-5-0	.167	2-7-0	.222
12.	Florida	0-3-1	.125	4-5-1	.450

Non-conference record: 41-13-1 .755

1948					
1.	Georgia	6-0-0	1.000	9-2-0	.818
2.	Ole Miss	6-1-0	.857	8-1-0	.889
3.	Tulane	5-1-0	.833	9-1-0	.900
4.	Vanderbilt	4-2-1	.643	8-2-1	.773
5.	Ga. Tech	4-3-0	.571	7-3-0	.700
6.	Alabama	4-4-1	.500	6-4-1	.591
6.	Miss. State	3-3-0	.500	4-4-1	.500
8.	Tennessee	2-3-1	.417	4-4-2	.500
9.	Kentucky	1-3-1	.300	5-3-2	.600
10.	Florida	1-5-0	.167	5-5-0	.500
10.	LSU	1-5-0	.167	3-7-0	.300
12.	Auburn	0-7-0	.000	1-8-1	.150

Non-conference record: 33-7-4 .795

1949					
1.	Tulane	5-1-0	.833	7-2-1	.750
2.	Kentucky	4-1-0	.800	9-3-0	.750
3.	Tennessee	4-1-1	.750	7-2-1	.750
4.	Ga. Tech	5-2-0	.714	7-3-0	.700
5.	LSU	4-2-0	.667	8-3-0	.727
6.	Alabama	4-3-1	.562	6-3-1	.650
7.	Vanderbilt	4-4-0	.500	5-5-0	.500
8.	Auburn	2-4-2	.375	2-4-3	.389
9.	Ole Miss	2-4-0	.333	4-5-1	.450
10.	Florida	1-4-1	.250	4-5-1	.450
10.	Georgia	1-4-1	.250	4-6-1	.591
12.	Miss. State	0-6-0	.000	0-8-1	.056

Non-conference record: 27-13-4 .659

1950		Conference		Overall	
1.	Kentucky	5-1-0	.833	11-1-0	.917
2.	Tennessee	4-1-0	.800	11-1-0	.917
3.	Alabama	6-2-0	.750	9-2-0	.818
4.	Tulane	3-1-1	.700	6-2-1	.722
5.	Ga. Tech	4-2-0	.667	5-6-0	.455
6.	Georgia	3-2-1	.583	6-3-3	.625
7.	Miss. State	3-4-0	.429	4-5-0	.444
7.	LSU	2-3-2	.429	4-5-2	.455
7.	Vanderbilt	3-4-0	.429	7-4-0	.636
10.	Florida	2-4-0	.333	5-5-0	.500
11.	Ole Miss	1-5-0	.167	5-5-0	.500
12.	Auburn	0-7-0	.000	0-10-0	.000

Non-conference record: 37-13-0 .740

1951		Conference		Overall	
1.	Ga. Tech	7-0-0	1.000	11-0-1	.958
2.	Tennessee	5-0-0	1.000	10-1-0	.909
3	Ole Miss	4-2-1	.642	6-3-1	.650
3	LSU	4-2-1	.642	7-3-1	.682
5.	Kentucky	3-3-0	.500	8-4-0	.667
6.	Auburn	3-4-0	.429	5-5-0	.500
7.	Vanderbilt	3-5-0	.375	6-5-0	.545
7.	Alabama	3-5-0	.375	5-6-0	.455
9.	Georgia	2-4-0	.333	5-5-0	.500
9.	Florida	2-4-0	.333	5-5-0	.500
11.	Miss. State	2-5-0	.286	4-5-0	.444
12.	Tulane	1-5-0	.167	4-6-0	.400

Non-conference record: 37-9-1 .798

1952		Conference		Overall	
1.	Ga. Tech	6-0-0	1.000	12-0-0	1.000
2.	Tennessee	5-0-1	.917	8-2-1	.773
3.	Ole Miss	4-0-2	.833	8-1-2	.818
4.	Alabama	4-2-0	.667	10-2-0	.833
5.	Georgia	4-3-0	.571	7-4-0	.636
6.	Florida	3-3-0	.500	8-3-0	.727
7.	Miss. State	3-4-0	.429	5-4-0	.556
8.	Tulane	3-5-0	.375	5-5-0	.500
9.	Kentucky	1-3-2	.333	5-4-2	.545
10.	LSU	2-5-0	.286	3-7-0	.300
11.	Vanderbilt	1-4-1	.250	3-5-2	.400
12.	Auburn	0-7-0	.000	2-8-0	.200

Non-conference record: 40-9-1 .810

1953					
1.	Alabama	4-0-3	.786	6-3-3	.625
2.	Ga. Tech	4-1-1	.750	9-2-1	.792
2.	Ole Miss	4-1-1	.750	7-2-1	.750
2.	Kentucky	4-1-1	.750	7-2-1	.750
5.	Auburn	4-2-1	.643	7-3-1	.682
5.	Miss. State	3-1-3	.643	5-2-3	.650
7.	Tennessee	3-2-1	.583	6-4-1	.591
8.	LSU	2-3-3	.438	5-3-3	.591
9.	Florida	1-3-2	.250	3-5-2	.400
10.	Vanderbilt	1-5-0	.167	3-7-0	.300
10.	Georgia	1-5-0	.167	3-8-0	.273
12.	Tulane	0-7-0	.000	1-8-1	.150

Non-conference record: 31-18-1 .630

1954		Conference		Overall	
1.	Ole Miss	5-1-0	.833	9-2-0	.818
2.	Ga. Tech	6-2-0	.750	8-3-0	.727
3.	Florida	5-2-0	.714	5-5-0	.500
3.	Kentucky	5-2-0	.714	7-3-0	.700
5.	Georgia	5-3-0	.625	6-3-1	.650
5.	Auburn	3-3-0	.500	8-3-0	.727
5.	Miss. State	3-3-0	.500	6-4-0	.600
5.	Alabama	3-3-2	.500	4-5-2	.455
9.	LSU	2-5-0	.286	5-6-0	.455
10.	Tulane	1-6-1	.188	1-6-3	.250
11.	Vanderbilt	1-5-0	.167	2-7-0	.222
11.	Tennessee	1-5-0	.167	4-6-0	.400

Non-conference record: 26-13-3 .655

1955		Conference		Overall	
1.	Ole Miss	5-1-0	.833	10-1-0	.909
2.	Auburn	5-1-1	.786	8-2-1	.773
3.	Ga. Tech	4-1-1	.750	9-1-1	.864
4.	Tennessee	3-2-1	.583	6-3-1	.650
5.	Vanderbilt	4-3-0	.571	8-3-0	.727
6.	Miss. State	4-4-0	.500	6-4-0	.600
6.	Kentucky	3-3-1	.500	6-3-1	.650
6.	Tulane	3-3-1	.500	5-4-1	.550
9.	LSU	2-3-1	.417	3-5-2	.400
10.	Florida	3-5-0	.375	4-6-0	.400
11.	Georgia	2-5-0	.286	4-6-0	.400
12.	Alabama	0-7-0	.000	0-10-0	.000

Non-conference record: 31-10-1 .750

1956		Conference		Overall	
1.	Tennessee	6-0-0	1.000	10-1-0	.909
2.	Ga. Tech	7-1-0	.875	10-1-0	.909
3.	Florida	5-2-0	.714	6-3-1	.650
4.	Ole Miss	4-2-0	.667	7-3-0	.700
5.	Auburn	4-3-0	.571	7-3-0	.700
6.	Kentucky	4-4-0	.500	6-4-0	.600
6.	Tulane	3-3-0	.500	6-4-0	.600
8.	Vanderbilt	2-5-0	.286	5-5-0	.500
8.	Alabama	2-5-0	.286	2-7-1	.250
8.	Miss. State	2-5-0	.286	4-6-0	.400
11.	LSU	1-5-0	.167	3-7-0	.300
12.	Georgia	1-6-0	.143	3-6-1	.350

Non-conference record: 28-8-3 .756

1957					
1.	Auburn	7-0-0	1.000	10-0-0	1.000
2.	Ole Miss	5-0-1	.917	9-1-1	.864
3.	Florida	4-2-1	.642	6-2-1	.722
3.	Miss. State	4-2-1	.642	6-2-1	.722
5.	Tennessee	4-3-0	.571	8-3-0	.727
6	Vanderbilt	3-3-1	.500	5-3-2	.600
6.	LSU	4-4-0	.500	5-5-0	.500
8.	Ga. Tech	3-4-1	.438	4-4-2	.500
9.	Georgia	3-4-0	.429	3-7-0	.300
10.	Tulane	1-5-0	.167	2-8-0	.200
11.	Alabama	1-6-1	.188	2-7-1	.250
12.	Kentucky	1-7-0	.125	3-7-0	.300

Non-conference record: 23-9-2 .706

1958		Conference		Overall	
1.	LSU	6-0-0	1.000	11-0-0	1.000
2.	Auburn	6-0-1	.929	9-0-1	.950
3.	Ole Miss	4-2-0	.667	9-2-0	.818
4.	Vanderbilt	2-1-3	.583	5-2-3	.650
5.	Tennessee	4-3-0	.571	4-6-0	.400
6.	Alabama	3-4-1	.438	5-4-1	.550
6.	Kentucky	3-4-1	.438	5-4-1	.550
8.	Florida	2-3-1	.417	6-4-1	.591
8.	Ga. Tech	2-3-1	.417	5-4-1	.550
10.	Georgia	2-4-0	.333	4-6-0	.400
11.	Tulane	1-5-0	.167	3-7-0	.300
12.	Miss. State	1-6-0	.143	3-6-0	.333

Non-conference record: 33-10-0 .767

1959					
1.	Georgia	7-0-0	1.000	10-1-0	.909
2.	LSU	5-1-0	.833	9-2-0	.818
2.	Ole Miss	5-1-0	.833	10-1-0	.909
4.	Alabama	4-1-2	.714	7-2-2	.727
5.	Auburn	4-3-0	.571	7-3-0	.700
5.	Vanderbilt	3-2-2	.571	5-3-2	.600
7.	Ga. Tech	3-3-0	.500	6-5-0	.545
8.	Tennessee	3-4-1	.438	5-4-1	.550
9.	Florida	2-4-0	.333	5-4-1	.550
10.	Kentucky	1-6-0	.143	4-6-0	.400
11.	Tulane	0-5-1	.083	3-6-1	.350
12.	Miss. State	0-7-0	.000	2-7-0	.222

Non-conference record: 36-7-1 .830

1960					
1.	Ole Miss	5-0-1	.917	10-0-1	.955
2.	Florida	5-1-0	.833	9-2-0	.818
3.	Alabama	5-1-1	.786	8-1-2	.818
4.	Auburn	5-2-0	.714	8-2-0	.800
5.	Tennessee	3-2-2	.571	6-2-2	.700
5.	Georgia	4-3-0	.571	6-4-0	.600
7.	Ga. Tech	4-4-0	.500	5-5-0	.500
8.	LSU	2-3-1	.417	5-4-1	.550
9.	Kentucky	2-4-1	.357	5-4-1	.550
10.	Tulane	1-4-1	.250	2-6-1	.278
11.	Miss. State	0-5-1	.083	2-6-1	.278
12.	Vanderbilt	0-7-0	.000	3-7-0	.300

Non-conference record: 33-7-1 .817

1961					
1.	Alabama	7-0-0	1.000	11-0-0	1.000
2.	LSU	6-0-0	1.000	10-1-0	.900
3.	Ole Miss	5-1-0	.833	9-2-0	.900
4.	Tennessee	4-3-0	.571	6-4-0	.600
4.	Ga. Tech	4-3-0	.571	7-4-0	.700
6.	Florida	3-3-0	.500	4-5-1	.450
7.	Auburn	3-4-0	.429	6-4-0	.600
8.	Kentucky	2-4-0	.333	5-5-0	.500
9.	Georgia	2-5-0	.286	3-7-0	.300
10.	Miss. State	1-5-0	.167	5-5-0	.500
10.	Tulane	1-5-0	.167	2-8-0	.200
12.	Vanderbilt	1-6-0	.143	2-8-0	.200

Non-conference record: 31-14-1 .685

1962		Conference		Overall	
1.	Ole Miss	6-0-0	1.000	10-0-0	1.000
2.	Alabama	6-1-0	.857	10-1-0	.909
3.	LSU	5-1-0	.833	9-1-1	.850
4.	Ga. Tech	5-2-0	.714	7-3-1	.750
5.	Florida	4-2-0	.667	7-4-0	.600
6.	Auburn	4-3-0	.571	6-3-1	.650
7.	Georgia	2-3-1	.417	3-4-3	.450
7.	Kentucky	2-3-1	.417	3-5-2	.400
9.	Miss. State	2-5-0	.286	3-6-0	.333
10.	Tennessee	2-6-0	.250	4-6-0	.400
11.	Vanderbilt	1-6-0	.143	1-9-0	.100
12.	Tulane	0-7-0	.000	0-10-0	.000

Non-conference record: 24-13-6 .628

1963					
1.	Ole Miss	5-0-1	.917	7-1-2	.889
2.	Auburn	6-1-0	.857	9-2-0	.818
3.	Alabama	6-2-0	.750	9-2-0	.818
	Miss. State	4-1-2	.714	7-2-2	.700
5.	LSU	4-2-0	.667	7-4-0	.700
6.	Ga. Tech	4-3-0	.571	7-3-0	.700
7.	Florida	3-3-1	.500	6-3-1	.650
8.	Tennessee	3-5-0	.375	5-5-0	.500
9.	Georgia	2-4-0	.333	4-5-1	.450
10.	Vanderbilt	0-5-2	.143	1-7-2	.200
11.	Kentucky	0-5-1	.083	3-6-1	.350
12.	Tulane	0-6-1	.072	1-8-1	.150

Non-conference record: 29-11-2 .714

1964					
1.	Alabama	8-0-0	1.000	10-1-0	.909
2.	Georgia	4-2-0	.667	7-3-1	.650
2.	Florida	4-2-0	.667	7-3-0	.700
2.	Kentucky	4-2-0	.667	5-5-0	.500
5.	LSU	4-2-1	.643	8-2-1	.750
6.	Auburn	3-3-0	.500	6-4-0	.600
7.	Ole Miss	2-4-1	.357	5-5-1	.550
8.	Miss. State	2-5-0	.286	4-6-0	.400
9.	Vanderbilt	1-4-1	.250	3-6-1	.350
10.	Tennessee	1-5-1	.214	4-5-1	.450
11.	Tulane	1-5-0	.167	3-7-0	.300

Ga. Tech leaves the SEC after the 1963 season.
Non-conference record: 28-13-1 .679

1965					
1.	Alabama	6-1-1	.812	9-1-1	.864
2.	Auburn	4-1-1	.750	5-5-1	.500
3.	Florida	4-2-0	.667	7-4-0	.636
3.	Tennessee	3-1-2	.667	8-1-2	.818
5.	Ole Miss	5-3-0	.625	7-4-0	.636
6.	LSU	3-3-0	.500	8-3-0	.727
6.	Kentucky	3-3-0	.500	6-4-0	.600
6.	Georgia	3-3-0	.500	6-4-0	.600
9.	Vanderbilt	1-5-0	.167	2-7-1	.250
9.	Tulane	1-5-0	.167	2-8-0	.200
9.	Miss. State	1-5-0	.167	4-6-0	.400

Non-conference record: 30-16-1 .649

1966		Conference		Overall	
1.	Alabama	6-0-0	1.000	11-0-0	1.000
1.	Georgia	6-0-0	1.000	10-1-0	.909
3.	Florida	5-1-0	.833	9-2-0	.818
4.	Ole Miss	5-2-0	.714	8-3-0	.727
5.	Tennessee	4-2-0	.667	8-3-0	.727
6.	LSU	3-3-0	.500	5-4-1	.550
7.	Kentucky	2-4-0	.333	3-6-1	.350
8.	Auburn	1-5-0	.167	4-6-0	.400
9.	Miss. State	0-6-0	.000	2-8-0	.200
9.	Vanderbilt	0-6-0	.000	1-9-0	.100

Tulane leaves SEC after the 1965 season.
Non-conference record: 29-13-2 .681

1967					
1.	Tennessee	6-0-0	1.000	9-2-0	.818
2.	Alabama	5-1-0	.833	8-2-1	.773
3.	Florida	4-2-0	.667	6-4-0	.600
3.	Georgia	4-2-0	.667	7-4-0	.636
5.	Ole Miss	4-2-1	.643	6-4-1	.591
6.	LSU	3-2-1	.583	7-3-1	.682
7.	Auburn	3-3-0	.500	6-4-0	.600
8.	Kentucky	1-6-0	.143	2-8-0	.200
9.	Vanderbilt	0-6-0	.000	2-7-1	.350
9.	Miss. State	0-6-0	.000	1-9-0	.100

Non-conference record: 24-17-2 .581

1968					
1.	Georgia	5-0-1	.917	8-1-2	.818
2.	Tennessee	4-1-1	.750	8-2-1	.773
3.	Alabama	4-2-0	.667	8-3-0	.727
3.	LSU	4-2-0	.667	8-3-0	.727
3.	Auburn	4-2-0	.667	7-4-0	.636
6.	Florida	3-2-1	.583	6-3-1	.650
6.	Ole Miss	3-2-1	.583	7-3-1	.682
8.	Vanderbilt	2-3-1	.417	5-4-1	.550
9.	Miss. State	0-4-2	.167	0-8-2	.100
10.	Kentucky	0-7-0	.000	3-7-0	.300

Non-conference record: 31-13-1 .700

1969					
1.	Tennessee	5-1-0	.833	9-2-0	.818
2.	LSU	4-1-0	.800	9-1-0	.900
3.	Auburn	5-2-0	.714	8-3-0	.727
4.	Florida	3-1-1	.700	9-1-1	.864
5.	Ole Miss	4-2-0	.667	8-3-0	.727
6.	Georgia	2-3-1	.417	5-5-1	.500
7.	Vanderbilt	2-3-0	.400	4-6-0	.400
8.	Alabama	2-4-0	.333	6-5-0	.545
9.	Kentucky	1-6-0	.143	2-8-0	.200
10.	Miss. State	0-5-0	.000	3-7-0	.300

Non-conference record: 35-13-0 .729

1970					
1.	LSU	5-0-0	1.000	9-3-0	.818
2.	Tennessee	4-1-0	.800	11-1-0	.909
3.	Auburn	5-2-0	.714	9-2-0	.818
4.	Ole Miss	4-2-0	.667	7-4-0	.700
5.	Florida	3-3-0	.500	7-4-0	.636
5.	Georgia	3-3-0	.500	5-5-0	.500
7.	Alabama	3-4-0	.429	6-5-1	.542
7.	Miss. State	3-4-0	.429	6-5-0	.545
9.	Vanderbilt	1-5-0	.167	4-7-0	.364
10.	Kentucky	0-7-0	.000	2-9-0	.182

Non-conference record: 35-14-1 .710

1971		Conference		Overall	
1.	Alabama	7-0-0	1.000	11-1-0	.917
2.	Auburn	5-1-0	.833	9-2-0	.818
2.	Georgia	5-1-0	.833	11-1-0	.917
4.	Ole Miss	4-2-0	.667	10-2-0	.833
4.	Tennessee	4-2-0	.667	10-2-0	.833
6.	LSU	3-2-0	.600	9-3-0	.750
7.	Vanderbilt	1-5-0	.167	4-6-1	.450
8.	Florida	1-6-0	.143	4-7-0	.364
8.	Kentucky	1-6-0	.143	3-8-0	.273
10.	Miss. State	1-7-0	.125	2-9-0	.182

Non-conference record: 41-9-1 .813

1972					
1.	Alabama	7-1-0	.875	10-2-0	.833
2.	Auburn	6-1-0	.857	10-1-0	.909
3.	LSU	4-1-1	.750	9-2-1	.792
4.	Tennessee	4-2-0	.667	10-2-0	.833
5.	Georgia	4-3-0	.571	7-4-0	.636
6.	Florida	3-3-1	.500	5-5-1	.500
7.	Ole Miss	2-5-0	.286	5-5-0	.500
7.	Kentucky	2-5-0	.286	3-8-0	.273
9.	Miss. State	1-6-0	.143	4-7-0	.364
10.	Vanderbilt	0-6-0	.000	3-8-0	.273

Non-conference record: 33-11-0 .750

1973					
1.	Alabama	8-0-0	1.000	11-1-0	.917
2.	LSU	5-1-0	.833	9-3-0	.750
3.	Ole Miss	4-3-0	.571	6-5-0	.545
4.	Tennessee	3-3-0	.500	8-4-0	.667
5.	Florida	3-4-0	.429	7-5-0	.583
5.	Kentucky	3-4-0	.429	5-6-0	.455
5.	Georgia	3-4-0	.429	7-4-1	.625
8.	Auburn	2-5-0	.286	6-6-0	.500
8.	Miss. State	2-5-0	.286	4-5-2	.455
10.	Vanderbilt	1-5-0	.167	5-6-0	.455

Non-conference record: 34-11-3 .740

1974					
1.	Alabama	6-0-0	1.000	11-1-0	.917
2.	Auburn	4-2-0	.667	10-2-0	.833
2.	Georgia	4-2-0	.667	6-6-0	.500
4.	Kentucky	3-3-0	.500	6-5-0	.545
4.	Florida	3-3-0	.500	8-4-0	.667
4.	Miss. State	3-3-0	.500	9-3-0	.750
7.	Vanderbilt	2-3-1	.417	7-3-2	.667
7.	Tennessee	2-3-1	.417	7-3-2	.667
9.	LSU	2-4-0	.333	5-5-1	.500
10.	Ole Miss	0-6-0	.000	3-8-0	.273

Non-conference record: 43-11-3 .781

1975					
1.	Alabama	6-0-0	1.000	11-1-0	.917
2.	Ole Miss	5-1-0	.833	6-5-0	.545
2.	Georgia	5-1-0	.833	9-3-0	.750
2.	Florida	5-1-0	.833	9-3-0	.750
5.	Tennessee	3-3-0	.500	7-5-0	.583
6.	Vanderbilt	2-4-0	.333	7-4-0	.636
6.	LSU	2-4-0	.333	5-6-0	.455
6.	Auburn	2-4-0	.333	4-6-1	.419
9.	Kentucky	0-6-0	.000	2-8-1	.227
9.	Miss. State	0-6-0	.000	2-9-0	.182

Non-conference record: 32-20-2 .611

1976		Conference		Overall	
1.	Georgia	5-1-0	.833	10-2-0	.833
1.	Kentucky	5-1-0	.833	9-3-0	.750
3.	Alabama	5-2-0	.714	9-3-0	.750
4.	Florida	4-2-0	.667	8-4-0	.667
5.	Ole Miss	4-3-0	.571	6-5-0	.545
6.	LSU	3-3-0	.500	7-3-1	.682
6.	Auburn	3-3-0	.500	4-7-0	.364
8.	Tennessee	2-4-0	.333	6-5-0	.545
9.	Vanderbilt	0-6-0	.000	2-9-0	.182
9.	Miss. State	0-6-0	.000	0-11-0	.000

Non-conference record: 30-21-1 .587

1977					
1.	Alabama	7-0-0	1.000	11-1-0	.917
2.	Kentucky	6-0-0	1.000	10-1-0	.909
3.	Auburn	5-1-0	.833	6-5-0	.545
4.	LSU	4-2-0	.667	8-4-0	.667
5.	Florida	3-3-0	.500	6-4-1	.591
6.	Ole Miss	3-4-0	.429	6-5-0	.545
7.	Georgia	2-4-0	.333	5-6-0	.455
8.	Tennessee	1-5-0	.167	4-7-0	.364
9.	Vanderbilt	0-6-0	.000	2-9-0	.182
9.	Miss. State	0-6-0	.000	0-11-0	.000

Non-conference record: 27-22-1 .550

1978					
1.	Alabama	6-0-0	1.000	11-1-0	.917
2.	Georgia	5-0-1	.917	9-2-1	.792
3	Auburn	3-2-1	.583	6-4-1	.591
4.	LSU	3-3-0	.500	8-4-0	.667
4.	Tennessee	3-3-0	.500	5-5-1	.500
4.	Florida	3-3-0	.500	4-7-0	.364
7.	Kentucky	2-4-0	.333	4-6-1	.409
7.	Ole Miss	2-4-0	.333	5-6-0	.455
7.	Miss. State	2-4-0	.333	6-5-0	.545
10.	Vanderbilt	0-6-0	.000	2-9-0	.182

Non-conference record: 30-21-2 .585

1979					
1.	Alabama	6-0-0	1.000	12-0-0	1.000
2.	Georgia	5-1-0	.833	6-5-0	.545
3.	Auburn	4-2-0	.667	8-3-0	.727
3.	LSU	4-2-0	.667	7-5-0	.583
4.	Tennessee	3-3-0	.500	7-5-0	.583
4.	Kentucky	3-3-0	.500	5-6-0	.455
4.	Ole Miss	3-3-0	.500	4-7-0	.364
8.	Miss. State	2-4-0	.333	3-8-0	.273
9.	Vanderbilt	0-6-0	.000	1-10-0	.091
9.	Florida	0-6-0	.000	0-10-1	.046

Non-conference record: 23-29-1 .443

1980					
1.	Georgia	6-0-0	1.000	12-0-0	1.000
2.	Miss. State	5-1-0	.833	9-3-0	.818
2.	Alabama	5-1-0	.833	10-2-0	.833
4.	LSU	4-2-0	.667	7-4-0	.636
4.	Florida	4-2-0	.667	8-4-0	.667
6.	Tennessee	3-3-0	.500	5-6-0	.455
7.	Ole Miss	2-4-0	.333	3-8-0	.273
8.	Kentucky	1-5-0	.167	3-8-0	.273
9.	Auburn	0-6-0	.000	5-6-0	.455
9.	Vanderbilt	0-6-0	.000	2-9-0	.182

Non-conference record: 34-20-0 .630

1981		Conference		Overall	
1.	Georgia	6-0-0	1.000	10-2-0	.833
1.	Alabama	6-0-0	1.000	9-2-1	.767
3.	Miss. State	4-2-0	.667	8-4-0	.667
4.	Florida	3-3-0	.500	7-5-0	.583
4.	Tennessee	3-3-0	.500	8-4-0	.667
6.	Auburn	2-4-0	.333	5-6-0	.455
6.	Kentucky	2-4-0	.333	3-8-0	.273
8.	Ole Miss	1-4-1	.250	4-6-1	.409
8.	LSU	1-4-1	.250	3-7-1	.318
10.	Vanderbilt	1-5-0	.167	4-7-0	.364

Non-conference record: 32-22-1 .591

1982					
1.	Georgia	6-0-0	1.000	11-1-0	.917
2.	LSU	4-1-1	.750	8-3-1	.708
3.	Auburn	4-2-0	.667	9-3-0	.750
3.	Vanderbilt	4-2-0	.667	8-4-0	.667
5.	Tennessee	3-2-1	.583	6-5-1	.542
6.	Florida	3-3-0	.500	8-4-0	.667
6.	Alabama	3-3-0	.500	8-4-0	.667
8.	Miss. State	2-4-0	.333	5-6-0	.455
9.	Ole Miss	0-6-0	.000	4-7-0	.364
9.	Kentucky	0-6-0	.000	0-10-1	.046

Non-conference record: 38-18-1 .675

1983					
1.	Auburn	6-0-0	1.000	11-1-0	.917
2.	Georgia	5-1-0	.833	10-1-1	.875
3.	Florida	4-2-0	.667	9-2-1	.792
3.	Tennessee	4-2-0	.667	9-3-0	.750
3.	Alabama	4-2-0	.667	8-4-0	.667
3.	Ole Miss	4-2-0	.667	7-5-0	.583
7.	Kentucky	2-4-0	.333	6-5-1	.542
8	Miss. State	1-5-0	.167	3-8-0	.273
9.	LSU	0-6-0	.000	4-7-0	.364
9.	Vanderbilt	0-6-0	.000	2-9-0	.182

Non-conference record: 39-15-2 .714

1984					
1.	Florida*	5-0-1	.917	9-1-1	.864
2.	LSU	4-1-1	.750	8-3-1	.708
3.	Auburn	4-2-0	.667	9-4-0	.692
3.	Georgia	4-2-0	.667	7-4-1	.625
5.	Kentucky	3-3-0	.500	9-3-0	.750
5.	Tennessee	3-3-0	.500	7-4-1	.625
7.	Vanderbilt	2-4-0	.333	5-6-0	.455
7.	Alabama	2-4-0	.333	5-6-0	.455
9.	Miss. State	1-5-0	.167	4-7-0	.364
9.	Ole Miss	1-5-0	.167	4-6-1	.409

*Title vacated

Non-conference record: 38-15-3 .705

1985					
1.	Tennessee	5-1-0	.833	9-1-2	.833
2.	LSU	4-1-1	.750	9-2-1	.792
2.	Alabama	4-1-1	.750	9-2-1	.792
4.	Georgia	3-2-1	.583	7-3-2	.667
5.	Auburn	3-3-0	.500	8-4-0	.667
6.	Ole Miss	2-4-0	.333	4-6-1	.409
7.	Vanderbilt	1-4-1	.250	3-7-1	.318
8.	Kentucky	1-5-0	.167	5-6-0	.455
9.	Miss. State	0-6-0	.000	5-6-0	.455
	Florida *	5-1-0	.833	9-1-1	.864

*Not eligible for conference title.

Non-conference record: 40-10-5 .773

1986		Conference		Overall	
1.	LSU	5-1-0	.833	9-3-0	.750
2.	Auburn	4-2-0	.667	10-2-0	.833
2.	Alabama	4-2-0	.667	10-3-0	.769
2.	Georgia	4-2-0	.667	8-4-0	.667
2.	Ole Miss	4-2-0	.667	8-3-1	.708
6.	Tennessee	3-3-0	.500	7-5-0	.583
7.	Florida	2-4-0	.333	6-5-0	.545
7.	Miss. State	2-4-0	.333	6-5-0	.545
7.	Kentucky	2-4-0	.333	5-5-1	.500
10.	Vanderbilt	0-6-0	.000	1-10-0	.091

Non-conference record: 40-15-2 .719

1987					
1.	Auburn	5-0-1	.917	9-1-2	.833
2.	LSU	5-1-0	.833	10-1-1	.875
3.	Tennessee	4-1-1	.750	10-2-1	.808
4.	Georgia	4-2-0	.667	9-3-0	.750
4.	Alabama	4-2-0	.667	7-5-0	.583
6.	Florida	3-3-0	.500	6-6-0	.500
7.	Kentucky	1-5-0	.167	5-6-0	.455
7.	Vanderbilt	1-5-0	.167	4-7-0	.364
7.	Miss. State	1-5-0	.167	4-7-0	.364
7.	Ole Miss	1-5-0	.167	3-8-0	.273

Non-conference record: 38-17-2 .684

1988					
1.	Auburn	6-1-0	.857	10-2-0	.833
1.	LSU	6-1-0	.857	8-4-0	.667
3.	Georgia	5-2-0	.714	9-3-0	.750
4.	Alabama	4-3-0	.571	9-3-0	.750
4.	Florida	4-3-0	.571	7-5-0	.583
6.	Ole Miss	3-4-0	.429	5-6-0	.455
6.	Tennessee	3-4-0	.429	5-6-0	.455
8.	Kentucky	2-5-0	.286	5-6-0	.455
8.	Vanderbilt	2-5-0	.286	3-8-0	.273
10.	Miss. State	0-7-0	.000	1-10-0	.091

Non-conference record: 27-18-0 .600

1989					
1.	Alabama	6-1-0	.857	10-2-0	.833
1.	Tennessee	6-1-0	.857	11-1-0	.917
1.	Auburn	6-1-0	.857	10-2-0	.833
4.	Florida	4-3-0	.571	7-5-0	.583
4.	Ole Miss	4-3-0	.571	8-4-0	.667
4.	Georgia	4-3-0	.571	6-6-0	.500
7.	Kentucky	2-5-0	.286	6-5-0	.545
7.	LSU	2-5-0	.286	4-7-0	.364
9.	Miss. State	1-6-0	.143	5-6-0	.455
10.	Vanderbilt	0-7-0	.000	1-10-0	.091

Non-conference record: 33-13-0 .717

1990					
1.	Tennessee	5-1-1	.786	9-2-2	.769
2.	Ole Miss	5-2-0	.714	9-3-0	.750
2.	Alabama	5-2-0	.714	7-5-0	.583
4.	Auburn	4-2-1	.643	8-3-1	.708
5.	Kentucky	3-4-0	.429	4-7-0	.364
6.	LSU	2-5-0	.286	5-6-0	.455
6.	Georgia	2-5-0	.286	4-7-0	.364
8.	Miss. State	1-6-0	.143	5-6-0	.455
8.	Vanderbilt	1-6-0	.143	1-10-0	.909
	Florida*	6-1-0	.857	9-2-0	.818

*Not eligible for conference title.
Non-conference record: 27-17-1 .611

1991		Conference		Overall	
1.	Florida	7-0-0	1.000	10-2-0	.833
2.	Alabama	6-1-0	.857	11-1-0	.917
3.	Tennessee	5-2-0	.714	9-3-0	.750
4.	Georgia	4-3-0	.571	9-3-0	.750
4.	Miss. State	4-3-0	.571	7-5-0	.583
6.	LSU	3-4-0	.429	5-6-0	.455
6.	Vanderbilt	3-4-0	.429	5-6-0	.455
8.	Auburn	2-5-0	.286	5-6-0	.455
9.	Ole Miss	1-6-0	.143	5-6-0	.455
10.	Kentucky	0-7-0	.000	3-8-0	.273

Non-conference record: 34-11-0 .756

1992

Eastern Division

1.	Florida	6-2-0	.750	9-4-0	.692
1.	Georgia	6-2-0	.750	10-2-0	.833
3.	Tennessee	5-3-0	.625	9-3-0	.750
4.	S. Carolina	3-5-0	.375	5-6-0	.455
5.	Kentucky	2-6-0	.250	4-7-0	.364
6.	Vanderbilt	2-6-0	.250	4-7-0	.364

Western Division

1.	Alabama	8-0-0	1.000	13-0-0	1.000
2.	Ole Miss	5-3-0	.625	9-3-0	.750
3.	Miss. State	4-4-0	.500	7-5-0	.583
4.	Arkansas	3-4-1	.438	3-6-1	.350
5.	Auburn	2-5-1	.312	5-5-1	.500
6.	LSU	1-7-0	.125	2-9-0	.182

South Carolina and Arkansas join the SEC, which goes to a two-division setup.
Championship game: Alabama 28, Florida 21.
Non-conference record: 32-9-0 .780

1993

Eastern Division

1.	Florida	7-1-0	.875	11-2-0	.846
1.	Tennessee	7-1-0	.875	10-2-0	.833
3.	Kentucky	4-4-0	.500	6-6-0	.500
4.	Georgia	2-6-0	.250	5-6-0	.445
5.	S. Carolina	3-5-0	.375	5-6-0	.445
6.	Vanderbilt	2-6-0	.250	5-6-0	.445

Western Division

Alabama forfeits all games, while Arkansas and Auburn are not eligible for title. After forfeits:

1.	Ole Miss	4-4-0	.500	6-5-0	.545
2.	Miss. State	3-4-1	.438	4-5-2	.455
3.	LSU	3-5-0	.375	5-6-0	.455
	Arkansas	4-3-1	.562	6-4-1	.591
	Alabama	0-8-0	.000	1-12-0	.077
	Auburn	8-0-0	1.000	11-0-0	1.000

Championship game: Florida 28, Alabama 13.
Non-conference record: 27-12-1 .688

1994

Eastern Division

1.	Florida	7-1-0	.875	10-2-1	.808
2.	Tennessee	5-3-0	.625	8-4-0	.667
3.	S. Carolina	4-4-0	.500	7-5-0	.583
4.	Georgia	3-4-1	.438	6-4-1	.591
5.	Vanderbilt	2-6-0	.250	5-6-0	.455
6.	Kentucky	0-8-0	.000	1-10-0	.091

Western Division

1.	Alabama	8-0-0	1.000	12-1-0	.923
2.	Miss. State	5-3-0	.625	8-4-0	.667
3.	LSU	3-5-0	.375	4-7-0	.364
4.	Ole Miss	2-6-0	.250	4-7-0	.364
4.	Arkansas	2-6-0	.250	4-7-0	.364
	Auburn*	6-1-1	.812	9-1-1	.864

*Not eligible for conference title.
Championship game: Florida 24, Alabama 23.
Non-conference record: 30-10-1 .744

1995		Conference		Overall	
Eastern Division					
1.	Florida	8-0-0	1.000	12-1-0	.923
2.	Tennessee	7-1-0	.875	11-1-0	.917
3.	Georgia	3-5-0	.375	6-6-0	.500
4.	S. Carolina	2-5-1	.312	4-6-1	.409
5.	Kentucky	2-6-0	.250	4-7-0	.364
6.	Vanderbilt	1-7-0	.125	2-9-0	.182
Western Division					
1.	Arkansas	6-2-0	.750	8-4-0	.667
2.	Auburn	5-3-0	.625	8-4-0	.667
3.	LSU	4-3-1	.562	7-4-1	.625
4.	Miss. State	1-7-0	.125	3-8-0	.273
Alabama*		5-3-0	.625	8-3-0	.727
Ole Miss*		3-5-0	.375	6-5-0	.545

*Not eligible for conference title.
Championship: Florida 35, Arkansas 24
Non-conference record: 31-10-0 .756

1996					
Eastern Division					
1.	Florida	8-0-0	1.000	12-1-0	.923
2.	Tennessee	7-1-0	.875	10-2-0	.833
3.	S. Carolina	4-4-0	.500	6-5-0	.545
4.	Georgia	3-5-0	.375	5-6-0	.455
4.	Kentucky	3-5-0	.375	4-7-0	.364
6.	Vanderbilt	0-8-0	.000	2-9-0	.182
Western Divison					
1.	Alabama	6-2-0	.750	10-3-0	.769
1.	LSU	6-2-0	.750	10-2-0	.833
3.	Auburn	4-4-0	.500	8-4-0	.667
4.	Miss. State	3-5-0	.375	5-6-0	.455
5.	Arkansas	2-6-0	.250	4-7-0	.364
Ole Miss*		2-6-0	.250	5-6-0	.455

*Not eligible for conference title.
Championship game: Florida 45, Alabama 30.
Non-conference record: 32-9-0 .780

1997					
Eastern Division					
1.	Tennessee	7-1-0	.875	11-2-0	.846
2.	Georgia	6-2-0	.750	10-2-0	.833
2.	Florida	6-2-0	.750	10-2-0	.833
4.	S. Carolina	3-5-0	.375	5-6-0	.455
5.	Kentucky	2-6-0	.250	5-6-0	.455
6.	Vanderbilt	0-8-0	.000	3-8-0	.273
Western Division					
1.	Auburn	6-2-0	.750	10-3-0	.769
1.	LSU	6-2-0	.750	9-3-0	.750
3.	Ole Miss	4-4-0	.500	8-4-0	.667
3.	Miss. State	4-4-0	.500	7-4-0	.636
5.	Arkansas	2-6-0	.250	4-7-0	.364
5.	Alabama	2-6-0	.250	4-7-0	.364

Championship game: Tennessee 30, Auburn 29.
Non-conference record: 35-5-0 .875

1998		Conference		Overall	
Eastern Division					
1.	Tennessee	8-0-0	1.000	13-0-0	1.000
2.	Florida	7-1-0	.875	10-2-0	.833
3.	Georgia	6-2-0	.750	9-3-0	.750
4.	Kentucky	4-4-0	.500	7-5-0	.583
5.	Vanderbilt	1-7-0	.125	2-9-0	.182
6.	S. Carolina	0-8-0	.000	1-10-0	.091
Western Divison					
1.	Miss. State	6-2-0	.750	8-5-0	.615
1.	Arkansas	6-2-0	.750	9-3-0	.750
3.	Alabama	4-4-0	.500	7-5-0	.583
4.	Ole Miss	3-5-0	.375	7-5-0	.583
5.	LSU	2-6-0	.250	4-7-0	.364
6.	Auburn	1-7-0	.125	3-8-0	.273

Championship game: Tennessee 24, Miss. State 14
Non-conference record: 31-13-0 .705

1999					
Eastern Division					
1.	Florida	7-1-0	.875	9-4-0	.692
2.	Tennessee	6-2-0	.750	9-3-0	.750
3.	Georgia	5-3-0	.625	8-4-0	.667
4.	Kentucky	4-4-0	.500	6-6-0	.500
5.	Vanderbilt	2-6-0	.250	5-6-0	.455
6.	S. Carolina	0-8-0	.000	0-11-0	.000
Western Division					
1.	Alabama	7-1-0	.875	10-3-0	.769
2	Miss. State	6-2-0	.750	10-2-0	.833
3.	Ole Miss	4-4-0	.500	8-4-0	.667
3.	Arkansas	4-4-0	.500	8-4-0	.667
5.	Auburn	2-6-0	.250	5-6-0	.455
6.	LSU	1-7-0	.125	3-8-0	.273

Championship game: Alabama 34, Florida 7.
Non-conference record: 32-12-0 .727

2000					
Eastern Division					
1.	Florida	7-1-0	.875	10-3-0	.769
2.	Tennessee	5-3-0	.625	8-4-0	.667
2.	Georgia	5-3-0	.625	8-4-0	.667
2.	S. Carolina	5-3-0	.625	8-4-0	.667
5.	Vanderbilt	1-7-0	.125	3-8-0	.273
6.	Kentucky	0-8-0	.000	2-9-0	.182
Western Division					
1.	Auburn	6-2-0	.750	9-4-0	.692
2.	LSU	5-3-0	.625	8-4-0	.667
3.	Ole Miss	4-4-0	.500	7-5-0	.583
3.	Miss. State	4-4-0	.500	8-4-0	.667
5.	Arkansas	3-5-0	.375	6-6-0	.500
5.	Alabama	3-5-0	.375	3-8-0	.273

Championship game: Florida 28, Auburn 6.
Non-conference record: 31-14-0 .689

2001		Conference		Overall	
Eastern Division					
1.	Tennessee	7-1-0	.875	11-2-0	.846
2.	Florida	6-2-0	.750	10-2-0	.833
3.	S. Carolina	5-3-0	.625	9-3-0	.750
3.	Georgia	5-3-0	.625	8-4-0	.667
5.	Kentucky	1-7-0	.125	2-9-0	.182
6.	Vanderbilt	0-8-0	.000	2-9-0	.182
Western Division					
1.	LSU	5-3-0	.625	10-3-0	.769
1.	Auburn	5-3-0	.625	7-5-0	.583
3.	Alabama	4-4-0	.500	7-5-0	.583
3.	Arkansas	4-4-0	.500	7-5-0	.583
3.	Ole Miss	4-4-0	.500	7-4-0	.636
6	Miss. State	2-6-0	.250	3-8-0	.273

Championship game: LSU 31, Tennessee 20
Non-conference record: 36-10-0 .783

2002		Conference		Overall	
Eastern Division					
1.	Georgia	7-1-0	.889	13-1-0	.929
2.	Florida	6-2-0	.750	8-5-0	.615
3.	Tennessee	5-3-0	.625	8-5-0	.615
4.	Kentucky	3-5-0	.375	7-5-0	.583
4.	South Carolina	3-5-0	.375	5-7-0	.417
6.	Vanderbilt	0-8-0	.000	2-10-0	.167
Western Division					
1.	Alabama*	6-2-0	.750	10-3-0	.769
2.	Auburn*	5-3-0	.625	9-4-0	.692
2.	LSU	5-3-0	.625	8-5-0	.615
2.	Arkansas	5-3-0	.625	9-5-0	.643
5.	Ole Miss	3-5-0	.375	7-6-0	.538
6.	Miss. State	0-8-0	.000	3-9-0	.250

*Alabama and Auburn ineligible for league title.
Championship game: Georgia 30, Arkansas 3
Non-conference record: 39-16-0 .709

2003		Conference		Overall	
Eastern Division					
1.	Georgia	6-2-0	.750	11-3-0	.786
1.	Tennessee	6-2-0	.750	10-3-0	.769
1.	Florida	6-2-0	.750	8-5-0	.615
4.	So. Carolina	2-6-0	.250	5-7-0	.417
5.	Kentucky	1-7-0	.125	4-8-0	333
6.	Vanderbilt	1-7-0	.125	2-10-0	.167
Western Division					
1.	LSU	7-1-0	.875	13-1-0	.929
1.	Ole Miss	7-1-0	.875	10-3-0	.769
3.	Auburn	5-3-0	.625	8-5-0	.615
4.	Arkansas	4-4-0	.500	9-4-0	.692
5.	Alabama	2-6-0	.250	4-9-0	.308
6.	Miss. State	1-7-0	.125	2-10-0	.167

Championship Game: LSU 34, Georgia 13
Non-conference record: 38-20-0 .654

Decade	Alabama	Auburn	Florida	Georgia	Ga. Tech	Kentucky	LSU	Miss.	Miss. St.	Sewanee	Tenn.
1933-39	33- 6-4	22-18-5	11-25-3	14-17-3	19-21-5	9-23-1	26-12-2	12-17-3	13-23-1	0-36-0	32-10-2
1940-49	39-19-4	12-37-4	7-32-3	34-19-3	33-20-0	11-31-3	29-25-2	25-25-1	26-20-2	0- 1-0	33-10-3
1950-59	30-35-9	36-30-3	29-31-4	30-36-1	46-16-4	30-34-5	30-31-7	41-15-5	25-41-4		38-20-4
1960-69	55-12-2	38-26-1	38-19-3	34-25-3	17-12-0	17-44-3	38-19-3	44-16-5	10-47-5		35-26-6
1970-79	61- 7-0	39-23-1	28-34-1	41-20-1		25-39-0	35-22-1	31-33-0	14-51-0		29-29-1
1980-89	42-19-1	40-21-1	37-24-1	47-14-1		16-46-0	35-23-4	22-39-1	17-45-0		37-23-2
1990-99	51-27-0	40-35-3	69- 9-0	40-37-1		24-54-0	31-46-1	33-45-0	37-40-1		62-15-0
2000-03	15-17-0	21-11-0	25- 7-0	24- 9-0		5-27-0	22-10-0	18-14-0	7-25-0		23- 9-0

Decade	Tulane	Vander.	S. Carol.	Arkansas
1933-39	28-12-4	21-20-3		
1940-49	21-25-3	22-28-2		
1950-59	16-45-4	23-37-7		
1960-69	4-32-2	8-51-4		
1970-79		7-52-1		
1980-89		11-50-1		
1990-99		14-64-0	19-44-1	29-33-2
2000-03		2-32-0	15-17-0	16-16-0

SEC W-L-T PERCENTAGES (1933-2003)

Alabama	326-142-20	.689	Mississippi State	149-292-13	.343
Auburn	250-201-18	.552	Sewanee	0- 37- 0	.000
Florida	244-181-15	.572	Tennessee	289-142-18	.661
Georgia	264-177-13	.596	Tulane	69-114-13	.385
Georgia Tech	115- 69- 9	.619	Vanderbilt	107-332-18	.254
Kentucky	137-298-12	.320	South Carolina	34- 61- 1	.359
LSU	246-188-20	.564	Arkansas	45- 49- 2	.474
Ole Miss	226-204-15	.525			

SEC TITLES BY DECADES (1933-2003)

Decade	Alabama	Auburn	Florida	Georgia	Ga. Tech	Kentucky	LSU	Miss.	Miss. St.	Sewanee	Tenn.
1933-39	2				.5		2				1.5
1940-49	1			2.5	2			1	1		1.5
1950-59	1	1		1	2	1	1	2			1
1960-69	3.5			1.5				3			2
1970-79	8			.5		.5	1				
1980-89	.83	2.83		2.5			2.5				1.33
1990-99	2		5								3
2000-02			1	1			2				
Totals	18.33	3.83	6	9	4	1.5	8.5	6	1		10.33

Decade	Tulane	Vander.	S. Carolina	Arkansas
1933-39	1			
1940-49	1			
1950-59				
1960-69				
1970-79				
1980-89				
1990-99				
2000-02				
Totals	2			

SOUTHERN CONFERENCE (1922–2002). This was the first major college conference organized in the South beginning play in 1922. After the 1932 season, thirteen SC members left to form the Southeastern Conference. After the 1953 season, six SC members left to join with Maryland and Virginia in forming the Atlantic Coast Conference. West Virginia and Virginia Tech continued as members through the 1967 season. East Carolina was a member through the 1976 season. In 1981, the Southern Conference was classified as a Division I-AA conference. Data are shown here only through the 1981 season. League standings are based on the rankings given in the 2001 Southern Conference Media Guide.

1922		Conference		Overall	
1.	N. Carolina	5-0-0	1.000	9-1-0	.900
2.	Ga. Tech	4-0-0	1.000	7-2-0	.778
2.	Vanderbilt	3-0-0	1.000	8-0-1	.944
2.	Virginia Tech	3-0-0	1.000	8-1-1	.850
2.	Florida	2-0-0	1.000	7-2-0	.778
6.	Auburn	2-1-0	.667	8-2-0	.800
7.	Tennessee	3-2-0	.600	8-2-0	.800
8.	Alabama	3-2-1	.583	6-3-1	.650
9.	Virginia	1-1-1	.500	4-4-1	.500
10.	Miss. State	2-3-0	.400	3-4-2	.444
11.	Kentucky	1-2-0	.333	6-3-0	.667
11.	Clemson	1-2-0	.333	5-4-0	.556
11.	Wash. & Lee	1-2-0	.333	5-3-1	.611
11.	Maryland	1-2-0	.333	4-5-1	.450
11.	LSU	1-2-0	.333	3-7-0	.300
16.	Georgia	1-3-1	.300	5-4-1	.550
17.	Tulane	1-4-0	.200	4-4-0	.500
18.	S. Carolina	0-2-0	.000	5-4-0	.556
18.	Ole Miss	0-2-0	.000	4-5-1	.450
18.	NC State	0-5-0	.000	4-6-0	.400

Non-conference record: 80-31-7 .702

1923					
1.	Wash. & Lee	4-0-1	.900	6-3-1	.650
2.	Vanderbilt	3-0-1	.875	5-2-1	.688
3.	Florida	1-0-2	.667	6-1-2	.833
4.	Ga. Tech	1-0-4	.600	3-2-4	.556
5.	VMI	5-1-0	.833	9-1-0	.900
6.	Alabama	4-1-1	.750	7-2-1	.750
7.	Virginia Tech	4-2-0	.667	6-3-0	.667
8.	Maryland	2-1-0	.667	7-2-1	.750
9.	Miss. State	2-1-1	.625	5-2-2	.667
10.	Georgia	3-2-0	.600	5-3-1	.611
11.	Tennessee	4-3-0	.571	5-4-1	.550
12.	Tulane	2-2-1	.500	6-3-1	.650
12.	N. Carolina	2-2-1	.500	5-3-1	.611
14.	Clemson	1-1-1	.500	5-2-1	.688
15.	NC State	1-5-0	.167	3-7-0	.300
16.	Auburn	0-1-3	.375	3-3-3	.500
17.	Kentucky	0-2-2	.250	4-3-2	.556
18.	Virginia	0-4-1	.100	3-5-1	.438
19.	LSU	0-3-0	.000	3-5-1	.438
19	Ole Miss	0-4-0	.000	4-6-0	.400
19.	S. Carolina	0-4-0	.000	4-6-0	.400

VMI joins the Southern Conference.
Non-conference record: 63-30-5 .638

1924		Conference		Overall	
1.	Alabama	5-0-0	1.000	8-1-0	.889
2.	Florida	2-0-1	.833	6-2-2	.700
2.	Georgia	5-1-0	.833	7-3-0	.700
4.	Tulane	4-1-0	.800	8-1-0	.889
5.	Wash. & Lee	4-1-1	.750	6-3-1	.650
6.	Miss. State	3-2-0	.600	5-4-0	.556
6.	Sewanee	3-2-0	.600	6-4-0	.600
6	S. Carolina	3-2-0	.600	7-3-0	.700
6.	Virginia	3-2-0	.600	5-4-0	.556
10.	Ga. Tech	3-2-1	.583	5-3-1	.688
11.	Virginia Tech	2-2-3	.500	4-2-3	.688
11.	Vanderbilt	3-3-0	.500	6-3-1	.650
13.	VMI	2-3-1	.417	6-3-1	.650
14.	N. Carolina	2-3-0	.400	4-5-0	.444
14.	Kentucky	2-3-0	.400	4-5-0	.444
16.	Maryland	1-2-1	.375	3-3-3	.500
16.	Auburn	2-4-1	.357	4-4-1	.500
18.	NC State	1-4-1	.250	2-4-2	.375
19.	LSU	0-3-0	.000	5-4-0	.556
19.	Ole Miss	0-3-0	.000	4-5-0	.444
19.	Clemson	0-3-0	.000	2-6-0	.333
19.	Tennessee	0-4-0	.000	3-5-0	.375

Sewanee joins the SC.
Non-conference record: 60-27-5 .679

1925					
1.	Alabama	7-0-0	1.000	10-0-0	1.000
2.	Tulane	5-0-0	1.000	9-0-1	.950
3.	N. Carolina	4-0-1	.900	7-1-1	.833
4.	Wash. & Lee	5-1-0	.833	5-5-0	.500
5.	Virginia	4-1-1	.750	7-1-1	.833
5.	Ga. Tech	4-1-1	.750	6-2-1	.722
7.	Kentucky	4-2-0	.667	6-3-0	.667
8.	Florida	3-2-0	.600	8-2-0	.800
9.	Auburn	3-2-1	.583	5-3-1	.611
10.	Virginia Tech	3-3-1	.500	5-3-2	.600
10.	Vanderbilt	3-3-0	.500	6-3-0	.667
10.	Tennessee	2-2-1	.500	5-2-1	.688
10.	S. Carolina	2-2-0	.500	7-3-0	.700
14.	Georgia	2-4-0	.333	4-5-0	.444
15.	Sewanee	1-4-0	.200	4-4-1	.500
15.	Miss. State	1-4-0	.200	3-4-1	.438
17.	VMI	2-4-0	.333	6-4-0	.600
18.	LSU	0-2-1	.167	5-3-1	.611
19.	NC State	0-4-1	.100	3-5-1	.389
20.	Ole Miss	0-4-0	.000	5-5-0	.500
20.	Clemson	0-4-0	.000	1-7-0	.125
20.	Maryland	0-4-0	.000	2-5-1	.312

Non-conference record: 64-17-5 .773

1926		Conference		Overall	
1.	Alabama	8-0-0	1.000	9-0-1	.950
2.	Tennessee	5-1-0	.833	8-1-0	.889
3.	Vanderbilt	4-1-0	.800	8-1-0	.889
4.	Georgia	4-2-0	.667	5-4-0	.556
4.	S. Carolina	4-2-0	.667	6-4-0	.600
6.	Virginia	4-2-1	.643	6-2-2	.700
7.	Virginia Tech	3-2-1	.583	5-3-1	.611
7.	Wash. & Lee	3-2-1	.583	4-3-2	.556
9.	Ga. Tech	4-3-0	.571	4-5-0	.444
10.	N. Carolina	3-3-0	.500	4-5-0	.444
10.	Auburn	3-3-0	.500	5-4-0	.556
10.	LSU	3-3-0	.500	6-3-0	.667
10.	Ole Miss	2-2-0	.500	5-4-0	.556
14.	Miss. State	2-3-0	.400	5-4-0	.556
15.	VMI	2-4-0	.333	5-5-0	.500
15.	Tulane	2-4-0	.333	3-5-1	.389
17.	Maryland	1-3-1	.300	5-4-1	.550
18.	Florida	1-4-1	.250	2-6-2	.300
18.	Kentucky	1-4-1	.250	2-6-1	.278
20.	Clemson	0-3-0	.000	2-7-0	.222
20.	NC State	0-4-0	.000	4-6-0	.400
20.	Sewanee	0-5-0	.000	2-6-0	.250

Non-conference record: 46-28-5 .614

1927		Conference		Overall	
1.	Ga. Tech	7-0-1	.938	8-1-1	.850
2.	Tennessee	5-0-1	.917	8-0-1	.944
3.	Vanderbilt	5-0-2	.857	8-1-2	.818
4.	NC State	4-0-0	1.000	9-1-0	.900
5.	Georgia	6-1-0	.857	9-1-0	.900
6.	Florida	5-2-0	.714	7-3-0	.700
7.	Ole Miss	3-2-0	.600	5-3-1	.611
8.	Virginia	4-4-0	.500	5-4-0	.556
8.	Clemson	2-2-0	.500	5-3-1	.611
10.	Alabama	3-4-1	.438	5-4-1	.550
11.	LSU	2-3-1	.417	4-4-1	.500
12.	Miss. State	2-3-0	.400	5-3-0	.625
12.	Wash. & Lee	2-3-0	.400	4-4-1	.500
12.	Virginia Tech	2-3-0	.400	5-4-0	.556
15.	Maryland	3-5-0	.375	4-7-0	.364
16.	S. Carolina	2-4-0	.333	4-5-0	.444
16.	VMI	2-4-0	.333	6-4-0	.600
18.	Tulane	2-5-1	.312	2-5-1	.312
18.	N. Carolina	2-5-0	.286	4-6-0	.400
20.	Sewanee	1-4-0	.200	2-6-0	.250
21.	Kentucky	1-5-0	.167	3-6-1	.350
22.	Auburn	0-6-1	.072	0-7-2	.111

Non-conference record: 48-15-5 .743

1928		Conference		Overall	
1.	Ga. Tech	7-0-0	1.000	10-0-0	1.000
2.	Tennessee	6-0-1	.929	9-0-1	.950
3.	Florida	6-1-0	.857	8-1-0	.889
4.	Virginia Tech	4-1-0	.800	7-2-0	.778
5.	Alabama	6-2-0	.750	6-3-0	.667
6.	LSU	3-1-1	.700	6-2-1	.722
7.	Clemson	4-2-0	.667	8-3-0	.727
7.	Vanderbilt	4-2-0	.667	8-2-0	.800
9.	Tulane	3-3-1	.500	6-3-1	.650
9.	Ole Miss	3-3-0	.500	5-4-0	.556
9.	N. Carolina	2-2-2	.500	5-3-2	.600
9.	Kentucky	2-2-1	.500	4-3-1	.562
9.	S. Carolina	2-2-1	.500	6-2-2	.700
14.	Maryland	2-3-1	.417	6-3-1	.650
14.	VMI	2-3-1	.417	5-3-2	.600
16.	Georgia	2-4-0	.333	4-5-0	.444
17.	NC State	1-3-1	.300	4-5-1	.450
18.	Miss. State	1-4-0	.200	2-4-2	.375
19.	Virginia	1-6-0	.143	2-6-1	.278
19.	Wash. & Lee	1-6-0	.143	2-8-0	.200
21.	Sewanee	0-5-0	.000	2-7-0	.222
21.	Auburn	0-7-0	.000	1-8-0	.111

Non-conference record: 54-15-4 .767

1929		Conference		Overall	
1.	Tulane	6-0-0	1.000	9-0-0	1.000
2.	Tennessee	6-0-1	.929	9-0-1	.950
3.	N. Carolina	7-1-0	.875	9-1-0	.900
4.	Florida	6-1-0	.857	8-2-0	.800
5.	Vanderbilt	5-1-0	.833	7-2-0	.778
6.	Kentucky	3-1-1	.700	6-1-1	.812
7.	Georgia	4-2-0	.667	6-4-0	.600
7.	VMI	4-2-0	.667	8-2-0	.800
7.	Duke	2-1-0	.667	4-6-0	.400
10.	LSU	3-2-0	.600	6-3-0	.667
11.	Alabama	4-3-0	.571	6-3-0	.667
12.	Clemson	3-3-0	.500	8-3-0	.727
12.	Virginia Tech	2-3-0	.400	5-4-0	.556
14.	Ga. Tech	3-5-0	.375	3-6-0	.333
15.	S. Carolina	2-5-0	.286	6-5-0	.545
16.	Virginia	1-3-2	.333	4-3-2	.556
17.	Maryland	1-3-1	.300	4-4-2	.500
18.	Wash. & Lee	1-4-1	.250	3-5-1	.389
19.	Ole Miss	0-4-2	.167	1-6-2	.222
20.	Miss. State	0-3-1	.125	1-5-2	.250
21.	Sewanee	0-4-1	.100	2-5-2	.333
22.	NC State	0-5-0	.000	1-8-0	.111
22.	Auburn	0-7-0	.000	2-7-0	.222

Duke joins the Southern Conference.
Non-conference record: 55-22-3 .706

1930

		Conference		Overall	
1.	Alabama	8-0-0	1.000	10-0-0	1.000
2.	Tulane	5-0-0	1.000	8-1-0	.889
3.	Tennessee	6-1-0	.857	9-1-0	.900
4.	Duke	4-1-1	.750	8-1-2	.818
5.	Vanderbilt	5-2-0	.714	8-2-0	.800
6.	Maryland	4-2-0	.667	7-5-0	.583
7.	Florida	4-2-1	.643	6-3-1	.650
8.	N. Carolina	4-2-2	.625	5-3-2	.600
9.	Clemson	3-2-0	.600	8-2-0	.800
10.	Georgia	3-2-1	.583	7-2-1	.750
11.	Kentucky	4-3-0	.571	5-3-0	.675
11.	S. Carolina	4-3-0	.571	6-4-0	.600
13.	Virginia Tech	2-3-1	.417	5-3-1	.611
14.	Miss. State	2-3-0	.400	2-7-0	.222
15.	Ga. Tech	2-4-1	.357	2-6-1	.278
16.	LSU	2-4-0	.333	2-6-1	.278
17.	Virginia	2-5-0	.286	4-6-0	400
18	Sewanee	1-4-0	.200	3-6-1	.350
19.	NC State	1-5-0	.167	2-8-0	.200
19.	Ole Miss	1-5-0	.167	3-5-1	.389
21.	Auburn	1-6-0	.143	3-7-0	.300
22.	Wash. & Lee	0-4-1	.100	3-6-1	.350
23.	VMI	0-5-0	.000	3-6-0	.333

Non-conference record: 51-25-4 .662

1931

		Conference		Overall	
1.	Tulane	8-0-0	1.000	11-1-0	.917
2.	Tennessee	6-0-1	.929	9-0-1	.950
3.	Alabama	7-1-0	.875	9-1-0	.900
4.	Georgia	6-1-0	.857	8-2-0	.800
5.	Maryland	4-1-1	.750	8-1-1	.850
6.	Kentucky	4-2-2	.625	5-2-2	.667
7.	LSU	3-2-0	.600	5-4-0	.556
8.	Duke	3-3-1	.500	5-3-2	.600
8.	S. Carolina	3-3-1	500	5-4-1	.550
8.	Auburn	3-3-0	.500	5-3-1	.688
8.	Sewanee	3-3-0	.500	6-3-1	.650
12.	Vanderbilt	3-4-0	.429	5-4-0	.556
13.	N. Carolina	2-3-3	.438	4-3-3	.550
14.	Wash. & Lee	2-3-0	.400	4-5-1	.450
15.	Florida	2-4-2	.375	2-6-2	.300
16.	Ga. Tech	2-4-1	.357	2-7-1	.250
17.	VMI	2-4-0	.333	3-6-1	.350
17.	NC State	2-4-0	.333	3-6-0	.333
19.	Virginia Tech	1-4-1	.250	3-4-2	.444
20.	Clemson	1-4-0	.200	1-6-2	.222
21.	Ole Miss	1-5-0	.167	2-6-1	.278
22.	Virginia	0-5-1	.083	1-7-2	.200
23.	Miss. State	0-5-0	.000	2-6-0	.250

Non-conference record: 40-22-10 .625

1932

		Conference		Overall	
1.	Tennessee	7-0-1	.938	9-0-1	.950
2.	Auburn	6-0-1	.929	9-0-1	.950
3.	LSU	4-0-0	1.000	6-3-1	.650
4.	Virginia Tech	6-1-0	.857	8-1-0	.889
5.	Vanderbilt	4-1-2	.714	6-1-2	.778
6.	NC State	3-1-1	.700	6-1-2	.778
7.	Alabama	5-2-0	.714	8-2-0	.800
8.	Tulane	5-2-1	.688	6-2-1	.778
9.	Duke	5-3-0	.625	7-3-0	.700
10.	Ga. Tech	4-4-1	.500	4-5-1	.450
10.	S. Carolina	2-2-2	.500	5-4-2	.545
12.	Kentucky	4-5-0	.444	4-5-0	.444
13.	Virginia	2-3-0	.400	5-4-0	.556
13.	Ole Miss	2-3-0	.400	5-6-0	.455
15.	Georgia	2-4-2	.375	2-5-2	.333
16.	Maryland	2-4-0	.333	5-6-0	.455
17.	N. Carolina	2-5-1	.312	3-5-2	.400
18.	VMI	1-4-0	.200	2-8-0	.200
18.	Wash. & Lee	1-4-0	.200	1-9-0	.100
20.	Florida	1-6-0	.143	3-6-0	.333
21.	Clemson	0-4-0	.000	3-5-1	.388
21.	Miss. State	0-4-0	.000	3-5-0	.375
21.	Sewanee	0-6-0	.000	2-7-1	.250

Non-conference record: 44-25-5 .628

Following the 1932 season, 13 members of the SC left to form a new conference, the Southeastern Conference. The SC continued on with the remaining ten members.

1933

		Conference		Overall	
1.	Duke	4-0-0	1.000	9-1-0	.900
2.	S. Carolina	3-0-0	1.000	6-3-1	.650
3.	N. Carolina	2-1-0	.667	4-5-0	.444
4.	VMI	2-1-1	.625	2-7-1	.250
5.	Wash. & Lee	1-1-1	.500	4-4-2	.500
5.	Clemson	1-1-0	.500	3-6-2	.364
5.	Virginia Tech	1-1-3	.500	4-3-3	.550
8.	Virginia	1-3-1	.300	2-6-2	.300
9.	Maryland	1-4-0	.200	3-7-0	.300
10.	NC State	0-4-0	.000	1-5-3	.278

Non-conference record 22-31-8 .426

1934

		Conference		Overall	
1.	Wash. & Lee	4-0-0	1.000	7-3-0	.700
2.	N. Carolina	2-0-1	.833	7-1-1	.833
3.	Duke	3-1-0	.750	7-2-0	.778
3.	Maryland	3-1-0	.750	7-3-0	.700
5.	Clemson	2-1-0	.667	5-4-0	.556
6.	Virginia Tech	3-3-0	.500	5-5-0	.500
7.	S. Carolina	2-3-0	.400	5-4-0	.556
8.	NC State	1-3-1	.300	2-6-1	.278
9.	Virginia	1-4-0	.200	3-6-0	.333
10.	VMI	0-5-0	.000	1-8-0	.111

Non-conference record: 28-21-0 .571

1935

		Conference		Overall	
1.	Duke	5-0-0	1.000	8-2-0	.800
2.	N. Carolina	4-1-0	.800	8-1-0	.889
3.	Maryland	3-1-1	.700	7-2-2	.727
4.	Clemson	2-1-0	.667	6-3-0	.667
5.	Virginia Tech	3-3-1	.500	4-3-2	.556
5.	NC State	2-2-0	.500	6-4-0	.600
7.	Wash. & Lee	1-3-1	.300	3-4-1	.438
8.	Virginia	0-3-2	.200	1-5-4	.300
8.	S. Carolina	1-4-0	.200	3-7-0	.300
10.	VMI	0-3-1	.125	2-7-1	.250

Non-conference record: 27-17-4 .604

1936

		Conference		Overall	
1.	Duke	7-0-0	1.000	9-1-0	.900
2.	N. Carolina	5-1-0	.833	8-2-0	.800
3.	Furman	4-1-0	.800	7-2-0	.778
4.	VMI	4-2-0	.667	6-4-0	.600
5.	Clemson	3-2-0	.600	5-5-0	.500
5.	Maryland	3-2-0	.600	6-5-0	.545
7.	Davidson	4-3-0	.571	5-4-0	.556
8.	Wash. & Lee	2-2-0	.500	4-6-0	.400
9.	Wake Forest	2-3-0	.400	5-4-0	.556
10.	NC State	2-4-0	.333	3-7-0	.300
11.	Virginia Tech	3-5-0	.375	5-5-0	.500
12.	S. Carolina	2-5-0	.286	5-7-0	.417
13.	Richmond	1-3-0	.250	4-4-2	.500
14.	The Citadel	0-4-0	.000	4-6-0	.400
14.	Wm. & Mary	0-4-0	.000	1-8-0	.111

Furman, Davidson, Wake Forest, Richmond, The Citadel, and William and Mary join the SC, and Virginia leaves.
Non-conference record: 35-29-2 .545

1937

		Conference		Overall	
1.	Maryland	2-0-0	1.000	8-2-0	.800
2.	N. Carolina	4-0-1	.900	7-1-1	.833
3.	Clemson	2-0-1	.833	4-4-1	.500
3.	Duke	5-1-0	.833	7-2-1	.750
5.	VMI	4-2-0	.667	5-5-0	.500
6.	NC State	4-2-1	.643	5-3-1	.611
7.	S. Carolina	2-2-1	.500	5-6-1	.458
8.	Wash. & Lee	2-3-0	.400	4-5-0	.444
8.	The Citadel	2-3-0	.400	7-4-0	.636
8.	Richmond	2-3-0	.400	5-4-1	.550
8.	Furman	1-2-2	.400	4-3-2	.556
12.	Virginia Tech	2-4-0	.333	5-5-0	.500
13.	Wm. & Mary	1-3-0	.250	4-5-0	.444
14.	Wake Forests	1-4-0	.200	3-6-0	.333
15.	Davidson	1-6-0	.143	2-8-0	.200

Non-conference record: 40-28-2 .586

1938

		Conference		Overall	
1.	Duke	5-0-0	1.000	9-1-0	.900
2.	Clemson	3-0-1	.875	7-1-1	.833
3.	VMI	4-0-3	.786	6-1-4	.727
4.	N. Carolina	4-1-0	.800	6-2-1	.722
5.	Richmond	3-2-1	.583	6-3-1	.650
6.	Wash. & Lee	2-2-0	.500	4-4-1	.500
6.	NC State	3-3-1	.500	3-7-1	.318
6.	S. Carolina	2-2-0	.500	6-4-1	.591
9.	Wake Forest	3-4-1	.438	4-5-1	.450
10.	Virginia Tech	2-3-2	.429	3-5-2	.400
11.	The Citadel	2-3-0	.400	6-5-0	.545
12.	Maryland	1-2-0	.333	2-7-0	.222
13.	Davidson	2-6-0	.250	4-6-0	.400
14.	Furman	0-4-1	.100	2-7-1	.250
15.	Wm. & Mary	0-4-0	.000	2-7-0	.222

Non-conference record: 34-29-4 .537

1939

		Conference		Overall	
1.	Duke	5-0-0	1.000	8-1-0	.889
2.	Clemson	4-0-0	1.000	9-1-0	.900
3.	N. Carolina	5-1-0	.833	8-1-1	.850
4.	VMI	3-1-1	.700	6-3-1	.650
4.	Richmond	3-1-1	.700	7-1-2	.800
6.	Furman	3-3-0	.500	5-4-0	.556
6.	Wake Forest	3-3-0	.500	7-3-0	.700
6.	Wm. & Mary	1-1-1	.500	6-2-1	.722
9.	NC State	2-4-0	.333	2-8-0	.200
10.	Wash. & Lee	1-2-0	.333	3-4-1	.438
11.	S. Carolina	1-3-0	.250	3-6-1	.350
11.	Virginia Tech	1-4-1	.250	4-5-1	.450
13.	Davidson	1-7-0	.125	2-7-0	.222
14.	Maryland	0-1-0	.000	2-7-0	.222
14.	The Citadel	0-4-0	.000	3-8-0	.272

Non-conference record: 42-26-4 .611

1940

		Conference		Overall	
1.	Clemson	4-0-0	1.000	6-2-1	.722
2.	Duke	4-1-0	.800	7-2-0	.778
3.	Wake Forest	4-2-0	.667	7-3-0	.700
4.	Wm. & Mary	2-1-1	.625	6-2-1	.722
5.	N. Carolina	3-2-0	.600	6-4-0	.600
5.	Richmond	3-2-0	.600	7-3-0	.700
7.	VMI	3-2-1	.583	7-2-1	.750
8.	Furman	4-3-0	.571	5-4-0	.556
9.	Wash. & Lee	1-1-1	.500	2-7-1	.250
10.	Virginia Tech	2-3-0	.400	5-5-0	.500
11.	NC State	3-5-0	.375	3-6-0	.333
12.	Maryland	0-1-1	.250	2-6-1	.278
12.	S. Carolina	1-3-0	.250	3-6-0	.333
14.	Davidson	1-5-0	.167	5-5-0	.500
15.	The Citadel	0-4-0	.000	4-5-0	.444

Non-conference record: 40-27-1 .596

1941		Conference		Overall	
1.	Duke	5-0-0	1.000	9-1-0	.900
2.	S. Carolina	4-0-1	.900	4-4-1	.500
3.	Clemson	5-1-0	.833	7-2-0	.778
4.	Wm. & Mary	4-1-0	.800	8-2-0	.800
5.	VMI	4-2-0	.667	4-6-0	.400
5.	Virginia Tech	4-2-0	.667	6-4-0	.600
7.	Wake Forest	4-2-1	.643	5-5-1	.500
8.	NC State	3-4-2	.444	4-5-2	.455
9.	Furman	2-3-2	.429	3-4-2	.444
10.	Wash. & Lee	1-2-2	.400	1-6-2	.222
11.	N. Carolina	2-4-0	.333	3-7-0	.300
11.	Maryland	1-2-0	.333	3-5-1	.389
13.	Davidson	1-5-2	.250	1-6-3	.250
14.	The Citadel	0-2-1	.167	4-3-1	.562
15.	G. Washington	0-4-1	.100	1-7-1	.167
16.	Richmond	0-6-0	.000	2-7-0	.222

George Washington joins the SC.
Non-conference record: 25-34-2 .426

1942					
1.	Wm. & Mary	4-0-0	1.000	9-1-1	.864
2.	Virginia Tech	5-1-0	.833	7-2-1	.750
3.	Wake Forest	6-1-1	.812	6-2-1	.722
4.	N. Carolina	3-1-1	.700	5-2-2	.667
4.	Duke	3-1-1	.700	5-4-1	.550
6.	NC State	3-1-2	.667	4-4-2	.500
7.	Furman	3-3-0	.500	3-6-0	.333
7.	The Citadel	2-2-0	.500	5-2-0	.714
9.	Clemson	2-3-1	.417	3-6-1	.350
10	Davidson	2-4-1	.357	2-6-1	.278
10.	VMI	2-4-1	.357	3-5-1	.389
12.	G. Washington	2-4-0	.333	3-6-0	.333
12.	Maryland	1-2-0	.333	7-2-0	.778
14.	S. Carolina	1-4-0	.200	1-7-1	.167
15.	Richmond	1-5-0	.167	3-6-1	.350
16.	Wash. & Lee	0-4-0	.000	1-8-0	.111

Non-conference record: 28-29-5 .492

1943					
1.	Duke	4-0-0	1.000	8-1-0	.889
2.	Maryland	2-0-0	1.000	4-5-0	.444
3.	S. Carolina	2-1-0	.667	5-2-0	.714
4.	Wake Forest	3-2-0	.600	4-5-0	.444
5.	N. Carolina	2-2-0	.500	6-3-0	.667
5.	Richmond	1-1-0	.500	6-1-0	.857
7.	Clemson	2-3-0	.400	2-6-0	.250
7.	VMI	2-3-0	.400	2-6-0	.250
9.	NC State	1-4-0	.200	3-6-0	.333
10.	Davidson	0-3-0	.000	0-5-0	.000

Six teams drop football for 1943.
Non-conference record: 21-21-0 .500

1944					
1.	Duke	4-0-0	1.000	6-4-0	.600
2.	Wake Forest	6-1-0	.857	8-1-0	.889
3.	Clemson	3-1-0	.750	4-5-0	.444
3.	NC State	3-1-0	.750	7-2-0	.778
5.	Wm. & Mary	2-1-1	.625	5-2-1	.688
6.	Maryland	1-1-0	.500	1-7-1	.167
7.	S. Carolina	1-3-0	.250	3-4-2	.444
8.	VMI	1-5-0	.167	1-8-0	.111
9.	N. Carolina	0-3-1	.125	1-7-1	.167
10.	Richmond	0-4-0	.000	2-6-0	.250

Davidson drops football, Wm. & Mary adds football.
Non-conference record: 17-26-3 .402

1945		Conference		Overall	
1.	Duke	4-0-0	1.000	6-2-0	.750
2.	Wake Forest	4-1-1	.750	5-3-1	.611
3.	Wm. & Mary	4-2-0	.667	6-3-0	.667
4.	Clemson	2-1-1	.625	6-3-1	.650
5.	Maryland	3-2-0	.600	6-2-1	.722
5.	VMI	3-2-0	.600	5-4-0	.556
7.	N. Carolina	2-2-0	.500	5-5-0	.500
8.	NC State	2-4-0	.333	3-6-0	.333
9.	Virginia Tech	2-5-0	.286	2-6-0	.250
10.	S. Carolina	0-3-2	.200	2-4-3	.389
11.	Richmond	0-4-0	.000	2-6-0	.250

Non-conference record: 22-18-2 .548

1946					
1.	N. Carolina	4-0-1	.900	8-2-1	.773
2.	Wm. & Mary	7-1-0	.875	8-2-0	.800
3.	NC State	6-1-0	.857	8-3-0	.727
4.	S. Carolina	4-2-0	.667	5-3-0	.625
5.	Duke	3-2-0	.600	4-5-0	.444
6.	Richmond	3-2-2	.571	6-2-2	.700
7.	Virginia Tech	3-3-3	.500	3-4-3	.350
8.	VMI	2-3-1	.416	4-5-1	.450
9.	G. Washington	1-1-0	.500	4-3-0	.571
10.	Clemson	2-3-0	.400	4-5-0	.444
10.	Wake Forest	2-3-0	.400	6-3-0	.667
12.	Maryland	2-5-0	.286	3-6-0	.333
13.	Furman	1-4-0	.200	2-8-0	.200
13.	Wash. & Lee	1-4-0	.200	2-6-0	.250
15.	The Citadel	1-5-0	.167	3-5-0	.375
15.	Davidson	1-5-0	.167	4-5-0	.444

All 1941 members now back playing football.
Non-conference record: 31-23-0 .574

1947					
1.	Wm. & Mary	7-1-0	.875	9-2-0	.818
2.	N. Carolina	4-1-0	.800	8-2-0	.800
3.	S. Carolina	4-1-1	.750	6-2-1	.722
4.	Duke	3-1-1	.700	4-3-2	.556
5.	Wash & Lee	3-2-0	.600	5-5-0	.500
6	Maryland	3-2-1	.583	7-2-2	.727
6.	NC State	3-2-1	.583	5-3-1	.611
8.	Virginia Tech	4-3-0	.571	4-5-0	.444
9.	Davidson	3-3-1	.500	6-3-1	.650
10.	Wake Forest	3-4-0	.429	6-4-0	.600
11.	VMI	2-3-1	.417	3-5-1	.389
12.	Clemson	1-3-0	.250	4-5-0	.444
13.	The Citadel	1-4-0	.200	3-5-0	.375
13.	Furman	1-4-0	.200	2-7-0	.222
15.	Richmond	1-5-0	.167	3-7-0	.300
16.	G. Washington	0-4-0	.000	1-7-1	.167

Non-conference record: 33-24-3 .575

1948		Conference		Overall	
1.	Clemson	5-0-0	1.000	11-0-0	1.000
2.	N. Carolina	4-0-1	.900	9-1-1	.864
3.	VMI	5-1-0	.833	6-3-0	.667
4.	Wm. & Mary	5-1-1	.917	7-2-2	.727
5.	Wake Forest	5-2-0	.714	6-4-0	.600
6.	Maryland	4-2-0	.667	6-4-0	.600
7.	Duke	3-2-1	.583	4-3-2	.556
8.	Richmond	3-3-1	.500	5-3-2	.600
9.	Wash. & Lee	2-2-0	.500	4-6-0	.400
10.	Furman	2-4-0	.333	2-6-1	.278
10.	G. Washington	2-4-0	.333	4-6-0	.400
12.	Davidson	2-5-0	.286	3-5-1	.389
13.	S. Carolina	1-3-0	.250	3-5-0	.375
14.	NC State	1-4-1	.250	3-6-1	.350
15.	Virginia Tech	0-6-1	.072	0-8-1	.055
16.	The Citadel	0-5-0	.000	2-7-0	.222

Non-conference record: 31-25-5 .549

1949					
1.	N. Carolina	5-0-0	1.000	7-4-0	.636
2.	Maryland	4-0-0	1.000	9-1-0	.900
3.	Wash. & Lee	3-1-1	.700	3-5-1	.389
4.	Duke	4-2-0	.667	6-3-0	.667
4.	Wm. & Mary	4-2-0	.667	6-4-0	.600
6.	VMI	3-2-1	.583	3-5-1	.389
7.	The Citadel	2-2-0	.500	4-5-0	.444
7.	Clemson	2-2-0	.500	4-4-2	.500
7.	Furman	3-3-0	.500	3-6-0	.667
7.	S. Carolina	3-3-0	.500	4-6-0	.400
7.	Wake Forest	3-3-0	.500	4-6-0	.400
12.	G. Washington	2-3-0	.400	4-5-0	.444
13.	NC State	3-6-0	.333	3-7-0	.300
14.	Virginia Tech	1-5-2	.250	1-7-2	.200
14.	Richmond	2-6-0	.250	3-7-0	.300
16.	Davidson	1-5-0	.167	2-8-0	.200

Non-conference record: 21-38-2 .361

1950					
1.	Wash. & Lee	6-0-0	1.000	8-3-0	.727
2.	Clemson	3-0-1	.875	9-0-1	.950
3.	VMI	5-1-0	.833	6-4-0	.600
4.	Wake Forest	6-1-1	.812	6-1-2	.778
5.	Maryland	4-1-1	.750	7-2-1	.750
6.	Duke	5-2-0	.714	7-3-0	.700
7.	N. Carolina	3-2-1	.583	3-5-2	.400
8.	G. Washington	4-3-0	.571	5-4-0	556
9.	NC State	4-4-1	.500	5-4-1	.550
9.	Wm. & Mary	3-3-0	.500	4-7-0	.364
11.	The Citadel	2-3-0	.400	4-6-0	.400
12.	S. Carolina	2-4-1	.357	3-4-2	.444
13.	Furman	2-4-0	.333	2-9-1	.208
14.	West Virginia	1-3-0	.250	2-8-0	.200
15.	Davidson	1-5-0	.167	3-6-0	.333
16.	Richmond	1-8-0	.111	2-8-0	.200
17.	Virginia Tech	0-8-0	.000	0-10-0	.000

West Virginia joins the SC.
Non-conference record: 24-32-4 .433

1951		Conference		Overall	
1.	Maryland	5-0-0	1.000	10-0-0	1.000
1.	VMI	5-0-0	1.000	7-3-0	.700
3.	Wash. & Lee	5-1-0	.833	6-4-0	.600
3.	Wm. & Mary	5-1-0	.833	7-3-0	.700
5.	Clemson	3-1-0	.750	7-3-0	.700
6.	Duke	4-2-0	.667	5-4-1	.550
7.	S. Carolina	5-3-0	.625	5-4-0	.556
7.	Wake Forest	5-3-0	.625	6-4-0	.600
9.	G. Washington	2-3-1	.417	2-6-1	.278
10.	N. Carolina	2-3-0	.400	2-8-0	.200
10.	W. Virginia	2-3-0	.400	5-5-0	.500
12.	NC State	2-6-0	.250	3-7-0	.300
12.	Richmond	2-6-0	.250	3-8-0	.273
12.	The Citadel	1-3-0	.250	4-6-0	.400
12.	Furman	1-4-1	.250	3-6-1	.350
16.	Davidson	1-5-0	.167	1-8-0	.111
17.	Virginia Tech	1-7-0	.125	2-8-0	.250

Non-conference record: 27-36-1 .430

1952					
1.	Duke	5-0-0	1.000	8-2-0	.800
2.	Wake Forest	5-1-0	.833	5-4-1	.550
2.	West Virginia	5-1-0	.833	7-2-0	.778
4.	Wm. & Mary	4-1-0	.800	4-5-0	.444
5.	G. Washington	4-2-0	.667	5-3-1	.611
6.	Virginia Tech	4-4-0	.500	5-6-0	.455
6.	Furman	2-2-1	.500	6-3-1	.650
8.	Wash. & Lee	3-4-0	.429	3-7-0	.300
9.	VMI	2-3-1	.417	3-6-1	.350
10.	NC State	2-4-0	.333	3-7-0	.300
10.	S. Carolina	2-4-0	.333	5-5-0	.500
10.	N. Carolina	1-2-0	.333	2-6-0	.333
13.	The Citadel	1-3-1	.300	3-5-1	.389
14.	Davidson	1-6-0	.143	2-7-0	.222
15.	Richmond	0-6-0	.000	1-9-0	.100
16.	Clemson	0-0-0	.000	2-6-1	.278

Maryland leaves the SC.
Non-conference record: 23-40-3 .371

Following the 1952 season, Duke, Wake Forest, NC State, S. Carolina, N. Carolina, and Clemson leave the SC to join with Virginia and Maryland in forming the ACC.

1953					
1.	West Virginia	4-0-0	1.000	8-2-0	.800
2.	Furman	2-0-0	1.000	7-2-0	.778
3.	G. Washington	4-2-0	.667	5-4-0	.556
4.	Wm. & Mary	3-2-0	.667	5-4-1	.550
5.	Richmond	3-3-0	.500	5-3-1	.611
5.	Virginia Tech	3-3-0	.500	5-5-0	.500
5.	VMI	3-3-0	.500	5-5-0	.500
8.	Wash. & Lee	2-4-0	.333	4-6-0	.400
9.	The Citadel	1-3-0	.250	2-7-0	.222
10.	Davidson	0-5-0	.000	0-9-0	.000

Non-conference record: 21-22-2 .489

1954					
1.	West Virginia	3-0-0	1.000	8-1-0	.889
2.	Furman	2-0-0	1.000	5-5-0	.500
3.	Virginia Tech	3-0-1	.875	8-0-1	.944
4.	Davidson	2-1-0	.667	6-3-0	.667
5.	VMI	4-3-0	.571	4-6-0	.400
6.	Richmond	2-3-0	.400	5-4-0	.556
6.	Wm. & Mary	1-2-2	.400	4-4-2	.500
8.	G. Washington	0-4-1	.100	1-7-1	.167
9.	The Citadel	0-4-0	.000	2-8-0	.200

Non-conference record: 26-20-0 .565

1955

1.	West Virginia	4-0-0	1.000	8-2-0	.800
2.	Virginia Tech	2-1-1	.625	6-3-1	.650
3.	Davidson	3-2-0	.600	5-4-0	.556
3.	G. Washington	3-2-0	.600	5-4-0	.556
5.	Richmond	3-2-2	.571	4-3-2	.556
6.	The Citadel	2-2-0	.500	5-4-0	.556
6.	Furman	1-1-0	.500	1-9-0	.100
8.	Wm. & Mary	1-3-1	.300	1-7-1	.167
9.	VMI	1-6-0	.143	1-9-0	.100
10.	Wash. & Lee	0-1-0	.000	0-7-0	.000

Non-conference record: 16-32-0 .333

1956

1.	West Virginia	5-0-0	1.000	6-4-0	.600
2.	Virginia Tech	3-0-0	1.000	7-2-1	.750
3.	G. Washington	5-1-0	.833	8-1-1	.850
4.	Davidson	2-2-1	.500	5-3-1	.611
4.	Furman	2-2-0	.500	2-8-0	.200
6.	VMI	2-3-1	.417	3-6-1	.350
7.	Richmond	2-5-0	.286	4-5-0	.444
8.	The Citadel	1-3-0	.250	3-5-1	.389
9.	Wash. & Lee	0-1-0	.000	1-7-0	.125
9.	Wm. & Mary	0-5-0	.000	0-9-1	.050

Non-conference record: 17-28-4 .388

1957

1.	VMI	6-0-0	1.000	9-0-1	.950
2.	West Virginia	3-0-0	1.000	7-2-1	.750
3.	The Citadel	4-2-0	.667	5-4-1	.550
3.	Furman	2-1-0	.667	3-7-0	.300
5.	Richmond	2-4-0	.333	4-6-0	.400
5.	Wm. & Mary	2-4-0	.333	4-6-0	.400
7.	Davidson	1-3-0	.250	5-3-0	.625
7.	Virginia Tech	1-3-0	.250	4-6-0	.400
9.	G. Washington	1-5-0	.167	2-7-0	.222
	Wash. & Lee	0-0-0	---	0-8-0	.000

Non-conference record: 21-27-3 .441
Washington and Lee withdraws from the conference.

1958

1.	West Virginia	4-0-0	1.000	4-5-1	.450
2.	Virginia Tech	3-1-0	.750	5-4-1	.550
3.	G. Washington	3-2-0	.600	3-5-0	.375
4.	VMI	2-2-1	.500	6-2-2	.700
5.	Richmond	3-4-0	.429	3-7-0	.300
6.	The Citadel	2-3-0	.400	4-6-0	.400
6.	Davidson	2-3-0	.400	5-4-0	.556
8.	Furman	1-2-0	.333	2-7-0	.222
9.	Wm. & Mary	1-4-1	.250	2-6-1	.278

Non-conference record: 13-25-3 .354

1959

1.	VMI	5-0-1	.917	8-1-1	.850
2.	The Citadel	5-1-0	.833	8-2-0	.800
3.	Virginia Tech	3-1-0	.750	6-4-0	.600
4.	Furman	3-2-0	.600	3-7-0	.300
5.	Richmond	4-3-1	.562	4-5-1	.450
6.	West Virginia	2-2-0	.500	3-7-0	.300
7.	Wm. & Mary	2-5-0	.286	4-6-0	.400
8.	Davidson	0-5-0	.000	1-8-0	.111
8.	G. Washington	0-5-0	.000	1-8-0	.111

Non-conference record: 14-24-0 .368

1960

1.	VMI	4-1-0	.800	7-2-1	.750
2.	The Citadel	4-2-0	.667	8-3-1	.708
2.	G. Washington	4-2-0	.667	5-3-1	.611
2.	Virginia Tech	4-2-0	.667	6-4-0	.600
5.	Furman	2-2-0	.500	5-4-1	.550
6.	Richmond	3-4-1	.438	3-6-1	.350
7.	Davidson	1-3-0	.250	3-5-0	.375
8.	Wm. & Mary	1-5-0	.167	2-8-0	.200
9.	West Virginia	0-2-1	.167	0-8-2	.100

Non-conference record: 16-20-5 .451

1961

1.	The Citadel	5-1-0	.833	7-3-0	.700
2.	Richmond	5-2-0	.714	5-5-0	.500
3.	VMI	4-2-0	.667	6-4-0	.600
3.	West Virginia	2-1-0	.667	4-6-0	.400
5.	Furman	2-2-0	.500	7-3-0	.700
6.	G. Washington	3-4-0	.429	3-6-0	.333
7.	Virginia Tech	2-3-0	.400	4-5-0	.444
8.	Davidson	1-4-0	.200	4-4-0	.500
9.	Wm & Mary	1-6-0	.143	1-9-0	.100

Non-conference record: 16-20-0 .444

1962

1.	VMI	6-0-0	1.000	6-4-0	.600
2.	West Virginia	4-0-0	1.000	8-2-0	.800
3.	Richmond	3-2-0	.600	6-3-0	.667
4.	Wm. & Mary	4-3-1	.562	4-5-1	.450
5.	Furman	2-2-0	.500	4-6-0	.400
6.	Virginia Tech	2-3-0	.400	5-5-0	.500
7.	The Citadel	1-4-0	.200	3-7-0	.300
8.	G. Washington	1-5-0	.167	3-7-0	.300
9.	Davidson	0-4-1	.100	3-5-1	.389

Non-conference record: 19-21-0 .475

1963

1.	Virginia Tech	5-0-0	1.000	8-2-0	.800
2.	West Virginia	3-1-0	.750	4-6-0	.400
3.	VMI	3-1-2	.667	3-5-2	.400
4.	Furman	3-2-0	.600	7-3-0	.700
5.	Wm. & Mary	4-4-0	.500	4-6-0	.400
5.	Richmond	2-2-1	.500	3-6-1	.350
7.	The Citadel	2-4-0	.333	4-6-0	.400
8.	G. Washington	1-5-0	.167	2-7-0	.222
9.	Davidson	0-4-1	.100	1-5-2	.250

Non-conference record: 13-23-1 .365

1964

1.	West Virginia	5-0-0	1.000	7-4-0	636
2.	Virginia Tech	3-1-0	.750	6-4-0	.600
3.	G. Washington	3-2-0	.600	5-4-0	.556
4.	The Citadel	4-3-0	.571	4-6-0	.400
4.	Wm & Mary	4-3-0	.571	4-6-0	.400
6.	Richmond	2-4-0	.333	3-7-0	.300
7.	Davidson	1-3-0	.250	3-6-0	.333
8.	Furman	1-4-0	.200	3-7-0	.300
8	VMI	1-4-0	.200	1-9-0	.100
	East Carolina			9-1-0	.900

East Carolina joins the Southern Conference, but plays no
SC games. Virginia Tech leaves the SC after the 1964 season.
Non-conference record: (excluding East Carolina):
12-29-0 .293

1965

1.	West Virginia	4-0-0	1.000	6-4-0	.600
2.	Wm. & Mary	5-1-0	.833	6-4-0	.600
3.	East Carolina	3-1-0	.750	9-1-0	.900
4.	VMI	3-2-0	.600	3-7-0	.300
5.	G. Washington	4-3-0	.571	5-5-0	.500
6.	Furman	2-3-0	.400	5-5-0	.500
6.	Davidson	2-3-0	.400	6-4-0	.600
8.	The Citadel	2-6-0	.250	2-8-0	.200
9.	Richmond	0-6-0	.000	0-10-0	.000

Non-conference record: 17-23-0 .425

1966

1.	East Carolina	4-1-1	.750	4-5-1	.450
1.	Wm. & Mary	4-1-1	.750	5-4-1	.550
3.	West Virginia	3-1-1	.700	3-5-2	.400
4.	G. Washington	4-3-0	.571	4-6-0	.400
5.	Davidson	2-3-0	.400	4-5-0	.444
6.	The Citadel	3-5-0	.375	4-6-0	.400
7.	Richmond	2-4-0	.333	2-8-0	.200
8.	Furman	1-4-0	.200	3-7-1	.318
8.	VMI	1-4-0	.200	2-8-0	.200

Non-conference record: 7-28-1 .208

George Washington withdraws from the conference after the 1966 season.

1967

1.	West Virginia	4-0-1	.900	5-4-1	.550
2.	East Carolina	4-1-0	.800	8-2-0	.800
3.	Richmond	5-2-0	714	5-5-0	.500
4.	Wm. & Mary	2-2-1	.500	5-4-1	.550
5.	VMI	2-3-0	.400	6-4-0	.600
5.	Furman	2-3-0	.400	5-5-0	.500
7.	The Citadel	2-4-0	.333	5-5-0	.500
8.	Davidson	1-5-0	.167	4-5-0	.444

Non-conference record: 21-14-0 .600

West Virginia withdraws from the Southern Conference after the 1967 season.

1968

1.	Richmond	6-0-0	1.000	8-3-0	.727
2.	The Citadel	4-2-0	.667	5-5-0	.500
3.	East Carolina	2-2-0	.500	4-6-0	.400
3.	Wm. & Mary	2-2-0	.500	3-7-0	.300
5.	Davidson	1-3-0	.250	3-6-0	.333
6.	VMI	1-3-0	.250	1-9-0	.100
7.	Furman	0-4-0	.000	1-9-0	.100

Non-conference record: 9-29-0 .237

1969

1.	Davidson	5-1-0	.833	7-4-0	.636
1.	Richmond	5-1-0	.833	6-4-0	.600
3.	The Citadel	4-2-0	667	7-3-0	.700
4.	Wm. & Mary	2-2-0	.500	3-7-0	.300
5.	East Carolina	1-3-0	.250	2-7-0	.222
6.	Furman	0-4-0	.000	1-8-1	.150
6.	VMI	0-4-0	.000	0-10-0	.000

Non-conference record: 9-26-1 .264

1970

1.	Wm. & Mary	3-1-0	.750	5-7-0	.417
2.	The Citadel	4-2-0	.667	5-6-0	.545
3.	Furman	3-2-0	.600	8-3-0	.727
4.	East Carolina	2-2-0	.500	3-8-0	.273
4.	Richmond	3-3-0	.500	4-6-0	.400
6.	Davidson	2-4-0	.333	2-8-0	.200
7	VMI	1-4-0	.200	1-10-0	.091

Non-conference record: 10-30-0 .250

1971

1.	Richmond	5-1-0	.833	5-6-0	.455
2.	Wm. & Mary	4-1-0	.800	5-6-0	.455
3.	The Citadel	4-2-0	.667	8-3-0	.727
4.	East Carolina	3-2-0	.609	4-6-1	.409
5.	Furman	2-3-0	.400	5-5-1	.500
6.	VMI	1-4-0	.200	1-10-0	.091
7.	Davidson	0-6-0	.000	1-9-0	.100
	Appal. State			7-3-1	.682

Non-conference record: 10-26-2 .289

Appalachian State joins the Southern Conference, but plays. no conference games.

1972

1.	East Carolina	6-0-0	1.000	9-2-0	.818
2.	Richmond	5-1-0	.833	6-4-0	.600
3.	Wm. & Mary	4-2-0	.667	5-6-0	.455
4.	The Citadel	4-3-0	.571	5-6-0	.455
5.	Davidson	2-3-1	.417	3-7-1	.318
6	VMI	1-5-0	.167	2-9-0	.182
7.	Furman	1-6-0	.143	2-9-0	.182
8.	Appal. State	0-3-1	.125	5-5-1	.500

Non-conference record: 14-25-0 .359

1973

1.	East Carolina	7-0-0	1.000	9-2-0	.818
2.	Richmond	5-1-0	.833	8-2-0	.800
3.	Wm. & Mary	3-2-0	.600	6-5-0	.545
4.	Furman	3-3-0	.500	7-4-0	.636
4.	App. State	2-2-0	.500	3-7-1	.318
6.	VMI	2-4-0	.333	3-8-0	.273
7.	Davidson	1-6-0	.143	2-8-0	.200
7.	The Citadel	1-6-0	.143	3-8-0	.273

Non-conference record: 17-20-1 461

1974

1.	VMI	5-1-0	.833	7-4-0	.636
2.	App. State	4-1-0	.800	6-5-0	.545
3.	East Carolina	3-3-0	.500	7-4-0	.636
3.	Richmond	3-3-0	.500	6-4-0	.600
5.	The Citadel	3-4-0	.429	4-7-0	.364
6.	Wm. & Mary	2-3-0	.400	4-7-0	.364
7.	Furman	2-4-0	.333	5-6-0	.455
8.	Davidson	0-3-0	.0-00	2-7-0	.222

Non-conference record: 19-22-0 .463

1975

1.	Richmond	5-1-0	.833	5-6-0	.455
2.	East Carolina	4-2-0	.667	8-3-0	.727
3.	App. State	3-2-0	.600	8-3-0	.727
4.	The Citadel	4-3-0	.571	6-5-0	.545
5.	Wm. & Mary	2-3-0	.400	2-9-0	.182
6.	Furman	2-4-0	.333	5-5-1	.500
6.	VMI	2-4-0	.333	3-8-0	.273
8.	Davidson	0-3-0	.000	1-8-0	.111

Non-conference record: 16-25-1 .393

1976

1.	East Carolina	4-1-0	.800	9-2-0	.818
2.	Wm. & Mary	3-2-0	.600	7-4-0	.636
3.	App. State	2-2-1	.500	6-4-1	.591
3.	Furman	2-2-1	.500	6-4-1	.591
5.	VMI	2-3-0	.400	5-5-0	.500
6.	The Citadel	1-4-0	.200	6-5-0	.545
	Davidson*			2-6-1	.278
	Marshall			5-6-0	.455
	Chattanooga			6-4-1	.591
	West. Carolina			6-4-0	.600

Marshall, Chattanooga, and West Carolina join the Conference, but play no SC games. Richmond leaves. Davidson is listed as an SC member, 1976-1981, but plays no conference games in those seasons.
Non-conference record: 25-10-0 .600

1977

1.	Chattanooga	4-1-0	.800	9-1-1	.864
1	VMI	4-1-0	.800	7-4-0	.636
3.	The Citadel	3-2-0	.600	5-6-0	.455
4.	Furman	3-2-1	.583	4-5-2	.455
5.	W. Carolina	2-2-1	.500	6-4-1	.591
6.	App. State	1-4-0	.200	2-9-0	.182
7.	Marshall	0-5-0	.000	2-9-0	.182
	Davidson*			4-6-0	.400

East Carolina and William and Mary leave the conference. Non-conference record: 22-27-2 .451

1978

1.	Furman	4-1-0	.800	8-3-0	.727
1.	Chattanooga	4-1-0	.800	7-3-1	.682
3.	App. State	4-2-0	.667	7-4-0	.636
3.	W. Carolina	4-2-0	.667	6-5-0	.545
5.	The Citadel	2-3-0	.400	5-6-0	.455
6.	VMI	1-4-0	.200	3-8-0	.273
7.	Marshall	0-5-0	.000	1-10-0	.091
	Davidson*			5-5-0	.500
	E. Tenn. State			4-7-0	.364

East Tennessee State joins the SC, but plays no SC games.
Non-conference record: 18-21-1 .463

1979

1.	Chattanooga	5-1-0	.833	9-2-0	.818
1.	East Carolina	4-1-0	.800	9-2-0	.818
2.	Wm. & Mary	3-2-0	.600	7-4-0	.636
3.	App. State	2-2-1	.500	6-4-1	.591
3.	Furman	2-2-1	.500	6-4-1	.591
5.	VMI	2-3-0	.400	5-5-0	.500
6.	The Citadel	1-4-0	.200	6-5-0	.545
	Davidson*			2-6-1	.278
	Marshall			5-6-0	.455
	Chattanooga			6-4-1	.591
	West Carolina			6-4-0	.600

Marshall, Chattanooga, and West Carolina join the Conference, but play no SC games. Richmond leaves. Davidson is listed as an SC member, 1976-1981, but plays no conference games in those seasons.
Non-conference record: 25-10-0 .600

1980

1.	Furman	7-0-0	1.000	9-1-1	.864
2.	Chattanooga	5-2-0	.714	8-3-0	.727
3.	App. State	4-2-1	.643	6-4-1	.591
4.	The Citadel	3-2-0	.600	7-4-0	.636
5.	W. Carolina	2-4-1	.357	3-7-1	.318
6.	VMI	1-4-1	.250	3-7-1	.318
7.	E. Tenn. State	1-4-0	.200	2-9-0	.182
8.	Marshall	0-5-1	.083	2-8-1	.227
	Davidson*			5-5-0	.500

Non-conference record: 17-20-1 .461

1981

1.	Furman	5-2-0	.714	8-3-0	.727
2.	VMI	3-1-1	.700	6-3-1	.650
3.	E. Tenn. State	4-2-0	.667	6-5-0	.545
4.	The Citadel	3-2-1	.583	7-3-1	.682
4.	Chattanooga	3-2-1	.583	7-3-1	.682
6.	W. Carolina	3-4-0	.429	4-7-0	.364
7.	App. State	1-5-1	214	3-7-1	.318
8.	Marshall	1-5-0	.167	2-9-0	.182
	Davidson*			4-6-0	.400

Non-conference record: 20-17-0 .541
The Southern Conference was classified I-AA in the NCAA restructuring of college football that became effective in 1981.

Decade	Alabama	Clemson	Duke	Ga. Tech	Maryland	N.Carol.	Tenn.	Tulane	Auburn	Sewanee	W.Forest
1922-29	40-12-3	11-20-1	2- 1-0	33-11-7	11-23-3	27-16-4	31-12-4	25-19-3	10-31-6	5-24-1	
1930-39	20- 3-0	21-15-3	46- 9-2	8-12-3	23-18-2	34-15-8	19- 1-2	18- 2-1	10- 9-1	4-13-0	9-14-1
1940-49		28-17-2	37- 9-3		21-17-2	29-15-4					40-21-3
1950-52		6- 1-1	14- 4-0		9- 1-1	6- 7-1					16- 5-1

Decade	Florida	Georgia	Kentucky	LSU	Miss.	Miss.St.	NC State	S.Carolina	Vanderb.	Virginia
1922-29	26-10-4	27-19-1	14-21-5	12-19-3	8-24-2	13-23-2	7-30-3	15-23-1	30-10-3	18-23-6
1930-39	7-12-3	11- 7-3	12-10-2	9- 6-0	4-13-0	2-12-0	20-32-4	22-27-4	12- 7-2	6-23-4
1940-49							28-32-6	21-23-4		
1950-52							8-14-1	9-11-1		

Decade	VMI	Va. Tech	Furman	Davidson	E.Carol.	Richmond	Citadel	G.Wash	W. Va.	W.&Lee	Wm&Mary.
1922-29	19-21-2	23-16-0								21-19-4	
1930-39	20-27-6	24-31-9	8-10-3	8-22-0		9- 9-2	4-14-0			16-24-3	2-12-1
1940-49	27-27-4	21-28-6	16-24-2	11-35-4		14-38-3	6-24-1	7-20-1		11-16-4	39-10-3
1950-52	12- 4-1	5-19-0	5-10-2	3-16-0		3-20-0	4- 9-1	10- 8-1	8- 7-0	14- 5-0	12- 5-0
1953-59	23-17-3	18- 9-2	13- 8-0	10-21-1		19-24-3	15-18-0	16-21-1	25- 2-0	2- 6-0	10-25-4
1960-69	25-24-2	16- 9-0	15-30-0	14-33-2	14- 8-1	33-27-2	31-33-0	20-24-0	25- 5-3		29-29-3
1970-79	23-31-0		26-30-2	5-25-1	29-10-0	26-10-0	30-31-0				21-14-0
1980-81	4- 5-2		12- 2-0				6- 4-1				

Decade	App.St.	Marsh.	Chatt	W. Carol.	E. Tenn. St
1950-52					
1953-39					
1960-69					
1970-79	19-20-2	0-16-0	13- 3-0	8- 8-1	2- 3-0
1980-81	5- 7-2	1-10-1	8- 4-1	5- 8-1	5- 6-0

SOUTHERN CONFERENCE W-L-T PERCENTAGES (1922-1952)

Team	Record	Pct.	Team	Record	Pct.
Alabama	60-15-3	.788	Mississippi State	15-35-2	.308
Clemson	66-53-7	.552	North Carolina State	63-108-14	.378
Duke	99-23-5	.799	South Carolina	67-84-10	.447
Georgia Tech	41-23-10	.622	Vanderbilt	42-17-5	.695
Maryland	64-59-8	.519	Virginia	24-46-10	.362
North Carolina	96-53-17	.630	Virginia Tech	73-94-20	.444
Tennessee	50-13-6	.768	VMI	78-79-13	.497
Tulane	43-21-4	.662	Sewanee	9-37-1	.202
Washington & Lee	62-64-11	.493	Furman	29-44-7	.406
William & Mary	53-27-4	.655	Davidson	21-73-4	.235
Auburn	20-40-7	.351	Wake Forest	65-40-5	.614
Florida	33-22-7	.589	Richmond	26-67-5	.291
Georgia	38-26-4	.588	The Citadel	14-47-2	.238
Kentucky	26-29-7	.476	George Washington	17-28-2	.383
LSU	21-25-3	.459	West Virginia	8- 7-0	.533
Mississippi	12-37-2	.255			

SOUTHERN CONFERENCE W-L-T PERCENTAGES (1953-1981)

Team	Record	Pct.	Team	Record	Pct.
VMI	75-77-7	.494	West Virginia	50- 7-3	.858
Va. Tech	34-18-2	.648	Wash. & Lee	2- 6-0	.250
Furman	66-70-2	.486	Wm. & Mary	60-63-7	.488
Davidson	29-79-4	.277	Appalachian State	24-27-4	.473
East Carolina	43-18-1	.702	Marshall	1-26-1	.026
Richmond	78-61-5	.559	Chattanooga	21- 7-1	.741
The Citadel	82-86-1	.488	Western Carolina	13-16-1	.450
George Washington	36-45-1	.445	East Tennessee State	7- 9-0	.438

SOUTHERN CONFERENCE TITLES BY DECADES (1922-1952)

Decade	Alabama	Clemson	Duke	Ga. Tech	Maryland	N.Carol.	Tenn.	Tulane	W&L	Wm&M	VMI
1922-29	3			2		1		1	1		
1930-39	1		5		1		1	1	1		
1940-49		2	4			2				2	
1950-52			1		.5				1		.5
Totals	4	2	10	2	1.5	3	1	2	3	2	.5

SOUTHERN CONFERENCE TITLES BY DECADES (1953-1981)

Decade	West Va.	VMI	Citadel	Va. Tech	E.Carol.	Wm&M.	Richmond	Davidson	Chatt.	Furman
1953-59	5	2								
1960-69	3	2	1	1	.5	.5	1.5	.5		
1970-79		1.5			3	1	2		2	.5
1980-81										2
Totals	8	5.5	1	1	3.5	1.5	3.5	.5	2	2.5

SOUTHWEST CONFERENCE (1915-1995). The Southwest Conference disbanded after the 1995 season, with four members (Texas, Texas Tech, Texas A&M, and Baylor) joining with the Big Eight members to form the Big Twelve Conference.

1915

Rank	School	SWC W-L-T	Pct.	Overall W-L-T	Pct.
1.	Oklahoma	3-0-0	1.000	10-0-0	1.000
2.	Arkansas	1-1-0	.500	4-2-1	.643
2.	Texas	2-2-0	.500	6-3-0	.667
2.	Texas A&M	1-1-0	.500	6-2-0	.750
5.	Rice	1-2-0	.333	5-3-0	.625
6.	Oklahoma A&M	0-3-0	.000	4-5-1	.450
6.	Southwestern	0-2-0	.000	4-3-0	.571
8.	Baylor*	3-0-0	1.000	7-1-0	.875

Non-conference record: 32-9-2 .767

*Baylor ineligible for title for using ineligible player

1916

Rank	School	SWC W-L-T	Pct.	Overall W-L-T	Pct.
1.	Texas	5-1-0	.833	7-2-0	778
2.	Baylor	3-1-0	.750	9-1-0	.900
3.	Oklahoma	2-1-0	.667	6-5-0	.545
3.	Texas A&M	2-1-0	.667	6-3-0	.667
5.	Okla. A&M	0-3-0	.000	4-4-0	.500
5.	Arkansas	0-2-0	.000	4-4-0	.500
5.	Southwestern	0-3-0	.000	3-5-1	389

Rice out of SWC.

Non-conference record: 27-12-1 .688

1917

Rank	School	SWC W-L-T	Pct.	Overall W-L-T	Pct.
1.	Texas A&M	2-0-0	1.000	8-0-0	1.000
2.	Baylor	2-1-0	.667	6-2-1	.722
3.	Oklahoma	1-1-1	.500	6-4-1	.591
4.	Texas	2-3-0	.400	4-4-0	.500
5.	Okla. A&M	1-2-0	.333	4-4-0	.500
6.	Arkansas	0-1-1	.250	5-1-1	.786

Non-conference record: 25-7-1 .797

1918

Rank	School	SWC W-L-T	Pct.	Overall W-L-T	Pct.
1.	Texas	4-0-0	1.000	9-0-0	1.000
1.	Oklahoma	2-0-0	1.000	6-0-0	1.000
3.	Texas A&M	1-1-0	.500	6-1-0	.857
3.	Rice	1-1-0	.500	1-5-1	.214
5.	SMU	1-2-0	.333	4-2-0	.667
6.	Arkansas	0-1-0	.000	3-2-0	.600
6.	Baylor	0-2-0	.000	0-4-0	.000
6.	Okla. A&M	0-2-0	.000	4-2-0	.667

Rice returns to SWC, and SMU joins SWC.

Non-conference record: 24-7-1 .766

1919

Rank	School	SWC W-L-T	Pct.	Overall W-L-T	Pct.
1.	Texas A&M	4-0-0	1.000	10-0-0	1.000
2.	Rice	3-1-0	.750	8-1-0	.889
3.	Oklahoma	2-1-0	.667	5-2-3	.650
4.	Texas	3-2-0	.600	6-3-0	.667
5.	Arkansas	1-2-0	.333	3-4-0	.429
6.	SMU	0-2-1	.167	5-4-1	.550
7.	Baylor	0-3-1	.125	5-3-1	.611
8.	Okla. A&M	0-2-0	.000	3-3-2	.500

Non-conference record: 32-7-5 .784

1920

Rank	School	SWC W-L-T	Pct.	Overall W-L-T	Pct.
1.	Texas	5-0-0	1.000	9-0-0	1.000
2.	Arkansas	2-0-1	.833	3-2-2	.571
2.	Texas A&M	5-1-0	.833	6-1-1	.812
4.	Rice	2-2-1	.500	4-2-2	.625
5.	Baylor	1-2-1	.375	4-4-1	.500
6.	Phillips	0-3-0	.000	4-5-1	.450
6.	Okla. A&M	0-3-0	.000	0-7-1	.062
6.	SMU	0-4-1	.100	3-5-2	.400

Oklahoma leaves SWC, and Phillips joins SWC.

Non-conference record: 18-11-6 .600

1921

Rank	School	SWC W-L-T	Pct.	Overall W-L-T	Pct.
1.	Texas A&M	3-0-2	.800	5-1-2	.750
2.	Texas	1-0-1	.750	6-1-1	.812
3.	Arkansas	2-1-0	.667	5-3-1	.611
4.	Baylor	2-2-0	.500	8-3-0	.727
4.	Okla. A&M	1-1-0	.500	5-4-1	.550
6.	Rice	1-2-1	.375	4-4-1	.500
7.	SMU	0-4-0	.000	1-6-1	.188

Phillips leaves the SWC.

Non-conference record: 24-12-3 .634

1922

Rank	School	SWC W-L-T	Pct.	Overall W-L-T	Pct.
1.	Baylor	5-0-0	1.000	8-3-0	.727
2.	Texas	2-1-0	.667	7-2-0	.778
3.	Texas A&M	2-2-0	.500	5-4-0	.556
3.	SMU	2-2-0	.500	6-3-1	.650
5.	Okla. A&M	2-3-0	.400	5-4-1	.550
6.	Arkansas	1-3-0	.250	5-4-0	.556
7.	Rice	1-4-0	.200	4-4-0	.500

Non-conference record: 25-9-2 .722

1923

Rank	School	SWC W-L-T	Pct.	Overall W-L-T	Pct.
1.	SMU	5-0-0	1.000	9-0-0	1.000
2.	Texas	2-0-1	.833	8-0-1	.944
3.	TCU	2-1-0	.667	4-5-0	.444
4.	Arkansas	2-2-0	.500	6-2-1	.722
4.	Baylor	1-1-2	.500	5-1-2	.750
6.	Okla. A&M	1-3-0	.250	2-8-0	.200
7.	Rice	1-4-0	.200	3-5-0	.375
8.	Texas A&M	0-3-1	.125	5-3-1	.688

TCU joins the SWC.

Non-conference record: 28-10-1 .731

1924

Rank	School	SWC W-L-T	Pct.	Overall W-L-T	Pct.
1.	Baylor	4-0-1	.900	7-2-1	.750
2.	SMU	2-0-4	.667	5-1-4	.700
3.	Rice	2-2-0	.500	4-4-0	.500
3.	Texas A&M	2-2-1	.500	7-2-1	.750
3.	Okla. A&M	1-1-1	.500	6-1-2	.778
6.	Texas	2-3-0	.400	5-3-1	.611
7.	Arkansas	1-2-1	.375	7-2-1	.750
8.	TCU	1-5-0	.167	4-5-0	.444

Non-conference record: 30-5-2 .838

1925

Rank	School	SWC W-L-T	Pct.	Overall W-L-T	Pct.
1.	Texas A&M	4-1-0	.800	7-1-1	.833
2.	Texas	2-1-1	.625	6-2-1	.722
2.	TCU	2-1-1	.625	7-1-1	.833
4.	SMU	1-1-2	.500	5-2-2	.667
4.	Arkansas	2-2-1	.500	4-4-1	.500
6.	Rice	1-2-1	.375	4-4-1	.500
7.	Baylor	0-3-2	.200	3-5-2	.400

Oklahoma A&M leaves the SWC.

Non-conference record: 24-8-1 .742

1926

Rank	School	SWC W-L-T	Pct.	Overall W-L-T	Pct.
1.	SMU	5-0-0	1.000	8-0-1	.944
2.	Baylor	3-1-0	.700	6-3-1	.650
3.	Texas	2-2-0	.500	5-4-0	.556
3.	Arkansas	2-2-0	.500	5-5-0	.500
3.	TCU	1-1-2	.500	6-1-2	.778
6.	Texas A&M	1-3-1	.300	5-3-1	.611
7.	Rice	0-4-0	.000	4-4-1	.500

Non-conference record: 25-7-2 .765

1927

Rank	School	SWC W-L-T	Pct.	Overall W-L-T	Pct.
1.	Texas A&M	4-0-1	.900	8-0-1	.944
2.	SMU	4-1-0	.800	7-2-0	.778
3.	Arkansas	3-1-0	.750	8-1-0	.889
4.	Texas	2-2-1	.500	6-2-1	.722
5.	TCU	1-2-2	.400	4-3-2	.556
6.	Rice	1-3-0	.250	2-6-1	.278
7	Baylor	0-5-0	.000	2-7-0	.222

Non-conference record: 22-7-1 .750

1928

Rank	School	SWC W-L-T	Pct.	Overall W-L-T	Pct.
1.	Texas	5-1-0	.833	7-2-0	.778
2.	Arkansas	3-1-0	.750	7-2-0	.778
3.	Baylor	3-2-0	.600	8-2-0	.800
3.	TCU	3-2-0	.600	8-2-0	.800
5.	SMU	2-2-1	.500	6-3-1	.650
6.	Texas A&M	1-3-1	.300	5-4-1	.550
7.	Rice	0-5-0	.000	2-7-0	.222

Non-conference record: 26-6-0 .812

1929

Rank	School	SWC W-L-T	Pct.	Overall W-L-T	Pct.
1.	TCU	4-0-1	.900	9-0-1	.950
2.	SMU	3-0-2	.800	6-0-4	.800
3.	Arkansas	3-2-0	.600	7-2-0	.778
4.	Texas	2-2-2	.500	5-2-2	.667
4.	Baylor	2-2-1	.500	7-3-1	.682
6.	Texas A&M	2-3-0	.400	5-3-0	.625
7.	Rice	0-5-0	.000	2-7-0	.222

Non-conference record: 25-3-2 .867

1930

Rank	School	SWC W-L-T	Pct.	Overall W-L-T	Pct.
1.	Texas	4-1-0	.800	8-1-1	.850
2.	Baylor	3-1-1	.700	6-3-1	.650
3.	TCU	4-2-0	.667	9-2-1	.792
4.	SMU	2-2-1	.500	6-3-1	.650
4.	Arkansas	2-2-0	.500	3-6-0	.333
6.	Rice	2-4-0	.333	8-4-0	.667
7.	Texas A&M	0-5-0	.000	2-7-0	.222

Non-conference record: 25-9-2 .722

1931

Rank	School	SWC W-L-T	Pct.	Overall W-L-T	Pct.
1.	SMU	5-0-1	.917	9-1-1	.864
2.	TCU	4-1-1	.750	9-2-1	.792
3.	Texas A&M	3-2-0	.600	7-3-0	.700
4.	Rice	3-3-0	.500	6-4-0	.600
5.	Texas	2-3-0	.400	6-4-0	.600
6.	Baylor	1-5-0	.167	3-6-0	.333
7.	Arkansas	0-4-0	.000	3-5-1	.389

Non-conference record: 25-7-1 .773

1932

Rank	School	SWC W-L-T	Pct.	Overall W-L-T	Pct.
1.	TCU	6-0-0	1.000	10-0-1	.955
2.	Texas	5-1-0	.833	8-2-0	.800
3.	Rice	3-3-0	.500	7-3-0	.700
4.	Texas A&M	1-2-2	.400	4-2-2	.625
5.	Baylor	1-4-1	.250	3-5-1	.389
5.	SMU	1-4-1	.250	3-7-2	.333
7.	Arkansas	1-4-0	.200	1-6-2	.222

Non-conference record: 18-7-4 .690

1933

Rank	School	SWC W-L-T	Pct.	Overall W-L-T	Pct.
1.	TCU	5-1-0	.833	10-1-1	.875
1.	Baylor	5-1-0	.833	7-3-0	.700
3.	Texas	3-2-1	.583	5-4-2	.545
4.	Texas A&M	2-2-1	.500	6-3-1	.650
5.	SMU	3-3-0	.500	5-6-1	.458
6.	Rice	1-5-0	.167	3-8-0	.273
	Arkansas*	0-5-0	.800	0-11-0	.000

*Records are after Arkansas forfeited all games.

Non-conference record: 17-17-3 .500

1934

Rank	School	SWC W-L-T	Pct.	Overall W-L-T	Pct.
1.	Rice	5-1-0	.833	9-1-1	.864
2.	Texas	4-1-1	.750	7-2-1	.750
3.	SMU	3-2-1	.583	8-2-2	.750
4.	TCU	3-3-0	.500	8-4-0	.667
5.	Arkansas	2-3-1	.417	4-4-2	.500
6.	Texas A&M	1-4-1	.250	2-7-2	.273
7.	Baylor	1-5-0	.167	3-7-0	.300

Non-conference record: 22-8-4 .706

1935

Rank	School	SWC W-L-T	Pct.	Overall W-L-T	Pct.
1.	SMU	6-0-0	1.000	12-1-0	.923
2.	TCU	5-1-0	.833	12-1-0	.923
3.	Rice	3-3-0	.500	8-3-0	.727
3.	Baylor	3-3-0	.500	8-3-0	.727
5.	Arkansas	2-4-0	.333	4-5-1	.450
6.	Texas	1-5-0	.167	4-6-0	.400
6.	Texas A&M	1-5-0	.1676	3-7-0	.300

Non-conference record: 30-5-1 .847

1936

Rank	School	SWC W-L-T	Pct.	Overall W-L-T	Pct.
1.	Arkansas	5-1-0	.833	7-3-0	.700
2.	TCU	4-1-1	.750	9-2-2	.769
3.	Texas A&M	3-2-1	.583	8-3-1	.708
3.	Baylor	3-2-1	.583	6-3-1	.650
5.	SMU	2-3-1	.417	5-4-1	.550
6.	Texas	1-5-0	.167	2-6-1	.278
7.	Rice	1-5-0	.167	5-7-0	.417

Non-conference record: 23-9-2 .706

1937

Rank	School	SWC W-L-T	Pct.	Overall W-L-T	Pct.
1.	Rice	4-1-1	.750	6-3-2	.636
2.	TCU	3-1-2	.667	4-4-2	.500
3.	Arkansas	3-2-1	.583	6-2-2	.700
4.	Baylor	3-3-0	.500	7-3-0	.700
4.	Texas A&M	2-2-2	.500	5-2-2	.667
6.	SMU	2-4-0	.667	5-6-0	.455
7.	Texas	1-5-0	.167	2-6-1	.278

Non-conference record: 17-8-3 .661

1938

Rank	School	SWC W-L-T	Pct.	Overall W-L-T	Pct.
1.	TCU	6-0-0	1.000	11-0-0	1.000
2.	SMU	4-2-0	.667	6-4-0	.600
3.	Baylor	3-2-1	.583	7-2-1	.750
4.	Rice	3-3-0	.500	4-6-0	.400
5.	Texas A&M	2-3-1	.417	4-4-1	.500
6.	Texas	1-5-0	.167	1-8-0	.111
6.	Arkansas	1-5-0	.167	2-7-1	.250

Non-conference record: 15-11-1 .574

1939		SWC		Overall	
Rank	School	W-L-T	Pct.	W-L-T	Pct.
1.	Texas A&M	6-0-0	1.000	11-0-0	1.000
2.	SMU	4-2-0	.667	6-3-1	.650
2.	Baylor	4-2-0	.667	7-3-0	.700
4.	Texas	3-3-0	.500	5-3-0	.625
5.	Arkansas	2-3-1	.417	4-5-1	.450
6.	TCU	1-5-0	.167	3-7-0	.300
7.	Rice	0-5-1	.083	1-9-1	.136

Non-conference record: 17-10-1 .625

1940					
1.	Texas A&M	5-1-0	.833	9-1-0	.900
1.	SMU	5-1-0	.833	8-1-1	.850
3.	Rice	4-2-0	.667	7-3-0	.700
3.	Texas	4-2-0	.667	8-2-0	.800
5.	TCU	2-4-0	.333	3-7-0	.300
6.	Arkansas	1-5-0	.167	4-6-0	.400
7.	Baylor	0-6-0	.000	4-6-0	.400

Non-conference record: 22-5-1 .804

1941					
1.	Texas A&M	5-1-0	.833	9-2-0	.818
2.	Texas	4-1-1	.750	8-1-1	.950
2.	TCU	4-1-1	.750	7-3-1	.682
4.	Rice	3-2-1	.583	6-3-1	.650
5.	SMU	2-4-0	.333	5-5-0	.500
6.	Baylor	1-4-1	.250	3-6-1	.350
7.	Arkansas	0-6-0	.000	3-7-0	.300

Non-conference record: 22-8-0 .733

1942					
1.	Texas	5-1-0	.833	9-2-0	.818
2.	Rice	4-1-1	.750	7-2-1	.750
3.	TCU	4-2-0	.667	7-3-0	.700
4.	Baylor	3-2-1	.583	6-4-1	.591
5.	Texas A&M	2-3-1	.417	4-5-1	.450
6.	SMU	1-4-1	.250	3-6-2	.364
7.	Arkansas	0-6-0	.000	3-7-0	.300

Non-conference record: 20-10-1 .661

1943					
1.	Texas	5-0-0	1.000	7-1-1	.833
2.	Texas A&M	4-1-0	.800	7-2-1	.750
3.	SMU	2-3-0	.400	2-7-0	.222
3.	Rice	2-3-0	.400	3-7-0	.300
5.	TCU	1-4-0	.200	2-6-0	.333
5.	Arkansas	1-4-0	.200	2-7-0	.222

Non-conference record: 8-15-2 .360
Baylor drops football during WW II.

1944					
1.	TCU	3-1-1	.700	7-3-1	.682
2.	Texas	3-2-0	.600	5-4-0	.556
3.	Arkansas	2-2-1	.500	5-5-1	.500
4.	Texas A&M	2-3-0	.400	7-4-0	.636
4.	Rice	2-3-0	.400	5-6-0	.455
4.	SMU	2-3-0	.400	5-5-0	.500

Non-conference record: 20-13-0 .606

1945					
1.	Texas	5-1-0	.833	10-1-0	.909
2.	SMU	4-2-0	.667	5-6-0	.455
3.	Rice	3-3-0	.500	5-6-0	.455
3.	Texas A&M	3-3-0	.500	6-4-0	.600
3.	TCU	3-3-0	.500	5-5-0	.500
6.	Baylor	2-4-0	.333	5-5-1	.500
7.	Arkansas	1-5-0	.167	3-7-0	.300

Non-conference record: 18-13-1 .578

1946		SWC		Overall	
Rank	School	W-L-T	Pct.	W-L-T	Pct.
1.	Rice	5-1-0	.833	9-2-0	.818
1.	Arkansas	5-1-0	.833	6-3-2	.636
3.	Texas	4-2-0	.667	8-2-0	.800
4.	Texas A&M	3-3-0	.500	4-6-0	.400
5.	SMU	2-4-0	.333	4-5-1	.450
5.	TCU	2-4-0	.333	2-7-1	.250
7.	Baylor	0-6-0	.000	1-8-0	.111

Non-conference record: 13-12-4 .517

1947					
1.	SMU	5-0-1	.917	9-0-2	.909
2.	Texas	5-1-0	.833	10-1-0	.909
3.	Rice	4-2-0	.667	6-3-1	.650
4.	TCU	2-3-1	.417	4-5-2	.455
5.	Texas A&M	1-4-1	.250	3-6-1	.350
5.	Arkansas	1-4-1	.250	6-4-1	.591
7.	Baylor	1-5-0	.167	5-5-0	.500

Non-conference record: 24-5-3 .797

1948					
1.	SMU	5-0-1	.917	9-1-1	.864
2.	Texas	4-1-1	.750	7-3-1	.682
3.	Rice	3-2-1	.583	5-4-1	.550
3.	Baylor	3-2-1	583	6-3-2	.636
5.	Arkansas	2-4-0	.333	5-5-0	.500
6.	TCU	1-4-1	.250	4-5-1	.450
7.	Texas A&M	0-5-1	.083	0-9-1	.050

Non-conference record: 18-12-1 .598

1949					
1.	Rice	6-0-0	1.000	10-1-0	.909
2.	Baylor	4-2-0	.667	8-2-0	.800
3.	Texas	3-3-0	.500	6-4-0	.600
3.	TCU	3-3-0	.500	6-3-1	.650
5.	SMU	2-3-1	.417	5-4-1	.550
6.	Arkansas	2-4-0	.333	5-5-0	.500
7.	Texas A&M	0-5-1	.083	1-8-1	.150

Non-conference record: 21-7-1 .741

1950		SWC		Overall	
Rank	School	W-L-T	Pct.	W-L-T	Pct.
1.	Texas	6-0-0	1.000	9-2-0	.818
2.	Baylor	4-2-0	.667	7-3-0	.700
3.	Texas A&M	3-3-0	.500	7-4-0	.636
3.	TCU	3-3-0	.500	5-5-0	.500
5.	Rice	2-4-0	.333	6-4-0	.600
5.	SMU	2-4-0	.333	6-4-0	.600
7.	Arkansas	1-5-0	.167	2-8-0	.200

Non-conference record: 21-9-0 .700

1951					
1.	TCU	5-1-0	.833	6-5-0	.545
2.	Baylor	4-1-1	.750	8-2-1	.773
3.	Texas	3-3-0	.500	7-3-0	.700
3.	Rice	3-3-0	.500	5-5-0	.500
5.	Texas A&M	1-3-2	.333	5-3-2	.600
5.	Arkansas	2-4-0	.333	5-5-0	.500
7.	SMU	1-4-1	.250	3-6-1	.350

Non-conference record: 20-10-0 .667

1952					
1.	Texas	6-0-0	1.000	9-2-0	.818
2.	Rice	4-2-0	.667	5-5-0	.500
3.	SMU	3-2-1	.583	4-5-1	.450
4.	TCU	2-2-2	.500	4-4-2	.500
5.	Baylor	1-3-2	.333	4-4-2	.500
6.	Texas A&M	1-4-1	.250	3-6-1	.350
7.	Arkansas	1-5-0	.167	2-8-0	.200

Non-conference record: 13-16-0 .448

1953					
1.	Rice	5-1-0	.833	9-2-0	.818
1.	Texas	5-1-0	.833	7-3-0	.700
3.	Baylor	4-2-0	.667	7-3-0	.700
4.	SMU	3-3-0	.500	5-5-0	.500
5.	Arkansas	2-4-0	.333	3-7-0	.300
6.	Texas A&M	1-5-0	.167	4-5-1	.450
6.	TCU	1-5-0	.167	3-7-0	.300

Non-conference record: 17-11-1 .603

1954					
1.	Arkansas	5-1-0	.833	8-3-0	.727
2.	SMU	4-1-1	.750	6-3-1	.650
3.	Baylor	4-2-0	.667	7-4-0	.636
3.	Rice	4-2-0	.667	7-3-0	.700
5.	Texas	2-3-1	.417	4-5-1	.450
6.	TCU	1-5-0	.167	4-6-0	.400
7.	Texas A&M	0-6-0	.000	1-9-0	.100

Non-conference record: 17-13-0 .567

1955					
1.	TCU	5-1-0	.833	9-2-0	.818
2.	Texas A&M	4-1-1	.750	7-2-1	.750
3.	Texas	4-2-0	.667	5-5-0	.500
4.	Arkansas	3-2-1	.583	5-4-1	.550
5.	Baylor	2-4-0	.333	5-5-0	.500
5.	SMU	2-4-0	.333	4-6-0	.400
7.	Rice	0-6-0	.000	2-7-1	.250

Non-conference record: 17-11-1 .603

1956		SWC		Overall	
Rank	School	W-L-T	Pct.	W-L-T	Pct.
1.	Texas A&M	6-0-0	1.000	9-0-1	.950
2.	TCU	5-1-0	.833	8-3-0	.727
3.	Baylor	4-2-0	.667	9-2-0	.818
4.	Arkansas	3-3-0	.500	6-4-0	.600
5.	SMU	2-4-0	.333	4-6-0	.400
6.	Rice	1-5-0	.167	4-6-0	.400
7.	Texas	0-6-0	.000	1-9-0	.100

Non-conference record: 20-9-1 .683

1957					
1.	Rice	5-1-0	.833	7-4-0	.636
2.	Texas	4-1-1	.750	6-4-1	.591
3.	Texas A&M	4-2-0	.667	8-3-0	.727
4	SMU	3-3-0	.500	4-5-1	.450
5.	Arkansas	2-4-0	.333	6-4-0	.600
5.	TCU	2-4-0	.333	5-4-1	.550
7.	Baylor	0-5-1	.083	3-6-1	350

Non-conference record: 19-10-2 .645

1958					
1.	TCU	5-1-0	.833	8-2-1	.773
2.	Rice	4-2-0	.667	5-5-0	.500
2.	SMU	4-2-0	.556	6-4-0	.600
4.	Texas	3-3-0	.500	7-3-0	.700
5.	Texas A&M	2-4-0	.333	4-6-0	.400
5.	Arkansas	2-4-0	.333	4-6-0	.400
7.	Baylor	1-5-0	.167	3-7-0	.300

Non-conference record: 16-12-1 .550

1959					
1.	Texas	5-1-0	.833	9-2-0	.818
1.	TCU	5-1-0	.833	8-3-0	.727
1.	Arkansas	5-1-0	.833	9-2-0	.818
4.	SMU	2-3-1	.417	5-4-1	.550
5.	Baylor	2-4-0	.333	4-6-0	.400
6.	Rice	1-4-1	.250	1-7-2	.200
7.	Texas A&M	0-6-0	.000	3-7-0	.300

Non-conference record: 19-11-1 .629

1960					
1.	Arkansas	6-1-0	.857	8-3-0	.727
2.	Baylor	5-2-0	.714	8-3-0	.727
2.	Texas	5-2-0	.714	7-3-1	.682
2.	Rice	5-2-0	.714	7-4-0	.636
5.	TCU	3-3-1	.500	4-4-2	.500
6.	Texas Tech	1-5-1	.214	3-6-1	.350
6.	Texas A&M	0-4-3	.214	1-6-3	.250
8.	SMU	0-6-1	.071	0-9-1	.050

Non-conference record: 13-13-2 .500

Texas Tech joins the SWC.

1961					
1.	Texas	6-1-0	.857	10-1-0	.909
1.	Arkansas	6-1-0	.857	8-3-0	.727
3.	Rice	5-2-0	.714	7-4-0	.636
4.	Texas A&M	3-4-0	.429	4-5-1	.450
5.	TCU	2-4-1	.357	3-5-2	.400
6.	Baylor	2-5-0	.286	6-5-0	.545
6.	Texas Tech	2-5-0	.286	4-6-0	.400
8.	SMU	1-5-1	.214	2-7-1	.250

Non-conference record: 17-9-2 .643

1962

Rank	School	SWC W-L-T	Pct.	Overall W-L-T	Pct.
1.	Texas	6-0-1	.929	9-1-1	.864
2.	Arkansas	6-1-0	.857	9-2-0	.818
3.	TCU	5-2-0	.714	6-4-0	.600
4.	Texas A&M	3-4-0	.429	3-7-0	.300
4.	Baylor	3-4-0	.429	4-6-0	.400
6.	Rice	2-4-1	.357	2-6-2	.300
7.	SMU	2-5-0	.286	2-8-0	.200
8.	Texas Tech	0-7-0	.000	1-9-0	.100

Non-conference record: 9-16-1 .365

1963

Rank	School	SWC W-L-T	Pct.	Overall W-L-T	Pct.
1.	Texas	7-0-0	1.000	11-0-0	1.000
2.	Baylor	6-1-0	.857	8-3-0	.727
3.	Rice	4-3-0	.571	6-4-0	.600
4.	Arkansas	3-4-0	.429	5-5-0	.500
5.	TCU	2-4-1	.357	4-5-1	.450
6.	Texas Tech	2-5-0	.286	5-5-0	.500
6.	SMU	2-5-0	.286	4-7-0	.364
8.	Texas A&M	1-5-1	.214	2-7-1	250

Non-conference record: 18-9-0 .667

1964

Rank	School	SWC W-L-T	Pct.	Overall W-L-T	Pct.
1.	Arkansas	7-0-0	1.000	11-0-0	1.000
2.	Texas	6-1-0	.857	10-1-0	.909
3.	Baylor	4-3-0	.571	5-5-0	.500
4.	Rice	3-3-1	.500	4-5-1	.450
4.	Texas Tech	3-3-1	.500	6-4-1	.591
6.	TCU	3-4-0	.429	4-6-0	.400
7.	Texas A&M	1-6-0	.143	1-9-0	.100
8.	SMU	0-7-0	.000	1-9-0	.100

Non-conference record: 15-12-0 .556

1965

Rank	School	SWC W-L-T	Pct.	Overall W-L-T	Pct.
1.	Arkansas	7-0-0	1.000	10-1-0	.909
2.	Texas Tech	5-2-0	.714	8-3-0	.727
2.	TCU	5-2-0	.714	6-5-0	.545
4.	Baylor	3-4-0	.429	5-5-0	.500
4.	SMU	3-4-0	.429	4-5-1	.450
4.	Texas	3-4-0	.429	6-4-0	.600
7.	Rice	1-6-0	.143	2-8-0	.200
7.	Texas A&M	1-6-0	.143	3-7-0	.300

Non-conference record: 16-10-1 .593

1966

Rank	School	SWC W-L-T	Pct.	Overall W-L-T	Pct.
1.	SMU	6-1-0	.857	8-3-0	.727
2.	Arkansas	5-2-0	.714	8-2-0	.800
2.	Texas	5-2-0	.714	7-4-0	.636
4.	Texas A&M	4-3-0	.571	4-5-1	.450
5.	Baylor	3-4-0	.429	5-5-0	.500
6.	TCU	2-5-0	.286	2-8-0	.200
6.	Texas Tech	2-5-0	.286	4-6-0	.400
8.	Rice	1-6-0	.143	2-8-0	.200

Non-conference record: 12-13-1 .481

1967

Rank	School	SWC W-L-T	Pct.	Overall W-L-T	Pct.
1.	Texas A&M	6-1-0	.857	7-4-0	.636
2.	Texas Tech	5-2-0	.714	6-4-0	.600
3.	TCU	4-3-0	.571	4-6-0	.400
3.	Texas	4-3-0	.571	6-4-0	.600
5.	Arkansas	3-3-1	.500	4-5-1	.450
6.	SMU	3-4-0	.429	3-7-0	.300
7.	Rice	2-5-0	.286	4-6-0	.400
8.	Baylor	0-6-1	.071	1-8-1	.150

Non-conference record: 8-17-0 .320

1968

Rank	School	SWC W-L-T	Pct.	Overall W-L-T	Pct.
1.	Texas	6-1-0	.857	9-1-1	.864
1.	Arkansas	6-1-0	.857	10-1-0	.909
3.	SMU	5-2-0	.714	8-3-0	.727
4.	Texas Tech	4-3-0	.571	5-3-2	.600
5.	Baylor	3-4-0	.429	3-7-0	.300
6.	Texas A&M	2-5-0	.286	3-7-0	.300
6.	TCU	2-5-0	.286	3-7-0	.300
8.	Rice	0-7-0	.000	0-9-1	.050

Non-conference record: 13-10-4 .556

1969

Rank	School	SWC W-L-T	Pct.	Overall W-L-T	Pct.
1.	Texas	7-0-0	1.000	11-0-0	1.000
2.	Arkansas	6-1-0	.857	9-2-0	.818
3.	Texas Tech	4-3-0	.571	5-5-0	.500
3.	TCU	4-3-0	.571	4-6-0	.400
5.	SMU	3-4-0	.429	3-7-0	.300
6.	Texas A&M	2-5-0	.286	3-7-0	.300
6.	Rice	2-5-0	.286	3-7-0	.300
8.	Baylor	0-7-0	.000	0-10-0	.000

Non-conference record: 10-16-0 .385

1970

Rank	School	SWC W-L-T	Pct.	Overall W-L-T	Pct.
1.	Texas	7-0-0	1.000	10-1-0	909
2.	Arkansas	6-1-0	.857	9-2-0	.818
3.	Texas Tech	5-2-0	.714	8-4-0	.667
4.	SMU	3-4-0	.429	5-6-0	.455
4	TCU	3-4-0	.429	4-6-1	.409
4.	Rice	3-4-0	.429	5-5-0	.500
7.	Baylor	1-6-0	.167	2-9-0	.182
8.	Texas A&M	0-7-0	.000	2-9-0	.182

Non-conference record: 17-14-1 .547

1971

Rank	School	SWC W-L-T	Pct.	Overall W-L-T	Pct.
1.	Texas	6-1-0	.857	8-3-0	.727
2	Arkansas	5-1-1	.786	8-3-1	.708
3.	TCU	5-2-0	.714	6-4-1	.591
4.	Texas A&M	4-3-0	.571	5-6-0	.455
5.	SMU	3-4-0	.429	4-7-0	.364
6.	Rice	2-4-1	.357	3-7-1	.318
7.	Texas Tech	2-5-0	.286	4-7-0	.364
8.	Baylor	0-7-0	.000	1-9-0	.100

Non-conference record: 12-19-1 .391

1972

Rank	School	SWC W-L-T	Pct.	Overall W-L-T	Pct.
1.	Texas	7-0-0	1.000	10-1-0	.909
2.	SMU	4-3-0	.571	7-4-0	.636
2.	Texas Tech	4-3-0	.571	8-4-0	.667
4.	Baylor	3-4-0	.429	5-6-0	.455
4.	Rice	3-4-0	.429	5-5-0	.500
4.	Arkansas	3-4-0	.429	6-5-0	.545
7.	TCU	2-5-0	.286	5-6-0	.455
7.	Texas A&M	2-5-0	.286	3-8-0	.273

Non-conference record: 21-11-0 .625

1973

Rank	School	SWC W-L-T	Pct.	Overall W-L-T	Pct.
1.	Texas	7-0-0	1.000	8-3-0	.727
2.	Texas Tech	6-1-0	.857	11-1-0	.917
3.	Rice	4-3-0	.571	5-6-0	.455
4.	SMU	3-3-1	.500	6-4-1	.591
4.	Arkansas	3-3-1	.500	5-5-1	.500
6.	Texas A&M	3-4-0	.429	5-6-0	.455
7.	TCU	1-6-0	.143	3-8-0	.273
8.	Baylor	0-7-0	.000	2-9-0	.182

Non-conference record: 18-15-0 .545

1974

Rank	School	SWC W-L-T	Pct.	Overall W-L-T	Pct.
1.	Baylor	6-1-0	.857	8-4-0	.667
2.	Texas	5-2-0	.714	8-4-0	.667
2.	Texas A&M	5-2-0	.714	8-3-0	.727
4.	Arkansas	3-3-1	.500	6-4-1	.591
4.	SMU	3-3-1	.500	6-4-1	.591
6.	Texas Tech	3-4-0	.429	6-4-2	.583
7.	Rice	2-5-0	.286	2-8-1	.227
8.	TCU	0-7-0	.000	1-10-0	.091

Non-conference record: 18-14-3 .557

1975

Rank	School	SWC W-L-T	Pct.	Overall W-L-T	Pct.
1.	Arkansas	6-1-0	.857	10-2-0	.833
1.	Texas A&M	6-1-0	.857	10-2-0	.833
1.	Texas	6-1-0	.857	10-2-0	.833
4.	Texas Tech	4-3-0	.571	6-5-0	.545
5.	SMU	2-5-0	.286	4-7-0	.364
5.	Baylor	2-5-0	.286	3-6-2	.364
7.	TCU	1-6-0	.143	1-10-0	.091
7.	Rice	1-6-0	.143	2-9-0	.182

Non-conference record: 18-15-2 .543

1976

Rank	School	SWC W-L-T	Pct.	Overall W-L-T	Pct.
1.	Houston	7-1-0	.875	10-2-0	.833
1.	Texas Tech	7-1-0	.875	10-2-0	.833
2.	Texas A&M	6-2-0	.750	10-2-0	.833
4.	Baylor	4-3-1	.562	7-3-1	.682
5.	Texas	4-4-0	.500	5-5-1	.500
6.	Arkansas	3-4-1	.438	5-5-1	.500
7.	Rice	2-6-0	.250	3-8-0	.272
7.	SMU	2-6-0	.250	3-8-0	.272
9.	TCU	0-8-0	.000	0-11-0	.000

Non-conference record: 18-11-1 .617
Houston joins the SWC.

1977

Rank	School	SWC W-L-T	Pct.	Overall W-L-T	Pct.
1.	Texas	8-0-0	1.000	11-1-0	.917
2.	Arkansas	7-1-0	.875	11-1-0	.917
3.	Texas A&M	6-2-0	.750	8-4-0	.667
4.	Houston	4-4-0	.500	6-5-0	.545
4.	Texas Tech	4-4-0	.500	7-5-0	.583
6.	Baylor	3-5-0	.375	5-6-0	.455
6.	SMU	3-5-0	.375	4-7-0	.364
8.	TCU	1-7-0	.125	2-9-0	.182
9.	Rice	0-8-0	.000	1-10-0	.091

Non-conference record: 19-12-0 .613

1978

Rank	School	SWC W-L-T	Pct.	Overall W-L-T	Pct.
1.	Houston	7-1-0	.875	9-3-0	.750
2.	Texas	6-2-0	.750	9-3-0	.750
2.	Arkansas	6-2-0	.750	9-2-1	.792
4.	Texas Tech	5-3-0	.625	7-4-0	.636
5.	Texas A&M	4-4-0	.500	8-4-0	.667
6.	SMU	3-5-0	.375	4-6-1	.409
6.	Baylor	3-5-0	.375	3-8-0	.273
8.	Rice	2-6-0	.250	2-9-0	.182
9.	TCU	0-8-0	.000	2-9-0	.182

Non-conference record: 17-12-2 .581

1979

Rank	School	SWC W-L-T	Pct.	Overall W-L-T	Pct.
1.	Houston	7-1-0	.875	11-1-0	.917
1.	Arkansas	7-1-0	.875	10-2-0	.833
3.	Texas	6-2-0	.750	9-3-0	.750
4.	Baylor	5-3-0	.625	8-4-0	.667
5.	Texas A&M	4-4-0	.500	6-5-0	.545
6.	SMU	3-5-0	.375	5-6-0	.455
7.	Texas Tech	2-5-1	.312	3-6-2	.364
8.	TCU	1-6-1	.188	2-8-1	.227
9.	Rice	0-8-0	.000	1-10-0	.091

Non-conference record: 20-10-1 .661

1980

Rank	School	SWC W-L-T	Pct.	Overall W-L-T	Pct.
1.	Baylor	8-0-0	1.000	10-2-0	.833
2.	SMU	5-3-0	.625	8-4-0	.667
2.	Houston	5-3-0	.625	7-5-0	.583
4.	Texas	4-4-0	.500	7-5-0	.583
4.	Rice	4-4-0	.500	5-6-0	.455
6.	Arkansas	3-5-0	.375	7-5-0	.583
6.	Texas Tech	3-5-0	.375	5-6-0	.455
6.	Texas A&M	3-5-0	.375	4-7-0	.364
9.	TCU	1-7-0	.125	1-10-0	.091

Non-conference record: 18-14-0 .562

1981

Rank	School	SWC W-L-T	Pct.	Overall W-L-T	Pct.
1.	SMU	7-1-0	.875	10-1-0	.909
2.	Texas	6-1-1	.812	10-1-1	.875
3.	Houston	5-2-1	.688	7-4-1	.625
4.	Arkansas	5-3-0	.625	8-4-0	.667
5.	Texas A&M	4-4-0	.500	7-5-0	.583
6.	Rice	3-5-0	.375	4-7-0	.364
6.	Baylor	3-5-0	.375	5-6-0	.455
8.	TCU	1-6-1	.188	2-7-2	.273
9.	Texas Tech	0-7-1	.062	1-9-1	.136

Non-conference record: 20-10-1 .661

1982

Rank	School	SWC W-L-T	Pct.	Overall W-L-T	Pct.
1.	SMU	7-0-1	.938	11-0-1	.958
2.	Texas	7-1-0	.875	9-3-0	.750
3.	Arkansas	5-2-1	.688	9-2-1	.792
4.	Houston	4-3-1	.562	5-5-1	.500
5.	Baylor	3-4-1	.438	4-6-1	.409
6.	Texas Tech	3-5-0	.375	4-7-0	.364
6.	Texas A&M	3-5-0	.375	5-6-0	.455
8.	TCU	2-6-0	.250	3-8-0	.272
9.	Rice	0-8-0	.000	0-11-0	.000

Non-conference record: 16-14-0 .533

1983

Rank	School	SWC W-L-T	Pct.	Overall W-L-T	Pct.
1.	Texas	8-0-0	1.000	11-1-0	.917
2.	SMU	7-1-0	.875	10-2-0	.833
3.	Baylor	4-3-1	.562	7-4-1	.625
3.	Texas A&M	4-3-1	.562	5-5-1	.500
5.	Arkansas	4-4-0	.500	6-5-0	.545
6.	Texas Tech	3-4-1	.436	3-7-1	.318
7.	Houston	3-5-0	.375	4-7-0	.364
8.	TCU	1-6-1	.188	1-8-2	.182
9.	Rice	0-8-0	.000	1-10-0	.091

Non-conference record: 14-15-1 .483

1984

Rank	School	SWC W-L-T	Pct.	Overall W-L-T	Pct.
1.	SMU	6-2-0	.750	10-2-0	.833
1.	Houston	6-2-0	.750	7-5-0	.583
3.	TCU	5-3-0	.625	8-4-0	.667
3	Texas	5-3-0	.625	7-4-1	.625
3.	Arkansas	5-3-0	.625	7-4-1	.625
6.	Baylor	4-4-0	.500	5-6-0	.455
7.	Texas A&M	3-5-0	.375	6-5-0	.545
8.	Texas Tech	2-6-0	.250	4-7-0	.364
9.	Rice	0-8-0	.000	1-10-0	.091

Non-conference record: 19-11-2 .625

1985

Rank	School	SWC W-L-T	Pct.	Overall W-L-T	Pct.
1.	Texas A&M	7-1-0	.875	10-2-0	.833
2.	Arkansas	6-2-0	.750	10-2-0	.833
2.	Baylor	6-2-0	.750	9-3-0	.750
2.	Texas	6-2-0	.750	8-4-0	.667
5.	Houston	3-5-0	.375	4-7-0	.364
6.	Rice	2-6-0	.250	3-8-0	.273
7.	Texas Tech	1-7-0	.125	4-7-0	.364
8.	TCU	0-8-0	.000	3-8-0	.273
	SMU*	5-3-0	.625	6-5-0	.545

*SMU ineligible for title.
Non-conference record: 21-10-0 .677

1986

Rank	School	SWC W-L-T	Pct.	Overall W-L-T	Pct.
1.	Texas A&M	7-1-0	.875	9-3-0	.750
2.	Arkansas	6-2-0	.750	9-3-0	.750
2.	Baylor	6-2-0	.750	9-3-0	.750
4.	Texas Tech	5-3-0	.625	7-5-0	.583
5.	Texas	4-4-0	.500	5-6-0	.455
6.	Rice	2-6-0	.250	4-7-0	.364
7.	Houston	0-8-0	.000	1-10-0	.091
	SMU*	5-3-0	.625	6-5-0	.545
	TCU*	1-7-0	.125	3-8-0	.273

*SMU and TCU ineligible for title.
Non-conference record: 17-14-0 .548

1987

Rank	School	SWC W-L-T	Pct.	Overall W-L-T	Pct.
1.	Texas A&M	6-1-0	.857	10-2-0	.833
2.	Texas	5-2-0	.714	7-5-0	.583
2.	Arkansas	5-2-0	.714	9-4-0	.692
4.	Texas Tech	3-3-1	.500	6-4-1	.591
5.	TCU	3-4-0	.429	5-6-0	.455
5.	Baylor	3-4-0	.429	6-5-0	.545
7.	Houston*	2-4-1	.357	4-6-1	.409
8.	Rice	0-7-0	.000	2-9-0	.182
	SMU**				

*Includes loss for forfeited win versus Temple.
**SMU did not play football in 1987.
Non-conference record: 22-14-0 .611

1988

Rank	School	SWC W-L-T	Pct.	Overall W-L-T	Pct.
1.	Arkansas	7-0-0	1.000	10-2-0	.833
2.	Houston	5-2-0	.714	9-3-0	.750
3.	Texas Tech	4-3-0	.571	5-6-0	.455
4.	Baylor	2-5-0	.286	6-5-0	.545
4.	Texas	2-5-0	.286	4-7-0	.364
4.	TCU	2-5-0	.286	4-7-0	.364
7.	Rice	0-7-0	.000	0-11-0	.000
	Texas A&M*	6-1-0	.857	7-5-0	.583
	SMU**				

*Texas A&M ineligible for league title.
**SMU did not play football in 1988.
Non-conference record 17-18-0 .486

1989

Rank	School	SWC W-:L-T	Pct.	Overall W-L-T	Pct.
1.	Arkansas	7-1-0	.875	10-2-0	.833
2.	Texas A&M	6-2-0	.750	8-4-0	.667
3.	Texas Tech	5-3-0	.625	9-3-0	.750
4.	Baylor	4-4-0	.500	5-6-0	.455
4.	Texas	4-4-0	.500	5-6-0	.455
6.	TCU	2-6-0	.250	4-7-0	.364
6.	Rice	2-6-0	.250	2-8-1	.227
8.	SMU	0-8-0	.000	2-9-0	.182
	Houston*	6-2-0	.750	9-2-0	.818

*Houston not eligible for title in 1989.
Non-conference record: 19-11-1 .629

1990

Rank	School	SWC W-L-T	Pct.	Overall W-L-T	Pct.
1.	Texas	8-0-0	1.000	10-2-0	.833
2.	Texas A&M	5-2-1	.688	9-3-1	.731
2.	Baylor	5-2-1	.688	6-4-1	.591
4.	Rice	3-5-0	.375	5-6-0	.455
4.	TCU	3-5-0	.375	6-6-0	.455
4.	Texas Tech	3-5-0	.375	7-5-0	.583
7.	Arkansas	1-7-0	.125	3-8-0	.273
8.	SMU	0-8-0	.000	1-10-0	.091
	Houston*	7-1-0	.875	10-1-0	.909

*Houston not eligible for titlc.
Non-conference record: 21-10-0 .677

1991

Rank	School	SWC W-L-T	Pct.	Overall W-L-T	Pct.
1.	Texas A&M	8-0-0	1.000	10-2-0	.833
2.	Baylor	5-3-0	.625	8-4-0	.667
2.	Texas Tech	5-3-0	.625	6-5-0	.545
2.	Arkansas	5-3-0	.625	6-6-0	.500
5.	Texas	4-4-0	.500	5-6-0	.455
5.	TCU	4-4-0	.500	7-4-0	.636
7.	Houston	3-5-0	.375	4-7-0	.364
8.	Rice	2-6-0	.250	4-7-0	.364
9.	SMU	0-8-0	.000	1-10-0	.091

Non-conference record: 15-15-0 .500

1992

Rank	School	SWC W-L-T	Pct.	Overall W-L-T	Pct.
1.	Texas A&M	7-0-0	1.000	12-1-0	.923
2.	Baylor	4-3-0	.571	7-5-0	.583
2.	Rice	4-3-0	.571	6-5-0	.545
2.	Texas	4-3-0	.571	6-5-0	.545
2.	Texas Tech	4-3-0	.571	5-6-0	.455
6.	SMU	2-5-0	.286	5-6-0	.455
6.	Houston	2-5-0	.286	4-7-0	.364
8.	TCU	1-6-0	.143	2-8-1	.227

Arkansas leaves SWC.
Non-conference record: 19-15-1 .557

1993

Rank	School	SWC W-L-T	Pct.	Overall W-L-T	Pct.
1.	Texas A&M	7-0-0	1.000	10-2-0	.833
2.	Texas Tech	5-2-0	.714	6-6-0	.500
2.	Texas	5-2-0	.714	5-5-1	.500
4.	Rice	3-4-0	.429	6-5-0	.545
4.	Baylor	3-4-0	.429	5-6-0	.455
6.	TCU	2-5-0	.286	4-7-0	.364
7.	SMU	1-5-1	214	2-7-2	.272
7.	Houston	1-5-1	.214	1-9-1	.136

Non-conference record: 12-20-2 .382

1994

Rank	School	W-L-T	Pct.	W-L-T	Pct.
1.	Texas Tech	4-3-0	.571	6-6-0	.500
1.	Baylor	4-3-0	.571	7-5-0	.583
1.	Rice	4-3-0	.571	5-6-0	.455
1.	Texas	4-3-0	.571	8-4-0	.667
1.	TCU	4-3-0	.571	7-5-0	.583
6.	Houston	1-6-0	.143	1-10-0	.091
7.	SMU	0-6-1	.072	1-9-1	.136
	Texas A&M*	6-0-1	.929	10-0-1	.955

*Texas A&M ineligible for title.
Non-conference record: 18-18-0   .500

1995

1.	Texas	7-0-0	1.000	10-2-1	.808
2.	Texas A&M	5-2-0	.714	9-3-0	.750
2.	Texas Tech	5-2-0	.714	9-3-0	.750
2.	Baylor	5-2-0	.714	7-4-0	.636
5.	TCU	3-4-0	.429	6-5-0	.545
6.	Houston	2-5-0	.286	2-9-0	.182
7.	Rice	1-6-0	.143	2-8-1	.227
8.	SMU	0-7-0	.000	1-10-0	.091

SWC disbands after 1995 season.
Non-conference record: 18-16-2   .528

SWC W-L-T RECORDS BY DECADES (1915-1995)

Decade	Arkansas	Baylor	Rice	Texas	TexA&M	SMU	TCU	Tex. Tech	Houston	Okla.	OklA&M
1915-19	2- 7-1	8- 7-1	5- 4-0	16- 8-0	10- 3-0	1- 4-1				10- 3-1	1-12-0
1920-29	21-16-3	21-18-8	9-33-3	25-12-6	24-18-7	24-14-10	14-12-6				5-11-1
1930-39	18-33-3	27-28-4	25-33-2	25-31-2	21-27-8	32-22-5	41-15-4				
1940-49	15-41-2	14-31-3	36-19-3	42-14-2	25-29-4	30-24-4	25-29-4				
1950-59	26-33-1	26-30-4	29-30-1	38-20-2	22-34-4	26-30-4	34-24-2				
1960-69	55-14-1	29-40-1	25-43-2	55-14-1	23-43-4	25-43-2	32-35-3	28-40-2			
1970-79	49-21-4	27-46-1	19-54-1	62-12-0	40-34-0	29-43-2	14-59-1	42-31-1	25- 7-0		
1980-89	53-24-1	43-33-2	13-65-0	51-26-1	49-28-1	42-21-1	18-58-2	29-46-3	39-36-3		
1990-95	6-10-0	26-17-1	17-27-0	32-12-0	38- 4-2	3-39-2	17-27-0	26-18-0	16-27-1		

Decade	Southwest	Phillips
1915-19	0- 5-0	
1920-29		0- 3-0

SWC W-L-T Percentages (1915-1995)

Team	Record	Pct.	Team	Record	Pct.
Arkansas	245-199-16	.550	Texas Tech	125-135-6	.481
Baylor	221-250-25	.471	Houston	80- 70-4	.532
Rice	178-308-12	.369	Oklahoma	10- 3-1	.750
Texas	346-149-14	.694	Oklahoma A&M	6- 23-1	.217
Texas A&M	252-220-30	.532	Southwest	0- 5-0	.000
SMU	212-240-31	.471	Phillips	0- 3-0	.000
TCU	195-259-22	.433			

SWC TITLES BY DECADES (1915-1995)

Decade	Arkansas	Baylor	Rice	Texas	TexA&M	SMU	TCU	Tex. Tech	Houston	Okla.
1915-19				2	2					1
1920-29		2		2	3	2	1			
1930-39	1		2	1	1	2	3			
1940-49	.5		1.5	3	1.5	3.5	1			
1950-59	1.33		1.5	2.83	1		3.33			
1960-69	4			4	1	1				
1970-79	.83	1		5.33	.33			.5	2	
1980-89	2	1		1	3	2.5			.5	
1990-95		.2	.2	2.2	3		.2	.2		
Totals	9.66	4.2	5.2	23.36	15.83	11	8.53	.7	2.5	

SUN BELT CONFERENCE (2001-2003). The Sun Belt football Conference was organized in 2001 after the Big West Conference disbanded and includes four of the members of that conference. After the 2003 season, the Sun Belt announced the loss of Utah State and New Mexico State to the WAC, and the addition of Troy State for the 2004 season, with Florida International and Florida Atlantic to join the Sun Belt later.

2001		Conference		Overall	
1.	North Texas	5-1-0	.833	5-6-0	.455
1.	Middle Tenn.	5-1-0	.833	8-3-0	.727
3.	N.M. State	4-2-0	.667	5-7-0	.417
4.	UL Lafayette	2-4-0	.333	3-8-0	.273
4.	Arkansas State	2-4-0	.333	2-9-0	.182
4.	UL Monroe	2-4-0	.333	2-9-0	.182
7.	Idaho	1-5-0	.167	1-10-0	.091

Non-conference record: 5-31-0 .139

2002		Conference		Overall	
1.	North Texas	6-0-0	1.000	8-5-0	.615
2.	N.M. State	5-1-0	.833	7-5-0	.583
3.	Arkansas State	3-3-0	.500	6-7-0	.462
4.	Middle Tenn.	2-4-0	.333	3-8-0	.273
4.	UL Lafayette	2-4-0	.333	3-9-0	.250
4.	UL Monroe	2-4-0	.333	3-9-0	.250
7.	Idaho	1-5-0	.167	2-10-0	.167

Non-conference record: 11-32-0 .262

2003		Conference		Overall	
1.	North Texas	7-0-0	1.000	9-4-0	.692
2.	Middle Tenn.	4-3-0	.571	4-8-0	.333
2.	UL Lafayette	4-3-0	.571	4-8-0	.333
4.	Arkansas State	3-4-0	.429	5-7-0	.417
4.	Idaho	3-4-0	.429	3-9-0	.250
4.	Utah State	3-4-0	.429	3-9-0	.250
7.	N.M. State	2-5-0	.286	3-9-0	.250
8.	UL Monroe	1-6-0	.143	1-11-0	.083

Non-conference record: 5-36-0 .122

WESTERN ATHLETIC CONFERENCE (1962 –2003). The WAC was organized in 1962 by teams leaving the Border Conference and the Mountain States (Skyline) Conference, both of which were disbanded after the 1961 season. After the 2003 season, the WAC announced the loss of Rice, SMU, and Tulsa to Conference USA, and added Utah State and New Mexico State from the Sun Belt.

1962		Conference		Overall	
1.	New Mexico	2-1-1	.625	7-2-1	.750
2.	Wyoming	2-2-0	.500	5-5-0	.500
2.	BYU	2-2-0	.500	4-6-0	.400
2.	Arizona	2-2-0	.500	5-5-0	.500
5.	Utah	1-2-1	.375	4-5-1	.450
	Arizona State*	1-1-0	.500	7-2-1	.750

*fewer than qualifying number of games.
Non-conference record: 22-15-1 .592

1963					
1.	New Mexico	3-1-0	.750	6-4-0	.600
2.	Arizona	2-2-0	.500	5-5-0	.500
2.	Utah	2-2-0	.500	4-6-0	.400
4.	Wyoming	2-3-0	.400	6-4-0	.600
5.	BYU	0-4-0	.000	2-8-0	.200
	Ariz. State*	3-0-0	1.000	8-1-0	.889

*fewer than qualifying number or games.
Non-conference record: 19-16-0 .543

1964					
1.	Arizona	3-1-0	.750	6-3-1	.650
1.	Utah	3-1-0	.750	9-2-0	.818
1.	New Mexico	3-1-0	.750	9-2-0	.818
4.	Wyoming	2-2-0	.500	6-2-2	.700
5.	BYU	0-4-0	.000	3-6-1	.350
	Ariz. State*	0-2-0	.000	8-2-0	.800

*fewer than qualifying number of games.
Non-conference record: 30-6-4 .800

1965					
1.	BYU	4-1-0	.800	6-4-0	.600
2.	Ariz. State	3-1-0	.750	6-4-0	.600
3.	Wyoming	3-2-0	.600	6-4-0	.600
4.	New Mexico	2-3-0	.400	3-7-0	.300
5.	Utah	1-3-0	.250	3-7-0	.300
6.	Arizona	1-4-0	.200	3-7-0	.300

Non-conference record: 13-19-0 .406

1966					
1.	Wyoming	5-0-0	1.000	10-1-0	.909
2.	BYU	3-2-0	.600	8-2-0	.800
2.	Ariz. State	3-2-0	.600	5-5-0	.500
2.	Utah	3-2-0	.600	5-5-0	.500
5.	Arizona	1-4-0	.200	3-7-0	.300
6.	New Mexico	0-5-0	.000	2-8-0	.200

Non-conference record: 18-13-0 .581

1967					
1.	Wyoming	5-0-0	1.000	10-1-0	.909
2.	Ariz. State	4-1-0	.800	8-2-0	.800
3.	BYU	3-2-0	.600	6-4-0	.600
4.	Utah	2-3-0	.400	4-7-0	.364
5.	Arizona	1-4-0	.200	3-6-1	.350
6.	New Mexico	0-5-0	.000	1-9-0	.100

Non-conference record: 17-14-1 .547

1968					
1.	Wyoming	6-1-0	.857	7-3-0	.700
2.	Ariz. State	5-1-0	.833	8-2-0	.800
2.	Arizona	5-1-0	.833	8-3-0	.727
4.	UTEP	3-3-0	.500	4-5-1	.450
5.	Utah	2-3-0	.400	3-7-0	.300
6.	Colo. State	1-2-0	.333	2-8-0	.200
7.	BYU	1-5-0	.167	2-8-0	.200
8.	New Mexico	0-7-0	.000	0-10-0	.100

UTEP and Colorado State join the WAC.
Non-conference record: 11-23-1 .329

1969		Conference		Overall	
1.	Ariz. State	6-1-0	.875	8-2-0	.800
2.	Utah	5-1-0	.833	8-2-0	.800
3.	BYU	4-3-0	.571	6-4-0	.600
3.	Wyoming	4-3-0	.571	6-4-0	.600
5.	Arizona	3-3-0	.500	3-7-0	.300
6.	UTEP	2-5-0	.286	4-6-0	.400
7.	New Mexico	1-5-0	.167	4-6-0	.400
8.	Colo. State	0-4-0	.000	4-6-0	.400

Non-conference record: 17-12-0 .586

1970					
1.	Ariz. State	7-0-0	1.000	11-0-0	1.000
2.	New Mexico	5-1-0	.833	7-3-0	.700
3.	Utah	4-2-0	.667	6-4-0	.600
4.	UTEP	4-3-0	.571	6-4-0	.600
5.	Arizona	2-4-0	.333	4-6-0	.400
6.	Colo. State	1-3-0	.250	4-7-0	.364
7.	BYU	1-6-0	.143	3-8-0	.273
7.	Wyoming	1-6-0	.143	1-9-0	.100

Non-conference record: 17-16-0 .515

1971					
1.	Ariz. State	7-0-0	1.000	11-1-0	.917
2.	New Mexico	5-1-0	.833	6-3-2	.636
3.	Arizona	3-3-0	.500	5-6-0	.455
4.	BYU	3-4-0	.429	5-6-0	.455
4.	Utah	3-4-0	.429	3-8-0	.273
4.	Wyoming	3-4-0	.429	5-6-0	.455
7.	Colo. State	1-4-0	.200	3-8-0	.273
8.	UTEP	1-6-0	.143	5-6-0	.455

Non-conference record: 17-16-2 .514

1972					
1.	Ariz. State	5-1-0	.833	10-2-0	.833
2.	BYU	5-2-0	.714	7-4-0	.636
2.	Utah	5-2-0	.714	6-5-0	.545
4.	Arizona	4-3-0	.571	4-7-0	.363
5.	Wyoming	3-4-0	.428	4-7-0	.363
6.	New Mexico	2-4-0	.333	3-8-0	.273
7.	Colo. State	1-4-0	.200	1-10-0	.091
8.	UTEP	1-6-0	.143	2-8-0	.200

Non-conference record: 11-25-0 .306

1973					
1.	Arizona	6-1-0	.857	8-3-0	.727
1.	Ariz. State	6-1-0	.857	11-1-0	.916
3.	Utah	4-2-0	.667	7-5-0	.583
4.	BYU	3-4-0	.429	5-6-0	.455
4.	New Mexico	3-4-0	.429	4-7-0	.363
4.	Wyoming	3-4-0	.429	4-7-0	.363
7.	Colo. State	2-4-0	.333	5-6-0	.455
8.	UTEP	0-7-0	.000	0-11-0	.000

Non-conference record: 17-19-0 .472

1974					
1.	BYU	6-0-1	.929	7-4-1	.625
2.	Arizona	6-1-0	.857	9-2-0	.818
3.	Ariz. State	4-3-0	.571	7-5-0	.583
4.	New Mexico	3-4-0	.429	4-6-1	.409
4.	UTEP	3-4-0	.429	4-7-0	.364
6.	Colo. State	2-3-1	.417	4-6-1	.409
7.	Utah	1-5-0	.167	1-10-0	.091
8.	Wyoming	1-6-0	.143	2-9-0	.182

Non-conference record: 12-23-1 .347

1975		Conference		Overall	
1.	Ariz. State	7-0-0	1.000	12-0-0	1.000
2.	Arizona	5-2-0	.714	9-2-0	.818
3.	Colo. State	4-2-0	.667	6-5-0	.545
4.	BYU	4-3-0	.571	6-5-0	.545
4.	New Mexico	4-3-0	.571	6-5-0	.545
6.	Utah	1-4-0	.200	1-10-0	.091
7.	Wyoming	1-6-0	.143	2-9-0	.182
8.	UTEP	0-6-0	.000	1-10-0	.091

Non-conference record: 17-20-0 .459

1976					
1.	BYU	6-1-0	.857	9-4-0	.692
1.	Wyoming	6-1-0	.857	8-4-0	.667
3.	Ariz. State	4-3-0	.571	4-7-0	.364
4.	Utah	3-3-0	.500	3-8-0	.273
5.	Arizona	3-4-0	.428	5-6-0	.455
5.	New Mexico	3-4-0	.428	4-7-0	.364
7.	Colo. State	2-4-0	.333	6-5-0	.545
8.	UTEP	0-7-0	.000	1-11-0	.083

Non-conference record: 13-25-0 .342

1977					
1.	Ariz. State	6-1-0	.857	9-3-0	.750
1.	BYU	6-1-0	.857	9-2-0	.818
3.	Colo. State	5-2-0	.714	9-2-1	.792
4.	Wyoming	4-3-0	.571	4-6-1	.409
5.	Arizona	3-4-0	.429	5-7-0	.417
6.	New Mexico	2-5-0	.286	5-7-0	.417
6.	Utah	2-5-0	.286	3-8-0	.273
8.	UTEP	0-7-0	.000	1-10-0	.091

Non-conference record: 17-17-2 .500

1978					
1.	BYU	5-1-0	.833	9-4-0	.692
2.	Utah	4-2-0	.667	8-3-0	.727
2.	Wyoming	4-2-0	.667	5-7-0	.417
4.	New Mexico	3-3-0	.500	7-5-0	.583
5.	Colo. State	2-4-0	.333	5-6-0	.455
5.	San Diego State	2-4-0	.333	4-7-0	.364
7.	UTEP	1-5-0	.167	1-11-0	.083

Arizona and Arizona State leave the WAC, and San Diego State joins the WAC.
Non-conference record: 18-22-0 .450

1979					
1.	BYU	7-0-0	1.000	11-1-0	.917
2.	S. Diego State	5-2-0	.714	8-3-0	.727
2.	Utah	5-2-0	.714	6-6-0	.500
4.	Hawaii	3-4-0	.429	6-5-0	.545
4.	New Mexico	3-4-0	.429	6-6-0	.500
4.	Colo. State	3-4-0	.429	4-7-1	.375
7.	Wyoming	2-5-0	.286	4-8-0	.333
8.	UTEP	0-7-0	.000	2-9-0	.182

Hawaii joins the WAC
Non-conference record: 19-17-1 .527

1980					
1.	BYU	6-1-0	.857	12-1-0	923
2.	Colo. State	5-1-1	.786	6-4-1	.591
3.	Hawaii	4-3-0	.571	8-3-0	.727
4.	Wyoming	4-4-0	.500	6-5-0	.545
4.	S. Diego State	4-4-0	.500	4-8-0	.333
6.	New Mexico	3-4-0	.429	4-7-0	.364
7.	Utah	2-3-1	.417	5-5-1	.500
8.	Air Force	1-6-0	.143	2-9-1	.208
8.	UTEP	1-6-0	.143	1-11-0	.083

Air Force joins the WAC.
Non-conference record 17-13-1 .565

1981		Conference		Overall	
1.	BYU	7-1-0	.875	11-2-0	.846
2.	Hawaii	6-1-0	.857	9-2-0	.818
3.	Utah	5-1-1	.786	8-2-1	.773
3.	Wyoming	6-2-0	.750	8-3-0	.727
5.	New Mexico	3-4-1	.437	4-7-1	.375
6.	S. Diego State	3-5-0	.375	6-5-0	.545
7.	Air Force	2-5-0	.285	4-7-0	.363
8.	UTEP	1-6-0	.143	1-10-0	.091
9.	Colo. State	0-8-0	.000	0-12-0	.000

Non-conference record: 18-17-0 .514

1982					
1.	BYU	7-1-0	.875	8-4-0	.667
2.	New Mexico	6-1-0	.857	10-1-0	.909
3.	Air Force	4-3-0	.571	8-5-0	.617
3.	S. Diego State	4-3-0	.571	7-5-0	.583
5.	Hawaii	4-4-0	.500	6-5-0	.545
6.	Colo. State	3-5-0	.375	4-7-0	.364
7.	Utah	2-4-0	.333	5-6-0	.455
8.	Wyoming	2-6-0	.250	5-7-0	.417
9.	UTEP	1-6-0	.143	2-10-0	.167

Non-conference record: 22-17-0 .564

1983					
1.	BYU	7-0-0	1.000	11-1-0	.917
2.	Air Force	5-2-0	.714	10-2-0	.833
3.	Wyoming	5-3-0	.625	7-5-0	.583
4.	New Mexico	4-3-0	.571	6-6-0	.500
5.	Hawaii	3-3-1	.500	5-5-1	.500
5.	Utah	4-4-0	.500	5-6-0	.455
5.	Colo. State	4-4-0	.500	5-7-0	.417
8.	S. Diego State	1-6-1	.187	2-9-1	.208
9.	UTEP	0-8-0	.000	2-10-0	.167

Non-conference record: 20-18-0 .526

1984					
1.	BYU	8-0-0	1.000	13-0-0	1.000
2.	Hawaii	5-2-0	.714	7-4-0	.636
3.	Air Force	4-3-0	.571	8-4-0	.667
4.	Utah	4-3-1	.562	6-5-1	.542
4.	S. Diego State	4-3-1	.562	4-7-1	.375
6.	Wyoming	4-4-0	.500	6-6-0	.500
7.	Colo. State	3-5-0	.375	3-8-0	.273
8.	New Mexico	1-7-0	.125	4-8-0	.333
8.	UTEP	1-7-0	.125	2-9-0	.182

Non-conference record: 19-15-0 .559

1985					
1.	Air Force	7-1-0	.875	12-1-0	.923
1.	BYU	7-1-0	.875	11-3-0	.786
3.	Utah	5-3-0	.625	8-4-0	.667
4.	Hawaii	4-3-1	.563	4-6-2	.417
5.	Colo. State	4-4-0	.500	5-7-0	.417
6.	S. Diego State	3-4-1	.438	5-6-1	.458
7.	New Mexico	2-6-0	.250	3-8-0	.273
7.	Wyoming	2-6-0	.250	3-8-0	.273
9.	UTEP	1-7-0	.125	1-10-0	.091

Non-conference record: 17-18-1 .486

1986		Conference		Overall	
1.	S. Diego State	7-1-0	.875	8-4-0	.667
2.	BYU	6-2-0	.750	8-5-0	.615
3.	Air Force	5-2-0	.714	6-5-0	.545
4.	Hawaii	4-4-0	.500	7-5-0	.583
4.	Colo. State	4-4-0	.500	6-5-0	.545
4.	Wyoming	4-4-0	.500	6-6-0	.500
7.	New Mexico	2-5-0	.286	4-8-0	.333
8.	UTEP	2-6-0	.250	4-8-0	.333
9.	Utah	1-7-0	.125	2-9-0	.182

Non-conference record: 16-20-0 .444

1987					
1.	Wyoming	8-0-0	1.000	10-3-0	.769
2.	BYU	7-1-0	.875	9-4-0	.692
3.	Air Force	6-2-0	.750	9-4-0	.692
4.	UTEP	5-3-0	.625	7-4-0	.636
5.	S. Diego State	4-4-0	.500	5-7-0	.417
6.	Hawaii	3-5-0	.375	5-7-0	.417
7.	Utah	2-6-0	.250	5-7-0	.417
8.	Colo. State	1-7-0	.125	1-11-0	.083
9.	New Mexico	0-8-0	.000	0-11-0	.000

Non-conference record: 15-22-0 .405

1988					
1.	Wyoming	8-0-0	1.000	11-2-0	.846
2.	UTEP	6-2-0	.750	10-3-0	.769
3.	Hawaii	5-3-0	.625	9-3-0	.750
3.	BYU	5-3-0	.625	9-4-0	.692
5.	Utah	4-4-0	.500	6-5-0	.545
6.	Air Force	3-5-0	.375	5-7-0	.417
6.	S. Diego State	3-5-0	.375	3-8-0	.273
8.	New Mexico	1-7-0	.125	2-10-0	.167
8.	Colo. State	1-7-0	.125	1-10-0	.091

Non-conference record: 20-16-0 .556

1989					
1.	BYU	7-1-0	.875	10-3-0	.769
2.	Air Force	5-1-1	.786	8-4-1	.654
3.	Hawaii	5-2-1	.688	9-3-1	.731
4.	Wyoming	5-3-0	.625	5-6-0	.455
5.	S. Diego State	4-3-0	.571	6-5-1	.542
5.	Colo. State	4-3-0	.571	5-5-1	.500
7.	Utah	2-6-0	.250	4-8-0	.333
8.	UTEP	1-7-0	.125	2-10-0	.167
9.	New Mexico	0-7-0	.000	2-10-0	.167

Non-conference record: 18-21-2 .463

1990					
1.	BYU	7-1-0	.875	10-3-0	.769
2.	Colo. State	6-1-0	.857	9-4-0	.692
3.	S. Diego State	5-2-0	.714	6-5-0	.545
4.	Wyoming	5-3-0	.625	9-4-0	.692
5.	Hawaii	4-4-0	.500	7-5-0	.583
6.	Air Force	3-4-0	.429	7-5-0	.583
7.	Utah	2-6-0	.250	4-7-0	.364
8.	New Mexico	1-6-0	.143	2-10-0	.167
9.	UTEP	1-7-0	.125	3-8-0	.273

Non-conference record: 23-17-0 .575

1991		Conference		Overall	
1.	BYU	7-0-1	.938	8-3-2	.692
2.	S. Diego State	6-1-1	.813	8-4-1	.654
3.	Air Force	6-2-0	.750	10-3-0	.769
4.	Utah	4-4-0	.500	7-5-0	.583
5.	Hawaii	3-5-0	.375	4-7-1	.375
6.	Wyoming	2-5-1	.313	4-6-1	.409
6.	UTEP	2-5-1	.313	4-7-1	.375
8.	Colo. State	2-6-0	.250	3-8-0	.273
8.	New Mexico	2-6-0	.250	3-9-0	.250

Non-conference record: 17-18-2 .486

1992					
1.	Hawaii	6-2-0	.750	11-2-0	.846
1.	Fresno State	6-2-0	.750	9-4-0	.692
1.	BYU	6-2-0	.750	8-5-0	.614
4.	S. Diego State	5-3-0	.625	5-5-1	.500
5.	Air Force	4-4-0	.500	7-5-0	.583
5.	Utah	4-4-0	.500	6-6-0	.500
7.	Wyoming	3-5-0	.375	5-7-0	.417
7.	Colo. State	3-5-0	.375	5-7-0	.417
9.	New Mexico	2-6-0	.250	3-8-0	.273
10.	UTEP	1-7-0	.125	1-10-0	.091

Fresno State joins the WAC.

Non-conference record: 20-19-1 .512

1993					
1.	Fresno State	6-2-0	.750	8-4-0	.667
1.	Wyoming	6-2-0	.750	8-4-0	.667
1.	BYU	6-2-0	.750	6-6-0	.500
4.	Utah	5-3-0	.625	7-6-0	.538
4.	Colo. State	5-3-0	.625	5-6-0	.455
6.	New Mexico	4-4-0	.500	6-5-0	.545
6.	S. Diego State	4-4-0	.500	6-6-0	.500
8.	Hawaii	3-5-0	.375	6-6-0	.500
9.	Air Force	1-7-0	.125	4-8-0	.333
10.	UTEP	0-8-0	.000	1-11-0	.083

Non-conference record: 17-22-0 .436

1994					
1.	Colo. State	7-1-0	.875	10-2-0	.833
2.	Utah	6-2-0	.750	10-2-0	.833
2.	BYU	6-2-0	.750	10-3-0	.769
2.	Air Force	6-2-0	.750	8-4-0	.667
5.	Wyoming	4-4-0	.500	6-6-0	.500
5.	New Mexico	4-4-0	.500	5-7-0	.417
7.	Fresno State	3-4-1	.438	5-7-1	.423
8.	S. Diego State	2-6-0	.250	4-7-0	.364
9.	UTEP	1-6-1	.188	3-7-1	.318
10.	Hawaii	0-8-0	.000	3-8-1	.292

Non-conference record: 25-14-1 .638

1995					
1.	Colo. State	6-2-0	.750	8-4-0	.667
1.	BYU	6-2-0	.750	7-4-0	.636
1.	Utah	6-2-0	.750	7-4-0	.636
1.	Air Force	6-2-0	.750	8-5-0	.615
5.	S. Diego State	5-3-0	.625	8-4-0	.667
6.	Wyoming	4-4-0	.500	6-5-0	.545
7.	Fresno State	2-6-0	.250	5-7-0	.417
7.	New Mexico	2-6-0	.250	4-7-0	.417
7.	Hawaii	2-6-0	.250	4-8-0	.333
10.	UTEP	1-7-0	.125	2-10-0	.167

Non-conference record: 19-18-0 .514

1996

Pacific Division

		Conference		Overall	
1.	Wyoming	7-1-0	.875	10-2-0	.833
2.	Colo. State	6-2-0	.750	7-5-0	.583
2.	S. Diego State	6-2-0	.750	8-3-0	.727
4.	Air Force	5-3-0	.625	6-5-0	.545
5.	Fresno State	3-5-0	.375	4-7-0	.364
5.	S. Jose State	3-5-0	.375	3-9-0	.250
7.	Hawaii	1-7-0	.125	2-10-0	.167
7.	UNLV	1-7-0	.125	1-11-0	.083

Mountain Division

1.	BYU	8-0-0	1.000	14-1-0	.933
2.	Rice	6-2-0	.750	7-4-0	.636
2.	Utah	6-2-0	.750	8-4-0	.667
4.	SMU	4-4-0	.500	5-6-0	.455
5.	New Mexico	3-5-0	.375	6-5-0	.545
5.	TCU	3-5-0	.375	4-7-0	.364
7.	Tulsa	2-6-0	.250	4-7-0	.364
8.	UTEP	0-8-0	.000	2-9-0	.182

San Jose State, Rice, SMU, TCU, and Tulsa join the WAC.
Non-conference record: 27-31-0 .466

1997

Pacific Division

		Conference		Overall	
1.	Colo. State	7-1-0	.875	11-2-0	.846
2.	Air Force	6-2-0	.750	10-3-0	.769
3.	Fresno State	5-3-0	.625	6-6-0	.500
4.	Wyoming	4-4-0	.500	8-5-0	.615
4.	S. Diego State	4-4-0	.500	5-7-0	.417
4.	S. Jose State	4-4-0	.500	4-7-0	.364
7.	UNLV	2-6-0	.250	3-8-0	.273
8.	Hawaii	1-7-0	.125	3-9-0	.250

Mountain Division

1.	New Mexico	6-2-0	.750	9-4-0	.692
2.	Rice	5-3-0	.625	7-4-0	.636
2.	SMU	5-3-0	.625	6-5-0	.545
2.	Utah	5-3-0	.625	6-5-0	.545
5.	BYU	4-4-0	.500	6-5-0	.545
6.	UTEP	3-5-0	.375	4-7-0	.364
7.	Tulsa	2-6-0	.250	2-9-0	.182
8.	TCU	1-7-0	.125	1-10-0	.091

Non-conference record: 22-32-0 .458

1998

Pacific Division

1.	BYU	7-1-0	.875	9-5-0	.643
1.	S. Diego State	7-1-0	.875	7-5-0	.583
3.	Utah	5-3-0	.625	7-4-0	.636
3.	Fresno State	5-3-0	.625	5-6-0	.455
5.	S. Jose State	3-5-0	.375	4-8-0	.333
5.	UTEP	3-5-0	.375	3-8-0	.273
7.	New Mexico	1-7-0	.125	3-9-0	.250
8.	Hawaii	0-8-0	.000	0-12-0	.000

Mountain Division

1.	Air Force	7-1-0	.875	12-1-0	.923
2.	Wyoming	6-2-0	.750	8-3-0	.727
3.	Colo. State	5-3-0	.625	8-4-0	.667
3.	Rice	5-3-0	.625	5-6-0	.455
5.	TCU	4-4-0	.500	7-5-0	.583
5.	SMU	4-4-0	.500	5-7-0	.417
7.	Tulsa	2-6-0	.250	4-7-0	.364
8.	UNLV	0-8-0	.000	0-11-0	.000

Non-conference record: 23-37-0 .383

1999

		Conference		Overall	
1.	Hawaii	5-2-0	.714	9-4-0	.692
1.	TCU	5-2-0	.714	8-4-0	.667
1.	Fresno State	5-2-0	.714	8-5-0	.615
4.	Rice	4-3-0	.571	5-6-0	.455
5.	SMU	3-3-0	.500	4-6-0	.400
6.	UTEP	3-4-0	.429	5-7-0	.417
7.	S. Jose State	1-5-0	.167	3-7-0	.300
8.	Tulsa	1-6-0	.143	2-9-0	.182

BYU, San Diego State, Utah, New Mexico, Air Force, Wyoming, Colorado State, and UNLV leave the WAC to form the Mountain West Conference.
Non-conference record: 17-21-0 .447

2000

1.	TCU	7-1-0	.875	10-2-0	.833
1.	UTEP	7-1-0	.875	8-4-0	.667
3.	Fresno State	6-2-0	.750	7-5-0	.583
4.	S. Jose State	5-3-0	.625	7-5-0	.583
5.	Tulsa	4-4-0	.500	5-7-0	.417
6.	Hawaii	2-6-0	.250	3-9-0	.250
6.	Rice	2-6-0	.250	3-8-0	.273
6.	SMU	2-6-0	.250	3-9-0	.250
9.	Nevada	1-7-0	.125	2-10-0	.167

Non-conference record: 12-23-0 .343
Nevada joins the WAC.

2001

1.	Louisiana Tech	7-1-0	.875	7-5-0	.583
2.	Fresno State	6-2-0	.750	11-3-0	.786
2.	Boise State	6-2-0	.750	8-4-0	.667
4.	Hawaii	5-3-0	.625	9-3-0	.750
4.	Rice	5-3-0	.625	8-4-0	.667
6.	SMU	4-4-0	.500	4-7-0	.364
7.	Nevada	3-5-0	.375	3-8-0	.273
7.	S. Jose State	3-5-0	.375	3-9-0	.250
9.	UTEP	1-7-0	.125	2-9-0	.182
10.	Tulsa	0-8-0	.000	1-10-0	.091

Louisiana Tech and Boise State join the WAC.
Non-conference record: 16-22-0 .421

2002

1.	Boise State	8-0-0	1.000	12-1-0	.923
2.	Hawaii	7-1-0	.875	10-4-0	.714
3.	Fresno State	6-2-0	.750	9-5-0	.643
4.	S. Jose State	4-4-0	.500	6-7-0	.462
4.	Nevada	4-4-0	.500	5-7-0	.417
6.	Rice	3-5-0	.375	4-7-0	.364
6.	Louisiana Tech	3-5-0	.375	4-8-0	.333
6.	SMU	3-5-0	.375	3-9-0	.250
9.	UTEP	1-7-0	.125	2-10-0	.167
9.	Tulsa`	1-7-0	.124	1-11-0	.083

Non-conference record: 16-29-0 .356

2003

1.	Boise State	8-0-0	1.000	13-1-0	.929
2.	Fresno State	6-2-0	.750	9-5-0	.643
2.	Tulsa	6-2-0	.750	8-5-0	.615
4.	Hawaii	5-3-0	.625	9-5-0	.643
4.	Rice	5-3-0	.625	5-7-0	.417
6.	Nevada	4-4-0	.500	6-6-0	.500
7.	Louisiana Tech	3-5-0	.375	5-7-0	.417
8.	San Jose State	2-6-0	.250	3-8-0	.273
9.	UTEP	1-7-0	.125	2-11-0	.154
10.	SMU	0-8-0	.000	0-12-0	.000

Non-conference record: 20-27-0 .574

Decade	Arizona	Ariz.St.	BYU	New Mex.	Utah	Wyoming	UTEP	Colo.St.	SD St.	Hawaii	Air Force
1962-69	18-21-0	25-- 9-0	17-23-0	11-28-1	19-17-1	29-13-0	5- 8-0	1- 6-0			
1970-79	32-22-0	46- 9-0	46-22-1	33-33-0	32-31-0	28-41-0	10-58-0	23-34-1	7- 6-0	3- 4-0	42-30-1
1980-89			67-11-0	22-52-1	32-41-3	48-32-0	19-58-0	29-49-1	37-38-3	43-30-3	42-30-1
1990-99			57-14-1	25-46-0	43-29-0	41-30-1	15-62-2	52-26-0	44-26-0	25-54-0	44-27-0
2000-03							10-22-0			19-13-0	

Decade	Fresno St.	S.Jose St.	UNLV	Rice	SMU	TCU	Tulsa	Nevada	La.Tech	Boise St.
1990-99	35-27-1	11-19-0	3-21-0	20-11-0	16-14-0	13-18-0	7-24-0			
2000-03	24- 8-0	14-18-0		15-17-0	9-23-0	7- 1-0	11-21-0	12-20-0	13-11-0	22- 2-0

WAC W-L-T PERCENTAGES (1962-2003)

Arizona	50- 43-0	.538	Fresno State	59-35-1	.626
Arizona State	71- 18-0	.798	San Jose State	25-37-0	.435
BYU	187- 70-2	.726	UNLV	3-21-0	.125
New Mexico	91-159-2	.365	Rice	35-28-0	.556
Utah	125-118-4	.514	SMU	25-37-0	.403
Wyoming	146-116-1	.557	TCU	20-19-0	.513
UTEP	59-208-2	.223	Tulsa	18-45-0	.286
Colorado State	100-111-2	.474	Nevada	12-20-0	.375
San Diego State	88- 70-4	.556	Louisiana Tech	13-11-0	.542
Hawaii	90-101-3	.472	Boise State	22- 2-0	.917
Air Force	86- 57-1	.597			

WAC TITLES BY DECADES (1962-2003)

Decade	Arizona	Ariz. St.	BYU	New Mex.	Utah	Wyoming	UTEP	Colo. St.	SD St.	Hawaii	Air Force
1962-69	.33	1	1	2.33	.33	3					
1970-79	.5	5	4			.5					
1980-89			6.5			2			1		.5
1990-99			3.41		.25	.33		2.25	.33	.83	.58
2000-03							.5				
Totals	.83	6	14.41	2.33	.58	5.83	.5	2.25	1.33	.83	1.08

Decade	Fresno St.	S. Jose St.	UNLV	Rice	SMU	TCU	Tulsa	Nevada	La. Tech	Boise St.
1990-99	.66					.33				
2000-03						.5			1	2
Totals						.83			1	2

PART VI

Records of Bowl Games

ACTIVE BOWLS (as of 2003 season)

ALAMO BOWL

Year	Winner		Loser	
1993	California	37	Iowa	3
1994	Wash. State	10	Baylor	3
1995	Texas A&M	22	Michigan	20
1996	Iowa	27	Texas Tech	0
1997	Purdue	33	Okla. State	20
1998	Purdue	37	Kansas State	34
1999	Penn State	24	Texas A&M	0
2000	Nebraska	66	Northwestern	17
2001	Iowa	19	Texas Tech	16
2002	Wisconsin	31	Colorado	28
2003	Nebraska	17	Mich. State	3

CAPITAL ONE BOWL
(TANGERINE BOWL, 1947-1982)

Year	Winner		Loser	
1947	Catawba	31	Maryville	6
1948	Catawba	7	Marshall	0
1949	Murray State	21	Sul-Ross St.	21
1950	St. Vincent	7	Em.&Henry	6
1951	Morris-Harv.	35	Em.&Henry	14
1952	Stetson	35	Ark. State	20
1953	East Texas	33	Texas Tech	0
1954	East Texas	7	Ark. State	7
1955	Neb-Omaha	7	East Ky.	6
1955	Juniata	6	Mo. Valley	6
1957	West Texas	20	So. Miss.	13
1958	East Texas	26	Mo. Valley	7
1958	East Texas	10	So. Miss.	9
1960	Mid. Tenn.	21	Presbyterian	12
1960	Citadel	27	Tenn. Tech	0
1961	Lamar	21	Mid. Tenn.	14
1962	Houston	49	Miami (OH)	21
1963	West Ky.	27	Coast Guard	0
1964	E. Carolina	14	UMass	13
1965	E. Carolina	31	Maine	0
1966	Morgan St.	14	Westchester	6
1967	Tenn-Martin	25	Westchester	8
1968	Richmond	49	Ohio	42
1969	Toledo	56	Davidson	33
1970	Toledo	40	Wm.&Mary	12
1971	Toledo	28	Richmond	3
1972	Tampa	21	Kent State	18
1973	Miami (OH)	16	Florida	7
1974	Miami (OH)	21	Georgia	10
1975	Miami (OH)	20	So. Carolina	7
1976	Okla. State	48	BYU	21
1977	Fla. State	40	Texas Tech	17
1978	NC State	30	Pittsburgh	17
1979	LSU	34	Wake Forest	10
1980	Florida	35	Maryland	20
1981	Missouri	19	So. Miss.	17
1982	Auburn	33	BC	26

CITRUS BOWL (1983-2002)

Year	Winner		Loser	
1983	Tennessee	30	Maryland	23
1984	Georgia	17	Fla. State	17
1985	Ohio State	10	BYU	7
1987	Auburn	16	USC	7
1988	Clemson	35	Penn State	10
1989	Clemson	13	Oklahoma	6
1990	Illinois	31	Virginia	21
1991	Ga. Tech	45	Nebraska	21
1992	California	37	Clemson	13
1993	Georgia	21	Ohio State	14
1994	Penn State	31	Tennessee	13
1995	Alabama	24	Ohio State	17
1996	Tennessee	20	Ohio State	14
1997	Tennessee	48	Northwestern	28
1998	Florida	21	Penn State	6
1999	Michigan	45	Arkansas	31

CAPITAL ONE BOWL (cont'd)

Year	Winner		Loser	
2000	Mich. State	37	Florida	34
2001	Michigan	31	Auburn	28
2002	Tennessee	45	Michigan	17

CAPITAL ONE BOWL

Year	Winner		Loser	
2003	Auburn	13	Penn State	9
2004	Georgia	34	Purdue	27

CONTINENTAL TIRE BOWL

Year	Winner		Loser	
2002	Virginia	48	West Va.	22
2003	Virginia	23	Pittsburgh	16

COTTON BOWL

Year	Winner		Loser	
1937	TCU	16	Marquette	6
1938	Rice	28	Colorado	14
1939	St. Mary's	20	Texas Tech	13
1940	Clemson	6	BC	3
1941	Texas A&M	13	Fordham	12
1942	Alabama	29	Texas A&M	21
1943	Texas	14	Ga. Tech	7
1944	Texas	7	Randolph Fld.	7
1945	Okla. State	34	TCU	0
1946	Texas	40	Missouri	27
1947	Arkansas	0	LSU	0
1948	SMU	13	Penn State	13
1949	SMU	21	Oregon	13
1950	Rice	27	No. Carolina	13
1951	Tennessee	20	Texas	14
1952	Kentucky	20	TCU	7
1953	Texas	16	Tennessee	0
1954	Rice	28	Alabama	6
1955	Ga. Tech	14	Arkansas	6
1956	Ole Miss	14	TCU	7
1957	TCU	28	Syracuse	27
1958	Navy	20	Rice	7
1959	TCU	0	Air Force	0
1960	Syracuse	23	Texas	14
1961	Duke	7	Arkansas	6
1962	Texas	12	Ole Miss	7
1963	LSU	13	Texas	0
1964	Texas	28	Navy	6
1965	Arkansas	10	Nebraska	7
1966	LSU	14	Arkansas	7
1967	Georgia	24	SMU	9
1968	Texas A&M	20	Alabama	16
1969	Texas	36	Tennessee	13
1970	Texas	21	Notre Dame	17
1971	Notre Dame	24	Texas	11
1972	Penn State	30	Texas	6
1973	Texas	17	Alabama	13
1974	Nebraska	19	Texas	3
1975	Penn State	41	Baylor	20
1976	Arkansas	31	Georgia	10
1977	Houston	30	Maryland	21
1978	Notre Dame	38	Texas	10
1979	Notre Dame	35	Houston	34
1980	Houston	17	Nebraska	14
1981	Alabama	30	Baylor	2
1982	Texas	14	Alabama	12
1983	SMU	7	Pittsburgh	3
1984	Georgia	10	Texas	0
1985	BC	45	Houston	28
1986	Texas A&M	36	Auburn	16
1987	Ohio State	28	Texas A&M	12
1988	Texas A&M	35	Notre Dame	10
1989	UCLA	17	Arkansas	3
1990	Tennessee	31	Arkansas	27
1991	Miami (FL)	46	Texas	3
1992	Fla. State	10	Texas A&M	2
1993	Notre Dame	28	Texas A&M	3

COTTON BOWL (cont'd)

Year	Winner		Loser	
1994	Notre Dame	24	Texas A&M	21
1995	USC	55	Texas Tech	14
1996	Colorado	38	Oregon	6
1997	BYU	19	Kansas State	15
1998	UCLA	29	Texas A&M	23
1999	Texas	38	Miss. State	11
2000	Arkansas	23	Texas	6
2001	Kansas State	35	Tennessee	21
2002	Oklahoma	10	Arkansas	3
2003	Texas	35	LSU	20
2004	Ole Miss	31	Okla. State	28

FIESTA BOWL

Year	Winner		Loser	
1971	Ariz. State	45	Fla. State	38
1972	Ariz. State	49	Missouri	35
1973	Ariz. State	28	Pittsburgh	7
1974	Okla. State	16	BYU	6
1975	Ariz. State	17	Nebraska	14
1976	Oklahoma	41	Wyoming	7
1977	Penn State	42	Ariz. State	30
1978	Arkansas	10	UCLA	10
1979	Pittsburgh	16	Arizona	10
1980	Penn State	31	Ohio State	19
1982	Penn State	26	USC	10
1983	Ariz. State	32	Oklahoma	21
1984	Ohio State	28	Pittsburgh	23
1985	UCLA	39	Miami (FL)	37
1986	Michigan	27	Nebraska	23
1987	Penn State	14	Miami (FL)	10
1988	Fla. State	31	Nebraska	28
1989	Notre Dame	34	West Va.	21
1990	Fla. State	41	Nebraska	17
1991	Louisville	34	Alabama	7
1992	Penn State	42	Tennessee	17
1993	Syracuse	26	Colorado	22
1994	Arizona	29	Miami (FL)	0
1995	Colorado	41	Notre Dame	24
1996	Nebraska	62	Florida	24
1997	Penn State	38	Texas	15
1997	Kansas State	35	Syracuse	18
1999	Tennessee	23	Fla. State	16
2000	Nebraska	31	Tennessee	21
2001	Oregon State	41	Notre Dame	9
2002	Oregon	38	Colorado	16
2003	Ohio State	31	Miami (FL)	24
2004	Ohio State	35	Kansas State	28

GATOR BOWL

Year	Winner		Loser	
1946	Wake Forest	26	So. Carolina	14
1947	Oklahoma	34	NC State	13
1948	Maryland	20	Georgia	20
1949	Clemson	24	Missouri	23
1950	Maryland	20	Missouri	7
1951	Wyoming	20	Wash.&Lee	7
1952	Miami (FL)	14	Clemson	0
1953	Florida	14	Tulsa	13
1954	Texas Tech	35	Auburn	13
1954	Auburn	33	Baylor	13
1955	Vanderbilt	25	Auburn	13
1956	Ga. Tech	21	Pittsburgh	14
1957	Tennessee	3	Texas A&M	0
1958	Ole Miss	7	Florida	3
1960	Arkansas	14	Ga. Tech	7
1960	Florida	13	Baylor	12
1961	Penn State	30	Ga. Tech	15
1962	Florida	17	Penn State	7
1963	No. Carolina	35	Air Force	0
1965	Fla. State	36	Oklahoma	19
1965	Ga. Tech	31	Texas Tech	21

Year	Winner	Score	Loser	Score
1966	Tennessee	18	Syracuse	12
1967	Penn State	17	Fla. State	17
1968	Missouri	35	Alabama	10
1969	Florida	14	Tennessee	13
1971	Auburn	35	Ole Miss	28
1971	Georgia	7	No. Carolina	3
1972	Auburn	24	Colorado	3
1973	Texas Tech	28	Tennessee	19
1974	Auburn	27	Texas	3
1975	Maryland	13	Florida	0
1976	Notre Dame	20	Penn State	9
1977	Pittsburgh	34	So. Carolina	3
1978	Clemson	17	Ohio State	15
1979	No. Carolina	17	Michigan	15
1980	Pittsburgh	37	So. Carolina	9
1981	No. Carolina	31	Arkansas	27
1982	Fla. State	31	West Va.	12
1983	Florida	14	Iowa	6
1984	Okla. State	21	So. Carolina	14
1985	Fla. State	34	Okla. State	23
1986	Clemson	27	Stanford	21
1987	LSU	30	So. Carolina	13
1989	Georgia	34	Mich. State	27
1989	Clemson	27	West Va.	7
1991	Michigan	35	Ole Miss	3
1991	Oklahoma	48	Virginia	14
1992	Florida	27	NC State	10
1993	Alabama	24	No. Carolina	10
1994	Tennessee	45	Va. Tech	23
1996	Syracuse	41	Clemson	0
1997	No. Carolina	20	West Va.	13
1998	No. Carolina	42	Va. Tech	3
1999	Ga. Tech	35	Notre Dame	28
2000	Miami (FL)	28	Ga. Tech	13
2001	Va. Tech	41	Clemson	20
2002	Fla. State	30	Va. Tech	17
2003	NC State	28	Notre Dame	6
2004	Maryland	41	West Va.	7

GMAC BOWL
(MOBILE BOWL, 1999-2000)

Year	Winner	Score	Loser	Score
1999	TCU	28	E. Carolina	14
2000	So. Miss.	28	TCU	21

GMAC BOWL

Year	Winner	Score	Loser	Score
2001	Marshall	64	E. Carolina	61
2002	Marshall	38	Louisville	15
2003	Miami	49	Louisville	28

HAWAII BOWL
(ALOHA BOWL, 1982-2000)

Year	Winner	Score	Loser	Score
1982	Washington	21	Maryland	20
1983	Penn State	13	Washington	10
1984	SMU	27	Notre Dame	20
1985	Alabama	24	USC	3
1986	Arizona	30	No. Carolina	21
1987	UCLA	20	Florida	16
1988	Washington	24	Houston	22
1989	Mich. State	33	Hawaii	13
1990	Syracuse	28	Arizona	0
1991	Ga. Tech	18	Stanford	17
1992	Kansas	23	BYU	20
1993	Colorado	41	Fresno State	30
1994	BC	12	Kansas State	7
1995	Kansas	51	UCLA	30
1996	Navy	42	California	38
1997	Washington	51	Mich. State	23
1998	Colorado	51	Oregon	43
1999	Wake Forest	23	Ariz. State	17
2000	BC	31	Ariz. State	17

O'AHU BOWL (1998-2000)

Year	Winner	Score	Loser	Score
1998	Air Force	45	Washington	25
1999	Hawaii	23	Oregon State	17
2000	Georgia	37	Virginia	14

HAWAII BOWL

Year	Winner	Score	Loser	Score
2002	Tulane	36	Hawaii	28
2003	Hawaii	54	Houston	48

HOLIDAY BOWL

Year	Winner	Score	Loser	Score
1978	Navy	23	BYU	16
1979	Indiana	38	BYU	37
1980	BYU	46	SMU	45
1981	BYU	38	Wash. State	36
1982	Ohio State	47	BYU	17
1983	BYU	21	Missouri	17
1984	BYU	24	Michigan	17
1985	Arkansas	18	Ariz. State	17
1986	Iowa	39	S. Diego St.	38
1987	Iowa	20	Wyoming	19
1988	Okla. State	62	Wyoming	14
1989	Penn State	50	BYU	39
1990	Texas A&M	65	BYU	14
1991	Iowa	13	BYU	13
1992	Hawaii	27	Illinois	17
1993	Ohio State	28	BYU	21
1994	Michigan	24	Col. State	14
1995	Kansas State	54	Col. State	21
1996	Colorado	33	Washington	21
1997	Col. State	35	Missouri	24
1998	Arizona	23	Nebraska	20
1999	Kansas State	24	Washington	20
2000	Oregon	35	Texas	30
2001	Texas	47	Washington	43
2002	Kansas State	34	Ariz. State	27
2003	Wash. State	28	Texas	20

HOUSTON BOWL
(GALLERYFURNITURE. COM BOWL 2000-2001)

Year	Winner	Score	Loser	Score
2000	E. Carolina	40	Texas Tech	27
2001	Texas A&M	28	TCU	9

HOUSTON BOWL

Year	Winner	Score	Loser	Score
2002	Okla. State	33	So. Miss.	23
2003	Texas Tech	38	Navy	14

HUMANITARIAN BOWL

Year	Winner	Score	Loser	Score
1997	Cincinnati	35	Utah State	19
1998	Idaho	42	So. Miss.	35
1999	Boise State	34	Louisville	31
2000	Boise State	38	UTEP	23
2001	Clemson	48	La. Tech	24
2002	Boise State	34	Iowa State	16
2004	Ga. Tech	52	Tulsa	10

INDEPENDENCE BOWL

Year	Winner	Score	Loser	Score
1976	McNeese St.	20	Tulsa	16
1977	La. Tech	24	Louisville	14
1978	E. Carolina	35	La. Tech	13
1979	Syracuse	31	McNeese St.	7
1980	So. Miss.	16	McNeese St.	14
1981	Texas A&M	33	Okla. State	16
1982	Wisconsin	14	Kansas State	3
1983	Air Force	9	Ole Miss	3
1984	Air Force	23	Va. Tech	7
1985	Minnesota	20	Clemson	13
1986	Ole Miss	20	Texas Tech	17
1987	Washington	24	Tulane	12
1988	So. Miss.	38	UTEP	18
1989	Oregon	27	Tulsa	24
1990	La. Tech	34	Maryland	34
1991	Georgia	24	Arkansas	15

Year	Winner	Score	Loser	Score
1992	Wake Forest	39	Oregon	35
1993	Va. Tech	45	Indiana	20
1994	Virginia	20	TCU	10
1995	LSU	45	Mich. State	26
1996	Auburn	32	Army	29
1997	LSU	27	Notre Dame	9
1998	Ole Miss	35	Texas Tech	18
1999	Ole Miss	27	Oklahoma	25
2000	Miss. State	43	Texas A&M	41
2001	Alabama	14	Iowa State	13
2002	Ole Miss	27	Nebraska	23
2003	Arkansas	27	Missouri	24

INSIGHT.COM BOWL
(COPPER BOWL, 1989-1996)

Year	Winner	Score	Loser	Score
1989	Arizona	17	NC State	10
1990	California	17	Wyoming	15
1991	Indiana	24	Baylor	0
1992	Wash. State	31	Utah	28
1993	Kansas State	62	Wyoming	17
1994	BYU	31	Oklahoma	6
1995	Texas Tech	55	Air Force	41
1996	Wisconsin	38	Utah	10

INSIGHT.COM BOWL

Year	Winner	Score	Loser	Score
1997	Arizona	30	New Mexico	14
1998	Missouri	34	West Va.	31
1999	Colorado	62	BC	28
2000	Iowa State	37	Pittsburgh	29
2001	Syracuse	26	Kansas State	3
2002	Pittsburgh	38	Oregon St.	13
2003	California	52	Va. Tech	49

LAS VEGAS BOWL
(CALIFORNIA BOWL, 1981-1991)

Year	Winner	Score	Loser	Score
1981	Toledo	27	San Jose St.	25
1982	Fresno State	29	Bowl. Green	28
1983	No. Illinois	20	CS Fullerton	13
1984	UNVL*	30	Toledo*	13
1985	Fresno State	51	Bowl. Green	7
1986	San Jose St.	37	Miami (OH)	7
1987	E. Michigan	30	San Jose St.	27
1988	Fresno State	35	W. Michigan	30
1989	Fresno State	27	Ball State	6
1990	San Jose St.	48	Cent. Mich.	24
1991	Bowl. Green	28	Fresno State	21

LAS VEGAS BOWL

Year	Winner	Score	Loser	Score
1992	Bowl. Green	35	Nevada	34
1993	Utah State	42	Ball State	33
1994	UNLV	52	Cent. Mich.	24
1995	Toledo	40	Nevada	37
1996	Nevada	18	Ball State	15
1997	Oregon	41	Air Force	13
1998	No. Carolina	20	San Diego St.	13
1999	Utah	17	Fresno State	16
2000	UNLV	31	Arkansas	14
2001	Utah	10	USC	6
2002	UCLA	27	New Mexico	13
2003	Oregon State	55	New Mexico	14.

*UNLV later forfeited the 1984 game

LIBERTY BOWL

Year	Winner	Score	Loser	Score
1959	Penn State	7	Alabama	0
1960	Penn State	41	Oregon	12
1961	Syracuse	15	Miami (FL)	14
1962	Oregon St.	6	Villanova	0
1963	Miss. State	16	NC State	12
1964	Utah	32	West Va.	6
1965	Ole Miss	13	Auburn	7
1966	Miami (FL)	14	Va. Tech	7
1967	NC State	14	Georgia	7

LIBERTY BOWL *(cont'd)*

1968 Ole Miss	34	Va. Tech	7
1969 Colorado	47	Alabama	33
1970 Tulane	17	Colorado	3
1971 Tennessee	14	Arkansas	13
1972 Ga. Tech	31	Iowa State	20
1973 NC State	31	Kansas	18
1974 Tennessee	7	Maryland	3
1975 USC	20	Texas A&M	0
1976 Alabama	36	UCLA	6
1977 Nebraska	21	No. Carolina	17
1978 Missouri	20	LSU	15
1979 Penn State	9	Tulane	6
1980 Purdue	28	Missouri	25
1981 Ohio State	31	Navy	28
1982 Alabama	21	Illinois	15
1983 Notre Dame	19	BC	18
1984 Auburn	21	Arkansas	15
1985 Baylor	21	LSU	7
1986 Tennessee	21	Minnesota	14
1987 Georgia	20	Arkansas	17
1988 Indiana	34	So. Carolina	10
1989 Ole Miss	42	Air Force	29
1990 Air Force	23	Ohio State	11
1991 Air Force	38	Miss. State	15
1992 Ole Miss.	13	Air Force	0
1993 Louisville	18	Mich. State	7
1994 Illinois	30	E. Carolina	0
1995 E. Carolina	19	Stanford	13
1996 Syracuse	30	Houston	17
1997 So. Miss.	41	Pittsburgh	7
1998 Tulane	41	BYU	27
1999 So. Miss.	23	Col. State	17
2000 Col. State	22	Louisville	17
2001 Louisville	28	BYU	10
2002 TCU	17	Col. State	3
2003 Utah	17	So. Miss	0

MOTOR CITY BOWL

1997 Ole Miss	34	Marshall	31
1998 Marshall	48	Louisville	29
1999 Marshall	21	BYU	3
2000 Marshall	25	Cincinnati	14
2001 Toledo	23	Cincinnati	16
2002 BC	51	Toledo	25
2003 Bowl. Green	28	Northwestern	24

MUSIC CITY BOWL

1998 Va. Tech	38	Alabama	7
1999 Syracuse	20	Kentucky	13
2000 West Va.	49	Ole Miss	38
2001 BC	20	Georgia	16
2002 Minnesota	29	Arkansas	14
2003 Auburn	28	Wisconsin	14

NEW ORLEANS BOWL

2001 Col. State	45	No. Texas	20
2002 No Texas	34	Cincinnati	19
2003 Memphis	27	No. Texas	17

ORANGE BOWL

1935 Bucknell	26	Miami (FL)	0
1936 Catholic U.	20	Ole Miss	19
1937 Duquesne	13	Miss. State	12
1938 Auburn	6	Mich. State	0
1939 Tennessee	17	Oklahoma	0
1940 Ga. Tech	21	Missouri	7
1941 Miss. State	14	Georgetown	7
1942 Georgia	40	TCU	26
1943 Alabama	37	BC	21
1944 LSU	19	Texas A&M	14
1945 Tulsa	26	Ga. Tech	12

ORANGE BOWL *(cont'd)*

1946 Miami (FL)	13	Holy Cross	6
1947 Rice	8	Tennessee	0
1948 Ga. Tech	20	Kansas	14
1949 Texas	41	Georgia	28
1950 Santa Clara	21	Kentucky	13
1951 Clemson	15	Miami (FL)	14
1952 Ga. Tech	17	Baylor	14
1953 Alabama	61	Syracuse	6
1954 Oklahoma	7	Maryland	0
1955 Duke	34	Nebraska	7
1956 Oklahoma	20	Maryland	6
1957 Colorado	27	Clemson	21
1958 Oklahoma	48	Duke	21
1959 Oklahoma	21	Syracuse	6
1960 Georgia	14	Missouri	0
1961 Missouri	21	Navy	14
1962 LSU	25	Colorado	7
1963 Alabama	17	Oklahoma	0
1964 Nebraska	13	Auburn	7
1965 Texas	21	Alabama	17
1966 Alabama	39	Nebraska	28
1967 Florida	27	Ga. Tech	12
1968 Oklahoma	26	Tennessee	24
1969 Penn State	15	Kansas	14
1970 Penn State	10	Missouri	3
1971 Nebraska	17	LSU	12
1972 Nebraska	38	Alabama	6
1973 Nebraska	40	Notre Dame	6
1974 Penn State	16	LSU	9
1975 Notre Dame	13	Alabama	11
1976 Oklahoma	14	Michigan	6
1977 Ohio State	27	Colorado	10
1978 Arkansas	31	Oklahoma	6
1979 Oklahoma	31	Nebraska	24
1980 Oklahoma	24	Fla. State	7
1981 Oklahoma	18	Fla. State	17
1982 Clemson	22	Nebraska	15
1983 Nebraska	21	LSU	20
1984 Miami (FL)	31	Nebraska	30
1985 Washington	28	Oklahoma	17
1986 Oklahoma	25	Penn State	10
1987 Oklahoma	42	Arkansas	8
1988 Miami (FL)	20	Oklahoma	14
1989 Miami (FL)	23	Nebraska	3
1990 Notre Dame	21	Colorado	6
1991 Colorado	10	Notre Dame	9
1992 Miami (FL)	22	Nebraska	0
1993 Fla. State	27	Nebraska	14
1994 Fla. State	18	Nebraska	16
1995 Nebraska	24	Miami (FL)	17
1996 Fla. State	31	Notre Dame	26
1996 Nebraska	41	Va. Tech	21
1998 Nebraska	42	Tennessee	17
1999 Florida	31	Syracuse	10
2000 Michigan	35	Alabama	34
2001 Oklahoma	13	Fla. State	2
2002 Florida	56	Maryland	23
2003 USC	38	Iowa	17
2004 Miami	16	Fla. State	14

OUTBACK BOWL
(HALL OF FAME BOWL, 1977-1995)

1977 Maryland	17	Minnesota	7
1978 Texas A&M	28	Iowa State	12
1979 Missouri	24	So. Carolina	14
1980 Arkansas	34	Tulane	15
1981 Miss. State	10	Kansas	0
1982 Air Force	36	Vanderbilt	28
1983 West Va.	20	Kentucky	16

HALL OF FAME (OUTBACK, 1996-)

1984 Kentucky	20	Wisconsin	19
1986 BC	27	Georgia	24
1988 Michigan	28	Alabama	24
1989 Syracuse	23	LSU	10
1990 Auburn	31	Ohio State	14
1991 Clemson	30	Illinois	0
1992 Syracuse	24	Ohio State	17
1993 Tennessee	38	BC	23
1994 Michigan	42	NC State	7
1995 Wisconsin	34	Duke	20
1996 Penn State	43	Auburn	14
1997 Alabama	17	Michigan	14
1998 Georgia	33	Wisconsin	6
1999 Penn State	26	Kentucky	14
2000 Georgia	28	Purdue	25
2001 So. Carolina	24	Ohio State	7
2002 So. Carolina	31	Ohio State	28
2003 Michigan	38	Florida	30
2004 Iowa	37	Florida	17

PEACH BOWL

1958 LSU	31	Fla. State	27
1969 West Va.	14	So. Carolina	3
1970 Ariz. State	48	No. Carolina	26
1971 Ole Miss	41	Ga. Tech	18
1972 NC State	49	West Va.	13
1973 Georgia	17	Maryland	16
1974 Vanderbilt	6	Texas Tech	6
1975 West Va.	13	NC State	10
1976 Kentucky	21	No. Carolina	0
1977 NC State	24	Iowa State	14
1978 Purdue	41	Ga. Tech	21
1970 Baylor	24	Clemson	18
1981 West Va.	26	Florida	6
1981 Miami (FL)	20	Va. Tech	10
1982 Iowa	28	Tennessee	22
1983 Fla. State	28	No. Carolina	3
1984 Virginia	27	Purdue	24
1985 Army	31	Illinois	29
1986 Va. Tech	25	NC State	24
1987 Tennessee	27	Indiana	22
1988 NC State	28	Iowa	23
1989 Syracuse	19	Georgia	18
1990 Auburn	27	Indiana	23
1991 E. Carolina	37	NC State	34
1993 No. Carolina	21	Miss. State	17
1994 Clemson	14	Kentucky	13
1995 NC State	28	Miss. State	24
1995 Virginia	34	Georgia	27
1996 LSU	10	Clemson	7
1998 Auburn	21	Clemson	17
1998 Georgia	35	Virginia	33
1999 Miss. State	17	Clemson	7
2000 LSU	28	Ga. Tech	14
2001 No. Carolina	16	Auburn	10
2002 Maryland	30	Tennessee	3
2004 Clemson	27	Tennessee	14

ROSE BOWL

1902 Michigan	49	Stanford	0
1916 Wash. State	14	Brown	0
1917 Oregon	14	Penn	0
1918 Mare Island	9	Camp Lewis	7
1919 Great Lakes	17	Mare Island	0
1920 Harvard	7	Oregon	6
1921 California	28	Ohio State	0
1922 Wash.&Jeff.	0	California	0
1923 USC	14	Penn State	3
1924 Navy	14	Washington	14

Year	Winner	Score	Loser	Score
1925	Notre Dame	27	Stanford	10
1926	Alabama	20	Washington	19
1927	Alabama	7	Stanford	7
1928	Stanford	7	Pittsburgh	6
1929	Ga. Tech	8	California	7
1930	USC	47	Pittsburgh	14
1931	Alabama	24	Wash. State	0
1932	USC	21	Tulane	12
1933	USC	35	Pittsburgh	0
1934	Columbia	7	Stanford	0
1935	Alabama	29	Stanford	13
1936	Stanford	7	SMU	0
1937	Pittsburgh	21	Washington	0
1938	California	13	Alabama	0
1939	USC	7	Duke	3
1940	USC	14	Tennessee	0
1941	Stanford	21	Nebraska	13
1942	Oregon St.	20	Duke	16
1943	Georgia	9	UCLA	0
1944	USC	29	Washington	0
1945	USC	25	Tennessee	0
1946	Alabama	34	USC	14
1947	Illinois	45	UCLA	14
1948	Michigan	48	USC	0
1949	Northwestern	20	California	14
1950	Ohio State	17	California	14
1951	Michigan	14	California	6
1952	Illinois	40	Stanford	7
1953	USC	7	Wisconsin	0
1954	Mich. State	28	UCLA	20
1955	Ohio State	20	USC	7
1956	Mich. State	17	UCLA	14
1957	Iowa	35	Oregon St.	19
1958	Ohio State	10	Oregon	7
1959	Iowa	38	California	12
1960	Washington	44	Wisconsin	8
1961	Washington	17	Minnesota	7
1962	Minnesota	21	UCLA	3
1963	USC	42	Wisconsin	37
1964	Illinois	17	Washington	7
1965	Michigan	34	Oregon St.	7
1966	UCLA	14	Mich. State	12
1967	Purdue	14	USC	13
1968	USC	14	Indiana	3
1969	Ohio State	27	USC	16
1970	USC	10	Michigan	3
1971	Stanford	27	Ohio State	17
1972	Stanford	13	Michigan	12
1973	USC	42	Ohio State	17
1974	Ohio State	42	USC	21
1975	USC	17	Ohio State	17
1976	UCLA	23	Ohio State	10
1977	USC	14	Michigan	6
1978	Washington	27	Michigan	20
1979	USC	17	Michigan	10
1980	USC	17	Ohio State	16
1981	Michigan	23	Washington	6
1982	Washington	28	Iowa	0
1983	UCLA	24	Michigan	14
1984	UCLA	45	Illinois	9
1985	USC	20	Ohio State	17
1986	UCLA	45	Iowa	28
1987	Ariz. State	22	Michigan	15
1988	Mich. State	20	USC	17
1989	Michigan	22	USC	14
1990	USC	17	Michigan	10
1991	Washington	46	Iowa	34

Year	Winner	Score	Loser	Score
1992	Washington	34	Michigan	14
1993	Michigan	38	Washington	31
1994	Wisconsin	21	UCLA	16
1995	Penn State	38	Oregon	20
1996	USC	41	Northwestern	32
1997	Ohio State	20	Ariz. State	17
1998	Michigan	21	Wash. State	16
1999	Wisconsin	38	UCLA	31
2000	Wisconsin	17	Stanford	9
2001	Washington	34	Purdue	24
2002	Miami (FL)	37	Nebraska	14
2003	Oklahoma	34	Wash. State	14
2004	USC	28	Michigan	14

SAN FRANCISCO BOWL*

Year	Winner	Score	Loser	Score
2000	Va. Tech	20	Air Force	13
2001	Ga. Tech	24	Stanford	14
2002	Wake Forest	38	Oregon	17
2003	BC	35	Colo. State	21

SILICON VALLEY CLASSIC

Year	Winner	Score	Loser	Score
2000	Air Force	37	Fresno State	34
2001	Mich. State	44	Fresno State	35
2002	Fresno State	30	Ga. Tech	21
2003	Fresno State	17	UCLA	9

SUGAR BOWL

Year	Winner	Score	Loser	Score
1935	Tulane	20	Temple	14
1936	TCU	3	LSU	2
1937	Santa Clara	21	LSU	14
1938	Santa Clara	6	LSU	0
1939	TCU	15	Carn.Tech	7
1940	Texas A&M	14	Tulane	13
1941	BC	19	Tennessee	13
1942	Fordham	2	Missouri	0
1943	Tennessee	14	Tulsa	7
1944	Ga. Tech	20	Tulsa	18
1945	Duke	29	Alabama	26
1946	Okla. State	33	St. Mary's	13
1947	Georgia	20	No. Carolina	10
1948	Texas	27	Alabama	7
1949	Oklahoma	14	No. Carolina	6
1950	Oklahoma	35	LSU	0
1951	Kentucky	13	Oklahoma	7
1952	Maryland	28	Tennessee	13
1953	Ga. Tech	24	Ole Miss	7
1954	Ga. Tech	42	West Va.	19
1955	Navy	21	Ole Miss	0
1956	Ga. Tech	7	Pittsburgh	0
1957	Baylor	13	Tennessee	7
1958	Ole Miss	39	Texas	7
1959	LSU	7	Clemson	0
1960	Ole Miss	21	LSU	0
1961	Ole Miss	14	Rice	6
1962	Alabama	10	Arkansas	3
1963	Ole Miss	17	Arkansas	13
1964	Alabama	12	Ole Miss	7
1965	LSU	13	Syracuse	10
1966	Missouri	20	Florida	18
1967	Alabama	34	Nebraska	7
1968	LSU	20	Wyoming	13
1969	Arkansas	16	Georgia	2
1970	Ole Miss	27	Arkansas	22
1971	Tennessee	34	Air Force	13
1972	Oklahoma	40	Auburn	22
1972	Oklahoma	14	Penn State	0
1973	Notre Dame	24	Alabama	23
1974	Nebraska	13	Florida	10
1975	Alabama	13	Penn State	6
1977	Pittsburgh	27	Georgia	3
1978	Alabama	35	Ohio State	6

Year	Winner	Score	Loser	Score
1979	Alabama	14	Penn State	7
1980	Alabama	24	Arkansas	9
1981	Georgia	17	Notre Dame	10
1982	Pittsburgh	24	Georgia	20
1983	Penn State	27	Georgia	23
1984	Auburn	9	Michigan	7
1985	Nebraska	28	LSU	10
1986	Tennessee	35	Miami (FL)	7
1987	Nebraska	30	LSU	15
1988	Syracuse	16	Auburn	16
1989	Fla. State	13	Auburn	7
1990	Miami (FL)	33	Alabama	25
1991	Tennessee	23	Virginia	22
1992	Notre Dame	39	Florida	28
1993	Alabama	34	Miami (FL)	13
1994	Florida	41	West Va.	7
1995	Fla. State	23	Florida	17
1995	Va. Tech	28	Texas	10
1997	Florida	52	Fla. State	20
1998	Fla. State	31	Ohio State	14
1999	Ohio State	24	Texas A&M	14
2000	Fla. State	46	Va. Tech	29
2001	Miami (FL)	37	Florida	20
2002	LSU	47	Illinois	34
2003	Georgia	26	Fla. State	13
2004	LSU	21	Oklahoma	14

SUN BOWL

Year	Winner	Score	Loser	Score
1936	Hard-Simm.	14	New Mex. St.	14
1937	Hard.-Simm.	34	UTEP	6
1938	West Va.	7	Texas Tech	6
1939	Utah	26	New Mexico	0
1940	Catholic U.	0	Ariz. State	0
1941	Case-Reserve	26	Ariz. State	13
1942	Tulsa	6	Texas Tech	0
1943	2nd Air Force	13	Hard.-Simm.	7
1944	Southwestern	7	New Mexico	0
1944	Southwestern	35	U. of Mexico	0
1946	New Mexico	34	Denver	24
1947	Cincinnati	18	Va. Tech	6
1948	Miami (OH)	13	Texas Tech	12
1949	West Va.	21	UTEP	12
1950	UTEP	33	Georgetown	20
1951	West Texas	21	Cincinnati	13
1953	Texas Tech	25	Pacific	14
1953	Pacific	26	So. Miss.	7
1954	UTEP	37	So. Miss.	14
1955	UTEP	47	Fla. State	20
1956	Wyoming	21	Texas Tech	14
1957	Geo. Wash	13	UTEP	0
1958	Wyoming	14	Hard.-Simm.	6
1958	Louisville	34	Drake	20
1959	New Mex. St.	28	North Texas	8
1960	New Mex. St.	20	Utah State	13
1961	Villanova	17	Wichita St.	9
1962	West Texas	15	Ohio U.	14
1963	Oregon	21	SMU	14
1964	Georgia	7	Texas Tech	0
1965	UTEP	13	TCU	12
1966	Wyoming	28	Fla. State	20
1967	UTEP	14	Ole Miss	7
1968	Auburn	34	Arizona	10
1969	Nebraska	45	Georgia	6
1970	Ga. Tech	17	Texas Tech	9
1971	LSU	33	Iowa State	15
1972	No. Carolina	32	Texas Tech	28
1973	Missouri	34	Auburn	17
1974	Miss. State	26	No. Carolina	24
1975	Pittsburgh	33	Kansas	19

*SF Bowl was Seattle Bowl, 2001-2002.

SUN BOWL (cont'd)

1977	Texas A&M	37	Florida	14
1977	Stanford	24	LSU	14
1978	Texas	42	Maryland	0
1979	Washington	14	Texas	7
1980	Nebraska	31	Miss. State	17
1981	Oklahoma	40	Houston	14
1982	No. Carolina	26	Texas	10
1983	Alabama	28	SMU	7
1984	Maryland	28	Tennessee	27
1985	Georgia	13	Arizona	13
1986	Alabama	28	Washington	6

JOHN HANCOCK BOWL, 1987-1993

1987	Okla. State	35	West Va.	33
1988	Alabama	29	Army	28
1989	Pittsburgh	31	Texas A&M	28
1990	Mich. State	17	USC	16
1991	UCLA	6	Illinois	3
1992	Baylor	20	Arizona	15
1993	Oklahoma	41	Texas Tech	10

SUN BOWL

1994	Texas	35	No. Carolina	31
1995	Iowa	38	Washington	18
1996	Stanford	38	Mich. State	0
1997	Ariz. State	17	Iowa	7
1998	TCU	28	USC	19
1999	Oregon	24	Minnesota	20
2000	Wisconsin	21	UCLA	20
2001	Wash. State	33	Purdue	27
2002	Purdue	34	Washington	24
2003	Minnesota	31	Oregon	30

TANGERINE BOWL
(see **CAPITAL ONE BOWL** for an early version of this bowl)

2001	Pittsburgh	34	NC State	19
2002	Texas Tech	55	Clemson	15
2003	NC State	56	Kansas	26

FORT WORTH BOWL (new, 2003)

2003	Boise State	34	TCU	31

INACTIVE BOWLS
ALL AMERICAN BOWL

1977	Maryland	17	Minnesota	7
1978	Texas A&M	28	Iowa State	12
1979	Missouri	24	So. Carolina	14
1980	Arkansas	34	Tulane	15
1981	Miss. State	10	Kansas	0
1982	Air Force	36	Vanderbilt	29
1983	West Va.	20	Kentucky	16
1984	Kentucky	20	Wisconsin	19
1985	Ga. Tech	17	Mich. State	14
1986	Fla. State	27	Indiana	13
1987	Virginia	22	BYU	16
1988	Florida	14	Illinois	10
1989	Texas Tech	49	Duke	21
1990	NC State	31	So. Miss.	27

AVIATION BOWL*

1961	New Mexico	28	West. Mich.	12

BACARDI BOWL*

1936	Auburn	7	Villanova	7

BLUEBONNET BOWL

1959	Clemson	23	TCU	7
1960	Texas	3	Alabama	3
1961	Kansas	33	Rice	7
1962	Missouri	14	Ga. Tech	10
1963	Baylor	14	LSU	7

BLUEBONNET BOWL (cont'd)

1965	Tulsa	14	Ole Miss	7
1966	Tennessee	27	Tulsa	6
1966	Texas	19	Ole Miss	0
1967	Colorado	31	Miami (FL)	21
1968	SMU	28	Oklahoma	27
1969	Houston	36	Auburn	7
1970	Alabama	24	Oklahoma	24
1971	Colorado	29	Houston	17
1972	Tennessee	24	LSU	17
1973	Houston	47	Tulane	7
1974	NC State	31	Houston	31
1975	Texas	38	Colorado	21
1976	Nebraska	27	Texas Tech	24
1977	USC	47	Texas A&M	28
1978	Stanford	25	Georgia	22
1979	Purdue	27	Tennessee	22
1980	No. Carolina	16	Texas	7
1981	Michigan	33	UCLA	14
1982	Arkansas	28	Florida	24
1983	Okla. State	24	Baylor	14
1984	West Va.	31	TCU	14
1985	Air Force	24	Texas	16
1986	Baylor	21	Colorado	9
1987	Texas	32	Pittsburgh	27

BLUEGRASS BOWL*

1958	Okla. State	15	Fla. State	6

CAMELIA BOWL*

1949	Hard.-Simm.	49	Wichita State	12
1966	San Diego St.	28	Montana State	7
1967	San Diego St.	28	S. Francisco St.	6
1968	Humboldt St.	29	Fresno State	14
1971	Boise State	32	Chico State	28

CHERRY BOWL*

1984	Army	10	Mich. State	6
1985	Maryland	35	Syracuse	18

CHRISTMAS FESTIVAL*

1924	USC	20	Missouri	9

CIGAR BOWL*

1950	Fla. State	19	Wofford	6

DELTA BOWL*

1948	Ole Miss	13	TCU	9
1949	Wm.&Mary	20	Okla. State	0

DIXIE CLASSIC*

1922	Texas A&M	22	Centre	14
1934	Arkansas	34	Centenary	7
1948	Arkansas	21	Wm.&Mary	19
1949	Baylor	20	Wake Forest	7

EASTERN BOWL*

1963	E. Carolina	27	Northeastern	6

EAST-WEST BOWL*

1922	West Va.	21	Gonzaga	13

ELKS BOWL*

1954	Morr-Harvey	12	E. Carolina	0

FREEDOM BOWL

1984	Iowa	55	Texas	17
1985	Washington	20	Colorado	17
1986	UCLA	31	BYU	10
1987	Ariz. State	33	Air Force	28
1988	BYU	20	Colorado	17
1989	Washington	34	Florida	7
1990	Colo. State	32	Oregon	31
1991	Tulsa	28	S. Diego St.	17
1992	Fresno State	24	USC	7
1993	USC	28	Utah	21
1994	Utah	16	Arizona	13

GARDEN STATE BOWL*

1979	Ariz. State	34	Rutgers	18
1980	Houston	35	Navy	0
1981	Tennessee	28	Wisconsin	21

GLASS BOWL*

1946	Toledo	21	Bates	12
1947	Toledo	20	New Hamp.	14
1948	Toledo	27	Okla. City	14
1949	Cincinnati	33	Toledo	13

GRAPE BOWL*

1947	Pacific	35	Utah State	21
1948	Hard.-Simm.	35	Pacific	35

GOTHAM BOWL*

1961	Baylor	24	Utah State	9
1962	Nebraska	36	Miami (FL)	34
1975	Penn State	41	Baylor	20

GREAT LAKES BOWL

1947	Kentucky	24	Villanova	14

HARBOR BOWL*

1947	New Mexico	13	Montana St.	13
1948	Hard.-Simm.	53	S. Diego St.	0
1949	Villanova	27	Nevada	7

LIONS BOWL*

1952	Clarion Coll.	13	E. Carolina	6

INDEPENDENCE BOWL*

1969	Oregon	27	Tulsa	24

LITTLE ALL AMERICAN BOWL*

1937	Fresno State	27	Ark. State	26

MERCY BOWL*

1961	Fresno State	36	Bowl. Green	6
1971	CS Fullerton	17	Fresno State	14

MICRON.COM BOWL
(BLOCKBUSTER BOWL, 1990-1994)

1990	Fla. State	24	Penn State	17
1991	Alabama	30	Colorado	25
1993	Stanford	24	Penn State	3
1994	BC	31	Virginia	13

(CARQUEST BOWL, 1995-1997)

1995	So. Carolina	24	West Va.	21
1995	No. Carolina	20	Arkansas	10
1996	Miami (FL)	31	Virginia	21
1997	Ga. Tech	35	West Va.	30

MICRON.COM BOWL *(cont'd)*
(MICRON.COM BOWL)

1998 Miami (FL)	46	NC State	23
1999 Illinois	62	Virginia	21
2000 NC State	38	Minnesota	30

MINERAL WATER BOWL*

1962 Adams State	23	No. Illinois	20
1963 No. Illinois	21	SW Mo. St.	14
1964 No. Dakota	37	No. Illinois	20

MIRAGE BOWL*

1977 Grambling	35	Temple	32
1978 Temple	28	BC	24

OIL BOWL*

1946 Georgia	20	Tulsa	6
1947 Ga. Tech	41	St. Mary's	19
1948 SW La.	24	Ark. A&M	7

OPTIMIST BOWL*

1946 No. Texas	14	Pacific	13

PALM FESTIVAL*

1933 Miami (FL)	7	Manhattan	0
1934 Duquesne	33	Miami (FL)	7

PAPER BOWL*

1948 Jacksonville	19	Troy State	9

PASADENA BOWL*

1969 S.Diego St.	28	Boston U.	7
1970 Louisville	34	LB State	24
1971 Memphis St.	28	San Jose St.	9

PECAN BOWL*

1968 No. Dak. St.	23	Ark. State	14
1969 Ark. State	29	Drake	21
1970 Ark. State	38	Cent. Mo. St.	21

PIONEER BOWL*

1971 La. Tech	14	East. Mich.	3

PINEAPPLE BOWL*

1938 Washington	53	Hawaii	13
1940 Fresno State	3	Hawaii	0
1940 Oregon State	39	Hawaii	6
1949 Oregon State	47	Hawaii	27
1950 Hawaii	28	Denver	27

PRESIDENTIAL CUP*

1950 Texas A&M	40	Georgia	20

RAISIN BOWL*

1945 Drake	13	Fresno State	12
1946 San Jose St.	20	Utah State	0
1947 Pacific	26	Wichita State	14
1949 Occidental	21	Colo. State	20
1949 San Jose St.	20	Texas Tech	13

REFRIGERATOR BOWL*

1947 Evansville	20	No. Illinois	0
1952 West Ky.	34	Ark. State	19
1954 Delaware	19	Kent State	7
1956 Sam Houston	27	Mid. Tenn. St.	13

SALAD BOWL*

1948 Nevada	13	North Texas	6
1949 Drake	14	Arizona	13
1950 Xavier	33	Ariz. State	21
1951 Miami (OH)	34	Ariz. State	21
1952 Houston	26	Miami (OH)	21

SHRINE BOWL

1948 Hard.-Simm.	40	Ouachita	12

TURKEY BOWL*

1946 Evansville	19	No. Illinois	7

Asterisked bowls are those for which histories might be incomplete.

PART VII

All American Teams (1883–2003)

ALL AMERICAN TEAMS (1889-2003)

Walter Camp Teams (1889-1924)

1889			1894			1899		
E	Arthur Cumnock, Harvard		E	Frank Hinkey, Yale		E	David Campbell, Harvard	
	Amos Alonzo Stagg, Yale			Charles Gelbert, Penn			Arthur Pie, Princeton	
T	Hector Cowan, Princeton		T	Bert Waters, Harvard		T	A.R.T. Hillebrand, Princeton	
	Charles Gill, Yale			Langdon Lea, Princeton			George Stillman, Yale	
G	John Cranston, Harvard		G	Arthur Wheeler, Princeton		G	Truxton Hare, Penn	
	Pudge Hefflefinger, Yale			Wiliam Hickok, Yale			Gordon Brown, Yale	
C	William George, Princeton		C	Phillip Stillman, Yale		C	Peter Overfield, Penn	
QB	Edgar Allen Poe, Princeton		QB	George Adee, Yale		QB	Charles Daly, Harvard	
HB	James Lee, Harvard		HB	Arthur Knipe, Penn		HB	Isaac Seneca, Carlisle	
	Roscoe Channing, Princeton			George Brooke, Penn			Josiah McCracken, Penn	
FB	Knowlton Ames, Princeton		FB	Frank Butterworth, Yale		FB	Malcolm McBride, Yale	

1890			1895			1900		
E	Frank Hallowell, Harvard		E	Norman Cabot, Harvard		E	David Campbell, Harvard	
	Ralph Warren, Princeton			Charles Gelbert, Penn			John Hallowell, Harvard	
T	Marshall Newell, Harvard		T	Langdon Lea, Princeton		T	James Bloomer, Yale	
	William Rhodes, Yale			Fred Murphy, Yale			George Stillman, Yale	
G	Jesse Riggs, Princeton		G	Charles Wharton, Penn		G	Gordon Brown, Yale	
	Pudge Hefflefinger, Yale			Dudley Riggs, Princeton			Truxton Hare, Penn	
C	John Cranston, Harvard		C	Al Bull, Penn		C	Herman Olcott, Yale	
QB	Dudley Dean, Harvard		QB	Clinton Wyckoff, Cornell		QB	William Fincke, Yale	
HB	John Corbett, Harvard		HB	Samuel Thorne, Yale		HB	George Chadwick, Yale	
	Lee McClung, Yale			Charles Brewer, Harvard			William Morley, Columbia	
FB	Sheppard Homans, Princeton		FB	George Brooke, Penn		FB	Perry Hale, Yale	

1891			1896			1901		
E	Frank Hinkey, Yale		E	Norman Cabot, Harvard		E	David Campbell, Harvard	
	John Hartwell, Yale			Charles Gelbert, Penn			Ralph Davis, Princeton	
T	Wallace Winter, Yale		T	William Church, Princeton		T	Oliver Cutts, Harvard	
	Marshall Newell, Harvard			Fred Murphy, Yale			Paul Bunker, Army	
G	Pudge Hefflefinger, Yale		G	Charles Wharton, Penn		G	William Warner, Cornell	
	Jesse Riggs, Princeton			Wiley Woodruff, Penn			William Lee, Harvard	
C	John Adams, Penn		C	Robert Gailey, Princeton		C	Henry Holt, Yale	
QB	Phillip King, Princeton		QB	William Fincke, Yale		QB	Charles Daly, Army	
HB	Everett Lake, Harvard		HB	Edgar Wrightington, Yale		HB	Robert Kernan, Harvard	
	Lee McClung, Yale			Addison Kelly, Princeton			Harold Weekes, Columbia	
FB	Sheppard Homans, Princeton		FB	John Baird, Princeton		FB	Thomas Graydon, Harvard	

1892			1897			1902		
E	Frank Hinkey, Yale		E	Garrett Cochran, Princeton		E	Thomas Shevlin, Yale	
	Frank Hallowell, Harvard			John Hall, Yale			Edward Bowditch, Harvard	
T	Hamilton Wallis, Yale		T	Burr Chamberlain, Yale		T	James Hogan, Yale	
	Marshall Newell, Harvard			John Outland, Penn			Gilbert Kinney, Yale	
G	Bert Waters, Harvard		G	Truxton Hare, Penn		G	John DeWitt, Princeton	
	Arthur Wheeler, Princeton			Gordon Brown, Yale			Edgar Glass, Yale	
C	William Lewis, Harvard		C	Alan Doucette, Harvard		C	Henry Holt, Yale	
QB	Vance McCormick, Yale		QB	Charles De Saulles, Yale		QB	Foster Rockwell, Yale	
HB	Charles Brewer, Yale		HB	Benjamin Dibblee, Harvard		HB	George Chadwick, Yale	
	Phillip King, Princeton			Addison Kelly, Princeton			Paul Bunker, Army	
FB	Harry Thayer, Penn		FB	John Minds, Penn		FB	Thomas Graydon, Harvard	

1893			1898			1903		
E	Frank Hinkey, Yale		E	Lew Palmer, Princeton		E	Howard Henry, Princeton	
	Thomas Trenchard, Princeton			John Hallowell, Harvard			Charles Rafferty, Yale	
T	Langdon Lea, Princeton		T	A.R. T. Hillebrand, Princeton		T	James Hogan, Yale	
	Marshall Newell, Harvard			Burr Chamberlain, Yale			Daniel Knowlton, Harvard	
G	Arthur Wheeler, Princeton		G	Truxton Hare, Penn		G	John DeWitt, Princeton	
	William Hickok, Yale			Gordon Brown, Yale			Andrew Marshall, Harvard	
C	William Lewis, Harvard		C	Peter Overfield, Penn		C	H.J. Hooper, Dartmouth	
QB	Phillip King, Princeton		QB	Charles Daly, Harvard		QB	James Johnson, Carlisle	
HB	Charles Brewer, Harvard		HB	John Outland, Penn		HB	Willie Heston, Michigan	
	Franklin Morse, Princeton			Benjamin Dibblee, Harvard			J. Dana Kafer, Princeton	
FB	Frank Butterworth, Yale		FB	Clarence Herschberger, Chicago		FB	Richard Smith, Columbia	

Water Camp Teams *(cont'd)*

1904
E   Thomas Shevlin, Yale
    Walter Eckersall, Chicago
T   James Cooney, Princeton
    James Hogan, Yale
G   Frank Piekarski, Penn
    Ralph Kinney, Yale
C   Arthur Tipton, Army
QB Vincent Stevenson, Penn
HB Daniel Hurley, Harvard
    Willie Heston, Michigan
FB Andrew Smith, Penn

1905
E   Thomas Shevlin, Yale
    Ralph Glaze, Dartmouth
T   Otis Lamson, Penn
    Beaton Squires, Harvard
G   Roswell Tripp, Yale
    Francis Burr, Harvard
C   Robert Torrey, Penn
QB Walter Eckersall, Chicago
HB Howard Roome, Yale
    John Hubbard, Amherst
FB James McCormick, Princeton

1906
E   Robert Forbes, Yale
    Caspar Wister, Princeton
T   Horatio Biglow, Yale
    Jamaes Cooney, Princeton
G   Francis Burr, Harvard
    Elmer Thompson, Cornell
C   W. T. Dunn, Penn State
QB Walter Eckersall, Chicago
HB John Mayhew, Brown
    William Knox, Yale
FB Paul Veeder, Yale

1907
E   W.H. Dague, Navy
    Clarence Alcott, Yale
T   Dexter Draper, Penn
    Horatio Biglow, Yale
G   Gus Ziegler, Penn
    William Erwin, Army
C   Adolph Schulz, Michigan
QB Dwight Jones, Yale
HB John Wendell, Harvard
    Edwin Harlan, Princeton
FB James McCormick, Princeton

1908
E   Hunter Scarlett, Penn
    George Schildmiller, Dartmouth
T   Hamilton Fish, Harvard
    Frank Horr, Syracuse
G   William Goebel, Yale
    Clarke Tobin, Dartmouth
C   Charles Nourse, Harvard
QB Walter Steffen, Chicago
HB Frederick Tibbott, Princeton
    William Hollenback, Penn
FB Ted Coy, Yale

1909
E   Adrien Regnier, Brown
    John Kilpatrick, Yale
T   Hamilton Fish, Harvard
    Henry Hobbs, Yale
G   Albert Benbrook, Michigan
    Hamlin Andrus, Yale
C   Carroll Cooney, Yale
QB John McGovern, Minnesota
HB Stephen Philbin, Yale
    W. W. Minot, Harvard
FB Ted Coy, Yale

1910
E   John Kilpatrick, Yale
    Stanfield Wells, Michigan
T   Robert McKay, Harvard
    James Walker, Minnesota
G   Albert Benbrook Michigan
    Robert Fisher, Harvard
C   Ernest Cozens, Penn
QB Earl Sprackling, Brown
HB Talbot Pendleton, Princeton
    Perry Wendell, Harvard
FB LeRoy Mercer, Penn

1911
E   Sanford White, Princeton
    Douglass Bomeisler, Yale
T   Edward Hart, Princeton
    Leland Devore, Army
G   Robert Fisher, Harvard
    Joseph Duff, Princeton
C   Henry Ketcham, Yale
QB Arthur Howe, Yale
HB Percy Wendell, Harvard
    Jim Thorpe, Carlisle
FB J.P. Dalton, Navy

1912
E   Samuel Felton, Harvard
    Douglass Bomeisler, Yale
T   Wesley Englehorn, Dartmouth
    Robert Butler, Wisconsin
G   Stanley Pennock, Harvard
    John Logan, Princeton
C   Henry Ketcham, Yale
QB George Crowther, Brown
HB Charles Brickley, Harvard
    Jim Thorpe, Carlisle
FB LeRoy Mercer, Penn

1913
E   Robert Hoggett, Dartmouth
    L.A. Merrilat, Army
T   Harold Ballin, Princeton
    Nelson Talbot, Yale
G   Stanley Pennock, Harvard
    J.H. Brown, Yale
C   Paul Des Jardien, Chicago
QB Ellery Huntingon, Colgate
HB James Craig, Michigan
    Charles Brickley, Harvard
FB Edward Mahan, Harvard

1914
E   Huntington Hardwick, Harvard
    John O'Hearn, Cornell
T   Harold Ballin, Princeton
    Walter Trumbull, Harvard
G   Stanley Pennock, Harvard
    Ralph Chapman, Illinois
C   John McEwan, Army
QB Milton Ghee, Dartmouth
HB John Maulbetsch, Michigan
    Frederick Bradlee, Harvard
FB Edward Mahan, Harvard

1915
E   Bert Baston, Minnesota
    Murray Shelton, Cornell
T   Joseph Gilman, Harvard
    Earl Abell, Colgate
G   Clarence Spears, Dartmouth
    Christopher Schlachter, Syracuse
C   Robert Peck, Pittsburgh
QB Charles Barrett, Cornell
HB Richard King, Harvard
    Bart Macomber, Illinois
FB Edward Mahan, Harvard

1916
E   Bert Baston, Minnesota
    George Moseley, Yale
T   Belford West, Colgate
    Clarence Horning, Colgate
G   Clinton Black, Yale
    Harrie Dadmun, Harvard
C   Robert Peck, Pittsburgh
QB Oscar Anderson, Colgate
HB Elmer Oliphant, Army
    Fritz Pollard, Brown
FB Chic Harley, Ohio State

1917: Camp did not issue a College
All American team, but did prepre a
list of "Stars of 1917", and a team of
college players in the service:
E   Paul Robeson, Rutgers
    Weeks, Brown
T   Fats Henry, Washington and Jefferson
    George Hauser, Minnesota
G   Dale Sies, Pittsburgh
    Rollins, Rutgers
C   Russell Bailey, West Virginia
QB Bell, Penn
HB Joe Guyon, Georgia Tech
    Tank McLaren, Pittsburgh
FB Berry, Penn

1917 Camp All Service Team
E   Rasmussen, Nebraska
    Gardiner, Carlisle
T   Beckett, Oregon
    West, Colgate
G   Black, Yale
    Allemdinger, Michigan
C   Callahan, Yale
QB Watkins, Colgate
HB Casey, Harvard
    Minot, Harvard
FB Smith, Michigan

Walter Camp Teams *(cont'd)*

1918

E	Paul Robeson, Rutgers	
	Robert Hopper, Penn	
T	Leonard Hillty, Pittsburgh	
	Lou Usher, Syracuse	
G	Joe Alexander, Syracuse	
	Lyman Perry, Navy	
C	Ashel Day, Georgia Tech	
QB	Frank Murray, Princeton	
HB	Thomas Davies, Pittsburgh	
	Wolcott Roberts, Navy	
FB	Frank Steketee, Michigan	

1919

E	Robert Higgins, Penn State
	Henry Miller, Penn
T	Belford West, Colgate
	Fats Henry, Wash. & Jeff.
G	Joe Alexander, Syracuse
	Adolf Youngstrom, Dartmouth
C	James Weaver, Centre
QB	Bo McMillin, Centre
HB	Edward Casey, Harvard
	Chic Harley, Ohio State
FB	Ira Rodgers, West Virginia

1920

E	Charles Carney, Illinois
	W.E. Fincher, Georgia Tech
T	Stanton Keck, Princeton
	Ralph Scott, Wisconsin
G	Timothy Callahan, Yale
	Thomas Woods, Harvard
C	Herbert Stein, Princeton
QB	Donald Lourie, Princeton
HB	Charles Way, Penn State
	Pete Stinchcomb, Ohio State
FB	George Gipp, Notre Dame

1921

E	Brick Muller, California
	James Roberts, Centre
T	Russell Stein, Washs. & Jeff.
	Charles McGuire, Chicago
G	Frank Schwab, Lafayette
	John Brown, Harvard
C	Henry Vick, Michigan
QB	Aubrey Devine, Iowa
HB	Glenn Killinger, Penn State
	Malcolm Aldrich, Yale
FB	Edgar Kay, Cornell

1922

E	W.H. Taylor, Navy
	Brick Muller, California
T	Herbert Treat, Princeton
	John Thurman, Penn
G	Frank Schwab, Lafayette
	Charles Hubbard, Harvard
C	Edgar Garbisch, Army
QB	Gordon Locke, Iowa
HB	Edgar Kay, Cornell
	Harry Kipke, Michigan
FB	John Thomas, Chicago

1923

E	Lynn Bomar, Vanderbilt
	Homer Hazel, Rutgers
T	Century Milstead, Yale
	Frank Sundstrom, Cornell
G	Charles Hubbard, Harvard
	Joseph Bedenk, Penn State
C	Jack Blott, Michigan
QB	George Pfann, Cornell
HB	Red Grange, Illinois
	Earl Martineau, Minnesota
FB	William Mallory, Yale

1924

E	Henry Bjorkman, Dartmouth
	Charles Berry, Lafayette
T	Edward McGinley, Penn
	Ed Weir, Nebraska
G	Edliff Slaughter, Michigan
	Edwin Horrell, California
C	Edgar Garbisch, Army
QB	Harry Stuhldreher, Notre Dame
HB	Red Grange, Illinois
	Walter Koppisch, Columbia
FB	Homer Hazel, Rutgers

Grantland Rice Teams (1925-1947)

1925

E	Bennie Oosterbaan, Michigan
	George Thayer, Penn
T	Ed Weir, Nebraska
	Ralph Chase, Pittsburgh
G	Carl Diehl, Dartmouth
	Ed Hess, Ohio State
C	Edward McMillan, Princeton
QB	Red Grange, Illinois
HB	Swede Oberlander, Dartmouth
	George Wilson, Washington
FB	Ernie Nevers, Stanford

1926

E	Bennie Oosterbaan, Michigan
	Vic Hanson, Syracuse
T	Bud Sprague, Army
	Frank Wickhorst, Navy
G	Bernie Shively, Illinois
	Harry Connaughton, Georgetown
C	Bud Boeringer, Notre Dame
QB	Benny Friedman, Michigan
HB	Morton Kaer, USC
	Ralph Baker, Northwestern
FB	Herb Joesting, Minnesota

1927

E	Bennie Oosterbaan, Michigan
	Thomas Nash, Georgia
T	Leo Raskowski, Ohio State
	John H. Smith, Penn
G	John P. Smith, Notre Dame
	Crane, Illinois
C	John Charlesworth, Yale
QB	Morley Drury, USC
HB	Red Cagle, Army
	Gilbert Welch, Pittsburgh
FB	Herb Joesting, Minnesota

1928

E	Wes Fesler, Ohio State
	Ken Haycraft, Minnesota
T	Michael Getto, Pittsburgh
	Otto Pommerening, Michigan
G	Seraphim Post, Stanford
	Ed Burke, Navy
C	Pete Pund, Georgia Tech
QB	Howard Harpster, Carnegie Tech
HB	Red Cagle, Army
	Paul Scull, Penn
FB	Ken Strong, NYU

1929

E	Josephy Donchess, Pittsburgh
	Wear Schoonover, Arkansas
T	Bronko Nagurski, Minnesota
	Elmer Sleight, Purdue
G	John Cannon, Notre Dame
	Ray Montgomery, Pittsburgh
C	Benjamin Ticknor, Harvard
QB	Frank Carideo, Notre Dame
HB	Red Cagle, Army
	Bill Glassgow, Iowa
FB	Pest Welch, Purdue

Grantland Rice Teams *(cont'd)*

1930

E	Wes Fesler, Ohio State	
	Jerry Dalrymple, Tulane	
T	Frederick Sington, Alabama	
	Hugh Rhea, Nebraska	
G	Barton Koch, Baylor	
	Theodore Beckett, California	
C	Benjamin Ticknor, Harvard	
QB	Frank Carideo, Notre Dame	
HB	Bobby Dodd, Tennessee	
	Erny Pinckett, USC	
FB	Len Macaluso, Colgate	

1931

E	Vernon Smith, Georgia
	Jerry Dalyrmple, Tulane
T	Jesse Quatse, Pittsburgh
	Paul Schwegler, Washington
G	Biggie Munn, Minnesota
	Herman Hickman, Tennessee
C	Doc Morrison, Michigan
QB	Barry Wood, Harvard
HB	Marchy Schwartz, Notre Dame
	Pug Rentner, Northwestern
FB	Gus Shaver, USC

1932

E	Paul Moss, Purdue
	Dave Nisbett, Washington
T	Ernest Smith, USC
	Joe Kurth, Notre Dame
G	Milt Summerfelt, Army
	William Corbus, Stanford
C	Lawrence Ely, Nebraska
QB	Harry Newman, Michigan
HB	Don Zimmerman, Tulane
	Jim Hitchcock, Auburn
FB	Warren Heller, Pittsburgh

1933

E	Joe Skaldany, Pittsburgh
	Butch Larson, Minnesota
T	Francis Wistert, Michigan
	Fred Crawford, Duke
G	William Corbus, Stanford
	Aaron Rosenberg, USC
C	Charles Bernard, Michigan
QB	Cotton Warburton, USC
HB	Duane Purvis, Purdue
	Beattie Feathers, Tennessee
FB	George Sauer, Nebraska

1934

E	Don Hutson, Alabama
	Butch Larson, Minnesota
T	Bill Lee, Alabama
	Horse Reynolds, Stanford
G	George Barclay, North Carolina
	Bill Bevan, Minnesota
C	George Shotwell, Pittsburgh
QB	Bobby Grayson, Stanford
HB	Bill Wallace, Rice
	Buzz Borries, Navy
FB	Pug Lund, Minnesota

1935

E	Gaynell Tinsley, LSU
	Monk Moscrip, Stanford
T	Dick Smith, Minnesota
	Truman Spain, SMU
G	John Weller, Princeton
	Inwood Smith, Ohio State
C	Darrell Lewis, TCU
QB	Riley Smith, Alabama
HB	Jay Berwanger, Chicago
	Bobby Wilson, SMU
FB	Robert Grayson, Stanford

1936

E	Gaynell Tinsley, LSU
	Larry Kelley, Yale
T	Ed Widseth, Minnesota
	Averell Daniell, Pittsburgh
G	Max Starcevich, Washington
	Steve Reid, Northwestern
C	Alex Wojciechowicz, Fordham
QB	Sammy Baugh, TCU
HB	Clint Frank, Yale
	Buzz Buivid, Marquiette
FB	Sam Francis, Nebraska

1937

E	Andy Bershak, North Carolina
	Brud Holand, Cornell
T	Ed Franco, Fordham
	Vic Markov, Washington
G	Leroy Monsky, Alabama
	Joe Routt, Texas A&M
C	Carl Hinkle, Vanderbilt
QB	Clint Frank, Yale
HB	Marshall Goldberg, Pittsburgh
	Whizzer White, Colorado
FB	Sam Chapman, California

1938

E	Bowden Wyatt, Tennessee
	Roland Young, Oklahoma
T	Ed Beinor, Notre Dame
	Bill McKeever, Cornell
G	Ralph Heikkinen, Michigan
	Sid Roth, Cornell
C	Ki Aldrich, TCU
QB	Davey O'Brien, TCU
HB	Bob MacCleod, Dartmouth
	Vic Bottari, California
FB	Marshall Goldberg, Pittsburgh

1939

E	Pop Ivy, Oklahoma
	Esco Sarkkinen, Ohio State
T	Nick Dahos, Cornell
	Joe Boyd, Texas A&M
G	Ed Molinski, Tennessee
	Harry Smith, USC
C	John Scheicht, Santa Clara
QB	Paul Christman, Missouri
HB	Nile Kinnick, Iowa
	Tom Harmon, Michigan
FB	Banks McFadden, Clemson

1940

E	Dave Rankin, Purdue
	Gene Goodreault, Boston College
T	Bob Reinhard, California
	Al Bauman, Northwestern
G	Bob Suffridge, Tennessee
	Augie Lio, Georgetown
C	Rudy Mucha, Washington
QB	Frankie Albert, Stanford
HB	Tom Harmon, Michigan
	Sonny Franck, Minnesota
FB	John Kimbrough, Texas A&M

1941

E	John Rokisky, Duquesne
	Mal Kutner, Texas
T	Ernie Blandin, Tulane
	Bob Reinhard, California
G	Chub Peabody, Harvard
	Benie Crimmins, Notre Dame
C	Vince Banonis, Detroit
QB	Frankie Albert, Stanford
HB	Bruce Smith, Minnesota
	Bill Dudley, Virginia
FB	Bob Westfall, Michigan

1942

E	Dave Schreiner, Wisconsin
	Don Currivan, Boston College
T	Robin Olds, Army
	Dick Wildung, Minnesota
G	Julie Francks, Michigan
	Lindell Houston, Ohio State
C	Joe Domnanovich, Alabama
QB	Paul Governali, Columbia
HB	Billy Hillenbrand, Indiana
	Frankie Sinkwich, Georgia
FB	Holovak, Boston College

1943

E	Herb Hein, Northwestern
	Pete Pihos, Indiana
T	Jim White, Notre Dame
	Art McCaffrey, Pacific
G	Merv Pregulman, Michigan
	Pat Filley, Notre Dame
C	Casimir Myslinski, Army
QB	Angelo Bertelli, Notre Dame
HB	Creighton Miller, Notre Dame
	Bob Odell, Penn
FB	Bill Daley, Michigan

1944

E	Paul Walker, Yale
	Phil Tinsley, Georgia Tech
T	John Ferraro, USC
	Don Whitmire, Navy
G	John Green, Army
	Bill Hackett, Ohio State
C	Tex Warrington, Auburn
QB	Doug Kenna, Army
HB	Bob Jenkins, Navy
	Bob Fennimore, Oklahoma A&M
FB	Les Horvath, Ohio State

Grantland Rice Teams *(cont'd)*   **Consensus Teams (1948-1990)**

1945

E	Dick Duden, Navy
	Hub Bechtol, Texas
T	Tex Coulter, Army
	George Savitsky, Penn
G	Warren Ambling, Ohio State
	John Green, Army
C	Vaughn Mancha, Alabama
QB	Herman Wedemeyer, St. Mary's
HB	Glenn Davis, Army
	Harry Gilmer, Alabama
FB	Doc Blanchard, Army

1946

E	Hank Foldberg, Army
	Burr Baldwin, UCLA
T	Richard Huffman, Tennessee
	George Connor, Notre Dame
G	Weldon Humble, Rice
	John Mastrangelo, Notre Dame
C	Paul Duke, Georgia Tech
QB	Johnny Lujack, Notre Dame
HB	Glen Davis, Army
	Charlie Trippi, Georgia
FB	Felix Blanchard, Army
UB	Arnold Tucker, Army

1947

E	Paul Cleary, USC
	Bill Siwacki, Columbia
T	George Connor, Notre Dame
	Bob Davis, Georgia Tech
G	Steve Sukey, Penn State
	Joe Steffy, Army
C	Dick Scott, Navy
QB	Johnny Lujack, Notre Dame
HB	Skippy Minisi, Penn
	Bob Chappuis, Michigan
B	Ray Evans, Kansas

1948

E	Dick Rifenburg, Michigan
	Leon Hart, Notre Dame
T	Al Wistert, Michigan
	Leo Nomellini, Minnesota
G	Bill Fischer, Notre Dame
	Paul Burris, Oklahoma
C	Chuck Bednarik, Penn
B	John Rauch, Georgia
B	Doak Walker, SMU
B	Charlie Justice, North Carolina
B	Jackie Jensen, California
B	Emil Sitko, Notre Dame
B	Clyde Scott, Arkansas

1949

E	James Wilson, Rice
	Leon Hart, Notre Dame
T	Leo Nomellini, Minnesota
	Al Wistert, Michigan
G	Rod Franz, California
	Ed Bagdon, Michigan State
C	Claryton Tonnemaker, Minnesota
B	Arnold Galiffa, Army
B	Bob Williams, Notre Dame
B	Emil Sitko, Notre Dame
B	Doak Walker, SMU

1950

E	Bill McColl, Stanford
	Dan Foldberg, Army
T	Bob Gain, Kentucky
	Jim Weatherall, Oklahoma
G	Bud McFadin, Texas
	Les Richter, California
C	Jerry Groom, Notre Dame
B	Babe Parilli, Kentucky
B	Vic Janowicz, Ohio State
B	Kyle Rote, SMU
B	Leon Heath, Oklahoma

1951

E	Bill McColl, Stanford
	Robert Carey, Michigan State
T	Don Coleman, Michigan State
	Jim Weatherall, Oklahoma
G	Robert Ward, Maryland
	Les Richter, California
C	Dick Hightower, SMU
B	Babe Parilli, Kentucky
B	Henry Lauricella, Tennessee
B	Dick Kazmaier, Princeton
B	John Karras, Illinois

1952

E	Frank McPhee, Princeton
	Bernie Flowers, Purdue
T	Dick Modzelewski, Maryland
	Harold Miller, Georgia Tech
G	Elmer Willhoite, USC
	John Michels, Tennessee
C	Donn Moomaw, UCLA
B	John Scarbath, Maryland
	Johnny Lattner, Notre Dame
	Jim Sears, USC
	Billy Vessels, Oklahoma

1953

E	Don Dohoney, Michigan State
	Carlton Massey, Texas
T	Stan Jones, Maryland
	Arthur Hunter, Notre Dame
G	J. D. Roberts, Oklahoma
	Crawford Mims, Mississippi
C	Larry Morris, Georgia Tech
B	Johnny Lattner, Notre Dame
	Paul Giel, Minnesota
	Paul Cameron, UCLA
	J. C. Caroline, Illinois

1954

E	Max Boydston, Oklahoma
	Ron Beagle, Navy
T	Jack Ellena, UCLA
	Sidney Fournet, LSU
G	Bud Brooks, Arkansas
	Calvin Jones, Iowa
C	Kurt Burris, Oklahoma
B	Ralph Guglielmi, Notre Dame
	Richard Moegle, Rice
	Howard Cassady, Ohio State
	Alan Ameche, Wisconsin

1955

E	Ron Beagle, Navy
	Ron Kramer, Michigan
T	Bruce Bosley, West Virginia
	Norm Masters, Michigan State
G	Bo Bolinger, Oklahoma
	Calvin Jones, Iowa
	Hardiman Cureton, UCLA
C	Bob Pellegrini, Maryland
B	Howard Cassady, Ohio State
	James Swink, TCU
	Earl Morrall, Michigan State
	Paul Hornung, Notre Dame

1956

E	Ron Kramer, Michigan
T.	John Witte, Oregon State
	Lou Michaels, Kentucky
G	Jim Parker, Ohio State
	William Glass, Baylor
C	Jerry Tubbs, Oklahoma
B	Jim Brown, Syracuse
	Johnny Majors, Tennessee
	Tom McDonald, Oklahoma
	John Brodie, Stanford

1957

E	Jim Phillips, Auburn
	Dick Wallen, UCLA
T	Lou Michaels, Kentucky
	Alex Karras, Iowa
G	William Krisher, Oklahoma
	Al Ecuyer, Notre Dame
C	Daniel Currie, Michigan State
B	John David Crow, Texas A&M
	Walter Kowalczyk, Michigan State
	Robert Anderson, Army
	Clendon Thomas, Oklahoma

Consensus Teams *(cont'd)*

1958

E   Buddy Dial, Rice
     Samuel Williams, Michigan State
T   Theodore Bates, Oregon State
     Brock Strom, Air Force
G   John Guzik, Pittsburgh
     Zeke Smith, Auburn
     George Deiderich, Vanderbilt
C   Robert Harrison, Oklahoma
B   Randy Duncan, Iowa
     Pete Dawkins, Army
     Billy Cannon, LSU
     Bob White, Ohio State

1959

E   Bill Carpenter, Army
     Monty Stickles, Notre Dame
T   Don Floyd, TCU
     Dan Lanphear, Wisconsin
G   Roger Davis, Syracuse
     William Burrell, Illinois
C   Maxie Baughan, Georgia Tech
B   Richard Lucas, Penn State
     Billy Cannon, LSU
     Ron Burton, Northwestern
     Charles Flowers, Mississippi

1960

E   Mike Ditka, Pittsburgh
     Dan LaRose, Missouri
T   Bob Lilly, TCU
     Ken Rice, Auburn
G   Joseph Romig, Colorado
     Tom Brown, Minnesota
C   E. J. Holub, Texas Tech
B   Jake Gibbs, Mississippi
     Joe Bellino, Navy
     Ernie Davis, Syracuse
     Bob Ferguson, Ohio State

1961

E   Gary Collins, Maryland
     Bill Miller, Miami (FL)
T   William Neighbors, Alabama
     Merlin Olsen, Utah State
G   Roy Winston, LSU
     Joseph Romig, Colorado
C   Alex Kroll, Rutgers
B   Ernie Davis, Syracuse
     Bob Ferguson, Ohio State
     Jim Saxton, Texas
     Sandy Stephens, Minnesota

1962

E   Hal Bedsole, USC
     Pat Richter, Wisconsin
T   Bobby Bell, Minnesota
     James Dunaway, Mississippi
G   John Cverko, Northwesten
     Jack Treadwell, Texas
C   Lee Roy Jordan, Alabama
B   Terry Baker, Oregon State
     Mel Renfro, Oregon
     George Saimes, Michigan State
     Jerry Stovall, LSU

1963

E   Vern Burke, Oregon State
     Lawrence Elkins, Baylor
T   Scott Appleton, Texas
     Carl Eller, Minnesota
G   Robert Brown, Nebraska
     Rick Redman, Washington
C   Dick Butkus, Illinois
B   Roger Staubach, Navy
     Sherman Lewis, Mich. State
     Gale Sayers, Kansas
     Paul Martha, Pittsburgh
     Jim Grisham, Oklahoma

1964

E   Jack Snow, Notre Dame
     Fred Biletnikoff, Fla. State
T   Larry Kramer, Minnesota
     Ralph Neely, Oklahoma
G   Rick Redman, Washington
     Glenn Ressler, Penn State
C   Dick Butkus, Illinois
B   John Huarte, Notre Dame
     Gale Sayers, Kansas
     Larry Elkins, Baylor
     Tucker Frederickson, Auburn

1965

Offense

E   Harold Twilley, Tulsa
     Freeman White, Nebraska
T   Sam Ball, Kentucky
     Glen Ray Hines, Arksnasas
G   Richard Arrington, Notre Dame
     Stas Maliszewski, Princetonn
C   Paul Crane, Alabama
B   Bob Griese, Purdue
     Donny Anderson, Texas Tech
     Mike Garrett, USC
     Jim Grabowski, Illinois

Defense

E   Aaron Brown, Minnesota
     Bubba Smith, Michigan State
T   Walter Barnes, Nebraska
     Lloyd Phillips, Arkansas
MG   Carl McAdams, Oklahoma
LB   Bill Yearby, Michigan
     Frank Emanuel, Tennessee
     Tommy Nobis, Texas
B   George Webster, Michigan State
     Johnny Roland, Missouri
     Nick Rassas, Notre Dame

1966

E   Jack Clancy, Michigan
     Ray Perkins, Alabama
T   Ron Yary, USC
     Cecil Dowdy, Alabama
G   Thomas Regner, Notre Dame
     LaVerne Allers, Nebraska
C   James Breland, Georgia Tech
B   Steve Spurrier, Florida
     Floyd Little, Syracuse
     Clinton Jones, Michigan State
     Nick Eddy, Notre Dame
     Mel Farr, UCLA

Defense

E   Alan Page, Notre Dame
     Bubba Smith, Michigan State
T   Thomas Greenlee, Washington
     Lloyd Phillips, Arkansas
MG   John LaGrone, SMU
     Wayne Meylan, Nebraska
LB   Paul Naumoff, Tennessee
     Jim Lynch, Notre Dame
B   George Webster, Michigan State
     Thomas Beier, Miami (FL)
     Nate Shaw, USC

1967

Offense

E   Dennis Homan, Alabama
     Jim Seymour, Notre Dame
     Ron Sellers, Fla. State
T   Edgar Chandler, Georgia
     Ron Yary, USC
G   Gary Cassells, Indiana
     Harry Olzewski, Clemson
     Rich Stotter, Houston
C   Bob Thomas, Tennessee
QB   Gary Beban, UCLA
B   Larry Csonka, Syracuse
     Leroy Keyes, Purdue
     O. J. Simpson, USC

Defense

E   Ted Hendricks, Miami (FL)
     Bob Stein, Minnesota
     Tim Rossovich, USC
T   Dennis Byrd, NC State
     Kevin Hardy, Notre Dame
MG   Granville Liggins, Oklahoma
LB   Don Manning, UCLA
     Wayne Meyland, Nebraska
     Adrian Young, USC
B   Bobby Johns, Alabama
     Tom Schoen, Notre Dame
     Frank Loria, Virginia Tech
     Dick Anderson, Colorado

1968

Offense

E	Jim Seymour, Notre Dame
	Ted Kwalick, Penn State
	Jerry LeVias, SMU
T	Dave Foley, Ohio State
	George Kunz, Notre Dame
G	Guy Dennis, Florida
	Charles Rosenfedler, Tennesee
	Mike Montler, Colorado
	Jim Barnes, Arkansas
C	John Didion, Oregon State
QB	Terry Hanratty, Notre Dame
B	Leroy Keyes, Purdue
	O.J. Simpson, USC
	Chris Gilbert, Texas

Defense

E	Ted Hendricks, Miami
	Bob Stein, Minnesota
	John Zook, Kansas
T	Bill Stanfill, Georgia
	Joe Greene, North Texas
MG	Chuck Kyle, Purdue
	Ed White, California
LB	Dennis Onkotz, Penn Stte
	Mike Hall, Alabama
	Steve Kiner, Tennessee
B	Jake Scott, Georgia
	Roger Wehrli, Missouri
	Tony Kyasky, Syracuse
	Mike Battle, USC
	Al Worley, Washington

1969

Offense

E	Jim Mandich, Michigan
	Charles Speyrer, Texas
	Walker Gillette, Richmond
FL	Carlos Alvarez, Florida
T	Sid Smith, USC
	Bob McKay, Texas
	John Ward, Oklahoma
G	Larry DiNardo, Notre Dame
	Chip Kell, Tennessee
	Bill Bridges, Houston
C	Rodney Brand, Arkansas
QB	Mike Phipps, Purdue
B	Steve Owens, Oklahoma
	Jim Otis, Ohio State
	Bob Anderson, Colorado

Defense

E	Jim Gunn, USC
	Phil Olsen, Utah
T	Mike Reid, Penn State
	Mike McCoy, Notre Dame
MG	Jim Stillwagon, Ohio State
LB	Dennis Onkotz, Penn State
	Steve Kiner, Tennessee
	Mike Ballou, UCLA
B	Jack Tatum, Ohio State
	Tom Curtis, Michigan
	Buddy McClinton, Auburn

1970

Offense

E	Chuck Dicus, Arkansas
	Tom Gatewood, Notre Dame
	Ernie Jennings, Air Force
	Elmo Wright, Houston
	Charles Speyrer, Texas
T	Dan Dierdorf, Michigan
	Bobby Weunsch, Texas
	Bob Newton, Nebraska
G	Larry DiNardo, Notre Dame
	Chip Kell, Tennessee
C	Don Popplewell, Colorado
QB	Jim Plunkett, Stanford
B	John Musso, Alabama
	Don McCauley, North Carolina
	Steve Worster, Texas

Defense

E	Jack Youngblood, Florida
	Charles Weaver, USC
	Bill Atessis, Texas
T	Rock Perdoni, Georgia Tech
	Tom Neville, Yale
	Dick Bumpas, Arkansas
MG	Jim Stillwagon, Ohio State
LB	Jerry Murtaugh, Nebraska
	Jack Ham, Penn State
	Mike Anderson, LSU
B	Larry Willingham, Auburn
	Pat Murphy, Colorado
	Murray Bowden, Dartmouth
	Jack Tatum, Ohio State
	Dave Elmendorf, Texas A&M
	Tommy Casanova, LSU

1971

Offense

E	Terry Beasley, Auburn
	Johnny Rodgers, Nebraska
T	Jerry Sisemore, Texas
	Dave Joyner, Penn State
G	Reggie McKenzie, Michigan
G	Royce Smith, Georgia
C	Tom Brahaney, Oklahoma
QB	Pat Sullivan, Auburn
B	Johnny Musso, Alabama
	Ed Marinaro, Cornell
	Greg Pruitt, Oklahoma

Defense

E	Walt Patulski, Notre Dame
	Willie Harper, Nebraska
T	Sherman White, California
	Herb Orvis, Colorado
	Larry Jacobson, Nebraska
	Mel Long, Toledo
MG	Rich Glover, Nebraska
LB	Mike Taylor, Michigan
	Jackie Walker, Tennessee
	Jeff Siemon, Stanford
B	Tommy Casanova, LSU
	Bobby Majors, Tennessee
	Clarence Ellis, Notre Dame
	Dickie Harris, South Carolina
	Ernie Jackson, Duke

1972

Offense

WR	Johnny Rodgers, Nebraska
TE	Charles Young, USC
T	Jerry Sisemore, Texas
	John Hicks, Ohio State
	Paul Seymour, Michigan
G	John Hannah, Alabama
	Skip Singletary, Temple
	Ron Rusnak, North Carolina
C	Tom Brahaney, Oklahoma
QB	John Hufnagel, Penn State
	Bert Jones, LSU
B	Greg Pruitt, Oklahoma
	Dick Jauron, Yale
	Otis Armstrong, Purdue
	Woody Green, Arizona State

Defense

E	Willie Harper, Nebraska
	Bruce Bannon, Penn State
T	Dave Butz, Purdue
	Greg Marx, Notre Dame
MG	Rich Glover, Nebraska
LB	Steve Brown, Oregon State
	Tom Jackson, Louisville
	Randy Gradishar, Ohio State
	Tom Skorupan, Penn State
B	Ray Guy, Southern Miss.
	Bob Popelka, SMU
	Brad Van Pelt, Michigan State
	Randy Logan, Michigan
	Cullen Bryant, Colorado

1973

Offense

TE	Dave Casper, Notre Dame
WR	Wayne Wheeler, Alabama
	Lynn Swann, USC
T	John Hicks, Ohio State
	Eddie Foster, Oklahoma
	Booker Brown, USC
G	Tyler Lafauci, LSU
	Bill Yoest, NC State
	Buddy Brown, Alabama
C	Bill Wyman, Texas
QB	David Jaynes, Kansas
B	John Cappelletti, Penn State
	Roosevelt Leaks, Texas
	Woody Green, Arizona State
	Kermit Johnson, UCLA

Defense

L	Lucious Selmon, Oklahoma
	Dave Gallagher, Michigan
	John Dutton, Nebraska
	Charlie Hall, Tulane
MG	Tony Christiani, Miami (FL)
LB	Randy Gradishar, Ohio State
	Richard Wood, USC
	Ed O'Neil, Penn State
	Rod Shoate, Oklahoma
B	Mike Townsend, Notre Dame
	Artimus Parker, USC
	Randy Rhino, Georgia Tech
	Dave Brown, Michigan

1974

Offense
WR	Patrick McInally, Harvard
	Peter Demmerle, Notre Dame
TE	Bennie Cunningham, Clemson
T	Kurt Schumacher, Ohio State
	Robert Simmons, Texas
	Marvin Crenshaw, Nebraska
G	John Nessel, Penn State
	Kenneth Huff, North Carolina
	John Roush, Oklahoma
C	Geoff Reece, Wash. State
	Steve Myers, Ohio State
QB	Steve Joachim, Temple
	Steve Bartkowski, California
RB	Joseph Washington, Oklahoma
	Archie Griffin, Ohio State
	Anthony Davis, USC

Defense
L	Mack Mitchell, Houston
	James Webb, Miss. State
	Randy White, Maryland
	Michael Fanning, Notre Dame
	Mike Hartenstine, Penn State
	Pat Donovan, Stanford
	Leroy Cook, Alabama
MG	Gary Burley, Pittsburgh
	Louie Kelcher, SMU
LB	Rod Shoate, Oklahoma
	Woodrow Lowe, Alabama
	Kenneth Bernich, Auburn
	Richard Wood, USC
B	John Provost, Holy Cross
	Dave Brown, Michigan
	Pat Thomas, Texas A&M
	Randy Rhino, Georgia Tech

1975

Offense
WR	Steve Rivera, California
	Larry Seivers, Tennessee
TE	Bennie Cunningham, Clemson
T	Dennis Lick, Wisconsin
	Bob Simmons, Texas
	Terry Webb, Oklahoma
	Randy Johnson, Georgia
	Ted Smith, Ohio State
C	Rik Bonness, Nebraska
QB	John Sciarra, UCLA
RB	Archie Griffin, Ohio State
	Ricky Bell, USC
	Tony Dorsett, Pittsburgh
	Chuck Muncie, California

Defense
E	Leroy Cook, Alabama
	Jimbo Elrod, Oklahoma
T	Leroy Selmon, Oklahoma
	Steve Niehaus, Notre Dame
MG	Dewey Selmon, Oklahoma
LB	Ed Simonini, Texas A&M
	Greg Buttle, Penn State
	Don Dufek, Michigan
	Sammy Green, Florida
B	Chet Moeller, Navy
	Pat Thomas, Texas A&M
	Tim Fox, Ohio State
P	Chris Bahr, Penn State

1976

Offense
SE	Larry Sievers, Tennessee
TE	Ken McAfee, Notre Dame
T	Warren Bryant, Kentucky
	Mike Vaughan, Oklahoma
	Chris Ward, Ohio State
G	Mark Donahue, Michigan
	Joel Parrish, Georgia
C	Derrel Gofourth, Oklahoma State
	Bill Bryan, Duke
QB	Tommy Kramer, Rice
RB	Tony Dorsett, Pittsburgh
	Ricky Bell, USC
	Rob Lytle, Michigan
K	Tony Franklin, Texas A&M

Defense
E	Ross Browner, Notre Dame
	Duncan McColl, Stanford
	Bob Brudzinski, Ohio State
T	Wilson Whitely, Houston
	Mike Fultz, Nebraska
	Gary Jeter, USC
	Joe Campbell, Maryland
MG	Al Romano, Pittsburgh
LB	Calvin O'Neal, Michigan
	Robert Jackson, Texas A&M
	Thomas Howard, Texas Tech
	Jerry Robinson, UCLA
B	Luther Bradley, Notre Dame
	Bill Armstrong, Wake Forest
	Dennis Thurman, USC
	David Butterfield, Nebraska
	Gary Green, Baylor

1977

Offense
SE	Ozzie Newsome, Alabama
	John Jefferson, Arizona State
TE	Ken McAfee, Notre Dame
T	Chris Ward, Ohio State
	Dan Irons, Texas Tech
G	Mark Donahue, Michigan
	Leotis Harris, Arkansas
C	Tom Brzoza, Pittsburgh
QB	Doug Williams, Grambling
	Guy Benjamin, Stanford
B	Earl Campbell, Texas
	Terry Miller, Oklahoma State
	Charles Alexander, LSU
	John Pagliaro, Yale
K	Steve Little, Arkansas

Defense
E	Ross Browner, Notre Dame
	Art Still, Kentucky
T	Brad Shearer, Texas
	Randy Holloway, Pittsburgh
	Dee Hardison, North Carolina
MG	Aaron Brown, Ohio State
LB	Jerry Robinson, UCLA
	Tom Cousineau, Ohio State
	Darryl Hunt, Oklahoma
	Gary Spani, Kansas State
B	Luther Bradley, Notre Dame
	Zac Henderson, Oklahoma
	Dennis Thurman, USC
	Bob Jury, Pittsburgh

1978

Offense
WR	Emanuel Tollbert, SMU
TE	Kellen Winslow, Missouri
T	Kelvin Clark, Nebraska
	Keith Dorney, Penn State
G	Pat Howell, USC
	Greg Roberts, Oklahoma
C	Dave Huffman, Notre Dame
QB	Chuck Fusina, Penn State
RB	Billy Sims, Oklahoma
	Charles White, USC
	Charles Alexander, LSU
	Ted Brown, NC State
K	Matt Bahr, Penn State
	Russell Erxleben, Texas

Defense
L	Al Harris, Arizona State
	Hugh Green, Pittsburgh
	Matt Millen, Penn State
	Mike Bell, Colorado State
	Bruce Clark, Penn State
	Marty Lyons, Alabama
MG	Reggie Kinlaw, Oklahoma
LB	Jerry Robinson, UCLA
	Tom Cousineau, Ohio State
	Bob Golic, Notre Dame
B	Jeff Nixon, Richmond
	Ken Easley, UCLA
	Johnnie Johnson, Texas

1979

Offense
WR	Ken Margerum, Stanford
TE	Junior Miller, Nebraska
T	Greg Kolenda, Arkansas
	Melvin Jones, Houston
	Jim Bunch, Alabama
G	Brad Budde, USC
	Ken Fritz, Ohio State
C	Jim Richter, NC State
QB	Marc Wilson, BYU
B	Charles White, USC
	Billy Sims, Oklahoma
	Vagas Ferguson, Notre Dame
PK	Dale Castro, Maryland

Defense
L	Hugh Green, Pittsburgh
	Jacob Green, Texas A&M
	Steve McMichael, Texas
	Bruce Clark, Penn State
	Jim Stuckey, Clemson
MG	Ron Simmons, Fla. State
LB	George Cumby, Oklahoma
	Mike Singletary, Baylor
	Ron Simpkins, Michigan
B	Ken Easley, UCLA
	Roland James, Tennessee
	Johnnie Johnson, Texas
	Jim Miller, Mississippi

1980
Offense
WR Ken Margerum, Stanford
TE Dave Young, Purdue
L   Louis Oubre, Oklahoma
    Keith Van Horne, USC
    Mark May, Pittsburgh
    Randy Schleusener, Nebraska
    Ron Wooten, North Carolina
C   George Lilja, Michigan
    John Scully, Notre Dame
QB Mark Herrmann, Purdue
B   George Rogers, So. Carolina
    Herschel Walker, Georgia
    Jarvis Redwine, Nebraska
PK Rex Robinson, Georgia
Defense
L   Hugh Green, Pittsburgh
    E.J. Junior, Alabama
    Kenneth Sims, Texas
    Len Mitchell, Houston
    Hosca Taylor, Houston
MB Ron Simmons, Fla. State
LB Mike Singletary, Baylor
    Tom Boyd, Alabama
    Bob Crable, Notre Dame
    Lawrence Taylor, N. Carolina
    David Little, Florida
B   Ken Easley, UCLA
    Ronnie Lott, USC
    Scott Woerner, Georgia
    John Simmons, SMU
P   Ray Stachowicz, Mich. State

1981
Offense
WR Anthony Carter, Michigan
TE Tim Wrightman, UCLA
L   Terry Tausch, Texas
    Bubba Paris, Michigan
    Sean Farrell, Penn State
    Roy Foster, USC
    Terry Crouch, Oklahoma
    Ed Muransky, Michigan
    Kurt Becker, Michigan
C   Dave Rimington, Nebraska
QB Dan Marino, Pittsburgh
    Jim McMahon, BYU
B   Marcus Allen, USC
    Herschel Walker, Georgia
    Curt Warner, Penn State
PK Morten Anderson, Mich. State
Defense
L   Billy Ray Smith, Arkansas
    Jimmy Williams, Nebraska
    Andre Tippett, Iowa
    Kenneth Sims, Texas
    Lester Williams, Miami (FL)
MG Tim Krumrie, Wisconsin
LB Bob Crable, Notre Dame
    Tom Boyd, Alabama
    Chip Banks, USC
    Jeff Davis, Clemson
    Sal Sunseri, Pittsburgh
B   Vann McElroy, Baylor
    Mike Richardson, Arizona State
    Tommy Wilcox, Alabama
    Terry Kinard, Clemson
    Fred Marion, Miami/ P Reggie Roby, Iowa

1982
Offense
WR Anthony Carter, Michigan
TE Gordon Hudson, BYU
L   Don Mosebar, USC
    Jimbo Covert, Pittsburgh
    Steve Korte, Arkansas
    Bruce Matthews, USC
    Dave Dreschler, No. Carolina
C   Dave Rimington, Nebraska
QB John Elway, Stanford
B   Herschel Walker, Georgia
    Eric Dickerson, SMU
    Ernest Anderson, Oklahoma State
    Mike Rozier, Nebraska
PK Chuck Nelson, Washington
Defense
L   Billy Ray Smith, Arkansas
    Jimmy Payne, Georgia
    Mike Pitts, Alabama
    Tim Krumrie, Wisconsin
    Wilber Marshall, Florida
    George Achica, USC
    Gabriel Rivera, Texas Tech
LB Mark Stewart, Washington
    Darryl Talley, West Virginia
    Marcus Marek, Ohio State
    Vernon Maxwell, Arizona State
    Rick Bryan, Oklahoma
B   Mike Richardson, Arizona State
    Terry Hoage, Georgia
    Tommy Wilcox, Alabama
    Terry Kinard, Clemson
P   Reggie Roby, Iowa
P   Jim Arnold, Vanderbilt

1983
Offense
WR Irving Fryar, Nebraska
TE Gordon Hudson, BYU
L   Bill Fralic, Pittsburgh
    Terry Long, E. Carolina
    Dean Steinkuhler, Nebrasks
    Doug Dawson, Texas
C   Tony Slaton, USC
QB Steve Young, BYU
B   Mike Rozier, Nebraska
    Bo Jackson, Auburn
    Greg Allen, Fla. State
    Napoleon McCallum, Navy
PK Luis Zendejas, Arizona State
Defense
L   Rick Bryan, Oklahoma
    William Fuller, No. Carolina
    Reggie White, Tennessee
    William Perry, Clemson
LB Jeff Leiding, Texas
    Ron Rivera, California
    Ricky Hunley, Arizona
    Wilber Marshall, Florida
B   Don Rogers, UCLA
    Jerry Gray, Texas
    Mossy Cade, Texas
    Russell Carter, SMU
    Terry Hoage, Georgia
    Jim Colquitt, Tennessee
    Jack Weil, Wyoming

1984
Offense
WR David Williams, Illinois
    Eddie Brown, Miami (FL)
TE Bob Bennett, West Virginia
    Jay Novacek, Wyoming
L   Will Fralic, Pittsburgh
    Lomas Brown, Florida
    Bill Mayo, Tennessee
    Jim Lachey, Ohio State
    Del Wilkes, So. Carolina
C   Mark Traynowicz, Nebraska
QB Doug Flutie, Boston College
B   Keith Byars, Ohio State
    Greg Allen, Fla. State
    Ken Davis, TCU
    Reuben Mayes, Wash. State
PK Kevin Butler, Georgia
Defense
L   William Perry, Clemson
    Tony Degrate, Texas
    Bruce Smith, Virginia Tech
    Ron Holmes, Washington
    Tony Casillas, Oklahoma
LB Jack Del Rio, USC
    Larry Station, Iowa
    Greg Carr, Auburn
B   Jeff Sanchez, Georgia
    Jerry Gray, Texas
    David Fulcher, Arizona State
    Tony Thurman, Boston College
    Rod Brown, Oklahoma State
    Ricky Anderson, Vanderbilt

1985
P   Barry Helton, Colorado
Offense
WR David Williams, Illinois
    Tim McGee, Tennessee
TE Willie Smith, Miami (FL)
L   Jim Drombowski, Virginia
    Jeff Bregel, USC
    Brian Jozwiak, West Virginia
    John Rienstra, Temple
    J.E. Maarleveld, Maryland
    Jamie Dukes, Fla. State
    Jeff Zimmerman, Florida
C   Gene Chilton, Texas
    Pete Anderson, Georgia
QB Chuck Long, Iowa
B   Bo Jackson, Auburn
    Lorenzo White, Mich. State
    Thurman Thomas, Oklahoma State
    Napoleon McCallum, Navy
    Reggie Dupard, SMU
PK John Lee, UCLA
Defense
L   Tony Casillas, Oklahoma
    Mike Ruth, Boston College
    Leslie O"Neal, Oklahoma State
    Tim Green, Syracuse
    Mike Hammerstein, Michigan
LB Larry Station, Iowa
    Cornelius Bennett, Alabama
    Brian Bosworth, Oklahoma
    John Holland, Texas A&M
B   Brad Cochran, Michigan
    Scott Thomas, Air Force
    Allen Druden, Arizona/David Fulcher, Ariz. State

1986
WR Cris Carter, Ohio State
TE Keith Jackson, Oklahoma
L John Clay, Missouri
    Danny Villa, Arizona State
    Randy Dixon, Pittsburgh
    Jeff Bregel, USC
    Jeff Zimmerman, Florida
C Ben Tamburello, Auburn
QB Vinny Testaverde, Miami (FL)
B D.J. Dozier, Penn State
    Brent Fullwood, Auburn
    Paul Palmer, Temple
    Terrence Flagler, Clemson
    Brad Muster, Stanford
PK Jeff Jaeger, Washington
Defense
L Jerome Brown, Miami (FL)
    Tim Johnson, Penn State
    Danny Noonan, Nebraska
    Reggie Rogers, Washington
    Tony Woods, Pittsburgh
    Jason Buck, BYU
LB Cornelius Bennett, Alabama
    Brian Bosworth, Oklahoma
    Shane Conlan, Penn State
    Chris Spielman, Ohio State
B Thomas Everett, Baylor
    John Little, Georgia
    Bennie Blades, Miami (FL)
    Tim McDonald, USC
    Garland Rivers, Michigan
    Rod Woodson, Purdue
P Bill Smith, Mississippi
    Barry Helton, Colorado

1987
P Tom Tupa, Ohio State

WR Tim Brown, Notre Dame
    Wendell Davis, LSU
TE Keith Jackson, Oklahoma
L Dave Cadigan, USC
    John Elliott, Michigan
    Mark Hutson, Oklahoma
    Randall McDaniel, Arizona State
C Nacho Albergamo, LSU
QB Don McPherson, Syracuse
B Gaston Green, UCLA
    Craig Heyward, Pittsburgh
    Bobby Humphrey, Alabama
    Lorenzo White, Mich. State
PK David Treadwell, Clemson
Defense
L Chad Hennings, Air Force
    Tracy Rocker, Auburn
    Daniel Stubbs, Miami
    Ted Gregory, Syracuse
    Broderick Thomas, Nebraska
    John Roper, Texas A&M
LB Aundray Bruce, Auburn
    Ken Norton, Jr., UCLA
    Dante Jones, Oklahoma
    Chris Spielman, Ohio State
B Bennie Blades, Miami (FL)
    Chuck Cecil, Arizona
    Ricky Dixon, Oklahoma
    Deion Sanders, Fla. State
    Jarvis Williams, Florida

1988
Offense
WR Hart Lee Dykes, Okla. State
    Jason Phillips, Houston
TE Troy Sadowski, Georgia
    Marv Cook, Iowa
L Tony Mandarich, Mich. State
    Pat Tomberlin, Fla. State
    Anthony Phillips, Oklahoma
    Mark Stepnoski, Pittsburgh
C Jake Young, Nebraska
    John Vitale, Michigan
QB Troy Aikman, UCLA
    Steve Walsh, Miami (FL)
B Barry Sanders, Okla. State
    Anthony Thompson, Indiana
    Tim Worley, Georgia
PK Kendall Trainor, Arkansas
Defense
L Dave Haight, Iowa
    Bill Hawkins, Miami (FL)
    Wayne Martin, Arkansas
    Mark Messner, Michigan
    Frank Stams, Notre Dame
    Tracy Rocker, Auburn
LB Mike Stonebreaker, Notre Dame
    Broderick Thomas, Nebraska
    Derrick Thomas, Alabama
B Darryl Henley, UCLA
    Louis Oliver, Florida
    Deion Sanders, Fla. State
    Donnell Woolford, Clemson
P Keith English, Colorado

1989

WR Clarkston Hines, Duke
    Terance Mathis, New Mexico
TE Mike Busch, Iowa State
L Doug Glaser, Nebraska
    Bob Kula, Mich. State
    Mohammed Elowinibi, BYU
    Jim Mabry, Arkansas
    Joe Garten, Colorado
    Ed King, Auburn
    Eric Still, Tennessee
C Jake Young, Nebraska
QB Andre Ware, Houston
B Emmitt Smith, Florida
    Blair Thomas, Penn State
    Anthony Thompson, Indiana
PK Jason Hanson, Wash. State
Defense
L Moe Gardner, Illinois
    Greg Mark, Miami (FL)
    Odell Haggins, Fla. State
    Tim Ryan, USC
    Chris Zorich, Notre Dame
LB Keith McCants, Alabama
    Alfred Williams, Colorado
    Kanavis McGhee, Colorado
    Percy Snow, Mich. State
B LeRoy Butler, Fla. State
    Mark Carrier, USC
    Todd Lyght, Notre Dame
    Tripp Wilborne, Michigan
P Tom Rouen, Colorado

1990
Offense
WR Raghib Ismail, Notre Dame
    Herman Moore, Virginia
TE Chris Smith, BYU
L Antone Davis, Tennessee
    Stacy Long, Clemson
    Greg Skrepenak, Michigan
    Joe Garten, Colorado
    Ed King, Auburn
C John Flannery, Syracuse
QB Ty Detmer, BYU
B Eric Bieniemy, Colorado
    Darren Lewis, Texas A&M
    Greg Lewis, Washington
PK Philip Doyle, Alabama
Defense
L Moe Gardner, Illinois
    Russell Maryland, Miami (FL)
    David Rocker, Auburn
    Chris Zorich, Notre Dame
LB Maurice Crum, Miami (FL)
    Michael Stonebreaker, Notre Dame
    Alfred Williams, Colorado
B Darryl Lewis, Arizona
    Todd Lyght, Notre Dame
    Ken Swilling, Georgia Tech
    Tripp Welborne, Michigan
P Brian Greenfield, Pittsburgh

1991
Offense
WR Desmond Howard, Michigan
    Mario Bailey, Washington
TE Derek Brown, Notre Dame
    Kelly Blackwell, TCU
L Greg Skrepenak, Michigan
    Bob Whitfield, Stanford
    Jeb Flesch, Clemson
    Jerry Ostroski, Tulsa
    Mirko Jurkovic, Notre Dame
C Jay Leeuwenburg, Colorado
QB Casey Weldon, Fla. State
    Ty Detmer, BYU
B Vaughn Dunbar, Indiana
    Amp Lee, Fla. State
    Trevor Cobb, Rice
    Russell White, California
PK Carlos Huerta, Miami (FL)
Defense
L Steve Emtman, Washington
    Santana Dotson, Baylor
    Brad Culpepper, Florida
    Joel Steef, Colorado
    Leroy Smith, Iowa
    Shane Dronett, Texas
LB Levon Kirkland, Clemson
    Marvin Jones, Fla. State
    Robert Jones, E. Carolina
B Terrell Buckley, Fla. State
    Darryl Williams, Miami (FL)
    Dale Carter, Tennessee
    Kevin Smith, Texas A&M
P Mark Bounds, Texas Tech

Consensus Teams *(cont'd)*

1992
Offense
WR Sean Dawkins, California
     O.J. McDuffie, Penn State
TE   Chris Gedney, Syracuse
L   Lincoln Kennedy, Washington
     Tony Boselli, USC
     Will Shields, Nebraska
     Willie Roaf, Louisiana Tech
     Aaron Taylor, Notre Dame
     Everett Lindsay, Mississippi
C   Mike Compton, West Virginia
QB Gino Torretta, Miami (FL)
B   Marshall Faulk, San Diego State
     Garrison Hearst, Georgia
PK   Scott Sisson, Georgia Tech
     Joe Allison, Memphis State
Defense
L   John Copeland, Alabama
     Rob Waldrop, Arizona
     Coleman Rudolph, Georgia Tech
     Eric Curry, Alabama
     Chris Slade, Virginia
LB   Marvin Jones, Fla. State
     Michael Barrow, Miami
     Marcus Buckley, Texas A&M
B   Deon Figures, Colorado
     Carlton Gray, UCLA
     Carlton McDonald, Air Force
     Ryan McNeil, Miami
P   Ed Bunn, UTEP
     Sean Snyder, Kansas State

1993
Offense
WR David Palmer, Alabama
     Johnnie Morton, USC
     J. J. Stokes, UCLA
TE   Carlester Crumpler, E. Carolina
L   Korey Stringer, Ohio State
     Aaron Taylor, Notre Dame
     Wayne Gandy, Auburn
     Rich Braham, West Virginia
     Mark Dixon, Virginia
     Stacy Seegars, Clemson
C   Jim Pyne, Virginia Tech
QB Charlie Ward, Fla. State
B   Marshall Faulk, San Diego State
     LeShon Johnson, Northern Illinois
PK   Bjorn Merten, UCLA
Defense
L   Sam Adams, Texas A&M
     Lou Benfatti, Penn State
     Rob Waldrop, Arizona
     Dan Wilkinson, Ohio State
     Kevin Patrick, Miami (FL)
LB   Trev Albert, Nebraska
     Derrick Brooks, Fla. State
     Jamir Miller, UCLA
     Dana Howard, Illinois
B   Jeff Burris, Notre Dame
     Aaron Glenn, Texas A&M
     Antonio Langham, Alabama
     Corey Sawyer, Fla. State
P   Terry Daniel, Auburn

1994
Offense
WR Michael Westbrook, Colorado
     Jack Jackson, Florida
     Bobby Engram, Penn State
TE   Pete Mitchell, Boston College
L   Zach Wiegert, Nebraska
     Tony Boselli, USC
     Korey Stringer, Ohio State
     Brenden Stai, Nebraska
     Jeff Hartings, Penn State
C   Corey Raymer, Wisconsin
QB Kerry Collins, Penn State
B   Rashaan Salaam, Colorado
     Ki-Jana Carter, Penn State
PK   Steve McLaughlin, Arizona
AP   Leeland McElroy, Texas A&M
Defense
L   Warren Sapp, Miami (FL)
     Tedy Bruschi, Arizona
     Kevin Carter, Florida
     Derrick Alexander, Fla. State
     Luther Elliss, Utah
LB   Dana Howard, Illinois
     Derrick Brooks, Fla. State
     Ed Stewart, Nebraska
B   Bobby Taylor, Notre Dame
     Tony Bouie, Arizona
     Brian Robinson, Auburn
     Chris Hudson, Colorado
     Clifton Abraham, Fla. State
     Ty Law, Michigan
P   Todd Sauerbrun, West Virginia

AP Teams (1995-2002)

1995
Offense
WR Terry Glenn, Ohio State
     Keyshawn Johnson, USC
TE   Marco Battaglia, Rutgers
L   Jason Odom, Florida
     Johnathan Ogden, UCLA
     Orlando Pace, Ohio State
     Heath Irwin, Colorado
C   Aaron Graham, Nebraska
QB Tommie Frazier, Nebraska
B   Eddie George, Ohio State
     Troy Davis, Iowa State
K   Michael Reeder, TCU
AP   Leeland McElroy, Texas A&M
Defense
L   Tedy Bruschi, Arizona
     Cornell Brown, Virginia Tech
     Marcus Jones, North Carolina
     Jared Tomich, Nebraska
LB   Pat Fitzgerald, Northwestern
     Ray Lewis, Miami (FL)
     Zach Thomas, Texas Tech
     Kevin Hardy, Illinois
B   Chris Canty, Kansas State
     Lawyer Milloy, Washington
     Greg Myers, Colorado State
P   Brad Maynard, Ball State

1996
Offense
WR Reidel Anthony, Florida
     Marcus Harris, Wyoming
TE   Pat Fitzgerald, Texas
L   Chris Naeole, Colorado
     Benji Olson, Washington
     Orlando Pace, Ohio State
     Juan Roque, Arizona State
C   K.C. Jones, Miami (FL)
QB Danny Wuerffel, Florida
B   Troy Davis, Iowa State
     Byron Hanspard, Texas Tech
K   Marc Primanti, NC State
AP   Kevin Faulk, LSU
Defense
L   Peter Boulware, Fla. State
     Derrick Rodgers, Arizona State
     Reinhard Wilson, Fla. State
     Grant Wistrom, Nebraska
LB   Pat Fitzgerald, Northwestern
     Jarrett Irons, Michigan
     Matt Russell, Colorado
     Canute Curtis, West Virginia
B   Dre' Bly, North Carolina
     Chris Canty, Kansas State
     Charles Woodson, Michigan
P   Noel Prefontaine, San Diego State

AP on offense refers to "All Purpose" player.

1997
Offense
WR	Jacques Green, Florida
	Randy Moss, Marshall
TE	Alonzo Mayes, Oklahoma State
L	Alan Faneca, LSU
	Benji Olson, Washington
	Chad Overhauser, UCLA
	Aaron Taylor, Nebraska
C	Olin Kreutz, Washington
QB	Peyton Manning, Tennessee
B	Curtis Enis, Penn State
	Ricky Williams, Texas
K	Martin Gramatica, Kansas State
AP	Tim Dwight, Iowa

Defense
L	Greg Ellis, North Carolina
	Jason Peter, Nebraska
	Andre Wadsworth, Fla. State
	Grant Wistrom, Nebraska
LB	Sam Cowart, Fla. State
	Andy Katzenmoyer, Ohio State
	Anthony Simmons, Clemson
	Brian Simmons, North Carolina
B	Drew Bly, North Carolina
	Donovin Darius, Syracuse
	Brian Lee, Wyoming
	Charles Woodson, Michigan
P	Chad Kessler, LSU

1998
Offense
WR	Torry Holt, NC State
	Peter Warwick, Fla. State
TE	Rufus French, Mississippi
L	Kris Farris, UCLA
	Aaron Gibson, Wisconsin
	Rob Murphy, Ohio State
	Matt Stinchcomb, Georgia
C	Craig Page, Georgia Tech
QB	Cade McNown, UCLA
B	Mike Cloud, Boston College
	Ricky Williams, Texas
K	Sebastian Janikowski, Fla. State
AP	David Allen, Kansas State

Defense
L	Tom Burke, Wisconsin
	Anthony McFarland, LSU
	Montae Reagor, Texas Tech
	Corey Simon, Fla. State
LB	Chris Claiborne, USC
	Jeff Kelly, Kansas State
	Dat Nguyen, Texas A&M
	Al Wilson, Tennessee
B	Champ Bailey, Georgia
	Chris McAlister, Arizona
	Anthony Poindexter, Virginia
	Antoine Winfield, Ohio State
P	Joe Kristosik, UNLV

1999
Offense
WR	Troy Walters, Stanford
	Peter Warrick, Fla. State
TE	James Whalen, Kentucky
L	Cosey Coleman, Tennessee
	Chris McIntosh, Wisconsin
	Chris Samuels, Alabama
	Jason Whitaker, Fla. State
C	Ben Hamilton, Minnesota
QB	Joe Hamilton, Georgia Tech
B	Ron Dayne, Wisconsin
	Thomas Jones, Virginia
K	Sebastian Janikowski, Fla. State
AP	Dennis Northcutt, Arizona

Defense
L	Courtney Brown, Penn State
	Casey Hampton, Texas
	Corey Moore, Virginia Tech
	Corey Simon, Fla. State
LB	Brandon Short, Penn State
	Mark Simoneau, Kansas State
	Raynoch Thompson, Tennessee
	LaVar Arrington, Penn State
B	Mike Brown, Nebraska
	Tyrone Carter, Minnesota
	Deltha O'Neal, California
	Brian Urlalcher, New Mexico
P	Shane Lechler, Texas A&M

2000
Offense
WR	Antonio Bryant, Pittsburgh
	Marvin Minnis, Fla. State
TE	Brian Natkin, UTEP
L	Chris Brown, Georgia Tech
	Leonard Davis, Texas
	Steve Hutchinson, Michigan
	Chad Ward, Washington
C	Dominic Raiola, Nebraska
QB	Chris Weinke, Fla. State
B	Damien Anderson, Northwestern
	LaDainian Tomlinson, TCU
K	Jonathan Ruffin, Cincinnati
AP	Santana Moss, Miami (FL)

Defense
L	Andre Carter, California
	Casey Hampton, Texas
	John Henderson, Tennessee
	Jamal Reynolds, Fla. State
LB	Keith Adams, Clemson
	Rocky Calmus, Oklahoma
	Dan Morgan, Miami
	Carlos Polk, Nebraska
B	Jamar Fletcher, Wisconsin
	Edward Reed, Miami
	Dwight Smith, Akron
	Fred Smoot, Miss. State
P	Nick Harris, California

2001
Offense
WR	Jabar Gaffney, Florida
	Josh Reed, LSU
TE	Dan Graham, Colorado
L	Toniu Fonoti, Nebraska
	Andre Gurode, Colorado
	Bryant McKinie, Miami (FL)
	Mike Pearson, Florida
C	LeCharles Bentley, Ohio State
QB	Rex Grossman, Florida
B	Luke Staley, BYU
	Travis Stephens, Tennessee
K	Damon Duval, Auburn
AP	Erich Cruuch, Nebraska

Defense
L	Alex Brown, Florida
	Dwight Feeney, Syracuse
	John Henderson, Tennessee
	Julius Peppers, North Carolina
LB	Rocky Calmus, Oklahoma
	Levar Fisher, NC State
	E.J. Henderson, Maryland
	Robert Thomas, UCLA
B	Quentin Jammer, Texas
	Edward Reed, Miami
	LaMont Thompson, Wash. State
	Roy Williams, Oklahoma
P	Travis Dorsch, Purdue

2002
Offense
WR	Charles Rogers, Mich. State
	Reggie Williams, Washington
TE	Dallas Clark, Iowa
L	Shawn Andrews, Arkansas
	Derrick Dockery, Texas
	Jordan Gross, Utah
	Eric Steinbach, Iowa
C	Brett Romberg, Miami
QB	Carson Palmer, USC
B	Larry Johnson, Penn State
	Willis McGhee, Miami (FL)
K	Mike Nugent, Ohio State
AP	Derek Abney, Kentucky

Defense
L	Tommie Harris, Oklahoma
	Rien Long, Wash. State
	David Pollack, Georgia
	Terrell Suggs, Arizona State
LB	E.J. Henderson, Maryland
	Teddy Lehman, Oklahoma
	Matt Wilhelm, Ohio State
B	Mike Doss, Ohio State
	Terence Newman, Kansas State
	Troy Polamalu, USC
	Shane Walton, Notre Dame
P	Mark Mariscal, Colorado

2003

Offense

WR Larry Fitzgerald, Pittsburgh
Mike Williams, USC
TE Kellen Winslow, Miami (FL)
L Shawn Andrews, Arkansas
Alex Barron, Florida State
Robert Gallery, Iowa
Jacob Rogers, USC
C Jake Grove, Virginia Tech
QB Jason White, Oklahoma
B Chris Perry, Michigan
Darren Sproles, Kansas State
K Nate Kaeding, Iowa
AP Antonio Perkins, Oklahoma

Defense

L David Ball, UCLA
Tommie Harris, Oklahoma
Chad Lavalais, LSU
Kenechi Udeze, USC
LB Derrick Johnson, Texas
Teddy Lehman, Oklahoma
Grant Wiley, West Virginia
B Will Allen, Ohio State
Keiwan Ratliff, Florida
Derrick Strait, Oklahoma
Sean Taylor, Miami (FL)
P Dutin Colquitt, Tennessee

PART VIII

Player Awards

HEISMAN TROPHY

1935 Jay Berwanger, Chicago
1936 Larry Kelley, Yale
1937 Clint Frank, Yale
1938 Davey O'Brien, TCU
1939 Nike Kinnick, Iowa
1940 Tom Harmon, Michigan
1941 Bruce Smith, Minnesota
1942 Frank Sinkwich, Georgia
1943 Angelo Bertelli, Notre Dame
1944 Les Horvath, Ohio State
1945 Doc Blanchard, Army
1946 Glenn Davis, Army
1947 John Lujack, Notre Dame
1948 Doak Walker, SMU
1949 Leon Hart, Notre Dame
1950 Vic Janowicz, Ohio State
1951 Dick Kazmaier, Princeton
1952 Billy Vessels, Oklahoma
1953 John Lattner, Notre Dame
1954 Alam Ameche, Wisconsin
1955 Howard Cassady, Ohio State
1956 Paul Hornung, Notre Dame
1957 John Crowe, Texas A & M
1958 Pete Dawkins, Army
1959 Billy Cannon, LSU
1960 Joe Bellino, Navy
1961 Ernie Davis, Syracuse
1962 Terry Baker, Oregon State
1963 Roger Stauback, Navy
1964 John Huarte, Notre Dame
1965 Mike Garrett, USC
1966 Steve Spurrier, Florida
1967 Gary Beban, UCLA
1968 Steve Owens, Oklahoma
1970 Jim Plunkett, Stanford
1971 Pat Sullivan, Auburn
1972 Johnny Rogers, Nebraska
1973 John Capelletti, Penn State
1974 Archie Griffin, Ohio State
1975 Archie Griffin, Ohio State
1976 Tony Dorsett, Pittsburgh
1977 Earl Campbell, Texas
1978 Billy Sims, Oklahoma
1979 Charles White, USC
1980 George Rogers, So. Carolina
1981 Marcus Allen, USC
1982 Herschel Walker, Georgia
1983 Mike Rozier, Nebraska
1984 Doug Flutie, Boston College
1985 Bo Jackson, Auburn
1986 Vinny Testaverde, Miami (FL)
1987 Tim Brown, Notre Dame
1988 Barry Sanders, Oklahoma State
1989 Andre Ware, Houston
1990 Ty Detmer, BYU
1991 Desmond Howard, Michigan
1992 Gina Toretta, Miami (FL)
1993 Charlie Ward, Florida State
1994 Rashaam Salam, Colorado
1995 Eddie George, Ohio State
1996 Danny Wuerffel, Florida
1997 Charles Woodson, Michigan
1998 Ricky Williams, Texas
1999 Ron Dayne, Wisconsin
2000 Chris Weinke, Florida
2001 Eric Crouch, Nebraska
2002 Carson Palmer, USC
2003 Jason White, Oklahoma

MAXWELL AWARD

1937 Clint Frank, Yale
1938 Davey O'Brien, TCU
1939 Nile Kinnick, Iowa
1940 Tom Harmon, Michigan
1941 Bill Dudley, Virginia
1942 Paul Governali, Columbia
1943 Bob Odell, Penn
1944 Glenn Davis, Army
1945 Doc Blanchard, Army
1946 Charley Trippi, Georgia
1947 Doak Walter, SMU
1948 Chuck Bednarik, Penn
1949 Leon Hart, Notre Dame
1950 Reds Bagnell, Penn
1951 Dick Kazmaier, Princeton
1952 John Lattner, Notre Dame
1953 John Lattner, Notre Dame
1954 Ron Beale, Navy
1955 Howard Cassady, Ohio State
1956 Tommy McDonald, Oklahoma
1957 Bob Reifsnyder, Army
1958 Pete Dawkins, Army
1959 Rich Lucas, Penn State
1960 Joe Bellino, Navy
1961 Bob Ferguson, Ohio State
1962 Terry Baker, Oregon State
1963 Roger Staubach, Navy
1964 Glenn Ressler, Penn State
1965 Tommy Nobis, Texas
1966 Jim Lynch, Notre Dame
1967 Gary Beban, UCLA
1968 O. J. Simpson, USC
1969 Mike Reid, Penn State
1970 Jim Plunkett, Stanford
1971 Ed Marinaro, Cornell
1972 Brad Van Pelt, Michigan State
1973 John Cappelletti, Penn State
1974 Steve Joachim, Temple
1975 Archie Griffin, Ohio State
1976 Tony Dorsett, Pittsburgh
1977 Ross Browner, Notre Dame
1978 Chuck Fusina, Penn State
1979 Charles White, USC
1980 Hugh Green, Pittsburgh
1981 Marcus Allen, USC
1982 Herschel Walker, Georgia
1983 Mike Rozier, Nebraska
1984 Doug Flutie, Boston College
1985 Chuck Long, Iowa
1986 Vinny Testaverde, Miami (FL)
1987 Don McPherson, Syracuse
1988 Barry Sanders, Oklahoma State
1989 Anthony Thompson, Indiana
1990 Ty Detmer, BYU
1991 Desmond Howard, Michigan
1992 Gino Toretta, Miami (FL)
1993 Charlie Ward, Florida State
1994 Kerry Collins, Penn State
1995 Eddie George, Ohio State
1996 Danny Wuerffel, Florida
1997 Peyton Manning, Tennessee

1998 Ricky Williams, Texas
1999 Ron Dayne, Wisconsin
2000 Drew Brees, Purdue
2001 Ken Dorsey, Miami (FL)
2002 Larry Johnson, Penn State
2003 Eli Manning, Mississippi

OUTLAND TROPHY

1946 George Connor, Notre Dame
1947 Joe Steffy, Army
1948 Bill Fischer, Notre Dame
1949 Ed Bagdon, Michigan State
1950 Bob Gain, Kentucky
1951 Jim Weatherall, Oklahoma
1952 Dick Modzelewski, Maryland
1953 J. D. Roberts, Oklahoma
1954 Bill Brooks, Arkansas
1955 Calvin Jones, Iowa
1956 Jim Parker, Ohio State
1957 Alex Karras, Iowa
1958 Zeke Smith, Auburn
1959 Mike McGee, Duke
1960 Tom Brown, Minnesota
1961 Merlin Olsen, Utah State
1962 Bobby Bell, Minnesota
1963 Scott Appleton, Texas
1964 Steve DeLong, Tennessee
1965 Tommy Nobis, Texas
1966 Lloyd Phillips, Arkansas
1967 Ron Yary, USC
1968 Bill Stanfill, Georgia
1969 Mike Reid, Penn State
1970 Jim Stillwagon, Ohio State
1971 Larry Jacobson, Nebraska
1972 Rich Glover, Nebraska
1973 John Hicks, Ohio State
1974 Randy White, Maryland
1975 Lee Roy Selmon, Oklahoma
1976 Ross Browner, Notre Dame
1977 Brad Shearer, Texas
1978 Greg Roberts, Oklahoma
1979 Jim Ritcher, NC State
1980 Mark May, Pittsburgh
1981 Dave Rimington, Nebraska
1982 Dave Rimington, Nebraska
1983 Dan Seinkuhler, Nebraska
1984 Bruce Smith, Va. Tech
1985 Mike Ruth, Boston College
1986 Jason Buck, BYU
1987 Chad Hennings, Air Force
1988 Tracy Rocker, Auburn
1989 Mohamed Edelwomibi, BYU
1990 Russell Maryland, Miami (FL)
1991 Steve Emtman, Washington
1992 Will Shields, Nebraska
1993 Rob Waldrop, Arizona
1994 Zack Wiegent, Nebraska
1995 Jonathon Ogden, UCLA
1996 Orlando Pace, Ohio State
1997 Aaron Taylor, Nebraska
1998 Kris Farris, UCLA
1999 Chris Samuels, Alabama
2000 John Henderson, Tennessee
2001 Bryant McKenzie, Miami (FL)
2002 Rien Long, Washington State
2003 Robert Gallery, Iowa

— 471 —

RAY GUY AWARD
2000 Kevin Stemke, Wisconsin
2001 Travis Dorsch, Purdue
2002 Mark Mariscal, Colorado
2003 B. J. Sander, Ohio State

DICK BUTKUS AWARD
1985 Brian Bosworth, Oklahoma
1986 Brian Bosworth, Oklahoma
1987 Paul McCowan, Fla. State
1988 Derrick Thomas, Alabama
1989 Percy Snow, Michigan State
1990 Alfred Williams, Colorado
1991 Erich Anderson, Michigan
1992 Marvin Jones, Florida State
1993 Trev Alberts, Nebraska
1994 Dana Howard, Illinois
1995 Kevin Hardy, Illinois
1996 Matt Russell, Colorado
1997 Andy Katzenmoyer, Ohio State
1998 Chris Claiborne, USC
1999 LaVar Arrington, Penn State
2000 Dan Morgan, Miami (FL)
2001 Rocky Calmus, Oklahoma
2002 E. J. Henderson, Maryland
2003 Teddy Lehman, Oklahoma

FRED BILETNIKOFF AWARD
1994 Bobby Engram, Penn State
1995 Terry Glenn, Ohio State
1996 Marcus Harris, Wyoming
1997 Randy Moss, Marshall
1998 Troy Edwards, La. Tech
1999 Troy Walters, Stanford
2000 Antonio Bryant, Pittsburgh
2001 Josh Reed, LSU
2002 Charles Rogers, Michigan State
2003 Larry Fitzgerald, Pittsburgh

DAVEY O'BRIEN AWARD
1981 Jim McMahon, BYU
1982 Todd Blackledge, Penn State
1983 Steve Young, BYU
1984 Doug Flutie, Boston College
1985 Chuck Long, Iowa
1986 Vinny Testaverde, Miami (FL)
1987 Don McPherson, Syracuse
1988 Troy Aikman, UCLA
1989 Andre Ware, Houston
1990 Ty Detmer, BYU
1991 Ty Detmer, BYU
1992 Gino Toretta, Miami (FL)
1993 Charlie Ward, Florida State
1994 Kerry Collins, Penn State
1995 Danny Wuerffel, Florida
1996 Danny Wuerffel, Florida
1997 Peyton Manning, Tennessee
1998 Tim Couch, Kentucky
1999 Joe Hamilton, Georgia Tech
2000 Chris Weinke, Florida State
2001 Eric Crouch, Nebraska
2002 Brad Banks, Iowa
2003 Jason White, Oklahoma

DOAK WALKER AWARD
1990 Greg Lewis, Washington

1991 Trevor Cobb, Rice
1992 Garrison Hearst, Georgia
1993 Byron Morris, Texas Tech
1994 Rashaan Salaam, Colorado
1995 Eddie George, Ohio State
1996 Byron Hanspard, Texas Tech
1997 Ricky Williams, Texas
1998 Ricky Williams, Texas
1999 Ron Dayne, Wisconsin
2000 LaDainian Tomlinson, UCLA
2001 Luke Staley, BYU
2002 Larry Johnson, Penn State
2003 Chris Perry, Michigan

LOMBARDI AWARD
1970 Jim Stillwagon, Ohio State
1971 Walt Patulski, Notre Dame
1972 Rich Glover, Nebraska
1973 John Hicks, Ohio State
1974 Randy White, Maryland
1975 Lee Roy Selmon, Oklahoma
1976 Wilson Whitley, Houston
1977 Ross Browner, Notre Dame
1978 Bruce Clark, Penn State
1979 Brad Budde, USC
1980 Hugh Green, Pittsburgh
1981 Kenneth Sims, Texas
1982 Dave Rimington, Nebraska
1983 Dave Rimington, Nebraska
1984 Tony Degrate, Texas
1985 Tony Casillas, Oklahoma
1986 Cornelius Bennett, Alabama
1987 Chris Spielman, Ohio State
1988 Tracy Rocker, Auburn
1989 Percy Snow, Michigan State
1990 Chris Zorich, Notre Dame
1991 Steve Emtman, Washington
1992 Marvin Jones, Florida State
1993 Aaron Taylor, Notre Dame
1994 Warren Sapp, Miami
1995 Orlando Pace, Ohio State
1996 Orlando Pace, Ohio State
1997 Grant Wistrom, Nebraska
1998 Dat Nguyen, Texas A&M
1999 Corey Moore, Virginia Tech
2000 Jamal Reynolds, Florida State
2001 Julius Pepper, North Carolina
2002 Terrell Suggs, Arizona State

JIM THORPE AWARD
1986 Thomas Everett, Baylor
1987 Bennie Blades, Miami (FL)
1988 Deion Sanders, Florida State
1989 Mark Carrier, USC
1990 Darryl Lewis, Arizona
1991 Terrell Buckley, Florida State
1992 Deon Figures, Colorado
1993 Antonio Langham, Alabama
1994 Chris Hudson, Colorado
1995 Greg Myers, Colorado State
1996 Lawrence Wright, Florida
1997 Charles Woodson, Michigan
1998 Antone Winfield, Ohio State
1999 Tyrone Carter, Minnesota
2000 Jamar Fletcher, Wisconsin
2001 Roy Williams, Oklahoma

2002 Terence Newman, Kansas State
2003 Derrick Strait, Oklahoma

LOU GROZA AWARD
1992 Joe Allison, Memphis State
1993 Judd Davis, Florida
1994 Steve McLaughlin, Arizona
1995 Michael Reeder, TCU
1996 Mark Primanti, North Carolina
1997 Martin Gramatica, Kansas State
1998 Sebastian Janikowski, Florida State
1999 Sebastian Janikowski, Florida State
2000 Jonathon Ruffin, Cincinnati
2001 Seth Marler, Tulane
2002 Nate Kaeding, Iowa

CHUCK BEDNARIK AWARD
1993 Rob Waldrop, Arizona
1994 Warren Sapp, Miami (FL)
1995 Pat Fitzgerald, Northwestern
1996 Pat Fitzgerald, Northwestern
1997 Charles Woodson, Michigan
1998 Dat Nguyen, Texas A&M
1999 LaVar Arrington, Penn State
2000 Dan Morgan, Miami (FL)
2001 Julius Peppers, North Carolina
2002 E. J. Henderson, Maryland
2003 Teddy Lehman, Oklahoma

JOHNNY UNITAS AWARD
1987 Don McPherson, Syracuse
1988 Rodney Peate, USC
1989 Tony Rice, Notre Dame
1990 Craig Erickson, Miami (FL)
1991 Casey Weldon, Florida State
1992 Gino Torretta, Miami (FL)
1993 Charlie Ward, Florida State
1994 Jay Barker, Alabama
1995 Tommie Frazer, Nebraska
1996 Danny Wuerffel, Florida
1997 Peyton Manning, Tennessee
1998 Cade McNown, UCLA
1999 Chris Redman, Louisville
2000 Chris Weinke, Florida State
2001 David Carr, Fresno State
2002 Carson Palmer, UCS
2003 Eli Manning, Mississippi

SAMMY BAUGH AWARD
1959 Dick Norman, Stanford
1960 Hayseed Stephens, Hardin-Simmons
1961 Ron Miller, Wisconsin
1962 Don Trull, Baylor
1963 Don Trull, Baylor
1964 Jerry Rhome, Tulsa
1965 Steve Sloan, Alabama
1966 Bob Greise, Purdue
1967 Terry Hanratty, Notre Dame
1968 Chuck Hickson, SMU
1969 Mike Phipps, Purdue
1970 Pat Sullivan, Auburn
1971 John Reaves, Florida
1972 Don Strock, Virginia Tech
1973 Jessee Freitas, San Diego State
1974 Gary Scheide, BYU
1975 Gene Swick, Toledo

SAMMY BAUGH TROPHY (cont'd)

1976 Tommy Kramer, Rice
1977 Guy Benjamin, Stanford
1978 Steve Dils, Stanford
1979 Marc Wilson, BYU
1980 Marc Herrmann, Purdue
1981 Jim McMahon, BYU
1982 John Elway, Stanford
1983 Steve Young, BYU
1984 Robbie Bosco, BYU
1985 Brian McClure, Bowling Green
1986 Vinny Testaverde, Miami (FL)
1987 Don McPherson, Syracuse
1988 Steve Walsh, Miami (FL)
1989 Jeff George, Illinois
1990 David Klinger, Houston
1991 Ty Detmer, BYU
1992 Elvis Brbac, Michigan
1993 Trent Dilfer, Fresno State
1994 Kerry Collins, Penn State
1995 Danny Wuerffel, Florida
1996 Steve Sarkisian, BYU
1997 Ryan Leaf, Washington State
1998 Duante Culpepper, Central Florida
1999 Chad Pennington, Marshall
2000 Chris Weinke, Florida State
2001 David Carr, Fresno State
2002 Kliff Kingsbury, Texas Tech

WALTER CAMP AWARD

1967 O. J. Simpson, USC
1968 O. J. Simpson, USC
1969 Steve Owens, Oklahoma
1970 Jim Plunkett, Stanford
1971 Pat Sullivan, Auburn
1972 Johnny Rogers, Nebraska
1973 John Cappelletti, Penn State
1974 Archie Griffin, Ohio State
1975 Archie Griffin, Ohio State
1976 Tony Dorsett, Pittsburgh
1977 Ken MacAfee, Notre Dame
1978 Billy Sims, Oklahoma
1979 Charles White, USC
1980 Hugh Green, Pittsburgh
1981 Marcus Allen, USC
1982 Herschel Walker, Georgia
1983 Mike Rozier, Nebraska
1984 Doug Flutie, Boston College
1985 Bo Jackson, Auburn
1986 Vinny Testaverde, Miami (FL)
1987 Tim Brown, Notre Dame
1988 Barry Sanders, Oklahoma State
1989 Anthony Thompson, Indiana
1990 Raghib Ismail, Notre Dame
1991 Desmond Howard, Michigan
1992 Gino Torretta, Miami (FL)
1993 Charlie Ward, Florida State
1994 Rashaan Salaam, Colorad
1995 Eddie George, Ohio State
1996 Danny Wuerffel, Florida
1997 Charles Woodson, Michigan
1998 Ricky Williams, Texas
1999 Ron Dayne, Wisconsin
2000 Josh Heupel, Oklahoma
2001 Eric Crouch, Nebraska
2002 Larry Johnson, Penn State
2003 Larry Fitzgerald, Pittsburgh

TED HENDRICKS AWARD

2002 Terrell Suggs, Arizona State

JOHN MACKEY AWARD

2000 Tim Stratton, Purdue
2001 Daniel Graham, Colorado
2002 Dallas Clark, Iowa
2003 Kellen Winslow, Miami (FL)

BRONKO NAGURSKI AWARD

1993 Rob Waldrop, Arizona
1994 Warren Sapp, Miami (FL)
1995 Pat Fitzgerald, Northwestern
1996 Pat Fitzgerald, Northwestern
1997 Charles Woodson, Michigan
1998 Champ Bailey, Georgia
1999 Corey Moore, Virginia Tech
2000 Dan Morgan, Miami (FL)
2001 Roy Williams, Oklahoma
2002 Terrell Suggs, Arizona State
2003 Dave Ball, UCLA

RIMINGTON TROPHY

2000 Dominic Raiola, Nebraska
2001 LeCharles Bently, Ohio State
2002 Brett Romberg, Miami
2003 Jake Grove, Virginia Tech

MOISI TATUPU AWARD

1997 Brock Olivo, Missouri
1998 Chris McAlister, Arizona
1999 Deltha O'Neal, California
2000 J. T. Thatcher, Oklahoma
2001 Kahlil Hill, Iowa
2002 Glen Pakulak, Kentucky

PART IX

National Rankings of Teams (1883–2003)

Helms Foundation Selection of Mythical National Champion (1883-1935)

1883. Yale	1892. Yale	1901. Michigan	1910. Harvard	1919. Harvard	1928. Ga. Tech
1884. Yale	1893. Princeton	1902. Michigan	1911. Princeton	1920. California	1929. Notre Dame
1885. Princeton	1894. Yale	1903. Princeton	1912. Harvard	1921. Cornell	1930. Notre Dame
1886. Yale	1895. Penn	1904. Penn	1913. Harvard	1922. Cornell	1931. USC
1887. Yale	1896. Princeton	1905. Chicago	1914. Army	1923. Illinois	1932. USC
1888. Yale	1897. Penn	1906. Princeton	1915. Cornell	1924. Notre Dame	1933. Michigan
1889. Princeton	1898. Harvard	1907. Yale	1916. Pittsburgh	1925. Alabama	1934. Minnesota
1890. Harvard	1899. Harvard	1908. Penn	1917. Ga. Tech	1926. Alabama	1935. Minnesota
1891. Yale	1900. Yale	1909. Yale	1918. Pittsburgh	1927. Illinois	

Rankings 1924-1935 (Dickinson Rankings)   **Rankings 1936-1940 (AP and Dickinson)**

1924:
1. Notre Dame
2. California
3. Yale
4. Illinois
5. Stanford
6. Iowa
7. USC
8. Pennsylvania
9. Dartmouth
10. Missouri
11. Chicago

1925:
1. Dartmouth
2. Michigan
3. Alabama
4. Colgate
5. Missouri
6. Tulane
7. Washington
8. Wisconsin
9. Stanford
10. Pittsburgh
11. Lafayette

1926:
1. Stanford
2. Navy
3. Notre Dame
3. Michigan
5. Lafayette
6. USC
7. Alabama
8. Ohio State
9. Army
10. Brown
10. Illinois
10. Pennsylvania

1927:
1. Illinois
2. Pittsburgh
3. Minnesota
4. Notre Dame
5. Yale
6. Army
7. Michigan
8. Georgia
9. Nebraska
10. USC
11. Texas A&M

1928:
1. USC
2. California
3. Georgia Tech
4. Stanford
4. Wisconsin
6. Carnegie Tech
6. Iowa
6. Illinois
9. Army
10. NYU
11. Pennsylvania

1929:
1. Notre Dame
2. Purdue
3. Pittsburgh
4. California
5. Illinois
6. USC
7. Nebraska
8. TCU
9. SMU
10. Tulane
11. Pennsylvania

1930:
1. Notre Dame
2. Wash. State
3. Alabama
4. Northwestern
5. Michigan
6. USC
7. Stanford
8. Dartmouth
9. Army
10. Tennessee
11. Tulane

1931:
1. USC
2. Tulane
3. Tennessee
4. Northwestern
5. St. Mary's
6. Georgia
7. Harvard
8. Yale
9. Pittsburgh
10. Purdue
11. Notre Dame

1932:
1. Michigan
2. USC
3. Pittsburgh
4. Purdue
5. Colgate
6. Ohio State
7. Notre Dame
8. Army
9. Tennessee
10. TCU
11. Wisconsin

1933:
1. Michigan
2. Nebraska
3. Minnesota
4. Pittsburgh
5. Ohio State
6. USC
7. Princeton
8. Oregon
9. Army
10. Purdue
11. Stanford

1934:
1. Minnesota
2. Pittsburgh
3. Navy
4. Illinois
5. Rice
6. Alabama
7. Columbia
8. Ohio State
9. Colgate
10. Stanford
11. Tulane

1935
1. SMU
2. Minnesota
3. Princeton
4. LSU
5. Stanford
5. California
7. Ohio State
8. TCU
9. Notre Dame
10. UCLA
11. Fordham

1936: AP
1. Minnesota
2. LSU
3. Pittsburgh
4. Alabama
5. Washington
6. Santa Clara
7. Northwestern
8. Notre Dame
9. Nebraska
10. Pennsylvania
11. Duke
12. Yale
13. Dartmouth
14. Duquesne
15. Fordham
16. TCU
17. Tennessee
18. Arkansas
18. Navy
20. Marquette

1936: Dickinson
1. Minnesota
2. LSU
3. PIttsburgh
4. Washington
5. Alabama
6. Northwestern
7. Notre Dame
8. Santa Clara
9. Duke
10. Pennsylvania
11. Nebraska

1937: AP
1. Pittsburgh
2. California
3. Fordham
4. Alabama
5. Minnesota
6. Villanova
7. Dartmouth
8. LSU
9. Notre Dame
9. Santa Clara
11. Nebraska
12. Yale
13. Ohio State
14. Holy Cross
15. Arkansas
16. TCU
17. Colorado
18. Rice
19. North Carolina
20. Duke

1937: Dickinson
1. Pittsburgh
2. Fordham
3. Dartmouth
4. Alabama
5. Nebraska
6. Yale
7. California
8. LSU
9. Santa Clara
10. Notre Dame
11. Minnesota

1938: AP	1938: Dickinson	1941	1944	1947
1.TCU	1.Notre Dame	1.Minnesota	1.Army	1.Notre Dame
2.Tennessee	2.Duke	2.Duke	2.Ohio State	2.Michigan
3.Duke	3.Tennessee	3.Notre Dame	3.Randolph Field	3.SMU
4.Oklahoma	4.USC	4.Texas	4.Navy	4.Penn State
5.Notre Dame	5.Oklahoma	5.Michigan	5.Bainbridge	5.Texas
6.Carnegie Tech	6.Michigan	6.Fordham	6.Iowa Pre Flight	6.Alabama
7.USC	7.Minnesota	7.Missouri	7.USC	7.Pennsylvania
8.Pittsburgh	8.TCU	8.Duquesne	8.Michigan	8.USC
9.Holy Cross	9.Alabama	9.Texas A&M	9.Notre Dame	9.North Carolina
10.Minnesota	10.Carnegie Tech	10.Navy	10.March Field	10.Georgia Tech
11.Texas Tech	11.Pittsburgh	11.Northwestern	11.Duke	11.Army
12.Cornell		12.Oregon State	12.Tennessee	12.Kansas
13.Alabama		13.Ohio State	13.Georgia Tech	13.Mississippi
14.California		14.Georgia	14. Norman P-F	14.Wm & Mary
15.Fordham		15.Pennsylvania	15.Illinois	15.California
16.Michigan		16.Mississippi State	16.El Toro Marines	16.Oklahoma
17.Northwestern		17.Mississippi	17.Great Lakes	17.NC State
18.Villanova		18.Tennessee	18.Fort Pierce	18.Rice
19.Tulane		19.Wash. State	19.St. Mary's P-F	19.Duke
20.Dartmouth		20.Alabama	20.2[nd] Air Force	20.Columbia

1939: AP	1939: Dickinson	1942:	1945:	1948:
1.Texas A&M	1.USC	1.Ohio State	1.Army	1.Michigan
2.Tennessee	2.Texas A&M	2.Georgia	2.Alabama	2.Notre Dame
3.USC	3.Cornell	3.Wisconsin	3.Navy	3.North Carolina
4.Cornell	4.Tulane	4.Tulsa	4.Indiana	4.California
5.Tulane	5.Tennessee	5.Georgia Tech	5.Oklahoma A&M	5.Oklahoma
6.Missouri	6.Notre Dame	6.Notre Dame	6.Michigan	6.Army
7.UCLA	7.Michigan	7.Tennessee	7.St. Mary's	7.Northwestern
8.Duke	8.Duke	8.Boston College	8.Pennsylvania	8.Georgia
9.Iowa	9.Missouri	9.Michigan	9.Notre Dame	9.Oregon
10.Duquesne	10.UCLA	10.Alabama	10.Texas	10.SMU
11.Boston College	11.Iowa	11.Texas	11.USC	11.Clemson
12.Clemson		12.Stanford	12.Ohio State	12.Vanderbilt
13.Notre Dame		13.UCLA	13.Duke	13.Tulane
14.Santa Clara		14.Wm. & Mary	14.Tennessee	14.Michigan State
15.Ohio State		15.Santa Clara	15.LSU	15.Mississippi
16. Georgia Tech		16.Auburn	16.Holy Cross	16.Minnesota
17.Fordham		17.Wash. State	17.Tulsa	17.Wm & Mary
18.Nebraska		18.Mississippi State	18.Georgia	18.Penn State
19.Oklahoma		19.Minnesota	19.Wake Forest	19.Cornell
20.Michigan		19.Holy Cross	20.Columbia	20.Wake Forest

1940: AP	1940: Dickinson	1943: AP	1946:	1949:
1.Minnesota	1.Minnesota	1.Notre Dame	1.Notre Dame	1.Notre Dame
2.Stanford	2.Michigan	2.Iowa Pre-Flight	2.Army	2.Oklahoma
3.Michigan	3.Stanford	3.Michigan	3.Georgia	3.California
4.Tennessee	4.Tennessee	4.Navy	4.UCLA	4.Army
5.Boston College	5.Texas A&M	5.Purdue	5.Illinois	5.Rice
6.Texas A&M	6.Pennsylvania	6.Great Lakes	6.Michigan	6.Ohio State
7.Nebraska	7.Mississippi State	7.Duke	7.Tennessee	7.Michigan
8.Northwestern	8.SMU	8.Del Monte P-F	8.LSU	8.Minnesota
9.Mississippi State	9.Texas	9.Northwestern	9.North Carolina	9.LSU
10.Washington	10.Nebraska	10.March Field	10.Rice	10.Pacific
11.Santa Clara	11.Northwestern	11.Army	11.Georgia Tech	11.Kentucky
12.Fordham		12.Washington	12.Yale	12.Cornell
13.Georgetown		13.Georgia Tech	13.Pennsylvania	13.Villanova
14.Pennsylvania		14.Texas	14.Oklahoma	14.Maryland
15.Cornell		15.Tulsa	15.Texas	15.Santa Clara
16.SMU		16.Dartmouth	16.Arkansas	16.North Carolina
17.Hardin-Simmons		17.Bainbridge	17.Tulsa	17.Tennessee
18.Duke		18.Colorado Coll.	18.NC State	18.Princeton
19.Lafayette		19.Pacific	19.Delaware	19.Michigan State
20.Penn State		20.Pennsylvania	20.Indiana	20.Missouri
				20.Baylor

Rankings, 1950-2003 AP and UPI (CNN-USA Today)

1950: AP	1950: UPI	1953: AP	1953: UPI	1956: AP	1956: UPI
1.Oklahoma	1.Oklahoma	1.Maryland	1.Maryland	1.Oklahoma	1.Oklahoma
2.Army	2.Texas	2.Notre Dame	2.Notre Dame	2.Tennessee	2.Tennessee
3.Texas	3.Tennessee	3.Michigan State	3.Michigan State	3.Iowa	3.Iowa
4.Tennessee	4.California	4.Oklahoma	4.UCLA	4.Georgia Tech	4.Georgia Tech
5.California	5.Army	5.UCLA	5.Oklahoma	5.Texas A&M	5.Texas A&M
6.Princeton	6.Michigan	6.Rice	6.Rice	6.Miami (FL)	6.Miami (FL)
7.Kentucky	7.Kentucky	7.Illinois	7.Illinois	7.Michigan	7.Michigan
8.Michigan State	8.Princeton	8.Georgia Tech	8.Texas	8.Syracuse	8.Syracuse
9.Michigan	9.Michigan State	9.Iowa	9.Georgia Tech	9.Michigan State	9.Minnesota
10.Clemson	10.Ohio State	10.West Virginia	10.Iowa	10.Oregon State	10.Michigan State
11.Washington	11.Illinois	11.Texas	11.Alabama	11.Baylor	11.Baylor
12.Wyoming	12.Clemson	12.Texas Tech	12.Texas Tech	12.Minnesota	12.Pittsburgh
13.Illinois	13.Miami (FL)	13.Alabama	13.West Virginia	13.Pittsburgh	13.Oregon State
14.Ohio State	14.Wyoming	14.Army	14.Wisconsin	14.TCU	14.TCU
15.Miami (FL)	15.Washington	15.Wisconsin	15.Kentucky	15.Ohio State	15.USC
16.Alabama	15.Baylor	16.Kentucky	16.Army	16.Navy	16.Wyoming
17.Nebraska	17.Alabama	17.Auburn	17.Stanford	17.G. Washington	17.Yale
18.Wash. & Lee	18.Wash. & Lee	18.Duke	18.Duke	18.USC	18.Colorado
19.Tulsa	19.Navy	19.Stanford	19.Michigan	19.Clemson	19.Navy
20.Tulane	20 Nebraska	20.Michigan	10.Ohio State	20.Colorado	20.Duke
	20.Cornell				
	20.Wisconsin				

1951: AP	1951: UPI	1954: AP	1954: UPI	1957: AP	1957: UPI
1.Tennessee	1.Tennessee	1.Ohio State	1.UCLA	1.Auburn	1.Ohio State
2.Michigan State	2.Michigan State	2.UCLA	2.Ohio State	2.Ohio State	2.Auburn
3.Maryland	3.Illinois	3.Oklahoma	3.Oklahoma	3.Michigan State	3.Michigan State
4.Illinois	4.Maryland	4.Notre Dame	4.Notre Dame	4.Oklahoma	4.Oklahoma
5.Georgia Tech	5.Georgia Tech	5.Navy	5.Navy	5.Navy	5.Iowa
6.Princeton	6.Princeton	6.Mississippi	6.Mississippi	6.Iowa	6.Navy
7.Stanford	7.Stanford	7.Army	7.Army	7.Mississippi	7.Rice
8.Wisconsin	8.Wisconsin	8.Maryland	8.Arkansas	8.Rice	8.Mississippi
9.Baylor	9.Baylor	9.Wisconsin	9.Miami (FL)	9.Texas A&M	9.Notre Dame
10.Oklahoma	10.TCU	10.Arkansas	10.Wisconsin	10.Notre Dame	10.Texas A&M
11.TCU	11.Oklahoma	11.Miami (FL)	11.USC	11.Texas	11.Texas
12.California	12.California	12.West Virgiinia	11.Maryland	12.Arizona State	12.Arizona State
13.Virginia	13.Notre Dame	13.Auburn	11.Georgia Tech	13.Tennessee	13.Army
14.San Francisco	14.Wash. State	14.Duke	14.Duke	14.Mississippi State	14.Duke
15.Kentucky	14.San Francisco	15.Michigan	15.Michigan	15.NC State	14.Wisconsin
16.Boston U.	14.Purdue	16.Virginia Tech	16.Penn State	16.Duke	16.Tennessee
17.UCLA	17.UCLA	17.USC	17.SMU	17.Florida	17.Oregon
18.Wash. State	17.Holy Cross	18.Baylor	18.Denver	18.Army	18.UCLA
19.Holy Cross	17.Kentucky	19.Rice	19.Rice	19.Wisconsin	18.Clemson
20.Clemson	20.Kansas	20.Penn State	20.Minnesota	20.VMI	20.NC State

1952: AP	1952: UPI	1955: AP	1955: UPI	1958: AP	1958: UPI
1.Michigan State	1.Michigan State	1.Oklahoma	1.Oklahoma	1.LSU	1.LSU
2.Georgia Tech	2.Georgia Tech	2.Michigan State	2.Michigan State	2.Iowa	2.Iowa
3.Notre Dame	3.Notre Dame	3.Maryland	3.Maryland	3.Army	3.Army
4.Oklahoma	4.USC	4.UCLA	4.UCLA	4.Auburn	4.Auburn
5.USC	4.Oklahoma	5.Ohio State	5.Ohio State	5.Oklahoma	5.Oklahoma
6.UCLA	6.UCLA	6.TCU	6.TCU	6.Air Force	6.Wisconsin
7.Mississippi	7.Mississippi	7.Georgia Tech	7.Georgia Tech	7.Wisconsin	7.Ohio State
8.Tennessee	8.Tennessee	8.Auburn	8.Auburn	8.Ohio State	8.Air Force
9.Alabama	9.Alabama	9.Notre Dame	9.Mississippi	9.Syracuse	9.TCU
10.Texas	10.Wisconsin	10.Mississippi	10.Notre Dame	10.TCU	10.Syracuse
11.Wisconsin	11.Texas	11.Pittsburgh	11.Pittsburgh	11.Mississippi	11.Purdue
12.Tulsa	12.Purdue	12.Michigan	12.USC	12.Clemson	12.Mississippi
13.Maryland	13.Maryland	13.USC	13.Michigan	13.Purdue	13.Clemson
14.Syracuse	14.Princeton	14.Miami (FL)	14.Texas A&M	14.Florida	14.Notre Dame
15.Florida	15.Ohio State	15.Miami (OH)	15.Army	15.South Carolina	15.Florida
16. Duke	16.Pittsburgh	16.Stanford	16.Duke	16.California	16.California
17.Ohio State	17.Navy	17.Texas A&M	17.West Virginia	17.Notre Dame	17.Northwestern
18.Purdue	18.Duke	18.Navy	18.Rice	18.SMU	18.SMU
19.Princeton	19.Houston	19.West Virginia	19.Iowa	19.Oklahoma State	
20.Kentucky	19.Kentucky	20.Army	20.Stanford	20.Rutgers	
			20.Navy/Miami (OH)		

1959: AP
1. Syracuse
2. Mississippi
3. LSU
4. Texas
5. Georgia
6. Wisconsin
7. TCU
8. Washington
9. Arkansas
10. Alabama
11. Clemson
12. Penn State
13. Illinois
14. USC
15. Oklahoma
16. Wyoming
17. Notre Dame
18. Missouri
19. Florida
20. Pittsburgh.

1959: UPI
1. Syracuse
2. Mississippi
3. LSU
4. Texas
5. Georgia
6. Wisconsin
7. Washington
8. TCU
9. Arkansas
10. Penn State
11. Clemson
12. Illinois
13. Alabama
13. USC
15. Auburn
16. Mich. State
17. Oklahoma
18. Notre Dame
19. Pittsburgh
20. Missouri
20. Florida

1962: AP
1. USC
2. Wisconsin
3. Mississippi
4. Texas
5. Alabama
6. Arkansas
7. LSU
8. Oklahoma
9. Penn State
10. Minnesota

1962: UPI
1. USC
2. Wisconsin
3. Mississippi
4. Texas
5. Alabama
6. Arkansas
7. Oklahoma
8. LSU
9. Penn State
10. Minnesota
11. Georgia Tech
12. Missouri
13. Ohio State
14. Duke
14. Washington
16. Northwestern
16. Oregon State
18. Arizona State
18. Miami (FL)

1965: AP
1. Alabama
2. Mich. State
3. Arkansas
4. UCLA
5. Nebraska
6. Missouri
7. Tennessee
8. LSU
9. Notre Dame
10. USC

1965: UPI
1. Mich. State
2. Arkansas
3. Nebraska
4. Alabama
5. UCLA
6. Missouri
7. Tennessee
8. Notre Dame
9. USC
10. Texas Tech
11. Ohio State
12. Florida
13. Purdue
14. LSU
15. Georgia
16. Tulsa
17. Mississippi
18. Kentucky
19. Syracuse
20. Colorado

1960: AP
1. Minnesota
2. Mississippi
3. Iowa
4. Navy
5. Missouri
6. Washington
7. Arkansas
8. Ohio State
9. Alabama
10. Duke
11. Kansas
12. Baylor
13. Auburn
14. Yale
15. Mich. State
16. .Penn State
17. New Mexico St.
18. Florida
19. Syracuse
19. Purdue

1960:UPI
1. Minnesota
2. Iowa
3. Mississippi
4. Missouri
5. Washington
6. Navy
7. Arkansas
8. Ohio State
9. Kansas
10. Alabama
11. Duke
11. Baylor
11. Mich. State
14. Auburn
15. Purdue
16. Florida
17. Texas
18. Yale
19. New Mexico St.
20. Tennessee

1963: AP
1. Texas
2. Navy
3. Illinois
4. Pittsburgh
5. Auburn
6. Nebraska
7. Mississippi
8. Alabama
9. Oklahoma
10. Mich. State

1963: UPI
1. Texas
2. Navy
3. Pittsburgh
4. Illinois
5. Nebraska
6. Auburn
7. Mississippi
8. Oklahoma
9. Alabama
10. Mich. State
11. Miss. State
12. Syracuse
13. Arizona State
14. Memphis
15. Washington
16. Penn State
16. USC
16. Missouri
19. North Carolina
20. Baylor

1966: AP
1. Notre Dame
2. Mich. State
3. Alabama
4. Georgia
5. UCLA
6. Nebraska
7. Purdue
8. Georgia Tech
9. Miami (FL)
10. SMU

1966: UPI
1. Notre Dame
2. Mich. State
3. Alabama
4. Georgia
5. UCLA
6. Purdue
7. Nebraska
8. Georgia Tech
9. SMU
10. Miami (FL)
11. Florida
12. Mississippi
13. Arkansas
14. Tennessee
15. Wyoming
16. Syracuse
17. Houston
18. USC
19. Oregon State
20. Virginia Tech

1961: AP
1. Alabama
2. Ohio State
3. Texas
4. LSU
5. Mississippi
6. Minnesota
7. Colorado
8. Mich. State
9. Arkansas
10. Utah State
11. Missouri
12. Purdue
13. Georgia Tech
14. Syracuse
15. Rutgers
16. UCLA
17. Rice
17. Penn State
18. Arizona
20. Duke

1961: UPI
1. Alabama
2. Ohio State
3. LSU
4. Texas
5. Mississippi
6. Minnesota
7. Colorado
8. Arkansas
9. Mich. State
10. Utah State
11. Purdue
11. Missouri
13. Georgia Tech
14. Duke
15. Kansas
16. Syracuse
17. Wyoming
18. Wisconsin
19. Miami (FL)
20. Penn State

1964: AP
1. Alabama
2. Arkansas
3. Notre Dame
4. Michigan
5. Texas
6. Nebraska
7. LSU
8. Oregon State
9. Ohio State
10. USC

1964: UPI
1. Alabama
2. Arkansas
3. Notre Dame
4. Michigan
5. Texas
6. Nebraska
7. LSU
8. Oregon State
9. Ohio State
10. USC
11. Florida State
12. Syracuse
13. Princeton
14. Penn State
14. Utah
16. Illinois
16. New Mexico
18. Tulsa
18. Missouri
20. Ole Miss

1967: AP
1. USC
2. Tennessee
3. Oklahoma
4. Indiana
5. Notre Dame
6. Wyoming
7. Oregon State
8. Alabama
9. Purdue
10. Penn State

1967: UPI
1. USC
2. Tennessee
3. Oklahoma
4. Notre Dame
5. Wyoming
6. Indiana
7. Alabama
8. Oregon State
9. Purdue
10. UCLA
11. Penn State
12. Syracuse
13. Colorado
14. Minnesota
15. Florida State
16. Miami (FL)
17. NC State
18. Georgia
19. Houston
20. Arizona State

1968: AP	1968: UPI	1971: AP	1971: UPI	1974: AP	1974: UPI
1.Ohio State	1.Ohio State	1.Nebraska	1.Nebraska	1.Oklahoma	1.USC
2.Penn State	2.USC	2.Oklahoma	2.Alabama	2.USC	2.Alabama
3.Texas	3.Penn State	3.Colorado	3.Oklahoma	3.Michigan	3.Ohio State
4.USC	4.Georgia	4.Alabama	4.Michigan	4.Ohio State	4.Notre Dame
5.Notre Dame	5.Texas	5.Penn State	5.Auburn	5.Alabama	5.Michigan
6.Arkansas	6.Kansas	6.Michigan	6.Arizona State	5.Notre Dame	6.Auburn
7.Kansas	7.Tennessee	7.Georgia	7.Colorado	7.Penn State	7.Penn State
8.Georgia	8.Notre Dame	8.Arizona State	8.Georgia	8.Auburn	8.Nebraska
9.Missouri	9.Arkansas	9.Tennessee	9.Tennessee	9.Nebraska	9.NC State
10.Purdue	10.Oklahoma	10.Stanford	10.LSU	10.Miami (OH)	10.Miami (OH)
11.Oklahoma	11.Purdue	11.LSU	11.Penn State	11.NC State	11.Houston
12.Michigan	12.Alabama	12.Auburn	12.Texas	12.Mich. State	12.Florida
13.Tennessee	13.Oregon State	13.Notre Dame	13.Toledo	13.Maryland	13.Maryland
14.SMU	14.Florida State	14.Toledo	14.Houston	14.Baylor	14.Baylor
15.Oregon State	15.Michigan	15.Mississippi	15.Notre Dame	15.Florida	15.Texas A&M
16.Auburn	16.SMU	16.Arkansas	16.Stanford	16.Texas A&M	15.Tennessee
17.Alabama	17.Missouri	17.Houston	17.Iowa State	17.Miss. State	17.Miss. State
18.Houston	18.Ohio U.	18.Texas	18.North Carolina	17.Texas	18.Mich. State
19.LSU	18.Minnesota	19.Wshington	19.Florida State	19.Houston	19.Tulsa
20.Ohio U.	20.Houston	20.USC	20.Arkansas	20.Tennessee	
	20.Stanford		20.Mississippi		

1969:AP	1969:UPI	1972: AP	1972: UPI	1975: AP	1975: UPI
1.Texas	1.Texas	1.USC	1.USC	1.Oklahoma	1.Oklahoma
2.Penn State	2.Penn State	2.Oklahoma	2.Oklahoma	2.Arizona State	2.Arizona State
3.USC	3.Arkansas	3.Texas	3.Ohio State	3.Alabama	3.Alabama
4.Ohio State	4.USC	4.Nebraska	4.Alabama	4.Ohio State	4.Ohio State
5.Notre Dame	5.Ohio State	5.Auburn	5.Texas	5.UCLA	5.UCLA
6.Missouri	6.Missouri	6.Michigan	6.Michigan	6.Texas	6.Arkansas
7.Arkansas	7.LSU	7.Alabama	7.Auburn	7.Arkansas	7.Texas
8.Mississippi	8.Michigan	8.Tennessee	8.Penn State	8.Michigan	8.Michigan
9.Michigan	9.Notre Dame	9.Ohio State	9.Nebraska	9.Nebraska	9.Nebraska
10.LSU	10.UCLA	10.Penn State	10.LSU	10.Penn State	10.Penn State
11.Nebraska	11.Tennessee	11.LSU	11.Tennessee	11.Texas A&M	11.Maryland
12.Houston	12.Nebraska	12.North Carolina	12.Notre Dame	12.Miami (OH)	12.Texas A&M
13.UCLA	13.Mississippi	13.Arizona State	13.Arizona State	13.Maryland	13.Arizona
14.Florida	14.Stanford	14.Notre Dame	14.Colorado	14.California	13.Pittsburgh
15.Tennessee	15.Auburn	15.UCLA	14.North Carolina	15.Pittsburgh	15.California
16.Colorado	16.Houston	16.Colorado	16.Louisville	16.Colorado	16.Miami (OH)
17.West Virginia	17.Florida	17.NC State	17.UCLA	17.USC	17.Notre Dame
18.Purdue	18.Purdue	18.Louisville	17.Wash. State	18.Arizona	17.West Virginia
19.Stanford`	18.San Diego St.	19.Wash. State	19.Utah State	19.Georgia	19.Georgia
20.Auburn	18.West Virginia	20.Georgia Tech	20.San Diego State	20.West Virginia	19.USC

1970:AP	1970: UPI	1973: AP	1973: UPI	1976: AP	1976: UPI
1.Nebraska	1.Texas	1.Notre Dame	1.Alabama	1.Pittsburgh	1.Pittsburgh
2.Notre Dame	2.Ohio State	2.Ohio State	2.Oklahoma	2.USC	2.USC
3.Texas	3.Nebraska	3.Oklahoma	3.Ohio State	3.Michigan	3.Michigan
4.Tennessee	4.Tennessee	4.Alabama	4.Notre Dame	4.Houston	4.Houston
5.Ohio State	5.Notre Dame	5.Penn State	5.Penn State	5.Oklahoma	5.Ohio State
6.Arizona State	6.LSU	6.Michigan	6.Michigan	6.Ohio State	6.Oklahoma
7.LSU	7.Michigan	7.Nebraska	7.USC	7.Texas A&M	7.Nebraska
8.Stanford	8.Arizona State	8.USC	8.Texas	8.Maryland	8.Texas A&M
9.Michigan	9.Auburn	9.Arizona State	9.UCLA	9.Nebraska	9.Alabama
10.Auburn	10.Stanford	9.Houston	10.Arizona State	10.Georgia	10.Georgia
11.Arkansas	11.Air Force	11.Texas Tech	11.Nebraska	11.Alabama	11.Maryland
12.Toledo	12.Arkansas	12.UCLA	11.Texas Tech	12.Notre Dame	12.Notre Dame
13.Georgia Tech	13.Houston	13.LSU	13.Houston	13.Texas Tech	13.Texas Tech
14.Dartmouth	13.Dartmouth	14.Texas	14.LSU	14.Oklahoma State	14.Oklahoma State
15.USC	15.Oklahoma	15.Miami (OH)	15.Kansas	15.UCLA	15.UCLA
16.Air Force	16.Colorado	16.NC State	17.Miami (OH)	16.Colorado	16.Colorado
17.Tulane	17.Georgia Tech	17.Missouri	17.Miami (OH)	17.Rutgers	17.Rutgers
18.Penn State	17.Toledo	18.Kansas	18.Maryland	18.Kentucky	18.Iowa State
19.Houston	19.Penn State	19.Tennessee	19.San Diego State	19.Iowa State	19.Baylor
20.Oklahoma	19.USC	20.Maryland	20.Florida	20.Miss. State	19.Kentucky
20.Mississippi		20.Tulane			

1977: AP	1977: UPI	1980: AP	1980: UPI
1.Notre Dame	1.Notre Dame	1.Georgia	1.Georgia
2.Alabama	2.Alabama	2.Pittsburgh	2.Pittsburgh
3.Arkansas	3.Arkanasa	3.Oklahoma	3.Oklahoma
4.Texas	4.Penn State	4.Michigan	4.Michigan
5.Penn State	5.Texas	5.Florida State	5.Florida State
6.Kentucky	6.Oklahoma	6.Alabama	6.Alabama
7.Oklahoma	7.Pittsburgh	7.Nebraska	7.Nebraska
8.Pittsburgh	8.Michigan	8.Penn State	8.Penn State
9.Michigan	9.Washington	9.Notre Dame	9.North Carolina
10.Washington	10.Nebraska	10.North Carolina	10.Notre Dame
11.Ohio State	11.Florida State	11.USC	11.BYU
12.Nebraska	12.Ohio State	12.BYU	12.USC
13.USC	12.USC	13.UCLA	13.Baylor
14.Florida State	14.North Carolina	14.Baylor	14.UCLA
15.Stanford	15.Stanford	15.Ohio State	15.Ohio State
16.San Diego State	16.North Texas	16.Washington	16.Purdue
17.North Carolina	16.BYU	17.Purdue	17.Washington
18.Arizona State	18.Arizona State	18.Miami (FL)	18.Miami (FL)
19.Clemson	19.San Diego State	19.Miss. State	19.Florida
20. BYU	19.NC State	20.SMU	20.SMU

1978: AP	1978: UPI	1981: AP	1981: UPI
1.Alabama	1.USC	1.Clemson	1.Clemson
2.USC	2.Alabama	2.Texas	2.Pittsburgh
3.Oklahoma	3.Oklahoma	3.Penn State	3.Penn State
4.Penn State	4.Penn State	4.Pittsburgh	4.Texas
5.Michigan	5.Michigan	5.SMU	5.Georgia
6.Clemson	6.Notre Dame	6.Georgia	6.Alabama
7.Notre Dame	7.Clemson	7.Alabama	7.Washington
8.Nebraska	8.Nebraska	8.Miami (FL)	8.North Carolina
9.Texas	9.Texas	9.North Carolina	9.Nebraska
10.Houston	10.Arkansas	10.Washington	10.Michigan
11.Arkansas	11.Houston	11.Nebraska	11.BYU
12.Mich. State	12.UCLA	12.Michigan	12.Ohio State
13.Purdue	13.Purdue	13.BYU	13.USC
14.UCLA	14.Missouri	14.USC	14.Oklahoma
15.Missouri	15.Georgia	15.Ohio State	15.Iowa
16.Georgia	16.Stanford	16.Arizona State	16.Arkansas
17.Stanford	17.Navy	17.West Virginia	17.Miss. State
18.NC State	18.Texas A&M	18.Iowa	18.West Virginia
19.Texas A&M	19.Arizona State	19.Missouri	19.Southern Miss.
20.Marryland	19.NC State	20.Oklahoma	20.Missouri

1979: AP	1979: UPI	1982: AP	1982: UPI
1.Alabama	1.Alabama	1.Penn State	1.Penn State
2.USC	2.USC	2.SMU	2.SMU
3.Oklahoma	3.Oklahoma	3.Nebraska	3.Nebraska
4.Ohio State	4.Ohio State	4.Georgia	4.Georgia
5.Houston	5.Houston	5.UCLA	5.UCLA
6.Florida State	6.Pittsburgh	6.Arizona State	6.Arizona State
7.Pittsburgh	7.Nebraksa	7.Washington	7.Washington
8.Arkansas	8.Florida State	8.Clemson	8.Arkansas
9.Nebraska	9.Arkansas	9.Arkansas	9.Pittsburgh
10.Purdue	10.Purdue	10.Pittsburgh	10.Florida State
11.Washington	11.Washington	11.LSU	11.LSU
12.Texas	12.BYU	12.Ohio State	12.Ohio State
13.BYU	13.Texas	13.Florida State	13.North Carolina
14.Baylor	14.North Carolina	14.Auburn	14.Auburn
15.NC State	15.Baylor	15.USC	15.Michigan
16.Auburn	16.Indiana	16.Oklahoma	16.Oklahoma
17.Temple	17.Temple	17.Texas	17.Alabama
18.Michigan	18.Penn State	18.North Carolina	18.Texas
19.Indiana	19.Michigan	19.West Virginia	19.West Virginia
20.Penn State	20.Missouri	20.Maryland	20.Maryland

1983: AP	1983: UPI	1986: AP	1986: UPI	1989: AP	1989: UPI
1.Miami (FL)	1.Miami (FL)	1.Penn State	1.Penn State	1.Miami (FL)	1.Miami (FL)
2.Nebraska	2.Nebraska	2.Miami (FL)	2.Miami (FL)	2.Notre Dame	2.Florida State
3.Auburn	3.Auburn	3.Oklahoma	3.Oklahoma	3.Florida State	3.Notre Dame
4.Georgia	4.Georgia	4.Arizona State	4.Nebraska	4.Colorado	4.Colorado
5.Texas	5.Texas	5.Nebraska	5.Arizona State	5.Tennessee	5.Tennessee
6.Florida	6.Florida	6.Auburn	6.Ohio State	6.Auburn	6.Auburn
7.BYU	7.BYU	7.Ohio State	7.Michigan	7.Michigan	7.Alabama
8.Michigan	8.Ohio State	8.Michigan	8.Auburn	8.USC	8.Michigan
9.Ohio State	9.Michigan	9.Alabama	9.Alabama	9.Alabama	9.USC
10.Illinois	10.Illinois	10.LSU	10.Arizona	10.Illinois	10.Illinois
11.Clemson	11.SMU	11.Arizona	11.LSU	11.Nebraska	11.Clemson
12.SMU	12.Alabama	12.Baylor	12.Texas A&M	12.Clemson	12.Nebraska
13.Air Force	13.UCLA	13.Texas A&M	13.Baylor	13.Arkansas	13.Arkansas
14.Iowa	14.Iowa	14.UCLA	14.UCLA	14.Houston	14.Penn State
15.Alabama	15.Air Force	15.Arkansas	15.Iowa	15.Penn State	15.Virginia
16.West Virginia	16.West Virginia	16.Iowa	16.Arkansas	16.Mich. State	16.Texas Tech
17.UCLA	17.Penn State	17.Clemson	17.Washington	17.Pittsburgh	16.Mich. State
18.Pittsburgh	18.Oklahoma State	18.Washington	18.Boston College	18.Virginia	18.BYU
19.Boston College	19.Pittsburgh	19.Boston College	19.Clemson	19.Texas Tech	19.Pittsburgh
20.E. Carolina	20.Boston College	20.Virginia Tech	20.Florida State	20.Texas A&M	20.Washington
				21.West Virginia	
1984: AP	1984: UPI	1987: AP	1987: UPI	22.BYU	
1.BYU	1.BYU	1.Miami (FL)	1.Miami (FL)	23.Washington	
2.Washington	2.Washington	2.Florida State	2.Florida State	24.Ohio State	
3.Florida	3.Nebraska	3.Oklahoma	3.Oklahoma	25.Arizona	
4.Nebraska	4.Boston College	4.Syracuse	4.Syracuse		
5.Boston College	5.Oklahoma State	5.LSU	5.LSU	1990: AP	1990: UPI
6.Oklahoma	6.Oklahoma	6.Nebraska	6.Nebraska	1.Colorado	1.Georgia Tech
7.Oklahoma State	7.Florida	7.Auburn	7.Auburn	2.Georgia Tech	2.Colorado
8.SMU	8.SMU	8.Mich. State	8.Mich. State	3.Miami (FL)	3.Miami (FL)
9.UCLA	9.USC	9.UCLA	9.Texas A&M	4.Florida State	4.Florida State
10.USC	10.UCLA	10.Texas A&M	10.Clemson	5.Washington	5.Washington
11.So. Carolina	11.Maryland	11.Oklahoma State	11.UCLA	6.Notre Dame	6.Notre Dame
12.Maryland	12.Ohio State	12.Clemson	12.Oklahoma State	7.Michigan	7.Tennessee
13.Ohio State	13.So. Carolina	13.Georgia	13.Tennessee	8.Tennessee	8.Michigan
14.Auburn	14.Auburn	14.Tennessee	14.Georgia	9.Clemson	9.Clemson
15.LSU	15.Iowa	15.So. Carolina	15.So. Carolina	10.Houston	10.Penn State
16.Iowa	16.LSU	16.Iowa	16.Iowa	11.Penn State	11.Texas
17.Florida State	17.Virginia	17.Notre Dame	17.USC	12.Texas	12.Louisville
18.Miami (FL)	18.West Virginia	18.USC	18.Michigan	13.Florida	13.Texas A&M
19.Kentucky	19.Kentucky	19.Michigan	19.Texas	14.Louisville	14.Mich. State
20.Virginia	20.Florida State	20.Arizona State	20.Indiana	15.Texas A&M	15.Virginia
				16.Mich. State	16.Iowa
1985: AP	1985: UPI	1988: AP	1988: UPI	17.Oklahoma	17.BYU
1.Oklahoma	1.Oklahoma	1.Notre Dame	1.Notre Dame	18.Iowa	17.Nebraska
2.Michigan	2.Michigan	2.Miami (FL)	2.Miami (Fl)	19.Auburn	19.Auburn
3.Penn State	3.Penn State	3.Florida State	3.Florida State	20.USC	20.San Jose State
4.Tennessee	4.Tennessee	4.Michigan	4.Michigan	21.Mississippi	21.Syracuse
5.Florida	5.Air Force	5.West Virginia	5.West Virginia	22.BYU	22.USC
6.Texas A&M	6.UCLA	6.UCLA	6.UCLA	23.Virginia	23.Mississippi
7.UCLA	7.Texas A&M	7.USC	7.Auburn	24.Nebraska	24.Illinois
8.Air Force	8.Miami (FL)	8.Auburn	8.Cclemson	25.Illinois	25.Virginia Tech
9.Miami (FL)	9.Iowa	9.Clemson	9.USC		
10.Iowa	10.Nebraska	10.Nebraska	10.Nebraska		
11.Nebraska	11.Ohio State	11.Oklahoma State	11.Oklahoma State		
12.Arkansas	12.Arkansas	12.Arkansas	12.Syracuse		
13.Alabama	13.Florida State	13.Syracuse	13.Arkansas		
14.Ohio State	14.Alabama	14.Oklahoma	14.Oklahoma		
15.Florida State	15.Baylor	15.Georgia	15.Georgia		
16.BYU	16.Fresno State	16.Wash. State	16.Wash. State		
17.Baylor	17.BYU	17.Alabama	17.NC State		
18.Maryland	18.Georgia Tech	18.Houston	17.Alabama		
19.Georgia Tech	19.Maryland	19.LSU	19.Indiana		
20.LSU	20.LSU	20.Indiana	20.Wyoming		

1991: AP	1991: CNN/USA	1993: AP	1993: CNN/USA	1995: AP	1995: CNN/USA
1.Miami (FL)	1.Washington	1.Florida State	1.Florida State	1.Nebraska	1.Nebraska
2.Washington	2.Miami (FL)	2.Notre Dame	2.Notre Dame	2.Florida	2.Tennessee
3.Penn State	3.Penn State	3.Nebraska	3.Nebraska	3.Tennessee	3.Florida
4.Florida State	4.Florida State	4.Auburn	4.Florida	4.Florida State	4.Colorado
5.Alabama	5.Alabama	5.Florida	5.Wisconsin	5.Colorado	5.Florida State
6.Michigan	6.Michigan	6.Wisconsin	6.West Virginia	6.Ohio State	6.Kansas State
7.Florida	7.California	7.West Virginia	7.Penn State	7.Kansas State	7.Northwestern
8.California	8.Florida	8.Penn State	8.Texas A&M	8.Northwestern	8.Ohio State
9.E. Carolina	9.E. Carolina	9.Texas A&M	9.Arizona	9.Kansas	9.Virginia Tech
10.Iowa	10.Iowa	10.Arizona	10.Ohio State	10.Virginia Tech	10.Kansas
11.Syracuse	11.Syracuse	11.Ohio State	11.Tennessee	11.Notre Dame	11.USC
12.Texas A&M	12.Notre Dame	12.Tennessee	12.Boston College	12.USC	12.Penn State
13.Notre Dame	13.Texas A&M	13.Boston College	13.Alabama	13.Penn State	13.Notre Dame
14.Tennessee	14.Oklahoma	14.Alabama	14.Oklahoma	14.Texas	14.Texas
15.Nebraska	15.Tennessee	15.Miami (FL)	15.Miami (FL)	15.Texas A&M	15.Texas A&M
16.Oklahoma	16.Nebraska	16.Colorado	16.Colorado	16.Virginia	16.Syracuse
17.Georgia	17.Clemson	17.Oklahoma	17.UCLA	17.Michigan	17.Virginia
18.Clemson	18.UCLA	18.UCLA	18.Kansas State	18.Oregon	18.Oregon
19.UCLA	19.Georgia	19.North Carolina	19.Michigan	19.Syracuse	19.Michigan
20.Colorado	20.Colorado	20.Kansas State	20.Virginia Tech	20.Miami (FL)	20.Texas Tech
21.Tulsa	21.Tulsa	21.Michigan	21.North Carolina	21.Alabama	21.Auburn
22.Stanford	22.Stanford	22.Virginia Tech	22.Clemson	22.Auburn	22.Iowa
23.BYU	23.BYU	23.Clemson	23.Louisville	23.Texas Tech	23.E. Carolina
24.NC State	24.Air Force	24.Louisville	24.California	24.Toledo	24.Toledo
25.Air Force	25.NC State	25.California	25.USC	25.Iowa	25.LSU

1992: AP	1992: CNN/USA	1994: AP	1994: CNN/USA	1996: AP	1996: CNN/USA
1.Alabama	1.Alabama	1.Nebraska	1.Nebraska	1.Florida	1.Florida
2.Florida State	2.Florida State	2.Penn State	2.Penn State	2.Ohio State	2.Ohio State
3.Miami (FL)	3.Miami (FL)	3.Colorado	3.Colorado	3.Florida State	3.Florida State
4.Notre Dame	4.Notre Dame	4.Florida State	4.Alabama	4.Arizona State	4.Arizona State
5.Michigan	5.Michigan	5.Alabama	5.Florida State	5.BYU	5.BYU
6.Syracuse	6.Texas A&M	6.Miami (FL)	6.Miami (FL)	6.Nebraska	6.Nebraska
7.Texas A&M	7.Syracuse	7.Florida	7.Florida	7.Penn State	7.Penn State
8.Georgia	8.Georgia	8.Texas A&M	8.Utah	8.Colorado	8.Colorado
9.Stanford	9.Stanford	9.Auburn	9.Ohio State	9.Tennessee	9.Tennessee
10.Florida	10.Washington	10.Utah	10.BYU	10.North Carolina	10.North Carolina
11.Washington	11.Florida	11.Oregon	11.Oregon	11.Alabama	11.Alabama
12.Tennessee	12.Tennessee	12.Michigan	12.Michigan	12.LSU	12.Virginia Tech
13.Colorado	13.Colorado	13.USC	13.Virginia	13.Virginia Tech	13.LSU
14.Nebraska	14.Nebraska	14.Ohio State	14.Colorado State	14.Miami (FL)	14.Miami (FL)
15.Wash. State	15.NC State	15.Virginia	15.USC	15.Northwestern	15.Washington
16.Mississippi	16.Mississippi	16.Colorado State	16.Kansas State	16.Washington	16.Northwestern
17.NC State	17.Wash. State	17.NC State	17.NC State	17.Kansas State	17.Kansas State
18.Ohio State	18.North Carolina	18.BYU	18.Tennessee	18.Iowa	18.Iowa
19.North Carolina	19.Ohio State	19.Kansas State	19.Washington State	19.Notre Dame	19.Syracuse
20.Hawaii`	20.Hawaii	20.Arizona	20.Arizona	20.Michigan	20.Michigan
21.Boston College	21.Boston College	21.Wash. State	21.North Carolina	21.Syracuse	21.Notre Dame
22.Kansas	22.Fresno State	22.Tennessee	22.Boston College	22.Wyoming	22.Wyoming
23.Miss. State	23.Kansas	23.Boston College	23.Texas	23.Texas	23.Texas
24.Fresno State	24.Penn State	24.Miss. State	24.Virginia Tech	24.Auburn	24.Army
25.Wake Forest	25.Wake Forest	25.Texas	25.Miss. State	25.Army	25.Auburn

1997-1999 / 2001

1997: AP	1997: USA/ESPN	1999: AP	1999: USA/ESPN	2001: AP	2001: USA/ESPN
1.Michigan	1.Nebraska	1.Florida State	1.Florida State	1.Miami (FL)	1.Miami (FL)
2.Nebraska	2.Michigan	2.Virginia Tech	2.Nebraska	2.Oregon	2.Oregon
3.Florida State	3.Florida State	3.Nebraska	3.Virginia Tech	3.Florida	3.Florida
4.Florida	4.North Carolina	4.Wisconsin	4.Wisconsin	4.Tennessee	4.Tennessee
5.UCLA	5.UCLA	5.Michigan	5.Michigan	5.Texas	5.Texas
6.North Carolina	6.Florida	6.Kansas State	6.Kansas State	6.Oklahoma	6.Oklahoma
7.Tennessee	7.Kansas State	7.Mich. State	7.Mich. State	7.LSU	7.Nebraska
8.Kansas State	8.Tennessee	8.Alabama	8.Alabama	8.Nebraska	8.LSU
9.Wash. State	9.Wash. State	9.Tennessee	9.Tennessee	9.Colorado	9.Colorado
10.Georgia	10.Georgia	10.Marshall	10.Marshall	10.Wash. State	10.Maryland
11.Auburn	11.Auburn	11.Penn State	11.Penn State	11.Maryland	11.Wash. State
12.Ohio State	12.Ohio State	12.Florida	12.Miss. State	12.Illinois	12.Illinois
13.LSU	13.LSU	13.Miss. State	13.So. Mississippi	13.So. Carolina	13.So. Carolina
14.Arizona State	14.Arizona State	14.So. Mississippi	14.Florida	14.Syracuse	14.Syracuse
15.Purdue	15.Purdue	15.Miami (FL)	15.Miami (FL)	15.Florida State	15.Florida State
16.Penn State	16.Colorado State	16.Georgia	16.Georgia	16.Stanford	16.Louisville
17.Colorado State	17.Penn State	17.Arkansas	17.Minnesota	17.Louisville	17.Stanford
18.Washington	18.Washington	18.Minnesota	18.Oregon	18.Virginia Tech	18.Virginia Tech
19.So. Mississippi	19.So. Mississippi	19.Oregon	19.Arkansas	19.Washington	19.Washington
20. Texas A&M	20.Syracuse	20.Georgia Tech	20.Texas A&M	20.Michigan	20.Michigan
21.Syracuse	21.Texas A&M	21.Texas A&M	21.Georgia Tech	21.Boston College	21.Marshall
22.Mississippi	22.Mississippi	22.Mississippi	22.Mississippi	22.Georgia	22.Toledo
23.Missouri	23.Missouri	23.Texas	23.Texas	23.Toledo	23.Boston College
24.Oklahoma State	24.Oklahoma State	24.Illinois	24.Stanford	24.Georgia Tech	24.BYU
25.Georgia Tech	25.Air Force	25.Purdue	25.Illinois	25.BYU	25.Georgia

1998 / 2000 / 2002

1998: AP	1998: USA/ESPN	2000: AP	2000: USA/ESPN	2002: AP	2002: USA/ESPN
1.Tennessee	1.Tennessee	1.Oklahoma	1.Oklahoma	1.Ohio State	1.Ohio State
2.Ohio State	2.Ohio State	2.Miami (FL)	2.Miami (FL)	2.Miami (FL)	2.Miami (FL)
3.Florida State	3.Florida State	3.Washington	3.Washington	3.Georgia	3.Georgia
4.Arizona	4.Arizona	4.Oregon State	4.Florida State	4.USC	4.USC
5.Florida	5.Wisconsin	5.Florida State	5.Oregon State	5.Oklahoma	5.Oklahoma
6.Wisconsin	6.Florida	6.Virginia Tech	6.Virginia Tech	6.Texas	6.Kansas State
7.Tulane	7.Tulane	7.Oregon	7.Nebraska	7.Kansas State	7.Texas
8.UCLA	8.UCLA	8.Nebraska	8.Kansas State	8.Iowa	8.Iowa
9.Georgia Tech	9.Kansas State	9.Kansas State	9.Oregon	9.Michigan	9.Michigan
10.Kansas State	10.Air Force	10.Florida	10.Michigan	10.Wash. State	10.Wash. Sate
11.Texas A&M	11.Georgia Tech	11.Michigan	11.Florida	11.Alabama	11.NC State
12.Michigan	12.Michigan	12.Texas	12.Texas	12.NC State	12.Boise State
13.Air Force	13.Texas A&M	13.Purdue	13.Purdue	13.Maryland	13.Maryland
14.Georgia	14.Georgia	14.Colorado State	14.Clemson	14.Auburn	14.Virginia Tech
15.Texas	15.Penn State	15.Notre Dame	15.Colorado State	15.Boise State	15.Penn State
16.Arkansas	16.Texas	16.Notre Dame	16.Notre Dame	16.Penn State	16.Auburn
17.Penn State	17.Arkansas	17.Georgia Tech	17.Georgia	17.Notre Dame	17.Notre Dame
18.Virgiinia	18.Virginia	18.Auburn	18.TCU	18.Virginia Tech	18.Pittsburgh
19.Nebraska	19.Virginia Tech	19.So. Carolina	19.Georgia Tech	19.Pittsburgh	19.Marshall
20.Miami (FL)	20.Nebraska	20.Georgia	20.Auburn	20.Colorado	20.West Virginia
21.Missouri	21.Miami (FL)	21.TCU	21.South Carolina	21.Florida State	21.Colorado
22.Notre Dame	22.Notre Dame	22.LSU	22.Miss. State	22.Virginia	22.TCU
23.Virginia Tech	23.Purdue	23.Wisconsin	23.Iowa State	23.TCU	23.Florida State
24.Purdue	24.Syracuse	24.Miss. State	24.Wisconsin	24.Marshall	24.Florida
25.Syracuse	25.Missouri	25.Iowa State	25.Tennessee	25.West Virginia	25.Virginia

2003:AP	2003:USA/ESPN
1.USC	1.LSU
2.LSU	2.USC
3.Oklahoma	3.Oklahoma
4.Ohio State	4.Ohio State
5.Miami (FL)	5.Miami (FL)
6.Michigan	6.Georgia
7.Georgia	7.Michigan
8.Iowa	8.Iowa
9.Wash. State	9.Wash. State
10.Miami (OH)	10.Fla. State
11.Fla. State	11.Texas
12.Texas	12.Miami (OH)
13.Ole Miss	13.Kansas State
14.Kansas State	14.Ole Miss
15.Tennessee	15.Boise State
16.Boise State	16.Tennessee
17.Maryland	17.Minnesota
18.Purdue	18.Nebraska
19.Nebraska	19.Purdue
20.Minnesota	20.Maryland
21.Utah	21.Utah
22.Clemson	22.Clemson
23.Bowling Green	23.Bowling Green
24.Florida	24.TCU
25.TCU	25.Florida

PART X

Changes in the Rules of College Football

The first football game was played on November 6, 1869, with Rutgers beating Princeton, 6-4. There were 25 players on each team, playing on a 120-yard field, with a rugby ball, in a game in which each goal counted one point. In games played over the next six or seven years, most teams used adaptations of the rules of Association ball, borrowed from England, but the details differed from team to team. Among other things, the Association rules banned the carrying or throwing of the ball. The first meeting to standardize the rules of football was held in 1873. The meeting was attended by delegates from Yale, Princeton, Columbia, and Rutgers, and its recommendations followed the Association rules in large part. Harvard was invited to the meeting, but declined to attend, because Harvard's version of football allowed running with the ball, as well as passing it. At the 1873 meeting, the number of players on a team was reduced to twenty, and there were to be two judges, one from each team, with disputes to be settled by a referee.

In 1876, there was another meeting, this time with Harvard in attendance. The rules adopted at this meeting made it permissible for a player to run with the ball, and changed the dimensions of the playing field to 110 yards long and 53½ yards wide. There was a further reduction in the number of players per team to fifteen. In 1877, a time dimension was introduced into the game, when the length of the game was set at ninety minutes. American college football was beginning to take shape.

Significant changes in rules from 1877 on include the following.

1879: The number of players on a team is reduced from fifteen to eleven, and the field size is standardized at four hundred feet by two hundred feet.

1881: Field size is set at one hundred yards by fifty-three yards.

1882: Rules concerning maintaining possession of the ball are introduced. A team could maintain possession only by gaining five yards in three downs.

1883: Point values were assigned to different scoring plays for the first time, with the winning team determined by the number of points scored. A safety was worth one point, a touchdown two points, a goal after a touchdown four points, and a field goal five points. The referee is now specified to be an alumnus of the home team.

1884: A safety is worth two points, a touchdown four, and a goal after touchdown two.

1894: Game time is reduced from ninety minutes to seventy minutes, divided into two thirty-five minute halves.

Prior to 1894, ten players could line up in the backfield and could be in motion when the ball was snapped. The 1894 rules change states that only three men can be five yards or more behind the line of scrimmage, and a maximum of three men can be in motion when the ball is snapped.

1895: A minimum of six players must be on the line of scrimmage when the ball is snapped. Only one man can be in motion when the ball is snapped, and he must be in motion towards his own goal. Lines five yards apart and parallel to the goal lines are to drawn on the field.

1896: Five players must be on the line of scrimmage when the ball is snapped.

1897: The rule on substitutes to this time was that a player could be substituted for only if he was injured or was disqualified for play. The 1897 rule permitted the substitution of one player for another at any time. The ball is standardized as a prolate sphere twenty-seven inches in circumference. The ball remains at this size until 1912. There are to be two officials, a referee to follow the ball, and an umpire to follow the players.

1898: Points are five for a touchdown, five for a field goal, two for a safety, and one point for a goal after a touchdown.

1903: There are to be either seven men or five men on the line of scrimmage, depending on the field position of the team with the ball.

1904: A field goal is worth four points.

1905: A player taken out for a substitute is out for the rest of the game.

1906: The Intercollegiate Athletic Association of the United States is formed and introduces a number of changes to reduce the brutality of football, responding to the criticisms of President Theodore Roosevelt. Among the most important are these:

The game is shortened to sixty minutes, divided into two thirty-minute halfs. To attain a first down, a team now has to gain ten yards in three plays. Tackling out of bounds, piling on, tackling below the knee, and striking another player are all made illegal. The forward pass is legalized, subject to severe limitations. An incomplete pass results in a turnover to the opposing team. A pass completed in the other team's end zone is a turnover to the other team, which gets the ball on its own twenty yard line. If a passer throws a pass when he is more than five yards to the right or left of where the ball was centered, the pass, whether completed or not, is a turnover to the other team. A pass that hits an ineligible receiver also results in a turnover. In addition, the first man receiving the ball from the center on a running play must not cross the line of scrimmage within five yards to the right or left of where the ball was centered. On the playing field, lines are to be drawn five yards apart, parallel to the sidelines, to assist the officials in determining whether a given run or pass play is legal or illegal. This gives rise to the term "gridiron" to describe a football field.

1908: Forfeited games enter the records with a score of 1-0 against the forfeiting team. The flying tackle is outlawed. There must be seven players on the line of scrimmage when the ball is centered.

1909: The point value of a field goal is reduced to three points.

1910: The rules regarding throwing a pass within five yards to the right or left of where the ball was centered, or the first back handling the ball not crossing the line of scrimmage within five yards to the right or left of the center, are dropped. The lines on the field running parallel to the sidelines are now dropped as well. The game is divided into four quarters of fifteen minutes each. Forward passes are limited to twenty yards in length and must be thrown from at least five yards behind the line of scrimmage. An on-side kick on a kickoff must travel at least twenty yards. Any player leaving the game for a substitute has to remain on the sidelines until the opening of the next quarter, and can only return at that time. The Intercollegiate Athletic Association of the U.S. changes its name to the National Collegiate Athletic Association (NCAA).

1912: The ball is slenderized. The ball is to be tightly inflated, and the circumference of the ball is set at 22½ to 23 inches around the middle, with a weight of between fourteen and fifteen ounces. The possession rule is changed to four downs to make ten yards. The value of a touchdown is increased from five points to six points. The twenty-yard restriction on passes is removed. A pass completed in the opponent's end zone is now a touchdown and not a turnover; and an incomplete pass is now the loss of a down, and not a turnover. If a player returns illegally after leaving the game, the team is charged a fifteen-yard penalty, and the player is suspended for the game. Field, including end zones, is set at 120 yards by 53⅓ yards.

1915: Any substitute entering a game may not communicate with any of his team's players until after the next play of the game. The penalty for communicating is fifteen yards.

1922: A player substituted for in the first half can return at any time in the second half, not just at the beginning of the second half. A player substituted for in the second half cannot be returned to the game.

1925: The winner of the coin toss can choose whether to defend or receive. A clipping violation costs a twenty-five yard penalty.

1926: The second (or third or fourth) incomplete pass in a row carries a penalty of five yards. Any pass incomplete in the opponent's end zone leads to a turnover to the opponent.

1927: A thirty-second time limit between plays is set, with a five-yard penalty for delay of game for exceeding the limit.

1930: Players may be substituted for at any time, but a player leaving the game in the first half cannot return until the second half, and a player leaving the game in the second half is out for the rest of the game.

1934: Ball is further slenderized, with the circumference around the middle at between 21¼ and 21½ inches. The penalties against incomplete passes enacted in 1926 are eliminated, except that if there are two successive passes incomplete in the end zone, this is a touchback, with the opponent receiving the ball at its twenty yard line, and a fourth down pass incomplete in the end zone is also a touchback

1937: All players are to be identified with numbers on their jerseys.

1938: Except for fourth down passes, passes incomplete in the end zone do not lead to a touchback, but simply loss of a down.

1939: All players are required to wear helmets. On a pass play, ineligible players cannot advance beyond the line of scrimmage until the ball is thrown.

1940: The thirty-second limit between plays is reduced to twenty-five seconds.

1941: Players can leave and return to the game at any time, except that one play has to take place before a player can return. A fourth down pass incomplete in the end zone results in the defending team taking over at the spot where it was put into play.

1945: The requirement that passes must be made from at least five yards behind the line of scrimmage is eliminated, thus freeing T-formation quarterbacks for passing.

1949: Offensive linemen cannot cross the line of scrimmage on a pass play until the pass is completed.

1953: Limited substitution ("one-platoon football") is reintroduced to college football. A player substituted for can return to the game only once in that quarter.

1958: Following a touchdown, a team has the choice of a kick for one point, or a run or pass for two points.

1965: Unlimited substitution and "two-platoon football" returns to the college game. Any number of players can enter the game at a change of possession. At other times, a maximum of two players can enter after each play.

1988: If, on a point after touchdown try, the defenders block a kick, intercept a pass, or otherwise obtain the ball legally, and return the ball across the offensive team's goal line, the defenders are awarded two points.

1992: Defenders can advance a recovered fumble anywhere on the field.

1996: If a game ends in a tie, there are overtime periods in each of which each team in turn gets the ball on the opponent's twenty-five yard line and attempts to score, the team scoring the most points wins the game. If the game is still tied after two overtime periods (two possessions by each team), then, in any later overtime period, the teams must attempt two-point tries for points after a touchdown.

Sources: L. H. Baker, the RSFC home page, and McCallum and Pearson, *College Football USA 1869–1971*.

James Quirk is a retired professor from Caltech. He is the author of several books in economics and co-author of *Paydirt: The Business of Pro Team Sports* and *Hardball: The Abuse of Power in Pro Team Sports.*

Sport and Society

A Sporting Time: New York City and the Rise of
    Modern Athletics, 1820–70—*Melvin L. Adelman*

Sandlot Seasons: Sport in Black Pittsburgh—*Rob Ruck*

West Ham United: The Making of a Football Club
    —*Charles Korr*

Beyond the Ring: The Role of Boxing in American
    Society—*Jeffrey T. Sammons*

John L. Sullivan and His America
    —*Michael T. Isenberg*

Television and National Sport: The United States and
    Britain—*Joan M. Chandler*

The Creation of American Team Sports: Baseball and
    Cricket, 1838–72—*George B. Kirsch*

City Games: The Evolution of American Urban
    Society and the Rise of Sports—*Steven A. Riess*

The Brawn Drain: Foreign Student-Athletes in
    American Universities—*John Bale*

The Business of Professional Sports—*Edited by
    Paul D. Staudohar and James A. Mangan*

Fritz Pollard: Pioneer in Racial Advancement
    —*John M. Carroll*

A View from the Bench: The Story of an Ordinary
    Player on a Big-Time Football Team (*formerly
    Go Big Red! The Story of a Nebraska Football
    Player*)—*George Mills*

Sport and Exercise Science: Essays in the History of
    Sports Medicine—*Edited by Jack W. Berryman and
    Roberta J. Park*

Minor League Baseball and Local Economic
    Development—*Arthur T. Johnson*

Harry Hooper: An American Baseball Life
    —*Paul J. Zingg*

Cowgirls of the Rodeo: Pioneer Professional Athletes
    —*Mary Lou LeCompte*

Sandow the Magnificent: Eugen Sandow and the
    Beginnings of Bodybuilding—*David Chapman*

Big-Time Football at Harvard, 1905: The Diary of
    Coach Bill Reid—*Edited by Ronald A. Smith*

Leftist Theories of Sport: A Critique and
    Reconstruction—*William J. Morgan*

Babe: The Life and Legend of Babe Didrikson
    Zaharias—*Susan E. Cayleff*

Stagg's University: The Rise, Decline, and Fall of
    Big-Time Football at Chicago—*Robin Lester*

Muhammad Ali, the People's Champ—*Edited by
    Elliott J. Gorn*

People of Prowess: Sport, Leisure, and Labor in Early
    Anglo-America—*Nancy L. Struna*

The New American Sport History: Recent Approaches
    and Perspectives—*Edited by S. W. Pope*

Making the Team: The Cultural Work of Baseball
    Fiction—*Timothy Morris*

Making the American Team: Sport, Culture, and the
    Olympic Experience—*Mark Dyreson*

Viva Baseball! Latin Major Leaguers and Their
    Special Hunger—*Samuel O. Regalado*

Touching Base: Professional Baseball and American
    Culture in the Progressive Era (rev. ed.)
    —*Steven A. Riess*

Red Grange and the Rise of Modern Football
    —*John M. Carroll*

Golf and the American Country Club
    —*Richard J. Moss*

Extra Innings: Writing on Baseball
    —*Richard Peterson*

Global Games—*Maarten Van Bottenburg*

The Sporting World of the Modern South—*Edited by
    Patrick B. Miller*

The End of Baseball As We Knew It: The Players
    Union, 1960–81—*Charles P. Korr*
Rocky Marciano: The Rock of His Times
    —*Russell Sullivan*
Saying It's So: A Cultural History of the Black Sox
    Scandal—*Daniel A. Nathan*
The Nazi Olympics: Sport, Politics, and Appeasement
    in the 1930s—*Edited by Arnd Krüger and*
    William Murray

The Unlevel Playing Field: A Documentary History
    of the African American Experience in Sport
    —*David K. Wiggins and Patrick B. Miller*
Sports in Zion: Mormon Recreation, 1890–1940
    —*Richard Ian Kimball*
The Nazi Olympics—*Richard D. Mandell*
Sports in the Western World (2d ed.)—*William J. Baker*
The Ultimate Guide to College Football: Rankings,
    Records, and Scores of the Major Teams and
    Conferences—*James Quirk*

The University of Illinois Press
is a founding member of the
Association of American University Presses.

———————————————————

Composed in 11/15.5 Times Roman
with Times Roman display
at the University of Illinois Press
Designed by Dennis Roberts
Manufactured by Sheridan Books, Inc.

University of Illinois Press
1325 South Oak Street
Champaign, IL 61820–6903
www.press.uillinois.edu